Your fully reengineered Mic[...]

MW00331906

The all-new learning format of your Microsoft study guide delivers in-dept[...]
by-objective review—along with great new study tools to help prepare you[...]

- Relevant exam objectives highlighted at the start of each chapter

- Chapter Scenarios and Real-World sidebars on how you can apply concepts presented on the job

- Case scenario exercises where you work through a multi-step, real-world solution

- Troubleshooting labs on a simulated operating system for practical field experience

---

Lesson 2: Creating Multiple User Objects

There occasionally situations that require you to create multiple user objects quickly, such as a new class of incoming students at a school, or a group of new hires at an organization. In these situations you need to know how to effectively facilitate or automate user object creation so that you are not approaching the task on an account-by-account basis. In Lesson 1, you learned how to create and manage user objects with Active Directory Users and Computers. This lesson will extend those concepts, skills, and tools to include user object creation through template objects, imported objects, and command line scripting of objects.

> **After this lesson, you will be able to**
> - Create and utilize user object templates
> - Import user objects from comma-delimited files
> - Leverage new command-line tools to create and manage user objects
>
> **Estimated lesson time: 15 minutes**

Creating and Using User Templates

It is common for objects to share similar properties. For example, all sales representatives may belong to the same security groups, are allowed to log on to the network during the same hours, and have home folders and roaming profiles on the same server. In such cases, it is helpful when creating a user object for that object to be pre-populated with common properties. This can be accomplished by creating a generic user object—often called a *template*—and then copying that object to create new users.

To generate a user template, create a user and populate its properties. Put the user into appropriate groups.

 Security Alert Be certain to disable the user, since it is just a template, to ensure that the account is not used for access to network resources.

To create a new user based on the template, select the template and choose Copy from the Action menu. You will be prompted for properties similar to those when you create a new user: first and last name, initials, logon names, password, and account options. When the object is created, you will find that properties are copied from the template based on the following property-page based description:

- **General** No properties copied.
- **Address** All properties except Street address are copied.

- "Off the Record" sidebars bridge the gap between how things *should* work and how they *do* work

- Security Alerts and Planning Tips you can apply in the real world

- 300-page objective-by-objective review section

- Exam highlights—key points and terms you should know

- Exam tips written by industry insiders

---

3 User Accounts

Exam Objectives in this Chapter:
- Create and manage user accounts.
  - Create and modify user accounts by using the Active Directory Users and Computers MMC snap-in.
  - Create and modify user accounts by using automation.
  - Import user accounts.
- Manage local, roaming, and mandatory user profiles.
- Troubleshoot user accounts.
  - Diagnose and resolve account lockouts.
  - Diagnose and resolve issues related to user account properties.
- Troubleshoot user authentication issues.

Why This Chapter Matters

Before individuals in your enterprise can begin to access resources they require, you must enable authentication of those individuals. Of course, the primary component of that authentication is the user's identity, maintained as an account in Active Directory. In this chapter, you will review and enhance your knowledge related to the creation, maintenance, and troubleshooting of user accounts and authentication.

Each enterprise, and each day, brings with it a unique set of challenges related to user management. The properties you configure for a standard user account are likely to be different from those you apply to the account of a Help Desk team member, which are different still from those configured on the built-in Administrator account. Skills that are effective to create or modify a single user account become clumsy and inefficient when you are working with masses of accounts, for example when managing the accounts for a number of new hires.

To effectively address a diverse sampling of account management scenarios, we will examine a variety of user management skills and tools including the Active Directory Users & Computers snap-in and powerful command-line utilities.

 Note Be sure to configure share permissions allowing Everyone Full Control. The Windows Server 2003 default share permissions allow Read, which is not sufficient for a roaming profile share.

On the Profile tab of the user's Properties dialog box, type the Profile Path in the format: **<server >****<share>****%username%**. The %username% variable will automatically be replaced with the user's logon name.

It's that simple. The next time the user logs on to their system, the system will identify the roaming profile location.

 Exam Tip Roaming user profiles are nothing more than a shared folder and a path to the user's profile folder, within that share, entered into the user object's profile path property. Roaming profiles are not, in any way, a property of a computer object.

When the user logs *off* of their system, it will upload the profile to the profile server. The user can now log on to their system, or any other system in the domain, and the documents and settings that are part of the RUP will be applied.

 Note Windows Server 2003 introduces a new policy: Only allow local user profiles. This policy, linked to an OU containing computer accounts, will prevent roaming profiles from being used on those computers. Users will, instead, maintain local profiles.

When a user with an RUP logs on to a new system for the first time, the system does not copy its Default User profile. Instead, it downloads the RUP from the network location. When a user logs off, or when a user logs on to a system on which they've worked before, the system copies only files that have changed.

 Real World   Roaming Profile Synchronization
Unlike previous versions of Microsoft Windows, Windows 2000, Windows XP, and Windows Server 2003 do not upload and download the entire user profile at logoff and logon. Instead, the user profile is *synchronized*. Only files that have changed are transferred between the local system and the network RUP folder. This means that logon and logoff with RUPs are significantly faster than with earlier Windows systems. Organizations that have not implemented RUPs for fear of their impact on logon and network traffic should reevaluate their configuration in this light.

Objective Card
Exam 70-270: Installing, Configuring, and Administering Microsoft Windows XP Professional

Skills Measured by Exam 70–270	Chapter	Lesson
1. Installing Microsoft Windows XP Professional		
1.1 Perform and troubleshoot an attended installation of Windows XP Professional.	2	2,3,4
1.2 Perform and troubleshoot an unattended installation of Windows XP Professional.		
■ 1.1.1 Install Windows XP Professional by using Remote Installation Services (RIS).	3	3
■ 1.1.2 Install Windows XP Professional by using the System Preparation Tool.	3	2
■ 1.1.3 Create unattended answer files by using Setup Manager to automate the installation of Windows XP Professional.	3	1
1.3 Upgrade from a previous version of Windows to Windows XP Professional.		
■ 1.3.1 Prepare a computer to meet upgrade requirements.	2	1
■ 1.3.2 Migrate existing user environments to a new installation.	2	4
1.4 Perform post-installation updates and product activation.	2	6
1.5 Troubleshoot failed installations.	2	5
2. Implementing and Conducting Administration of Resources		
2.1 Monitor, manage, and troubleshoot access to files and folders.		
■ 2.1.1 Configure, manage, and troubleshoot file compression.	10	2
■ 2.1.2 Control access to files and folders by using permissions.	8	1, 2
■ 2.1.3 Optimize access to files and folders.	10	1, 3, 5, 6
2.2 Manage and troubleshoot access to shared folders.		
■ 2.2.1 Create and remove shared folders.	9 17	1 2
■ 2.2.2 Control access to shared folders by using permissions.	9	2
■ 2.2.3 Manage and troubleshoot Web server resources.	5	5
2.3 Connect to local and network print devices.		
■ 2.3.1 Manage printers and print jobs.	11, 12	2, 3, 4 2, 3
■ 2.3.2 Control access to printers by using permissions.	12	2
■ 2.3.2 Connect to an Internet printer.	11	3
■ 2.3.4 Connect to a local print device.	11	2
2.4 Configure and manage file systems.		
■ 2.4.1 Convert from one file system to another file system. Create and modify user accounts by using automation.	10	1
■ 2.4.2 Configure NTFS, FAT32, or FAT file systems.	10	1
2.5 Manage and troubleshoot access to and synchronization of offline files.	10	6
3. Implementing, Managing, Monitoring, and Troubleshooting Hardware Devices and Drivers		
3.1 Implement, manage, and troubleshoot disk devices.		
■ 3.1.1 Install, configure, and manage DVD and CD-ROM devices.	10	1
■ 3.1.2 Monitor and configure disks.	10	1
■ 3.1.3 Monitor, configure, and troubleshoot volumes.	10	1
■ 3.1.4 Monitor and configure removable media, such as tape devices.	10	1
3.2 Implement, manage, and troubleshoot display devices.		
■ 3.2.1 Configure multiple-display support.	5	1
■ 3.2.2 Install, configure, and troubleshoot a video adapter.	5	1
3.3 Configure Advanced Configuration Power Interface (ACPI).	5	2
3.4 Implement, manage, and troubleshoot input and output (I/O) devices.		
■ 3.4.1 Monitor, configure, and troubleshoot I/O devices, such as printers, scanners, multimedia devices, mouse, keyboard, and smart card reader.	6	2
■ 3.4.2 Monitor, configure, and troubleshoot multimedia hardware, such as cameras.	6	2
■ 3.4.3 Install, configure, and manage modems.	15	2
■ 3.4.4 Install, configure, and manage Infrared Data Association (IrDA) devices.	6	2
■ 3.4.5 Install, configure, and manage wireless devices.	15	3
■ 3.4.6 Install, configure, and manage universal serial bus (USB) devices.	6	2
■ 3.4.7 Install, configure, and manage hand held devices.	6	2
■ 3.4.8 Install, configure, and manage network adapters.	15	1

	Chapter	Lesson
3. Implementing, Managing, Monitoring, and Troubleshooting Hardware Devices and Drivers (cont.)		
3.5 Manage and troubleshoot drivers and driver signing.	6	4
3.6 Monitor and configure multiprocessor computers.	19	1
4. Monitoring and Optimizing System Performance and Reliability		
4.1 Monitor, optimize, and troubleshoot performance of the Windows XP Professional desktop.		
■ 4.1.1 Optimize and troubleshoot memory performance.	19	1, 2
■ 4.4.2 Optimize and troubleshoot processor utilization.	19	1, 2
■ 4.4.3 Optimize and troubleshoot disk performance.	19	1, 2
■ 4.4.4 Optimize and troubleshoot application performance.	19	1, 2
■ 4.4.5 Configure, manage, and troubleshoot Scheduled Tasks.	18	3
4.2 Manage, monitor, and optimize system performance for mobile users.	19	1, 2
4.3 Restore and back up the operating system, System State data, and user data.		
■ 4.3.1 Recover System State data and user data by using Windows Backup.	20	2, 3
■ 4.3.2 Troubleshoot system restoration by starting in safe mode.	4	3
■ 4.3.3 Recover System State data and user data by using the Recovery console.	4	3
■ 4.4.4 Optimize and troubleshoot application performance.	20	4
5. Configuring and Troubleshooting the Desktop Environment		
5.1 Configure and manage user profiles and desktop settings.		
5.2 Configure support for multiple languages or multiple locations.		
■ 5.2.1 Enable multiple-language support.	5	4
■ 5.2.2 Configure multiple-language support for users.	5	4
■ 5.2.3 Configure local settings.	5	4
■ 5.2.4 Configure Windows XP Professional for multiple locations.	5	4
5.3 Manage applications by using Windows Installer packages.	3	4
6. Implementing, Managing, and Troubleshooting Network Protocols and Services		
6.1 Configure and troubleshoot the Transmission Control Protocol/Internet Protocol (TCP/IP) protocol.	13	1, 2
6.2 Connect to computers by using dial-up networking.		
■ 6.2.1 Connect to computers by using a virtual private network (VPN) connection.	15	1, 2
■ 6.2.2 Create a dial-up connection to connect to a remote access server.	15	2
■ 6.2.3 Connect to the Internet by using dial-up networking.	15	2
■ 6.2.4 Configure and troubleshoot Internet Connection Sharing (ICS).	15	4
6.3 Connect to resources by using Internet Explorer.	16	6
6.4 Configure, manage, and implement Internet Information Services (IIS).	5	5
6.5 Configure, manage, and troubleshoot Remote Desktop and Remote Assistance.	18	5
6.6 Configure, manage, and troubleshoot an Internet Connection Firewall (ICF).	15	5
7. Configuring, Managing, and Troubleshooting Security		
7.1 Configure, manage, and troubleshoot Encrypting File System (EFS).	10	4
7.2 Configure, manage, and troubleshoot a security configuration and local security policy.	16	1, 2, 3, 4
7.3 Configure, manage, and troubleshoot local user and group accounts.		
■ 7.3.1 Configure, manage, and troubleshoot auditing.	16	5
■ 7.3.2 Configure, manage, and troubleshoot account settings.	7	3, 4
■ 7.3.3 Configure, manage, and troubleshoot account policy.	16	2
■ 7.3.4 Configure, manage, and troubleshoot user and group rights.	16	3
7.4 Configure, manage, and troubleshoot Internet Explorer security settings.	16	6

Note Exam objectives are subject to change at any time without prior notice and at Microsoft's sole discretion. Please visit Microsoft's Training & Certification Web site (*www.microsoft.com/traincert*) for the most current listing of exam objectives.

Microsoft

MCSA/MCSE Self-Paced Training Kit (Exam 70-270): Installing, Configuring, and Administering Microsoft® Windows® XP Professional, Second Edition

Walter Glenn
Tony Northrup

PUBLISHED BY
Microsoft Press
A Division of Microsoft Corporation
One Microsoft Way
Redmond, Washington 98052-6399

Copyright © 2005 by Microsoft Corporation

All rights reserved. No part of the contents of this book may be reproduced or transmitted in any form or by any means without the written permission of the publisher.

Library of Congress Control Number 2004118216

Printed and bound in the United States of America.

13 14 15   QWT   9 8

Distributed in Canada by H.B. Fenn and Company Ltd.

A CIP catalogue record for this book is available from the British Library.

Microsoft Press books are available through booksellers and distributors worldwide. For further information about international editions, contact your local Microsoft Corporation office or contact Microsoft Press International directly at fax (425) 936-7329. Visit our Web site at www.microsoft.com/learning/. Send comments to *tkinput@microsoft.com*.

Microsoft, Active Directory, ActiveSync, ActiveX, DirectSound, DirectX, FrontPage, IntelliMirror, Microsoft Press, MSDN, MS-DOS, MSN, NetMeeting, Outlook, Visual InterDev, Visual Studio, Win32, Windows, Windows Media, Windows Mobile, Windows NT, and Windows Server are either registered trademarks or trademarks of Microsoft Corporation in the United States and/or other countries.

The example companies, organizations, products, domain names, e-mail addresses, logos, people, places, and events depicted herein are fictitious. No association with any real company, organization, product, domain name, e-mail address, logo, person, place, or event is intended or should be inferred.

Product Planner: Martin DelRe
Content Development Managers: Marzena Makuta, Elise Morrison
Technical Editor: Karena Lynch
Project Manager: Julie Pickering
Copy Editor: Nancy Sixsmith
Indexer: Julie Hatley

Body Part No. X10-87059

For my wife, Susan
Walter Glenn

For my wife, Erica
Tony Northrup

About the Authors

Walter Glenn, Microsoft Certified System Engineer (MCSE) and Microsoft Certified Trainer (MCT), has been a part of the computer industry for more than 17 years. He currently works in Huntsville, Alabama, as a consultant, trainer, and writer. Walter is the author or coauthor of more than 20 computer books, including *Microsoft Exchange Server 2003 Administrator's Companion* (Microsoft Press, 2003), *MCDST Self-Paced Training Kit (Exam 70-271): Supporting Users and Troubleshooting a Microsoft Windows XP Operating System* (Microsoft Press, 2004), *MCDST Self-Paced Training Kit (Exam 70-272): Supporting Users and Troubleshooting Desktop Applications on a Microsoft Windows XP Operating System* (Microsoft Press, 2004), and *MCSE Self-Paced Training Kit (Exam 70-297): Designing a Microsoft Windows Server 2003 Active Directory and Network Infrastructure* (Microsoft Press, 2003). He has also written a number of Web-based courses that are geared toward Microsoft certification training.

Tony Northrup, Certified Information Systems Security Professional (CISPP), MCSE, and Microsoft Most Valuable Professional (MVP), is a networking consultant and author living in the Boston, Massachusetts area. During his seven years as principal systems architect at BBN/Genuity, he was ultimately responsible for the reliability and security of hundreds of Windows servers and dozens of Windows domains—all directly connected to the Internet. Needless to say, Tony learned the hard way how to keep Windows systems safe and reliable in a hostile environment. As a consultant, Tony has provided networking guidance to a wide variety of businesses, from Fortune 100 enterprises to small businesses. When he is not consulting or writing, Tony enjoys cycling, hiking, and nature photography.

Contents at a Glance

Contents

What do you think of this book?
We want to hear from you!

Microsoft is interested in hearing your feedback about this publication so we can continually improve our books and learning resources for you. To participate in a brief online survey, please visit: *www.microsoft.com/learning/booksurvey/*

2   Installing Windows XP Professional   2-1

8   Securing Resources with NTFS Permissions   8-1

9   Administering Shared Folders   9-1

10   Managing Data Storage   10-1

13   Supporting TCP/IP   13-1

14   Overview of Active Directory Service   14-1

16   Configuring Security Settings and Internet Options   16-1

18   Using Windows XP Tools   18-1

Part 2   Prepare for the Exam

21   Installing Windows XP Professional (1.0)   21-3

What do you think of this book?   Microsoft is interested in hearing your feedback about this publication so we can
We want to hear from you!   continually improve our books and learning resources for you. To participate in a brief
                                 online survey, please visit: *www.microsoft.com/learning/booksurvey/*

Acknowledgments

A book like this is a big project and it would not get done without the help of a lot of people. I have worked on many books over the years with a lot of different people. Without question, the team at Microsoft Learning is the best. Team members are exacting and conscientious, and they take pride in producing the best books they can.

I want to extend my thanks to everyone who worked on this book. Julie Pickering, our project manager, did a great job of coordinating everyone's effort—and that can be a pretty tough assignment when you are working with writers. Our editors—Elise Morrison, Lori Kane, and Marzena Makuta—pored over every detail to make sure that the book was of the highest quality and that everyone involved turned in their best effort. And Tony Northrup, our technical editor of part 1, gave a detailed technical review and helped to make sure that I actually knew what I was talking about. I also want to thank Randall Galloway at Microsoft for his technical guidance and support along the way.

And as always, I want to thank Neil Salkind and everyone else at StudioB for helping put this project together.

Walter Glenn

I'd like to thank my friends, especially Chris and Diane Geggis, Bob Hogan, Kurt and Beatriz Dillard, Eric and Alyssa Faulkner, John and Tara Banks, Kristin Casciato, Samuel Jackson, and Eric John Parucki. They each helped me enjoy my time away from the keyboard. I have to thank my wife, Erica, more than anyone, for being so patient during many long days of writing.

Tony Northrup

About This Book

Welcome to *MCSE Self-Paced Training Kit (Exam 70-270): Installing, Configuring, and Administering Microsoft Windows XP Professional, Second Edition.* This book introduces you to the Microsoft Windows XP Professional operating system and prepares you to install, configure, and support Windows XP Professional.

You will learn how to work with Windows XP Professional in a networked environment. This book focuses on the following:

- Installing Windows XP Professional
- Implementing and managing resources
- Installing, managing, and troubleshooting hardware devices and drivers
- Monitoring and optimizing system performance and reliability
- Configuring and troubleshooting the desktop environment
- Implementing, managing, and troubleshooting network protocols and services

 Note For more information about becoming a Microsoft Certified Professional, see the section titled "The Microsoft Certified Professional Program" later in this introduction.

Intended Audience

Anyone who wants to learn about Windows XP Professional will find this book useful. This book was developed for information technology (IT) professionals who need to design, plan, implement, and support Windows XP Professional or who plan to take the related Microsoft Certified Professional Exam 70-270, *Installing, Configuring, and Administering Microsoft Windows XP Professional.*

 Note Exam skills are subject to change without prior notice and at the sole discretion of Microsoft.

Prerequisites

This training kit requires that students meet the following prerequisites:

- Have a working knowledge of the Windows XP operating system
- Have a basic understanding of computer hardware
- Have a basic understanding of networking technologies

About the CD-ROM

For your use, this book includes a Supplemental CD-ROM, which contains a variety of informational aids to complement the book content:

- The Microsoft Press Readiness Review Suite Powered by MeasureUp. This suite of practice tests and objective reviews contains questions of varying degrees of complexity and offers multiple testing modes. You can assess your understanding of the concepts presented in this book and use the results to develop a learning plan that meets your needs.

- An electronic version of this book (eBook). For information about using the eBook, see the "The eBook" section later in this introduction.

- Tools recommended in the book.

A second CD-ROM contains a 180-day Evaluation Edition of Microsoft Windows XP Professional with Service Pack 2.

Caution   The 180-day Evaluation Edition provided with this training kit is not the full retail product and is provided only for the purposes of training and evaluation. Microsoft Technical Support does not support this evaluation edition.

For additional support information regarding this book and the CD-ROM (including answers to commonly asked questions about installation and use), visit the Microsoft Learning Technical Support Web site at *http://www.microsoft.com/learning/support/*. You can also e-mail tkinput@microsoft.com or send a letter to Microsoft Learning, Attn: Microsoft Learning Technical Support, One Microsoft Way, Redmond, WA 98052-6399.

Features of This Book

This book has two parts. Use Part I to learn at your own pace and practice what you have learned with practical exercises. Part II contains questions and answers you can use to test yourself on what you have learned.

Part I: Learn at Your Own Pace

Each chapter identifies the exam objectives that are covered within the chapter, provides an overview of why the topics matter by identifying how the information is applied in the real world, and lists any prerequisites that must be met to complete the lessons presented in the chapter.

The chapters are divided into lessons. Most lessons contain practices that include one or more hands-on exercises. These exercises give you an opportunity to use the skills being presented or to explore the part of the application being described.

After the lessons, you are given an opportunity to apply what you have learned in a case scenario exercise. In this exercise, you work through a multistep solution for a realistic case scenario. You are also given an opportunity to work through a troubleshooting lab that explores difficulties you might encounter when applying what you have learned on the job.

Each chapter ends with a short summary of key concepts and a short section that lists key topics and terms you need to know before taking the exam. This section summarizes the key topics you have learned, with a focus on demonstrating that knowledge on the exam.

> **Real World**   **Helpful Information**
>
> You will find sidebars like this one that contain related information you might find helpful. "Real World" sidebars contain specific information gained through the experience of IT professionals just like you.

Part II: Prepare for the Exam

Part II helps to familiarize you with the types of questions you will encounter on the Microsoft Certified Professional (MCP) exam. By reviewing the objectives and sample questions, you can focus on the specific skills you need to improve before taking the exam.

> **See Also**   For a complete list of MCP exams and their related objectives, go to *http://www.microsoft.com/learning/mcp/*.

Part II is organized by the exam's objectives. Each chapter covers one of the primary groups of objectives, referred to as *Objective Domains*. Each chapter lists the tested skills you need to master to answer the exam questions, and it includes a list of further readings to help you improve your ability to perform the tasks or skills specified by the objectives.

Within each Objective Domain, you will find the related objectives that are covered on the exam. Each objective provides you with several practice exam questions. The answers are accompanied by explanations of each correct and incorrect answer.

> **On the CD**   These questions are also available on the companion CD as a practice test.

Informational Notes

Several types of reader aids appear throughout the training kit.

- **Tip** contains methods of performing a task more quickly or in a not-so-obvious way.

- **Important** contains information that is essential to completing a task.

- **Note** contains supplemental information.

- **Caution** contains valuable information about possible loss of data; be sure to read this information carefully.

- **Warning** contains critical information about possible physical injury; be sure to read this information carefully.

- **See Also** contains references to other sources of information.

- **On the CD** points you to supplementary information or files you need that are on the companion CD.

- **Security Alert** highlights information you need to know to maximize security in your work environment.

- **Exam Tip** flags information you should know before taking the certification exam.

- **Off the Record** contains practical advice about the real-world implications of information presented in the lesson.

Notational Conventions

The following conventions are used throughout this book:

- Characters or commands that you type appear in **bold** type.

- *Italic* in syntax statements indicates placeholders for variable information. *Italic* is also used for book and exam titles.

- Names of files and folders appear in Title caps, except when you are to type them directly. Unless otherwise indicated, you can use all lowercase letters when you type a file name in a dialog box or at a command prompt.

- File name extensions appear in all uppercase.

- Acronyms appear in all uppercase.

- Monospace type represents code samples, examples of screen text, or entries that you might type at a command prompt or in initialization files.

- Square brackets [ ] are used in syntax statements to enclose optional items. For example, [*filename*] in command syntax indicates that you can choose to type a file name with the command. Type only the information within the brackets, not the brackets themselves.

- Braces { } are used in syntax statements to enclose required items. Type only the information within the braces, not the braces themselves.

Keyboard Conventions

- A plus sign (+) between two key names means that you must press those keys at the same time. For example, "Press ALT+TAB" means that you hold down ALT while you press TAB.

- A comma (,) between two or more key names means that you must press each of the keys consecutively, not together. For example, "Press ALT, F, X" means that you press and release each key in sequence. "Press ALT+W, L" means that you first press ALT and W at the same time, and then release them and press L.

Getting Started

This training kit contains hands-on exercises to help you learn about supporting applications in Windows XP. Use this section to prepare your self-paced training environment.

Hardware Requirements

To follow the practices in this book, it is recommended that you use a computer that is not your primary workstation because you will be called on to make changes to the operating system and application configuration. The computer you use must have the following minimum configuration. All hardware should be listed in the Windows Catalog.

- Personal computer with an Intel Pentium 233 MHz or faster processor (300 MHz or faster processor recommended)

- 64 MB of RAM or higher (128 MB or higher recommended)

- 1.5 GB of available hard disk space

- CD-ROM drive or DVD drive

- Super VGA (800 x 600) or higher resolution monitor
- Microsoft Mouse or compatible pointing device
- Internet connection

Software Requirements

The following software is required to complete the procedures in this training kit. (A 120-day Evaluation Edition of Microsoft Windows XP Professional with Service Pack 2 is included on the CD-ROM.)

- Windows XP Professional with Service Pack 2

> **Caution**   The 120-day Evaluation Edition provided with this training is not the full retail product and is provided only for the purposes of training and evaluation. Microsoft Technical Support does not support this evaluation edition. For additional support information regarding this book and the CD-ROMs (including answers to commonly asked questions about installation and use), visit the Microsoft Learning Technical Support Web site at *http://mspress.microsoft.com/learning/support/*. You can also e-mail tkinput@microsoft.com or send a letter to Microsoft Learning, Attn: Microsoft Learning Technical Support, One Microsoft Way, Redmond, WA 98502-6399.

Setup Instructions

Set up your computer according to the manufacturer's instructions.

> **Caution**   If your computer is part of a larger network, you *must* verify with your network administrator that the computer name, domain name, and other information used in configuring Windows XP in several chapters of this book do not conflict with network operations. If they do conflict, ask your network administrator to provide alternative values and use those values throughout all the exercises in this book. It is better if you can configure your computer as a stand-alone computer with Internet access.

The Readiness Review Suite

The CD-ROM includes a practice test made up of 300 sample exam questions and an objective-by-objective review with an additional 125 questions. Use these tools to reinforce your learning and to identify any areas in which you need to gain more experience before taking the exam.

▶ **To install the practice test and objective review**

1. Insert the Supplemental CD-ROM into your CD-ROM drive.

> **Note**   If AutoRun is disabled on your machine, refer to the Readme.txt file on the CD-ROM.

2. Click Readiness Review Suite on the user interface menu.

The eBook

The CD-ROM includes an electronic version of the Training Kit. The eBook is in Portable Document Format (PDF) and can be viewed by using Adobe Acrobat Reader.

▶ **To use the eBook**

1. Insert the Supplemental CD-ROM into your CD-ROM drive.

> **Note**   If AutoRun is disabled on your machine, refer to the Readme.txt file on the CD-ROM.

2. Click Training Kit eBook on the user interface menu. You can also review any of the other eBooks that are provided for your use.

The Microsoft Certified Professional Program

The Microsoft Certified Professional (MCP) program provides the best method to prove your command of current Microsoft products and technologies. The exams and corresponding certifications are developed to validate your mastery of critical competencies as you design and develop, or implement and support, solutions with Microsoft products and technologies. Computer professionals who become Microsoft-certified are recognized as experts and are sought after industry-wide. Certification brings a variety of benefits to the individual and to employers and organizations.

> **See Also**   For a full list of MCP benefits, go to *http://www.microsoft.com/learning/itpro/ default.asp.*

Certifications

The Microsoft Certified Professional program offers multiple certifications, based on specific areas of technical expertise:

- *Microsoft Certified Professional (MCP).* Demonstrated in-depth knowledge of at least one Microsoft Windows operating system or architecturally significant platform. An MCP is qualified to implement a Microsoft product or technology as part of a business solution for an organization.

- *Microsoft Certified Desktop Support Technician (MCDST).* Individuals who support end users and troubleshoot desktop environments running on the Windows operating system.

- *Microsoft Certified Solution Developer (MCSD).* Professional developers qualified to analyze, design, and develop enterprise business solutions with Microsoft development tools and technologies including the Microsoft .NET Framework.

- *Microsoft Certified Application Developer (MCAD).* Professional developers qualified to develop, test, deploy, and maintain powerful applications using Microsoft tools and technologies including Microsoft Visual Studio .NET and XML Web services.

- *Microsoft Certified Systems Engineer (MCSE).* Qualified to effectively analyze the business requirements and design and implement the infrastructure for business solutions based on the Microsoft Windows Server 2003 operating system.

- *Microsoft Certified Systems Administrator (MCSA).* Individuals with the skills to manage and troubleshoot existing network and system environments based on the Microsoft Windows Server 2003 operating systems.

- *Microsoft Certified Database Administrator (MCDBA).* Individuals who design, implement, and administer Microsoft SQL Server databases.

- *Microsoft Certified Trainer (MCT).* Instructionally and technically qualified to deliver Microsoft Official Curriculum through a Microsoft Certified Technical Education Center (CTEC).

Requirements for Becoming a Microsoft Certified Professional

The certification requirements differ for each certification and are specific to the products and job functions addressed by the certification.

To become a Microsoft Certified Professional, you must pass rigorous certification exams that provide a valid and reliable measure of technical proficiency and expertise. These exams are designed to test your expertise and ability to perform a role or task with a product and are developed with the input of professionals in the industry.

Questions in the exams reflect how Microsoft products are used in actual organizations, giving them "real-world" relevance.

■ Microsoft Certified Professional (MCP) candidates are required to pass one current Microsoft certification exam. Candidates can pass additional Microsoft certification exams to further qualify their skills with other Microsoft products, development tools, or desktop applications.

■ Microsoft Certified Solution Developers (MCSDs) are required to pass three core exams and one elective exam. (MCSD for Microsoft .NET candidates are required to pass four core exams and one elective.)

■ Microsoft Certified Application Developers (MCADs) are required to pass two core exams and one elective exam in an area of specialization.

■ Microsoft Certified Systems Engineers (MCSEs) are required to pass five core exams and two elective exams.

■ Microsoft Certified Systems Administrators (MCSAs) are required to pass three core exams and one elective exam that provide a valid and reliable measure of technical proficiency and expertise.

■ Microsoft Certified Database Administrators (MCDBAs) are required to pass three core exams and one elective exam that provide a valid and reliable measure of technical proficiency and expertise.

■ Microsoft Certified Trainers (MCTs) are required to meet instructional and technical requirements specific to each Microsoft Official Curriculum course they are certified to deliver. The MCT program requires ongoing training to meet the requirements for the annual renewal of certification. For more information about becoming a Microsoft Certified Trainer, visit *http://www.microsoft.com/learning/mcp/mct/* or contact a regional service center near you.

Technical Support

Every effort has been made to ensure the accuracy of this book and the contents of the companion disc. If you have comments, questions, or ideas regarding this book or the companion disc, please send them to Microsoft Learning using either of the following methods:

E-mail: tkinput@microsoft.com

Postal Mail: Microsoft Learning
                   Attn: *MCSE Self-Paced Training Kit (Exam 70-270): Installing,
                   Configuring, and Administering Microsoft Windows XP Professional,
                   Second Edition,* Editor
                   One Microsoft Way
                   Redmond, WA 98052-6399

For additional support information regarding this book and the CD-ROM (including answers to commonly asked questions about installation and use), visit the Microsoft Learning Technical Support Web site at *http://www.microsoft.com/learning/support/*. To connect directly to the Microsoft Press Knowledge Base and enter a query, visit *http://www.microsoft.com/mspress/support/search.asp*. For support information regarding Microsoft software, please connect to *http://support.microsoft.com/*.

Evaluation Edition Software Support

The 120-day Evaluation Edition provided with this training is not the full retail product and is provided only for the purposes of training and evaluation. Microsoft and Microsoft Technical Support do not support this evaluation edition.

> **Caution**   The Evaluation Edition of Windows XP Professional with Service Pack 2 included with this book should not be used on a primary work computer. The Evaluation Edition is unsupported. For online support information relating to the full version of Windows XP Professional that *might* also apply to the Evaluation Edition, you can connect to *http://support.microsoft.com/*.

Information about any issues relating to the use of this Evaluation Edition with this training kit is posted to the Support section of the Microsoft Learning Web site (*http://www.microsoft.com/learning/support/*). For information about ordering the full version of any Microsoft software, please call Microsoft Sales at (800) 426-9400 or visit *http://www.microsoft.com*.

Part I
Learn at Your Own Pace

1 Introduction to Windows XP Professional

Exam Objectives in this Chapter:

- This first chapter serves as an introduction to Windows XP Professional and does not specifically cover any exam objective.

Why This Chapter Matters

This book prepares you to install, configure, and support Microsoft Windows XP Professional. This chapter introduces you to the various editions of Microsoft Windows that make up the Windows XP family. It also provides a look at some of the areas in which Microsoft has enhanced Windows XP with Windows XP Service Pack 2. This chapter introduces the concepts of workgroups and domains and also explains how to log on and off Windows XP Professional. By the time you are finished reading this chapter, you should have a firm understanding of where and why Windows XP Professional is used.

Lessons in this Chapter:

Before You Begin

There are no special requirements to complete this chapter.

Lesson 1: Explaining Windows XP

This lesson introduces the various editions of Windows XP, including Windows XP Professional, Windows XP Home Edition, Windows XP Tablet PC Edition, Windows XP Home Media Edition, and Windows XP 64-Bit Edition.

After this lesson, you will be able to

- Identify the available editions of Windows XP.
- Explain the differences between Windows XP editions.

Estimated lesson time: 10 minutes

Available Windows XP Editions

There are a number of different editions of Windows XP, each of which is designed for different users and computing devices. The following editions are part of the Windows family:

- Windows XP Professional Edition
- Windows XP Home Edition
- Windows XP Media Center Edition
- Windows XP Tablet PC Edition
- Windows XP 64-Bit Edition

Windows XP Professional Edition

Windows XP Professional Edition is intended for computers that are part of a corporate network, for the majority of computers on small networks, and for home users who need certain advanced capabilities. Windows XP Professional sets the standard for desktop performance, security, and reliability.

Windows XP Professional is also the focus of both this book and Exam 70-270: *Installing, Configuring, and Administering Microsoft Windows XP Professional*.

Windows XP Home Edition

Windows XP Home Edition, which is intended for home users, simplifies many aspects of networking and file management so that home users have a cleaner experience. In particular, Windows XP Home Edition has the following limitations compared with Windows XP Professional:

- Computers running Windows XP Home Edition cannot join a domain.

- Windows XP Home Edition does not support the use of NTFS or print permissions. Instead, Windows XP Home Edition supports only Simple File Sharing. You will learn more about NTFS permissions in Chapter 8, "Securing Resources with NTFS Permissions." You will learn more about print permissions in Chapter 12, "Managing Printers and Documents."

- Windows XP Home Edition does not support the use of dynamic disks, which you will learn about in Chapter 10, "Managing Data Storage."

- Windows XP Home Edition does not support the Encrypting File System (EFS), which you will learn about in Chapter 10.

- Windows XP Home Edition supports only one processor, whereas Windows XP Professional supports two processors.

- Windows XP Home Edition does not include Internet Information Services.

- Windows XP Home Edition does not include Remote Desktop.

- Windows XP Home Edition does not provide Remote Installation Services (RIS) support (which you will learn about in Chapter 3, "Deploying Windows XP Professional").

See Also   You can learn more about Windows XP Home Edition and find a detailed feature comparison with Windows XP Professional at *http://www.microsoft.com/windowsxp/home/*.

Windows XP Media Center Edition

The Windows XP Media Center Edition 2004 operating system is available only on new Media Center PCs—computers with special hardware features that enable users to connect the computer as an integral part of a home entertainment system. Because of its special requirements, Media Center PCs running Windows XP Media Center Edition are available only from Microsoft PC manufacturer partners.

See Also   For more information about Windows XP Media Center Edition, visit *http:// www.microsoft.com/windowsxp/mediacenter/*.

Windows XP Tablet PC Edition

The Windows XP Tablet PC Edition operating system expands on Windows XP Professional, providing all the features and performance of Windows XP Professional, while also providing additional capabilities designed to take advantage of a touch-screen interface: pen input, handwriting recognition, and speech recognition.

Windows XP Tablet PC Edition offers users the efficiency and dependability of Windows XP Professional. For developers, it offers a rich platform for creating new applications or extending their current applications to take advantage of Tablet PC handwriting and speech capabilities.

> **See Also**   For more information about Windows XP Tablet PC Edition, visit *http://www.microsoft.com/windowsxp/tabletpc/*.

Windows XP 64-Bit Edition

Microsoft Windows XP 64-Bit Edition, which provides support for the 64-bit computing platforms, is designed to meet the demands of advanced technical workstation users who require large amounts of memory and floating point performance in areas such as mechanical design and analysis, 3D animation, video editing and composition, and scientific and high-performance computing applications. One of the key differences between the 64-bit and 32-bit platforms is that the 64-bit platform supports considerably more system memory—up to 16 GB of physical RAM.

> **See Also**   For more information about Windows XP 64-Bit Edition, visit *http://www.microsoft.com/windowsxp/64bit/*.

Lesson Review

Use the following questions to help determine whether you have learned enough to move on to the next lesson. If you are unable to answer a question, review the lesson materials and try the question again. You can find answers to the questions in the "Questions and Answers" section at the end of this chapter.

1. Windows XP _Mobie_ Edition and Windows XP _64 bit_ Edition are available only on supported hardware devices and are not available as stand-alone products. Fill in the blanks.

2. Which features supported in Windows XP Professional are not supported in Windows XP Home Edition?

   NTFS, EFS, Dual Proc, Domain, IIS
   Dynamic Disks, Remote Install
   Remote Desktop, print perm

Lesson Summary

- The Windows XP family includes Windows XP Professional Edition, Windows XP Home Edition, Windows XP Media Center Edition, Windows XP Tablet PC Edition, and Windows XP 64-Bit Edition.

- Features provided in Windows XP Professional that are not provided in Windows XP Home Edition include dynamic disks, Remote Desktop, NTFS and print permissions, Encrypting File System, domain membership, dual processors, and IIS.

Lesson 2: Identifying Major Features of Windows XP Service Pack 2

As part of a major effort to increase the security of desktop computers, in 2004, Microsoft is releasing an update to Windows XP named **Windows XP Service Pack 2**. As with all Windows service packs, Windows XP Service Pack 2 includes all of the critical updates released for Windows XP to date. In addition, Service Pack 2 includes a large number of new enhancements to Windows XP—enhancements aimed at increasing the default level of security for the operating system.

In addition to a new **Security Center** that provides at-a-glance security status for a computer, Service Pack 2 provides enhancements to the built-in software firewall in Windows XP (now named Microsoft Windows Firewall), to the Automatic Updates feature, and to Microsoft Internet Explorer.

After this lesson, you will be able to

- Determine whether Service Pack 2 is installed on a computer running Windows XP Professional.
- Identify the major enhancements included in Windows XP Service Pack 2.

Estimated lesson time: 20 minutes

How to Determine Whether Service Pack 2 Is Installed

Aside from simply looking for new enhancements to the interface (such as the Security Center), you can determine whether Service Pack 2 (or any Service Pack, for that matter) is installed in one of two ways:

- From the Start menu, right-click My Computer and click Properties. The General tab of the System Properties dialog box (in the System section) allows you to know which version of Windows and which Service Pack is installed.

- From the Start menu, click Run. In the Run dialog box, type **winver.exe** and click OK. The About Windows dialog box shows you the exact version of Windows (including Service Pack), down to the build number.

Note   This section presents an overview of the most important and obvious features of Windows XP Service Pack 2. The procedures and discussions in this book assume that you have Windows XP Service Pack 2 installed. You can learn more about Windows XP Service Pack 2 at *http://www.microsoft.com/technet/prodtechnol/winxppro/maintain/winxpsp2.mspx*. You can download and install Service Pack 2 from the Windows Update site at *http://www.windowsupdate.com*.

Major Enhancements Included in Windows XP Service Pack 2

The major enhancements in Windows XP Service Pack 2 include Security Center, Automatic Updates, Windows Firewall, and Internet Explorer. This section describes these enhancements in detail.

Security Center

Security Center is an entirely new feature provided by Windows XP Service Pack 2. The Security Center service runs as a background process in Windows XP and routinely checks the status of the following components:

Windows Firewall   Security Center detects whether **Windows Firewall** is enabled or disabled. Security Center can also detect the presence of some third-party software firewall products.

Automatic Updates   Security Center detects the current **Automatic Updates** setting in Windows XP. If Automatic Updates is turned off or not set to the recommended settings, the Security Center provides appropriate recommendations.

Virus Protection   Security Center detects the presence of antivirus software from many third-party organizations. If the information is available, the Security Center service also determines whether the software is up-to-date and whether real-time scanning is turned on.

When Security Center is running, its presence is indicated by an icon in the notification area on the Windows taskbar, as shown in Figure 1-1. When Security Center detects an important security condition (such as improper settings), it displays a pop-up notice in the notification area.

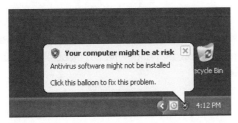

Figure 1-1   The Security Center icon in the notification area provides access to the Security Center window and alerts the user to security conditions.

You can also double-click the Security Center icon in the notification area to open the main Security Center window, shown in Figure 1-2. The Security Center window provides the following information:

- Resources where you can learn more about security-related issues.

- An indication of whether Windows Firewall is enabled or disabled, as well as a shortcut for opening the Windows Firewall dialog box.

- The current configuration for Automatic Updates, as well as a link for changing Automatic Updates settings.

- The current status of antivirus software installed on the computer. For some antivirus products, Security Center can also determine whether the antivirus software is up-to-date.

- Additional shortcuts for opening the Internet Options and System dialog boxes.

Figure 1-2   The Security Center window provides a central interface for managing security on a computer running Windows XP.

Note   If you are running firewall or antivirus software that is not detected by Security Center, Security Center presents options for bypassing alerts for that component. If you see a Recommendations button, you can use it to open a window that allows you to disable alerts or research any appropriate third-party products.

Automatic Updates

Software updates help keep computers protected from new vulnerabilities that are discovered (and new threats that are created) after the initial shipping of an operating system. Updates are crucial to keeping computers secure and functioning properly. Updates provided by Microsoft provide solutions to known issues, including patches for security vulnerabilities, and updates to the operating system and some applications.

Windows XP features an automatic updating service named Automatic Updates that can download and apply updates automatically in the background. Automatic Updates connects periodically to Windows Update on the Internet (or possibly to a Windows Update Services server on a corporate network). When Automatic Updates discovers new updates that apply to the computer, it can be configured to install all updates automatically (the preferred method) or to notify the computer's administrator (or other users configured to receive notifications) that an update is available.

Windows XP Service Pack 2 provides several enhancements to the Automatic Updates feature, including the following:

- The latest version of Automatic Updates offers expanded support for Microsoft products, including Microsoft Office.

- Previous versions of Automatic Updates could download only critical updates. Now Automatic Updates can download updates in the following categories: security updates, critical updates, update roll-ups, and service packs.

- Automatic Updates now prioritizes the download of available updates based on the importance and size of the updates. For example, if a large service pack is being downloaded, and a smaller security update is released to address an exploit, that security update will be downloaded more quickly than the service pack.

- Automatic Updates is now more automated. The need for users to accept End-User License Agreements (EULAs) has been eliminated. Also, the user now has a choice of whether to restart the computer following the installation of updates that might require a restart. Updates that do require a restart can now be consolidated into a single installation so that only one restart is required.

> **Real World   A New Windows Update Site**
>
> A forthcoming update to the online Windows Update Web site will provide many of the same features that Automatic Updates provides to users of Windows XP Service Pack 2 who choose not to use Automatic Updates. These features include the ability to download updates for Microsoft applications in addition to operating system updates, to perform express installations that require minimal user input, and to research updates more easily.

The Windows Update site offers a more hands-on approach to updating Windows than Automatic Updates. If a user resists using the Automatic Updates feature, teach the user to frequently visit the Windows Update site and perform an Express Install that scans for, downloads, and then installs critical and security updates.

Windows Firewall

A firewall protects a computer from attacks originating outside the computer (specifically, the Internet) by blocking all incoming network traffic except that which you specifically configure the firewall to allow through. Any computer connected directly to any network—whether it is a stand-alone computer, a computer that provides Internet Connection Sharing (ICS) services for other computers on a network, or even a computer that is already on a network protected by perimeter firewalls—should have a firewall enabled.

Previous versions of Windows XP include a software-based firewall named Internet Connection Firewall (ICF). After installing Windows XP Service Pack 2, this firewall is replaced by Windows Firewall. Windows Firewall is a stateful, host-based firewall that drops all incoming traffic that does not meet one of the following conditions:

■ Solicited traffic (valid traffic that is sent in response to a request by the computer) is allowed through the firewall.

■ Excepted traffic (valid traffic that you have specifically configured the firewall to accept) is allowed through the firewall.

In addition to its new name, Windows Firewall also boasts a number of enhancements, including the following:

Enabled by default   Windows Firewall is now enabled by default on all network connections. This includes LAN (wired and wireless), dial-up, and virtual private network (VPN) connections that exist when Windows XP Service Pack 2 is installed. When a new connection is created, Windows Firewall is also enabled by default.

Global settings   In Windows XP (prior to installing Windows XP Service Pack 2), ICF settings must be configured individually for each connection. After installing Windows XP Service Pack 2, Windows Firewall provides an interface for configuring global settings that apply to all the connections of the computer. When you change a global Windows Firewall setting, the change is applied to all the connections on which Windows Firewall is enabled. Of course, you can still apply configurations to individual connections as well.

New interface   In previous versions, ICF is enabled by selecting a single check box on the Advanced tab of the Properties dialog box for a connection. A Settings button opens a separate dialog box, in which you can configure services, logging, and Internet Control Message Protocol (ICMP) allowances. In Windows XP Service Pack 2, the check box on the Advanced tab has been replaced with a Settings button that launches the new Windows Firewall Control Panel applet, which consolidates global and connection-specific settings, service, and ICMP allowances and log settings in a single updated interface.

Prevent excepted traffic   In previous versions, ICF is either enabled or disabled. When enabled, solicited traffic and excepted traffic are allowed. When disabled, all traffic is allowed. In Windows XP Service Pack 2, Windows Firewall supports a new feature that allows you to keep Windows Firewall enabled and also not allow any exceptions; only solicited traffic is allowed. This new feature is intended to create an even more secure environment when connecting to the Internet in a public location or other unsecured location.

Startup security   In previous versions, ICF becomes active on connections only when the ICF/ICS service is started successfully. This means that when a computer is started, there is a delay between when the computer is active on the network and when the connections are protected with ICF. In Windows XP Service Pack 2, a startup Windows Firewall policy performs stateful packet filtering during startup, so that the computer can perform basic network tasks (such as contacting Dynamic Host Configuration Protocol [DHCP] and Domain Name System [DNS] servers) and still be protected.

> **Exam Tip**   Remember that the new Windows Firewall policy performs packet filtering during Windows startup, meaning that connections are protected from the moment they become active on the network.

Traffic source restrictions   In previous versions, you could not apply firewall rules based on Internet Protocol (IP) addresses. In Windows XP Service Pack 2, you can configure Windows Firewall so that firewall rules apply to IP addresses (or IP address ranges), meaning that only traffic from computers with valid IP addresses is allowed through the firewall.

Create exceptions using application file names   In previous versions, you configure permitted traffic by specifying the Transmission Control Protocol (TCP) and User Datagram Protocol (UDP) ports used by a service or application. In Windows XP Service Pack 2, you can also configure permitted traffic by specifying the file name of the application. When the application runs, Windows Firewall monitors the ports on which the application listens and automatically adds them to the list of allowed incoming traffic.

Internet Explorer

Windows XP Service Pack 2 introduces a number of new security features to Internet Explorer 6. As with the rest of the enhancements introduced with Windows XP Service Pack 2, most of the updates to Internet Explorer are intended to provide better security. Internet Explorer enhancements provided by Windows XP Service Pack 2 include the following:

Information bar   The Internet Explorer Information bar in Windows XP Service Pack 2 replaces many of the common dialog boxes that prompt users for information and provides a common area for displaying information. Notifications such as blocked ActiveX installs, blocked pop-up windows, and downloads all appear in the Information bar, which appears below the toolbars and above the main browsing window. Either clicking or right-clicking on the Information bar brings up a menu that relates to the notification that is presented. A new custom security zone setting allows users to change the settings of the Information bar for each security zone, including the ability to disable the Information bar and return to using separate dialog boxes.

Pop-up blocker   When Windows XP Service Pack 2 is installed, Internet Explorer provides a pop-up blocker for blocking pop-up windows. Internet Explorer displays a notification in the Information bar when a pop-up is blocked. Clicking the information bar allows you to show the blocked pop-up, allow all pop-ups on the current site, and configure other settings.

File download prompt   With Windows XP Service Pack 2 installed, Internet Explorer presents a new dialog box when a user downloads a file, as shown in Figure 1-3. The new dialog box displays publisher information for the file (if available) and a section with information on the risks of downloading the file.

Figure 1-3   The Internet Explorer File Download dialog box provides more file information.

Add-on management   With Windows XP Service Pack 2 installed, Internet Explorer prompts users when add-on software tries to install itself into Internet Explorer. Users can also view and control the list of add-ons that can be loaded by Internet Explorer. Internet Explorer also attempts to detect crashes in Internet Explorer that are related to add-ons. If an add-on is identified, this information is presented to the user; the user can then disable the add-ons to prevent future crashes.

Lesson Review

Use the following questions to help determine whether you have learned enough to move on to the next lesson. If you are unable to answer a question, review the lesson materials and try the question again. You can find answers to the questions in the "Questions and Answers" section at the end of this chapter.

1. After Windows XP Service Pack 2 is installed, Internet Explorer combines many of the common dialog boxes that prompt users for information into a common area named the _____. Fill in the blank.

2. Which of the following is true of Windows Firewall? Choose all that apply.

   a. Windows Firewall is enabled by default.

   b. Windows Firewall is disabled by default.

   c. Windows Firewall must be configured individually for each connection.

   d. Windows Firewall protects a network connection as soon as the connection is active on the network.

Lesson Summary

- You can determine whether Service Pack 2 is installed by viewing the General tab of the System Properties dialog box or by typing **winver.exe** in the Run dialog box to open the About Windows dialog box.

- Windows XP Service Pack 2 includes four major enhancements:

  ❑ Security Center, an entirely new feature, provides real-time status and alerts for Windows Firewall, Automatic Updates, and some antivirus software.

  ❑ Enhancements to Automatic Updates allow it to download updates for more Microsoft products, download all types of updates, and prioritize update importance.

  ❑ Enhancements to Windows Firewall enable the firewall for each connection by default, allow the inspection of traffic from the moment the connection becomes active, and let you make global configuration settings for all connections.

  ❑ Enhancements to Internet Explorer include a new Information bar that consolidates many user prompts, a pop-up blocker, and better add-on management.

Lesson 3: Identifying Key Characteristics of Workgroups and Domains

Windows XP Professional supports two types of network environments in which users can share common resources, regardless of network size. A **workgroup** consists of a number of peer-based computers, with each maintaining its own security. A **domain** consists of servers that maintain centralized security and directory structures and workstations that participate in those structures.

After this lesson, you will be able to

- Identify the key characteristics of workgroups and explain how they work.
- Identify the key characteristics of domains and explain how they work.

Estimated lesson time: 15 minutes

How Workgroups Work

A Windows XP Professional workgroup is a logical grouping of networked computers that share resources, such as files and printers. A workgroup is also called a peer-to-peer network because all computers in the workgroup can share resources as equals (peers) without requiring a dedicated server.

Each computer in the workgroup maintains a local security database, which is a list of user accounts and resource security information for the computer on which it resides. Using a local security database on each workstation decentralizes the administration of user accounts and resource security in a workgroup. Figure 1-4 shows a local security database.

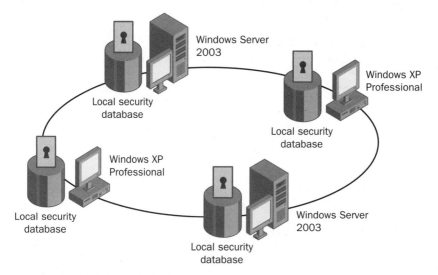

Figure 1-4   A Windows XP Professional workgroup is also called a peer-to-peer network.

Note   A workgroup can contain computers running a server operating system, such as Windows Server 2003, as long as the server is not configured as a domain controller (in other words, as long as no domain is present). In a workgroup, a computer running Windows Server 2003 is called a **stand-alone server**.

Because workgroups have decentralized administration and security, the following are true:

- A user must have a user account on a local computer if that user wants to log on to that computer locally (that is, by sitting down at that computer).

- Any changes to user accounts, such as changing a user's password or adding a new user account, must be made on each computer in the workgroup. If you forget to add a new user account to one of the computers in your workgroup, the new user cannot log on to that computer and cannot access resources on it.

Workgroups provide the following advantages:

- Workgroups do not require a domain controller to hold centralized security information, making workgroups much simpler to configure and manage.

- Workgroups are simple to design and implement. Workgroups do not require the extensive planning and administration that a domain requires.

- Workgroups provide a convenient networking environment for a limited number of computers in close proximity. However, a workgroup becomes impractical in environments with more than 10 computers.

How Domains Work

A domain is a logical grouping of network computers that share a central directory database. (See Figure 1-5.) A directory database contains user accounts and security information for the domain. This database, which is known as the directory, is the database portion of **Active Directory** service—the Windows 2003 directory service.

In a domain, the directory resides on computers that are configured as domain controllers. A domain controller is a server that manages all security-related aspects of user and domain interactions, centralizing security and administration.

Exam Tip   You can designate only a computer running Microsoft Windows 2000 Server or Windows Server 2003 as a domain controller. If all computers on the network are running Windows XP Professional, the only type of network available is a workgroup.

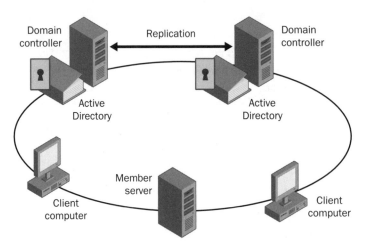

Figure 1-5   A Windows 2003 domain relies on Active Directory to provide user authentication.

A domain does not refer to a single location or specific type of network configuration. The computers in a domain can share physical proximity on a small LAN or they can be located in different corners of the world. They can communicate over any number of physical connections, including dial-up connections, Integrated Services Digital Network (ISDN) circuits, Ethernet networks, token ring connections, frame relay networks, satellite links, and leased lines.

The benefits of a domain include the following:

- Centralized administration because all user information is stored in the Active Directory database. This centralization allows users to manage only a single user name and password, and enables domain administrators to control which users can access resources on any computer that is a member of the domain.

- A single logon process for users to gain access to network resources (such as file, print, and application resources) for which they have permissions. In other words, you can log on to one computer and use resources on another computer in the network as long as you have appropriate permissions to access the resource.

- Scalability, so that you can create very large networks with hundreds or thousands of computers.

A typical Windows 2003 domain includes the following types of computers:

Domain controllers running Windows Server 2003   Each **domain controller** stores and maintains a copy of Active Directory. In a domain, you create a user account in Active Directory only once. When a user logs on to a computer in the domain, a domain controller authenticates the user by checking the directory for the user name, password, and logon restrictions. When there are multiple domain controllers in a domain, they periodically replicate their directory information so that each domain controller has a copy of Active Directory. Domain controllers do not maintain a local user database.

Member servers running Windows Server 2003   A **member server** is a server that is a member of a domain, but is not configured as a domain controller. A member server does not store directory information and cannot authenticate users. Member servers provide shared resources such as shared folders or printers.

Client computers running Windows XP Professional or Windows 2000 Professional   Client computers run a user's desktop environment and allow the user to gain access to resources in the domain.

Lesson Review

Use the following questions to help determine whether you have learned enough to move on to the next lesson. If you are unable to answer a question, review the lesson materials and try the question again. You can find answers to the questions in the "Questions and Answers" section at the end of this chapter.

1. Which of the following statements about a Windows XP Professional workgroup are correct? Choose all that apply.

   a. A workgroup is also called a peer-to-peer network.

   b. A workgroup is a logical grouping of network computers that share a central directory database.

   c. A workgroup is practical in environments with up to 100 computers.

   d. A workgroup can contain computers running Windows Server 2003 as long as the server is not configured as a domain controller.

2. What is a domain controller?

   _____

   _____

   _____

3. A directory database contains user accounts and security information for the domain and is known as the _____. This directory database is the database portion of _____, which is the Windows 2000 directory service. Fill in the blanks.

4. A(n) _____ provides a single logon for users to gain access to network resources that they have permission to access—such as file, print, and application resources. Fill in the blank.

Lesson Summary

- To explain how workgroups work, you must know the following things:

  - ❏ A Windows XP Professional workgroup is a logical grouping of networked computers that share resources such as files and printers.

  - ❏ A workgroup is referred to as a peer-to-peer network because all computers in the workgroup can share resources as equals (peers) without a dedicated server.

  - ❏ Each computer in the workgroup maintains a local security database, which is a list of user accounts and resource security information for the computer on which it resides.

- To explain how domains work, you must know the following things:

  - ❏ A domain is a logical grouping of network computers that share a central directory database containing user accounts and security information for the domain.

  - ❏ This central directory database, known as the directory, is the database portion of Active Directory service, which is the Windows 2003 directory service.

  - ❏ The computers in a domain can share physical proximity on a small LAN or can be distributed worldwide, communicating over any number of physical connections.

  - ❏ You can designate a computer running Windows Server 2003 as a domain controller. If all computers on the network are running Windows XP Professional, the only type of network available is a workgroup.

Lesson 4: Logging On and Off Windows XP Professional

This lesson explains the Welcome screen and the Enter Password dialog box, which are the two options that you use to log on to Windows XP Professional. It also explains how Windows XP Professional authenticates a user during the logon process. This mandatory authentication process ensures that only valid users can gain access to resources and data on a computer or the network.

After this lesson, you will be able to

- Log on locally to the computer running Windows XP Professional.
- Identify how Windows XP Professional authenticates a user when the user logs on to a local computer or to a domain.
- Create and use a password reset disk to recover a forgotten password.
- Run programs using different credentials than the currently logged-on user.
- Use Fast Logon Optimization.
- Log off or turn off a computer that is running Windows XP Professional.
- Identify the features of the Windows Security dialog box.

Estimated lesson time: 15 minutes

How to Log On Locally to the Computer Running Windows XP Professional

Windows XP Professional offers two options for logging on locally: the Welcome screen and the Log On To Windows dialog box.

The Welcome Screen

By default, if a computer is a member of a workgroup, Windows XP Professional uses the Welcome screen to allow users to log on locally, as shown in Figure 1-6. To log on, click the icon for the user account you want to use. If the account requires a password, you are prompted to enter it. If the account is not password-protected, you are logged on to the computer. You can also use CTRL+ALT+DELETE at the Welcome screen to get the Log On To Windows dialog box. This dialog box enables you to log on to the Administrator account, which is not displayed on the Welcome screen when other user accounts have been created. To use CTRL+ALT+DELETE, you must enter the sequence twice to get the logon prompt.

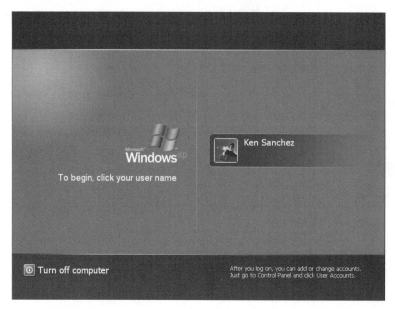

Figure 1-6   The Welcome screen is used by default on computers in workgroups.

> **See Also**   For more information about creating user accounts during installation, see Chapter 2, "Installing Windows XP Professional." For more information about setting up user accounts (including turning on and off the Welcome screen), see Chapter 7, "Setting Up and Managing User Accounts."

A user can log on locally to either of the following:

- A computer that is a member of a workgroup
- A computer that is a member of a domain but is not a domain controller

> **Note**   Because domain controllers do not maintain a local security database, local user accounts are not available on domain controllers. Therefore, a user cannot log on locally to a domain controller.

The User Accounts program in the Control Panel includes a Change The Way Users Log On Or Off task, which allows you to configure Windows XP Professional to use the Log On To Windows dialog box instead of the Welcome screen.

The Log On To Windows Dialog Box

To use the Log On To Windows dialog box (shown in Figure 1-7) to log on locally to a computer running Windows XP Professional, you must supply a valid user name; if the user name is password-protected, you must also supply the password. Windows

XP Professional authenticates the user's identity during the logon process. Only valid users can access resources and data on a computer or a network. Windows XP Professional authenticates users who log on locally to the computer at which they are seated; a domain controller authenticates users who log on to a domain.

Figure 1-7   Use the Log On To Windows dialog box in domains or as an alternative to the Welcome screen.

When a user starts a computer running Windows XP Professional that is configured to use the Log On To Windows dialog box, an Options button also appears. Table 1-1 describes the options in the Log On To Windows dialog box for a computer that is part of a domain.

Table 1-1   Log On To Windows Dialog Box Options

Option	Description
User Name	A unique user logon name that is assigned by an administrator. To log on to a domain with the user name, the user must have an account that resides in the directory.
Password	The password that is assigned to the user account. Users must enter a password to prove their identity. Passwords are case sensitive. For security purposes, the password appears on the screen as asterisks (*). To prevent unauthorized access to resources and data, users must keep passwords secret.
Log On To	Allows the user to choose to log on to the local computer or to log on to the domain.
Log On Using Dial-Up Connection	Permits a user to connect to a domain server by using dial-up networking. Dial-up networking allows a user to log on and perform work from a remote location.
Shutdown	Closes all files, saves all operating system data, and prepares the computer so that a user can safely turn it off.
Options	Toggles on and off between the Log On To option and the Log On Using Dial-Up Connection option. The Options button appears only if the computer is a member of a domain.

> **Note**   If your computer is not part of a domain, the Log On To option is not available.

Windows XP Professional Authentication Process

To gain access to a computer running Windows XP Professional or to any resource on that computer (whether the computer is configured to use the Welcome screen or the Log On To Windows dialog box), you must provide a user name and possibly a password. (You will learn more about using passwords effectively in Chapter 7.)

The way Windows XP Professional authenticates a user depends on whether the user is logging on to a domain or logging on locally to a computer (see Figure 1-8).

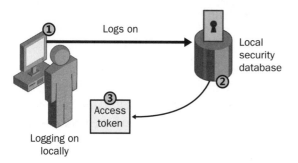

Figure 1-8   Windows XP Professional grants an access token based on user credentials during the authentication process.

The steps in the authentication process are as follows:

1. The user logs on by providing logon credentials—typically user name and password—and Windows XP Professional forwards this information to the security subsystem of that local computer.

2. Windows XP Professional compares the logon credentials with the user information in the local security database, which resides in the security subsystem of the local computer.

3. If the credentials are valid, Windows XP Professional creates an **access token** for the user, which is the user's identification for that local computer. The access token contains the user's security settings, which allow the user to gain access to the appropriate resources on that computer and to perform specific system tasks.

> **Note**   In addition to the logon process, any time a user makes a connection to a computer, that computer authenticates the user and returns an access token. This authentication process is invisible to the user.

If a user logs on to a domain, Windows XP Professional contacts a domain controller in the domain. The domain controller compares the logon credentials with the user information that is stored in Active Directory. If the credentials are valid, the domain controller creates an access token for the user. The security settings contained in the access token allow the user to gain access to the appropriate resources in the domain.

How to Use a Password Reset Disk

A **password reset disk** allows a user to recover a user account when the user forgets his or her password. You create a password reset disk using the Forgotten Password Wizard, which you can start in the following ways:

- If your computer is a member of a domain, press CTRL+ALT+DELETE to open the Windows Security dialog box. Click Change Password, select your local account from the "Log on to" drop down menu, and then click Backup to start the wizard.

- If your computer is in a workgroup, and you are using a computer administrator account, open the User Accounts tool in Control Panel, click your account name, and then click Prevent A Forgotten Password.

- If your computer is in a workgroup, and you are using a limited account, open the User Accounts tool in Control Panel, and in the Relate Tasks section on the left side of the window, click Prevent A Forgotten Password.

No matter which way you start the Forgotten Password Wizard, the wizard walks you through the steps necessary to create a password reset disk. You can store your password reset key on any removable disk, including floppy (in which case you will need one, blank, formatted 1.44 MB floppy disk) and universal serial bus (USB) flash drives.

> **Warning**   You can have only one password reset disk at a time. If you create a new disk, any previous disk becomes invalid.

If you forget your logon password, you can use a password reset disk in one of the following ways:

- If your computer is a member of a domain, simply try to log on to Windows by using an invalid password. In the Logon Failed dialog box that appears, click Reset to start the Password Reset Wizard, which will walk you through the recovery process.

- If your computer is a member of a workgroup, on the Windows XP logon screen, click the user name that you want to use to make the Type Your Password box appear. Press ENTER or click the right arrow button. In the pop-up error message that appears, click Use Your Password Reset Disk to start the Password Reset Wizard.

How to Run Programs with Different User Credentials

Windows XP Professional allows you to run programs using user credentials that are different from the currently logged-on user. Using different credentials is useful if you are troubleshooting a user's computer and do not want to log off and log back on using administrative permissions just to perform a troubleshooting task or run a particular program. Using this method is also more secure than logging on to a user's computer with administrative credentials.

Running a program with different credentials in Windows XP Professional relies on a built-in service named the **Secondary Logon service**. This service must be running (and it is by default on computers running Windows XP) to run a program with alternate credentials.

To determine whether the Secondary Logon service is running (and enable the service if it is not running), follow these steps:

1. Log on to the computer as Administrator or as a user with administrative permissions.

2. From the Start menu, click Control Panel.

3. In the Control Panel window, click Performance and Maintenance.

4. In the Performance and Maintenance window, click Administrative Tools.

5. In the Administrative Tools window, double-click Services.

6. In the Services window, locate the Secondary Logon service on the list of Services.

7. If the status for the Secondary Logon service is listed as Started, the service is enabled, and you can close the Services window. If the status is listed as Manual or Disabled, right-click the Secondary Logon service and click Properties.

8. On the General tab of the Secondary Logon Properties dialog box, on the Startup type drop-down list, click Automatic.

9. In the Service Status section, click Start.

10. Click OK to close the Secondary Logon Properties dialog box, and then close the Services window.

If the Secondary Logon service is running, you can run a program using different user credentials than the currently logged-on user. On the Start menu, right-click the shortcut for the program you want to run. On the shortcut menu, click Run As. In the Run As dialog box that opens, you can run the program as the current user, or you can enter an alternative user name and password. Microsoft recommends logging on with a limited user account and using this technique to run applications that require administrative privileges.

The Purpose of Fast Logon Optimization

Windows XP Professional includes a feature named Fast Logon Optimization. Enabled by default, this feature allows existing users to log on by using cached credentials instead of waiting for the network to become fully initialized before allowing logon. This features enables faster logons from the user perspective. Group Policy and other settings are applied in the background after logon and after the network is initialized.

Fast Logon Optimization is always turned off in the following situations:

- The first time a user logs on to a computer
- When a user logs on using a roaming profile, a home directory, or a user logon script (you will learn more in Chapter 7)

How to Log Off Windows XP Professional

To log off a computer running Windows XP Professional, click Start and then click Log Off. Notice that the Start menu, shown in Figure 1-9, also allows you to turn off the computer.

Figure 1-9   The Start menu provides a way to log off Windows XP Professional.

Features of the Windows Security Dialog Box

The Windows Security dialog box provides information such as the user account currently logged on, and the domain or computer to which the user is logged on. This information is important for users with multiple user accounts, such as a user who has a regular user account as well as a user account with administrative privileges.

If a computer running Windows XP Professional is joined to a domain (or if the Welcome screen is disabled even when the computer is a member of a workgroup), you can access the Windows Security dialog box by pressing CTRL+ALT+DELETE at any time while Windows is running. If the Welcome screen is enabled, pressing CTRL+ALT+DELETE activates Task Manager instead. Figure 1-10 shows the Windows Security dialog box, and Table 1-2 describes the Windows Security dialog box options.

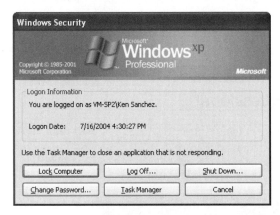

Figure 1-10   Use the Windows Security dialog box for many security activities.

Table 1-2   The Windows Security Dialog Box Options

Option	Description
Lock Computer	Allows users to secure the computer without logging off. All programs remain running. Users should lock their computers when they leave for a short time. The user who locks the computer can unlock it by pressing CTRL+ALT+DELETE and entering the valid password. An administrator can also unlock a locked computer. This process logs off the current user. Whether the Windows Security dialog box is available or not, you can also press WINDOWS KEY+L to immediately lock the computer.
Log Off	Allows a user to log off as the current user and close all running programs, but leaves Windows XP Professional running. You can also log off Windows by choosing Log Off from the Start menu.
Shut Down	Allows a user to close all files, save all operating system data, and prepare the computer so that it can be safely turned off. You can also log off Windows by choosing Turn Off Computer from the Start menu.
Change Password	Allows a user to change his or her user account password. The user must know the current password to create a new one. This is the only way users can change their own passwords. Administrators can also change the password.

Table 1-2   The Windows Security Dialog Box Options

Option	Description
Task Manager	Provides a list of the programs that are running and a summary of overall central processing unit (CPU) and memory usage, as well as a quick view of how each program, program component, or system process is using the CPU and memory resources. Users can also use Task Manager to switch between programs and to stop a program that is not responding. You can also access Task Manager by right-clicking any open space on the taskbar and clicking Task Manager.
Cancel	Closes the Windows Security dialog box.

Practice: Creating a Password Reset Disk

In this practice, you will create a password reset disk. Complete either Exercise 1 or Exercise 2. If you are working on a computer that is a member of a domain, use the steps in Exercise 1 to create the disk. If you are working on a computer that is a member of a workgroup, use the steps in Exercise 2 to create the disk. For either exercise, you will need a blank, formatted, 1.44-MB floppy disk.

Exercise 1: Creating a Password Reset Disk on a Computer That Is a Member of a Domain

1. Log on as the user for whom you are creating a password reset disk.

2. Press CTRL+ALT+DELETE.

3. In the Windows Security dialog box, click Change Password.

4. In the Change Password dialog box, click Backup. If the Backup button does not appear click the "Log on to" drop-down menu and select a "Local Computer" or "This Computer" profile.

5. On the Welcome page of the Forgotten Password Wizard, click Next.

6. On the Create A Password Reset Disk page, make sure that the correct floppy drive is selected; ensure that a blank, formatted, 1.44-MB floppy disk is inserted in the drive; and then click Next.

7. On the Current User Account Password page, type the current password for the account, and then click Next.

8. After Windows writes the key information to the disk, click Next.

9. Click Finish. Remove the disk, label it, and store it in a secure location. If an attacker gains access to this disk, he can log on to your computer without a password.

Exercise 2: Creating a Password Reset Disk on a Computer That Is a Member of a Workgroup

1. Log on as the user for whom you are creating a password reset disk.

2. From the Start menu, click Control Panel.

3. In the Control Panel window, click User Accounts.

4. In the User Accounts window, click the account you want to use if you are logged on as an Administrator. Otherwise, continue to the next step.

5. In the Related Tasks section, click Prevent A Forgotten Password.

6. On the Welcome page of the Forgotten Password Wizard, click Next.

7. On the Create A Password Reset Disk page, make sure that the correct floppy drive is selected; ensure that a blank, formatted, 1.44 MB floppy disk is inserted in the drive; and then click Next.

8. On the Current User Account Password page, type the current password for the account, and then click Next.

9. After Windows writes the key information to the disk, click Next.

10. Click Finish. Remove the disk and label it.

Lesson Review

Use the following questions to help determine whether you have learned enough to move on to the next lesson. If you are unable to answer a question, review the lesson materials and try the question again. You can find answers to the questions in the "Questions and Answers" section at the end of this chapter.

1. What can you do when you log on locally to a computer, and what determines what you can do when you log on locally to a computer?

---

2. What is the main difference in the authentication process for logging on locally to a computer and logging on to a domain?

_____

_____

_____

_____

3. Which of the following computers can a user log on to locally? Choose all that apply.

   a. A computer running Windows XP Professional that is in a workgroup

   b. A computer running Windows XP Professional that is in a domain

   c. A computer running Windows Server 2003 that is configured as a domain controller

   d. A computer running Windows Server 2003 that is a member server in a domain

4. Which of the following statements about the Windows Security dialog box are correct? Choose all that apply.

   a. You can access it by pressing CTRL+ALT+DELETE.

   b. The dialog box tells you how long the current user has been logged on.

   c. The dialog box allows you to log off the computer or domain.

   d. The dialog box allows a user with administrative permissions to change other users' passwords.

Lesson Summary

- By default, Windows XP Professional uses the Welcome screen to allow users to log on locally to the computer. You can configure Windows XP Professional to use the Log On To Windows dialog box instead of the Welcome screen. When a user logs on, she can log on to the local computer; if the computer is a member of a domain, the user can log on to the domain.

- When a user logs on locally, the local computer does the authentication. When a user logs on to a domain, a domain controller must do the authentication. In a workgroup environment, an access token is the user's identification for that local computer, and it contains the user's security settings. These security settings allow the user to gain access to the appropriate resources on that computer and to perform specific system tasks.

- An administrator or a user can create a password reset disk for a user that allows the user to recover a forgotten password and log on to Windows XP Professional.

- Instead of logging on as Administrator, you can specify administrative credentials when you run a program no matter what user account you are logged on with. This provides a way to run programs that requires administrative rights without the risks associated with logging on using an Administrator account.

- Fast Logon Optimization allows existing users to log on by using cached credentials instead of waiting for the network to become fully initialized before allowing logon. This features enables faster logons from the user perspective.

- You can log off Windows XP (and should whenever you leave your computer for an extended period) by using the Log Off command on the Start menu.

- The Windows Security dialog box allows you to lock your computer, change your password, log off your computer, shut down your computer, and access Task Manager.

Case Scenario Exercises

Read the following two scenarios and answer the associated questions. You can use the scenarios to help determine whether you have learned enough to move on to the next chapter. If you have difficulty completing this work, review the material in this chapter before beginning the next chapter. You can find answers to these questions in the "Questions and Answers" section at the end of this chapter.

Scenario 1.1

You are working as an administrator who supports users by telephone. One of your users says that she has recently installed Windows XP Professional on her home computer, which she uses to connect to her company's corporate network. She is used to having to press CTRL+ALT+DELETE to log on to Windows, but instead her new computer shows a Welcome screen with her user name listed. She would feel more comfortable using the Log On To Windows dialog box instead of the Welcome screen. How should you configure the computer?

_____

_____

_____

_____

Scenario 1.2

You are an administrator for a corporate network that runs a Windows Server 2003–based domain. All client workstations run Windows XP Professional. A user complains to you that when he logs on to his computer, his desktop does not look right and he cannot access any network resources. What do you suspect might be the problem?

_____

_____

Troubleshooting Lab

Using what you have learned in this chapter, provide the following information about your own computer:

- What edition of Windows XP are you running?

- Which Service Pack, if any, is applied to your installation of Windows XP? What tools can you use to determine which one you have?

- Is your computer a member of a workgroup or a domain? What is the name of the workgroup or domain?

- If your computer is a member of a domain, can you also log on to your computer locally?

Chapter Summary

- The Windows XP family includes Windows XP Professional Edition, Windows XP Home Edition, Windows XP Media Center Edition, Windows XP Tablet PC Edition, and Windows XP 64-Bit Edition. Features provided in Windows XP Professional that are not provided in Windows XP Home Edition include dynamic disks, Remote Desktop, NTFS and print permissions, EFS, domain membership, dual processors, and IIS.

- You can determine whether Service Pack 2 is installed by viewing the General tab of the System Properties dialog box or by typing **winver.exe** in the Run dialog box to open the About Windows dialog box. Enhancements provided by Service Pack 2 include:

  - ❏ Security Center provides real-time status and alerts for Windows Firewall, Automatic Updates, and some antivirus software.

  - ❏ Enhancements to Automatic Updates allow it to download updates for more Microsoft products, download all types of updates, and prioritize update importance.

❏ Enhancements to Windows Firewall enable the firewall for each connection by default, allow the inspection of traffic from the moment the connection becomes active, and let you make global configuration settings for all connections.

❏ Enhancements to Internet Explorer include a new Information bar that consolidates many user prompts, a pop-up blocker, and better add-on management.

■ A computer running Windows XP Professional can be a member of two types of networks: a workgroup or a domain. You can designate a computer running Windows Server 2003 as a domain controller. If all computers on the network are running Windows XP Professional, the only type of network available is a workgroup. Features of workgroups and domains include:

❏ A Windows XP Professional workgroup is a logical grouping of networked computers that share resources such as files and printers. A workgroup is referred to as a peer-to-peer network because all computers in the workgroup can share resources as equals (peers) without a dedicated server. Each computer in the workgroup maintains a local security database, which is a list of user accounts and resource security information for the computer on which it resides.

❏ A domain is a logical grouping of network computers that share a central directory database containing user accounts and security information for the domain. This central directory database is known as the directory; it is the database portion of Active Directory service, which is the Windows 2003 directory service. The computers in a domain can share physical proximity on a small LAN or can be distributed worldwide, communicating over any number of physical connections.

■ By default, Windows XP Professional uses the Welcome screen to allow users to log on locally to the computer. You can configure Windows XP Professional to use the Log On To Windows dialog box instead of the Welcome screen. When a user logs on, he can log on to the local computer; if the computer is a member of a domain, the user can log on to the domain.

❏ When a user logs on locally, the local computer does the authentication.

❏ When a user logs on to a domain, a domain controller must do the authentication.

Exam Highlights

Before taking the exam, review the key points and terms that are presented in this chapter. You need to know this information.

Key Points

- The new Windows Firewall policy performs packet filtering during Windows startup, meaning that connections are protected from the moment they become active on the network.

- You can designate only a computer running Microsoft Windows 2000 Server or Windows Server 2003 as a domain controller. If all computers on the network are running Windows XP Professional, the only type of network available is a workgroup.

Key Terms

access token   An object that describes the security context for a user. When a user logs on, Windows verifies the user's credentials. After the user is authenticated, Windows assigns an access token that defines the user's rights and permissions.

Active Directory   A directory structure that allows any object on a network to be tracked and located. Active Directory is the directory service used in Windows 2000 Server and Windows Server 2003. Active Directory provides the foundation for Windows-based distributed networks.

Automatic Updates   A Windows service that scans for, downloads, and installs available updates for Windows XP and other Microsoft programs.

domain   A group of computers that consists of servers that maintain centralized security and directory structures, and workstations that participate in those structures.

domain controller   A server in an Active Directory domain that stores a copy of the Active Directory database and runs the Active Directory service.

member server   A server that is a member of an Active Directory domain but is not a domain controller.

password reset disk   A disk that allows a user to recover a user account when the user forgets her password.

Secondary Logon service   A service that allows a user to run a program (by using the Run As command) with credentials different from the currently logged-on user.

Security Center   A software interface that provides at-a-glance security status for a computer, including information on Windows Firewall, Automatic Updates, and antivirus software.

stand-alone server   A computer running Windows Server 2003 or Windows 2000 Server that is a member of a workgroup.

Windows Firewall   A software-based firewall built in to Windows XP Service Pack 2 that replaces the ICF built into Windows XP prior to Service Pack 2.

Windows XP Service Pack 2   An update that includes all the critical updates released for Windows XP to date. In addition, Service Pack 2 includes a large number of new enhancements to Windows XP—enhancements aimed at increasing the default level of security for the operating system.

workgroup   A group of computers that consists of a number of peer-based computers, each of which maintains its own security.

Questions and Answers

Lesson 1 Review

Page
1-6

1. Windows XP _____ Edition and Windows XP _____ Edition are available only on supported hardware devices and are not available as stand-alone products. Fill in the blanks.

Tablet PC and Media Center

2. Which features supported in Windows XP Professional are not supported in Windows XP Home Edition?

Features provided in Windows XP Professional that are not provided in Windows XP Home Edition include dynamic disks, Remote Desktop, NTFS and print permissions, EFS, domain membership, dual processors, and IIS.

Lesson 2 Review

Page
1-14

1. After Windows XP Service Pack 2 is installed, Internet Explorer combines many of the common dialog boxes that prompt users for information into a common area named the _____. Fill in the blanks.

Information bar

2. Which of the following is true of Windows Firewall? Choose all that apply.

  a. Windows Firewall is enabled by default.

  b. Windows Firewall is disabled by default.

  c. Windows Firewall must be configured individually for each connection.

  d. Windows Firewall protects a network connection as soon as the connection is active on the network.

A and D are correct. Windows Firewall is enabled by default and begins protecting a network connection as soon as the connection is active on the network. B is not correct because Windows Firewall is enabled by default. C is not correct because you can configure global settings for Windows Firewall that affect all connections (although you can configure connections individually if you want to).

Lesson 3 Review

Page
1-19

1. Which of the following statements about a Windows XP Professional workgroup are correct? Choose all that apply.

  a. A workgroup is also called a peer-to-peer network.

  b. A workgroup is a logical grouping of network computers that share a central directory database.

   c. A workgroup is practical in environments with up to 100 computers.

   d. A workgroup can contain computers running Windows Server 2003 as long as the server is not configured as a domain controller.

A and D are correct. A is correct because in a workgroup, computers act as equals (or peers), and the arrangement is also called a peer-to-peer network. D is correct because computers running a server product might be part of a workgroup (such computers are called stand-alone servers) as long as no server is acting as a domain controller. B is not correct because each computer in a workgroup maintains its own security database instead of relying on a centralized security database. C is not correct because a workgroup begins to become impractical with more than 10 workstations—not 100 workstations.

2. What is a domain controller?

A domain controller is a computer running Windows 2000 Server that is configured as a domain controller so that it can manage all security-related aspects of user and domain interactions.

3. A directory database contains user accounts and security information for the domain and is known as the _____. This directory database is the database portion of _____, which is the Windows 2000 directory service. Fill in the blanks.

directory, Active Directory service

4. A(n) _____ provides a single logon for users to gain access to network resources that they have permission to access—such as file, print, and application resources. Fill in the blanks.

domain

Lesson 4 Review

Page
1-30

1. What can you do when you log on locally to a computer, and what determines what you can do when you log on locally to a computer?

When you log on locally to a computer, you can access the appropriate resources on that computer and you can perform specific system tasks. What you can do when logged on locally to a computer is determined by the access token assigned to the user account you used to log on. The access token is your identification for that local computer; it contains your security settings. These security settings allow you to access specific resources on that computer and to perform specific system tasks.

2. What is the main difference in the authentication process for logging on locally to a computer and logging on to a domain?

When you log on locally to a computer, its security subsystem uses the local security database to authenticate the user name and password you entered. When you log on to a domain, a domain controller uses the directory to authenticate the user name and password you entered.

3. Which of the following computers can a user log on to locally? Choose all that apply.

   a. A computer running Windows XP Professional that is in a workgroup

   b. A computer running Windows XP Professional that is in a domain

   c. A computer running Windows Server 2003 that is configured as a domain controller

   d. A computer running Windows Server 2003 that is a member server in a domain

   A, B, and D are correct. C is not correct because domain controllers do not maintain a local security database, so you cannot log on locally to a domain controller.

4. Which of the following statements about the Windows Security dialog box are correct? Choose all that apply.

   a. You can access it by pressing CTRL+ALT+DELETE.

   b. The dialog box tells you how long the current user has been logged on.

   c. The dialog box allows you to log off the computer or domain.

   d. The dialog box allows a user with administrative permissions to change other users' passwords.

   A and C are correct. B is not correct because the Windows Security dialog box does not tell you how long you have been logged on. D is not correct because the Windows Security dialog box does not allow you to change other users' passwords.

Case Scenario Exercises: Scenario 1.1

Page 1-32

You are working as an administrator who supports users by telephone. One of your users says that she has recently installed Windows XP Professional on her home computer, which she uses to connect to her company's corporate network. She is used to having to press CTRL+ALT+DELETE to log on to Windows, but instead her new computer shows a Welcome screen with her user name listed. She would feel more comfortable using the Log On To Windows dialog box instead of the Welcome screen. How should you configure the computer?

In the Windows Control Panel, you should open the User Accounts tool. In the User Accounts window, you should click Change The Way Users Log On Or Off, and then clear the Use The Welcome Screen check box.

Case Scenario Exercises: Scenario 1.2

Page
1-33
You are an administrator for a corporate network that runs a Windows Server 2003–based domain. All client workstations run Windows XP Professional. A user complains to you that when he logs on to his computer, his desktop does not look right and he cannot access any network resources. What do you suspect might be the problem?

Most likely, the user is logging on to the workstation locally instead of logging on to the domain.

2 Installing Windows XP Professional

Exam Objectives in this Chapter:

- Perform and troubleshoot an attended installation of Windows XP.
- Upgrade from a previous version of Windows to Windows XP Professional.
  - ❑ Prepare a computer to meet upgrade requirements.
  - ❑ Migrate existing user environments to a new installation.
- Troubleshoot failed installations.

Why This Chapter Matters

This chapter prepares you to install Windows XP Professional. You will learn some preinstallation tasks that help ensure that your installation of Windows XP Professional will go smoothly. These tasks include verifying that your hardware and any software installed on the computer are compatible with Windows XP Professional, determining which file system to use, and deciding whether your computer will join a workgroup or a domain. You will learn about installing Windows XP Professional from a CD-ROM and over the network, and about upgrading from a previous version of Windows. You will learn how to modify an installation using switches and how to troubleshoot failed installations. Finally, you will learn how to perform post-installation tasks such as activating and updating Windows XP.

Lessons in this Chapter:

Before You Begin

To complete this chapter, you must have a computer that meets or exceeds the minimum hardware requirements listed in the preface, "About This Book." You must also have a Windows XP Professional installation CD-ROM.

Lesson 1: Preparing for Installation

When you install Windows XP Professional, the Windows XP Professional Setup program allows you to specify how to install and configure the operating system. Preparing in advance helps you avoid problems during and after installation.

After this lesson, you will be able to

- Verify that your computer meets the minimum hardware requirements for installing Windows XP Professional.
- Verify that hardware is compatible with Windows XP Professional.
- Create a partitioning scheme appropriate for an installation.
- Choose a file system appropriate for an installation.
- Join a domain or workgroup during installation.
- Update installation files using Dynamic Updates.
- Explain how Microsoft grants software licenses.

Estimated lesson time: 70 minutes

Overview of Preinstallation Tasks

Before you start the installation, you should complete the following tasks:

- Ensure that your hardware meets the requirements for installing Windows XP Professional.
- Determine whether your hardware is in the Windows Catalog.
- Decide how you will partition the hard disk on which you will install Windows XP Professional.
- Choose a file system for the installation partition.
- Determine whether your computer will join a domain or a workgroup.
- Complete a preinstallation checklist.

Windows XP Professional Hardware Requirements

Before installing Windows XP Professional, you must determine whether your hardware meets or exceeds the minimum requirements for installing and operating Windows XP Professional, as shown in Table 2-1.

Table 2-1   Windows XP Professional Hardware Requirements

Component	Requirements
Central processing unit (CPU)	Pentium 233 megahertz (MHz) or equivalent.
Memory	64 megabytes (MB) minimum; 128 MB recommended; 4 gigabytes (GB) of random access memory (RAM) maximum.
Hard disk space	1.5 GB of free disk space for installing Windows XP Professional. You should also have several additional gigabytes of hard disk space to allow for updates, additional Windows components, applications, and user data.
Networking	Network adapter card and a network cable, if necessary.
Display	Video display adapter and monitor with Super Video Graphics Adapter (SVGA) resolution or higher.
Other drives	CD-ROM drive, 12X or faster recommended (not required for installing Windows XP Professional over a network), or DVD drive. High-density 3.5-inch disk drive as drive A, unless the computer supports starting the Setup program from a CD-ROM or DVD drive.
Accessories	Keyboard and Microsoft-compatible mouse or other pointing device.

Exam Tip   You should memorize the basic hardware requirements for running Windows XP. A 233 MHz processor, 64 MB RAM, and a 2 GB hard disk with 1.5 GB free space are required.

How to Verify Hardware Compatibility with the Windows Catalog

Although the Windows XP Professional Setup Wizard automatically checks your hardware and software for potential conflicts, before you install Windows XP Professional, you should verify that your hardware is listed in the **Windows Catalog**. Microsoft provides tested drivers for the listed devices only. Using hardware not listed in the Windows Catalog could cause problems during or after installation. To find the Windows Catalog, go to the Windows Catolog page of the Microsoft Web site at *http://www.microsoft.com/windows/catalog/*.

Note   If your hardware is not in the Windows Catalog, the hardware manufacturer might be able to provide you with a Windows XP Professional driver for the component.

What Are Disk Partitions?

The Windows XP Professional Setup program examines the hard disk to determine its existing configuration. Setup then allows you to install Windows XP Professional on an existing partition or to create a new partition on which to install it.

A **disk partition** is a logical section of a hard disk on which the computer can write data. Partitions offer a way to divide the space on a single physical hard disk into multiple areas, each of which is treated as a different disk within Windows. Some people create separate partitions to help organize their files. For example, you might store the Windows system files and application files on one partition, user-created documents on another partition, and backup files on another partition.

Another reason to use multiple partitions is to isolate operating systems from one another when you install more than one operating system on a computer. Although it is technically possible to install some operating systems on the same partition, Microsoft does not recommend or support this practice. You should always create a separate partition for each operating system.

Depending on the hard disk configuration, do one of the following procedures during installation:

- If the hard disk is not partitioned, create and size the Windows XP Professional partition. Unless you have a specific reason to create multiple partitions (such as for multiple operating systems or to have a separate partition for document storage), you should create one partition that uses all available drive space.

- If an existing partition is large enough, install Windows XP Professional on that partition. Installing on an existing partition might overwrite any existing operating system files.

- If the existing partition is not large enough, delete it and combine it with other partitions on the same physical disk to provide more unpartitioned disk space for creating the Windows XP Professional partition.

Although you can use Setup to create other partitions, you should create and size only the partition on which you will install Windows XP Professional. After you install Windows XP Professional, use the Disk Management snap-in of the Computer Management console to partition any remaining unpartitioned space on the hard disk. Disk Management is much easier to use for disk partitioning than Setup. You will learn more about partitions and the Disk Management tool in Chapter 10, "Managing Data Storage."

Guidelines for Choosing a File System

After you create the installation partition, Setup prompts you to select the file system with which to format the partition. Windows XP Professional can be installed on two file systems:

File allocation table (FAT)   Although Windows Setup references only **file allocation table (FAT)**, there are actually two versions of FAT: FAT and FAT32. FAT is a 16-bit file system used in older versions of Windows. FAT32 is a 32-bit file system supported by Windows 95 original equipment manufacturer (OEM) Service Release 2, Windows 98, Windows Me, Windows 2000, and Windows XP.

NTFS   The preferred file system for Windows XP, NTFS provides more security and flexibility than FAT32. Microsoft recommends that you always use NTFS unless there is a specific reason to use another file system (such as when you are installing more than one operating system on a computer and one of those operating systems does not recognize NTFS partitions). NTFS is supported by Windows NT 4.0, Windows 2000, Windows XP, and Windows 2003 Server.

Figure 2-1 summarizes some of the features of these file systems.

- File-level and folder-level security
- Disk compression
- File encryption

- Dual boot configuration support
- No file-level security

Figure 2-1   NTFS offers more features than FAT.

> **Exam Tip**   Unless you are installing Windows XP Professional on a multiple-boot computer that also has an operating system that cannot access NTFS partitions (such as Windows 98), you should always use NTFS.

Using NTFS

Use NTFS when the partition on which Windows XP Professional will reside requires any of the following features:

File- and folder-level security   NTFS allows you to control access to files and folders. For additional information, see Chapter 8, "Securing Resources with NTFS Permissions."

Disk compression   NTFS can compress files to store more data on the partition. For additional information, see Chapter 10.

Disk quota   NTFS allows you to control disk usage on a per-user basis. For additional information, see Chapter 10.

Encryption   NTFS allows you to encrypt file data on the physical hard disk by using the Microsoft Encrypting File System (EFS). For additional information, see Chapter 10.

The version of NTFS in Windows XP Professional supports remote storage, dynamic volumes, and mounting volumes to folders. Windows XP Professional, Windows Server 2003, Windows 2000, and Windows NT are the only operating systems that can access data on a local hard disk formatted with NTFS.

FAT and FAT32

FAT and FAT32 offer compatibility with other operating systems. You must format the system partition with either FAT or FAT32 if you will dual boot Windows XP Professional and another operating system that requires FAT or FAT32.

FAT and FAT32 do not offer many of the features (for example, file-level security) that NTFS supports. Therefore, in most situations, you should format the hard disk with NTFS. The only reason to use FAT or FAT32 is for dual booting with an older operating system that does not support NTFS. If you are setting up a computer for dual booting, you need to format the boot partition that contains the older version of Windows with FAT or FAT32. For example, if drive C is the boot partition that holds Windows 98, you could format drive C as FAT or FAT32. You should then format the boot partition that will hold Windows XP as NTFS. Finally, for multiple booting to be successful, the system partition must be formatted using a file system that all installed operating systems can access. For example, if you are dual-booting between Windows XP and Windows 95, the system partition (as well as the boot partition on which Windows 95 is installed) would have to be formatted with FAT.

Converting a FAT or FAT32 Volume to NTFS

Windows XP Professional provides the Convert command for converting a partition to NTFS without reformatting the partition and losing all the information on the partition. To use the Convert command, click Start, click Run, type **cmd** in the Open text box, and then click OK. This opens a command prompt, which you use to request the Convert command. The following example shows how you might use switches with the Convert command.

```
Convert volume /FS:NTFS [/V] [/CvtArea:filename] [/NoSecurity] [/X]
```

Table 2-2 lists the switches available in the Convert command and describes their functions.

Table 2-2   Convert Command Switches

Switch	Function	Required
Volume	Specifies the drive letter (followed by a colon), volume mount point, or volume name that you want to convert	Yes
/FS:NTFS	Specifies converting the volume to NTFS	Yes
/V	Runs the Convert command in verbose mode	No
/CvtArea:*filename*	Specifies a contiguous file in the root directory to be the placeholder for NTFS system files	No
/NoSecurity	Sets the security settings to make converted files and directories accessible by everyone	No
/X	Forces the volume to dismount first, if necessary, and all open handles to the volume are then not valid	No

If you convert a system volume (or any volume that has files that are currently in use), the Convert command might not be able to convert the drive right away. Instead, Windows schedules the conversion to happen the next time Windows is restarted.

> **Note**   For help with any command-line program, at the command prompt, type the command followed by **/?** and then press ENTER. For example, to receive help on the Convert command, type **Convert /?** and then press ENTER.

Guidelines for Choosing Domain or Workgroup Membership

During installation, you must choose the type of network security group that the computer will join: a domain or a workgroup. Figure 2-2 shows the requirements for joining a domain or workgroup.

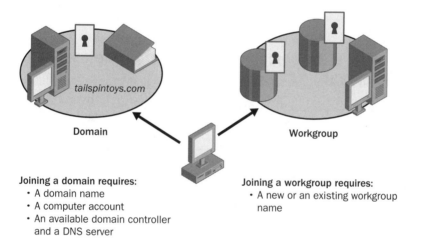

Joining a domain requires:
- A domain name
- A computer account
- An available domain controller and a DNS server

Joining a workgroup requires:
- A new or an existing workgroup name

Figure 2-2   Joining a domain requires more planning than joining a workgroup.

Joining a Domain

When you install Windows XP Professional on a computer, you can add that computer to an existing domain. Adding a computer to a domain is referred to as joining a domain. You can join a computer to a domain during or following installation. Joining a domain during installation requires the following:

Domain name   Ask the domain administrator for the Domain Name System (DNS) name for the domain that the computer will join. An example of a DNS-compatible domain name is *microsoft.com*, in which *microsoft* is the name of the organization's DNS identity.

Computer account   Before a computer can join a domain, you must create a computer account in the domain. You can ask a domain administrator to create the computer account before installation or, if you have been assigned the Add Workstations To Domain right, you can create the computer account during installation. If you create the computer account during installation, Setup prompts you for the name and password of a user account with authority to add domain computer accounts.

Available domain controller and a server running the DNS service (called the DNS server)   At least one domain controller in the domain that you are joining and one DNS server must be online when you install a computer in the domain.

Joining a Workgroup

When you install Windows XP Professional on a computer, you can add that computer to an existing workgroup. This process is referred to as joining a workgroup.

You can join a computer to a workgroup during installation simply by assigning a workgroup name to the computer. The workgroup name you assign can be the name of an existing workgroup or the name of a new workgroup that you create during installation.

How to Ensure You Have the Necessary Information Before Installing Windows XP Professional

Complete the following preinstallation checklist to ensure that you have all the necessary information available before you begin installing Windows XP Professional.

Task	Done
Verify that your components meet the minimum hardware requirements.	❑
Verify that all your hardware is listed in the Windows Catalog.	❑
Verify that the hard disk on which you will install Windows XP Professional has a minimum of 1.5 GB of free disk space.	❑
Select the file system for the Windows XP Professional partition. Format this partition with NTFS unless you need to dual boot operating systems with an operating system that requires a FAT partition.	❑
Determine the name of the domain or workgroup that each computer will join. If the computer joins a domain, write down the domain name in the DNS format: *server.subdomain.domain*. If the computer joins a workgroup, use the 15-character NetBIOS naming convention: *Server_name*.	❑
Determine the name of the computer before installation. If TCP/IP is installed on your computer, the maximum length for the computer name you can specify during installation is 63 characters.	❑
If the computer will join a domain, create a computer account in that domain. You can create a computer account during installation if you have been granted the Add Workstations To Domain right.	❑
Determine a password for the Administrator account.	❑

How Microsoft Grants Software Licenses

A software license grants a user the right to run an application. Microsoft grants software licenses in one of three ways:

Full Packaged Product   A Full Packaged Product is boxed software like you would buy in a retail store. Full Packaged Products are intended for consumers who need to purchase a small quantity of software licenses. When you install the Full Packaged Product version of Windows XP Professional, Setup asks you to enter a product ID (a 25-digit code found on the product packaging) during installation. You must also activate Windows XP Professional after installation.

Original Equipment Manufacturer or System Builder   Original Equipment Manufacturer (OEM) and System Builder licenses are acquired when you buy a computer that already has software installed. Typically, you do not have to activate this type of license.

Volume Licensing   Microsoft Volume Licensing programs are intended for consumers who need to purchase large quantities of software licenses, such as in a small business or corporate environment. When a company has a volume license for Windows XP Professional, the installation files are typically made available for installation over the network. Product IDs and product activation are not required.

Practice: Prepare for Installation

In this practice, you will determine whether your computer meets the minimum requirements specified by Microsoft to run Windows XP Professional and whether the hardware in your computer is in the Windows Catalog. Complete the two exercises that follow.

Exercise 1: Gather Information About Your Computer

1. From the Start menu, click Run.

2. In the Run dialog box, type **msinfo32** and click OK.

3. The System Information utility opens to show a summary of your system. Use this information to fill out the following table and determine whether your computer meets the minimum hardware requirements.

Component	Minimum Required	Your Computer
CPU	233 MHz Pentium- or AMD-compatible	
Memory	64 MB RAM	
Hard disk space	2GB hard disk with 1.5 GB free disk space	
Display	Super Video Graphics Array (SVGA)–compatible (800 x 600)	
Input devices	Keyboard and Microsoft mouse (or other pointing device)	
Other	CD-ROM or DVD-ROM	

Exercise 2: Verify Your Hardware in the Windows Catalog

1. Locate the documentation that came with your computer, including any information about the motherboard, expansion cards, network adapters, video display adapters, and sound cards.

2. Compare your findings with those in the Windows Catalog.

3. If any of your current hardware is not on the list, contact the manufacturer to determine whether Windows XP supports the product.

Lesson Review

Use the following questions to help determine whether you have learned enough to move on to the next lesson. If you have difficulty answering these questions, review the material in this lesson before beginning the next lesson. You can find answers to these questions in the "Questions and Answers" section at the end of this chapter.

1. What are the minimum and recommended memory requirements for installing Windows XP Professional?

_____

_____

2. What is the minimum hard disk space required for installing Windows XP Professional? Choose the correct answer.

   a. 500 MB

   b. 1 GB

   c. 1.5 GB

   d. 2 GB

3. What information is required when joining a domain during the Windows XP Professional installation? Choose all that apply.

   a. You must know the DNS name for the domain the computer will join.

   b. You must have a user account in the domain.

   c. At least one domain controller in the domain must be online when you install a computer in the domain.

   d. At least one DNS server must be online when you install a computer in the domain.

4. Which of the following statements about file systems are correct? Choose all that apply.

   a. File- and folder-level security is available only with NTFS.

   b. Disk compression is available with FAT, FAT32, and NTFS.

   c. Dual booting between Windows 98 and Windows XP Professional is available only with NTFS.

   d. Encryption is available only with NTFS.

Lesson Summary

- The first preinstallation task is to ensure that your hardware meets the hardware requirements for installing Windows XP Professional.

- The next preinstallation task is to ensure that your hardware is in the Windows Catalog. Additional preinstallation tasks include determining how to partition the hard disk on which you will install Windows XP Professional and deciding whether to format the partition as NTFS, FAT, or FAT32.

- Your computer can join a domain or a workgroup during or after installation.

Lesson 2: Installing Windows XP Professional from a CD-ROM

This lesson covers the four-stage process of installing Windows XP Professional from a CD-ROM. After you learn about these four stages, you will install Windows XP Professional on your computer.

After this lesson, you will be able to

- Describe the Windows XP Professional setup process
- Initiate text mode setup
- Run the setup wizard
- Install Windows XP Professional networking components
- Explain how the installation process is completed
- Describe the purpose of the Dynamic Update feature

Estimated lesson time: 70 minutes

Overview of Windows XP Professional Setup

The installation process for Windows XP Professional combines the Setup program with wizards and informational screens. Installing Windows XP Professional from a CD-ROM to a clean hard disk consists of these four stages:

Text mode setup   During the text mode phase of installation, Setup prepares the hard disk for the later installation stages and copies the files necessary to run the Setup Wizard.

Setup Wizard   The Setup Wizard requests setup information about the computer, such as names, and passwords.

Network setup   After gathering information about the computer, the Setup Wizard prompts you for networking information and then installs the networking components that allow the computer to communicate with other computers on the network.

Completing the installation   Setup copies files to the hard disk and configures the computer. The system restarts after installation is complete.

The following sections cover the four stages in more detail.

How to Initiate Text Mode Setup

If a computer's basic input/output system (BIOS) supports booting directly from CD-ROM, you can initiate text mode setup by inserting the Windows XP Professional installation CD-ROM in your CD-ROM drive and starting your computer. If a computer does not support booting from CD, you can create a set of floppy disks that will start the computer and then initiate setup from the CD. After the installation has started, this method proceeds just like booting from CD.

See Also   Microsoft makes the tools for creating boot floppy disks for Windows XP Professional Edition and Windows XP Home Edition available for download. Visit *http:// www.microsoft.com/downloads* and search by using the keywords **Windows XP boot floppy** to locate these utilities.

If a computer is already running a previous version of Windows, you can simply insert the Windows XP installation CD and use a setup wizard to begin the installation. Setup gives you the choice of upgrading the existing operating system or performing a clean installation.

Figure 2-3 shows the six steps involved in the text mode stage of Setup.

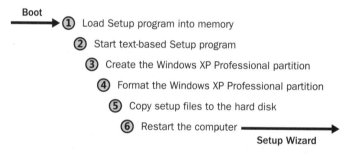

Figure 2-3   There are six steps in the text mode stage of Setup.

Running the Setup program involves the following steps:

1. After the computer starts, a minimal version of Windows XP Professional is copied into memory. This version of Windows XP Professional starts the Setup program.

2. Setup then starts the text mode portion of Setup, which loads storage device drivers and then prompts you to read and accept a licensing agreement. If you have a storage device for which Windows XP does not provide drivers, you can press F6 during the initial setup and supply drivers for your device.

3. Setup prompts you to select the partition on which to install Windows XP Professional, as shown in Figure 2-4. You can select an existing partition or create a new partition by using unpartitioned space on the hard disk.

```
Windows XP Professional Setup

   The following list shows the existing partitions and
   unpartitioned space on this computer.

   Use the UP and DOWN ARROW keys to select an item in the list.

        • To set up Windows XP on the selected item, press ENTER.

        • To create a partition in the unpartitioned space, press C.

        • To delete the selected partition, press D.

   4095 MB Disk 0 at Id 0 on bus 0 on atapi [MBR]

        Unpartitioned space                  4095 MB




   ENTER=Install   C=Create Partition   F3=Quit
```

Figure 2-4   Select the partition on which to install Windows XP Professional.

4. Setup prompts you to select a file system for the new partition. Next, Setup formats the partition with the selected file system.

5. Setup copies files to the hard disk and saves configuration information.

6. Setup restarts the computer and then starts the Windows XP Professional Setup Wizard, the graphical user interface (GUI) portion of Setup. By default, the Setup Wizard installs the Windows XP Professional operating system files in the C:\Windows folder.

How to Run the Setup Wizard

The graphical Windows XP Professional Setup Wizard leads you through the next stage of the installation process. It gathers information about you, your organization, and your computer, including the following information:

Regional settings   Customize language, locale, and keyboard settings. You can configure Windows XP Professional to use multiple languages and regional settings.

> **See Also**   You can add another language or change the locale and keyboard settings after installation is complete. For more information, see Chapter 5, "Configuring Windows XP Professional."

Name and organization   Enter the name of the person and the organization to which this copy of Windows XP Professional is licensed.

Computer name   Enter a computer name of up to 15 characters. The computer name must be different from other computer, workgroup, or domain names on the network. The Setup Wizard displays a default name (the organization name you entered earlier in the process).

> **Note**   To change the computer name after installation is complete, click Start, click My Computer, and then click View System Information. In the System Properties dialog box, click the Computer Name tab, and then click Change.

Password for Administrator account   Specify a password for the Administrator user account, which the Setup Wizard creates during installation. The Administrator account provides the administrative privileges required to manage the computer. Securely store this password in case you or another administrator at your organization needs to use it later to access the computer.

Time and date   Select the time zone, adjust the date and time settings if necessary, and determine whether you want Windows XP Professional to automatically adjust for daylight-savings time.

After you complete this step, the Setup Wizard starts to install the Windows networking components.

How to Install Windows XP Professional Networking Components

After gathering information about your computer, the Setup Wizard guides you through installing the Windows XP Professional networking components, as shown in Figure 2-5.

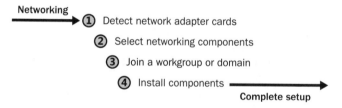

Figure 2-5   The Setup Wizard installs Windows networking components.

Installing Windows XP Professional networking components involves the following steps:

1. Detect network adapter cards.

   The Windows XP Professional Setup Wizard detects and configures any network adapter cards installed on the computer. After configuring network adapters, it attempts to locate a server running the Dynamic Host Configuration Protocol (DHCP) service (called the DHCP server) on the network.

2. Select networking components.

   The Setup Wizard prompts you to choose typical or customized settings for the networking components it installs. The typical installation includes the following options:

❑ **Client For Microsoft Networks**   Allows your computer to access network resources.

❑ **File And Printer Sharing For Microsoft Networks**   Allows other computers to access file and print resources on your computer.

❑ **QoS Packet Scheduler**   Helps provide a guaranteed delivery system for network traffic, such as Transmission Control Protocol/Internet Protocol (TCP/IP) packets.

❑ **Internet Protocol (TCP/IP)**   Allows your computer to communicate over local area networks (LANs) and wide area networks (WANs). TCP/IP is the default networking protocol.

Note   You can install other clients, services, and network protocols during the Windows XP Professional installation; or you can wait until after the installation has completed. You will learn more about networking with TCP/IP in Chapter 13, "Supporting TCP/IP."

3. Join a workgroup or domain.

If you choose to join a domain for which you have sufficient privileges, you can create the computer account during installation. The Setup Wizard prompts you for the name and password of a user account with authority to add domain computer accounts.

Note   To change the domain or workgroup for your computer after you have installed Windows XP Professional, click Start, click My Computer, click View System Information, click the Computer Name tab, and then click Change.

4. Install components.

The Setup Wizard installs and configures the Windows networking components you selected.

How the Installation Is Completed

After installing the networking components, the Setup Wizard automatically starts the final step in the installation process. (See Figure 2-6.)

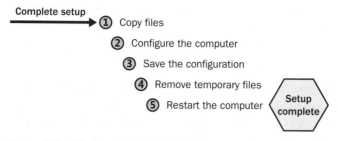

Figure 2-6   Windows completes the installation with these steps.

To complete the installation, the Setup Wizard performs the following tasks:

Installs Start menu items   The Setup Wizard sets up shortcuts that will appear on the Start menu.

Registers components   The Setup Wizard applies the configuration settings that you specified earlier.

Saves the configuration   The Setup Wizard saves your configuration settings to the local hard disk. The next time you start Windows XP Professional, the computer uses this configuration automatically.

Removes temporary files   To save hard disk space, the Setup Wizard deletes any files used for installation only.

Restarts the computer   The Setup Wizard restarts the computer. This finishes the installation.

What Is Dynamic Update?

Dynamic Update is a feature of the Windows XP Professional Setup program that allows you to download updated files that are used during the installation of Windows XP. Setup uses Dynamic Update to query the Windows Update site prior to installing Windows XP to obtain the following files:

Critical Updates   Setup downloads any available replacements for files on the Windows XP Professional installation CD.

Device Drivers   Setup also downloads any available hardware driver replacement files for drivers found on the Windows XP Professional installation CD.

To use Dynamic Update during Setup, your computer must have a working Internet connection. For this reason, Dynamic Update is available only when you start a clean installation or upgrade from within an existing installation of Windows. When Setup asks whether it should look for updates, click Yes to have Setup search for and install available updates.

Dynamic Update is also enabled by default during unattended installations. You will learn more about unattended installations in Chapter 3, "Deploying Windows XP Professional."

Important   Setup does not use Dynamic Update to download any updates that are not already included on the installation CD, so even if you use Dynamic Update, you should still use the Windows Update site or the Windows Automatic Updates feature to obtain critical updates following installation. You will learn more about updating Windows in Lesson 6, "Activating and Updating Windows XP Professional."

Practice: Installing Windows XP Professional

In this practice, you install Windows XP Professional. In Exercise 1, you will install Windows XP Professional from a CD-ROM onto a computer that contains no partitions or operating systems by booting the computer using the CD-ROM. If your computer does not boot from a CD-ROM or if there is already an operating system loaded on your computer, go to Exercise 2 to install Windows XP Professional from a CD-ROM without having to boot from the Windows XP Professional installation CD-ROM.

Exercise 1: Installing Windows XP Professional from a CD-ROM

1. Make sure that your computer is set up to start from the CD-ROM drive. If you are not sure how to do this, consult your computer documentation for information about accessing the BIOS settings.

2. Insert the Windows XP Professional installation CD into your CD-ROM drive and restart the computer. When the computer restarts, the text mode portion of the installation begins.

   During this time, you will be asked if you need to install any third-party drivers. You only have a few seconds to press the F6 key and install the drivers before the installation continues.

Note   Some computers will require you to press a key to boot from the CD-ROM drive. If you are prompted to press any key to boot from the CD, press the spacebar.

3. Windows loads a number of files needed for setup, and the Welcome To Setup screen appears after a few minutes. You can use this screen to set up Windows XP or to repair an existing installation. Press ENTER to continue with the installation.

4. The Windows XP Licensing Agreement appears. After reading the terms of the license, press F8 to accept the terms and continue the installation. If you do not accept the agreement, Setup does not continue.

5. After you accept the Licensing Agreement, Setup proceeds to the Disk Partitioning portion. If you have multiple partitions, Setup will list them and allow you to you choose which one to install XP Professional to. If you have no partitions configured, you can create one at this point.

6. After you have determined which partition to install to, press ENTER to continue.

7. The Format screen appears, which is where you decide how the drive should be formatted (FAT or NTFS). Select Format The Partition Using The NTFS File System and press ENTER.

> **Caution**   If you are planning on dual booting your computer with an operating system that does not support NTFS, your C drive cannot be formatted with NTFS. You might want to install Windows XP Professional in a different drive and format that drive with NTFS.

8. Setup displays a screen warning that formatting the disk will delete all files from it. Press F to format the drive and continue.

9. After the format process is complete, Setup copies the files needed to complete the next phase of the install process and then restarts the computer.

10. After the computer restarts, Setup enters the GUI mode portion of the installation.

11. Setup continues the installation for several minutes, and then displays the Regional And Language Options page. Make sure that the settings are correct for your area, and then click Next.

12. The Personalize Your Software page appears. Fill in the appropriate information and click Next.

13. The Product Key entry page appears. Enter the 25-digit product ID and click Next.

14. The Computer Name And Administrator Password page appears. Enter a name for your computer, choose a password for the Administrator account, and click Next.

15. The Date And Time Settings page appears. Make sure that the information is correct for your area and click Next.

    If Setup detects an installed network adapter, Setup will install network components next.

16. The Network Settings page appears. You should select the Typical Settings option if you want Setup to automatically configure networking components. Typical components include Client For Microsoft Networks, File And Print Sharing For Microsoft Networks, QoS Packet Scheduler, and TCP/IP. Click Next.

17. After you choose the network settings, Setup displays the Workgroup Or Computer Domain name page. Enter the appropriate information and click Next.

18. After you click Next in the Workgroup Or Computer Domain page, Setup continues with the final portion of the installation. It might take from 15 to 60 minutes for the process to finish. When the installation is complete, the computer restarts and you are prompted to log on for the first time.

Exercise 2: Installing Windows XP Professional from an Existing Operating System

If your computer does not boot from a CD-ROM, or if there is already an operating system loaded on your computer, you can install Windows XP Professional from a CD-ROM without having to boot from the Windows XP Professional installation CD-ROM.

> **Important** If you have completed Exercise 1, do not do this practice.

1. If there is an operating system currently installed on your computer, start the computer, log on as an administrator, and insert the Windows XP Professional CD-ROM into the CD-ROM drive.

2. When the Welcome To Microsoft Windows XP page appears, click Install Windows XP.

3. If you see a Windows Setup message box indicating that the version of the operating system cannot be upgraded and that option to upgrade will not be available, click OK.

4. On the Welcome To Setup page in the Installation Type box, click New Installation (Advanced), and then click Next.

5. On the License Agreement page, read the license agreement, select I Accept This Agreement, and then click Next.

6. On the Your Product Key page, type in your 25-character product key, and then click Next.

7. The Setup Options page allows you to configure the following three options:

   ❑ **Advanced Options** Allows you to control where the installation files are obtained, where the installation files are copied to, whether or not to copy all installation files to the hard disk, and whether or not you want to specify the drive letter and partition during Setup.

   ❑ **Accessibility Options** Gives you the option of using the Microsoft Magnifier during Setup to display an enlarged portion of the screen in a separate window for users with limited vision and the option of using the Microsoft Narrator to read the contents of the screen for users who are blind.

   ❑ **Select The Primary Language And Region You Want To Use** Allows you to specify the primary language and region you use.

8. After you have configured any required Setup options, click Next.

9. Setup displays the Get Updated Setup Files dialog box. If your computer has access to the Internet, you might want to ensure that the Yes, Download The Updated Setup Files (Recommended) check box is selected, and then click Next. Otherwise, select No, Skip This Step And Continue Installing Windows, and then click Next.

10. If your partition is not currently formatted with Windows XP Professional NTFS, the Setup Wizard displays the Upgrade To The Windows NTFS File System page.

   If you get the Upgrade To The Windows NTFS File System page, ensure that Yes, Upgrade My Drive is selected, and then click Next.

> **Caution**   If you plan to dual boot your computer with an operating system that does not support NTFS, your C drive cannot be formatted with NTFS. You might want to install Windows XP Professional in a different drive, and then format that drive with NTFS. If you install Windows XP Professional on a drive other than the C drive, you must be sure you are using the correct drive for the rest of the practices in the training kit.

11. If you are installing an Evaluation Edition of Windows XP Professional, the Setup Wizard displays the Setup Notification page, informing you that this is an evaluation version. If Setup displays the Setup Notification screen, press ENTER to continue.

12. On the Welcome To Setup page, press ENTER to install Windows XP Professional.

> **Note**   You can also delete partitions at this time. If you have a C partition, you might not be able to delete it because Setup has already loaded some files onto it. The partition you choose to use must be at least 2000 MB in size. If you cannot use the C partition to install Windows XP Professional, you must replace the C partition in all following practices in this training kit with the appropriate partition, the one on which you install Windows XP Professional.

13. The Setup Wizard prompts you to select an area of free space on an existing partition to install Windows XP Professional. Select the C partition.

   The Setup Wizard displays the following message: You Chose To Install Windows XP On A Partition That Contains Another Operating System. Installing Windows XP Professional On This Partition Might Cause The Other Operating System To Function Improperly.

14. Press C to have Setup continue and use this partition.

Caution Depending on the operating system currently installed on the C partition, Setup might display the following message: A Windows Folder Already Exists That May Contain A Windows Installation. If You Continue, The Existing Windows Installation Will Be Overwritten. If You Want To Keep Both Operating Systems, Press Esc And Specify A Different Folder To Use.

15. If you get a warning about a Windows folder already existing, press L to use the folder and delete the installation in it.

    If your partition was not formatted with NTFS and you choose to have the partition formatted as NTFS, Setup formats it as NTFS, and then copies files. Otherwise, Setup examines the partition and then copies files.

16. The Setup Wizard reboots the computer and continues to copy files in GUI mode, after which it displays the Regional And Language Options page. Select the appropriate system locale, user locale, and keyboard layout (or ensure that they are correct for your language and location), and then click Next.

17. Setup displays the Personalize Your Software page, prompting you for your name and your organization name. The Setup Wizard uses your organization name to generate the default computer name.

    Many applications that you install later will use this information for product registration and document identification. In the Name text box, type your name. In the Organization text box, type the name of your organization, and then click Next.

18. The Setup Wizard displays the Computer Name And Administrator Password page. Type a name for the computer in the Computer Name text box.

Caution If your computer is on a network, check with the network administrator before assigning a name to your computer.

19. In the Administrator Password text box and in the Confirm Password text box, type a password, and then click Next.

20. Depending on your computer configuration, the Setup Wizard might display the Modem Dialing Information page. Configure the following information:

    ❑ Ensure that the correct country or region is selected.

    ❑ Type the correct area code or city code.

    ❑ If you dial a number to get an outside line, type the number.

    ❑ Ensure that the correct dialing tone is selected, and then click Next.

21. The Setup Wizard displays the Date And Time Settings page. If necessary, select the time zone for your location from the Time Zone drop-down list, and adjust the date and the time. Ensure that the Automatically Adjust Clock For Daylight Saving

Changes check box is selected if you want Windows XP Professional to automatically adjust the time on your computer for daylight savings time, and then click Next.

22. Ensure that Typical Settings is selected, and then click Next.

23. On the Workgroup Or Computer Domain page, ensure that the No, This Computer Is Not On A Network, Or Is On A Network Without A Domain option is selected, make sure that the workgroup name is Workgroup, and then click Next.

24. The Setup Wizard configures the networking components and then copies files, installs Start menu items, registers components, saves settings, and removes temporary files. This process takes several minutes.

25. The computer restarts, and Windows XP Professional starts for the first time.

Lesson Review

Use the following questions to help determine whether you have learned enough to move on to the next lesson. If you have difficulty answering these questions, review the material in this lesson before beginning the next lesson. You can find answers to these questions in the "Questions and Answers" section at the end of this chapter.

1. If TCP/IP is installed on your computer, what is the maximum length for the computer name you specify during installation?

   _____

2. Can you change the computer name after installation without having to reinstall Windows XP Professional? If you can change the name, how do you do it? If you cannot change the name, why not?

   _____

   _____

3. Which of the following statements about joining a workgroup or a domain are correct? Choose all that apply.

   a. You can add your computer to a workgroup or a domain only during installation.

   b. If you add your computer to a workgroup during installation, you can join the computer to a domain later.

   c. If you add your computer to a domain during installation, you can join the computer to a workgroup later.

   d. You cannot add your computer to a workgroup or a domain during installation.

4. When you install networking components with typical settings, what components are installed? What does each component do?

_____

_____

_____

_____

_____

_____

Lesson Summary

■ If your computer does not support booting from a CD-ROM, you can install Windows XP Professional by booting another operating system first and then accessing the Windows XP Professional installation CD-ROM.

■ The Setup Wizard asks you to provide regional settings, your name and your organization's name, a computer name, and a password for the Administrator account. It also asks you to specify the time zone, time, and date; and to decide whether you want Windows XP Professional to automatically adjust for daylight savings time.

■ Choosing to install networking components using typical settings installs the Client For Microsoft Networks, File And Printer Sharing For Microsoft Networks, and TCP/IP.

■ You can customize the networking components during installation or any time after installation.

Lesson 3: Installing Windows XP Professional over the Network

You can install Windows XP Professional over the network. This lesson discusses the similarities and differences between installing from a CD-ROM and installing over the network. The major difference is the location of the source files needed for installation. This lesson also lists the requirements for an over-the-network installation.

After this lesson, you will be able to

- Prepare for a network installation
- Install Windows XP Professional over a network
- Modify the setup process using Winnt.exe
- Modify the setup process using Winnt32.exe

Estimated lesson time: 10 minutes

How to Prepare for a Network Installation

In a network installation, the Windows XP Professional installation files are located in a shared location on a network file server, which is called a distribution server. From the computer on which you want to install Windows XP Professional (the target computer), you connect to the distribution server, and then run the Setup program.

Figure 2-7 shows the requirements for a network installation.

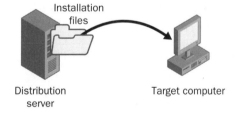

Distribution
server

Target computer

Requirements for a network installation:
- Distribution server
- FAT partition on the target computer
- Network client

Figure 2-7   A network client contacts a distribution server for installation files.

Installing Windows XP Professional requires you to do the following:

1. Locate a distribution server. The distribution server contains the installation files from the I386 folder on the Windows XP Professional CD-ROM. These files reside in a common network location in a shared folder that allows computers on the network to access the installation files. Contact a network administrator to obtain the path to the installation files on the distribution server.

> **Note**   After you have created or located a distribution server, you can use the over-the-network installation method to concurrently install Windows XP Professional on multiple computers.

2. Create a FAT partition on the target computer. The target computer requires a formatted partition to copy the installation files to. Create a partition containing at least 1.5 GB of disk space or more, and format it with the FAT file system.

3. Install a network client. A network client is software that allows the target computer to connect to the distribution server. On a computer without an operating system, you must boot from a client disk that includes a network client that enables the target computer to connect to the distribution server.

How to Install over the Network

The Setup program copies the installation files to the target computer and creates the Setup boot disks. After Setup copies the installation files, you start the installation on the target computer by booting from the Setup boot disks. From this point, you install Windows XP Professional as you would from a CD-ROM.

Figure 2-8 shows the process for installing Windows XP Professional over the network.

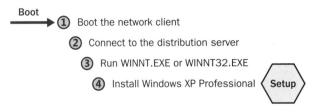

Figure 2-8   Install Windows XP Professional over the network.

Installing Windows XP Professional over the network involves the following steps:

1. Boot the network client.

    On the target computer, boot from a floppy disk that includes a network client or start another operating system that can be used to connect to the distribution server.

2. Connect to the distribution server.

    After you start the network client on the target computer, connect to the shared folder on the distribution server that contains the Windows XP Professional installation files.

3. Run Winnt.exe or Winnt32.exe to start the Setup program.

    Winnt.exe and Winnt32.exe reside in the shared folder on the distribution server.

    ❑ Use Winnt.exe for an installation using MS-DOS or Windows 3.0 or later versions on the source system.

    ❑ Use Winnt32.exe for an installation using Windows 95, Windows 98, Windows Me, Windows NT 4.0, or Windows 2000 Professional.

Exam Tip   You can use Winnt.exe and Winnt32.exe to install Windows XP Professional from the command line, using optional parameters to modify the installation. Winnt.exe runs under MS-DOS and Windows 3.0/3.1. Winnt32.exe runs under the 32-bit Windows operating systems such as Windows 95, Windows 98, Windows Me, Windows NT 4.0, and Windows 2000.

Running Winnt.exe or Winnt32.exe from the shared folder does the following:

❑ Creates the Win_nt.~ls temporary folder on the target computer

❑ Copies the Windows XP Professional installation files from the shared folder on the distribution server to the Win_nt.~ls folder on the target computer

4. Install Windows XP Professional.

Setup restarts the local computer and begins installing Windows XP Professional.

How to Modify the Setup Process Using Winnt.exe

You can modify an over-the-network installation by changing how Winnt.exe runs Setup. Table 2-3 lists the parameters you can use with Winnt.exe and describes their functions.

Table 2-3   Winnt.exe Parameters

Switch	Function
/a	Enables accessibility options.
/r[:*folder*]	Specifies an optional folder to be copied and saved. The folder remains after Setup finishes.
/rx[:*folder*]	Specifies the optional folder to be copied. The folder is deleted after Setup finishes.
/s[:*sourcepath*]	Specifies the source location of Windows XP Professional files. This must be a full path of the form *x*:\[*path*] or *server**share*\[*path*]. The default is the current folder location.
/t[:*tempdrive*]	Specifies a drive to contain temporary setup files and directs Setup to install Windows XP Professional on that drive. If you do not specify a drive, Setup attempts to locate the drive with the most available space.
/u[:*script_file*]	Performs an unattended installation by using an optional script file. Unattended installations also require using the /s switch. The answer file provides answers to some or all of the prompts that the end user normally responds to during Setup.
/udf:id[,*UDF_file*]	Indicates an identifier (id) that Setup uses to specify how a uniqueness database file (UDF) modifies an answer file. The /udf parameter overrides values in the answer file, and the identifier determines which values in the UDF file are used. If you do not specify a *UDF_file*, Setup prompts you to insert a disk that contains the $UNIQUE$.UDB file.

How to Modify the Setup Process Using Winnt32.exe

You can modify an over-the-network installation by changing how Winnt32.exe runs Setup. Table 2-4 lists the parameters you can use with Winnt32.exe and describes their functions.

Table 2-4 Winnt32.exe Parameters

Switch	Function
/checkupgradeonly	Checks your computer for upgrade compatibility for Windows XP Professional. If you use this option with /unattend, no user input is required. Otherwise, the results are displayed onscreen and you can save them under the file name you specify. For Windows 98 or Windows Me upgrades, the default filename is Upgrade.txt in the %systemroot% folder (the folder that contains the Windows XP Professional system files). For Windows NT 4.0 or Windows 2000 upgrades, the default file name is Ntcompat.txt in the %systemroot% folder.
/cmd:*command_line*	Specifies a specific command that Setup is to run. This command is run after the computer restarts and after Setup collects the necessary configuration information.
/cmdcons	Copies to the hard disk the additional files necessary to load a command-line interface, the Recovery Console, which is used for repair and recovery. The Recovery Console is installed as a Startup option. You can use the Recovery Console to stop and start services and to access the local drive, including drives formatted with NTFS. You can use this option only after you install Windows XP Professional.
/copydir:*foldername*	Creates an additional folder within the %systemroot% folder, which contains the Windows XP Professional system files. For example, if your source folder contains a folder called My_drivers, type **/copydir:My_drivers** to copy the My_drivers folder to your system folder. You can use the /copydir switch to create as many additional folders as you want. /copysource:*foldername* creates an additional folder within the %systemroot% folder. Setup deletes folders created with /copysource after installation is complete.
/debug[*level*] [:*file_name*]	Creates a debug log at the specified level. By default, the debug log file is C:\Winnt32.log, and the default level is 2. Includes the following levels: ■ 0 (severe errors) ■ 1 (errors) ■ 2 (warnings) ■ 3 (information) ■ 4 (detailed information for debugging) Each level includes the level below it.

Table 2-4   Winnt32.exe Parameters

Switch	Function
/dudisable	Prevents Dynamic Update from running. Without Dynamic Update, Setup runs only with the original Setup files. This option disables Dynamic Update even if you use an answer file and specify Dynamic Update options in that file.
/dushare:*pathname*	Specifies a share on which you previously downloaded Dynamic Update files (updated files for use with Setup) from the Microsoft Download Center. When run from your installation share and used with /duprepare, it prepares the updated files for use in network-based client installations. When used without /duprepare and run on a client, it specifies that the client installation will use the updated files on the share specified in the path.
/duprepare:*pathname*	Prepares an installation share for use with Dynamic Update files that you downloaded from the Microsoft Download Center. You can use this share for installing Windows XP Professional for multiple clients (used only with /dushare).
/m:*foldername*	Instructs Setup to copy replacement files from an alternate location. Directs Setup to look in the alternate location first and, if files are present, to use them instead of the files from the default location.
/makelocalsource	Instructs Setup to copy all installation source files to the local hard disk. Use this switch when installing from a CD-ROM to provide installation files when the CD-ROM is not available later in the installation.
/noreboot	Prevents Setup from restarting the computer after completing the file-copy phase. This allows you to execute another command.
/s:*sourcepath*	Specifies the source location of Windows XP Professional installation files. To simultaneously copy files from multiple paths, use a separate /s switch for each source path. If you type multiple /s switches, the first location specified must be available or the installation will fail. You can use a maximum of eight /s switches.
/syspart:[*drive_letter*]	Copies Setup startup files to a hard disk and marks the drive as active. You can then install the drive in another computer. When you start that computer, Setup starts at the next phase. Using /syspart requires the /tempdrive switch. You can use /syspart on computers running Windows NT 4.0, Windows 2000, Windows XP Professional, or Windows 2000 Server. You cannot use it on computers running Windows 95, Windows 98, or Windows Me.
/tempdrive:*drive_letter*	Places temporary files on the specified drive and installs Windows XP Professional on that drive.

Table 2-4   Winnt32.exe Parameters

Switch	Function
/udf:id[,*udb_file*]	Indicates an identifier (id) that Setup uses to specify how a UDF modifies an answer file. The UDF file overrides values in the answer file, and the identifier determines which values in the UDF file are used. For example, /udf:RAS_user, Our_company.udf overrides settings that are specified for the RAS_user identifier in the Our_company.udf file. If you do not specify a UDF file, Setup prompts you to insert a disk that contains the $Unique$.udf file.
/unattend	Upgrades your previous version of Windows 98, Windows Me, Windows NT 4.0, or Windows 2000 in unattended mode (without user input). Setup downloads the Dynamic Update files from Windows Update and includes these files in the installation. All user settings are taken from the previous installation, so no user intervention is required during Setup.
/unattend[*num*]:[*answer_file*]	Performs a fresh installation of Windows in unattended mode using the specified answer file. Setup downloads the Dynamic Update files from the Windows Update website and includes these files in the installation. The specified *num* value indicates the number of seconds between the time that Setup finishes copying the files and when Setup restarts. You can use *num* on any computer running Windows 98, Windows Me, Windows NT Workstation 4.0, Windows 2000, or Windows XP. The specified *answer_file* provides Setup with your custom specifications.

Lesson Review

Use the following questions to help determine whether you have learned enough to move on to the next lesson. If you have difficulty answering these questions, review the material in this lesson before beginning the next lesson. You can find answers to these questions in the "Questions and Answers" section at the end of this chapter.

1. On which of the following operating systems running on the client computer do you use Winnt32.exe to install Windows XP Professional? Choose all that apply.

   a. Windows 3.0

   b. Windows 95

   c. Windows 98

   d. Windows NT 4.0

2. Which Windows XP Professional command allows you to verify that your computer is compatible with Windows XP Professional before you begin installing it?

_____

3. You use the _____ switch with Winnt32.exe to prevent Setup from restarting the computer after completing the file-copy phase.

4. You use the _____ switch with Winnt32.exe to tell Setup to copy all installation source files to your local hard disk.

Lesson Summary

- When you install Windows XP Professional, the main difference between an over-the-network installation and an installation from CD-ROM is the location of the source files.

- After you connect to the shared folder containing the source files and start Winnt.exe or Winnt32.exe, the installation proceeds as an installation from CD-ROM.

- Several switches for Winnt.exe and Winnt32.exe allow you to modify the installation process.

- The /checkupgradeonly switch specifies that Winnt32.exe should check your computer only for upgrade compatibility with Windows XP Professional.

Lesson 4: Upgrading Earlier Versions of Windows to Windows XP Professional

You can upgrade many earlier versions of Windows operating systems directly to Windows XP Professional. Before upgrading, however, you must do the following:

■ Ensure that the computer hardware meets the minimum Windows XP Professional hardware requirements.

■ Check the Windows Catalog or test the computer for hardware compatibility using the Windows XP Professional Compatibility tool. Using compatible hardware prevents problems when you start the upgrade on a large number of client computers.

After this lesson, you will be able to
- Identify client upgrade paths to Windows XP Professional.
- Generate a hardware compatibility report.
- Upgrade earlier Windows client operating systems to Windows XP Professional.

Estimated lesson time: 10 minutes

Client Upgrade Paths

You can upgrade most client computers running earlier versions of Windows directly to Windows XP Professional. However, computers running some earlier versions of Windows (including Windows 95, Windows NT 3.1, and Windows NT 3.5) require an additional step. Table 2-5 lists the Windows XP Professional upgrade paths for various client operating systems.

Table 2-5   Windows XP Professional Upgrade Paths for Client Operating Systems

Upgrade From	Upgrade To
Windows NT 3.1, 3.5, or 3.51	Windows NT 4.0 Workstation first, and then upgrade to Windows XP Professional
Windows 95	Windows 98 first, and then upgrade to Windows XP Professional
Windows 98	Windows XP Professional
Windows Me	Windows XP Professional
Windows NT Workstation 4.0 with Service Pack 6 or later	Windows XP Professional
Windows 2000 Professional	Windows XP Professional
Windows XP Home Edition	Windows XP Professional

Real World   Upgrading Older Computers

Microsoft provides a number of upgrade paths to Windows XP Professional—even from operating systems as old as Windows 95. However, although upgrades from these operating systems are supported, it is unlikely that the computer hardware running the older operating systems will support Windows XP Professional. Even if the hardware and applications on the computers prove compatible with Windows XP Professional, it is not likely that the computers will run Windows XP Professional or any modern applications with acceptable performance.

How to Generate a Hardware Compatibility Report

Before you upgrade a client computer to Windows XP Professional, ensure that it meets the minimum hardware requirements by using the Windows XP Compatibility tool to generate a hardware and software compatibility report. This tool runs automatically during the actual upgrade process, but running it before beginning the upgrade should identify any hardware and software problems and allow you to fix compatibility problems ahead of time.

Generating the Compatibility Report

To run the Windows XP Compatibility tool and generate a compatibility report, perform the following steps:

1. Insert the Windows XP Professional CD-ROM into the CD-ROM drive.

2. From the Start menu, select Run.

3. In the Run dialog box, type **d:\i386\winnt32 /checkupgradeonly** (where *d* is the drive letter of your CD-ROM drive) and click OK.

Note   Generating the upgrade report can take several minutes. The tool checks only for compatible hardware and software, and generates a report that you can analyze to determine the system components that are compatible with Windows XP Professional.

Reviewing the Report

The winnt32 /checkupgradeonly command generates a report that appears as a text document, which you can view from within the Compatibility tool or save as a text file and view with any text editor. The report documents the system hardware and software that are incompatible with Windows XP Professional. It also specifies whether you need to obtain an upgrade pack for software installed on the system and recommends additional system changes or modifications to maintain functionality in Windows XP Professional.

How to Upgrade Compatible Computers Running Windows 98

For client computers running Windows 98 that test as compatible with Windows XP Professional, you can upgrade using a setup wizard or by running Winnt32.exe to complete the upgrade.

To upgrade a computer running Windows 98 to Windows XP Professional using Winnt32.exe, complete the following steps:

1. Insert the Windows XP Professional CD-ROM in the CD-ROM drive.

2. The Autorun program on the Windows XP Professional CD-ROM displays the Welcome To Microsoft Windows XP screen.

> **Note**   If you do not want to use any switches with Winnt32.exe, click Install Windows XP and follow the prompts on your screen. These steps are the same as Exercise 1 in Lesson 2, "Installing Windows XP Professional from a CD-ROM."

3. Open the Command Prompt window, type **d:\i386\winnt32.exe** with any appropriate switches, and press ENTER.

4. Accept the license agreement.

5. If the computer is already a member of a domain, create a computer account in that domain. Windows 98 clients do not require a computer account, but Windows XP Professional clients do.

6. Provide upgrade packs for applications that need them. Upgrade packs update the software to work with Windows XP Professional. These packs are available from the software vendor.

7. Upgrade to NTFS when prompted. Select the upgrade if you do not plan to set up the client computer to dual boot.

8. Continue with the upgrade if the Windows XP Professional Compatibility tool generates a report showing that the computer is compatible with Windows XP Professional. The upgrade finishes without further intervention, and adds your computer to a domain or workgroup.

If the report shows that the computer is incompatible with Windows XP Professional, terminate the upgrade process, and then upgrade your hardware or software.

How to Upgrade Compatible Computers Running Windows NT 4.0

The upgrade process for computers running Windows NT 4.0 is similar to the upgrade process for computers running Windows 98. Before you perform the upgrade, use the Windows XP Professional Compatibility tool to verify that the systems are compatible with Windows XP Professional and to identify any potential problems.

Windows NT 4.0 computers that meet the hardware compatibility requirements can upgrade directly to Windows XP Professional. To upgrade a computer running Windows NT 4.0 to Windows XP Professional using Winnt32.exe, complete the following steps:

1. Insert the Windows XP Professional CD-ROM in the CD-ROM drive. The Autorun program on the Windows XP Professional CD-ROM displays the Welcome To Microsoft Windows XP screen.

> **Note**   If you do not want to use any switches with Winnt32.exe, click Install Windows XP and follow the prompts on your screen. These steps are the same as those in Practice 2 in Lesson 2.

2. Open the Command Prompt window, type **d:\i386\winnt32.exe** with any appropriate switches, and press ENTER.

3. On the Welcome To Windows page, in the Installation Type drop-down list, select Upgrade, and then click Next.

4. On the License Agreement page, read the license agreement, click I Accept This Agreement, and then click Next.

5. On the Product Key page, enter your 25-character product key, which is located on the back of the Windows XP Professional CD-ROM case.

6. On the Windows XP Professional NTFS File System page, click Yes, Upgrade My Drive, and then click Next.

7. After Setup copies installation files, the computer restarts and the upgrade finishes without further user intervention necessary.

Lesson Review

Use the following questions to help determine whether you have learned enough to move on to the next lesson. If you have difficulty answering these questions, review the material in this lesson before beginning the next lesson. You can find answers to these questions in the "Questions and Answers" section at the end of this chapter.

1. Which of the following operating systems can be upgraded directly to Windows XP Professional? Choose all that apply.

    a. Windows NT Workstation 4.0

    b. Windows NT 3.51

    c. Windows 2000 Professional

    d. Windows NT Server 4.0

2. How can you upgrade a computer running Windows 95 to Windows XP Professional?

_____

_____

3. Before you upgrade a computer running Windows NT 4.0 Workstation, which of the following actions should you perform? Choose all that apply.

    a. Create a 2 GB partition on which to install Windows XP Professional.

    b. Verify that the computer meets the minimum hardware requirements.

    c. Generate a hardware and software compatibility report.

    d. Format the partition containing Windows NT 4.0 so that you can install Windows XP Professional.

4. How can you verify that your computer is compatible with Windows XP Professional and therefore can be upgraded?

Lesson Summary

- Before you upgrade a client computer to Windows XP Professional, ensure that it meets the minimum hardware requirements.

- Use the Windows XP Professional Compatibility tool to generate a hardware and software compatibility report.

- For client systems that test as compatible with Windows XP Professional, run the Windows XP Professional Setup program (Winnt32.exe) to complete the upgrade.

Lesson 5: Troubleshooting Windows XP Professional Setup

The best way to avoid problems when installing Windows XP Professional is to fully prepare a computer for installation, choose the right kind of installation for your needs, and make sure that the hardware in the computer is compatible with Windows XP Professional prior to beginning the installation. Although installations of Windows XP Professional complete without any problems most of the time, this lesson introduces you to some common reasons why an installation might fail and what you can to do solve the problem.

After this lesson, you will be able to

- Identify common setup failures and their solutions.
- Troubleshoot setup failures by using setup logs.

Estimated lesson time: 15 minutes

Guidelines for Resolving Common Problems

Fortunately, most installation problems are relatively minor issues that are simple to correct. Table 2-6 lists some common installation problems and offers solutions to those problems.

Table 2-6   Troubleshooting Tips

Problem	Solution
Media errors occur.	If you are installing from a CD-ROM, use a different CD-ROM. To request a replacement CD-ROM, contact Microsoft or your vendor. Try using a different computer and CD-ROM drive. If you can read the CD-ROM on a different computer, you can perform an over-the-network installation. If one of your Setup disks is not working, try using a different set of Setup disks.
CD-ROM drive is not supported.	Replace the CD-ROM drive with a supported drive. If replacement is impossible, try another installation method such as installing over the network. After you complete the installation, install the driver for the adapter card driver for the CD-ROM drive if it is available.
Computer cannot copy files from the CD-ROM.	Test the CD-ROM on another computer. If you can copy the files using a different CD-ROM drive on a different computer, use the CD-ROM to copy the files to a network share or to the hard drive of the computer on which you want to install Windows XP Professional. Sometimes, when you get an error stating that Setup cannot copy a particular file, the problem can actually be a failed RAM module. If you test the CD and CD-ROM drive successfully, testing your memory should be the next step.

Table 2-6   Troubleshooting Tips

Problem	Solution
Insufficient disk space.	Do one of the following: ■ Use the Setup program to create a partition by using existing free space on the hard disk. ■ Delete and create partitions as needed to create a partition that is large enough for installation. ■ Reformat an existing partition to create more space.
Setup failure during early text mode portion of Setup.	Verify that Windows XP supports the mass storage devices on the computer. If not, press F6 when prompted and supply the necessary drivers for these devices from floppy disk.
Dependency service fails to start.	In the Windows XP Professional Setup Wizard, return to the Network Settings page and verify that you installed the correct protocol and network adapter. Verify that the network adapter has the proper configuration settings, such as transceiver type, and that the local computer name is unique on the network.
During Setup, the computer's BIOS-based virus scanner gives an error message indicating that a virus is attempting to infect the boot sector. Setup fails.	When Setup attempts to write to the boot sector to make the hard disk Windows XP-bootable, BIOS-based virus scanners might interpret the action as an attempt by a virus to infect the system. Disable the virus protection in the BIOS and enable it again after Windows XP is fully installed.
Setup cannot connect to the domain controller.	Verify the following: ■ The domain name is correct. ■ The server running the DNS service and the domain controller are both running and online. If you cannot locate a domain controller, install Windows XP Professional into a workgroup and then join the domain after installation. ■ The network adapter card and protocol settings are set correctly. If you are reinstalling Windows XP Professional and are using the same computer name, delete the computer account and re-create it.
Windows XP Professional fails to install or start.	Verify the following: ■ Windows XP Professional is detecting all the hardware. ■ All the hardware is in the Windows Catalog. Try running Winnt32 /checkupgradeonly to verify that the hardware is compatible with Windows XP Professional. Remove unsupported devices in an attempt to get past the error. If you are unsure about which devices are unsupported, consider removing all devices during the installation (except those necessary to run the system, such as the motherboard, display adapter, memory, and so on) and then reconnecting them after Windows is installed.

Guidelines for Troubleshooting Setup Failures Using the Windows XP Setup Logs

During Setup, Windows XP Professional generates a number of log files containing installation information that can help you resolve any problems that occur after Setup is completed. The action log and the error log are especially useful for troubleshooting. Both are located in the installation folder (C:\Windows by default).

> **Tip**   The logs are text documents that you can view in Notepad, WordPad, or Word. Some of the documents are very large. Consider searching the document for the word **fail**, which can help you locate instances in the log files that contain information on failed operations.

Action Log

The action log records the actions that the Setup program performs in chronological order. It includes actions such as copying files and creating Registry entries. It also contains entries that are written to the Setup error log. The action log is named Setupact.log. If an installation fails, you can often pinpoint what was going on (for example, what file was being copied) when the installation failed. Searching the Microsoft Knowledge Base using the description of the action as a keyword often yields solutions to the problem at hand.

Error Log

The error log describes errors (and their severity) that occur during Setup. Because the contents of this log are also included in the action log, you can think of the error log as a subset of the action log. The error log is named Setuperr.log. If errors occur, the log viewer displays the error log at the end of Setup. If no errors occurred during installation, this file is empty.

> **See Also**   For additional information about troubleshooting installations, see Lesson 3, "Using Startup and Recovery Tools," in Chapter 4, "Modifying and Troubleshooting the Startup Process."

Troubleshooting Stop Errors

Stop errors, also referred to as blue screen errors, occur when the system detects a condition from which it cannot recover. The system stops responding and displays a screen of information on a blue background. The most likely time during installation that you might experience stop errors is when the text mode stage of setup has finished, your computer restarts, and the Setup Wizard stage begins. During this transition, Windows XP loads the newly installed operating system kernel for the first time and initializes new hardware drivers.

Stop errors are identified by a 10-digit hexadecimal number. The two most common stop errors you will encounter during Windows XP installation are described as follows:

Stop: 0x0000000A Error   This error usually indicates that Windows attempted to access a particular memory address at too high an internal request level (IRQL). This error usually occurs when a hardware driver uses an incorrect memory address, but can also indicate an incompatible device driver or a general hardware problem. To troubleshoot this error, confirm that your hardware is listed in the Windows Catalog, make sure that your BIOS is compatible with Windows XP Professional, and perform general hardware troubleshooting. You can learn more about troubleshooting this stop error by reading Microsoft Knowledge Base article 314063, "Troubleshooting a Stop 0x0000000A Error in Windows XP."

Stop: 0x0000007B Error   This error normally indicates that you have an inaccessible boot device, meaning that Windows cannot access your hard disk. The common causes for this type of error are a boot sector virus, bad or incompatible hardware, or missing hardware drivers. You can learn more about troubleshooting this stop error by reading Microsoft Knowledge Base article 324103, "How to Troubleshoot 'Stop 0x0000007B' Errors in Windows XP."

Tip   Although these are the two most common Stop errors you will see during Windows XP installation, you might encounter other Stop errors. If you get a Stop error, write down the Stop error number. Search the Microsoft Knowledge Base using the number as your keyword, and you can find information on how to resolve the error. You can learn more about troubleshooting Stop errors by reading the article "Windows Server 2003 Troubleshooting Stop Errors," which is available at *http://www.microsoft.com/technet/prodtechnol/ windowsserver2003/operations/system/sptcestp.mspx*. Although the article is written for Windows Server 2003, it also applies to Windows XP.

Lesson Review

Use the following questions to help determine whether you have learned enough to move on to the next lesson. If you have difficulty answering these questions, review the material in this lesson before beginning the next lesson. You can find answers to these questions in the "Questions and Answers" section at the end of this chapter.

1. If you encounter an error during setup, which of the following log files should you check? Choose all that apply.

   a. Setuperr.log

   b. Netsetup.log

   c. Setup.log

   d. Setupact.log

2. If your computer cannot connect to the domain controller during installation, what should you do?

   _____

   _____

   _____

   _____

   _____

3. If your computer cannot connect to read the CD-ROM during installation, what should you do?

   _____

   _____

   _____

   _____

Lesson Summary

- The action log, Setupact.log, records and describes in chronological order the actions that Setup performs.

- The error log, Setuperr.log, describes errors that occur during Setup and indicates the severity of each error.

- If a failed installation results in a stop error, you can search the Microsoft Knowledge Base for information on troubleshooting the problem.

Lesson 6: Activating and Updating Windows XP Professional

After installing Windows XP for a home or small business user, you will need to activate Windows. Unless activated, Windows can only be used only for 30 days. Corporate installations typically do not need to be activated because most corporations use a volume licensing system. You will also need to install any available updates and preferably configure Windows to download and install critical updates automatically.

After this lesson, you will be able to

- Activate Windows XP following installation.
- Scan a system and display available updates by using the Windows Update site.
- Configure Automatic Updates to download and install updates automatically.
- Explain the purpose of Software Update Services.
- Explain the purpose of service packs.

Estimated lesson time: 30 minutes

Guidelines for Activating Windows Following Installation

Unless you are working with an installation that is part of a volume licensing plan, Windows XP Professional requires that the operating system be activated with Microsoft within 30 days of installation. Typically, if you install Windows XP Professional using an original installation CD, you need to activate it. If the operating system is not activated within this time, Windows ceases to function until it is activated. You are not allowed to log on to the system until you contact one of Microsoft's product activation centers.

The first time you log on to Windows following installation, Windows prompts you to activate the product if activation is necessary. If you do not perform the activation, Windows continues to prompt you at regular intervals until you activate the product.

Windows Product Activation (WPA) requires each installation to have a unique product key. When you enter the 25-character product key during Windows installation, the Setup program generates a 20-character product ID (PID). During activation, Windows combines the PID and a hardware ID to form an installation ID. Windows sends this installation ID to a Microsoft license clearinghouse, where the PID is verified to ensure that it is valid and that it has not already been used to activate another installation. If this check passes, the license clearinghouse sends a confirmation ID to your computer, and Windows XP Professional is activated. If the check fails, activation fails.

How to Scan a System and Display Available Updates Using the Windows Update Site

Windows Update is an online service that provides enhancements to the Windows family of operating systems. Product updates such as critical and security updates, general Windows updates, and device driver updates are all easily accessible. When you connect to the Windows Update website, the site scans your system (a process that happens locally without sending any information to Microsoft) to determine what is already installed, and then presents you with a list of available updates for your system.

You can access Windows Update in the following ways:

- Through Internet Explorer by clicking Windows Update from the Tools menu
- Through any Web browser by using the URL *http://www.microsoft.com/windows-update*
- Through the Help And Support Center by clicking Windows Update
- Through the Start menu by clicking All Programs and then Windows Update
- Through Device Manager by clicking Update Driver in the Properties dialog box of any device

▶   **Using the Windows Update Site**

To perform an Express Install from the Windows Update site, follow these steps:

1. From the Start menu, click All Programs, and then click Windows Update.

2. On the Microsoft Windows Update website, click Express Install.

3. After the scan is complete (a process that is performed locally—no information is sent to Microsoft's servers), click Install.

4. If you are prompted with an End User License Agreement (EULA), read the agreement and click I Accept.

5. Wait while the updates are downloaded and installed. If you are prompted to restart your computer, click Restart Now. If you are not prompted to restart, click Close.

How to Configure Automatic Updates

Windows XP also supports **Automatic Updates**, a feature that automatically downloads and installs new updates when they become available. You should configure the Automatic Updates feature in Windows XP to automatically download and install new updates according to a regular schedule.

To configure Automatic Updates, follow these steps:

1. From the Start menu, click Control Panel.

2. In the Control Panel window, click Performance And Maintenance.

3. In the Performance And Maintenance window, click System.

4. On the Automatic Updates tab, click the Automatic option, as shown in Figure 2-9.

5. Select how often and at what time of day updates should be downloaded and installed. For users with dedicated connections (such as a cable modem), you should configure Windows to check for updates daily at a time when the user is not using the computer. Users with dial-up connections might want to check less frequently if they are concerned about allowing their computers to connect to the Internet automatically.

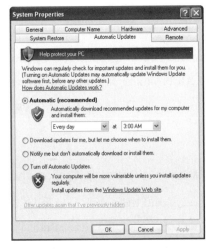

Figure 2-9 You should schedule Automatic Updates to download and install updates automatically.

6. Click OK.

> **Exam Tip** Enabling Automatic Update and configuring it to download and install updates automatically according to a preset schedule is the recommended way for handling critical updates for Windows XP.

What Is Software Update Services?

By default, Automatic Updates locates and downloads updates from Microsoft's public update servers. As an alternative, you can configure an update service to run on the local network and supply updates to clients. This procedure provides better control over the specific updates made available to client computers.

Software Update Services (SUS) is a server component installed on a Windows 2000 or Windows 2003 server inside the corporate firewall. SUS allows for the distribution of critical updates and security updates; it does not allow the distribution of Service Packs or driver updates, and it does not have a mechanism to deploy software packages outright.

SUS synchronizes with the public Windows Update site at Microsoft on behalf of your clients. SUS, which is designed to support up to 15,000 clients, serves as a distribution point of updates to the clients in your organization in two ways:

Automatically   You can create an automatic content distribution point on the SUS server that will synchronize its content with the content from the Windows Update website. This option offers clients the same updates as the public server, but cuts down on Internet traffic by providing the updates locally.

Manually   You can also create a content distribution point on a server running Microsoft Internet Information Services (IIS) version 5.0 or later. This option lets you specify which updates are available.

You can also control which server each Windows client connects to for updates (if you are running more than one SUS server across multiple sites), as well as schedule when the client should perform the installations of critical updates.

Installing SUS

You can install the Software Update Services server component on a server running either Windows 2000 Server or Windows Server 2003. The computer should meet the following system requirements:

- Pentium III 700 MHz or better processor
- 512 MB of RAM
- 6 GB of available hard disk space formatted with NTFS
- Windows 2000 Server (with Service Pack 2 or later) or Windows Server 2003
- IIS 5.0 or later
- Internet Explorer 6.0 or later

The SUS component is available for download from (*http://www.microsoft.com/ windows2000/windowsupdate/sus/default.asp*). After the download is complete, double-click the setup file to begin the installation process and simply follow the menu prompts for a Typical installation (a Custom installation lets you choose the folder where the service is installed and the location where updates are stored).

To Use Group Policy to Configure Clients to Access SUS

After SUS is installed in your environment, you need to configure the client systems to use it—otherwise, they will just keep using the Windows Update public server instead.

You must use Group Policy to configure clients to use the SUS server. You can set the policy at either the domain or organizational unit level. Group Policy is explained in more detail in Chapter 16, "Configuring Security Settings and Internet Options."

To set the Group Policy, follow these steps:

1. Log on as a domain administrator or open the Active Directory Users And Computers tool using the Run As command to enter the appropriate credentials.

2. Right-click the domain or organizational unit and choose Properties from the shortcut menu.

3. Switch to the Group Policy tab.

4. You could edit the default domain policy, but it is normally recommended that you create another one for these types of secondary settings. To do this, choose the New button and name the new policy that appears in the window.

5. After you have named the policy, click the Edit button to open the Group Policy Object Editor window.

6. Expand the Computer Configuration node, then the Administrative Templates node, then the Windows Components node, and then the Windows Update node.

7. Double-click the Configure Automatic Updates setting to specify any of the following:

   ❑ Notify The User Before Download And Before Installation

   ❑ Automatically Download And Notify The User Before Installation

   ❑ Automatically Download And Schedule An Automatic Installation

8. Double-click the Specify Intranet Microsoft Update Service Location setting. Change the setting to Enabled and enter the name of the internal SUS server that the clients in the domain should use into both fields. This information can be entered by name or by IP address.

9. Double-click the Reschedule Automatic Updates scheduled installations setting to change the schedule for automatic installation on clients.

10. Double-click the No Auto-Restart For Scheduled Automatic Updates installations to prevent clients from restarting after an automatic installation.

Note   After Automatic Updates is configured by Group Policy, the Automatic Updates settings become unavailable to the user of the client computer.

What Are Service Packs?

Microsoft periodically releases service packs for Windows XP. A **service pack** is a collection of all updates released to that point, and often includes new features, as well.

You should be familiar with the deployment of service packs to ensure that all operating systems on the network are up-to-date and to avoid issues that you might encounter in the future.

Windows XP ships with a utility called Winver.exe, which you can use to determine what version of Windows you are running and what level of service pack (if any) is installed. Figure 2-10 displays the output of Winver.exe prior to any service pack being installed. If a service pack has been installed, the version will be noted after the build number.

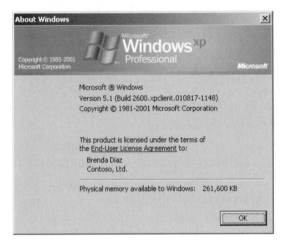

Figure 2-10   Use Winver.exe to determine the current Windows version and service pack.

To Obtain a Service Pack

Service packs are free, and you can get them in the following ways:

- Use Windows Update to update a single computer with a service pack.

- Download the service pack from Windows Update to deploy to many computers. The download is a single large self-extracting executable, which will have a different name depending on the service pack version that you are installing. The file is quite large (85 MB or more), so be sure that you have sufficient bandwidth available to support the download.

- Order the service pack CD. You can order the service pack CD from Microsoft for a nominal fee that covers the cost of manufacture and shipping. In addition to containing the service pack, the CD contains operating system enhancements and other advanced utilities.

- Use Microsoft subscription services. Microsoft has several subscription services, such as Microsoft TechNet, which automatically provide you with service packs with the next issue after the release of the service pack.

To Install a Service Pack

Service pack setup programs can have various names, though most Windows Service Packs use a program named Update.exe. Regardless of the file name, though, most Windows updates support the same command-line parameters, which control how the service pack deploys. Table 2-7 lists these parameters.

Table 2-7 Common Command-Line Parameters for Windows Updates

Switch	Function
/f	Forces all applications to close prior to restarting the system.
/n	Does not back up uninstall files. You cannot uninstall the service pack if this switch is used.
/o	Overwrites OEM-provided files without prompting the user.
/q	Installation runs in quiet mode with no user interaction required (requires /o to update OEM-supplied files).
/s:[*path to distribution folder*]	Creates an integration installation point.
/u	Unattended installation (requires /o to update OEM-supplied files).
/x	Extracts files without starting Setup. This is useful if you want to move installation files to another location.
/z	Disables automatic restart when installation is finished.

Service pack installations require a significant amount of disk space (hundreds of megabytes). The uninstall folder consumes the majority of this disk space. You can install a service pack without saving uninstall files by using the /n switch when installing the service pack.

You must choose an installation method from the following options:

Update installation   The service pack executable is started locally, across the network, or through Windows Update. The service pack is installed on the existing operating system.

Integrated installation   Also called slipstreaming, an integrated installation is one in which the service pack is applied to the installation files on a distribution server using the /s switch, integrating the installation files and the service pack into a single set of updated installation files. New installations that included the service pack can then be performed from the integrated distribution point. This eliminates the need to apply the service pack after the installation. However, the service pack cannot be uninstalled if it is applied in this fashion.

Combination installation   This involves installation using a combination of an integrated installation, an answer file to control the installation process, and a Cmdlines.txt file to launch additional application setup programs after the operating system setup has completed.

When you install new operating system components after a service pack has been installed, Setup requires both the operating system and service pack installation files. This allows Setup to install the updated version of the component.

To Uninstal a Service Pack

By default, the service pack setup program automatically creates a backup of the files and settings that are changed during the service pack installation and places them in an uninstall folder named \$NTServicepackUninstall\$\ in %systemroot%. You can uninstall the service pack through Add/Remove Programs on Control Panel or from a command line by running Spuninst.exe from the %systemroot%\$NTServicepackUninstall\Spuninst\ folder.

Note   If you installed a service pack without creating a backup, you cannot uninstall the service pack.

Practice: Configuring Automatic Updates

In this practice, you will configure Automatic Updates to download and install critical updates automatically.

1. From the Start menu, click Control Panel.

2. In the Control Panel window, click Performance And Maintenance.

3. In the Performance And Maintenance window, click System.

4. On the Automatic Updates tab, click the Automatic option.

5. Click OK.

Lesson Review

Use the following questions to help determine whether you have learned enough to move on to the next lesson. If you have difficulty answering these questions, review the material in this lesson before beginning the next lesson. You can find answers to these questions in the "Questions and Answers" section at the end of this chapter.

1. A(n) _____ is a collection of all updates released to a particular point, and often includes new features.

2. What is the recommended way to configure the Automatic Updates feature in Windows XP?

_____

_____

3. For how many days does Windows XP function if you do not activate Windows or are not part of a volume licensing agreement? Choose the correct answer.

    a. 10 days

    b. 14 days

    c. 30 days

    d. 60 days

    e. 120 days

Lesson Summary

- You can use the Windows Update site to scan a computer and display available critical, Windows, and driver updates.

- Automatic Updates is a Windows XP feature that downloads and installs critical updates automatically. Although you can specify that Automatic Updates prompt users before downloading or installing, Microsoft recommends that you configure it to download and install automatically according to a preset schedule.

- Service packs are collections of updates (and sometimes new features) that have been tested to ensure that they work together correctly. Microsoft occasionally issues new service packs for its products.

Case Scenario Exercises

Read the following two scenarios and answer the associated questions. You can use the scenarios to help determine whether you have learned enough to move on to the next chapter. If you have difficulty completing this work, review the material in this chapter before beginning the next chapter. You can find answers to these questions in the "Questions and Answers" section at the end of this chapter.

Scenario 2.1

You have been given a computer running Windows 98 Second Edition with the following hardware installed:

- 200 MHz Pentium II processor

- 32 MB of RAM

- 4 GB hard disk, 500 MB free

- 24x CD-ROM drive

- Floppy drive, mouse, keyboard

- SVGA monitor and video card

- 10 Mbps Ethernet network card

You will reformat the hard disk, create one partition that uses the entire hard disk, and install Windows XP Professional.

Question

What additional hardware do you need to install onto the computer prior to installing Windows XP?

_____

_____

_____

_____

_____

Scenario 2.2

One of your users wants you to install Windows XP Professional on his workstation. Currently, the workstation is running Windows 98. The user wants to continue having Windows 98 running on the computer because he often must test the software he develops on that system. The user's computer is configured with the following hardware:

- 2.4 GHz Pentium 4 processor

- 512 MB of RAM

- 60 GB hard disk

    There are currently 2 partitions on the hard disk: a 20 GB partition on which Windows 98 and the user's current applications are installed and a 15 GB partition on which the user stores his documents. Both partitions are formatted using the FAT32 file system. There is 25 GB of unpartitioned space.

- 24x CD-ROM drive

- Floppy drive, mouse, keyboard

- SVGA monitor and video card

- 10 Mbps Ethernet network card

Question

How should you configure this computer to run both Windows 98 and Windows XP Professional?

_____

_____

_____

_____

_____

Troubleshooting Lab

Read the following troubleshooting scenario and then answer the question that follows. You can use this lab to help determine whether you have learned enough to move on to the next chapter. If you have difficulty completing this work, review the material in this chapter before beginning the next chapter. You can find the answer to this question in the "Questions and Answers" section at the end of this chapter.

Scenario

One of your users is attempting to upgrade to Windows XP Professional on a computer that has been running Windows 98. Her computer has one hard disk that is configured with a single partition. She has already backed up her computer and plans to reformat the partition, and then perform a clean installation of Windows XP Professional. She has configured her BIOS to start the computer from CD-ROM. When she starts the computer, the text mode stage of Windows XP Professional Setup begins as expected. However, when the user tries to reformat the partition, her computer presents an error message stating that a virus is attempting to infect the boot sector of her hard disk. She is certain that she is using a genuine Windows XP Professional installation CD.

Question

What do you suspect is the problem?

_____

_____

_____

_____

_____

Chapter Summary

- Before installing Windows XP Professional, you should first ensure that your hardware meets the minimum hardware requirements and that your hardware is in the Windows Catalog. Additional preinstallation tasks include determining how to partition the hard disk on which you will install Windows XP Professional and deciding whether to format the partition as NTFS, FAT, or FAT32.

- Your computer can join a domain or a workgroup during or after installation.

- When you install Windows XP Professional, the main difference between an over-the-network installation and an installation from CD-ROM is the location of the source files.

- After you connect to the shared folder containing the source files and start Winnt.exe or Winnt32.exe, the installation proceeds as an installation from CD-ROM. Several switches for Winnt.exe and Winnt32.exe allow you to modify the installation process. The /checkupgradeonly switch specifies that Winnt32.exe should check your computer only for upgrade compatibility with Windows XP Professional.

- Before you upgrade a client computer to Windows XP Professional, use the Windows XP Professional Compatibility tool to generate a hardware and software compatibility report. For client systems that test as compatible with Windows XP Professional, run the Windows XP Professional Setup program (Winnt32.exe) to complete the upgrade.

- The Setupact.log action log records and describes in chronological order the actions that Setup performs. The Setuperr.log error log describes errors that occur during Setup and indicates the severity of each error.

- You can use the Windows Update site to scan a computer and display available critical, Windows, and driver updates. Automatic Updates is a Windows XP feature that downloads and installs critical updates automatically. Although you can specify that Automatic Updates prompt users before downloading or installing, Microsoft recommends that you configure it to download and install automatically according to a preset schedule. Service packs are collections of updates (and sometimes new features) that have been tested to ensure that they work together correctly. Microsoft issues new service packs for its products occasionally.

Exam Highlights

Before taking the exam, review the key points and terms that are presented in this chapter. You need to know this information.

Key Points

- You should memorize the basic hardware requirements for running Windows XP. A 233MHz processor, 64MB RAM, and a 2GB hard disk with 1.5GB of free space are required.

- Unless you are installing Windows XP Professional on a multiple-boot computer that also has an operating system that cannot access NTFS partitions (such as Windows 98), you should always use NTFS.

- You can use Winnt.exe and Winnt32.exe to install Windows XP Professional from the command line by using optional parameters to modify the installation. Winnt.exe runs under MS-DOS and Windows 3.0/3.1. Winnt32.exe runs under the 32-bit Windows operating systems such as Windows 95, Windows 98, Windows Me, Windows NT 4.0, and Windows 2000.

Key Terms

Automatic Update   A feature that automatically downloads and installs new updates when they become available.

boot partition   The disk partition that possesses the system files required to load the operating system into memory.

disk partition   A logical section of a hard disk on which the computer might write data.

File Allocation Table (FAT)   A file system used in older versions of Windows and still supported in Windows XP Professional. The 16-bit FAT system for older versions of Windows is called FAT16, and the 32-bit system for newer versions of Windows is called FAT32.

Files And Settings Transfer Wizard   One of two methods used by administrators to transfer user configuration settings and files from systems running Windows 95 or later to a clean Windows XP installation.

NTFS   The native file management system for Windows XP. However, Windows XP is also capable of working with FAT and FAT32 file systems so that it can remain compatible with older Microsoft operating systems.

service pack   A collection of all updates for a Microsoft product released to a certain point. Service packs sometimes include new features, as well.

stop errors   Occur when the system detects a condition from which it cannot recover. (Also referred to as blue screen errors.)

system partition   Normally the same partition as the boot partition, this partition contains the hardware-specific files required to load and start Windows XP.

User State Migration Tools (USMT)   Tools that let administrators transfer user configuration settings and files from systems running Windows 95 or later to a clean Windows XP installation.

Windows Catalog   A site that lists all hardware and software tested for compatibility with Windows XP by Microsoft.

Windows Product Activation (WPA)   The process of activating a copy of Windows with Microsoft after installation. Windows XP Professional requires that the operating system be activated with Microsoft within 30 days of installation.

Windows Update   An online service that provides enhancements to the Windows family of operating systems.

Winnt.exe   The command used for starting Windows XP Professional installation in MS-DOS and Windows 3.0/3.1.

Winnt32.exe   The command used for starting Windows XP Professional installation in Windows 95, Windows 98, Windows Me, Windows NT 4.0, or Windows 2000 Professional.

Questions and Answers

Lesson 1 Review

Page
2-10

1. What are the minimum and recommended memory requirements for installing Windows XP Professional?

   The minimum amount of memory required to install Windows XP Professional is 64 MB, and the recommended amount of memory is 128 MB.

2. What is the minimum hard disk space required for installing Windows XP Professional? Choose the correct answer.

   a. 500 MB

   b. 1 GB

   c. 1.5 GB

   d. 2 GB

   C is the correct answer. Windows XP Professional requires 1.5 GB of free disk space.

3. What information is required when joining a domain during the Windows XP Professional installation? Choose all that apply.

   a. You must know the DNS name for the domain the computer will join.

   b. You must have a user account in the domain.

   c. At least one domain controller in the domain must be online when you install a computer in the domain.

   d. At least one DNS server must be online when you install a computer in the domain.

   A, C, and D are correct. To join a domain during the installation of Windows XP Professional, you must know the DNS name for the domain the computer will join. To add an account for the computer to the domain, a domain controller must be available. Also, a DNS server must be available so that the computer on which you are installing Windows XP can locate the domain controller for the domain. B is not correct because you do not need to have a user account to join a computer to a domain. However, the computer must already have an account in the domain, or you must have sufficient privileges in the domain so that you can create a computer account during the installation.

4. Which of the following statements about file systems are correct? Choose all that apply.

   a. File- and folder-level security is available only with NTFS.

   b. Disk compression is available with FAT, FAT32, and NTFS.

c. Dual booting between Windows 98 and Windows XP Professional is available only with NTFS.

d. Encryption is available only with NTFS.

A and D are correct. NTFS provides file-level security and encryption. B is not correct because only NTFS offers disk compression; FAT and FAT32 do not. C is not correct because Windows 98 cannot access a drive formatted with NTFS.

Lesson 2 Review

Page
2-22

1. If TCP/IP is installed on your computer, what is the maximum length for the computer name you specify during installation?

   63 characters

2. Can you change the computer name after installation without having to reinstall Windows XP Professional? If you can change the name, how do you do it? If you cannot change the name, why not?

   Yes. To change the computer name after installation is complete, click Start, click My Computer, click View System Information, click the Computer Name tab, and then click Change.

3. Which of the following statements about joining a workgroup or a domain are correct? Choose all that apply.

   a. You can add your computer to a workgroup or a domain only during installation.

   b. If you add your computer to a workgroup during installation, you can join the computer to a domain later.

   c. If you add your computer to a domain during installation, you can join the computer to a workgroup later.

   d. You cannot add your computer to a workgroup or a domain during installation.

   B and C are correct. You can join a domain or a workgroup during installation or at any time following installation. A and D are not correct because you can join a domain or workgroup during or after installation.

4. When you install networking components with typical settings, what components are installed? What does each component do?

   There are four components. Client For Microsoft Networks allows your computer to access network resources. File And Printer Sharing For Microsoft Networks allows other computers to access file and print resources on your computer. The QoS Packet Scheduler helps provide a guaranteed delivery system for network traffic, such as TCP/IP packets. TCP/IP is the default networking protocol that allows your computer to communicate over LANs and WANs.

Lesson 3 Review

Page
2-30

1. On which of the following operating systems running on the client computer do you use Winnt32.exe to install Windows XP Professional? Choose all that apply.

   a. Windows 3.0

   b. Windows 95

   c. Windows 98

   d. Windows NT 4.0

   B, C, and D are correct. A is not correct because you use the Winnt.exe command with MS-DOS and Windows 3.0.

2. Which Windows XP Professional command allows you to verify that your computer is compatible with Windows XP Professional before you begin installing it?

   Winnt32.exe with the /checkupgradeonly switch

3. You use the _____ switch with Winnt32.exe to prevent Setup from restarting the computer after completing the file-copy phase.

   /noreboot

4. You use the _____ switch with Winnt32.exe to tell Setup to copy all installation source files to your local hard disk.

   /makelocalsource

Lesson 4 Review

Page
2-35

1. Which of the following operating systems can be upgraded directly to Windows XP Professional? Choose all that apply.

   a. Windows NT Workstation 4.0

   b. Windows NT 3.51

   c. Windows 2000 Professional

   d. Windows NT Server 4.0

   A and C are correct. B is not correct because you must first upgrade Windows NT 3.51 to Windows NT 4.0 Workstation, and then upgrade to Windows XP Professional. D is not correct because you cannot upgrade to Windows XP Professional from a server product.

2. How can you upgrade a computer running Windows 95 to Windows XP Professional?

   Upgrade the computer to Windows 98 first, and then upgrade to Windows XP Professional.

3. Before you upgrade a computer running Windows NT 4.0 Workstation, which of the following actions should you perform? Choose all that apply.

   a. Create a 2 GB partition on which to install Windows XP Professional.

b. Verify that the computer meets the minimum hardware requirements.

c. Generate a hardware and software compatibility report.

d. Format the partition containing Windows NT 4.0 so that you can install Windows XP Professional.

B and C are correct. A is not correct because you do not need to create a new partition to upgrade the operating system. D is not correct because you should not reformat the partition containing Windows NT 4.0 in order to perform an upgrade. If you did reformat, you would lose all data, including current configuration information and installed applications.

4. How can you verify that your computer is compatible with Windows XP Professional and therefore can be upgraded?

Use the Windows XP Professional Compatibility tool. You can start this tool by typing **winnt32 /checkupgradeonly** at the command prompt.

Lesson 5 Review

Page 2-40

1. If you encounter an error during setup, which of the following log files should you check? Choose all that apply.

a. Setuperr.log

b. Netsetup.log

c. Setup.log

d. Setupact.log

A and D are correct. During installation, Windows XP Professional Setup creates an action log (Setupact.log) and an error log (Setuperr.log). B and C are not correct because they are not valid installation log files.

2. If your computer cannot connect to the domain controller during installation, what should you do?

First, verify that a domain controller is running and online, and then verify that the server running the DNS service is running and online. If both servers are online, verify that the network adapter card and protocol settings are correctly set and that the network cable is plugged into the network adapter card.

3. If your computer cannot connect to read the CD-ROM during installation, what should you do?

Use a different CD-ROM. (To request a replacement CD-ROM, contact Microsoft or your vendor.) You can also try using a different computer and CD-ROM drive. If you can read the CD-ROM on a different computer, you can do an over-the-network installation.

Lesson 6 Review

Page 2-49

1. A(n) _____ is a collection of all updates released to a particular point, and often includes new features.

service pack

2. What is the recommended way to configure the Automatic Updates feature in Windows XP?

Microsoft recommends that you configure Automatic Updates to download and install updates automatically according to a preset schedule.

3. For how many days does Windows XP function if you do not activate Windows or are not part of a volume licensing agreement? Choose the correct answer.

a. 10 days

b. 14 days

c. 30 days

d. 60 days

e. 120 days

C is correct. Windows functions normally for 30 days following installation. If you do not activate Windows within 30 days of installation, you cannot start Windows until you activate it.

Case Scenario Exercises: Scenario 2.1

Page 2-50

What additional hardware do you need to install onto the computer prior to installing Windows XP?

According to the minimum requirements for installing Windows XP Professional, you would need to upgrade the processor to at least a 233 MHz processor. Ideally, though, if you want to upgrade this processor, you should consider upgrading to something significantly faster. Although Windows XP Professional also requires a minimum of 64 MB RAM, 128 MB of RAM is recommended for adequate performance.

Case Scenario Exercises: Scenario 2.2

Page 2-51

How should you configure this computer to run both Windows 98 and Windows XP Professional?

You can install Windows XP Professional either by starting the installation from within Windows 98 or by starting the system using the Windows XP installation CD. You should create a new partition from the unpartitioned space on which to install Windows XP Professional. You should probably format the new partition using the FAT 32 file system. If you format the partition using NTFS, Windows 98 cannot access any data on that partition.

Troubleshooting Lab

Page 2-52

What do you suspect is the problem?

Because Setup is failing when trying to write to the boot sector of the disk (which happens when Setup tries to reformat the disk), it is likely that the user's computer has virus detection enabled in her computer's BIOS. She must disable the BIOS-based protection while installing Windows XP Professional. She should re-enable the BIOS-based virus protection after the installation of Windows XP Professional is complete.

3 Deploying Windows XP Professional

Exam Objectives in this Chapter:

- Perform and troubleshoot an unattended installation of Microsoft Windows XP Professional
    - ❏ Install Windows XP Professional by using Remote Installation Services (RIS).
    - ❏ Install Windows XP Professional by using the System Preparation Tool.
    - ❏ Create unattended answer files by using Windows Setup Manager to automate the installation of Windows XP Professional.
- Manage applications by using Windows Installer packages

Why This Chapter Matters

This chapter prepares you to automate the process of installing Microsoft Windows XP Professional. Automated deployments can be done in three ways. The decision to use a specific method instead of another is usually determined by the resources, infrastructure, and deployment time required. The three automated deployment methods include the following:

- Small deployments or situations involving many different hardware configurations often use an **unattended installation**, in which the Winnt32 and Winnt commands are used along with an unattended answer file to script the installation. This file is created with Windows Setup Manager.

- Many larger enterprise deployments use **disk duplication** to deploy systems, a process in which you use the System Preparation Tool to create an image from a computer running Windows XP Professional, and then clone that image on other computers. Using disk duplication usually requires third-party software.

- Microsoft provides **Remote Installation Services** (RIS) for use in environments in which Active Directory service is available. The RIS server software (which resides on a server computer running Windows 2000 Server or Windows Server 2003) stores images of Windows XP installations and makes those images available over the network. A client computer boots from the network (or by using a special RIS boot disk), contacts the RIS server, and then installs an image from that server.

This chapter will also look at some tools in Windows XP Professional that help make your deployment of Windows XP Professional easier. These tools include the File and Transfer Wizard, the User State Migration Tool (USMT), and Windows Installer.

Lessons in this Chapter:

Before You Begin

To complete this chapter, you must have a computer that meets or exceeds the minimum hardware requirements listed in the preface, "About This Book." You must also have Windows XP Professional installed on a computer on which you can make changes.

Lesson 1: Creating Unattended Installations by Using Windows Setup Manager

This lesson presents methods that will help you create unattended Windows XP Professional installations. When you must install Windows XP Professional on computers with varying configurations, scripting provides automation with increased flexibility. You will learn how Windows Setup Manager makes it easy to create the answer files that are necessary for scripted installations.

After this lesson, you will be able to

- Describe unattended installations.
- Find the Windows XP deployment tools.
- Explain what Windows Setup Manager is used for.
- Use Windows Setup Manager to create an answer file.
- Explain how to start an unattended installation.

Estimated lesson time: 45 minutes

Overview of Unattended Installations

At several points during a standard installation, Setup requires that the user provide information, such as the time zone, network settings, and so on. One way to automate an installation is to create an **answer file** that supplies the required information. Answer files are really just text files that contain responses to some, or all, of the questions that Setup asks during the installation process. After creating an answer file, you can apply it to as many computers as necessary.

However, there also are certain settings that must be unique to each computer, such as the computer name. To answer this need, Windows Setup Manager also allows the creation of a file called a **uniqueness database file** (UDF), which is used in conjunction with the standard answer file. The UDF contains the settings that are unique to each computer.

Exam Tip   Remember that a standard answer file is used to provide the common configuration settings for all computers that are affected during an unattended installation. A UDF provides the unique settings that each computer needs to distinguish it from other computers.

How to Find the Windows XP Deployment Tools

Windows Setup Manager is one of the Windows XP deployment tools included on the Windows XP Professional installation CD-ROM. The tools that concern this chapter are as follows:

- **Deploy.chm**   A compiled Hypertext Markup Language (HTML) help named "Microsoft Windows Corporate Deployment Tools User's Guide" that provides detailed information on using all the deployment tools

- **Setupmgr.chm**   Compiled HTML help file for using Windows Setup Manager

- **Setupmgr.exe**   The Windows Setup Manager Wizard tool

- **Sysprep.exe**   The System Preparation Tool (covered in Lesson 2, "Deploying Windows XP Professional by Using Disk Duplication")

To extract the Windows XP deployment tools to your hard disk, use these steps:

1. Insert the Windows XP Professional CD-ROM in the CD-ROM drive.

2. If the Welcome To Microsoft Windows XP screen is displayed automatically, click Exit to close that screen.

3. In Windows Explorer, create a folder to hold the deployment tools.

4. In Windows Explorer, locate the \Support\Tools folder on the Windows XP Professional CD-ROM.

5. In the \Support\Tools folder, double-click the Deploy.cab file to open it.

    Windows XP Professional displays the contents of Deploy.cab.

6. Select all the files listed in Deploy.cab, and then copy them to the folder you created on your hard disk.

> **Tip**   To select all the files in any folder quickly, press CTRL+A.

7. Open the folder you created on your hard disk to view the contents and access the deployment tools.

What Windows Setup Manager Does

Windows Setup Manager provides a wizard-based interface that allows you to quickly create an answer file for an unattended installation of Windows XP Professional. Windows Setup Manager (see Figure 3-1) enables you to create scripts to perform customized installations on workstations and servers that meet the specific hardware and network requirements of your organization.

Figure 3-1 Use Windows Setup Manager to create unattended answer files.

You can create or modify an answer file, typically named unattend.txt, by using Windows Setup Manager. You can also create answer files with a simple text editor, such as Notepad, but using the Windows Setup Manager reduces errors in syntax.

Windows Setup Manager does the following:

- Provides a wizard with an easy-to-use graphical interface with which you can create and modify answer files

- Makes it easy to create UDFs (typically named unattend.udb)

Note A uniqueness database file (UDF) provides the ability to specify per-computer parameters. The UDF modifies an installation by overriding values in the answer file. When you run Setup with Winnt32.exe, you use the /udf:id[,*UDF_filename*] switch. The UDF overrides values in the answer file, and the identifier (id) determines which values in the .udb file are used.

- Makes it easy to specify computer-specific or user-specific information
- Simplifies the inclusion of application setup scripts in the answer file
- Creates the distribution folder that you use for the installation files

Note If you are upgrading systems to Windows XP Professional, you can add any application upgrades or update packs to the distribution folder and enter the appropriate commands in the Additional Commands page of the Windows Setup Manager Wizard so that these upgrades or update packs are applied to the application as part of the upgrade.

How to Use the Windows Setup Manager to Create an Answer File

Windows Setup Manager provides a straightforward wizard interface. To create an answer file for a fully automated installation by using Windows Setup Manager, use these steps:

1. In Windows Explorer, locate the folder where you extracted Windows Setup Manager (setupmgr.exe). Double-click setupmgr.exe.

   Windows XP Professional starts the Windows Setup Manager Wizard.

2. Click Next.

   The New Or Existing Answer File page appears.

3. Ensure that the Create A New Answer File is selected, and then click Next.

   The Windows Setup Manager Wizard displays the Product To Install page, which provides the following three options:

   ❑ Windows Unattended Installation

   ❑ Sysprep Install

   ❑ Remote Installation Services

4. Ensure that Windows Unattended Installation is selected, and then click Next.

   The Windows Setup Manager Wizard displays the Platform page.

5. Ensure that Windows XP Professional is selected, and then click Next.

   The Windows Setup Manager Wizard displays the User Interaction Level page, shown in Figure 3-2, which has the following five options:

   ❑ **Provide Defaults.** The answers you provide in the answer file are the default answers that the user sees. The user can accept the default answers or change any of the answers supplied by the script.

   ❑ **Fully Automated.** The installation is fully automated. The user does not have the chance to review or change the answers supplied by the script.

   ❑ **Hide Pages.** The answers provided by the script are supplied during the installation. Any page for which the script supplies all answers is hidden from the user, so the user cannot review or change the answers supplied by the script.

   ❑ **Read Only.** The script provides the answers, and the user can view the answers on any page that is not hidden, but the user cannot change the answers.

   ❑ **GUI Attended.** The text-mode portion of the installation is automated, but the user must supply the answers for the graphical user interface (GUI) mode portion of the installation.

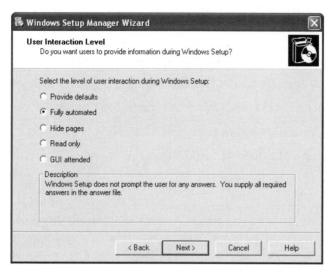

Figure 3-2   Select the level of user interaction you want.

6. Select Fully Automated, and then click Next.

   The Windows Setup Manager Wizard displays the Distribution Folder page. The Setup Manager Wizard can create a distribution folder on your computer or network containing the required source files. You can add files to this distribution folder to further customize your installation.

7. Select No, This Answer File Will Be Used To Install From A CD, and then click Next.

   The Windows Setup Manager Wizard displays the License Agreement page.

8. Select I Accept The Terms Of The License Agreement, and then click Next.

   The Windows Setup Manager Wizard displays the Customize The Software page, shown in Figure 3-3.

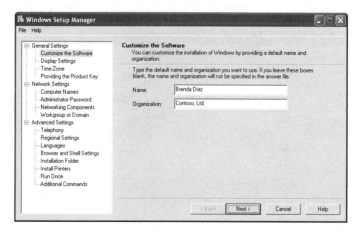

Figure 3-3   Use the Customize The Software Page to provide details for the answer file that will be used during installation.

9. Type your name in the Name box and your organization in the Organization box, and then click Next.

   The Windows Setup Manager Wizard displays the Display Settings page.

10. Leave the default settings on the Display Settings page, and then click Next.

    The Windows Setup Manager displays the Time Zone page.

11. Select the appropriate time zone, and then click Next.

    The Windows Setup Manager Wizard displays the Providing The Product Key page.

12. Type in the appropriate product key.

> **Note**   The product key identifies your copy of Windows XP Professional, so you need a separate license for each copy that you install. Note, however, that in many corporate environments a volume licensing system is in place, so you might need a special key for that. Also, Setup Manager does not validate the product key when you enter it, so you won't actually find out until installing Windows XP Professional with the answer file whether the key is valid. Make sure that you use a valid key.

13. Click Next.

    The Windows Setup Manager Wizard displays the Computer Names page, shown in Figure 3-4. Notice that you have three choices:

    ❑ Enter a series of names to be used during the various iterations of the script.

    ❑ Click Import and provide the name of a text file that has one computer name per line listed. Setup imports and uses these names as the computer names in the various iterations of the script.

    ❑ Select Automatically Generate Computer Names Based On Organization Name to allow the system to automatically generate the computer names to be used.

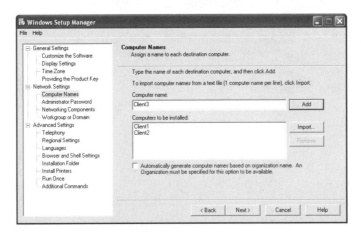

Figure 3-4   Add the names of the computers that will use the installation.

14. In the Computer Name text box, type a name for the computer, and then click Add. Repeat this step to add additional computers to the installation.

15. Click Next.

The Windows Setup Manager Wizard displays the Administrator Password page, which appears with the following two options:

❏ Prompt The User For An Administrative Password

❏ Use The Following Administrative Password (127 Characters Maximum)

 Note   You selected the User Interaction level of Fully Automated, so the Prompt The User For An Administrative Password option is unavailable.

Notice that you have the option to encrypt the Administrator's password in the answer file. You also have the option to have the Administrator log on automatically, and you can set the number of times you want the Administrator to log on automatically when the computer is restarted.

16. Ensure that Use The Following Administrative Password (127 Characters Maximum) is selected, and then type a password in the Password text box and the Confirm Password box.

17. Select Encrypt Administrator Password In Answer File, and then click Next.

The Windows Setup Manager Wizard displays the Networking Components page, shown in Figure 3-5, with the following two options:

❏ **Typical Settings.** Installs Transmission Control Protocol/Internet Protocol (TCP/IP), enables Dynamic Host Configuration Protocol (DHCP), installs the Client For Microsoft Networks protocol, and installs File And Printer Sharing For Microsoft Networks for each destination computer

❏ **Customize Settings.** Allows you to select and configure the networking components to be installed

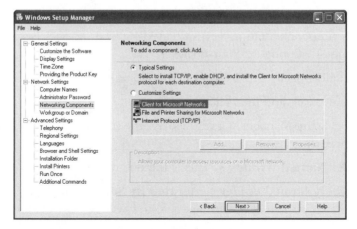

Figure 3-5   Choose network settings for the installation.

18. Configure network settings as appropriate for your network, and then click Next.

    The Windows Setup Manager Wizard displays the Workgroup Or Domain page.

19. If the computer will join a workgroup, type the workgroup name. If the computer will join a domain, click Windows Server Domain, and then type the name of the domain. If a computer that will join a domain does not already have a computer account in that domain, you can have Windows Setup create such an account during installation. Click Create A Computer Account In The Domain, and then enter the credentials for an account that has permission to create new computer accounts in the domain. Click Next to continue.

    The Windows Setup Manager Wizard displays the Telephony page.

20. Select the appropriate setting for What Country/Region Are You In.

21. Type the appropriate setting for What Area (Or City) Code Are You In.

22. If necessary, type the appropriate setting for If You Dial A Number To Access An Outside Line, What Is It.

23. Select the appropriate setting for The Phone System At This Location Uses, and then click Next.

    The Windows Setup Manager Wizard displays the Regional Settings page. The default selection is Use The Default Regional Settings For The Windows Version You Are Installing, but you can also specify different regional settings.

24. Configure the regional settings, and then click Next.

    The Windows Setup Manager Wizard displays the Languages page, which allows you to add support for additional languages.

25. Select additional languages if they are required for the computers on which you will install Windows XP Professional, and then click Next.

    The Windows Setup Manager Wizard displays the Browser And Shell Settings page with the following three options:

    ❑ Use Default Internet Explorer Settings

    ❑ Use An Autoconfiguration Script Created By The Internet Explorer Administration Kit To Configure Your Browser

    ❑ Individually Specify Proxy And Default Home Page Settings

26. Make your selection, and then click Next.

    The Windows Setup Manager Wizard displays the Installation Folder page with the following three options:

    ❑ **A Folder Named Windows.** This is the default selection.

    ❑ **A Uniquely Named Folder Generated By Setup.** Setup generates a unique folder name so that the installation folder will be less obvious. This folder name is recorded in the Registry, so programs and program installations can easily access the Windows XP Professional system files and folders.

❏ **This Folder.** If you select this option, you must specify a path and folder name.

27. Make your selection, and then click Next.

The Windows Setup Manager Wizard displays the Install Printers page, shown in Figure 3-6, which allows you to specify a network printer to be installed the first time a user logs on after Setup.

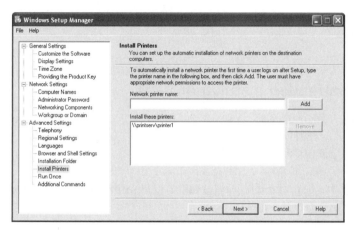

Figure 3-6   Specify printers to be installed during setup.

28. Add any printers that you want to configure during installation, and then click Next.

The Windows Setup Manager Wizard displays the Run Once page. This page allows you to configure Windows to run one or more commands the first time a user logs on.

29. To add a command, type the command in the Command To Run text box, and then click Add. Click Next when you are finished adding commands.

The Windows Setup Manager Wizard displays the Additional Commands page. This page allows you to specify additional commands to be run at the end of the unattended setup before any user logs on to the computer.

30. To add a command, type the command in the Command To Run text box, and then click Add. Click Finish when you are finished adding commands.

The Windows Setup Manager Wizard displays a dialog box indicating that the Windows Setup Manager has successfully created an answer file. It also prompts you for a location and a name for the script. The default is a file named unattend.txt in the folder from which you launched Windows Setup Manager.

Note   If multiple computer names were specified, the wizard also creates a .udb file.

31. Accept the default name and location, or type an alternate name and location. Click OK to continue.

The Windows Setup Manager Wizard displays the Setup Manager Complete page, indicating that new files were created:

❏ unattend.txt is the answer file.

❏ unattend.udb is the uniqueness database file created if you supply multiple computer names.

❏ unattend.bat is a batch script that will launch the Windows installation using the answer file and uniqueness database file.

32. On the File menu, click Exit.

How to Start an Unattended Installation

To perform an installation, you can use the unattend.bat file created by the Windows Setup Manager. This batch file simply uses the winnt32.exe command to start the installation, supplying parameters based on the location you saved the files to when you ran Windows Setup Manager. You can modify this batch file to suit your needs or simply start Setup from the command line yourself (the most common way to start an unattended installation). To start Setup from the command line (or modify the batch file), you must use a specific parameter and indicate the location of the answer file.

To use the **winnt.exe** command from a Microsoft MS-DOS or Windows 3.x command prompt to perform a clean installation of Windows XP, you must use the following syntax:

winnt [/**s**:*SourcePath*] [/**u**:*answer file*] [/**udf**:*ID* [,*UDB_file*]]

To use the **winnt32.exe** command from a Windows 95, Windows 98, Windows Me, or Windows 2000 command prompt to perform a clean installation of Windows XP, you must use the following syntax:

winnt32 [/**unattend**[*num*]:[*answer_file*] [/**udf**:*ID* [,*UDB_file*]]

See Also   For more information on answer file structure, syntax, and configurable options, see the Deployment User Tools Guide on the Windows XP Professional CD. You can find it in the following location: \Support\Tools\Deploy.cab\Deploy.chm.

On the CD   At this point, you should view the multimedia presentation, "How Setup Uses Answer Files and UDFs," included in the Multimedia folder on the CD accompanying this book. This presentation will help deepen your understanding of unattended installations.

Practice: Creating Unattended Installations with Windows Setup Manager

In this practice, you extract the Windows XP Professional deployment tools from the Windows XP Professional CD-ROM you used for program installation, and then you use the Windows System Manager to create a fully automated unattended answer file.

Exercise 1: Extract the Windows XP Deployment Tools

In this exercise, you extract the Windows deployment tools from the CD-ROM you used to install Windows XP Professional and copy them to your hard drive.

1. Insert the Windows XP Professional CD-ROM in the CD-ROM drive.

2. If the Welcome To Microsoft Windows XP screen opens automatically, click Exit to close the screen.

3. In Windows Explorer, locate the root of the C drive and create a folder named **Deploy**.

   The C:\Deploy folder will be used to contain the files extracted from DEPLOY.CAB on the Windows XP Professional CD-ROM.

4. In Windows Explorer, open your CD-ROM drive and locate the Support\Tools\ folder. In the Tools folder, double-click Deploy.cab.

> **Note**   If D is not the correct drive letter for your CD-ROM drive, replace the *D* with the letter representing your CD-ROM drive.

   Windows XP Professional displays the contents of Deploy.cab.

5. Press CTRL+A to select all of the files listed in Deploy.cab.

6. Press CTRL+C to copy the selected files.

7. In Windows Explorer, locate and open the Deploy folder that you created on the C drive.

8. In the Deploy folder that you created, press CTRL+V to paste (copy) the files.

9. Double-click Readme.txt.

10. Take a moment to view the topics covered in the Readme.txt file, and then close Notepad.

Exercise 2: Create an Answer File by Using Windows Setup Manager

In this exercise, you use Windows Setup Manager to create an answer file for a fully automated unattended installation. At the same time, the Windows Setup Manager Wizard creates a distribution folder and a .udb file.

1. In Windows Explorer, locate the C:\Deploy folder.

2. Double-click Setupmgr.exe

   Windows XP Professional starts the Windows Setup Manager Wizard.

3. Click Next.

   The New Or Existing Answer File page appears.

4. Ensure that Create A New Answer File is selected, and then click Next.

   The Windows Setup Manager Wizard displays the Product To Install page.

5. Ensure that Windows Unattended Installation is selected, and then click Next.

   The Windows Setup Manager Wizard displays the Platform page.

6. Ensure that Windows XP Professional is selected, and then click Next.

   The Windows Setup Manager Wizard displays the User Interaction Level page.

7. Click Fully Automated, and then click Next.

   The Windows Setup Manager Wizard displays the Distribution Folder page.

8. Select No, This Answer File Will Be Used To Install From A CD, and then click Next.

   The Windows Setup Manager Wizard displays the License Agreement page.

9. Select I Accept The Terms Of The License Agreement, and then click Next.

   The Windows Setup Manager Wizard displays the Customize The Software page.

10. Type your name in the Name box and your organization in the Organization box, and then click Next.

    The Windows Setup Manager Wizard displays the Display Settings page.

11. Leave the default settings on the Display Settings page, and then click Next.

    Windows Setup Manager displays the Time Zone page.

12. Select the appropriate time zone, and then click Next.

    The Windows Setup Manager Wizard displays the Providing The Product Key page.

13. Enter your Windows XP Professional product key, and then click Next.

    The Windows Setup Manager Wizard displays the Computer Names page.

14. In the Computer Name text box, type **Client1**, and then click Add. Repeat this step to add Client2 and Client3 to the list of names.

    Notice that the names Client1, Client2, and Client3 appear in the Computers To Be Installed box.

15. Click Next.

The Windows Setup Manager Wizard displays the Administrator Password page.

16. Ensure that Use The Following Administrative Password (127 Characters Maximum) is selected, and then type **password** in the Password text box and the Confirm Password text box.

17. Click Encrypt Administrator Password In Answer File, and then click Next.

The Windows Setup Manager Wizard displays the Networking Components page.

18. Leave Typical Settings selected, and then click Next.

The Windows Setup Manager Wizard displays the Workgroup Or Domain page.

19. Click Next to accept the default of the computers joining a workgroup named WORKGROUP.

The Windows Setup Manager Wizard displays the Telephony page.

20. Select the appropriate setting for What Country/Region Are You In.

21. Type the appropriate setting for What Area (Or City) Code Are You In.

22. If necessary, type the appropriate setting for If You Dial A Number To Access An Outside Line, What Is It.

23. Select the appropriate setting for The Phone System At This Location Uses, and then click Next.

The Windows Setup Manager Wizard displays the Regional Settings page.

24. Click Next to accept the default settings.

The Windows Setup Manager Wizard displays the Languages page.

25. Click Next to accept the default setting.

The Windows Setup Manager Wizard displays the Browser And Shell Settings page.

26. Click Next to accept the default setting: Use Default Internet Explorer Settings.

The Windows Setup Manager Wizard displays the Installation Folder page.

27. Select This Folder. In the This Folder text box, type **WINXPPro**, and then click Next.

The Windows Setup Manager Wizard displays the Install Printers page.

28. Click Next to continue without having the script install any network printers.

The Windows Setup Manager Wizard displays the Run Once page.

29. Click Next to continue without having the script run any additional commands.

The Windows Setup Manager Wizard displays the Additional Commands page.

30. Click Finish to complete the script without having the script run any additional commands.

   The Windows Setup Manager Wizard displays a dialog box indicating that the Windows Setup Manager has successfully created an answer file.

31. Click OK to accept the default file name and location.

   The Windows Setup Manager Wizard displays the Setup Manager Complete page.

32. On the File menu, click Exit.

Lesson Review

The following questions are intended to reinforce key information presented in this lesson. If you are unable to answer a question, review the lesson materials and try the question again. You can find answers to the questions in the "Questions and Answers" section at the end of this chapter.

1. What is the purpose of Windows Setup Manager?

   _____

   _____

2. How can you apply an application update pack as part of the Windows XP Professional installation?

   _____

   _____

   _____

3. What type of answer files does Windows Setup Manager allow you to create?

   _____

4. Why would you use a UDF?

   _____

   _____

Lesson Summary

- The Windows Setup Manager Wizard makes it easy to create the answer files that are necessary for unattended installations.

- To use the Windows Setup Manager, you must extract the files located in the \Support\Tools\Deploy.cab file on the Windows XP Professional CD-ROM.

■ Windows Setup Manager provides a wizard with an easy-to-use graphical interface with which you can create and modify answer files and UDFs. The Windows Setup Manager makes it easy to specify computer-specific or user-specific information and to include application setup scripts in the answer file. The Windows Setup Manager can also create the distribution folder and copy the installation files to it.

■ You run Windows Setup Manager by launching the setupmgr.exe file that you extracted from the Deploy.cab file. The wizard walks you through choosing the type of installation you want to create and how much detail you want to provide in the answer file.

■ To perform an installation, you can use the Unattend.bat file created by the Windows Setup Manager. You can also start Setup from the command line by using the Winnt.exe command (from an MS-DOS or Windows 3.1 command line) or the Winnt32.exe command (from a Windows 95 or later command line).

Lesson 2: Using Disk Duplication to Deploy Windows XP Professional

When you install Windows XP Professional on several computers with identical hardware configurations, the most efficient installation method to use is disk duplication. By creating a disk image of a Windows XP Professional installation and copying that image onto multiple destination computers, you save time in the rollout of Windows XP Professional. This method also creates a convenient baseline that you can easily recopy onto a computer that is experiencing significant problems.

After this lesson, you will be able to

- Explain the purpose of disk duplication.
- Extract the System Preparation Tool that is used to prepare a disk image for duplication.
- Prepare a computer for the creation of a master image by using the System Preparation Tool.
- Install Windows XP Professional from a master disk image.

Estimated lesson time: 40 minutes

Overview of Disk Duplication

Windows XP Professional includes a program named **System Preparation** (sysprep.exe) that allows you to prepare master images of an existing Windows XP installation for distribution to other computers by removing machine-specific information from the image. The first step of creating a disk image is for the administrator to install Windows XP Professional onto a reference computer. The reference computer can contain just the Windows XP Professional operating system, or it can contain the operating system and any number of installed applications.

After the reference computer is configured properly, you will use the System Preparation Tool to prepare the computer for imaging. Many settings on a Windows XP Professional computer must be unique, such as the Computer Name and the Security Identifier (SID), which is a number used to track an object through the Windows security subsystem. The System Preparation Tool removes the SID and all other user- and computer-specific information from the computer, and then shuts down the computer so that you can use can use a disk duplication utility to create a disk image. The disk image is simply a compressed file that contains the contents of the entire hard disk on which the operating system is installed.

When a client computer starts Windows XP Professional for the first time after loading a disk image that has been prepared with Sysprep, Windows automatically generates a unique SID, initiates Plug-and-Play detection, and starts the Mini Setup Wizard. The

Mini Setup Wizard prompts the user for user- and computer-specific information, such as the following:

- End-User License Agreement (EULA)

- Regional options

- User name and company

- Product key

- Computer name and administrator password

- Time zone selection

> **Note** When you create a disk image, all the hardware settings of the reference computer become part of the image. Thus, the reference computer should have the same (or similar) hardware configuration as the destination computers. If the destination computers contain Plug and Play devices that are not present in the reference computer, they are automatically detected and configured at the first startup following installation. The user must install any non–Plug and Play devices manually.

To install Windows XP Professional using disk duplication, you first need to install and configure Windows XP Professional on a test computer. You then need to install and configure any applications and software updates on the test computer.

How to Extract the Windows System Preparation Tool

Before you can use the Windows System Preparation Tool, you must copy the necessary files onto the computer you are using to create the master image. To copy the System Preparation Tool, you must extract the files from \Support\Tools\Deploy.cab on the Windows XP Professional CD-ROM. For the steps to do this, see Lesson 1, "Creating Unattended Installations by Using Windows Setup Manager."

Preparing a Computer for the Creation of a Master Image by Using the System Preparation Tool

The System Preparation Tool was developed to eliminate problems encountered in disk copying. First of all, every computer must have a unique security identifier (SID). If you copied an existing disk image to other computers, every computer on which the image was copied would have the same SID. To prevent this problem, the System Preparation Tool adds a system service to the master image that creates a unique local domain SID the first time the computer to which the master image is copied is started.

The hard drive controller device driver and the hardware abstraction layer (HAL) on the computer on which the disk image was generated and on the computer to which the disk image was copied must be identical. The other peripherals, such as the network adapter, the video adapter, and sound cards on the computer on which the disk image was copied, need not be identical to the ones on the computer on which the image was generated because the computer will run a full Plug and Play detection when it starts the first time following installation from the image.

You can run the System Preparation Tool in its default mode by simply double-clicking the Sysprep.exe file that you extracted from Windows XP deployment tools. Table 3-1 describes some of the optional parameters you can use when running Sysprep.exe.

Table 3-1 Optional Parameters for Sysprep.exe

Switch	Description
/quiet	Runs with no user interaction because it does not show the user confirmation dialog boxes
/nosidgen	Does not regenerate SID on reboot
/pnp	Forces Setup to detect Plug and Play devices on the destination computers on the next reboot
/reboot	Restarts the source computer after Sysprep.exe has completed
/noreboot	Shuts down without a reboot
/forceshutdown	Forces a shutdown instead of powering off

> **Note** For a complete list of the switches for Sysprep.exe, start a command prompt, change to the Deploy folder or the folder where you installed Sysprep.exe, type **sysprep.exe/?**, and press ENTER.

How to Install Windows XP Professional from a Master Disk Image

After running Sysprep on your test computer, you are ready to run a non-Microsoft disk image copying tool to create a master disk image. Save the new disk image on a shared folder or CD-ROM, and then copy this image to the multiple destination computers.

End users can then start the destination computers. The Mini-Setup Wizard prompts the user for computer-specific variables, such as the administrator password for the computer and the computer name. If a sysprep.inf file was provided, the Mini-Setup Wizard is bypassed, and the system loads Windows XP Professional without user intervention. You can also automate the completion of the Mini-Setup Wizard further by creating a sysprep.inf file.

Practice: Deploying Windows XP Professional by Using Disk Duplication

In this practice, you use the Windows System Preparation Tool to prepare a master image for disk duplication. You will then use that master image to perform an installation.

Exercise 1: Prepare a Master Image

Important   If you have not completed Exercise 1 of Lesson 1 in this chapter, you must complete that exercise and extract the System Preparation Tool from the Windows XP Professional CD-ROM before you can complete the following exercise.

Caution   You should perform this procedure only on a test computer that does not contain valuable data. After completing the following exercise, you will have to reinstall Windows XP Professional on your computer.

1. Click Start, point to All Programs, point to Accessories, and then click Command Prompt.

2. In the Command Prompt window, type **cd \Deploy**, and then press ENTER.

Note   If you extracted the sysprep.exe file to a different location, use that location instead.

3. Type **sysprep.exe /pnp /noreboot** and then press ENTER.

4. What do the optional parameters /pnp and /noreboot do?

_____

_____

_____

_____

_____

_____

Note   You should run Sysprep only if you are preparing your computer for duplication.

5. If you are certain that you do not mind having to reinstall Windows XP Professional, click OK to continue.

   Sysprep displays a System Preparation Tool dialog box that allows you to configure Sysprep.

> **Note** To quit Sysprep, in the Flags box, click the down-pointing arrow in the Shutdown box, select Quit, and then click Reseal to stop System Preparation from running on your computer.

6. In the Flags box, select Mini-Setup.

7. In the Shutdown list, click Shut Down, and then click Reseal.

   Sysprep displays a Windows System Preparation Tool message box, telling you that you have chosen to regenerate the SIDs on the next reboot. You need to regenerate SIDs only if you plan to image after shutdown.

> **Note** If you did not want to regenerate SIDs, you would click Cancel, select the NoSIDGEN check box in the Flags box, and then click Reseal.

8. Click OK.

   Sysprep displays a Sysprep Is Working message box, telling you that the tool is removing the system-specific data on your computer. When Sysprep is finished, your computer shuts down.

9. If your computer does not turn off automatically after shutting down, turn your computer off.

Exercise 2: Install Windows XP Professional from a Master Image

In this exercise, you use a master disk image that you created in the previous exercise to install Windows XP Professional. Normally, you would use a third-party tool to copy this disk image to another computer. For the purposes of this practice, you reinstall by using the master disk image as if it were a computer that had the disk image copied to it.

1. Turn on your computer.

   Setup displays the following message: Please Wait While Windows Prepares To Start. After a few minutes, Setup displays the Welcome To The Windows XP Setup Wizard page.

2. Click Next to continue with Setup.

   The Windows XP Professional Setup Wizard displays the License Agreement page.

3. Read through the license agreement, click I Accept This Agreement, and then click Next.

   The Windows XP Professional Setup Wizard displays the Regional And Language Options page.

4. Ensure that the Regional And Language Options and Text Input Languages settings are correct, and then click Next.

   The Windows XP Professional Setup Wizard displays the Personalize Your Software page.

5. In the Name text box, type your name. In the Organization text box, type your organization name, and then click Next.

   The Windows XP Professional Setup Wizard displays the Your Product Key page.

6. Enter your product key, and then click Next.

   The Windows XP Professional Setup Wizard displays the Computer Name And Administrator Password page.

7. In the Computer Name text box, type the name for your computer.

8. In the Password and Confirm Password text boxes, type a password, and then click Next.

   The Windows XP Professional Setup Wizard displays the Modem Dialing Information page.

> **Note**   If you do not have a modem, you might not see this page. If you do not get the Modem Dialing Information page, skip to Step 13.

9. Select the appropriate setting for What Country/Region Are You In.

10. Type the appropriate setting for What Area Or City Code Are You In.

11. If necessary, type the appropriate setting for If You Dial A Number To Access An Outside Line, What Is It.

12. Select the appropriate setting for The Phone System At This Location Uses, and then click Next.

    The Windows XP Professional Setup Wizard displays the Date And Time Settings page.

13. Ensure that the settings for Date, Time, Time Zone, and Daylight Saving Changes are correct, and then click Next.

    The Windows XP Professional Setup Wizard displays the Networking Settings page.

14. Ensure that the default setting of Typical Settings is selected, and then click Next.

    The Windows XP Professional Setup Wizard displays the Workgroup Or Computer Domain page.

15. Ensure that No, This Computer Is Not On A Network Or Is On A Network Without A Domain is selected.

16. Ensure that WORKGROUP appears in the Workgroup Or Computer Domain Box, and then click Next.

    The Windows XP Professional Setup Wizard displays the Performing Final Tasks page, and then it displays the Completing The Windows XP Setup Wizard page.

17. Click Finish.

    The system will reboot, and the Welcome screen appears.

18. Log on as you normally would.

Lesson Review

The following questions are intended to reinforce key information presented in this lesson. If you are unable to answer a question, review the lesson materials and try the question again. You can find answers to the questions in the "Questions and Answers" section at the end of this chapter.

1. What is disk duplication?

_____

_____

2. What is the purpose of the System Preparation Tool?

_____

_____

_____

_____

_____

_____

_____

3. What does the /quiet switch do when you run Sysprep.exe?

_____

Lesson Summary

■ The first step in disk duplication is preparing a computer running Windows XP Professional that will serve as a reference computer. This preparation includes installing, updating, and configuring the operating system, as well as installing other applications. After the reference computer is configured, the next step is using the System Preparation Tool to prepare the computer for imaging. The final step is using a non-Microsoft disk duplication utility to create a hard disk image.

■ To use the System Preparation Tool, you must extract the files located in the \Support\Tools\Deploy.cab file on the Windows XP Professional CD-ROM.

■ One of the primary functions of the System Preparation Tool is to delete security identifiers (SIDs) and all other user-specific or computer-specific information.

■ When the user restarts the destination computer, the Windows Setup Wizard appears, but requires very little input to complete. You can automate the completion of the Windows Setup Wizard by creating a sysprep.inf file.

Lesson 3: Performing Remote Installations

Remote Installation Services (RIS) is a service that is available for servers running Windows 2000 Server and Windows Server 2003 in a Microsoft Active Directory directory service environment. The RIS server is a disk image server that contains as many disk images as are necessary to support the different configurations of Windows XP Professional on a network. A RIS client is a computer that connects to the RIS server and downloads an image for installation. The RIS server might be preconfigured to download a particular image to a client computer, or the user might be able to select an image manually from a special RIS Administration menu.

After this lesson, you will be able to

- Describe how RIS is used
- Install and configure RIS on a server running Windows Server 2003
- Explain requirements for RIS client computers

Estimated lesson time: 60 minutes

Overview of RIS

RIS provides the best features of unattended installations and disk duplication and also provides a powerful way to make remote installations possible in large network environments. The basic RIS process works as follows:

1. In an Active Directory domain, you install RIS on a server running Windows 2000 Server or Windows Server 2003. The methods for installation on each version are different, and each method is covered in this lesson.

2. You load disk images on the RIS server. RIS supports two types of images:

   ❑ A CD-based image that contains the Windows XP Professional operating installation files. You can create answer files for these images to automate the installation process on the client end.

   ❑ A Remote Installation Preparation (RIPrep) image that can contain the Windows XP Professional operating system along with other applications. This image is based on a preconfigured reference computer, much like the computer used in creating images for disk duplication.

3. A client computer connects to the RIS server over the network. Clients must conform to the Net PC specification or have a network adapter that supports the **Preboot eXecution Environment** (PXE) standard for network booting. This type of adapter allows the client to boot the computer with no pre-existing operating system installed, locate a RIS server, and start the installation process using an image on the RIS server. For clients who do not have a PXE-compliant network adapter, you can create a special boot floppy disk that will allow the client to boot up and contact the RIS server.

4. The client begins the installation of Windows XP Professional from an image on the RIS server. A RIS server can support many different disk images, and the user of the client computer can choose the image they want to use to install Windows XP Professional. You can also configure a RIS server so that installation choices are made automatically when a client computer contacts the RIS server. The user of the client computer sees a screen that indicates the operating system being installed, but is not prompted to make any choices or provide any information. If only one image is available on the RIS server, the user also does not get to make a choice.

5. Windows XP Professional is installed on the client computer. Depending on the image and type of installation, the user might be or might not be prompted for personal information during the installation.

RIS provides the following benefits:

■ It enables remote installation of Windows XP Professional.

■ It simplifies server image management by eliminating hardware-specific images and by detecting Plug and Play hardware during setup.

■ It supports recovery of the operating system and computer in the event of computer failure.

■ It retains security settings after restarting the destination computer.

■ It reduces total cost of ownership (TCO) by allowing either users or technical staff to install the operating system on individual computers.

Installing and Configuring RIS

RIS is available only on computers running Windows 2000 Server or Windows Server 2003. The RIS server can be a domain controller or a member server. Table 3-2 lists the network services required for RIS and their RIS function. These network services do not have to be installed on the same computer as RIS, but they must be available somewhere on the network.

Table 3-2   Network Services Requirements for RIS

Network Service	RIS Function
DNS Service	RIS relies on the Domain Name System (DNS) server for locating both the directory service and client computer accounts.
DHCP service	Client computers that can perform a network boot receive an Internet Protocol (IP) address from the DHCP server.
Active Directory	RIS relies on the Active Directory service in Windows XP Professional for locating existing client computers as well as existing RIS servers.

Note   This chapter covers installing RIS on a computer running Windows Server 2003. The method for installing RIS on a computer running Windows 2000 Server is different, but you make many of the same choices.

Exam Tip   Remember that RIS requires an Active Directory environment so that RIS clients can locate RIS servers. Active Directory requires that DNS be used on a network; DNS is used to locate services in Active Directory. DHCP is also required for RIS because RIS clients must be able to contact a DHCP server to obtain an IP address so that they can communicate with other devices on the network.

Remote installation requires that RIS be installed on a volume that is shared over the network. This shared volume must meet the following criteria:

- The shared volume cannot be on the same volume that holds the Windows 2000 Server or Windows Server 2003 system files.
- The shared volume must be large enough to hold the RIS software and the various Windows XP Professional images.
- The shared volume must be formatted with the NTFS file system.

To install RIS on a computer running Windows Server 2003, use the following steps:

1. Click Start, point to Control Panel, and then click Add Or Remove Programs.
2. In the Add Or Remove Programs window, click Add/Remove Windows Components.
3. In the Windows Components Wizard, in the Components list, select the Remote Installation Services check box, and then click Next.

   Windows Server 2003 builds a list of necessary files, and then installs RIS.
4. Click Finish to exit the Windows Components Wizard.

   Windows prompts you to restart your computer.
5. Click Yes.

   The computer restarts.
6. After the computer restarts, log on as an administrator, click Start, point to Administrative Tools, and then click Remote Installation Services Setup.
7. On the Welcome page of the Remote Installation Services Setup Wizard, click Next.

   Windows displays the Remote Installation Folder Location page, shown in Figure 3-7. You must specify a path for the location in which to create the installation folder structure—the folders that will contain the RIS images. This path cannot be on the system volume. The path must be on an NTFS-formatted volume that has enough space to hold the images.

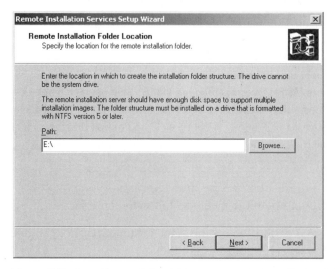

Figure 3-7   Specify a path in which to create the installation folder structure.

8. Type a path, and then click Next.

Windows displays the Initial Settings page, as shown in Figure 3-8. By default, the RIS server will not support client computers until you specifically configure it to do so following Setup. This gives you the chance to configure the server before accepting client connections. However, you can select the Respond To Client Computers Requesting Service check box if you want the server to begin responding immediately.

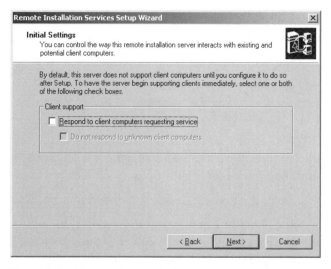

Figure 3-8   Choose whether the server should respond to client requests immediately or after configuration.

9. Choose whether you want the server to begin responding to client requests immediately, and then click Next.

   Windows displays the Installation Source Files Location page, which you can use to
   specify the path to the Windows XP Professional installation files you want to use.

10. Type the path into the Path text box, and then click Next to continue.

11. On the Windows Installation Image Folder Name page, type the name for the
    folder to which the Windows installation files will be copied. This folder is created
    in the path you specified on the Remote Installation Folder Location page.

12. On the Friendly Description And Help Text page, shown in Figure 3-9, type a
    description and help text that helps users on RIS clients identify the operating system.
    Click Next to continue.

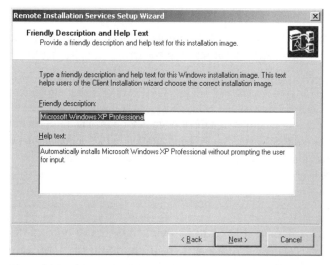

Figure 3-9   Enter a friendly description for the operating system and any help text that might
assist users.

13. On the Review Settings page, make sure that the settings you have selected look
    okay, and then click Finish.

    The Remote Installation Services Setup Wizard begins copying Windows installation
    files, and then performs a number of additional tasks that include the following:

    ❑ Creating the remote installation folder

    ❑ Copying files needed by RIS

    ❑ Copying the Windows XP Professional installation files to the server

    ❑ Configuring the Client Installation Wizard screens that appear during a
    remote installation

    ❑ Creating an unattended installation answer file

❑ Creating remote installation services

❑ Updating the Registry

❑ Creating the Single-Instance Store volume

❑ Starting the required RIS services

❑ Authorizing the RIS server in DHCP

14. When the wizard is finished, click Done.

Requirements for RIS Client Computers

To support remote installation from a RIS server, client computers must have one of the following configurations:

■ A configuration meeting the Net PC specification

■ A network adapter card with a PXE-compliant network adapter and basic input/output system (BIOS) support for starting the computer from PXE

■ A supported network adapter card and a remote installation boot disk

> **Exam Tip**   For the exam, remember the three options for enabling a RIS client to boot from the network and locate a RIS server: Net PC configuration, a PXE-compliant network adapter, or a supported network adapter card and a remote installation boot disk.

Net PCs

The Net PC is a highly manageable platform with the capability to perform a network boot, manage upgrades, and prevent users from changing the hardware or operating system configuration. Additional requirements for the Net PC are as follows:

■ The network adapter must be set as the primary boot device within the system BIOS.

■ The user account that will be used to perform the installation must be assigned the user right Log On As A Batch Job. For more information on assigning user rights, see Chapter 16, "Configuring Security Settings and Internet Options."

> **Note**   The Administrator group does not have the right to log on to a batch job by default. You should create a new group for performing remote installations, assign that group the Log On As A Batch Job user right, and then add users to that group prior to attempting a remote installation.

■ Users must be assigned permission to create computer accounts in the domain they are joining. The domain is specified in the Advanced Settings on the RIS server.

PXE-Compliant Network Adapters

Computers that do not directly meet the Net PC specification can still interact with the RIS server. To enable remote installation on a computer that does not meet the Net PC specification, perform the following steps:

1. Install a PXE-compliant network adapter card.

2. Set the BIOS to start from the PXE boot ROM.

3. The user account that will be used to perform the installation must be assigned the user right Log On As A Batch Job.

4. Users must be assigned permission to create computer accounts in the domain they are joining. The domain is specified in the Advanced Settings on the RIS server.

RIS Boot Floppy Disk

If the network adapter card in a client is not equipped with a PXE boot ROM, or the BIOS does not allow starting from the network adapter card, create a remote installation boot disk. The boot disk simulates the PXE boot process. After installing RIS, you can use the Remote Boot Disk Generator (see Figure 3-10), which allows you to easily create a boot disk.

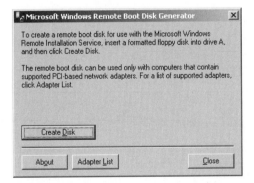

Figure 3-10   Use the Remote Boot Disk Generator to create RIS boot floppy disks.

You can run the Remote Boot Disk Generator (rbfg.exe) to create a boot disk. The rbfg.exe file is located in the Admin\i386 folder in the remote installation folder location you specified when installing RIS. These boot floppies support only the Peripheral Component Interconnect (PCI)–based network adapters listed in the Adapters List. To see the list of the supported network adapters, click Adapter List, as shown in Figure 3-10. A partial listing of the supported network adapter cards is shown in Figure 3-11.

You also need to set the user rights and permissions. The user account that will be used to perform the installation must be assigned the user right Log On As A Batch Job. The users must be assigned permission to create computer accounts in the domain they are joining. The domain is specified in the Advanced Settings on the RIS server.

Figure 3-11   View network adapters that are supported by boot floppies.

Lesson Review

The following questions are intended to reinforce key information presented in this lesson. If you are unable to answer a question, review the lesson materials and try the question again. You can find answers to the questions in the "Questions and Answers" section at the end of this chapter.

1. What is a RIS server and what is it used for?

_____

_____

_____

_____

_____

2. What network services are required for RIS?

_____

3. What can you do if the network adapter card in a client is not PXE-compliant? Does this solution work for all network adapter cards? Why or why not?

_____

_____

_____

_____

4. Which user rights must be assigned to the user account that will be used to perform the remote installation?

_____

_____

Lesson Summary

- Remote installation is the process of connecting to a Remote Installation Services (RIS) server and starting an automated installation of Windows XP Professional on a local computer. Remote installation enables administrators to install Windows XP Professional on client computers throughout a network from a central location.

- RIS is available only on computers running Windows 2000 Server or Windows Server 2003. The RIS server can be a domain controller or a member server. In Windows Server 2003, you use the Add/Remove Windows Components Wizard to add the RIS service. After adding the service, you use the Remote Installation Services Setup Wizard to configure RIS.

- Client computers that support remote installation must have one of the following configurations:

  - ❑ A configuration that meets the Net PC specification, and the network adapter must be set as the primary boot device within the system BIOS

  - ❑ A network adapter card with a PXE boot ROM, and BIOS support for starting from the PXE boot ROM

  - ❑ A supported network adapter card and a remote installation boot disk

Real World   Automating Installations in Large Networks

In large network environments, users typically are not responsible for installing Windows XP Professional themselves. Most IT departments have dedicated staff whose job it is to purchase or build computers, install the operating system and applications, configure the computer, and deliver the computers to users. Most often, this process happens by using disk duplication or RIS.

After installation of the operating system, most large companies use software like Microsoft Systems Management Server (SMS) to distribute and upgrade software (SMS cannot be used to install an operating system to new computers because the client computer must have SMS client components installed). SMS not only automates installations and upgrades; it also monitors the distribution of software throughout the network, helps resolve problems related to installations, and generates reports on the rate and success of deployments.

Lesson 4: Using Tools to Simplify Deployment

There are some additional tools in Windows XP Professional that will help make your deployment of the operating system easier. These tools include the Files And Settings Transfer Wizard, the User State Migration Tool (USMT), and Windows Installer.

After this lesson, you will be able to

- Use the Files And Settings Transfer Wizard
- Explain the purpose of the USMT
- Manage applications by using Windows Installer

Estimated lesson time: 60 minutes

How to Use the Files And Settings Transfer Wizard

Windows XP Professional provides the **Files And Settings Transfer Wizard** to simplify the task of moving data files and personal settings from your old computer to your new one. You do not have to configure all your personal settings on your new computer because you can move your old settings—including display settings, Microsoft Internet Explorer and Microsoft Outlook Express options, dial-up connections, and your folder and taskbar options—to your new computer. The wizard also helps you move specific files and folders to your new computer as well.

The best way to connect your old computer to your new computer is to use a network connection, but you can also use a direct cable connection. To directly connect your computers using a cable, you must have the following items:

- An available COM port (serial port) on both computers
- A null modem cable long enough to connect the two computers

Tip Null modem cables are sometimes called serial file transfer cables. The null modem cable must be serial. You cannot use parallel cables for file transfers using the Direct cable option. Most older computers have 25-pin serial ports, and most newer ones have 9-pin serial ports. Before you purchase your cable, check what type of serial ports are on your computers.

To connect your computers and use a network, check out Chapter 15, "Configuring Network and Internet Connections." After you have connected your computers, you are ready to run the Files And Settings Transfer Wizard.

To open the Files And Settings Transfer Wizard, do the following:

1. Click Start, point to All Programs, point to Accessories, and point to System Tools.

2. Click Files And Settings Transfer Wizard.

   Windows XP Professional starts the Files And Settings Transfer Wizard.

3. In the Welcome To The Files And Settings Transfer Wizard page, click Next.

   The Files And Settings Transfer Wizard displays the What Computer Is This page, which has the following two options:

   ❑ **New Computer.** Select this option if you want to transfer your files and settings to this computer.

   ❑ **Old Computer.** Select this option if you want to transfer the files and settings on this computer to your new computer.

> **Note**   The old computer can be running Windows 95 or later.

4. Select the Old Computer option and click Next. If you have Service Pack 2 installed, a Windows Security Alert dialog box appears. Click Unblock.

   The Files And Settings Transfer Wizard displays the Select The Transfer Method page, which has the following four options:

   ❑ **Direct Cable.** A cable that connects your computer's serial ports.

   ❑ **Home Or Small Office Network.** Both computers must be connected to a network.

   ❑ **Floppy Drive Or Other Removable Media.** Both computers must have the same type of drive.

   ❑ **Other.** You can save files and settings to any disk drive or folder on your computer or on the network.

> **Note**   If you are saving the files and settings to your computer, you can click Browse to locate or create a new folder to hold the files and settings.

5. Select the appropriate option and click Next. Depending on your choice, you might be asked to configure your connection. Configure the connection, and then click Next.

   The Files And Settings Transfer Wizard displays the What Do You Want To Transfer page, which has the following three options:

   ❑ **Settings Only.** The following settings are transferred: Accessibility, Command Prompt Settings, Display Properties, Internet Explorer Settings, Microsoft Messenger, Microsoft NetMeeting, Mouse And Keyboard, MSN Explorer, Network Printer And Drives, Outlook Express, Regional Settings, Sounds And Multimedia, Taskbar Options, Windows Media Player, and Windows Movie Maker.

❑ **Files Only.** The following folders are transferred: Desktop, Fonts, My Documents, My Pictures, Shared Desktop, and Shared Documents. The following files types are transferred: *.asf (Windows Media Audio/Video file), *.asx (Windows Media Audio/Video shortcut), *.AU (AU format sound), *.avi (video clip), *.cov (fax cover page file), *.cpe (fax cover page file), *.doc (WordPad document), *.dvr-ms (Microsoft Recorded TV Show), *.eml (Internet e-mail message), *.m3u (M3U file), *.mid (MIDI sequence), *.midi (MIDI sequence), *.mp2 (Movie File MPEG), *.mp3 (MP3 Format Sound), *.mpa (Movie File MPEG), *.mpeg and *.mpg (Movie File MPEG), *.MSWMM (Windows Movie Maker Project), *.nws (Internet News Message), *.ppi (Microsoft Passport configuration), *.rft (Rich Text Format), *.snd (AU Sound Format), *.wav (Wave Sound), *.wm (Windows Media Audio/Video file), *.wma (Windows Media Audio file), *.wpl (Windows Media Playlist), *.wri (Write document).

❑ **Both Files And Settings.**

Tip   You can select the Let Me Select A Custom List Of Files And Settings When I Click Next check box if you do not want all the default folders, file types, and settings to be transferred.

6. Select the appropriate option and click Next.

Unless you select the Let Me Select A Custom List Of Files And Settings When I Click Next check box, the Files And Settings Transfer Wizard displays the Collection In Progress page. The Files And Settings Transfer Wizard displays the Completing The Collection Phase page.

Important   This page indicates any files and settings that the wizard could not collect. You must manually transfer these files and settings or they will not be transferred to your new computer.

7. Click Finish to complete the wizard on your old computer.

8. Move to your new computer and run the Files And Settings Transfer Wizard on it to complete the transfer of files and settings.

What Is the User State Migration Tool?

The **User State Migration Tool** (USMT) provides all the same functionality as the Files And Settings Transfer Wizard plus the ability to fully customize specific settings such as unique modifications to the Registry. Where the Files And Settings Transfer Wizard is designed for a single user to migrate settings and files from an old computer to a new computer, the USMT is designed for administrators to facilitate large-scale deployments of Windows XP Professional in an Active Directory setting.

The USMT consists of two executable files (ScanState.exe, LoadState.exe), and four migration rule information files (Migapp.inf, Migsys.inf, Miguser.inf, and Sysfiles.inf). ScanState.exe collects user data and settings based on the information contained in Migapp.inf, Migsys.inf, Miguser.inf and Sysfiles.inf. LoadState.exe deposits this user state data on a computer running a fresh (not upgraded) installation of Windows XP Professional.

See Also   For more information on using the USMT, visit *http://www.microsoft.com/technet/ prodtechnol/winxppro/deploy/usermigr.mspx.*

How to Manage Applications by Using Windows Installer

Windows Installer and installation packages (.msi files) simplify the installation and removal of software applications. An installation package contains all the information that the Windows Installer requires to install or uninstall an application or product and to run the setup user interface. Each installation package includes an .msi file that contains an installation database, a summary information stream, and data streams for various parts of the installation. The .msi file can also contain one or more transforms, internal source files, and external source files or cabinet files required by the installation.

If there is a problem during the installation of a software application, or if the installation fails, Windows Installer can restore or roll back the operating system to its previous state. Windows Installer also reduces conflicts between applications by preventing the installation of an application from overwriting a dynamic-link library (DLL) used by another application. Windows Installer can determine if an application you installed using it has any missing or corrupted files, and can then replace them to resolve the problem.

To preserve users' disk space, Windows Installer allows you to install only the essential files required to run an application. It supports the installation of application features on demand, which means that the first time a user accesses any feature not included in the minimal installation, the necessary files are automatically installed. Windows Installer allows you to configure unattended application installations and it supports both 32-bit and 64-bit applications.

The Windows Installer can advertise the availability of an application to users or other applications without actually installing the application. If an application is advertised, only the interfaces required for loading and launching the application are presented to the user or other applications. If a user or application activates an advertised interface, the installer then proceeds to install the necessary components.

The two types of advertising are assigning and publishing. An application appears installed to a user when that application is assigned to the user. The Start menu contains the appropriate shortcuts, icons are displayed, files are associated with the application, and Registry entries reflect the application's installation. When the user tries to open an assigned application, it is installed upon demand.

You can also publish a Windows Installer application from within Active Directory. A published application becomes available to the user for installation, but is not advertised to the user. The user can locate and install the application by using the Add Or Remove Programs tool in Control Panel.

Windows Installer supports Microsoft's .NET framework technology. The .NET framework gives developers code reuse, code specialization, resource management, multi-language development, improved security, deployment, and administration. Windows Installer also provides software restriction policies that provide virus protection, including protection from Trojan horse viruses and worms propagated through e-mail and the Web.

The way you troubleshoot a Windows Installer package depends on the problem you are having. If a Windows Installer package does not install correctly, you need to determine whether the package has become corrupted. To repair a corrupted Windows Installer package, use the Windows Installer repair option. Open a command prompt and type the following command:

```
msiexec /f[p][o][e][d][c][][a][u][m][s][v] {package|ProductCode}
```

For an explanation of the parameters used with the /f switch in the Msiexec.exe command, see Table 3-3.

Table 3-3   Parameters for the /f Switch for Msiexec.exe

Parameters	Description
P	Reinstall only if the file is missing
O	Reinstall if the file is missing or if an older version is installed
E	Reinstall if the file is missing or if an equal or older version is installed
D	Reinstall if the file is missing or if a different version is installed
C	Reinstall if the file is missing or if the stored checksum does not match the calculated value
A	Force all the files to be reinstalled
U	Rewrite all the required user-specific Registry entries
M	Rewrite all the required computer-specific Registry entries
S	Overwrite all the existing shortcuts
V	Run from source and recache the local package

There are several additional switches for the Msiexec.exe command. These switches include the ones explained in Table 3-4. In this table, package is the name of the

Windows Installer Package file, and *ProductCode* is the globally unique identifier (GUID) of the Windows Installer package. For a complete listing of switches, see Help And Support Center.

Table 3-4   Switches for Msiexec.exe

Switch	Parameter	Description
/I	{package | *ProductCode*}	Installs or configures a product For example: msiexec /i a:\sample.msi
/a	Package	Administrative installation option For example: msiexec /a a:\sample.msi
/x	{package | *ProductCode*}	Uninstalls a product For example: msiexec /x sample.msi
/j	[u | m]package]	Advertises a product, as follows: **u** Advertises to the current user **m** Advertises to all users For example: msiexec /jm sample.msi
/L	[i][w][e][a][r][u] [c][m][p][v][+][!]logfile	The path to the log file. The parameters specify what to log, as follows: **i** Log status messages **w** Log nonfatal warnings **e** Log all error messages **a** Log all startup actions r Log action-specific records u Log user requests c Log initial user interface parameters m Log out of memory p Log terminal properties v Log verbose output + Append to existing file ! Flush each line to the log * Log all information except the v option (wildcard) To include the v options, specify /L*v

If the installation process stops before completing, either Windows Installer was unable to read the package, or conditions on your computer prevented it from installing the application. Open Event Viewer and review the Application log.

See Also   For more information about how to use Event Viewer, see Chapter 18, "Using Windows XP Tools."

Lesson Review

The following questions are intended to reinforce key information presented in this lesson. If you are unable to answer a question, review the lesson materials and try the question again. You can find answers to the questions in the "Questions and Answers" section at the end of this chapter.

1. When do you use the Files And Settings Transfer Wizard?

   _____

   _____

   _____

   _____

   _____

2. Which of the following statements are true for the Files And Settings Transfer Wizard? (Choose all that apply.)

   a. You run the Files And Settings Transfer Wizard only on your old computer.

   b. You must run the Files And Settings Transfer Wizard on both your old and your new computers.

   c. You can use a standard 25-pin cable to connect the parallel ports on your old and new computers to run the Files And Settings Transfer Wizard.

   d. You can use serial ports to directly connect your old and new computers to run the Files And Settings Transfer Wizard.

3. How can Windows Installer help you minimize the amount of disk space taken up on a user's disk when you install a new application on that user's disk?

   _____

   _____

   _____

   _____

Lesson Summary

- The Files And Settings Transfer Wizard simplifies the task of moving data files and personal settings from your old computer to your new one. The Files And Settings Transfer Wizard can move your display settings, Internet Explorer and Outlook Express options, dial-up connections, and your folder and taskbar options to your new computer.

- The USMT offers all the advantages of the Files And Settings Transfer Wizard, but is geared toward large-scale deployments of multiple users in an Active Directory setting.

- Windows Installer has a client-side installer service, Msiexec.exe, which allows the operating system to control the installation. Windows Installer uses the information stored in the package file, an .msi file, to install the application.

Case Scenario Exercise

In this exercise, you will read a scenario about deploying Windows XP Professional, and then answer the questions that follow. If you have difficulty completing this work, review the material in this chapter before beginning the next chapter. You can find answers to these questions in the "Questions and Answers" section at the end of this chapter.

Scenario

You are working as an administrator for the School of Fine Art, which has a large campus in San Francisco. The school's network consists of 75 client computers running Windows XP Professional and six servers running Windows Server 2003. All computers are members of the same Active Directory domain. Two of the servers are configured as domain controllers. The rest are configured as member servers that serve various roles on the network. The company is adding 25 computers to its network, and you have been given the responsibility of installing Windows XP Professional on these computers. All 25 of these computers are the same model computer from the same manufacturer and have similar hardware. Your company has a volume licensing arrangement and has purchased an additional 25 licenses of Windows XP Professional for the computers.

Questions

1. What automated methods could you use to install Windows XP Professional on these computers?

   _____

   _____

   _____

2. Because all the computers have the same hardware configuration, you have decided to use disk duplication to install Windows XP Professional on the computers. What component will you need to obtain that does not come with Windows XP Professional?

   _____

   _____

3. How should you prepare the reference computer?

_____

_____

_____

_____

_____

Troubleshooting Lab

You are working as an administrator for a company named Wide World Importers, which has recently hired a number of new employees. The company has purchased a number of new computers and placed them in the appropriate locations. You do not have time to install Windows XP Professional for every new user, so you have installed a RIS server that will enable users to install the operating system when they first start their computers. The new users have been briefed on the process, but you decide to test the process on one of the new computers. When you turn on his computer, the process does not work.

List the network, server, and client requirements for using a RIS server and why those requirements are important.

The requirements for using a RIS server are as follows:

- RIS requires an Active Directory environment with DNS and DHCP service. RIS clients must be able to contact a DHCP server to obtain an IP address so they can communicate with other devices on the network. RIS clients require DNS so that they can locate the appropriate services in Active Directory. RIS clients require Active Directory so that they can locate RIS servers.

- RIS must be installed on a server running Windows 2000 Server or Windows Server 2003 that is a member of an Active Directory domain. You must add the RIS service to the computer, and then set the service up.

- RIS clients must be able to boot from the network. To do this, the client must support the Net PC specification or have a PXE-compliant network adapter, or you must create a floppy boot disk for the client with drivers for the client's network adapter.

Chapter Summary

■ Small deployments or situations involving many different hardware configurations often use an unattended installation, in which the Winnt32 and Winnt commands are used along with an unattended answer file to script the installation. This file is created with Windows Setup Manager.

■ Many larger enterprise deployments use disk duplication to deploy systems, a process in which you use the System Preparation Tool to create an image from a computer running Windows XP Professional, and then clone that image on other computers. Using disk duplication usually requires third-party software.

■ Microsoft provides RIS for use in environments in which Active Directory service is available. The RIS server software (which resides on a server computer running Windows 2000 Server or Windows Server 2003) stores images of Windows XP installations and makes those images available over the network. A client computer boots from the network (or using a special RIS boot disk), contacts the RIS server, and then installs an image from that server.

■ Windows XP Professional also provides tools that help make your deployment of Windows XP Professional easier. These tools include the Files And Settings Transfer Wizard, the USMT, and Windows Installer.

Exam Highlights

Before taking the exam, review the key points and terms that are presented in this chapter. You need to know this information.

Key Points

■ An answer file is used to provide the common configuration settings for all computers that are affected during an unattended installation. A UDF provides the unique settings that each computer needs to distinguish it from other computers.

■ RIS requires an Active Directory environment so that RIS clients can locate RIS servers. Active Directory requires that DNS be used on a network; DNS is used to locate services in Active Directory. DHCP is also required for RIS because RIS clients must be able to contact a DHCP server to obtain an IP address so that they can communicate with other devices on the network.

■ There are three ways that a RIS client can boot from the network and locate a RIS server: by being compliant with the Net PC configuration, having a PXE-compliant network adapter, or having a supported network adapter card and using a RIS boot disk.

Key Terms

answer file   A text file that supplies Windows XP Professional Setup with information necessary during the installation process.

disk duplication   An automated installation in which you use the System Preparation Tool to create an image from a computer running Windows XP Professional, and then clone that image on other computers. Using disk duplication usually requires third-party software.

Files And Settings Transfer Wizard   A Windows XP Professional wizard that simplifies the task of moving data files and personal settings from your old computer to your new one.

Preboot eXecution Environment (PXE)   A standard for network booting that is supported by some network adapters. Using a PXE-compliant network adapter is one of three configurations that allow a RIS client to boot from the network and locate a RIS server. (RIS clients can also be compliant with the Net PC specification or use a RIS boot disk.)

Remote Installation Services (RIS)   Software stores images of Windows XP installations and makes those images available over the network.

System Preparation   A utility that allows you to prepare master images of an existing Windows XP installation for distribution to other computers by removing machine-specific information from the computer.

unattended installation   An automated installation in which the Winnt32 and Winnt commands are used along with an unattended answer file to script the installation.

uniqueness database file (UDF)   A text file that is used in conjunction with an answer file and contains the settings that are unique to each computer.

User State Migration Tool (USMT)   A utility that provides all the same functionality as the Files And Settings Transfer Wizard plus the ability to fully customize specific settings such as unique modifications to the Registry. The USMT is designed for administrators to facilitate large-scale deployments of Windows XP Professional in an Active Directory setting.

Windows Setup Manager   A wizard-based program that allows you to quickly create a script for a unattended installation of Windows XP Professional.

winnt.exe   A command-line utility used to start Windows Setup from the MS-DOS or Windows 3.1 command prompt.

winnt32.exe   A command-line utility used to start Windows Setup from the Windows 95 or later command prompt.

Questions and Answers

Lesson 1 Review

Page
3-16

1. What is the purpose of Windows Setup Manager?

Windows Setup Manager makes it easy to create the answer files and uniqueness database files that you use to run unattended installations.

2. How can you apply an application update pack as part of the Windows XP Professional installation?

You need to add the commands to execute in the Additional Commands page of the Windows Setup Manager Wizard so that the update packs will be applied to the application as part of the Windows XP Professional installation.

3. What type of answer files does Windows Setup Manager allow you to create?

Windows Unattended Installation, Sysprep Install, and RIS

4. Why would you use a UDF?

A UDF allows you to specify per-computer parameters for an unattended installation. This file overrides values in the answer file.

Lesson 2 Practice: Exercise 1

Page
3-21

4. What do the optional parameters /pnp and /noreboot do?

The /pnp parameter forces the destination computer to detect Plug and Play devices on their first reboot following installation. The /noreboot parameter prevents the computer on which you are running Sysprep.exe from rebooting after running Sysprep.exe.

A Windows System Preparation Tool dialog box appears, warning you that running Sysprep might modify some of the security parameters of this system.

Lesson 2 Review

Page
3-24

1. What is disk duplication?

Creating a disk image of a Windows XP Professional installation and copying that image to multiple computers with identical hardware configurations.

2. What is the purpose of the System Preparation Tool?

The System Preparation Tool was developed to prepare a master image for disk copying. Every computer must have a unique SID. The System Preparation Tool adds a system service to the master image that will create a unique local domain SID the first time the computer to which the master image is copied is started. The System Preparation Tool also adds a Mini-Setup Wizard to the master copy that runs the first time the computer to which the master image is copied is started and guides you through entering user-specific information.

3. What does the /quiet switch do when you run Sysprep.exe?

The /quiet switch causes Sysprep.exe to run without any user intervention.

Lesson 3 Review

Page
3-32

1. What is a RIS server and what is it used for?

A RIS server is a computer running Windows 2000 Server or Windows Server 2003, on which you have installed RIS. The RIS server is used to perform remote installations of Windows XP Professional. Remote installation enables administrators to install Windows XP Professional on client computers throughout a network from a central location.

2. What network services are required for RIS?

DNS Service, DHCP, and Active Directory

3. What can you do if the network adapter card in a client is not PXE-compliant? Does this solution work for all network adapter cards? Why or why not?

If the network adapter card in a client is not PXE-compliant, you can create a remote installation boot disk that simulates the PXE boot process. A remote installation boot disk does not work for all network adapter cards; it works only for those cards supported by the Windows 2000 Remote Boot Disk Generator.

4. Which user rights must be assigned to the user account that will be used to perform the remote installation?

The user account that will be used to perform the installation must be assigned the user right Log On As A Batch Job.

Lesson 4 Review

Page
3-40

1. When do you use the Files And Settings Transfer Wizard?

The Files And Settings Transfer Wizard helps you move data files and personal settings when you upgrade your hardware. The settings you can move include display settings, Internet Explorer and Outlook Express options, dial-up connections, and your folder and taskbar options. The wizard also helps you move specific files and folders to your new computer.

2. Which of the following statements are true for the Files And Settings Transfer Wizard? (Choose all that apply.)

   a. You run the Files And Settings Transfer Wizard only on your old computer.

   b. You must run the Files And Settings Transfer Wizard on both your old and your new computers.

   c. You can use a standard 25-pin cable to connect the parallel ports on your old and new computers to run the Files And Settings Transfer Wizard.

   d. You can use serial ports to directly connect your old and new computers to run the Files And Settings Transfer Wizard.

The correct answers are B and D. A is not correct because you run the wizard on both the old and new computers. C is not correct because you use parallel ports to directly connect the old and new computers.

3. How can Windows Installer help you minimize the amount of disk space taken up on a user's disk when you install a new application on that user's disk?

Windows Installer allows you to install only the essential files required to run an application to reduce the amount of space used on a user's hard disk. The first time a user accesses any feature not included in the minimal installation, the necessary files are automatically installed.

Case Scenario Exercise Questions

Page 3-41

1. What automated methods could you use to install Windows XP Professional on these computers?

You could use one of the three methods discussed in this chapter: use Setup Manager to create an answer file, use the System Preparation Tool to prepare images for disk duplication, or configure RIS on one of the server computers.

2. Because all the computers have the same hardware configuration, you have decided to use disk duplication to install Windows XP Professional on the computers. What component will you need to obtain that does not come with Windows XP Professional?

You will need to obtain a disk duplication utility to copy the disk images to the new computers.

3. How should you prepare the reference computer?

You should first install Windows XP Professional on the reference computer, and then apply all available software updates. You should then configure Windows as it should be configured on all the computers. You should also install any other applications that all of the computers will need. After you have done this, you should run the System Preparation Tool on the reference computer to prepare it for disk imaging.

4 Modifying and Troubleshooting the Startup Process

Exam Objectives in this Chapter:

- Restore and back up the operating system, System State data, and user data.
    - ❏ Troubleshoot system restoration by starting in safe mode.
    - ❏ Recover System State data and user data by using the Recovery Console.

Why This Chapter Matters

Troubleshooting startup problems in Microsoft Windows XP Professional is an important skill. To effectively troubleshoot startup problems, you must have a clear understanding of how the startup process works. This chapter introduces the Windows XP Professional startup process. It also teaches how the Windows Registry works and how to use the startup and recovery tools that Windows XP Professional provides.

Lessons in this Chapter:

Before You Begin

To complete this chapter, you must have a computer that meets the minimum hardware requirements listed in the preface, "About This Book." You must also have Windows XP Professional installed on your computer.

Lesson 1: Explaining the Startup Process

In this lesson, you learn about the files that Windows XP Professional uses during the startup process. You also learn the five stages of startup: preboot sequence, boot sequence, kernel load, kernel initialization, and logon. You also learn how to effectively troubleshoot the Windows XP Professional startup process.

After this lesson, you will be able to

- Describe the files used in the startup process.
- Explain what happens during the preboot sequence.
- Explain what happens during the boot sequence.
- Explain the purpose and function of the BOOT.INI file.
- Explain what happens during the kernel load phase.
- Explain what happens during the kernel initialization phase.
- Explain what happens during the logon phase.

Estimated lesson time: 40 minutes

Files Used in the Startup Process

Windows XP Professional requires certain files during startup. Table 4-1 lists the files used in the Windows XP Professional startup process, the appropriate location of each file, and the phases of the startup process associated with each file.

Note   %systemroot% represents the path of your Windows XP Professional installation directory, which by default is a folder named \Windows on the system partition.

Table 4-1   Files Used in the Windows XP Professional Startup Process

File	Location	Startup Phase
NTLDR	System partition root (C:\ )	Preboot and boot
BOOT.INI	System partition root	Boot
BOOTSECT.DOS	System partition root	Boot (optional)
NTDETECT.COM	System partition root	Boot
NTBOOTDD.SYS	System partition root	Boot (optional)
NTOSKRNL.EXE	%systemroot%\System32	Kernel load
HAL.DLL	%systemroot%\System32	Kernel load
SYSTEM	%systemroot%\System32	Kernel initialization
Device drivers (.sys)	%systemroot%\System32\Drivers	Kernel initialization

Note   To view the files listed in Table 4-1, open Windows Explorer and click Folder Options on the Tools menu. In the View tab of the Folder Options dialog box, under Hidden Files And Folders, click Show Hidden Files And Folders. Clear the Hide Protected Operating System Files (Recommended) check box. A Warning message box appears, indicating that it is not a good idea to display the protected operating system files. Click Yes to display them. Click OK to close the Folder Options dialog box.

What Happens During the Preboot Sequence

During startup, a computer running Windows XP Professional initializes and then locates the boot portion of the hard disk.

The following four steps occur during the preboot sequence:

1. The computer runs power-on self test (POST) routines to determine the amount of physical memory, whether the hardware components are present, and so on. If the computer has a Plug and Play–compatible basic input/output system (BIOS), enumeration and configuration of hardware devices occurs at this stage.

2. The computer BIOS locates the boot device, and then loads and runs the **Master Boot Record (MBR)**.

3. The MBR scans the partition table to locate the active partition, loads the boot sector on the active partition into memory, and then executes it.

4. The computer loads and initializes the **NTLDR** file, which is the operating system loader.

Note   Windows XP Professional Setup modifies the boot sector during installation so that NTLDR loads during system startup.

There are a number of problems that can occur during the preboot sequence, including the following:

Improper hardware configuration or malfunctioning hardware   If the BIOS cannot detect a hard drive during its POST routine, startup fails early during the preboot sequence and usually presents a message stating that a hard drive cannot be located.

Corrupt MBR   If your MBR becomes corrupt (a fairly common action taken by viruses), you can generally repair it by using the Recovery Console, which is covered in Lesson 3, "Troubleshooting Problems Using Startup and Recovery Tools." Antivirus software can prevent and often repair a corrupt MBR.

Floppy or USB disk inserted   If you see an error message stating that there is a non-system disk or a disk error, or stating that no operating system could be found, a common reason is that a floppy disk or a universal serial bus (USB) flash memory disk is inserted in the drive during startup. On most computers, BIOS is configured by default to try starting using the floppy drive or an available USB drive before it attempts to start by using the hard drive.

What Happens During the Boot Sequence

After the computer loads NTLDR into memory, the boot sequence gathers information about hardware and drivers in preparation for the Windows XP Professional load phases. The boot sequence uses the following files: NTLDR, **BOOT.INI**, BOOT-SECT.DOS (optional), NTDETECT.COM, and NTOSKRNL.EXE.

The boot sequence has four phases: initial boot loader phase, operating system selection, hardware detection, and configuration selection (described in the following sections).

Initial Boot Loader Phase

During the initial boot loader phase, NTLDR switches the microprocessor from real mode to 32-bit flat memory mode, which NTLDR requires to carry out any additional functions. Next, NTLDR starts the appropriate minifile system drivers. The minifile system drivers are built into NTLDR so that NTLDR can find and load Windows XP Professional from partitions formatted with file allocation table (FAT), FAT32, or NT file system (NTFS).

Operating System Selection

During the boot sequence, NTLDR reads the BOOT.INI file. If more than one operating system selection is available in the BOOT.INI file, a Please Select The Operating System To Start screen appears, listing the operating systems specified in the BOOT.INI file. If you do not select an entry before the timer reaches zero, NTLDR loads the operating system specified by the default parameter in the BOOT.INI file. Windows XP Professional Setup sets the default parameter to the most recent Windows XP Professional installation. If there is only one entry in the BOOT.INI file, the Please Select The Operating System To Start screen does not appear, and the default operating system is automatically loaded.

> **Note**   If the BOOT.INI file is not present, NTLDR attempts to load Windows XP Professional from the first partition of the first disk—typically C:\.

Hardware Detection

NTDETECT.COM and NTOSKRNL.EXE perform hardware detection. NTDETECT.COM executes after you select Windows XP Professional on the Please Select The Operating System To Start screen (or after the timer times out).

> **Note**   If you select an operating system other than Windows XP Professional (such as Windows 98), NTLDR loads and executes BOOTSECT.DOS, which is a copy of the boot sector that was on the system partition at the time Windows XP Professional was installed. Passing execution to BOOTSECT.DOS starts the boot process for the selected operating system.

NTDETECT.COM collects a list of currently installed hardware components and returns this list to NTLDR for later inclusion in the Registry under the HKEY_LOCAL_MACHINE\HARDWARE key.

NTDETECT.COM detects the following components:

- Bus/adapter type
- Communication ports
- Floating-point coprocessor
- Floppy disks
- Keyboard
- Mouse/pointing device
- Parallel ports
- SCSI adapters
- Video adapters

Configuration Selection

After NTLDR starts loading Windows XP Professional and collects hardware information, the operating system loader presents you with the Hardware Profile/Configuration Recovery menu, which contains a list of the hardware profiles that are set up on the computer. The first hardware profile is highlighted. You can press the DOWN arrow key to select another profile. You also can press L to invoke the Last Known Good configuration.

If there is only a single hardware profile, NTLDR does not display the Hardware Profile/Configuration Recovery menu and loads Windows XP Professional using the default hardware profile configuration.

Troubleshooting the Boot Sequence

There are a number of problems that can occur during the boot sequence, including the following:

Missing or corrupt boot files   If the NTLDR, BOOT.INI, BOOTSECT.DOS, NTDE-TECT.COM, or NTOSKRNL.EXE files become corrupt or are missing, you see an error message indicating the situation, and Windows startup fails. You should use the Recovery Console (described in Lesson 3) to restore the files.

Improperly configured BOOT.INI   An improperly configured BOOT.INI file generally results from an error while manually editing the file or from a change to disk configuration. It is also possible for the BOOT.INI file to become corrupt or missing. In this case, you should use the Recovery Console to restore the files.

Improperly configured hardware   NTDETECT.COM can fail during its detection of hardware if a hardware device is incorrectly configured, a bad driver is installed, or the device is malfunctioning. If startup fails during hardware detection, you should begin troubleshooting hardware by removing unnecessary devices from the computer and adding them back one at a time until you discover the source of the problem. You can also try the Last Known Good configuration if you suspect that a new configuration or driver is at fault.

What Is the BOOT.INI File?

When you install Windows XP Professional on a computer, Windows Setup saves the BOOT.INI file in the active partition. NTLDR uses information in the BOOT.INI file to display the boot loader screen, from which you select the operating system to start.

The BOOT.INI file includes two sections, *[boot loader]* and *[operating systems]*, which contain information that NTLDR uses to create the Boot Loader Operating System Selection menu. A typical BOOT.INI might contain the following lines:

```
[boot loader]
timeout=30
default=multi(0)disk(0)rdisk(0)partition(2)\WINDOWS
[operating systems]
multi(0)disk(0)rdisk(0)partition(2)\WINDOWS="Microsoft Windows XP Professional" /fast-
detect
multi(0)disk(0)rdisk(0)partition(1)\WINNT="Windows NT Workstation Version 4.00"
multi(0)disk(0)rdisk(1)partition(1)\ WINNT="Windows NT Server Workstation 4.00 [VGA mo
de]" /basevideo /sos
C:\CMDCONS\BOOTSECT.DAT="Microsoft Windows Recovery Console" /cmdcons
```

The *[operating systems]* section of a BOOT.INI file that is created during a default installation of Windows XP Professional contains a single entry for Windows XP Professional. If your computer is a Windows 95–based or Windows 98–based dual-boot system, the *[operating systems]* section also contains an entry for starting the system by using the other operating system. If you installed Windows XP Professional on a computer and kept an installation of Windows NT 4.0 on another partition of the same computer, the *[operating systems]* section also contains an entry for starting the system using this version of Windows NT.

ARC Paths

During installation, Windows XP Professional generates the BOOT.INI file, which contains Advanced RISC Computing (ARC) paths pointing to the computer's boot partition. (RISC stands for Reduced Instruction Set Computing, a microprocessor design that uses a small set of simple instructions for fast execution.) The following is an example of an ARC path:

```
multi(0)disk(0)rdisk(1)partition(2)
```

Table 4-2 describes the naming conventions for ARC paths.

Table 4-2   ARC Path Naming Conventions

Convention	Description
multi(x) | scsi(x)	The adapter/disk controller. Use scsi to indicate a Small Computer System Interface (SCSI) controller on which SCSI BIOS is not enabled. For all other adapter/disk controllers, use multi, including SCSI disk controllers with BIOS enabled. Here, x represents a number that indicates the load order of the hardware adapter. For example, if you have two SCSI adapters in a computer, the first to load and initialize receives number 0, and the next SCSI adapter receives number 1.
Disk(y)	The SCSI ID. For multi, this value is always 0.
Rdisk(z)	A number that identifies the disk (ignored for SCSI controllers).
Partition(a)	A number that identifies the partition.

In both multi and scsi conventions, multi, scsi, disk, and rdisk numbers are assigned starting with 0. Partition numbers start with 1. All primary partitions are assigned numbers first, followed by logical volumes in extended partitions.

Exam Tip   Learn the syntax of ARC paths and how to determine which disk and partition a particular path refers to. Most disk types use the multi convention. The value following multi indicates the disk number. The value following partition indicates the partition number on that disk.

See Figure 4-1 for some examples of how to determine the ARC path.

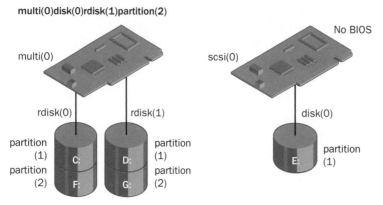

Figure 4-1   ARC paths list the available partitions.

The scsi ARC naming convention varies the disk(y) parameter for successive disks on one controller, whereas the multi format varies the rdisk(z) parameter.

BOOT.INI Switches

You can add a variety of switches to the entries in the *[operating systems]* section of the BOOT.INI file to provide additional functionality. Table 4-3 describes some of these optional switches that you can use for entries in the BOOT.INI file.

Table 4-3   BOOT.INI Optional Switches

Switch	Description
/basevideo	Boots the computer using the standard Video Graphics Adapter (VGA) video driver. If a new video driver is not working correctly, use this switch to start Windows XP Professional, and then change to a different driver.
/fastdetect=[com$x$ | comx,y,z.]	Disables serial mouse detection. Without a port specification, this switch disables peripheral detection on all COM ports. This switch is included in every entry in the BOOT.INI file by default.
/maxmem:n	Specifies the amount of random access memory (RAM) that Windows XP Professional uses. Use this switch if you suspect that a memory chip is bad.
/noguiboot	Boots the computer without displaying the graphical boot status screen.
/sos	Displays the device driver names as they are loading. Use this switch when startup fails while loading drivers to determine which driver is triggering the failure.

Modifications to BOOT.INI

You can modify the timeout and default parameter values in the BOOT.INI file using the Startup And Recovery dialog box (which you can open from the Advanced tab of the System Properties dialog box). In addition, you can manually edit these and other parameter values in the BOOT.INI file. For example, you might modify the BOOT.INI file to add more descriptive entries for the Boot Loader Operating System Selection menu or to include various switches to aid in troubleshooting the boot process.

During Windows XP Professional installation, Windows Setup sets the read-only and system attributes for the BOOT.INI file. Before editing the BOOT.INI file with a text editor, you must make the file visible and turn off the read-only attribute. You can change file attributes using My Computer, Windows Explorer, or the command prompt.

To change file attributes by using My Computer or Windows Explorer, complete the following steps:

1. From the Start menu, click My Computer.

2. In the My Computer window, double-click the icon for the drive containing the BOOT.INI file.

3. On the Tools menu, click Folder Options.

4. In the Folder Options dialog box, on the View tab, click Show Hidden Files And Folders. Clear the Hide Protected Operating System Files check box and click Yes when prompted. Click OK.

5. Click Show The Contents Of This Drive. In the window showing the contents of the drive, right-click the file named BOOT, and then click Properties.

6. On the General tab, under Attributes, clear the Read-Only check box, and then click OK.

To change file attributes using the command prompt, switch to the directory containing the BOOT.INI file if necessary, and then type

```
attrib -s -r boot.ini
```

After you have changed the attributes of the BOOT.INI file, you can open and modify the file using a text editor.

What Happens During the Kernel Load Phase

After configuration selection, the Windows XP Professional kernel (NTOSKRNL.EXE) loads and initializes. NTOSKRNL.EXE also loads and initializes device drivers and loads services. If you press ENTER when the Hardware Profile/Configuration Recovery menu appears, or if NTLDR makes the selection automatically, the computer enters the kernel load phase. The screen clears, and a series of white rectangles appears across the bottom of the screen, indicating startup progress.

During the kernel load phase, NTLDR does the following:

■ Loads NTOSKRNL.EXE, but does not initialize it.

■ Loads the hardware abstraction layer file (HAL.DLL).

■ Loads the HKEY_LOCAL_MACHINE\SYSTEM Registry key.

■ Selects the control set it will use to initialize the computer. A control set contains configuration data used to control the system, such as a list of the device drivers and services to load and start.

■ Loads device drivers with a value of 0x0 for the Start entry. These typically are low-level hardware device drivers, such as those for a hard disk. The value for the List entry, which is specified in the HKEY_LOCAL_MACHINE\SYSTEM\Current-ControlSet\Control\ServiceGroupOrder subkey of the Registry, defines the order in which NTLDR loads these device drivers.

Problems during the kernel load phase of startup often occur because of corrupted system files or because of a hardware malfunction. In the case of corrupted system files, you can try to replace those files using the Recovery Console, which is covered in Lesson 3. In the case of a hardware problem, you will likely need to troubleshoot by removing or replacing hardware components until you identify the problem. You may be able to isolate the hardware device causing the problem by enabling boot logging (which is also covered in Lesson 3).

What Happens During the Kernel Initialization Phase

When the kernel load phase is complete, the kernel initializes, and then NTLDR passes control to the kernel. At this point, the system displays a graphical screen with a status bar that indicates load status. Four tasks are accomplished during the kernel initialization stage:

The Hardware key is created.   On successful initialization, the kernel uses the data collected during hardware detection to create the Registry key HKEY_LOCAL_MACHINE\HARDWARE. This key contains information about hardware components on the system board and the interrupts used by specific hardware devices.

The Clone control set is created.   The kernel creates the Clone control set by copying the control set referenced by the value of the Current entry in the

HKEY_LOCAL_MACHINE\SYSTEM\Select subkey of the Registry. The Clone control set is never modified because it is intended to be an identical copy of the data used to configure the computer and should not reflect changes made during the startup process.

Device drivers are loaded and initialized.   After creating the Clone control set, the kernel initializes the low-level device drivers that were loaded during the kernel load phase. The kernel then scans the HKEY_LOCAL_MACHINE\ SYSTEM\CurrentControlSet\Services subkey of the Registry for device drivers with a value of 0x1 for the Start entry. As in the kernel load phase, a device driver's value for the Group entry specifies the order in which it loads. Device drivers initialize as soon as they load. If an error occurs while loading and initializing a device driver, the boot process proceeds based on the value specified in the ErrorControl entry for the driver. Table 4-4 describes the possible ErrorControl values and the resulting boot sequence actions.

Table 4-4   ErrorControl Values and Resulting Action

ErrorControl Value	Action
0x0 (Ignore)	The boot sequence ignores the error and proceeds without displaying an error message.
0x1 (Normal)	The boot sequence displays an error message, but ignores the error and proceeds.
0x2 (Severe)	The boot sequence fails and then restarts using the Last Known Good control set. If the boot sequence is currently using the Last Known Good control set, the boot sequence ignores the error and proceeds.
0x3 (Critical)	The boot sequence fails and then restarts using the Last Known Good control set. However, if the Last Known Good control set is causing the critical error, the boot sequence stops and displays an error message.

Note   ErrorControl values appear in the Registry under the subkey HKEY_LOCAL_MACHINE\ SYSTEM\CurrentControlSet\Services*name_of_service_or_driver*\ErrorControl.

Services are started.   After the kernel loads and initializes device drivers, Session Manager (SMSS.EXE) starts the higher-order subsystems and services for Windows XP Professional. Session Manager executes the instructions in the BootExecute data item, and in the Memory Management, DOS Devices, and SubSystems keys. Table 4-5 describes the function of each instruction set and the resulting Session Manager action.

Table 4-5   Session Manager Reads and Executes These Instruction Sets

Data Item or Key	Action
BootExecute data item	Session Manager executes the commands specified in this data item before it loads any services.
Memory Management key	Session Manager creates the paging file information required by the Virtual Memory Manager.
DOS Devices key	Session Manager creates symbolic links that direct certain classes of commands to the correct component in the file system.
SubSystems key	Session Manager starts the Win32 subsystem, which controls all input/output (I/O) and access to the video screen, and starts the WinLogon process.

What Happens During the Logon Phase

The logon phase begins at the conclusion of the kernel initialization phase. The Win32 subsystem automatically starts WINLOGON.EXE, which in turn starts the Local Security Authority (LSASS.EXE) and displays the Logon dialog box. You can log on at this time, even though Windows XP Professional might still be initializing network device drivers.

Next, the Service Control Manager executes and makes a final scan of the HKEY_ LOCAL_MACHINE\SYSTEM\CurrentControlSet\Services subkey, looking for services with a value of 0x2 for the Start entry. These services, including the Workstation service and the Server service, are marked to load automatically.

The services that load during this phase do so based on their values for the DependOn-Group or DependOnService entries in the HKEY_LOCAL_MACHINE\ SYSTEM\CurrentControlSet\Services Registry subkey.

A Windows XP Professional startup is not considered good until a user successfully logs on to the system. After a successful logon, the system copies the Clone control set to the Last Known Good control set.

> **Note**   For more information on Last Known Good configuration, see Lesson 3 later in this chapter.

Lesson Review

Use the following questions to help determine whether you have learned enough to move on to the next lesson. If you are unable to answer a question, review the lesson materials and try the question again. You can find answers to the questions in the "Questions and Answers" section at the end of this chapter.

1. Windows XP Professional modifies the boot sector during installation so that _____ loads during system startup. Fill in the blank.

2. What is the purpose of the BOOT.INI file, and what happens if it is not present?

_____

_____

_____

3. What does the BOOTSECT.DOS file contain and when is it used?

_____

_____

_____

_____

4. A user calls you and tells you that Windows XP Professional does not appear to be loading correctly. The Hardware Profile/Configuration Recovery menu does not appear when the computer is restarted, but it does appear on the computer of the person sitting in the next cubicle when that computer is restarted. What would you tell the user?

_____

_____

_____

_____

Lesson Summary

- Files used during the Windows XP Professional startup process include NTLDR, BOOT.INI, BOOTSECT.DOS, NTDETECT.COM, NTBOOTDD.SYS, NTOSKRNL.EXE, HAL.DLL, SYSTEM, and Device drivers (.sys).

- During the preboot sequence, the BIOS runs a POST test, locates a boot device, and loads the MBR found on that boot device. The MBR loads the boot sector on the active partition into memory and then initializes NTLDR.

- The boot sequence has four phases: initial boot loader phase, operating system selection, hardware detection, and configuration selection. The boot sequence uses the following files: NTLDR, BOOT.INI, BOOTSECT.DOS (optional), NTDETECT.COM, and NTOSKRNL.EXE.

- NTLDR uses information in the BOOT.INI file to display the boot loader screen, from which you select the operating system to start. You can edit the BOOT.INI file, including modifying ARC paths and using the optional BOOT.INI switches.

- During the kernel load phase, the Windows XP Professional kernel (NTOSKRNL.EXE) loads and initializes. NTOSKRNL.EXE also loads and initializes device drivers and loads services.

- During the kernel initialization phase, the kernel initializes, and then NTLDR passes control to the kernel. At this point, the system displays a graphical screen with a status bar that indicates load status. Four tasks are accomplished during the kernel initialization phase:

  ❑ The Hardware key is created.

  ❑ The Clone control set is created.

  ❑ Device drivers are loaded and initialized.

  ❑ Services are started.

- During the logon phase, the Win32 subsystem automatically starts WINLOGON.EXE, which in turn starts the Local Security Authority (LSASS.EXE) and displays the Logon dialog box. You can log on at this time, even if Windows XP Professional might still be initializing network device drivers.

Lesson 2: Editing the Registry

Windows XP Professional stores hardware and software settings centrally in a hierarchical database called the Registry, which replaces many of the .ini, .sys, and .com configuration files used in earlier versions of Windows. The Registry controls the Windows XP Professional operating system by providing the appropriate initialization information to boot Windows XP Professional, to start applications, and to load components such as device drivers and network protocols.

Most users of Windows XP Professional never need to access the Registry. However, management of the Registry is an important part of the system administrator's job, and includes viewing, editing, backing up, and restoring the Registry. You use Registry Editor to view and change the Registry configuration.

After this lesson, you will be able to

- Identify the purpose of the Registry.
- Define the hierarchical structure of the Registry.
- View and edit the Registry by using Registry Editor.

Estimated lesson time: 40 minutes

What Is the Registry?

The Registry is a hierarchical database that contains a variety of different types of data, including descriptions of the following:

- The hardware installed on the computer, including the central processing unit (CPU), bus type, pointing device or mouse, and keyboard.
- Installed device drivers.
- Installed applications.
- Installed network protocols.
- Network adapter card settings. Examples include the interrupt request (IRQ) number, memory base address, I/O port base address, I/O channel ready, and transceiver type.

The Registry structure provides a secure set of records. The data in the Registry is read, updated, or modified by many of the Windows XP Professional components. Table 4-6 describes some of the components that access and store data in the Registry.

Table 4-6   Components That Use the Registry

Component	Description
Windows XP Professional kernel	During startup, the Windows XP Professional kernel (NTOSKRNL.EXE) reads information from the Registry, including the device drivers to load and the order in which they should be loaded. The kernel writes information about itself to the Registry, such as the version number.
Device drivers	Device drivers receive configuration parameters from the Registry. They also write information to the Registry. A device driver informs the Registry which system resources it is using, such as hardware interrupts or direct memory access (DMA) channels. Device drivers also report discovered configuration data.
User profiles	Windows XP Professional creates and maintains user work environment settings in a user profile. When a user logs on, the system caches the profile in the Registry. Windows XP Professional first writes user configuration changes to the Registry and then to the user profile.
Setup programs	During setup of a hardware device or application, a setup program can add new configuration data to the Registry. It can also query the Registry to determine whether required components have been installed.
Hardware profiles	Computers with two or more hardware configurations use hardware profiles. When Windows XP Professional starts, the user selects a hardware profile, and Windows XP Professional configures the system accordingly.
NTDETECT.COM	During system startup, NTDETECT.COM performs hardware detection. This dynamic hardware configuration data is stored in the Registry.

The Hierarchical Structure of the Registry

The Registry is organized in a hierarchical structure similar to the hierarchical structure of folders and files on a disk. Figure 4-2 shows the hierarchical structure of the Registry as displayed by the Registry Editor.

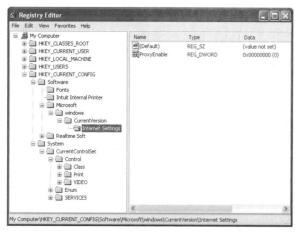

Figure 4-2   Registry Editor displays the hierarchical structure of the Registry.

Table 4-7 describes the components that make up the hierarchical structure of the Registry.

Table 4-7   Components That Make Up the Registry

Component	Description
Subtree	A subtree (or subtree key) is analogous to the root folder of a disk. The Windows XP Professional Registry has two subtrees: HKEY_LOCAL_MACHINE and HKEY_USERS. However, to make the information in the Registry easier to find and view, there are five predefined subtrees that can be seen in the editor: HKEY_CLASSES_ROOT HKEY_CURRENT_USER HKEY_LOCAL_MACHINE HKEY_USERS HKEY_CURRENT_CONFIG
Keys	Keys, which are analogous to folders and subfolders, correspond to hardware or software objects and groups of objects. Subkeys are keys within higher-level keys.
Entries	Keys contain one or more entries. An entry has three parts: name, data type, and value (data or configuration parameter).
Hive	A hive is a discrete body of keys, subkeys, and entries. Each hive has a corresponding Registry file and .log file located in %systemroot%\System32\Config. Windows XP Professional uses the .log file to record changes and ensure the integrity of the Registry.
Data types	Each entry's value is expressed as one of these data types: ■ **REG_SZ (String value).** One value; Windows XP Professional interprets it as a string to store. ■ **REG_BINARY (Binary value).** One value; it must be a string of hexadecimal digits. Windows XP Professional interprets each pair as a byte value. ■ **REG_DWORD (DWORD value).** One value; must be a string of 1–8 hexadecimal digits. ■ **REG_MULTI_SZ (Multistring value).** Multiple values allowed; Windows XP Professional interprets each string as a component of MULTI_SZ separate entries. ■ **REG_EXPAND_SZ (Expandable string value).** Similar to REG_SZ, except the text can contain a replaceable variable. For example, in the string %systemroot%\NTVDM.EXE, Windows XP Professional replaces the systemroot environmental variable with the path to the Windows XP Professional System32 folder. ■ **REG_FULL_RESOURCE_DESCRIPTOR.** Stores a resource list for hardware components or drivers. You cannot add or modify an entry with this data type.

Registry Subtrees

Understanding the purpose of each subtree can help you locate specific keys and values in the Registry. The following five subtrees or subtree keys are displayed in the Registry Editor (refer to Figure 4-2):

HKEY_CLASSES_ROOT   Contains software configuration data: object linking and embedding (OLE) and file-class association data. This subtree points to the Classes subkey under HKEY_LOCAL_MACHINE\SOFTWARE.

HKEY_CURRENT_USER   Contains data about the current user. Retrieves a copy of each user account used to log on to the computer from the NTUSER.DAT file and stores it in the %systemroot%\Profiles*username* key. This subkey points to the same data contained in HKEY_USERS*SID_currently_logged_on_user*. This subtree takes precedence over HKEY_LOCAL_MACHINE for duplicated values.

HKEY_LOCAL_MACHINE   Contains all configuration data for the local computer, including hardware and operating system data such as bus type, system memory, device drivers, and startup control data. Applications, device drivers, and the operating system use this data to set the computer configuration. The data in this subtree remains constant regardless of the user.

HKEY_USERS   Contains the .DEFAULT subkey, which holds the system default settings (system default profile) used to display the CTRL+ALT+DELETE logon screen, and the Security Identifier (SID) of the current user.

HKEY_CURRENT_CONFIG   Contains data on the active hardware profile extracted from the SOFTWARE and SYSTEM hives. This information is used to configure settings such as the device drivers to load and the display resolution to use.

The HKEY_LOCAL_MACHINE Subtree

HKEY_LOCAL_MACHINE provides a good example of the subtrees in the Registry for two reasons:

■ The structure of all subtrees is similar.

■ HKEY_LOCAL_MACHINE contains information specific to the local computer and is always the same, regardless of the user who is logged on.

The HKEY_LOCAL_MACHINE root key has five subkeys, which are explained in Table 4-8.

Table 4-8   HKEY_LOCAL_MACHINE Subkeys

Subkey	Description
HARDWARE	The type and state of physical devices attached to the computer. This subkey is volatile, meaning that Windows XP Professional builds it from information gathered during startup. Because the values for this subkey are volatile, it does not map to a file on the disk. Applications query this subkey to determine the type and state of physical devices attached to the computer.

Table 4-8   HKEY_LOCAL_MACHINE Subkeys

Subkey	Description
SAM	The directory database for the computer. The SAM hive maps to the SAM and SAM.LOG files in the %systemroot%\System32\Config directory. Applications that query SAM must use the appropriate application programming interfaces (APIs). This hive is a pointer to the same one accessible under HKEY_LOCAL_MACHINE\SECURITY\SAM.
SECURITY	The security information for the local computer. The SECURITY hive maps to the Security and SECURITY.LOG files in the %systemroot%\System32\Config directory. Applications cannot modify the keys contained in the SECURITY subkey. Instead, applications must query security information by using the security APIs.
SOFTWARE	Information about the local computer software that is independent of per-user configuration information. This hive maps to the Software and SOFTWARE.LOG files in the %systemroot%\System32\Config directory. It also contains file associations and OLE information.
SYSTEM	Information about system devices and services. When you install or configure device drivers or services, they add or modify information under this hive. The SYSTEM hive maps to the System and SYSTEM.LOG files in the %systemroot%\System32\Config directory. The Registry keeps a backup of the data in the SYSTEM hive in the SYSTEM.ALT file.

Control Sets

A typical Windows XP Professional installation contains the following control set subkeys: Clone, ControlSet001, ControlSet002, and CurrentControlSet. Control sets are stored as subkeys of the Registry key HKEY_LOCAL_MACHINE\SYSTEM (see Figure 4-3). The Registry might contain several control sets, depending on how often you change or have problems with system settings.

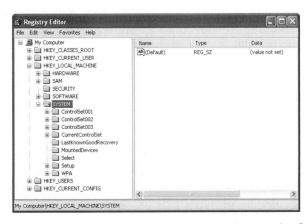

Figure 4-3   You can view the current control sets using Registry Editor.

The CurrentControlSet subkey is a pointer to one of the ControlSet00*x* keys. The Clone control set is a clone of the control set used to initialize the computer (either Default or Last Known Good), and is created by the kernel initialization process each time you start your computer. The Clone control set is not available after you log on.

To better understand control sets, you should know about the Registry subkey HKEY_LOCAL_MACHINE\SYSTEM\Select. The entries contained in this subkey include the following:

Current   Identifies which control set is the CurrentControlSet. When you use Control Panel options or the Registry Editor to change the Registry, you modify information in the CurrentControlSet.

Default   Identifies the control set to use the next time Windows XP Professional starts unless you select the Last Known Good configuration. Default and Current typically contain the same control set number.

Failed   Identifies the control set that was designated as failed the last time the computer was started using the Last Known Good control set.

LastKnownGood   Identifies a copy of the control set that was used the last time the computer started Windows XP Professional successfully. After a successful logon, the Clone control set is copied to the Last Known Good control set.

Each of these entries in HKEY_LOCAL_MACHINE\SYSTEM\Select takes a REG_DWORD data type, and the value for each entry refers to a specific control set. For example, if the value for the Current entry is set to 0x1, the CurrentControlSet points to ControlSet001. Similarly, if the value for the Last Known Good entry is set to 0x2, the Last Known Good control set points to ControlSet002.

How to View and Edit the Registry Using the Registry Editor

Setup installs Registry Editor (REGEDIT.EXE) in the %systemroot%\System32 directory during installation. However, because most users do not need to use Registry Editor, it does not appear on the Start menu. To start Registry Editor, click Run on the Start menu, type **Regedit**, and then click OK.

Although Registry Editor allows you to perform manual edits on the Registry, it is intended for troubleshooting and problem resolution. You should make most configuration changes through either Control Panel or Administrative Tools. However, some configuration settings can be made only directly through the Registry.

Caution   Using Registry Editor incorrectly can cause serious, system-wide problems that could require reinstallation of Windows XP Professional. When using Registry Editor to view or edit data, use a program such as Windows Backup to save a backup copy of the Registry file before viewing. In Windows XP Professional, you can use Backup to back up the System State, which includes the Registry, the COM class registration database, and the system boot files.

Registry Editor saves data automatically as you make entries or corrections. New Registry data takes effect immediately.

You can select Find Key on the View menu to search the Registry for a specific key. Key names appear in the left pane of Registry Editor. The search begins at the currently selected key and parses all descendant keys for the specified key name. The search is local to the subtree in which the search begins. For example, a search for a key in the HKEY_LOCAL_MACHINE subtree does not include keys under HKEY_CURRENT_USER.

Practice: Modifying the Registry

In this practice, you use Registry Editor to view the information in the Registry. Complete Exercise 1 to determine information such as the BIOS, the processor on your computer, and the version of the operating system. Complete Exercise 2 to use Registry Editor's Find Key command to search the Registry for a specific word with key names. Complete Exercise 3 to modify the Registry by adding a value to it, and save a subtree as a file so that you can use an editor such as Notepad to search the file.

Exercise 1: Exploring the Registry

1. Ensure that you are logged on as Administrator.

2. From the Start menu, click Run.

3. In the Run dialog box, type **Regedit** and then click OK.

> **Security Alert**   You should make it a practice not to log on as an administrator when performing non-administrative functions. It is better to log on as a normal user and use the Run As command when you need to perform an administrative function. If you prefer to run the Registry Editor without logging on as an administrator, at the command prompt, type
> **runas /user:administrator regedit**.

4. Maximize the Registry Editor window, and then expand HKEY_LOCAL_MACHINE.

5. Under HKEY_LOCAL_MACHINE, expand HARDWARE.

6. Expand DESCRIPTION and then double-click the System subkey. Find the following information:

   ❑ The SystemBiosDate and SystemBiosVersion of your computer

   ❑ The computer type of your local machine according to the Identifier entry

7. Expand SOFTWARE\Microsoft\WindowsNT.

8. Click CurrentVersion, and then fill in the following information.

Software Configuration	Value and String
Current build number	
Current version	
Registered organization	
Registered owner	

Exercise 2: Using the Find Command

In this exercise, you use the Registry Editor's Find command to search the Registry to find a specific word in the keys, values, and data in the Registry.

1. In Registry Editor, click the HKEY_LOCAL_MACHINE subkey to ensure that the entire subtree is searched.

2. On the Edit menu, click Find.

3. In the Find dialog box, in the Find What text box, type **serial** and then clear the Values and Data check boxes. Click Find Next.

4. The Registry Editor locates and highlights the first entry containing serial. Press F3 to find the next entry containing serial. Continue pressing F3 until a Registry Editor dialog box appears, indicating that Registry Editor has finished searching the Registry. Notice that serial appears in many locations in the Registry.

5. Click OK to close the Registry Editor dialog box.

Exercise 3: Modifying the Registry

1. In Registry Editor, expand HKEY_CURRENT_USER.

2. Under HKEY_CURRENT_USER, click Environment. The values in the Environment key appear in the right pane of the Registry Editor window.

3. Click the Edit menu, point to New, and then click String Value. The Registry Editor adds a New Value #1 entry in the right pane of the Registry Editor window.

4. Name the new value **Test** and then press ENTER.

5. Right-click the Test value, and then click Modify.

6. In the Edit String dialog box, in the Value Data text box, type **%windir%\system32** and then click OK. Test REG_SZ %windir%\ system32 is now an entry in the right pane of the Registry Editor window.

7. Minimize the Registry Editor window.

8. From the Start menu, right-click My Computer, and then click Properties.

9. In the System Properties dialog box, on the Advanced tab, click Environment Variables.

10. In the Environment Variables dialog box, ensure that the test variable appears in the User Variables For Administrator list.

11. Close the Environment Variables dialog box, and then close the System Properties dialog box.

Lesson Review

Use the following questions to help determine whether you have learned enough to move on to the next lesson. If you are unable to answer a question, review the lesson materials and try the question again. You can find answers to these questions in the "Questions and Answers" section at the end of this chapter.

1. What is the Registry and what does it do?

   _____

   _____

   _____

   _____

2. What are some of the Windows XP Professional components that use the Registry?

   _____

   _____

3. How do you access the Registry Editor?

   _____

4. Why should you make most of your configuration changes through either Control Panel or Administrative Tools rather than by editing the Registry directly with the Registry Editor?

   _____

   _____

   _____

   _____

   _____

Lesson Summary

- Windows XP Professional stores hardware and software settings in the Registry, a hierarchical database that replaces many of the .ini, .sys, and .com configuration files used in earlier versions of Windows. The Registry provides the appropriate initialization information to boot Windows XP Professional, to start applications, and to load components such as device drivers and network protocols.

- The Registry structure provides a secure set of records that can be read, updated, or modified by many of the Windows XP Professional components. The Registry has two subtrees: HKEY_LOCAL_MACHINE and HKEY_USERS. However, additional parts of the Registry (including HKEY_CLASSES_ROOT, HKEY_CURRENT_USER, and HKEY_CURRENT_CONFIG) are represented in the top level of the visible structure in Registry Editor to make important areas easier to locate.

- The Registry Editor (REGEDIT.EXE) allows you to view and change the Registry. The Registry Editor is primarily intended for troubleshooting. For most configuration changes, you should use either Control Panel or Administrative Tools, not Registry Editor.

Lesson 3: Troubleshooting Problems Using Startup and Recovery Tools

In this lesson, you learn about the tools and options Windows XP Professional provides to help you troubleshoot problems with starting your computer and recovering from disasters. These tools include **safe mode**, the **Last Known Good configuration**, and the **Recovery Console** (which are all covered in this lesson), and the Automated System Restore Wizard (which is covered in Chapter 20, "Backing Up and Restoring Data").

After this lesson, you will be able to

- Troubleshoot startup using safe mode.
- Troubleshoot startup using the Last Known Good configuration.
- Describe additional advanced boot options.
- Perform troubleshooting and recovery tasks using the Windows XP Professional Recovery Console.

Estimated lesson time: 40 minutes

Guidelines for Troubleshooting Startup Using Safe Mode

If your computer does not start normally, you might be able to start it by using safe mode. Pressing F8 during the operating system selection phase of startup (just after the POST screen disappears) displays a screen with advanced options for booting Windows XP Professional. If you select safe mode, Windows XP Professional starts with limited device drivers and system services. These basic device drivers and system services include the mouse, standard VGA monitor, keyboard, mass storage, default system services, and no network connections. Safe mode also ignores programs that automatically start up, user profiles, programs listed in the Registry to automatically run, and all local group policies.

Safe mode provides access to Windows XP Professional configuration files, so you can make configuration changes. You can disable or delete a system service, a device driver, or an application that automatically starts that prevents the computer from starting normally.

If you choose to start your computer in safe mode, the background will be black and "Safe Mode" appears in all four corners of the screen (see Figure 4-4). If your computer does not start using safe mode, you can try Windows XP Professional Automatic System Recovery.

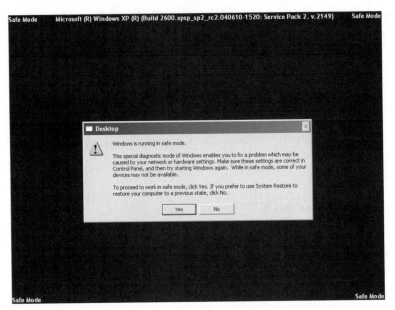

Figure 4-4   Use safe mode to troubleshoot drivers and services that prevent Windows from starting normally.

Safe Mode with Networking

One variation of safe mode is safe mode with networking, which is identical to safe mode except that it adds the drivers and services necessary to enable networking to function when you restart your computer. Safe mode with networking allows Group Policy to be implemented, including settings that are implemented by the server during the logon process and those configured on the local computer.

Safe Mode with Command Prompt

A second variation of safe mode is safe mode with command prompt, which is similar to safe mode, but it loads the command interpreter as the user shell instead of the graphical interface, so when the computer restarts, it displays a command prompt.

> **See Also**   After starting a computer in safe mode, you can use the tools built into Windows XP Professional to troubleshoot any problems you are having. Coverage of specific trouble-shooting tools appears throughout this book. You can learn more about troubleshooting hardware devices and drivers in Chapter 6, "Installing, Managing, and Troubleshooting Hardware Devices and Drivers." You can learn more about using the Windows Event Viewer to view important event logs in Chapter 18, "Using Windows XP Tools."

Guidelines for Troubleshooting Startup Using the Last Known Good Configuration

Selecting the Last Known Good configuration advanced boot option starts Windows XP Professional using the control set saved to the Registry following the last successful logon. If you change the Windows XP Professional configuration to load a driver and have problems rebooting, you can use the Last Known Good configuration to recover your working configuration.

Windows XP Professional provides two configurations for starting a computer, Default and Last Known Good. Figure 4-5 shows the events that occur when you make configuration changes to your system. Any configuration changes (for example, adding or removing drivers) are saved in the Current control set.

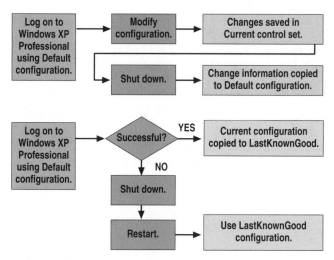

Figure 4-5   Default and Last Known Good are the two available startup configurations.

After you reboot the computer, the kernel copies the information in the Current control set to the Clone control set during the kernel initialization phase. When you successfully log on to Windows XP Professional, the information in the Clone control set is copied to the Last Known Good control set, as shown in the lower part of Figure 4-5.

If you experience startup problems that you think might relate to Windows XP Professional configuration changes, shut down the computer without logging on, and then restart it. When you are prompted to select the operating system to start from a list of the operating systems specified in the BOOT.INI file, press F8 to open the Windows Advanced Options Menu screen. Then select the Last Known Good Configuration option.

> **Exam Tip**   The Safe Mode and Last Known Good Configuration options are two of the most useful tools to try first when troubleshooting Windows startup. Enabling Boot Logging is also useful, typically when you are having trouble locating the source of the problem.

The next time you log on, the Current configuration is copied to the Default configuration. If your configuration changes work correctly, the next time you log on, the Current configuration is copied to the Default configuration. If your configuration changes do not work, you can restart and use the Last Known Good Configuration option to log on.

Table 4-9 summarizes the purpose of the Default and Last Known Good configurations.

Table 4-9   Default and Last Known Good Configurations

Configuration	Description
Default	Contains information that the system saves when a computer shuts down. To start a computer using the default configuration, select Windows XP Professional on the Please Select The Operating System To Start menu.
Last Known Good	Contains information that the system saves after a successful logon. The Last Known Good configuration loads only if the system is recovering from a severe or critical device driver loading error or if it is selected during the boot process.

Table 4-10 lists situations in which you can use the Last Known Good configuration and the related solutions.

Table 4-10   When to Use the Last Known Good Configuration

Situation	Solution
After a new device driver is installed, Windows XP Professional restarts, but the system stops responding.	Use the Last Known Good configuration option to start Windows XP Professional because the Last Known Good configuration does not contain any reference to the new (possibly faulty) driver.
You accidentally disable a critical device driver (such as the Scsiport driver).	Some critical drivers are written to keep users from making the mistake of disabling them. With these drivers, the system automatically reverts to the Last Known Good control set if a user disables the driver. If the driver does not automatically cause the system to revert to the Last Known Good control set, you must manually select the Last Known Good Configuration option.

Using the Last Known Good configuration does not help in the following situations:

- When the problem is not related to Windows XP Professional configuration changes. Such a problem might arise from incorrectly configured user profiles or incorrect file permissions.

- After you log on. The system updates the Last Known Good control set with Windows XP Professional configuration changes after a successful logon.

- When startup failures relate to hardware failures or missing or corrupted files.

Important   Starting Windows XP Professional using the Last Known Good configuration overwrites any changes made since the last successful boot of Windows XP Professional.

Additional Advanced Boot Options

Pressing F8 during the operating system selection phase displays a screen with the Windows Advanced Options menu. This menu provides the following additional options:

Enable Boot Logging   Selecting the Enable Boot Logging advanced boot option logs the loading and initialization of drivers and services for troubleshooting boot problems. All drivers and services that are loaded and initialized or that are not loaded in a file are logged. The log file, NTBTLOG.TXT, is located in the %windir% folder. All three versions of safe mode automatically create this boot log file.

See Also   You can learn more about using boot logging to troubleshoot by reading Appendix D of the Microsoft Windows XP Professional Resource Kit Documentation on the Microsoft Web site at *http://www.microsoft.com/resources/documentation/Windows/XP/all/reskit/en-us/*.

Enable VGA Mode   Selecting the Enable VGA Mode advanced boot option starts Windows XP Professional with a basic VGA driver. Use this setting if you are experiencing problems with the video card, video driver, or monitor.

Directory Services Restore Mode   Selecting the Directory Services Restore Mode advanced boot option is applicable only to domain controllers, so it does not apply to computers running Windows XP Professional.

Debugging Mode   Selecting the Debugging Mode advanced boot option starts Windows XP Professional in kernel debug mode, which allows a debugger to break into the kernel for troubleshooting and system analysis.

Disable Automatic Restart On System Failure   By default, Windows XP Professional automatically restarts the computer when there is a system failure. Normally, this default setting works well, but you might want to disable automatic restarts when you are troubleshooting certain problems. A good example of this is when troubleshooting stop errors. If automatic restarting is enabled, Windows restarts the computer before you can get a chance to read the error message. Use the Disable Automatic Restart On System Failure setting to prevent Windows from restarting when the computer fails (using this setting gives you the chance to read the error or perform any actions you need to perform before a restart).

Note When using the advanced boot options in Windows XP, logging is enabled with every option except Last Known Good Configuration. The system writes the log file (NTBTLOG.TXT) to the %systemroot% folder. In addition, each option except Last Known Good Configuration loads the default VGA driver.

Using an advanced boot option to boot the system sets the environment variable %SAFEBOOT_OPTION% to indicate the mode used to boot the system.

How to Perform Troubleshooting and Recovery Tasks Using the Recovery Console

The Windows XP Professional Recovery Console is a text mode command interpreter that you can use to access NTFS, FAT, and FAT32 volumes without starting Windows XP Professional. The Recovery Console allows you to perform a variety of troubleshooting and recovery tasks, including the following:

- Copying files between hard disks and from a floppy disk to a hard disk (but not from hard disk to a floppy disk), which allows you replace or remove items that might be affecting the boot process, or to retrieve user data from an unsalvageable computer

- Starting and stopping services

- Adding, removing, and formatting partitions on the hard disk

- Repairing the MBR or boot sector of a hard disk or volume

- Restoring the Registry

This section explains how to install, start, and use the Recovery Console and presents the major Recovery Console commands.

Exam Tip The Recovery Console provides an excellent way to access hard disks when the operating system will not boot. You can use the Recovery Console to access all partitions on a drive, regardless of the file system.

How to Install the Recovery Console

To install the Recovery Console, insert the Windows XP Professional CD-ROM into your CD-ROM drive, and close the Windows XP Professional CD dialog box if it opens. Open a Run dialog box or a Command Prompt window in Windows XP Professional, and run the command *drive*:\i386\Winnt32.exe /cmdcons, where *drive* represents the letter of the CD-ROM or network drive that holds the Windows XP installation files. After installation, you can start the Recovery Console by choosing it from the list of installed operating systems—you do not need to have the installation CD.

How to Start the Windows XP Professional Recovery Console

You can also run the Recovery Console from the Windows XP Professional CD-ROM without installing it. The Recovery Console provides a limited set of administrative commands that you can use to repair your Windows XP Professional installation. You can use the following steps to start the Recovery Console from the Windows XP Professional CD-ROM:

1. Insert the Windows XP Professional CD-ROM into the CD-ROM drive and restart the computer. If your computer or the workstation you want to repair does not have a bootable CD-ROM drive, you need to insert your Windows XP Professional Setup Boot disk into your floppy disk drive. Insert the additional Windows XP Professional Setup disks when you are prompted to do so.

2. When Setup displays the Setup Notification message, read it, and then press Enter to continue.

3. Setup displays the Welcome To Setup screen. In addition to the initial installation of Windows XP Professional, you can use Windows Setup to repair or recover a damaged Windows XP Professional installation. Press R to repair a Windows XP Professional installation.

4. The Windows XP Recovery Console screen appears. Press C to start the Recovery Console.

5. If you have more than one installation of Windows XP Professional on the computer, you are prompted to select which installation you want to repair. Type **1** and then press ENTER.

6. Type the Administrator's password, and then press ENTER.

7. Setup displays a command prompt. Type **help** and then press ENTER for a list of the commands available.

8. When you have completed the repair process, type **exit** and then press ENTER. The computer will restart.

The Major Recovery Console Commands

There are a number of commands available in the Recovery Console, some of which are described in Table 4-11.

Table 4-11 Major Recovery Console Commands

Command	Description
Attrib	Changes the attributes of a file or folder. – Clears an attribute + Sets an attribute **c** Compressed file attribute **h** Hidden file attribute **r** Read-only attribute **s** System file attribute
Chdir (cd)	Displays the name of the current folder or changes the current folder.
Chkdsk	Checks a disk and displays a status report.
Cls	Clears the screen.
Copy	Copies a single file to another location. You cannot copy a file from a hard drive to a floppy disk, but you can copy a file from a floppy disk or a CD-ROM to a hard drive or from a hard drive to another hard drive. This command allows you to access and recover user data when you cannot otherwise start the computer.
Delete (Del)	Deletes one or more files.
Dir	Displays a list of files and subfolders in a folder. The wildcard characters * and ? are permitted.
Disable	Disables a system service or a device driver.
Diskpart	Creates, deletes, and manages partitions on your hard disk. **/add** Creates a new partition **/delete** Deletes an existing partition Do not modify the structure of dynamic disks with this command because you might damage your partition table.
Enable	Starts or enables a system service or a device driver.
Exit	Exits the Recovery Console and restarts your computer.
Expand	Expands a compressed file stored on the Windows XP Professional CD-ROM or from within a .cab file and copies it to a specified destination.
Fdisk	Manages partitions on your hard disk.
Fixboot	Writes a new partition boot sector onto the system partition.
Fixmbr	Repairs the MBR of the partition boot sector. This command overwrites only the master boot code, leaving the existing partition table intact. If corruption in the MBR affects the partition table, running fixmbr might not resolve the problem.
Format	Formats a disk. If no file system is specified, NTFS is used by default.
Help	Lists the commands you can use in the Recovery Console.
Logon	Logs on to a Windows XP Professional installation.
Map	Displays the drive letter mappings.
Mkdir (md)	Creates a folder.

Table 4-11   Major Recovery Console Commands

Command	Description
More	Displays a text file.
Rmdir (rd)	Deletes a folder.
Rename (ren)	Renames a single file.
Systemroot	Sets the current folder to the %systemroot% folder of the system you are currently logged on to.
Type	Displays a text file.

See Also   You can also use Recovery Console to restore System and Software files, which are stored in the %systemroot%\System32\Config folder, with a backup copy that is stored in the %systemroot%\repair folder. Windows XP Professional uses these files to create the registry keys HKEY_LOCAL_MACHINE\SYSTEM and HKEY_LOCAL_MACHINE\SOFTWARE. The Windows Backup program automatically backs up these files when you back up the System State. For more information about backups and about restoring these files by using Recovery Console, see Chapter 20, "Backing Up and Restoring Data."

Real World   Fixing Corrupted Boot Files

Although the Recovery Console is useful for replacing missing and corrupted boot files such as NTLDR and for fixing problematic MBRs, this is an area in which you should be careful. One of the most common reasons for MBR and NTLDR problems is a type of virus known as a boot sector virus—a virus that resides in the MBR. Once entrenched, boot sector viruses can set about corrupting other files, such as NTLDR. Boot sector viruses can also be difficult to get rid of because they can often survive even a full reformatting of a hard disk. Even if you use the Recovery Console to fix a corrupted boot file, you should not assume that you have gotten to the root of the problem.

Fortunately, there are some fairly simple steps you can take to help prevent boot sector viruses from ever becoming a problem. First, all computers should be running good antivirus software that is kept up-to-date with the latest virus information. You should configure the antivirus software to perform full system scans regularly—scans that include the MBR. On most computers, you can also configure BIOS to prevent virus-like activity (which essentially means that it will prompt you before it allows any program to write information to the boot sector).

Practice: Installing and Accessing the Windows XP Professional Recovery Console

In this practice, you install and then start the Recovery Console, and you look at Help to determine which commands are available in the Recovery Console. You also use the Listsvc command to view the services, and then use the Disable command to disable the Server service. Complete Exercises 1, 2, and 3.

Exercise 1: Installing the Windows XP Professional Recovery Console

In this exercise, you install the Recovery Console.

1. Log on as Administrator.

2. Insert the Windows XP Professional CD into the CD-ROM drive.

3. When the Windows XP Professional CD splash screen appears, close it.

4. From the Start menu, click Run.

5. In the Run dialog box, type **<cd-drive>:\i386\winnt32 /cmdcons** (where *<cd-drive>* represents the letter assigned to your CD-ROM drive), and then click OK.

> **Security Alert**   If you have installed Windows XP Service Pack 2 on your computer and you try to install the Recovery Console you may receive the following error: Setup cannot continue because the version of Windows on your computer is newer than the version on the CD. Workarounds for this error can be found on the following Knowledge Base article: http://support.microsoft.com/kb/898594.

6. In the Windows Setup message box that appears, click Yes to install the Windows XP Professional Recovery Console. Windows Setup next attempts to contact Microsoft and confirm that you have the latest version of Setup; it then installs the Windows XP Recovery Console on your hard disk. Windows XP Professional then displays a Windows XP Professional Setup message box indicating that the Windows Recovery Console has been successfully installed.

7. Click OK to close the Microsoft Windows XP Professional Setup dialog box.

Exercise 2: Using the Recovery Console to Disable the Server Service

In this exercise, you start the Recovery Console and use the Help command to view the available commands. You then use the Listsvc and Disable commands.

1. Restart your computer.

2. In the Please Select The Operating System To Start screen, select Windows Recovery Console.

3. The Windows XP Recovery Console starts and prompts you to select which Windows installation you want to log on to. If you had more than one Windows XP Professional installation on this computer, all of them would be listed here. Type **1** and then press ENTER.

4. When prompted for the Administrator password, enter your password and press ENTER.

5. At the prompt, type **help** and then press ENTER to see the list of available commands.

6. Scroll through the list of commands.

7. The Listsvc command allows you to view all the available services. Type **listsvc** and press ENTER, and then scroll through the list of available services.

8. Press ESC to stop viewing services.

9. Type **disable** and press ENTER.

   The Disable command allows you to disable a Windows system service or driver.

10. Type **disable server** and then press ENTER.

    Recovery Console displays several lines of text describing how the Registry entry for the Server service has been changed from Service_Demand_Start to Service_Disabled. The Server service is now disabled.

11. Type **exit** and then press ENTER to restart your computer.

Exercise 3: Restarting the Server Service

In this exercise, you confirm that the Server service is disabled and then restart it.

1. Log on as Administrator.

2. Click Start, click All Programs, click Administrative Tools, and then click Computer Management.

3. In the Computer Management window, expand Services And Applications.

4. Under Services And Applications, click Services.

5. Double-click Server.

6. In the Server Properties dialog box, change the Startup Type option to Automatic and click OK.

7. Right-click Server and click Start.

8. Close the Computer Management window.

Lesson Review

Use the following questions to help determine whether you have learned enough to move on to the next lesson. If you are unable to answer a question, review the lesson materials and try the question again. You can find answers to these questions in the "Questions and Answers" section at the end of this chapter.

1. What is safe mode and why do you use it?

_____

_____

_____

_____

_____

_____

_____

_____

_____

_____

2. How do you start Windows XP Professional in safe mode?

_____

_____

3. When is the Last Known Good configuration created?

_____

_____

_____

_____

4. When do you use the Last Known Good configuration?

_____

_____

_____

5. How can you install the Windows XP Professional Recovery Console on your computer?

_____

_____

_____

_____

Lesson Summary

- If your computer does not start, you might be able to start it by using safe mode because Windows XP Professional starts with limited device drivers and system services.

- If you change the Windows XP Professional configuration to load a driver and have problems rebooting, you can use the Last Known Good process to recover your working configuration.

- Pressing F8 during the operating system selection phase displays a screen with the Windows Advanced Options menu that provides the following options: Safe Mode, Safe Mode With Networking, Safe Mode With Command Prompt, Enable Boot Logging, Enable VGA Mode, Last Known Good Configuration, Directory Services Restore Mode, and Debugging Mode.

- The Windows XP Professional Recovery Console is a command-line interface that you can use to perform a variety of troubleshooting and recovery tasks.

Case Scenario Exercise

In this exercise, you will read a scenario about a user who is experiencing a startup problem and then answer the questions that follow. If you have difficulty completing this work, review the material in this chapter before beginning the next chapter. You can find answers to these questions in the "Questions and Answers" section at the end of this chapter.

Scenario

You are an administrator working for a company named Contoso, Ltd. You receive a call from one of your users. She tells you that this morning, on advice from a friend, she downloaded and installed the newest drivers for her video card. After the installation, the setup program prompted her to restart the computer. When the computer restarted, the user could log on, but the computer stopped responding shortly thereafter. The user tells you that she has made no other changes to her system.

Questions

1. What is the likely problem?

   _____

   _____

   _____

2. You decide to remove the new driver. However, the computer stops responding before you can do so. What should you do? Choose the correct answer.

   a. Start the computer using the Last Known Good configuration.

   b. Start the computer in safe mode and try to roll back the driver.

   c. Use the Recovery Console to roll back the new driver.

   d. Use the Recovery Console to edit the BOOT.INI file.

Troubleshooting Lab

In this lab, you will create a system boot failure, and then repair that failure using the Recovery Console. Complete Exercises 1 and 2.

> **Important**   To complete this exercise, you must have a computer that is capable of booting using the CD-ROM drive. You must also know the password for the local Administrator account. If you do not meet these requirements, do not attempt this exercise. You should also not attempt this exercise on a production computer.

▶   **Exercise 1: Creating a System Boot Failure**

To create a system boot failure, use the following steps:

1. From the Start menu, right-click My Computer, and then click Explore.

2. In the Explorer window, in the Folders list, click Local Disk (C:), and then click Show The Contents Of This Folder.

3. Click the Tools menu, and then click Folder Options.

4. In the Folder Options dialog box, on the View tab, in the Advanced Settings list, click Show Hidden Files And Folders. Also clear the Hide Protected Operating System Files (Recommended) check box. Click OK.

5. In the right pane of the Explorer window, right-click the file named NTLDR and then click Rename.

6. Type **oldntldr** and then press ENTER.

7. Windows XP Professional displays a Confirm File Rename dialog box asking if you are sure you want to rename the system file NTLDR to OLDNTLDR. Click Yes.

8. Restart the computer.

   When you restart the computer, you should see an error message stating that NTLDR is missing. Windows startup will fail at this point.

Restart your computer, start the Recovery Console, and try to repair the installation. If you need assistance, you can use the following procedure.

▶ **Exercise 2: Using the Recovery Console to Repair an Installation**

1. Insert the Windows XP Professional installation CD into the CD-ROM drive and press CTRL+ALT+DELETE to restart the computer.

2. If your computer requires you to press a key to boot from the CD-ROM, press SPACEBAR when prompted.

3. Setup displays the Welcome To Setup screen. Press R to repair a Windows XP Professional installation.

4. Setup starts the Recovery Console. Type **1** and press ENTER.

5. You are prompted to enter the Administrator's password. Type your password and press ENTER.

6. Setup displays a C:\Windows command prompt. Type *d:* (where *d* is the letter of your CD-ROM drive) and press ENTER.

7. Type **cd i386** to change to the i386 folder and press ENTER.

8. Type **dir** and press ENTER.

9. Most of the files on the CD-ROM end with an _ (for example, NTOSKRNL.EX_). Press SPACEBAR to scroll through the files and locate NTLDR. NTLDR is not compressed, so you can copy it directly to your computer.

10. Type **copy ntldr c:\ntldr** and then press ENTER.

11. When the copy is complete, Setup displays a 1 File(s) Copied message. If there is a disk in your floppy drive, remove it. If your computer is capable of booting from the CD-ROM drive, remove the Windows XP Professional CD from your CD-ROM drive. Type **exit** and press ENTER. The computer reboots and should start normally.

Chapter Summary

- Files used during the Windows XP Professional startup process include NTLDR, BOOT.INI, BOOTSECT.DOS, NTDETECT.COM, NTBOOTDD.SYS, NTOSK-RNL.EXE, HAL.DLL, SYSTEM, and Device drivers (.sys). The startup sequence occurs in five major stages:

  - ❏ Preboot sequence

  - ❏ Boot sequence

  - ❏ Kernel load

  - ❏ Kernel initialization

  - ❏ Logon

- Windows XP Professional stores hardware and software settings in the Registry, a hierarchical database that replaces many of the .ini, .sys, and .com configuration files used in earlier versions of Windows. The Registry provides the appropriate initialization information to boot Windows XP Professional, to start applications, and to load components such as device drivers and network protocols. The Registry Editor (REGEDIT.EXE) allows you to view and change the Registry.

- Pressing F8 during the operating system selection phase displays a screen with the Windows Advanced Options menu that provides the following options: Safe Mode, Safe Mode With Networking, Safe Mode With Command Prompt, Enable Boot Logging, Enable VGA Mode, Last Known Good Configuration, Directory Services Restore Mode, and Debugging Mode. The Windows XP Professional Recovery Console is a command-line interface that you can use to perform a variety of troubleshooting and recovery tasks.

Exam Highlights

Before taking the exam, review the key points and terms that are presented in this chapter. You need to know this information.

Key Points

- Learn the syntax of ARC paths and how to determine which disk and partition a particular path refers to. Most disk types use the multi convention. The value following multi indicates the disk number. The value following partition indicates the partition number on that disk.

- The Safe Mode and Last Known Good Configuration options are two of the most useful tools to try first when troubleshooting Windows startup. Enabling Boot Logging is also useful, typically when you are having trouble locating the source of the problem.

■ The Recovery Console provides an excellent way to access hard disks when the operating system will not boot. You can use the Recovery Console to access all partitions on a drive, regardless of the file system.

Key Terms

BOOT.INI   A file used to build the operating system choices that are displayed during startup.

Last Known Good configuration   A hardware configuration that is available by pressing the F8 key during startup. The Last Known Good configuration contains the configuration information saved after the last successful logon.

master boot record (MBR)   The first sector on a hard disk, which begins the process of starting a computer. The MBR contains the partition table for the disk.

NTLDR   A file used to control the Windows startup process until control is passed to the Windows kernel.

Recovery Console   A command-line console interface that provides access to the hard disks and a limited set of administrative commands useful for recovering a computer.

Registry   A hierarchical database that controls the Windows XP Professional operating system by providing the appropriate initialization information to boot Windows XP Professional, to start applications, and to load components.

safe mode   A method of starting Windows using only basic files and drivers and without networking support.

Questions and Answers

Lesson 1 Review

Page
4-12

1. Windows XP Professional modifies the boot sector during installation so that _____ loads during system startup. Fill in the blank.

   NTLDR

2. What is the purpose of the BOOT.INI file, and what happens if it is not present?

   NTLDR reads BOOT.INI to determine the operating system selections to be loaded. If BOOT.INI is missing, NTLDR attempts to load Windows XP Professional from the Windows folder on the first partition of the first disk—typically C:\Windows.

3. What does the BOOTSECT.DOS file contain and when is it used?

   BOOTSECT.DOS is a copy of the boot sector that was on the system partition at the time Windows XP Professional was installed. BOOTSECT.DOS is used if you are booting more than one operating system and you choose to load an operating system other than Windows XP Professional.

4. A user calls you and tells you that Windows XP Professional does not appear to be loading correctly. The Hardware Profile/Configuration Recovery menu does not appear when the computer is restarted, but it does appear on the computer of the person sitting in the next cubicle when that computer is restarted. What would you tell the user?

   The user probably has only one hardware profile. If there is a single hardware profile, NTLDR does not display the Hardware Profile/Configuration Recovery menu and instead loads Windows XP Professional using the default hardware profile configuration.

Lesson 2 Review

Page
4-23

1. What is the Registry and what does it do?

   The Registry is a hierarchical database in which Windows XP Professional stores hardware and software settings. The Registry provides the appropriate initialization information to boot Windows XP Professional, to start applications, and to load components such as device drivers and network protocols.

2. What are some of the Windows XP Professional components that use the Registry?

   Windows NT kernel, device drivers, user profiles, setup programs, hardware profiles, and NTDETECT.COM.

3. How do you access the Registry Editor?

   On the Start menu, click Run, type **Regedit** and then click OK.

4. Why should you make most of your configuration changes through either Control Panel or Administrative Tools rather than by editing the Registry directly with the Registry Editor?

Using the Registry Editor to modify the Registry is dangerous because the Registry Editor saves data automatically as you make entries or corrections, so new Registry data takes effect immediately. If you incorrectly edit the Registry it can cause serious, system-wide problems that could require you to reinstall Windows XP Professional.

Lesson 3 Review

Page 4-36

1. What is safe mode and why do you use it?

Starting Windows XP Professional in safe mode uses limited device drivers and system services, and no network connections. Safe mode also ignores programs that automatically start up, user profiles, programs listed in the Registry to automatically run, and all local group policies. Safe mode allows Windows to start successfully when the normal Windows XP startup fails.

You use safe mode because it provides access to Windows XP Professional configuration files so you can make configuration changes. You can disable or delete a system service, a device driver, or application that automatically starts that prevents the computer from starting normally.

2. How do you start Windows XP Professional in safe mode?

To start Windows XP Professional in safe mode, restart or boot the computer and press F8 during the operating system selection phase.

3. When is the Last Known Good configuration created?

After you reboot the computer, the kernel copies the information in the Current control set to the Clone control set during the kernel initialization phase. When you successfully log on to Windows XP Professional, the information in the Clone control set is copied to the Last Known Good control set.

4. When do you use the Last Known Good configuration?

If you change the Windows XP Professional configuration to load a driver and have problems rebooting, you use the Last Known Good process to recover your working configuration.

5. How can you install the Windows XP Professional Recovery Console on your computer?

To install the Recovery Console, insert the Windows XP Professional CD-ROM into your CD-ROM drive. Open a Command Prompt window, change to the i386 folder on the Windows XP Professional CD, and then run the winnt32 command with the /cmdcoms switch.

Case Scenario Exercise

Page
4-37

1. What is the likely problem?

   Because the user has made no other configuration changes, and because the problem started after the new driver installation, the most likely problem is the new driver.

2. You decide to remove the new driver. However, the computer stops responding before you can do so. What should you do? Choose the correct answer.

   a. Start the computer using the Last Known Good configuration.

   b. Start the computer in safe mode and try to roll back the driver.

   c. Use the Recovery Console to roll back the new driver.

   d. Use the Recovery Console to edit the BOOT.INI file.

   The correct answer is B. Starting the computer in safe mode loads only a generic video driver. You should then be able to roll back the new driver. A is not correct because the Last Known Good configuration is created after a successful logon. Because the user could log on following the driver installation, reverting to the Last Known Good configuration would not roll back the new driver. C is not correct because you cannot use the Recovery Console to roll back drivers. D is not correct because editing the BOOT.INI file does not help in this situation.

5 Configuring Windows XP Professional

Exam Objectives in this Chapter:

- Manage and troubleshoot Web server resources.
- Implement, manage, and troubleshoot display devices.
    - Configure multiple-display support.
    - Install, configure, and troubleshoot a video adapter.
- Configure Advanced Configuration Power Interface.
- Configure and manage user profiles and desktop settings.
- Configure support for multiple languages or multiple locations.
    - Enable multiple-language support.
    - Configure multiple-language support for users.
    - Configure local settings.
    - Configure Microsoft Windows XP Professional for multiple locations.

Why This Chapter Matters

The Microsoft Windows XP Professional desktop environment provides a user interface that is easily customized. Appropriate configuration of the desktop enhances a user's experience with the operating system and can increase productivity. Configuration information on a computer running Windows XP Professional is stored in the Windows Registry. On computers that are part of a domain, configuration information might also be stored in Active Directory or on other server computers. Each user on a computer has a profile that contains that user's desktop configuration settings and also governs the location in which configuration information is stored.

It is important that you understand the options that are available for desktop configuration and management. This chapter covers configuring and troubleshooting display settings, power management, basic operating system settings, the desktop environment, and Windows components.

Lessons in this Chapter:

Before You Begin

To complete this chapter, you must have a computer that meets the minimum hardware requirements listed in the preface, "About This Book." You must also have Windows XP Professional installed on a computer on which you can make changes.

Lesson 1: Configuring and Troubleshooting the Display

Users can configure and clean up the icons that appear on their computer's desktop. Users with permission to load and unload device drivers can also install and test video drivers. Windows XP Professional allows you to change video resolutions dynamically without restarting the system and also supports multiple display configurations.

After this lesson, you will be able to

- Configure display and desktop properties.
- Configure a computer to use multiple displays.

Estimated lesson time: 30 minutes

How to Configure Display and Desktop Properties

To view or modify the display or the Desktop properties, in Control Panel, click Appearance And Themes, and then click Display. The tabs in the Display Properties dialog box (see Figure 5-1) are described in Table 5-1.

Figure 5-1 Use the Display Properties dialog box to control display and desktop settings.

Table 5-1 Display Properties Dialog Box Tabs

Tab	Description
Themes	Allows you to choose a theme. A theme is a collection of settings that include desktop background, sounds, icons, and other elements to help you personalize your computer.
Desktop	Allows you to choose a background and color for your desktop. The Customize Desktop button allows you to add or remove some Windows program icons and determine which icons represent those programs. You can also include Web content on your desktop (see Figure 5-2).

Table 5-1 Display Properties Dialog Box Tabs

Tab	Description
Screen Saver	Allows you to choose a screen saver to appear on your screen when the computer is idle. The default time after which a screen saver initiates is 10 minutes. On older CRT monitors, screen savers prevented damage to monitors by preventing an image from becoming burned into the monitor. Although this is no longer a problem on newer cathode-ray tube (CRT) and liquid crystal display (LCD) monitors, screen savers are still useful. When a computer is left unattended, a screen saver protects the information on the screen from casual eavesdropping. If you configure the screen saver to prompt for a password to return to the desktop, you can also prevent more deliberate intrusion. You can also click Power to adjust monitor power settings and save energy. See Lesson 2, "Configuring Power Options."
Appearance	Allows you to configure the windows and buttons styles, the color scheme, and the font size. Click Effects to configure the following options: ■ Use The Following Transition Effect For Menus And Tooltips. Options include a fade effect or scroll effect. Although these features look nice to some people, many people find that it slows the perceived responsiveness of Windows. ■ Use The Following Method To Smooth Edges Of Screen Fonts. Options include Standard (best for CRT monitors) and Clear Type (best for LCD monitors). ■ Use Large Icons. This option can help users who have trouble seeing smaller icons. However, using this option can reduce performance on slow computers. ■ Show Shadows Under Menus. This option gives menus a three-dimensional appearance. ■ Show Windows Contents While Dragging. This option causes Windows to redraw folders as you drag them. Although useful, this option can reduce performance on slow computers. ■ Hide Underlined Letters For Keyboard Navigation Until I Press The Alt Key. Windows provides keyboard access to many menu commands when you press the ALT key. Clear this check box if users find the underlined letters in commands bothersome. ■ If you select Windows Classic as your theme, you can click Advanced to customize the look of windows, menus, fonts, and icons.
Settings	Allows you to configure display options including the number of colors, video resolution, font size, and refresh frequency, as shown in Figure 5-3 and explained in Table 5-2.

Important You can enable security settings that restrict access to Display options. For example, you can remove the Appearance tab or the Settings tab from the Display Properties dialog box. For more information about security settings, see Chapter 16, "Configuring Security Settings and Internet Options."

Figure 5-2   Use the Desktop Items dialog box to control what appears on your desktop.

To access the Desktop Items dialog box, on the Desktop tab, click Customize Desktop. The Desktop Items dialog box allows you to include or exclude an icon for My Documents, My Computer, My Network Places, and the Internet Explorer on your desktop, as well as to customize the icons used to represent these items. You can also configure the frequency with which the **Desktop Cleanup Wizard** runs. The default setting for running the Desktop Cleanup Wizard is every 60 days. Click Clean Desktop Now to run the Desktop Cleanup Wizard immediately. The Desktop Cleanup Wizard removes icons from the desktop that have not been used in the last 60 days, but it does not remove any programs from your computer.

To include Web content on your desktop, in the Desktop Items dialog box, click the Web tab. Any Web page listed in the Web Pages text box can be included on your desktop by selecting it. Click New to add a Web page and click Delete to remove a Web page from the list. Click Properties to view the Properties dialog box for the Web page. The Properties dialog box allows you to make the Web page available offline, synchronize immediately or schedule the synchronization of this offline Web page with the content on the Internet, and specify whether you want Internet Explorer to download more than just the top-level page of this Web site.

> **Note**   If you want Internet Explorer to download more than just the top-level page, you can specify up to three levels deep, but specifying three levels deep downloads all the pages linked to the second-level pages. This process can quickly result in hundreds of pages, depending on how many links are on each page.

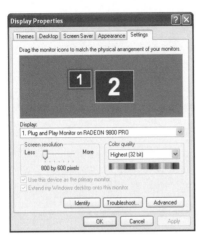

Figure 5-3 Use the Settings tab to control the color quality and screen resolution of the desktop.

Table 5-2 describes the options available in the Settings tab for configuring the display settings.

Table 5-2 Settings Tab Options for Configuring the Display

Option	Description
Color Quality	The **Color Quality** setting displays the current color configuration for the monitor attached to the video adapter listed under Display. This option allows you to change the color quality for the display adapter. You should set this value to the highest quality available for your chosen screen resolution because using a higher-quality color depth does not significantly affect performance.
Screen Resolution	**Screen Resolution** controls the current resolution settings for the monitor attached to the video adapter listed under Display. This option allows you to set the resolution for the display adapter. As you increase the number of pixels, you display more information on the screen, but you decrease the size of the fonts and pictures. Users will need to experiment with resolutions until they find one that strikes a good balance between amount of information displayed and the size of that information. You should also note that many LCD monitors operate at a fixed native resolution. Changing the resolution on these monitors might make the information displayed look bad.
Identify	Identify displays large numbers on the desktop of each monitor in a multiple-display configuration. This helps you identify which physical monitor corresponds to each displayed monitor on the Settings tab. For more information on using multiple displays, see the section "How to Configure Multiple Displays," later in this lesson.
Troubleshoot	Troubleshoot opens the Video Display Troubleshooter to aid you in diagnosing display problems.
Advanced	Advanced opens the Properties dialog box for the display adapter, as described next.

To open the Properties dialog box for the display adapter, click Advanced. Table 5-3 describes the display adapter options.

Table 5-3   Display Adapter Advanced Options

Tab	Option	Description
General	Display	Provides small, large, or other display font option. The other option lets you choose any custom font size you want.
General	Compatibility	Determines the action that the Windows XP operating systems should take when you make changes to display settings. After you change the color settings, you must choose one of the following options: ■ Restart The Computer Before Applying The New Display Settings ■ Apply The New Display Settings Without Restarting ■ Ask Me Before Applying The New Display Settings You should use Restart The Computer Before Applying The New Display Settings only if you experience problems changing resolution.
Adapter	Adapter Type	Provides the manufacturer and model number of the installed adapter. Clicking Properties displays the Properties dialog box for your adapter. The General tab of the Properties dialog box provides additional information, including device status, resource settings, and any conflicting devices. The Driver tab of the Properties dialog box provides details about the driver and allows you to update the driver, roll back to the previously installed driver, and uninstall the driver. The Resources tab of the Properties dialog box indicates resources, such as areas of memory being used by the adapter.
Adapter	Adapter Information	Provides additional information about the display adapter, such as video chip type, digital-to-analog converter (DAC) type, memory size, and basic input/output system (BIOS).
Adapter	List All Modes	Displays all compatible modes for your display adapter and lets you select resolution, color depth, and refresh frequency in one step.
Monitor	Monitor Type	Provides the manufacturer and model number of the monitor currently installed. The Properties button provides additional information and gives access to the Video Display Troubleshooter to help resolve problems with this device.

Table 5-3   Display Adapter Advanced Options

Tab	Option	Description
Monitor	Monitor Settings	Configures the refresh rate frequency. This option applies only to high-resolution drivers. Do not select a refresh rate and screen resolution combination that is unsupported by the monitor. If you are unsure, refer to your monitor documentation or select the lowest refresh rate option.
Troubleshoot	Hardware Acceleration	Lets you progressively decrease your display hardware's acceleration features to help you isolate and eliminate display problems. Lets you select whether to use write combining, which improves video performance by speeding up the display of information to your screen. Increased speed can lead to screen corruption, however. If you experience trouble with your display, try clearing the Enable Write Combining check box.
Color Management		Chooses the color profile for your monitor.
Other tabs		Some video adapters create additional tabs with other options for controlling the adapter features.

Exam Tip   Understand how to control color quality and screen resolution. Also understand how to control advanced display settings, such as adapter type, monitor type, and compatibility.

How to Configure Multiple Displays

Windows XP Professional supports using multiple displays simultaneously, which means that you can attach more than one monitor to your computer and have your desktop spread across all attached monitors, as shown in Figure 5-4. Windows XP Professional supports the extension of your display across a maximum of 10 monitors.

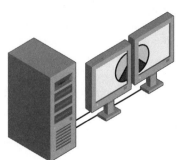

- Use of multiple displays extends the desktop across a maximum of 10 monitors.
- Multiple displays must use Peripheral Component Interconnect (PCI) or Accelerated Graphics Port (AGP) devices.
- Hardware requirements for primary (main) and secondary displays differ.

Figure 5-4   Windows XP Professional can spread your desktop across multiple displays.

Important   You must use Peripheral Component Interconnect (PCI) or Accelerated Graphics Port (AGP) video adapters when configuring multiple displays.

If one of the display adapters is built into the motherboard, note these additional considerations:

- The motherboard adapter always becomes the secondary adapter. It must be multiple-display compatible.

- You must set up Windows XP Professional before installing another adapter. Windows XP Professional Setup disables the motherboard adapter if it detects another adapter. Some systems completely disable the onboard adapter on detecting an add-in adapter. If you are unable to override this detection in the BIOS, you cannot use the motherboard adapter with multiple displays.

Typically, the system BIOS selects the **primary display** based on PCI slot order. However, on some computers, the BIOS allows the user to select the primary display device.

You cannot stop the primary display (in other words, there will always be a primary display, although you can switch the monitor that is the primary display). This caveat is an important consideration for laptop computers with docking stations. For example, some docking stations contain a display adapter; they often disable, or turn off, a laptop's built-in display. Multiple display support does not function on these configurations unless you attach multiple adapters to the docking station.

How to Install Multiple Monitors

Before you can configure multiple displays, you must install them. When you configure multiple displays, you must configure each one in a multiple-display environment.

To install multiple monitors, complete the following steps:

1. Turn off your computer and insert one or more additional PCI or AGP video adapters into available slots on your computer.

2. Plug an additional monitor into each PCI or AGP video adapter that you installed.

3. Turn on your computer and allow Windows XP Professional to detect the new adapters and install the appropriate device drivers.

4. In Control Panel, click Appearance And Themes, and then click Display.

5. In the Settings tab, click the monitor icon that represents the monitor you want to use in addition to your primary monitor. Click Identify if you are not sure which monitor corresponds to which display.

6. Select the Extend My Windows Desktop Onto This Monitor check box and then click OK.

To configure your display in a multiple-display environment, complete the following steps:

1. In Control Panel, click Appearance And Themes, and then click Display.

2. In the Display Properties dialog box, click the Settings tab.

3. Click the monitor icon for the primary display device.

4. Select the color depth and resolution.

5. Click the monitor icon for the secondary display device.

6. Select the Extend My Windows Desktop Onto This Monitor check box.

7. Select the color depth and resolution for the secondary display.

8. Repeat Steps 5 through 7 for each additional display.

Windows XP Professional uses the virtual desktop concept to determine the relationship of each display. The virtual desktop uses coordinates to track the position of each individual display desktop.

The coordinates of the top-left corner of the primary display always remain 0, 0. Windows XP Professional sets secondary display coordinates so that all the displays adjoin each other on the virtual desktop, which allows the system to maintain the illusion of a single large desktop in which users can cross from one monitor to another without losing track of the mouse.

To change the display positions on the virtual desktop, in the Settings tab click Identify and drag the display representations to the desired position. The positions of the icons dictate the coordinates and the relative positions of the displays to one another.

Real World   Using Multiple Displays

Using multiple displays is a great way to increase your desktop space (although it can quickly consume the space on your actual desk). Many video adapter manufacturers have adapters that already have ports for more than one monitor—an easy way to set up a multiple-display configuration. Some of these adapters come with extra software to help manage the displays that provides features like controlling the particular display on which applications appear, limiting the appearance of dialog boxes to the display on which the parent application is shown, using separate screen savers for each display, and so on.

When you are purchasing extra monitors, you should try to use monitors that are roughly the same size and set them to use the same resolution. The reason for this decision is that when you arrange your displays on the Settings tab, the location of the monitor icons accurately predicts what happens when you move your mouse pointer between displays. For example, assume that you have two displays side by side. One of the displays is a 19-inch monitor and one is a 15-inch monitor. You can arrange these displays on the Settings tab so that either the tops or the bottoms of the displays are aligned. If the tops were aligned, whenever you move your mouse pointer from the bottom of the bigger display toward the second display, the pointer would get "stuck." To get the pointer over to the smaller display, you would have to move the pointer upward to the point where the bottom of the smaller display was. Although it seems as if it might not be a big deal, losing track of your mouse pointer because of this arrangement is a common complaint among multiple-display users.

How to Troubleshoot Multiple Displays

If you encounter problems with multiple displays, use the troubleshooting guidelines in Table 5-4 to help resolve them.

Table 5-4   Troubleshooting Tips for Multiple Displays

Problem	Solution
You cannot see any output on the secondary displays.	Activate the device in the Display Properties dialog box. Confirm that you chose the correct video driver.
	Restart the computer to confirm that the secondary display initialized. If not, check the status of the video adapter in Device Manager.
	Switch the order of the adapters in the slots. (The primary adapter must qualify as a secondary adapter.)
The Extend My Windows Desktop Onto This Monitor check box is unavailable.	Select the secondary display rather than the primary one in the Display Properties dialog box.
	Confirm that the secondary display adapter is supported.
	Confirm that Windows XP Professional can detect the secondary display.
An application fails to display on the secondary display.	Run the application on the primary display.
	Run the application in full-screen mode (for Microsoft MS-DOS-based programs) or maximized (for older Windows-based programs).
	Disable the secondary display to determine whether the problem is specific to multiple-display support.

Lesson Review

The following questions are intended to reinforce key information presented in this lesson. If you are unable to answer a question, review the lesson materials and try the question again. You can find answers to the questions in the "Questions and Answers" section at the end of this chapter.

1. You can enable _____ to restrict access to Display options.

2. Which of the following items does the Desktop Items dialog box allow you to choose to include or exclude an icon on your desktop? (Choose all that apply.)

   a. My Documents

   b. Control Panel

   c. My Network Places

   d. Recycle Bin

3. Windows XP Professional supports extension of your display across a maximum of _____ monitors.

4. You must use _____ or _____ video adapters when configuring multiple displays.

5. If one of the display adapters is built into the motherboard, the motherboard adapter always becomes the _____ (primary/secondary) adapter.

Lesson Summary

- You can use the Display Properties dialog box to control most settings that govern the appearance of your desktop and the settings for your video adapter and monitor.

- Windows XP Professional supports the use of up to 10 displays, extending the Windows desktop so that it is spread across all available displays. You must use PCI or AGP video adapters when configuring multiple displays.

Lesson 2: Configuring Power Options

Windows XP Professional contains a number of features that allow the operating system to manage the use of power by your computer and the hardware devices attached to it. Power management features included in Windows XP Professional include System Power Management, Device Power Management, Processor Power Management, System Events, and Battery Management.

After this lesson, you will be able to

- Select a power scheme.
- Configure advanced power options.
- Enable hibernate mode.
- Configure Advanced Power Management.
- Configure an uninterruptible power supply.

Estimated lesson time: 40 minutes

How to Select a Power Scheme

Power Options allows you to configure Windows XP Professional to turn off the power to your monitor and your hard disk, or put the computer in hibernate mode. To configure Power Options, in Control Panel, click Performance And Maintenance, and then click Power Options. The Power Options Properties dialog box allows you to configure Power Options (see Figure 5-5).

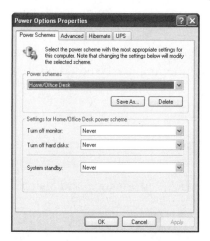

Figure 5-5 Use the Power Schemes tab of the Power Options Properties dialog box to control automatic power-saving options.

> **Note** Your hardware must support powering off the monitor and hard disk for you to config-ure power schemes. Almost all modern monitors and hard disks support this feature. How-ever, some applications (particularly older applications) do not respond well to monitors and hard disks being turned off, causing loss of data or even crashing.

Power schemes allow you to configure Windows XP Professional to turn off the power to your monitor and your hard disk, conserving energy. In the Power Options Properties dialog box, click the Power Schemes tab. Windows XP Professional provides the following six built-in power schemes:

- **Home/Office Desk** This power scheme is designed for a desktop computer. After 20 minutes of inactivity, the monitor is turned off, but the hard disks are never turned off.

- **Portable/Laptop** This power scheme is optimized for portable computers that will be running on batteries. After 15 minutes of inactivity, the monitor is turned off; after 30 minutes of inactivity, the hard disks are turned off.

- **Presentation** This power scheme is designed for use with presentations for which the computer display is always to remain on. The monitor and the hard disks are never turned off.

- **Always On** This power scheme is designed for use with personal servers. After 20 minutes of inactivity, the monitor is turned off, but the hard disks are never turned off.

- **Minimal Power Management** This power scheme disables some power man-agement features such as timed hibernation. After 15 minutes of inactivity, the monitor is turned off, but the hard disks are never turned off.

- **Max Battery** This power scheme is designed to conserve as much battery power as possible. After 15 minutes of inactivity, the monitor is turned off, but the hard disks are never turned off.

To select a power scheme, use the following steps:

1. Ensure that you are logged on with a user account that is a member of the Admin-istrators local group.

2. Click Start, click Control Panel, and then click Performance And Maintenance.

3. Click Power Options.

   Windows XP Professional displays the Power Options Properties dialog box with the Power Schemes tab active.

4. Click the arrow at the end of the Power Schemes box to display the pull-down menu listing the available power schemes. Click the power scheme you want to use.

5. Click OK to close the Power Options Properties dialog box.

If none of these power schemes is appropriate for your computer environment, you can modify one of the built-in power schemes or configure a new power scheme. To modify a power scheme or to create a new power scheme, use the following steps:

1. Ensure that you are logged on with a user account that is a member of the Administrators group.

2. Click Start, click Control Panel, and then click Performance And Maintenance.

3. Click Power Options.

   Windows XP Professional displays the Power Options Properties dialog box with the Power Schemes tab active.

4. Click the arrow at the end of the Power Schemes box to display the pull-down menu listing the available power schemes. Click the power scheme you want to base your new power scheme on.

5. In the Settings For *Power_Scheme_Name* Power Scheme text box, modify the amount of inactive time before the monitor or hard drives are turned off.

6. Do one of the following:

   ❑ Click OK to modify the existing power scheme and close the Power Options Properties dialog box.

   ❑ Click Save As to create a new power scheme.

How to Configure Advanced Power Options

To configure your computer to use advanced power options, open the Power Options Properties dialog box and click the Advanced tab. There are two options that always appear on the Advanced tab. If you want an icon to appear in the notification area that displays the current power status for your computer (plugged-in or on battery power) and provides quick power-management access, select the Always Show Icon On The Taskbar check box. The second check box on the Advanced tab is Prompt For Password When Computer Resumes From Standby. Selecting this check box causes Windows to prompt you for your Windows password when your computer comes out of standby mode.

If you have a portable computer, you will also see a Power Buttons section on the Advanced tab. This section allows you to configure what happens when you press the power button on the computer, when you close the lid (thereby pressing the small button signaling that the lid is closed, and when you press the sleep button (if your computer has one). Options that you can choose for each of these buttons include shutting down the computer, sending the computer to standby mode, and having the computer enter hibernation.

Note   The Prompt For Password When Computer Resumes From Standby box will not be displayed if the computer does not support standby mode (this is the case with many desktop computers).

How to Enable Hibernate Mode

Hibernate mode works in a way that is a bit different from standby mode. When a computer enters standby mode, Windows XP turns off most of the devices in the computer (including the display, hard disks, and peripherals), but keeps just enough power flowing to keep the information in memory intact—information that includes open windows and running programs. When you exit standby mode (typically by moving the mouse or pressing a key), Windows is returned to the state in which you left it. However, when a computer is in standby mode, it is still reliant on a power source. If the power source is interrupted (for example, if the battery runs out), information in memory is lost.

When your computer enters hibernate mode, Windows saves the information in memory (including open programs and windows) to your hard disk, and then your computer shuts down. When you start the computer after it has been hibernating, Windows returns to its previous state. Restarting to the previous state includes automatically restarting any programs that were running when it went into hibernate mode, and it even restores any network connections that were active at the time. The advantage of hibernation mode over standby mode is that when a computer is in hibernation mode, it is not reliant on a power source—the computer is completely shut down.

To configure your computer to use hibernate mode, use the Power Options Properties dialog box. Click the Hibernate tab and select the Enable Hibernation check box. If the Hibernate tab is unavailable, your computer does not support this mode.

Hibernation works by saving the information currently stored in your computer's memory to hard disk. To do this, Windows creates a hibernation file on the root of your system partition. This file changes size, depending on the amount of memory you have, but always consumes the amount of space it will need—even if you have never hibernated. Unless you plan to use hibernation, you should disable this option to save disk space.

How to Configure Advanced Power Management

Windows XP Professional supports **Advanced Power Management (APM)**, which helps reduce the power consumption of your system. To configure your computer to use APM, use the Power Options Properties dialog box. Click the APM tab and select the Enable Advanced Power Management Support check box. If the APM tab is unavailable, your computer is compliant with a newer standard named **Advanced**

Configuration and Power Interface (ACPI), which automatically enables Advanced Power Management Support and disables the APM tab. You must be logged on as a member of the Administrators group to configure APM.

If your computer does not have an APM BIOS installed, Windows XP Professional does not install APM, so there will not be an APM tab in the Power Options Properties dialog box. However, your computer can still function as an ACPI computer if it has an ACPI-based BIOS, which takes over system configuration and power management from the Plug and Play BIOS.

Note   If your laptop has an ACPI-based BIOS, you can insert and remove PC cards on the fly, and Windows XP Professional automatically detects and configures them without requiring you to restart your machine. This is known as dynamic configuration of PC cards. There are two other important features for mobile computers that rely on dynamic Plug and Play: hot and warm docking/undocking and hot swapping of Integrated Device Electronics (IDE) and floppy devices. Hot and warm docking/undocking means you can dock and undock from the Windows XP Professional Start menu without turning off your computer. Windows XP Professional automatically creates two hardware profiles for laptop computers: one for the docked state and one for the undocked state. (For more information about hardware profiles see Chapter 6, "Installing, Managing, and Troubleshooting Hardware Devices and Drivers.") Hot swapping of IDE and floppy devices means that you can remove and swap devices such as floppy drives, DVD/CD drives, and hard drives without shutting down your system or restarting your system. Windows XP Professional automatically detects and configures these devices.

How to Configure an Uninterruptible Power Supply

An **uninterruptible power supply** (UPS) is a device connected between a computer or another piece of electronic equipment and a power source, such as an electrical outlet. The UPS ensures that the electrical flow to the computer is not interrupted because of a power outage and, in most cases, protects the computer against potentially damaging events such as power surges and brownouts. When a power outage occurs, the UPS provides a limited amount of time for you to save documents, exit applications, and turn off the computer. Different UPS models offer different levels of protection.

To configure your UPS, click the UPS tab in the Power Options Properties dialog box. The UPS tab shows the current power source, the estimated UPS run time, the estimated UPS capacity, and the battery condition. In the UPS tab, click Configure to display the UPS Selection dialog box. It displays a list of manufacturers from which you can select the manufacturer of your UPS.

Note   Check the Windows Catalog to make sure that the UPS you are considering is compatible with Windows XP Professional before you purchase it.

If you want to configure a custom simple-signaling UPS, in the Select Manufacturer list box, click Generic. In the Select Model list box, click Generic, and then click Next. You can configure the conditions that trigger the UPS device to send a signal in the UPS Interface Configuration dialog box (see Figure 5-6). These conditions include power failures, a low battery, and the UPS shutting down.

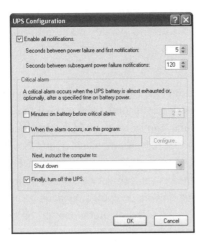

Figure 5-6   Configure the UPS by using the UPS Configuration dialog box.

After you have configured the UPS service for your computer, you should test the configuration to ensure that your computer is protected from power failures. Disconnect the main power supply to simulate a power failure. During your test, the computer and the devices connected to the computer should remain operational. You should let the test run long enough for the UPS battery to reach a low level so that you can verify that an orderly shutdown occurs.

Off the Record   Although Windows XP Professional provides some level of support for UPSs, a good UPS usually comes with software of its own. The manufacturer's software is often better than Windows XP Professional at determining battery levels and estimated run time. In addition, some software includes extra features such as the capability to automatically save documents, exit programs, and shut down the computer (or even to send the computer into hibernation) when a power outage occurs.

Practice: Configuring Power Options

In this practice, you use Control Panel to configure Power Options.

1. Ensure that you are logged on with a user account that is a member of the Administrators group.

2. Click Start, click Control Panel, and then click Performance And Maintenance.

3. Click Power Options.

   Windows XP Professional displays the Power Options Properties dialog box with the Power Schemes tab active.

4. In the Power Schemes list, select Portable/Laptop.

5. In the Turn Off Monitor box, select After 10 Mins.

6. In the Turn Off Hard Disks box, select After 20 Mins.

7. Click Save As, and then in the Save Scheme text box, type **Airplane**.

8. Click OK.

   You have just created a new power scheme. If you click the arrow at the end of the Power Scheme box, Airplane is now included in the list of available power schemes. If you want to use this power scheme, click Apply.

9. Click the Advanced tab and select the Always Show Icon On The Taskbar check box.

10. Click the Hibernate tab.

11. If the Enable Hibernation check box is not selected, select it, and then click Apply.

12. Click the APM tab.

13. If you do not see an APM tab on your computer, what are two reasons why it might not be there?

   _____

   _____

   _____

14. If the Enable Advanced Power Management Support check box is not selected, select it, and then click Apply.

15. To apply these changes you would click OK. Click Cancel.

   Windows XP Professional closes the Power Options Properties dialog box.

16. Close all open windows.

Lesson Review

The following questions are intended to reinforce key information presented in this lesson. If you are unable to answer a question, review the lesson materials and try the question again. You can find answers to the questions in the "Questions and Answers" section at the end of this chapter.

1. What is a power scheme and why would you use one?

   _____

   _____

2. Which of the following statements about Windows XP Professional power schemes are true? (Choose all that apply.)

   a. Windows XP Professional ships with six built-in power schemes.

   b. Windows XP Professional allows you to create your own power schemes.

   c. Windows XP Professional allows you to modify existing power schemes, but you cannot create new ones.

   d. Windows XP Professional does not ship with any built-in power schemes.

3. A(n) _____ is a device that connects between a computer and a power source to ensure that the electrical flow to the computer is not abruptly stopped because of a blackout.

   _____

4. What does hibernate mode do?

   _____

   _____

   _____

   _____

Lesson Summary

- A power scheme is a collection of energy-saving power options. You can configure a power scheme to turn off your monitor or hard disk, or even send the computer to standby after a certain amount of idle time.

- The advanced power management options allow you to add an icon for quick access to Power Management to the taskbar and choose to be prompted for your Windows password when your computer comes out of standby mode.

- When your computer hibernates, it saves the current system state to your hard disk, and then your computer shuts down. When you start the computer after it has been hibernating, it returns to its previous state.

- APM is a power standard that helps reduce the power consumption of your computer. To support APM, you must have an APM-compatible BIOS in your computer. A newer standard, ACPI, automatically enables APM support.

- A UPS is a device that ensures that the electrical flow to a computer is not interrupted because of power loss.

Lesson 3: Configuring System Settings

You use the System Properties dialog box (available in the Control Panel window) to configure operating system settings. These system settings affect the operating system environment regardless of which user is logged on to the computer.

After this lesson, you will be able to

- Configure system performance options.
- Create, modify, and manage user profiles.
- Configure startup and recovery settings.
- Configure environmental variables.
- Configure error reporting.

Estimated lesson time: 70 minutes

How to Configure System Performance Options

To configure system settings, in Control Panel, click Performance And Maintenance. To view operating system performance configuration options, in the Performance And Maintenance window, click System, and then click the Advanced tab. The Advanced tab of the System Properties dialog box (see Figure 5-7) allows you to configure performance options, user profiles, startup and recovery settings, environment variables, and error reporting.

Tip   You can open the System Properties dialog box quickly by right-clicking the My Computer icon and clicking Properties.

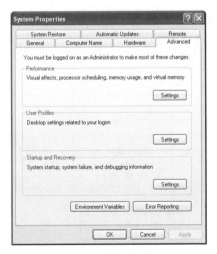

Figure 5-7   Use the Advanced tab of the System Properties dialog box to configure a number of system settings.

On the Advanced tab, in the Performance section, click Settings to display the Performance Options dialog box. There are three tabs on the Performance Options dialog box: Visual Effects, Advanced, and Data Execution Prevention.

Visual Effects Tab

The **Visual Effects** tab of the Performance Options dialog box is shown in Figure 5-8. There are a number of options that you can select to manually control the visual effects on your computer. Windows XP Professional provides four options to help you control the visual effects: Let Windows Choose What's Best For My Computer, Adjust For Best Appearance, Adjust For Best Performance, and Custom. If you want to manually indicate which visual effects to apply, click Custom.

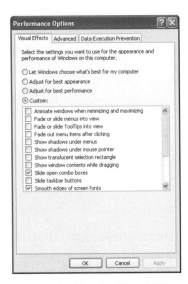

Figure 5-8 Use the Visual Effects tab to control performance options.

Table 5-5 lists the visual effects along with descriptions of those that are not self-explanatory.

Table 5-5 Windows XP Visual Effects

Visual Effect	Description
Animate windows when minimizing and maximizing	Causes a zoom effect when you minimize or maximize a window. Disabling this effect makes windows minimize and maximize faster.
Fade or slide menus into view	Causes menus to fade or slide into view instead of simply appearing. Disabling this effect makes menus appear faster.
Fade or slide ToolTips into view	Causes ToolTips to fade or slide into view instead of simply appearing. ToolTips are the pop-up descriptions that appear beside certain items when you hold your pointer over them. Disabling this effect makes ToolTips appear faster.

Table 5-5   Windows XP Visual Effects

Visual Effect	Description
Fade-out menu items after clicking	Causes menus to fade out after you select a command. Disabling this effect makes menus disappear instantly after selecting a command.
Show shadows under menus	Causes Windows to display a drop shadow behind menus for a three-dimensional effect. Disabling this effect makes menus appear more quickly.
Show shadows under mouse pointer	Causes Windows to display a drop shadow behind the mouse pointer. Disabling this effect can make the mouse more responsive. Also, some older applications do not work well when this feature is enabled.
Show translucent selection rectangle	Draws a filled-in rectangle when selecting multiple items on the desktop instead of just a rectangle outline. Disabling this effect slightly increases the speed with which you can select items.
Show window contents while dragging	Causes Windows to redraw a window while the window is being moved. Disabling this command makes dragging open windows noticeably faster.
Slide open combo boxes	Causes combo boxes to slide open instead of simply appear. A combo box is a drop-down list of items that you open from within a dialog box. Disabling this effect makes combo boxes appear more quickly.
Slide taskbar buttons	Causes taskbar buttons to slide to the left when other programs are closed or to the right when new programs are opened. Disabling this effect makes taskbar buttons appear instantly in the new location instead of sliding. Disabling this effect makes taskbar buttons available more quickly when they change locations.
Smooth edges of screen fonts	Makes screen fonts easier to read, especially at higher resolutions. Disabling this effect increases the speed at which Windows displays windows and dialog boxes.
Smooth-scroll list boxes	Causes the contents of a list box to scroll smoothly when you click the scroll bar rather than just jump down a few items in the list. Disabling this effect makes scrolling list boxes faster, but often disorienting.
Use a background image for each folder type	Different types of folders in Windows XP can use different background images. Many of the special Windows folders, such as Control Panel, make use of this effect.
Use common tasks in folders	Causes folders in Windows to display a task pane on the left side of the folder that lists tasks that are related to the files in the folder.
Use drop shadows for icon labels on the desktop	Creates a transparency effect on text labels for icons, but this transparency really allows you to see only any other icons obscured by an icon on top. The transparency does not allow you to "see through" to the actual desktop background. Disabling this effect causes Windows to display the desktop more quickly.
Use visual styles on windows and buttons	This setting is an important one in that it controls the new look of Windows XP. If you disable it, your desktop will look like previous versions of Windows.

Advanced Performance Options

The Advanced tab of the Performance Options dialog box is shown in Figure 5-9. The options in this dialog box allow you to adjust the application response, which is the priority of foreground programs versus background programs, and virtual memory.

Figure 5-9   Configure additional settings on the Advanced tab of the Performance Options dialog box.

Processor Scheduling   Windows XP Professional uses the Processor Scheduling settings to distribute microprocessor resources among running programs. Selecting Programs assigns more resources to the foreground program (the active program that is responding to user input). Windows XP Professional assigns more resources to the foreground program by allocating short, variable time slices, or quanta, to running programs. A time slice, or quantum, is a brief period of time during which a particular task is given control of the microprocessor. When you select Background Services, Windows assigns an equal number of resources to all programs by assigning long fixed quanta instead. You should select Background Services only when a computer is used as a server.

> **Exam Tip**   Understand the difference between the Programs and Background Services options.

Memory Usage   Windows XP Professional uses the Memory Usage settings to distribute memory resources between running programs. Select Programs if your computer is being used primarily as a workstation. With the Programs option, your programs will work faster, and your system cache will be the default size for Windows XP

Professional. Select System Cache if you are using your computer as a server or if the programs you are running require a large system cache.

Virtual Memory   For virtual memory, Windows XP Professional uses a process called demand paging to exchange data between random access memory (RAM) and paging files on the hard disk. When you install Windows XP Professional, Setup creates a virtual-memory **paging file**, PAGEFILE.SYS, on the partition in which you installed Windows XP Professional. The default or recommended paging file size for Windows XP Professional is equal to 1.5 times the total amount of RAM. For best results, never set the value of the paging file size to less than the recommended amount. Typically, you can leave the size of the paging file set to the default value and let Windows XP Professional manage the file size. In some circumstances, such as when you run a large number of applications simultaneously, you might find it advantageous to use a larger paging file or multiple paging files.

> **Exam Tip**   By default, Windows XP manages the paging file size, but you can designate a file size for special circumstances. The recommended paging file size is equal to 1.5 times the total amount of RAM.

To configure the paging file, in the Performance Options dialog box, click the Change button in the Virtual Memory section. The Virtual Memory dialog box (see Figure 5-10) identifies the drives in which the paging files reside and allows you to modify the paging file size for the selected drive.

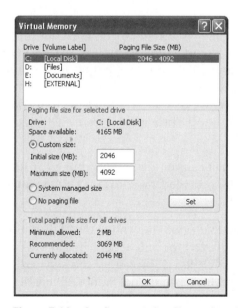

Figure 5-10   Configure paging file settings in the Virtual Memory dialog box.

Important   Only users with administrative rights can use the Performance Options dialog box to increase the paging file size.

Paging files never decrease below the value found in the Initial Size text box that was set during installation. Unused space in the paging file remains available to the internal Windows XP Professional Virtual Memory Manager (VMM). As needed, a paging file grows from its initial size to the maximum configured size, which is listed in the Maximum Size text box. When a paging file reaches the maximum size, but a running program still needs to allocate more virtual memory, Windows XP Professional will refuse that allocation, which can cause an error, or even a crash, in applications.

When you restart a computer running Windows XP Professional, the system resizes all paging files to the initial size.

Data Execution Prevention

Data Execution Prevention (DEP) is a set of hardware and software technologies that perform additional checks on memory to help prevent malicious code from running on a computer. In Windows XP Professional, DEP can be enforced by compatible hardware and by software.

Note   DEP is an update included with Windows XP Service Pack 2. Hardware DEP is available with compatible devices and runs only on the 32-bit version of Windows XP Professional and Home Edition.

Hardware DEP works by marking all pages in memory as non-executable unless the page explicitly contains executable code. This process helps prevent malicious attacks that try to insert and run executable code into memory. To use hardware DEP, a computer must have a compatible processor that allows Windows to mark memory pages as non-executable. Both Intel and AMD provide hardware DEP–compatible processors.

Software DEP is a set of security checks that can run on any processor capable of running Windows XP. However, the security provided by software DEP is limited compared to that provided by hardware DEP.

You can configure DEP by using the Data Execution Prevention tab of the Performance Options dialog box. By default, DEP is enabled for only essential Windows programs and services. However, you can turn DEP on for all programs and services, and then select specific programs and services for which you do not want DEP enabled.

How to Enhance System Performance

You can enhance system performance in several ways. First, if your computer has multiple hard disk controllers, you can create a paging file on a disk on each controller. Distributing information across multiple paging files improves performance because Windows can read and write from disks on different controllers simultaneously. When attempting to write to the paging file, VMM tries to write the page data to the paging file on the controller that is the least busy.

Second, you can enhance performance by moving the paging file off the drive that contains the Windows XP Professional *%systemroot%* folder (by default, the Windows folder), which avoids competition between the various reading and writing requests. If you place a paging file on the Windows XP Professional system partition to facilitate the recovery feature, which is discussed in the section entitled "How to Configure Startup and Recovery Settings" later in this lesson, you can still increase performance by creating multiple paging files. Because the VMM alternates write operations between paging files, the paging file on the boot partition is accessed less frequently.

Third, you can enhance system performance by setting the initial size of the paging file to the value displayed in the Virtual Memory dialog box's Maximum Size box, which eliminates the time required to enlarge the file from the initial size to the maximum size.

> **Note**   When applying new settings, be sure to click Set before clicking OK.

How to Configure User Profiles

Each user account in Windows XP has an associated **user profile** that stores user-specific configuration settings, such as a customized desktop or personalized application settings. Understanding how user profiles function and how to control them lets you effectively manage the user's desktop environment.

Windows XP supports three types of user profiles:

- **Local**   A local user profile is available only on the system on which it was created. A unique local user profile is created and stored on each computer that a user logs on to.

- **Roaming**   Roaming profiles, which are stored in a shared folder on a network server, are accessible from any location in the network.

- **Mandatory**   Mandatory user profiles are roaming user profiles that users cannot make permanent changes to. Mandatory profiles are used to enforce configuration settings.

Where Local User Profiles Are Stored

Windows stores local user profiles in the Documents And Settings folder hierarchy on the *%systemroot%* drive. When a user logs on to a Windows XP system for the first time, Windows creates a folder in Documents And Settings that matches the user's user name. Within each user profile, several files and folders contain configuration information and data. These files and folders include the following:

- **Application Data**   Contains application configuration information. Applications that are Windows XP–aware can take advantage of this folder to store user-specific configuration settings. This folder is hidden.

- **Cookies**   Contains cookie files, which Web sites usually create to store user information and preferences on the local system. When you return to a site, the cookie files allow the site to provide you with customized content and track your activity within the site.

- **Desktop**   Contains files, folders, and shortcuts that have been placed on the Windows XP desktop.

- **Favorites**   Used to store shortcuts to locations that a user has added to the Favorites list in Windows Explorer or Internet Explorer.

- **Local Settings**   Holds application data, history, and temporary files (including temporary Internet files). This folder is hidden.

- **My Documents**   Used to store documents and other user data. My Documents is easily accessible from the Start menu.

- **My Recent Documents**   Contains shortcuts to recently accessed documents and folders. You can also access My Recent Documents from the Start Menu. This folder is hidden.

- **NetHood**   Holds shortcuts created by the Add Network Place option in My Network Places. This folder is hidden.

- **PrintHood**   Contains shortcuts to printer folder items. This folder is hidden.

- **SendTo**   Contains shortcuts to document-handling utilities, such as e-mail applications. These shortcuts are displayed on the Send To option on the action menu for files and folders. This folder is hidden.

- **Start Menu**   Holds the shortcuts to programs that are displayed in the Start menu. One way to modify the Start Menu is to add or delete folders and shortcuts to the Start Menu folder within a user's profile folder.

- **Templates**   Contains template items. Created by user applications and are used by those applications when a user creates a new document. This folder is hidden.

- **NTUSER.DAT**   The user-specific portion of the Registry. This file contains configuration changes made to Windows Explorer and the taskbar, as well as user-specific

Control Panel and Accessories settings. These settings are visible under HKEY_CURRENT_USER in the Registry.

- **NTUSER.DAT.LOG**   A log file used as part of the process of committing changes to Ntuser.dat and also in the recovery of Ntuser.dat if the system crashes.

Built-In User Profiles

Windows stores user profiles locally by default. A local user profile is available only on the system on which it was created. Windows creates two built-in local user profiles during installation:

- **Default User profile**   Windows uses the Default User profile as a template to create all new profiles on the system. When a new user logs on, the user receives a copy of the Default User profile as her own personal user profile. You can customize the Default User profile to control which options and settings a new user will receive. Modifications to the Default User profile will affect only the profiles of new users; existing personal profiles will not be affected. The Default User profile is stored in the \Documents and Settings\Default User folder. This folder is hidden. To view and work with it, you must set the Folder Options in Windows Explorer to include hidden files and folders.

- **All Users profile**   The All Users profile contains settings that apply to every user who logs on to the system. Windows merges the settings in All Users with the current user's profile for the duration of the logon session, but the settings are not made a permanent part of the user's profile. You can modify the All Users profile to contain settings that all users logging on to the system should have. For example, many applications create shortcuts in the Start menu or desktop of the All Users profile during installation, which ensures that all users who log on to the system have easy access to those applications. As the Administrator, you can directly edit the All Users profile to add and remove items as necessary. The All Users profile is stored in the \Documents and Settings\All Users folder. The folder contains only a subset of the folders contained in other profiles on the system because it is concerned only with settings that could potentially apply to everyone.

How to Use Multiple Profiles for the Same User Account

If a computer running Windows XP Professional is a member of a Windows domain, there is the potential for two users with the same user account name to log on to the same system. An example of this is the local Administrator account (stored in the local accounts database of the Windows XP computer) and the domain Administrator account (stored in the centralized accounts database on the domain controllers). The local account and the domain account are discrete entities, each maintaining a different user profile.

Windows XP does not permit two user accounts with the same name to share the same profile folder (for example, C:\Documents and Settings\Administrator). If Windows did allow this to happen, the profile of one user would overwrite the profile of the other. Instead, Windows creates the profile of the first user to log on using the user name of the user in \Documents and Settings*%username%*. Windows stores subsequent user accounts with the same name using the path \Documents and Settings*%username%.x*. The folder extension (*x*) varies as follows:

- If the additional user to log on with the same user name is a domain account, Windows creates the folder extension using the name of the domain.

- If the additional user to log on with the same user name is a local account, Windows creates the folder extension using the name of the computer.

For example, if the local Administrator logs on first, and the domain Administrator logs on second, Windows stores the local Administrator's profile in the Administrator folder, and the domain Administrator's profile would be stored in a folder named Administrator.*<domain_name>*.

Multiple user profiles are an issue only when the system is a member of a domain because domain membership enables both local and domain accounts to log on. In a workgroup environment, Windows XP relies solely on the local accounts database, and you cannot create two user accounts of the same name on the same computer.

How to Work with Local User Profiles

To view, create, delete, and change the type of user profiles, in Control Panel, click Performance And Maintenance, click System, and then click the Advanced tab (refer to Figure 5-7). In the User Profiles box, click Settings to display the User Profiles dialog box (see Figure 5-11).

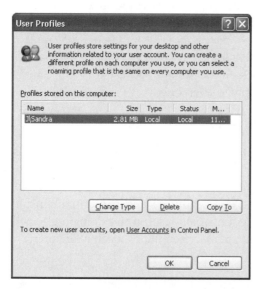

Figure 5-11   Use the User Profiles dialog box to control local user profiles.

The User Profiles dialog box lists the profiles stored on the computer you are sitting at. You can perform the following tasks:

- **Change Type**   Allows you to change the type of profile to local or roaming.

- **Delete**   Allows you to delete user profiles.

- **Copy To**   Allows you to create user profiles by copying an existing user profile and assigning it to another user.

After you click Copy To, the Copy Profile To text box allows you to specify a path for the location to which the user profile is to be copied. You can click Browse to locate the appropriate path. The Permitted To Use box allows you to specify the user or users who can use the user profile.

How to Configure Startup and Recovery Settings

The System Properties dialog box also controls the startup and recovery settings for a computer. Click Settings in the Startup And Recovery section of the Advanced Tab of the System Properties dialog box to display the Startup And Recovery dialog box, as shown in Figure 5-12. The System Startup options control the behavior of the Please Select The Operating System To Start menu that appears when your computer starts. The System Failure options control the actions that Windows XP Professional performs in the event of a stop error, which is a severe error that causes Windows XP Professional to stop all processes.

Figure 5-12   Use the Startup And Recovery dialog box to control startup and system failure settings.

   Off the Record   Stop errors are often referred to as fatal system errors or blue screen errors.

System Startup

When you first turn on the computer, the system displays the Please Select The Operating System To Start screen, which lists the available operating systems if more than one is installed. By default, the system chooses one of the operating systems and displays a countdown timer. If you do not choose another operating system, the system starts the preselected operating system when the countdown timer reaches zero or when you press ENTER. Modify the options under System Startup to determine which operating system is preselected, how long the countdown timer runs, and whether to display the boot menu. You are also given the option of modifying the BOOT.INI file manually, but it is usually better to allow Windows XP Professional to modify the file rather than attempting to do so manually.

System Failure

The four recovery options that Windows XP Professional provides to assist administrators in the event of a system failure are described in Table 5-6.

> **Important** You must be logged on as a member of the Administrators group to set the options in the Startup And Recovery dialog box.

Table 5-6 Recovery Options

Option	Additional Information
Write An Event To The System Log	Select this check box to have Windows XP Professional write an event to the system log when a system stops unexpectedly. Read Chapter 18, "Using Windows XP Tools," for more on events and the system log.
Send An Administrative Alert	Select this check box to have Windows XP Professional send an administrative alert to administrators when the system stops unexpectedly.
Automatically Restart	Select this check box to have Windows XP Professional reboot whenever the system stops unexpectedly. Clear this check box if you are troubleshooting a computer that continually reboots itself due to a startup error.
Write Debugging Information	This section allows you to specify whether Windows XP Professional should record the contents of memory to a debugging file when there is a system failure and how much of the memory contents to write. Typically, debugging information is used by Microsoft support technicians to help identify and solve problems. The first option allows you to specify what information Windows XP Professional should write to the dump file: Memory.dmp. The following four choices are available: ■ **None** Nothing is written to the dump file.

Table 5-6   Recovery Options

Option	Additional Information
	■ **Small Memory Dump** The minimum amount of useful information will be dumped. This option (the default setting) requires a paging file of at least 2 MB on the boot volume of your computer. A new dump file will be created every time the system stops unexpectedly. The small dump directory stores a history of these dumps. By default, the small dump directory is %Systemroot%\Minidump. A small memory dump can be useful when troubleshooting stop errors because it allows you to see the actual stop error and often determines the driver causing the error.
	■ **Kernel Memory Dump** Only kernel memory is written to the dump file. Depending on the amount of RAM on your computer, you must have from 50 MB to 800 MB available in the paging file on the boot volume. A kernel memory dump can be useful when debugging more complicated system failures. Typically, providing a kernal memory to Microsoft support technicians allows them to determine the cause of most errors.
	■ **Complete Memory Dump** Records the entire contents of system memory when the system stops unexpectedly. You must have a paging file on the boot volume large enough to hold all the RAM on your system plus 1 MB. A complete memory dump is quite large and usually contains more information than you will find useful for simple debugging. You should enable this option only when a Microsoft support technician requests it.
	There are also two additional options:
	■ **Small Dump Directory** Specifies the name and location of the small memory dump file. By default, it is %Systemroot%\Memory.dmp.
	■ **Overwrite Any Existing File** By default, if you choose Complete Memory Dump or Kernel Memory Dump, Windows XP Professional always writes to the same dump file: Memory.dmp. Clear this check box to prevent Windows from overwriting Memory.dmp.

The following requirements must be met for the Write Debugging Information recovery option to work:

■ A paging file must be on the system partition (the partition that contains the %systemroot% folder).

■ The paging file must be at least 1 MB larger than the amount of physical RAM in your computer if you choose Complete Memory Dump.

■ You must have enough disk space to write the file to the location you specify.

How to Configure Environment Variables

Environment variables define the system and user environment information, and they contain information such as a drive, path, or file name. Environment variables provide information that Windows XP Professional uses to control various applications. For example, the TEMP environment variable specifies where some applications place temporary files.

In the Advanced tab of the System Properties dialog box, click Environment Variables to display the system and user environment variables that are currently in effect in the Environment Variables dialog box (see Figure 5-13).

Figure 5-13 Environment variables control the system and user environment.

System Environment Variables

Because system environment variables apply to the entire computer, they also affect all users of the computer. During installation, Setup configures the default system environment variables, including the path to the Windows XP Professional files. Only an administrator can add, modify, or remove a system environment variable.

User Environment Variables

The user environment variables differ for each user of a particular computer. The user environment variables include any user-defined settings (such as a desktop pattern) and any variables defined by applications (such as the path to the location of the application files). Users can add, modify, or remove their user environment variables in the System Properties dialog box.

How Windows XP Professional Sets Environment Variables

Windows XP Professional sets environment variables in the following order:

1. By default, Windows XP Professional searches the AUTOEXEC.BAT file, if it exists, and sets any environment variables.

2. Next, the system environment variables are set. If any system environment variables conflict with environment variables set from the search of the AUTOEXEC.BAT file, the system environment variables override them.

3. Finally, the user environment variables are set. If any user environment variables conflict with environment variables set from the search of the AUTOEXEC.BAT file or from the system environment variables, the user environment variables override them.

For example, if you add the line SET TMP=C:\ in AUTOEXEC.BAT, and a TMP=X:\TEMP user variable is set, the user environment variable setting (X:\TEMP) overrides the prior setting C:\.

> **Note**   You can prevent Windows XP Professional from searching the AUTOEXEC.BAT file by editing the registry and setting the value of the ParseAutoexec entry to 0. The ParseAutoexec entry is located in the registry under the following subkey:
>
> \HKEY_CURRENT_USER\SOFTWARE\Microsoft\Windows NT\ CurrentVersion\Winlogon. See Chapter 4, "Modifying and Troubleshooting the Startup Process," for more information on the Windows Registry.

How to Configure Error Reporting

Error reporting helps Microsoft improve future products and resolve any difficulties you might encounter with Windows XP Professional. To configure error reporting, in the Advanced tab of the System Properties dialog box, click Error Reporting. This displays the Error Reporting dialog box. Notice that Enable Error Reporting is selected by default. To turn off error reporting, click Disable Error Reporting.

If you do not want to turn off error checking, you can configure reporting to indicate which errors to report. Under Enable Error Reporting there are two check boxes selected by default. Clear the Windows Operating System check box if you do not want errors in the operating system to be reported. Clear the Programs check box if you do not want errors in any of the programs running on your system to be reported. If you want to specify the programs for which Windows XP Professional reports errors, click Select Programs.

> **Note**   If a system or program error occurs and you have configured your system to report it, Windows XP Professional displays a dialog box that allows you to indicate whether you want to send the report to Microsoft.

Practice: Configuring System Settings by Using Control Panel

In this practice, you use the System program to change some of the system settings. First, you change the paging file size. Then, you add a new system environment variable.

Exercise 1: Change the Paging File Size

In this exercise, you use the System Properties dialog box to change the size of the Windows XP Professional paging file.

1. In the System Properties dialog box, click the Advanced tab.

2. In the Performance box, click Settings.

   Windows XP Professional displays the Performance Options dialog box with the Visual Effects tab active.

3. Click the Advanced tab.

   By default, both Processor Scheduling and Memory Usage are optimized for applications.

4. In the Virtual Memory box, click Change.

   Windows XP Professional displays the Virtual Memory dialog box.

5. In the Drive list, click the drive that contains your paging file, if necessary.

6. In the Initial Size text box, increase the value by 10, and then click Set.

   You have just increased the initial size of the paging file.

7. Click OK to close the Virtual Memory dialog box.

8. Click OK to close the Performance Options dialog box.

   Leave the System Properties dialog box open for the next exercise.

Exercise 2: Add a System Environment Variable

In this exercise, you use the System Properties dialog box to add a new system environment variable. You then test the new variable by using it at the command prompt.

1. In the System Properties dialog box, in the Advanced tab, click Environment Variables.

   Windows XP Professional displays the Environment Variables dialog box.

2. Under System Variables, click New.

   Windows XP Professional displays the New System Variable dialog box.

3. In the Variable Name text box, type **WinXPdir**.

4. In the Variable Value text box, type the path to the folder containing the Windows XP Professional system files, for example, **C:\Windows**.

   If you are not sure of the path to the Windows XP Professional system files, use Windows Explorer to locate the Windows directory.

5. Click OK.

   You are returned to the Environment Variables dialog box.

6. Scroll through the System Environment Variables and verify that WinXPdir is listed.

7. Click OK to close the Environment Variables dialog box, and then click OK to close the System Properties dialog box.

8. Close the Performance And Maintenance window.

9. From the Start menu, click Run.

10. In the Open text box, type **cmd**, and then click OK.

11. What does typing the cmd command do?

    _____

12. At the command prompt, type **set | more**, and then press ENTER.

    The list of current environment variables is displayed, and WinXPdir is listed. (You might need to press SPACEBAR to scroll down to see WinXPdir listed.)

13. If necessary, type **c:** and then press ENTER to switch to the drive on which you installed Windows XP Professional. (Adjust the drive letter, if necessary.)

14. Type **cd** and then press ENTER to switch to the root directory.

15. Type **cd %WinXPdir%**, and then press ENTER.

    You should now be in the Windows directory.

16. Type **exit** and press ENTER to close the command prompt.

Lesson Review

The following questions are intended to reinforce key information presented in this lesson. If you are unable to answer a question, review the lesson materials and try the question again. You can find answers to the questions in the "Questions and Answers" section at the end of this chapter.

1. What performance options can you control with the tabs of the Performance Options dialog box?

   _____

   _____

   _____

   _____

   _____

2. Which of the following statements about the use of virtual memory in Windows XP Professional are correct? (Choose all that apply.)

   a. When you install Windows XP Professional, Setup creates a virtual memory paging file, PAGEFILE.SYS, on the partition where you installed Windows XP Professional.

   b. In some environments, you might find it advantageous to use multiple paging files.

   c. If the entire paging file is not in use, it can decrease below the initial size that was set during installation.

   d. Unused space in the paging file remains unavailable to all programs, even the internal Windows XP Professional VMM.

3. When you first turn on the computer, the system displays a Please Select The Operating System To Start screen, which lists the available operating systems. What happens if a user does not select an operating system before the countdown timer reaches zero?

   _____

   _____

4. Which requirements must be met for the Write Debugging Information recovery option to work?

   _____

   _____

   _____

   _____

   _____

   _____

_____

_____

_____

Lesson Summary

■ The Advanced tab of the System Properties dialog box allows you to configure performance options for a computer. You can enable and disable visual effects that affect performance, as well as configure processor scheduling, memory usage, virtual and memory settings.

■ Each user account in Windows XP has an associated user profile that stores user-specific configuration settings. There are three types of user profiles: local, roaming, and mandatory. Local user profiles are stored in the Documents And Settings folder hierarchy on the %systemroot% drive.

■ You can also use the System Properties dialog box to control the startup and recovery settings for a computer. Startup settings include which operating system is loaded by default during Windows Startup and how long Windows waits for you to choose an operating system before loading the default automatically. Recovery settings allow you to control Windows behavior in the event of a system failure.

■ Environment variables define the system and user environment information. Environment variables provide information that Windows XP Professional uses to control various applications.

■ When Error Reporting is enabled, Windows collects information after an application or operating system error and offers to send that information to Microsoft. Error reporting assists Microsoft in improving future products and in resolving any difficulties you might encounter with Windows XP Professional.

Lesson 4: Configuring Languages, Locations, and Accessibility Options

Windows XP Professional provides great flexibility when configuring the desktop. You can configure your computer for multiple languages and multiple locations. This is especially important for international companies that deal with customers in more than one country or users who live in a country in which more than one language is spoken. Windows XP Professional also provides accessibility options that allow you to make the operating system easier to use.

After this lesson, you will be able to

- Configure and troubleshoot regional and language options.
- Configure and troubleshoot accessibility options.

Estimated lesson time: 40 minutes

How to Configure and Troubleshoot Regional and Language Options

Regional And Language Options, available from Date, Time, Language, And Regional Options in Control Panel, define the standards and formats that the computer uses to perform calculations; provide information such as date and time; and display the correct format for currency, numbers, dates, and other units. These settings also define a user's location, which enables help services to provide local information such as news and weather. Language options define the **input languages** (one computer can accept input in many different languages); therefore, the computer must be configured with the proper settings.

In many instances, users need to add a region or an input language because they travel, work, or live in two different countries or regions; an input language needs to be added because users who share a computer speak different languages; or a currency, time, and date need to be changed temporarily on a user's laptop while he is on a business trip.

You will perform almost all regional and language configuration and troubleshooting tasks in Control Panel by clicking Date, Time, Language, And Regional Options; and then clicking Regional And Language Options. Figure 5-14 shows the Regional And Language Options dialog box.

Configuring Correct Currency, Time, and Date

When a user requests a change to the currency, time, or date standards and formats on a computer, you make those changes in the Regional And Language Options dialog box on the Regional Options tab. Changing the standard and format is as simple as clicking the drop-down list in the Standards And Formats section and selecting a new option. In Figure 5-15, English (United States) is no longer selected; French (France) is. Notice that the date is written in French, that the currency has changed, and that the date, November 4, 2004, is written 04/11/2004—different from the English version, which is 11/04/2004.

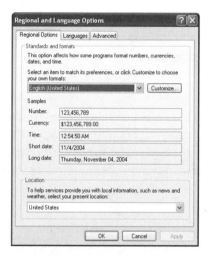

Figure 5-14   The Regional And Language Options dialog box allows you to select available languages and customize formatting.

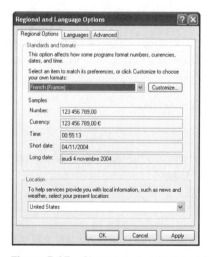

Figure 5-15   Changing standard and format options changes the currency, date, language, and more.

To make changes and to access the other regional and language options, use these steps:

1. Click Start, and then click Control Panel.

2. In the Control Panel window, click Date, Time, Language, And Regional Options; and then click Regional And Language Options.

3. In the Regional And Language Options dialog box, on the Regional Options tab, in the Standards And Formats section, click the drop-down list to view the additional choices. Select one of these choices.

4. In the Location section, choose a country or region from the list to change the default location.

5. To further customize the settings, click Customize.

6. When finished, click OK in each open dialog box to exit.

How to Customize Regional Options

If you need to change the default settings—such as changing the currency symbol, the time or date format, or the system of measurement—but need to keep other default settings intact, click Customize (refer to Figure 5-14) and make the appropriate changes. Each option has a drop-down list, and selecting a different option requires only selecting it from the list.

How to Configure Input Languages

The input language that is configured for the computer tells Windows how to react when a user types text using the keyboard. A user might want you to add a language if he works in or travels between two or more countries that use different languages and he needs to work in those languages or perform calculations with the currencies in those countries. With multiple languages configured, the user can toggle between them as needed. In addition, users might want to change language settings even if they do not travel because they do work with an international group or conduct business with other countries.

To add (or remove) an input language, use these steps:

1. Click Start menu, and then click Control Panel.

2. In the Control Panel window, click Date, Time, Language, And Regional Options; and then click Regional And Language Options.

3. In the Regional And Language Options dialog box, on the Languages tab, click Details.

4. In the Text Services And Input Languages dialog box, click Add to add a language.

5. In the Add Input Language dialog box, click the language you want to add. To choose a specific keyboard layout, select the Keyboard Layout/IME check box and choose the appropriate layout. (To add a keyboard layout or input method editor [IME], you need to have installed it on your computer first.) Click OK.

6. In the Text Services And Input Languages dialog box, select which language should be the default language from the Default Input Language drop-down list and click OK.

Figure 5-16 shows two available languages: English [United States]-US and French [France]-France. You can now switch between these languages by using the Language toolbar located on the taskbar.

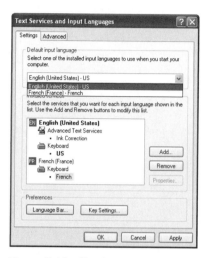

Figure 5-16 Two languages are now available.

How to Troubleshoot Language-Related Problems

When users have multiple languages configured, language-related problems will probably occur. A common problem occurs when a user who has multiple languages configured changes the default language in use by accidentally pressing the key combination that switches between them. By default, pressing LEFT ALT + SHIFT switches between languages. If you press this combination accidentally, it might suddenly seem that the keyboard does not act as it is supposed to. You must press the key combination again (or use the Language toolbar) to switch back to the default language. You might want to disable this feature if it becomes a regular problem.

Exam Tip Consider regional settings as a possibility when keyboard errors are reported or when users report that symbols do not look correct.

How to Configure and Troubleshoot Accessibility Options

Windows XP Professional provides the ability to configure accessibility options through the Accessibility Options icon in Control Panel.

Keyboard Options

To configure keyboard options, in Control Panel, click Accessibility Options. In the Accessibility Options window, click Accessibility Options to display the Accessibility Options dialog box. The Keyboard tab of the Accessibility Options dialog box, shown in Figure 5-17, allows you to configure the keyboard options StickyKeys, FilterKeys, and ToggleKeys.

Figure 5-17   Configure keyboard accessibility options.

StickyKeys   Turning on StickyKeys allows you to press a multiple-key combination, such as CTRL+ALT+DELETE, one key at a time. This is useful for people who have difficulty pushing more than one key at a time. This is a check box selection, so it is either on or off. You can configure StickyKeys by clicking Settings to activate the Settings For StickyKeys dialog box (see Figure 5-18).

Figure 5-18   StickyKeys allows you to press a multiple-key combination one key at a time.

You can also configure a shortcut key for StickyKeys. You can use the default shortcut key, pressing SHIFT five times, to turn on StickyKeys. This option is activated by default.

Two other options can also be configured for StickyKeys: Press Modifier Key Twice To Lock and Turn StickyKeys Off If Two Keys Are Pressed At Once. The modifier keys are CTRL, ALT, SHIFT, and the Windows Logo key. If you select the modifier key option, pressing one of the modifier keys twice will cause that key to remain active until you press it again. This is useful for people who have difficulty pressing key combinations. If you choose to use the second option, StickyKeys is disabled if two keys are pressed simultaneously.

Two Notification settings can be configured for StickyKeys: Make Sounds When Modifier Key Is Pressed and Show StickyKeys Status On Screen. The first notification setting causes a sound to be made when any of the modifier keys—CTRL, ALT, SHIFT, or the Windows Logo key—is pressed. The second notification setting causes a StickyKeys icon to be displayed in the taskbar when StickyKeys is turned on.

FilterKeys   The Keyboard tab also allows you to configure FilterKeys. Turning on FilterKeys causes the keyboard to ignore brief or repeated keystrokes. This option also allows you to configure the keyboard repeat rate, which is the rate at which a key continuously held down repeats the keystroke. This is a check box selection, so it is either on or off. You can configure FilterKeys by clicking Settings to activate the Settings For FilterKeys dialog box (see Figure 5-19).

Figure 5-19   FilterKeys causes the keyboard to ignore brief or repeated keystrokes.

You can also configure a shortcut key for FilterKeys. You can use the default shortcut key, holding down the RIGHT SHIFT key for eight seconds, to turn on FilterKeys. This setting is activated by default.

Two other Filter options can also be configured for FilterKeys: Ignore Repeated Keystrokes and Ignore Quick Keystrokes And Slow Down The Repeat Rate. Ignore Repeated Keystrokes is inactive by default; Ignore Quick Keystrokes And Slow Down The Repeat Rate is active by default. Only one of these two filter options can be active at a time. Configure each of them by clicking Settings.

Two Notification settings can be configured for FilterKeys: Beep When Keys Pressed Or Accepted and Show FilterKey Status On Screen. The first notification setting causes a beep when you press a key and another beep when the keystroke is accepted. The second notification option causes a FilterKeys icon to be displayed in the taskbar when FilterKeys is turned on. These settings are check boxes, so one of the settings, both of the settings (the default), or neither of the settings can be selected.

ToggleKeys   You can also configure ToggleKeys in the Keyboard tab. Turning on ToggleKeys causes the computer to make a high-pitched sound each time the CAPS LOCK, NUM LOCK, or SCROLL LOCK key is switched on. Turning on ToggleKeys also causes the computer to make a low-pitched sound each time these three keys are turned off.

You can configure a shortcut key for ToggleKeys by clicking Settings. You can use the shortcut key, holding down NUM LOCK for five seconds, to turn on ToggleKeys. This setting is activated by default.

> **Note**   There is one more check box on the Keyboard tab: Show Extra Keyboard Help In Programs. When activated, this check box causes other programs to display additional keyboard help if available.

Sound Options

The Sound tab provides the Use SoundSentry check box, which allows you to configure Windows XP Professional to generate visual warnings when your computer makes a sound. The Sound tab also provides the Use ShowSounds check box, which allows you to configure Windows XP Professional programs to display captions for the speech and sounds they make.

Display Options

The Display tab of the Accessibility Options dialog box provides the Use High Contrast check box, which allows you to configure Windows XP Professional to use color and fonts designed for easy reading. You can click Settings to turn off or on the use of a shortcut, LEFT ALT+LEFT SHIFT+PRTSCN, which is enabled by default. Clicking Settings also allows you to select the high-contrast appearance scheme that you want to use. The Display tab also provides cursor options that allow you to set the blink rate and the width of the cursor.

Mouse Options

The Mouse tab provides the Use MouseKeys check box, which allows you to configure Windows XP Professional to control the pointer with the numeric keypad on your keyboard. You can click Settings to configure MouseKeys in the Settings For MouseKeys dialog box (see Figure 5-20).

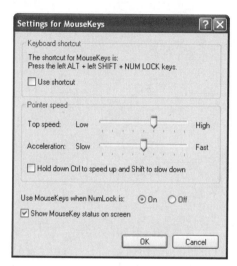

Figure 5-20   MouseKeys allows you to control the pointer with the numeric keypad.

MouseKeys uses a shortcut, LEFT ALT+LEFT SHIFT+NUM LOCK, which is enabled by default. You can also configure the pointer speed and acceleration speed. There is even a check box, Hold Down Ctrl To Speed Up And Shift To Slow Down, that allows you to temporarily speed up or slow down the mouse pointer speed when you are using MouseKeys. To speed up the mouse pointer movement, hold down CTRL while you press the numeric keypad directional keys. To slow down the mouse pointer movement, hold down SHIFT while you press the numeric keypad directional keys.

General Tab

The General tab of the Accessibility Options dialog box (see Figure 5-21) allows you to configure Automatic Reset. This feature turns off all the accessibility features, except the SerialKeys devices, after the computer has been idle for a specified amount of time.

The General tab also includes the Notification feature, which allows you to configure Windows XP Professional to give a warning message when a feature is activated and to make a sound when turning a feature on or off.

The General tab also allows you to activate the SerialKeys Devices feature, which configures Windows XP Professional to support an alternative input device (also called an augmentative communication device) to your computer's serial port.

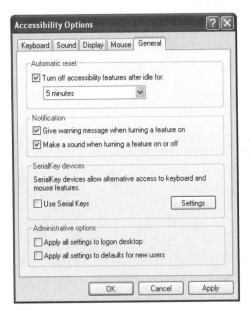

Figure 5-21   Configure general accessibility options.

The Administrative Options feature provides two check boxes, Apply All Settings To Logon Desktop and Apply All Settings To Defaults For New Users, which allow you to configure Windows XP Professional to apply all configured accessibility options to this user at logon and to apply all configured accessibility options to all new users.

Practice: Configuring Multiple Languages by Using Control Panel

In this practice, you use the Regional And Language Options icon in Control Panel to configure multiple languages and multiple locations.

1. In Control Panel, click the Date, Time, Language, And Regional Options icon.

2. Click Regional And Language Options.

    Windows XP Professional displays the Regional And Language Options dialog box with the Regional Options tab active.

3. Click the Languages tab.

4. In the Text Services And Input Languages box, click Details.

    Windows XP Professional displays the Text Services And Input Languages dialog box.

5. In the Installed Services box, click Add.

    Windows XP Professional displays the Add Input Language dialog box.

6. Click the down-pointing arrow at the end of the Input Languages box to scroll through the listed languages and select French (France).

   The French Keyboard Layout/IME is selected automatically.

7. Click OK to close the Add Input Language dialog box.

   Windows XP Professional displays the Text Services And Input Languages dialog box. Notice that there are now two Installed Services.

8. Click OK to close the Text Services And Input Languages dialog box.

9. Click OK to close the Regional And Language Options dialog box.

10. Close all open programs.

Lesson Review

The following questions are intended to reinforce key information presented in this lesson. If you are unable to answer a question, review the lesson materials and try the question again. You can find answers to the questions in the "Questions and Answers" section at the end of this chapter.

1. How can you configure Windows XP Professional to use multiple languages?

   _____

   _____

   _____

   _____

   _____

   _____

   _____

   _____

   _____

2. Which of the following features allows you to press a multiple-key combination, such as CTRL+ALT+DELETE, one key at a time. (Choose the correct answer.)

   a. FilterKeys

   b. StickyKeys

   c. ToggleKeys

   d. MultiKeys

3. Turning on _____ causes the keyboard to ignore brief or repeated keystrokes. This option also allows you to configure the keyboard repeat rate, which is the rate at which a key continuously held down repeats the keystroke.

4. When using MouseKeys, to speed up the mouse pointer movement, hold down the _____ key while you press the numeric keypad directional keys. To slow down the mouse pointer movement, hold down the _____ key while you press the numeric keypad directional keys.

Lesson Summary

- Regional and language options, available from Control Panel, define the standards and formats that the computer uses to perform calculations; provide information such as date and time; and display the correct format for currency, numbers, dates, and other units.

- Windows XP also provides a number of accessibility options that make Windows easier to work with for some people. Some of these features are as follows:

  - StickyKeys allows you to press a multiple-key combination, such as CTRL+ALT+DELETE, one key at a time.

  - FilterKeys causes the keyboard to ignore brief or repeated keystrokes.

  - ToggleKeys causes the computer to make a high-pitched sound each time the CAPS LOCK, NUM LOCK, or SCROLL LOCK key is switched on.

  - SoundSentry causes Windows XP Professional to generate visual warnings when your computer makes a sound.

  - ShowSounds causes Windows XP Professional programs to display captions for the speech and sounds they make.

  - MouseKeys allows you to configure Windows XP Professional to control the pointer with the numeric keypad on your keyboard.

Lesson 5: Managing Windows Components

Windows XP Professional provides the Add or Remove Programs tool in Control Panel to make it easy for you manage programs and Windows components on your computer. You use it to add applications, such as Microsoft Word, from CD-ROM, floppy disk, or network shares. You also use it to add Windows components to a Windows XP Professional installation. The Add Or Remove Programs tool also allows you to remove applications or Windows components.

After this lesson, you will be able to

- Add Windows components
- Remove Windows components
- Manage Microsoft Internet Information Services (IIS)

Estimated lesson time: 20 minutes

How to Add Windows Components

You can install Windows components that you did not select when you installed Windows XP Professional on your computer. The components you can install include Fax Services, **Internet Information Services (IIS)**, Management and Monitoring Tools, Message Queuing, and additional Network Services. If you want to install one of the Windows components, select it, and then click Next.

To install or remove Windows components, use the Add Or Remove Programs tool. In the Add Or Remove Programs window, click Add/Remove Windows Components to open the Windows Components Wizard (see Figure 5-22).

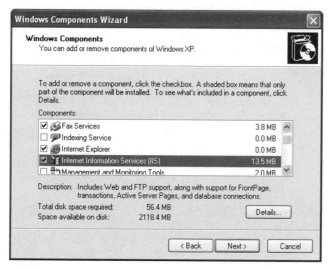

Figure 5-22   Use the Windows Components Wizard to add or remove components from a Windows XP Professional installation.

Adding components works pretty much the same way no matter what component you install, so this chapter focuses on IIS: Web server software that is included with Windows XP.

To install IIS, use these steps:

1. Click Start, and then click Control Panel

2. In the Control Panel window, click Add Or Remove Programs.

3. In the Add Or Remove Programs window, click Add/Remove Windows Components.

   Windows XP Professional starts the Windows Components Wizard.

4. Select the Internet Information Services (IIS) check box.

5. Click Details.

   The Windows Components Wizard displays the Internet Information Services page, which shows the components included when you install IIS. Table 5-7 lists these components.

Table 5-7   Components Included with IIS

Component	Selected by Default	Description
Common Files	Yes	Installs the required IIS program files
Documentation	Yes	Installs documentation about publishing site content, and Web and FTP Server Administration
File Transfer Protocol (FTP) Service	No	Provides support to create FTP sites used to upload and download files
FrontPage 2000 Server Extensions	Yes	Enables authoring and administration of Web sites with Microsoft FrontPage and Microsoft Visual InterDev
Internet Information Services Snap-In	Yes	Installs the IIS Administrative interface into Microsoft Management Console
SMTP Service	Yes	Supports the transfer of electronic mail
World Wide Web Service	Yes	Uses the Hypertext Transfer Protocol (HTTP) to respond to Web client requests on a TCP/IP network

6. Click OK to close the Internet Information Services (IIS) page.

7. In the Windows Components page, click Next to continue with the installation of IIS.

   The Windows Components Wizard displays the Configuring Components page while the appropriate files are copied and the components are configured. This might take a few minutes.

8. In the Completing The Windows Components Wizard page, click Finish.

9. Click Close to close the Add Or Remove Programs tool.

How to Remove Windows Components

The Windows Components Wizard is also used to uninstall or remove Windows components from your computer. If you want to remove a Windows component, on the Windows Component page of the Windows Components Wizard, clear the check box for the component you want to remove, and then click Next. The Windows Components Wizard displays the Configuring Components page as the files are removed from your computer. When the component is removed, the Windows Components Wizard displays the Completing The Windows Components Wizard page; click Finish to close the wizard. Click Close to close the Add Or Remove Programs tool, and then close Control Panel.

How to Manage Internet Information Services

IIS allows you to easily publish information on the Internet, or on your or your company's intranet. You place your Web files in directories on your server and users establish HTTP connections and view your files with a Web browser. IIS for Windows XP Professional is designed for home or small business networks and allows only 10 simultaneous client connections. It also does not provide all the features that the version included with Windows Server 2003 provides.

You will use the Internet Information Services snap-in to manage IIS. The Internet Information Services snap-in helps you manage the content of and access to your Web and FTP sites. To access the Internet Information Services snap-in, click Start, point to All Programs, point to Administrative Tools, and then click Internet Information Services. The Internet Information Services snap-in lets you handle all aspects of administration for IIS. For example, every Web and FTP site must have a home directory. When you install IIS, a default home directory is created. When you create a new Web site, you can use the Internet Information Services snap-in to change your home directory.

To change your home directory, in the Internet Information Services snap-in, right-click a Web or FTP site, and then click Properties. In the site's Properties dialog box, click the Home Directory tab. You can specify a directory on this computer, a shared directory located on another computer, or a redirection to a URL, and then type the path in the Local Path text box. Click OK and you have changed your home directory.

If your Web site contains files that are located in directories other than your home directory (for example, on another computer), you must create virtual directories to include these files on your Web site. You use the IIS console to create these virtual directories. In the console, select the Web or FTP site to which you want to add a directory. On the Action menu, point to New, and click Virtual Directory. This starts the Virtual Directory Creation Wizard, which will guide you through creating the new directory.

When IIS is installed on a computer running Windows XP Professional, an additional tab named Web Sharing becomes available on the Properties dialog box of any folder, as shown in Figure 5-23. You can use this tab to quickly make any folder accessible via your personal Web site.

Figure 5-23   IIS makes the Web Sharing tab available on the Properties dialog box for folders.

To share a folder on a personal Web site by using the Web Sharing tab, use these steps:

1. In Windows Explorer, right-click the folder you want to share through your Web site, and then click Properties.

2. In the Properties dialog box for the folder, on the Web Sharing tab, use the Share On menu to select the site on which you want to share the folder. By default, the Default Web Site is selected. If you have only one Web site, there are no other choices on the menu.

3. Click Share This Folder.

   Windows XP displays the Edit Alias dialog box.

4. In the Edit Alias dialog box, type an Alias for the folder. The alias is the name by which the folder is displayed on the Web site. By default, Windows creates an alias that is the same as the folder name.

5. Configure access permissions for the folder. Available access permissions are as follows:

   ❑ The Read permission allows users to open or download files in the folder.

   ❑ The Write permission allows users to modify files in the folder.

   ❑ The Script Source Access permission allows users to access source code for scripts in the folder.

   ❑ The Directory Browsing permission allows users to view the files in the folder.

6. Configure Application Permissions for the folder. This setting determines whether applications can run scripts or executable files in the folder.

7. Click OK to exit the Edit Alias dialog box.

8. Click OK again to apply settings and exit the Properties dialog box for the folder.

You can also use the Web Sharing tab to create additional aliases for a folder, edit the properties of existing aliases, and remove an alias from a folder.

Lesson Review

The following questions are intended to reinforce key information presented in this lesson. If you are unable to answer a question, review the lesson materials and try the question again. You can find answers to the questions in the "Questions and Answers" section at the end of this chapter.

1. How do you add Windows components to your Windows XP Professional installation?

   _____

   _____

   _____

   _____

   _____

2. What service does IIS provide?

   _____

   _____

   _____

3. How many simultaneous client connections can you have by using IIS for Windows XP Professional?

   a. 8

   b. 10

   c. 20

   d. 32

4. How do you administer IIS for Windows XP Professional?

_____

_____

Lesson Summary

- Use the Add or Remove Programs tool in Control Panel to add applications and Windows components. To add a Windows component, in the Add or Remove Programs window, select Add/Remove Windows Components.

- You will also use the Add/Remove Windows Components dialog box to remove components from a Windows XP Professional installation.

- IIS allows you to publish information on the Internet or on your intranet. IIS for Windows XP Professional is designed for home or small business networks and only allows 10 simultaneous client connections.

Case Scenario Exercise

In this exercise, you will read a scenario about configuring Windows XP and then answer the questions that follow. If you have difficulty completing this work, review the material in this chapter before beginning the next chapter. You can find answers to these questions in the "Questions and Answers" section at the end of this chapter.

Scenario

You are working as an administrator for a company named Trey Research, a manufacturer of wireless tracking devices. You are working with Olinda, a technical writer and translator who is creating a user manual in English and French for the software interface to one of the company's products.

Questions

1. The software interface for the products uses the metric system instead of the U.S. system of measurement. Olinda's regional settings are configured to use the English (United States) standard. How would you change the default system of measurement on her computer from U.S. to metric?

_____

_____

2. Because Olinda is documenting how to run the software interface in Windows XP, she needs to be able to use Windows XP in both English and French. How should you configure this feature?

_____

_____

_____

_____

3. After adding French to Olinda's computer, how can she switch between English and French?

_____

_____

_____

4. After working with the software interface for the company's product, Olinda reports that sometimes after she leaves her computer for a while, her monitor goes blank. When she moves her mouse, she says the monitor comes back, but the program crashes. She wants to stop her monitor from going blank when she leaves it unattended. What should you do?

_____

_____

5. After working with the creators of the software interface, Olinda discovers that the program does not respond well to certain visual effects. In particular, the programmers tell her that displaying shadows under the mouse pointer can cause problems with the program. Olinda wants to include instructions in her manual for disabling this feature and has asked you to provide those instructions. What do you tell her?

_____

_____

_____

_____

_____

Troubleshooting Lab

You are working as an administrator for a company named Contoso, Ltd., a national distributor of paper products. Marcel, a user in the Sales department, reports that he is having a problem with his computer running Windows XP Professional. When he starts his computer, the startup process gets as far as the Windows logo screen and then fails. Marcel sees a blue screen with a lot of text on it, and then the computer restarts. The computer does this over and over again.

1. What is happening to Marcel's computer?

_____

_____

2. You can start Marcel's computer successfully in safe mode. You want to see the Stop error. What should you do?

_____

_____

_____

_____

3. After researching the Stop error on Marcel's computer, you have determined that a damaged paging file is causing the stop error. You need to remove the paging file from Marcel's computer. How would you do this?

_____

_____

_____

_____

4. After removing the damaged paging file, you need to create a new paging file. You want Windows to manage the paging file size. How would you do this?

_____

_____

_____

Chapter Summary

- You can use the Display Properties dialog box to control most settings that govern the appearance of your desktop and the settings for your video adapter and monitor. Windows XP Professional supports the use of up to 10 displays, extending the Windows Desktop so that it is spread across all available displays. You must use PCI or AGP video adapters when configuring multiple displays.

- Power Options allows you to configure Windows XP Professional to turn off the power to your monitor and your hard disk, configure APM support, enable hibernation, and configure support for a UPS.

- The Advanced tab of the System Properties dialog box allows you to configure performance options for a computer. You can enable and disable visual effects that affect performance, as well as configure processor scheduling, memory usage, and virtual and memory settings. You can also use the System Properties dialog box to control the startup and recovery settings for a computer, user profiles, and environmental variables.

- Regional and language options, available from Control Panel, define the standards and formats that the computer uses to perform calculations; provide information such as date and time; and display the correct format for currency, numbers, dates, and other units. Windows XP also provides a number of accessibility options that make Windows easier to work with for some people.

- You can use the Add Or Remove Programs tool in Control Panel to add and remove applications and Windows components. IIS, Web server software built into Windows XP Professional, is an example of a component you can add.

Exam Highlights

Before taking the exam, review the key points and terms that are presented in this chapter. You need to know this information.

Key Points

- Understand how to control color quality and screen resolution. Also understand how to control advanced display settings, such as adapter type, monitor type, and compatibility.

- You can configure processor scheduling to favor Programs or Background Services. Selecting Programs assigns more resources to the foreground program (the active program that is responding to user input). When you select Background Services, Windows assigns an equal number of resources to all programs.

- By default, Windows XP manages the paging file size, but you can designate a file size for special circumstances. The recommended paging file size is equal to 1.5 times the total amount of RAM.

- Consider regional settings as a possibility when keyboard errors are reported or when users report that symbols do not look correct.

Key Terms

Advanced Configuration and Power Interface (ACPI)   A newer power standard than APM that allows Windows to control power settings for a computer. A computer that supports ACPI automatically supports APM.

Advanced Power Management (APM)   A power standard that allows Windows to manage the power settings on a computer.

Color Quality   A setting that affects the number of colors used to display objects on the Desktop.

Desktop Cleanup Wizard   A wizard that runs every 60 days by default, offering to remove unused Desktop icons.

Environment variables   Variables that define the system and user environment information, and contain information such as a drive, path, or file name.

hibernate mode   A state in which Windows saves the current system state (including open programs and windows) to your hard disk, and then shuts the computer down. When you restart the computer, the open programs and windows are restored.

input languages   Languages installed on a computer running Windows XP Professional from which the computer can accept input.

Internet Information Services (IIS)   Web server software built into Windows XP Professional that allows you to easily publish information on the Internet, or on your or your company's intranet.

paging file   The file Windows uses to swap pages of data between physical memory and hard disk to augment the memory on a computer. This augmentation is known as virtual memory.

Power schemes   Schemes that allow you to configure Windows XP Professional to turn off the power to your monitor and your hard disk, conserving energy.

primary display   The default display in a multiple display configuration. You can often change which video adapter controls the primary display by changing settings in the computer's BIOS.

Screen Resolution   A setting that allows you to set the number of pixels Windows uses to display the Desktop.

uninterruptible power supply (UPS)   A device connected between a computer or another piece of electronic equipment and a power source to ensure that the electrical flow to the computer is not interrupted because of a power outage.

user profile   A collection of user-specific settings, such as a customized desktop or personalized application settings.

Visual Effects   Desktop display features that look nice, but often degrade a computer's performance.

Questions and Answers

Lesson 1 Review

Page 5-12

1. You can enable _____ to restrict access to Display options.

   Group Policy settings

2. Which of the following items does the Desktop Items dialog box allow you to choose to include or exclude an icon on your desktop? (Choose all that apply.)

   a. My Documents

   b. Control Panel

   c. My Network Places

   d. Recycle Bin

   The correct answers are A and C. B is not correct because you cannot include the Control Panel icon on your Desktop. D is not correct because you cannot remove the Recycle Bin icon from your Desktop.

3. Windows XP Professional supports extension of your display across a maximum of _____ monitors.

   10

4. You must use _____ or _____ video adapters when configuring multiple displays.

   PCI, AGP

5. If one of the display adapters is built into the motherboard, the motherboard adapter always becomes the _____ (primary/secondary) adapter.

   Secondary

Lesson 2 Practice: Configuring Power Options

Page 5-19

13. If you do not see an APM tab on your computer, what are two reasons why it might not be there?

    The APM tab is not shown if your computer does not have an APM-capable BIOS. Also, if your computer supports the newer ACPI standard, the APM tab is not shown because Windows XP Professional automatically enabled APM support.

Lesson 2 Review

Page 5-19

1. What is a power scheme and why would you use one?

   Power schemes allow you to configure Windows XP Professional to turn off the power to your monitor and your hard disk to conserve energy.

2. Which of the following statements about Windows XP Professional power schemes are true? (Choose all that apply.)

   a. Windows XP Professional ships with six built-in power schemes.

   b. Windows XP Professional allows you to create your own power schemes.

   c. Windows XP Professional allows you to modify existing power schemes, but you cannot create new ones.

   d. Windows XP Professional does not ship with any built-in power schemes.

   The correct answers are A and B. C is not correct because Windows XP Professional does allow you to create new power schemes. D is not correct because Windows XP Professional comes with several power schemes built in.

3. A(n) _____ is a device that connects between a computer and a power source to ensure that the electrical flow to the computer is not abruptly stopped because of a blackout.

   UPS

4. What does hibernate mode do?

   When your computer hibernates, it saves the current system state to your hard disk, and then your computer shuts down. When you start the computer after it has been hibernating, it returns to its previous state, restarts any programs that were running, and restores any active network connections.

Lesson 3 Practice: Exercise 2

Page
5-37

11. What does typing the cmd command do?

   Typing cmd in the Run dialog box opens the Command Prompt window.

Lesson 3 Review

Page
5-37

1. What performance options can you control with the tabs of the Performance Options dialog box?

   The Visual Effects tab of the Performance Options dialog box provides a number of options that allow you to manually control the visual effects on your computer. The Advanced tab of the Performance Options dialog box allows you to adjust the application response, which is the priority of foreground applications versus background applications, and virtual memory.

2. Which of the following statements about the use of virtual memory in Windows XP Professional are correct? (Choose all that apply.)

   a. When you install Windows XP Professional, Setup creates a virtual memory paging file, PAGEFILE.SYS, on the partition where you installed Windows XP Professional.

   b. In some environments, you might find it advantageous to use multiple paging files.

c. If the entire paging file is not in use, it can decrease below the initial size that was set during installation.

d. Unused space in the paging file remains unavailable to all programs, even the internal Windows XP Professional VMM.

The correct answers are A and B. C is not correct because the paging file size will never decrease below the initial size. D is not correct because unused space in the paging file is available to all programs.

3. When you first turn on the computer, the system displays a Please Select The Operating System To Start screen, which lists the available operating systems. What happens if a user does not select an operating system before the countdown timer reaches zero?

If a user does not choose an operating system, the system starts the preselected operating system when the countdown timer reaches zero.

4. Which requirements must be met for the Write Debugging Information recovery option to work?

A paging file must be on the system partition (the partition that contains the %systemroot% folder). You must have enough disk space to write the file to the location you specify. A small memory dump requires a paging file of at least 2 MB on the boot volume. A kernel memory dump requires 50 MB to 800 MB available in the paging file on the boot volume. A complete memory dump requires a paging file on the boot volume large enough to hold all the RAM on your computer plus 1 MB. With a small memory dump, a new dump file will be created every time the system stops unexpectedly. For a complete memory dump or kernel memory dump, if you want the new dump file to overwrite an existing file, select the Overwrite Any Existing File check box.

Lesson 4 Review

Page 5-49

1. How can you configure Windows XP Professional to use multiple languages?

To configure multiple languages, in Control Panel, click Date, Time, Language, And Regional Options. In the Date, Time, Language, And Regional Options window, click Regional And Language Options to open the Regional And Language Options dialog box. In the Languages tab of the Regional And Languages Options dialog box, click Details. Windows XP Professional displays the Text Services And Input Languages dialog box. Click Add. Click the down-pointing arrow at the end of the Input Language list box. Scroll through the list of languages and select the ones you want to add. If you added at least one language to the one already installed on your computer, your computer is now supporting multiple languages.

2. Which of the following features allows you to press a multiple key combination, such as CTRL+ALT+DELETE, one key at a time. (Choose the correct answer.)

a. FilterKeys

b. StickyKeys

c. ToggleKeys

d. MultiKeys

The correct answer is B. A, C, and D are not correct because it is the StickyKeys feature that allows you to press a multiple key combination one key at a time.

3. Turning on _____ causes the keyboard to ignore brief or repeated keystrokes. This option also allows you to configure the keyboard repeat rate, which is the rate at which a key continuously held down repeats the keystroke.

FilterKeys

4. When using MouseKeys, to speed up the mouse pointer movement, hold down the _____ key while you press the numeric keypad directional keys. To slow down the mouse pointer movement, hold down the _____ key while you press the numeric keypad directional keys.

CTRL; SHIFT

Lesson 5 Review

Page
5-55

1. How do you add Windows components to your Windows XP Professional installation?

In Control Panel, click Add Or Remove Programs. In the Add Or Remove Windows Programs window, click Add/Remove Windows Components to start the Windows Components Wizard. You use the Windows Components Wizard to select the Windows components that you want to add to or remove from your Windows XP Professional installation.

2. What service does IIS provide?

IIS allows you to publish information on the Internet or on your intranet. You place your files in directories on your server, and IIS allows users to establish HTTP connections and view the files with their Web browsers.

3. How many simultaneous client connections can you have by using IIS for Windows XP Professional?

a. 8

b. 10

c. 20

d. 32

The correct answer is B. Windows XP Professional allows up to 10 concurrent connections.

4. How do you administer IIS for Windows XP Professional?

You use the Internet Information Services snap-in to manage IIS and the content of and access to your Web and FTP sites.

Case Scenario Exercise

Page
5-56

1. The software interface for the products uses the metric system instead of the U.S. system of measurement. Olinda's regional settings are configured to use the English (United States) standard. How would you change the default system of measurement on her computer from U.S. to metric?

   You should keep the English (United States) setting, but customize the measurement system to use the metric system.

2. Because Olinda is documenting how to run the software interface in Windows XP, she needs to be able to use Windows XP in both English and French. How should you configure this feature?

   You should add the French input language to Olinda's computer. To do this, use the Regional And Language Options dialog box. On the Languages tab, click Details to show the languages installed on Olinda's computer. Click Add to add French to Olinda's computer.

3. After adding French to Olinda's computer, how can she switch between English and French?

   Olinda can switch between installed input languages by using the Language toolbar on the taskbar or by pressing left ALT+SHIFT—the default key combination for switching languages.

4. After working with the software interface for the company's product, Olinda reports that sometimes after she leaves her computer for a while, her monitor goes blank. When she moves her mouse, she says the monitor comes back, but the program crashes. She wants to stop her monitor from going blank when she leaves it unattended. What should you do?

   You should configure Olinda's current power scheme so that Windows does not attempt to turn off the monitor after an idle period.

5. After working with the creators of the software interface, Olinda discovers that the program does not respond well to certain visual effects. In particular, the programmers tell her that displaying shadows under the mouse pointer can cause problems with the program. Olinda wants to include instructions in her manual for disabling this feature and has asked you to provide those instructions. What do you tell her?

   You should tell her to open the System Properties dialog box by right-clicking the My Computer icon and clicking Properties. She should click the Advanced tab and, in the Performance section, click Settings. In the Performance Options dialog box that opens, Olinda should click Custom, and then clear the Show Shadows Under Mouse Pointer check box. She should then click OK to close the Performance Options dialog box, and then click OK again to close the System Properties dialog box.

Troubleshooting Lab

Page
5-58

1. What is happening to Marcel's computer?

Marcel's computer is experiencing a Stop error when it starts. However, the computer is restarting each time it encounters this error, causing an endless loop.

2. You can start Marcel's computer successfully in safe mode. You want to see the Stop error. What should you do?

You should use the Startup and Recovery dialog box to clear the Automatically Restart check box in the System Failure section. This action will prevent Marcel's computer from restarting when it encounters the error, giving you time to see the actual error.

3. After researching the Stop error on Marcel's computer, you have determined that a damaged paging file is causing the stop error. You need to remove the paging file from Marcel's computer. How would you do this?

You should use the Virtual Memory dialog box (available via the Advanced tab in the Performance Options dialog box). In the Paging File Size For Selected Drive section, you should click No Paging File, click Set, and then exit the dialog boxes that are open. You should then restart the computer.

4. After removing the damaged paging file, you need to create a new paging file. You want Windows to manage the paging file size. How would you do this?

You should open the Virtual Memory dialog box again. In the Paging File Size For Selected Drive section, you should click System Managed Size, click Set, and then exit the dialog boxes that are open. You should then restart the computer.

6 Installing, Managing, and Troubleshooting Hardware Devices and Drivers

Exam Objectives in this Chapter:

- Implement, manage, and troubleshoot input and output (I/O) devices.
  - ❑ Monitor, configure, and troubleshoot I/O devices, such as printers, scanners, multimedia devices, mouse, keyboard, and smart card reader.
  - ❑ Monitor, configure, and troubleshoot multimedia hardware, such as cameras.
  - ❑ Install, configure, and manage Infrared Data Association (IrDA) devices.
  - ❑ Install, configure, and manage universal serial bus (USB) devices.
  - ❑ Install, configure, and manage handheld devices.
- Manage and troubleshoot drivers and driver signing.

Why This Chapter Matters

Microsoft Windows XP Professional provides features that make installing, configuring, and managing hardware devices easier than ever. The Plug and Play specification, taken advantage of by most modern hardware, makes installation and configuration of devices nearly automatic. Device Manager provides a single interface for configuring and troubleshooting hardware devices on a computer. This chapter introduces the installation, configuration, and troubleshooting of hardware devices in Windows XP Professional. It also teaches how to configure hardware profiles and work with hardware drivers.

Lessons in this Chapter:

Before You Begin

To complete this chapter, you must have a computer that meets the minimum hardware requirements listed in the preface, "About This Book." You must also have Windows XP Professional installed on the computer.

Lesson 1: Installing a Hardware Device

Windows XP Professional supports both **Plug and Play** and non–Plug and Play hardware. This lesson introduces you to the automatic hardware-installation features of Windows XP Professional. Occasionally, Windows XP Professional fails to automatically detect a hardware device. When this occurs, you must install the hardware device manually. You might also have to do this if the device requires a specific hardware resource to ensure that it is installed properly.

After this lesson, you will be able to

- Install a hardware device automatically.
- Install a hardware device manually.

Estimated lesson time: 30 minutes

How to Install Hardware Automatically

Windows XP Professional supports Plug and Play hardware. For most devices that are Plug and Play–compliant, as long as the appropriate driver is available and the basic input/output system (BIOS) on the computer is Plug and Play–compatible or supports Advanced Configuration and Power Interface (ACPI), Windows XP Professional automatically detects, installs, and configures the device. When Windows XP Professional detects a new piece of hardware for which it does not have a hardware driver, it displays the Found New Hardware Wizard, shown in Figure 6-1.

Figure 6-1   Use the Found New Hardware Wizard to configure devices for which Windows does not have a hardware driver.

> **Exam Tip**   Windows XP Professional automatically detects, installs, and configures most Plug and Play and some non–Plug and Play hardware. If Windows does not detect Plug and Play hardware, you can often force the detection by restarting the computer or running the Add Hardware Wizard. For many non–Plug and Play devices, you must use the Add Hardware Wizard to manually configure the device.

To Use the Add Hardware Wizard

Occasionally, Windows does not detect a new Plug and Play hardware device automatically, so you might need to initiate the installation process by using the Add Hardware Wizard. You can also use the Add Hardware Wizard to initiate automatic hardware installation for undetected hardware devices (both Plug and Play and non–Plug and Play) and to troubleshoot devices.

To use the Add Hardware Wizard to have Windows automatically detect and install Plug and Play hardware, complete the following steps:

1. From the Start menu, select Control Panel.

2. In the Control Panel window, click Printers And Other Hardware.

3. In the Printers And Other Hardware window, in the See Also section, click Add Hardware.

4. On the Welcome To The Add Hardware Wizard page, click Next.

5. Windows XP Professional searches for new devices and one of the following three events occurs:

   ❏ If Windows XP Professional detects any new Plug and Play hardware for which it has a hardware driver built in, Windows installs the new hardware.

   ❏ If Windows XP Professional detects new hardware for which it does not have a hardware driver, Windows starts the Found New Hardware Wizard.

   ❏ If the wizard cannot find a new device, it displays the Is The Hardware Connected page. If you have already connected the new device, click Yes, I Have Already Connected The Hardware, and then click Next. The wizard displays the The Following Hardware Is Already Installed On Your Computer page, as shown in Figure 6-2. To add hardware that is not in the list, click Add A New Hardware Device.

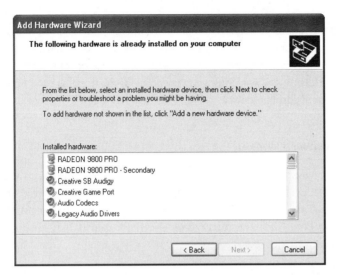

Figure 6-2   Add hardware or troubleshoot with the Add Hardware Wizard.

Note   To use the Add Hardware Wizard to troubleshoot a hardware device, click the device in the list of installed hardware devices and click Next. The Completing The Add Hardware Wizard page appears. Click Finish to launch a troubleshooter to help resolve any problems you might be having with that hardware device.

To Confirm Hardware Installation

After installing hardware, you should confirm the installation by using **Device Manager**.

To start Device Manager, follow these steps:

1. From the Start menu, select Control Panel.

2. In the Control Panel window, click Performance And Maintenance.

3. In the Performance And Maintenance window, click System.

4. In the System Properties dialog box, on the Hardware tab, click Device Manager. Device Manager allows you to view the hardware installed on a computer, as shown in Figure 6-3.

Figure 6-3   Device Manager shows devices listed by type.

Windows XP Professional uses icons in the Device Manager window to identify each installed hardware device. If Windows XP Professional does not have an icon for the device type (usually because the hardware device is unidentified), Device Manager displays a question mark as the icon for the device.

Expand the device tree to locate the newly installed hardware device. The device icon indicates whether the hardware device is operating properly. You can use the information in Table 6-1 to determine the hardware status.

Table 6-1   Device Manager Hardware Status

Icon	Hardware Status
Normal icon	Hardware is operating properly.
Stop sign on icon	Windows XP Professional disabled the hardware device because of hardware conflicts.
Exclamation point on icon	The hardware device is incorrectly configured or its drivers are missing.
Red "x" on icon	The hardware device is disabled in the current hardware profile.

How to Install Hardware Manually

Most non–Plug and Play hardware requires manual installation. Although it is rare these days to find computers running Windows XP Professional that still use non–Plug and Play hardware, it does happen on occasion, so you should understand how to install and configure hardware manually. To manually install hardware, first determine which hardware resource is required by the hardware device. Next, you must determine the available hardware resources. In some cases, you have to change hardware resources. Finally, you might have to troubleshoot any problems you encounter.

Hardware Device Communication Resources

With older, non–Plug and Play devices, you often must configure the device itself to specify which hardware resources the device will use. This configuration mostly happens by changing jumpers or switches on the device, but sometimes happens through a software interface. Again, it is extremely rare that you will encounter a device made within the last few years that you will have to configure manually, but it is still handy information to have.

When installing new hardware, you need to know which resources the hardware can use. You can reference the product documentation to determine the resources that a hardware device requires. Table 6-2 describes the resources that hardware devices use to communicate with an operating system.

Table 6-2   Hardware Device Resources

Resource	Description
Interrupt	Hardware devices use interrupts to send messages. The microprocessor knows this as an interrupt request (IRQ). The microprocessor uses this information to determine which device needs its attention and the type of attention that it needs. There are 16 IRQs (numbered 0 to 15) that Windows XP assigns to devices. For example, Windows XP Professional assigns IRQ 1 to the keyboard.
Input/output (I/O) port	I/O ports are a section of memory that a hardware device uses to communicate with the operating system. When a microprocessor receives an IRQ, the operating system checks the I/O port address to retrieve additional information about what the hardware device wants it to do. An I/O port is represented as a hexadecimal number.
Direct memory access (DMA)	DMAs are channels that allow a hardware device, such as a floppy disk drive, to access memory directly, without interrupting the microprocessor. DMA channels speed up access to memory. Windows XP Professional assigns eight DMA channels, numbered 0 through 7.
Memory	Many hardware devices, such as a network interface card (NIC), use onboard memory or reserve system memory. This reserved memory is unavailable for use by other devices or Windows XP Professional.

To Determine Available Hardware Resources

After you determine which resources a hardware device requires, you can look for an available resource. Device Manager provides a list of all hardware resources and their availability, as shown in Figure 6-4.

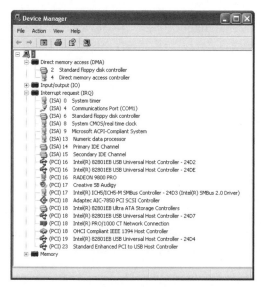

Figure 6-4   Device Manager can also list resources by connection type.

To view the hardware resource lists in Device Manager, follow these steps:

1. In Device Manager, click the View menu, and then click Resources By Connection.

2. The Device Manager displays the resources that are currently in use (for example, IRQs). To view a list of resources for another type of hardware resource, on the View menu, click the type of hardware resource you want to see.

After you know which hardware resources are available, you can configure the device to use those resources and then install the hardware manually with the Add Hardware Wizard.

> **Note**   If you select a hardware resource during manual installation, you might need to configure the hardware device so that it can use the resource. For example, for a network adapter to use IRQ 5, you might have to set a jumper on the adapter and configure Windows XP Professional so that it recognizes that the adapter now uses IRQ 5.

To Change Hardware Resource Assignments

In some circumstances, you might need to change the resource assignments for a device. For example, a hardware device might require a specific resource presently in use by another device. You might also encounter two hardware devices requesting the same hardware resource, resulting in a conflict.

To change a resource setting, in Device Manager, open the device's Properties dialog box and switch to the Resources tab.

When you change a hardware resource, print the content of Device Manager, which provides you with a record of the hardware configuration. If you encounter problems, you can use the printout to verify the hardware resource assignments.

From this point, follow the same procedures that you used to choose a hardware resource during a manual installation.

> **Note**   Changing the resource assignments for non–Plug and Play devices in Device Manager does not change the resources used by that device. You use Device Manager only to instruct the operating system on device configuration. To change the resources used by a non–Plug and Play device, consult the device documentation to see whether switches or jumpers must be configured on the device.

Practice: Running the Add Hardware Wizard

In this practice, you will manually install the software for a printer that is not actually connected to your computer. Complete the following steps.

> **Important**   This practice assumes that you do not already have a hardware device connected to a parallel port named LPT2 on your computer. Do not worry if you do not have an LPT2 port; the exercise will work anyway.

1. From the Start menu, click Control Panel.

2. In the Control Panel window, click Printers And Other Hardware.

3. In the Printers And Other Hardware window, in the See Also section, click Add Hardware.

4. On the Welcome To The Add Hardware Wizard page of the Add Hardware Wizard, click Next.

5. The Add Hardware Wizard searches for any new Plug and Play devices, and then displays the Is The Hardware Connected page. Click Yes, I Have Already Connected The Hardware, and then click Next.

6. In the list of installed hardware, scroll to the bottom and click Add A New Hardware Device. Click Next.

7. Click Install The Hardware That I Manually Select From A List (Advanced), and then click Next.

8. In the list of common hardware types, click Printers and then click Next.

9. On the Select A Printer Port page, in the Use The Following Port drop-down list, click LPT2: (Printer Port), and then click Next.

10. On the Install Printer Software page, in the Manufacturer list, click Royal. In the Printers list, select Royal CJP 450. Click Next.

11. On the Name Your Printer page, click Next.

12. On the Print Test Page page, select No and then click Next.

13. If you are using Windows XP Professional and you have Simple File Sharing disabled, you next will see a page asking whether you want to share the new printer. Select Do Not Share This Printer, and then click Next.

14. Click Finish to exit the Add Hardware Wizard.

Lesson Review

Use the following questions to help determine whether you have learned enough to move on to the next lesson. If you have difficulty answering these questions, review the material in this lesson before beginning the next lesson. You can find answers to these questions in the "Questions and Answers" section at the end of this chapter.

1. When you initiate automatic hardware installation by starting the Add Hardware Wizard, what does Windows XP Professional query the hardware about?

   _____

2. _____ are channels that allow a hardware device, such as a floppy disk drive, to access memory directly (without interrupting the microprocessor). Fill in the blank.

3. Why would you install a hardware device manually?

   _____

   _____

Lesson Summary

■ For most Plug and Play hardware, you connect the device to the computer, and Windows XP Professional automatically configures the new settings. For non–Plug and Play hardware, Windows XP Professional often identifies the hardware and automatically installs and configures it. For the occasional Plug and Play hardware device and for any non–Plug and Play hardware that Windows XP Professional does not identify, install, and configure, you initiate automatic hardware installation with the Add Hardware Wizard.

■ When you manually install hardware, you must determine any resources required by that hardware device. Hardware resources include interrupts, I/O ports, and memory. The Device Manager snap-in provides a list of all hardware resources and their availability.

Lesson 2: Configuring and Troubleshooting Hardware Devices

Device Manager is one of the tools you use to manage and troubleshoot devices—you learn how to use it and how it helps you manage your computer. You also learn to install and configure fax support in Windows XP Professional, as well as how to manage various I/O devices.

After this lesson, you will be able to

- Configure and troubleshoot devices by using Device Manager.
- Install, configure, and troubleshoot fax support.
- Manage and troubleshoot I/O devices.

Estimated lesson time: 40 minutes

How to Configure and Troubleshoot Devices Using Device Manager

Device Manager provides you with a graphical view of the hardware installed on your computer and helps you manage and troubleshoot hardware devices. You can use Device Manager to configure, disable, and uninstall devices as well as to update device drivers. Device Manager also helps you determine whether the hardware on your computer is working properly.

Tip   Windows XP Professional also provides the Hardware Troubleshooter to troubleshoot hardware problems. It should appear automatically if you have problems. To start it manually, on the Start menu, click Help And Support. In the Help And Support Center, under Pick A Help Topic, click Hardware. In the Hardware list, click Fixing A Hardware Problem. Under Fixing A Hardware Problem, click Hardware Troubleshooter. The Hardware Troubleshooter walks you through the troubleshooting process.

When you change device configurations manually, Device Manager can help you avoid problems by allowing you to identify free resources, assign devices to those resources, disable devices to free resources, and reallocate resources used by devices to free a required resource. You must be logged on as a member of the Administrators group to change resource settings. Even if you are logged on as Administrator, if your computer is connected to a network, policy settings on the network might prevent you from changing resources.

> **Caution**   Improperly changing resource settings on devices can disable your hardware and cause your computer to stop working.

Windows XP Professional automatically identifies Plug and Play devices and arbitrates their resource requests. However, the resource allocation among Plug and Play devices is not permanent. If another Plug and Play device requests a resource that has already been allocated, Windows XP Professional again arbitrates the requests to satisfy all the devices.

You should not change resource settings for a Plug and Play device manually because Windows XP Professional is then unable to arbitrate the assigned resources if requested by another Plug and Play device. In Device Manager, Plug and Play devices have a Resources tab in their Properties dialog box. To free the resource settings you manually assigned and to allow Windows XP Professional to again arbitrate the resources, select the Use Automatic Settings check box in the Resources tab.

You can use the following procedure to configure or troubleshoot a device using Device Manager:

1. From the Start menu, right-click My Computer, and then click Manage. The Computer Management window opens, as shown in Figure 6-5.

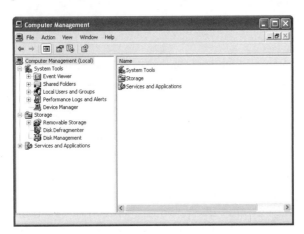

Figure 6-5   You can access Device Manager through the Computer Management window.

2. Expand the System Tools node, and then click Device Manager.

3. In the right pane, expand the device category (Network adapters, for example), and then double-click the device you want to configure. The Properties dialog box for the device appears, as shown in Figure 6-6.

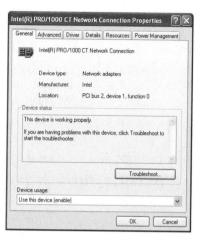

Figure 6-6 Use the Properties dialog box to configure the device.

Although the tabs available in a device's Properties dialog box vary depending on the device, they usually include some of the tabs listed in Table 6-3.

Table 6-3 A Device's Properties Dialog Box Tabs

Tab	Functionality
Advanced or Advanced Properties	The properties listed vary depending on the device selected.
General	Displays the device type, manufacturer, and location. It also displays the device status and provides a troubleshooter to help you troubleshoot any problems you are having with the device. The troubleshooter steps you through a series of questions to determine the problem and provide a solution.
Device Properties	The properties listed vary depending on the device selected.
Driver	Displays the driver provider, driver date, driver version, and digital signer. This tab also provides the following three additional buttons: Driver Details, Uninstall, and Driver Update. These buttons allow you to get additional information on the driver, uninstall the driver, or update the driver with a newer version, respectively.
Port Settings	In a communications port (COM1) Properties dialog box, displays and allows you to configure settings for bits per second, data bits, parity, stop bits, and flow control.
Properties	Determines the way Windows uses the device. For example, on the CD-ROM, the properties could include volume and a feature named Digital CD Playback, which allows you to to enable digital instead of analog playback. These settings determine how Windows uses the CD-ROM for playing CD music.
Resources	Displays the resource type and setting, whether there are any resource conflicts, and whether or not you can change the resource settings.

Viewing Hidden Devices

By default, Device Manager does not display all devices. Some devices are hidden, such as non–Plug and Play devices and devices that are not currently connected to the computer (phantom devices). To view any hidden non–Plug and Play devices, on the Device Manager View menu, click Show Hidden Devices.

To view phantom devices, follow these steps:

1. Click Start and then click Run. In the Open text box, type **cmd** and click OK.

2. At the command prompt, type **set DEVMGR_SHOW_NONPRESENT_ DEVICES=1**.

3. Press ENTER.

4. Start Device Manager by typing **start devmgmt.msc** and pressing ENTER.

To set Device Manager to always show phantom devices, add the following system environment variable: **set DEVMGR_SHOW_NONPRESENT_DEVICES=1**. For information on adding system environment variables, see Chapter 5, "Configuring Windows XP Professional."

How to Install, Configure, Manage, and Troubleshoot Fax Support

Windows XP Professional can provide complete fax facilities from your computer. It provides you with the capability to send and receive faxes with a locally attached fax device, or with a remote fax device connected on your network. You can track and monitor fax activity as well. However, the Fax component of Windows XP Professional is not installed by default, so you must install it.

You can use the following procedure to install the Fax component:

1. From the Start menu, click Control Panel.

2. In the Control Panel window, click Add Or Remove Programs.

3. In the Add Or Remove Programs window, click Add/Remove Windows Components.

4. In the Windows Components Wizard, select Fax Services, and then click Next. The Configuring Components page appears while the Windows Components Wizard examines the components, copies the necessary files, and configures the Fax Service.

5. On the Completing The Windows Components Wizard page, click Finish.

6. Close the Add Or Remove Programs window.

7. In the Control Panel window, click Printers And Other Hardware.

8. In the Printers And Other Hardware window, click Printers And Faxes. Notice that a new printer named Fax has been added.

> **Note**   If there is no Fax icon, click Install A Local Fax Printer to add one.

After installing the Fax Service, a new icon named Fax appears in the Control Panel window. You can use this tool to add, monitor, and troubleshoot fax devices, including fax modems and fax printers.

You can use the following procedure to configure how Windows sends and receives faxes:

1. From the Start menu, select Printers And Faxes.

2. In the Printers And Faxes window, double-click the Fax icon.

3. On the Welcome To The Fax Configuration Wizard page, click Next.

4. On the Sender Information page, enter information in the following text boxes: Your Full Name, Fax Number, E-Mail Address, Title, Company, Office Location, Department, Home Phone, Work Phone, Address, and Billing Code. When you are done, click Next.

5. On the Completing The Fax Configuration Wizard page, click Finish. Windows XP Professional displays the Fax Console.

> **Tip**   To configure a fax, click Configure Fax on the Tools menu of the Fax Console. To open the Fax Console, click Start, point to All Programs, point to Accessories, point to Communications, point to Fax, and then click Fax Console.

To Manage and Troubleshoot Fax Support

Windows XP Professional provides the Fax Console to help you manage and troubleshoot faxes.

To manage and troubleshoot faxes, complete the following steps:

1. From the Start menu, point to All Programs, point to Accessories, point to Communications, point to Fax, and then click Fax Console.

2. Windows XP Professional displays the Fax Console, as shown in Figure 6-7.

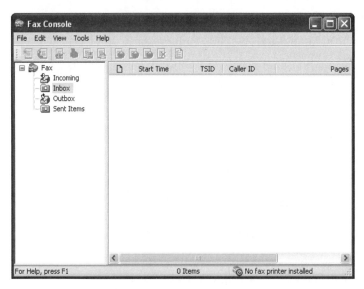

Figure 6-7   Use the Fax Console to manage and troubleshoot faxes.

The Outbox contains all faxes waiting to be sent or in the process of being sent, whether the faxes were sent using a locally attached fax device or a network fax device. You can right-click any fax shown, and then press DELETE or click Delete on the File menu to delete the fax. When you right-click a fax, you can also click Pause to prevent it from being sent or click Resume to place a fax that you paused back in the queue to be sent. If a fax fails, you can right-click the fax and click Restart to attempt to resend the fax. Finally, when you right-click a fax, you can click Save As to save a copy of the fax, Mail To to mail a copy of the fax to someone, or Print to print a copy of the fax.

The Incoming box allows you to manage incoming faxes in the same manner that the Outgoing box helps you manage outgoing faxes. You can click the Incoming box, and then right-click a fax to delete, pause, resume, save, mail to someone, and print the fax. You can also click Properties to view the properties of an incoming fax.

Table 6-4 discusses some common troubleshooting scenarios for faxes.

Table 6-4   Common Fax Troubleshooting Scenarios

Problem	Cause	Solution
When I click the Print button on my application's toolbar, my fax does not print to a fax printer.	The print button on the toolbar of some Windows applications does not use the Print dialog box, causing your document to be printed on the last printer used.	On the File menu of your Windows application, click Print to access the Print dialog box so that you can select your fax printer.

Table 6-4   Common Fax Troubleshooting Scenarios

Problem	Cause	Solution
A fax I sent is pending in the Outbox.	There is a problem with the local fax device.	Either there is no local fax device configured to send faxes or there is a problem with the local fax device. Verify that there is a local fax device and that it is configured for sending faxes. On the Tools menu of the Fax Console, click Fax Printer Status.
	The remote fax device is busy.	On the Tools menu of the Fax Console, click Fax Printer Status.
Someone sent me a fax, and my incoming fax device is not detecting the call.	There is a problem with your local fax device.	Verify that your local fax device is configured to receive faxes. If you have an external modem, turn it off and on. If you have an internal modem, shut down your computer and restart it.
I am using dialing rules with calling cards, but the calling card information is not working.	Calling card information is defined on a per-user basis. Ensure that the Fax Service is running by using the same user account as the calling card information.	Right-click My Computer, click Manage, and then click Services And Applications. In the Services list, double-click Fax. Click Log On. Set the Fax Service to run under the calling card user account.

To Send a Fax

Windows XP Professional makes it simple for you to use your computer to send faxes.

You can use the following procedure to send a fax:

1. From the Start menu, point to All Programs, point to Accessories, point to Communications, point to Fax, and then click Send A Fax.

2. On the Welcome To The Send Fax Wizard page (which indicates that if you want to fax a document, you create or open the document in a Windows-based application and print it to a fax printer), click Next.

3. On the Recipient Information page, enter the name and number of the person to whom you want to send a fax, and then click Next.

> **Tip**   To send the fax to multiple recipients, enter the first person's name and phone number, and then click Add. Enter the information for each recipient and click Add until all recipients have been entered.

4. On the Preparing The Cover Page page, select a cover page template. You can also enter a subject line, a note, and sender information. Click Next.

> **Note**   Either the Subject Line or Note text boxes must be filled in to proceed.

5. On the Schedule page, choose when to send the fax (Now, When Discount Rates Apply, or A Specific Time In The Next 24 Hours). You can also specify a priority of High, Normal, or Low. Click Next.

6. On the Completing The Send Fax Wizard page, review the information. If the information is correct, click Finish to send the fax.

How to Manage and Troubleshoot the Most Common I/O Devices

The list of possible devices that you can install is too long to include here. Instead, the following sections include some of the most common devices and how they are installed, configured, and managed.

Scanners and Cameras

Most digital cameras, scanners, and other imaging devices are Plug and Play devices, and Windows XP Professional installs them automatically when you connect them to your computer. If your imaging device is not installed automatically when you connect it, or if it does not support Plug and Play, use the Scanner And Camera Installation Wizard. To open this wizard, in Control Panel, click Printers And Other Hardware, and then click Scanners And Cameras. In the Scanners And Cameras window, double-click Add An Imaging Device to start the Scanners And Camera Installation Wizard. Click Next and follow the onscreen instructions to install your digital camera, scanner, or other imaging device.

In Device Manager, select the appropriate device, and then click Properties. The standard color profile for Integrated Color Management (ICM 2.0) is RGB, but you can add, remove, or select an alternate color profile for a device. To change the color profile, click the Color Management tab on the device's Properties dialog box. If you are having problems with your scanner or camera, click Troubleshoot in the Scanners And Cameras Properties dialog box.

You use the Scanners And Cameras tool in Control Panel to manage imaging devices. Configuration options vary depending on the device that is connected, but at a minimum you can test the device to verify that it is functioning, set the rate at which data is transferred from the camera or scanner to the computer, and control color profiles. It is important to not set the data transfer rate higher than what the device supports. If the transfer rate is set too high, image transfer might fail.

Mouse Devices

Mouse devices are generally Plug and Play, and Windows generally recognizes mouse devices when they are connected to the computer or, at the least, when Windows starts up. In some cases, though, you must install a mouse using the Add Hardware Wizard. Mouse devices connect to computers through a mouse (PS/2) port, serial port, or USB port. Wireless mouse devices are also available, although they usually communicate with a receiver that connects to the computer using a USB port.

Click the Mouse icon in the Printers And Other Hardware window of Control Panel to configure and troubleshoot your mouse. The Buttons tab (see Figure 6-8) allows you to configure your mouse for a left-handed or right-handed user. It also allows you to set a single mouse click as select or open and to control the double-click speed.

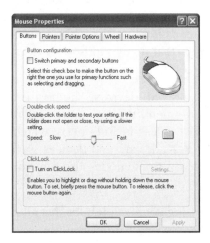

Figure 6-8   Configure button properties using the Buttons tab of the Mouse Properties dialog box.

The Pointers tab allows you to select or create a custom scheme for your pointer. The Pointer Options tab allows you to adjust the speed and acceleration of your pointer and to set the Snap To Default option, which moves the pointer automatically to the default button in dialog boxes.

The Hardware tab allows you to access the troubleshooter if you are having problems with your mouse. The Hardware tab also has a Properties button that allows you to do an advanced configuration for your mouse. This includes uninstalling or updating your driver, viewing or changing the resources allocated to your mouse, and increasing or decreasing the sensitivity of your mouse by varying the sample rate, which changes how often Windows XP Professional determines the position of your mouse.

Keyboards

Like mouse devices, keyboards are generally Plug and Play devices. Keyboards are usually connected to the computer through a (PS/2) keyboard port or a USB port.

Wireless keyboards are also available, although (like wireless mouse devices) they typically communicate with a receiver that connects to the computer using a USB port.

Click Keyboard in the Printers And Other Hardware window of Control Panel to configure or troubleshoot a keyboard. In the Speed tab, you can configure the character repeat delay and the character repeat rate. You can also control the cursor blink rate. The Hardware tab shows you the device properties for the installed keyboard and allows you to access the troubleshooter if you are having problems with your keyboard. You can also install a device driver, roll back to a previous device driver, or uninstall a device driver.

USB Devices

Universal serial bus (USB) is a type of connection developed to provide a fast, flexible method of attaching up to 127 peripheral devices to a computer. USB provides a connection format designed to replace the computer's traditional serial-port and parallel-port connections. The term "universal" indicates that many kinds of devices can take advantage of USB. USB is fully Plug and Play–compliant.

The USB system comprises a single USB host and USB devices. The host is at the top of the USB hierarchy. In a Windows XP environment, the operating system and the hardware work together to form the USB host. Devices include hubs, which are connection points for other USB devices and nodes. Nodes are end devices such as printers, scanners, mouse devices, keyboards, and so on. Some nodes also function as hubs, allowing additional USB devices to be connected to them.

You can connect USB peripherals together by using connection hubs that allow the bus to branch out through additional port connections. In this example, some of the peripheral devices are simply devices, whereas others serve as both devices and connection hubs. The computer provides a USB host connection that serves as the main USB connection.

A special hub, called the root hub, is an integral part of the host system (typically built into the motherboard), and provides one or more attachment points for USB devices (the ports available on the computer). The built-in USB ports on computers function as the root hub. USB provides for a total of up to five levels of devices. The root hub is at the first level. Regular hubs can form up to three additional levels, and nodes can function as the last level.

You can add or remove most USB devices from a computer while the computer is turned on. This practice is often referred to as hot-plugging the device. Plug and Play detects the presence (or absence) of the device and configures it for operation.

The USB interface provides power to the peripheral that is attached to it. The root hub provides power from the host computer to directly connected devices. Hubs also supply power to connected devices. Even if the interface supplies power to the USB devices, USB devices also can have their own power sources, if necessary. Many devices, such as digital cameras and scanners, draw more power than a USB hub can provide.

> **Exam Tip**   Some USB hubs are self-powered, and some are not. Hubs that are not self-powered draw power from the hub to which they are connected or from the computer itself. If you find that a USB device that is connected to an unpowered USB hub is not working as expected, try replacing the unpowered USB hub with a self-powered hub.

Because you can add nearly any type of peripheral device to the PC through the USB port, the range of symptoms that are associated with USB devices include all the symptoms that are listed for peripheral devices in this chapter. Problems that are associated specifically with the USB technology occur in the following general areas:

- USB hardware device
- USB controller
- USB drivers

The first step in troubleshooting USB problems is to check the BIOS setup to make sure that the USB function is enabled for the computer. Table 6-5 describes basic USB troubleshooting procedures.

Table 6-5   Basic USB Troubleshooting

If This Happens	Do This
USB functionality is enabled in the BIOS.	Check Device Manager to make sure that the USB controller appears there. In Windows XP, the USB controller should be listed under the Universal Serial Bus Controllers entry (using the default Devices By Type view in Device Manager).
The controller does not appear in Device Manager, or a yellow warning icon appears next to the controller.	Contact the BIOS manufacturer for an updated copy of the BIOS because the computer's BIOS might be outdated.
The controller is present in Device Manager.	Right-click the USB controller, and then select Properties. If there are any problems, a message should appear in the Device Status section on the General tab of the controller's Properties dialog box.
The BIOS and controller settings appear to be correct.	Check the USB port drivers next. USB ports are listed in Device Manager as USB Root Hubs. Right-click a USB Root Hub entry, and then select Properties. Use the Driver tab of the USB Root Hub Properties dialog box to update or roll back drivers, if necessary.

When troubleshooting USB devices, you must be aware that the problem could be a result of general USB issues or be a problem with the device itself. Usually, but not always, general USB issues affect more than one device. If you suspect a problem with a specific device, uninstall the device by using Device Manager, disconnect the device from the computer, and then restart the computer. After the computer restarts, reconnect the device and let Plug and Play detect, install, and configure it again. If the device still does not function correctly, investigate the possibility that the device is damaged in some way or that you need to obtain updated drivers from Microsoft or the device manufacturer.

Smart Card Readers

Smart cards are small, credit card–sized devices that are used to store information. Smart cards are generally used to store authentication credentials, such as public and private keys, and other forms of personal information. They are highly portable, allowing users to easily carry their credentials and other personal information with them.

A computer must have a smart card reader to access a smart card. The reader is generally a PS/2, USB, or PC Card device, although some computers have smart card readers built in. Windows XP supports Plug and Play smart card readers that follow the Personal Computer/Smart Card (PC/SC) standards. A manufacturer might provide a device driver for its legacy smart card device, but Microsoft recommends using only Plug and Play smart card readers.

In addition to installing drivers for a smart card reader, you must enable the Smart Card service for Windows XP Professional to read smart cards. After you have installed and configured the smart card reader, make sure that the Smart Card service is started by using the Services snap-in in Computer Management.

Modems

Analog modems connect a computer to a remote device through the Public Switched Telephone Network (PSTN). Modems are often used to connect to the Internet through an Internet service provider (ISP) or to connect to a remote private network, such as a corporate network.

A modem can be either an internal or an external device. Internal modems connect to one of the computer's internal expansion slots. External modems connect to one of the computer's serial or USB ports.

You can manage modems through the Phone And Modem Options tool in Control Panel and through Device Manager. In Control Panel, select Printers And Other Hardware; then select Phone And Modem Options. In the Phone and Modem Options dialog box, on the Modems tab, double-click a modem to open a modem's Properties dialog box. The Properties dialog box allows you to control speaker volume for the modem or to disable modem sound entirely. This is actually a common request from users who do not like hearing the modem sounds every time they connect to the Internet.

The Maximum Port Speed list controls how quickly communications programs are permitted to send information to the modem. This is not the same as the modem's connection speed, which is negotiated when the modem dials out and establishes a connection. The maximum port speed is generally configured during installation and does not need to be reconfigured to match the modem's connection speed.

The Wait For Dial Tone Before Dialing check box is enabled by default. The telephone systems of some countries do not use a dial tone, in which case this option must be disabled or else the modem will never dial.

The Diagnostics tab of the modem's Properties dialog box lets you query the modem to see whether it can respond to standard modem commands. When you are troubleshooting, this is a useful way to determine whether the modem is initializing and functioning correctly.

During installation, Windows XP often installs a standard modem driver rather than the specific driver for the modem. This happens in cases where Windows cannot find a device-specific driver. The standard modem driver provides basic functionality, but does not support advanced modem features. You can use this driver temporarily until you obtain the appropriate driver from the manufacturer.

Game Controllers

Click Game Controllers in the Printers And Other Hardware window of Control Panel to install, configure, or troubleshoot your game controller. Attach the game controller to the computer (for example, if it is USB game controller, attach it to a USB port). If it does not install properly, in Device Manager, look under Human Interface Devices. If the controller is not listed, then check to make sure that USB is enabled in the BIOS. When prompted during system startup, access BIOS setup and enable USB. If USB is enabled in BIOS, contact the maker or vendor for your computer and obtain the current version of BIOS.

To configure the controller, select a device, and then click Properties. To troubleshoot a device, select it, and then click Troubleshoot.

IrDA and Wireless Devices

Most internal Infrared Data Association (IrDA) devices should be installed by Windows XP Professional Setup or when you start Windows XP Professional after adding one of these devices. If you attach an IrDA transceiver to a serial port, you must install it using the Add Hardware Wizard. In Control Panel, click Printers And Other Hardware, and then click Add Hardware to start the Add Hardware Wizard. Click Next to close the

Welcome To The Add Hardware Wizard page. Select Yes, I Have Already Connected The Hardware, and then click Next. Select Add A New Hardware Device and then click Next, and follow the directions onscreen.

To configure an IrDA device, in Control Panel click Wireless Link. In the Hardware tab, click the device you want to configure, and then click Properties. The Properties dialog box shows the status of the device, driver files, and any power management settings.

> **Note** The Wireless Link icon appears in Control Panel only if you have already installed an infrared device on your computer.

Handheld Devices

Most handheld devices support either IrDA standards or connect to the computer through a serial or USB port. For handheld devices that use a port, some connect directly to the port, and some connect to a cradle, which in turn is connected to the port.

You will need to install software so that Windows XP can communicate correctly with the handheld device. For example, Palm-based personal digital assistants (PDAs) require you to install the Palm desktop software to allow the PDA to transfer data to and from a Windows-based PC. Handheld devices running Windows Mobile software, such as the Pocket PC, require that you install a program named ActiveSync on the computer.

> **See Also** For more information about supporting handheld devices running Windows Mobile software, visit the Windows Mobile page of the Microsoft Web site at *http://www.microsoft.com/windowsmobile/*.

Practice: Disabling and Re-enabling a Hardware Device

In this practice, you use Device Manager to disable and re-enable a hardware device. Complete the following steps.

1. From the Start menu, click Control Panel.

2. In the Control Panel window, click Performance And Maintenance.

3. In the Performance And Maintenance window, click System.

4. In the System Properties dialog box, on the Hardware tab, click the Device Manager button.

5. In the Device manager window, expand the Ports (COM & LPT) category, right-click the parallel port—almost always named Printer Port (LPT1)—and click Properties.

6. In the Printer Port (LPT1) Properties dialog box, on the General tab, in the Device Usage drop-down list, select Do Not Use This Device (Disable). Click OK.

7. In the Device Manager window, note that the icon for Printer Port (LPT1) has a red "x" on it, indicating that the device is disabled. Right-click the Printer Port (LPT1) and click Properties.

8. In the Printer Port (LPT1) Properties dialog box, on the General tab, in the Device Usage drop-down list, select Use This Device (Enable). Click OK.

9. Close all open windows.

Lesson Review

Use the following questions to help determine whether you have learned enough to move on to the next lesson. If you have difficulty answering these questions, review the material in this lesson before beginning the next lesson. You can find answers to these questions in the "Questions and Answers" section at the end of this chapter.

1. Windows XP Professional automatically identifies Plug and Play devices and arbitrates their resource requests; the resource allocation among these devices is _____ (permanent/not permanent).

2. How can you free any resource settings that you manually assigned to a Plug and Play device?

3. You get a call on the help desk from a user wondering why there is no Wireless Link icon in Control Panel on her desktop computer like the one on her laptop computer. What should you tell the user?

Lesson Summary

- Device Manager provides you with a graphical view of the hardware installed on your computer and helps you manage and troubleshoot it. Device Manager flags each device with an icon that indicates the device type and the status of the device. By default, Device Manager does not display non–Plug and Play devices and devices that are not currently connected to the computer (phantom devices).

- You can use the Windows XP Professional Fax Service to send and receive faxes with a locally attached fax device or with a remote fax device connected on your network. The Fax Service is not installed by default, so you must install it.

- Windows XP Professional supports a number of different types of I/O devices, including the following:

  - ❑ Most imaging devices are installed automatically when you connect them. If your device is not installed, Windows XP Professional provides the Scanner and Camera Installation Wizard to help you install it.

  - ❑ Use the Mouse option in the Printers And Other Hardware window of Control Panel to configure and troubleshoot your mouse.

  - ❑ Use the Phone And Modem Options option in the Printers And Other Hardware window of Control Panel to install, configure, or troubleshoot your modem.

  - ❑ Use the Game Controllers option in the Printers And Other Hardware window of Control Panel to install, configure, or troubleshoot your game controller.

  - ❑ Use the Add Hardware Wizard to install an IrDA transceiver you attach to a serial port.

  - ❑ The Wireless Link icon that you use to configure an infrared device does not appear in Control Panel until you have installed an infrared device on your computer.

  - ❑ Use the Keyboard option in the Printers And Other Hardware window of Control Panel to configure or troubleshoot a keyboard.

Lesson 3: Viewing and Configuring Hardware Profiles

A hardware profile is a collection of configuration information about the hardware that is installed on your computer. Within a profile, you can enable or disable each piece of hardware (such as networking adapters, ports, monitors, and so on) or provide specific configuration information. You can have many hardware profiles on a computer and switch between different profiles when booting into Windows XP.

After this lesson, you will be able to

- Explain when to use hardware profiles.
- Create a hardware profile.
- Manage hardware profiles.
- Configure hardware settings in a hardware profile.
- Select a hardware profile during Windows startup.

Estimated lesson time: 15 minutes

When to Use Hardware Profiles

With Windows XP Professional's capability to reconfigure network settings when it detects a new network, hardware profiles are not as important as they used to be, and it is likely that you will never need to use them. Nonetheless, hardware profiles are still used, and you should understand how to create and configure them.

Hardware profiles are useful when you have one or more hardware devices that you want to disable sometimes and enable other times. Rather than enabling and disabling the devices using Device Manager each time you start Windows, you can create hardware profiles in which the devices are enabled or disabled, and then just choose the correct hardware profile during startup.

This functionality is particularly useful when you have an older portable computer that does not support hot docking (the capability for Windows XP to automatically determine whether the portable computer is docked and reconfigure devices appropriately).

How to Create a Hardware Profile

Hardware profiles provide a way to configure a single computer for different situations. Within a profile, you can enable or disable specific hardware devices and configure those devices differently. As an example, assume that you have a user with a portable computer. When he is at home, the computer is connected to an external monitor, keyboard, mouse, and printer. When the user takes the computer away from home, none of these devices is connected. You could set his computer up with two hardware profiles: one in which those devices were enabled, and one in which they were disabled.

Whenever the computer starts, the user would choose the hardware profile to use, preventing him from having to make configuration changes or be notified of missing devices.

By default, Windows creates one hardware profile named Profile 1 during installation. To create an additional hardware profile, perform the following steps:

1. From the Start menu, select Control Panel.

2. In the Control Panel window, select Performance And Maintenance.

3. In the Performance And Maintenance window, select System.

4. In the System Properties dialog box, on the Hardware tab, click the Hardware Profiles button.

5. In the Hardware Profiles dialog box, shown in Figure 6-9, select Profile 1 (Current), and then click the Copy button. You cannot create a new profile directly; you must copy an existing profile and then modify the copy.

Figure 6-9   Copy and modify an existing hardware profile.

6. In the Copy Profile dialog box, type a name for the new profile, and then click OK.

7. In the Hardware Profiles dialog box, select the new profile you just named, and then click the Properties button.

8. In the Properties dialog box for the profile, you can configure two options:

   ❑ Select the This Is A Portable Computer check box if the computer is a portable computer that uses a docking station (and if that docking station is one that Windows XP supports). When a supported docking station is used, Windows

XP can determine whether a portable computer is docked or undocked, and then apply the correct profile automatically. If you do not use a docking station (or just prefer to set up and control your own profiles), leave this option deselected.

❑   Select the Always Include This Profile As An Option When Windows Starts check box if you want the profile to appear on the boot menu as a selectable profile.

9. In the Properties dialog box for the profile, click OK to return to the Hardware Profiles dialog box.

10. Click OK to return to the System Properties dialog box, and then click OK again to return to Windows.

How to Manage Hardware Profiles

After you have created a profile, you can control generally how Windows XP treats profiles by using the same Hardware Profiles dialog box you used to create the profile. (Open the System Properties dialog box, switch to the Hardware tab, and then click the Hardware Profiles button to access the dialog box.)

First, you can specify how Windows uses hardware profiles during startup. You have the following options:

■   Have Windows wait until you select a hardware profile before it continues booting.

■   Have Windows automatically select the first hardware profile in the list and continue booting after a specified amount of time. If you select this option, you can specify how long Windows should wait before going on without you. The default is 30 seconds.

You also can specify the order in which hardware profiles appear in the list during startup. The order is important, mostly because it is the first profile on the list that Windows will boot if you configure Windows to select a profile automatically. Select any profile on the list and use the up or down buttons on the right to move the profile around.

How to Configure Hardware Settings in a Profile

After you have created the necessary profiles and configured Windows to display and start them the correct way, the next step is to configure hardware settings for each profile. To configure hardware for a profile, you must start the computer by using that profile. After you have started Windows by using a profile, use Device Manager to enable, disable, and configure individual devices. The settings you make will affect the currently loaded profile.

The only tricky part of setting up hardware devices in profiles is actually remembering which profile you are currently using because neither Device Manager nor a device's Properties dialog box provides information on the current profile. You can always switch back to the System Properties dialog box and open the Hardware Profiles window to determine your current profile.

How to Select a Hardware Profile During Startup

If there are two or more profiles in the Available Hardware Profiles list, Windows XP Professional prompts the user to make a selection during startup. You can configure how long the computer waits before starting the default configuration. To adjust this time delay, click the Select The First Profile Listed If I Don't Select A Profile option, and then specify the number of seconds in the Seconds text box within the Hardware Profiles Selection group. You can configure Windows XP Professional to start the default profile by setting the number of seconds to 0. To override the default during startup, press SPACEBAR during the system prompt. You can also select the Wait Until I Select A Hardware Profile option to have Windows XP Professional wait for you to select a profile.

Lesson Review

Use the following questions to help determine whether you have learned enough to move on to the next lesson. If you have difficulty answering these questions, review the material in this lesson before beginning the next lesson. You can find answers to these questions in the "Questions and Answers" section at the end of this chapter.

1. What is the minimum number of hardware profiles you can have on your computer?

   _____

   _____

   _____

2. Windows XP Professional creates an initial profile during installation and assigns it the name of _____ in the list of hardware profiles available on the computer. Fill in the blank.

3. Which of the following statements are true about hardware profiles in Windows XP Professional? Choose all that apply.

   a. Windows XP Professional prompts the user to select a hardware profile during startup only if there are two or more profiles in the Available Hardware Profiles list.

   b. It is a good idea to delete the default profile when you create a new profile to avoid confusion.

c. You can configure Windows XP Professional to always start the default profile by selecting the Do Not Display The Select Hardware Profile check box.

d. You can select the Wait Until I Select A Hardware Profile option to have Windows XP Professional wait for you to select a profile at startup.

Lesson Summary

■ A hardware profile stores configuration settings for a set of devices and services. Windows XP Professional uses hardware profiles to determine which drivers to load when system hardware changes. To create or modify a hardware profile, in the System Properties dialog box, click the Hardware tab and then click Hardware Profiles to view the Available Hardware Profiles list.

■ After you have created a profile, you can control whether Windows displays available profiles during startup and whether Windows automatically selects a particular profile after a specified amount of time.

■ After you have created a profile and configured how Windows uses profiles, you can configure hardware for a profile by starting Windows using that profile and configuring the hardware using Device Manager.

■ If there are two or more profiles in the Available Hardware Profiles list, Windows XP Professional prompts the user to make a selection during startup.

Lesson 4:   Configuring and Troubleshooting Device Drivers

Hardware drivers are software that govern the interactions between Windows and a hardware device. Device Manager provides a simple method of viewing and updating drivers for any device in the system. Windows XP also supports **driver signing**, which provides a method to verify that Microsoft has tested the designated device drivers for reliability.

After this lesson, you will be able to

- Explain the purpose of the Driver.cab file.
- Update device drivers.
- Configure and monitor driver signing.

Estimated lesson time: 20 minutes

What Is the Driver.cab File?

Drivers that ship with Windows XP are stored on the installation CD in a single cabinet file called Driver.cab. Windows XP Setup copies this file to the %systemroot%\Driver Cache\i386 folder on the local hard disk during installation. Windows uses this file during and after installation to install drivers when new hardware is detected. This process helps by ensuring that users do not have to provide the installation CD whenever drivers are installed. All drivers in the Driver.cab file are digitally signed.

Actions You Can Take to Update Drivers

It is important to keep device drivers updated for all devices in a system. Using up-to-date drivers ensures optimum functionality and reduces the chance of an outdated device driver causing problems.

The Driver tab of a device's Properties dialog box (shown in Figure 6-10) displays basic information about the device driver, such as the date of the driver and version number. You can also perform the following actions on the Driver tab:

- View the names of the actual driver files by clicking the Driver Details button.

- Update a device driver to a more recent version by clicking the Update Driver button. Windows prompts you for the location of the newer version of the driver. You can obtain new drivers from the device's manufacturer. You can also use the Update Driver option to reinstall drivers for a device that has ceased to function correctly because of a driver problem. If updating the drivers does not successfully restore device functionality, consider removing the device by using Device Manager and then restarting the computer. If the device supports Plug and Play, Windows will recognize the device when the computer restarts. Non–Plug and Play devices require manual reinstallation.

■ Revert to a previous version of a driver by clicking the Roll Back Driver button. This feature restores the last device driver that was functioning before the current driver was installed. Windows supports driver rollback for all devices *except* printers. In addition, driver rollback is available only on devices that have had new drivers installed. When a driver is updated, the previous version is stored in the %systemroot%\system32\reinstallbackups folder.

■ Remove the device from the computer by clicking the Uninstall button.

Security Alert   To work with device drivers, your user account must have the Load And Unload Device Drivers user right.

Figure 6-10   Use the Driver tab of a device's Properties dialog box to view driver details.

Exam Tip   You should consider rolling back a driver when you are sure that a new driver is causing a problem and you do not want to affect other system configurations or drivers with a tool such as System Restore.

How to Configure and Monitor Driver Signing

Hardware drivers can often cause a computer running Windows XP to become unstable or to fail entirely. Windows XP implements driver signing as a method to reduce the likelihood of such problems. Driver signing allows Windows XP to identify drivers that have passed all Windows Hardware Quality Labs (WHQL) tests, and have not been altered or overwritten by any program's installation process.

To configure how the system responds to unsigned files, click System in the Performance And Maintenance window in Control Panel. In the System Properties dialog box, on the Hardware tab, click Driver Signing to open the Driver Signing Options dialog box (see Figure 6-11).

Figure 6-11 Configure driver signing in the Driver Signing Options dialog box.

You can configure the following three driver signing settings:

- **Ignore** This option allows any files to be installed regardless of their digital signature or the lack thereof.

- **Warn** This option, the default, displays a warning message before allowing the installation of an unsigned file.

- **Block** This option prevents the installation of unsigned files.

Real World   Driver Signing

Because of the time that it takes for Microsoft to test device drivers before signing them, the most recent drivers available from a manufacturer are rarely signed. If you are managing a small number of computers, you are usually better off not worrying too much about driver signing and just using the most recent driver available from the manufacturer of a device because newer drivers are likely to have bug fixes and improvements that are worth having. Just make sure that you acquire the drivers directly from the vendor.

If you are managing a large installation of computers, though, the small risk associated with using unsigned drivers becomes significant enough that it is probably better to wait for the signed drivers to come out.

If you are logged on as Administrator or as a member of the Administrators group, you can select the Make This Action The System Default check box to apply the driver signing configuration you set up to all users who log on to the computer.

The **File Signature Verification utility (Sigverif.exe)** in Windows scans a computer running Windows XP and notifies you if there are any unsigned drivers on the computer. You can start the utility by typing **sigverif.exe** at the command prompt or at the Run dialog box. After the File Signature Verification utility scans your computer, the utility displays the results in a window similar to the one shown in Figure 6-12. Note that you cannot use the utility to remove or modify unsigned drivers; the utility scans only for unsigned drivers and shows you their location.

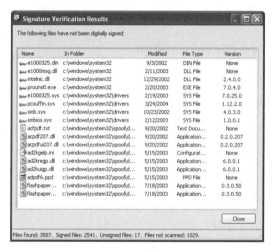

Figure 6-12   The File Signature Verification utility scans a system for unsigned drivers.

The File Signature Verification utility also writes the results of the scan to a log file named Segverif.txt, which is found in the %systemroot% folder. You can change this log file's name and location, as well as configure advanced search options, by clicking the Advanced button on the File Signature Verification dialog box.

Practice: Configuring Driver Signature Settings and Scanning for Unsigned Drivers

In this practice, you will configure settings for unsigned drivers and use the File Signature Verification utility to scan your computer for unsigned drivers. Complete the following two exercises.

Exercise 1: Configure Settings for Driver Signatures

1. From the Start menu, click Control Panel.

2. In the Control Panel window, click Performance And Maintenance.

3. In the Performance And Maintenance window, click System.

4. In the System Properties dialog box, on the Hardware tab, click the Driver Signing button.

5. In the Driver Signing Options dialog box, ensure that the Warn option is selected so that you are prompted whenever Windows detects drivers that have not been digitally signed. Click OK to close the Driver Signing Options dialog box.

6. Click OK again to close the System Properties dialog box.

Exercise 2: Using the Windows File Signature Verification Tool

1. From the Start menu, click Run.

2. In the Run dialog box, type **sigverif.exe** and click OK.

3. In the File Signature Verification dialog box, click Start.

4. The File Signature Verification utility scans your system for unsigned drivers, a process that can take anywhere from a few seconds to a few minutes. When the scan is finished, a list of unsigned drivers is displayed.

5. Click Close to exit the Signature Verification Results window. Click Close again to exit the File Signature Verification dialog box.

Lesson Review

Use the following questions to help determine whether you have learned enough to move on to the next lesson. If you have difficulty answering these questions, review the material in this lesson before beginning the next lesson. You can find answers to these questions in the "Questions and Answers" section at the end of this chapter.

1. Why does Microsoft digitally sign the files in Windows XP Professional?

   _____

   _____

   _____

   _____

   _____

2. Which of the following tools would you use to block the installation of unsigned files? Choose the correct answer.

    a. File Signature Verification utility

    b. Driver Signing Options in the System Control Panel

    c. System File Checker

    d. Sigverif

3. How can you view the file signature verification log file?

_____

_____

_____

_____

Lesson Summary

■ The Driver.cab file contains all the device drivers that ship with Windows XP Professional. Windows uses this file during and after installation to install drivers when new hardware is detected.

■ You can use the Driver tab of a device's Properties dialog box in Device Manager to view driver details for a device. Windows XP Professional also allows you to roll back a driver to a previous version if a new driver causes instability in a system.

■ Digitally signed drivers indicate that a driver has passed quality testing at Microsoft and has not been altered since testing. You can configure Windows to ignore or accept unsigned drivers, or to notify you if an unsigned driver is about to be installed. Windows XP Professional provides two tools to verify the digital signatures of system files: SFC and File Signature Verification.

Case Scenario Exercise

In this exercise, you will read a scenario about a user who is trying to install a device driver for a new sound card that he has purchased for his computer; you will then answer the questions that follow. If you have difficulty completing this work, review the material in this chapter before beginning the next chapter. You can find answers to these questions in the "Questions and Answers" section at the end of this chapter.

Scenario

You are an administrator working for Contoso, Ltd., a nationwide insurance company. You receive an e-mail from Darren Parker, one of your users, that says "After receiving authorization from the IT support staff, I purchased a sound card for my desktop computer running Windows XP Professional. The IT support staff created a temporary administrator account so that I could install the drivers for the card. I followed the instructions provided by the manufacturer for physically installing the sound card in the computer. After restarting Windows, I continued to follow the manufacturer's instructions and canceled the Found New Hardware Wizard when it appeared. Then I inserted the CD-ROM that came with the sound card. The Setup program on the CD ran automatically and notified me that it would first install device drivers and then install other related applications. But then early during the installation, I received an error message, stating that the drivers I am trying to install are unsigned and cannot be installed. The Setup program ended with an error message. I have a big video presentation to finish today, and if I do not get this problem fixed in the next hour, I am totally hosed. Help!"

Questions

1. What is the likely problem?

   _____

   _____

2. What should you tell Darren to do to allow driver signing?

   _____

   _____

   _____

   _____

3. If the IT staff had not provided Darren with a temporary administrator account, what might have prevented Darren from being able to allow driver signing?

   _____

   _____

   _____

4. Aside from assigning Darren a temporary administrator account, in what two ways might the IT support staff allow Darren to install unsigned drivers?

   _____

   _____

   _____

   _____

Troubleshooting Lab

In this lab, you will use Device Manager to simulate troubleshooting an unterminated Small Computer System Interface (SCSI) chain. Complete the following steps.

1. From the Start menu, right-click My Computer, and then click Manage.

2. In the Computer Management window, under the System Tools node, click Device Manager.

3. In the right pane, expand the Disk Drives category, and then double-click one of the drives listed.

4. In the Properties dialog box for the drive you selected, on the General tab, the Device Status field indicates whether there are any problems with the device. Click Troubleshoot. (Normally, you would do this only if a problem was indicated with this device.)

5. Windows XP Professional displays the Help And Support Center window with the Drives And Network Adapters Troubleshooter displayed.

6. Click I Am Having A Problem With A Hard Disk Drive Or Floppy Disk Drive, and then click Next.

7. Read the information about SCSI devices; click Yes, I Am Having A Problem With A SCSI Device; and then click Next.

8. Read the information provided, click Yes, My Hardware Is On The HCL, and then click Next.

9. On the Does The SCSI Adapter Or A Device In The Chain Need Power page, you are asked, "Does Your Drive Work When All The SCSI Components Have The Power They Need?" Click No, My Drive Does Not Work, and then click Next.

10. On the Does Device Manager Show A Problem With Your Device page, you are asked, "Does This Information Help You To Solve The Problem?" Click No, My Device Still Does Not Work, and then click Next.

11. On the Did You Recently Install A New Driver page, you are asked, "Does Rolling Back To A Previous Driver Solve The Problem?" Click No, I Still Have A Problem, and then click Next.

12. On the Is There A Problem With The Driver For Your Device page, you are asked, "Does Reinstalling Or Updating Your Driver Solve The Problem?" Click No, I Still Have A Problem, and then click Next.

13. On the Is Your SCSI Cable Connected Correctly page, you are asked, "Does Your Drive Work When You Replace Any Faulty Cables Or Adapters?" Click No, My Drive Does Not Work.

14. On the Is the SCSI Chain Terminated page, you are asked, "Does Your Drive Work When You Terminate The SCSI Chain?" Click Yes, Terminating The SCSI Chain Solves The Problem, and then click Next.

15. Close Help And Support Center, close the Properties dialog box for the selected disk drive, and close Computer Management.

Chapter Summary

- For most Plug and Play hardware, you connect the device to the computer, and Windows XP Professional automatically configures the new settings. For non–Plug and Play hardware, Windows XP Professional often identifies the hardware and automatically installs and configures it. For the occasional Plug and Play hardware device and for any non–Plug and Play hardware that Windows XP Professional does not identify, install, and configure, you initiate automatic hardware installation with the Add Hardware Wizard. When you manually install hardware, you must determine any resources required by that hardware device. Hardware resources include interrupts, I/O ports, and memory. The Device Manager snap-in provides a list of all hardware resources and their availability.

- Device Manager provides you with a graphical view of the hardware installed on your computer, and helps you manage and troubleshoot it. Device Manager flags each device with an icon that indicates the device type and the status of the device. Windows XP Professional supports a number of different types of I/O devices, including the following:

    ❑ Most imaging devices are installed automatically when you connect them, but if your device is not, Windows XP Professional provides the Scanner and Camera Installation Wizard to help you install it.

    ❑ Use the Mouse option in the Printers And Other Hardware window of Control Panel to configure and troubleshoot your mouse.

    ❑ Use the Phone And Modem Options option in the Printers And Other Hardware window of Control Panel to install, configure, or troubleshoot your modem.

    ❑ Use the Game Controllers option in the Printers And Other Hardware window of Control Panel to install, configure, or troubleshoot your game controller.

    ❑ Use the Add Hardware Wizard to install an IrDA transceiver you attach to a serial port.

    ❑ The Wireless Link icon that you use to configure an infrared device does not appear in Control Panel until you have installed an infrared device on your computer.

    ❑ Use the Keyboard option in the Printers And Other Hardware window of Control Panel to configure or troubleshoot a keyboard.

- A hardware profile stores configuration settings for a set of devices and services. Windows XP Professional uses hardware profiles to determine which drivers to load when system hardware changes. To create or modify a hardware profile, in the System Properties dialog box, click the Hardware tab, and then click Hardware Profiles to view the Available Hardware Profiles list.

- You can use the Driver tab of a device's Properties dialog box in Device Manager to view driver details for a device. Windows XP Professional also allows you to roll back a driver to a previous version if a new driver causes instability in a system. Digitally signed drivers indicate that a driver has passed quality testing at Microsoft and has not been altered since testing. You can configure Windows to ignore or accept unsigned drivers, or to notify you if an unsigned driver is about to be installed. Windows XP Professional provides two tools to verify the digital signatures of system files: SFC and File Signature Verification.

Exam Highlights

Before taking the exam, review the key points and terms that are presented in this chapter. You need to know this information.

Key Points

- Windows XP Professional automatically detects, installs, and configures most Plug and Play (and some non–Plug and Play) hardware. If Windows does not detect Plug and Play hardware, you can often force the detection by restarting the computer or running the Add Hardware Wizard. For many non–Plug and Play devices, you must use the Add Hardware Wizard to manually configure the device.

- Some USB hubs are self-powered, and some are not. Hubs that are not self-powered draw power from the hub to which they are connected or from the computer itself. If you find that a USB device that is connected to an unpowered USB hub is not working as expected, try replacing the unpowered USB hub with a self-powered hub.

- You should consider rolling back a driver when you are sure that a new driver is causing a problem and you do not want to affect other system configurations or drivers with a tool such as System Restore.

Key Terms

Device Manager   An administrative tool that you can use to manage the devices on your computer. Using Device Manager, you can view and change device properties, update device drivers, configure device settings, and uninstall devices.

driver signing A process in which device drivers that have passed a series of tests by Microsoft are digitally signed, enabling the operating system to determine whether the drivers are acceptable for use.

File Signature Verification utility (Sigverif.exe) A utility that is used to scan a Windows XP system for unsigned files, providing a simple method to identify unsigned drivers.

Plug and Play A technology that enables the computer to automatically determine which hardware devices are installed on the computer and then to allocate system resources to those devices as required to configure and manage the devices.

Roll Back Driver A feature in Windows XP that permits you to reinstall (roll back) a previously installed driver. The uninstalled drivers are stored in the systemroot\system32\reinstallbackups folder.

Questions and Answers

Lesson 1 Review

Page
6-9

1. When you initiate automatic hardware installation by starting the Add Hardware Wizard, what does Windows XP Professional query the hardware about?

The resources the hardware requires and the settings for those resources.

2. _____ are channels that allow a hardware device, such as a floppy disk drive, to access memory directly (without interrupting the microprocessor). Fill in the blank.

DMAs

3. Why would you install a hardware device manually?

You install a hardware device manually if Windows XP Professional fails to automatically detect a hardware device.

Lesson 2 Review

Page
6-25

1. Windows XP Professional automatically identifies Plug and Play devices and arbitrates their resource requests; the resource allocation among these devices is _____ (permanent/not permanent).

Not permanent

2. How can you free any resource settings that you manually assigned to a Plug and Play device?

To free the resource settings you manually assigned and allow Windows XP Professional to again arbitrate the resources, in Device Manager, select the Use Automatic Settings check box in the Resources tab of the Properties dialog box for the device.

3. You get a call on the help desk from a user wondering why there is no Wireless Link icon in Control Panel on her desktop computer like the one on her laptop computer. What should you tell the user?

Tell the user that the Wireless Link icon appears in Control Panel only if she has already installed an infrared device on her computer. Apparently, infrared devices are not installed on her desktop computer.

Lesson 3 Review

Page
6-30

1. What is the minimum number of hardware profiles you can have on your computer?

Windows XP Professional creates an initial profile during installation, which is listed as Profile 1 (Current), so one is the minimum number of hardware profiles you can have on a computer.

2. Windows XP Professional creates an initial profile during installation and assigns it the name of _____ in the list of hardware profiles available on the computer. Fill in the blank.

Profile 1 (Current)

3. Which of the following statements are true about hardware profiles in Windows XP Professional? Choose all that apply.

   a. Windows XP Professional prompts the user to select a hardware profile during startup only if there are two or more profiles in the Available Hardware Profiles list.

   b. It is a good idea to delete the default profile when you create a new profile to avoid confusion.

   c. You can configure Windows XP Professional to always start the default profile by selecting the Do Not Display The Select Hardware Profile check box.

   d. You can select the Wait Until I Select A Hardware Profile option to have Windows XP Professional wait for you to select a profile at startup.

A and D are the correct answers. B is not correct because you cannot delete the default profile. C is not correct because you must choose the Select The First Profile Listed If I Don't Select A Profile In xx Seconds option to always start a particular profile.

Lesson 4 Review

Page
6-36

1. Why does Microsoft digitally sign the files in Windows XP Professional?

Windows XP Professional drivers and operating system files have been digitally signed by Microsoft to ensure their quality and to simplify troubleshooting of altered files. Some applications overwrite existing operating files as part of their installation process, which might cause system errors that are difficult to troubleshoot.

2. Which of the following tools would you use to block the installation of unsigned files? Choose the correct answer.

   a. File Signature Verification utility

   b. Driver Signing Options in the System Control Panel

   c. System File Checker

   d. Sigverif

B is the correct answer. A and D are not correct because the File Signature Verification Utility (sigverif.exe) scans a computer for unsigned files. C is not correct because the System File Checker scans a computer for Windows files that have been modified since the installation of Windows.

3. How can you view the file signature verification log file?

By default, the Windows File Signature Verification tool saves the file signature verification to a log file. To view the log file, click Start, click Run, type sigverif, and then press ENTER. Click Advanced, click the Logging tab, and then click View Log.

Case Scenario Exercise

Page
6-37

1. What is the likely problem?

Driver signing on Darren's computer is configured so that unsigned drivers might not be installed.

2. What should you tell Darren to do to allow driver signing?

He should open the Driver Signing Options dialog box. He can do this by clicking the Driver Signing button on the Hardware tab of the System Properties dialog box. In the Driver Signing Options dialog box, he should select either the Warn or Ignore option.

3. If the IT staff had not provided Darren with a temporary administrator account, what might have prevented Darren from being able to allow driver signing?

If an administrator has configured a system default for the computer so that Windows blocks unsigned drivers, Darren could not configure Windows to allow the installation of unsigned drivers.

4. Aside from assigning Darren a temporary administrator account, in what two ways might the IT support staff allow Darren to install unsigned drivers?

The IT support staff could have Darren use the Run As command to enable Driver Signing without actually logging on with an administrator account. Also, the IT support staff could assign Darren's account the Load And Unload Device Drivers user right.

7 Setting Up and Managing User Accounts

Exam Objectives in this Chapter:

- Configure, manage, and troubleshoot local user and group accounts.
  - ❑ Configure, manage, and troubleshoot account settings.

Why This Chapter Matters

One of the most important functions that you will undertake as an administrator is the creation and management of user accounts. User accounts allow a person to log on to a computer or a network. User accounts also govern the access that person has to various resources and the ability a person has to perform certain actions on the computer. Groups make the administration of user accounts easier by allowing you to group together users who share common security and access needs.

This chapter explains how to plan, establish, and maintain local user accounts and local groups on computers running Microsoft Windows XP Professional.

Lessons in this Chapter:

Before You Begin

To complete this chapter, you must have a computer that meets the minimum hardware requirements listed in the preface, "About This Book." You must also have Windows XP Professional installed on your computer.

Lesson 1: Introduction to User Accounts

A user logs on to a computer or a network by supplying a user name and password that identify that user's user account. There are two types of user accounts.

■ A **local user account** allows you to log on to a specific computer to access resources on that computer.

■ A **domain user account** allows you to log on to a domain to access network resources.

After this lesson, you will be able to

■ Describe how a local user account works

■ Describe how a domain user account works

■ Identify the built-in local user accounts in Windows XP Professional

■ Enable or disable the built-in Guest account

Estimated lesson time: 30 minutes

Local User Accounts

Local user accounts allow users to log on only to the computer on which the local user account has been created and to access resources only on that computer. When you create a local user account, Windows XP Professional creates the account only in that computer's security database, called the **local security database**, shown in Figure 7-1. Windows XP Professional uses the local security database to authenticate the local user account, which allows the user to log on to that computer. Windows XP Professional does not replicate local user account information on any other computer.

Local user accounts
• Provide access to resources on the local computer
• Are created only on computers that are not in a domain
• Are created in the local security database

Figure 7-1 Local user accounts provide access to local resources only and should be used in work-group settings.

Microsoft recommends that you use local user accounts only on computers in workgroups. If you create a local user account in a workgroup of five computers running Windows XP Professional—for example, User1 on Computer1—you can only log on to Computer1 with the User1 account. If you need to be able to log on as User1 to all five computers in the workgroup, you must create a local user account, User1, on each of the five computers. Furthermore, if you decide to change the password for User1, you must change the password for User1 on each of the five computers because each computer maintains its own local security database.

> **Exam Tip**   A domain does not recognize local user accounts, so do not create local user accounts on computers running Windows XP Professional that are part of a domain. Doing so restricts users from accessing resources on the domain and prevents the domain administrator from administering the local user account properties or assigning access permissions for domain resources.

Domain User Accounts

Domain user accounts allow you to log on to the domain and access resources anywhere on the network. When you log on, you provide your logon information, which is your user name and password. A domain controller running Windows 2000 Server or Windows Server 2003 uses this logon information to authenticate your identity and build an access token that contains your user information and security settings. The access token identifies you to the computers in the domain on which you try to access resources. The access token is valid throughout the logon session.

> **Note**   You can have domain user accounts only if you have a domain. You can have a domain only if you have at least one computer running Windows 2000 Server or later that is configured as a domain controller (which means that the server has the Active Directory directory service installed).

You create a domain user account in the Active Directory database (the directory) on a domain controller, as shown in Figure 7-2. The domain controller replicates the new user account information to all domain controllers in the domain. After the domain controller replicates the new user account information to other domain controllers, all the domain controllers in the domain tree and other computers that are members of the domain can authenticate the user during the logon process.

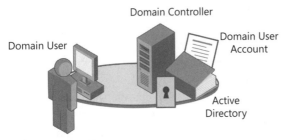

Domain user accounts
- Provide access to network resources
- Provide the access token for authentication
- Are created in Active Directory directory services on a domain controller

Figure 7-2   Domain user accounts

Built-In User Accounts

Windows XP Professional automatically creates a number of built-in local user accounts. Table 7-1 describes these accounts.

Table 7-1   Built-In Local User Accounts

Account	Description
Administrator	Use the built-in Administrator account to manage the overall computer. You can perform tasks to create and modify user accounts and groups, manage security policies, create printer resources, and assign the permissions and rights that allow user accounts to access resources.
Guest	Use the built-in Guest account to allow occasional users to log on and access resources. For example, an employee who needs access to resources for a short time can use the Guest account. This account is disabled by default to protect your computer from unauthorized use.
InitialUser	The *InitialUser* account is named based on the registered user and is created during Windows Activation (directly following installation) only if the computer is a member of a workgroup. For example, if a user named Sandra installed and activated Windows XP Professional as a member of a workgroup, an account named Sandra is created following installation. This account is made a member of the Administrators local group.
HelpAssistant	The HelpAssistant account is not available for standard logon. Instead, this account is used to authenticate users who connect by using Remote Assistance. Windows enables this account automatically when a user creates a Remote Assistance invitation and disables the account automatically when all invitations have expired. You will learn more about Remote Assistance in Chapter 18, "Using Windows XP Tools."

Table 7-1   Built-In Local User Accounts

Account	Description
SUPPORT_*xxxxxxxx*	The SUPPORT_*xxxxxxxx* account (where *xxxxxxxx* is a random number generated during Windows setup) is used by Microsoft when providing remote support through the Help And Support Service account. It is not available for logon or general use

Although you cannot delete any of the built-in user accounts, you can rename or disable them. To rename a user account, right-click the account in the Computer Management window and then select Rename. You will learn more about disabling accounts later in this section.

> **Real World   Using *RunAs* to Start a Program**
>
> As you might expect, administrators require more permissions and user rights to perform their duties than other users. However, logging on using an administrator account as a regular practice is not a good idea because it makes the computer (and the network) more vulnerable to security risks such as viruses, Trojan horses, spyware, and other malicious programs. A much safer practice is to log on routinely using a normal account that is a member of the Users or Power Users group and to use the *RunAs* command to perform tasks that require administrative rights or permissions. For example, you could log on using your normal user account and then launch the Computer Management tool using administrative credentials.
>
> Windows XP Professional provides this functionality using the Secondary Logon service, which must be enabled for the *RunAs* command to work. To learn how to enable this service, read Chapter 1, "Introduction to Windows XP Professional."
>
> After the Secondary Logon service is enabled, you can use the *RunAs* command in one of two ways.
>
> - In Windows Explorer (or on the Start menu), hold down the SHIFT key, right-click the program (or shortcut) you want to run, and click Run As. In the Run As dialog box, provide your administrative credentials.
>
> - At the command prompt, type **runas /user: *domain_name\administrator_ account program name***. For example, you might type **runas /user: contoso\administrator compmgmt.msc** to start the Computer Management tool using an account named Administrator in a domain named Contoso.

How to Enable or Disable the Guest Account

The Guest account has limited privileges on a computer and is used to provide access to users who do not have a user account on the computer. Although the Guest account can be useful for providing limited access to a computer, the account does present security problems because by design the Guest account allows anyone to log on to the computer. Fortunately, the Guest account is turned off (also known as disabled) by default. For a more secure environment, leave the Guest account turned off and create a normal user account for anyone who needs to use the computer.

Exam Tip Allow Guest access only in low-security workgroups, and always assign a password to the Guest account. Also, you can rename the Guest account, but you cannot delete it.

Log on with a user account that is a member of the Administrators group, and use the User Accounts tool in the Control Panel (shown in Figure 7-3) to turn the Guest account on or off. The User Accounts window displays the user accounts that can log on to the computer. The User Accounts window in Figure 7-3 indicates that Guest access is on.

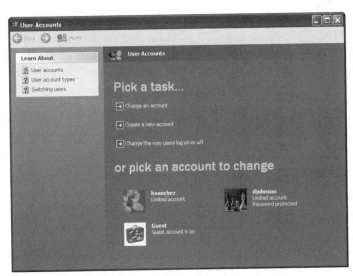

Figure 7-3 Use the User Accounts window to enable and disable the Guest account.

To enable or disable the Guest account, complete the following steps:

1. Click Start, click Control Panel, and then click User Accounts.

2. In the User Accounts window, click User Accounts.

3. If the Guest account is turned off, in the User Accounts window (a different window from the one in step 2), click the Guest icon to access the Do You Want To Turn On The Guest Account window (shown in Figure 7-4). Click Turn On The Guest Account. The Guest account is now turned on.

   If the Guest account is turned on, click the Guest icon to access the What Do You Want To Change About The Guest Account page. Click Turn Off The Guest Account.

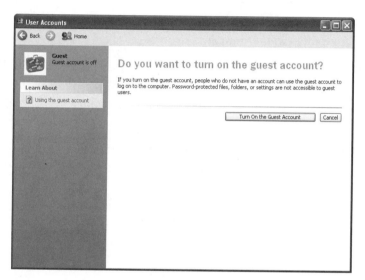

Figure 7-4   The Do You Want To Turn On The Guest Account window

4. Close the User Accounts window and the Control Panel window.

Lesson Review

Use the following questions to help determine whether you have learned enough to move on to the next lesson. If you have difficulty answering these questions, review the material in this lesson before beginning the next lesson. You can find answers to these questions in the "Questions and Answers" section at the end of this chapter.

1. Where do local user accounts allow users to log on and gain access to resources?

   _____

2. Where should you create user accounts for computers running Windows XP Professional that are part of a domain?

   _____

   _____

3. Which of the following statements about domain user accounts are correct? (Choose all that apply.)

   a. Domain user accounts allow users to log on to the domain and gain access to resources anywhere on the network, as long as the users have the required access permissions.

   b. If at least one computer on the network is configured as a domain controller, you should use domain user accounts only.

   c. The domain controller replicates the new user account information to all other computers in the domain.

   d. A new domain user account is established in the local security database on the domain controller on which you created the account.

4. Which of the following statements about built-in accounts are correct? (Choose all that apply.)

   a. You can delete the Guest account.

   b. You cannot delete the Administrator account.

   c. You cannot rename the Guest account.

   d. You can rename the Administrator account.

5. How do you disable the Guest account?

   _____

   _____

   _____

   _____

Lesson Summary

- Local user accounts allow users to log on at and access resources on only the computer on which you create the local user account. When you create a local user account, Windows XP Professional creates the account only in that computer's security database, which is called the local security database.

- Domain user accounts allow users to log on to the domain and access resources anywhere on the network. You create a domain user account in the copy of the Active Directory database (the *directory*) on a domain controller.

- Windows XP Professional automatically creates a number of built-in local user accounts. The two most important built-in local user accounts are Administrator and Guest. You cannot delete built-in accounts, but you can rename them or disable them.

- You can use the User Accounts tool to enable or disable the Guest account.

Lesson 2: Planning New User Accounts

On networks with more than just a few computers, you should take the time to create a plan for user accounts. In particular, you should establish a naming convention so that user account names are consistent. You should also establish password requirements for users.

After this lesson, you will be able to

- Establish an effective naming convention for your organization's local user accounts
- Create password requirements for protecting access to computers running Windows XP Professional

Estimated lesson time: 10 minutes

Naming Conventions

A **naming convention** is an organization's established standard for identifying users. Following a consistent naming convention, especially on large networks, helps administrators and users remember logon names. It also makes it easier for administrators to locate specific user accounts to add them to groups or perform account administration. Table 7-2 summarizes some guidelines for determining an effective naming convention for your organization.

Table 7-2   Naming Convention Guidelines

Guideline	Explanation
Create unique user logon names.	Local user account names must be unique on the computer on which you create the local user account. User logon names for domain user accounts must be unique to the directory. Common practices include the following: ■ Use the first and middle initials and the last name. A user named Kevin F. Browne, for example, would have the user name kfbrowne. ■ Separate first and last name with a period (.). A user named David Johnson would have the user name David.Johnson.
Use a maximum of 20 characters.	User account names can contain up to 20 uppercase or lowercase characters. The field accepts more than 20 characters, but Windows XP Professional recognizes only the first 20.
Remember that user logon names are not case sensitive.	You can use a combination of special and alphanumeric characters to establish unique user accounts. User logon names are not case sensitive, but Windows XP Professional preserves the case for display purposes.
Avoid characters that are not valid.	The following characters are not valid: " / \ [ ] : ; | = , + * ? < >

Table 7-2   Naming Convention Guidelines

Guideline	Explanation
Accommodate employees with duplicate names.	If two users have the same name, you could create a user logon name consisting of the first name, the last initial, and additional letters from the last name to differentiate the users. For example, if two users are named John Evans, you could create one user account logon as johne and the other as johnev. You could also number each user logon name—for example, johne1 and johne2.
Identify the type of employee.	Some organizations prefer to identify temporary employees in their user accounts. You could add a T and a dash in front of the user's logon name (T-johne) or use parentheses at the end—for example, johne(Temp).
Rename the Administrator and Guest built-in user accounts.	You should rename the Administrator and Guest accounts to provide greater security.

Password Guidelines

To protect access to the computer, every user account should have a password. Consider the following guidelines for passwords:

- Always assign a password to the Administrator account to prevent unauthorized access to the account.

- Determine whether the Administrator or the users will control passwords. You can assign unique passwords to user accounts and prevent users from changing them, or you can allow users to enter their own passwords the first time they log on. In most cases, users should control their passwords.

- Use passwords that are hard to guess. For example, avoid using passwords with an obvious association, such as a family member's name. Using a real name, a user name, or a company name makes for an easy-to-guess password. Also avoid using common passwords such as "letmein" or "password."

- Using a common dictionary word makes you vulnerable to automated programs that are designed to guess passwords.

- Using any password that you write down or that you share with someone else is not secure.

- Passwords can contain up to 128 characters; a minimum length of 8 characters is recommended.

- Include both uppercase and lowercase letters (unlike user names, user passwords are case sensitive), numerals, and the valid nonalphanumeric characters (such as punctuation).

- Using no password at all is not a good practice because it is then easy for other users to just walk up to an unsecured computer and log on.

If users find that complex passwords are difficult to remember, tell them that Windows XP allows the use of pass phrases instead of passwords. For example, a perfectly valid password in Windows XP is "My dog ate 2 turkeys last Thanksgiving." Another technique is to join together simple words with numbers and symbols. An example of a password that uses this technique is "2eggs+2bacon=1breakfast".

Exam Tip   You should understand the guidelines for creating strong passwords. In particular, remember that a password should be a minimum of eight characters and should include a mix of uppercase and lowercase letters, numbers, and symbols.

Security Alert   You can use a blank password by default on Windows XP Professional if the computer is a member of a workgroup. However, you will only be able to use this password to log on and access local resources on the computer. By default, the local security policy in Windows XP prohibits you from logging on to a remote computer if you have a blank password. The name of this security setting is Accounts: Limit Local Account Use Of Blank Passwords To Console Logon Only. You will learn more about local security policy in Chapter 16, "Configuring Security Settings and Internet Options."

Creating Strong Passwords

Weak passwords are a big security risk. You should encourage users to select and use strong passwords, even if they do not really want to. You can use the following guidelines to create strong passwords:

- Passwords should be at least eight characters long—and longer is better.

- Passwords should use a combination of lowercase and uppercase letters, numbers, and symbols (for example, ` ~ ! @ # $ % ^ & * ( ) _ + - = { } | [ ] \ : " ; ' < > ? , . / or a space character).

- Passwords should be changed regularly.

An example of a strong password using these guidelines is J5!if^8D.

Lesson Review

Use the following questions to help determine whether you have learned enough to move on to the next lesson. If you have difficulty answering these questions, review the material in this lesson before beginning the next lesson. You can find answers to these questions in the "Questions and Answers" section at the end of this chapter.

1. The maximum number of characters that Windows XP Professional recognizes in a local user account name is _____.

2. When are duplicate local user accounts valid in a network of computers running Windows XP Professional?

   _____

   _____

   _____

3. Passwords can be up to _____ characters long with a minimum length of _____ characters recommended.

Lesson Summary

- Local user account names must be unique on the computer on which you create the account, and domain user accounts must be unique to the directory. User logon names can contain up to 20 uppercase or lowercase characters. The User Name text box in the Log On To Windows dialog box accepts more than 20 characters, but Windows XP Professional recognizes only the first 20. The following characters are not valid: " / \ [ ] : ; | = , + * ? < >

- Passwords can be up to 128 characters long; a minimum of 8 characters is recommended. Use a mixture of uppercase and lowercase letters, numerals, and valid nonalphanumeric characters in creating passwords.

Lesson 3: Modifying, Creating, and Deleting User Accounts

Windows XP Professional provides two tools for modifying, creating, and deleting user accounts: the User Accounts tool in the Control Panel (for creating and managing user accounts in a workgroup) and the Computer Management snap-in (for creating and managing user accounts in a workgroup or domain).

After this lesson, you will be able to

- Manage users by using the User Accounts tool
- Manage users by using the Computer Management snap-in
- Create a password reset disk

Estimated lesson time: 50 minutes

User Accounts Tool

The User Accounts tool in the Control Panel (shown in Figure 7-5) is one of the tools that you use to modify, create, and delete local user accounts when working in a workgroup environment.

Figure 7-5   Use the User Accounts tool to perform limited user account tasks.

If you are logged on with an account that is a member of the Administrators group, the Pick A Task portion of the User Accounts tool allows you to perform the following tasks:

- Change an account (which includes deleting the account)
- Create a new user account
- Change the way users log on or log off

How to Modify an Existing User Account by Using the User Accounts Tool

If you are an administrator, the Change An Account task allows you to make changes to any user account on the computer. If you are logged on with a limited user account, you do not see the same Pick A Task page as an administrator; you see only a Pick A Task page that contains some of the following options that an administrator can perform:

- **Change My/The Name**   Changes the user account name of an account on the computer. You see this option only if you are logged on as an administrator because only an administrator can perform this task.

- **Create A Password**   Creates a password for your account. You only see this option if your user account does not have a password. Only an administrator can create passwords for other user accounts.

- **Change My/The Password**   Changes the password for your account. You only see this option if your user account already has a password signed to it; you see this option instead of the Create A Password option. Only an administrator can change passwords for other user accounts.

- **Remove My/The Password**   Removes the password for your account or any other account on the computer. You only see this option if your user account already has a password assigned to it. Only an administrator can remove passwords for other user accounts.

- **Change My/The Picture**   Changes the picture that appears on the Welcome screen. Only an administrator can change the pictures for other user accounts.

- **Change My/The Account Type**   Changes the account type for a specified account. Only an administrator can change the account type for a user account.

- **Set Up My Account To Use A .NET Passport**   Starts the Add A .NET Passport To Your Windows XP Professional Account Wizard. A passport allows you to have online conversations with family and friends, create your own personal Web pages, and sign in instantly to all Microsoft .NET–enabled sites and services. You can set up only your own account to use a .NET Passport.

■ **Delete The Account**   Deletes a specified user account. You only see this option if you are logged on as an administrator because only an administrator can perform this task.

> **Caution**   When you delete a user account, there is no way to recover the permissions and the rights that are associated with that account. Also, when you delete a user account, Windows XP Professional displays the Do You Want To Keep *local_user_account's* Files window. If you click Keep Files, Windows XP Professional saves the contents of the user's desktop and My Documents folder to a new folder named *local_user_account* on your desktop. However, it cannot save user's e-mail messages, Internet Favorites, or other settings.

To modify an account while logged on with a limited user account, complete the following steps:

1. Click Start, click Control Panel, and then click User Accounts.

   The Pick A Task page appears.

2. Click the appropriate option for the modification that you want to make, and then follow the prompts on the screen.

To change an account while logged on as an administrator, complete the following steps:

1. Click Start, click Control Panel, and then click User Accounts.

2. In the User Accounts window, click Change An Account.

   The Pick An Account To Change page appears. The account modifications that you can make on this page depend on the account type and how it is configured.

3. Click the account you want to change.

   The What Do You Want To Change About *account_name* Account page appears.

4. Click the appropriate option for the modification that you want to make, and then follow the prompts on the screen.

How to Change the Way That Users Log On or Off by Using the User Accounts Tool

Only administrators can change the way users log on or log off the computer. This option is available on the Pick A Task page only if you are logged on with a user account that is a member of the Administrators group.

The following options control how all users log on and log off the computer. Remember that these options are only available if the computer is a member of a workgroup and not if the computer is part of a domain.

- **Use The Welcome Screen**   This check box, enabled by default, allows you to click your user account on the Welcome screen to log on to the computer. If you clear this check box, you must type your user name and password at a logon prompt to log on.

- **Use Fast User Switching**   This check box, enabled by default, allows you to quickly switch to another user account without first logging off and closing all programs.

To change the way users log on or log off, complete the following steps:

1. Click Start, click Control Panel, and then click User Accounts.

2. In the User Accounts window, click Change The Way Users Log On Or Off. The Select Logon And Logoff Options window appears.

3. Select or clear the appropriate check boxes.

How to Create a New User Account in the User Accounts Tool

Only administrators can create new user accounts. This option is only available on the Pick A Task screen if you are logged on with a user account that is a member of the Administrators group.

To create a new user account, complete the following steps:

1. Click Start, click Control Panel, and then click User Accounts.

2. In the User Accounts window, click Create A New Account.

   The Name The New Account page appears.

3. In the Type A Name For The New Account box, type a user logon name (up to 20 characters), and then click Next.

> **Note**   The user's logon name appears in the Welcome screen and on the Start menu. For information about valid characters for creating user accounts, see Table 7-2.

The Pick An Account Type window appears. Windows XP Professional provides two account types: Computer Administrator and Limited. Table 7-3 lists the capabilities of each account type.

4. Select the appropriate account type, and then click Create Account.

Table 7-3   User Account Types and Capabilities

Capability	Computer Administrator	Limited Account
Change your own picture	X	X
Create, change, or remove your password	X	X
Change your own account type	X	
Change your own account name	X	
Change other users' pictures, passwords, account types, and account names	X	
Have full access to other user accounts	X	
Create user accounts on this computer	X	
Delete user accounts on this computer	X	
Access and read all files on this computer	X	
Install programs and hardware	X	
Make system-wide changes to the computer	X	

Computer Management Snap-In

The Computer Management snap-in, shown in Figure 7-6, provides a more sophisticated means of managing local users than the User Accounts tool. Using Computer Management, you can create, delete, and disable local user accounts. You can also create and manage local groups.

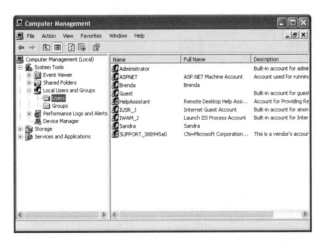

Figure 7-6   Use the Computer Management snap-in for a more detailed set of user account tasks.

How to Create a Local User Account by Using Computer Management

To create local user accounts by using the Computer Management snap-in complete the following steps:

1. From the Start menu, click Control Panel.

2. In the Control Panel window, click Performance And Maintenance.

3. In the Performance And Maintenance window, click Administrative Tools.

4. In the Administrative Tools window, double-click Computer Management.

> **Tip**   You can also access the Computer Management window by right-clicking the My Computer icon on the desktop or Start menu and clicking Manage.

5. In the console tree of the Computer Management window, click the Computer Management plus sign (+) icon to expand the tree. Computer Management contains three folders: System Tools, Storage, and Services And Applications.

6. In the console tree, expand System Tools, and then click Local Users And Groups.

7. In the details pane, right-click Users, and then click New User.

8. Fill in the appropriate text boxes in the New User dialog box (shown in Figure 7-7), click Create, and then click Close.

Figure 7-7   Create a new user.

Table 7-4 describes the user account options shown in Figure 7-8.

Table 7-4   Local User Account Options

Option	Action
User Name	Type the user's logon name. This field is required.
Full Name	Type the user's full name. You can include the user's first and last names, but you can also include the middle name or initial. This field is optional.
Description	Type descriptive text about the user account or the user. This field is optional.
Password	Type the account password that is used to authenticate the user. For greater security, always assign a password. As an additional security measure, the password appears as a string of asterisks as you type it.
Confirm Password	Confirm the password by typing it a second time. This field is required if you assign a password.
User Must Change Password At Next Logon	Select this check box if you want the user to change his or her password the first time that he or she logs on. This ensures that only the user knows the password. This option is selected by default.
User Cannot Change Password	Select this check box if more than one person uses the same user account (such as Guest), or if you want only administrators to control passwords. If you have selected the User Must Change Password At Next Logon check box, this option is not available.
Password Never Expires	Select this check box if you never want the password to change—for example, for a domain user account that a program or a Windows XP Professional service uses. The User Must Change Password At Next Logon option overrides this option, so if you have selected the User Must Change Password At Next Logon check box, this option is not available.
Account Is Disabled	Select this check box to prevent use of this account—for example, for a new employee who has not yet started working for your organization.

> **Security Alert**   Always require new users to change their passwords the first time they log on. This forces them to use passwords that only they know. For added network security, use a combination of letters and numbers to create unique initial passwords for all new user accounts.

How to Delete a User by Using Computer Management

You can also delete users in Computer Management. To delete a user by using the Computer Management snap-in, use these steps:

1. From the Start menu, click Control Panel.

2. In the Control Panel window, click Performance And Maintenance.

3. In the Performance And Maintenance window, click Administrative Tools.

4. In the Administrative Tools window, double-click Computer Management.

5. In the console tree of the Computer Management window, click the Computer Management plus sign (+) icon to expand the tree. Computer Management contains three folders: System Tools, Storage, and Services And Applications.

6. In the console tree, expand System Tools, and then click Local Users And Groups.

7. Under Local Users And Groups, click Users.

8. In the Details pane, right-click the user you want to delete and click Delete.

   Windows displays the Local Users And Groups dialog box, which warns you that when you delete a user, all permissions and rights associated with that user account are also lost.

9. In the Local Users And Groups dialog box, click Yes.

How to Create a Password Reset Disk

The **password reset disk** is a floppy disk that contains encrypted password information and allows users to change their password without knowing the old password. As standard practice, you should encourage users to create a password reset disk and keep it in a secure location.

To create a password reset disk for a domain-based user account, follow these steps:

1. Press CTRL+ALT+DEL, and then click Change Password.

2. In the User Name box, type the user name of the account for which you want to create a password reset disk.

3. In the Log On To box, click *ComputerName*, where *ComputerName* is your assigned computer name, and then click Backup.

4. Follow the steps in the Forgotten Password Wizard until the procedure is complete. Store the password reset disk in a secure place.

To create a password reset disk for a local user account, follow these steps:

1. From the Start menu, click Control Panel.

2. In Control Panel, click User Accounts.

3. If you are logged on using a Computer Administrator account, click the account name and then, in the Related Tasks list, select Prevent A Forgotten Password. If you are logged on using a Limited account, the Prevent A Forgotten Password option is located on the main page of the User Accounts window. (You do not have to click the account name first.)

4. Follow the steps in the Forgotten Password Wizard until the procedure is complete. Store the password reset disk in a secure place.

Users cannot change their password and create a password reset disk at the same time. If a user types a new password in the New Password and Confirm New Password boxes before the user clicks Backup, the new password information is not saved. When the wizard prompts a user for his current user account password, the user must type the old password.

A user can change a password anytime after creating a password reset disk. The user does not have to create a new password disk after changing a password or resetting a password manually.

When logging on, if a user forgets the password and has previously created a password reset disk, the user is presented with an option to reset his password by using the password reset disk. Select the option on the logon screen to launch the Password Reset Wizard. The Password Reset Wizard asks user to create a new password and hint. Log on with the new password and then return the password reset disk to its safe storage place. The user does not need to make a new password reset disk.

Practice: Modifying, Creating, and Deleting Local User Accounts

In this practice, you create a new local user account and assign it a password using the User Accounts tool. You then create a custom Microsoft Management Console (MMC) that contains the Computer Management snap-in and use the snap-in to create two more new user accounts. Then you test one of the newly created local user accounts. You complete the practice by using the User Accounts tool to delete a local user account.

After completing this practice, you will be able to accomplish the following tasks:

- Use the User Accounts tool to create a new local user account
- Create a customized MMC containing the Computer Management snap-in
- Use the Computer Management snap-in to create a new local user account

Exercise 1: Creating a New Local User Account by Using the User Accounts Tool

1. Log on with a user account that is a member of the Administrators group.
2. Click Start, click Control Panel, and then click User Accounts.
3. In the User Accounts window, under Pick A Task, click Create A New Account.
4. On the Name The New Account page, in the Type A Name For The New Account text box, type **User1**, and then click Next.
5. On the Pick An Account Type page, click Limited.

> **Note** If your account is a limited account type, you can change or remove your password, change the picture displayed with your account, and change your theme and other desktop settings. You can also view files that you created and files in the shared documents folder.

6. Click Create Account.

   Windows XP Professional displays the User Accounts window; User1 appears in the list of accounts.

7. Create an account named User2 using steps 3 through 6.

   Leave the User Accounts window open for the next exercise.

Exercise 2: Assigning a Password to a Local User Account by Using the User Accounts Tool

1. In the User Accounts window, click User1.

2. Click Create A Password.

3. Type **password** in both the Type A New Password text box and the Type The New Password Again To Confirm text box.

4. Type **the most commonly used password** in the Type A Word Or Phrase To Use As A Password Hint text box.

5. Click Create Password.

6. What two new options appear for User1's account? What option is no longer available?

   _____

   _____

   _____

7. Click the Home icon to return to the User Accounts window.

8. Assign User2 the password User2.

9. Close the User Accounts window and Control Panel.

Exercise 3: Creating a Customized MMC That Contains the Computer Management Snap-In

1. Click Start, and then click Run.

2. In the Open text box, type **mmc** and then click OK.

   The MMC starts and displays an empty console.

3. Maximize the Console1 window by clicking Maximize.

4. Maximize the Console Root window by clicking Maximize.

5. On the File menu, click Add/Remove Snap-In.

   The MMC displays the Add/Remove Snap-In dialog box.

6. Click Add.

   The MMC displays the Add Standalone Snap-In dialog box.

7. In the Available Standalone Snap-Ins list, click Computer Management and then click Add.

   The MMC displays the Computer Management dialog box, which allows you to specify the computer that you want to administer. The Local Computer option is selected by default.

8. In the Computer Management dialog box, click Finish.

   The MMC creates the console that contains the Computer Management snap-in for managing the local computer.

9. In the Add Standalone Snap-In dialog box, click Close.

10. In the Add/Remove Snap-In dialog box, click OK to place the Computer Management snap-in in your customized MMC.

    Computer Management (Local) now appears in the console tree.

11. On the File menu, click Save As.

    The MMC displays the Save As dialog box.

12. In the File Name text box, type **Computer Management Local**, and then click Save.

    The title bar is now Computer Management Local. You have just created a customized MMC containing the Computer Management snap-in and have named it Computer Management Local.

Exercise 4: Creating a New Local User Account by Using the Computer Management Snap-In

1. In the Computer Management Local window, in the console pane, click the plus sign in front of Computer Management (Local) to expand it.

   Computer Management contains three folders: System Tools, Storage, and Services And Applications.

2. In the console pane, expand System Tools, and then click Local Users And Groups.

3. In the details pane, right-click Users, and then select New User.

   The New User dialog box appears.

4. In the User Name text box, type **User3**.

5. In the Full Name text box, type **User Three**.

   Do not assign a password to the user account.

6. Confirm that the User Must Change Password At Next Logon check box is selected.

7. Click Create to create the new user, and then click Close.

8. Click Start, click Control Panel, and then click User Accounts.

   The User Accounts window appears.

9. What type of account is User3? (Get answer.)

   The account type for User3 is Limited Account.

10. Close the User Accounts window, and then close Control Panel.

11. In the Computer Management Local window, in the details pane, right-click Users, and then click New User.

12. In the User Name text box, type **User4**.

13. In the Full Name text box, type **User Four**.

14. In the Password and Confirm Password text boxes, type **User4**.

15. How does the password appear on the screen? Why?

   _____

   _____

> **Security Alert**   In high-security environments, assign initial passwords to user accounts and then require users to change their passwords the next time they log on. This accomplishes two goals: it prevents a user account from existing without a password and ensures that only the user knows the password. The password assigned in this exercise was for ease of use in the exercise. The passwords you assign should be difficult to guess and should include both uppercase and lowercase letters, numerals, and valid nonalphanumeric characters. For information about valid characters for creating user accounts, see Table 7-2.

16. Confirm that the User Must Change Password At Next Logon check box is selected, and then click Create.

17. Close the New User dialog box.

18. In the Computer Management console, on the File menu, click Exit to close the Computer Management custom MMC.

   The Microsoft Management Console dialog box appears, in which you indicate whether you want to save Console settings to Computer Management.

Note   If you click Yes, the next time you open the Computer Management console, it appears as it does now. If you click No, Windows XP Professional does not save the settings.

19. Click Yes to save the console settings.

20. Click Start, and then click Log Off.

    Windows XP Professional displays a Log Off Windows dialog box telling you to click Switch User if you want to leave programs running and switch to another user. Your other options are to click Log Off or Cancel.

21. In the Log Off Windows dialog box, click Log Off.

22. On the Welcome screen, click User Three.

23. What happens?

    _____

    _____

24. Click OK. The Change Password dialog box appears.

25. Leave the Old Password text box blank, and in the New Password and Confirm New Password text boxes, type **User3**, and then click OK.

    Windows XP Professional displays a Change Password dialog box indicating that the password has been changed.

26. Click OK to close the Change Password dialog box.

    The User3 user account that you created using the Computer Management snap-in allowed you to log on. Because you left the default check box, User Must Change Password At Next Logon, selected when you created the account, you were prompted to change passwords when you logged on as User3. You confirmed that the User3 user account was created with a blank password when you left the Old Password box blank and successfully changed the password to User3.

27. Log off the computer.

Exercise 5: Deleting a Local User Account

1. Log on with a user account that is a member of the Administrators group.

2. In the Control Panel, click User Accounts.

3. Click User Three.

    Windows XP Professional displays the What Do You Want To Change About User Three's Account window.

4. Click Delete The Account.

    Windows XP Professional displays the Do You Want To Keep User Three's Files window.

Exam Tip After you delete a user account, there is no way to recover the rights and permissions associated with that user account. A better practice than deleting user accounts is to disable them until you are sure they are no longer needed.

5. Click Delete Files.

   Windows XP Professional displays the Are You Sure You Want To Delete User Three's Account window.

6. Click Delete Account.

   Windows XP Professional displays the User Accounts window. Notice that the User3 account is no longer listed under Or Pick An Account To Change.

7. Close the User Accounts tool, and then close the Control Panel.

8. Log off the computer.

Lesson Review

Use the following questions to help determine whether you have learned enough to move on to the next lesson. If you have difficulty answering these questions, review the material in this lesson before beginning the next lesson. You can find answers to these questions in the "Questions and Answers" section at the end of this chapter.

1. Which of the following statements about the Windows XP Professional User Accounts tool are correct? (Choose all that apply.)

   a. The User Accounts tool allows you to remotely create, modify, and delete user accounts on all computers in the network running Windows XP Professional.

   b. The User Accounts tool allows you to view and modify all accounts on the computer.

   c. The tasks you can perform with the User Accounts tool depend on the type of account you use to log on to the local computer.

   d. The User Accounts tool allows users to delete, create, or remove their individual passwords.

2. Which of the following tasks can both account types (Computer Administrator and Limited) perform? (Choose all that apply.)

   a. Change your picture

   b. Change your account type

   c. Create, change, or remove your password

   d. Change your account name

3. Which of the following statements about logging on or logging off a computer running Windows XP Professional are true? (Choose all that apply.)

    a. When you use the Welcome screen to log on the local computer, you can quickly switch to another user account without logging off and closing all programs that you are running.

    b. The User Accounts tool allows you to disable a local user account to prevent users from using the disabled account to log on.

    c. When you use the Welcome screen to log on the local computer, you can log on using only one of the accounts displayed on the Welcome screen.

    d. The User Accounts tool allows you to replace the Welcome screen with a logon prompt that requires users to type their individual user names and passwords.

4. When you use the Computer Management snap-in to create a new user account, which check box do you select to prevent a new employee from using the new account until the employee starts working for the company?

_____

Lesson Summary

- The User Accounts tool allows administrators to create a new user account, change an existing account, and change the way a user logs on or logs off. The two check boxes that control the way users log on and log off the computer, Use The Welcome Screen and Use Fast User Switching, are available only on computers that are workgroup members and apply to all users. You cannot configure them for individual local user accounts.

- The Computer Management snap-in allows you to create, modify, and delete user accounts for the local computer on which you are working. If your computer is part of a network, you can use the Computer Management snap-in on a remote computer. The Computer Management snap-in provides all the functionality of the User Accounts tool and additional functionality, including the ability to view all accounts in the local security database and to disable accounts.

Lesson 4: Configuring Properties for User Accounts

Windows XP Professional creates a set of default account properties for each local user account. After you create a local user account, you can configure the account properties by using the Computer Management snap-in. The account properties are grouped under three tabs in the Properties dialog box for a user account: General, Member Of, and Profile.

After this lesson, you will be able to

■ Configure general properties for user accounts by using the General tab

■ Add a user account to groups by using the Members tab

■ Configure a user profile by using the Profile tab

Estimated lesson time: 30 minutes

The General Tab

The General tab in the Properties dialog box for a user account (shown in Figure 7-8) allows you to configure or edit all the fields from the New User dialog box except User Name, Password, and Confirm Password. In addition, it provides an Account Is Locked Out check box.

Figure 7-8   Configure basic user properties by using the General tab of the Properties dialog box for a user account.

If the account is active and is not locked out of the system, the Account Is Locked Out check box is unavailable. The system locks out a user who exceeds the limit for the number of failed logon attempts. This security feature makes it more difficult for an unauthorized user to break into the system by guessing passwords. If the system locks out an account, the Account Is Locked Out check box becomes available, and an administrator can clear the check box to allow user access. You will learn more about account lockout in Chapter 16.

The Member Of Tab

The Member Of tab in the Properties dialog box for a user account allows you to add the user account to or remove the user account from a group. For information about groups, see Lesson 5, "Implementing Groups."

The Profile Tab

The Profile tab in the Properties dialog box for a user account allows you to enter a path for the user profile, the logon script, and home folder (shown in Figure 7-9).

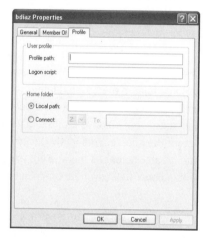

Figure 7-9   Configure user profiles, logon scripts, and home folders by using the Profile tab.

User Profile

A **user profile** is a collection of folders and data that stores your current desktop environment, application settings, and personal data. It also contains all the network connections that are established when you log on to a computer, such as Start menu items and drives mapped to network servers. The user profile maintains consistency by providing the same desktop environment every time you log on to the computer.

Windows XP Professional creates a user profile the first time you log on to a computer and stores it on that computer. This user profile is also known as a local user profile.

User profiles on client computers running Windows XP Professional operate in the following way:

- User profiles are stored locally in a subfolder of the Documents And Settings folder. The subfolder has the same name as the user account and contains important user folders, such as My Documents, Favorites, and Desktop. The user profile folder also stores application data and Windows settings pertinent to the user.

- When you log on the client computer, you always receive your desktop settings and connections, regardless of how many users share the same client computer.

- The first time you log on to the client computer, Windows XP Professional creates a default user profile for you. The default user profile is stored in the *system_partition_root*\Documents and Settings*user_logon_name* folder (typically C:\Documents and Settings*user_logon_name*), where *user_logon_name* is the name you enter when logging on to the system.

- The user profile contains the My Documents folder, which provides a place to store personal files. My Documents is the default location for the *File Open* and *Save As* commands. My Documents appears on the Start menu, which makes it easier to locate personal documents.

Important   Users can store their documents in My Documents or in home folders, such as a home directory that is located on a network server. Home folders are covered later in this lesson. Windows XP Professional automatically sets up My Documents as the default location for storing data for Microsoft applications. If there is adequate room on drive C or the drive where Windows XP Professional was installed, users can store their documents in My Documents. However, using My Documents to store personal data greatly increases the amount of space required on a hard disk for installing Windows XP Professional well beyond the minimum.

- You can change your user profile by changing desktop settings. For example, if you make a new network connection or add a file to My Documents, Windows XP Professional incorporates the changes into your user profile when you log off. The next time you log on, the new network connection and the file are present.

Logon Script

A logon script is a file that you can create and assign to a user account to configure the user's working environment. For example, you can use a logon script to establish network connections or start applications. Each time a user logs on, the assigned logon script is run.

Home Folder

In addition to the My Documents folder, Windows XP Professional allows you to create home folders for users to store their personal documents. You can store a home folder on a client computer, in a shared folder on a file server, or in a central location on a network server.

Storing all home folders on a file server provides the following advantages:

■ Users can access their home folders from any client computer on the network.

■ You can centralize backing up and administering user documents by moving the responsibility for backing up and managing the documents out of the hands of the users and into the hands of one of the network backup operators or network administrators.

Note   The home folders are accessible from a client computer running any Microsoft operating system, including MS-DOS, Windows 95, Windows 98, Windows 2000 Professional, and Windows XP Professional.

Important   Store home folders on an NTFS volume so that you can use NTFS permissions to control access to user documents. If you store home folders on a file allocation table (FAT) volume, you can restrict home folder access only by using shared folder permissions.

To create a home folder on a network file server, complete the following steps:

1. Create and share a folder for storing all users' home folders on a network server.

   The home folder for each user will reside in this shared folder.

2. For the shared folder, remove the default Full Control permission from the Everyone group and assign Full Control to the Users group.

   This ensures that only users with domain user accounts can access the shared folder.

3. In the Properties dialog box for the user account, on the Profile tab, click Connect and select or type a drive letter with which to connect to the user account home folder on the network.

4. In the To text box, type a Universal Naming Convention (UNC) name (*server_ name**shared_folder_name**user_logon_name*).

   Type the *username* variable as the user's logon name to automatically give each user's home folder the user logon name (for example, \\server_name\Users\ %*username*%). Naming a folder on an NTFS volume with the *username* variable assigns the NTFS Full Control permission to the user and removes all other permissions for the folder, including those for the Administrator account.

To configure User Account properties, complete the following steps:

1. Click Start, point to All Programs, point to Administrative Tools, and click Computer Management.

2. Under System Tools, expand Local Users And Groups, and then click Users.

3. In the details pane, right-click the appropriate user account and then click Properties.

4. Click the appropriate tab for the properties that you want to configure or modify, and then enter a value for each property.

Practice: Modifying User Account Properties

This practice presents exercises that allow you to modify user account properties and test them.

1. Log on with a user account that is a member of the Administrators group.

2. Click Start, click Run, type **mmc** and then click OK.

   The MMC starts and displays an empty console.

3. On the File menu, click Computer Management Local.

4. Expand Local Users And Groups, and then click Users.

   The MMC displays the user accounts in the details pane.

5. Right-click User1, and then click Properties.

6. In the User1 Properties dialog box, on the General tab, select User Cannot Change Password, and then clear all other check boxes.

> **Tip**   When you select the User Cannot Change Password check box, the User Must Change Password At Next Logon option is unavailable.

7. Click OK to close the User1 Properties dialog box.

8. Right-click User2, and then click Properties.

9. In the User2 Properties dialog box, on the General tab, select the Account Is Disabled check box and clear all other check boxes.

10. Click OK to close the User2 Properties dialog box.

11. Close the Computer Management window, and if you are prompted about saving the console settings, click No.

12. Log off the computer.

13. On the Welcome screen, click User1.

14. In the Type Your Password dialog box, click the question mark icon for your password hint.

    Windows XP Professional displays the password hint you entered.

15. In the Type Your Password text box, type **password** and then press ENTER.

16. In the Control Panel, click User Accounts.

    Windows XP Professional starts the User Accounts tool.

17. Click Change My Password.

18. In the Type Your Current Password text box, type **password**.

19. In the Type A New Password and Type The New Password Again To Confirm text boxes, Type **User1**.

20. Click Change Password.

21. What happens? Why?

    _____

    _____

    _____

22. Log off as User1.

    Notice that disabled accounts such as User2 do not appear on the Welcome screen.

Lesson Review

Use the following questions to help determine whether you have learned enough to move on to the next lesson. If you have difficulty answering these questions, review the material in this lesson before beginning the next lesson. You can find answers to these questions in the "Questions and Answers" section at the end of this chapter.

1. When can you select the Account Is Locked Out check box for a user and why?

    _____

    _____

    _____

2. Which of the following statements about local user account properties are correct? (Choose all that apply.)

   a. You can configure all of the default properties associated with each local user account using the User Accounts tool located in the Control Panel.

   b. In Computer Management, the General tab in a user account's Properties dialog box allows you to disable the account.

   c. In Computer Management, the General tab in a user account's Properties dialog box allows you to select the Account Is Locked Out check box to prevent the user from logging on to the computer.

   d. You can use the Computer Management snap-in to configure all of the default properties associated with each local user account.

3. Which of the following statements about user profiles are correct? (Choose all that apply.)

   a. A user profile is a collection of folders and data that stores the user's current desktop environment, application settings, and personal data.

   b. A user profile contains all the network connections that are established when a user logs on to a computer.

   c. Windows XP Professional creates a user profile when you create a new local user account.

   d. You must create each user profile by copying and modifying an existing user profile.

4. Which of the following statements about user profiles are correct? (Choose all that apply.)

   a. Users should store their documents in home directories rather than in their My Documents folders.

   b. The Profile tab in the account-name Properties dialog box for a user account allows you to create a path for the user profile, logon script, and home folder.

   c. A user profile contains the My Documents folder, which provides a place for users to store personal files.

   d. When users change their desktop settings, the changes are reflected in their user profiles.

5. What three tasks must you perform to create a home folder on a network server?

_____

_____

_____

_____

_____

_____

Lesson Summary

- The General tab in a user account's Properties dialog box allows you to configure or edit all the fields from the New User dialog box except for User Name, Password, and Confirm Password. In addition, it provides an Account Is Locked Out check box.

- The Member Of tab in a user account's Properties dialog box allows you to add the user account to or remove the user account from a group.

- The Profile tab in a user account's Properties dialog box for a user account allows you to create a path for the user profile, logon script, and home folder.

Lesson 5: Implementing Groups

In this lesson, you will learn what groups are and how you can use them to simplify user account administration. You will also learn about built-in groups, which have a predetermined set of user rights and group membership, and about special groups, which you cannot add members to yourself but for which Windows creates memberships dynamically. Windows XP Professional has two categories of built-in groups, local and system, which it creates for you to simplify the process of assigning rights and permissions for commonly used functions.

After this lesson, you will be able to
- Explain the purpose of a group
- Identify guidelines for using local groups
- Create a local group
- Add members to a local group
- Delete a local group
- Identify the built-in local groups
- Identify the built-in system groups

Estimated lesson time: 40 minutes

What Is a Group?

A **group** is a collection of user accounts. Groups simplify administration by allowing you to assign permissions and rights to a group of users rather than to each user account individually (shown in Figure 7-10).

Permissions control what users can do with a resource such as a folder, a file, or a printer. When you assign permissions, you allow users to gain access to a resource and you define the type of access that they have. For example, if several users need to read the same file, you can add their user accounts to a group and then give the group permission to read the file. **Rights** allow users to perform system tasks, such as changing the time on a computer and backing up or restoring files.

See Also For more information about permissions, see Chapter 8, "Securing Resources with NTFS Permissions." For more information about rights, see Chapter 16.

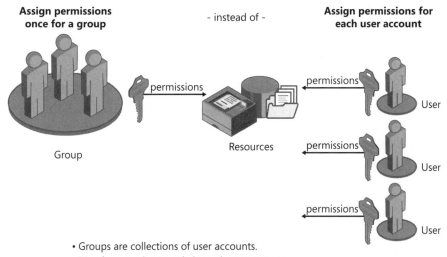

Assign permissions once for a group   - instead of -   **Assign permissions for each user account**

permissions

Group

Resources

permissions → User

permissions → User

permissions → User

- Groups are collections of user accounts.
- Members receive permissions given to groups.
- Users can be members of multiple groups.
- Groups can be members of other groups.

Figure 7-10   Groups simplify administration.

Guidelines for Using Local Groups

A local group is a collection of user accounts on a computer. Use local groups to assign permissions to resources residing on the computer on which the local group is created. Windows XP Professional creates local groups in the local security database.

Guidelines for using local groups include the following:

- Before creating a new group, determine whether a built-in group (or other existing group) fits your needs. For example, if all users need access to a resource, use the built-in Users group.

- Use local groups on computers that do not belong to a domain. You can use local groups only on the computer on which you create them. Although local groups are available on member servers and domain computers running Windows 2000 Server or later, do not use local groups on computers that are part of a domain. Using local groups on domain computers prevents you from centralizing group administration. Local groups do not appear in the Active Directory service, and you must administer them separately for each computer.

- You can assign permissions to local groups to access only the resources on the computer on which you create the local groups.

Note   You cannot create local groups on domain controllers because domain controllers cannot have a security database that is independent of the database in Active Directory.

Membership rules for local groups include the following:

- Local groups can contain local user accounts from the computer on which you create the local groups. On a domain-joined system, local groups can also contain domain users, domain computers, and all three types of domain groups (or, in short, any domain security principal).

- Local groups cannot belong to any other group.

How to Create Local Groups

Use the Computer Management snap-in to create local groups in the Groups folder.

To create a local group, complete the following steps:

1. In Computer Management, expand Local Users And Groups.

2. Right-click Groups, and then click New Group.

   The MMC displays the New Group dialog box (shown in Figure 7-11). Table 7-5 describes the available options.

Figure 7-11 Create a new group using the Computer Management snap-in.

3. Enter the appropriate information, and then click Create.

Table 7-5 New Local Group Options

Option	Description
Group Name	Requires a unique name for the local group. This is the only required entry. Use any character except for the backslash (\). The name can contain up to 256 characters, but very long names might not display in some windows.
Description	Describes the group.

Table 7-5   New Local Group Options

Option	Description
Members	Lists the user accounts belonging to the group.
Add	Adds a user to the list of members.
Remove	Removes a user from the list of members.
Create	Creates the group.
Close	Closes the New Group dialog box.

How to Add Members to a Local Group

You can add members to a local group when you create the group by clicking Add in the New Group dialog box. In addition, Windows XP Professional provides two methods for adding members to a group that has already been created: by using the Properties dialog box of the group or by using the Member Of tab in the Properties dialog box for a user account.

To add members to a group by using the Properties dialog box of the group, follow these steps:

1. Start the Computer Management snap-in.

2. Expand Local Users And Groups, and then click Groups.

3. In the details pane, right-click the appropriate group and then click Properties.

   Computer Management displays Properties dialog box for the group.

4. Click Add.

   Computer Management displays the Select Users dialog box, as shown in Figure 7-12.

Figure 7-12   Type a user name in the Select Users dialog box.

5. In the From This Location text box, ensure that the computer on which you created the group is selected.

6. In the Select Users dialog box, in the Enter The Object Names To Select text box, type the user account names that you want to add to the group, separated by semicolons, and then click OK.

> **Tip**   The Member Of tab in Properties dialog box of a user account allows you to add a user account to multiple groups. Use this method to quickly add the same user account to multiple groups.

How to Delete Local Groups

Use the Computer Management snap-in to delete local groups. Each group that you create has a unique identifier that cannot be used again. Windows XP Professional uses this value to identify the group and its assigned permissions. When you delete a group, Windows XP Professional does not use the identifier again, even if you create a new group with the same name as the group that you deleted. Therefore, you cannot restore access to resources by re-creating the group.

When you delete a group, you remove only the group and its associated permissions and rights. Deleting a group does not delete the user accounts that are members of the group. To delete a group, right-click the group name in the Computer Management snap-in and then click Delete.

Built-In Local Groups

All computers running Windows XP Professional have built-in local groups. These groups give rights to perform system tasks on a single computer, such as backing up and restoring files, changing the system time, and administering system resources. Windows XP Professional places the built-in local groups in the Groups folder in Computer Management.

Table 7-6 lists the most commonly used built-in local groups and describes their capabilities. Except where noted, these groups do not include initial members.

Table 7-6   Built-In Local Group Capabilities

Local Group	Description
Administrators	Members can perform all administrative tasks on the computer. By default, the built-in Administrator account is a member. When a member server or a computer running Windows XP Professional joins a domain, the domain controller adds the Domain Admins group to the local Administrators group.
Backup Operators	Members can use Windows Backup to back up and restore the computer.
Guests	Members can do the following: ■ Perform only the tasks for which they have been specifically granted rights ■ Access only those resources for which they have assigned permissions Members cannot make permanent changes to their desktop environment. By default, the built-in Guest account is a member. When a member server or a computer running Windows XP Professional joins a domain, the domain controller adds the Domain Guests group to the local Guests group.
Power Users	Members can create and modify local user accounts on the computer and share resources.
Replicator	Supports file replication in a domain.
Users	Members can do the following: ■ Perform only the tasks for which they have been specifically granted rights ■ Access only those resources for which they have assigned permissions By default, Windows XP Professional adds to the Users group all local user accounts that an administrator creates on the computer. When a member server or a computer running Windows XP Professional joins a domain, the domain controller adds the Domain Users group to the local Users group.

Built-In System Groups

Built-in system groups exist on all computers running Windows XP Professional. System groups do not have specific memberships that you can modify; instead, they represent different users at different times, depending on how a user gains access to a computer or resource. You do not see system groups when you administer groups, but they are available when you assign rights and permissions to resources. Windows XP Professional bases system group membership on how the computer is accessed, not on who uses the computer. Table 7-7 lists the most commonly used built-in system groups and describes their capabilities.

Table 7-7 Built-In System Group Capabilities

System Group	Description
Everyone	All users who access the computer. By default, when you format a volume with NTFS, the Full Control permission is assigned to the Everyone group. This presented a problem in earlier versions of Windows, including Windows 2000. In Windows XP Professional, the Anonymous Logon is no longer included in the Everyone group. When a Windows 2000 Professional system is upgraded to a Windows XP Professional system, resources with permission entries for the Everyone group and not explicitly for the Anonymous Logon group are no longer available to the Anonymous Logon group.
Authenticated Users	All users with valid user accounts on the computer. (If your computer is part of a domain, it includes all users in Active Directory.)
Creator Owner	The user account for the user who created or took ownership of a resource. If a member of the Administrators group creates a resource, the Administrators group owns the resource.
Network	Any user with a current connection from another computer on the network to a shared resource on the computer.
Interactive	The user account for the user who is logged on at the computer. Members of the Interactive group can access resources on the computer at which they are physically located. They log on and access resources by "interacting" with the computer.
Anonymous Logon	Any user account that Windows XP Professional cannot authenticate.
Dialup	Any user who currently has a dial-up connection.

Practice: Creating and Managing Local Groups

In this practice, you create two local groups, and then add members to the local groups after you create them. You delete a member from one of the groups, and then delete one of the local groups that you created.

Exercise 1: Creating Local Groups

In this exercise, you create two local groups, Accounting and Marketing.

1. Log on with a user account that is a member of the Administrators group.

2. Click Start, point to All Programs, point to Administrative Tools, and then click Computer Management.

   Windows XP Professional starts Computer Management.

3. Under System Tools, if necessary, expand Local Users And Groups, right-click Groups, and then click New Group.

4. In the New Group dialog box, in the Group Name text box, type **Accounting**.

5. In the Description text box, type **Access to Accounts Receivable Files**.

6. Click Add.

7. In the Select Users dialog box, in the Name text box, type **User1; User2; User4** and then click OK.

   User1, User2, and User4 appear in the Members list in the New Group dialog box.

8. Click Create.

   Windows XP Professional creates the group and adds it to the list of groups in the details pane. Notice that the New Group dialog box is still open and might block your view of the list of groups.

9. Repeat steps 4 through 8 to create a group named Marketing with a description of Access To Mailing Lists and User2 and User4 as group members.

10. When you finish creating both the Accounting and the Marketing groups, click Close to close the New Group dialog box.

    The Accounting and the Marketing groups now appear in the details pane.

Exercise 2: Adding and Removing Members

In this exercise, you add members to both groups that you created in the previous exercise. You add a member to the existing Marketing group, and then remove a member from the Marketing group.

1. In the details pane of the Computer Management window, double-click Marketing.

   The Marketing Properties dialog box displays the properties of the group. Notice that User2 and User4 are in the Members list.

2. To add a member to the group, click Add.

   Computer Management displays the Select Users dialog box.

3. In the Name text box, type **User1**, and then click OK.

   The Marketing Properties dialog box now displays User1, User2, and User4 in the Members list.

4. Select User4, and then click Remove.

   Notice that User4 is no longer in the Members list. User4 still exists as a local user account, but it is no longer a member of the Marketing group.

5. Click OK.

Exercise 3: Deleting a Local Group

1. In the details pane of the Computer Management window, right-click Marketing, and then click Delete.

   Computer Management displays a Local Users And Groups dialog box asking whether you are sure that you want to delete the group.

2. Click Yes.

   Marketing is no longer listed in the details pane indicating that the Marketing group was successfully deleted.

3. In the console pane of the Computer Management window, click Users.

   User1 and User2 are still listed in the details pane indicating that the group was deleted, but the members of the group were not deleted from the Users folder.

4. Close Computer Management.

Lesson Review

Use the following questions to help determine whether you have learned enough to move on to the next lesson. If you have difficulty answering these questions, review the material in this lesson before beginning the next lesson. You can find answers to these questions in the "Questions and Answers" section at the end of this chapter.

1. What are groups, and why do you use them?

   _____

   _____

   _____

2. An administrator or owner of a resource uses _____ to control what users can do with a resource such as a folder, a file, or a printer.

3. You use local groups to assign permissions to resources residing _____

   _____.

4. Which of the following statements about deleting local groups are correct? (Choose all that apply.)

    a. Each group that you create has a unique identifier that cannot be reused.

    b. You can restore access to resources by re-creating the group.

    c. When you delete a group, you also remove the permissions and rights associated with it.

    d. Deleting a group deletes the user accounts that are members of the group.

5. What is the difference between built-in system groups and built-in local groups found on computers running Windows XP Professional? Give at least two examples of each type of group.

    _____

    _____

    _____

    _____

    _____

    _____

    _____

    _____

    _____

    _____

    _____

Lesson Summary

- Groups simplify administration by allowing you to assign permissions and rights to a group of users rather than to individual user accounts. Permissions control what users can do with a resource such as a folder, file, or printer. Rights allow users to perform system tasks, such as changing the time on a computer and backing up or restoring files.

- Windows XP Professional creates local groups in the local security database, so you can use local groups only on the computer on which you create them.

- You can use the Computer Management snap-in to create, add members to, and delete local groups.

- All computers running Windows XP Professional have built-in local groups that give rights to perform system tasks on a single computer.

- Computers running Windows XP Professional also have built-in system groups whose membership is determined dynamically.

Case Scenario Exercise

In this exercise, you will read a scenario about creating users and groups and then answer the questions that follow. If you have difficulty completing this work, review the material in this chapter before beginning the next chapter. You can find answers to these questions in the "Questions and Answers" section at the end of this chapter.

Scenario

You are an administrator working for the Baldwin Museum of Science. The museum has hired a number of temporary workers that will be researching information for a new exhibit on the history of coal use in northern Europe. Each of these workers has been assigned a workstation in a small workgroup that the museum has set up in the exhibit room. One computer in the workgroup is acting as a file server where the workers will store their research files. All workstations and the file server are running Windows XP Professional.

The temporary researchers' names are as follows:

- Cat Francis
- David Jaffe
- Mary North
- Jeff Teper
- Bernhard Tham

Questions

1. Your first task is to create a naming convention for these workers. The museum management would like the user names to reflect that these are temporary workers, but not require too complicated a user name for the workers to type. Use the following table to create names for the workers.

Full Name	User Account Name
Cat Francis	
David Jaffe	
Mary North	
Jeff Teper	
Bernhard Tham	

2. Where should you create these user names?

_____

_____

_____

3. The file server in the workgroup contains a folder named Coal Research, to which each of the workers needs access. You would like to minimize the number of times you have to assign permissions to the Research folder. How would you do this?

_____

_____

_____

_____

4. When creating passwords for the users on their workstations, what must you ensure so that the users can access the file server?

_____

_____

_____

_____

_____

_____

Troubleshooting Lab

You are working as an administrator for Tailspin Toys, a manufacturer of remote-controlled airplanes. Raymond, one of your junior administrators, tells you that he received a call from Martin, a user in the Sales department, who shares a workstation with two other users. Martin complained to Raymond that he had forgotten the password for his local user account and could not log on to his computer. Raymond intended to use Computer Management to reset Martin's password, but accidentally deleted the user account instead. He says that he clicked Yes in the dialog box that warned him about the deletion, thinking that the message was warning him about resetting the password instead.

1. Martin's user account was assigned permissions to access a number of resources on the computer and Raymond is not sure exactly what permissions were assigned. He wants to recover the deleted user account. Can he do this? If so, how?

   _____

   _____

2. If you really mean to delete the user account, what is often a better way to handle the situation than simply deleting the user account?

   _____

   _____

   _____

   _____

3. To prevent a situation like the one that happened with Raymond (in which rights and permissions to resources were assigned directly to Martin's user account and were thus difficult to reconstruct), what is a better way to assign rights and permissions?

   _____

   _____

   _____

   _____

   _____

   _____

   _____

4. Soon after creating a new user account for Martin, Raymond contacts you and tells you that Martin has forgotten his new password. Can you reset his password? How?

   _____

   _____

   _____

   _____

5. What should you tell Martin to do so that he can recover his own password should this happen again?

   _____

Chapter Summary

- Local user accounts allow users to log on at and access resources on only the computer on which you create the local user account. Domain user accounts allow users to log on to the domain and access resources anywhere on the network.

- Local user account names must be unique on the computer on which you create the account, and domain user accounts must be unique to the directory. Passwords can be up to 128 characters long; a minimum of 8 characters is recommended. Use a mixture of uppercase and lowercase letters, numerals, and valid nonalphanumeric characters in creating passwords.

- You can administer local user accounts using the following two tools:

  ❏ The User Accounts tool allows administrators to create a new user account, change an existing account, and change the way a user logs on or logs off.

  ❏ The Computer Management snap-in allows you to create, modify, and delete user accounts for the local computer on which you are working. If your computer is part of a network, you can use the Computer Management snap-in on a remote computer.

- After creating a user account, you can modify the properties for the account by using the Properties dialog box for the user account in Computer Management.

- Groups simplify administration by allowing you to assign permissions and rights to a group of users rather than to individual user accounts. Windows XP Professional creates local groups in the local security database, so you can use local groups only on the computer on which you create them.

Exam Highlights

Before taking the exam, review the key points and terms that are presented in this chapter. You need to know this information.

Key Points

- A domain does not recognize local user accounts, so do not create local user accounts on computers running Windows XP Professional that are part of a domain. Doing so restricts users from accessing resources in the domain and prevents the domain administrator from administering the local user account properties or assigning access permissions for domain resources.

- Allow Guest access only in low-security workgroups, and always assign a password to the Guest account. You can rename the Guest account, but you cannot delete it.

- You should understand the guidelines for creating strong passwords. In particular, remember that a password should be a minimum of eight characters and should include a mix of uppercase and lowercase letters, numbers, and symbols.

- After you delete a user account, there is no way to recover the rights and permissions associated with that user account. A better practice than deleting user accounts is to disable them until you are sure they are no longer needed.

Key Terms

Computer Management A console that provides access to a number of management utilities for administering a computer, including the ability to create, manage, and monitor shared folders.

domain user account An account that allows you to log on to a domain to access network resources.

group A collection of user accounts. Groups simplify administration by allowing you to assign permissions and rights to a group of users rather than to each user account individually.

local security database A database on a computer running Windows XP Professional that holds local user accounts and groups.

local user account An account that allows you to log on to a specific computer to access resources on that computer.

naming convention An organization's established standard for identifying users.

password reset disk A floppy disk that contains encrypted password information and allows users to change their password without knowing the old password.

Permissions Permissions control what users can do with a resource such as a folder, a file, or a printer.

Rights Rights allow users to perform system tasks, such as changing the time on a computer and backing up or restoring files.

user profile A collection of folders and data that stores your current desktop environment, application settings, and personal data.

Questions and Answers

Lesson 1 Review

Page
7-7

1. Where do local user accounts allow users to log on and gain access to resources?

Only on the computer on which the local user account is created.

2. Where should you create user accounts for computers running Windows XP Professional that are part of a domain?

You should create it on one of the domain controllers. You should not use local user accounts on Windows XP Professional computers that are part of a domain.

3. Which of the following statements about domain user accounts are correct? (Choose all that apply.)

   a. Domain user accounts allow users to log on to the domain and gain access to resources anywhere on the network, as long as the users have the required access permissions.

   b. If at least one computer on the network is configured as a domain controller, you should use domain user accounts only.

   c. The domain controller replicates the new user account information to all other computers in the domain.

   d. A new domain user account is established in the local security database on the domain controller on which you created the account.

The correct answers are A and B. C is not correct because the domain controller replicates user account information only to other domain controllers in a domain—not to every computer. D is not correct because a domain user account is established in Active Directory, not in the local security database. A local user account is established in the local security database.

4. Which of the following statements about built-in accounts are correct? (Choose all that apply.)

   a. You can delete the Guest account.

   b. You cannot delete the Administrator account.

   c. You cannot rename the Guest account.

   d. You can rename the Administrator account.

The correct answers are B and D. A is not correct because you cannot delete the Guest account (or any built-in local user accounts, for that matter). C is not correct because you can rename the Guest account.

5. How do you disable the Guest account?

Click Start, click Control Panel, and then click User Accounts. In the User Accounts window, click the Guest icon. In the What Do You Want To Change About The Guest Account window, click Turn Off The Guest Account. The Guest Account is now disabled.

Lesson 2 Review

Page
7-12
1. The maximum number of characters that Windows XP Professional recognizes in a local user account name is _____.

20

2. When are duplicate local user accounts valid in a network of computers running Windows XP Professional?

They are valid as long as they are not on the same computer. In fact, in a workgroup, you must create the same user account on each computer in the workgroup that you want the user to be able to access.

3. Passwords can be up to _____ characters long with a minimum length of _____ characters recommended.

128, 8

Page
7-22
Lesson 3 Practice: Exercise 2

6. What two new options appear for User1's account? What option is no longer available?

The list of changes you can make to the user's account includes two new options: Change The Password and Remove The Password. The Create A Password option is gone.

Lesson 3 Practice: Exercise 4

Page
7-23
1. What type of account is User3? (Get answer.)

The account type for User3 is Limited Account.

15. How does the password appear on the screen? Why?

The password is displayed as large dots as you type. This prevents others from viewing the password as you type it.

23. What happens?

A Logon Message dialog box appears, informing you that you are required to change your password at first logon.

Lesson 3 Review

Page
7-26
1. Which of the following statements about the Windows XP Professional User Accounts tool are correct? (Choose all that apply.)

a. The User Accounts tool allows you to remotely create, modify, and delete user accounts on all computers in the network running Windows XP Professional.

b. The User Accounts tool allows you to view and modify all accounts on the computer.

c. The tasks you can perform with the User Accounts tool depend on the type of account you use to log on to the local computer.

d. The User Accounts tool allows users to delete, create, or remove their individual passwords.

The correct answers are C and D. A is not correct because you cannot use the User Accounts tool to administer a remote computer. B is not correct because the User Accounts tool does not allow you to administer certain built-in accounts.

2. Which of the following tasks can both account types (Computer Administrator and Limited) perform? (Choose all that apply.)

a. Change your picture

b. Change your account type

c. Create, change, or remove your password

d. Change your account name

The correct answers are A and C. B and D are not correct because only computer administrators can change the account type and account name.

3. Which of the following statements about logging on or logging off a computer running Windows XP Professional are true? (Choose all that apply.)

a. When you use the Welcome screen to log on the local computer, you can quickly switch to another user account without logging off and closing all programs that you are running.

b. The User Accounts tool allows you to disable a local user account to prevent users from using the disabled account to log on.

c. When you use the Welcome screen to log on the local computer, you can log on using only one of the accounts displayed on the Welcome screen.

d. The User Accounts tool allows you to replace the Welcome screen with a logon prompt that requires users to type their individual user names and passwords.

The correct answers are A and D. B is not correct because the User Accounts tool allows you to disable the Guest account, but not to disable other user accounts. C is not correct because you can press CTRL+ALT+DELETE at the Welcome screen to access the traditional logon dialog box, which allows you to type in a user name.

4. When you use the Computer Management snap-in to create a new user account, which check box do you select to prevent a new employee from using the new account until the employee starts working for the company?

Account Disabled

Lesson 4 Practice: Modifying User Account Properties

Page
7-32

1. What happens? Why?

A User Accounts dialog box appears with the message Windows Cannot Change The Password. This happens because you enabled the User Cannot Change Password option for User1.

Lesson 4 Review

Page
7-33

1. When can you select the Account Is Locked Out check box for a user and why?

Never because the Account Is Locked Out check box is unavailable when the account is active and is not locked out of the system. The system locks out a user if the user exceeds the limit for the number of failed logon attempts.

2. Which of the following statements about local user account properties are correct? (Choose all that apply.)

a. You can configure all of the default properties associated with each local user account using the User Accounts tool located in Control Panel.

b. In Computer Management, the General tab in a user account's Properties dialog box allows you to disable the account.

c. In Computer Management, the General tab in a user account's Properties dialog box allows you to select the Account Is Locked Out check box to prevent the user from logging on to the computer.

d. You can use the Computer Management snap-in to configure all of the default properties associated with each local user account.

The correct answers are B and D. A is not correct because the User Accounts tool only provides a limited subset of the available options for a user account. You must use the Computer Management snap-in to access all options for a user account. C is not correct because you cannot select the Account Is Locked Out check box manually. This check box is selected automatically when an account is locked out.

3. Which of the following statements about user profiles are correct? (Choose all that apply.)

a. A user profile is a collection of folders and data that stores the user's current desktop environment, application settings, and personal data.

b. A user profile contains all the network connections that are established when a user logs on to a computer.

c. Windows XP Professional creates a user profile when you create a new local user account.

d. You must create each user profile by copying and modifying an existing user profile.

The correct answers are A and B. C is not correct because Windows XP does not create a user profile when you create a user account, but rather the first time someone logs on using that user account. D is not correct because a user profile is created automatically the first time a person logs on with a user account.

4. Which of the following statements about user profiles are correct? (Choose all that apply.)

a. Users should store their documents in home directories rather than in their My Documents folders.

b. The Profile tab in the account-name Properties dialog box for a user account allows you to create a path for the user profile, logon script, and home folder.

c. A user profile contains the My Documents folder, which provides a place for users to store personal files.

d. When users change their desktop settings, the changes are reflected in their user profiles.

The correct answers are B, C, and D. A is not correct because the My Documents folder is located within a user's home directory automatically when a home directory is created. Users do not need to go looking for their home directory.

5. What three tasks must you perform to create a home folder on a network server?

First, create and share a folder in which to store all home folders on a network server. Second, for the shared folder, remove the default Full Control permission from the Everyone group and assign Full Control to the Users group for users that will reside in this shared folder. Third, provide the path to the user's home folder in the shared home directory folder on the Profile tab of the Properties dialog box for the user account.

Lesson 5 Review

Page
7-44

1. What are groups, and why do you use them?

A group is a collection of user accounts. A group simplifies administration by allowing you to assign permissions and rights to a group of users rather than to each individual user account.

2. An administrator or owner of a resource uses _____ to control what users can do with a resource such as a folder, a file, or a printer.

Permissions

3. You use local groups to assign permissions to resources residing _____ _____.

On the computer on which the local group is created

4. Which of the following statements about deleting local groups are correct? (Choose all that apply.)

   a. Each group that you create has a unique identifier that cannot be reused.

   b. You can restore access to resources by re-creating the group.

   c. When you delete a group, you also remove the permissions and rights associated with it.

   d. Deleting a group deletes the user accounts that are members of the group.

   The correct answers are A and C. B is not correct because re-creating a group does not re-create the membership of that group or any of the rights or permissions associated with that group. D is not correct because deleting a group does not delete the user accounts that are members of the group. Deleting a group does remove any rights and permissions that were extended to the members of the group by virtue of their membership.

5. What is the difference between built-in system groups and built-in local groups found on computers running Windows XP Professional? Give at least two examples of each type of group.

   Built-in local groups give rights to perform system tasks on a single computer, such as backing up and restoring files, changing the system time, and administering system resources. Some examples of built-in local groups are Administrators, Backup Operators, Guests, Power Users, Replicator, and Users. Built-in system groups do not have specific memberships that you can modify, but they can represent different users at different times, depending on how a user gains access to a computer or resource. You do not see system groups when you administer groups, but they are available for use when you assign rights and permissions to resources. Some examples of built-in system groups are Everyone, Authenticated Users, Creator Owner, Network, Interactive, Anonymous Logon, and Dialup.

Case Scenario Exercise

Page
7-46

1. Your first task is to create a naming convention for these workers. The museum management would like the user names to reflect that these are temporary workers, but not require too complicated a user name for the workers to type. Use the following table to create names for the workers.

Full Name	User Account Name
Cat Francis	
David Jaffe	
Mary North	
Jeff Teper	
Bernhard Tham	

There are a number of ways you could create these user names. One way would be to use the first initial and last name of each person to create the user name and then to prepend each user name with a T to indicate the workers' temporary status. This could give you the following user names:

- ❑   T_cfrancis

- ❑   T_djaffe

- ❑   T_mnorth

- ❑   T_jteper

- ❑   T_btham

2. Where should you create these user names?

You must create a local user name for each user on the user's workstation. You must also create a local user name for each user on the file server so that you can assign permissions.

3. The file server in the workgroup contains a folder named Coal Research, to which each of the workers needs access. You would like to minimize the number of times you have to assign permissions to the Research folder. How would you do this?

You should create a local group on the file server. You should name the group something simple like Coal Researchers and then add each of the workers' user names to that group. You can then assign permissions to the group for the Coal Research folder rather than assigning permissions to each user name.

4. When creating passwords for the users on their workstations, what must you ensure so that the users can access the file server?

You must not create blank passwords for the users on their workstations. Although blank passwords would allow the users to log on to their workstations and access local resources, the default security configuration on the file server is to enable the Accounts: Limit Local Account Use Of Blank Passwords To Console Logon Only security setting, which would prevent users with blank passwords from being able to access resources on the file server remotely.

Troubleshooting Lab

Page
7-47

1. Martin's user account was assigned permissions to access a number of resources on the computer and Raymond is not sure exactly what permissions were assigned. He wants to recover the deleted user account. Can he do this? If so, how?

After a user account is deleted, it cannot be recovered. All permissions and rights assigned to the user account are lost.

2. If you really mean to delete the user account, what is often a better way to handle the situation than simply deleting the user account?

It is usually better to disable the account instead of deleting it. When an account is disabled, no user can log on by using it. If the account is needed again, you can re-enable it, and all rights and permissions are retained. When you are sure that you no longer need a disabled account, you can then delete it.

3. To prevent a situation like the one that happened with Raymond (in which rights and permissions to resources were assigned directly to Martin's user account and were thus difficult to reconstruct), what is a better way to assign rights and permissions?

You should assign rights and permissions to local groups rather than directly to local user accounts. You should then make the user accounts members of the appropriate groups. This way, if a user account is accidentally deleted, you can create a new user account and place it in the appropriate groups again, rather than having to reconstruct rights and permissions on the user account. Using groups also helps to manage rights and permissions better in other situations, such as when a user no longer needs access to particular resources or when a new user joins the company.

4. Soon after creating a new user account for Martin, Raymond contacts you and tells you that Martin has forgotten his new password. Can you reset his password? How?

Yes. You must log on to Martin's computer and use the Computer Management snap-in (or use the Computer Management snap-in remotely) to reset the password. You should also configure Martin's user account so that he must change the password the next time he logs on, so that the password is known only to him.

5. What should you tell Martin to do so that he can recover his own password should this happen again?

You should show Martin how to create a password reset disk.

8 Securing Resources with NTFS Permissions

Exam Objectives in this Chapter:

- Monitor, manage, and troubleshoot access to files and folders.
  - ❏ Control access to files and folders by using permissions.

Why This Chapter Matters

This chapter introduces you to NT file system (NTFS) folder and file permissions for Windows XP Professional. You will learn how to assign NTFS folder and file permissions to user accounts and groups, and you will see how moving or copying files and folders affects NTFS file and folder permissions. You will also learn how to troubleshoot common resource access problems.

Lessons in this Chapter:

Before You Begin

To complete this chapter, you must have a computer that meets the minimum hardware requirements listed in the preface, "About This Book." You must also have Microsoft Windows XP Professional installed on the computer.

Lesson 1: Introduction to NTFS Permissions

You use **NTFS permissions** to specify which users and groups can access files and folders and what they can do with the contents of the files or folders. NTFS permissions are available only on NTFS volumes; they are *not* available on volumes formatted with file allocation table (FAT) or FAT32 file systems. NTFS security is effective whether a user accesses the file or folder at the local computer or over the network.

The permissions you assign for folders are different from the permissions you assign for files. Administrators, the owners of files or folders, and users with Full Control permission can assign NTFS permissions to users and groups to control access to files and folders.

After this lesson, you will be able to

- Identify the standard NTFS folder permissions
- Identify the standard NTFS file permissions
- Describe how Windows XP Professional uses access control lists (ACLs)
- Explain how effective permissions are calculated when multiple sets of NTFS permissions are in effect
- Explain how permissions inheritance is controlled

Estimated lesson time: 30 minutes

Standard NTFS Folder Permissions

You assign folder permissions to control the access that users have to folders and to the files and subfolders that are contained within the folders. Table 8-1 lists the standard NTFS folder permissions that you can assign and the type of access that each provides.

Table 8-1   NTFS Folder Permissions

This NTFS Folder Permission	Allows the User To
Read	See files and subfolders in the folder and view folder permissions, and attributes (such as Read-Only, Hidden, Archive, and System)
Write	Create new files and subfolders within the folder, change folder attributes, and view folder ownership and permissions
List Folder Contents	See the names of files and subfolders in the folder
Read & Execute	Move through folders to reach other files and folders, even if the users do not have permission for those folders, and perform actions permitted by the Read permission and the List Folder Contents permission
Modify	Delete the folder plus perform actions permitted by the Write permission and the Read & Execute permission
Full Control	Change permissions, take ownership, and delete subfolders and files; plus perform actions permitted by all other NTFS folder permissions

You can deny permission to a user account or group. To deny all access to a user account or group for a folder, deny the Full Control permission.

Standard NTFS File Permissions

You assign file permissions to control the access that users have to files. Table 8-2 lists the standard NTFS file permissions that you can assign and the type of access that each provides.

Table 8-2   NTFS File Permissions

This NTFS File Permission	Allows the User to
Read	Read the file and view file attributes, ownership, and permissions
Write	Overwrite the file, change file attributes, and view file ownership and permissions
Read & Execute	Run applications, plus perform the actions permitted by the Read permission
Modify	Modify and delete the file, plus perform the actions permitted by the Write permission and the Read & Execute permission
Full Control	Change permissions and take ownership, plus perform the actions permitted by all other NTFS file permissions

How Windows XP Professional Uses Access Control Lists

NTFS stores an **access control list (ACL)** with every file and folder on an NTFS volume. The ACL contains a list of all user accounts and groups that have been assigned permissions for the file or folder, as well as the permissions that they have been assigned. When a user attempts to gain access to a resource, the ACL must contain an entry, called an **access control entry (ACE)**, for the user account or a group to which the user belongs. The entry must allow the type of access that is requested (for example, Read access) for the user to gain access. If no ACE exists in the ACL, the user cannot access the resource.

How Effective Permissions Are Calculated When Multiple Sets of NTFS Permissions Are in Effect

It is possible for multiple sets of NTFS permissions to apply to a user for a particular resource. For example, a user might be a member of two different groups, each of which is assigned different permissions to access a resource. To assign permissions effectively, you must understand the rules and priorities by which NTFS assigns and combines multiple permissions and NTFS permissions inheritance.

What Are Effective Permissions?

A user's **effective permissions** for a resource are the sum of the NTFS permissions that you assign to the individual user account and to all the groups to which the user belongs. If a user is granted Read permission for a folder and is a member of a group with Write permission for the same folder, the user has both Read and Write permissions for that folder.

> **Exam Tip** To manually calculate effective NTFS permissions, first combine all allow permissions from all sources. Next, determine any deny permissions the user has. Deny permissions override allow permissions. The result is the user's effective permissions for the resource.

How File Permissions Override Folder Permissions

NTFS permissions assigned to files take priority over NTFS permissions assigned to the folder that contains the file. If you have access to a file, you can access the file if you have the Bypass Traverse Checking security permission—even if you do not have access to the folder containing the file. You can access the files for which you have permissions by using the full Universal Naming Convention (UNC) or local path to open the file from its respective application, even if you have no permission to access the folder that contains the file. In other words, if you do not have permission to access the folder containing the file you want to access, you must have the Bypass Traverse Checking security permission and you have to know the full path to the file to access it. Without permission to access the folder, you cannot see the folder, so you cannot browse for the file.

> **See Also** The Bypass Traverse Checking security permission is described further in Lesson 2, "Assigning NTFS Permissions and Special Permissions."

How Deny Permissions Override Allow Permissions

In addition to granting a permission, you can also specifically deny a permission (although this is not the recommended method of controlling access to resources). Denying a permission overrides all instances in which that permission is allowed. Even if a user has permission to access a file or folder as a member of a group, denying permission to the user blocks any other permissions the user might have (see Figure 8-1).

In Figure 8-1, User1 has Read permission for FolderA and is a member of Group A and Group B. Group B has Write permission for FolderA. Group A has been denied Write permission for File2.

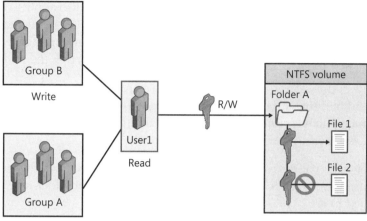

- NTFS permissions are cumulative.
- File permissions override folder permissions.
- Deny overrides other permissions.

Figure 8-1   You must be able to calculate effective NTFS permissions.

The user can read and write to File1. The user can also read File2, but cannot write to File2 because she is a member of Group A, which has been denied Write permission for File2.

How NTFS Permissions Inheritance Is Controlled

By default, permissions that you assign to the parent folder are inherited by and propagated to the subfolders and files contained in the parent folder. However, you can prevent **permissions inheritance**, as shown in Figure 8-2.

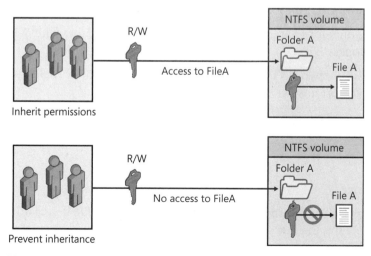

Figure 8-2   Files and folders inherit permissions from their parent folder.

By default, whatever permissions you assign to the parent folder also apply to subfolders and files contained within the parent folder. When you assign NTFS permissions to give access to a folder, you assign permissions for the folder and for any existing files and subfolders, as well as for any new files and subfolders that are created in the folder.

You can prevent permissions that are assigned to a parent folder from being inherited by subfolders and files that are contained within the folder. That is, you can change the default inheritance behavior and cause subfolders and files to not inherit permissions that have been assigned to the parent folder containing them.

The folder for which you prevent permissions inheritance becomes the new parent folder. The subfolders and files contained within this new parent folder inherit the permissions assigned to it.

Lesson Review

Use the following questions to help determine whether you have learned enough to move on to the next lesson. If you have difficulty answering these questions, review the material in this lesson before beginning the next lesson. You can find answers to these questions in the "Questions and Answers" section at the end of this chapter.

1. Which of the following statements correctly describe NTFS file and folder permissions? Choose all that apply.

   a. NTFS security is effective only when a user gains access to the file or folder over the network.

   b. NTFS security is effective when a user gains access to the file or folder on the local computer.

   c. NTFS permissions specify which users and groups can gain access to files and folders and what they can do with the contents of the file or folder.

   d. NTFS permissions can be used on all file systems available with Windows XP Professional.

2. Which of the following NTFS folder permissions allow you to delete the folder? Choose the correct answer.

   a. Read

   b. Read & Execute

   c. Modify

   d. Administer

3. Which of the NTFS file permissions should you assign to a file if you want to allow users to delete the file but do not want to allow users to take ownership of a file?

4. What is an access control list (ACL), and what is the difference between an ACL and an access control entry (ACE)?

_____

_____

_____

_____

5. What are a user's effective permissions for a resource?

_____

_____

_____

_____

_____

6. By default, what inherits the permissions that you assign to the parent folder?

_____

_____

Lesson Summary

- NTFS folder permissions are Read, Write, List Folder Contents, Read & Execute, Modify, and Full Control.

- The NTFS file permissions are Read, Write, Read & Execute, Modify, and Full Control.

- NTFS stores an ACL, which contains a list of all user accounts and groups that have been granted access to the file or folder, as well as the type of access that they have been granted, with every file and folder on an NTFS volume.

- It is possible for multiple sets of NTFS permissions to apply to a user for a particular resource. A user's effective permissions for a resource are the sum of the NTFS permissions that you assign to the individual user account and to all the groups to which the user belongs.

- By default, permissions that you assign to the parent folder are inherited by and propagated to the subfolders and files contained in the parent folder. However, you can prevent permissions inheritance.

Lesson 2: Assigning NTFS Permissions and Special Permissions

You should follow certain guidelines for assigning NTFS permissions. Assign permissions according to group and user needs, which include allowing or preventing permissions to be inherited from parent folders to subfolders and files that are contained in the parent folder.

After this lesson, you will be able to

- Assign or modify NTFS folder and file permissions to user accounts and groups
- Grant or deny special permissions
- Take ownership of files and folders
- Prevent permissions inheritance
- Identify guidelines for planning NTFS permissions

Estimated lesson time: 70 minutes

How to Assign or Modify Permissions

Administrators, users with the Full Control permission, and owners of files and folders can assign permissions to user accounts and groups.

To assign or modify NTFS permissions for a file or a folder, in the Security tab of the Properties dialog box for the file or folder, configure the options that are shown in Figure 8-3 and described in Table 8-3.

Table 8-3   Security Tab Options

Option	Description
Group Or User Names	Allows you to select the user account or group for which you want to change permissions or that you want to remove from the list.
Permissions For *group or user name*	Allows and denies permissions. Select the Allow check box to allow a permission. Select the Deny check box to deny a permission.
Add	Opens the Select Users Or Groups dialog box, which you use to select user accounts and groups to add to the Group Or User Names list (see Figure 8-4).
Remove	Removes the selected user account or group and the associated permissions for the file or folder.
Advanced	Opens the Advanced Security Settings dialog box for the selected folder so that you can grant or deny special permissions (see Figure 8-5).

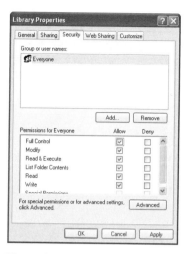

Figure 8-3   Use the Security tab of the Properties dialog box for a folder to set NTFS permissions.

Clicking the Add button on the Security tab of a file or folder's Properties dialog box displays the Select Users Or Groups dialog box (see Figure 8-4). Use this dialog box to add users or groups so that you can assign them permissions for accessing a folder or file. The options available in the Select Users Or Groups dialog box are described in Table 8-4.

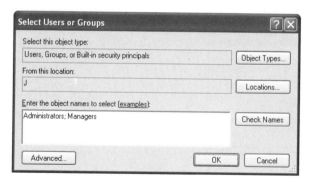

Figure 8-4   Use the Select Users or Groups dialog box to add additional users and groups.

Table 8-4   Select Users Or Groups Dialog Box Options

Option	Description
Select This Object Type	Allows you to select the types of objects you want to look for, such as built-in user accounts, groups, and computer accounts.
From This Location	Indicates where you are currently looking; for example, in the domain or on the local computer.
Locations	Allows you to select where you want to look; for example, in the domain or on the local computer.

Table 8-4   Select Users Or Groups Dialog Box Options

Option	Description
Enter The Object Names To Select	Allows you to type in a list of built-in users or groups to be added.
Check Names	Verifies the selected list of built-in users or groups to be added.
Advanced	Allows you access to advanced search features, including the ability to search for deleted accounts, accounts with passwords that do not expire, and accounts that have not logged on for a certain number of days.

How to Grant or Deny Special Permissions

Click the Advanced button on the Security tab of a file or folder's Properties dialog box to display the Advanced Security Settings dialog box (shown in Figure 8-5), which lists the users and groups and the permissions they have on this object. The Permissions Entries box also shows where the permissions were inherited from and where they are applied.

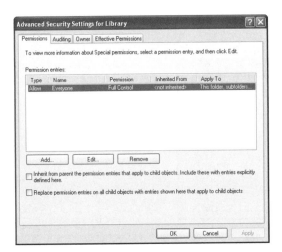

Figure 8-5   Assign special permissions using the Permissions tab of the Advanced Security Settings dialog box.

You can use the Advanced Security Settings dialog box to change the permissions set for a user or group. To change the permissions set for a user or group, select a user and click Edit to display the Permission Entry For dialog box (see Figure 8-6). You can then select or clear the specific permissions, explained in Table 8-5, that you want to change.

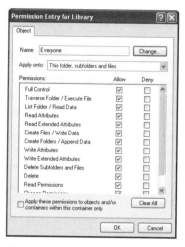

Figure 8-6   Select special permissions by using the Permission Entry For dialog box.

Table 8-5   Special Permissions

Permission	Description
Full Control	Full Control applies all permissions to the user or group.
Traverse Folder/ Execute File	**Traverse Folder** is applied only to folders and allows a user to move (or denies a user from moving) through folders even when the user has no permissions set on the traversed folder (the folder that the user is moving through). For example, a user might not have permissions set on a folder named Sales, but might have permission to access a subfolder named Brochures that is in the Sales folder. If allowed the Traverse Folder permission, the user could access the Brochures folder. The Traverse Folder permission has no affect on users for whom the Bypass Traverse Checking user right is assigned. Execute File is applied only to files and allows or denies running executable files (application files). Execute File applies only to files.
List Folder/Read Data	List Folder allows or denies viewing file names and subfolder names within the folder. List Folder applies only to folders. Read Data allows or denies viewing the contents of a file. Read Data applies only to files.
Read Attributes	Read Attributes allows or denies the viewing of the attributes of a file or folder. These attributes are defined by NTFS.
Read Extended Attributes	Read Extended Attributes allows or denies the viewing of extended attributes of a file or a folder. These attributes are defined by programs.
Create Files/ Write Data	Create Files allows or denies the creation of files within a folder. Create Files applies to folders only. Write Data allows or denies the making of changes to a file and the overwriting of existing content. Write Data applies to files only.

Table 8-5   Special Permissions

Permission	Description
Create Folders/ Append Data	Create Folders allows or denies the creation of folders within the folder. Create Folders applies only to folders. Append Data allows or denies making changes to the end of the file, but not changing, deleting, or overwriting existing data. Append Data applies to files only.
Write Attributes	Write Attributes allows or denies the changing of the attributes of a file or folder. These attributes are defined by NTFS.
Write Extended Attributes	Write Extended Attributes allows or denies the changing of the extended attributes of a file or a folder. These attributes are defined by programs.
Delete Subfolders And Files	Delete Subfolders And Files allows or denies the deletion of subfolders or files within a folder, even if the Delete permission has not been granted on the particular subfolder or file.
Delete	Delete allows or denies the deletion of a file or folder. A user can delete a file or folder even without having the Delete permission granted on that file or folder, if the Delete Subfolder And Files permission has been granted to the user on the parent folder.
Read Permissions	Read Permissions allows or denies the reading of the permissions assigned to the file or folder.
Change Permissions	Change Permissions allows or denies the changing of the permissions assigned to the file or folder. You can give other administrators and users the ability to change permissions for a file or folder without giving them the Full Control permission over the file or folder. In this way, the administrator or user cannot delete or write to the file or folder, but can assign permissions to the file or folder.
Take Ownership	Take Ownership allows or denies taking ownership of the file or folder. The owner of a file can always change permissions on a file or folder, regardless of the permissions set to protect the file or folder.
Synchronize	Synchronize allows or denies different threads in a multithreaded program to synchronize with one another. A multithreaded program performs multiple actions simultaneously by using both processors in a dual-processor computer. This permission is not assigned to users, but instead applies only to multithreaded programs.

Exam Tip   When you grant permissions, grant users the minimum permissions that they need to get their job done. This is referred to as the principle of least privilege.

How to Take Ownership of Files and Folders

Every object (file or folder) on an NTFS volume has an owner who controls how permissions are set on the object and to whom permissions are granted. When a user creates an object, that user automatically becomes the object's owner.

You can transfer ownership of files and folders from one user account or group to another. You can give someone the ability to take ownership and, as an administrator, you can take ownership of a file or folder.

The following rules apply for taking ownership of a file or folder:

- The current **owner** or any user with Full Control permission can assign the Full Control standard permission or the Take Ownership special access permission to another user account or group, allowing the user account or any member of the group to take ownership.

- An administrator can take ownership of a folder or file, regardless of assigned permissions. If an administrator takes ownership, the Administrators group becomes the owner, and any member of the Administrators group can change the permissions for the file or folder and assign the Take Ownership permission to another user account or group.

For example, if an employee leaves the company, an administrator can take ownership of the employee's files and assign the Take Ownership permission to another employee, and then that employee can take ownership of the former employee's files.

> **Note**   You cannot assign anyone ownership of a file or folder. The owner of a file, an administrator, or anyone with Full Control permission can assign Take Ownership permission to a user account or group, allowing them to take ownership. To become the owner of a file or folder, a user or group member with Take Ownership permission must explicitly take ownership of the file or folder.

To take ownership of a file or folder, the user or a group member with Take Ownership permission must explicitly take ownership of the file or folder, as follows:

1. In the Security tab of the Properties dialog box for the file or folder, click Advanced.

2. In the Advanced Security Settings dialog box, in the Owner tab, in the Change Owner To list, select your name.

3. Select the Replace Owner On Subcontainers And Objects check box to take ownership of all subfolders and files that are contained within the folder, and then click OK.

How to Prevent Permissions Inheritance

By default, subfolders and files inherit permissions that you assign to their parent folder. This is indicated in the Advanced Security Settings dialog box (refer to Figure 8-5) when the Inherit From Parent The Permission Entries That Apply To Child Objects check box is selected. To prevent a subfolder or file from inheriting permissions from a parent folder, clear the check box. You are then prompted to select one of the options described in Table 8-6.

Table 8-6   Preventing Permissions Inheritance Options

Option	Description
Copy	Copy the permission entries that were previously applied from the parent to the child and then deny subsequent permissions inheritance from the parent folder.
Remove	Remove the permission entries that were previously applied from the parent to the child and retain only the permissions that you explicitly assign here. Clicking this button removes all permissions from the file or folder; if you do not grant yourself permissions immediately afterward, you could lose access to the file. To recover access to the file, you would need to take ownership.
Cancel	Cancel the dialog box.

Guidelines for Planning NTFS Permissions

If you take the time to plan your NTFS permissions and follow a few guidelines, you will find that permissions are more straightforward to manage than you might imagine. Use the following guidelines when you assign NTFS permissions:

- To simplify administration, organize files into folders so that you can assign permissions to folders instead of directly to files.

- Allow users only the level of access that they require. If a user only needs to read a file, assign the Read permission to his or her user account for the file. This reduces the possibility of users accidentally modifying or deleting important documents and application files.

- Create groups according to the access that the group members require for resources, and then assign the appropriate permissions to the group. Assign permissions to individual user accounts only when necessary.

- When you assign permissions to application folders, assign the Read & Execute permission to the Users group and the Administrators group. This prevents application files from being accidentally deleted or damaged by users or viruses.

- When you assign permissions for public data folders, assign the Read & Execute permission and the Write permission to the Users group and the Full Control permission to the CREATOR OWNER. By default, the user who creates a file is also the owner of the file. The owner of a file can grant another user permission to take ownership of the file. This grants users the ability to read and modify documents that other users create (and the ability to read, modify, and delete the files and folders that they create).

■ Do not make denying permissions a part of your permissions plan. Deny permissions only when it is essential to deny specific access to a specific user account or group.

■ Encourage users to assign permissions to the files and folders that they create and teach them how to do so.

> **Real World   Managing Permissions Structures**
>
> The availability of so many different permissions often lures administrators into creating permission structures that are much more complicated than necessary. In addition to following the guidelines set out in this chapter (such as applying permissions to folders instead of files, and assigning permissions to groups instead of user accounts), you can make a permissions structure more manageable by doing the following:
>
> ■ For most companies, you will want to err on the side of being too secure. Make it a practice to lock everything down with permissions and then grant access only to those that need it. Also, grant only the level of permission that users need. It is often tempting to grant Full Control to users just to avoid complaints from those users about not being able to perform tasks, but avoid that temptation. On smaller networks, you might want to take an opposite approach—one in which you allow access to everything and then secure only those resources that need to be secured.
>
> ■ Document your security decisions and encourage users to do so, as well. You should record which folders and files have which permissions, and make notes on why you made the decision. Although it seems an extra burden (and does require more work upfront), this documentation is invaluable when the time comes to change or troubleshoot the permissions structure.

Practice: Planning and Assigning NTFS Permissions

In this practice, you will plan NTFS permissions for folders and files based on a business scenario. Then you will apply NTFS permissions for folders and files on your computer running Windows XP Professional in a workgroup environment, based on a second scenario. Finally, you will test the NTFS permissions that you set up to make sure that they are working properly.

Complete the following six exercises, and answer any questions that are asked. You can find answers to these questions in the "Questions and Answers" section at the end of this chapter.

Exercise 1: Preparing for This Practice

To prepare for subsequent exercises, log on with an account that is a member of the Administrators group and create the Limited users listed in the following table.

User Account	Type
User81	Limited
User82	Limited
User83	Limited
User84	Limited

Create the following folders:

- C:\Public
- C:\Public\Library

Exercise 2: Determining the Default NTFS Permissions for a Folder

In this exercise, you determine the default NTFS permissions for the newly created Public folder located on a computer running Windows XP Professional in a workgroup environment.

1. Log on with a user account that is a member of the Administrators group.

2. On the Start menu, right-click My Computer, and then click Explore.

3. Expand Local Disk (C:), right-click the Public folder, and then click Properties.

4. In the Public Properties dialog box, on the Security tab, note the default groups and users that have permissions for the Public folder.

Tip If you do not see a Security tab, there are two things to check: Is your partition formatted as NTFS or FAT? Only NTFS partitions use NTFS permissions, so only NTFS partitions have a Security tab. Are you using Simple File Sharing? Click Cancel to close the Public Properties dialog box. On the Tools menu, click Folder Options. In the Folder Options dialog box, click View. Under Advanced Settings, clear the Use Simple File Sharing (Recommended) check box and click OK. Repeat Steps 3 and 4 and continue with this practice.

5. Click each user and group in the Group Or User Names list, noting the default permissions assigned to each.

6. What are the existing folder permissions?

_____

_____

_____

_____

_____

7. Click OK to close the Public Properties dialog box.

8. Close Windows Explorer and log off.

Exercise 3: Testing the Folder Permissions for the Public Folder

1. Log on as **User81**, and then start Windows Explorer.

2. Expand the Public folder.

3. In the Public folder, create a text document named **USER81** and type in the following text: **The first four letters in the alphabet are a, b, c, and d.**

> **Tip**   With the Public folder selected in the folder tree (the left pane), on the File menu, click New, and then click Text Document to create the text document.

4. Were you successful? Why or why not?

_____Yes_____

_____

5. Attempt to perform the following tasks for the file that you just created:

☑ Open the file

☑ Modify the file

☑ Delete the file

6. Were you able to complete all of these tasks and why?

_____Yes_____Owner_____

_____

7. In the Public folder, re-create the text file named User81.

8. Log off Windows XP Professional.

9. Log on as **User82** and attempt to perform the following tasks on the USER81 text document:

   ☑ Open the file

   ❑ Modify the file *No*

   ❑ Delete the file

10. Which tasks were you able to perform and why?

Open = yes

Modify = No —

Delete = No —

Exercise 4: Assigning NTFS Permissions

In this exercise, you assign NTFS permissions for the Public folder.

The permissions that you assign are to be based on the following criteria:

■ All users should be able to read documents and files in the Public folder.

■ All users should be able to create documents in the Public folder.

■ All users should be able to modify the contents, properties, and permissions of the documents that they create in the Public folder.

■ User82 is responsible for maintaining the Public folder and should be able to modify and delete all files in the Public folder.

1. Based on what you learned in Exercise 1, what changes in permission assignments do you need to make to meet each of these four criteria? Why?

2. You are currently logged on as User82. Can you change the permissions assigned to User82 while logged on as User82? Why or why not?

No - User82 cannot change permissions of User82

3. Log on with a user account that is a member of the Administrators group, and then start Windows Explorer.

4. Expand the Public folder.

5. Right-click the Public folder, and then click Properties.

6. In the Properties dialog box for the folder, on the Security tab, click Add.

7. In the Select Users Or Groups dialog box, in the Enter The Object Names To Select text box, type **User82**, and then click Check Names.

8. *Computer_name*\User82 should now appear in the Enter The Object Names To Select text box, indicating that Windows XP Professional located User82 on the computer and it is a valid user account. Click OK to close the Select Users Or Groups dialog box.

9. User82 now appears in the Group Or User Name box in the Public Properties dialog box. Click User82 and note the assigned permissions.

10. Which permissions are assigned to User82?

Read & Execute, List Folders, Read

11. Click Advanced.

12. In the Advanced Security Settings For Public dialog box, ensure that User82 is selected, and then click Edit.

13. In the Permission Entry For Public dialog box (with User82 displayed in the Name text box), in the Allow column, click Full Control.

14. Click OK to close the Permission Entry For Public dialog box.

15. Click OK to close the Advanced Security Settings For Public dialog box.

16. Click OK to close the Public Properties dialog box.

17. Close Explorer and log off Windows XP Professional.

Exercise 5: Testing the New NTFS Permissions for the Folder

1. Log on as **User82**.

2. Start Windows Explorer.

3. Expand Local Disk (C:), and then expand the Public folder.

4. Attempt to perform the following tasks on the USER81 text document:

   ❑ Modify the file

   ❑ Delete the file

5. Which tasks were you able to record and why?

   All - User82 has full control

6. Close Windows Explorer and then log off Windows XP Professional.

Exercise 6: Testing NTFS Permissions

In this exercise, you create a file in a subfolder and test how NTFS permissions are inherited through a folder hierarchy.

1. Log on as **User81**, and then start Windows Explorer.

2. In Windows Explorer, expand the Public\Library folder.

3. Create a text document named **USER81** in the Library folder.

4. Log off Windows XP Professional.

5. Log on as **User82**, and then start Windows Explorer.

6. Expand the Public\Library folder.

7. Attempt to perform the following tasks on the USER81 file:

   ❑ Open the file

   ❑ Modify the file

   ❑ Delete the file

8. Which tasks were you able to perform and why?

   All

9. Log off Windows XP Professional.

Lesson Review

Use the following questions to help determine whether you have learned enough to move on to the next lesson. If you have difficulty answering these questions, review the material in this lesson before beginning the next lesson. You can find answers to these questions in the "Questions and Answers" section at the end of this chapter.

1. By default, when you format a volume with NTFS, the _____ permission is assigned to the Everyone group. Fill in the blank.

2. When you assign permissions for public data folders, it is recommended that you assign the _____ permission and the _____ permission to the Users group, and the _____ permission to the CREATOR OWNER user. Fill in the blanks.

3. Which of the following users or groups can assign permissions to user accounts and groups? Choose all that apply.

    a. Administrators

    b. Power Users

    c. Users with the Full Control permission

    d. Owners of files and folders

4. Which of the following tabs in the Properties dialog box for the file or folder do you use to assign or modify NTFS permissions for a file or a folder? Choose the correct answer.

    a. Advanced

    b. Permissions

    c. Security

    d. General

5. What is the purpose of the Traverse Folder/Execute File special permission?

    _____

    _____

    _____

6. What is the difference between the Delete permission and Delete Subfolder And Files permission?

    _____

    _____

    _____

    _____

Lesson Summary

- To assign or modify NTFS permissions for a file or a folder, you use the Security tab of the Properties dialog box for the file or folder.

- You can use the Advanced Security Settings dialog box to configure specific permissions for a user or group.

- The current owner or any user with Full Control permission can assign the Full Control standard permission or the Take Ownership special access permission to another user account or group, allowing the user account or a member of the group to take ownership. You cannot assign anyone ownership of a file or folder; you can only give them permission to take ownership.

- By default, subfolders and files inherit permissions that you assign to their parent folder. To stop subfolders and files from inheriting permissions that you assign to their parent folder, clear the Inherit From Parent The Permission Entries That Apply To Child Objects check box in the Advanced Security Settings dialog box.

- Take the time to properly plan NTFS permissions following best-practice guidelines. A well-planned permission structure is easier to administer and causes fewer problems.

Lesson 3: Supporting NTFS Permissions

When you assign or modify NTFS permissions to files and folders, problems might arise. When you copy or move files and folders, the permissions you set on the files or folders might change. Specific rules control how and when permissions change. Understanding these rules helps you solve permissions problems. Troubleshooting these problems is important to keep resources available for the appropriate users and protected from unauthorized users.

After this lesson, you will be able to

- Describe the effect on NTFS file and folder permissions when files and folders are copied
- Describe the effect on NTFS file and folder permissions when files and folders are moved
- Troubleshoot resource access problems

Estimated lesson time: 40 minutes

Effect on NTFS File and Folder Permissions When Files and Folders Are Copied

When you copy files or folders from one folder to another or from one volume to another, permissions change (as shown in Figure 8-7).

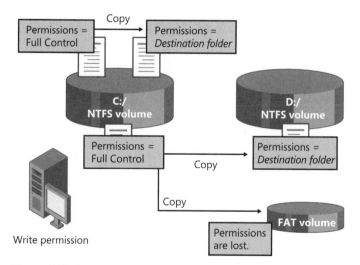

Figure 8-7   Copy files or folders between folders or volumes.

When you copy a file within a single NTFS volume or between NTFS volumes, note the following:

- Windows XP Professional treats it as a new file. As a new file, it takes on the permissions of the destination folder.

- You must have Write permission for the destination folder to copy files and folders.

- You become the creator and owner.

> **Security Alert**   When you copy files or folders to FAT volumes, the folders and files lose their NTFS permissions because FAT volumes do not support NTFS permissions.

Effect on NTFS File and Folder Permissions When Files and Folders Are Moved

When you move a file or folder, permissions might or might not change, depending on where you move the file or folder (see Figure 8-8).

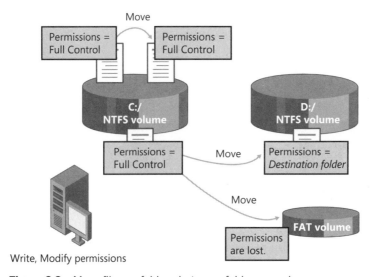

Figure 8-8   Move files or folders between folders or volumes.

Facts to Know About Moving Within a Single NTFS Volume

When you move a file or folder within a single NTFS volume, note the following things:

- The file or folder retains the original permissions.

- You must have the Write permission for the destination folder to move files and folders into it.

- You must have the Modify permission for the source file or folder. The Modify permission is required to move a file or folder because Windows XP Professional deletes the file or folder from the source folder after it is copied to the destination folder.

- You become the creator and owner.

Facts to Know About Moving Between NTFS Volumes

When you move a file or folder between NTFS volumes, note the following:

- The file or folder inherits the permissions of the destination folder.

- You must have the Write permission for the destination folder to move files and folders into it.

- You must have the Modify permission for the source file or folder. The Modify permission is required to move a file or folder because Windows XP Professional deletes the file or folder from the source folder after it is copied to the destination folder.

- You become the creator and owner.

Security Alert   When you move files or folders to FAT volumes, the folders and files lose their NTFS permissions because FAT volumes do not support NTFS permissions.

Exam Tip   When you move files or folders within an NTFS volume, permissions that have been directly assigned to the file or folder carry over to the new location. In all other cases of moving and copying, existing permissions are lost, and the object will inherit permissions from the new parent. When moving to a FAT volume, permissions are lost entirely.

How to Troubleshoot Common Permissions Problems

Table 8-7 describes some common permissions problems that you might encounter and provides solutions that you can use to try to resolve these problems.

Table 8-7   Permissions Problems and Troubleshooting Solutions

Problem	Solution
A user cannot gain access to a file or folder.	If the file or folder was copied or moved to another NTFS volume, the permissions might have changed. Check the permissions that are assigned to the user account and to groups to which the user belongs. The user might not have permission, or might be denied access either individually or as a member of a group.
You add a user account to a group to give that user access to a file or folder, but the user still cannot gain access.	For access permissions to be updated to include the new group to which you have added the user account, the user must either log off and then log on again, or close all network connections to the computer on which the file or folder resides, and then make new connections.
A user with Full Control permission to a folder deletes a file in the folder, although that user does not have permission to delete the file itself. You want to stop the user from being able to delete more files.	You have to clear the special access permission, the Delete Subfolders And Files check box, for that folder to prevent users with Full Control of the folder from being able to delete files in it.

Practice: Managing NTFS Permissions

In this practice, you will observe the effects of taking ownership of a file. Then you will determine the effects of permission and ownership when you copy or move files. Finally, you will determine what happens when a user with Full Control permission to a folder has been denied all access to a file in that folder but attempts to delete the file.

Complete the following two exercises, and answer any questions that are asked. You can find answers to these questions in the "Questions and Answers" section at the end of this chapter.

> **Important**   To successfully complete this practice, you must have completed all exercises in the Lesson 2 practice.

Exercise 1: Taking Ownership of a File

In this exercise, you observe the effects of taking ownership of a file. To do this, you must determine permissions for a file, assign the Take Ownership permission to a user account, and then take ownership as that user.

▶ **To determine the permissions for a file**

1. Log on with a user account that is a member of the Administrators group, and then start Windows Explorer.

2. In the Public folder, create a text document named OWNER.

3. Right-click OWNER, and then click Properties.

4. In the Owner Properties dialog box, click the Security tab. Note the permissions for the OWNER file.

5. Click Advanced.

6. In the Advanced Security Settings For Owner dialog box, on the Owner tab, note the current owner of the file.

7. Who is the current owner of the OWNER file?

▶ **To assign permission to a user to take ownership**

1. In the Advanced Security Settings For Owner dialog box, on the Permissions tab, click Add.

2. In the Select User Or Group dialog box, in the Enter The Object Names To Select text box, type **User81**, and then click Check Names.

3. User81 should now appear in the Enter The Object Names To Select text box, indicating that Windows XP Professional located User81 on the computer and it is a valid user account. Click OK.

4. In the Permission Entry For Owner dialog box, notice that all the permission entries for User81 are blank.

5. Under Permissions, select the Allow check box next to Take Ownership, and then click OK.

6. In the Advanced Security Settings For Owner dialog box, click OK to return to the Owner Properties dialog box.

7. Click OK to apply your changes and close the Owner Properties dialog box.

8. Close Windows Explorer, and then log off Windows XP Professional.

▶ **To take ownership of a file**

1. Log on as **User81**, and then start Windows Explorer.

2. Select the Public folder.

3. Right-click OWNER, and then click Properties.

4. In the Owner Properties dialog box, on the Security tab, notice the permissions for the OWNER folder. Click Advanced.

5. In the Advanced Security Settings For Owner dialog box, on the Owner tab, in the Change Owner To list, select User81, and then click Apply.

6. Who is now the owner of the OWNER file?

_____

7. Click OK to close the Advanced Security Settings For Owner dialog box.

8. Click OK to close the Owner Properties dialog box.

▶ **To test permissions for a file as the owner**

1. While you are logged on as User81, assign User81 the Full Control permission for the OWNER text document and click Apply.

2. Click Advanced and clear the Inherit From Parent The Permission Entries That Apply To Child Objects check box.

3. In the Security dialog box, click Remove.

4. Click OK to close the Advanced Security Settings For Owner dialog box.

5. Click OK to close the Owner Properties dialog box.

6. Delete the OWNER text document.

Exercise 2: Copying and Moving Folders

In this exercise, you see the effects of permissions and ownership when you copy and move folders.

▶ **To create a folder while logged on as a user**

1. While you are logged on as User81, in Windows Explorer, in the root folder of drive C, create a folder named **Temp1**.

2. What are the permissions that are assigned to the folder?

User or Group	Permissions

3. Who is the owner? Why?

_____

4. Close all applications, and then log off Windows XP Professional.

▶ **To create a folder while logged on as a member of the Administrators group**

   1. Log on as Administrator, or as a user account that is a member of the Administrators group, and then start Windows Explorer.

   2. In the root folder of drive C, create the folders **Temp2** and **Temp3**.

   3. What are the permissions for the Temp2 and Temp3 folders that you just created?

User or Group	Permissions

   4. Who is the owner of the Temp2 and Temp3 folders? Why?

_____

_____

_____

_____

   5. Assign the following permissions to the Temp2 and Temp3 folders. Clear the Inherit From Parent The Permission Entries That Apply To Child Objects check box. When prompted, click Remove to remove all permissions except those explicitly set.

Folder	Assign These Permissions
Temp2	Administrators: Full Control Users: Read & Execute
Temp3	Administrators: Full Control Backup Operators: Read & Execute Users: Full Control

▶   **To copy a folder to another folder within a Windows XP Professional NTFS volume**

1. While logged on with an account that is a member of the Administrators group, in Windows Explorer, copy C:\Temp2 to C:\Temp1 by selecting C:\Temp2, holding down CTRL, and then dragging C:\Temp2 to C:\Temp1.

> **Note**   Because this is a copy, C:\Temp2 and C:\Temp1\Temp2 should both exist.

2. Select C:\Temp1\Temp2, and then compare its permissions and ownership with those of C:\Temp2.

3. Who is the owner of C:\Temp1\Temp2 and what are the permissions? Why?

_____

_____

_____

_____

▶   **To move a folder within the same NTFS volume**

1. Log on as **User81**.

2. In Windows Explorer, select C:\Temp3, and then move it to C:\Temp1.

3. What happens to the permissions and ownership for C:\Temp1\Temp3? Why?

_____

4. Close all windows and log off.

Lesson Review

Use the following questions to help determine whether you have learned enough to move on to the next lesson. If you have difficulty answering these questions, review the material in this lesson before beginning the next lesson. You can find answers to these questions in the "Questions and Answers" section at the end of this chapter.

1. Which of the following statements about copying a file or folder are correct? Choose all that apply.

   a. When you copy a file from one folder to another folder on the same volume, the permissions on the file do not change.

   b. When you copy a file from a folder on an NTFS volume to a folder on a FAT volume, the permissions on the file do not change.

   c. When you copy a file from a folder on an NTFS volume to a folder on another NTFS volume, the permissions on the file match those of the destination folder.

   d. When you copy a file from a folder on an NTFS volume to a folder on a FAT volume, the permissions are lost.

2. Which of the following statements about moving a file or folder are correct? Choose all answers that are correct.

    a. When you move a file from one folder to another folder on the same volume, the permissions on the file do not change.

    b. When you move a file from a folder on an NTFS volume to a folder on a FAT volume, the permissions on the file do not change.

    c. When you move a file from a folder on an NTFS volume to a folder on another NTFS volume, the permissions on the file match those of the destination folder.

    d. When you move a file from a folder on an NTFS volume to a folder on the same volume, the permissions on the file match those of the destination folder.

3. When you assign NTFS permissions you should assign the _____ (least/most) restrictive permissions. Fill in the blank.

4. If you do not want a user or group to gain access to a particular folder or file, should you deny access permissions to that folder or file?

_____

_____

_____

Lesson Summary

■ When you copy or move files and folders, the permissions you set on the files or folders might change. When you copy files or folders from one folder to another or from one volume to another, the object takes on the permissions of the destination folder. You must have Write permission for the destination folder to copy files and folders. When you copy a file, you become the creator and owner of the file.

■ When you move a file or folder within a single NTFS volume, the file or folder retains its original permissions. When you move a file or folder between NTFS volumes, the file or folder inherits the permissions of the destination folder.

■ There are a number of common problems associated with NTFS permissions that you should learn to troubleshoot. In particular, you should make sure that the permissions are configured the way you think they are (particularly if the object has been moved or copied). Also, if you have recently assigned permissions, a user must log off and back on for the permissions to become effective.

Case Scenario Exercise

In this exercise, you will read a scenario about applying NTFS permissions to folders and files, and then answer the questions that follow. If you have difficulty completing this work, review the material in this chapter before beginning the next chapter. You can find answers to these questions in the "Questions and Answers" section at the end of this chapter.

Scenario

You are an administrator working for a company named Fabrikam, Inc., a regional advertising company with a headquarters office in Memphis, TN, and several branch locations throughout the Southeast. Members of the company's Accounting department, which is located in the main office, keep accounting information for the company's clients on a file server located within the department. On that file server is a folder named Client Accounts, to which all members of the Accounting department need access. Due to confidentiality agreements, there are certain documents within the Client Accounts folder that should be accessible only by employees, not by temporary or contract workers.

You have configured the Client Accounts folder in the following manner:

- You removed the Everyone group entirely.
- You added the Users group and assigned that group Full Control.

In addition, you have performed the following actions:

- You made all part-time employees members of a group named Part Time.
- You made all contract workers members of a group named Contractors.
- You assigned the Deny Full Control permission to the Part Time And Contractors groups for the files that are protected by the confidentiality agreement.

Questions

1. Will users in the Part Time And Contractors group be able to open the files protected by the confidentiality agreement?

_____

_____

2. Even if users of the Part Time And Contractors groups cannot access the file, there is a risk that they will delete the file. Why?

_____

_____

_____

_____

3. How could you solve this problem by changing permissions on the Client Accounts folder?

_____

_____

4. What would have been a better way to approach this problem from the beginning?

_____

_____

_____

_____

Troubleshooting Lab

Read the following troubleshooting scenario and then answer the questions that follow. You can use this lab to help determine whether you have learned enough to move on to the next chapter. If you have difficulty completing this work, review the material in this chapter before beginning the next chapter. You can find the answers to these questions in the "Questions and Answers" section at the end of this chapter.

Scenario

You are an administrator for a company named Contoso, Ltd., and are working with the Sales, Marketing, and Accounting departments to help set up permissions for folders that all departments use.

Both the Sales and Marketing departments access the Brochures folder. A group named Sales contains users that are in the Sales department, and a group named Marketing contains users that are in the Marketing department. Your boss gives you the following tables. The first table shows the permissions assigned to the Sales group for the Brochures folder. The second table shows the permissions assigned to the Marketing group for the Brochures folder. A user named David is a member of both the Sales and Marketing groups.

Permissions Assignments for Sales Group

Permission	Allow	Deny
Full Control		
Modify		
Read & Execute	X	
List Folder Contents	X	
Read	X	
Write		

Permissions Assignments for Marketing Group

Permission	Allow	Deny
Full Control		
Modify		
Read & Execute		
List Folder Contents		
Read	X	
Write		

Questions

1. Based on the information in tables that your boss gave you, what are David's effective permissions on the Brochures folder?

   _____

   _____

   _____

2. Your boss stops by and says, "Whoops, here is the other table I meant to give you." The table shows the permissions assigned to the Accounting group for the Brochures folder. A user named Yvette is a member the Sales, Marketing, and Accounting groups.

   Permissions Assignments for Accounting Group

Permission	Allow	Deny
Full Control		
Modify		
Read & Execute		
List Folder Contents		X
Read	X	
Write		X

Based on the information in all the tables that you received, what are Yvette's effective permissions on the Brochures folder?

_____

_____

_____

_____

_____

_____

Chapter Summary

■ You use NTFS permissions to specify which users and groups can access files and folders, and what they can do with the contents of the files or folders. NTFS permissions are available only on NTFS volumes. It is possible for multiple sets of NTFS permissions to apply to a user for a particular resource. A user's effective permissions for a resource are the sum of the NTFS permissions that you assign to the individual user account and to all of the groups to which the user belongs.

■ To assign or modify NTFS permissions for a file or a folder, you use the Security tab of the Properties dialog box for the file or folder. You can use the Advanced Security Settings dialog box to configure specific permissions for a user or group. You should also note the following:

❑ You cannot assign a user ownership of a file or folder; you can only give a user permission to take ownership.

❑ By default, subfolders and files inherit permissions that you assign to their parent folder. You can prevent a folder from propagating permissions to subfolders and items in the folder. You can also prevent a file or subfolder from inheriting permissions from its parent folder.

■ You should be aware of the following behaviors when you copy or move files and folders to which NTFS permissions are applied:

❑ When you copy files or folders from one folder to another or from one volume to another, the object takes on the permissions of the destination folder.

❑ When you move a file or folder within a single NTFS volume, the file or folder retains its original permissions.

❑ When you move a file or folder between NTFS volumes, the file or folder inherits the permissions of the destination folder.

Exam Highlights

Before taking the exam, review the key points and terms that are presented in this chapter. You need to know this information.

Key Points

■ To calculate effective NTFS permissions, first combine all allow permissions from all sources. Next, determine any deny permissions the user has. Deny permissions override allow permissions. The result is the user's effective permissions for the resource.

■ When you grant permissions, grant users the minimum permissions that they need to get their jobs done. This is referred to as the principle of least privilege.

■ When you move files or folders within an NTFS volume, permissions that have been directly assigned to the file or folder carry over to the new location. In all other cases of moving and copying, existing permissions are lost, and the object will inherit permissions from the new parent. When moving to a FAT volume, permissions are lost entirely.

Key Terms

access control entry (ACE)   A specific entry on the ACL that grants or denies a user or group access to a resource.

access control list (ACL)   A list of all user accounts and groups that have been assigned permissions for the file or folder, as well as the permissions that they have been assigned.

effective permissions   The permissions level that a user actually has, taking all permission sources into account.

NTFS permissions   Assignments that specify which users and groups can access files and folders and what they can do with the contents of the files or folders. NTFS permissions are available only on NTFS volumes.

owner   The user who created a file, folder, or printer.

permissions inheritance   The process of a file or folder receiving permissions based on the permissions assigned to the object's parent folder.

Traverse Folder   A permission that allows or denies moving through folders to access other files or folders, even when the user has no permissions for the traversed folder (the folder that the user is moving through).

Questions and Answers

Lesson 1 Review

Page
8-6

1. Which of the following statements correctly describe NTFS file and folder permissions? Choose all that apply.

    a. NTFS security is effective only when a user gains access to the file or folder over the network.

    b. NTFS security is effective when a user gains access to the file or folder on the local computer.

    c. NTFS permissions specify which users and groups can gain access to files and folders and what they can do with the contents of the file or folder.

    d. NTFS permissions can be used on all file systems available with Windows XP Professional.

The correct answers are B and C. NTFS security is locally based and so affects all users accessing a resource, whether those users are logged on locally or accessing the resource from the network. A is not correct because NTFS security does not *only* apply to network users. D is not correct because NTFS permissions can be used only on partitions formatted with NTFS.

2. Which of the following NTFS folder permissions allow you to delete the folder? Choose the correct answer.

    a. Read

    b. Read & Execute

    c. Modify

    d. Administer

The correct answer is C. A and B are not correct because these permissions do not allow you to delete a folder. D is not correct because Administer is not a valid permission.

3. Which of the NTFS file permissions should you assign to a file if you want to allow users to delete the file but do not want to allow users to take ownership of a file?

Modify

4. What is an access control list (ACL), and what is the difference between an ACL and an access control entry (ACE)?

An ACL, which is stored with every file and folder on an NTFS volume, contains a list of all user accounts or groups that have been assigned permissions to that file or folder. An ACE is an entry in an ACL that contains the operations that a user or group is allowed or specifically denied to perform on that file or folder.

5. What are a user's effective permissions for a resource?

A user's effective permissions for a resource are the sum of the NTFS permissions assigned to the individual user account and to all of the groups to which the user belongs. If there are any Deny permissions set, they override all instances in which that permission is allowed and must be removed from the user's effective permissions.

6. By default, what inherits the permissions that you assign to the parent folder?

By default, the permissions that you assign to the parent folder are inherited by and propagated to the subfolders and files that are contained in the parent folder.

Lesson 2 Practice: Planning and Assigning NTFS Permissions

Page
8-15

Exercise 2: Determining the Default NTFS Permissions for a Folder

6. What are the existing folder permissions?

The Administrators group has Full Control. The CREATOR OWNER has special permissions, Full Control. The account that created the folder has special permissions, Full Control of subfolders and files only. SYSTEM has Full Control. The Users group has Read & Execute, List Folder Contents, Read, and special permissions of Create Files/Write Data and Create Folders/Append Data.

Exercise 3: Testing the Folder Permissions for the Public Folder

4. Were you successful? Why or why not?

Yes, because the Users group is assigned the special permissions of Create Files/Write Data and Create Folders/Append Data for the Public folder.

6. Were you able to complete all of these tasks and why?

Yes, because the Users group is assigned the special permissions of Create Files/Write Data and Create Folders/Append Data for the Public folder.

10. Which tasks were you able to perform and why?

You can open the file because the Users group has Read permission for the Public folder. When you attempt to modify the file, you get an error message. You cannot modify the file because the Users group does not have either Full Control or Modify permissions for the Public folder. Users can create files and folders in the Public folders, and they have Full Control permission for the file and folders that they created, but they cannot modify files and folders for which they are not the creator or owner. You cannot delete the file because only the owner of a file and members of the Administrators group have Full Control of the file by default.

Exercise 4: Assigning NTFS Permissions

1. Based on what you learned in Exercise 1, what changes in permission assignments do you need to make to meet each of these four criteria? Why?

   The first three criteria are met by the default permission assignments. To allow User82 the ability to modify or delete all files in the Public folder, you could change the special permission assigned to User82 to Full Control.

2. You are currently logged on as User82. Can you change the permissions assigned to User82 while logged on as User82? Why or why not?

   No, you cannot change the permissions assigned User82 while logged on as User82 because User82 is not a member of the Administrators group, is not the owner of the Public folder, and does not have the Full Control permission for the Public folder. Only Administrators, the owners of files or folders, and users with Full Control permission can assign NTFS permissions to users and groups to control access to files and folders.

10. Which permissions are assigned to User82?

    Read & Execute, List Folder Contents, and Read

Exercise 5: Testing the New NTFS Permissions for the Folder

5. Which tasks were you able to record and why?

   User82 can open, modify, and delete the file because User82 has been assigned the Full Control permission for the Public folder.

Exercise 6: Testing NTFS Permissions

8. Which tasks were you able to perform and why?

   User82 can open, modify, and delete the file because User82 has been assigned the Full Control permission for the Library folder. The Inherit From Parent The Permission Entries That Apply To Child Objects check box is selected by default. Therefore, the Full Control permission was inherited by the Library folder from the Public folder.

Lesson 2 Review

Page
8-21

1. By default, when you format a volume with NTFS, the _____ permission is assigned to the Everyone group. Fill in the blank.

   Full Control

2. When you assign permissions for public data folders, it is recommended that you assign the _____ permission and the _____ permission to the Users group, and the _____ permission to the CREATOR OWNER user. Fill in the blanks.

   Read & Execute; Write; Full Control

3. Which of the following users can assign permissions to user accounts and groups? Choose all that apply.

   a. Administrators

   b. Power users

   c. Users with the Full Control permission

   d. Owners of files and folders

   The correct answers are A, C, and D. B is not correct because members of the Power users group cannot assign permissions.

4. Which of the following tabs in the Properties dialog box for the file or folder do you use to assign or modify NTFS permissions for a file or a folder? Choose the correct answer.

   a. Advanced

   b. Permissions

   c. Security

   d. General

   The correct answer is C. A, B, and D are incorrect because you use the Security tab to modify NTFS permissions.

5. What is the purpose of the Traverse Folder/Execute File special permission?

   Traverse Folder allows or denies moving through folders to access other files or folders, even when the user has no permissions for the traversed folder. Execute File allows or denies running executable files (application files).

6. What is the difference between the Delete permission and Delete Subfolder And Files permission?

   Delete allows or denies the deleting of a file or folder. Even if a user does not have the Delete permission for a file or folder, the user can still delete the file or folder if the Delete Subfolder And Files permission has been granted to the user on the parent folder.

Lesson 3 Practice: Managing NTFS Permissions

Page
8-26 **Exercise 1: Taking Ownership of a File**

▶ **To determine the permissions for a file**

7. Who is the current owner of the OWNER file?

   The user account you used to log on to Windows XP.

▶ **To take ownership of a file**

6. Who is now the owner of the OWNER file?

   User81

Exercise 2: Copying and Moving Folders

▶ **To create a folder while logged on as a user**

2. What are the permissions that are assigned to the folder?

User or Group	Permissions
Creator Owner	Special Permissions: Full control for subfolders and files only
System	Full Control
User81	Full Control
Users	Special Permissions: Traverse Folder/Execute File, List Folder/Read Data, Read Attributes, Read Extended Attributes, Read Permissions, Create Files/Write Data, and Create Folders/Append Data

3. Who is the owner? Why?

   User81 is the owner because the person who creates a folder or file is the owner.

▶ **To create a folder while logged on as a member of the Administrators group**

3. What are the permissions for the Temp2 and Temp3 folders that you just created?

User or Group	Permissions
Administrators	Full Control
Creator Owner	Special Permissions: Full control for subfolders and files only
System	Full Control
the name of the user account you used to create the folders	Special Permissions: Full control for this folder only
Users	Special Permissions: Traverse Folder/Execute File, List Folder/Read Data, Read Attributes, Read Extended Attributes, Read Permissions, Create Files/Write Data and Create Folders/Append Data

4. Who is the owner of the Temp2 and Temp3 folders? Why?

   The Administrators group or the name of the user account you used to create the folders (if you did not log on as Administrator) is the owner because the person who creates a folder or file is the owner. If the person is a member of the Administrators group, the Administrators group is the owner.

▶ **To copy a folder to another folder within a Windows XP Professional NTFS volume**

3. Who is the owner of C:\Temp1\Temp2 and what are the permissions? Why?

   The owner of C:\Temp1\Temp2 is the user account that performed the copy. The permissions for C:\Temp1\Temp2 are now the same as the permissions of Temp1. When you copy a folder or file into another folder, the permissions assigned to it are always the same as the permissions on the destination folder.

▶ **To move a folder within the same NTFS volume**

3. What happens to the permissions and ownership for C:\Temp1\Temp3? Why?

Nothing; they do not change.

Lesson 3 Review

Page
8-30
1. Which of the following statements about copying a file or folder are correct? Choose all that apply.

a. When you copy a file from one folder to another folder on the same volume, the permissions on the file do not change.

b. When you copy a file from a folder on an NTFS volume to a folder on a FAT volume, the permissions on the file do not change.

c. When you copy a file from a folder on an NTFS volume to a folder on another NTFS volume, the permissions on the file match those of the destination folder.

d. When you copy a file from a folder on an NTFS volume to a folder on a FAT volume, the permissions are lost.

The correct answers are C and D. A is not correct because when you copy a file to a folder on the same volume, the file inherits the permissions assigned to the target folder. B is not correct because when you copy a file to a FAT volume, permissions are lost.

2. Which of the following statements about moving a file or folder are correct? Choose all answers that are correct.

a. When you move a file from one folder to another folder on the same volume, the permissions on the file do not change.

b. When you move a file from a folder on an NTFS volume to a folder on a FAT volume, the permissions on the file do not change.

c. When you move a file from a folder on an NTFS volume to a folder on another NTFS volume, the permissions on the file match those of the destination folder.

d. When you move a file from a folder on an NTFS volume to a folder on the same volume, the permissions on the file match those of the destination folder.

The correct answers are A and C. B is not correct because when you move a file to a FAT partition, all permissions are lost. D is not correct because when you move a file to a folder on the same volume, the original permissions are retained.

3. When you assign NTFS permissions you should assign the _____ (least/most) restrictive permissions. Fill in the blank.

Most

4. If you do not want a user or group to gain access to a particular folder or file, should you deny access permissions to that folder or file?

You should assign permissions to the folder or file rather than deny permission to access the folder or file. Denying permissions should be an exception, not common practice.

Case Scenario Exercise

Page
8-32

1. Will users in the Part Time And Contractors group be able to open the files protected by the confidentiality agreement?

No. The Deny Full Control permission will prevent users from being able to access the file.

2. Even if users of the Part Time And Contractors groups cannot access the file, there is a risk that they will delete the file. Why?

Full Control includes the Delete Subfolders And Files special permission for POSIX compliance. This special permission allows a user to delete files in the root of a folder to which the user has been assigned Full Control permission. This permission overrides the file permissions.

3. How could you solve this problem by changing permissions on the Client Accounts folder?

Allow users all of the individual permissions, and then deny users the Delete Subfolders And Files special permission.

4. What would have been a better way to approach this problem from the beginning?

It is better to not use Deny permissions unless absolutely necessary. The simplest and most secure way to approach this problem would be to put the files that are protected by a confidentiality agreement into a separate folder from the Client Accounts folder. You could then grant permissions on the separate folder only to users that need permissions.

Troubleshooting Lab

Page
8-33

1. Based on the information in tables that your boss gave you, what are David's effective permissions on the Brochures folder?

To determine David's effective permissions, you must combine all the permissions that have been assigned. Thus, David's effective permissions on the Brochures folder are Read & Execute, List Folder Contents, and Read.

2. Your boss stops by and says, "Whoops, here is the other table I meant to give you." The table shows the permissions assigned to the Accounting group for the Brochures folder. A user named Yvette is a member the Sales, Marketing, and Accounting groups.

Permissions Assignments for Accounting Group

Permission	Allow	Deny
Full Control		
Modify		
Read & Execute		
List Folder Contents		X
Read	X	
Write		X

Based on the information in all the tables that you received, what are Yvette's effective permissions on the Brochures folder?

To determine Yvette's effective permissions, you must combine all the permissions that have been granted. Yvette's cumulative granted permissions are Read & Execute, List Folder Contents, and Read. You must then apply any denied permissions. Based on membership in the Accounting group, Yvette is denied the List Folder Contents and Write permissions. Denying the List Folder Contents permission effectively denies the Read & Execute permission (because Read & Execute depends on List Folder Contents). This results in effective permissions of Read for Yvette.

9 Administering Shared Folders

Exam Objectives in this Chapter:

- Manage and troubleshoot access to shared folders.

    - ❏ Create and remove shared folders.

    - ❏ Control access to shared folders by using permissions.

Why This Chapter Matters

In Chapter 8, "Securing Resources with NTFS Permissions," you learned about NTFS File System permissions for Microsoft Windows XP Professional. You use NTFS permissions to specify which users and groups are allowed to access files and folders and how NTFS permissions control what users are allowed to do with the contents of the file or folder. Remember that NTFS permissions are available only on NTFS volumes and that NTFS security is in effect whether a user gains access to the file or folder at the local computer or over the network.

In this chapter, you will learn how to share folders and make the folders accessible over the network. You access a computer's folders and their contents by first sharing the folders, and then accessing the folders across the network from a remote computer. Shared folders provide a way to restrict access to file resources that are located on file allocation table (FAT) or FAT32 partitions. In this chapter, you will learn how to share folders and how to restrict access to **shared folders** by using permissions.

Lessons in this Chapter:

Before You Begin

To complete this chapter, you must have a computer that meets the minimum hardware requirements listed in the preface, "About This Book." You must also have Windows XP Professional installed on the computer.

Lesson 1: Introduction to Shared Folders

You use shared folders to provide network users with access to file resources. When a folder is shared, users with appropriate permissions can access the folder over the network.

After this lesson, you will be able to

- Explain Simple File Sharing
- Identify shared folder permissions
- Identify the requirements for sharing a folder
- Identify the characteristics of shared folder permissions
- Share a folder
- Assign shared folder permissions
- Create multiple share names for a shared folder
- Modify a shared folder
- Connect to a shared folder
- Explain the use of administrative shares
- Manage shared folders by using the Computer Management utility
- Explain guidelines for assigning shared folder permissions

Estimated lesson time: 60 minutes

Simple File Sharing

Simple File Sharing, as its name implies, is a simplified sharing model that allows users to easily share folders and files with other local users on the same computer or with users in a workgroup without configuring NTFS permissions and standard shared folders. On computers running Windows XP Professional that are members of a workgroup, you can use Simple File Sharing or you can disable Simple File Sharing and use shared folder permissions. On computers running Windows XP Professional that are members of a domain, Simple File Sharing is not available.

> **Exam Tip**   If you are not able to access the Security tab of a file or folder's Properties dialog box or if you cannot assign shared folder permissions to a folder, Simple File Sharing is probably enabled.

When Simple File Sharing is enabled, users have only one choice to make—whether a folder is shared or not. When a user shares a folder, that folder is accessible to all network users. Also, with Simple File Sharing, the user cannot assign shared folder permissions. To enable or disable Simple File Sharing, in any open folder, click Tools and then click Folder Options. In the Folder Options dialog box, on the View tab, in the Advanced Settings list, select or clear the Use Simple File Sharing (Recommended) check box.

> **Note**   The remainder of this chapter assumes that you are *not* using Simple File Sharing.

Shared Folder Permissions

When Simple File Sharing is disabled, you can control how users gain access to a shared folder by assigning **shared folder permissions**. Shared folder permissions are simpler than NTFS permissions. Table 9-1 explains what each of the shared folder permissions allows a user to do, presented from most restrictive to least restrictive.

Table 9-1   Shared Folder Permissions

This Shared Folder Permission	Allows the User to
Read	Display folder names, file names, file data, and attributes; run program files; and change folders within the shared folder
Change	Create folders, add files to folders, change data in files, append data to files, change file attributes, and delete folders and files; also allows the user to perform actions that are permitted by the Read permission
Full Control	Change file permissions, take ownership of files, and perform all tasks that are permitted by the Change permission

You grant or deny shared folder permissions. Generally, it is best to grant permissions to a group rather than to individual users. You should deny permissions only when it is necessary to override permissions that are otherwise applied, for example, when it is necessary to deny permission to a specific user who belongs to a group to which you have granted the permission. If you deny a shared folder permission to a user, the user will not have that permission. For example, to deny all remote access to a shared folder, deny the Full Control permission.

Requirements for Sharing a Folder

To create shared folders on a computer running Windows XP Professional, you must be a member of the Administrators or Power Users groups. Also, users who are granted the Create Permanent Shared Objects user right are allowed to share folders. You can share only folders; you cannot share individual files. If you need to provide users network access to files, you must share the folder that contains the files.

Exam Tip   Users of the Administrators or Power Users groups can share a folder. Users who have been assigned the Create Permanent Shared Objects user right can also share folders.

Characteristics of Shared Folder Permissions

You can share any folder on a computer so that network users can access the folder. The following are characteristics of shared folder permissions:

■ Shared folder permissions apply to folders, not individual files. Because you can apply shared folder permissions only to the entire shared folder and not to individual files or subfolders in the shared folder, shared folder permissions provide less detailed security than NTFS permissions.

■ Shared folder permissions do not restrict users who access the folder locally by logging on to the computer. They apply only to users who connect to the folder over the network.

■ Shared folder permissions are the only way to secure network resources on a FAT volume, because NTFS permissions are not available on FAT volumes.

■ The default shared folder permission is Read, and it is assigned to the Everyone group when you share the folder.

Security Alert   If you share a folder and do not change the default shared folder permissions (where the Everyone group is assigned the Read permission), the shared folder is effectively not protected from people reading the contents of the folder across the network. In this case, restriction from reading the folder depends entirely on local NTFS permissions.

How to Share a Folder

When you share a folder, you can give it a share name, provide comments to describe the folder and its content, control the number of users who have access to the folder, assign permissions, and create multiple share names for the folder.

To share a folder, complete the following steps:

1. Log on with a user account that is able to share folders.

2. Right-click the folder that you want to share, and then click Properties.

3. On the Sharing tab of the Properties dialog box, click Share This Folder and configure the options shown in Figure 9-1 and described in Table 9-2.

Figure 9-1   Use the Sharing tab of a folder's Properties dialog box to share a folder.

Table 9-2   Sharing Tab Options

Option	Description
Share Name	The name that users from remote locations use to connect to the shared folder. You must enter a share name. By default, this is the same name as the folder. You can type in a different name up to 80 characters long.
Comment	An optional description for the share name. The comment appears in addition to the share name when users at client computers browse the server for shared folders. This comment can be used to identify contents of the shared folder.
User Limit	The number of users who can concurrently connect to the shared folder. If you click Maximum Allowed as the user limit, Windows XP Professional supports up to 10 connections.
Permissions	The shared folder permissions that apply only when the folder is accessed over the network. By default, the Everyone group is assigned Read for all new shared folders.
Caching	The settings to configure offline access to this shared folder. This feature is covered in Chapter 10, "Managing Data Storage."
New Share	The settings to configure more than one share name and set of permissions for this folder. This button appears only when the folder has already been shared. You will learn how to create multiple shares in the section "How to Create Multiple Share Names for a Shared Folder."

How to Assign Shared Folder Permissions

After you share a folder, the next step is to specify which users have access to the shared folder by assigning shared folder permissions to selected user accounts and groups. To assign permissions to user accounts and groups for a shared folder, use the following steps:

1. On the Sharing tab of the Properties dialog box of the shared folder, click Permissions.

2. In the Permissions dialog box for the folder, ensure that the Everyone group is selected and then click Remove.

3. In the Permissions dialog box, click Add.

4. In the Select Users Or Groups dialog box (shown in Figure 9-2), in the Enter The Object Names To Select text box, type the name of the user or group to which you want to assign permissions. Repeat this step for all user accounts and groups to which you want to assign permissions.

Tip   If you want to enter more than one user account or group at a time, separate the names by a semicolon. If you want to ensure the names are correct, click Check Names.

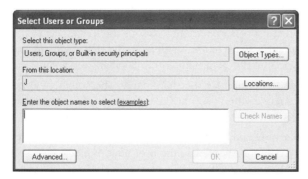

Figure 9-2   Select a user or a group to which to assign permissions.

5. Click OK.

6. In the Permissions dialog box for the shared folder, click the user account or group, and then, under Permissions, select the Allow check box or the Deny check box for the appropriate permissions for the user account or group.

How to Create Multiple Share Names for a Shared Folder

You might want to grant different permissions on a shared folder. You can create multiple share names for the same folder and assign each a different set of permissions. To share a folder with multiple share names, open the folder's Properties dialog box and then click New Share. In the New Share dialog box (shown in Figure 9-3), you assign a new share name, limit the number of connections to the share, and click Permissions to grant the permissions for the shared folder.

Figure 9-3   Create an additional share name for a shared folder.

How to Modify a Shared Folder

For existing shared folders, you can stop sharing the folder, modify the share name, and modify shared folder permissions.

To modify a shared folder, complete the following steps:

1. In the Properties dialog box of the shared folder, click the Sharing tab.
2. To complete the appropriate task, use the steps in Table 9-3.

Table 9-3   Steps to Modify a Shared Folder

To	Do This
Stop sharing a folder	Click Do Not Share This Folder.
Modify the share name	Click Do Not Share This Folder to stop sharing the folder, and click Apply. Then click Share This Folder, and type the new share name in the Share Name text box.
Modify shared folder permissions	Click Permissions. In the Permissions dialog box, click Add to add a user account or group so that you can specify permissions for a specific user or group, or click Remove to remove a user account or group. In the Select Users, Computers, Or Groups dialog box, click the user account or the group whose permissions you want to modify, and then select Allow or Deny for the appropriate permissions.

Caution   If you stop sharing a folder while a user has a file open, the user might lose data. If you click Do Not Share This Folder and a user has an open connection to the shared folder, Windows XP Professional displays a dialog box notifying you of that fact.

How to Connect to a Shared Folder

You can access a shared folder on another computer by using My Network Places, the Add Network Place Wizard, or the *Run* command.

To connect to a shared folder using My Network Places, complete the following steps:

1. Click Start, and then click Control Panel.

> **Note**   When you first use My Network Places, Windows XP Professional adds it to your Start
> menu. If My Network Places is listed on your Start menu, click it and proceed to step 4.

2. In the Control Panel window, click Network And Internet Connections.
3. In the Network And Internet Connections window, under See Also, click My Network Places.
4. Double-click the share you want to access.

> **Note**   If the share you want to connect to is listed, when you double-click it, you are con-
> nected. If the share that you want to connect to is not listed, go to step 5.

5. If the share you want to connect to is not listed, click Add A Network Place.
   The Welcome To The Add Network Place Wizard page is displayed.
6. Click Next.
7. On the Where Do You Want To Create This Network Place page, select Choose Another Network Location, and then click Next.
8. On the What Is The Address Of This Network Place page, shown in Figure 9-4, you can type a Universal Naming Convention (UNC) path to the folder (for example, *computer_name**sharedfolder_name*) and click Next.

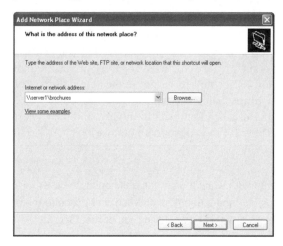

Figure 9-4   Type the UNC for the share that you want to access.

> **Tip**   You can also use the Other Locations On Your Network page to make a network connec-
> tion shortcut to a Web share (http://*Webserver*/*share*) or a File Transfer Protocol (FTP) site
> (ftp://ftp.microsoft.com).

9. On the What Do You Want To Name This Place page, type a friendly name for this page and then click Next.

10. In the Completing The Add Network Place Wizard, click Finish.

To connect to a shared folder using the *Run* command, complete the following steps:

1. Click Start, click Run, type ***computer_name*** in the Open text box, and then click OK.

   Windows XP Professional displays shared folders for the computer.

2. Double-click the shared folder to which you want to connect.

What Are Administrative Shares?

Windows XP Professional automatically shares some folders for administrative purposes. These **administrative shares** are marked with a dollar sign ($) at the end of the share name. Administrative shares are hidden from users who browse the computer. The root of each volume, the system root folder, and the location of the printer drivers are hidden shared folders that you can access across the network by typing in the exact name of the share.

Table 9-4 describes the purpose of the administrative shared folders that Windows XP Professional automatically provides.

Table 9-4   Windows XP Professional Administrative Shared Folders

Share	Purpose
C$, D$, E$, and so on	The root of each volume on a hard disk is automatically shared, and the share name is the drive letter with a dollar sign ($). When you connect to this folder, you have access to the entire volume. You use the administrative shares to remotely connect to the computer to perform administrative tasks. Windows XP Professional assigns the Full Control permission to the Administrators group.
Admin$	The system root folder, which is C:\Windows by default, is shared as Admin$. Administrators can access this shared folder to administer Windows XP Professional without knowing in which folder it is installed. Only members of the Administrators group have access to this share. Windows XP Professional assigns the Full Control permission to the Administrators group.
Print$	When you install the first shared printer, the %systemroot%\System32\Spool\Drivers folder is shared as Print$. This folder provides access to printer driver files for clients. Only members of the Administrators and Power Users groups have the Full Control permission. The Everyone group has the Read permission.

Hidden shared folders are not limited to those that the system automatically creates. You can share an additional **hidden share** by simple adding a dollar sign to the end of the share name. Only users who know the folder name can access it if they also possess the proper permissions.

> **Exam Tip** You often can use the built-in administrative shares to access resources on a computer when you cannot otherwise gain access. In particular, the Admin$ share is useful because it allows you to access the system root folder of a computer. You can also type the drive letter followed by a dollar sign (for example, C$) to access a particular drive.

How to Manage Shared Folders by Using Computer Management

You can also manage shared folders by using the **Computer Management** utility. Available shared folder management options are as follows:

- View a list of all folders that are currently shared
- Create additional shared folders
- View and edit the properties of shared folders
- Stop sharing a folder
- Manage users that are connected to shared folders
- Remotely manage shared folders on other computers

How to View a List of Shared Folders in Computer Management

You can view all folders that are currently shared in a single location within Computer Management. To view shared folders, follow these steps:

1. Start Computer Management, either by right-clicking My Computer and selecting Manage, or from the Administrative Tools folder in Control Panel.

2. Expand the System Tools node.

3. Under the System Tools node, expand the Shared Folders node, and then select the Shares folder. Shared folders are displayed in the details pane, as shown in Figure 9-5.

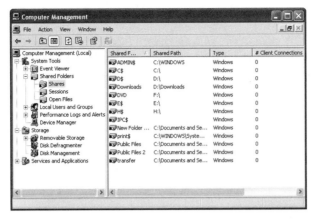

Figure 9-5   View shared folders in Computer Management.

How to Create Additional Shared Folders by Using Computer Management

You can easily share folders by using Computer Management. To share a folder, complete the following steps:

1. In Computer Management, right-click the Shares folder (in the Shared Folders node) and select New File Share.

   The Create A Shared Folder Wizard appears.

2. Click Next.

3. On the Set Up A Shared Folder page, type the path to be shared, the share name, and the share description. Click Next to continue.

4. If the folder to be shared does not exist, Windows opens a dialog box asking whether or not you want to create the folder. Click Yes to create the folder and continue.

5. On the Shared Folder Permissions page, select the appropriate permissions option and click Next.

6. Finally, click Finish to create the shared folder.

View and Edit the Properties of Shared Folders by Using Computer Management

You can view and edit the properties of any shared folder through Computer Management by right-clicking the shared folder and selecting Properties. Figure 9-6 shows the Properties dialog box of a shared folder named Public Files. On the Security tab of new shares that you create, you can also manage the NTFS permissions of the folder.

Figure 9-6 Use Computer Management to modify the properties of a shared folder.

How to Stop Sharing a Folder

You can also use Computer Management to stop sharing a folder (or a particular share name for a folder). To stop sharing a folder in Computer Management, use the following steps:

1. Start Computer Management, either by right-clicking My Computer and selecting Manage, or from the Administrative Tools folder in Control Panel.

2. Expand the System Tools node.

3. Under the System Tools node, expand the Shared Folders node, and then select the Shares folder.

4. In the Details pane, right-click the share that you want to stop, and then click Stop Sharing.

   This action does not delete the folder; it merely stops sharing the folder under the particular share name.

Manage Users That Are Connected to Shared Folders

To view the users that are connected to the server, expand the Shared Folders node in Computer Management and then select the Sessions folder. Occasionally, you might need to disconnect users from the computer so that you can perform maintenance tasks on hardware or software. To disconnect users from the server, do one of the following:

- To disconnect a single user, right-click the user name in the Sessions folder, and then select the Close Session option from the action menu.

- To disconnect all users from the server, right-click the Sessions folder, and then select the Disconnect All Sessions option from the action menu.

To view users that have shared files and folders open, under Shared Files, select the Open Files option. The details pane displays the files and folders that are currently in use on the server. This information is valuable if you are trying to work with a shared folder or file and need to know who is currently accessing the resource so that you can ask that person to disconnect.

Guidelines for Shared Folder Permissions

The following list provides some general guidelines for managing your shared folders and assigning shared folder permissions:

- Determine which groups need access to each resource and the level of access that they require. Document the groups and their permissions for each resource.

- Assign permissions to groups instead of user accounts to simplify access administration.

- Assign to a resource the most restrictive permissions that still allow users to perform required tasks. This practice is known as the **principle of least privilege**. For example, if users only need to read information in a folder and they will never delete or create files, assign the Read permission.

- Organize resources so that folders with the same security requirements are located within a folder. For example, if users require Read permission for several application folders, store those folders within the same folder. Then share this folder instead of sharing each individual application folder.

- Use intuitive share names so that users can easily recognize and locate resources. For example, for the Application folder, use Apps for the share name. You should also use share names that all client operating systems can use.

Table 9-5 describes share and folder naming conventions for different client computer operating systems.

Table 9-5   Client Computer Operating Systems and Share Name Length

Operating System	Share Name Length
Windows 2000 and later	80 characters
Windows NT, Windows 98, and Windows 95	12 characters
MS-DOS, Windows 3.*x*, and Windows for Workgroups	8.3 characters

Windows XP Professional provides 8.3-character equivalent names, but the resulting names might not be intuitive to users. For example, a Windows XP Professional folder named Accountants Database would appear as Accoun~1 on client computers running MS-DOS, Windows 3.*x*, and Windows for Workgroups.

> **Real World**   **Shared Folder Permissions on Large Networks**
>
> On small networks, you are likely to find that either Simple File Sharing or shared folder permissions are used to control access to files and folders on the network. Even when drives are formatted with the NTFS file system, most people on small networks just do not use NTFS permissions.
>
> On large company networks, you find just the opposite. Administrators typically rely on NTFS permissions and leave the default shared folder permissions (or remove the Everyone group and provide the Users group full access) in place because NTFS permissions do a much better job of securing data. Because of the way that shared folder permissions and NTFS permissions interact, NTFS permissions secure data for both local and network access. Adding shared folder permissions is really unnecessary and in fact complicates the permissions that administrators must work with. The exception to this is on computers running older versions of Windows (for example, Windows 98 or Windows Me) that do not support the NTFS file system; these systems must use shared folder permissions if their data is to be shared on the network.

Practice: Managing Shared Folders

In this practice, you will determine the effective shared permissions of users, share a folder, create an additional share name for a shared folder, and stop the sharing of a folder.

Exercise 1: Calculate Effective Shared Permissions

In the following exercise, User101 has been assigned permissions to access resources as an individual and as a member of a group, as shown in Figure 9-7.

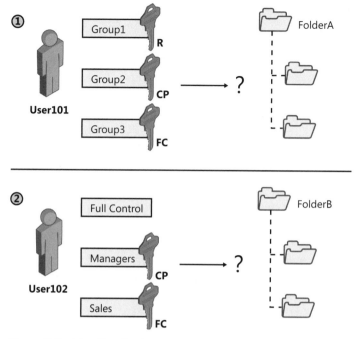

Figure 9-7   Identify effective permissions.

Determine which effective permissions are assigned for User101 and User102.

1. User101 is a member of Group1, Group2, and Group3. Group1 has Read permission. Group2 has change permission for FolderA, and Group3 has Full Control permissions assigned for FolderA. What are User101's effective permissions for FolderA?

_____

_____

_____

2. User102 has been granted the Full Control shared folder permission for FolderB as an individual user. User102 is a member of the Managers group, which has been granted Change permission for FolderB, and a member of the Sales group, which has been denied all access to FolderB. What are User102's effective permissions for FolderB?

_____

_____

_____

_____

Exercise 2: Create a Shared Folder

1. Click Start, and then click My Documents.

2. In the My Documents window, click the File menu, point to New, and then click Folder.

3. The new folder appears in the window with the name highlighted. Type **Public Files** for the name of the folder.

4. Right-click the Public Files folder, and click Sharing and Security.

5. In the Public Files Properties dialog box, on the Sharing tab, click Share This Folder, and then click Apply.

6. What new button appears on the dialog box after you click Apply?

   _____

   _____

   _____

7. Click Permissions.

8. In the Permissions for Public Files dialog box, in the Group Or User Names list, click Everyone and then click Remove.

9. Click Add.

10. In the Select Users Or Groups dialog box, type **Users** and then click OK.

11. In the Permissions for Public Files dialog box, in the Group Or User Names list, click Users.

12. In the Permissions for Users list, in the Allow column, select the Change check box.

13. Click OK, and leave the Public Files dialog box open for the next exercise.

Exercise 3: Create an Additional Share Name for a Folder

1. In the Public Files dialog box, click New Share.

2. In the New Share dialog box, in the Share Name text box, type **Public Files 2**.

3. In the Comment text box, type **Power Users**.

4. Click Permissions.

5. In the Permissions for Public Files 2 dialog box, in the Group Or User Names list, click Everyone and then click Remove.

6. Click Add.

7. In the Select Users Or Groups dialog box, type **Power Users** and then click OK.

8. In the Permissions for Public Files dialog box, in the Group Or User Names list, click Power Users.

9. In the Permissions for Users list, in the Allow column, select the Full Control check box, and then click OK.

10. In the New Share dialog box, click OK.

11. What new button is added to the Public Files Properties dialog box?

_____

_____

12. Click OK.

Lesson Review

Use the following questions to help determine whether you have learned enough to move on to the next lesson. If you have difficulty answering these questions, review the material in this lesson before beginning the next lesson. You can find answers to these questions in the "Questions and Answers" section at the end of this chapter.

1. Because you use NTFS permissions to specify which users and groups can access files and folders and what these permissions allow users to do with the contents of the file or folder, why do you need to share a folder or use shared folder permissions?

_____

_____

_____

_____

_____

_____

_____

2. Which of the following permissions are shared folder permissions? (Choose all that apply.)

a. Read

b. Write

c. Modify

d. Full Control

3. _____ (Denied /Allowed) permissions take precedence over _____ (denied /allowed) permissions on a shared folder.

4. When you copy a shared folder, the original folder is _____ (no longer shared /still shared) and the copy is _____ (not shared / shared).

5. When you move a shared folder, the folder is _____ (no longer shared /still shared).

6. When you rename a shared folder, the folder is _____ (no longer shared /still shared).

7. Windows XP Professional automatically shares folders for administrative purposes. These shares are marked with a _____, which hides them from users who browse the computer.

8. The system root folder, which is C:\Windows by default, is shared as _____. Administrators can access this shared folder to administer Windows XP Professional without knowing in which folder it is installed. Only members of the Administrators group have access to this share. Windows XP Professional assigns the Full Control permission to the Administrators group.

Lesson Summary

- Simple File Sharing is a simplified sharing model that allows users to share or not share a folder instead of applying NTFS and shared folder permissions. Simple File Sharing is enabled by default on computers running Windows XP Professional that are members of a workgroup. Simple File Sharing is not available on computers that are members of a domain.

- The three shared folder permissions are Read, Change, and Full Control.

- To share a folder, you must be a member of the Administrators or Power Users groups, or have the Create Permanent Shared Objects user right assigned to your account.

- The characteristics of shared folder permissions include:
  - ❏ Shared folder permissions apply to folders, not individual files.
  - ❏ Shared folder permissions apply only to users who connect to the folder over the network.
  - ❏ Using shared folder permissions is the only way to secure file resources on FAT volumes.
  - ❏ The default shared folder permission is Read, and it is assigned to the Everyone group when you share the folder.

- When you share a folder, you can give it a share name, provide comments to describe the folder and its content, control the number of users who have access to the folder, assign permissions, and share the same folder multiple times.

- After sharing a folder, control access to that folder by assigning shared folder permissions.

- You can create multiple share names for a single folder and assign different permissions to each share name.

- For existing shared folders, you can stop sharing the folder, modify the share name, and modify shared folder permissions.

- You can connect to a shared folder by using My Network Places, My Computer, or the Run dialog box.

- Windows XP Professional automatically shares folders for administrative purposes. These shares are marked with a dollar sign ($), which hides them from users who browse the computer.

- You can use Computer Management to view, create, and modify shared folders, as well as to view users that are connected to each share. You can also use Computer Management to remotely manage shared folders on other computers.

- You should practice the principle of least privilege when assigning shared folder permissions by allowing users only the access they need to do their job. You should grant permissions to groups rather than users. You should also try to arrange folders so that resources with the same security requirements are grouped.

Lesson 2: Combining Shared Folder Permissions and NTFS Permissions

You share folders to provide network users with access to resources. If you are using a FAT volume, the shared folder permissions are the only resource available to provide security for the folders that you have shared and the folders and files they contain. If you are using an NTFS volume, you can assign NTFS permissions to individual users and groups to better control access to the files and subfolders in the shared folders. When you combine shared folder permissions and NTFS permissions, the more restrictive permission is always the overriding permission.

After this lesson, you will be able to

■ Calculate effective permissions for folders that have shared folder and NTFS permissions

■ Explain the rules when combining shared folder permissions and NTFS permissions

■ Combine shared folder permissions and NTFS permissions

Estimated lesson time: 15 minutes

How to Calculate Effective Permissions for Folders That Have Shared Folder and NTFS Permissions

When users connect to shared folders that are located on NTFS volumes, share permissions and NTFS permissions will combine to control the actions that a user can perform. Determining effective permissions can be somewhat difficult when both NTFS and shared permissions are involved.

Calculating effective permissions for resources within a shared folder on an NTFS partition is a three-step process.

1. Calculate the NTFS effective permissions for the user.

2. Calculate the shared folder effective permissions for the user.

3. Analyze the results of steps 1 and 2, and select the result that is the more restrictive of the two. This will be the user's effective permission for the shared folder.

Rules When Combining Shared Folder Permissions and NTFS Permissions

When you use shared folder permissions on an NTFS volume, the following rules apply:

- You can apply NTFS permissions to files and subfolders in the shared folder. You can apply different NTFS permissions to each file and subfolder contained in a shared folder.

- In addition to shared folder permissions, users must have NTFS permissions for the files and subfolders contained in shared folders to access those files and subfolders. This is in contrast to FAT volumes, in which permissions for a shared folder are the only permissions protecting files and subfolders in the shared folder.

- When you combine shared folder permissions and NTFS permissions, the more restrictive permission is always the overriding permission.

In Figure 9-8, the Users group has the shared folder Full Control permission for the Public folder and the NTFS Read permission for FileA. The Users group's effective permission for FileA is the more restrictive Read permission. The effective permission for FileB is Full Control because both the shared folder permission and the NTFS permission allow this level of access.

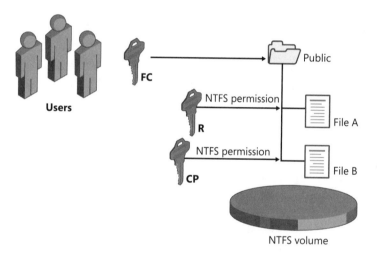

Figure 9-8   Combine shared folder permissions and NTFS permissions.

Practice: Combining Permissions

Figure 9-9 shows examples of shared folders on NTFS volumes. These shared folders contain subfolders that have also been assigned NTFS permissions. Determine a user's effective permissions for each example.

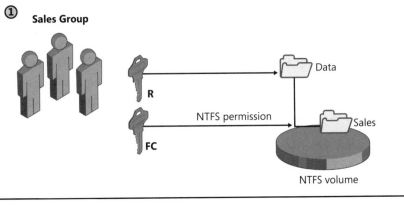

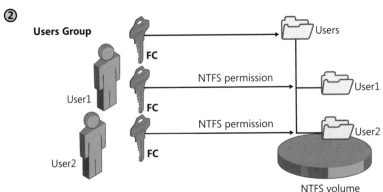

Figure 9-9   Combine permissions for each group.

1. In the first example, the Data folder is shared. The Sales group has the shared folder Read permission for the Data folder and the NTFS Full Control permission for the Sales subfolder. What are the Sales group's effective permissions for the Sales subfolder when they gain access to the Sales subfolder by making a connection to the Data shared folder?

_____

_____

_____

2. In the second example, the Users folder contains user home folders. Each user home folder contains data accessible only to the user for whom the folder is named. The Users folder has been shared, and the Users group has the shared folder Full Control permission for the Users folder. User1 and User2 have the NTFS Full Control permission for their home folder only and no NTFS permissions for other folders. These users are all members of the Users group. What permissions does User1 have when he or she accesses the User1 subfolder by making a con-

nection to the Users shared folder? What are User1's permissions for the User2 subfolder?

_____

_____

_____

_____

Lesson Review

Use the following questions to help determine whether you have learned enough to move on to the next lesson. If you have difficulty answering these questions, review the material in this lesson before beginning the next lesson. You can find answers to these questions in the "Questions and Answers" section at the end of this chapter.

1. If you are using both shared folder and NTFS permissions, the _____ (least/most) restrictive permission is always the overriding permission.

2. Which of the following statements about combining shared folder permissions and NTFS permissions are true? (Choose all that apply.)

   a. You can use shared folder permissions on all shared folders.

   b. The Change shared folder permission is more restrictive than the Read NTFS permission.

   c. You can use NTFS permissions on all shared folders.

   d. The Read NTFS permission is more restrictive than the Change shared folder permission.

3. Which of the following statements about shared folder permissions and NTFS permissions are true? (Choose all that apply.)

   a. NTFS permissions apply only when the resource is accessed over the network.

   b. NTFS permissions apply whether the resource is accessed locally or over the network.

   c. Shared folder permissions apply only when the resource is accessed over the network.

   d. Shared folder permissions apply whether the resource is accessed locally or over the network.

4. If needed, you can apply different _____ permissions to each folder, file, and subfolder.

Lesson Summary

- To combine shared folder and NTFS permissions, you should take the following steps:

    a. Calculate the NTFS effective permissions for the user.

    b. Calculate the shared folder effective permissions for the user.

    c. Analyze the results of steps 1 and 2, and select the result that is the more restrictive of the two. This will be the user's effective permission for the shared folder.

- On a FAT volume, the shared folder permissions are the only available way to provide security for the folders you have shared and for the folders and files they contain. On an NTFS volume, you can assign NTFS permissions to individual users and groups to better control access to the files and subfolders in the shared folders. On an NTFS volume, you can apply different NTFS permissions to each file and subfolder in a shared folder.

Case Scenario Exercise

In this exercise, you will read a scenario about planning shared folders and then answer the questions that follow. If you have difficulty completing this work, review the material in this chapter before beginning the next chapter. You can find answers to these questions in the "Questions and Answers" section at the end of this chapter.

Scenario

You are an administrator working for a company named Contoso, Ltd., a manufacturer of telephone systems used in airplanes. You are planning how to share resources on servers in the company's main office. Record your decisions in the table at the end of this exercise. Figure 9-10 illustrates a partial folder structure for the servers at the manufacturing company.

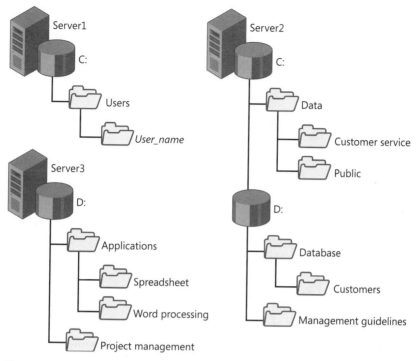

Figure 9-10   A partial folder structure for the servers at a manufacturing company

You need to make resources on these servers available to network users. To do this, determine which folders to share and which permissions to assign to groups, including the appropriate built-in groups. Base your planning decisions on the following criteria:

- Members of the Managers group need to read and revise documents in the Management Guidelines folder. Nobody else should have access to this folder.

- Administrators need complete access to all shared folders, except for Management Guidelines.

- The customer service department needs its own network location to store working files. All customer service representatives are members of the Customer Service group.

- All employees need a network location to share information with each other.

- All employees need to use the spreadsheet, database, and word processing software.

- Only members of the Managers group should have access to the project management software.

- Members of the CustomerDBFull group need to read and update the customer database.

- Members of the CustomerDBRead group need to read only the customer database.

- Each user needs a private network location to store files, which must be accessible only to that user.

- Share names must be accessible from computers running Windows 95 and later, as well as from non-Windows-based platforms.

Questions

Record your answers in this table.

Folder Name and Location	Shared Name	Groups and Permissions
Example: Management Guidelines	MgmtGd	Managers: Full Control

Troubleshooting Lab

You are an administrator for a company named Contoso, Ltd., which is a distributor of high-end fabrics sold at custom furniture retailers across the United States. You are working with Sandra, a manager in the Sales department. Sandra is trying to work with a file named Winter Products, which is located in a shared folder named Brochures. She can access the file in a shared folder, but cannot save the file after making changes.

Sandra is a member of the following groups:

- Sales

- Users

- Sales Managers

NTFS permissions are configured as shown in Figure 9-11.Shared folder permissions are configured as shown in Figure 9-12.

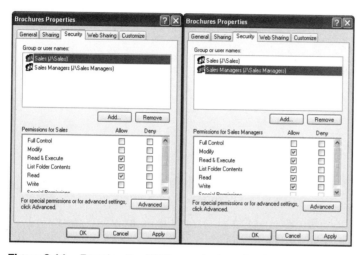

Figure 9-11   Examine the NTFS permissions for the Brochures folder.

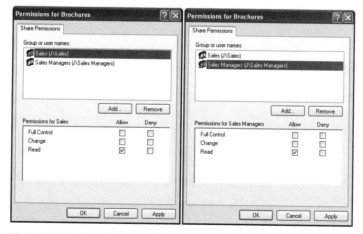

Figure 9-12   Examine the shared folder permissions for the Brochures folder.

Why can Sandra open the file but not save it in the shared folder? How would you solve the problem?

_____

_____

_____

_____

_____

_____

_____

_____

_____

Chapter Summary

- Sharing a folder makes the folder available to users on the network. You should understand the following points about shared folders:

  - ❑ Simple File Sharing is enabled by default on computers running Windows XP Professional that are members of a workgroup. Simple File Sharing is not available on computers that are members of a domain.

  - ❑ The three shared folder permissions are Read, Change, and Full Control.

  - ❑ To share a folder, you must be a member of the Administrators or Power Users groups, or have the Create Permanent Shared Objects user right assigned to your account.

  - ❑ You can share folders, but not individual files.

  - ❑ You can share folders on NTFS or FAT volumes.

  - ❑ You can create multiple share names for a single folder.

  - ❑ Windows XP Professional automatically shares folders for administrative purposes. These shares are marked with a dollar sign ($), which hides them from users who browse the computer.

  - ❑ You can use Computer Management to view, create, and modify shared folders, as well as to view users that are connected to each share. You can also use Computer Management to remotely manage shared folders on other computers.

- When shared folder permissions and NTFS permissions exist on a folder, you can calculate the overall effective permissions by calculating the effective shared folder permissions, then calculating the effective NTFS permissions, and then applying the more restrictive of those two.

Exam Highlights

Before taking the exam, review the key points and terms that are presented in this chapter. You need to know this information.

Key Points

- If you cannot access the Security tab of a file or folder's Properties dialog box or if you cannot assign shared folder permissions to a folder, Simple File Sharing is probably enabled.

- Users of the Administrators or Power Users groups can share a folder. Users who have been assigned the Create Permanent Shared Objects user right can also share folders.

- You often can use the built-in administrative shares to access resources on a computer when you cannot otherwise gain access. In particular, the Admin$ share is useful because it allows you to access the system root folder of a computer. You can also type the drive letter followed by a dollar sign (for example, C$) to access a particular drive.

Key Terms

administrative share   Hidden shares that Windows XP Professional creates automatically so that administrators can access resources on a computer.

Computer Management   A console that provides access to a number of management utilities for administering a computer, including the ability to create, manage, and monitor shared folders.

effective permissions   The permissions level that a user actually has, taking all permission sources into account.

hidden share   A method of preventing users who are browsing the network from viewing the share. If you append the dollar sign ($) to a share name, it becomes hidden. Built-in administrative shares are examples of hidden shares.

shared folder permissions   Permissions assigned to shared folders that control access to the folder over the network. Shared folder permissions include Read, Change, and Full Control.

shared folders   Folders made accessible to users on the network.

Simple File Sharing   A type of sharing that is used when a Windows XP computer has not joined a domain or is running Windows XP Home Edition.

Questions and Answers

Lesson 1 Practice: Exercise 1

Page 9-14

1. User101 is a member of Group1, Group2, and Group3. Group1 has Read permission. Group2 has Full Control permission for FolderA, and Group3 has change permissions assigned for FolderA. What are User101's effective permissions for FolderA?

   Because User101 is a member of Group1, Group2, and Group3, User101's effective permission is Full Control, which includes all capabilities of the Read permission and the Change permission.

2. User102 has been granted the Full Control shared folder permission for FolderB as an individual user. User102 is a member of the Managers group, which has been granted Change permission for FolderB, and a member of the Sales group, which has been denied all access to FolderB. What are User102's effective permissions for FolderB?

   User102 has been granted Full Control to FolderB, but because User102 is a member of the Managers group and the Sales group, User102's effective permission is denied Full Control access to FolderB. Denied permission overrides all other permissions.

Lesson 1 Practice: Exercise 2

Page 9-16

1. What new button appears on the dialog box after you click Apply?

   A button named New Share appears in the Properties dialog box for a folder after you share the folder for the first time. This button allows you to create additional shares.

Lesson 1 Practice: Exercise 3

Page 9-16

1. What new button is added to the Public Files Properties dialog box?

   After creating an additional share, a button named Remove Share is added to the dialog box. You can use this button to remove the additional share name.

Lesson 1 Review

Page 9-17

1. Because you use NTFS permissions to specify which users and groups can access files and folders and what these permissions allow users to do with the contents of the file or folder, why do you need to share a folder or use shared folder permissions?

   Although NTFS security is effective whether a user gains access to the file or folder at the computer or over the network, NTFS permissions do not make folders available over the network. Sharing folders is the only way to make folders and their contents available over the network. Shared folder permissions provide another way to secure file resources. They can be used on FAT or FAT32 partitions, as well as NTFS partitions, whereas NTFS permissions are available only on NTFS volumes.

2. Which of the following permissions are shared folder permissions? (Choose all that apply.)

   a. Read

   b. Write

   c. Modify

   d. Full Control

   The correct answers are A and D. The available shared folder permissions are Read, Change, and Full Control. B and C are not correct because Write and Modify are not valid shared folder permissions.

3. _____ (Denied /Allowed) permissions take precedence over _____ (denied /allowed) permissions on a shared folder.

   Denied permissions take precedence over allowed permissions on a shared folder.

4. When you copy a shared folder, the original folder is _____ (no longer shared /still shared) and the copy is _____ (not shared / shared).

   When you copy a folder, the original folder is still shared and the copy is not shared.

5. When you move a shared folder, the folder is _____ (no longer shared /still shared).

   When you move a shared folder, the folder is no longer shared.

6. When you rename a shared folder, the folder is _____ (no longer shared /still shared).

   When you rename a shared folder, the folder is no longer shared.

7. Windows XP Professional automatically shares folders for administrative purposes. These shares are marked with a _____, which hides them from users who browse the computer.

   Dollar sign ($)

8. The system root folder, which is C:\Windows by default, is shared as _____. Administrators can access this shared folder to administer Windows XP Professional without knowing in which folder it is installed. Only members of the Administrators group have access to this share. Windows XP Professional assigns the Full Control permission to the Administrators group.

   Admin$

Lesson 2 Practice: Combining Permissions

Page
9-21

1. In the first example, the Data folder is shared. The Sales group has the shared folder Read permission for the Data folder and the NTFS Full Control permission for the Sales subfolder. What are the Sales group's effective permissions for the Sales subfolder when they gain access to the Sales subfolder by making a connection to the Data shared folder?

The Sales group has the Read permission for the Sales subfolder because when shared folder permissions are combined with NTFS permissions, the more restrictive permission applies.

2. In the second example, the Users folder contains user home folders. Each user home folder contains data accessible only to the user for whom the folder is named. The Users folder has been shared, and the Users group has the shared folder Full Control permission for the Users folder. User1 and User2 have the NTFS Full Control permission for their home folder only and no NTFS permissions for other folders. These users are all members of the Users group. What permissions does User1 have when he or she accesses the User1 subfolder by making a connection to the Users shared folder? What are User1's permissions for the User2 subfolder?

User1 has the Full Control permission for the User1 subfolder because both the shared folder permission and the NTFS permission allow Full Control. User1 cannot access the User2 subfolder because she or he has no NTFS permission to gain access to it.

Lesson 2 Review

Page
9-23

1. If you are using both shared folder and NTFS permissions, the _____ (least/most) restrictive permission is always the overriding permission.

Most

2. Which of the following statements about combining shared folder permissions and NTFS permissions are true? (Choose all that apply.)

a. You can use shared folder permissions on all shared folders.

b. The Change shared folder permission is more restrictive than the Read NTFS permission.

c. You can use NTFS permissions on all shared folders.

d. The Read NTFS permission is more restrictive than the Change shared folder permission.

The correct answers are A and D. B is not correct because the Read NTFS permission is more restrictive than the Change shared folder permission. C is not correct because you can use NTFS permissions only on volumes formatted with NTFS, whereas you can use shared folder permissions on volumes formatted with NTFS or FAT.

3. Which of the following statements about shared folder permissions and NTFS permissions are true? (Choose all that apply.)

    a. NTFS permissions apply only when the resource is accessed over the network.

    b. NTFS permissions apply whether the resource is accessed locally or over the network.

    c. Shared folder permissions apply only when the resource is accessed over the network.

    d. Shared folder permissions apply whether the resource is accessed locally or over the network.

The correct answers are B and C. A is not correct because NTFS permissions apply whether the resource is accessed locally or over the network. D is not correct because shared folder permissions are applied only when a folder is accessed remotely over the network.

4. If needed, you can apply different _____ permissions to each folder, file, and subfolder.

NTFS

Case Scenario Exercise Questions

Page
9-24

Folder Name and Location	Shared Name	Groups and Permissions
Example: Management Guidelines	MgmtGd	Managers: Full Control

You have two choices for permissions: you can rely entirely on NTFS permissions and assign Full Control for all shared folders to the Everyone group, or you can use shared folder permissions according to resource needs. The following suggested shared folders include required permissions if you decide to assign shared folder permissions.

■ Share Management Guidelines as MgmtGd. Assign the Full Control permission to the Managers group.

■ Share Data as Data. Assign the Full Control permission to the Administrators built-in group.

- Share Data\Customer Service as CustServ. Assign the Change permission to the Customer Service group.

- Share Data\Public as Public. Assign the Change permission to the Users built-in group.

- Share Applications as Apps. Assign the Read permission to the Users built-in group and the Full Control permission to the Administrators built-in group.

- Share Project Management as ProjMan. Assign the Change permission to the Managers group and the Full Control permission to the Administrators built-in group.

- Share Database\Customers as CustDB. Assign the Change permission to the CustomerDBFull group, the Read permission to the CustomerDBRead group, and the Full Control permission to the Administrators built-in group.

- Share Users as Users. Create a folder for every employee below this folder. Assign the Full Control permission to each employee for his or her own folder. Preferably, have Windows XP Professional create the folder and assign permission automatically when you create each user account

Troubleshooting Lab

Page 9-26

Why can Sandra open the file but cannot save it in the shared folder? How would you solve the problem?

Sandra has the effective NTFS permissions necessary to open and save the file. The Sales group has the Read & Execute, List Folder Contents, and Read permissions. The Sales Managers group has these permissions plus the Modify and Write permissions. To determine effective NTFS permissions, combine permissions from all sources.

For shared folder permissions, both the Sales and Sales Managers groups have only the Read permission. Because you choose the most restrictive permission when combining NTFS and shared folder permissions, Sandra ends up being able to read—but not change—files in the Brochures folder. To solve this problem, you should select the Change check box in the Allow column of the Permissions for Sales Managers list (see Figure 9-12).

10 Managing Data Storage

Exam Objectives in this Chapter:

- Monitor, manage, and troubleshoot access to files and folders
    - Configure, manage, and troubleshoot file compression
    - Optimize access to files and folders
- Manage and troubleshoot access to and synchronization of offline files
- Implement, manage, and troubleshoot disk devices
    - Install, configure, and manage DVD and CD-ROM devices
    - Monitor and configure disks
    - Monitor, configure, and troubleshoot volumes
    - Monitor and configure removable media, such as tape drives
- Configure, manage, and troubleshoot the Encrypting File System (EFS)

Why This Chapter Matters

This chapter introduces data storage management on different types of volumes. You will learn about the different types of disk devices and volumes, as well as how to manage and troubleshoot them in Windows XP Professional. You will learn about compression, which allows you to store more data on a disk, and you will learn about disk quotas, which allow you to control how much space a user can use on a disk. You will learn how you can increase the security of files and folders on your computer by using the Microsoft Encrypting File System (EFS). You will also learn about defragmenting a disk, which allows your system to access and save files and folders more efficiently.

Lessons in this Chapter:

Before You Begin

To complete this chapter, you must have a computer that meets the minimum hardware requirements listed in the preface, "About This Book." You must also have Windows XP Professional installed on the computer.

Lesson 1: Managing and Troubleshooting Disks and Volumes

Hard disks are fixed storage devices that are connected to a computer by Integrated Device Electronics (IDE) or Small Computer System Interface (SCSI) controllers. Portable hard disks are also available, and they can be connected with universal serial bus (USB) and Institute of Electrical and Electronics Engineers (IEEE) 1394 (also known as FireWire) interfaces. Windows typically treats portable hard disks, CD-ROM drives, and DVDs as removable storage devices. This lesson focuses on configuring and troubleshooting hard disks in Windows XP. You should also be able to use the tools that Windows XP provides for managing, maintaining, and troubleshooting hard disks.

After this lesson, you will be able to

- Explain the use of basic and dynamic disks.
- Manage hard disks by using the Disk Management tool.
- Manage hard disks on a remote computer in Computer Management.
- Manage disks from the command line by using the Diskpart command.
- Troubleshoot disks and volumes.
- Work with removable media.

Estimated lesson time: 70 minutes

Overview of Basic and Dynamic Disks

Windows XP Professional supports two types of hard disk storage on desktop computers: **basic disks** and **dynamic disks**. (You cannot use dynamic disks on portable computers.)

Basic Disks

Basic disks are the traditional type of storage that is available in earlier versions of Microsoft Windows. Basic disks are also the default storage type in Windows XP, so all hard disks begin as basic disks. Windows XP recognizes all disks as basic by default, including all new installations and upgrades from previous versions of Windows. To use a dynamic disk, you must convert a basic disk to a dynamic disk.

On a basic disk, you must create one or more partitions (also called basic volumes). Partitions were covered in detail in Chapter 2, "Installing Windows XP Professional," but a brief review is in order.

You must configure a basic disk with at least one partition. In fact, most computers that you will encounter have a single hard disk with one partition that takes up all the physical space on the disk. You can also divide a hard disk into multiple partitions for the purpose of organizing file storage or supporting multiple operating systems on a single computer. You can create the following three types of partitions on a basic hard disk:

Primary You can configure up to four **primary partitions** on a computer running a Windows operating system (three partitions if you also have an extended partition on the disk). You can configure any primary partition as the active (or bootable) drive, but only one primary partition is active at a time. Other primary drives are typically hidden from the operating system and are not assigned a drive letter.

Extended An **extended partition** provides a way to exceed the four primary partition limit. You cannot format an extended partition with any file system. Rather, extended partitions serve as a shell in which you can create any number of logical partitions.

Logical You can create any number of **logical partitions** inside an extended partition. Logical partitions are normally used for organizing files. All logical partitions are visible, no matter which operating system is started.

Windows stores partition information for basic disks in the partition table, which is not part of any operating system (it is an area of the drive that is accessible by all operating systems). Other configuration options, such as drive letter assignments, are controlled by the operating system and are stored in the Windows Registry.

Dynamic Disks

Windows XP Professional supports dynamic disks (except on portable computers). Dynamic disks offer several advantages over basic disks:

- You can divide a dynamic disk into many volumes. The basic disk concept of primary and extended partitions does not exist when using dynamic disks.

- Windows stores configuration information for dynamic disks entirely on the disk. If there are multiple dynamic disks, Windows replicates information to all other disks so that each disk has a copy of the configuration information. This information is stored in the last 1 MB of the disk.

- You can extend dynamic volumes by using contiguous or noncontiguous disk space. Dynamic volumes can also be made up of areas of disk space on more than one disk.

Windows XP supports the following types of dynamic volumes

Simple volume   A **simple volume** can contain disk space from a single disk and can be extended if necessary.

Spanned volume   A **spanned volume** can contain disk space from 2 or more (up to a maximum of 32) disks. The amount of disk space from each disk can vary. You will most often use spanned volumes when a simple volume is running low on disk space and you need to extend the volume by using space on another hard disk. You can continue to extend spanned volumes to include areas from additional hard disks as necessary. When Windows writes data to a spanned volume, it writes data to the area on the first disk until the area is filled, and then writes data to the area on the second disk, and so on. There is no fault tolerance in spanned volumes. If any of the disks containing the spanned volume fail, you lose all data in the entire spanned volume.

Striped volume   A **striped volume** can contain disk space from 2 or more (up to a maximum of 32) disks. Unlike spanned volumes, striped volumes require that you use an identical amount of disk space from each disk. When Windows writes data to a striped volume, it divides the data into 64 KB chunks and writes to the disks in a fixed order. Thus, Windows will split a 128 KB file into two 64 KB chunks, and then stores each chunk on a separate disk. Striped volumes provide increased performance because it is faster to read or write two smaller pieces of a file on two drives than to read or write the entire file on a single drive. However, you cannot extend striped volumes, and they provide no fault tolerance. If any of the disks that contain the striped volume fail, you lose all data on the volume. Striped volumes are also referred to as RAID-0.

> **Exam Tip**   Windows XP Professional does not support fault-tolerant disk configurations. Spanned volumes simply allow you to use different amounts of disk space from multiple hard disks in a single volume. Striped volumes allow you use an identical amount of disk space from multiple hard disks. The advantage of using striped volumes is that Windows can write information to the disk more quickly.

Real World   **Supporting Multiple Operating Systems**

Basic disks are generally sufficient for a computer with a single hard disk. There are really two situations in which you might want to use a dynamic disk. The first is if you need to extend a volume to contain unallocated disk space that is not contiguous (for example, if you have extra free space on the same disk, but not directly adjacent to the volume you need to extend, or if you have free space on another disk). The second reason is if you want to configure a striped volume to increase read/write speed.

If you plan to use multiple operating systems on the same computer, your choice of disk types will be limited by the operating systems you want to install. Although multibooting is not used as much as it used to be, it continues to be a useful feature if you are using Windows XP but occasionally need to replicate older computing environments. (You will probably find an alternate solution such as Microsoft Virtual PC more efficient and easy to configure.) If you decide to use multibooting, you are limited in the following ways:

- If you need to install Windows XP Professional along with any operating system other than Windows 2000 Professional, you must use a basic disk. You should create a primary disk partition for each operating system.

- If you have a single dynamic disk, you can install only one operating system: Windows XP Professional or Windows 2000 Professional (the only desktop operating systems that support dynamic disks).

- If you have two or more hard disks installed in your computer, each dynamic disk can contain one installation of Windows XP Professional or Windows 2000. No other operating systems can start from a dynamic disk. Windows XP Home Edition does not support dynamic disks.

Managing Hard Disks by Using the Disk Management Tool

You will use the **Disk Management** tool to create and manage volumes on fixed and removable disks. You access Disk Management from within the Computer Management window, as shown in Figure 10-1. You can access Computer Management by using the Administrative Tools icon in Control Panel or by right-clicking My Computer and selecting Manage.

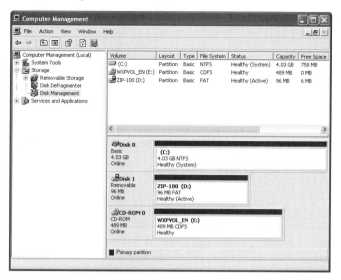

Figure 10-1   Use the Disk Management tool to manage fixed and removable storage.

Working with Basic Disks

You make unallocated space on basic disks available to the operating system by creating a partition and then formatting that partition with the file system of your choice.

How to Create a Primary Partition   To create a primary partition, follow these steps:

1. Click Start, and then click Control Panel.

2. In the Control Panel window, click Performance And Maintenance.

3. In the Performance And Maintenance window, click Administrative Tools.

4. In the Administrative Tools menu, double-click Computer Management.

> **Tip**   You can also open Computer Management by right-clicking the My Computer icon on the desktop or Start menu, and then clicking Manage.

5. In the Computer Management window, expand the Storage container, and then click Disk Management.

6. In Disk Management, right-click the unallocated space in which you want to create the primary partition, as shown in Figure 10-2, and then select New Partition.

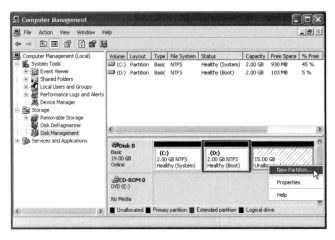

Figure 10-2 Create a partition on a basic disk.

7. On the Welcome page for the New Partition Wizard, click Next.

8. On the Select Partition Type page, shown in Figure 10-3, click Primary Partition and click Next.

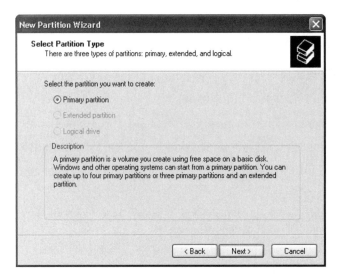

Figure 10-3 Select a partition type on the basic disk.

9. On the Specify Partition Size page, enter the amount of disk space in megabytes (MB) that you want to use for this partition, and then click Next.

10. On the Assign Drive Letter Or Path page, choose an available drive letter or a path for a volume mount point, and then click Next.

11. On the Format Partition page, click Format This Partition, select a file system, and then assign a volume label. Click Next.

12. On the Completion page, click Finish to create and format the partition. Be patient: Windows must perform a number of functions, which can take several minutes.

How to Create Extended Partitions To create an extended partition, follow these steps:

1. In Disk Management, right-click the unallocated space in which you want to create the extended partition and select New Partition.

2. On the Welcome page for the Create Partition Wizard, click Next.

3. On the Select Partition Type page, click Extended Partition, and then click Next.

4. On the Specify Partition Size page, enter the amount of disk space in MB that you want to use for this partition, and then click Next.

5. On the Completion page, click Finish to create the extended partition.

You are not prompted to assign a drive letter or to format an extended partition because the extended partition serves only as a shell to contain logical drives. You will format and assign drive letters to logical drives.

How to Create Logical Drives To create a logical drive inside an extended partition, follow these steps:

1. In Disk Management, right-click the free space in the extended partition in which you want to create the logical drive, and then click New Logical Drive.

2. On the Welcome page for the Create Partition Wizard, click Next.

3. On the Select Partition Type page, click Logical Drive, and then click Next.

4. On the Specify Partition Size page, enter the amount of disk space in MB that you want to use for this logical drive, and then click Next.

5. On the Assign Drive Letter Or Path page, choose an available drive letter, and then click Next.

6. On the Format Partition page, click Format This Partition, select a file system, and then assign a volume label. Click Next.

7. On the completion page, click Finish to create and format the logical drive.

Figure 10-4 shows an extended partition on Disk 1 that contains a 502 MB logical drive and 612 MB of remaining free space.

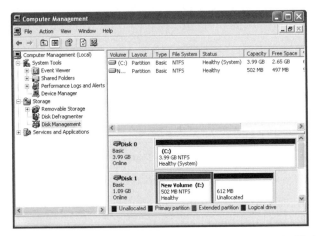

Figure 10-4   Viewing extended and logical partitions in Disk Management.

Formatting Volumes

Formatting a basic or dynamic volume with a file system prepares the volume to accept data. Unformatted volumes contain no file system and are not accessible by using Windows Explorer or any other application.

You can format volumes in the following ways:

■   By using Disk Management and formatting the new volume as it is being created

■   By using Disk Management, right-clicking an existing volume, and then selecting Format

■   By using Windows Explorer, right-clicking the drive letter, and then selecting Format

■   By using a command prompt, using the Format.exe command, and selecting the appropriate parameters

If you format an existing volume that contains data, all data is lost. Windows XP protects itself by preventing you from formatting the system and boot partition for the operating system by using any of the built-in Windows utilities.

Formatting options, shown in Figure 10-5, include the following:

Volume Label   The character name for a volume of up to 11 characters. This is the name that is displayed in Disk Management and Windows Explorer. You should choose a label that describes the type of information that is stored on the volume, such as System for the volume that contains the operating system or Documents for a volume that contains user documents.

File System   Allows you choose from the FAT (for FAT16), FAT32, or NTFS file systems (see Chapter 2 for more information on file systems).

Allocation Unit Size   Allows you change the default cluster size for any of the file systems. Microsoft recommends leaving this value at its default setting.

Perform A Quick Format   Specifies that you want to format the drive without having Windows perform an exhaustive scan of the drive to check for bad sectors. Select this option only if you have previously performed a full format and are certain that the disk is not damaged.

Enable File And Folder Compression   Specifies that all files placed on the disk will be compressed by default. Compression is always available on an NTFS volume, and you can enable or disable it at any time through the properties of the files and folders on the volume. File And Folder Compression is available only when you format a volume with NTFS. Read Lesson 2, "Managing Compression," for more information.

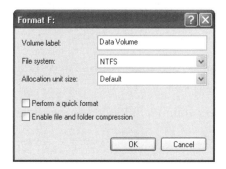

Figure 10-5   You can format a partition by using the Disk Management tool.

Drive Letters

When you create a basic or dynamic volume, you assign it a **drive letter**, such as C or D. The drive letter is used to access the volume through Windows Explorer and other applications. Floppy drives, CD-ROM and DVD drives, removable drives, and tape devices are also assigned drive letters.

To change the currently assigned drive letter for a volume, right-click the volume in Disk Management, select Change Drive Letter And Paths from the Action menu, and then click Change. Note that you can change a volume only to a drive letter that is not already being used.

Note   Windows XP Professional does not allow you to modify the drive letter for the system and boot partitions.

Volume Mount Points

Windows XP also allows you to mount a volume by using a path instead of assigning a drive letter. For example, you could create a folder named C:\Files. You could then assign the C:\Files path to a new volume labeled Files. When you open the C:\Files folder within Windows Explorer, you would actually see the information that is stored on the Files volume. This type of volume is referred to as a **mounted volume**, and the folder that the mounted volume is attached to is referred to as a volume mount point. You can create multiple volume mount points for a single volume. You can dismount and move a mounted volume to another volume mount point if necessary.

Mounted volumes provide a method of extending the perceived available space on an existing volume without extending the volume's actual size. Technically, a mounted volume is a separate volume, but in the user's eyes it appears to be an extension of an existing volume. Therefore, you can use mounted volumes to increase the amount of disk space that is available on a basic volume to include disk space on another hard disk (remember that you cannot actually extend a basic volume to include space on another disk). Also, mounted volumes provide a method for managing multiple volumes of information from the same drive letter.

Volume mount points are supported on NTFS volumes only. The volume that is being mounted can be formatted with any supported file system.

To add a mounted volume to an existing volume, follow these steps:

1. In Windows Explorer, create a folder on an NTFS volume to serve as the volume mount point.

2. In Disk Management, locate the volume for which you want to modify the drive letter or path information.

3. Right-click the volume and select Change Drive Letter And Path from the Action menu.

4. In the Change Drive Letter And Paths For New Volume dialog box, click Add to create a new mounted volume.

5. In the Add Drive Letter Or Path dialog box, click Mount In The Following Empty NTFS Folder and enter the path to the volume mount point, as shown in Figure 10-6.

Figure 10-6   A mounted volume is actually a path on an existing volume.

6. Click OK.

Mounted volume paths have a different icon in Windows Explorer, as shown in Figure 10-7, and are represented by the <JUNCTION> identifier when viewed at a command prompt, as shown in Figure 10-8.

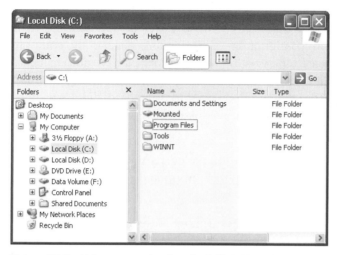

Figure 10-7   Volume mount points look like drives in Windows Explorer.

Figure 10-8   Volume mount points are labeled <JUNCTION> at a command prompt.

The following list contains some additional information about drive letters and paths:

- You cannot assign multiple drive letters to a single volume.

- You cannot assign the same drive letter to multiple volumes on the same computer.

- You can mount a volume into multiple paths simultaneously.

- A volume can exist without a drive letter or mount path assigned; however, the volume will not be accessible by applications.

How to Convert a Basic Disk to a Dynamic Disk

All disks are basic disks by default. When you need to take advantage of the functionality that dynamic disks provide, you must convert the basic disks to dynamic disks. You can convert a basic disk to a dynamic disk without losing existing data.

For the conversion to be successful, there must be at least 1 MB of free unpartitioned space available on the basic disk. This 1 MB is necessary to store the dynamic disk database, which tracks the configuration of all dynamic disks in the computer. If Windows XP Professional created the existing partitions, it will have automatically reserved the 1 MB of space required for the conversion. If another operating system or a third-party utility program created the partitions prior to upgrading, there is a chance that no free space is available. In that case, you will likely have to repartition the drive so that 1 MB of space is reserved as blank space.

During the conversion, all primary and extended partitions become simple dynamic volumes, and the disk will join the local disk group and receive a copy of the dynamic disk database.

To convert a basic disk to a dynamic disk, follow these steps:

1. In Disk Management, right-click the basic disk that you want to convert and select Convert To Dynamic Disk, as shown in Figure 10-9. Make sure that you right-click the actual disk (to the left of the partitions where the Disk number is located), not one of the partitions on the disk.

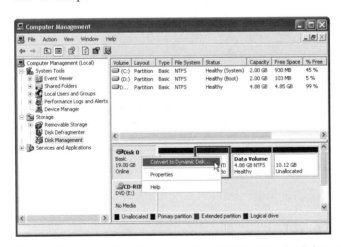

Figure 10-9   Use Disk Management to convert a basic disk to a dynamic disk.

2. In the Convert To Dynamic Disk box dialog box, verify the disks that you want to convert, and then click OK.

3. In the Disks To Convert dialog box, click Convert, and then click Yes to confirm. If you are warned that the file system must be dismounted, click Yes again.

Windows returns you to the Disk Management tool and begins the conversion.

> **Note**   If the disk contains the system or boot volume or any part of the paging file, you will have to restart the computer to complete the conversion process.

You can verify that Windows completed the conversion by viewing the disk type in Disk Management, as shown in Figure 10-10.

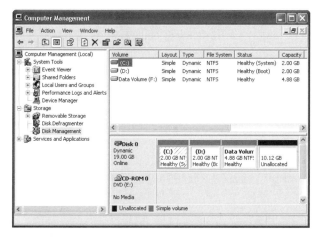

Figure 10-10   The dynamic disk type is displayed in Disk Management.

If you right-click the disk and do not see the Convert To Dynamic Disk option, one of the following conditions might exist:

- The disk has already been converted to dynamic.

- You have right-clicked a volume instead of the disk.

- The disk is in a portable computer. Portable computers do not support dynamic disks.

- There is not 1 MB of available space at the end of the disk to hold the dynamic disk database.

- The disk is a removable disk, such as a Zip disk or a detachable USB disk device. Dynamic disks are not supported on removable disks.

- The sector size on the disk is larger than 512 bytes. Windows XP Professional supports dynamic disks only on disks with a sector size of 512 bytes. The vast majority of hard disks use this sector size.

How to Revert from a Dynamic Disk to a Basic Disk

To make a dynamic disk locally accessible by an operating system other than Windows XP Professional (for example, to allow a computer running Windows 98 to access the hard disk when you install the hard disk in that computer), you must convert the dynamic disk back to a basic disk. Data is *not* preserved when reverting to a basic disk; the downgrade process requires that all data be removed from the disk.

> **Note**   Whether a disk is dynamic or basic has no effect on whether clients running any oper-ating system can connect to shared folders on that disk remotely over the network. Comput-ers running previous versions of Windows cannot locally access a dynamic disk when you install the disk into the computer.

To revert from a dynamic disk back to a basic disk, follow these steps:

1. Back up all files and folders on the entire disk.

2. In Disk Management, delete all the volumes from the disk.

3. Right-click the dynamic disk you want to convert and select Convert To Basic Disk.

4. Follow the on-screen instructions.

5. Create an appropriate partition scheme on the disk and format the newly created drives.

6. Restore data as necessary.

> **Exam Tip**   When you convert a basic disk to a dynamic disk, data on the disk is preserved. When you revert a dynamic disk to a basic disk, data on the disk is lost.

How to Create a Simple Dynamic Volume

A simple dynamic volume contains space on a single disk. Although similar to a pri-mary basic volume, there are no limits to how many simple volumes you can create on a single disk.

To create a simple volume, follow these steps:

1. In Disk Management, right-click the unallocated space on which you want to cre-ate the simple volume, and then select New Volume.

2. On the New Volume Wizard welcome page, click Next.

3. On the Select Volume Type page, click Simple, and then click Next.

4. On the Select Disks page, enter the desired size in MB, and then click Next.

5. On the Assign A Drive Letter Or Path page, select a drive letter or enter a path for a mounted volume, and then click Next.

6. On the Format Volume page, select the file system and enter a volume label. Click Next.

7. On the Completion page, click Finish to create the volume.

How to Create a Striped Dynamic Volume

Striped volumes can contain from 2 to 32 disks. Data is written to and read from multiple disks simultaneously, increasing disk performance. Data is written (striped) in 64 KB blocks. Striped volumes do not provide any fault tolerance. If one or more of the disks in a striped volume fails, all data on the entire volume is lost. Striped volumes are also known as RAID 0.

To create a striped volume, complete the following steps:

1. In Disk Management, right-click the unallocated space on one of the disks on which you want to create the striped volume, and then select New Volume.

2. On the New Volume Wizard welcome page, click Next.

3. On the Select Volume Type page, click Striped, and then click Next. Note that you must have multiple dynamic disks with unallocated space for Striped to be an option.

4. On the Select Disks page, select the disks to be included in the striped volume. Adjust the size of the striped volume accordingly, and then click Next.

5. On the Assign Drive Letter Or Path page, select a drive letter or enter a path for a mounted volume, and then click Next.

6. On the Format Volume page, select the file system and enter a volume label. Click Next.

7. On the Completion page, click Finish to create the volume.

The amount of disk space that is consumed on each disk in the striped volume must be equal. The disk with the smallest amount of available space limits the maximum amount of space available on a striped volume. For example, assume that you have the following drive configuration on your computer:

- Disk 0—No space available
- Disk 1—2 GB available
- Disk 2—2 GB available
- Disk 3—1 GB available

If you attempt to create a striped volume with Disks 1, 2, and 3, the maximum volume size that you can create is 3 GB. Because Disk 3 has only 1 GB of space available, you are limited to using only 1 GB from each of the disks in the set. However, if you create a striped volume using only Disks 1 and 2, the maximum volume size you can create is 4 GB because both disks have 2 GB of available space.

Extending Volumes

Windows XP Professional supports extending volumes on both basic and dynamic disks. You extend volumes on basic disks by using the **Diskpart** command-line utility. You can extend volumes on dynamic disks by using either the Disk Management utility or the Diskpart command-line utility.

Extending Volumes on Basic Disks   You can extend primary partitions and logical drives on basic disks if the following conditions are met:

- The volume to be extended is formatted with the NTFS file system.

- The volume is extended into contiguous unallocated space (adjacent free space) that follows the existing volume (as opposed to coming before it).

- The volume is extended on the same hard disk. Volumes on basic disks cannot be extended to include disk space on another hard disk.

- The volume is not the system or boot volume. The system or boot volumes cannot be extended.

You extend volumes by running the Diskpart utility from the command line, selecting the appropriate volume, and then executing the following command:

```
extend [size=n] [noerr]
```

See Also   For further information on the use of Diskpart, refer to the section entitled "How to Manage Disks from the Command Line by Using Diskpart" later in this chapter.

Extending Volumes on Dynamic Disks   You can extend a simple volume as long as it has been formatted with NTFS. You do this by attaching additional unallocated space from the same disk, or from a different disk, to an existing simple volume. Disk space that is used to extend a simple volume does not have to be contiguous. If the additional space comes from a different disk, the volume becomes a **spanned volume**. Spanned volumes can contain disk space from 2 to 32 disks.

If the volume is not formatted with NTFS, you must convert the volume to NTFS before you can extend it.

You extend simple volumes by using Disk Management or the Diskpart command-line utility. Perform extensions of simple volumes with Diskpart the same way that you perform extensions of basic volumes.

To extend a simple volume using Disk Management, follow these steps:

1. In Disk Management, right-click the simple volume that you want to extend, and then click Extend Volume.

2. On the Extend Volume Wizard welcome page, click Next.

3. On the Select Disks page, select the disk(s) that contain free space that you want to attach to this volume, enter the amount of space for each disk, and then click Next.

4. On the Completion page, click Finish to extend the volume.

Figure 10-11 shows the Select Disks page on a single-drive system. In this case, the maximum available space on the selected disk that you can use to extend the volume is 2048 MB.

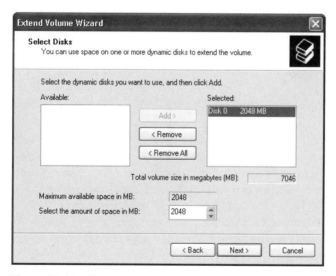

Figure 10-11   Extend a simple dynamic volume in Disk Management.

You are not prompted for any information concerning drive lettering or formatting because the added space assumes the same properties as the existing volume.

Moving Disks to Another Computer

If a computer fails but the hard disks are still functional, you can install the disks into another computer to ensure that the data is still accessible. However, you need to consider the following issues that are associated with moving disks:

- You cannot move dynamic disks to computers running Windows 95, Windows 98, Windows Millennium Edition (Windows Me), Windows NT 4.0 or earlier, or Windows XP Home Edition because these operating systems do not support dynamic disks. To move a disk to these operating systems, you must first convert it to a basic disk.

- When moving spanned or striped volumes, move all disks that are associated with the volume at the same time. If one disk is missing from a spanned or striped volume, none of the data on the entire volume is accessible.

- Windows XP Professional does not support volume sets or stripe sets that were created in Windows NT 4.0. You must back up the data, delete the volumes, install the disks into the Windows XP Professional computer, create new volumes, and then restore the data. Alternatively, you can install the disks into a computer running Windows 2000 (which does support Windows NT volume and stripe sets), convert the disks to dynamic disks (which converts volume sets to spanned volumes and stripe sets to striped volumes), and then install the disks into a computer running Windows XP Professional.

After moving disks, the disks appear in Disk Management on the new computer. Basic disks are immediately accessible. Dynamic disks initially appear as foreign disks and need to be imported before you can access them.

How to Import Foreign Disks

All dynamic disks on a computer running Windows XP Professional are members of the same disk group. Each disk in the group contains the dynamic disk database for the entire group stored in the 1 MB reserved disk area at the end of the disk. When you move a dynamic disk from one computer to another, Windows displays it as a foreign disk because it does not belong to the local disk group. You must import foreign disks, which merge the disk's information into the dynamic disk database on the new computer and place a copy of the database on the newly installed disk.

To import a foreign disk, follow these steps:

1. In Disk Management, right-click the disk that is marked Foreign and click Import Foreign Disks from the Action menu.

2. Select the disk group that you want to import. (There might be more than one foreign disk group if you have moved multiple disks from different computers into the same computer running Windows XP Professional.)

3. In the Foreign Disk Volumes dialog box, review the information to ensure that the condition for the volumes in the disk group being imported is displayed as OK. If all the disks for a spanned or striped volume are not present, the condition

is displayed as incomplete. You should resolve incomplete volume conditions before continuing with the import.

4. If you are satisfied with the information that is in the Foreign Disk Volumes dialog box, click OK to import the disks.

Removing Disks from the Dynamic Disk Database

If you remove a dynamic disk from a computer running Windows XP, Disk Management displays the disk as either Offline or Missing because the disk's configuration is still present in the dynamic disk database stored on the other disks on the computer. You can remove the missing disk's configuration from the dynamic disk database by right-clicking the disk and selecting Remove Disk.

How to Manage Disks Remotely By Using Computer Management

You can perform disk functions on a remote computer by connecting to that computer through Computer Management. To connect to a remote computer in Computer Management, follow these steps:

1. From the Start menu, right-click My Computer and select Manage to open the Computer Management window.

2. In the Computer Management window, right-click Computer Management and select Connect To Another Computer from the Action menu.

3. In the Select Computer dialog box, select the computer that you want to manage remotely, and then click OK. Computer Management displays the remote computer's information, and you can manage the disks on that computer by using the Disk Management tool.

How to Manage Disks from the Command Line by Using Diskpart

You can use the Diskpart.exe command to execute disk-management tasks from a command prompt and to create scripts for automating those tasks that you need to perform frequently or on multiple computers.

Executing Diskpart from a command prompt opens the Diskpart command interpreter. When you are in the Diskpart command interpreter, the command prompt changes to DISKPART>. You can view available commands for the Diskpart tool by typing **commands** at the Diskpart command prompt, as shown in Figure 10-12. Note that you type **exit** to close the Diskpart command interpreter and return to the normal command prompt.

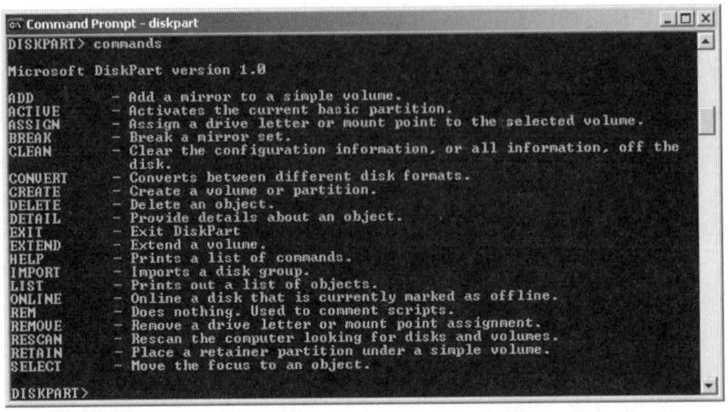

Figure 10-12   Viewing Diskpart command options.

One feature that is not available in Diskpart is the capability to format volumes. To format volumes, you must use the format.exe command from the standard command prompt.

How to Troubleshoot Disks and Volumes

Disk Management displays the status of each disk and volume. If you refer to Figure 10-1, you notice that all disks are online and all volumes are showing the desired status of Healthy.

Disk status types are as follows:

Online   Displayed by basic and dynamic disks. The disk is accessible. No user action is required.

Online (Errors)   Displayed by dynamic disks only. The disk is accessible, but input/output (I/O) errors have been detected. If the I/O errors are intermittent, right-click the disk and select Reactivate Disk. This normally returns the disk to Online status.

Offline Or Missing   Displayed by dynamic disks only. This disk is not accessible. Attempt to rescan the disks on the computer by selecting Rescan Disks from the Action menu in Disk Management. If the scan is unsuccessful, look for a physical reason for the drive failure (cables disconnected, no power to disk, failed disk). If you must replace a failed drive, first delete all volumes on the disk, right-click the disk, and select Remove Disk.

Foreign   Displayed by dynamic disks only. The disk has been moved to this computer from another computer. Right-click the disk, and then select Import Foreign Disk. If you do not want to keep the information on the disk, you can select Convert To Basic Disk, and all information on the disk will be lost.

Unreadable   Displayed by basic and dynamic disks. The disk is not accessible. Disks might show this status while they are initializing. If a disk continues to show this status, the disk might have failed entirely. Restart the computer to determine whether the disk will become accessible. If it is a dynamic disk, attempt to repair the disk by right-clicking it and selecting Rescan Disks.

Unrecognized   The disk is an unknown type, and Windows XP cannot recognize it.

No Media   This status is on drives with removable media, such as a CD-ROM drive, when the drive is empty.

Volume status types and the recommended action (if required) are as follows:

Healthy   The volume is accessible and has no detected problems.

Healthy (At Risk)   If the disk status is Online (Errors), the volumes will be accessible, but all volumes will display this status. Restoring the disk to Online will clear this status from the volume.

Initializing   The volume is in the process of initializing. No action is required. After the initialization is complete, the volume should show a status of Healthy.

Removable Media

Windows XP contains built-in support for both CD-ROM and DVD-ROM devices. Windows XP also supports a number of other removable media types, such as tape drives and memory storage. This section covers the monitoring and troubleshooting of removable media.

CD-ROM and DVD Devices

Most CD-ROM and DVD-ROM devices are Plug and Play–compliant and therefore require little configuration. To view the status and configuration of these types of devices, access the device's Properties dialog box through Device Manager. The General tab of the device's Properties dialog box indicates whether the device is functioning properly within Windows.

If Device Manager indicates that the device is installed and functioning, yet the device does not appear to be working properly, there might be a physical problem with the device installation, or the device itself might be faulty. If the disk tray does not eject properly, or if the power/usage light-emitting diode (LED) indicators are not illuminated, open the computer and verify that all connections have been properly established.

If a CD or DVD device appears to read data correctly but does not play back audio, there is most likely a device driver problem, or additional required components are not currently configured. Always verify that the device is listed in the Windows Catalog. Also, make sure that the latest version of the device driver and associated software is installed.

To troubleshoot an audio playback problem, take the following additional steps:

- Verify that the sound card is properly configured and functional.

- Verify that the speakers are plugged in and turned on.

- Verify that the sound has not been muted.

- Verify that the audio cables connecting the CD/DVD to the sound card are properly connected.

- Make sure that the CD is clean.

If the CD device supports it, you can enable the digital CD playback feature in the drive's Properties dialog box in Device Manager. On the Properties tab, select the Enable Digital CD Audio For This CD-ROM Device check box. Digital CD playback requires that CD devices support digital audio extraction (DAE), which older devices might not support. When digital CD playback is enabled, the CD-ROM drive does not have to be connected to the sound card, and audio output from the headphone jack on the CD-ROM drive is disabled.

Removable Storage Media

Removable storage media consist of devices such as disks, tape, and optical media, which are stored either online in the form of information libraries or offline on a shelf or in a file drawer. These media are used primarily for backup of applications and data. They are also used to archive data that is not accessed frequently.

Previous versions of Windows (pre–Windows 2000) did not provide strong support for removable devices. Each application that required access to a removable device needed a custom solution for accessing and managing removable storage media. Windows XP centralizes the management of these devices with Removable Storage technology. Removable Storage allows the operating system to manage removable media centrally, and applications gain access to removable devices through the Removable Storage interface. Devices with drivers that have been written to take advantage of Removable Storage are easily accessible and sharable by both the operating system and applications.

Removable Storage uses the concept of media pools to organize removable media. *Media pools* group media by usage, allow media to be shared by multiple applications, control media access, and provide for tracking of media usage. Other concepts of removable storage include the following:

Media units   The actual devices that store information, such as a CD-ROM, tape cartridge, or removable disk.

Media libraries   Encompass both online libraries and offline media physical locations. Online libraries, which include robotic libraries and stand-alone drives, are data-storage devices that provide a method of reading and writing to media when necessary. Offline media physical locations are holding places for media units that are cataloged by Removable Storage, but are not currently immediately available through an online library.

Work queues   Hold library requests until resources become available. For example, a robotic tape library has a fixed number of tape drives to access media. A request submitted to the library is held in a work queue until a tape drive becomes available and the requested tape is mounted.

Operator (administrator) requests   Hold requests for offline media. The operator must make the media available before processing can continue. Other situations that generate operator requests include the failure of a device or a device needing to be cleaned when no cleaner cartridge is available. After a request is satisfied, the administrator must inform Removable Storage so that processing can continue.

> **Note**   Removable storage devices can contain primary partitions only, and those partitions cannot be marked as active.

The Removable Storage Utility

You perform initial installation, configuration, and troubleshooting of removable storage devices by using the Add Hardware Wizard and Device Manager. After being recognized by the operating system, removable storage devices are available for management through the Removable Storage utility. Access Removable Storage by expanding the Storage node in the Computer Management window.

By using the Removable Storage utility, you can insert and eject removable media, control access to media, and manage the use of media by applications. Systems with standard, stand-alone, removable devices (such as a CD-ROM or DVD-ROM drive, Zip drive, or tape drive) do not require management and configuration by using Removable Storage. Removable Storage is required for computers with more complex configurations, which can include tape or optical disk libraries, especially if multiple applications will access those devices. You should always consult the documentation for the removable device to determine how it is best managed.

> **See Also**   Removable Storage devices that require management through the Remote Storage utility are most likely attached to Windows servers in a network environment. Further discussion of Removable Storage management is beyond the scope of this text. For more information, see *http://www.microsoft.com* and search for "Removable Storage."

Practice: Managing Hard Disks

In this practice, you will check the status of existing volumes on your computer by using Disk Management and also change the drive letter for a volume.

Exercise 1: Check the status of existing volumes

1. From the Start menu, right-click My Computer, and then select Manage.

2. In the Computer Management window, click Disk Management.

3. After the Disk Management display initializes, record the description in the Status column for each volume on your computer.

Exercise 2: Change the drive letter for a volume

1. From the Start menu, right-click My Computer, and then select Manage.

2. In the Computer Management window, click Disk Management.

3. Right-click a volume in the Disk Management display and select Change Drive Letter And Paths.

4. In the Change Drive Letter And Paths dialog box, click Change.

5. In the Change Drive Letter Or Path dialog box, select a new drive letter from the Assign The Following Drive letter drop-down list, and then click OK.

6. When prompted to confirm, click Yes.

Lesson Review

Use the following questions to help determine whether you have learned enough to move on to the next lesson. If you have difficulty answering these questions, review the material in this lesson before beginning the next lesson. You can find answers to these questions in the "Questions and Answers" section at the end of this chapter.

1. On which types of computers can you use dynamic disks?

   _____

   _____

2. What actions must you take to revert from a dynamic disk to a basic disk? What limitations does this process impose?

   _____

   _____

   _____

   _____

Lesson Summary

- Windows XP Professional supports two types of disk storage: basic disks and dynamic disks. Portable computers support only basic disks. All disks are basic disks by default. When you need to take advantage of the functionality that dynamic disks provide, you must upgrade the basic disks to dynamic disks (remember that this feature is available only in Windows XP Professional and Windows 2000 Professional). You can perform this operation with no loss of data.

- Windows XP Professional provides the Disk Management utility to configure, manage, and monitor hard disks and volumes. Using this utility, you can accomplish tasks such as the creation and formatting of volumes, moving disks from one computer to another, and remote disk management.

- You can manage disks on a remote computer by using Computer Management to connect to that computer. After connecting to the remote computer, you can use the Disk Management tool in the same way as on a local computer.

- You can manage disks from the command line by using the Diskpart command.

- Disk Management displays the status of disks and volumes. Using this status display, you can quickly determine whether disks are healthy, have errors, or are offline or missing.

Lesson 2: Managing Compression

Windows XP Professional supports two types of compression: **NTFS compression** and the **Compressed Folders** feature. NTFS compression enables you to compress files, folders, or an entire drive. NTFS compressed files and folders occupy less space on an NTFS-formatted volume, which enables you to store more data. Each file and folder on an NTFS volume has a compression state, which is either compressed or uncompressed. The Compressed Folders feature allows you to create a compressed folder so that all files you store in that folder are automatically compressed.

After this lesson, you will be able to

- Explain the purpose of compressed folders.
- Compress files, folders, or volumes by using NTFS compression.

Estimated lesson time: 60 minutes

What Is the Compressed Folders Feature?

The Compressed Folders feature is new in Windows XP Professional and allows you to compress folders, while retaining the ability to view and work with their contents.

To create a compressed folder, start Windows Explorer, click File, click New, and then click Compressed (Zipped) Folder. This creates a compressed folder in the current folder. You can drag and drop files into the compressed folder and the files are automatically compressed. If you copy a file from the compressed folder to another that is not compressed, that file will no longer be compressed. A zipper icon is shown, marking compressed folders (see Figure 10-13), and these folders are labeled Compressed Folder.

Benefits of using compressed folders generated with the Compressed Folders feature include the following:

- You can create and use compressed files and folders on both file allocation table (FAT) and NTFS volumes.

- You can open files directly from the compressed folders and you can run some programs directly from compressed folders.

- You can move these compressed files and folders to any drive or folder on your computer, the Internet, or your network and they are compatible with other zip programs.

- You can encrypt compressed folders that you created using this feature.

- You can compress folders without decreasing performance.

- You can compress individual files only by storing them in a compressed folder. If you move or extract the files into an uncompressed folder, they will be uncompressed.

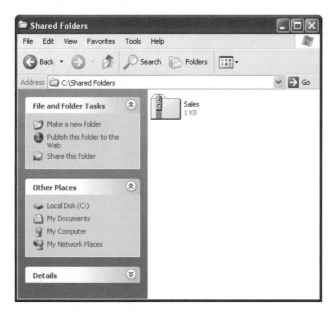

Figure 10-13   Compressed folders are labeled with a zipper icon.

How to Compress Files, Folders, or Volumes by Using NTFS Compression

Unlike compressed folders, NTFS compression is a function of the NTFS file system and as such is available only on volumes formatted with NTFS. Files compressed with NTFS compression can be read and written to by any Windows-based or MS-DOS–based application without first being uncompressed by another program. When an application or an operating system command requests access to a compressed file, NTFS automatically uncompresses the file before making it available. When you close or explicitly save a file, NTFS compresses it again.

> **Note**   NTFS allocates disk space based on uncompressed file size. If you copy a compressed file to an NTFS volume with enough space for the compressed file, but not enough space for the uncompressed file, you might get an error message stating that there is not enough disk space for the file, and the file will not be copied to the volume.

How to Compress a Folder or File

You will use Windows Explorer to set the compression state of folders and files. To set the compression state of a folder or file, right-click the folder or file in Windows Explorer, click Properties, and then click Advanced. In the Advanced Attributes dialog box, shown in Figure 10-14, select the Compress Contents To Save Disk Space check box. Click OK, and then click Apply in the Properties dialog box.

Note   NTFS encryption and compression are mutually exclusive. For that reason, if you select the Encrypt Contents To Secure Data check box, you cannot compress the folder or file.

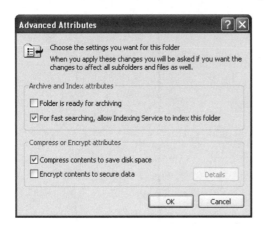

Figure 10-14   Use the Advanced Attributes dialog box to compress a file or folder.

Important   To change the compression state for a file or folder, you must have Write permission for that file or folder.

The compression state for a folder does not reflect the compression state of the files and subfolders in that folder. A folder can be compressed, yet all the files in that folder can be uncompressed. Alternatively, an uncompressed folder can contain compressed files. When you compress a folder that contains one or more files, folders, or both, Windows XP Professional displays the Confirm Attribute Changes dialog box, shown in Figure 10-15.

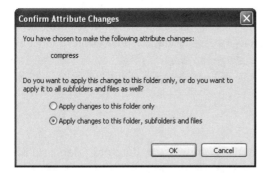

Figure 10-15   Use the Confirm Attribute Changes dialog box to control what happens to files and subfolders inside a folder you are compressing.

The Confirm Attribute Changes dialog box has the two additional options explained in Table 10-1.

Table 10-1   Confirm Attribute Changes Dialog Box Options

Option	Description
Apply Changes To This Folder Only	Compresses only the folder that you have selected
Apply Changes To This Folder, Subfolders, And Files	Compresses the folder and all subfolders and files that are contained within it and subsequently added to it

How to Compress a Drive or Volume

You can also set the compression state of an entire NTFS drive or volume. To do so, in Windows Explorer, right-click the drive or volume, and then click Properties. In the Properties dialog box, select the Compress Drive To Save Disk Space check box, as shown in Figure 10-16, and then click OK.

Figure 10-16   Use the Properties dialog box of a drive or volume to apply compression to the entire drive or volume.

How to Control Whether Windows Displays NTFS Compressed Files and Folders in a Different Color

Windows Explorer makes it easy for you to see whether a file or folder is compressed. By default, Windows displays the names of compressed files and folders in blue to distinguish them from those that are uncompressed.

To control whether Windows display compressed files and folders in a different color, use the following steps:

1. In Windows Explorer, click the Tools menu, and then click Folder Options.

2. In the Folder Options dialog box, on the View tab, clear or select the Show Encrypted Or Compressed Files In Color check box.

> **Note** When you clear the Show Encrypted Or Compressed Files In Color check box, Windows will no longer show compressed or encrypted files in color. There is no way to disable the color display of just-compressed or just-encrypted files.

Copying and Moving NTFS Compressed Files and Folders

There are rules that determine whether the compression state of files and folders is retained when you copy or move them within and between NTFS and FAT volumes. The following list describes how Windows XP Professional treats the compression state of a file or folder when you copy or move a compressed file or folder within or between NTFS volumes or between NTFS and FAT volumes.

Copying a file within an NTFS volume   When you copy a file within an NTFS volume (shown as A in Figure 10-17), the file inherits the compression state of the target folder. For example, if you copy a compressed file to an uncompressed folder, the file is automatically uncompressed.

Moving a file or folder within an NTFS volume   When you move a file or folder within an NTFS volume (shown as B in Figure 10-17), the file or folder retains its original compression state. For example, if you move a compressed file to an uncompressed folder, the file remains compressed.

Copying a file or folder between NTFS volumes   When you copy a file or folder between NTFS volumes (shown as C in Figure 10-17), the file or folder inherits the compression state of the target folder.

Moving a file or folder between NTFS volumes   When you move a file or folder between NTFS volumes (shown as C in Figure 10-17), the file or folder inherits the compression state of the target folder. Because Windows XP Professional treats a move as a copy and a delete, the files inherit the compression state of the target folder.

Moving or copying a file or folder to a FAT volume   Windows XP Professional supports compression only for NTFS files, so when you move or copy a compressed NTFS file or folder to a FAT volume, Windows XP Professional automatically uncompresses the file or folder.

Moving or copying a compressed file or folder to a floppy disk   When you move or copy a compressed NTFS file or folder to a floppy disk, Windows XP Professional automatically uncompresses the file or folder.

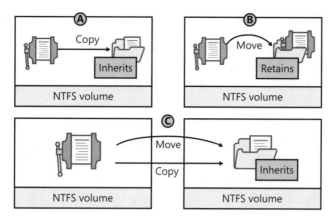

Figure 10-17   Copying and moving compressed folders and files have different results.

> **Note**   When you copy a compressed NTFS file, Windows XP Professional uncompresses the file, copies the file, and then compresses the file again as a new file. This might take considerable time.

NTFS Compression Guidelines

The following list provides best practices for using compression on NTFS volumes:

- Because some file types compress more than others, select file types to compress based on the anticipated resulting file size. For example, because Windows bitmap files contain more redundant data than application executable files, this file type compresses to a smaller size. Bitmaps often compress to less than 50 percent of the original file size, whereas application files rarely compress to less than 75 percent of the original size.

- Do not store compressed files, such as PKZIP files, in a compressed folder. Windows XP Professional will attempt to compress the file, wasting system time and yielding no additional disk space.

- Compress static data rather than data that changes frequently. Compressing and uncompressing files incurs some system overhead. By choosing to compress files that are infrequently accessed, you minimize the amount of system time dedicated to compression and uncompression activities.

- NTFS compression can cause performance degradation when you copy and move files. When a compressed file is copied, it is uncompressed, copied, and then compressed again as a new file. Compress data that is not copied or moved frequently.

Practice: Managing Compression

In this practice, you use NTFS compression to compress files and folders. You uncompress a file and test the effects that copying and moving files have on compression. In the last portion of the practice, you create a compressed folder using the Compressed Folders feature.

> **Important**   In this practice, it is assumed that you installed Windows XP Professional on the C drive, and that the C drive is formatted with NTFS. If you installed Windows XP Professional on a different partition and that partition is formatted with NTFS, use that drive letter when the practice refers to drive C.

Exercise 1: Create Compressed Folders by Using the Compressed Folders Feature

1. Click Start, point to All Programs, point to Accessories, and then click Windows Explorer.

2. In Windows Explorer, click File and then point to New.

   Compressed Folder is an option on the New menu.

3. Click Compressed Folder.

4. Name the compressed folder **My Compressed Files**.

   You have just created a compressed folder. Notice the zipper icon that identifies compressed folders. You can drag and drop files into the compressed folder, and they will automatically be compressed. If you copy a file from the compressed folder to another that is not compressed, the file will no longer be compressed.

5. Close Windows Explorer.

Exercise 2: Compress a Folder by Using NTFS Compression

1. Click Start, point to All Programs, point to Accessories, and then click Windows Explorer.

2. In Windows Explorer, click Local Disk (C:). If necessary, click Show The Contents Of This Folder.

3. In Windows Explorer, click File, point to New, and then click Folder.

   Windows creates a new folder and selects the name automatically so that you can simply start typing to rename the folder

4. Type **Compressed** for the name of the new folder and press ENTER.

5. Double-click the Compressed folder to open it.

6. In the Compressed folder, create a new folder and name it **Compressed2**.

7. Click the Up button on the toolbar to return to viewing the C drive.

8. Right-click the Compressed folder, and then click Properties.

   Windows XP Professional displays the Compressed Properties dialog box with the General tab active.

9. On the General tab, click Advanced.

   Windows XP Professional displays the Advanced Attributes dialog box.

10. Select the Compress Contents To Save Disk Space check box.

11. Click OK to return to the Compressed Properties dialog box.

12. Click Apply to apply your settings.

    Windows XP Professional displays the Confirm Attribute Changes dialog box, prompting you to specify whether to compress only this folder or this folder and all subfolders.

13. Select the Apply Changes To This Folder, Subfolders, And Files check box, and then click OK.

    Windows XP Professional displays the Applying Attributes message box, indicating the progress of the operation, and the paths and names of folders and files as they are compressed. Because there is no data in the folder, compression will likely complete too quickly for you to view this dialog box.

14. Click OK to close the Properties dialog box.

15. What color is the name of the Compressed folder?

    _____

Exercise 3: Remove Compression from a Folder

1. In Windows Explorer, double-click the Compressed folder to open it.

2. Is the Compressed2 folder compressed or not compressed? Why?

   _____

   _____

3. Right-click the Compressed2 folder, and then click Properties.

   Windows XP Professional displays the Compressed2 Properties dialog box with the General tab active.

4. On the General tab, click Advanced.

   Windows XP Professional displays the Advanced Attributes dialog box.

5. Clear the Compress Contents To Save Disk Space check box, and then click OK to return to the Compressed2 Properties dialog box.

6. Click OK to apply settings and close the Compressed2 Properties dialog box.

   Because the Compressed2 folder is empty, Windows XP Professional does not display the Confirm Attributes Changes dialog box that asks you to specify whether to uncompress only this folder or this folder and all subfolders.

7. What indication do you have that the Compressed2 folder is no longer compressed?

   _____

Exercise 4: Copy and Move Files

In this exercise, you see the effects that copying and moving files has on compressed files.

▶ **To create a compressed file**

1. In Windows Explorer, double-click the Compressed folder to open it.

2. On the File menu, click New, and then click Text Document.

3. Type **Text1.txt**, and then press ENTER.

4. How can you verify that the Text1.txt file is compressed?

   _____

▶ **To copy a compressed file to an uncompressed folder**

1. Copy (hold down CTRL and drag the file) the Text1.txt file to the Compressed2 folder.

2. Double-click the Compressed2 folder to open it.

3. Is the Text1.txt file in the Compressed2 folder compressed or uncompressed? Why?

   _____

   _____

4. Delete the Text1.txt file in the Compressed2 folder by right-clicking it and then clicking Delete.

▶ **To move a compressed file to an uncompressed folder**

1. Click the Up button on the toolbar to return to the Compressed folder.

2. Is the Text1.txt file in the Compressed folder compressed or uncompressed?

   _____

3. Move Text1.txt to the Compressed2 folder by dragging it there.

4. Double-click the Compressed2 folder to open it.

5. Is the Text1.txt file in the Compressed2 folder compressed or uncompressed? Why?

_____

_____

Lesson Review

Use the following questions to help determine whether you have learned enough to move on to the next lesson. If you have difficulty answering these questions, review the material in this lesson before beginning the next lesson. You can find answers to these questions in the "Questions and Answers" section at the end of this chapter.

1. When Sandra tried to copy a compressed file from one NTFS volume to another, the file was not copied, and she got an error message stating that there was not enough disk space for the file. Before she attempted to copy the file, Sandra verified that there was enough room for the compressed bitmap on the destination volume. Why did she get the error message?

_____

_____

_____

_____

2. When you move a file between NTFS volumes, does the file retain the compression state of the source folder, or does the file inherit the compression state of the target folder? Why?

_____

_____

_____

_____

3. What does Windows XP Professional do when you try to copy a compressed file to a floppy disk? Why?

_____

_____

_____

4. Which of the following types of files or data are good candidates for NTFS compression? (Choose all that apply.)

   a. Encrypted data

   b. Frequently updated data

   c. Bitmaps

   d. Static data

Lesson Summary

- A compressed folder created by the Compressed Folders feature appears in Windows Explorer as an icon of a zipper across a folder. You can drag and drop files into a compressed folder created by using the Compressed Folders feature, and the files are automatically compressed.

- NTFS compression is a function of the NTFS file system that allows you to compress files, folders, or an entire volume. You cannot apply both compression and encryption to a file or folder at the same time.

Lesson 3: Managing Disk Quotas

You use **disk quotas** to manage storage growth in distributed environments. Disk quotas allow you to allocate disk space to users based on the files and folders that they own. You can set disk quotas, quota thresholds, and quota limits for all users and for individual users. You can also monitor the amount of hard disk space that users have used and the amount that they have left against their quota.

> **After this lesson, you will be able to**
> - Describe the purpose of disk quotas
> - Set disk quotas for users
> - Determine the status of disk quotas
> - Monitor disk quotas
> - Identify guidelines for using disk quotas
>
> **Estimated lesson time: 30 minutes**

Overview of Disk Quotas

Windows XP Professional tracks disk quotas and controls disk usage on a per-user, per-volume basis. Windows XP Professional tracks disk quotas for each volume, even if the volumes are on the same hard disk. Because quotas are tracked on a per-user basis, every user's disk space is tracked regardless of the folder in which the user stores files. Disk quotas can be applied only to Windows XP Professional NTFS volumes.

Table 10-2 describes the characteristics of Windows XP Professional disk quotas.

Table 10-2   Disk Quota Characteristics and Descriptions

Characteristic	Description
Disk usage is based on file and folder ownership.	Windows XP Professional calculates disk space usage for users based on the files and folders that they own. When a user copies or saves a new file to an NTFS volume or takes ownership of a file on an NTFS volume, Windows XP Professional charges the disk space for the file against the user's quota limit.
Disk quotas do not use compression.	Windows XP Professional ignores compression when it calculates hard disk space usage. Users are charged for each uncompressed byte, regardless of how much hard disk space is actually used. This is done partially because file compression produces different degrees of compression for different types of files. Different uncompressed file types that are the same size might end up being very different sizes when they are compressed.
Free space for applications is based on quota limit.	When you enable disk quotas, the free space that Windows XP Professional reports to applications for the volume is the amount of space remaining within the user's disk quota limit.

You use disk quotas to monitor and control hard disk space usage. System administrators can do the following:

- Set a disk quota limit to specify the amount of disk space for each user.

- Set a disk quota warning to specify when Windows XP Professional should log an event, indicating that the user is nearing his or her limit.

- Enforce disk quota limits and deny users access if they exceed their limit, or allow them continued access.

- Log an event when a user exceeds a specified disk space threshold. The threshold could be when users exceed their quota limit or when they exceed their warning level.

After you enable disk quotas for a volume, Windows XP Professional collects disk usage data for all users who own files and folders on the volume, which allows you to monitor volume usage on a per-user basis. Even if you do not limit the disk space available to users, disk quotas provide an effective means of monitoring the disk space consumed by users.

By default, only members of the Administrators group can view and change quota settings. However, you can allow users to view quota settings.

How to Set Disk Quotas

You can enable disk quotas and enforce disk quota warnings and limits for all users or for individual users. If you want to enable disk quotas, open the Properties dialog box for a disk, click the Quota tab, and configure the options that are described in Table 10-3 and displayed in Figure 10-18.

Table 10-3   Quota Tab Options

Option	Description
Enable Quota Management	Select this check box to enable disk quota management.
Deny Disk Space To Users Exceeding Quota Limit	Select this check box so that when users exceed their hard disk space allocation, they receive an Out Of Disk Space message and cannot write to the volume.
Do Not Limit Disk Usage	Click this option when you do not want to limit the amount of hard disk space for users.
Limit Disk Space To	Configure the amount of disk space that users can use.
Set Warning Level To	Configure the amount of disk space that users can fill before Windows XP Professional logs an event, indicating that a user is nearing his or her limit.

Table 10-3   Quota Tab Options

Option	Description
Log Event When A User Exceeds Their Quota Limit	Select this option if you want Windows XP Professional to log an event in the System log every time a user exceeds his or her quota limit.
Log Event When A User Exceeds Their Warning Level	Select this option if you want Windows XP Professional to log an event in the Security log every time a user exceeds the warning level.
Quota Entries	Click this button to open the Quota Entries For window, in which you can add a new entry, delete an entry, and view the per-user quota information.

Figure 10-18   Use the Quota tab of the Properties dialog box for a disk to set disk quotas for users.

To enforce identical quota limits for all users, follow these steps:

1. In Windows Explorer, right-click the volume on which you want to set disk quotas, and then click Properties.

   Windows opens the Properties dialog box for the volume.

2. Click the Quota tab.

3. Select the Enable Quota Management check box.

4. Select the Deny Disk Space To Users Exceeding Quota Limit check box.

   Windows XP Professional will monitor usage and will not allow users to create files or folders on the volume when they exceed the limit.

5. Click Limit Disk Space To. In the Limit Disk Space To text box and in the Set Warning Level To text box, enter the values for the limit and warning levels that you want to set.

6. Click OK.

To enforce different quota limits for one or more specific users, use these steps:

1. In Windows Explorer, right-click the volume on which you want to set disk quotas, and then click Properties.

   Windows opens the Properties dialog box for the volume.

2. Click the Quota tab.

3. Select the Enable Quota Management check box.

4. Select the Deny Disk Space To Users Exceeding Quota Limit check box.

5. Click Quota Entries.

6. In the Quota Entries For window shown in Figure 10-19, click the Quota menu, and then click New Quota Entry.

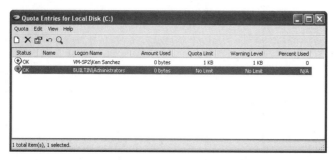

Figure 10-19   Use the Quota Entries For dialog box to enter quotas for specific users.

7. In the Select Users dialog box, type the name of the user for which you want to set a quota, and then click OK. (You can also click Advanced to search for a user.)

8. In the Add New Quota Entry dialog box shown in Figure 10-20, click Limit Disk Space To, enter the limit and warning levels, and then click OK.

Figure 10-20   Use the Add New Quota Entry dialog box to specify limits for a user.

How to Determine the Status of Disk Quotas

You can determine the status of disk quotas in the Properties dialog box for a disk by checking status message to the right of the traffic light icon (refer to Figure 10-18). The color shown on the traffic light icon indicates the status of disk quotas as follows:

- A red traffic light indicates that disk quotas are disabled.

- A yellow traffic light indicates that Windows XP Professional is rebuilding disk quota information.

- A green traffic light indicates that the disk quota system is active.

How to Monitor Disk Quotas

You use the Quota Entries For dialog box (refer to Figure 10-19) to monitor usage for all users who have copied, saved, or taken ownership of files and folders on the volume. Windows XP Professional scans the volume and monitors the amount of disk space in use by each user. Use the Quota Entries For dialog box to view the following:

- The amount of hard disk space that each user uses

- Users who are over their quota warning threshold, signified by a yellow triangle

- Users who are over their quota limit, signified by a red circle

- The warning threshold and the disk quota limit for each user

Guidelines for Using Disk Quotas

Use the following guidelines for using disk quotas:

- If you enable disk quota settings on the volume where Windows XP Professional is installed, and your user account has a disk quota limit, log on as Administrator to install additional Windows XP Professional components and applications. In this way, Windows XP Professional will not charge the disk space that you use to install applications against the disk quota allowance for your user account.

- You can monitor hard disk usage and generate hard disk usage information without preventing users from saving data. To do so, clear the Deny Disk Space To Users Exceeding Quota Limit check box when you enable disk quotas.

- Set more-restrictive default limits for all user accounts, and then modify the limits to allow more disk space to users who work with large files.

- If multiple users share computers running Windows XP Professional, set disk quota limits on computer volumes so that disk space is shared by all users who share the computer.

- Generally, you should set disk quotas on shared volumes to limit storage for users. Set disk quotas on public folders and network servers to ensure that users share hard disk space appropriately. When storage resources are scarce, you might want to set disk quotas on all shared hard disk space.

- Delete disk quota entries for users who no longer store files on a volume. You can delete quota entries for a user account only after all files that the user owns have been removed from the volume or after another user has taken ownership of the files.

Practice: Managing Disk Quotas

In this practice, you configure default quota management settings to limit the amount of data users can store on drive C (their hard disk drive). Next, you configure a custom quota setting for a user account. You increase the amount of data the user can store on drive C to 10 MB with a warning level set to 6 MB. Finally, you turn off quota management for drive C.

Note   If you did not install Windows XP Professional on drive C, substitute the NTFS partition on which you did install Windows XP Professional whenever drive C is referred to in the practice.

Exercise 1: Configure Quota Management Settings

In this exercise, you configure the quota management settings for drive C to limit the data that users can store on the volume. You then configure custom quota settings for a user account.

▶ **To configure default quota management settings**

1. Log on with an account that is a member of the Administrators group.

2. Use the User Accounts tool in Control Panel to create a user account named **User5** and assign it a Limited account type.

3. In Windows Explorer, right-click the drive C icon, and then click Properties.

   Windows XP Professional displays the Local Disk (C:) Properties dialog box with the General tab active.

4. Click the Quota tab.

   Notice that disk quotas are disabled by default.

5. In the Quota tab, select the Enable Quota Management check box.

   Notice that by default, the Do Not Limit Disk Usage option is selected.

6. Click Limit Disk Usage To.

7. What is the default disk space limit for new users?

_____

8. Click Do Not Limit Disk Usage.

If you want to place the same quota limit on all users of this computer, you use the Limit Disk Usage To option.

9. Select the Deny Disk Space To Users Exceeding Quota Limit check box.

10. Select the Log Event When A User Exceeds Their Quota Limit and Log Event When A User Exceeds Their Warning Limit check boxes, and then click Apply.

Windows XP Professional displays the Disk Quota dialog box, telling you that you should enable the quota system only if you will use quotas on this disk volume and warning you that the volume will be rescanned to update disk usage statistics if you enable quotas.

11. Click OK to enable disk quotas.

12. What happens to the quota status indicator?

_____

_____

▶ **To configure quota management settings for a user**

1. In the Quota tab of the Local Disk (C:) Properties dialog box, click Quota Entries.

Windows XP Professional displays the Quota Entries For Local Disk (C:) dialog box.

2. Are any user accounts listed? Why or why not?

_____

_____

3. On the Quota menu, click New Quota Entry.

Windows XP Professional displays the Select Users dialog box.

4. In the Name text box, type **User5**, and then click OK.

Windows XP Professional displays the Add New Quota Entry dialog box.

5. Click Limit Disk Space To. What are the default settings for the user you just set a quota limit for?

_____

_____

6. Increase the amount of data that the user can store on drive C by changing the Limit Disk Space To setting to 10 MB and the Set Warning Level To setting to 6 MB.

7. Click OK to return to the Quota Entries For Local Disk (C:) window.

8. Close the Quota Entries For Local Disk (C:) window.

9. Click OK to close the Local Disk (C:) Properties dialog box.

10. Log off.

11. Log on as **User5**.

12. Start Windows Explorer and create a User5 folder on drive C.

13. Insert the CD-ROM you used to install Windows XP Professional into your CD-ROM drive.

14. If a dialog box appears as a result of inserting the CD-ROM, close it.

15. Copy the i386 folder from your CD-ROM to the User5 folder.

    Windows XP Professional begins copying files from the i386 folder on the CD-ROM to a new i386 folder in the User5 folder on drive C. After copying some files, Windows XP Professional displays the Error Copying File Or Folder dialog box, indicating that there is not enough room on the disk.

16. Why did you get this error message?

    _____

    _____

    _____

17. Click OK to close the dialog box.

18. Right-click the User5 folder, and then click Properties.

    Notice that the Size On Disk value is slightly less than your quota limit of 10 MB.

19. Delete the User5 folder.

20. Close all open windows and log off.

Exercise 2: Disable Quota Management

1. Log on with an account that is a member of the Administrators group.

2. Start Windows Explorer.

3. Right-click the drive C icon, and then click Properties.

    Windows XP Professional displays the Local Disk (C:) Properties dialog box with the General tab active.

4. Click the Quota tab.

5. In the Quota tab, clear the Enable Quota Management check box.

   All quota settings for drive C are no longer available.

6. Click Apply.

   Windows XP Professional displays the Disk Quota dialog box, warning you that if you disable quotas, the volume will be rescanned if you enable them later.

7. Click OK to close the Disk Quota dialog box.

8. Click OK to close the Local Disk (C:) Properties dialog box.

9. Close all windows and log off Windows XP Professional.

Lesson Review

Use the following questions to help determine whether you have learned enough to move on to the next lesson. If you have difficulty answering these questions, review the material in this lesson before beginning the next lesson. You can find answers to these questions in the "Questions and Answers" section at the end of this chapter.

1. What is the purpose of disk quotas?

   _____

   _____

   _____

2. Which of the following statements about disk quotas in Windows XP Professional is correct? (Choose the correct answer.)

   a. Disk quotas track and control disk usage on a per-user, per-disk basis.

   b. Disk quotas track and control disk usage on a per-group, per-volume basis.

   c. Disk quotas track and control disk usage on a per-user, per-volume basis.

   d. Disk quotas track and control disk usage on a per-group, per-disk basis.

3. Which of the following statements about disk quotas in Windows XP Professional is correct? (Choose all that apply.)

   a. Disk quotas can be applied only to Windows XP Professional NTFS volumes.

   b. Disk quotas can be applied to any Windows XP Professional volume.

   c. You must be logged on with the Administrator user account to configure default quota management settings.

   d. Members of the Administrators and Power Users groups can configure quota management settings.

4. You get a call from an administrator who cannot delete a quota entry for a user account. What would you tell the administrator to check?

_____

_____

_____

Lesson Summary

- Use Windows XP Professional disk quotas to allocate disk space usage to users. Windows XP Professional disk quotas track and control disk usage on a per-user, per-volume basis. You can set disk quotas, quota thresholds, and quota limits for all users and for individual users. You can apply disk quotas only to Windows XP Professional NTFS volumes.

- You can set identical quotas for all users or you can configure different quotas for individual users.

- You can determine the basic status of the quota management system by looking at the traffic light indicator and the status text display on the Quota tab of a volume's Properties dialog box.

- You can monitor disk quotas by using the Quota Entries For dialog box, which you access by clicking Quota Entries on the Quota tab of a volume's Properties dialog box.

- There are a number of guidelines you should follow when using disk quotas. The most important guideline is that installing applications can use up disk quotas rapidly, so you should log on as an administrator without quota limits to install applications.

Lesson 4: Increasing Security by Using EFS

Encryption is the process of making information indecipherable to protect it from unauthorized viewing or use. A key is required to decode the information. The **Encrypting File System** (EFS) provides encryption for data in NTFS files stored on disk. This encryption is public key–based and runs as an integrated system service, making it easy to manage, difficult to attack, and transparent to the file owner. If a user who attempts to access an encrypted NTFS file has the private key to that file (which is assigned when the user logs on), the file can be decrypted so that the user can open the file and work with it transparently as a normal document. A user without the private key is denied access.

Windows XP Professional also includes the **Cipher** command, which provides the capability to encrypt and decrypt files and folders from a command prompt. Windows XP Professional also provides a recovery agent, a specially designated user account that can still recover encrypted files if the owner loses the private key.

After this lesson, you will be able to

- Describe EFS.
- Encrypt folders and files.
- Decrypt folders and files.
- Control encryption from the command line by using the Cipher command.
- Create an EFS recovery agent.

Estimated lesson time: 40 minutes

Overview of EFS

EFS allows users to encrypt NTFS files by using a strong public key–based cryptographic scheme that encrypts all files in a folder. Users with roaming profiles can use the same key with trusted remote systems. No administrative effort is needed to begin, and most operations are transparent. Backups and copies of encrypted files are also encrypted if they are in NTFS volumes. Files remain encrypted if you move or rename them, and temporary files created during editing and left unencrypted in the paging file or in a temporary file do not defeat encryption.

You can set policies to recover EFS-encrypted data when necessary. The recovery policy is integrated with overall Windows XP Professional security policy (see Chapter 16, "Configuring Security Settings and Internet Options," for more on security policy). Control of this policy can be delegated to individuals with recovery authority, and different recovery policies can be configured for different parts of the enterprise. Data recovery discloses only the recovered data, not the key that was used to encrypt the file. Several protections ensure that data recovery is possible and that no data is lost in the case of total system failure.

EFS is configured either from Windows Explorer or from the command line. It can be enabled or disabled for a computer, domain, or organizational unit (OU) by resetting recovery policy in the Group Policy console in Microsoft Management Console (MMC).

You can use EFS to encrypt and decrypt files on remote file servers but not to encrypt data that is transferred over the network. Windows XP Professional provides network protocols, such as Secure Sockets Layer (SSL) authentication, to encrypt data over the network.

Table 10-4 lists the key features provided by Windows XP Professional EFS.

Table 10-4   EFS Features

Feature	Description
Transparent encryption	In EFS, file encryption does not require the file owner to decrypt and re-encrypt the file on each use. Decryption and encryption happen transparently on file reads and writes to disk.
Strong protection of encryption keys	Public key encryption resists all but the most sophisticated methods of attack. Therefore, in EFS, the file encryption keys are encrypted by using a public key from the user's certificate. (Note that Windows XP Professional and Windows 2000 use X.509 v3 certificates.) The list of encrypted file encryption keys is stored with the encrypted file and is unique to it. To decrypt the file encryption keys, the file owner supplies a private key, which only he or she has.
Integral data-recovery system	If the owner's private key is unavailable, the recovery agent can open the file using his or her own private key. There can be more than one recovery agent, each with a different public key.
Secure temporary and paging files	Many applications create temporary files while you edit a document, and these temporary files can be left unencrypted on the disk. On computers running Windows XP Professional, EFS can be implemented at the folder level, so any temporary copies of an encrypted file are also encrypted, provided that all files are on NTFS volumes. EFS resides in the Windows operating system kernel and uses the nonpaged pool to store file encryption keys, ensuring that they are never copied to the paging file.

Security Alert   Even when you encrypt files, an intruder who accesses your computer can access those files if your user account is still logged on to the computer. Be sure to lock your console when you are not using the computer, or configure a screensaver to require a password when the computer is activated. If the computer is configured to go to standby mode when it is idle, you should require a password to bring the computer out of standby. These precautions are particularly important on portable computers, which people are more likely to leave unattended while the user is logged on.

How to Encrypt a Folder

The recommended method to encrypt files is to create an encrypted folder and place files in that folder. To encrypt a folder, use these steps:

1. In Windows Explorer, right-click the folder and click Properties.

2. In the Properties dialog box for the folder, on the General tab, click Advanced.

3. In the Advanced Attributes dialog box (refer to Figure 10-14), select the Encrypt Contents To Secure Data check box, and then click OK.

4. Click OK to close the Properties dialog box for the folder.

The folder is now marked for encryption, and all files placed in the folder are encrypted. Folders that are marked for encryption are not actually encrypted; only the files within the folder are encrypted.

> **Exam Tip**   Compressed files cannot be encrypted, and encrypted files cannot be compressed with NTFS compression.

After you encrypt the folder, when you save a file in that folder, the file is encrypted using file encryption keys, which are fast symmetric keys designed for bulk encryption. The file is encrypted in blocks, with a different file encryption key for each block. All the file encryption keys are stored and encrypted in the Data Decryption field (DDF) and the Data Recovery field (DRF) in the file header.

> **Caution**   If an administrator removes the password on a user account, the user account will lose all EFS-encrypted files, personal certificates, and stored passwords for Web sites or network resources. Each user should make a password reset disk to avoid this situation. To create a password floppy disk, open User Accounts and, under Related Tasks, click Prevent A Forgotten Password. The Forgotten Password Wizard steps you through creating the password reset disk.

How to Decrypt a Folder

Decrypting a folder or file refers to clearing the Encrypt Contents To Secure Data check box in a folder's or file's Advanced Attributes dialog box, which you access from the folder's or file's Properties dialog box. Once decrypted, the file remains decrypted until you select the Encrypt Contents To Secure Data check box. The only reason you might want to decrypt a file is if other people need access to the folder or file—for example, if you want to share the folder or make the file available across the network.

How to Control Encryption From the Command Line by Using the Cipher Command

The Cipher command provides the capability to encrypt and decrypt files and folders from a command prompt. The following example shows the available switches for the Cipher command, which are described in Table 10-5:

```
cipher [/e | /d] [/s:folder_name] [/a] [/i] [/f] [/q] [/h] [/k] [file_name [...]]
```

Table 10-5   Cipher Command Switches

Switch	Description
/e	Encrypts the specified folders. Folders are marked so any files that are added later are encrypted.
/d	Decrypts the specified folders. Folders are marked so any files that are added later are not encrypted.
/s	Performs the specified operation on files in the given folder and all subfolders.
/a	Performs the specified operation on files as well as folders. Encrypted files could be decrypted when modified if the parent folder is not encrypted. Encrypt the file and the parent folder to avoid problems.
/i	Continues performing the specified operation even after errors have occurred. By default, Cipher stops when an error is encountered.
/f	Forces the encryption operation on all specified files, even those that are already encrypted. Files that are already encrypted are skipped by default.
/q	Reports only the most essential information.
/h	Displays files with the hidden or system attributes, which are not shown by default.
/k	Creates a new file encryption key for the user running the Cipher command. Using this option causes the Cipher command to ignore all other options.
file_name	Specifies a pattern, file, or folder.

If you run the Cipher command without parameters, it displays the encryption state of the current folder and any files that it contains. You can specify multiple file names and use wildcards. You must put spaces between multiple parameters.

How to Create an EFS Recovery Agent

If you lose your file encryption certificate and associated private key through disk failure or for any other reason, a user account designated as the **recovery agent** can open the file using his or her own certificate and associated private key. If the recovery agent is on another computer in the network, send the file to the recovery agent.

Security Alert   The recovery agent can bring his or her private key to the owner's computer, but it is never a good security practice to copy a private key onto another computer.

It is a good security practice to rotate recovery agents. However, if the agent designation changes, access to the file is denied. For this reason, you should keep recovery certificates and private keys until all files that are encrypted with them have been updated.

The person designated as the recovery agent has a special certificate and associated private key that allow data recovery. To recover an encrypted file, the recovery agent does the following:

- Uses Backup or another backup tool to restore a user's backup version of the encrypted file or folder to the computer where his or her file recovery certificate is located.

- In Windows Explorer, opens the Properties dialog box for the file or folder, and in the General tab, clicks Advanced.

- Clears the Encrypt Contents To Secure Data check box.

- Makes a backup version of the decrypted file or folder and returns the backup version to the user.

Practice: Increasing Security by Using EFS

In this practice, you log on as an administrator and encrypt a folder and its files. You then log on using a different user account, and attempt to open an encrypted file and disable encryption on the encrypted file.

1. In Windows Explorer, create a folder named **Secret** on the C drive.

2. In the Secret folder, create a text file named **SecretFile.txt**.

3. Right-click the Secret folder, and then click Properties.

   Windows XP Professional displays the Secret Properties dialog box with the General tab active.

4. Click Advanced.

   The Advanced Attributes dialog box appears.

5. Select the Encrypt Contents To Secure Data check box, and then click OK.

6. Click OK to close the Secret Properties dialog box.

   The Confirm Attribute Change dialog box informs you that you are about to encrypt a folder. You have two choices: You can encrypt only this folder, or you can encrypt the folder and all subfolders and files in the folder.

7. Select the Apply Changes To This Folder, Subfolders And Files option, and then click OK.

8. Open the Secret folder.

9. What color is the SecretFile.txt text file? Why?

_____

_____

10. In the Secret folder, right-click the SecretFile.txt text file, and then click Properties.

   The SecretFile.txt Properties dialog box appears.

11. Click Advanced.

   The Advanced Attributes dialog box appears. Notice that the Encrypt Contents To Secure Data check box is selected.

12. Close the Advanced Attributes dialog box.

13. Close the Properties dialog box.

14. Close all windows and log off.

15. Log on as User5.

16. In Windows Explorer, locate and open the SecretFile.txt text file.

17. What happens?

_____

18. Close Notepad.

19. Right-click the SecretFile.txt text file, and then click Properties.

20. Click Advanced.

21. Clear the Encrypt Contents To Secure Data check box, and then click OK.

22. Click OK to close the SecretFile.txt Properties dialog box.

   The Error Applying Attributes dialog box appears and informs you that access to the file is denied.

23. Click Cancel.

24. Close all open windows and dialog boxes.

25. Log off.

Lesson Review

Use the following questions to help determine whether you have learned enough to move on to the next lesson. If you have difficulty answering these questions, review the material in this lesson before beginning the next lesson. You can find answers to these questions in the "Questions and Answers" section at the end of this chapter.

1. What is encryption and what is the EFS?

_____

_____

_____

_____

2. Which of the following files and folders does Windows XP Professional allow you to encrypt? (Choose all that apply.)

    a. A file on an NTFS volume

    b. A folder on a FAT volume

    c. A file stored on a floppy

    d. A folder on an NTFS volume

3. How do you encrypt a folder? Is the folder actually encrypted?

_____

_____

_____

_____

_____

4. If the private key belonging to the owner of an encrypted file is not available, how can you decrypt the file?

_____

_____

5. By default, the recovery agent for a computer running Windows XP Professional in a workgroup is _____, and the recovery agent for a computer running Windows XP Professional in a domain environment is _____.

Lesson Summary

■ EFS allows users to encrypt files and folder on an NTFS volume by using a strong public key–based cryptographic scheme that encrypts all files in a folder. Backups and copies of encrypted files are also encrypted if they are in NTFS volumes. Files remain encrypted if you move or rename them, and encryption is not defeated by leakage to paging files.

■ To encrypt a folder, select the Encrypt Contents To Secure Data check box in the Advanced Attributes dialog box, which you can access by clicking Advanced on the General tab of the folder's Properties dialog box.

■ To decrypt a folder, clear the Encrypt Contents To Secure Data check box in the Advanced Attributes dialog box.

■ You can control file and folder encryption from the command line using the Cipher command.

■ Windows XP Professional also provides a recovery agent. If an owner loses the private key, the recovery agent can still recover the encrypted file.

Lesson 5: Maintaining Disks with Disk Defragmenter, Check Disk, and Disk Cleanup

Windows XP Professional saves files and folders in the first available space on a hard disk and not necessarily in an area of contiguous space. The parts of the files and folders are scattered over the hard disk rather than being in a contiguous area. This scattering of files and folders across a hard disk is known as **fragmentation**. When your hard disk contains numerous fragmented files and folders, your computer takes longer to access them because it requires several additional disk reads to collect the various pieces. Creating new files and folders also takes longer because the available free space on the hard disk is scattered. Your computer must save a new file or folder in various locations on the hard disk.

Temporary files, Internet cache files, and unnecessary programs also take up space on your computer's hard drive. Sometimes there are file system errors, and sometimes sectors on your hard disk go bad, which can cause you to lose data that you have stored on your hard disk. This lesson introduces three Windows XP Professional tools—**Disk Defragmenter**, **Check Disk**, and **Disk Cleanup**—that help you organize your hard disks, recover readable information from damaged areas on your hard disk, and clean up any temporary files and unnecessary programs taking up space on your hard drive.

After this lesson, you will be able to

- Use Disk Defragmenter to organize your hard disks
- Use Check Disk to search for and repair file system errors and to recover readable information from bad sectors
- Use Disk Cleanup to remove unnecessary files from your hard disks

Estimated lesson time: 60 minutes

How to Analyze and Defragment Disks with Disk Defragmenter

The process of finding and consolidating fragmented files and folders is called defragmenting. Disk Defragmenter locates fragmented files and folders, and then defragments them by moving the pieces of each file or folder to one location so that each occupies a single contiguous space on the hard disk. Consequently, your system can access and save files and folders more efficiently. By consolidating files and folders, Disk Defragmenter also consolidates free space, making it less likely that new files will be fragmented. Disk Defragmenter can defragment FAT, FAT32, and NTFS volumes.

You access Disk Defragmenter by selecting Start, pointing to All Programs, pointing to Accessories, pointing to System Tools, and then clicking Disk Defragmenter. The Disk Defragmenter dialog box is split into three areas, as shown in Figure 10-21.

Figure 10-21 Use Disk Defragmenter to defragment a volume.

The upper portion of the dialog box lists the volumes that you can analyze and defragment. The middle portion provides a graphic representation of how fragmented the selected volume is. The lower portion provides a dynamic representation of the volume that continuously updates during defragmentation. The display colors indicate the condition of the volume as follows:

- Red indicates fragmented files.

- Blue indicates contiguous (nonfragmented) files.

- Green indicates system files, which Disk Defragmenter cannot move.

- White indicates free space on the volume.

By comparing the Analysis Display band to the Defragmentation Display band during and after defragmentation, you can easily see the improvement in the volume.

You can also open Disk Defragmenter by selecting a drive you want to defragment in Windows Explorer or My Computer. On the File menu, click Properties, click the Tools tab, and click Defragment Now. Then select one of the options described in Table 10-6.

Table 10-6   Disk Defragmenter Options

Option	Description
Analyze	Click this button to analyze the disk for fragmentation. After the analysis, the Analysis Display band provides a graphic representation of how fragmented the volume is.
Defragment	Click this button to defragment the disk. Defragmenting automatically performs an analysis. After defragmentation, the Defragmentation Display band provides a graphic representation of the defragmented volume. Additionally, you can view a report showing files that could not be defragmented.

Figure 10-22 shows the Disk Defragmenter dialog box after you have analyzed the C drive. Windows XP Professional displays another Disk Defragmenter dialog box, indicating that you need to defragment the volume. You can view a report that shows more details about the fragmentation on your volume, close the dialog box and run the defragmenter at a later time, or defragment the volume now.

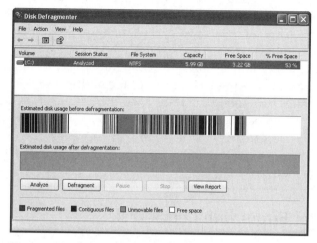

Figure 10-22   Use the Disk Defragmenter window to analyze the fragmentation on a volume.

If there is not enough fragmentation to require you to defragment the volume, Windows XP Professional displays a Disk Defragmenter dialog box, indicating that there is no need to defragment the volume at this time.

The following list provides some recommended guidelines for using Disk Defragmenter:

- Run Disk Defragmenter when the computer will receive the least usage. During defragmentation, data is moved around on the hard disk, and that process is microprocessor-intensive. The defragmentation process will adversely affect access time to other disk-based resources.

- Educate users to defragment their local hard disks at least once a month to prevent accumulation of fragmented files.

- Analyze the target volume before you install large applications and defragment the volume if necessary. Installations complete more quickly when the target media has adequate contiguous free space. Additionally, accessing the application after installation is faster.

- When you delete a large number of files or folders, your hard disk might become excessively fragmented, so be sure that you analyze it afterward. Generally, you should defragment hard disks on busy file servers more often than those on single-user client computers.

Real World   When to Defragment

Windows XP actually uses volumes formatted with NTFS pretty efficiently, so the need to routinely defragment a disk is not as great as it used to be. In fact, several recent tests have shown that there is not really a significant improvement in computer performance after defragmenting even a very fragmented drive. Nonetheless, defragmentation is a quick safe process that, simply put, just makes users feel better. Consider defragmenting drives two or three times per year. Better yet, show users how to do it themselves. You can also use Scheduled Tasks to schedule Disk Defragmenter to run automatically. Just configure a task to run at the desired times and launch the defrag.exe program located in the %systemroot%\system32 folder. After scheduling the task, open the advanced properties for the task and add the drive you want to defragment to the command line. An example command line would look something like %System-Root%\System32\Defrag.exe d. For more information on using Scheduled Tasks, see Chapter 18, "Using Windows XP Tools."

How to Scan a Hard Disk for Errors with Check Disk

Check Disk attempts to repair file system errors, locate bad sectors, and recover readable information from those bad sectors. All files must be closed for this program to run. To access Check Disk, select the drive you want to check in Windows Explorer or My Computer. Click the File menu, click Properties, click the Tools tab, and click Check Now. Select one of the options on the Check Disk dialog box shown in Figure 10-23. The options are explained in Table 10-7.

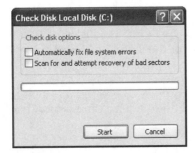

Figure 10-23   Use Check Disk to analyze and fix the file structure on a volume.

Table 10-7   Check Disk Options

Check box	Description
Automatically Fix File System Errors	Select this check box to have Windows XP Professional attempt to repair file system errors found during disk checking. All files must be closed for this program to run. If the drive is currently in use, a message asks if you want to reschedule the disk-checking for the next time you restart your computer. Your drive is not available to run other tasks while the disk is being checked.
Scan For And Attempt Recovery Of Bad Sectors	Select this check box to have Windows XP Professional attempt to repair file system errors found during disk checking, locate bad sectors, and recover any readable information located in those bad sectors. All files must be closed for this program to run. If the drive is currently in use, a message asks if you want to reschedule the disk-checking for the next time you restart your computer. Your drive is not available to run other tasks while the disk is being checked. If you select this check box, you do not need to select Automatically Fix File System Errors because Windows XP Professional attempts to fix any errors on the disk.

Note   Check Disk runs in five phases: file verification, index verification, security descriptor verification, file data verification, and free space verification.

You can also use the command-line version of Check Disk. The command-line syntax for Chkdsk is as follows:

```
Chkdsk [volume[[path]filename]]] [/f] [/v] [/r] [/x] [/i] [/c] [/l[:size]]
```

The switches used by Chkdsk are explained in Table 10-8.

Table 10-8   Chkdsk Switches

Switch	Description
filename	Specifies the file or set of files to check for fragmentation. You can use the wild-cards * and ?. This switch is valid only on volumes formatted with FAT12, FAT16, and FAT32 file systems.
path	Specifies the location of a file or set of files within the folder structure of the volume. This switch is valid only on volumes formatted with FAT12, FAT16, and FAT32 file systems.
size	Changes the log file size. You must use the /l switch with this switch. This switch is valid only on volumes formatted with NTFS.
volume	Specifies the drive letter (followed by a colon), mount point, or volume name. This switch is valid only on volumes formatted with FAT12, FAT16, and FAT32 file systems.
/c	Skips the checking of cycles within the folder structure. This switch is valid only on volumes formatted with NTFS.
/f	Fixes errors on the volume. If Chkdsk cannot lock the volume, you are prompted to have Chkdsk check it the next time the computer starts.
/i	Performs a less-vigorous check of index entries. This switch is valid only on volumes formatted with NTFS.
/l	Displays the current size of the log file. This switch is valid only on volumes formatted with NTFS.
/r	Locates bad sectors and recovers readable information. If Chkdsk cannot lock the volume, you are prompted to have Chkdsk check it the next time the computer starts.
/v	On volumes formatted with FAT12, FAT16, or FAT32, displays the full path and name of every file on the volume. On volumes formatted with NTFS, displays any cleanup messages.
/s	Forces the volume to dismount first, if necessary.
/?	Displays this list of switches.

Used without parameters, Chkdsk displays the status of the disk in the current volume.

How to Free Up Disk Space with Disk Cleanup

You can use Disk Cleanup to free up disk space by deleting temporary files and uninstalling programs. Disk Cleanup lists the temporary files, Internet cache files, and unnecessary programs that you can safely delete. To access Disk Cleanup, select the drive you want to check in Windows Explorer or My Computer. On the File menu, click Properties, and in the General tab, click Disk Cleanup. The Disk Cleanup dialog box is shown in Figure 10-24, and its options are explained in Table 10-9.

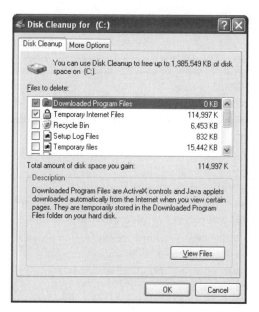

Figure 10-24   Use Disk Cleanup to remove unnecessary files from a volume.

Table 10-9   Disk Cleanup Deletion Options

Check box	Description
Downloaded Program Files	Select this check box to have Windows XP Professional delete the ActiveX controls and Java applets that have been downloaded automatically from the Internet when users viewed certain pages. These files are temporarily stored in the Downloaded Program Files folder on the computer's hard disk.
Temporary Internet Files	Select this check box to have Windows XP Professional delete the files in the Temporary Internet Files folder on the computer's hard drive. These files are Web pages stored on the hard disk for quick viewing. Users' personalized settings for Web pages are not deleted.
Recycle Bin	Select this check box to have Windows XP Professional delete the files in the Recycle bin. When you delete a file from your computer, it is not permanently removed from the computer until the Recycle Bin is emptied (by deleting the files contained in the Recycle Bin).
Temporary Files	Select this check box to have Windows XP Professional delete any Temporary files on this volume. Programs sometimes store temporary information in a Temp folder. Before a program closes, it usually deletes this information. You can safely delete temporary files that have not been modified in more than a week.

Table 10-9   Disk Cleanup Deletion Options

Check box	Description
WebClient/Publisher Temporary Files	Select this check box to have Windows XP Professional delete any temporary WebClient/Publisher files. The WebClient/Publisher service maintains a cache of accessed files on this disk. These files are kept locally for performance reasons only and can be deleted safely.
Compress Old Files	Select this check box to compress files that have not been accessed in a while. No files are deleted and all files are still accessible. Because files compress at different rates, the value displayed for the amount of space you will recover is an approximation.
Catalog Files For The Content Indexer	Select this check box to have Windows XP Professional delete any old catalog files left over from previous indexing operations. The Indexing Service speeds up and enriches file searches by maintaining an index of the files on this disk.

There are additional ways to free up space on your hard disk using Disk Cleanup. Click the More Options tab in the Disk Cleanup For dialog box (see Figure 10-25). The available options are explained in Table 10-10.

Figure 10-25   Use the More Options tab of the Disk Cleanup For dialog box to access additional features.

Table 10-10   Additional Features on the Disk Cleanup More Options Tab

Option	Description
Windows Components	Click Clean Up under Windows Components to launch the Windows Components Wizard, which allows you to add and remove Windows components from your installation. The Windows Components include Accessories and Utilities, Fax Services, Indexing Services, Microsoft Internet Explorer, Internet Information Services (IIS), Management and Monitoring Tools, Message Queuing, MSN Explorer, Networking Services, Other Network File and Print Services, and Update Root Certificates.
Installed Programs	Click Clean Up under Installed Programs to launch Add Or Remove Programs, which allows you to install programs and to uninstall programs that are no longer in use. The list of programs available to be uninstalled depends on which programs are installed on your computer.
System Restore	Click Clean Up under System Restore to delete all but the most recent restore points. For more information about restore points and System Restore, see Chapter 4, "Modifying and Troubleshooting the Startup Process."

Practice: Maintaining Disks

In this practice, you use the Disk Defragmenter to determine whether your hard disk is fragmented. If it is, you will defragment your hard disk. You then use Check Disk to examine your hard disk for file system errors, fix them, locate any bad sectors, and recover any readable information from those bad sectors. Finally, you use Disk Cleanup to free up disk space by deleting temporary files and uninstalling programs.

Note   If you started with a clean hard disk and installed Windows XP Professional in Chapter 2, these disk maintenance tools will probably not find much to clean up or repair.

Exercise 1: Defragment a Hard Drive

1. Click Start, point to All Programs, point to Accessories, point to System Tools, and then click Disk Defragmenter.

   Windows XP Professional displays the Disk Defragmenter dialog box.

2. If there are multiple volumes on your computer, select C, and then click Analyze.

3. If Windows XP Professional displays a dialog box, indicating that there is no need to defragment your volume at this time, click Close, and then read through Steps 6 through 12.

4. If Windows XP Professional displays a Disk Defragmenter dialog box, indicating that you need to defragment your volume now, click View Report.

5. In the Analysis Report dialog box, scroll through the Volume Information box.

6. Scroll through the Most Fragmented Files box, and then click Save As.

    Windows XP Professional displays the Save Defragmentation Report dialog box. Notice that the default title for the report is VolumeC, and the default location for the report is in the My Documents folder.

7. Click Save to save the report as VolumeC in the My Documents folder.

    You are returned to the Analysis Report dialog box.

8. Click Defragment.

    Disk Defragmenter defragments the volume. This process could take a long time to complete, depending on the size of the volume and the amount of fragmentation.

9. Compare the Analysis Display with the Defragmentation Display.

10. Close Disk Defragmenter.

    Leave the Local Disk (C:) Properties dialog box open for the next exercise.

Exercise 2: Run Check Disk

In Exercise 2, you run Check Disk to examine your hard disk for file system errors. If any errors are found, you fix them. You also locate any bad sectors and recover any readable information from those bad sectors.

1. In the Local Disk (C:) Properties dialog box, click the Tools tab.

2. In the Tools tab, click Check Now.

    Windows XP Professional displays the Check Disk Local Disk (C:) dialog box.

3. Select Scan For And Attempt Recovery Of Bad Sectors.

4. Click Start.

    It might take a few minutes to complete all five phases.

5. When prompted that the Disk Check is complete, click OK.

    Leave the Local Disk (C:) Properties dialog box open for the next exercise.

Exercise 3: Run Disk Cleanup

1. In the General tab of the Local Disk (C:) Properties dialog box, click Disk Cleanup.

    A Disk Cleanup dialog box appears, indicating that it is calculating how much space you can free on the C drive.

2. In the Files To Delete list box in the Disk Cleanup For (C:) dialog box, review the files that Disk Cleanup is recommending you delete.

> **Security Alert**   If you started with a clean hard disk and installed Windows XP Professional in Chapter 2, there might be few, if any, files that Disk Cleanup found to delete. If you want to delete any files that Disk Cleanup recommends that you delete, make sure that the files you want to delete are selected (a check mark is in the check box in front of the files), and then click OK.

3. Click the More Options tab.

4. When would you use the options available in the More Options tab?

_____

_____

_____

_____

5. Click Cancel.

6. Close Disk Cleanup and all open windows.

Lesson Review

Use the following questions to help determine whether you have learned enough to move on to the next lesson. If you have difficulty answering these questions, review the material in this lesson before beginning the next lesson. You can find answers to these questions in the "Questions and Answers" section at the end of this chapter.

1. What is fragmentation and what problems does it cause?

_____

_____

_____

_____

_____

2. The process of finding and consolidating fragmented files and folders is called _____. The Windows XP Professional system tool that locates fragmented files and folders and arranges them in contiguous space is _____.

3. Windows XP Professional provides a tool to locate fragmented files and folders and arrange them in contiguous space on volumes formatted with which file systems?

_____

4. Which of the following functions does Check Disk perform? (Choose all that apply.)

   a. Locates fragmented files and folders and arranges contiguously

   b. Locates and attempts to repair file system errors

   c. Locates bad sectors and recovers readable information from those bad sectors

   d. Deletes temporary files and offline files

Lesson Summary

- Windows XP Professional saves files and folders in the first available space on a hard disk and not necessarily in an area of contiguous space, which can lead to file and folder fragmentation. Disk Defragmenter, a Windows XP Professional system tool, locates fragmented files and folders and defragments them, which enables your system to access and save files and folders more efficiently.

- Check Disk attempts to repair file system errors, locate bad sectors, and recover readable information from those bad sectors.

- Disk Cleanup frees up disk space by locating temporary files, Internet cache files, and unnecessary programs that you can safely delete; and it also deletes temporary files and uninstalls programs.

Lesson 6: Configuring Offline Folders and Files

When the network is unavailable, or when you are on the road and your laptop is undocked, offline folders and files allow you to continue working on files that are stored on shared folders on the network. These network files are cached on your local disk so that they are available even if the network is not. When the network becomes available or when you dock your laptop, your connection to the network is re-established. The **Offline Files** feature synchronizes the cached files and folders on your local disk with those stored on the network.

After this lesson, you will be able to

- Enable the Offline Files feature on your computer
- Make folders and files available offline
- Configure your computer to share folders for use offline
- Synchronize offline folders and files

Estimated lesson time: 30 minutes

How to Enable the Offline Files Feature On Your Computer

Before you can use offline folders and files, you must configure your computer to use them. You configure offline folders and files by using the Folder Options selection located on the Tools menu of My Computer. In the Offline Files tab of Folder Options, you must select the Enable Offline Files and the Synchronize All Offline Files Before Logging Off check boxes (see Figure 10-26).

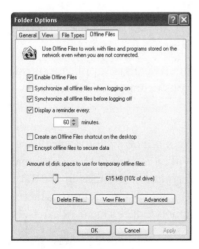

Figure 10-26   Use the Offline Files tab in the Folder Options dialog box to enable offline files.

On the Offline Files tab, you can click Delete Files to delete the locally cached copy of a network file. Click View Files to view the files stored in the Offline Files folder; these are the locally cached files that you have stored on your system. Click Advanced to configure how your computer responds when a network connection is lost. For example, when a network connection is lost, you can configure your computer to notify you and allow you to begin working offline.

> **Note**   To use Offline Files, you must disable the Fast User Switching feature in Windows. If your computer is a member of a domain, Fast User Switching is already turned off, anyway. If your computer is a member of a workgroup, you can disable Fast User Switching by opening the User Accounts tool in Control Panel and clicking Change The Way Users Log On Or Off. For more details on Fast User Switching, see Chapter 7, "Setting up and Managing User Accounts."

How to Make Folders and Files Available Offline

To make a specific file or folder available offline and enable automatic synchronization with the network, follow these steps:

1. In My Network Places, right-click the shared folder or file that you want to make available offline, and then select the Make Available Offline option.

2. In the Offline Files Wizard's Welcome page, click Next.

3. Select the Automatically Synchronize The Offline Files When I Log On And Log Off My Computer check box, and then click Next.

4. Optionally, you can enable reminders and create a shortcut to the Offline Files folder on your desktop. Click Finish.

    The files will be synchronized to your computer.

Files with extensions that are associated with certain database applications initially cannot be cached. By default, the following files types cannot be cached:

*.slm; *.mdb; *.ldb; *.mdw; *.mde; *.pst; *.db

When you make network resources available offline, Windows automatically copies them to the computer's local hard disk drive, along with a reference to the original network path. Windows stores offline files and information about the files in a database in the %systemroot%\CSC folder. (CSC is an acronym for client-side caching, which is another name for offline files.) The database emulates the network resource when it is offline.

When a user works offline, she continues to access offline resources as if she were connected to the network, but she is actually using the local copy of the file. When the network share becomes available again, the client will switch from the local offline files to the live files automatically, provided that the following conditions are met:

- The user does not have any files currently open from that network share.

- Synchronization is not required for any offline files in the share.

- The user is not connecting to the network over a slow link.

If any of these conditions are not met, the user will continue to work with the offline version of the share until all files are closed and synchronization occurs.

> **Note**   Users have the same permissions to the locally stored versions of offline files as they do to the original network versions.

How to Configure Your Computer to Share Offline Folders and Files

Before other users on the network can use shared folders and files on your computer offline, you must configure the resource to allow caching for offline use. You configure offline folders and files through Windows Explorer or My Computer. Figure 10-27 shows the Allow Caching Of Files In This Shared Folder check box in Windows Explorer.

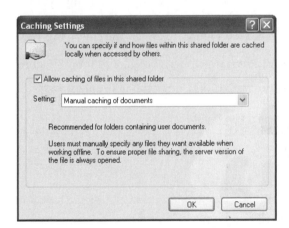

Figure 10-27   Configure shared files for offline use.

Windows XP Professional provides the following three settings for caching:

Manual Caching Of Documents   The default setting. Users must manually specify any files that they want available when they are working offline. To ensure proper file sharing, the server version of the file is always open.

Automatic Caching Of Documents   Every file a user opens is automatically downloaded and cached on the user's hard drive so that it will be available offline. If an earlier version of a file is already loaded on the user's hard drive, it is automatically replaced with the newer version. To ensure proper file sharing, the server version of the file is always opened.

Automatic Caching Of Programs and Documents   Opened files are automatically downloaded and cached on the user's hard drive so that they will be available offline. If an earlier version of a file is already loaded on the user's hard drive, it is automatically replaced with the newer version. File sharing is not ensured.

How to Synchronize Offline Folders and Files

By default, synchronization of offline files is configured to happen at logoff when offline files are initially made available on the client. File synchronization is straightforward if the copy of the file on the network does not change while you are editing a cached version of the file. Your edits are incorporated into the copy on the network. However, it is possible that another user could edit the network version of the file while you are working offline. If both your cached offline copy of the file and the network copy of the file are edited, you must decide what to do. You are given a choice of retaining your edited version and not updating the network copy with your edits, of overwriting your cached version with the version on the network, or of keeping a copy of both versions of the file. In the last case, you must rename your version of the file, and both copies will exist on your hard disk and on the network.

You can reconfigure or manually launch synchronization by using Synchronization Manager, which is available from the Items To Synchronize dialog box. You can access the Items To Synchronize dialog box (see Figure 10-28) in the following ways:

■ From the Start menu, select All Programs, Accessories, and then Synchronize.

■ From the Tools menu in Windows Explorer, select Synchronize.

Figure 10-28   Choose an item to synchronize manually.

Notice that you can manually synchronize your offline files with those on the network by clicking Synchronize. You can also configure the Synchronization Manager by clicking Setup.

When configuring the Synchronization Manager, you have three sets of options to configure synchronization. The first set of options is accessed through the Logon/Logoff tab (see Figure 10-29). You can configure synchronization to occur when you log on, when you log off, or both. You can also specify that you want to be prompted before synchronization occurs. You can specify the items to be synchronized at log on or log off, or both, and you can specify the network connection.

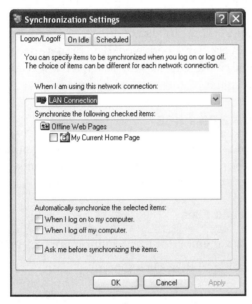

Figure 10-29   Logon/Logoff tab of the Synchronization Settings dialog box.

The second set of options in configuring the Synchronization Manager is accessed through the On Idle tab. The items configurable are similar to those configurable through the Logon/Logoff tab. The following items are configurable through the On Idle tab:

When I Am Using This Network Connection   This option allows you to specify the network connection and which items to synchronize.

Synchronize The Following Checked Items   This option allows you to specify which items you want to synchronize.

Synchronize The Selected Items While My Computer Is Idle   This option allows you to turn synchronization off or on during idle time.

Click Advanced on the On Idle tab to configure the following options: Automatically Synchronize The Specified Items After My Computer Has Been Idle For *X* Minutes; While My Computer Remains Idle, Repeat Synchronization Every *X* Minutes; and Prevent Synchronization When My Computer Is Running On Battery Power.

The third set of options for scheduling synchronization is accessed through the Scheduled tab. You can click Add to start the Scheduled Synchronization Wizard. After the welcome page, the first page of the Scheduled Synchronization Wizard allows you to specify the connection, specify the items to synchronize, and whether you want the computer to automatically connect if you are not connected when the scheduled time for synchronization arrives. The second page of the wizard is the Select The Time And Day You Want The Synchronization To Start page. It allows you to configure the starting time and date for the synchronization. You can also configure the frequency of the synchronization, which can be set for every day, every weekday, or at a specified interval measured in days. On the third page of the wizard, you assign a name to this scheduled synchronization, and on the final page, you review your settings.

Practice: Configuring Offline Folders and Files

In this practice, you configure your computer running Windows XP Professional just as you would if it were a laptop computer running Windows XP Professional so that you can use offline folders and files.

Exercise 1: Configure Offline Folders and Files

1. Log on with a user account that is a member of the Administrators group.

2. Click Start, right-click My Computer, and then click Open.

3. On the Tools menu, click Folder Options.

   Windows XP Professional displays the Folder Options dialog box.

4. Click the Offline Files tab.

> **Important** If Fast User Switching is enabled, Offline Files cannot be enabled. Click Cancel to close the Folder Options dialog box. Open User Accounts in Control Panel, and select Change The Way Users Log On Or Off. Clear the Use Fast User Switching check box and click Apply Options. Close User Accounts. In My Computer, on the Tools menu, click Folder Options, and then click the Offline Files tab. Go to Step 5.

5. Select the Enable Offline Files check box.

6. Ensure that the Synchronize All Offline Files Before Logging Off check box is selected, and then click OK.

   Your computer is now configured so that you can use offline folders and files.

7. Close the My Computer window.

Exercise 2: Configure Offline Folders for Sharing

In this exercise, you configure a network share on a computer running Windows XP Professional so that users can access the files in the share and use them offline.

1. Ensure that you are still logged on as Administrator, and start Windows Explorer.

2. Create a folder on the C drive named **Offline**.

3. Right-click the Offline folder, and then click Sharing And Security.

Windows Explorer displays the Offline Properties dialog box with the Sharing tab active.

4. Click Share This Folder, and then click Caching.

Windows Explorer displays the Caching Settings dialog box.

5. From the Setting list, ensure that Manual Caching Of Documents is selected, and then click OK.

6. Click OK to close the Offline Properties dialog box.

Leave Windows Explorer open.

Exercise 3: Configure Synchronization Manager

1. Click Tools, and then click Synchronize.

Windows XP Professional displays the Items To Synchronize dialog box, which allows you to specify which folders you want to synchronize.

2. If nothing is selected, click My Current Home Page, and then click Setup.

Windows XP Professional displays the Synchronization Settings dialog box with the Logon/Logoff tab selected.

3. Review the options on the Logon/Logoff tab, and then review the options on the On-Idle tab and the Scheduled tab.

4. On the Logon/Logoff tab, select My Current Home Page.

5. Ensure that both the When I Log On To My Computer and When I Log Off My Computer check boxes are checked.

6. Select the Ask Me Before Synchronizing The Items check box, and then click OK.

7. Click Close to close the Items To Synchronize dialog box, and then close Windows Explorer.

Lesson Review

Use the following questions to help determine whether you have learned enough to move on to the next lesson. If you have difficulty answering these questions, review the material in this lesson before beginning the next lesson. You can find answers to these questions in the "Questions and Answers" section at the end of this chapter.

1. How do you configure your computer to use offline folders and files?

   _____

   _____

   _____

   _____

2. Which tools does Windows XP Professional provide for you to configure your computer to provide offline files? What must you do to allow others to access files on your computer?

   _____

   _____

3. What does Synchronization Manager do?

   _____

   _____

   _____

Lesson Summary

- Before you can use offline files, you must use the Folders Options selection on the Tools menu of My Computer or Windows Explorer to configure your computer to use offline files.

- After enabling the Offline Files feature, you can use My Network Places to make any network-accessible folder for which offline caching is enabled available offline.

- To make shared folders on your own computer available for other users to use offline, you must use the Sharing tab of the folder's Properties dialog box to configure the offline caching for the folder. By default, shared folders are configured for offline use.

- Synchronization Manager allows you to configure synchronization to occur when you log on, when you log off, or both; and you can specify that you want to be asked before synchronization occurs.

Case Scenario Exercise

In this exercise, you will read a scenario about working with data storage, and then answer the questions that follow. If you have difficulty completing this work, review the material in this chapter before beginning the next chapter. You can find answers to these questions in the "Questions and Answers" section at the end of this chapter.

Scenario

You are an administrator working for a company named Fabrikam, Inc., a manufacturer of neon dyes used in safety clothing for various industries. You are working with a user named Iris, who plans and oversees exhibits that the company puts on at trade shows across the country. The company has just given Iris a new notebook computer, which she will use when traveling.

Questions

1. Iris' new notebook computer has a 16 GB hard disk that you want to configure as a single volume. It is the only hard disk on the computer. Should you create a basic or dynamic disk?

   _____

   _____

   _____

2. When she is running the exhibit booth at tradeshows, Iris' attention is often diverted, and she is worried that she cannot always keep an eye on her notebook computer. The computer contains trade secrets that she does not want to see compromised. Iris wants to secure the files on her computer, even if the computer is stolen. Can you configure encryption on her notebook computer? If so, what precautions should you take?

   _____

   _____

   _____

   _____

   _____

3. Iris' notebook computer does not have the biggest hard drive. She often works on large sales documents and also stores many picture files of the products she sells. She wants to compress these files to save space. What should you tell Iris to do?

_____

_____

_____

_____

4. What utility should you teach Iris to use that might also help maximize the free space on her hard disk?

_____

_____

5. You have configured Iris' notebook computer to connect securely via the Internet to the company network so that Iris can access the company e-mail server and file servers. Iris also wants to be able to access certain shared files on the company network when she cannot connect to the network. What should you do?

_____

_____

_____

_____

_____

_____

Troubleshooting Lab

You are an administrator for a company named Humongous Insurance, a provider of group medical insurance policies throughout the Midwest. On Friday morning, you receive a call from Jonas, a user in the claims department who has a workstation running Windows XP Professional. Jonas says that on his computer, he always stores documents on drive E. However, when he tried to transfer a large document to his local computer and store it on drive E, he received an error message stating that the drive could not be located. He checked My Computer, and the drive is not listed.

You use Computer Management to connect to Jonas' computer, and then open the Disk Management tool. You see the following configuration:

- Disk 0 is configured as a basic disk and it contains one partition. The drive letter for the partition is C, and the partition is labeled as the System partition. Disk Management reports the disk as online and the C partition as healthy.

- Disk 1 is configured as a dynamic disk, but Disk Management reports the disk as missing.

- Disk 2 is configured as a CD-ROM drive with the drive letter D.

What do you suspect is the problem? What would you do to help Jonas?

_____

_____

_____

_____

_____

_____

_____

_____

Chapter Summary

■ Windows XP Professional supports two types of disk storage: basic disks and dynamic disks. All disks are basic disks by default, but you can upgrade the basic disks to dynamic disks with no loss of data. You can also downgrade a dynamic disk to a basic disk, but all data on the disk is lost. Windows XP Professional provides the Disk Management utility to configure, manage, and monitor hard disks and volumes. You can also manage disks from the command line by using the Diskpart command.

■ Windows XP Professional provides two types of compression: Compressed Folders and NTFS compression. A compressed folder appears in Windows Explorer as an icon of a zipper across a folder. NTFS compression is a function of the NTFS file system that allows you to compress files, folders, or an entire volume.

■ Use Windows XP Professional disk quotas to allocate disk space usage to users. Windows XP Professional disk quotas track and control disk usage on a per-user, per-volume basis. You can set disk quotas, quota thresholds, and quota limits for all users and for individual users. You can apply disk quotas only to Windows XP Professional NTFS volumes.

■ EFS allows users to encrypt files and folder on an NTFS volume by using a strong public key–based cryptographic scheme that encrypts all files in a folder. You cannot apply both compression and encryption to a file or folder at the same time. Files remain encrypted if you move or rename them, or if you back them up.

■ Windows XP Professional provides three utilities for maintaining disks:

❑ Windows XP Professional saves files and folders in the first available space on a hard disk and not necessarily in an area of contiguous space, which can lead to file and folder fragmentation. Disk Defragmenter, a Windows XP Professional system tool, locates fragmented files and folders and defragments them, enabling your system to access and save files and folders more efficiently.

❑ Check Disk attempts to repair file system errors, locate bad sectors, and recover readable information from those bad sectors.

❑ Disk Cleanup frees up disk space by locating temporary files, Internet cache files, and unnecessary programs that you can safely delete.

■ The Offline Files feature allows Windows to create a temporary copy of shared files on the network so that you can use them when you are disconnected from the network. Before you can use offline files, you must use the Folders Options selection on the Tools menu of Windows Explorer to enable the feature. After enabling Offline Files, you can use My Network Places to make any network accessible folder for which offline caching is enabled available offline.

Exam Highlights

Before taking the exam, review the key points and terms that are presented in this chapter. You need to know this information.

Key Points

■ Windows XP Professional does not support fault-tolerant disk configurations. Spanned volumes simply allow you to use different amounts of disk space from multiple hard disks in a single volume. Striped volumes allow you use an identical amount of disk space from multiple hard disks. The advantage of using striped volumes is that Windows can write information to the disk more quickly.

■ When you convert a basic disk to a dynamic disk, data on the disk is preserved. When you revert a dynamic disk to a basic disk, data on the disk is lost.

■ Compressed files cannot be encrypted, and encrypted files cannot be compressed with NTFS compression.

■ NTFS allocates disk space based on uncompressed file size. If you copy a compressed file to an NTFS volume with enough space for the compressed file, but not enough space for the uncompressed file, you might get an error message that states that there is not enough disk space for the file, and the file will not be copied to the volume.

Key Terms

basic disk   A physical disk that can be accessed locally by MS-DOS and all Windows-based operating systems. Basic disks can contain up to four primary partitions or three primary partitions and an extended partition with multiple logical drives. If you want to create partitions that span multiple disks, you must first convert the basic disk to a dynamic disk using Disk Management or the Diskpart.exe command-line utility. Note that whether a disk is basic or dynamic has no bearing on whether computers running other operating systems can connect to shared folders on the disk.

Check Disk A command-line utility that verifies and repairs the integrity of the file system on a volume.

Cipher A command-line utility that provides the capability to encrypt and decrypt files and folders from a command prompt.

compressed folders A feature that allows you to compress folders on volumes formatted with NTFS or FAT. Compressed folders are compatible with other zip programs.

defragmentation The process of rearranging the various pieces of files and folders on the disk into contiguous spaces, thereby improving performance.

Disk Cleanup A utility that calculates the amount of space that you can gain by deleting certain types of files, such as temporary files and downloaded program files.

Disk Defragmenter The program used in Windows XP to defragment a disk.

Disk Management The name of the Windows XP utility used to manage fixed and removable disks, as well as to create and manage volumes and partitions.

disk quota A feature that allows you to allocate disk space to users based on the files and folders that they own.

Diskpart A command used to execute disk-management tasks from a command prompt and to create scripts for automating tasks that you need to perform frequently or on multiple computers.

drive letter Used to access the volume through Windows Explorer and other applications. Hard disks, floppy drives, CD-ROM and DVD drives, removable drives, and tape devices are assigned drive letters.

dynamic disk A physical disk that can be accessed locally only by Windows 2000 and Windows XP. Dynamic disks provide features that basic disks do not, such as support for volumes that span multiple disks. Dynamic disks use a hidden database to track information about dynamic volumes on the disk and other dynamic disks in the computer. You convert basic disks to dynamic disks by using the Disk Management snap-in or the Diskpart command-line utility. When you convert a basic disk to a dynamic disk, all existing basic volumes become dynamic volumes. Note that whether a disk is basic or dynamic has no bearing on whether computers running other operating systems can connect to shared folders on the disk.

Encrypting File System (EFS) A Windows XP Professional feature that provides encryption for data in NTFS files stored on disk.

encryption The process of making information indecipherable to protect it from unauthorized viewing or use.

extended partition A partition that provides a way to exceed the four primary partition limit. You cannot format an extended partition with any file system. Rather, extended partitions serve as a shell in which you can create any number of logical partitions.

fixed storage A storage device that is not removable, such as a hard drive.

formatting   Preparing a hard disk to accept data by creating a file system (such as NTFS or FAT) on that disk.

fragmentation   Occurs when files are frequently added and removed from the disk, or when the disk begins to fill up. In both of these cases, it can be difficult for the operating system to locate a contiguous area of the disk to write to, and data can become fragmented.

logical partition   A disk storage area that you create within an extended partition on a basic Master Boot Record (MBR) disk. Logical drives are similar to primary partitions, except that you can create an unlimited number of logical drives per disk. A logical drive can be formatted and assigned a drive letter.

mounted volume   A volume to which you assign a path on an existing volume rather than a drive letter.

NTFS compression   A function of the NTFS file system that performs dynamic compression and decompression on folders and files marked with the compression attribute.

Offline Files   A feature of Windows XP Professional that makes temporary copies of shared network files on a local computer so that you can access those files when the local computer is disconnected from the network.

primary partition   A partition that you can configure as the active, or bootable, drive. You can configure up to four primary partitions on a computer running a Windows operating system (three partitions if you also have an extended partition on the disk).

recovery agent   A user account that is given the capability to decrypt an encrypted file or folder in case the owner of the resource loses the file encryption certificate that allows decryption.

removable storage   A storage device that allows you to remove either the device itself or the storage media that the device uses.

simple volume   A dynamic volume that contains disk space from a single disk and can be extended if necessary.

spanned volume   A dynamic volume that contains disk space from 2 or more (up to a maximum of 32) disks. The amount of disk space from each disk can vary. There is no fault tolerance in spanned volumes. If any of the disks containing the spanned volume fail, you lose all data in the entire spanned volume.

striped volume   A dynamic volume that contains disk space from 2 or more (up to a maximum of 32) disks. Unlike spanned volumes, striped volumes require that you use an identical amount of disk space from each disk. Striped volumes provide increased performance because it is faster to read or write two smaller pieces of a file on two drives than to read or write the entire file on a single drive. However, you cannot extend striped volumes and they provide no fault tolerance.

Questions and Answers

Lesson 1 Review

Page
10-26

1. On which types of computers can you use dynamic disks?

To use a dynamic disk, you must be running Windows XP Professional or Windows 2000 Professional. Portable computers do not support dynamic disks.

2. What actions must you take to revert from a dynamic disk to a basic disk? What limitations does this process impose?

By using Disk Management, you must delete all volumes on the disk. You must then right-click the disk and select Revert To Basic Disk. All data is lost when reverting a dynamic disk to a basic disk. You must repartition and reformat the basic disk following the conversion.

Lesson 2 Practice: Exercise 2

Page
10-34

1. What color is the name of the Compressed folder?

Blue. This is the default color used by Windows XP to denote a compressed folder.

Lesson 2 Practice: Exercise 3

Page
10-35

1. Is the Compressed2 folder compressed or not compressed? Why?

The Compressed2 folder is compressed because in Exercise 2, you specified that all subfolders and files should also be compressed.

7. What indication do you have that the Compressed2 folder is no longer compressed?

The folder name is now displayed in the original color (typically black).

Page
10-36

Lesson 2: Exercise 4

▶ **To create a compressed file**

4. How can you verify that the Text1.txt file is compressed?

The folder name is displayed in blue.

▶ **To copy a compressed file to an uncompressed folder**

3. Is the Text1.txt file in the Compressed2 folder compressed or uncompressed? Why?

Uncompressed. A new file inherits the compression attribute of the folder in which it is created.

▶   **To move a compressed file to an uncompressed folder**

2. Is the Text1.txt file in the Compressed folder compressed or uncompressed?

Uncompressed. A new file inherits the compression attribute of the folder in which it is created.

3. Is the Text1.txt file in the Compressed2 folder compressed or uncompressed? Why?

Compressed. When a file is moved to a new folder on the same partition, its compression attribute does not change.

Lesson 2 Review

Page
10-37

1. When Sandra tried to copy a compressed file from one NTFS volume to another, the file was not copied, and she got an error message stating that there was not enough disk space for the file. Before she attempted to copy the file, Sandra verified that there was enough room for the compressed bitmap on the destination volume. Why did she get the error message?

If you copy a compressed file to an NTFS volume with enough space for the compressed file, but not enough space for the uncompressed file, you might get an error message stating that there is not enough disk space for the file. The file will not be copied to the volume.

2. When you move a file between NTFS volumes, does the file retain the compression state of the source folder, or does the file inherit the compression state of the target folder? Why?

When you move a file or folder between NTFS volumes, the file or folder inherits the compression state of the target folder. Windows XP Professional treats a move as a copy and then a delete, so the files inherit the compression state of the target folder.

3. What does Windows XP Professional do when you try to copy a compressed file to a floppy disk? Why?

When you copy a compressed file to a floppy disk, Windows XP Professional automatically uncompresses the file because floppy disks cannot be formatted with NTFS and cannot use NTFS compression.

4. Which of the following types of files or data are good candidates for NTFS compression? (Choose all that apply.)

a. Encrypted data

b. Frequently updated data

c. Bitmaps

d. Static data

The correct answers are C and D. A is not correct because you cannot apply both compression and encryption to a file. B is not correct because compression does add some overhead when accessing files, so you should not use it on files that you access frequently.

Page
10-44
Lesson 3 Practice: Exercise 1

▶ **To configure default quota management settings**

    7. What is the default disk space limit for new users?

    1 KB

    12. What happens to the quota status indicator?

    The traffic light indicator turns yellow momentarily, indicating that it is rebuilding the disk quotas for the disk.

▶ **To configure quota management settings for a user**

    2. Are any user accounts listed? Why or why not?

    Yes. The accounts listed are those that have logged on and gained access to drive C.

    5. Click Limit Disk Space To. What are the default settings for the user you just set a quota limit for?

    Limit Disk Space To 1 KB and Set The Warning Level To 1 KB are the default settings.

    16. Why did you get this error message?

    You have exceeded your quota limit, and because the Deny Disk Space To Users Exceeding Quota Limit check box is selected, you cannot use more disk space after you exceed your quota limit.

Lesson 3 Review

Page
10-47
    1. What is the purpose of disk quotas?

    Disk quotas allow you to allocate disk space to users and monitor the amount of hard disk space that users have used and the amount that they have left against their quota.

    2. Which of the following statements about disk quotas in Windows XP Professional is correct? (Choose the correct answer.)

        a. Disk quotas track and control disk usage on a per-user, per-disk basis.

        b. Disk quotas track and control disk usage on a per-group, per-volume basis.

        c. Disk quotas track and control disk usage on a per-user, per-volume basis.

        d. Disk quotas track and control disk usage on a per-group, per-disk basis.

    The correct answer is C. Answer A is not correct because disk quotas do not track usage on a per-disk basis. Answers B and D are not correct because disk quotas track usage on a per-user basis, not a per-group basis.

3. Which of the following statements about disk quotas in Windows XP Professional is correct? (Choose all that apply.)

   a. Disk quotas can be applied only to Windows XP Professional NTFS volumes.

   b. Disk quotas can be applied to any Windows XP Professional volume.

   c. You must be logged on with the Administrator user account to configure default quota management settings.

   d. Members of the Administrators and Power Users groups can configure quota management settings.

   The correct answers are A and C. B is not correct because the volume must be formatted with NTFS. D is not correct because members of the Power Users group cannot configure quota management settings.

4. You get a call from an administrator who cannot delete a quota entry for a user account. What would you tell the administrator to check?

   Tell the administrator to verify that all files owned by the user are removed or that another user has taken ownership of the files. You cannot delete a quota entry for a user account if there are files owned by that user on the volume.

Lesson 4 Practice: Increasing Security by Using EFS

Page
10-53

1. What color is the SecretFile.txt text file? Why?

   Green. Windows displays the names of encrypted files and folders as green by default.

17. What happens?

   A Notepad dialog box appears indicating that access is denied.

Lesson 4 Review

Page
10-54

1. What is encryption and what is the EFS?

   Encryption makes information indecipherable to protect it from unauthorized viewing or use. The EFS provides encryption for data in NTFS files stored on disk. This encryption is public key–based and runs as an integrated system service, making it easy to manage, difficult to attack, and transparent to the file owner.

2. Which of the following files and folders does Windows XP Professional allow you to encrypt? (Choose all that apply.)

   a. A file on an NTFS volume

   b. A folder on a FAT volume

   c. A file stored on a floppy

   d. A folder on an NTFS volume

   The correct answers are A and D. B is not correct because encryption is not available on volumes formatted with FAT. C is not correct because you cannot format a floppy disk with NTFS.

3. How do you encrypt a folder? Is the folder actually encrypted?

To encrypt a folder, in the Properties dialog box for the folder, click the General tab. In the General tab, click Advanced, and then select the Encrypt Contents To Secure Data check box. All files placed in the folder are encrypted, and the folder is now marked for encryption. Folders that are marked for encryption are not actually encrypted; only the files within the folder are encrypted.

4. If the private key belonging to the owner of an encrypted file is not available, how can you decrypt the file?

If the owner's private key is unavailable, a recovery agent can open the file by using his or her own private key.

5. By default, the recovery agent for a computer running Windows XP Professional in a workgroup is _____, and the recovery agent for a computer running Windows XP Professional in a domain environment is _____.

The administrator of the local computer; the domain administrator.

Lesson 5 Practice: Exercise 3

Page
10-66

1. When would you use the options available in the More Options tab?

When running Disk Cleanup did not free up enough space on your hard drive, and you need to find some additional space. The More Options tab allows you to delete Windows components, installed programs, and saved system restore points to free up additional space.

Lesson 5 Review

Page
10-67

1. What is fragmentation and what problems does it cause?

Fragmentation is the scattering of the parts of a file over the disk rather than having all parts of the file located in contiguous space. Over time, a hard disk will contain fragmented files and folders that cause Windows XP Professional to take longer to access the files. Creating new files and folders also takes longer because the available free space on the hard disk is scattered.

2. The process of finding and consolidating fragmented files and folders is called _____. The Windows XP Professional system tool that locates fragmented files and folders and arranges them in contiguous space is

_____.

Defragmenting or defragmentation; Disk Defragmenter

3. Windows XP Professional provides a tool to locate fragmented files and folders and arrange them in contiguous space on volumes formatted with which file systems?

NTFS, FAT, and FAT32

4. Which of the following functions does Check Disk perform? (Choose all that apply.)

    a. Locates fragmented files and folders and arranges contiguously

    b. Locates and attempts to repair file system errors

    c. Locates bad sectors and recovers readable information from those bad sectors

    d. Deletes temporary files and offline files

The correct answers are B and C. A is not correct because this is a function of Disk Defragmenter. D is not correct because this is a function of Disk Cleanup.

Lesson 6 Review

Page
10-76

1. How do you configure your computer to use offline folders and files?

To configure your computer to use offline folders and files, on the Tools menu of My Computer, click Folder Options. In the Offline Files tab of Folder Options, you enable the Enable Offline Files and the Synchronize All Offline Files Before Logging Off check boxes.

2. Which tools does Windows XP Professional provide for you to configure your computer to provide offline files? What must you do to allow others to access files on your computer?

Windows Explorer and My Computer. You must share the folder containing the file.

3. What does Synchronization Manager do?

Synchronization Manager allows you to manually synchronize or schedule the synchronization of the files on your computer with the ones on the network resource.

Case Scenario Exercise Questions

Page
10-77

1. Iris' new notebook computer has a 16 GB hard disk that you want to configure as a single volume. It is the only hard disk on the computer. Should you create a basic or dynamic disk?

Windows XP Professional does not support dynamic disks on notebook computers, so you must configure a basic disk. You should configure the basic disk with a single primary partition.

2. When she is running the exhibit booth at tradeshows, Iris' attention is often diverted, and she is worried that she cannot always keep an eye on her notebook computer. The computer contains trade secrets that she does not want to see compromised. Iris wants to secure the files on her computer, even if the computer is stolen. Can you configure encryption on her notebook computer? If so, what precautions should you take?

Iris can encrypt files on the notebook computer as long as the hard disk is formatted with NTFS. Iris should designate an EFS Recovery Agent that can recover the files if she is unable to. Iris should also be sure to lock her console when she is not using the computer, or configure her screensaver to require a password when the computer is activated. If the computer is configured to go to standby mode when it is idle, Iris should require a password to bring the computer out of standby.

3. Iris' notebook computer does not have the biggest hard drive. She often works on large sales documents and also stores many picture files of the products she sells. She wants to compress these files to save space. What should you tell Iris to do?

You should show Iris how to use the Compressed Folders feature in Windows XP Professional. Although she could use NTFS compression on her notebook, she cannot use NTFS compression on the same files that she encrypts, so NTFS compression is not a good solution for Iris.

4. What utility should you teach Iris to use that might also help maximize the free space on her hard disk?

You should teach Iris to use the Disk Cleanup utility to remove temporary and cached files from her computer.

5. You have configured Iris' notebook computer to connect securely via the Internet to the company network so that Iris can access the company e-mail server and file servers. Iris also wants to be able to access certain shared files on the company network when she cannot connect to the network. What should you do?

You should enable the Offline Files feature on Iris' notebook computer. While the computer is connected to the network, you should show Iris how make a shared folder available offline. You should also caution her that if she makes changes to a file while she is disconnected from the network, and another user changes the same file in the actual network folder, there might be a conflict when Iris' notebook synchronizes her offline files.

Troubleshooting Lab

Page 10-78

What do you suspect is the problem? What would you do to help Jonas?

Disk Management reports dynamic disks as either Offline or Missing when it cannot detect the disk. The cause of a missing dynamic disk can be an operating system error or a problem with the drive itself. You should first have Windows attempt to find the missing disk by selecting Rescan Disks from the Action menu of Disk Management. If that does not resolve the issue, you should have Jonas restart his computer. If Disk Management continues to report the disk as missing, you should check to make sure that the drive is properly connected in the computer. It is also possible that the drive has failed and must be replaced.

11 Setting Up, Configuring, and Troubleshooting Printers

Exam Objectives in this Chapter:

- Connect to local and network print devices.
- Manage printers and print jobs.
- Connect to an Internet printer.
- Connect to a local print device.

Why This Chapter Matters

This chapter introduces you to setting up and configuring network printers so that users can print over the network. You will also learn how to troubleshoot common printing problems associated with setting up network printers.

Lessons in this Chapter:

- Lesson 1: Introduction to Windows XP Professional Printing
- Lesson 2: Setting Up Network Printers
- Lesson 3: Connecting to Network Printers
- Lesson 4: Configuring Network Printers
- Lesson 5: Troubleshooting Setup and Configuration Problems

Before You Begin

To complete this chapter, you must have a computer that meets the minimum hardware requirements listed in the preface, "About This Book." You must also have Microsoft Windows XP Professional installed on a computer on which you can make changes.

Note You do not need a printer to complete the exercises in this chapter.

Lesson 1: Introduction to Windows XP Professional Printing

With Windows XP Professional printing, you can easily configure and share printers across an entire network. After a printer is shared on a computer running Windows XP Professional, you can then set up client computers running Windows XP, Windows 2000 Professional, Windows NT 4.0, Windows Me, Windows 98, and Windows 95 to use that shared printer.

After this lesson, you will be able to

■ Define Windows XP Professional printing terms.

■ Identify the requirements for network printing.

■ Develop a network-wide printing strategy.

Estimated lesson time: 15 minutes

Important Printing Terms

Before you start setting up printers, you should be familiar with some important Windows XP Professional printing terms that will help you understand how the different printing components work together, as shown in Figure 11-1.

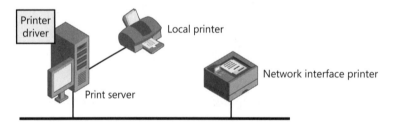

Figure 11-1   Several printing components work together to make printing happen.

The following list defines some Windows XP Professional printing terms:

Logical printer   The **logical printer** is the software configuration that is created in Windows XP and is represented by an icon in the Printers And Faxes window. It controls the printer's configuration and the way in which Windows sends documents to the printer.

Printer   The **printer** is a hardware device that puts text or images on paper or on other print media. You will encounter two types of printers:

  ❑ A **local printer** is connected to a physical port on the print server. A logical printer created on the print server provides tools for managing and sharing the printer.

❏ A **network interface printer** is connected directly to the network via an internal network adapter. You create a logical printer on a print server that you can use to manage and share the printer.

> **Note**   In previous versions of Windows, Microsoft made an important distinction between the terms "printer" and "print device." Prior to Windows XP, a "printer" was the software on the computer that controlled printing, and a "print device" was the actual hardware device. The two terms were not used interchangeably. In Windows XP, that terminology has changed. The Windows XP documentation generally defines the "printer" as "a device that puts text or images on paper or other print media," and the "logical printer" as the "collection of software components that interface between the operating system and the printer." Thus, the printer is the physical device connected to a computer, and the logical printer is the icon in the Printers And Faxes window that represents the printer.

Printer port   The **printer port** is a software interface through which a computer communicates with a printer by means of a locally attached interface. For example, if a computer has a parallel port, the printer port configured in Windows might be named LPT 1. Windows XP Professional supports the following interfaces: line printer (LPT), COM, universal serial bus (USB) 1.1 and 2.0, IEEE 1394 (FireWire), and network-attached devices such as HP JetDirect and Intel NetPort.

Print server   The **print server** is the computer that manages a printer on a network. The print server receives and processes documents from client computers. Note that any computer (a laptop or a desktop) can act as a print server.

Printer driver   The **printer driver** is a file or set of files containing information that Windows XP Professional requires to convert print commands into a specific printer language, such as Adobe PostScript. This conversion makes it possible for a printer to print a document. A printer driver is specific to each printer model.

Print job   A **print job** is a document that Windows has prepared for printing. Print jobs wait in a printer's print queue until it is their turn to be printed. While a print job is waiting in the queue, users can manage or delete the print job.

Requirements for Network Printing

The requirements for setting up printing on a Windows network include the following:

■ At least one computer to act as the print server. If the print server is to manage many heavily used printers, the task of printing documents can use 100 percent of the computer's processing or network capacity. This will slow down other services running on the computer. Therefore, Microsoft recommends using a dedicated print server if the server will be placed under a heavy load. The computer can run almost every Windows operating system, including the following:

❑ Windows Server 2003, which can handle a large number of connections, and supports Apple Macintosh and UNIX computers as well as Novell NetWare clients.

❑ Windows XP Professional, which is limited to 10 concurrent connections from other computers for file and print services. It does not support Macintosh computers or NetWare clients but does support UNIX computers.

■ Sufficient random access memory (RAM) to process documents. If a print server manages a large number of printers or many large documents, the server might require additional RAM beyond what Windows XP Professional or Windows Server 2003 requires for other tasks. If a print server does not have sufficient RAM for its workload, printing performance deteriorates. Given the modern prevalence of inexpensive memory, RAM is typically not an issue unless you expect a print server to be heavily utilized. Even having 64 MB of RAM beyond what the computer requires for other tasks should be sufficient.

■ Sufficient disk space on the print server to ensure that the print server can store documents that are sent to it until it sends the documents to the printer. This is critical when documents are large or likely to accumulate. For example, if 10 users send large documents to print at the same time, the print server must have enough disk space to hold all the documents until it can send them to the print device. If there is not enough space to hold all the documents, users get error messages and cannot print. As with memory, hard disk space really becomes an issue only on heavily used print servers. Having an extra 500 MB to 1 GB of disk space (or, even better, moving the print queue to a spare hard disk) ensures that disk space does not become an issue when printing.

Exam Tip   Windows XP Professional supports up to 10 simultaneous network connections. Windows XP Professional supports printing from the following clients: MS-DOS, Windows 3.1, Windows 95, Windows 98, Windows Me, Windows NT, Windows 2000, Windows Server 2003, Windows XP, and UNIX. Windows XP Professional does not support printing from NetWare or older Macintosh clients. Clients using newer Macintosh operating systems can communicate directly with Windows clients by using special built-in file and print services named Samba.

Guidelines for Developing a Network-wide Printing Strategy

Before you set up network printing, develop a network-wide printing strategy to meet users' printing needs without unnecessary duplication of resources or delays in printing. Table 11-1 provides some guidelines for developing such a strategy.

Table 11-1 Network Printing Environment Guidelines

Guideline	Explanation
Determine users' printing requirements	Determine the number of users who print and the printing workload. For example, 10 people in a billing department who print invoices continually will have a larger printing workload and might require more printers and possibly more print servers than 10 software developers who do all their work online.
Determine company's printing requirements	Determine the printing needs of your company, including the number and types of printers that are required. In addition, consider the type of workload that each printer will handle. Do not use a personal printer for network printing.
Determine the number of print servers required	Determine the number of print servers that your network requires to handle the number and types of printers that your network will contain.
Determine where to locate printers	Determine where to put the printers so that it is easy for users to pick up their printed documents. Think about how the print servers will connect to the printers. Typically, it is more cost-effective to choose network interface printers than to locate print servers physically close to each printer.

Lesson Review

Use the following questions to help determine whether you have learned enough to move on to the next lesson. If you are unable to answer a question, review the lesson materials and try the question again. You can find answers to the questions in the "Questions and Answers" section at the end of this chapter.

1. _____ are connected to a physical port on the print server. Fill in the blank.

2. Do you have to have a computer running one of the Windows Server products to have a print server on your network? Why or why not?

_____

_____

_____

_____

_____

_____

3. How many concurrent connections from other computers for file and print services can Windows XP Professional provide? Choose the correct answer.

   a. 20

   b. 10

   c. Unlimited

   d. 30

4. A(n) _____ is one file or a set of files containing information that Windows XP Professional requires to convert print commands into a specific printer language, such as PostScript. Fill in the blank.

5. Windows XP Professional printing supports which of the following types of computers? Choose all that apply.

   a. Macintosh computers

   b. UNIX computers

   c. NetWare clients

   d. Windows 98 computers

Lesson Summary

- To work with printers in Windows XP Professional, you should know the following terms:
  - ❑ A **printer** is a hardware device that puts text or images on paper or on other print media.
  - ❑ **Local printers** are connected to a physical port on the print server, and network interface printers are connected to a print server through the network.
  - ❑ **Network interface printers** require their own network interface cards (NICs) and have their own network address, or they are attached to an external network adapter.
  - ❑ A **printer driver** is one file or a set of files containing information that Windows XP Professional requires to convert print commands into a specific printer language.
- The requirements for setting up printing on a network include at least one computer to operate as a printer server, sufficient RAM to process documents, and sufficient disk space to ensure that the print server can store documents until it sends the documents to the printer.
- Before you set up network printing, you should take the time to determine the users' and company's printing requirements, the number of print servers needed, and where to locate printers.

Lesson 2: Setting Up Network Printers

Setting up and sharing a network printer makes it possible for multiple users to utilize it. You can set up a local printer that is connected directly to the print server, or you can set up a network interface printer that is connected to the print server over the network. In larger organizations, most printers are network interface printers.

After this lesson, you will be able to

- Add and share a local printer.
- Add and share a network interface printer.
- Add a Line Printer Remote (LPR) port.
- Configure client computers to print to a network printer.

Estimated lesson time: 30 minutes

How to Add and Share a Local Printer

The steps for adding a local printer or a network interface printer are similar. You use the following steps to add a local printer:

1. Log on as Administrator or with a user account that is a member of the Administrators group on the print server.

2. From the Start menu, click Printers And Faxes.

3. In the Printers And Faxes window, in the Printer Tasks section, click Add A Printer to start the Add Printer Wizard.

4. On the Welcome To The Add Printer Wizard page, click Next.

5. On the Local Or Network Printer page, shown in Figure 11-2, select Local Printer Attached To This Computer, and then click Next.

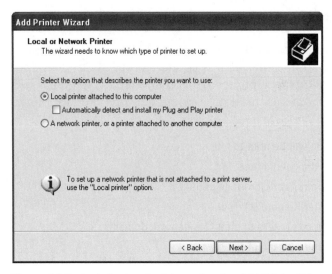

Figure 11-2   Install a local printer using the Add Printer Wizard.

> **Exam Tip**   Users running Windows XP Professional must be members of the Administrators or Power Users group to install a printer, and must have permission to load and unload device drivers.

The Add Printer Wizard guides you through the steps to add a printer that is connected to the print server. The number of local printers that you can connect to a print server through physical ports depends on your hardware configuration. Table 11-2 describes the Add Printer Wizard pages and options for adding a local printer.

Table 11-2   Add Printer Wizard Pages and Options for a Local Printer

Page	Option	Description
Local Or Network Printer	Local Printer Attached To This Computer	You are adding a printer to the computer at which you are sitting, which is the print server.
	Automatically Detect And Install My Plug And Play Printer	A check box that allows you to specify whether you want Windows XP Professional to automatically detect and install the Plug and Play printer.
Select A Printer Port	Use The Following Port	The port on the print server to which you attached the printer.

Table 11-2   Add Printer Wizard Pages and Options for a Local Printer

Page	Option	Description
Install Printer Software	Manufacturer And Printers	Select the appropriate manufacturer and printer so that the correct printer driver for the local printer will be installed. If your printer is not on the list, you must provide a printer driver from the manufacturer or select a model that is similar enough so the printer can use it.
Name Your Printer	Printer Name	A name that identifies the printer to the users. Some applications might not support more than 31 characters in the server and printer name combinations.
	Do You Want To Use This Printer As The Default Printer?	Select Yes to make this printer the default printer for all Windows-based applications and so that users do not have to set a printer for each application. This option does not appear the first time that you add a printer to the print server because the printer is automatically set as the default printer.
Printer Sharing	Share Name	Users (with the appropriate permissions) can use the share name to connect to the printer over the network. This name appears when users browse for a printer or supply a path to a printer. The share name must be compatible with the naming conventions for all client computers on the network. By default, the share name is the printer name truncated to an 8.3-character file name.
Location And Comment	Location	Describe the location of the printer.
	Comment	Provide information that helps users determine whether the printer meets their needs. If your computer is in a domain, users can search the Active Directory service for the information that you enter here.
Print Test Page	Do You Want To Print A Test Page?	Select Yes to print a test page and verify that you have installed the printer correctly.
Completing The Add Printer Wizard	Finish	If the information about how you configured the printer to be installed is correct, click Finish.

Real World **Plug and Play Printers**

If you have a Plug and Play printer that connects through a USB port, an IEEE 1394 interface, or any other port that allows you to attach or remove devices without having to shut down and restart your computer, you probably do not need to use the Add Printer Wizard. If Windows has the drivers for your printer, you can often connect the printer's cable to your computer (or point the printer toward your computer's infrared port) and turn on the printer. Windows automatically installs the printer for you.

However, you should always read the installation instructions provided by the manufacturer. With some printers, you must install the software provided by the manufacturer before you connect and turn on the printer. This process helps ensure that Windows has the proper drivers available when it first detects the printer.

How to Add and Share a Network Interface Printer

In larger companies, most printers are network interface printers. These printers offer a distinct advantage: Because you do not need to connect printers directly to the print server, you can place printers where you need them instead of where the print server is.

To add a network interface printer, select Local Printer Attached To This Computer on the Local Or Network Printer page of the Add Printer Wizard. The main difference between adding a local printer and adding a network interface printer is that you provide additional port and network protocol information for a typical network interface printer.

The default network protocol for Windows XP Professional is Transmission Control Protocol/Internet Protocol (TCP/IP), which many network interface printers use. For TCP/IP, you provide additional port information in the Add Standard TCP/IP Printer Port Wizard.

Figure 11-3 shows the Select A Printer Port page of the Add Printer Wizard, and Table 11-3 describes the options on this page that pertain to adding a network interface printer.

Table 11-3 Options on the Select A Printer Port Page That Affect Adding a Network Interface Printer

Option	Description
Create A New Port	This selection starts the process of creating a new port for the print server to which the network interface print device is connected. In this case, the new port points to the network connection of the print device.
Type Of Port	This selection determines the network protocol to use for the connection. If you select Standard TCP/IP, it starts the Add Standard TCP/IP Printer Port Wizard.

Figure 11-3   Configure the connection to the network printer on the Select A Printer Port page of the Add Printer Wizard.

Figure 11-4 shows the Add Port page of the Add Standard TCP/IP Printer Port Wizard, and Table 11-4 describes the options on this page.

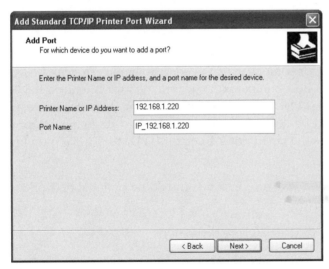

Figure 11-4   Enter the network printer's information on the Add Port page of the Add Standard TCP/IP Printer Port Wizard.

Table 11-4   Options on the Add Port Page That Affect Adding a Network Interface Printer

Option	Description
Printer Name Or IP Address	The network location of the printer. You must enter either the Internet Protocol (IP) address or a Domain Name System (DNS) name of the network interface printer. If you provide an IP address, Windows XP Professional automatically supplies a suggested port name for the print device in the form IP_*IPaddress*. If Windows XP Professional cannot connect to and identify the network interface printer, you must supply additional information about the type of printer. To enable automatic identification, make sure that the printer is powered on and connected to the network.
Port Name	The name that Windows XP Professional assigns to the port that you created and defined. You can enter a different name. After you create the port, Windows XP Professional displays it on the Select A Printer Port page of the Add Printer Wizard.

Note   If your printer uses a network protocol other than TCP/IP, you must install that network protocol before you can add additional ports that use it. The tasks and setup information required to configure a printer port depend on the network protocol.

How to Add an LPR Port

The LPR port is designed for computers that need to communicate with UNIX or virtual address extension (VAX) host computers in accordance with Request for Comments (RFC) 1179. For computers that need to submit print jobs to host computers, the standard TCP/IP port should be used in most cases. A network-connected printer must have a card that supports the Line Printer Daemon (LPD) for TCP/IP printing to work properly.

If you want to add an LPR port, you must first install the optional networking component, Print Services For UNIX.

To install Print Services For UNIX, follow these steps:

1. From the Start menu, click Control Panel.

2. In the Control Panel window, click Network And Internet Connections.

3. In the Network And Internet Connections window, click Network Connections.

4. On the Advanced menu, click Optional Networking Components.

5. In the Windows Optional Networking Components Wizard, on the Windows Components page, click the Other Network File And Print Services check box, and then click Details.

6. In the Other Network File And Print Services dialog box, select the Print Services For UNIX check box, and then click OK.

7. In the Windows Optional Networking Components Wizard, click Next.

8. When the installation completes, close the Network Connections window.

To connect to an LPR network printer, follow these steps:

1. From the Start menu, click Printers And Faxes.

2. In the Printers And Faxes window, click Add A Printer.

3. In the Add Printer Wizard, on the Welcome To The Add Printer Wizard page, click Next.

4. On the Local Or Network Printer page, click Local Printer Attached To This Computer, and clear the Automatically Detect And Install My Plug And Play Printer check box. Click Next.

5. On the Select A Printer Port page, click Create A New Port, and on the Type Of Port drop-down list, select LPR Port. Click Next.

> **Note**   If LPR Port is not available, make sure that the optional networking component Print Services For UNIX is installed. Click Cancel to exit the Add Printer Wizard.

6. In the Add LPR Compatible Printer dialog box, in the Name Or Address Of Server Providing LPD text box, type the DNS name or IP address of the host of the printer you are adding. In the Name Of Printer Or Print Queue On That Server text box, type the name of the print queue. Click OK.

> **Note**   The host can be the direct-connect TCP/IP printing device or the UNIX computer to which the printer is connected. The DNS name can be the name specified for the host in the HOSTS file. LPD is a service on the print server that receives documents (print jobs) from the LPR utilities running on client systems.

7. Follow the directions onscreen to complete the installation of the TCP/IP printer.

How to Configure Client Computers So Users Can Print

After you add and share a printer, you need to set up client computers so that users can print. Although the tasks to set up client computers vary depending on which operating systems are running on the client computers, all client computers require installation of a printer driver. The following points summarize the installation of printer drivers according to the computer's operating system:

- Windows XP Professional automatically downloads the printer drivers for client computers running Windows 2000, Windows NT versions 4.0 and earlier, Windows ME, Windows 95, or Windows 98.

- Client computers running other Microsoft operating systems require installation of printer drivers.

- Client computers running non-Microsoft operating systems require installation of printer drivers. For clients using LPR, you must install Print Services For UNIX.

To Set Up Client Computers Running Windows 2000, Windows NT, Windows Me, Windows 95, or Windows 98

Users of client computers running Windows XP Professional, Windows XP Home Edition, Windows 2000, Windows NT, Windows Me, Windows 98, and Windows 95 only need to connect to the shared printer. The client computer automatically downloads the appropriate printer driver, as long as there is a copy of it on the print server.

If your client computer is running Windows XP Professional and you want to connect to the shared printer, start the Add Printer Wizard on the client computer. On the Local Or Network Printer page (see Figure 11-2), select A Network Printer, Or A Printer Attached To Another Computer, and then click Next. The Specify A Printer page appears, as shown in Figure 11-5.

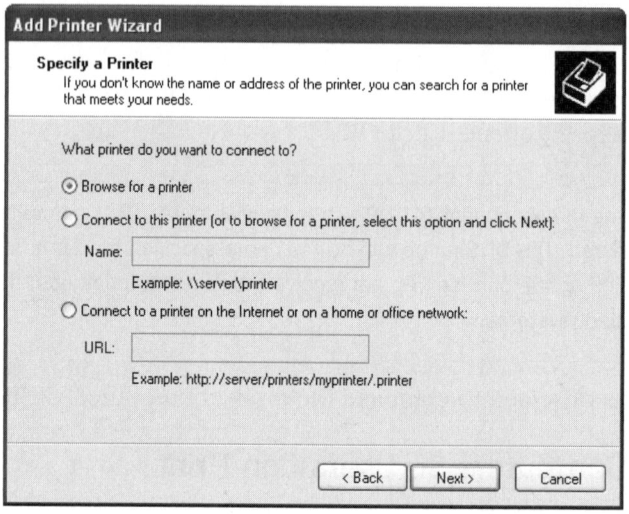

Figure 11-5 Choose the shared printer to connect to.

If you are not sure what the name of the shared printer is, you can browse for it by selecting the Browse For A Printer option, and then clicking Next. After you have located the shared printer and selected it, click Next. You are then asked whether it should be the default printer. If you want it to be the default printer, click Yes; otherwise, select No and click Next. The Completing The Add Printer Wizard page appears. Check over the information and then click Finish. You have successfully made a connection from your client computer to the shared printer.

What You Must Do to Set Up Client Computers Running Other Microsoft Operating Systems

To enable client computers running other Microsoft operating systems (such as Windows 3.1 or MS-DOS) to print to a shared printer on a computer running Windows XP Professional, you must manually install a printer driver on the client computer. To do this, you must get the appropriate printer driver for a Windows-based client computer from the installation disks for that client computer or from the printer manufacturer.

Practice: Installing a Network Printer

In this practice, you use the Add Printer Wizard to install and share a local printer. Sharing the printer makes it available to other users on the network. You also take the printer offline and then print a document, which loads the document into the print queue. Complete the five exercises that follow.

> **Important**   Before you can share a printer or a folder on a computer running Windows XP Professional in a workgroup environment, you must run the Network Setup Wizard to properly configure the network. You can learn more about setting up a network connection in Chapter 15, "Configuring Network and Internet Connections."

Exercise 1: Adding a Local Printer

1. Log on as Administrator or with a user account that is a member of the Administrators group on the print server.

2. From the Start menu, click Printers And Faxes.

3. In the Printers And Faxes window, click Add A Printer to launch the Add Printer Wizard.

4. On the Welcome To The Add Printer Wizard page, click Next.

5. On the Local Or Network Printer page, click Local Printer. Make sure that the Automatically Detect And Install My Plug And Play Printer check box is cleared, and then click Next.

6. On the Select A Printer Port page, in the Use The Following Port drop-down list, select LPT1: (Recommended Printer Port), and then click Next.

> **Note**   If you already have a printer connected to the LPT1 port, select LPT2: (Printer Port) in step 6.

7. On the Install Printer Software page, in the Manufacturer list, select HP. In the Printers list, select HP Color LaserJet 4550 PS printer. Click Next.

> **Note**   The selected driver is digitally signed to ensure reliability and to protect your system. Driver signing is covered in Chapter 6, "Installing, Managing, and Troubleshooting Hardware Devices and Drivers."

8. On the Name Your Printer page, in the Printer Name list box, the Add Printer Wizard suggests a printer name based on the printer model. For this exercise, do not change this name.

9. If other printers are already installed, the wizard also asks whether you want to make this the default printer. If the Add Printer Wizard displays the Do You Want To Use This Printer As The Default Printer message, click Yes.

10. Click Next to continue.

11. On the Printer Sharing page, click Share Name.

12. In the Share Name box, type **Printer1**, and then click Next.

> **Note**   The Add Printer Wizard suggests a share name that is a shortened version of the printer name. The shared printer name is used to identify a printer on the network. Some operating systems (such as Windows 3.1) recognize share names up to only 12 characters. If such clients will connect to the printer, you should use a name that is 12 characters or fewer; otherwise, you can use a longer name.

13. On the Location And Comment page, type **second floor west** and in the Comment text box type **mail room–room 2624**. Click Next.

> **Note**   If your computer running Windows XP Professional is part of a domain, Windows 2000 displays the values that you enter for Location and Comment when a user searches Active Directory for a printer. Entering this information is optional, but it can help users locate the printer more easily.

14. On the Print Test Page page, you can specify whether to print a test page to confirm that your printer is set up properly. Because this exercise does not require that you have a printer, click No, and then click Next. When you are actually setting up a printer, you should print a test page to confirm that it is working properly.

15. On the Completing The Add Printer Wizard page, click Finish.

16. In the Printers And Faxes window, notice that there is a new icon for the shared HP Color LaserJet 4550 PS printer. Windows XP Professional displays an open hand on the printer icon to indicate that the printer is shared. The check mark just above the printer indicates that printer as the default printer.

Exercise 2: Taking a Printer Offline

In this exercise, you take the printer that you created in Exercise 1 offline.

> **Note** Taking a printer offline causes documents that you send to this printer to be held on the computer while the print device is not available. This process eliminates error messages about unavailable printers in later exercises. Windows XP Professional displays such error messages when it attempts to send documents to a printer that is not connected to the computer. When a printer is offline, Windows XP Professional dims the icon and changes the status of the printer from Ready to Offline to reflect that the printer is not available.

1. From the Start menu, click Printers And Faxes.

2. Right-click the HP Color LaserJet 4550 PS icon.

3. On the shortcut menu, click Use Printer Offline.

Exercise 3: Printing a Test Document

1. In the Printers And Faxes folder, double-click the HP Color LaserJet 4550 PS icon.

2. In the HP Color LaserJet 4550 PS–Use Printer Offline dialog box, notice that there are no documents waiting to be printed.

3. Click Start, point to All Programs, point to Accessories, and then click Notepad.

4. In Notepad, type any text that you want.

5. Arrange the Notepad window and the HP Color LaserJet 4550 PS–Use Printer Offline dialog box on the desktop so that you can see the contents of both.

6. In Notepad, on the File menu, click Print.

7. In the Print dialog box, notice that the location and comment information that you entered when you created the printer are shown, and that the Status for the printer shows that it is currently offline.

8. Make sure that the HP Color LaserJet 4550 PS is selected as the printer, and then click Print.

9. Notepad briefly displays a message on your computer, stating that the document is printing. On a fast computer, you might not be able to see this message. Close Notepad and click No when prompted to save changes to your document.

10. In the HP Color LaserJet 4550 PS–Use Printer Offline dialog box, you will see the document waiting to be sent to the printer. Windows XP Professional holds the document because you took the printer offline. Otherwise, Windows XP Professional would have sent the document to the printer immediately.

11. Close the HP Color LaserJet 4550 PS–Use Printer Offline dialog box.

12. Close all open windows.

Exercise 4: Installing Print Services For UNIX

1. From the Start menu, click Control Panel.

2. In the Control Panel window, click Network And Internet Connections.

3. In the Network And Internet Connections window, click Network Connections.

4. On the Advanced menu, click Optional Networking Components.

5. In the Windows Optional Networking Components Wizard, on the Windows Components page, click the Other Network File And Print Services check box, and then click Details.

6. In the Other Network File And Print Services dialog box, click the Print Services For UNIX check box, and then click OK.

7. In the Windows Optional Networking Components Wizard, click Next.

8. When the installation completes, close the Network Connections window.

Exercise 5: Installing an LPR Port

1. From the Start menu, click Printers And Faxes.

2. In the Printers And Faxes window, click Add A Printer.

3. In the Add Printer Wizard, on the Welcome To The Add Printer Wizard page, click Next.

4. On the Local or Network Printer page, click Local Printer Attached To This Computer and clear the Automatically Detect And Install My Plug And Play Printer check box. Click Next.

5. On the Select A Printer Port page, click Create A New Port; and on the Type Of Port drop-down list, select LPR Port. Click Next.

6. In the Add LPR Compatible dialog box, in the Name Or Address Of Server Providing LPD text box, type the DNS name or IP address of the host of the printer you are adding. Click OK.

7. On the Install Printer Software page, in the Manufacturer list, select HP. In the Printers list, select HP Color LaserJet. Click Next.

8. On the Name Your Printer page, in the Printer Name list box, the Add Printer Wizard suggests a printer name based on the printer model. For this exercise, do not change this name. If other printers are already installed, the wizard also asks whether you want to make this the default printer. If the Add Printer Wizard displays the Do You Want To Use This Printer As The Default Printer message, click Yes.

9. Click Next to continue.

10. On the Printer Sharing page, click Do Not Share This Printer, and then click Next.

11. On the Print Test Page page, click No, and then click Next.

12. On the Completing The Add Printer Wizard page, click Finish.

Lesson Review

Use the following questions to help determine whether you have learned enough to move on to the next lesson. If you have difficulty answering these questions, review the material in this lesson before beginning the next lesson. You can find answers to these questions in the "Questions and Answers" section at the end of this chapter.

1. Which of the following tasks can you perform with the Add Printer Wizard? Choose all that apply.

   a. Taking a local printer offline

   b. Printing multiple copies of a document

   c. Adding an LPR port

   d. Making a printer that is connected to your computer available to other network users

2. What is the default printer in Windows XP Professional?

   _____

   _____

   _____

   _____

3. After you get home from the store, you unpack your new computer and printer. You install Windows XP Professional, and you want to install your printer. You want to set up the printer as your default printer. During the installation, you are not prompted to use the printer as your default printer for all Windows-based applications. You know you have seen this option at work when you install local printers. Why can you not see it on your home computer?

_____

_____

Lesson Summary

■ Local printers are directly connected to a print server. To install and share a local printer, use the Add Printer Wizard on the print server. Sharing a local printer makes it possible for multiple users on the network to utilize it.

■ In larger companies, most printers are network interface printers. To install a network interface printer, use the Add Printer Wizard and specify the port information for the printer (such as a network address).

■ The LPR port is designed for computers that need to communicate with UNIX or VAX host computers. For computers that need to submit print jobs to host computers, the standard TCP/IP port should be used in most cases. To install an LPR port, you must first install Print Services For UNIX.

■ Users of client computers running Windows XP Professional, Windows 2000, Windows Me, Windows NT, Windows 98, or Windows 95 only need to connect to the shared printer to be able to print. To enable users of client computers that use the LPR protocol to print, the print server must have Print Services For UNIX installed.

Lesson 3: Connecting to Network Printers

After you have installed and shared a printer on the print server, and installed appropriate drivers, users on client computers running Windows 95 and later can easily connect to the shared printer. For most Windows-based client computers, if the appropriate printer drivers are on the print server, the client computer automatically downloads the drivers when the user makes a connection to the printer. For information on how you can install additional drivers on a print server, see Lesson 4, "Configuring Network Printers," later in this chapter.

When you add and share a printer, by default, all users can connect to that printer and print documents. The method used to connect to a printer depends on the client computer. Client computers running Windows 95 and later can use the Add Printer Wizard. Client computers running Windows XP Professional, Windows XP Home Edition, or Windows 2000 can also use a Web browser to connect to the printer.

After this lesson, you will be able to

- Identify the options available when using the Add Printer Wizard to connect to a network printer.
- Connect directly to a shared printer.
- Connect to a network printer by using a Web browser.
- Find a printer using the Search Assistant.

Estimated lesson time: 15 minutes

Add Printer Wizard Options

The Add Printer Wizard is one method that client computers running Windows XP Professional, Windows XP Home Edition, Windows 2000, Windows Me, Windows NT, Windows 98, or Windows 95 can use to connect to a printer. This is the same wizard that you use to add and share a printer. The options that are available in the Add Printer Wizard that allow you to locate and connect to a printer vary depending on the operating system that the client computer is running.

Options for Client Computers Running Windows 2000 and Later

By using the Add Printer Wizard on client computers running Windows 2000 and later, you can connect to a printer through the following methods:

Use the Universal Naming Convention (UNC) name   You can use the UNC name (*print_server**printer_name*) to make connections by selecting Type The Printer Name Or Click Next To Browse For A Printer on the Locate Your Printer page of the Add Printer Wizard. If you know the UNC name, this is a quick method.

Browse the network   You can also browse the network for the printer by selecting Type The Printer Name Or Click Next To Browse For A Printer on the Locate Your Printer page of the Add Printer Wizard, leaving the Name text box blank, and clicking Next.

Use the Uniform Resource Locator (URL) name   You can also connect to a printer on the Internet or your intranet by selecting Connect To A Printer On The Internet Or On Your Local Intranet on the Locate Your Printer page of the Add Printer Wizard.

Search Active Directory   If your computer running Windows 2000 or later is a member of a domain, you can find the printer by using Microsoft Active Directory service search capabilities. You can search either the entire Active Directory or just a portion of it. You can also narrow the search by providing features of the printer, such as color printing.

Options for Client Computers Running Windows NT 4.0, Windows 95, or Windows 98

On client computers running Windows NT 4.0, Windows 95, or Windows 98, the Add Printer Wizard allows you only to enter a UNC name or to browse Network Neighborhood to locate the printer.

Options for Client Computers Running Other Microsoft Operating Systems

Users at client computers running early versions of Windows—such as Windows 3.1, Windows 3.5, and Windows for Workgroups—use Print Manager instead of the Add Printer Wizard to make a connection to a printer.

How to Connect Directly to a Shared Printer

Instead of using the Add Printer Wizard, an often simpler way to connect to a shared printer is to connect directly by using any of the following techniques:

Browse My Network Places or Network Neighborhood   In Windows 95, Windows 98, and Windows NT, Network Neighborhood provides a way to browse computers on the local network. In Windows 2000 and Windows XP, My Network Places provides this same functionality. After browsing to the computer that shares the printer, right-click the printer and click Connect to initiate a connection to the printer. You can also drag the printer icon to the Printers And Faxes folder on the client computer.

Use the Run dialog box   Click Start and then click Run to open the Run dialog box. Type the UNC of any printer (*print_server**printer_name*) into the Open text box, and then click OK to initiate a connection to the printer. If the print server does not have the appropriate drivers for the operating system running on the client, Windows asks you to provide the drivers.

Use the command prompt   Users of any Windows-based client computer can connect to a network printer by typing **net use lpt*x*: *print_server**printer_name***, where x is the number of the printer port. The Net Use command is also the only method available for making a connection to a network printer from client computers running MS-DOS or IBM OS/2 with Microsoft LAN Manager client software installed.

How to Use a Web Browser

If you are using a client computer running Windows XP Professional, Windows XP Home Edition, or Windows 2000, you can connect to a printer through your corporate intranet. You can type a URL in your Web browser, and you do not have to use the Add Printer Wizard. In Windows XP Professional, you can use Microsoft Internet Explorer, the Printers And Faxes folder, My Computer, or any other window or folder that has an address bar. After you make a connection, Windows XP Professional copies the correct printer drivers to the client computer automatically.

A Web designer can customize this Web page, for example, to display a floor plan that shows the location of print devices to which users can connect. There are two ways to connect to a printer using a Web browser:

- If you do not know the printer's name, type **http://*print_server*/printers**. The Web page lists all the shared printers on the print server that you have permission to use. The page provides information about the printers, including printer name, status of print jobs, location, model, and any comments that were entered when the printer was installed. This information helps you select the correct printer for your needs. Click the printer that you want to use.

- If you know the printer's name, type **http://*print_server*/*printer_name***. You provide the intranet path for a specific printer. You must have permission to use the printer.

Windows automatically copies the appropriate printer driver to your computer and the icon appears in Printers And Faxes. When you have connected to a shared printer from a Web browser, you can use the printer as if it were attached to your computer.

> **Note**   For Internet printing, you must have Internet Information Services (IIS) and the Internet Printing Windows component installed on the print server. You must use Internet Explorer version 4.0 or later to connect to a printer.

How to Find a Printer Using the Search Assistant

In the Search Assistant, the Find Printers feature allows you to search for printers in Active Directory when you are logged on to an Active Directory domain. To activate the Search Assistant, click Start, and then click Search. When the Search Assistant has started, click Find Printers. When you have located a printer using Find Printers, you can double-click the printer; or you can right-click it, and then click Connect to make a connection to the printer. The Find Printers dialog box has three tabs to help you locate a printer (see Figure 11-6).

Figure 11-6   Search for printers in Active Directory with the Find Printers dialog box.

The following list describes the three tabs of the Find Printers dialog box:

Printers tab   Allows you to enter and search for specific information, such as the name, location, and model of the printer.

Features tab   Allows you to select from a prepared list of additional search options, such as whether the printer can print double-sided copies or at a specific resolution.

Advanced tab   Allows you to use custom fields and Boolean operators to define complex searches, such as whether the printer supports collation and a specific printer language such as PostScript.

If you want to search for all available printers, you can leave all search criteria blank and click Find Now. All the printers in the domain will be listed.

Note   The Find Printers feature is not available in the Search Assistant unless you are logged on to a Windows domain. If you are using a computer that is in a workgroup, the Find Printers feature is not available.

Lesson Review

Use the following questions to help determine whether you have learned enough to move on to the next lesson. If you have difficulty answering these questions, review the material in this lesson before beginning the next lesson. You can find answers to these questions in the "Questions and Answers" section at the end of this chapter.

1. When you add and share a printer, who can connect to that printer by default?

   _____

2. Which of the following operating systems running on a client computer allow you to connect to a network printer by using Active Directory search capabilities? Choose all that apply.

   a. Windows 2000

   b. Windows Me

   c. Windows NT 4.0

   d. Windows XP Professional

3. You have a small workgroup consisting of five computers running Windows XP Professional at your house. You are giving your friend, who has never seen Windows XP Professional, a tour around the operating system. You are demonstrating how the Search Assistant works, but the Find Printers feature is missing. Why?

   _____

   _____

   _____

Lesson Summary

- Client computers running Windows XP Professional, Windows XP Home Edition, Windows 2000, Windows Me, Windows NT, Windows 98, or Windows 95 can use the Add Printer Wizard to connect to a printer. On client computers running Windows NT 4.0, Windows 95, or Windows 98, the Add Printer Wizard only allows you to enter a UNC name or to browse Network Neighborhood to locate the printer. Users on client computers running early versions of Windows (such as Windows 3.1, Windows 3.5, and Windows for Workgroups) use Print Manager to connect to a printer.

- You can also install a printer by connecting to it with My Network Places (or Network Neighborhood), the Run dialog box, or the command prompt.

- If you are using a client computer running Windows XP Professional, Windows XP Home Edition, or Windows 2000, you can connect to a printer through your corporate intranet by typing a URL in your Web browser.

- On client computers running Windows XP Professional, Windows XP Home Edition, or Windows 2000 that are part of a Active Directory domain, you can connect to a printer using Active Directory search capabilities.

Lesson 4: Configuring Network Printers

After you have set up and shared network printers, user and company printing needs might require you to configure printer settings so that your printing resources better fit these needs.

The five most common configuration changes you can make are as follows:

- You can share an existing nonshared printer if your printing load increases.

- You can download additional print drivers so that clients running other versions of Windows can use the shared printer.

- You can stop sharing an existing shared printer.

- You can create a printer pool with multiple printers so that print jobs are automatically distributed to the first available printer. In this way, users do not have to search for an available printer.

- You can set priorities among printers so that critical documents always print before noncritical documents.

After this lesson, you will be able to

- Share an existing printer.
- Install additional printer drivers.
- Stop sharing a printer.
- Create a printer pool.
- Set priorities among printers.

Estimated lesson time: 25 minutes

How to Share an Existing Printer

If the printing demands on your network increase, and if your network has a printer that is already installed as a local printer but not yet shared, you can share the printer with the network.

When you share a printer, you need to assign the printer a share name, which appears in My Network Places. Use an intuitive name to help users when they are browsing for a printer. You can also add printer drivers for all versions of Windows XP Professional, Windows XP Home Edition, Windows 2000, Windows NT, Windows 95, and Windows 98.

In the Properties dialog box for the printer, you can use the Sharing tab to share an existing printer (see Figure 11-7).

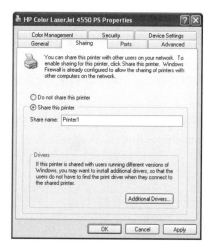

Figure 11-7   Use the Sharing tab of a printer's Properties dialog box to configure sharing.

You use the following steps to share an existing printer using the Sharing tab:

1. From the Start menu, click Printers And Faxes.

2. In the Printers And Faxes window, right-click the icon for the printer that you want to share and click Sharing.

> **Note**   If this is the first time you have shared a printer or a file on the computer, Windows XP Professional prompts you to either run the Network Setup Wizard or just enable sharing. For the purposes of this exercise, you should just enable sharing if Windows presents you with the choice. For more information on using the Network Setup Wizard, see Chapter 15.

3. In the Properties dialog box for the printer, on the Sharing tab, click Share This Printer.

4. In the Share Name text box, type in a share name, and then click OK.

After you have shared the printer, Windows XP Professional puts an open hand under the printer icon, indicating that the printer is shared.

How to Install Additional Printer Drivers

If you expect network users of a shared printer to have computers that are running different versions of Windows, you can install different drivers so that they are automatically available to users who connect to the printer. Making drivers available prevents users from having to find and install the drivers themselves. To verify which printer drivers are downloaded or to download printer drivers to your print server, use the following steps:

1. On the print server, click Start, and then click Printers And Faxes.

2. In the Printers And Faxes window, right-click the shared printer you want to manage, and then click Sharing.

3. In the Properties dialog box for the printer, on the Sharing tab, click Additional Drivers.

4. In the Additional Drivers dialog box, shown in Figure 11-8, select the check boxes for any environments for which you want to make drivers available, and then click OK.

Figure 11-8   Install additional drivers by using the Sharing tab.

5. If you are prompted for the Windows XP Professional installation files, enter the path to those files or insert the Windows XP Professional CD-ROM into the CD-ROM drive, and then click OK.

Note   If Windows XP Professional does not have the necessary drivers, you will be prompted to provide the drivers yourself.

6. The drivers are installed. Click OK to close the Properties dialog box for the printer.

How to Stop the Sharing of a Printer

If the printing demands on your network change, you can stop sharing an existing shared printer. Use the Sharing tab of the Properties dialog box for that printer to stop sharing it. The steps to stop sharing a printer are similar to those for sharing a printer. However, in the steps to stop sharing a printer, in the Properties dialog box for the printer, in the Sharing tab, click Do Not Share This Printer (refer to Figure 11-7), and then click OK.

How to Create a Printer Pool

A **printer pool** consists of two or more identical printers that are connected to one print server and are configured with a single logical printer. The printers can be local or network interface printers. Although the printers should be identical, you can use printers that are not identical but use the same printer driver. After you install a printer, you can create a printer pool using the Ports tab of the Properties dialog box for that printer. In the Ports tab, select the Enable Printer Pooling check box and select additional ports on the printer server (see Figure 11-9).

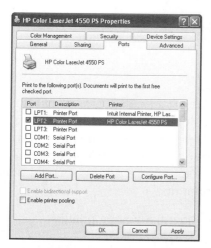

Figure 11-9   Enable printer pooling using the Properties dialog box for the printer.

When you create a printer pool, users can print documents without checking to see which printer is available. The document prints on the first available printer in the printing pool.

Tip   When you set up a printer pool, you should place the printers in the same physical area so that users can easily locate their documents.

A printing pool has the following advantages:

- In a network with a high volume of printing, it decreases the time that documents wait on the print server.

- It simplifies administration because you can administer multiple printers simultaneously.

After connecting the printers to the print server, you can create a printing pool by completing the following steps:

1. Click Start, and then click Printers And Faxes.

2. In the Printers And Faxes window, right-click the printer icon and click Properties.

3. In the Properties dialog box for the printer, on the Ports tab, select the Enable Printer Pooling check box.

4. Select the check box for each port to which a printer that you want to add to the pool is connected, and then click OK.

How to Set Priorities Among Printers

Although creating a printer pool involves creating a single logical printer for multiple printers, setting priorities involves creating multiple logical printers for a single printer. The **printer priority** you set on each logical printer governs the order in which print jobs are printed. For example, you could create a high-priority logical printer for some users and a lower-priority logical printer for other users. All users would print to the same printer, but some users would get to print first.

There are two things that you must do to set priorities among printers:

- Add a printer and share it. Then add a second printer and point it to the same physical printer or port. The port can be either a physical port on the print server or a port that points to a network interface print device.

- Set a different priority for each of the printers that is pointing to the physical printer or hardware device. Have different groups of users print to different virtual printers, or have users send different types of documents to different virtual printers.

For an example of printer priority, see Figure 11-10. User1 sends documents to a printer with the lowest priority of 1, and User2 sends documents to a printer with the highest priority of 99. In this example, User2's documents always print before User1's documents.

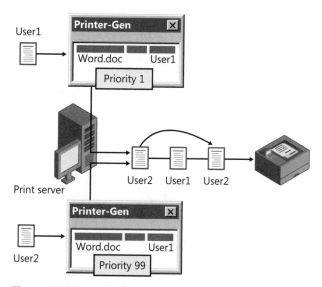

Figure 11-10   Logical printers with higher priorities print before logical printers with lower priorities.

Use the following steps to set the priority for a printer:

1. Click Start, and then click Printers And Faxes.

2. In the Printers And Faxes window, right-click the icon for the printer, and then click Properties.

3. In the Properties dialog box for the printer, on the Advanced tab, adjust the Priority setting for the printer. This value for a printer can be set from 1 through 99— the higher the number, the higher the priority of the printer.

4. Click OK.

Exam Tip   You can configure multiple logical printers for a single printer to control how the printer is used in different circumstances or by different users. You can also create a printer pool to configure multiple printers for a single logical printer.

Lesson Review

Use the following questions to help determine whether you have learned enough to move on to the next lesson. If you have difficulty answering these questions, review the material in this lesson before beginning the next lesson. You can find answers to these questions in the "Questions and Answers" section at the end of this chapter.

1. What are two advantages of sharing a printer?

_____

_____

2. How do you share a printer?

    _____

    _____

3. Which of the following statements about a printing pool in Windows XP Professional are correct? Choose all that apply.

    a. All printers in a printing pool must be network interface printers.

    b. A printing pool consists of two or more identical printers that are connected to one print server and act as a single printer.

    c. If you use printers that are not identical, they must use the same printer driver.

    d. If you use printers that are not identical, you must install all the required printer drivers on the print server.

4. Why would you create virtual printers and vary the priorities on them?

    _____

    _____

    _____

    _____

    _____

Lesson Summary

- To share an existing printer, use the Sharing tab of the Properties dialog box for the printer and select Share This Printer.

- If you expect network users of a shared printer to have computers that are running different versions of Windows, you can install different drivers so that they are automatically available to users who connect to the printer.

- To stop sharing a printer, in the Properties dialog box for the printer, on the Sharing tab, click Not Shared.

- A printer pool consists of two or more identical printers that are connected to one print server and act as a single printer.

- Setting priorities on virtual printers makes it possible for users to send critical documents to a high-priority printer and noncritical documents to a lower-priority printer, even when there is only one physical printer.

Lesson 5: Troubleshooting Setup and Configuration Problems

During setup and configuration of a printer, problems can occur. This lesson introduces you to a few common problems that you might encounter and provides some suggested solutions.

After this lesson, you will be able to

- Troubleshoot a printer setup problem by using the Windows troubleshooters
- Offer possible solutions to common troubleshooting scenarios

Estimated lesson time: 5 minutes

How to Use Windows Troubleshooters

Windows XP Professional helps you interactively troubleshoot problems you encounter. To troubleshoot problems with a printer, click Start, click Control Panel, and then click Printers And Other Hardware. In the Printers And Other Hardware window, under Troubleshooters, click Printing. The Help And Support Center window appears with the printing troubleshooter displayed, as shown in Figure 11-11.

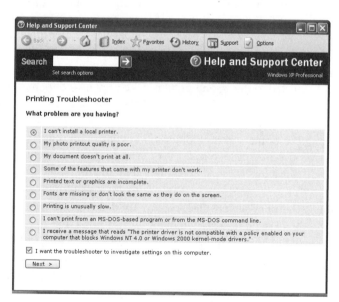

Figure 11-11   Use Windows troubleshooters to troubleshoot printing problems.

Notice the series of questions on the page. As you respond to these questions, the troubleshooter asks additional questions and makes suggestions to resolve your problem based on the answers you provide.

Possible Solutions to Common Troubleshooting Scenarios

Table 11-5 lists some of the common setup and configuration problems that you might encounter. It also gives probable causes of the problems and possible solutions.

Table 11-5   Common Printer Problems and Possible Solutions

Problem	Probable Cause	Possible Solution
Test page does not print. You have confirmed that the printer is connected and turned on.	The selected port is not correct.	Configure the printer for the correct port. For a printer that uses a network interface printer, make sure that the network address is correct.
Test page or documents print incorrectly as garbled text.	The installed printer driver is not correct.	Reinstall the printer with the correct printer driver.
Pages are only partially printing.	There might not be enough memory to print the document.	Consider adding memory to the print server.
	The printer might not have enough toner.	Try replacing the printer's toner cartridge.
Users report an error message that asks them to install a printer driver when they print to a print server running Windows XP Professional.	Printer drivers for the client computers are not installed on the print server.	On the print server, add the appropriate printer drivers for the client computers. Use the client computer operating system CD-ROM or a printer driver from the vendor.
Documents from one client computer do not print, but documents from other client computers do.	The client computer is connected to the wrong printer.	On the client computer, remove the printer, and then add the correct printer.
Documents print correctly on some (but not all) printers in a printer pool.	The printers in the printer pool are not identical.	Verify that all printers in the printer pool are identical or that they use the same printer driver. Remove inappropriate devices.
Printing is slow because the print server is taking a long time to render the job.	The print server's disk could be in need of defragmenting or could be getting close to capacity.	Try defragmenting the print server's disk and check that there is adequate space for temporary files on the hard disk.
Printing is slow, and print jobs are taking a long time to reach the top of the queue.	If you are using a printing pool, you might not have enough printers in the pool.	Add printers to the printing pool.
Documents do not print in the right priority.	The printing priorities among printers are set incorrectly.	Adjust the printing priorities for the printer associated with the printers.

Lesson Review

Use the following questions to help determine whether you have learned enough to move on to the next lesson. If you have difficulty answering these questions, review the material in this lesson before beginning the next lesson. You can find answers to these questions in the "Questions and Answers" section at the end of this chapter.

1. How do you access and use the printing troubleshooter?

    _____

    _____

    _____

    _____

2. What should you check if documents print correctly on some printers in a printing pool, but not on all of them?

    _____

    _____

3. What should you check if printing is slow because the print server is taking a long time to render the job?

    _____

    _____

4. What should you check if pages are only partially printing?

    _____

    _____

    _____

Lesson Summary

- Windows XP Professional helps you interactively troubleshoot problems you encounter. To troubleshoot printing problems, use the printing troubleshooter.
- There are a number of common setup and configuration problems that you should learn how to solve. The most common solutions include making sure that
    - The proper port is selected.
    - The proper printer driver is installed, as well as drivers for any clients running other operating systems.
    - The print server has enough memory.
    - The printer has enough toner.
    - The correct printer is being printed to.

Case Scenario Exercise

Read the following scenario and answer the associated questions. You can use this exercise to help determine whether you have learned enough to move on to the next chapter. If you have difficulty completing this work, review the material in this chapter before beginning the next chapter. You can find answers to these questions in the "Questions and Answers" section at the end of this chapter.

Scenario

You are an administrator for a company named Contoso, Ltd., which provides landscaping services for government-owned property. You are working with Jeff, a manager in the Marketing department who has just purchased 10 identical laser printers at an auction. The printers all have a built-in network interface that uses TCP/IP. You have verified that the printers are functional and have already attached each printer to the network. Jeff wants to configure these printers so that they are all accessible to the users in the department as a single printer, preventing users from having to install multiple printers.

Questions

1. What feature in Windows XP Professional allows you to configure all these printers so that users will have to install only one printer on their local computers.?

   _____

2. How will you configure this feature?

   _____

   _____

   _____

   _____

   _____

   _____

   _____

3. What steps will users have to take to connect to the printers?

   _____

   _____

   _____

Troubleshooting Lab

Read the following troubleshooting scenario and then answer the question that follows. You can use this lab to help determine whether you have learned enough to move on to the next chapter. If you have difficulty completing this work, review the material in this chapter before beginning the next chapter. You can find the answer to this question in the "Questions and Answers" section at the end of this chapter.

Scenario

You are working as an administrator for a company named Margie's Travel, one of the largest travel agents in the southeast United States. Angela, one of your users, has a color laser printer that is connected to her computer running Windows XP Professional. Angela shares the printer with other users on the network. Sometimes, the other users on the network print large documents that take a long time to print. Angela wants to keep the printer available to other users because it is the only color printer available in the department, but she often has important documents that need to be printed before any long documents that are waiting to be printed.

Question

How would you solve Angela's problem?

_____

_____

_____

_____

_____

_____

_____

Chapter Summary

- A printer is a hardware device that puts text or images on paper or on other print media. Local printers are connected to a physical port on the print server, and network interface printers are connected to a print server through the network. Network interface printers require their own NICs and have their own network address, or they are attached to an external network adapter. Before configuring a print server, you should make sure that the computer has sufficient RAM to process documents and sufficient disk space to ensure that the print server can store documents until it sends the documents to the printer.

- To install and share a local printer, use the Add Printer Wizard on the print server. Sharing a local printer makes it possible for multiple users on the network to utilize it. In larger companies, most printers are network interface printers. To install a network interface printer, use the Add Printer Wizard and specify the port information for the printer (such as a network address).

- Clients can connect to a shared printer by using the Add Printer Wizard, by connecting directly to the printer (using My Network Places, the Run dialog box, or the Command Prompt), by using a Web browser, or by searching Active Directory.

- To share an existing printer, use the Sharing tab of the Properties dialog box for the printer and select Share This Printer. If you expect network users of a shared printer to have computers that are running different versions of Windows, you can install different drivers so that they are automatically available to users who connect to the printer. You can also create two advanced printer configurations:

  ❑ A printer pool consists of two or more identical printers that are connected to one print server and act as a single printer.

  ❑ Setting priorities on virtual printers makes it possible for users to send critical documents to a high-priority printer and noncritical documents to a lower-priority printer, even when there is only one physical printer.

- Windows XP Professional helps you interactively troubleshoot problems you encounter. To troubleshoot printing problems, you can use the printing troubleshooter. You should also learn to resolve common problems such as improper printer drivers, improper ports, and low ink or toner.

Exam Highlights

Before taking the exam, review the key points and terms that are presented in this chapter. You need to know this information.

Key Points

- Windows XP Professional supports up to 10 simultaneous network connections. Windows XP Professional supports printing from the following clients: MS-DOS, Windows 3.1, Windows 95, Windows 98, Windows Me, Windows NT, Windows 2000, Windows Server 2003, Windows XP, and UNIX. Windows XP Professional does not support printing from NetWare or Macintosh clients.

- Users running Windows XP Professional must be members of the Administrators or Power Users groups to install a printer.

- You can configure multiple logical printers for a single printer to control how the printer is used in different circumstances or by different users. You can also create a printer pool to configure multiple printers for a single logical printer.

Key Terms

local printer   A printer that is connected to a physical port on the print server.

logical printer   The software configuration that is created in Windows and displayed in Printers And Faxes.

network interface printer   A printer that is connected directly to the network via an internal network adapter.

print job   A document that Windows has prepared for printing.

print server   The computer or other remote device that has a network printer physically connected to it.

printer   The physical device used for printing. This device is usually a standard printer, but it can also be a fax device, a plotter, or a file. It might also refer to the combination of the physical and logical printer.

printer driver   A file or set of files containing information that Windows XP Professional requires to convert print commands into a specific printer language.

printer pool   A printing option that permits you to attach two or more printers to a single printer configuration.

printer port   A software interface through which a computer communicates with a printer by means of a locally attached interface.

printer priority   Governs the order in which print jobs are printed relative to other logical printers configured for the same printer.

Questions and Answers

Lesson 1 Review

Page
11-5

1. _____ are connected to a physical port on the print server. Fill in the blank.

   Local printers

2. Do you have to have a computer running one of the Windows Server products to have a print server on your network? Why or why not?

   No. A print server is a computer that manages one or more printers on a network. The print server receives and processes documents from client computers. If you have a computer running Windows XP Professional and it has a shared printer attached to it, it is by definition a print server. However, if the print server will manage many heavily used printers, Microsoft recommends a dedicated print server, and most dedicated print servers run one of the Windows Server products.

3. How many concurrent connections from other computers for file and print services can Windows XP Professional provide? Choose the correct answer.

   a. 20

   b. 10

   c. Unlimited

   d. 30

   B is the correct answer. Windows XP Professional allows 10 concurrent connections from network users.

4. A(n) _____ is one file or a set of files containing information that Windows XP Professional requires to convert print commands into a specific printer language, such as PostScript. Fill in the blank.

   Printer driver

5. Windows XP Professional printing supports which of the following types of computers? Choose all that apply.

   a. Macintosh computers

   b. UNIX computers

   c. NetWare clients

   d. Windows 98 computers

   The correct answers are B and D. A and C are not correct because Windows XP Professional does not support printing from Macintosh or NetWare clients. Windows Server 2003 does support printing from these clients.

Lesson 2 Review

Page
11-19

1. Which of the following tasks can you perform with the Add Printer Wizard? Choose all that apply.

    a. Taking a local printer offline

    b. Printing multiple copies of a document

    c. Adding an LPR port

    d. Making a printer that is connected to your computer available to other network users

The correct answers are C and D. A is not correct because you take a printer offline by right-clicking the printer in the Printers And Faxes window and clicking Use Printer Offline. B is not correct because you print documents from within applications and not during the installation of the printer.

2. What is the default printer in Windows XP Professional?

The default printer is the printer used for all Windows-based applications. You select this option so that you do not have to set a printer for each application. The first time that you add a printer to the print server, this option does not appear because the printer is automatically selected as the default printer.

3. After you get home from the store, you unpack your new computer and printer. You install Windows XP Professional, and you want to install your printer. You want to set up the printer as your default printer. During the installation, you are not prompted to use the printer as your default printer for all Windows-based applications. You know you have seen this option at work when you install local printers. Why can you not see it on your home computer?

The first time that you add a printer to a computer, this option does not appear. The printer is automatically selected as the default printer.

Lesson 3 Review

Page
11-24

1. When you add and share a printer, who can connect to that printer by default?

By default, all users can connect to that printer.

2. Which of the following operating systems running on a client computer allow you to connect to a network printer by using Active Directory search capabilities? Choose all that apply.

    a. Windows 2000

    b. Windows Me

    c. Windows NT 4.0

    d. Windows XP Professional

The correct answers are A and D. B and C are not correct because Windows Me and Windows NT 4.0 do not allow you to search for computers using Active Directory.

3. You have a small workgroup consisting of five computers running Windows XP Professional at your house. You are giving your friend, who has never seen Windows XP Professional, a tour around the operating system. You are demonstrating how the Search Assistant works, but the Find Printers feature is missing. Why?

    The Find Printers feature is not available in the Search Assistant unless you are logged on to an Active Directory domain. If you are using a stand-alone computer or one that is in a workgroup, the Find Printers component is not available.

Lesson 4 Review

Page
11-31

1. What are two advantages of sharing a printer?

    Sharing a printer allows other users on the network to use the printer. It also simplifies administration because you can administer printers remotely.

2. How do you share a printer?

    In the Properties dialog box for the printer, in the Sharing tab, click Share This Printer and type in a share name.

3. Which of the following statements about a printing pool in Windows XP Professional are correct? Choose all that apply.

    a. All printers in a printing pool must be network interface printers.

    b. A printing pool consists of two or more identical printers that are connected to one print server and act as a single printer.

    c. If you use printers that are not identical, they must use the same printer driver.

    d. If you use printers that are not identical, you must install all the required printer drivers on the print server.

    The correct answers are B and C. A is not correct because you can also include local printers in a printer pool. D is not correct because you should use identical printers, but must at least use printers that use the same driver.

4. Why would you create virtual printers and vary the priorities on them?

    Creating virtual printers that print to the same physical printer and varying the printer priority allows you to set priorities among groups of documents that all print on the same physical printer. Users can send critical documents to a high-priority virtual printer and noncritical documents to a lower-priority virtual printer. The critical documents always print first, even if there is only one physical printer.

Lesson 5 Review

Page
11-35

1. How do you access and use the printing troubleshooter?

    Click Start, click Control Panel, and click Printers And Other Hardware. In the Printers And Other Hardware window, under Troubleshooters, click Printers. The Help And Support Services window appears with the printing troubleshooter displayed.

2. What should you check if documents print correctly on some printers in a printing pool, but not on all of them?

Verify that all print devices in the printer pool are identical or that they use the same printer driver.

3. What should you check if printing is slow because the print server is taking a long time to render the job?

Try defragmenting the print server's disk and check that there is adequate space for temporary files on the hard disk.

4. What should you check if pages are only partially printing?

There might not be enough memory to print the document, so consider adding memory to the print server. The printer might not have enough toner, so try replacing the printer's toner cartridge.

Case Scenario Exercise

Page
11-36
1. What feature in Windows XP Professional allows you to configure all these printers so that users will have to install only one printer on their local computers.?

Printer pooling

2. How will you configure this feature?

You must designate a computer to act as the print server. On this computer, you should install a logical printer that is configured with the IP address of one of the printers. Once the printer is installed, you should use the Ports tab of the printer's Properties dialog box to enable printer pooling. You should then add ports for the IP addresses of each of the other printers. Finally, you should share the logical printer with the network and install any additional drivers the client computers might need.

3. What steps will users have to take to connect to the printers?

After a printer pool is configured, users only need to connect to the single logical printer on the print server to use the printer pool. If drivers are configured appropriately, the printer installation should happen automatically.

Troubleshooting Lab

Page
11-37
How would you solve Angela's problem?

You should suggest that Angela configure two logical printers for the printer. She should assign one of the logical printers a higher priority than the other printer. She should also name the logical printers to indicate their use. (For example, she might name the logical printer with the lower priority "Long Document Printer" and name the printer with the higher priority "Normal Use Printer.") She should share each of the printers with the network and explain to the other users on the network how the printers are configured.

12 Managing Printers and Documents

Exam Objectives in this Chapter:

- Connect to local and network print devices.
    - ❑ Manage printers and print jobs.
    - ❑ Control access to printers by using permissions.

Why This Chapter Matters

In Chapter 11, "Setting Up, Configuring, and Troubleshooting Printers," you learned how to install and configure printers. This chapter focuses on the management of printers and of documents waiting to print. You will learn how to manage printers and documents, how to restrict access to printers by using permissions, and how to troubleshoot common printing problems.

Lessons in this Chapter:

- Lesson 1: Introduction to Printer Administration
- Lesson 2: Managing Printers
- Lesson 3: Managing Documents
- Lesson 4: Administering Printers by Using a Web Browser
- Lesson 5: Troubleshooting Common Printing Problems

Before You Begin

To complete this chapter, you must have a computer that meets the minimum hardware requirements listed in the preface, "About This Book." You must also have Microsoft Windows XP Professional installed on a computer on which you can make changes. To complete the practices in this chapter, you must have installed the drivers for an HP Color LaserJet 4550 PS printer as directed in Chapter 11.

Note You do *not* need a printer to complete the exercises in this chapter. You just need to have installed the software for the HP Color LaserJet 4550 PS printer.

Lesson 1: Introduction to Printer Administration

After your printing network is set up, you will be responsible for administering it. You can administer network printers at the print server or remotely over the network. This lesson introduces you to the concepts involved in administering network printers: managing printers, managing documents, troubleshooting printers, and performing tasks that require the Manage Printers permission. You will also learn how to access printers and how to control access by using print permissions.

After this lesson, you will be able to

- Identify tasks involved in printer management.
- Identify tasks involved in document management.
- Identify common troubleshooting tasks.
- Gain access to printers for administration.
- Assign print permissions to user accounts and groups.

Estimated lesson time: 30 minutes

Printer Management Tasks

Managing printers, which is one of the most important aspects of printer administration, includes the following tasks:

- Assigning forms to paper trays
- Setting a separator page
- Pausing, resuming, and canceling documents on a printer
- Redirecting documents
- Taking ownership of a printer

Document Management Tasks

A second major aspect of printer administration is managing documents, which includes the following tasks:

- Pausing and resuming a document
- Setting notification, priority, and printing time
- Restarting and deleting a document

Common Printer Problems that Require Troubleshooting

Troubleshooting printers, which means identifying and resolving all printer problems, is a third major aspect of printer administration. The types of problems you will commonly need to troubleshoot include the following:

- Printers that are off or offline
- Printers that are out of paper or out of ink
- Printers that are incorrectly configured
- Users who cannot print or cannot print correctly
- Users who cannot access a printer

How to Access Printers

You can perform most administrative tasks for printers by using the Printers And Faxes window. When you select a printer icon, Windows XP Professional displays many of the common printer management and document management tasks for you in the Printer Tasks list, as shown in Figure 12-1.

Figure 12-1   Manage printers and documents using the Printers And Faxes window.

> **Note**   These tasks, as well as some additional printer management and document management tasks, are covered in later lessons in this chapter.

To access printers by using the Printers And Faxes window, complete the following steps:

1. From the Start menu, click Printers And Faxes.

2. In the Printers And Faxes window, click the appropriate printer icon to select it.

3. After you have selected a printer icon, you can do the following:

   ❑ Click any of the tasks in the Printer Tasks list.

   ❑ Click the File menu and then click Open (or just double-click the printer icon) to open the printer window, which allows you to perform document management tasks.

   ❑ Click the File menu (or right-click the printer icon) and then click Properties to open the Properties dialog box, which allows you to perform printer-management tasks such as changing print permissions or editing Microsoft Active Directory service information about the printer.

Windows XP Professional Print Permissions

Windows XP Professional allows you to control printer usage and administration by assigning **print permissions**. With print permissions, you can control who can use a printer, who can manage the printer, and who can manage documents in the print queue.

For security reasons, you might need to limit user access to certain printers. You can also use print permissions to delegate responsibilities for specific printers to users who are not administrators. Windows XP Professional provides three levels of print permissions: Print, Manage Documents, and Manage Printers. Table 12-1 lists the capabilities of each level of permission.

Exam Tip   The Print permission offers the fewest rights, basically allowing users to print to the printer and manage their own documents. The Manage Documents permission allows all the rights offered by the Print permission and also allows users to manage other users' documents. The Manage Printers permission includes all the rights offered by the Manage Documents permission and allows users to configure printer settings.

You can allow or deny print permissions. Denied permissions always override allowed permissions. For example, if you select the Deny check box next to Manage Documents for the Everyone group, no one can manage documents, even if you grant this permission to another user account or group because all user accounts are members of the Everyone group.

See Also   For more information about using permissions, read Chapter 8, "Securing Resources with NTFS Permissions."

Table 12-1   Printing Capabilities of Windows XP Professional Print Permissions

Capabilities	Print	Permissions Manage Documents	Manage Printer
Print documents	✔	✔	✔
Pause, resume, restart, and cancel the user's own document	✔	✔	✔
Connect to a printer	✔	✔	✔
Control job settings for all documents		✔	✔
Pause, resume, restart, and cancel all other users' documents		✔	✔
Cancel all documents			✔
Share a printer			✔
Change printer properties			✔
Delete a printer			✔
Change print permissions			✔

To Assign Print Permissions

By default, Windows XP Professional assigns the Print permission for each printer to the built-in Everyone group, allowing all users to send documents to the printer. You can also assign print permissions to users or groups.

Security Alert   Because the Everyone group includes all users, you should remove the Everyone group from the list of groups with print permissions for a printer and instead use the Users group to provide general network access to a printer.

To assign print permissions, complete the following steps:

1. Click Start, and then click Printers And Faxes.

2. In the Printers And Faxes window, right-click the appropriate printer icon, and then click Properties.

3. Click the Security tab.

> **Note**   If your computer running Windows XP Professional is in a workgroup environment and you do not have a Security tab in your printer's Properties dialog box, close the Properties dialog box. In the Printers And Faxes window or in Explorer on the Tool menu, click Folder Options and click the View tab. Clear the Use Simple File Sharing (Recommended) check box, click OK, and then display your Printer's Properties dialog box.

4. In the Security tab, click Add.

5. In the Select Users, Groups, Or Computers dialog box, select the appropriate user account or group, and then click OK. Repeat this step for all users or groups that you are adding.

6. Click OK.

7. In the Security tab, shown in Figure 12-2, select a user account or group, and then do one of the following:

   ❏ Select the permissions in the bottom part of the dialog box that you want to assign.

   ❏ Click Advanced and assign additional print permissions that do not fit into the predefined permissions in the Security tab, and then click OK.

   The bottom part of the dialog box shows the permissions granted to the user or group selected in the upper part.

8. Click OK to close the Properties dialog box.

Figure 12-2   Assign print permissions on the Security tab of a printer's Properties dialog box.

To Modify Print Permissions

You can change the default print permissions that Windows XP Professional assigned or that you previously assigned for any user or group.

To modify print permissions, complete the following steps:

1. In the Printers And Faxes window, right-click the appropriate printer icon, and then click Properties.

2. In the Properties dialog box for the printer, on the Security tab, select the appropriate user account or group, and then do one of the following:

   ❑ Select the permissions that you want to change for the user or group.

   ❑ Click Advanced to modify additional print permissions that do not fit into the predefined permissions in the Security tab.

3. Click OK.

> ### Real World   **Encouraging Expert Users**
>
> In just about any size organization or department, you are likely to find users who are more interested in computing than others, and you should take advantage of these users when you find them. In larger companies in particular, users within a department often have a better understanding of how the people in the department use printing resources than the IT support staff. At the least, you should encourage these people to participate when planning the location and access of printing resources. You might also find that some users are willing to manage documents, or even manage printers and use IT support as a backup. This practice offloads some of the administrative overhead and can result in more efficient use of resources.

Practice: Changing the Default Permissions on a Printer

In this practice, you will change the default permissions on the HP Color LaserJet 4550 PS printer that you installed in Chapter 11. If you have not yet installed that printer, follow the instructions in Chapter 11 to install the printer before continuing with this practice. Complete the following steps.

1. Click Start, and then click Printers And Faxes.

2. In the Printer And Faxes window, right-click the HP Color LaserJet 4550 PS printer and click Properties.

3. In the HP Color LaserJet 4550 PS Properties dialog box, on the Security tab, in the Group Or User Names list, click Everyone, and then click Remove.

4. Click Add.

5. In the Select Users Or Groups dialog box, click Advanced.

6. In the Select Users Or Groups dialog box, click Find Now.

7. In the list of Names that appears, click Users and then click OK. Click OK again to close the Select Users Or Groups dialog box.

8. In the HP Color LaserJet 4550 PS Properties dialog box, in the Group Or User Names list, click Users. Make sure that the Users group is assigned only the Print permission.

9. Click OK.

Lesson Review

Use the following questions to help determine whether you have learned enough to move on to the next lesson. If you have difficulty answering these questions, review the material in this lesson before beginning the next lesson. You can find answers to these questions in the "Questions and Answers" section at the end of this chapter.

1. What are the four major types of tasks involved with administering network printers?

   _____

   _____

2. Windows XP Professional allows you to control printer usage and administration by assigning _____. Fill in the blank.

3. Which level of print permissions provided by Windows XP Professional grants users the ability to perform the most printing tasks? Choose the correct answer.

   a. Manage Printers

   b. Manage Documents

   c. Print

   d. Full Control

4. Which Windows XP Professional print permission allows users to pause, resume, restart, and cancel all other users' documents? Choose all that apply.

   a. Print

   b. Manage Printers

   c. Full Control

   d. Manage Documents

Lesson Summary

- Printer management involves assigning forms to paper trays, setting separator pages, redirecting documents, and taking ownership of printers.

- Document management involves pausing and resuming documents, configuring notifications, and deleting documents from the print queue.

- Troubleshooting printers involves identifying and resolving printer problems such as offline printers, printers that are out of paper or ink, printers that are incorrectly configured, and situations in which users are not using a printer properly.

- You can gain access to printers for administration by using the Printers And Faxes window accessed through Control Panel.

- Windows XP Professional allows you to control printer usage and administration by assigning permissions.

Lesson 2: Managing Printers

Managing printers includes assigning forms to paper trays and setting a separator page. In addition, you can pause a printer so that it does not try to print documents while you troubleshoot or make configuration changes. If a printer is faulty, or if you add printers to your network, you might need to redirect documents to a different printer. You might also need to change which users have administrative responsibility for printers, which involves changing ownership.

After this lesson, you will be able to

- Assign forms to paper trays.
- Set a separator page.
- Pause and resume a printer, and cancel all documents on a printer.
- Redirect documents to a different printer.
- Select a different print processor.
- Adjust print spooling settings.
- Take ownership of a printer.

Estimated lesson time: 40 minutes

How to Assign Forms to Paper Trays

If a printer has multiple trays that regularly hold different paper sizes, you can assign a form to a specific tray. A form defines a paper size. Users can then select the paper size from within their application. When the user prints, Windows XP Professional automatically selects the paper tray that holds the correct form. Examples of forms include the following: Legal, A4, Envelopes #10, and Letter Small.

To assign a form to a paper tray, complete the following steps:

1. Click Start, and then click Printers And Faxes.

2. In the Printers And Faxes window, right-click the icon of the appropriate printer, and then click Properties.

3. In the printer's Properties dialog box, on the Device Settings tab, in the box next to each paper tray, click the form for the paper type for the tray, as shown in Figure 12-3.

4. Click OK.

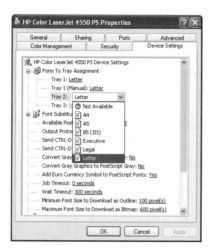

Figure 12-3   Set forms for a printer to make paper selection automatic.

After you have set up a paper tray, users specify the paper size from within applications. Windows XP Professional knows in which paper tray the form is located.

How to Set Up a Separator Page

This section explains what a separator page is, describes its functions, lists separator page files included in Windows XP Professional, and then describes how to set up a separator page.

What Is a Separator Page?

A separator page is a file that contains print device commands. Separator pages have two functions:

- To identify and separate printed documents, making it easier for users to find their documents on printers used by more than one person.

- To switch a printer to a different print mode. Some printers support different print modes that take advantage of different device features. You can use separator pages to specify the correct page description language. For example, you can specify PostScript or Printer Control Language (PCL) for a printer that can switch between different print modes but cannot automatically detect which language a print job uses.

Separator Page Files Included in Windows XP Professional

Windows XP Professional includes four separator page files, which are located in the %systemroot%\System32 folder. Table 12-2 lists the file name and describes the function for each of the included separator page files.

Table 12-2   Separator Page Files

File Name	Function
Sysprint.sep	Prints a page before each document; compatible with PostScript print devices
Pcl.sep	Switches the print mode to PCL for HP-series print devices and prints a page before each document
Pscript.sep	Switches the print mode to PostScript for HP-series print devices but does not print a page before each document
Sysprtj.sep	A version of SYSPRINT.SEP that uses Japanese characters

> **Exam Tip**   Separator pages identify and separate print jobs, and can also be used to switch a printer to a different print mode. Windows XP includes four separator pages: sysprint.sep, pcl.sep, pscript.sep, and sysprtj.sep. Sysprint.sep is the most commonly used page.

To Set Up a Separator Page

When you have decided to use a separator page and have chosen an appropriate one, use the Advanced tab in the printer's Properties dialog box to have the separator page printed at the beginning of each print job.

To set up a separator page, complete the following steps:

1. In the Properties dialog box for the printer, on the Advanced tab (see Figure 12-4), click Separator Page.

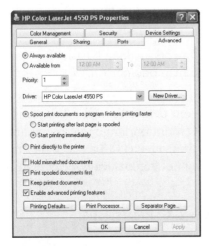

Figure 12-4   Configure a separator page by using the Advanced tab of a printer's Properties dialog box.

2. In the Separator Page dialog box, type the name of or browse for the separator page file.

3. Click OK to close the Separator Page box, and then click OK again to close the printer's Properties dialog box.

How to Pause a Printer and Cancel Documents

Pausing and resuming a printer or canceling all documents on a printer might be necessary if there is a printing problem. To pause or cancel all documents, right-click the icon for the printer in the Printers And Faxes window, and then click the appropriate command. To resume printing on a printer, right-click the printer and click Resume Printing.

Table 12-3 describes the tasks that you might perform when you manage printers, lists how to perform the tasks, and gives examples of situations in which you might perform these tasks.

Table 12-3   Managing Printer Tasks

Task	Action	Example
To pause printing	Click Pause Printing. The Pause Printing command changes to Resume Printing.	Pause the printer if there is a problem with the printer until you fix the problem.
To resume printing	Click Resume Printing. The Resume Printing command changes to Pause Printing.	Resume printing after you fix a problem with a printer.
To cancel all documents	Click Cancel All Documents. All documents are deleted from the printer.	Cancel all documents when you need to clear a print queue after old documents that no longer need to print have accumulated.

Tip   You can also pause a printer by taking the printer offline. To take a printer offline, open the printer window, and on the Printer menu, click Use Printer Offline.

How to Redirect Documents to a Different Printer

You can redirect documents to a different printer. For example, if a printer is not working, you should redirect the documents so that users do not need to resubmit them. You can redirect all print jobs for a printer, but you cannot redirect specific documents. The new printer must use the same printer driver as the current printer.

To redirect documents to a different printer, complete the following steps:

1. Open the Printers And Faxes window, right-click the printer, and then click Properties.

2. In the Properties dialog box, on the Ports tab, click the Add Port button.

3. In the Available Port Types list, click Local Port, and then click the New Port button.

4. In the Port Name dialog box, in the Enter A Port Name text box, type the Universal Naming Convention (UNC) name for the printer to which you are redirecting documents (for example, **\\prntsrv6\HPCLJ4550**), as shown in Figure 12-5.

Figure 12-5   Redirect documents to another printer so users do not have to print again.

5. Click OK to accept the change and close the Port Name dialog box.

6. Click Close to close the Printer Ports dialog box.

7. Click OK to close the printer's Properties dialog box.

If another printer is available for the current print server, you can redirect the documents to that printer. To redirect documents to another local or network printer that uses the same printer driver, select the appropriate port on the print server and cancel the selection of the current port.

Exam Tip   Remember that you can redirect all documents for a printer, but not individual documents. Also, the new printer must use the same printer driver as the current printer.

Formats Supported by the WinPrint Print Processor

The **print processor** is software that is responsible for processing print documents into a format that is suitable to be sent to the printer, and Windows XP contains only the Win-Print processor by default. The default print processor and data types are suitable for the vast majority of printing, and you should not change them unless you have an application that specifies the need for a different print processor or additional data type.

The WinPrint print processor supports the following formats:

RAW   RAW is a common data type for clients other than Windows. When using the RAW format, the spooler does not modify the print data; data is sent directly to the printer for processing. There are two additional versions of RAW:

❑ RAW [FF appended] is the same as the RAW format, except that a form feed character is appended to the end of each print job, which is necessary for certain types of printers.

❑ RAW [FF auto] works like RAW [FF appended], except that the processor checks to see if there is a form feed character at the end of a document and if there is not one already, the processor adds one.

EMF   Enhanced Metafile (EMF) is the default format used by WinPrint. The instructions for the print job are assembled on the client computer that prints the document when the spooler processes the print job.

Text   Text is a standard ANSI text format that prints using only the printer's default font.

How to Configure Spooling Options

Spooling is the process of saving a print job to the hard disk before sending it to the printer. The process increases user productivity because after the job has been spooled, the application is released, and the user can continue working while the printing process continues in the background. Print spooling also ensures that print jobs will be saved in the event of a computer, application, or printer failure. In addition, when a client is printing to a printer on the network, print spooling also manages the routing of the print job from the client to the appropriate print server.

On the Advanced tab of a printer's Properties dialog box, select the Spool Print Documents So The Program Finishes Printing Faster option to enable printer spooling. Select the Print Directly To The Printer option to disable spooling. If spooling is enabled, you need to decide whether you want the document to be spooled in its entirety before printing (the best option for remote printers) or to start printing immediately upon receiving the first page (the best option for local printers).

How to Move the Print Spool Folder

Windows XP uses the spool folder to store print jobs while they are waiting to be sent to the printer. By default, Windows stores this file on the same partition as the Windows system files, in %systemroot%\System32\spool\PRINTERS. Moving the print spool folder to a partition different from the system partition increases free space on the system partition.

To move the print spool folder, follow these steps:

1. From the Start menu, click Printers And Faxes.

2. In the Printers And Faxes window, click the File menu, and then click Server Properties.

3. In the Print Server Properties dialog box, on the Advanced tab, in the Spool Folder text box, type a new location for the print spool folder. This location should be on a different partition from the Windows system files.

4. Click OK.

How to Take Ownership of a Printer

There might be times when the owner of a printer can no longer manage that printer and you need to take ownership. Taking ownership of a printer enables you to change administrative responsibility for it. By default, the user who installed the printer owns it. If that user can no longer administer the printer, you should take ownership of it—for example, if the current owner leaves the company.

This section describes which users can take ownership of a printer and then explains how to do it.

Users Who Can Take Ownership of a Printer

The following users can take ownership of a printer:

- A user or a member of a group who has the Manage Printers permission for the printer.

- Members of the Administrators and Power Users groups. By default, these groups have the Manage Printers permission, which allows them to take ownership.

To Take Ownership of a Printer

To take ownership of a printer, complete the following steps:

1. In the Properties dialog box for the printer, on the Security tab, click Advanced.

2. In the Advanced Security Settings dialog box, on the Owner tab, click your user account under Change Owner To, as shown in Figure 12-6.

Figure 12-6   Take ownership of a printer when the current owner no longer manages the printer.

3. Click OK to change ownership and to close the Advanced Security Settings dialog box.

4. Click OK to close the Properties dialog box for the printer.

Practice: Managing Printers

In this practice, you perform three tasks that are part of managing printers. In the first exercise, you assign forms to paper trays. In the second exercise, you set up a separator page. In the third exercise, you learn how to take ownership of a printer. Complete the following exercises.

Exercise 1: Assigning Forms to Paper Trays

In this exercise, you assign a paper type (form) to a paper tray so that when users print to a specified form, the print job is automatically routed to and adjusted for the correct tray.

1. Log on with the user account you used to create the HP Color LaserJet 4550 PS printer in Chapter 11 or with any user account that is a member of the Administrators group.

2. Click Start, and then click Printers And Faxes.

3. Right-click the HP Color LaserJet 4550 PS printer, and then click Properties.

4. In the HP Color LaserJet 4550 PS Properties dialog box, on the Device Settings tab, click Tray 2, and then select Legal.

5. Click Apply and leave the HP Color LaserJet 4550 PS Properties dialog box open for the next exercise.

Exercise 2: Setting Up Separator Pages

In this exercise, you set up a separator page to print between documents. You use the Sysprint.sep separator page that ships with Windows XP Professional. This separator page includes the user's name and the date and time the document was printed.

1. On the Advanced tab of the HP Color LaserJet 4550 PS Properties dialog box, click Separator Page.

2. In the Separator Page dialog box, click Browse.

3. Windows XP Professional displays a Separator Page dialog box that lists the contents of the System32 folder, which contains the separator pages that ship with Windows XP Professional. This dialog box also allows you to search in additional folders. Select Sysprint.sep, and then click Open.

4. Click OK. Windows XP Professional is now set to print a separator page between print jobs.

5. Leave the Properties dialog box open for the next exercise.

Exercise 3: Taking Ownership of a Printer

In this exercise, you practice taking ownership of a printer.

1. On the Security tab of the Properties dialog box, click Advanced.

2. In the Advanced Security Settings For HP Color LaserJet 4550 dialog box, on the Owner tab, in the Change Owner To list, click Administrators to become the owner of the printer.

3. If you actually wanted to take ownership, you would click Apply, but for the purposes of this exercise, click Cancel and leave the ownership unchanged.

4. Click OK to close the Properties dialog box.

Lesson Review

Use the following questions to help determine whether you have learned enough to move on to the next lesson. If you have difficulty answering these questions, review the material in this lesson before beginning the next lesson. You can find answers to these questions in the "Questions and Answers" section at the end of this chapter.

1. If a printer has multiple trays that regularly hold different paper sizes, you can assign a form to a specific tray. How do you assign a form to a paper tray?

   _____

   _____

   _____

2. A(n) _____ is a file that contains print device commands that identify and separate printed documents. Fill in the blank.

3. Which of the following tabs do you use to redirect documents to a different printer? Choose the correct answer.

   a. Advanced tab of the Properties dialog box for the printer

   b. Security tab of the Properties dialog box for the printer

   c. Ports tab of the Properties dialog box for the printer

   d. Device Settings tab of the Properties dialog box for the printer

4. Which of the following tabs do you use to take ownership of a printer? Choose the correct answer.

   a. Advanced tab of the Properties dialog box for the printer

   b. Security tab of the Properties dialog box for the printer

   c. Ports tab of the Properties dialog box for the printer

   d. Permissions tab of the Properties dialog box for the printer

Lesson Summary

- If a printer has multiple trays that regularly hold different paper sizes, you can assign a form to a specific tray. A form defines a paper size.

- A separator page is a file that contains print device commands. Separator pages identify and separate printed documents, and they can be used to switch print devices between print modes.

- To pause a printer, cancel all documents, or to resume a paused printer, right-click the icon for the printer in the Printers And Faxes window and then click the appropriate command.

- You can redirect all print jobs for a printer to a different printer that uses the same printer driver. You cannot redirect specific documents in the print queue.

- The print processor prepares a document for printing before it sends the document to the printer. The WinPrint processor is shipped with Windows and supports the following formats: RAW, EMF, and Text.

- By default, print jobs are spooled to disk before the print processor sends them to the printer. This allows users to access their applications again more quickly.

- To take ownership of a printer, a user must have or be a member of a group that has the Manage Printers permission for the printer. By default, members of the Administrators and Power Users groups have the Manage Printers permission.

Lesson 3: Managing Documents

In addition to managing printers, you can use Windows XP Professional to manage documents that are in a printer's print queue waiting to be printed. Managing documents includes pausing, resuming, restarting, and canceling documents. In addition, you can set users to be notified when a print job is finished, a priority that allows a critical document to print before other documents, and a specific time for a document to print.

After this lesson, you will be able to

■ Pause, resume, restart, and cancel the printing of a document.

■ Set a notification, priority, and printing time.

Estimated lesson time: 20 minutes

How to Pause, Restart, and Cancel a Document

If a printer problem occurs during the printing of a document, you can pause that document while you resolve the problem and then resume printing. If you suspect that the printing problem is related to the document itself, you can restart or cancel the printing of the document. You must have the Manage Documents permission for the appropriate printer to perform these actions. Because the creator of a document has the default permissions to manage that document, users can perform any of these actions on their own documents.

To manage a document, right-click the icon representing the printer for the document in the Printers And Faxes window, and then click Open. Select the appropriate documents; click the Document menu; and then click the appropriate command to pause, resume, and restart from the beginning, or cancel a document, as shown in Figure 12-7.

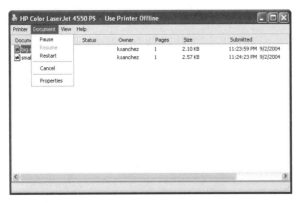

Figure 12-7 Manage documents by opening the print queue window.

Table 12-4 describes the tasks that you might perform when you manage individual documents, how to perform the tasks, and examples of situations in which you might perform them.

Table 12-4   Document Management Tasks

Task	Action	Example
To pause printing of a document	Select the documents for which you want to pause printing, and then click Pause. (The status changes to Paused.)	Pause printing of a document when there is a problem with the document.
To resume printing a document	Select the documents for which you want to resume printing, and then click Resume. (The status changes to Printing.)	Resume printing of the document after you fix the problem with the paused document.
To restart printing a document	Select the documents for which you want to restart printing, and then click Restart. Restart causes printing to start from the beginning of the document.	Restart printing of a partially printed document after you fix a problem with the document or the print device.
To cancel printing a document	Select the documents for which you want to cancel printing, and then click Cancel. You can also cancel a document by pressing the DELETE key.	When a document has the wrong printer settings or is no longer needed, you can cancel it so it is deleted before it prints.

How to Set Notification, Priority, and Printing Time

You can control print jobs by setting the notification, priority, and printing time. To perform these document management tasks, you must have the Manage Documents permission for the appropriate printer.

You can set the notification, priority, and printing time for a document in the General tab of the Properties dialog box for the document, as shown in Figure 12-8. To open the Properties dialog box for one or more documents, first select the documents in the Printer window, click Document on the Printer window menu bar, and then click Properties.

Figure 12-8   Set notification, priority, and printing time for a document.

Table 12-5 describes the tasks that you might perform when you control print jobs, how to perform the tasks, and examples of situations in which you might perform them.

Table 12-5   Setting a Notification, Changing Priority, and Scheduling Print Times

Task	Action	Example
Set a notification	In the Notify text box, type the logon name of the user who should receive the notification. By default, Windows XP Professional enters the name of the user who printed the document.	Change the print notification when someone other than the user who printed the document needs to retrieve it.
Change a document priority	Move the Priority slider to the priority level that you want. The highest priority is 99, and the lowest is 1.	Change a priority so that a critical document prints before other documents.
Schedule print times	To restrict print times, select Only From in the Schedule section, and then set the hours between which you want the document to print.	Set the print time for a large document so that it prints during off-hours, such as late at night.

Practice: Managing Documents

In this practice, you manage documents by printing a document, setting a notification for a document, changing the priority for a document, and then canceling a document. Complete the following exercises, and answer any questions that are asked. You can find answers to these questions in the "Questions and Answers" section at the end of this chapter. To complete this practice, you must have completed the exercises in Chapter 11.

Exercise 1: Verifying that a Printer is Offline

1. Log on with the user account you used to create the HP Color LaserJet 4550 PS printer in Chapter 11 or with any user account that is a member of the Administrators group.

2. Click Start, and then click Printers And Faxes.

3. In the Printers And Faxes window, click the HP Color LaserJet 4550 PS printer icon. Do one of the following to verify that the printer is offline:

   ❑ On the File menu, verify that the Use Printer Online option is listed because that indicates that the printer is currently offline.

   ❑ Right-click the printer icon and verify that the Use Printer Online command is listed because that indicates that the printer is currently offline.

   ❑ If the Printers And Faxes window is displayed in Web view, verify that Use Printer Offline is displayed in the left portion of the window.

4. Verify that a check mark appears above the printer icon indicating that it is the default printer.

5. Minimize the Printers And Faxes window.

> **Note**   Keep the printer offline so that documents enter the print queue, but are not sent to the printer. This eliminates error messages in later exercises.

Exercise 2: Printing a Document

1. Click Start, point to All Programs, point to Accessories, and then click WordPad.

2. Type **How big is big?**, and then, on the File menu, click Save.

3. In the File Name text box, type **big.rtf**, and then click Save.

4. Click File, and then click Print.

5. In the Print dialog box, make sure that the file will be printed on the HP Color LaserJet 4550 PS printer. Click Print, and then close WordPad.

Exercise 3: Setting a Notification

1. Restore the Printers And Faxes window that you minimized in Exercise 1.

2. Double-click HP Color LaserJet 4550 PS.

3. In the printer window, click the big document. On the Document menu, click Properties.

   Windows XP Professional displays the BIG Document Properties dialog box with the General tab active.

4. Which user is specified in the Notify text box? Why?

_____

_____

5. In the Notify text box, type **Fred**, and then click Apply.

Exercise 4: Increasing the Priority of a Document

1. In the big.rtf Document Properties dialog box, on the General tab, notice the default priority.

2. What is the current priority? Is it the lowest or highest priority?

_____

3. Move the Priority slider to the right to increase the priority of the document to 38, and then click OK.

Exercise 5: Canceling a Document

1. In the Printer window, select the big document.

2. On the Document menu, click Cancel.

3. In the Printers dialog box, click Yes to confirm the cancellation.

   The big document is removed from the document list.

4. Notice that for larger documents, you might see the document status change to Deleting for a period before the document is removed from the list.

> **Note**   You can also cancel a document by selecting the document and pressing the DELETE key.

5. Close the Printer window, and then close the Printers And Faxes window.

Lesson Review

Use the following questions to help determine whether you have learned enough to move on to the next lesson. If you have difficulty answering these questions, review the material in this lesson before beginning the next lesson. You can find answers to these questions in the "Questions and Answers" section at the end of this chapter.

1. What is the difference between resuming printing of a document and restarting printing of a document?

_____

_____

2. Which of the following statements about the range of priorities for a document to be printed is correct? Choose the correct answer.

   a. Priorities for a document range from 1 to 10, with 1 being the highest priority.

   b. Priorities for a document range from 1 to 10, with 10 being the highest priority.

   c. Priorities for a document range from 1 to 99, with 1 being the highest priority.

   d. Priorities for a document range from 1 to 99, with 99 being the highest priority.

3. You set the notification, priority, and printing time for a document on the _____ tab of the Properties dialog box for the document. Fill in the blank.

4. By default, Windows XP Professional enters which of the following user accounts in the Notify text box of a document?

   a. Administrator

   b. Owner of the printer

   c. All users with the Manage Documents permissions

   d. Person who printed the document

Lesson Summary

■ Managing documents includes pausing, resuming, restarting, and canceling documents. You must have the Manage Documents permission for the appropriate printer to perform these document-management tasks. The creator of a document has the default permissions to manage that document, so users can perform any of these actions on their own documents.

■ In the Notify text box for a document, you can set who is notified when the print job is finished. Setting the document priority allows a critical document to print before other documents. Setting a specific time for a document to print allows large documents to print only during off-hours, such as late at night.

Lesson 4: Administering Printers by Using a Web Browser

You can use Windows XP Professional to manage printers from any computer running a Web browser, regardless of whether the computer is running Windows XP Professional or has the correct printer driver installed. To access a printer using a Web browser, a print server running Windows 2000 Server or Windows XP Professional must have Microsoft Internet Information Services (IIS) installed. All management tasks that you perform with Windows XP Professional management tools are the same when you use a Web browser. The only difference in administering with a Web browser is the interface, which is a Web-based interface.

> **See Also**   For information about installing IIS, see Chapter 5, "Configuring Windows XP Professional."

After this lesson, you will be able to

- Describe the advantages of administering printers using a Web browser.
- Administer printers using a Web browser.

Estimated lesson time: 5 minutes

The Advantages of Using a Web Browser to Manage Printers

The following are the advantages of using a Web browser, such as Microsoft Internet Explorer, to manage printers:

- You can administer printers from any computer with a Web browser, regardless of whether the computer is running Windows XP Professional or has the correct printer driver installed.

- You can customize the Web interface. For example, you can create your own Web page containing a floor plan with the locations of the printers and the links to the printers.

- You can view a summary page that lists the status of all printers on a print server.

- You can view real-time print device data, such as whether the print device is in power-saving mode, if the printer driver makes such information available. This information is not available in the Printers And Faxes window.

How to Access Printers Using a Web Browser

You can access all printers on a print server by using a Web browser or you can use any of the windows or folders within the Windows XP Professional interface that has an address bar, such as the Printers And Faxes window or Internet Explorer. In the

Address text box, type **http://*print_server_name*/printers**. This command displays a page listing all the printers on the print server, as shown in Figure 12-9. Click the name of the printer that you want to use. When you are on that printer's page, under Printer Actions, click Connect to connect to the printer. Windows XP automatically copies the appropriate printer drivers to your computer and adds an icon for the printer to the Printers And Faxes window.

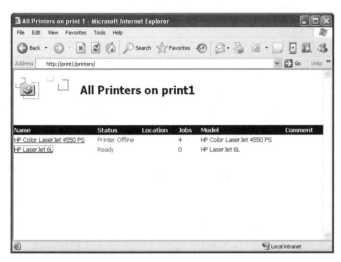

Figure 12-9   Manage printers remotely using Internet Explorer.

If you want to gain access to a specific printer by using a Web browser, open the Web browser, and then in the Address text box, type **http://*server_name*/ printer_share_name**. You are directed to that printer's page. Under Printer Actions, click Connect to connect to the printer.

From the printer's URL page, you can view information about the printer, such as its model, its location, and the number of documents waiting to print. You can manage any document you have sent to the printer, and if you have the Manage Printers permission for the printer, you can also pause or resume operation of the printer.

Lesson Review

Use the following questions to help determine whether you have learned enough to move on to the next lesson. If you have difficulty answering these questions, review the material in this lesson before beginning the next lesson. You can find answers to these questions in the "Questions and Answers" section at the end of this chapter.

1. If you are using a computer running Windows XP Professional as your print server, users can gain access to the printers on it by using a Web browser only if the print server has _____ installed. Fill in the blank.

2. How can you gain access to all printers on a print server?

_____

_____

3. Can you pause and resume operation of a printer that you have used Internet Explorer to connect to?

_____

_____

Lesson Summary

- The advantages of managing printers from a Web browser are:

  - It does not matter whether the print server is running Windows XP Professional.

  - All management tasks that you perform with Windows XP Professional management tools are the same when you use a Web browser.

  - You can customize the Web interface.

  - You can view a summary page and real-time device information.

- You can access all printers on a print server running IIS by typing **http://*print_server_name*/printers**. You can access a particular printer by typing **http://*print_server_name*/*printer_share_name***.

Lesson 5: Troubleshooting Common Printing Problems

In this lesson, you will learn about some common printing problems and how to troubleshoot them. This chapter also shows you to how to troubleshoot printer and document problems by using the built-in Printing Troubleshooter, which was introduced in Chapter 11.

After this lesson, you will be able to

- Examine a printing problem and know the appropriate troubleshooting questions to ask.
- Identify and solve common printing problems.
- Solve printing problems using the Printing Troubleshooter in Windows XP Professional.

Estimated lesson time: 10 minutes

Guidelines for Examining a Printing Problem

When you detect a printing problem, always verify that the printer is plugged in, turned on, and connected to the print server. For a network interface printer, verify that there is a network connection between the printer and the print server.

To determine the cause of a problem, first try printing from a different program to verify that the problem is with the printer, not with the program. If the problem is with the printer, ask the following questions:

- Can other users print normally? If so, the problem is most likely caused by insufficient permissions, no network connection, or client computer problems.
- Does the print server use the correct printer driver for the printer? If not, you should install the appropriate printer driver.
- Is the print server operational, and is there enough disk space for spooling?
- Does the client computer have the correct printer driver?

Solutions to Common Printing Problems

There are some printing problems that are common to most network printing environments. Table 12-6 describes some of these common printing problems, as well as some possible causes and solutions.

Table 12-6   Common Printing Problems, Causes, and Solutions

Problem	Possible Cause	Solution
A user receives an Access Denied message when trying to configure a printer from an application (for example, from earlier versions of Microsoft Excel).	The user does not have the appropriate permission to change printer configurations.	Change the user's permission or configure the printer for the user.
The document does not print completely or comes out garbled.	The printer driver is incorrect (if it is the first time you have used the printer since installation or updating the driver).	Install the correct printer driver.
	A user has changed the printer configuration or placed the printer into a separate mode.	Cancel the print job, reset the printer, and resubmit the print job.
Pages print only partially.	The printer is out of ink or toner, or the print server is low on memory. If specific parts of a page do not print and those parts are the same each time you print, the printer may not be able to print a particular font, or the margins of the document may be outside the printable range.	Replace the ink or toner cartridge. Check the memory on the print server. Change the font in a document or adjust the margins of the document.
The hard disk starts working too hard, the document does not reach the print server, or printing is very slow.	There is insufficient hard disk space for spooling.	Create more free space on the hard disk, or move the print spool folder to a different partition.
There is a problem printing graphics.	EMF format can occasionally cause problems with printing, especially with the printing of graphics.	Consider disabling EMF spooling on the Advanced tab of the printer's Properties dialog box by clearing the Enable Advanced Printing Features check box.

How to Solve Printing Problems Using the Windows XP Professional Printing Troubleshooter

Windows XP Professional has a built-in troubleshooter to help you resolve your printing problems. For example, in the Printers And Faxes window, you can click Troubleshoot Printing.

When you click Troubleshoot Printing, Windows XP Professional presents you with a series of potential printing problems. After you make a selection from the list of potential problems and click Next, the troubleshooter takes you through a series of suggestions and questions to help you resolve the problem. You can also perform a search to help resolve your problem or you can select the I Want The Troubleshooter To Investigate Settings On This Computer option.

Lesson Review

Use the following questions to help determine whether you have learned enough to move on to the next lesson. If you have difficulty answering these questions, review the material in this lesson before beginning the next lesson. You can find answers to these questions in the "Questions and Answers" section at the end of this chapter.

1. When you detect a printing problem, what three things should you always check before you start troubleshooting the problem?

   _____

   _____

2. If a user reports to you that he or she cannot print, what are some of the areas you should check?

   _____

   _____

   _____

Lesson Summary

- When there is a printing problem, always verify that the printer is plugged in, turned on, and connected to the print server. For a network interface print device, verify that there is a network connection between the printer and the print server. Ask questions to help determine whether the problem is with the application, the document, or the printer.

- There are a number of common printing problems that you should know how to solve, including problems arising from printer configuration, printer drivers, and print permissions.

- You can access the Windows XP Professional built-in Printing Troubleshooter from the Printers And Faxes window by clicking Troubleshoot Printing.

Case Scenario Exercise

In this exercise, you will read a scenario about a user who is trying to manage documents on a network printer, and then answer the questions that follow. If you have difficulty completing this work, review the material in this chapter before beginning the next chapter. You can find answers to these questions in the "Questions and Answers" section at the end of this chapter.

Scenario

You are working as an administrator for Fabrikam, Inc., a company that makes prebuilt cabinetry that people can install in their own homes. Erin, a user from the Sales department, calls at 4:45 p.m. to tell you that one of the other people in her department has printed a very long document to the department's only color laser printer. The printer is a network printer that is used by many people, and Erin does not think the long document has started printing yet.

Erin tells you that her manager, Jesper, has asked her to print several copies of an important memo to distribute to other people in her department before 5:00 p.m. She does not want to stop the long document from being printed because the person who printed it has already left for the afternoon and will need the printed document in the morning. Erin says that she has accessed the print server using her Web browser in the past but cannot remember how she did it. You determine that the print server is named SLS-PR1 and that the printer's share name is ColorLaser.

Questions

1. What URL should Erin type into her Web browser to access the printer directly?

_____

2. What action should Erin take to ensure that all printing on the printer stops while she figures out what to do, but that no documents need to be reprinted?

_____

3. What permission will Erin need to take this action?

_____

4. What action should Erin take to make sure that her document prints before the long document?

_____

_____

_____

_____

5. How else could Erin handle this situation?

_____

_____

_____

_____

_____

Troubleshooting Lab

In this lab, you will use the Printing Troubleshooter to simulate troubleshooting a printing problem.

1. From the Start menu, click Control Panel.

2. In the Control Panel window, click Printers And Other Hardware.

3. In the Printers And Other Hardware window, in the Troubleshooters list, click Printing.

4. In the Help And Support Center window, select Printed Text Or Graphics Are Incomplete, and then click Next.

5. On the Are You Having Trouble Printing Text Or Graphics? page, click I Am Having Trouble With Graphics, and then click Next.

6. On the Are The Page Size And Orientation Settings Correct? page, you are asked, "Does Adjusting Your Page Size And Orientation Settings Solve The Problem?" Click No, My Page Size And Orientation Settings Are Correct, But Part Of My File Still Does Not Print, and then click Next.

7. On the Are Your Printer Resolution Settings Correct? page, you are asked, "Does Changing Your Printer Resolution Solve The Problem?" Click No, I Still Have A Problem Printing Graphics, and then click Next.

8. On the Does The File Or Graphic That You Are Trying To Print Require Too Much Memory? page, you are asked, "Does Freeing Memory On Your Computer Solve The Problem?" Click No, I Still Have A Problem, and then click Next.

9. On the Does Your Printer Have Enough Memory? page, you are asked, "Do These Suggestions Help You To Solve The Problem?" Click No, I Still Have A Problem, and then click Next.

10. On the Is Your Graphic Damaged? page, you are asked, "Can You Print Your Graphic In WordPad?" Click No, I Cannot Print My Graphic In WordPad, and then click Next.

11. On the Is There A Problem With Your Printer Driver? page, you are asked, "Does Reinstalling Or Updating Your Printer Driver Solve The Problem?" Click Yes, This Solves The Problem, and then click Next.

12. Close Help And Support Center.

Chapter Summary

- Printer management involves assigning forms to paper trays, setting separator pages, redirecting documents, and taking ownership of printers. Document management involves pausing and resuming documents, configuring notifications, and deleting documents from the print queue.

- There are a number of tasks associated with managing printers, including the following:

  ❑ If a printer has multiple trays that regularly hold different paper sizes, you can assign a form to a specific tray. A form defines a paper size.

  ❑ A separator page is a file that contains print device commands. Separator pages identify and separate printed documents, and they can be used to switch print devices between print modes.

  ❑ To pause a printer, cancel all documents, or resume printing, right-click the icon for the printer in the Printers And Faxes window, and then click the appropriate command.

  ❑ You can redirect all print jobs for a printer to a different printer that uses the same printer driver. You cannot redirect specific documents in the print queue.

  ❑ The print processor prepares a document for printing before it sends the document to the printer. The WinPrint processor is shipped with Windows and supports the following formats: RAW, EMF, and Text.

  ❑ By default, print jobs are spooled to disk before the print processor sends them to the printer. This allows users to access their applications again more quickly.

  ❑ To take ownership of a printer, a user must have or be a member of a group that has the Manage Printers permission for the printer. By default, members of the Administrators and Power Users groups have the Manage Printers permission.

■ Managing documents includes pausing, resuming, restarting, and canceling documents. You must have the Manage Documents permission for the appropriate printer to perform these document management tasks. The creator of a document has the default permissions to manage that document, so users can perform any of these actions on their own documents.

■ You can also manage printers from a Web browser in Windows XP Professional. The print server must be running IIS for Web management to work. You can access all printers on a print server running IIS by typing **http:// print_server_name/printers**. You can access a particular printer by typing **http://*print_server_name/printer_share_name*.**

■ When there is a printing problem, always verify that the printer is plugged in, turned on, and connected to the print server. For a network interface print device, verify that there is a network connection between the printer and the print server. Ask questions that help determine whether the problem is with the application, the document, or the printer.

Exam Highlights

Before taking the exam, review the key points and terms that are presented in this chapter. You need to know this information.

Key Points

■ The general categories of print permissions are inclusive at progressive levels. The Print permission offers the least number of rights, basically allowing users to print to the printer and manage their own documents. The Manage Documents permission allows all the rights offered by the Print permission and also allows users to manage other users' documents. The Manage Printers permission includes all the rights offered by the Manage Documents permission and allows users to configure printer settings.

■ Separator pages identify and separate print jobs, and can also be used to switch a printer to a different print mode. Windows XP includes four separator pages: sysprint.sep, pcl.sep, pscript.sep, and sysprtj.sep. Sysprint.sep is the most commonly used separator page.

■ You can redirect all documents for a printer, but not individual documents. Also, the new printer must use the same printer driver as the current printer.

Key Terms

print spooling   The process of saving a print job to the hard disk before sending it to the printer.

print permissions   Permissions that enable you to control which users can access a printer and which actions they can perform.

print processor   Software that is responsible for processing print documents into a format that is suitable to be sent to the printer. Windows XP contains only the Win-Print processor by default.

redirecting   The process of sending a document to another printer. You can redirect only all documents for a printer, not individual documents. Also, you can redirect documents only to printers that use the same printer driver as the original printer.

separator page   A file that contains print device commands. Separator pages identify and separate print jobs and can also be used to switch a printer to a different print mode.

Questions and Answers

Lesson 1 Review

Page
12-8
1. What are the four major types of tasks involved with administering network printers?

Managing printers, managing documents, troubleshooting printers, and performing tasks that require the Manage Printers permission

2. Windows XP Professional allows you to control printer usage and administration by assigning _____. Fill in the blank.

permissions

3. Which level of print permissions provided by Windows XP Professional grants users the ability to perform the most printing tasks? Choose the correct answer.

    a. Manage Printers

    b. Manage Documents

    c. Print

    d. Full Control

The correct answer is A. Granting the Manage Printers permission also allows users to manage documents and print to the printer. B and C are not correct because these rights are included in the Manage Printers permission. D is not correct because Full Control is not a permission associated with printers.

4. Which Windows XP Professional print permission allows users to pause, resume, restart, and cancel all other users' documents? Choose all that apply.

    a. Print

    b. Manage Printers

    c. Full Control

    d. Manage Documents

The correct answers are B and D. Both the Manage Printers and Manage Documents permissions allow users to manage documents in the print queue. A is not correct because the Print permission allows users to print to a printer and to manage their own documents, but not to manage all documents in a printer queue. C is not correct because Full Control is not a permission associated with printers.

Lesson 2 Review

Page
12-18
1. If a printer has multiple trays that regularly hold different paper sizes, you can assign a form to a specific tray. How do you assign a form to a paper tray?

In the Properties dialog box for the printer, click the Device Settings tab. In the box next to each paper tray, select the form for the paper type you want to assign to that tray.

2. A(n) _____ is a file that contains print device commands that identify and separate printed documents. Fill in the blank.

separator page

3. Which of the following tabs do you use to redirect documents to a different printer? Choose the correct answer.

   a. Advanced tab of the Properties dialog box for the printer

   b. Security tab of the Properties dialog box for the printer

   c. Ports tab of the Properties dialog box for the printer

   d. Device Settings tab of the Properties dialog box for the printer

   The correct answer is C. The Ports tab defines the port (or address) that the logical printer uses to direct the document to the printer. A, B, and D are not correct because you do not use these tabs to redirect documents.

4. Which of the following tabs do you use to take ownership of a printer? Choose the correct answer.

   a. Advanced tab of the Properties dialog box for the printer

   b. Security tab of the Properties dialog box for the printer

   c. Ports tab of the Properties dialog box for the printer

   d. Permissions tab of the Properties dialog box for the printer

   The correct answer is B. The Security tab defines the permissions associated with the printer, so it is a logical place to change the owner of the printer. A, C, and D are not correct because you do not use these tabs to take ownership of a printer.

Lesson 3 Practice: Exercise 3

Page
12-22

1. Which user is specified in the Notify text box? Why?

   The user account that you are logged on with is specified because that is who created the print job.

Lesson 3 Practice: Exercise 4

2. What is the current priority? Is it the lowest or highest priority?

   The current priority is 1, which is the lowest priority.

Lesson 3 Review

Page
12-24

1. What is the difference between resuming printing of a document and restarting printing of a document?

   When you restart a document, it begins printing again from the beginning of the document. When you resume printing a document, it continues from where it left off printing.

2. Which of the following statements about the range of priorities for a document to be printed is correct? Choose the correct answer.

   a. Priorities for a document range from 1 to 10, with 1 being the highest priority.

   b. Priorities for a document range from 1 to 10, with 10 being the highest priority.

   c. Priorities for a document range from 1 to 99, with 1 being the highest priority.

   d. Priorities for a document range from 1 to 99, with 99 being the highest priority.

The correct answer is D. You can set a priority from 1 to 99 for any document. 99 is the highest priority; 1 is the lowest priority.

3. You set the notification, priority, and printing time for a document on the _____ tab of the Properties dialog box for the document. Fill in the blank.

General

4. By default, Windows XP Professional enters which of the following user accounts in the Notify text box of a document?

   a. Administrator

   b. Owner of the printer

   c. All users with the Manage Documents permissions

   d. Person who printed the document

The correct answer is D. By default, the person who printed the document is notified when the document prints or fails to print.

Lesson 4 Review

Page
12-27

1. If you are using a computer running Windows XP Professional as your print server, users can gain access to the printers on it by using a Web browser only if the print server has _____ installed. Fill in the blank.

Internet Information Services (IIS)

2. How can you gain access to all printers on a print server?

In a Web browser or any of the windows or folders within the Windows XP Professional interface that has an address bar, type **http://*print_server_name*/printers**.

3. Can you pause and resume operation of a printer that you have used Internet Explorer to connect to?

Yes, if you have the Manage Printers permission for the printer, you can also pause or resume operation of a printer that you used Internet Explorer to connect to.

Lesson 5 Review

Page
12-31

1. When you detect a printing problem, what three things should you always check before you start troubleshooting the problem?

   Always verify that the printer is plugged in, turned on, and connected to the print server or network.

2. If a user reports to you that he or she cannot print, what are some of the areas you should check?

   Answers may vary. Suggested questions to ask include the following: Can other users print normally? Is the print server operational, and is there enough disk space for spooling? Does the client computer have the correct printer driver?

Case Scenario Exercise

Page
12-32

1. What URL should Erin type into her Web browser to access the printer directly?

   http://SLS-PR1/ColorLaser

2. What action should Erin take to ensure that all printing on the printer stops while she figures out what to do, but that no documents need to be reprinted?

   She should either pause the printer or take it offline.

3. What permission will Erin need to take this action?

   She will need the Manage Printer permission (or will need to be in a group that has that permission).

4. What action should Erin take to make sure that her document prints before the long document?

   She should first make sure that the long document has not started printing. She should then open the Properties dialog box for her document and assign it a higher priority than the long document. She should then resume the printer.

5. How else could Erin handle this situation?

   Instead of pausing the printer itself, Erin could also pause the long document, which would allow other documents (including hers) to continue printing. After her document printed, she could resume printing of the long document. However, when talking a user through a situation like this, it is usually easier to pause the printer while the user gets her bearings.

13 Supporting TCP/IP

Exam Objectives in this Chapter:

- Configure and troubleshoot the TCP/IP protocol.

Why This Chapter Matters

A protocol is a set of rules and conventions for sending information over a network. Microsoft Windows XP Professional relies on the **Transmission Control Protocol/Internet Protocol** (TCP/IP) for logon, file, and print services; network and Internet access; and other common functions. This chapter presents the skills and knowledge necessary to configure and troubleshoot TCP/IP. The chapter also discusses Domain Name System (DNS), how Windows XP Professional performs name resolution, and how to configure a computer running Windows XP Professional as a DNS client.

Lessons in this Chapter:

Before You Begin

To complete this chapter, you must have a computer that meets the minimum hardware requirements listed in the preface, "About This Book." You must also have Windows XP Professional installed on a computer on which you can make changes.

Lesson 1: Configuring and Troubleshooting TCP/IP

On a TCP/IP network, each device (computer, router, or other device with a connection to the network) is referred to as a host. Each TCP/IP host is identified by a logical **IP address** that identifies a computer's location on the network in much the same way as a street address identifies a house on a street. Microsoft's implementation of TCP/IP enables a TCP/IP host to use a static Internet Protocol (IP) address or to obtain an IP address automatically from a **Dynamic Host Configuration Protocol** (DHCP) server. For simple network configurations based on local area networks (LANs), Windows XP also supports automatic assignment of IP addresses. Windows XP Professional includes many tools that you can use to troubleshoot TCP/IP and test connectivity.

After this lesson, you will be able to

■ Explain the use of IP addresses.

■ Configure TCP/IP to use a static IP address.

■ Configure TCP/IP to obtain an IP address automatically.

■ Explain the use of Automatic Private IP Addressing.

■ Specify an alternate TCP/IP configuration for a computer running Windows XP Professional.

■ Use TCP/IP tools to troubleshoot a connection.

Estimated lesson time: 60 minutes

What Is an IP Address?

Every interface on a TCP/IP network is given a unique IP address that identifies it on that network. IP handles this addressing, defining how the addresses are constructed and how packets are routed using those addresses.

An IP address consists of a set of four numbers, each of which can range from 0 to 255. Each of these numbers is separated from the others by a decimal point, so a typical IP address in decimal form might look something like 192.168.1.102. The reason that each number ranges only up to 255 is that each number is actually based on a binary octet, or an eight-digit binary number. The IP address 192.168.1.102 represented in binary form is 11000000 10101000 00000001 01100110. Computers work with the binary format, but it is much easier for people to work with the decimal representation.

An IP address consists of two distinct portions:

■ The **network ID** is a portion of the IP address starting from the left that identifies the network segment on which a host is located. Using the example 192.168.1.102, the portion 192.168.1 might be the network ID. When representing a network ID, it is customary to fill in the missing octets with zeroes. So, the proper network ID would be 192.168.1.0.

■ The **host ID** is the portion of the IP address that identifies a particular host on a network segment. The host ID for each host must be unique within the network ID. Continuing the example of the IP address 192.168.1.102 (where 192.168.1.0 is the network ID), the host ID is 102.

Two computers with different network IDs can have the same host ID. However, the combination of the network ID and the host ID must be unique to all computers in communication with each other.

Hosts depend on a second number called a **subnet mask** to help determine which portion of an IP address is the network ID and which portion is the host ID. The subnet mask defines where the network ID stops and the host ID starts. It is easier to see why this works if you step away from the decimal representation for a moment and look at the numbers in their binary format.

Figure 13-1 depicts a single IP address shown in both decimal and binary format. A subnet mask is also shown in both formats. In binary format, a subnet mask always represents a string of unbroken ones followed by a string of unbroken zeroes. The position of the change from ones to zeroes indicates the division of network ID and host ID in an IP address.

	Decimal	Binary
IP Address	135.109.15.42	10000111 01101101 00001111 00101010
Subnet Mask	255.255.0.0	11111111 11111111 00000000 00000000
Network ID	135.109.0.0	10000111 01101101 00000000 00000000
Host ID	0.0.15.42	00000000 00000000 00001111 00101010

Figure 13-1   The subnet mask separates the host ID and the network ID.

Classful IP Addressing

IP addresses are organized into classes that help define the size of the network being addressed, a system referred to as classful IP addressing. Five different classes of IP addresses define different-sized networks that are capable of holding varying numbers of hosts.

Classful IP addressing is based on the structure of the IP address and provides a systematic way to differentiate network IDs from host IDs. As you learned earlier, there are four numerical segments of an IP address, ranging from 0 to 255. Here, those segments are represented as w.x.y.z. Based on the value of the first octet (w), IP addresses are categorized into the five address classes listed in Table 13-1.

Table 13-1 IP Address Classes

Class	Network ID	Range of First Octet	Number of Available Network Segments	Number of Available Hosts	Subnet Mask
A	w.0.0.0	1–126	126	16,777,214	255.0.0.0
B	w.x.0.0	128–191	16,384	65,534	255.255.0.0
C	w.x.y.0	192–223	2,097,152	254	255.255.255.0
D	N/A	224–239	N/A	N/A	N/A
E	N/A	240–255	N/A	N/A	N/A

Classes A, B, and C are available for registration by public organizations. Actually, most of these addresses were snapped up long ago by major companies and Internet service providers (ISPs), so the actual assignment of an IP address to your organization will likely come from your chosen ISP. Classes D and E are reserved for special use.

The address class determines the subnet mask used, and therefore determines the division between the network ID and the host ID. For class A, the network ID is the first octet in the IP address (for example, the 98 in the address 98.162.102.53 is the network ID). For class B, it is the first two octets; and for class C, it is the first three octets. The remaining octets not used by the network ID identify the host ID.

Exam Tip Remember the IP address ranges that fall into each class and the default subnet mask for each class. This information not only helps to determine how a classful IP addressing scheme will apply to a situation, but also how to customize a scheme using the classless method (discussed next).

Classless Interdomain Routing (CIDR)

In the classful method of IP addressing, the number of networks and hosts available for a specific address class is predetermined by the default subnet mask for the class. As a result, an organization that is allocated a network ID has a single fixed network ID and a specific number of hosts. With the single network ID, the organization can have only one network connecting its allocated number of hosts. If the number of hosts is large, the network cannot perform efficiently. To solve this problem, the concept of classless interdomain routing (CIDR) was introduced.

CIDR allows a single classful network ID to be divided into smaller network IDs. The idea is that you take the default subnet mask used for the class to which your IP address range belongs, and then borrow some of the bits used for the host ID to use as an extension to the network ID, creating a custom subnet mask.

A custom subnet mask is not restricted by the same rules used in the classful method. Remember that a subnet mask consists of a set of four numbers, similar to an IP address. Consider the default subnet mask for a class B network (255.255.0.0), which in binary format would be the following:

11111111 11111111 00000000 00000000

This mask specifies that the first 16 bits of an IP address are to be used for the network ID and the second 16 bits are to be used for the host ID. To create a custom subnet mask, you would just extend the mask into the host ID portion. However, you must extend this by adding ones from left to right. Remember that a subnet mask must be an unbroken string of ones followed by an unbroken string of zeroes. For example, a custom subnet mask might look like this:

11111111 11111111 11111000 00000000

The value 11111000 in decimal format would be 248, making this IP address 255.255.248.0. Table 13-2 shows the possible values for an octet in a custom subnet mask.

Table 13-2   Custom Subnet Mask Values

Binary Value	Decimal Value
10000000	128
11000000	192
11100000	224
11110000	240
11111000	248
11111100	252
11111110	254

In the classful method, each of the four numbers in a subnet mask can be only the maximum value 255 or the minimum value 0. The four numbers are then arranged as contiguous octets of 255, followed by contiguous octets of 0. For example, 255.255.0.0 is a valid subnet mask, whereas 255.0.255.0 is not. The 255 octets identify the network ID, and the 0 octets identify the host ID. For example, the subnet mask 255.255.0.0 identifies the network ID as the first two numbers in the IP address.

When subnetting an existing network ID to create additional subnets, you can use any of the preceding subnet masks with any IP address or network ID. So the IP address 184.12.102.20 could have the subnet mask 255.255.255.0 and network ID 184.12.102.0, as opposed to the default subnet mask 255.255.0.0 with the network ID 184.12.0.0. This allows an organization to subnet an existing class B network ID of 184.12.0.0 into smaller subnets to match the actual configuration of their network.

> **Real World   Classful Addressing and CIDR**
>
> Although classful IP addressing is important to understand, it is primarily interesting only from a historical perspective. Most modern networks that use public class A or B addresses are no longer organized by using the traditional classful subnet mask. Originally, routers and routing protocols did not separately track network IDs and subnet masks because memory for these devices was scarce and expensive. Instead, classful routing was necessary because devices had to assume the subnet mask based on the first octet. Today, memory is cheap, and every router (and routing protocol) stores both network IDs and subnet masks in the routing tables.

Private Addressing

Every network interface that is connected directly to the Internet must have an IP address registered with the Internet Assigned Numbers Authority (IANA), which prevents IP address conflicts between devices. If you are configuring a private network that is not connected to the Internet or one that exists behind a firewall or proxy server, you can configure devices on your network with private addresses and have only the public address configured on the interface that is visible to the Internet.

Each address class has a range of private addresses available for general use:

- Class A: 10.0.0.0 through 10.255.255.255
- Class B: 172.16.0.0 through 172.31.255.255
- Class C: 192.168.0.0 through 192.168.255.255

You can choose whichever range you like to use for your network and implement custom subnets as you see fit. None of these addresses is ever officially assigned to a publicly accessible Internet host.

> **On the CD**   At this point, you should view three multimedia presentations: "Components of an IP Address," "How IP Addresses are Wasted," and "How Subnet Masks Work." These presentations are available in the Multimedia folder on the CD-ROM accompanying this book. Together, these presentations will strengthen your understanding of how IP addresses and subnet masks work.

How to Configure TCP/IP to Use a Static IP Address

By default, client computers running Windows 95 and later are configured to obtain TCP/IP configuration information automatically. Automatic TCP/IP information is provided on a network using a DHCP server. When a client computer starts, it sends a broadcast message to the network looking for a DHCP server that can provide IP addressing information. Typically, most computers on a network should be configured to obtain IP addresses automatically because automatic addressing eliminates most of the errors and administrative overhead associated with assigning static IP addresses to clients. However, even in a DHCP-enabled environment, you should assign a static IP address to selected network computers. For example, the computer running the DHCP Service cannot be a DHCP client, so it must have a static IP address. If the DHCP Service is not available, you can also configure TCP/IP to use a static IP address. For each network adapter card that uses TCP/IP in a computer, you can configure an IP address, subnet mask, and default gateway, as shown in Figure 13-2.

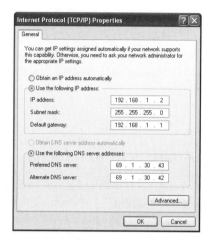

Figure 13-2 Configuring a static TCP/IP address in Windows XP Professional

Table 13-3 describes the options used in configuring a static TCP/IP address.

Table 13-3   Options for Configuring a Static TCP/IP Address

Option	Description
IP address	A logical 32-bit address that identifies a TCP/IP host. Each network adapter card in a computer running TCP/IP requires a unique IP address.
Subnet mask	Subnets divide a large network into multiple physical networks connected with routers. A subnet mask blocks out part of the IP address so that TCP/IP can distinguish the network ID from the host ID. When TCP/IP hosts try to communicate, the subnet mask determines whether the destination host is on a local or remote network. To communicate on a local network, computers must have the same subnet mask.
Default gateway	The router (also known as a gateway) on the local network. The router is responsible for forwarding traffic to and from remote networks.

To configure TCP/IP to use a static IP address, complete the following steps:

1. Click Start, and then click Control Panel.

2. In the Control Panel window, click Network And Internet Connections.

3. In the Network And Internet Connections window, click Network Connections, double-click Local Area Connection, and then click Properties.

4. In the Local Area Connection Properties dialog box, click Internet Protocol (TCP/IP), verify that the check box to its left is selected, and then click Properties.

5. In the Internet Protocol (TCP/IP) Properties dialog box, in the General tab, click Use The Following IP Address, type the TCP/IP configuration parameters, and then click OK.

6. Click OK to close the Local Area Connection Properties dialog box, and then close the Network And Dial-Up Connections window.

> **Caution**   IP communications can fail if duplicate IP addresses exist on a network. There-fore, you should always check with the network administrator to obtain a valid static IP address.

How to Configure TCP/IP to Obtain an IP Address Automatically

If a server running the DHCP Service is available on the network, it can automatically assign TCP/IP configuration information to the DHCP client, as shown in Figure 13-3. You can then configure any clients running Windows 95 and later to obtain TCP/IP configuration information automatically from the DHCP Service. This can simplify administration and ensure correct configuration information.

> **Note**   Windows XP Professional does not include the DHCP Service; it can act only as a DHCP client. Only the Windows 2000 Server products provide the DHCP Service.

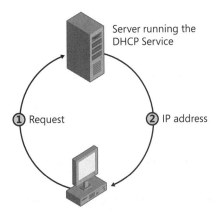

Figure 13-3   A server running the DHCP Service assigns TCP/IP addresses.

You can use the DHCP Service to provide clients with TCP/IP configuration information automatically. However, you must configure a computer as a DHCP client before it can interact with the DHCP Service.

To configure a computer running Windows XP Professional to obtain an IP address automatically, complete the following steps:

1. Click Start, and then click Control Panel.

2. In the Control Panel window, click Network And Internet Connections.

3. In the Network And Internet Connections window, click Network Connections, double-click Local Area Connection, and then click Properties.

4. In the Local Area Connection Properties dialog box, click Internet Protocol (TCP/IP), verify that the check box to its left is selected, and then click Properties.

5. In the Internet Protocol (TCP/IP) Properties dialog box, in the General tab, click Obtain An IP Address Automatically.

6. Click OK to close the Local Area Connection Properties dialog box, and then close the Network And Dial-Up Connections window.

On the CD   At this point, you should view the multimedia presentation "The Role of DHCP in the Network Infrastructure," which is available in the Multimedia folder on the CD-ROM accompanying this book. This presentation provides valuable insight into how DHCP works on a network.

What Is Automatic Private IP Addressing?

The Windows XP Professional implementation of TCP/IP supports automatic assignment of IP addresses for simple LAN-based network configurations. This addressing mechanism is an extension of dynamic IP address assignment for LAN adapters, enabling configuration of IP addresses without using static IP address assignment or using a DHCP server. **Automatic Private IP Addressing** (APIPA) is enabled by default in Windows XP Professional so that home users and small business users can create a functioning, single-subnet, TCP/IP-based network without having to configure the TCP/IP protocol manually or set up a DHCP server.

Note   The IANA has reserved 169.254.0.0 through 169.254.255.255 for APIPA. As a result, APIPA provides an address that is guaranteed not to conflict with routable addresses.

APIPA assigns an IP address and subnet mask only, and configures no additional parameters. This service is very useful in smaller, single-network environments in which there is no need for connectivity to other networks. APIPA provides a very simple way to configure TCP/IP; the network administrator does not need any knowledge of the necessary configuration parameters. However, if connectivity to other networks is required, or if the client requires name-resolution services, APIPA is not sufficient. APIPA does not provide a default gateway or name server address to the client.

The process for the APIPA feature, shown in Figure 13-4, is explained in the following steps:

1. Windows XP Professional TCP/IP attempts to find a DHCP server on the attached network to obtain a dynamically assigned IP address.

2. In the absence of a DHCP server during startup (for example, if the server is down for maintenance or repairs), the client cannot obtain an IP address.

3. APIPA generates an IP address in the form of 169.254.$x.y$ (where $x.y$ is the client's randomly generated unique identifier) and a subnet mask of 255.255.0.0.

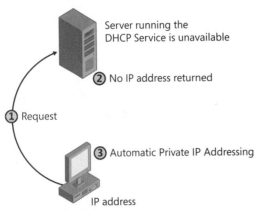

Figure 13-4 APIPA assigns IP addresses automatically.

After the computer generates the address, it broadcasts to this address, and then assigns the address to itself if no other computer responds. The computer continues to use this address until it detects and receives configuration information from a DHCP server. This allows two computers to be plugged into a LAN hub to restart without any IP address configuration and to use TCP/IP for local network access.

If the computer is a DHCP client that has previously obtained a lease from a DHCP server and the lease has not expired at boot time, the sequence of events is slightly different. The client tries to renew its lease with the DHCP server. If the client cannot locate a DHCP server during the renewal attempt, it attempts to ping the default gateway listed in the lease.

If pinging the default gateway succeeds, the DHCP client assumes that it is still on the same network in which it obtained its current lease, so it continues to use the lease. By default, the client attempts to renew its lease when 50 percent of its assigned lease time has expired. If pinging the default gateway fails, the client assumes that it has been moved to a network that has no DHCP services currently available and it autoconfigures itself, as previously described. After being automatically configured, the client continues to try to locate a DHCP server every five minutes.

APIPA can assign a TCP/IP address to DHCP clients automatically. However, APIPA does not generate all the information that typically is provided by DHCP, such as the address of a default gateway. Consequently, computers enabled with APIPA can communicate only with computers on the same subnet that also have addresses of the form 169.254.*x.y*.

> **Exam Tip**   If you are troubleshooting a network problem and discover that a client computer has an IP address on the 169.254.0.0 network, the computer has assigned itself that address using APIPA because the computer could not locate a DHCP server.

By default, the APIPA feature is enabled. However, you can disable it by specifying an alternate configuration to use if a DHCP server cannot be located (see Figure 13-5), as discussed in the next section.

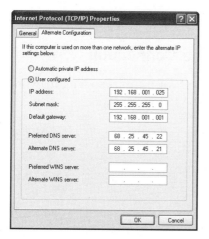

Figure 13-5   Specify an alternate TCP/IP configuration.

How to Specify an Alternate Configuration for TCP/IP

A feature in Windows XP Professional named Auto-Configuration For Multiple Networks Connectivity provides easy access to network devices and the Internet. It also allows a mobile computer user to seamlessly operate both office and home networks without having to manually reconfigure TCP/IP settings.

You specify an alternate configuration for TCP/IP if a DHCP server is not found. The alternate configuration is useful when a computer is used on multiple networks, one of which does not have a DHCP server and does not use an automatic private IP addressing configuration.

To configure Auto-Configuration For Multiple Networks Connectivity, use these steps:

1. Click Start and then click Control Panel.

2. In the Control Panel window, click Network And Internet Connections.

3. In the Network And Internet Connections window, click Network Connections, and then click Local Area Connection.

4. Click Change Settings Of This Connection.

   Windows XP Professional displays the Local Area Connection Properties dialog box.

5. Click Internet Protocol (TCP/IP), and then click Properties.

   Windows XP Professional displays the Internet Protocol (TCP/IP) Properties dialog box with the General tab active.

6. Click Alternate Configuration.

7. Specify the alternate TCP/IP configuration (refer to Figure 13-5).

How to Use TCP/IP Tools to Troubleshoot a Connection

Windows XP provides a number of TCP/IP tools for troubleshooting network connectivity problems. You should be familiar with the following tools:

- Ping
- Ipconfig
- Net View
- Tracert
- Pathping

Ping

When the problem appears to be with TCP/IP, start the troubleshooting process with the **Ping** command, which allows you to check for connectivity between devices on a network.

When you use the Ping command, you ping from the inside out. You want to find out where the communication and connection fail. For example, you ping the loopback address first, then a local computer on the same network, then a DNS or DHCP server on the local subnet if one exists, then the default gateway, then a remote computer on another network, and finally a resource on the Internet. You should be able to find out where the breakdown occurs by compiling the results of these checks.

> **Note**   When using the Ping command, you can use either the computer name or the computer's IP address.

Pinging the Loopback Address   The **loopback address** (127.0.0.1) is the first thing you should check when a TCP/IP problem appears. If this check fails, the TCP/IP configuration for the local machine is not correct. To ping the loopback address, follow these steps:

1. From the Start menu, point to All Programs, point to Accessories, and select Command Prompt.

2. Type **ping 127.0.0.1**. A successful ping to a loopback address is shown in Figure 13-6.

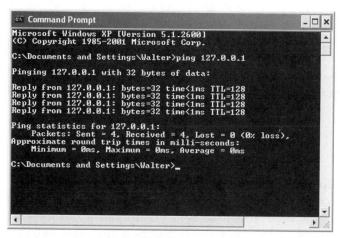

Figure 13-6   Ping the loopback address to verify that TCP/IP is configured correctly.

If pinging the loopback address fails, check the configuration of TCP/IP by following these steps:

1. Open the Network Connections window, right-click the configured connection, and choose Properties.

2. Select Internet Protocol (TCP/IP), and click Properties to view the configuration. If a static address is configured and a DHCP server is available, select Obtain An IP Address Automatically. If Obtain An IP Address Automatically is selected but a static IP address is necessary, select Use The Following IP Address; then enter the address, subnet mask, and gateway to use. If the configuration is correct, you might have to reset TCP/IP.

3. Click OK in the Properties dialog box and OK in the connection's Properties dialog box. Reboot the computer if prompted.

Pinging Other Resources   To ping any other computer on the network, simply replace the loopback address with the TCP/IP address of the resource on the network. Ping a local computer on the same subnet first, and then ping the gateway address. If you can ping the loopback address (a local computer on the same subnet), but the Ping command to the gateway fails, you probably found the problem. In this case, check the configuration on the local computer for the gateway address and verify that the gateway (or router) is operational.

If the ping to the gateway address is successful, continue to ping outward until you find the problem. For instance, ping a computer on a remote subnet and verify that the DNS server is operational.

> **Note**   Although pinging remote computers is a useful troubleshooting technique, many hosts and routers filter out incoming Internet Control Message Protocol (ICMP) echo requests (which are the basis of ping). Such hosts do not respond to a ping request, making it appear that the host cannot be reached. By default, computers protected with Windows Firewall also filter out such requests to protect the computers from intruders that would use ICMP-based denial of service (DoS) attacks or use ICMP to map a remote network.

Using Ipconfig

You can use the **Ipconfig** command-line utility to view current TCP/IP configuration information for a computer. To use Ipconfig, open the command prompt window and type **Ipconfig** to view basic TCP/IP parameters, **Ipconfig /all** to view the complete TCP/IP configuration (as shown in Figure 13-7), or **Ipconfig /?** to view additional options.

```
Command Prompt                                                          _ □ x
Microsoft Windows XP [Version 5.1.2600]
(C) Copyright 1985-2001 Microsoft Corp.

C:\Documents and Settings\Walter>ipconfig /all

Windows IP Configuration

        Host Name . . . . . . . . . . . . : j
        Primary Dns Suffix  . . . . . . . :
        Node Type . . . . . . . . . . . . : Unknown
        IP Routing Enabled. . . . . . . . : No
        WINS Proxy Enabled. . . . . . . . : No

Ethernet adapter Local Area Connection:

        Connection-specific DNS Suffix  . :
        Description . . . . . . . . . . . : Intel(R) PRO/1000 CT Network Connect
ion
        Physical Address. . . . . . . . . : 00-07-E9-45-C4-2D
        Dhcp Enabled. . . . . . . . . . . : No
        IP Address. . . . . . . . . . . . : 192.168.1.2
        Subnet Mask . . . . . . . . . . . : 255.255.255.0
        Default Gateway . . . . . . . . . : 192.168.1.1
        DNS Servers . . . . . . . . . . . : 69.1.30.43
                                            69.1.30.42

C:\Documents and Settings\Walter>_
```

Figure 13-7 Use the Ipconfig /all command to display a complete TCP/IP configuration.

Note You must run Ipconfig from a command prompt. If you try to execute it by using the Run command on the Start menu, the command window will close before you have a chance to read the information that is displayed.

Additional Ipconfig options include the following:

/release Releases DHCP-supplied configuration information

/renew Renews DHCP-supplied configuration information

/flushdns Purges the local DNS cache (the area of memory that stores recently resolved names so that the client does not have to contact the DNS server each time)

/registerdns Renews DHCP-supplied configuration information and registers the DNS name to IP address information with DNS

/displaydns Displays the contents of the local DNS cache

/setclassid Provides for the configuration of DHCP user classes, which can control the way IP addresses are assigned

Exam Tip Understand the various options available with the Ipconfig command. In particular, you should remember what /renew, /release, and /flushdns do.

Using Net View

The Net View command is another command that you can use to test TCP/IP connections. To use the command, log on with the proper credentials that are required to view shares on a remote or local computer, open a command prompt, and type **net view ***ComputerName* or **net view ***IP Address*. The resulting report lists the file and print shares on the computer. If there are no file or print shares on the computer, you see the message There Are No Entries In The List.

If the Net View command fails, check the following:

- The computer name in the System Properties dialog box

- The gateway or router address in the TCP/IP Properties dialog box

- The gateway or router status

- The remote computer is running the File And Printer Sharing For Microsoft Networks Service (this service can be added in the TCP/IP Properties dialog box)

Using Tracert

When a route breaks down on the way from the destination computer to its target computer, communication fails. The **Tracert** command-line utility can help you figure out exactly where along the route the breakdown happened. Sometimes the connection breaks down at the gateway on the local network and sometimes at a router on an external network.

To use Tracert, at the command prompt type **tracert** followed by the IP address of the remote computer. The resulting report shows where the packets were lost. You can use this information to uncover the source of the problem.

Using Pathping

The Ping command is used to test communication between one computer and another; Tracert is used to follow a particular route from one computer to another. The **Pathping** command is a combination of both Ping and Tracert, displaying information about packet loss at every router between the host computer and the remote one. The Pathping command provides information about data loss between the source and the destination, allowing you to determine which particular router or subnet might be having network problems. To use the Pathping command, at the command prompt, type **pathping** followed by the target name or IP address.

Note   The Windows Help And Support Center offers a list of all of the commands that you can perform by using the command line. Search for Command-Line Reference A–Z. Each command reference includes a description of the command and how to use it.

The TCP/IP Protocol Suite

The TCP/IP suite of protocols provides a set of standards for how operating systems and applications communicate and how networks are interconnected. The TCP/IP suite of protocols maps to a four-layer conceptual model known as the Department of Defense (DoD) model. The four layers are as follows:

- **Network access layer**   The network access layer is responsible for placing data on the network medium and receiving data off the network medium. This layer contains physical devices such as network cables and network adapters.

- **Internet layer**   The Internet layer is responsible for addressing, packaging, and routing the data that is handed down to it from the transport layer. There are four core protocols in this layer: IP, Address Resolution Protocol (ARP), Internet Control Message Protocol (ICMP), and Internet Group Management Protocol (IGMP).

- **Transport layer**   The transport layer protocols provide communication sessions between computers. The desired method of data delivery determines the transport protocol. The two transport layer protocols are TCP and User Datagram Protocol (UDP).

- **Application layer**   At the top of the model is the application layer, in which applications gain access to the network. There are many standard TCP/IP tools and services in the application layer, such as File Transfer Protocol (FTP), Telnet, Simple Network Management Protocol (SNMP), DNS, and so on.

The purpose of this layering is to provide a level of abstraction between an application or protocol in one layer and the functioning of the entire network. For example, an application in the application layer needs to know only where to pass information into the transport layer (and how to format that information); it does not need to take into account any specific network configuration beyond that point. Packets of data are passed down the layers on the sending host and back up the layers on the receiving host.

If you are interested in learning more about how layering works, you should view two multimedia presentations: "OSI Model" and "TCP/IP Protocol Suite." Both presentations are available in the Multimedia folder on the CD-ROM accompanying this book.

Practice: Configuring and Troubleshooting TCP/IP

In this practice, you will use two TCP/IP tools to verify your computer's configuration. Then you will configure your computer to use a static IP address and verify your computer's new configuration. Next, you will configure your computer to use a DHCP server to automatically assign an IP address to your computer (whether or not there is a DHCP server available on your network). Finally, you will test the APIPA feature in Windows XP Professional by disabling the DHCP server, if there is one on your network.

If your computer is part of an existing network, use the following table to record the IP address, subnet mask, and default gateway that your network administrator provides for you to use during this practice. Ask your network administrator whether there is another computer that you can use to test your computer's connectivity and record the IP address of that computer as well. If you are not on a network, you can use the suggested values.

Variable Value	Suggested Value	Your Value
Static IP address	192.168.1.201	
Subnet mask	255.255.0.0	
Default gateway (if required)	None	
Computer to test connectivity	N/A	

Exercise 1: Verify a Computer's TCP/IP Configuration

In this exercise, you will use two TCP/IP tools, Ipconfig and Ping, to verify your computer's configuration.

Tip   As you complete the exercises in this practice, you will use the command prompt and Network Connections windows frequently. For the sake of efficiency, open the windows one time, and then minimize and restore them as necessary.

1. Click Start, point to All Programs, point to Accessories, and then click Command Prompt.

2. At the command prompt, type **ipconfig /all**, and then press ENTER.

   The Windows XP Professional IP Configuration tool displays the TCP/IP configuration of the physical and logical adapters configured on your computer.

3. Use the information displayed to complete as much of the following table as possible.

Local Area Connection Setting	Value
Host name	
Primary DNS suffix	
Connection-specific DNS suffix description	
Physical address	
DHCP enabled	
Autoconfiguration enabled	
Autoconfiguration IP address	
Subnet mask	
Default gateway	

4. To verify that the IP address is working and configured for your adapter, type **ping 127.0.0.1**, and then press ENTER.

A response similar to the following indicates a successful ping:

```
Pinging 127.0.0.1 with 32 bytes of data:
Reply from 127.0.0.1: bytes=32 time<1ms TTL=128
Reply from 127.0.0.1: bytes=32 time<1ms TTL=128
Reply from 127.0.0.1: bytes=32 time<1ms TTL=128
Reply from 127.0.0.1: bytes=32 time<1ms TTL=128
Ping statistics for 127.0.0.1:
Packets: Sent = 4, Received = 4, Lost = 0 <0% loss>,
Approximate round trip times in milliseconds:
Minimum = 0ms, Maximum = 0ms, Average = 0ms
```

5. Minimize the Command Prompt window.

Exercise 2: Configure TCP/IP to Use a Static IP Address

1. Click Start, and then click Control Panel.

2. In the Control Panel window, click Network And Internet Connections.

3. In the Network And Internet Connections window, click Network Connections, and then click Local Area Connection.

4. Under Network Tasks, click Change Settings Of This Connection (you can also right-click the connection and then click Properties).

The Local Area Connection Properties dialog box appears, displaying the network adapter in use and the network components used in this connection.

5. Click Internet Protocol (TCP/IP), and then verify that the check box to the left of the entry is selected.

6. Click Properties.

The Internet Protocol (TCP/IP) Properties dialog box appears.

7. Click Use The Following IP Address.

Important In the next step, if the computer you are using is on a network, enter the IP address, subnet mask, and default gateway values you recorded in the table in Exercise 1. If you are on a stand-alone computer, complete the next step as it is written.

8. In the IP Address text box, type **198.168.1.201**; in the Subnet Mask text box, type **255.255.255.0**.

Important Be careful when entering IP configuration settings manually, especially numeric addresses. The most frequent cause of TCP/IP connection problems is incorrectly entered IP address information.

9. Click OK to return to the Local Area Connection Properties dialog box.

10. Click Close to close the Local Area Connection Properties dialog box and return to the Network Connections window.

11. Minimize the Network Connections window.

12. Restore the command prompt.

13. At the command prompt, type **ipconfig /all** and then press Enter.

The Windows XP Professional IP Configuration tool displays the physical and logical adapters configured on your computer.

14. Record the current TCP/IP configuration settings for your local area connection in the following table.

Setting	Value
IP address	
Subnet mask	

15. To verify that the IP address is working and configured for your adapter, type **ping 127.0.0.1**, and then press ENTER.

If the address is working and configured, you receive the following result:

```
Reply from 127.0.0.1: bytes=32 time<1ms TTL=128
Reply from 127.0.0.1: bytes=32 time<1ms TTL=128
Reply from 127.0.0.1: bytes=32 time<1ms TTL=128
Reply from 127.0.0.1: bytes=32 time<1ms TTL=128
```

16. If you have a computer that you are using to test connectivity, type **ping** **ip_address** (where *ip_address* is the IP address of the computer you are using to test connectivity), and then press ENTER. Minimize the command prompt.

Exercise 3: Configure TCP/IP to Automatically Obtain an IP Address

In this exercise, you will configure TCP/IP to automatically obtain an IP address, and then test the configuration to verify that the DHCP Service has provided the appropriate IP addressing information. Be sure to perform the first part of this exercise even if you have no DHCP server because these settings are also used in Exercise 4.

1. Restore the Network Connections window, right-click Local Area Connection, and then click Properties.

The Local Area Connection Properties dialog box appears.

2. Click Internet Protocol (TCP/IP) and verify that the check box to the left of the entry is selected.

3. Click Properties.

The Internet Protocol (TCP/IP) Properties dialog box appears.

4. Click Obtain An IP Address Automatically, and then click Obtain DNS Server Address Automatically.

5. Click OK to close the Internet Protocol (TCP/IP) Properties dialog box.

6. Click Close to close the Local Area Connection Properties dialog box.

7. Minimize the Network Connections window.

> **Note**   If there is not an available server running the DHCP Service to provide an IP address, skip the remainder of this exercise and continue with Exercise 4.

8. Restore the command prompt, type **ipconfig /release**, and then press ENTER.

9. At the command prompt, type **ipconfig /renew**, and then press ENTER.

10. At the command prompt, type **ipconfig**, and then press ENTER.

11. Record the current TCP/IP configuration settings for your local area connection in the following table.

Setting	Value
IP address	
Subnet mask	
Default gateway	

12. To test that TCP/IP is working and bound to your adapter, type **ping 127.0.0.1**, and then press ENTER.

The internal loopback test displays four replies if TCP/IP is bound to the adapter.

Exercise 4: Obtaining an IP Address Using APIPA

In this exercise, if you have a server running the DHCP Service, you need to disable it on that server so that a DHCP server is not available to provide an IP address for your computer (you can also disconnect the networking cable from your computer). Without a DHCP server available to provide an IP address, the Windows XP Professional APIPA feature provides unique IP addresses for your computer.

1. At the command prompt, type **ipconfig /release**, and then press ENTER.

2. At the command prompt, type **ipconfig /renew**, and then press ENTER.

There is a pause while Windows XP Professional attempts to locate a DHCP server on the network.

3. Which message appears, and what does it indicate?

_____

_____

_____

_____

4. Click OK to close the dialog box.

5. At the command prompt, type **ipconfig**, and then press ENTER.

6. Record the current TCP/IP settings for your local area connection in the following table.

Setting	Value
IP address	
Subnet mask	
Default gateway	

7. Is this the same IP address assigned to your computer in Exercise 3? Why or why not?

_____

_____

_____

8. To verify that TCP/IP is working, type **ping 127.0.0.1**, and then press ENTER. The internal loopback test displays four replies if TCP/IP is bound to the adapter.

9. If you have a computer to test TCP/IP connectivity with your computer, type **ping** ***ip_address*** (where *ip_address* is the IP address of the computer that you are using to test connectivity), and then press ENTER. If you do not have a computer to test connectivity, skip this step and proceed to Exercise 5.

10. Were you successful? Why or why not?

_____

_____

Exercise 5: Obtain an IP Address by Using DHCP

Before you begin this exercise, you will need to enable the DHCP Service running on the computer that is acting as a DHCP server (or reconnect your network cable if you disconnected it in Exercise 4). In this exercise, your computer obtains IP addressing information from the DHCP server.

> **Note**   If there is not an available server running the DHCP Service to provide an IP address, skip this exercise.

1. At the command prompt, type **ipconfig /release,** and then press ENTER.

2. At the command prompt, type **ipconfig /renew**, and then press ENTER.

    After a short wait, a message box indicates that a new IP address was assigned.

3. Click OK to close the message box.

4. At the command prompt, type **ipconfig /all**, and then press ENTER.

    Verify that the DHCP server has assigned an IP address to your computer.

5. Close the command prompt.

Lesson Review

The following questions are intended to reinforce key information presented in this lesson. If you are unable to answer a question, review the lesson materials and try the question again. You can find answers to the questions in the "Questions and Answers" section at the end of this chapter.

1. Why would you assign a computer a static IP address?

   _____

   _____

   _____

   _____

   _____

2. Which of the following statements correctly describe IP addresses? (Choose all that apply.)

   a. IP addresses are logical 64-bit addresses that identify a TCP/IP host.

   b. Each network adapter card in a computer running TCP/IP requires a unique IP address.

   c. 192.168.0.108 is an example of a class C IP address.

   d. The host ID in an IP address is always the last two octets in the address.

3. What is the purpose of a subnet mask?

   _____

   _____

4. By default, client computers running Windows XP Professional, Windows 95, or Windows 98 obtain TCP/IP configuration information automatically from the DHCP Service: True or false?

   _____

5. Your computer running Windows XP Professional was configured manually for TCP/IP. You can connect to any host on your own subnet, but you cannot connect to or even ping any host on a remote subnet. What is the likely cause of the problem and how would you fix it?

   _____

   _____

   _____

   _____

6. Your computer's Computer Name is Pro1, and you ping Pro1. The local address for Pro1 is returned as 169.254.128.71. What does this tell you?

   _____

   _____

   _____

Lesson Summary

- Each TCP/IP host is identified by a logical IP address that identifies a computer's location on the network. The IP address is composed of a network ID and a host ID. A subnet mask determines which portion of the IP address is the network ID and which portion is the host ID.

- A static IP address is a manually entered address. You should assign a static IP address to selected network computers, such as the computer running the DHCP Service.

- Windows XP Professional can obtain an IP address automatically from a DHCP server on the network. Using automatic addressing reduces the likelihood of errors being introduced when configuring static addresses.

- Windows XP Professional can assign itself an IP address using APIPA if a DHCP server is not available. Computers enabled with APIPA can communicate only with computers on the same subnet that also have addresses of the form 169.254.x.y.

- Specifying an alternate TCP/IP configuration is useful when a computer is used on multiple networks, one of which does not have a DHCP server and does not use an automatic private IP addressing configuration.

- Windows XP Professional includes a number of tools that you can use to trouble-shoot TCP/IP configurations. These tools include the following:

  - Ping
  - Ipconfig
  - Net View
  - Tracert
  - Pathping

Lesson 2: Understanding the Domain Name System

The **Domain Name System** (DNS) is used on the Internet and on many private networks. Private networks using Microsoft Active Directory directory service use DNS extensively to resolve computer names and to locate computers within their local networks and the Internet. In fact, networks based on Windows 2000 Server and Windows Server 2003 use DNS as a primary means of locating resources in Active Directory (which you will learn about in Chapter 14, "Overview of Active Directory Service").

After this lesson, you will be able to

- Explain how the domain namespace works.
- Identify domain-naming guidelines.
- Explain the purpose of zones.
- Explain the purpose of name servers.

Estimated lesson time: 20 minutes

What Is the Domain Namespace?

The domain namespace is the naming scheme that provides the hierarchical structure for the DNS database. Each node, referred to as a domain, represents a partition of the DNS database.

The DNS database is indexed by name, so each domain must have a name. As you add domains to the hierarchy, the name of the parent domain is added to its child domain (called a subdomain). Consequently, a domain's name identifies its position in the hierarchy. For example, in Figure 13-8, the domain name sales.microsoft.com identifies the sales domain as a subdomain of the microsoft.com domain and microsoft as a subdomain of the com domain.

The hierarchical structure of the domain namespace consists of a root domain, top-level domains, second-level domains, and host names.

Note   The term *domain*, in the context of DNS, does not correlate precisely to the term as used on the Active Directory network. A Windows domain is a grouping of computers and devices that are administered as a unit.

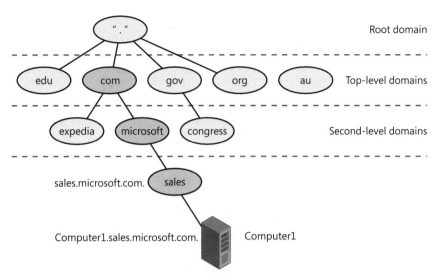

Figure 13-8   The domain namespace is hierarchical in structure.

Root Domain

At the top of the DNS hierarchy, there is a single domain called the root domain, which is represented by a single period.

Top-Level Domains

Top-level domains are two-, three-, or four-character name codes. Top-level domains are grouped by organization type or geographic location. Top-level domains are controlled by the Internet Architecture Board (IAB), an Internet authority controlling the assignment of domain names, among other things. Table 13-4 provides some examples of top-level domain names.

Table 13-4   Top-Level Domains

Top-Level Domain	Description
gov	Government organizations
com	Commercial organizations
edu	Educational institutions
org	Noncommercial organizations
au	Country code of Australia

Top-level domains can contain second-level domains and host names.

Second-Level Domains

Anyone can register a second-level domain name. Second-level domain names are registered to individuals and organizations by a number of different domain registry companies. A second-level name has two name parts: a top-level name and a unique second-level name. Table 13-5 provides some examples of second-level domains. After registering a second-level domain name, you can create as many subdomains of that domain name as you want. For example, if you registered the domain name contoso.com, you could create subdomains such as north.contoso.com, south.contoso.com, and so on.

Table 13-5   Second-Level Domains

Second-Level Domain	Description
ed.gov	United States Department of Education
Microsoft.com	Microsoft Corporation
Stanford.edu	Stanford University
w3.org	World Wide Web Consortium
pm.gov.au	Prime Minister of Australia

Host Names

Host names refer to specific computers on the Internet or a private network. For example, in Figure 13-8, Computer1 is a host name. A host name is the leftmost portion of a fully qualified domain name (FQDN), which describes the exact position of a host within the domain hierarchy. In Figure 13-8, Computer1.sales.microsoft.com. (including the end period, which represents the root domain) is an FQDN.

DNS uses a host's FQDN to resolve a name to an IP address.

> **Note**   The host name does not have to be the same as the computer name. By default, TCP/IP setup uses the computer name for the host name, replacing illegal characters, such as the underscore (_), with a hyphen (-).

> **On the CD**   At this point, you should view the multimedia presentation "Role of DNS," which is available in the Multimedia folder on the CD-ROM accompanying this book. This presentation provides valuable insight into how DNS works on a network.

Domain-Naming Guidelines

When you create a domain namespace, consider the following domain guidelines and standard naming conventions:

- Limit the number of domain levels. Typically, DNS host entries should be three or four levels down the DNS hierarchy and no more than five levels down the hierarchy. The numbers of levels increase the administrative tasks.

- Use unique names. Each subdomain must have a unique name within its parent domain to ensure that the name is unique throughout the DNS namespace.

- Use simple names. Simple and precise domain names are easier for users to remember. They also enable users to search intuitively and locate Web sites or other computers on the Internet or an intranet.

- Avoid lengthy domain names. Domain names can be up to 63 characters, including periods. The total length of an FQDN cannot exceed 255 characters. Case-sensitive naming is not supported.

- Use standard DNS characters and Unicode characters.

- Windows 2000 Server and Windows Server 2003 support the following standard DNS characters: a–z, 0–9, and the hyphen (-), as defined in RFC 1035.

- The DNS Service also supports the Unicode character set. The Unicode character set includes additional characters not found in the American Standard Code for Information Interchange (ASCII) character set; these additional characters are required for languages such as French, German, and Spanish.

 Note   Use Unicode characters only if all servers running the DNS Service in your environment support Unicode. For more information about the Unicode character set, read RFC 2044 by searching for "RFC 2044" with your Web browser.

What Are Zones?

A zone represents a discrete portion of the domain namespace. Zones provide a way to partition the domain namespace into manageable sections, and they provide the following functions:

- Multiple zones in a domain namespace are used to distribute administrative tasks to different groups. For example, Figure 13-9 depicts the microsoft.com domain namespace divided into two zones. These zones allow one administrator to manage the microsoft and sales domains, and another administrator to manage the development domain.

■ A zone must encompass a contiguous domain namespace. For example, in Figure 13-9, you cannot create a zone that consists of only the sales.microsoft.com and development.microsoft.com domains because these two domains are not contiguous.

> **Note**   For more information about contiguous namespaces, see Chapter 14.

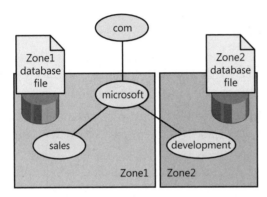

Figure 13-9   A domain namespace is divided into zones.

The name-to-IP address mappings for a zone are stored in the zone database file. Each zone is anchored to a specific domain, referred to as the zone's root domain. The zone database file does not necessarily contain information for all subdomains of the zone's root domain, only those subdomains within the zone.

In Figure 13-9, the root domain for Zone1 is microsoft.com, and its zone file contains the name-to-IP address mappings for the microsoft and sales domains. The root domain for Zone2 is development, and its zone file contains the name-to-IP address mappings only for the development domain. The zone file for Zone1 does not contain the name-to-IP address mappings for the development domain, although development is a subdomain of the microsoft domain.

What Are Name Servers?

A DNS name server stores the zone database file. Name servers can store data for one zone or multiple zones. A name server is said to have authority for the domain name space that the zone encompasses.

One name server contains the master zone database file, referred to as the primary zone database file, for the specified zone. As a result, there must be at least one name server for a zone. Changes to a zone, such as adding domains or hosts, are performed on the server that contains the primary zone database file.

Multiple name servers act as a backup to the name server containing the primary zone database file. Multiple name servers provide the following advantages:

■ They perform zone transfers. The additional name servers obtain a copy of the zone database file from the name server that contains the primary database zone file. This process is called a zone transfer. These name servers periodically query the name server containing the primary zone database file for updated zone data.

■ They provide redundancy. If the name server containing the primary zone database file fails, the additional name servers can provide service.

■ They improve access speed for remote locations. If there are a number of clients in remote locations, use additional name servers to reduce query traffic across slow wide area network (WAN) links.

■ They reduce the load on the name server containing the primary zone database file.

> **Real World   Active Directory and DNS**
>
> Active Directory and DNS are tightly integrated—they even share a common namespace. It is essential, therefore, that you understand how each system works and how they work together.
>
> DNS is the locator service used by Active Directory (and by many other Windows components). Active Directory makes its services available to the network by publishing them in DNS. When a domain controller is installed (or when services are added to it), the domain controller uses dynamic updates to register its services as SRV records in DNS. Clients can then locate services through simple DNS queries. The Microsoft DNS Service runs on every Windows Server 2003 domain controller by default.

Lesson Review

The following questions are intended to reinforce key information presented in this lesson. If you are unable to answer a question, review the lesson materials and try the question again. You can find answers to the questions in the "Questions and Answers" section at the end of this chapter.

1. What is DNS and what is it used for?

_____

_____

_____

2. Which of the following statements correctly describes DNS root domains? (Choose all that apply.)

   a. The root domain is at the top of the hierarchy.

   b. The root domain is at the bottom of the hierarchy.

   c. The root domain is represented by a two- or three-character name code.

   d. The root domain is represented by a period (.).

3. Which of the following are second-level domain names? (Choose all that apply.)

   a. gov

   b. Microsoft.com

   c. au

   d. ed.gov

4. _____ provide a way to partition the domain namespace into manageable sections, and each _____ represents a discrete portion of the domain namespace.

Lesson Summary

- The DNS database is indexed by name, so each domain (node) must have a name. The hierarchical structure of the domain namespace consists of a root domain, top-level domains, second-level domains, and host names.

- When creating a domain namespace, you should use certain guidelines, such as limiting the number of domain levels and using unique and simple names.

- Zones provide a way to partition the domain namespace into smaller sections, so a zone represents a discrete portion of the domain namespace.

- A DNS name server stores the zone database file. Name servers can store data for one zone or multiple zones. A name server is said to have authority for the domain namespace that the zone encompasses.

Lesson 3: Overview of Name Resolution

Name resolution is the process of resolving names to IP addresses. It is similar to looking up a name in a telephone book, in which the name is associated with a telephone number. For example, when you connect to the Microsoft Web site, you use the name www.microsoft.com. DNS resolves www.microsoft.com to its associated IP address. The mapping of names to IP addresses is stored in the DNS distributed database.

DNS name servers resolve forward and reverse lookup queries. A forward lookup query resolves a name to an IP address, and a reverse lookup query resolves an IP address to a name. A name server can resolve a query only for a zone for which it has authority. If a name server cannot resolve the query, it passes the query to other name servers that can resolve it. The name server caches the query results to reduce the DNS traffic on the network.

After this lesson, you will be able to

- Explain how a forward lookup query works.
- Explain the purpose of name server caching.
- Explain how a reverse lookup query works.

Estimated lesson time: 10 minutes

How a Forward Lookup Query Works

The DNS Service uses a client/server model for name resolution. To resolve a forward lookup query, which resolves a name to an IP address, a client passes a query to a local name server. The local name server either resolves the query and provides an IP address or queries another name server for resolution.

Figure 13-10 represents a client querying the name server for an IP address of www.microsoft.com.

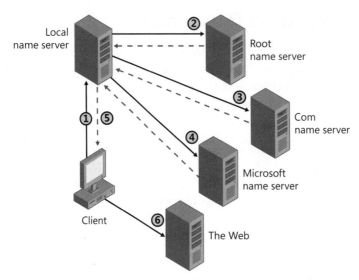

Figure 13-10   A forward lookup query resolves a name to an IP address.

The numbers in Figure 13-10 depict the following activities:

1. The client passes a forward lookup query for *www.microsoft.com* to its local name server.

2. The local name server checks its zone database file to determine whether it contains the name-to-IP address mapping for the client query. The local name server does not have authority for the microsoft.com domain, so it passes the query to one of the DNS root servers, requesting resolution of the host name. The root name server sends back a referral to the com name server.

3. The local name server sends a request to a com name server, which responds with a referral to the Microsoft name server.

4. The local name server sends a request to the Microsoft name server. Because the Microsoft name server has authority for that portion of the domain namespace, when it receives the request, it returns the IP address for *www.microsoft.com* to the local name server.

5. The local name server sends the IP address for *www.microsoft.com* to the client.

6. The name resolution is complete, and the client can access *www.microsoft.com*.

What Is Name Server Caching?

When a name server is processing a query, it might be required to send out several queries to find the answer. With each query, the name server discovers other name servers that have authority for a portion of the domain namespace. The name server caches these query results to reduce network traffic.

When a name server receives a query result, the following process takes place (see Figure 13-11):

1. The name server caches the query result for a specified amount of time, which is referred to as Time to Live (TTL).

> **Note**   The zone that provided the query results specifies the TTL. The default value is 60 minutes.

2. After the name server caches the query result, TTL starts counting down from its original value.

3. When TTL expires, the name server deletes the query result from its cache.

Caching query results enables the name server to resolve other queries to the same portion of the domain namespace quickly.

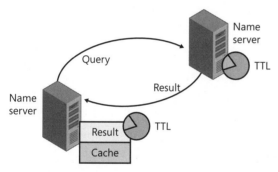

Figure 13-11   Names servers can cache query results for quicker subsequent access.

> **Note**   Shorter TTL values ensure that data about the domain namespace is more current across the network. However, shorter TTL values cause the cached values to expire sooner and increase the DNS traffic. A longer TTL value causes the cached values to be retained longer, which decreases the DNS traffic but increases the risk of the entries becoming stale. If a change does occur, the client does not receive the updated information until the TTL expires and a new query to that portion of the domain namespace is resolved.

How a Reverse Lookup Query Works

A reverse lookup query maps an IP address to a name. Troubleshooting tools, such as the nslookup command-line tool, use reverse lookup queries to report back host names. Additionally, certain applications implement security based on the capability to connect to names, not IP addresses.

Because the DNS distributed database is indexed by name and not by IP address, a reverse lookup query would require an exhaustive search of every domain name. To solve this problem, in-addr.arpa was created. This special second-level domain follows the same hierarchical naming scheme as the rest of the domain namespace; however, it is based on IP addresses, not domain names, as follows:

- Subdomains are named after the numbers in the dotted-decimal representation of IP addresses.

- The order of the IP address octets is reversed.

- Companies administer subdomains of the in-addr.arpa domain based on their assigned IP addresses and subnet mask.

For example, Figure 13-12 shows a dotted-decimal representation of the IP address 192.168.16.200. A company that has an assigned IP address range of 192.168.16.0 to 192.168.16.255 with a subnet mask of 255.255.255.0 has authority over the 16.168.192.in-addr.arpa domain.

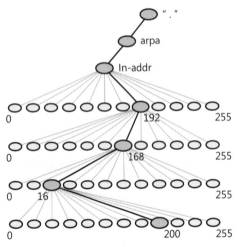

Figure 13-12   The in-addr.arpa domain is used in reverse lookup queries.

On the CD   At this point, you should view the multimedia presentation "The Name Resolution Process," which is available in the Multimedia folder on the CD-ROM accompanying this book. This presentation will give you a deeper understanding of the name resolution process.

Lesson Review

The following questions are intended to reinforce key information presented in this lesson. If you are unable to answer a question, review the lesson materials and try the question again. You can find answers to the questions in the "Questions and Answers" section at the end of this chapter.

1. What is a forward lookup query and how is it resolved?

_____

_____

_____

_____

_____

_____

_____

_____

_____

2. In DNS name resolution, which of the following statements about TTL are correct? (Choose all that apply.)

    a. TTL is the length of time a query can exist before it is discarded.

    b. Shorter TTL values help ensure that data about the domain namespace is more current across the network.

    c. Longer TTL values increase the amount of DNS traffic.

    d. Longer TTL values cause the cached values to be retained longer.

3. Which of the following statements about DNS name and address resolution are correct? (Choose all that apply.)

    a. The DNS distributed database is indexed by both names and IP addresses.

    b. The top-level domain in-addr.arpa is used for both forward and reverse queries.

    c. In the in-addr.arpa domain, the order of the IP address octets is reversed.

    d. Troubleshooting tools, such as the nslookup command-line tool, use reverse lookup queries to report back host names.

Lesson Summary

- A forward lookup query resolves a name to an IP address, and a reverse lookup query resolves an IP address to a name.

- Name servers cache query results to reduce DNS traffic on the network.

- The DNS distributed database is indexed by name, not by IP address, so in-addr.arpa (a special second-level domain) was created. It is based on IP addresses instead of domain names.

Lesson 4: Configuring a DNS Client

There are several methods available for configuring TCP/IP name resolution on Windows XP Professional clients. The method covered in this lesson uses DNS to provide name resolution. A second method is to use a HOSTS file. For networks without access to a DNS name server, creating a HOSTS file, which is a manually maintained local file, can provide host-to-IP address name resolution for applications and services. HOSTS files can also be used in environments in which name servers are available, but not all hosts are registered, perhaps because some hosts are only available to a limited number of clients.

If there is a computer on your network that is running Windows 2000 Server or Windows Server 2003 and has the DNS Service installed and configured on it, you should use DNS for name resolution. This lesson shows you how to configure your computer as a DNS client.

After this lesson, you will be able to

- Configure DNS server addresses on a computer running Windows XP Professional.
- Configure DNS query settings.

Estimated lesson time: 25 minutes

How to Configure DNS Server Addresses

Because DNS is a distributed database that is used in TCP/IP networks to translate computer names to IP addresses, you must first ensure that TCP/IP is enabled on a client running Windows XP Professional. Internet Protocol (TCP/IP) is enabled by default during Windows XP Professional installation. After you have confirmed that TCP/IP is enabled on your client, you are ready to configure your computer as a DNS client.

To configure your computer as a DNS client, use the following steps:

1. Click Start, and then click Control Panel.
2. In the Control Panel window, click Network And Internet Connections.
3. In the Network And Internet Connections window, click Network Connections.
4. Right-click Local Area Connection, and then click Properties.

   Windows XP Professional displays the Local Area Connection Properties dialog box.
5. Click Internet Protocol (TCP/IP), and then click Properties.

   Windows XP Professional displays the Internet Protocol (TCP/IP) Properties dialog box (see Figure 13-13).

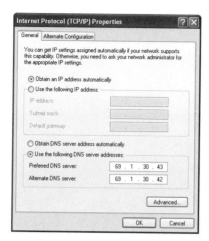

Figure 13-13   Configure DNS server addresses on a client computer.

6. Select one of the two following options:

   ❑ **Obtain DNS Server Address Automatically.** If you select this option, you must have a DHCP server available on your network to provide the IP address of a DNS server.

   ❑ **Use The Following DNS Server Addresses.** If you select this option, you must type in the IP addresses of the DNS servers you want this client to use. You can enter a Preferred DNS Server address and an Alternate DNS Server address.

In the Internet Protocol (TCP/IP) Properties dialog box, you can also click Advanced to open the Advanced TCP/IP Settings dialog box. Click the DNS tab, on which you can set additional configurations for DNS (see Figure 13-14). Additional options include the following:

■ Click Add to enter additional DNS server addresses to the list of servers that service this computer to resolve DNS domain names.

■ Click Edit to modify the addresses listed (for example, to correct an error you made in entering an IP address).

■ Click Remove to delete the address of a DNS server from the list.

■ Click the up-pointing arrow or down-pointing arrow to change the order of the servers listed. These arrows work like the up-pointing and down-pointing arrows you use to change the binding order. The order in which the addresses are listed is the order in which the servers are used. If you use the up-pointing arrow to move an address higher on the list, that server is used before all the servers listed after it. Conversely, using the down-pointing arrow to move a server lower on the list causes all servers that are listed above it to be used first to resolve DNS domain names.

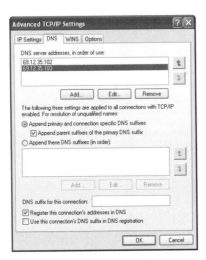

Figure 13-14   Use the Advanced TCP/IP Settings dialog box to configure additional DNS options.

How to Configure DNS Query Settings

In the Advanced TCP/IP Settings dialog box, you can also configure the way suffixes are added to queries.

Append Primary And Connection Specific DNS Suffixes Option

By default, the Append Primary And Connection Specific DNS Suffixes option (refer to Figure 13-14) is selected. This option causes the DNS resolver to append the client name to the primary domain name, as well as the domain name defined in the DNS Domain Name field of each network connection. The resolver then queries for that FQDN. If this query fails and you have specified a connection-specific DNS suffix in the DNS Suffix For This Connection text box, it causes the DNS resolver to append the client name to the name you specified there.

For example, assume that an organization's domain name is contoso.com. Querying for the FQDN of a specific computer in the domain (say, client1.contoso.com) would resolve that computer's IP address. If you were to configure the contoso.com suffix to be appended to queries, a user could query for an unqualified name (for example, by typing **client1** into the Internet Explorer address box). The computer would automatically append the suffix contoso.com to the query, creating the FQDN client1.contoso.com.

If a DHCP server configures this connection, and you do not specify a DNS suffix, a DNS suffix for the connection is assigned by an appropriately configured DHCP server. If you specify a DNS suffix, it is used instead of one assigned by a DHCP server.

The Append Parent Suffixes Of The Primary DNS Suffix check box is also selected by default. If it is selected, the DNS resolver strips off the leftmost portion of the primary DNS suffix and attempts the resulting domain name. If this fails, it continues stripping off the leftmost label and attempting the resulting domain name until only two labels remain.

For example, assume again that an organization uses the domain name north.contoso.com, and that the Append Primary And Connection Specific DNS Suffixes option is enabled. Normally, the suffix north.contoso.com would be added to unqualified queries, so that a user typing in **client1** would have the query appended to client1.north.contoso.com. If you enable the Append Parent Suffixes Of The Primary DNS Suffix option, DNS first uses the suffix north.contoso.com in the normal way. If that did not resolve, DNS would use the parent suffix contoso.com, and finally the parent suffix of that: .com. So when the user types **client1**, DNS would first try client1.north.contoso.com, then client1.contoso.com, and finally client1.com.

Append These DNS Suffixes (In Order) Option

By default, the Append Primary And Connection Specific DNS Suffixes option is selected, so the Append These DNS Suffixes (In Order) option is not selected; only one of these two options can be selected at one time. This option allows you to specify a list of domains to try. The DNS resolver adds each one of these suffixes one at a time and in the order you specified. Queries for unqualified names that are used on this computer are limited to the domains that you listed in Append These DNS Suffixes (In Order). Continuing the example from the previous section, you could specify that DNS suffixes be appended in the order .com, then contoso.com, and then north.contoso.com.

Register This Connection's Addresses In DNS Option

Selecting the Register This Connection's Addresses In DNS check box causes the computer to attempt to dynamically register the IP addresses (through DNS) of this computer with its full computer name. To view the computer name for this computer, click Start, click My Computer, click View System Information, and click the Computer Name tab.

Use This Connection's DNS Suffix In DNS Registration Option

Selecting the Use This Connection's DNS Suffix In DNS Registration check box causes the computer to use DNS dynamic updates to register the IP addresses and the connection-specific domain name of the connection. The connection-specific name of this DNS connection is the computer name, which is the first label of the full computer name specified in the Computer Name tab located in View System Information, and the DNS suffix of this connection. If the Register This Connection's Addresses In DNS check box is selected, this registration is in addition to the DNS registration of the full computer name.

Practice: Configuring a DNS Client

After completing this practice, you will be able to configure computers running Windows XP Professional as DNS clients.

1. Click Start, and then click Control Panel.

2. In the Control Panel window, click Network And Internet Connections.

3. Click Network Connections.

4. Right-click Local Area Connection, and then click Properties.

5. Click Internet Protocol (TCP/IP), and then click Properties.

6. In the Internet Protocol (TCP/IP) Properties dialog box, click Use The Following DNS Server Addresses.

7. In the Preferred DNS Server text box, type the IP address of the primary name server for this client.

Note If you are on a network, ask your network administrator the IP address of a primary and secondary DNS server you can use, and then type that address in the Preferred DNS Server text box. If you are not on a network, or if you do not have a DNS server on your network, type **192.168.1.203** as the Preferred DNS Server IP address and type **192.168.1.205** as the Alternate DNS Server IP address.

8. If there is a second name server available for this client, in the Alternate DNS Server text box, type the IP address of the second name server for this client.

    A client attempts to send its query requests to the preferred name server. If that name server is not responding, the client sends the query request to the alternate name server.

9. Click Advanced, and then in the Advanced TCP/IP Settings dialog box, click the DNS tab.

10. Under DNS Server Addresses, In Order Of Use, click Add.

11. If there is a third name server available for this client, in the TCP/IP DNS Server text box, type the IP address of the third available name server for this client.

Note If you are on a network, ask your network administrator for the IP address of a third DNS server you can use and type that address in the TCP/IP DNS Server text box. If you are not on a network or if you do not have a DNS server on your network, you can type **192.168.1.207** as an additional DNS Server IP address.

12. Click Add to add the third DNS server address and to close the TCP/IP DNS Server dialog box.

    There are now three addresses in the DNS Server Addresses, In Order Of Use list box.

13. Click OK to close the Advanced TCP/IP Settings dialog box.

14. Click OK to close the Internet Protocol (TCP/IP) Properties dialog box.

15. Click Close to close the Local Connection Properties dialog box.

16. Close the Network Connections window.

Lesson Review

The following questions are intended to reinforce key information presented in this lesson. If you are unable to answer a question, review the lesson materials and try the question again. You can find answers to the questions in the "Questions and Answers" section at the end of this chapter.

1. What is a HOSTS file, and when would you create one?

   _____

   _____

   _____

   _____

2. Which of the following functions do you perform by using the Advanced TCP/IP Settings dialog box? (Choose all that apply.)

   a. Edit the IP address of a DNS server.

   b. Delete the IP address of a DNS server.

   c. Enter additional IP addresses for other available DNS servers.

   d. Edit the IP addresses of the DHCP servers on the network.

3. What does selecting the Append These DNS Suffixes (In Order) option do?

   _____

   _____

Lesson Summary

- When configuring a DNS client in an environment in which there are DNS name servers, you can configure the client to obtain the address of the DNS server automatically from a DHCP server or you can manually enter multiple addresses for DNS servers.

- In the Advanced TCP/IP Settings dialog box, you can configure the way suffixes are added to queries.

Case Scenario Exercise

In this exercise, you will read a scenario about configuring TCP/IP on a client computer running Windows XP Professional, and then answer the questions that follow. If you have difficulty completing this work, review the material in this chapter before beginning the next chapter. You can find answers to these questions in the "Questions and Answers" section at the end of this chapter.

Scenario

You are working as an administrator for a company named Adventure Works, a leading supplier of skiing and snowboarding equipment. You are working with Andrew, a manager in the Engineering department who has recently made the decision to work several days each week from home. The company has provided Andrew with a new notebook computer that is running Windows XP Professional.

Questions

1. Andrew's notebook has a network adapter built-in. When he is at work, Andrew will connect the notebook to the company network. The company uses a DHCP server to provide IP addresses to computers on the network. How should you configure Andrew's computer to connect to the company network?

   _____

   _____

   _____

   _____

2. When Andrew is at home, he will connect his notebook computer to a digital subscriber line (DSL) modem supplied by his ISP. The ISP has issued Andrew a static IP address. How should you configure Andrew's computer so that it will use the static IP address when he is at home without interfering with the DHCP service on the company network?

_____

_____

_____

_____

_____

_____

_____

_____

_____

_____

_____

Troubleshooting Lab

You are working as an administrator for a company named Coho Vineyard, a national distributor of wines. Diane, a user in the Sales department, calls you on Tuesday morning to report that she cannot connect to any resources on the local network or on the Internet. After verifying that other users in her department can connect to the network, you visit Diane's computer, open the Command Prompt window, and type **ipconfig /all**. You get the following results:

Ethernet adapter Local Area Connection:

Connection-specific DNS Suffix

Description . . . . : Intel(R) PRO/1000 CT

Physical Address. . . . . : 1D-03-D2-E2-1A-2C

DHCP Enabled. . . . . : Yes

IP Address. . . . . : 169.254.103.52

Subnet Mask . . . . : 255.255.0.0

Default Gateway . . . . :

DNS Servers . . . . :

1. What do these results tell you?

_____

_____

_____

2. What would be your first troubleshooting step? What should you do if that first step does not work?

_____

_____

_____

_____

_____

_____

_____

_____

Chapter Summary

■ Microsoft's implementation of TCP/IP provides a robust, scalable, cross-platform client/server framework that is supported by most large networks, including the Internet. The TCP/IP suite of protocols maps to a four-layer conceptual model that includes the following layers: network access, Internet, transport, and application.

■ Each TCP/IP host is identified by a logical IP address that identifies a computer's location on the network. The IP address is composed of a network ID and a host ID. A subnet mask determines which portion of the IP address is the network ID and which portion is the host ID. You can configure Windows XP to use a static IP address or to obtain an IP address automatically. When configured to obtain an address automatically, Windows first attempts to lease an IP address from a DHCP server. If a DHCP server is unavailable, Windows XP assigns itself an IP address using APIPA.

■ The DNS database is indexed by name, so each domain (node) must have a name. The hierarchical structure of the domain namespace consists of a root domain, top-level domains, second-level domains, and host names.

■ DNS name servers resolve forward and reverse lookup queries. A forward lookup query resolves a name to an IP address, and a reverse lookup query resolves an IP address to a name. A name server can resolve a query only for a zone for which it has authority. If a name server cannot resolve the query, it passes the query to other name servers that can resolve it. The name server caches the query results to reduce the DNS traffic on the network.

■ When configuring a DNS client in an environment in which there are DNS name servers, you can configure the client to obtain the address of the DNS server automatically from a DHCP server or you can manually enter multiple addresses for DNS servers.

Exam Highlights

Before taking the exam, review the key points and terms that are presented in this chapter. You need to know this information.

Key Points

- Learn the IP address ranges that fall into each of the major classes (A, B, and C) and the default subnet mask for each class. This information will not only help determine how a classful IP addressing scheme will apply to a situation, but also how to customize a scheme using the classless method.

- If you are troubleshooting a network problem and discover that a client computer has an IP address on the 169.254.0.0 network, the computer has assigned itself that address using APIPA because the computer could not locate a DHCP server.

- Understand the various options available with the Ipconfig command. In particular, you should remember the following: /renew causes the computer to release and then attempt to renew an IP address lease from a DHCP server; /release causes the computer to release its IP address lease and not attempt to renew that lease; and /flushdns purges the local DNS cache.

Key Terms

Automatic Private IP Addressing (APIPA) A feature that allows Windows XP Professional to assign itself an IP address should the computer not be able to locate a DHCP server. Addresses in the range 169.254.0.0 through 169.254.255.255 are reserved for APIPA.

Domain Name System (DNS) A service that resolves domain names to IP addresses.

Dynamic Host Configuration Protocol (DHCP) A protocol for assigning IP addresses automatically to hosts on a TCP/IP network.

host ID The portion of an IP address that identifies the network segment on which a host is located.

IP address A 32-bit binary address (usually represented as four decimal numbers ranging from 0 to 255) that uniquely identifies a network interface on a TCP/IP network.

Ipconfig A command-line tool that allows you to view current TCP/IP configuration information for a computer.

loopback address A special reserved IP address that represents the local computer.

network ID The portion of the IP address that identifies a particular host on a network segment.

Pathping   A command-line tool that is a combination of both Ping and Tracert, which displays information about packet loss at every router between the host computer and the remote one.

Ping   A TCP/IP tool that allows you to check for connectivity between devices on a network.

subnet mask   A number similar to an IP address in a structure that defines which portion of an IP address is the network ID and which portion is the host ID.

Tracert   A command-line tool that shows the route that data moves along a network.

Transmission Control Protocol/Internet Protocol (TCP/IP)   The network protocol used on Windows networks and the Internet for communications between computers and other devices.

Questions and Answers

Lesson 1 Practice: Exercise 4

Page
13-18

1. Which message appears, and what does it indicate?

The message is as follows: An Error Occurred While Renewing Interface Local Area Connection: The Semaphore Timeout Period Has Expired. This error message indicates that Windows XP Professional could not renew the TCP/IP configuration.

7. Is this the same IP address assigned to your computer in Exercise 3? Why or why not?

No, this is not the same IP address assigned to the computer in Exercise 3. It is not the same address because this address is assigned by the Windows XP Professional APIPA.

10. Were you successful? Why or why not?

No, you would not be successful. Your computer has an address assigned by APIPA, and the test computer is on a different subnet.

Lesson 1 Review

Page
13-23

1. Why would you assign a computer a static IP address?

You can assign static IP addresses if there are no DHCP servers on the network, or you can use the APIPA feature. You should assign a static IP address to selected network computers, such as the computer running the DHCP Service. The computer running the DHCP Service cannot be a DHCP client, so it must have a static IP address.

2. Which of the following statements correctly describe IP addresses? (Choose all that apply.)

a. IP addresses are logical 64-bit addresses that identify a TCP/IP host.

b. Each network adapter card in a computer running TCP/IP requires a unique IP address.

c. 192.168.0.108 is an example of a class C IP address.

d. The host ID in an IP address is always the last two octets in the address.

The correct answers are B and C. A is not correct because IP addresses are 32-bit, not 64-bit addresses. D is not correct because the host ID in an IP address is determined by the subnet mask and is not always a fixed number of octets.

3. What is the purpose of a subnet mask?

A subnet mask blocks out part of the IP address so that TCP/IP can distinguish the network ID from the host ID.

4. By default, client computers running Windows XP Professional, Windows 95, or Windows 98 obtain TCP/IP configuration information automatically from the DHCP Service: True or false?

   True

5. Your computer running Windows XP Professional was configured manually for TCP/IP. You can connect to any host on your own subnet, but you cannot connect to or even ping any host on a remote subnet. What is the likely cause of the problem and how would you fix it?

   The default gateway might be missing or incorrect. You specify the default gateway in the Internet Protocol (TCP/IP) Properties dialog box (in the Network And Internet Connections dialog box under Network Connections). Other possibilities are that the default gateway is offline or the subnet mask is incorrect.

6. Your computer's Computer Name is Pro1, and you ping Pro1. The local address for Pro1 is returned as 169.254.128.71. What does this tell you?

   APIPA of Windows XP Professional has assigned your computer Pro1. This means that the local DHCP server is not configured properly or cannot be reached from your computer.

Lesson 2 Review

Page
13-31

1. What is DNS and what is it used for?

   DNS is a naming system that is used in TCP/IP networks to translate computer names to IP addresses. DNS makes it easy to locate computers and other resources on IP-based networks.

2. Which of the following statements correctly describes DNS root domains? (Choose all that apply.)

   a. The root domain is at the top of the hierarchy.

   b. The root domain is at the bottom of the hierarchy.

   c. The root domain is represented by a two- or three-character name code.

   d. The root domain is represented by a period (.).

   The correct answers are A and D. B is not correct because the root domain is at the top of the hierarchy. C is not correct because the root domain is represented by a period (.); top-level domains are represented by a two- or three-character name code.

3. Which of the following are second-level domain names? (Choose all that apply.)

   a. gov

   b. Microsoft.com

   c. au

   d. ed.gov

   The correct answers are B and D. A and C are not correct because these are representative of top-level domains.

4. _____ provide a way to partition the domain namespace into manageable sections, and each _____ represents a discrete portion of the domain namespace.

Zones; zone

Lesson 3 Review

Page
13-36

1. What is a forward lookup query and how is it resolved?

A forward lookup query is the resolving of a user-friendly DNS domain name to an IP address. To resolve a forward lookup query, a client passes a lookup query to its local name server. If the local name server can resolve the query, it returns the IP address for the name so the client can contact it. If the local name server cannot resolve the query, it passes the query on to one of the DNS root servers. The DNS root server sends back a referral to a name server that can resolve the request. The local name server sends the request to the name server it was referred to by the DNS root server. An IP address is returned to the local name server and the local name server sends the IP address to the client.

2. In DNS name resolution, which of the following statements about TTL are correct? (Choose all that apply.)

   a. TTL is the length of time a query can exist before it is discarded.

   b. Shorter TTL values help ensure that data about the domain namespace is more current across the network.

   c. Longer TTL values increase the amount of DNS traffic.

   d. Longer TTL values cause the cached values to be retained longer.

The correct answers are A, B, and D. C is not correct because longer TTL values do not increase DNS traffic, but shorter TTL values can increase it.

3. Which of the following statements about DNS name and address resolution are correct? (Choose all that apply.)

   a. The DNS distributed database is indexed by both names and IP addresses.

   b. The top-level domain in-addr.arpa is used for both forward and reverse queries.

   c. In the in-addr.arpa domain, the order of the IP address octets is reversed.

   d. Troubleshooting tools, such as the nslookup command-line tool, use reverse lookup queries to report back host names.

The correct answers are C and D. A is not correct because the DNS database is indexed by name, not by IP address. B is not correct because the top-level domain in-addr.arpa is used for reverse lookup queries, but not for forward lookup queries.

Lesson 4 Review

Page
13-43

1. What is a HOSTS file, and when would you create one?

A HOSTS file is a manually maintained local file that provides host-to-IP address resolution. You use a HOSTS file for networks without access to a DNS name server to provide host-to-IP address and NetBIOS-to-IP name resolution for applications and services.

2. Which of the following functions do you perform by using the Advanced TCP/IP Settings dialog box? (Choose all that apply.)

   a. Edit the IP address of a DNS server.

   b. Delete the IP address of a DNS server.

   c. Enter additional IP addresses for other available DNS servers.

   d. Edit the IP addresses of the DHCP servers on the network.

The correct answers are A, B, and C. D is not correct because you do not configure addresses for DHCP servers by using the Advanced TCP/IP Settings dialog box.

3. What does selecting the Append These DNS Suffixes (In Order) option do?

This option allows you to specify a list of domains to try when there is a query for an unqualified name. Queries are limited to the domains that you listed.

Case Scenario Exercise

Page
13-44

1. Andrew's notebook has a network adapter built-in. When he is at work, Andrew will connect the notebook to the company network. The company uses a DHCP server to provide IP addresses to computers on the network. How should you configure Andrew's computer to connect to the company network?

You should configure Andrew's computer to obtain an IP address automatically. You can do this by opening the Properties dialog box for the LAN connection, opening the Properties dialog box for the TCP/IP protocol, and then selecting the Obtain IP Address Automatically option.

2. When Andrew is at home, he will connect his notebook computer to a digital subscriber line (DSL) modem supplied by his ISP. The ISP has issued Andrew a static IP address. How should you configure Andrew's computer so that it will use the static IP address when he is at home without interfering with the DHCP service on the company network?

You should configure an alternate TCP/IP configuration on Andrew's computer. To do this, you must first make sure that his computer is configured to use automatic IP addressing as its primary configuration method. You can do this by opening the Properties dialog box for the LAN connection, opening the Properties dialog box for the TCP/IP protocol, and then selecting the Obtain IP Address Automatically option. When Windows XP Professional is configured to obtain an address automatically, an Alternate Configuration tab becomes available in the Internet Protocol (TCP/IP) Properties dialog box. On this tab, select the User Configured option and enter the appropriate IP address, subnet mask, default gateway, and DNS server addresses provided by the ISP.

Troubleshooting Lab

Page
13-45

1. What do these results tell you?

The computer is configured to connect to a DHCP server. However, the computer is not getting an IP address from a DHCP server successfully. You know this because the IP address is in the range assigned by APIPA.

2. What would be your first troubleshooting step? What should you do if that first step does not work?

You should type **ipconfig /renew** at the command prompt to force the computer to attempt to renew its lease with an available DHCP server. If the command is successful and the computer obtains a valid IP address, you have solved the problem. If the computer cannot obtain a valid IP address, you should first verify that the DHCP server is working. (It is likely that the DHCP is working because other users on the network can access the network.) If DHCP is functioning properly, you should check to make sure that the network cable is connected to the network adapter and that the network adapter is functioning properly.

14 Overview of Active Directory Service

Exam Objectives in this Chapter:

- This chapter does not cover any specific exam objectives. It is intended to introduce you to Active Directory directory service.

Why This Chapter Matters

A directory service uniquely defines users and resources on a network. Directory services based on **Active Directory** technology in Microsoft Windows 2000 Server or Windows Server 2003 provide a single point of network management, allowing you to add, remove, and relocate users and resources easily. This chapter introduces you to the Active Directory directory service.

Lessons in this Chapter:

> **Note** Active Directory is not a service that you can run on a computer running Windows XP Professional. Active Directory runs on a computer running Windows 2000 Server or Windows Server 2003 that is part of a domain. After the Active Directory service is installed on a server, that server becomes a domain controller. Computers running Windows XP Professional can become members of the domain.

Before You Begin

To complete this chapter, you must have a computer that meets the minimum hardware requirements listed in the preface, "About This Book." You must also have Windows XP Professional installed on your computer. You do not need access to an Active Directory domain in order to complete this chapter.

Lesson 1: Overview of Active Directory

Most computers running Windows XP Professional on large networks are clients in an Active Directory domain running Windows 2000 Server or Windows Server 2003. Much like a phone book acts as a directory of people's phone numbers and street addresses, Active Directory acts as a directory for resources on a network. Active Directory catalogs information about all the objects on a network, including users, computers, and printers, and makes that information available throughout a network. Active Directory provides a consistent way to name, find, manage, and secure information about these resources.

After this lesson, you will be able to

- Identify the advantages of Active Directory
- Describe the logical structure of Active Directory
- Describe the physical structure of Active Directory
- Describe replication within an Active Directory site

Estimated lesson time: 15 minutes

The Advantages of Active Directory

In a workgroup environment, each computer running Windows XP Professional is responsible for maintaining its own security database. Local user accounts are used to log on to the computer and to control access to resources on the computer. Security and administration in a workgroup are distributed. You must create local user accounts on each computer, and although you can often manage a computer remotely, you must manage each computer separately. The larger the network you are working with, the more overhead this distributed management creates.

Active Directory simplifies the security and administration of resources throughout a network (including the computers that are part of the network) by providing a single point of administration for all objects on the network. Active Directory organizes resources hierarchically in **domains**, which are logical groupings of servers and other network resources. Each domain includes one or more domain controllers. A **domain controller** is a computer running Windows 2000 Server or Windows Server 2003 on which Active Directory is installed. The domain controller stores a complete replica of the domain directory. To simplify administration, all domain controllers in the domain are peers. You can make changes to any domain controller, and the updates are replicated to all other domain controllers in the domain.

One big advantage that Active Directory provides is a single logon point for all network resources, so a user can log on to the network with a single user name and password, and then access any resources to which the user account is granted access. An administrator can log on to one computer and administer objects on any computer in the network.

Windows XP Professional provides a wide range of security settings that you can enforce (you will learn all about them in Chapter 16, "Configuring Security Settings and Internet Options"). You can enforce these settings locally by configuring them on each computer (and that is the way you have to do it in a workgroup environment). In an Active Directory environment, you can use a feature named Group Policy to enforce settings on all computers on the network. This allows the network administrator to make changes faster and improve network functionality without requiring user intervention to invoke changes.

On the CD   To learn more about how Active Directory provides single logon for network users, view the multimedia presentation "How Active Directory Enables a Single Sign-On," which is included in the Multimedia folder on the CD accompanying this book.

Logical Structure of Active Directory

What makes Active Directory so configurable and so scalable is that it separates the **logical structure** of the administrative hierarchy—which is made up of domains, trees, forests, organizational units (OUs), and objects—from the physical structure of the network itself. The logical structure of Active Directory does not rely on the physical location of servers or the network connectivity throughout the domain. This abstraction of the logical structure from the physical structure provides the powerful ability to structure domains according to your administrative and organizational needs.

Because Active Directory separates the logical structure of network resources from the physical structure of the network itself, it is useful to break the discussion of Active Directory along those same lines. The logical components of the Active Directory structure include the following (see Figure 14-1):

- Objects
- Organizational units
- Domains
- Trees
- Forests

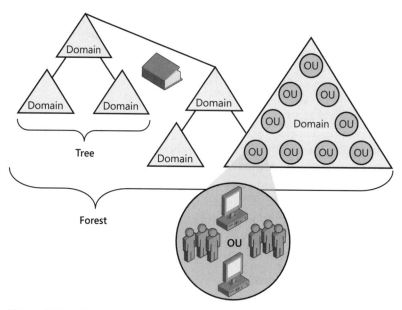

Figure 14-1 Resources are organized in a logical, hierarchical structure.

Objects

An **object** is a distinct named set of attributes that represents a network resource. Object attributes are characteristics of objects in the directory. For example, the attributes of a user account might include the user's first and last names, department, and e-mail address (see Figure 14-2). Objects are stored in the Active Directory in a hierarchical structure of containers and subcontainers, making the objects easier to find, access, and manage—much like organizing files in a set of Windows folders.

In Active Directory, you can organize objects in classes, which are logical groupings of objects. Object classes help organize objects by their similarities. For example, all user objects fall under the object class Users. When you create a new object, it automatically inherits attributes from its class. When you create a new user account, the information you can enter about that user account (its attributes) are derived from the object class Users. Microsoft defines a default set of object classes (and the attributes they define) used by Active Directory. Of course, because Active Directory is extensible, administrators and applications can modify the object classes available and the attributes that those classes define.

The classes and the attributes that they define are collectively referred to as the **Active Directory schema**—in database terms, a schema is the structure of the tables and fields and how they are related to one another. You can think of the Active Directory schema as a collection of data (object classes) that defines how the real data of the directory (the attributes of an object) is organized and stored.

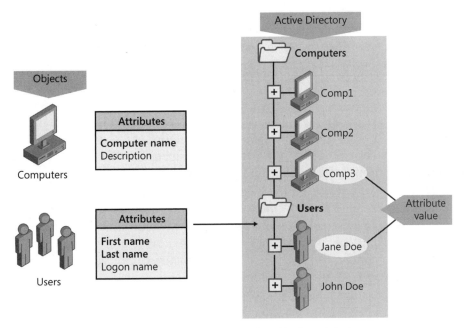

Figure 14-2   Each Active Directory object is defined by its attributes.

> **Note**   Some objects, known as containers, can contain other objects. For example, a domain is a container object.

Organizational Units

Enterprises often have thousands of computers, groups, and users. If you had several thousand computers in a single list, it would be very difficult to identify all the computers belonging to, say, the Accounting department, or located within the Boston office. Enterprises need a way to organize these objects. An **organizational unit** (OU) is a container used to organize objects within a domain into logical administrative groups. OUs provide a way to create administrative boundaries within a domain, allowing you to delegate administrative tasks within the domain. An OU can contain objects such as user accounts, groups, computers, printers, applications, file shares, and other OUs (refer to Figure 14-1).

The OU hierarchy within a domain is independent of the OU hierarchy structure of other domains—each domain can implement its own OU hierarchy. There are no restrictions on the depth of the OU hierarchy. However, a shallow hierarchy performs better than a deep one, so you should not create an OU hierarchy any deeper than necessary.

> **Exam Tip**   You can delegate administrative tasks by assigning permissions to OUs. OUs provide a way to structure the administrative needs of an organization without using excessive numbers of domains.

Domains

The core unit of logical structure in Active Directory is the domain. Using domains allows administrators to divide the network into manageable boundaries. In addition, administrators from different domains can establish their own security models (including password complexity and password-length requirements); security from one domain can then be isolated so that other domains' security models are not affected. Primarily, domains provide a way to logically partition a network along the same administrative lines as an organization. Organizations that are large enough to have more than one domain usually have divisions that are responsible for maintaining and securing their own resources. Grouping objects into one or more domains enables your network to reflect your company's organization. Domains share the following characteristics:

- All network objects exist within a domain, and each domain stores information only about the objects that it contains. Theoretically, a domain directory can contain up to 10 million objects, but 1 million objects per domain is a more practical amount.

- A domain is a administrative boundary. Access control lists (ACLs) control access to domain objects. ACLs contain the permissions associated with objects that control which users can gain access to an object and what type of access users can gain. In Active Directory, objects include files, folders, shares, printers, and Active Directory objects. All security policies and settings—such as administrative rights, security policies, and ACLs—do not cross from one domain to another.

Trees

A **tree** is a hierarchical arrangement of one or more domains that share a common schema and a contiguous namespace. In the example shown in Figure 14-3, all the domains in the tree under the microsoft.com root domain share the namespace microsoft.com.

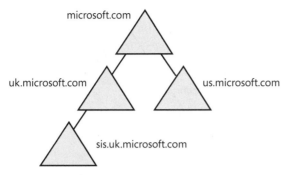

Figure 14-3   A domain tree is a hierarchical grouping of domains that share a contiguous namespace.

The first domain you create in a tree is called the root domain. The next domain that you add becomes a child domain of that root. Trees have the following characteristics:

- Following DNS standards, the domain name of a child domain is the relative name of that child domain appended with the name of the parent domain.

- All domains within a single tree share a common schema, which is a formal definition of all object types that you can store in an Active Directory deployment.

- All domains within a single tree share a common Global Catalog, which is the central repository of information about objects in a tree.

Forests

A **forest** is a grouping or hierarchical arrangement of one or more domain trees that form a disjointed namespace, but might share a common schema and Global Catalog (see Figure 14-4). In the example shown in Figure 14-4, the namespace microsoft.com is represented in one tree, and the namespace msn.com is represented in another. There is always at least one forest on a network, and it is created when the first Active Directory–enabled computer (domain controller) on a network is installed. This first domain in a forest, called the forest root domain, is special because it holds the schema and controls domain naming for the entire forest. It cannot be removed from the forest without removing the entire forest itself. Also, no other domain can ever be created above the forest root domain in the forest domain hierarchy.

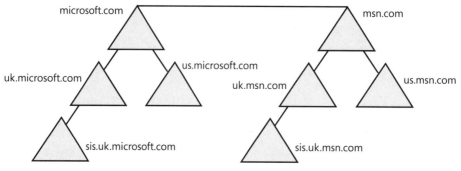

Figure 14-4   A forest is a group of one or more domain trees.

Forests have the following characteristics:

■ All trees in a forest share a common schema.

■ Trees in a forest have different naming structures, according to their domains.

■ All domains in a forest share a common Global Catalog.

■ Domains in a forest operate independently, but the forest enables communication across the entire organization.

A forest is the outermost boundary of Active Directory; the directory cannot be larger than the forest. However, you can create multiple forests and then create trust relationships between specific domains in those forests; this process would let you grant access to resources and accounts that are outside of a particular forest.

On the CD   At this point, you should view the multimedia presentation "The Logical Structure of Active Directory," which is included in the Multimedia folder on the CD accompanying this book. This presentation will help deepen your understanding of Active Directory.

Real World   Using a Simple Structure

What with domains, trees, forests, and OUs, you can see how enticing it could be to try to use all these components to organize your Active Directory implementation. However, you are best served by keeping your design as simple as your organizational needs allow. The details involved in designing and implementing an Active Directory setup are challenging enough without unnecessary complication. If you can work with a single domain and a couple of OUs to help organize administrative tasks, then do it. The whole purpose of Active Directory is to ease the burden of administration. A simple, well-thought-out design goes a long way toward achieving this purpose.

Physical Structure of Active Directory

The physical components of Active Directory, domain controllers and sites, are used to mirror the physical structure of an organization.

Domain Controllers

A domain controller is a computer running Windows 2000 Server or Windows Server 2003 that stores a replica of the domain directory (local domain database). You can create any number of domain controllers in a domain. Each domain controller in a given domain has a complete replica of that domain's directory partition. Domain controllers locally resolve queries for information about objects in their domain and refer queries regarding information they do not hold to domain controllers in other domains. Domain controllers also manage changes to directory information and are responsible for replicating those changes to other domain controllers.

Because each domain controller holds a full replica of the directory partition for their domain, domain controllers follow what is known as a multimaster model: Every domain controller holds a master copy of the partition that can be used to modify that information.

The functions of domain controllers include the following:

- Each domain controller stores a complete copy of all Active Directory information for that domain, manages changes to that information, and replicates those changes to other domain controllers in the same domain.

- Domain controllers in a domain automatically replicate all objects in the domain to each other. When you perform an action that causes an update to Active Directory, you are actually making the change at one of the domain controllers. That domain controller then replicates the change to all other domain controllers within the domain. You can control replication of traffic between domain controllers in the network by specifying how often replication occurs and the amount of data that Active Directory replicates at one time.

- Domain controllers immediately replicate certain important updates, such as the disabling of a user account.

- Active Directory uses multimaster replication, in which no one domain controller is the master domain controller. Instead, all domain controllers within a domain are peers, and each domain controller contains a copy of the directory database that can be written to. Domain controllers can hold different information for short periods of time until all domain controllers have synchronized changes to Active Directory.

- Domain controllers detect collisions, which can occur when an attribute is modified on a domain controller before a change to the same attribute on another domain controller is completely propagated. Collisions are detected by comparing each attribute's property version number, a number specific to an attribute that is initialized on creation of the attribute. Active Directory resolves the collision by replicating the changed attribute with the higher property version number.

- Having more than one domain controller in a domain provides fault tolerance. If one domain controller is offline, another domain controller can provide all required functions, such as recording changes to Active Directory.

- Domain controllers manage all aspects of user domain interaction, such as locating Active Directory objects and validating user logon attempts.

In general, there should be at least one domain controller for each domain in each site for authentication purposes. However, authentication requirements for your organization determine the number of domain controllers and their locations.

Sites

A **site** is a combination of one or more Internet Protocol (IP) subnets connected by a highly reliable, fast link to localize as much network traffic as possible. Typically, a site has the same boundaries as a local area network (LAN). When you group subnets on your network, you should combine only those subnets that have fast, cheap, and reliable network connections with one another. Fast network connections are at least 512 kilobits per second (Kbps). An available bandwidth of 128 Kbps and higher is sufficient.

With Active Directory, sites are not part of the namespace. When you browse the logical namespace, you see computers and users grouped into domains and OUs, not sites. Sites contain only computer objects and connection objects used to configure replication between sites.

Note   A single domain can span multiple geographical sites, and a single site can include user accounts and computers belonging to multiple domains.

On the CD   At this point, you should view the multimedia presentation "The Physical Structure of Active Directory," which is included in the Multimedia folder on the CD accompanying this book.

Replication Within an Active Directory Site

Active Directory also includes a replication feature. **Replication** ensures that changes to a domain controller are reflected in all domain controllers within a domain. To understand replication, you must understand domain controllers. A domain controller stores a replica of the domain directory. Each domain can contain one or more domain controllers.

Within a site, Active Directory automatically generates a ring topology for replication among domain controllers in the same domain. The topology defines the path for directory updates to flow from one domain controller to another until all receive the directory updates (see Figure 14-5).

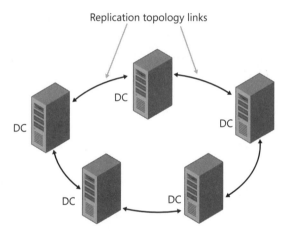

Replication topology links

DC

DC

DC

DC

DC

Figure 14-5 Within a site, replication between domain controllers happens automatically.

The ring structure ensures that there are at least two replication paths from one domain controller to another. Therefore, if one domain controller is down temporarily, replication still continues to all other domain controllers.

Active Directory periodically analyzes the replication topology within a site to ensure that it is still efficient. If you add or remove a domain controller from the network or a site, Active Directory reconfigures the topology to reflect the change.

On the CD At this point, please view the multimedia presentation "Replication Within Sites," which is included in the Multimedia folder on the CD accompanying this book.

Lesson Review

Use the following questions to help determine whether you have learned enough to move on to the next lesson. If you have difficulty answering these questions, review the material in this lesson before beginning the next lesson. You can find answers to these questions in the "Questions and Answers" section at the end of this chapter.

1. In Active Directory, you organize resources in a logical structure. What advantage does this provide?

   _____

   _____

   _____

2. A(n) _____ is a distinct, named set of attributes that represents a network resource.

3. What component do you use to organize objects into logical administrative groups? (Choose the correct answer.)

   a. Site

   b. Tree

   c. Domain

   d. OU

4. A(n) _____ is a grouping or hierarchical arrangement of one or more _____ that form a disjointed namespace.

5. The physical components of Active Directory are _____ and _____.

Lesson Summary

■ The logical structure of Active Directory is made up of domains, trees, forests, OUs, and objects. The logical structure is separated from the physical structure of the network itself, and does not rely on the physical location of servers or the network connectivity throughout the domain. The major components of the logical structure include the following:

   ❑ The core unit of logical structure in Active Directory is the domain. All network objects exist within a domain, and each domain stores information only about the objects that it contains.

❑ An OU is a container used to organize objects within a domain into logical administrative groups. An OU can contain objects such as user accounts, groups, computers, printers, applications, file shares, and other OUs.

❑ A tree is a grouping or hierarchical arrangement of one or more Active Directory domains that share a contiguous namespace.

❑ A forest is a grouping or hierarchical arrangement of one or more trees that forms a disjointed namespace.

■ The physical structure of Active Directory is based the underlying network. Major components of the physical structure include the following:

❑ A domain controller is a computer running Windows 2000 Server or Windows Server 2003 that stores a replica of the domain directory (local domain database). You can create any number of domain controllers in a domain. Each domain controller in a given domain has a complete replica of that domain's directory partition.

❑ A site is a combination of one or more IP subnets connected by a high-speed link.

■ Within a site, Active Directory automatically generates a ring topology for replication among domain controllers in the same domain. The ring structure ensures that there are at least two replication paths from one domain controller to another; if one domain controller is down temporarily, replication continues to all other domain controllers.

Lesson 2: Important Active Directory Concepts

There are several new concepts introduced with Active Directory. It is important that you understand their meaning as applied to Active Directory.

After this lesson, you will be able to

- Describe the purpose of the Active Directory schema
- Describe the purpose of a Global Catalog
- Explain the concept of a namespace
- Identify naming conventions used in Active Directory

Estimated lesson time: 30 minutes

What Is the Active Directory Schema?

The Active Directory schema defines objects that can be stored in Active Directory. The schema is a list of definitions that determines the kinds of objects and the type of information about those objects that can be stored in Active Directory.

The schema contains two types of definition objects: schema class objects and schema attribute objects. Class objects and attribute objects are defined in separate lists within the schema (see Figure 14-6). Schema class and attribute objects are also referred to as schema objects.

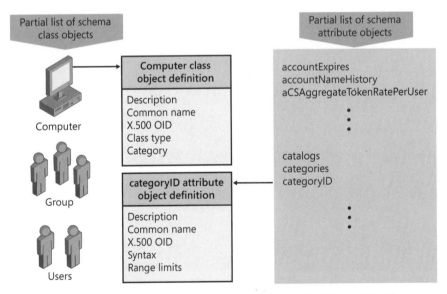

Figure 14-6 The schema is made up of class objects and attribute objects.

Schema class objects describe the possible Active Directory objects that can be created. Each schema class is a collection of schema attribute objects. For each object class, the schema defines which attributes an instance of the class must have, which additional attributes it can have, and which object class can be a parent of the current object class. Every object in Active Directory is an instance of a schema class object.

Schema attribute objects define the schema class objects with which they are associated. Each schema attribute is defined only once and can be used in multiple schema classes. Because the schema definitions are themselves stored as objects in Active Directory, they can be administered in the same manner as the rest of the objects in Active Directory.

Installing Active Directory on the first domain controller in a network creates a default schema that contains a set of basic schema class attributes. The default schema also contains definitions of objects and properties that Active Directory uses internally to function.

The Active Directory schema is extensible, which means that you can define new directory object types and attributes and new attributes for existing objects. For example, Microsoft Exchange Server extends the schema to add e-mail properties to user account information in Active Directory. You can also extend the schema directly by using the Schema Manager snap-in or the Active Directory Service Interface (ADSI). Only experienced developers or network administrators should dynamically extend the schema by defining new classes and attributes for existing classes.

The schema is implemented and stored within Active Directory itself (in the Global Catalog), and it can be updated dynamically. As a result, an application can extend the schema with new attributes and classes and use the extensions immediately.

Note   Write access to the schema is limited to members of the Schema Admins group by default.

What Is the Global Catalog?

Active Directory allows users and administrators to find objects (such as files, printers, or users) in their own domain. However, finding objects outside of the domain and across the enterprise requires a mechanism that allows the domains to act as one entity. A catalog service contains selected information about every object in all domains in the directory, which is useful for performing searches across an enterprise. The catalog service provided by Active Directory services is called the **Global Catalog**.

The Global Catalog is the central repository of information about objects in a tree or forest, as shown in Figure 14-7. By default, a Global Catalog is created automatically on the first domain controller in the first domain in the forest, and the domain controller containing the Global Catalog is known as the Global Catalog server. Using Active Directory service's multimaster replication, the Global Catalog information is replicated between Global Catalog servers in other domains.

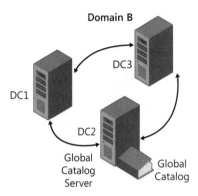

Figure 14-7   The Global Catalog is the central repository of information about objects in a forest.

By default, the attributes stored in the Global Catalog are those most frequently used in search operations (such as a user's first and last name, logon name, and so forth) and those necessary to locate a full replica of the object. As a result, you can use the Global Catalog to locate objects anywhere in the network without replication of all domain information between domain controllers.

Note   You use the Schema Manager snap-in to define which attributes are included in the Global Catalog replication process.

You can designate additional domain controllers as Global Catalog servers by using the Active Directory Sites and Services Management snap-in. When considering which domain controllers to designate as Global Catalog servers, base your decision on the capability of your network structure to handle replication and query traffic. The more Global Catalog servers you have, the greater is the replication traffic. However, the availability of additional servers can provide quicker responses to user inquiries. Every major site in your enterprise should have a Global Catalog server.

On the CD   At this point, please view the multimedia presentation "The Role of Universal Groups in the Logon Process," which is included in the Multimedia folder on the CD accompanying this book. This presentation will help you understand better how Global Catalog servers are used in Active Directory.

What Is a Namespace?

Active Directory, like all directory services, is primarily a **namespace**, which is any bounded area in which a name can be resolved. Name resolution is the process of translating a name into some object or information that the name represents. The Active Directory namespace is based on the DNS naming scheme, which allows for interoperability with Internet technologies. An example namespace is shown in Figure 14-8.

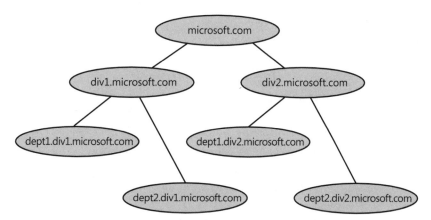

Figure 14-8   A namespace is a bounded area in which a name can be resolved.

Using a common namespace allows you to unify and manage multiple hardware and software environments in your network. There are two types of namespaces:

Contiguous namespace   The name of the child object in an object hierarchy always contains the name of the parent domain. A tree is a contiguous namespace.

Disjointed namespace   The names of a parent object and a child of the same parent object are not directly related to one another. A forest is a disjointed namespace.

> **Exam Tip**   The word *namespace* is often used. Remember that, at its simplest, a namespace is a structure (often a database) in which all objects are named similarly but are still uniquely identified.

Naming Conventions

Every object in Active Directory is identified by a name. Active Directory uses a variety of naming conventions: distinguished names, relative distinguished names, globally unique identifiers, and user principal names.

Distinguished Name

Every object in Active Directory has a **distinguished name** (DN), which uniquely identifies an object and contains sufficient information for a client to retrieve the object from the directory. The DN includes the name of the domain that holds the object, as well as the complete path through the container hierarchy to the object.

For example, the following DN identifies the *Firstname Lastname* user object in the microsoft.com domain (where *Firstname* and *Lastname* represent the actual first and last names of a user account):

/DC=COM/DC=microsoft/OU=dev/CN=Users/CN=*Firstname Lastname*

Table 14-1 describes the attributes in the example.

Table 14-1   Distinguished Name Attributes

Attribute	Description
DC	The DC, or DomainComponentName, indicates the domain in which the object is defined.
OU	The OU, or OrganizationalUnitName, indicates the organizational unit in which the object exists.
CN	The CN, or CommonName, is the actual name of the object.

DNs must be unique because Active Directory does not allow duplicate DNs.

Relative Distinguished Name

Active Directory supports querying by attributes, so you can locate an object even if the exact DN is unknown or has changed. The **relative distinguished name** (RDN) of an object is the part of the name that is an attribute of the object itself. In the preceding example, the RDN of the Firstname Lastname user object is *Firstname Lastname*. The RDN of the parent object is Users.

You can have duplicate RDNs for Active Directory objects, but you cannot have two objects with the same RDN in the same OU. For example, if a user account is named Jane Doe, you cannot have another user account called Jane Doe in the same OU. However, objects with duplicate RDNs can exist in separate OUs because they have different DNs (see Figure 14-9).

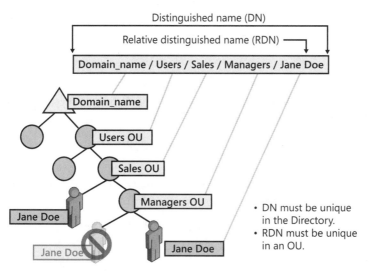

Figure 14-9   DNs must be unique to a directory, whereas RDNs are unique within an OU.

Globally Unique Identifier

A **globally unique identifier** (GUID) is a 128-bit number that is guaranteed to be unique. GUIDs are assigned to objects when they are created. The GUID never changes, even if you move or rename the object. Applications can store the GUID of an object and use it to retrieve that object regardless of its current DN.

User Principal Name

User accounts have a "friendly" name, the **user principal name** (UPN). The UPN is composed of a "shorthand" name for the user account and the DNS name of the tree in which the user account object resides. For example, user *Firstname Lastname* (substitute the first and last names of an actual user) in the microsoft.com tree might have a UPN of FirstnameL@microsoft.com (using the full first name and the first letter of the last name).

Lesson Review

Use the following questions to help determine whether you have learned enough to move on to the next lesson. If you have difficulty answering these questions, review the material in this lesson before beginning the next lesson. You can find answers to these questions in the "Questions and Answers" section at the end of this chapter.

1. What is the Active Directory schema?

   _____

   _____

   _____

2. Which of the following statements are correct for Active Directory Global Catalogs? (Choose all that apply.)

   a. The Global Catalog is the central repository of information about objects in a tree or forest.

   b. By default, a Global Catalog is created automatically on the first domain controller in the first domain in the forest.

   c. The Global Catalog is a list of definitions that determines the kinds of objects and the type of information about those objects that can be stored in Active Directory.

   d. You can have only one Global Catalog server in each domain.

3. Every object in Active Directory has a(n) _____ that uniquely identifies an object and contains sufficient information for a client to retrieve the object from the Directory.

4. A(n) _____ is a 128-bit number that is assigned to an object when it is created and is guaranteed to be unique.

5. What is the difference between a contiguous namespace and a disjointed namespace? Give an example of each type of namespace.

   _____

   _____

   _____

   _____

   _____

Lesson Summary

- The schema contains a formal definition of the contents and structure of Active Directory, including all classes and attributes. Installing Active Directory on the first domain controller in a network creates a default schema.

- The Global Catalog contains selected information about every object in all domains in the directory.

- In a contiguous namespace, the name of the child object in an object hierarchy always contains the name of the parent domain. A tree is an example of a contiguous namespace. In a disjointed namespace, the names of a parent object and of a child of the same parent object are not directly related to one another. A forest is an example of a disjointed namespace.

- Every object in Active Directory is identified by a name. Active Directory uses a variety of naming conventions: DNs, RDNs, GUIDs, and UPNs.

Case Scenario Exercise

In this exercise, you will read a scenario about Active Directory concepts and then answer the questions that follow. If you have difficulty completing this work, review the material in this chapter before beginning the next chapter. You can find answers to these questions in the "Questions and Answers" section at the end of this chapter.

Scenario

You are an administrator who has just been hired by a small company named Fabrikam, Inc., a marketing company with its headquarters in Memphis, TN, and one branch office in Chicago, IL. The company is building its network from scratch and has already decided on the following:

- Because the Memphis headquarters is located in a single building, the company will deploy a single high-speed LAN.

- It will deploy another single high-speed LAN in the branch office in Chicago.

- The two LANs will be connected by a high-speed, dedicated wide area network (WAN) connection.

- The main IT staff will be located in Memphis. A smaller IT staff will be located in Chicago and will need administrative authority over the Chicago network.

- The company has acquired the domain name fabrikam.com and wants to use that name throughout its implementation in both Memphis and Chicago.

- Users should be able to log on easily anywhere within the company (both locations) without having to specify where they are logging on.

Questions

1. Would you suggest a single domain or multiple domains for this organization? Why?

   _____

   _____

   _____

   _____

   _____

   _____

2. How many sites should you suggest? Why?

   _____

   _____

   _____

   _____

3. Which logical Active Directory structure would allow you to group objects in the Chicago location so that local administrators could manage those objects?

   _____

   _____

4. How many Global Catalog servers should you suggest and where would you place them?

   _____

   _____

Troubleshooting Lab

You are working as an administrator for a company named Contoso, Ltd., which produces specialized product-labeling machines for large manufacturing companies. You are working with a group of administrators and managers who are trying to determine the best Active Directory structure for a new network. The company is structured in the following manner:

- Contoso, Ltd. has a main office in Dallas, TX, and a branch office in Houston, TX.

- Contoso, Ltd. has recently acquired another company named Litware, Inc. Litware is located in Austin, TX.

Contoso, Ltd. has registered the domain name contoso.com and wants to use it for the main and branch office (in Dallas and Houston). However, they want the domain structure to reflect the different locations.

The company also owns the domain name litware.com and wants to continue using that name in the domain structure to reflect the acquired company, so that the acquired company maintains its own identity.

1. One of the managers has proposed a model that uses a single domain tree with two domains. Why would this type of model not meet the requirements?

    _____

    _____

    _____

2. Using what you have learned in this chapter, sketch a diagram of a domain structure that meets these requirements.

Chapter Summary

- Active Directory is the directory service included in the Windows 2000 Server and Windows Server 2003 networks. A directory service is a network service that identifies all resources on a network and makes them accessible to users and applications. Active Directory offers simplified administration, scalability, and open standards support.

- The logical structure of Active Directory is made up of domains, trees, forests, OUs, and objects. The logical structure is separated from the physical structure of the network itself, and does not rely on the physical location of servers or the network connectivity throughout the domain. The physical structure of Active Directory is based on the underlying network and is made up of domain controllers and sites.

- There are a number of concepts important to your understanding of Active Directory. These concepts include:

  - The schema contains a formal definition of the contents and structure of Active Directory, including all classes and attributes. Installing Active Directory on the first domain controller in a network creates a default schema.

  - The Global Catalog contains selected information about every object in all domains in the directory.

  - In a contiguous namespace, the name of the child object in an object hierarchy always contains the name of the parent domain. A tree is an example of a contiguous namespace. In a disjointed namespace, the names of a parent object and of a child of the same parent object are not directly related to one another. A forest is an example of a disjointed namespace.

  - Every object in Active Directory is identified by a name. Active Directory uses a variety of naming conventions: distinguished names, relative distinguished names, globally unique identifiers, and user principal names.

Exam Highlights

Before taking the exam, review the key points and terms that are presented in this chapter. You need to know this information.

Key Points

- You can delegate administrative tasks by assigning permissions to OUs, which provide a way to structure the administrative needs of an organization without using excessive numbers of domains.

- At its simplest, a namespace is a structure in which all objects are named similarly, but are still uniquely identified.

Key Terms

Active Directory   The directory service included in Windows 2000 Server and Windows Server 2003 that identifies all resources on a network and makes them accessible to users and applications.

Active Directory schema   The structure of the tables and fields and how they are related to one another. In Active Directory, the schema is a collection of data (object classes) that defines how the real data of the directory (the attributes of an object) is organized and stored.

distinguished name (DN) A name that uniquely identifies an object within Active Directory and contains sufficient information for a client to retrieve the object from the directory.

domain A logical grouping of servers and other network resources under a single domain name. The domain is the basic unit of replication and security in an Active Directory network.

domain controller A computer running Windows 2000 Server or Windows Server 2003 on which the Active Directory service is installed. The domain controller stores a complete replica of the domain directory.

forest A grouping or hierarchical arrangement of one or more domain trees that form a disjointed namespace but can share a common schema and Global Catalog.

Global Catalog The central repository of information about objects in a tree or forest.

globally unique identifier (GUID) A 128-bit number, guaranteed to be unique, that is assigned to an object created in Active Directory.

logical structure The administrative structure of Active Directory that includes domains, trees, organizational units, and objects.

namespace Any bounded area in which a name can be resolved.

object A distinct named set of attributes that represents a network resource.

organizational unit (OU) A container used to organize objects within a domain into logical administrative groups. OUs provide a way to create administrative boundaries within a domain.

relative distinguished name (RDN) A name that uniquely identifies an object within a particular OU.

replication The process of copying information from one location to another. In Active Directory, replication of directory information happens automatically between domain controllers in the same site.

site A combination of one or more IP subnets connected by a highly reliable and fast link to localize as much network traffic as possible.

tree A hierarchical arrangement of one or more domains that share a common schema and a contiguous namespace.

user principal name (UPN) A "shorthand" name representing the user account and the DNS name of the tree where the user account object resides.

Questions and Answers

Lesson 1 Review

Page
14-12

1. In Active Directory, you organize resources in a logical structure. What advantage does this provide?

Grouping resources logically enables you to find a resource by its name rather than its physical location. Because you group resources logically, Active Directory makes the network's physical structure transparent to users.

2. A(n) _____ is a distinct, named set of attributes that represents a network resource.

object

3. What component do you use to organize objects into logical administrative groups? (Choose the correct answer.)

   a. Site

   b. Tree

   c. Domain

   d. OU

The correct answer is D. OUs are user-created containers used to organize resources for administration. A is not correct because a site is a physical structure that relies on the underlying network architecture. B is not correct because a tree is a hierarchical grouping of domains that share a contiguous namespace. C is not correct because a domain represents computers, users, and other objects that share a common security database.

4. A(n) _____ is a grouping or hierarchical arrangement of one or more _____ that form a disjointed namespace.

Forest; domain trees

5. The physical components of Active Directory are _____ and _____.

Domain controllers; sites

Lesson 2 Review

Page
14-19

1. What is the Active Directory schema?

The Active Directory schema defines objects that can be stored in Active Directory. The schema is a list of definitions that determines the kinds of objects and the type of information about those objects that can be stored in Active Directory.

2. Which of the following statements are correct for Active Directory Global Catalogs? (Choose all that apply.)

   a. The Global Catalog is the central repository of information about objects in a tree or forest.

   b. By default, a Global Catalog is created automatically on the first domain controller in the first domain in the forest.

   c. The Global Catalog is a list of definitions that determines the kinds of objects and the type of information about those objects that can be stored in Active Directory.

   d. You can have only one Global Catalog server in each domain.

   The correct answers are A and B. C is not correct because this statement describes the Active Directory schema, not a Global Catalog. D is not correct because you can have multiple Global Catalog servers in a domain.

3. Every object in Active Directory has a(n) _____ that uniquely identifies an object and contains sufficient information for a client to retrieve the object from the Directory.

   DN

4. A(n) _____ is a 128-bit number that is assigned to an object when it is created and is guaranteed to be unique.

   GUID

5. What is the difference between a contiguous namespace and a disjointed namespace? Give an example of each type of namespace.

   In a contiguous namespace, the name of the child object in an object hierarchy always contains the name of the parent domain. A tree is a contiguous namespace. In a disjointed namespace, the names of a parent object and of a child of the same parent object are not directly related to one another. A forest is a disjointed namespace.

Case Scenario Exercise

Page 14-22

1. Would you suggest a single domain or multiple domains for this organization? Why?

   You should suggest a single domain for the company. Because the company is relatively small and is connected by a high-speed, dedicated link there is no real need to use separate domains for the locations. Also, the company wants users to be able to log on anywhere in the company without specifying a logon location, which requires a single domain. With two domains, users would sometimes need to specify the domain to which they were logging on.

2. How many sites should you suggest? Why?

You should suggest that this company create two sites: one for the Memphis network and one for the Chicago network. Sites are based on the underlying network structure. Because there are two distinct high-speed LANs, it would be best to create a site for each.

3. Which logical Active Directory structure would allow you to group objects in the Chicago location so that local administrators could manage those objects?

OUs would allow you to create administrative boundaries for each location.

4. How many Global Catalog servers should you suggest and where would you place them?

At a minimum, you should place one Global Catalog server in each site so that users can access the Global Catalog even if the link between the two sites is down.

Troubleshooting Lab

Page
14-22

1. One of the managers has proposed a model that uses a single domain tree with two domains. Why would this type of model not meet the requirements?

The company wants to maintain two distinct namespaces (contoso.com and litware.com). Because all domains in a single tree must share a contiguous namespace, the manager's model will not work.

2. Using what you have learned in this chapter, sketch a diagram of a domain structure that meets these requirements.

Because there are two distinct namespaces (contoso.com and litware.com), you must use a separate tree to represent each namespace. Within the litware.com tree, you could create a single domain named litware.com. Within the contoso.com tree, you could create a root domain named contoso.com, and then create child domains named dallas.contoso.com and houston.contoso.com. This would satisfy the requirement that the domain structure represent the different locations of the Dallas and Houston offices. An example sketch is shown in Figure 14-10.

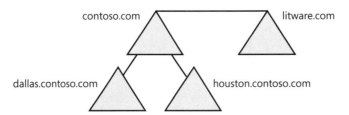

Figure 14-10   A disjointed namespace requires multiple domain trees.

15 Configuring Network and Internet Connections

Exam Objectives in this Chapter:

- Implement, manage, and troubleshoot input and output (I/O) devices.
    - ❏ Implement, configure, and manage modems.
    - ❏ Install, configure, and manage wireless devices.
    - ❏ Install, configure, and manage network adapters.
- Connect to computers by using dial-up networking.
    - ❏ Connect to computers by using a virtual private network (VPN) connection.
    - ❏ Create a dial-up connection to connect to a remote access server.
    - ❏ Connect to the Internet by using dial-up networking.
    - ❏ Configure and troubleshoot Internet Connection Sharing (ICS).
- Configure, manage, and troubleshoot an Internet Connection Firewall.

> **Note** Internet Connection Firewall is the software firewall built into versions of Windows XP Professional prior to applying the Service Pack 2 update. After installing Service Pack 2, the firewall is updated to the new (and much more robust) Windows Firewall. This chapter focuses on Windows Firewall, and the exam has been updated for Windows Firewall, as well. However, the official objectives still list Internet Connection Firewall.

Why This Chapter Matters

Microsoft Windows XP Professional provides many new features to simplify the configuration of network and Internet connections for home and small business environments. In this chapter, you learn how to configure local area network (LAN), dial-up, and wireless connections. You also learn about **Windows Firewall**, which protects your computer from unwanted traffic, and **Internet Connection Sharing** (ICS), which allows you to share one connection to the Internet with all computers on your network.

Lessons in this Chapter:

Before You Begin

To complete this chapter, you must have a computer that meets the minimum hardware requirements listed in the preface, "About This Book." You must also have installed Microsoft Windows XP Professional on the computer and have a network adapter and modem installed.

Lesson 1: Configuring Local Area Network (LAN) Connections

Windows XP Professional makes configuring LAN connections easy. When you install a network adapter, Windows creates a LAN connection automatically; it is just up to you to configure it. This lesson shows you how to view the LAN connections on a computer and how to configure those connections.

After this lesson, you will be able to

- View LAN connections on a computer running Windows XP Professional.
- Configure a LAN connection.
- Troubleshoot a LAN connection.
- Use the New Connection Wizard to configure a connection.

Estimated lesson time: 60 minutes

Viewing LAN Connections

Windows XP Professional provides a central location for viewing and configuring network connections: the Network Connections window, shown in Figure 15-1. You can open the Network Connections window in several ways, including the following:

- In Control Panel, click Network And Internet Connections, and then click Network Connections.

- In the Start menu or the desktop (if it is displayed), right-click My Network Places, and then select Properties.

- Directly from the Start menu if you first configure the Start menu to display the Network Connections folder.

The icons that are used for each connection provide visual clues for the type and status of the connection. These visual clues include the following:

- Dial-up connections (such as the Contoso.com connection in Figure 15-1) have a small picture of a phone and modem.

- LAN or high-speed Internet connections (such as the Local Area Connection in Figure 15-1) have a small picture meant to represent a network cable connection.

- Disabled or disconnected connections (such as the Contoso.com connection in Figure 15-1) are dimmed to show that they are disabled or disconnected.

- Connections that are protected with Windows Firewall have a small picture of a lock (such as the Contoso.com connection in Figure 15-1). You will learn more about Windows Firewall in Lesson 5, "Configuring Windows Firewall."

Figure 15-1   The Network Connections window shows LAN and dial-up connections.

Configuring a LAN Connection

Much of the configuration of a LAN connection happens in the Network Connections window. Right-clicking a particular connection provides a shortcut menu with commands for working with the connection.

How to View the Status of a Connection

To view the current status of a connection, right-click the connection, and then click Status. This action opens the Local Area Connection Status dialog box. The General tab of this dialog box (see Figure 15-2) shows the connection status and the activity on the connection since it was last enabled (the number of data packets sent and received over the connection).

The Support tab of the Local Area Connection Status dialog box (see Figure 15-3) shows you the Transmission Control Protocol/Internet Protocol (TCP/IP) configuration information (Internet Protocol [IP] address, subnet mask, and so on) for the connection. Click Details to view extended TCP/IP information, including the physical address of the network adapter, Dynamic Host Configuration Protocol (DHCP) server and lease information, and Domain Name System (DNS) server addresses.

Tip   As you learned in Chapter 13, "Supporting TCP/IP" you can also view the TCP/IP information for connections using the ipconfig command-line utility. The advantage of using ipconfig is that by typing **ipconfig /all** at the command prompt, you can view information for all connections on the computer at once. See Chapter 13 for more information on using this command.

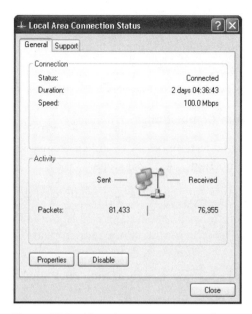

Figure 15-2   View the current status of a connection.

Figure 15-3   View the TCP/IP information for a connection.

How to Rename a Local Area Connection

If you have more than one network adapter installed, Windows names the first connection Local Area Connection, the second connection Local Area Connection 2, and so on. For clarity, consider using a naming scheme that makes it easy to identify what the different connections are for. To rename a connection, use these steps:

1. In the Network Connections window, right-click the connection, and then click Rename.

2. Type the new name for the connection, and then press ENTER.

How to Disable and Enable a Local Area Connection

There might be cases in which you will want to temporarily disable a connection without deleting it. To disable and enable a connection, use these steps:

1. In the Network Connections window, right-click the connection, and then click Disable.

   Windows disables the connection. The icon for the connection appears dimmed in the Network Connections window.

2. To enable a connection, right-click the connection, and then click Enable.

How to Bridge a Connection

The **Network Bridge** feature allows you to connect network segments (groups of networked computers) without having to use a router or bridge. The feature essentially turns the computer running Windows XP Professional into a router by allowing it to pass data between network adapters installed on the computer, each of which is attached to a different network segment. Network Bridge allows you to connect different types of network media. Before Network Bridge, if you were using more than one media type, you needed a different subnet for each media type. Packet forwarding would be required because different protocols are used on different media types. Network Bridge automates the configuration that is required to forward information from one media type to another.

To configure Network Bridge, do the following:

1. In the Network Connections window, select each of the network connections that you want to make part of the bridge.

2. Right-click one of the selected network connections, and then click Bridge Connections.

The following are important Network Bridge considerations:

■ Only Ethernet adapters, IEEE-1394 adapters, or Ethernet-compatible adapters, such as wireless or home phone network adapter (HPNA), can be part of the Network Bridge.

■ Adapters that have Windows Firewall or ICS enabled cannot be included in the Network Bridge.

- You can add connections to the Network Bridge after it has been created by using the Add To Bridge menu command.

- Only one bridge can exist on a Windows XP Professional computer, but it can be used to connect as many different media types as the computer can physically accommodate.

- You cannot create a bridge connection on computers running Windows 2000 or earlier.

How to Repair a Connection

Sometimes LAN connections stop working. This problem can happen for many reasons, including problems with the configuration of the network connection. When you are troubleshooting a networking problem, a good place to start is by using the Repair function provided by Windows XP Professional.

To repair a LAN connection, in the Network Connections window, right-click the connection, and then click Repair. When you use the Repair command, Windows takes the following actions:

1. Attempts to renew the connections DHCP lease, which is equivalent to using the ipconfig /renew command at the command prompt.

2. Flushes the Address Resolution Protocol (ARP) cache, which is equivalent to using the arp -d command at the command prompt.

3. Reloads the NetBIOS name cache, which is equivalent to using the nbtstat -R command at the command prompt. A NetBIOS name update is also sent, which is equivalent to using the nbtstat –RR command.

4. Flushes the Domain Name System (DNS) cache, which is equivalent to using the ipconfig /flushdns command at the command prompt.

5. Registers the computer's DNS name, which is equivalent to using the ipconfig /registerdns command at the command prompt.

See Also   For more information on the way the actions taken by the Repair command work, see Chapter 13.

6. Restarts IEEE 802.1x Authentication (which you will learn more about in the section "Authentication," later in this chapter).

Exam Tip   For the exam, be aware of the actions that happen when you repair a network connection. In particular, know that repairing a connection (or using ipconfig /renew at the command prompt) forces the computer to release its current IP address and attempt to renew its lease with a DHCP server.

Setting Options for a Connection

To configure options for LAN connection, you will open the Properties dialog box for that connection, shown in Figure 15-4. To do so, in the Network Connections window, right-click a connection, and then click Properties. The Connect Using section shows the network adapter associated with the LAN connection. Click the Configure button to open the Properties dialog box for the adapter; this is the same Properties dialog box you see if you view the properties for the network adapter through Device Manager (which is covered in Chapter 6, "Installing, Managing, and Troubleshooting Hardware Devices and Drivers").

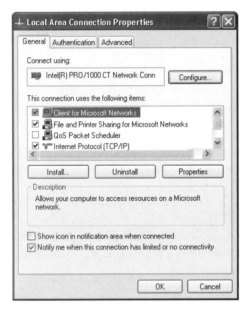

Figure 15-4   Configure a connection by using its Properties dialog box.

The Local Area Network Connection Properties dialog box also lists networking components installed on the computer. The components listed are available to all connections. Uninstalling a component makes the component unavailable to any network connection. Clearing the check box next to a component disables that component for only the connection you are viewing. The following networking components are installed by default for all LAN connections:

- **Client For Microsoft Networks**   This component provides the capability to access a Microsoft-based network.

- **File And Printer Sharing for Microsoft Networks**   This component provides the capability to share files and printers on the local computer with network users that access the computer through the given connection. If you have multiple connections on a computer, you can select or clear this check box for each connection individually, thus controlling the connections on which File And Printer Sharing is enabled.

- **QoS Packet Scheduler**   Quality of service (QoS) is a set of standards and mechanisms that improves quality data transmission for QoS-enabled programs by smoothing bursts and peaks in network traffic to an even flow and prioritizing more-important traffic over less-important traffic.

- **Internet Protocol (TCP/IP)**   This component indicates that the TCP/IP protocol is installed for the connection. You cannot uninstall TCP/IP for a LAN connection, but you can disable the protocol. Select the protocol and click Properties to open the Internet Protocol (TCP/IP) Properties dialog box, which you can use to configure the TCP/IP settings for the connection. You can learn more configuring TCP/IP settings in Chapter 13.

How to Install, Disable, and Uninstall Network Components   You can install and remove network components, such as additional network clients and protocols, by using the properties box of the network connection. You can have multiple clients, services, and protocols loaded and functioning simultaneously on a single connection.

To install a network component, follow these steps:

1. Open the Properties dialog box for the network connection.

2. Click Install. The Select Network Component Type dialog box appears, as shown in Figure 15-5.

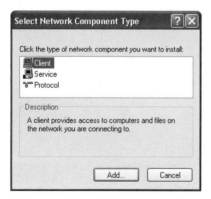

Figure 15-5   Choose network components to install.

3. Select the type of network component that you want to install, and then click Add.

4. In the dialog box that appears, select the desired component and click OK, or click Have Disk to install a component that does not appear on the list.

When you install a network component, the component becomes available to all connections automatically. You should disable components that are not used by a particular network connection. This process reduces the amount of network traffic generated on the connection, therefore increasing overall performance. To disable a component without uninstalling it, open the Properties dialog box for the network connection and clear the check box.

When a component is no longer required by any connection, you can uninstall it. Uninstalling a component removes it from *all* connections.

To uninstall a network component, follow these steps:

1. Open the Properties dialog box of the network connection.

2. Select the network component that you want to remove.

3. Click Uninstall, and then click Yes to confirm the uninstall operation.

Authentication   The Authentication tab of the Local Area Connection Properties dialog box, shown in Figure 15-6, allows you to configure **IEEE 802.1x authentication** for a connection. The IEEE 802.1x standard allows authentication and access to 802.11 wireless networks and wired Ethernet networks. When a user wants access to services through a particular LAN connection, the connection adopts one of two roles: authenticator or supplicant. As an authenticator, the connection enforces user authentication before it allows user access. As a supplicant, the connection requests access to the services that the user wants access to. An authentication server checks the supplicant's credentials, and then lets the authenticator know if the supplicant is authorized to access the authenticator's services.

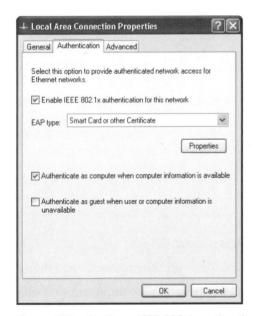

Figure 15-6   Configure IEEE 802.1x authentication.

The Authentication tab provides the following options:

■ **Enable IEEE 802.1x Authentication For This Network**   Select this check box to enable authentication. If you clear this check box, the rest of the options on this tab become unavailable. When authentication is enabled, you can choose from three types of authentication (referred to as EAP, or Extensible Authentication Protocol):

❑ Smart Card Or Other Certificate

❑ MD5-Challenge

❑ Protected EAP (PEAP)

■ **Authenticate As Computer When Computer Information Is Available**   This option specifies whether the computer attempts authentication within an Active Directory domain environment when a user is not logged on. This option requires that a computer account for the computer exists in the domain.

■ **Authenticate As Guest When User Or Computer Information Is Unavailable**   If a user account or computer account does not exist within a domain, this option allows the computer to attempt authentication as a guest. If you authenticate as a guest, the network infrastructure might limit the number of computers on the network that you can communicate with.

Note   The Advanced tab of the of the Local Area Connection Properties dialog box allows you to configure Windows Firewall and ICS. These options are the focus of Lesson 4, "Configuring Internet Connection Sharing (ICS)," and Lesson 5 "Configuring Windows Firewall."

The New Connection Wizard

Although it is not hard to configure a network connection in Windows XP Professional manually, Windows does offer a wizard (the **New Connection Wizard**) that can perform much of the work of configuring a network connection for different uses. Understanding the options found in this wizard will help you configure connections efficiently. You can start the New Connection Wizard from the Network Connections window by clicking Create A New Connection.

You can configure four types of connections by using the New Connection Wizard:

■ Connect To The Internet

■ Connect To The Network At My Workplace

■ Set Up A Home Or Small Office Network

■ Set Up An Advanced Connection

Note   This section covers the following options: Connect To The Internet, Connect To The Network At My Workplace, and Set Up An Advanced Connection. Selecting Set Up A Home Or Small Office Network allows you to configure ICS, which is covered in Lesson 4.

Connect To The Internet

To set up an Internet connection, start the New Connection Wizard, and then click Next to skip the Welcome page. The next page you see is Network Connection Type (see Figure 15-7).

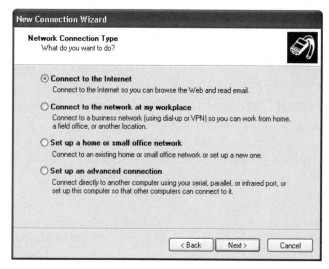

Figure 15-7   Use the Network Connection Type page to select the type of network connection to create.

Select Connect To The Internet on the Network Connection Type page and click Next. The New Connection Wizard displays the Getting Ready page, which has the following three options:

- Choose From A List Of Internet Service Providers (ISPs)

- Set Up My Connection Manually

- Use The CD I Got From An ISP

Choose From A List Of Internet Service Providers (ISPs)   If you select Choose From A List Of Internet Service Providers (ISPs) on the Getting Ready page, and then click Next, the New Connection Wizard displays the Completing The New Connection Wizard page. You can select Get Online With MSN or Select From A List Of Other ISPs. When you have made your selection, click Finish.

Set Up My Connection Manually   If you select Set Up My Connection Manually on the Getting Ready page, and then click Next, the New Connection Wizard displays the Internet Connection page. The following three options are available in the Internet Connection page:

- Connect Using A Dial-Up Modem

Select this option if your connection uses a modem and a regular or Integrated Services Digital Network (ISDN) phone line. If you select Connect Using A Dial-Up Modem and click Next, you are prompted to enter the information in Table 15-1.

Table 15-1   Connect Using A Dial-Up Modem

New Connection Wizard Page	Description
Connection Name	The name of your ISP is typically used as the connection name for dial-up connections to the Internet.
Phone Number To Dial	The phone number you use to connect to your ISP.
Internet Account Information	You will be prompted to enter the ISP account name and password. You can select or clear the following two check boxes:
	■ Use This Account Name And Password When Anyone Connects To The Internet From This Computer
	■ Make This The Default Internet Connection

Note   The New Connection Wizard automatically enables Windows Firewall for all new connections. See Lesson 5 for more information.

When you have entered the information on each of the pages listed in Table 15-1, the New Connection Wizard displays the Completing The New Connection Wizard page, which displays a summary of the information you entered to manually create a connection to the Internet. If you want a shortcut to appear on your desktop, select the Add A Shortcut To This Connection To My Desktop check box. Click Finish to create the connection.

■ Connect Using A Broadband Connection That Requires A User And Password

Select this option if your high-speed connection uses either a digital subscriber line (DSL) or cable modem. This type of connection is also known as Point-to-Point Protocol over Ethernet (PPPoE). If you select Connect Using A Broadband Connection That Requires A User And Password and click Next, you are also prompted to enter the information in Table 15-1.

■ Connect Using A Broadband Connection That Is Always On

Select this option if your high-speed connection uses a cable modem, DSL, or LAN connection. If you select Connect Using A Broadband Connection That Is Always On, the New Connection Wizard displays the Completing The New Connection Wizard page because the connection should already be configured and working.

Use The CD I Got From An ISP   If you select Use The CD I Got From An ISP on the Getting Ready page, and then click Next, the New Connection Wizard displays the Completing The New Connection Wizard page. You are instructed to click Finish and then insert the CD-ROM you received from your ISP. The Setup program on the CD-ROM should start automatically to assist you in connecting to the Internet.

Connect to a Private Network at Your Workplace

If you want to connect to a private network, select Connect To The Network At My Workplace on the Network Connection Type page (refer to Figure 15-7) and click Next. The New Connection Wizard displays the Network Connection page, which has the following two options:

- Dial-Up Connection
- Virtual Private Network Connection

Dial-Up Connection   Select this option if you want to connect to the network at your office using a modem and phone line or an ISDN phone line. If you select Dial-Up Connection and click Next, you are prompted to enter the information in Table 15-2.

Table 15-2   Dial-Up Connection Information

New Connection Wizard Page	Description
Connection Name	The name of your company or the name of the server to which you will be connecting is typically used as the connection name for dial-up connections when you are connecting to a private network.
Phone Number To Dial	The phone number used to make the connection.

When you have entered the information on each of the pages listed in Table 15-2, the New Connection Wizard displays the Completing The New Connection Wizard page, which displays a summary of the information you entered to create the connection. If you want a shortcut to appear on your desktop, select the Add A Shortcut To The Connection To My Desktop check box. Click Finish to create the connection.

Virtual Private Network Connection   Select this option if you want to connect to the network at your office using a virtual private network (VPN) connection over the Internet. If you select Virtual Private Network Connection and click Next, you are prompted to enter the information in Table 15-3.

Table 15-3   Virtual Private Network Connection Information

New Connection Wizard Page	Description
Connection Name	The name of your company or the name of the server to which you will be connecting is typically used as the connection name.
VPN Server Selection	The host name or IP address of the VPN server to which you are connecting.

When you have entered the information on each of the pages listed in Table 15-3, the New Connection Wizard displays the Completing The New Connection Wizard page, which displays a summary of the information you entered to create the connection. If you want a shortcut to appear on your desktop, select the Add A Shortcut To The Connection To My Desktop check box. Click Finish to create the connection.

Set Up An Advanced Connection

If you want to connect directly to another computer using a serial, parallel, or infrared port or to set up this computer so that other computers can connect to it, select Set Up An Advanced Connection on the Network Connection Type page (refer to Figure 15-7). The New Connection Wizard displays the Advanced Connection Options page, which offers two options:

- **Accept Incoming Connections** This option allows you to configure and administer inbound connections on a computer running Windows XP Professional. For more information about this option, see Lesson 2, "Configuring Dial-Up Connections," later in this chapter.

- **Connect Directly To Another Computer** This option allows you to create a direct cable connection to another computer. If you select this option and click Next, you must provide the information in Table 15-4.

Table 15-4   Connect Directly To Another Computer

New Connection Wizard Page	Description
Host Or Guest	Select Host if your computer contains information that other computers will access; select Guest if your computer will be accessing information on a computer configured as a host.
Connection Device	Select the device you want to use to make this connection. Possible choices include Direct Parallel (LPT1), Communications Port (COM1), and Communications Port (COM2).
User Permissions	Select the users who can connect to this computer.

When you have entered the information on each of the pages listed in Table 15-4, the New Connection Wizard displays the Completing The New Connection Wizard page, which displays a summary of the information you entered to create the connection. If you want a shortcut to appear on your desktop, select the Add A Shortcut To The Connection To My Desktop check box. Click Finish to create the connection.

Practice: Configuring a LAN Connection

In this practice, you use the New Connection Wizard to configure an outbound connection to a private network.

1. Click Start, and then click Control Panel.

2. In the Control Panel window, click Network And Internet Connections.

3. In the Network And Internet Connections window, click Network Connections.

4. In the Network Connections window, click Create A New Connection.

   Windows XP Professional starts the New Connection Wizard.

5. On the Welcome To The New Connection Wizard page, click Next.

   The New Connection Wizard displays the Network Connection Type page.

6. Click Connect To The Network At My Workplace, and then click Next.

   The New Connection Wizard displays the Network Connection page.

7. Click Virtual Private Network Connection, and then click Next.

   The New Connection Wizard displays the Connection Name page.

8. In the Company Name text box, type **Work**, and then click Next.

   The New Connection Wizard displays the Public Network page.

9. Click Do Not Dial The Initial Connection, and then click Next.

   The New Connection Wizard displays the VPN Server Selection page.

10. In the Host Name Or IP Address text box, type **192.168.1.202**, and then click Next.

> **Note**   If your computer is on a network and there is a valid address that you can use to test your outbound connection, use that address instead of 192.168.1.202.

   The New Connection Wizard displays the Completing The New Connection Wizard page.

11. Review the information summary, and then click Finish.

   Windows XP Professional displays the Connect Work dialog box.

12. In the User Name text box, type **Administrator** and type **password** for the password.

> **Note**   If your computer is on a network and you entered a valid IP address in Step 8, enter a valid user name and password in Step 12.

13. Click Connect.

Note   If your computer is a stand-alone computer, this operation will fail. If your computer is on a network and you entered a valid address in Step 8 and a valid user name and password in Step 11, a message will be displayed indicating that a connection has been made.

14. If your connection failed, in the Error Connecting to Work dialog box, click Cancel. If you connected successfully to another computer, double-click the connection icon in the notification area, click Disconnect, and then click Yes.

15. Close all windows and log off.

Lesson Review

Use the following questions to help determine whether you have learned enough to move on to the next lesson. If you have difficulty answering these questions, review the material in this lesson before beginning the next lesson. You can find answers to these questions in the "Questions and Answers" section at the end of this chapter.

1. What are the four outbound connection types that you can configure using the New Connection Wizard?

   _____

   _____

2. In which two ways can you force a network connection to attempt to renew its DHCP lease?

   _____

   _____

   _____

3. How can you tell the duration that a network connection has been successfully connected?

   _____

   _____

   _____

   _____

   _____

Lesson Summary

- You can view all network connections configured on a computer in the Network Connections window, which you can access through Control Panel.

- In the Network Connections window, you can right-click a connection to access a command for working with the connection. These commands include the following:

  - Viewing the status of a connection

  - Renaming a connection

  - Disabling or enabling a connection

  - Bridging connections

  - Repairing a connection

  - Setting options for a connection

- The New Connection Wizard can configure a network connection for different uses. You can use the wizard to configure a connection for connecting to the Internet, connecting to a private network, setting up a home or small office network, or configuring an advanced connection.

Lesson 2: Configuring Dial-Up Connections

A **dial-up connection** connects you to a private network or the Internet by using a device that transfers data over a public telephone network. This device can be a modem that uses a standard phone line, an ISDN card with a high-speed ISDN line, or a DSL modem that requires a dial-up connection. In this lesson, you learn to configure a modem in Windows XP Professional and create a dial-up connection. You also learn to configure Windows XP Professional to allow an incoming connection.

After this lesson, you will be able to

- Configure a modem in Windows XP Professional.
- Create a dial-up connection.
- Configure Windows XP Professional to allow incoming connections.

Estimated lesson time: 30 minutes

Configuring Modems

The most common dial-up connection uses a standard analog telephone line and a modem. Standard analog phone lines are available worldwide and meet most requirements of a mobile user. Standard analog phone lines are also referred to as a Public Switched Telephone Network (PSTN) or Plain Old Telephone Service (POTS).

Windows automatically detects and installs most modern modems that are Plug and Play–compliant. For the most part, users can create a dial-up connection that uses a modem without ever having to configure the modem itself. There are times, however, when you might need to configure or troubleshoot a modem. You will do so by using the Modems tab of the Phone And Modem Options dialog box, shown in Figure 15-8. To open this dialog box, use the following steps:

1. Click Start, and then click Control Panel.

2. In the Control Panel window, click Printers And Other Hardware.

3. In the Printers And Other Hardware window, click Phone And Modem Options. If prompted, provide your location information.

4. Click the Modems tab.

The Modems tab shows a list of modems installed on the computer. Select a modem, and then click Properties to open the Properties dialog box for the modem, shown in Figure 15-9. This is the same Properties dialog box that you see when you open the properties for a modem in Device Manager.

Figure 15-8   The Modems tab of the Phone And Modem Options dialog box shows installed modems.

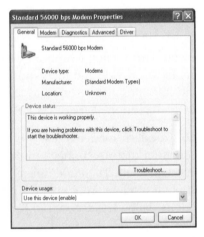

Figure 15-9   Use the Properties dialog box for a modem to configure and troubleshoot the modem.

The Properties dialog box for a modem always contains the following tabs (though you may see additional tabs depending on the type of modem you have installed):

- **General**   The General tab shows basic information about the modem, whether Windows reports the modem as working or not, and whether the modem is enabled.

- **Modem**   The Modem tab lets you control the speaker volume for the modem or turn the sound off. Many users prefer not to hear the modem each time it dials, although some users rely on hearing that sound to feel sure that their modem is working properly. The Modem tab also lets you control the maximum port speed for the modem, although because Windows negotiates the speed of the port you should not need to alter the default setting. The final option on the Modem tab lets you specify whether Windows should wait for a dial tone before dialing numbers. Users in some locations might find that their modem does not recognize the dial tone used in that area, or users might need to dial the phone manually.

- **Diagnostics**   The Diagnostics tab lets you issue a query to the modem to determine whether it is receiving and sending commands properly. Click Query Modem and wait a few moments to see the result. This command is the single most useful modem troubleshooting tool in Windows because it helps you determine whether a modem is working properly. If the query returns an error stating that it cannot communicate with the modem, you know you must troubleshoot the modem itself. If the query returns results, you know the modem is working and the problem lies elsewhere—most likely in the dial-up connection configuration or in the application trying to make the connection. The Diagnostics tab also lets you enable logging for the modem.

- **Advanced**   The Advanced tab lets you configure initialization commands for the modem—commands that control how the modem sends and receives data. Mostly, you do not need to worry about using extra initialization commands because the most common uses for these commands (such as waiting for a dial tone, dialing 9 to get an outside line, or using a code to disable call waiting) are all configurable options within Windows.

- **Driver**   The Driver tab displays version information about the modem driver; and provides tools for updating, rolling back, and uninstalling drivers. For more information about using the options on this tab, see Chapter 6.

 Note   Many modems are compatible with Windows XP. However, many difficult-to-detect problems are the result of older, incompatible modems. Plug and Play modems are cheap enough these days that it is usually easier and more cost-effective to replace an old modem than troubleshoot it. To find hardware that is supported by Windows operating systems, visit the Windows Catalog on the Microsoft Web site.

Configuring a Dial-Up Connection

Dial-up connections work much like LAN connections, but have additional options that let you control when the connection is dialed, the number for the connection, and other criteria for use. To create a dial-up connection, you use the New Connection Wizard (which was covered in Lesson 1, "Configuring Local Area Network (LAN) Connections") to create a connection to the Internet or to a private network.

After the dial-up connection is created, you can view the connection in the Network Connections window, as shown in Figure 15-10. Right-clicking a particular connection provides a shortcut menu with commands for working with the connection.

Figure 15-10   Dial-up connections are shown in the Network Connections window.

Setting Options for a Dial-Up Connection

To configure options for a dial-up connection, right-click the connection and click Properties. The Properties dialog box for the connection, shown in Figure 15-11, contains the following tabs:

■ **General**   The General tab shows the modem associated with the connection. Click Configure to open a Modem Configuration dialog box that allows you to set the maximum port speed, configure hardware options for the modem, and enable or disable the modem speaker (although not control the volume level). The General tab also allows you to configure the phone number for the connection. Configuring the phone number entails the following:

   ❑ Typing the phone number itself. You can also click Alternates to open an Alternate Phone Numbers dialog box that lets you enter additional phone numbers for the connection to try if the primary number is busy. The Phone Number text box is the only option available in the Phone Number section unless you enable dialing rules.

   ❑ Enabling dialing rules. When you select the Use Dialing Rules check box, the other options in the Phone Number section become available. Click the Dialing Rules button to create new dialing locations. Each location you configure can use an entirely different set of dialing rules, such as area code, number dialed for access to an outside line, and even calling card information.

   ❑ Selecting an area code. The list of area codes available is derived from the dialing locations you configure.

   ❑ Selecting a country/region code.

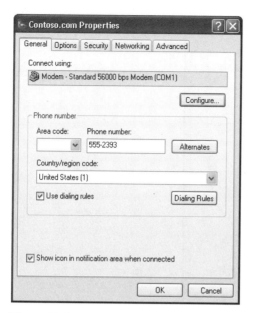

Figure 15-11   General options for a dial-up connection include modem configuration, phone number, and dialing rules.

- **Options**   The Options tab, shown in Figure 15-12, provides access to dialing and redialing options. You can configure Windows to display a dialog box during dialing so that you can see the dialing status. You can also have Windows prompt you for a user name and password each time it dials, include a Windows domain text box so that you can log on to a domain when you connect to a private network, and even prompt you for the phone number instead of automatically displaying it. The Options tab also lets you configure how many times Windows should attempt to redial a number if it is busy, how long to wait between dialing attempts, and the number of minutes after which Windows should disconnect if no network traffic is transmitted over the connection.

- **Security**   The Security tab allows you to configure authentication settings for the dial-up connection, which are used when dialing in to a private network.

- **Networking**   The Networking tab displays the type of dial-up server being dialed and the networking components enabled for the connection. This tab works just like the General tab of a LAN connection (refer to Figure 15-4).

- **Advanced**   The Advanced tab allows you to enable Windows Firewall and ICS, which are covered in Lessons 4 and 5.

Figure 15-12 The Options tab for a dial-up connection allows you to configure numerous dialing options.

How to Connect by using a Dial-Up Connection

After creating and configuring a dial-up connection, you can establish the connection by double-clicking the connection in the Network Connections window (or by right-clicking the connection and then clicking Connect). This action opens the Connect dialog box, as shown in Figure 15-13. The options you see here (such as entering a domain name) depend on how you configured the dial-up connection, as does the information (such as the user name and password) that is already filled in. Click Dial to establish the connection.

Figure 15-13 Establish a dial-up connection.

Allowing Incoming Dial-Up Connections

To configure and administer incoming connections on a computer running Windows XP Professional, you use the New Connection Wizard (which was discussed in detail in Lesson 1). On the Network Connection Type page (refer to Figure 15-7), click Set Up An Advanced Connection, and then click Next. The New Connection Wizard displays the Advanced Connection Options page (see Figure 15-14).

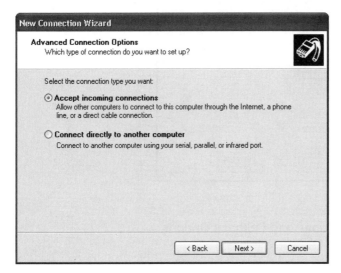

Figure 15-14   Use the Advanced Connection Options page to set up an inbound connection.

On the Advanced Connection Options page, click Accept Incoming Connections, and then click Next to display the Devices For Incoming Connection page.

Configuring Devices for Incoming Connections

The Devices For Incoming Connections page allows you to choose one of the available devices on your computer to accept incoming calls. If the device you select is configurable, click Properties to configure it. For example, if you have selected a modem, the possible options to configure in the device's Properties dialog box include port speed, error correction, use of compression, and the type flow control. The Advanced tab contains additional configurable options, which might include the number of data bits, the parity, the number of stop bits, and the modulation type.

Allowing VPN Connections

When you are finished configuring the device, click OK to close the Properties dialog box, and then click Next in the Devices For Incoming Connection page (see Figure 15-15). The New Connection Wizard displays the Incoming Virtual Private Network (VPN) Connection page. If you click Allow Virtual Private Connections, Windows XP Professional modifies Windows Firewall so that your computer can send and receive VPN traffic. Select the option either to allow or not allow VPN connections, and then click Next.

Figure 15-15   Configure the device that the incoming connection will use.

Specifying User Permissions and Callback Options

You must specify which users can use this inbound connection in the User Permissions page. After you select a user, click Properties. In the *user-name* Properties dialog box, click the Callback tab to set the callback options. You can choose Do Not Allow Callback, Allow The Caller To Set The Callback Number, or Always Use The Following Callback Number. Enabling callback causes the remote server, in this case your computer, to disconnect from the client calling in, and then to call the client computer back. By using callback, you can have the bill for the phone call charged to the office phone number rather than to the phone number of the user who called in. Callback can also be used to increase security because if you specify the callback number you do not have to worry about someone trying to break in. Even if an unauthorized user calls in, the system calls back at the number you specified, not the number of the unauthorized user.

Selecting Networking Software

After you specify the callback options, click Next. The New Connection Wizard displays the Networking Software page. You can choose the networking software you want to enable for incoming connections. You can also install additional networking software by clicking Install. Click Finish to create the connection.

Practice: Configuring an Inbound Connection

In this practice, you use the New Connection Wizard to configure an inbound connection.

1. Click Start, and then click Control Panel.

2. In the Control Panel window, click Network And Internet Connections.

3. In the Network And Internet Connections window, click Network Connections.

4. In the Network Connections window, click Create A New Connection.

   Windows XP Professional starts the New Connection Wizard.

5. On the Welcome To The New Connection Wizard page, click Next.

   The New Connection Wizard displays the Network Connection Type page.

6. Click Set Up An Advanced Connection, and then click Next.

   The New Connection Wizard displays the Advanced Connection Options page.

7. Ensure that Accept Incoming Connections is selected, and then click Next.

   The New Connection Wizard displays the Devices For Incoming Connections page.

8. Select the modem device option for your computer in the Connection Devices list, and then click Next.

> **Note**   If you do not have a modem, select Direct Parallel.

The New Connection Wizard displays the Incoming Virtual Private Network (VPN) Connection page.

9. Ensure that Do Not Allow Virtual Private Connections is selected, and then click Next.

   The New Connection Wizard displays the User Permissions page.

10. Select Administrator, and then click Properties.

    The New Connection Wizard displays the Administrator Properties dialog box with the General tab selected.

11. Click the Callback tab.

    The New Connection Wizard displays the Callback tab of the Administrator Properties dialog box.

12. Review the callback options, leave the default setting of Do Not Allow Callback, and then click OK.

13. In the User Permissions page, click Next.

The New Connection Wizard displays the Networking Software page.

14. Review the available networking components, click Internet Protocol (TCP/IP), and then click Properties.

The New Connection Wizard displays the Incoming TCP/IP dialog box.

15. Select Specify TCP/IP Addresses.

16. In the From text box, type **192.168.1.201**, in the To text box, type **192.168.1.205**, and then click OK.

17. On the Networking Software page, click Next.

The New Connection Wizard displays the Completing The New Connection Wizard page. The name assigned to the connection is Incoming Connections.

18. Click Finish.

Notice that an Incoming Connections icon now appears in the Network Connections window.

Lesson Review

Use the following questions to help determine whether you have learned enough to move on to the next lesson. If you have difficulty answering these questions, review the material in this lesson before beginning the next lesson. You can find answers to these questions in the "Questions and Answers" section at the end of this chapter.

1. A user complains to you that she does not want to hear her modem each time she connects to the company network from her portable computer. What should you do?

_____

_____

2. Other than allowing VPN connections, what does Windows XP Professional do when you configure a new connection to allow virtual private connections?

_____

_____

3. What is callback and why would you enable it?

_____

_____

_____

_____

_____

_____

Lesson Summary

■ You can access a list of installed modems by using the Modems tab of the Phone And Modem Options dialog box, which is available in Control Panel. From the list of modems, you can open the Properties dialog box for any modem. You can use a modem's Properties dialog box to configure speaker and port options and to perform diagnostics on the modem.

■ Dial-up connections work much like LAN connections, but have additional options that let you control when the connection is dialed, the number for the connection, and other criteria for use. To create a dial-up connection, you use the New Connection Wizard.

■ You can configure Windows XP Professional to accept incoming dial-up connections over a modem or by using VPN. You can choose which of the available devices on your computer you will allow to accept incoming calls. You can also specify which user accounts can use the incoming connections.

Lesson 3: Configuring Wireless Connections

Wireless networking offers a degree of freedom—freedom for users of portable and handheld computers to roam where they will and freedom for companies to place computers in new locations without having to run network cabling. With that freedom, however, comes increased vulnerability. Because wireless networking does not share the same physical security of a wired network, understanding the security options for a wireless network is of paramount importance. This lesson introduces you to the standards, implementations, and security options for wireless networks. This lesson also shows you how to configure a computer running Windows XP Professional to participate as a client in a wireless network.

After this lesson, you will be able to

- Identify the standards used in wireless networking.
- Explain the basic architecture of wireless networks.
- Identify the security concerns and options of wireless networks.
- Configure a computer running Windows XP Professional as a wireless networking client.

Estimated lesson time: 30 minutes

Introduction to Wireless Networking Standards

The primary wireless networking standard is known as 802.11. This standard is developed and maintained by the Institute of Electrical and Electronics Engineers (IEEE), so you will often see the standard referred to as IEEE 802.11.

The original 802.11 specification defines data rates of 1 Mbps and 2 Mbps, and uses a radio frequency of 2.45 GHz. 802.11 provides the foundation for a number of variations of the standard that IEEE has developed over the years, and it is these variations you will see implemented in wireless devices on the market today. These variations include the following:

- **802.11b**   The first real standard to market, which is called 802.11b, was originally developed in 1999, although it is still in wide use today. 802.11b supports additional data rates of 5.5 Mbps and 11 Mbps (comparable to the rated speed of traditional Ethernet) and still uses the 2.45 GHz radio frequency. The advantages of 802.11b over other standards are that it is typically available at a lower cost and it has the best overall signal range. However, 802.11b also has the lowest data transfer rate of the available standards.

- **802.11a**   802.11a was developed around the same time as 802.11b, but 802.11b was adopted by hardware manufacturers much faster than 802.11a. As a result, most manufacturers did not start providing wireless devices using 802.11a until 2003. 802.11a boasts a data transfer rate of 54 Mbps and operates in the 5.8 GHz radio frequency. 802.11a also provides greater resistance to electrical interference than 802.11b. Advantages of 802.11a are that it provides the highest speed of the available standards and also supports more simultaneous users in the same area than 802.11b. Disadvantages are that 802.11a devices have the highest cost and a shorter range than other standards. Also, 802.11a devices are not compatible with 802.11b devices.

- **802.11g**   The development of 802.11g was finalized in 2002. 802.11g supports data transfer rates up to 54 Mbps and operated in the 2.4 GHz radio frequency. 802.11g devices are compatible with 802.11b devices, but that compatibility comes at a price. If a network uses only 802.11g devices, all wireless devices can operate at up to 54 Mbps. If a network has even a single 802.11b device, 802.11g devices must operate in mixed mode, which lowers the data transfer for 802.11g devices by about 30 percent.

Note   Some manufacturers make hybrid devices that support both 802.11a and 802.11g, and such devices can connect to networks using any of the three standards mentioned here.

Real World   Rated Speeds

Although the standards covered in this lesson have rated speeds (up to 11 Mbps for 802.11b and up to 54 Mbps for 802.11a and 802.11g), these are mostly theoretical values. In practice, you will never actually get that kind of data transfer rate. Typical throughput for 802.11b products, for example, tops out around 4–5 Mbps. The 802.11g products have an actual capacity of about 20 Mbps, and 802.11a products have a capacity of 22 Mbps. In addition, even these more realistic transfer rates are often further limited in the real world by interference from electrical devices and materials in building structures.

Introduction to Wireless Networking Architecture

The 802.11 standard defines a number of main architectural components. These components include the following:

- **Station (STA)**   A station (STA) is a client device on a wireless network—typically a computer that has a wireless network adapter installed.

■ **Access point (AP)**   An access point (AP) provides an interface with which stations can communicate. APs are the bridge between the wireless stations and an existing network backbone, allowing wireless clients to communicate with the network. APs can be stand-alone devices, but are often combined with other network devices such as routers.

■ **Independent Basic Service Set (IBSS)**   An independent basic service set (IBSS) represents a wireless network that consists of two or more stations, but does not have an AP. This type of network, shown in Figure 15-16, is often referred to as an **ad-hoc wireless network**. Ad-hoc networks offer the advantage of being able to spontaneously create wireless network connections between stations with little configuration required. However, ad-hoc networks are considerably less secure and configurable than basic service set networks that include an AP.

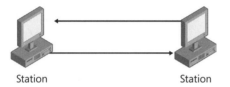

Figure 15-16   An IBSS, or ad-hoc wireless network, has wireless stations but no AP.

■ **Basic Service Set**   A basic service set (BSS) represents a network that allows stations to communicate through an AP, as shown in Figure 15-17. This type of network is often referred to as an **infrastructure wireless network**. In a BSS, all stations communicate through the AP. The AP provides connectivity to the wired LAN and provides bridging functionality when one station initiates communication to another station.

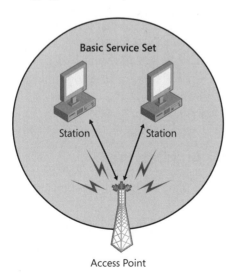

Figure 15-17   A BSS, or infrastructure wireless network, has wireless stations that communicate through an AP.

- **Extended Service Set**   An extended service set (ESS) represents a network in which multiple APs (and thus multiple BSSs) are used, as shown in Figure 15-18. This allows for increased mobility because stations can move from one BSS to another. APs can be interconnected with or without network cable (although most of the time they are connected to one another with cables).

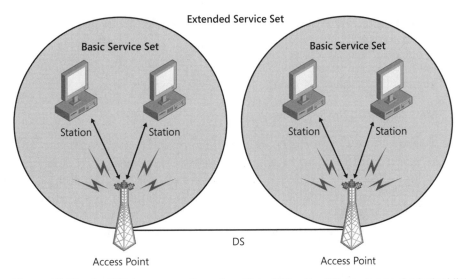

Figure 15-18   An ESS is a connection of multiple BSSs, the DS serving as the logical link between BSSs.

- **Distribution System**   The distribution system (DS) is a logical component used to interconnect BSSs in an ESS. The DS provides distribution services to allow for the roaming of STAs between BSSs.

> **Exam Tip**   Although the architectural elements of 802.11 networking sound a bit intimidating, it is important to understand the underlying components of the two modes in which you can configure a wireless client to operate: ad-hoc mode, in which there is no AP, and infrastructure mode, in which an AP is used. An ad-hoc network offers fewer configuration options and is sometimes used in small workgroup environments. An infrastructure network provides greater security and configurability and is the most common mode for wireless networking.

Introduction to Wireless Networking Security

When a wireless network is used, security becomes of greater concern. On traditional wired networks, there is a certain level of security to be had simply because you can physically protect the networking cables. On a wireless network, you cannot physically protect the radio frequencies used and so must rely on logical protection in the form of authentication and encryption.

One of the biggest threats to wireless networks is that operating systems such as Windows XP Professional make it very easy to locate and connect to wireless networks—so easy, in fact, that people often connect to unsecured wireless networks without even realizing that it has happened. There are also more deliberate threats to wireless networks. Attackers can gain access to unsecured (or improperly secured) networks by connecting with their wireless stations, or even by installing unauthorized APs on an existing wired network. Once connected, attackers can inspect, modify, or damage vital resources.

Fortunately, there are a number of ways to secure a wireless network against such threats. These methods are the focus of the next few sections.

MAC Address Filtering

A very basic way to protect an infrastructure wireless network is to implement media access control (MAC) filtering. Every network adapter (wireless network adapters included) contains an address known as a MAC address. An administrator can configure an AP so that it accepts communications only from specified MAC addresses. Although MAC filtering does offer some level of protection from casual intrusion, it is far from useful as a single security solution. Following are some concerns about using MAC filtering:

- It is relatively easy to spoof a MAC address. Many software products exist that let an intruder modify the MAC address on a wireless network adapter.

- Most APs require that you manually enter MAC addresses. For networks with large numbers of wireless clients, this means a lot of work for administrators. In addition, most APs have a limit to the number of MAC addresses you can authorize.

- MAC filtering can stop an unauthorized computer, but not an unauthorized user. If an intruder gains access to a computer that has an approved MAC address, the intruder can gain access to the wireless network.

Service Set Identifier (SSID) Broadcasting

Every infrastructure network is named with a service set identifier (SSID). This name distinguishes the network from other wireless networks. By default, most APs broadcast their SSID so that wireless clients can easily locate and connect to the network. SSID broadcasting provides a great deal of convenience because wireless clients (especially those that roam among different wireless networks) can easily detect networks without requiring much configuration from the user.

You can disable SSID broadcasting on most APs, which can prevent casual intruders from discovering a network. However, intruders who are looking for your network will likely be able to find it anyway. Several software programs exist that can scan for wireless networks and identify the SSID of a network, even if SSID broadcasting is disabled.

Typically, the convenience of using SSID broadcasting outweighs the slight security advantage that disabling broadcasting offers.

> **Note**   Several tools exist that can help users locate wireless networks, even if SSID broadcasting is turned off. As an administrator, you can use these tools to help evaluate the security of your own wireless network and identify rogue wireless networks in your organization. Two popular tools include NetStumbler, which you can find at *http://www.netstumbler.com*, and AirSnare, which you can find at *http://home.comcast.net/~jay.deboer/airsnare*.

Wired Equivalent Privacy (WEP)

Wired networks normally require a physical connection in order to be compromised. In wireless networks, because the data is broadcast using radio, intruders can intercept the signals. If those signals are not encrypted, intruders can view the data being transmitted. **Wired Equivalent Privacy** (WEP) is one of two wireless encryption standards supported by Windows XP Professional (the other being Wi-Fi Protected Access, which is covered in the next section). WEP is the encryption standard that is specified by the IEEE 802.11 standard.

WEP provides encryption services to protect authorized users of a wireless LAN from eavesdroppers. WEP functions by using a shared key to encrypt packets of data before transmitting them over a wireless network. This shared key is generated by using 40-bit or 64-bit secret key encryption, and then adding a 24-bit initialization vector (IV) to the end of that key. The shared key is set in place for a network, but a new IV is generated randomly for each packet of data that is transmitted over the network.

Unfortunately, WEP is not as strong as its designers had hoped. There are two basic shortcomings in the standard WEP protocol:

■ Most networks do not change the shared key often because the basic WEP standard does not provide a way to dynamically assign the shared key to APs and stations. Instead, administrators must manually enter the shared key.

> **Note**   To make cracking WEP more difficult, most AP vendors avoid using a handful of known-weak IVs that cracking tools specifically look for. When these IVs are disabled (by default for most up-to-date APs) and 128 bit encryption is used, WEP is actually a very secure encryption protocol. A newer implementation of WEP, known as Dynamic WEP, is designed to address the problem with manual entry of the shared key. Although Dynamic WEP is much more secure than WEP, the newer and stronger WPA standard and the bad reputation that WEP has gained probably means that Dynamic WEP will not gain wide acceptance.

■ The random IV is only 24 bits and is reused. On large networks, APs and stations reuse the IV pretty frequently (even as often as every hour). Many programs exist that can capture network traffic and examine the details of the data packets being transmitted, including details about the IV.

Wi-Fi Protected Access

To help address the security limitations of WEP, a group of wireless equipment known as the Wi-Fi Alliance developed a new encryption standard named **Wi-Fi Protected Access** (WPA). WPA builds upon the security in WEP in two main ways:

■ WPA provides stronger data encryption. WPA uses Temporal Key Integrity Protocol (TKIP), a protocol that provides per-packet key mixing, a message integrity check, and a stronger IV with keys that are not reused for longer periods of time.

■ WPA requires 802.1x authentication to ensure that only authorized users or computers are allowed to connect to a wireless network. 802.1x authentication is optional with WEP.

Configuring Wireless Networking in Windows XP Professional

Windows XP Professional includes a feature called Zero Client Configuration that eases the detection of and connection to wireless networks, and also makes transitions from one wireless network to another more transparent to users. Windows XP Professional supports both ad-hoc and infrastructure wireless networking, and also supports both WEP and WPA encryption.

> **Note** When Windows XP Professional first shipped, it did not include support for WPA. Support was provided later via the Windows WPA Client Update, available at *http://support.microsoft .com/Default.aspx?kbid=815485*. However, WPA support is also included with Windows XP Service Pack 2 without needing to use this client update.

How to Connect to a Wireless Network

After installing a wireless network adapter, Windows XP Professional attempts to locate wireless networks in the area automatically. When Windows locates a network, it displays an icon in the notification area (a picture of a computer with wireless "waves" coming out of it). Windows also displays a ScreenTip (a pop-up notification balloon) above that icon, letting you know that it has detected wireless networks.

To connect to a wireless network, use these steps:

1. Right-click the wireless connection icon in the notification area, and then click View Available Wireless Networks.

Windows displays the Wireless Network Connection dialog box, shown in Figure 15-19. This dialog box shows you each network Windows XP has detected and also the security status of the network (whether it is unsecured or secured).

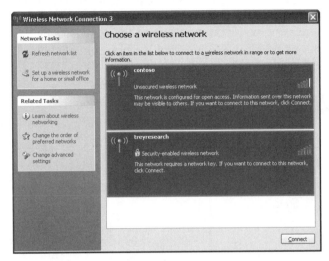

Figure 15-19   The Wireless Network Connections dialog box shows whether detected networks are secured or unsecured.

2. Click the wireless network to which you want to connect, and then click Connect.

   If the network to which you are connecting is unsecured (which means unencrypted), Windows displays a warning to that effect and asks whether you are sure you want to connect.

3. Click Yes.

   Windows refreshes the Wireless Network Connection window to show that you are now connected to the wireless network. Proceed to Step 5.

   If the wireless network to which you want to connect is secure, Windows displays a dialog box asking you to type the appropriate network key.

4. Type and confirm the network key, and then click Connect.

   Windows refreshes the Wireless Network Connection window to show that you are now connected to the wireless network.

5. Close the Wireless Network Connection window.

After making the connection to a network, you can right-click the connection icon in the notification area to disable or repair the connection, or to view open network connections.

Wireless Connection Options

In the Wireless Network Connection dialog box (refer to Figure 15-19), you can click Change Advanced Settings to bring up the Properties dialog box for the wireless connection, shown in Figure 15-20. You can also open the Properties dialog box for a wireless connection the same way you would for a local area connection: by opening the Network Connections window (via Control Panel), right-clicking the connection, and choosing Properties.

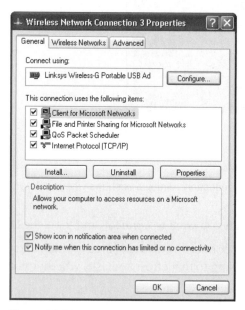

Figure 15-20   The Properties dialog box for a wireless connection works much like that of a LAN connection.

For the most part, this dialog box works the same way in which the Properties dialog box for local area connections works. On the General tab, you can control whether components are enabled or disabled for the connection. You can also configure TCP/IP options. On the Advanced tab, you can control Windows Firewall settings. However, ICS is not available for wireless connections.

On the Wireless Network tab, shown in Figure 15-21, you can click View Wireless Networks to return to the Wireless Network Connection window. The Preferred Networks shows you networks to which you have successfully connected. Windows automatically tries to connect to networks in the order in which they are listed, although you can adjust that order.

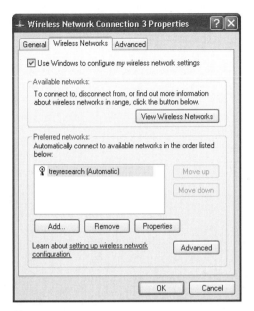

Figure 15-21   The Wireless Networking tab shows wireless networks to which you have connected.

To configure a specific network, click the network, and then click Properties. You can use the Properties dialog box for a network, shown in Figure 15-22, to configure the following:

■ On the Association tab (see Figure 15-22), you can change the SSID for the network connection, and change the wireless network key options used for network security. These options include settings for both data encryption and network authentication. For authentication, choose WPA or WPA-PSK if you are using WPA. If you are using WEP, you should use open authentication. Because WEP uses the same key for authentication and encryption, using open authentication is actually stronger than using WEP for authentication because an attacker that has cracked the WEP key would be able to access authentication information. For data encryption, select the type of encryption that matches the encryption used on your network.

■ On the Authentication tab, you can enable 802.1x authentication for the network.

■ On the Connection tab, you can specify whether Windows should connect to the wireless network when within range to do so.

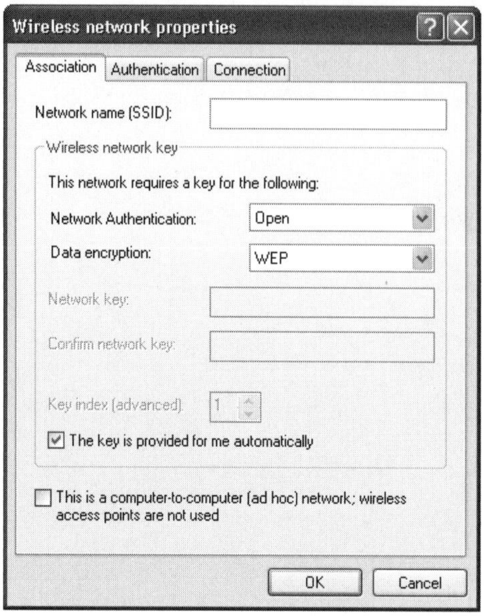

Figure 15-22 The Wireless Networking tab shows wireless networks to which you have connected.

Lesson Review

Use the following questions to help determine whether you have learned enough to move on to the next lesson. If you have difficulty answering these questions, review the material in this lesson before beginning the next lesson. You can find answers to these questions in the "Questions and Answers" section at the end of this chapter.

1. Which two modes of networking are available for connecting to a wireless network in Windows XP Professional?

   _____

   _____

2. What are four ways to protect a wireless network?

   _____

   _____

3. When you configure 802.1x authentication for wireless networking in Windows XP Professional, all wireless connections use the same authentication settings. (True/False)

   _____

   _____

Lesson Summary

- 802.11 standards include the following:
    - 802.11b, which offers data transfer rates of 5.5 Mbps and 11 Mbps, and operates in the 2.45 GHz radio frequency.
    - 802.11a, which offers data transfer rates up to 54 Mbps and operates in the 5.8 GHz frequency.
    - 802.11g, which offers data transfer rates up to 54 Mbps and operates in the 2.4 GHz frequency.
- Windows XP Professional can operate in two wireless networking modes:
    - Ad-hoc wireless networking, in which there are multiple stations but no AP. Ad-hoc wireless networks are technically known as independent basic service sets.
    - Infrastructure wireless networking, in which stations connect to an AP. Infrastructure wireless networks are technically known as basic service sets. Basic service sets can be network together to create extended service sets.
- You can protect wireless networks in the following ways:
    - By filtering MAC addresses so that only specified computers can connect to an AP.
    - By disabling SSID broadcasts so that casual intruders cannot detect the wireless network.
    - By using WEP encryption, which is widely supported but also has widely recognized flaws.
    - By using WPA encryption, which provides stronger encryption than WEP.
- Windows XP Professional supports Zero Client Configuration, which means that Windows can automatically detect and connect to wireless networks. For secured networks, you must configure the client to access the network properly, but connection after that configuration is also automatic.

Lesson 4: Configuring Internet Connection Sharing (ICS)

ICS offers a simple way to configure computers in a small home office network to share a single Internet connection. For small networks, ICS offers a cost-effective way to provide Internet access to multiple computers.

> **After this lesson, you will be able to**
>
> - Configure ICS.
> - Identify the limitations of ICS.
> - Troubleshoot ICS on a computer running Windows XP Professional.
>
> **Estimated lesson time: 10 minutes**

Introducing Internet Connection Sharing (ICS)

When you set up ICS on a network, the computer with the physical connection to the Internet (whether that is a modem, cable, or other type of connection) is designated as the ICS host. Other computers on the network connect to the Internet through the ICS host, as shown in Figure 15-23. In addition to providing Internet access, the ICS host computer also dynamically allocates IP addresses to the clients on the network, provides name resolution, and serves as the gateway for the other computers.

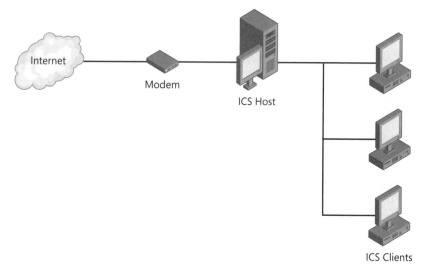

Figure 15-23   The ICS host has a shared Internet connection and acts as a DHCP server for network clients that obtain their IP addresses automatically.

Setting up ICS on a small network consists of the following general steps:

1. Make sure that the computer that will become the ICS computer is properly connected to the Internet.

2. Make sure that the ICS computer and the other computers are properly connected to one another via a local network.

3. On the ICS computer, enable Internet Connection Sharing on the network connection for the Internet.. This is done by selecting the Allow Other Network Users To Connect Through This Computer's Internet Connection option on the Advanced tab of the network connection's Properties dialog box. When you enable ICS, the ICS computer configures itself with the IP address 192.168.0.1 and also becomes a DHCP server for the network, so that it can provide IP addressing information to other computers.

4. Configure the remaining computers to obtain their IP address and DNS server information automatically and restart the computers. When each computer restarts, it will obtain addressing information from the ICS computer and should be able to connect to the Internet. IP addresses of the computers will fall in the range 192.168.0.2–192.168.0.254.

ICS Limitations

Because of what ICS does for a network (IP address allocation, name resolution, and acting as the network's gateway), and because the IP address the host computer uses is always 192.168.0.1 with a subnet mask of 255.255.255.0, several conditions must be met while ICS is used:

■ The IP addresses of the computers on the network must also be in the 192.168.0.x range, and the subnet mask must always be 255.255.255.0. If network computers cannot use these addresses, ICS does not work properly.

■ Windows 2000 Server or Windows Server 2003 servers configured as domain controllers, DNS servers, gateways, and DHCP servers cannot be used on the network. ICS is intended for use only in a workgroup environment.

■ Computers with static IP addresses that do not fall in the ICS range do not work with ICS.

■ If more than one network adapter is available, and if two or more LAN connections are configured and all of them connect to computers on the network, those connections need to be bridged. Bridging a connection is as simple as right-clicking the connection and selecting Bridge Connections.

■ ICS must be enabled from the dial-up, VPN, broadband, or other connection to the Internet.

Problems can also occur with ICS if the host computer originally had a static IP address on the network or if the address 192.168.0.1 is being used by another computer on the network.

 Note   If you are having problems with an ICS configuration, check the items in the preceding bulleted list. Make the appropriate changes to the network to resolve the problem.

Troubleshooting ICS

Although you can troubleshoot ICS by using many of the connectivity troubleshooting methods already covered in this chapter, if the network is small (10 or fewer computers), it is generally easiest to start over with ICS than to troubleshoot it. After you know that you have removed any offending DHCP or DNS servers or any computers with static IP addresses, simply reconfigure ICS on the host computer, and then reconfigure and restart the other computers on the network.

Lesson Review

Use the following questions to help determine whether you have learned enough to move on to the next lesson. If you have difficulty answering these questions, review the material in this lesson before beginning the next lesson. You can find answers to these questions in the "Questions and Answers" section at the end of this chapter.

1. A user has set up ICS on a host computer that runs Windows XP Professional, but is experiencing problems with clients being able to connect to both the Internet and other computers on the network. Which of the following items could be the cause of the problems? Choose all that apply.

   a. There is a DHCP server on the network.

   b. There is a DNS server on the network.

   c. There are computers on the network with static IP addresses.

   d. There is a Windows 2000 server on the network.

2. What IP address is assigned to the ICS host?

   _____

3. After enabling ICS on the host computer, how should you configure other computers in the workgroup to connect to the Internet through the ICS computer?

   _____

   _____

   _____

Lesson Summary

- ICS lets one computer with an Internet connection share that connection with other computers on the network. The computer running ICS always configures itself with the IP address 192.168.0.1. That computer also acts as a DHCP server and gives other computers on the network addresses in the 192.168.0.2 through 192.168.0.254 range.

- ICS is intended for workgroup environments. Windows 2000 Server or Windows Server 2003 servers configured as domain controllers, DNS servers, gateways, and DHCP servers cannot be used on the network. Also, computers with static IP addresses that do not fall in the ICS range do not work with ICS.

- ICS does not provide many troubleshooting options (although you can perform basic network connectivity troubleshooting on the network). The best option is almost always to reconfigure ICS on the network.

Lesson 5: Configuring Windows Firewall

A firewall protects a computer from the outside world (specifically, the Internet) by blocking all network traffic except that which you specifically configure the firewall to allow through. This section introduces firewalls and looks at the software-based firewall that is included with Windows XP Professional: Windows Firewall.

After this lesson, you will be able to

- Explain how firewalls protect computers.
- Enable or disable Windows Firewall for all network connections.
- Enable or disable Windows Firewall for a specific network connection.
- Configure advanced options for Windows Firewall.
- Troubleshoot connectivity problems that are associated with Windows Firewall.

Estimated lesson time: 40 minutes

Introducing Windows Firewall

A firewall acts as a security system that creates a border between the computer or network and the Internet. This border determines what traffic is allowed in the local network or computer. Firewalls help keep hackers, viruses, and other malicious activity from infiltrating the computer and network. A network-based firewall is a device that protects an entire network. A host-based firewall is a program that protects a single computer. Windows XP Professional includes a software firewall named Windows Firewall.

Windows Firewall is installed when you install Windows XP Service Pack 2, and is an updated version of the Internet Connection Firewall found on versions of Windows XP with Service Pack 1 and previous. Windows Firewall is a stateful, host-based firewall that drops all incoming traffic that does not meet one of the following conditions:

- Solicited traffic (valid traffic that is sent in response to a request by the computer) is allowed through the firewall.

- Expected traffic (valid traffic that you have specifically configured the firewall to accept) is allowed through the firewall.

Windows Firewall has the following characteristics:

- Is enabled by default for all network connections. This differs from Internet Connection Firewall, which was not enabled by default.

- Limits the network traffic that comes into a computer by blocking transmission over all ports except those specifically configured to allow traffic to reach the computer. When you allow a specific type of traffic into a computer through Windows Firewall, this is called creating an **exception**. You can create exceptions by specifying the file name of an application or by configuring specified ports for which to allow traffic. Windows Firewall lets you create exceptions for each network connection. This differs from Internet Connection Firewall, which only allowed you to create global exceptions that affected all connections.

- Can restrict traffic by IP address (or IP address range), meaning that only traffic from computers with valid IP addresses is allowed through the firewall.

- Allows you to enable or disable Windows Firewall on each connection configured on a computer running Windows XP Professional, whether that connection is a LAN connection, dial-up connection, or wireless connection. You can also set global configurations that affect all connections. This differs from Internet Connection Firewall, which only allowed you to enable or disable the firewall globally for all connections.

- Allows you to keep a security log of blocked traffic so that you can view firewall activity.

- Performs stateful packet filtering during startup, so that the computer can perform basic network tasks (such as contacting DHCP and DNS servers) and still be protected. This differs from Internet Connection Firewall, which did not perform any filtering during startup.

How to Enable or Disable Windows Firewall for all Network Connections

The only users who can make changes to Windows Firewall settings are those who log on to the computer with a user account that is a member of the local Administrators group. To enable or disable Windows Firewall for all network connections, use these steps:

1. Click Start, and then click Control Panel.

2. In the Control Panel window, click Network And Internet Connections.

3. In the Network And Internet Connections window, click Windows Firewall.

4. On the General tab of the Windows Firewall dialog box, shown in Figure 15-24, click On (Recommended) to enable the firewall for all connections. Click Off (Not Recommended) to disable the firewall for all connections.

5. Click OK.

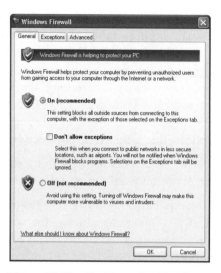

Figure 15-24   Enable or disable Windows Firewall for all network connections.

How to Enable or Disable Windows Firewall for a Specific Network Connection

In addition to begin able to enable or disable Windows Firewall for all connections, you can control whether Windows Firewall is enabled on each connection on a computer. To enable or disable Windows Firewall for a specific network connection, use these steps:

1. Click Start, and then click Control Panel.

2. In the Control Panel window, click Network And Internet Connections.

3. In the Network And Internet Connections window, click Windows Firewall.

4. In the Windows Firewall dialog box, click the Advanced tab, shown in Figure 15-25.

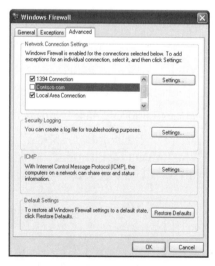

Figure 15-25   Enable or disable Windows Firewall for specific network connections.

5. To enable Windows Firewall for a connection, select the check box for that connection. To disable Windows Firewall for a connection, clear the check box for that connection.

6. Click OK to close the Windows Firewall dialog box.

7. Click OK to close the Properties dialog box for the network connection.

Windows Firewall Advanced Options

After enabling Windows Firewall, you might need to configure it for a specific situation. You have several options for configuring Windows Firewall options, including the following:

■ Enabling Windows Firewall logging to log network activity

■ Creating an exception for a service or application to allow traffic through the firewall

■ Creating a custom service definition when a built-in exception does not suit your needs

■ Creating an Internet Control Message Protocol (ICMP) exception so that the computer responds to traffic from certain network utilities

How to Enable Windows Firewall Logging

You can configure Windows Firewall to log network activity, including any dropped packets or successful connections to the computer. Security logging is not enabled by default for Windows Firewall. To enable security logging for Windows Firewall, use these steps:

1. Click Start, and then click Control Panel.

2. In the Control Panel window, click Network And Internet Connections.

3. In the Network And Internet Connections window, click Windows Firewall.

4. In the Windows Firewall dialog box, on the Advanced tab, in the Security Logging section, click Settings.

   Windows displays the Log Settings dialog box, shown in Figure 15-26.

5. In the Logging Options section, select one or both of the following check boxes:

   ❑ Log Dropped Packets. Logs all dropped packets originating from the local network or the Internet.

   ❑ Log Successful Connections. Logs all successful connections originating from the network or the Internet.

Figure 15-26   Enable security logging for Windows Firewall.

6. Note the location of the security log. By default, the log file is named pfirewall.log and is located in the %systemroot% folder. Click OK to close the Log Settings dialog box. Click OK again to close the Windows Firewall dialog box.

How to Access the Windows Firewall Log File

After you enable logging, you can access the log file by browsing to its location and opening the file. Log entries provide insight about which packets have been successful in getting into the network and which have been rejected. There are two sections of the log: the header and the body. The header includes information about the version of Windows Firewall, the full name of the Windows Firewall, where the time stamp on the log learned of the time, and the field names used by the body of the log entry to display data. The body details the log data.

There are 16 data entries per logged item, which include information about the date and time the log was written and information about the data that passed. This information tells which types of packets were opened, closed, dropped, and lost; which **protocol** was used in the data transmission; the destination IP address of the data; the **port** used by the sending computer; the port of the destination computer; and the size of the packet logged.

To locate and open the Windows Firewall log file, use these steps:

1. Click Start, and then click Control Panel.

2. In the Control Panel window, click Network And Internet Connections.

3. In the Network And Internet Connections window, click Windows Firewall.

4. In the Windows Firewall dialog box, on the Advanced tab, in the Security Logging section, click Settings.

5. In the Log Settings dialog box, in the Log File Options section, click Save As.

6. In the Browse dialog box, right-click the pfirewall.txt file, and then click Open.

7. After reviewing the firewall log, close the Notepad window, click OK to exit the Log Settings dialog box, and then click OK again to close the Windows Firewall dialog box.

Exam Tip   You should know where Windows Firewall log files are stored, whether logging is available, and what kind of information you can learn from log files.

▶ How to Create an Exception for a Service or Application

By default, Windows Firewall blocks all unsolicited traffic. You can create exceptions so that particular types of unsolicited traffic are allowed through the firewall. For example, if you want to allow sharing of files and printers on a local computer, you must enable the File And Printer Sharing exception in Windows Firewall so that requests for the shared resources are allowed to reach the computer.

Windows Firewall includes a number of common exceptions, such as Remote Assistance, Remote Desktop, File And Printer Sharing, and Windows Messenger. Windows Firewall also automatically extends the exceptions available for you to enable according to the programs installed on a computer. You can manually add exceptions to the list by browsing for program files.

To create a global exception that applies to all network connections for which Windows Firewall is enabled, use these steps:

1. Click Start, and then click Control Panel.

2. In the Control Panel window, click Network And Internet Connections.

3. In the Network And Internet Connections window, click Windows Firewall.

4. In the Windows Firewall dialog box, click the Exceptions tab, shown in Figure 15-27.

Figure 15-27   Create a global exception for all connections in Windows Firewall.

5. In the Programs And Services list, select the check box for the service you want to allow. If you need to add an exception for an installed program that does not appear on the list, click Add Program to locate the executable file for the program, and then enable the exception after the program is added to the list.

6. Click OK to close the Windows Firewall dialog box.

▶ **How to Create an Exception for a Particular Port**

If Windows Firewall does not include an exception for the traffic you need to allow, and adding an executable file to the list does not produce the results you need, you can also create an exception by unblocking traffic for a particular port.

To create a global exception for a port that applies to all network connections for which Windows Firewall is enabled, use these steps.

1. Click Start, and then click Control Panel.

2. In the Control Panel window, click Network And Internet Connections.

3. In the Network And Internet Connections window, click Windows Firewall.

4. In the Windows Firewall dialog box, on the Exceptions tab, click Add Port.

   Windows displays the Add A Port dialog box. To create an exception based on a Transmission Control Protocol (TCP) or User Datagram Protocol (UDP) port number, you must know the proper port number used by an application or service to use this option.

5. Type a name for the exception, type the port number you want to allow access for, and then select whether the port is a TCP or UDP port.

   You can also change the scope to which the exception applies. Your options are to have the exception apply to any computer (including computers on the Internet), the local network only, or a custom list of IP addresses.

6. To change the scope of the exception, click Change Scope to open the Change Scope dialog box, where you can configure the scope options. Click OK to return to the Add A Port dialog box.

7. Click OK again to add the exception and return to the Windows Firewall dialog box.

   After you have added the exception, it appears in the Programs And Services list on the Exceptions tab of the Windows Firewall dialog box.

8. Select the check box for the exception to enable it.

9. Click OK to close the Windows Firewall dialog box.

To create a service exception for a particular network connection for which Windows Firewall is enabled, use these steps.

1. Click Start, and then click Control Panel.

2. In the Control Panel window, click Network And Internet Connections.

3. In the Network And Internet Connections window, click Windows Firewall.

4. In the Windows Firewall dialog box, on the Advanced tab, in the Network Connection Settings section, click the connection for which you want to configure an exception, and then click Settings.

   Windows displays the Advanced Settings dialog box, shown in Figure 15-28.

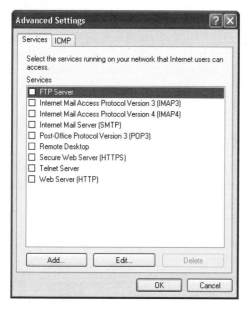

Figure 15-28   Create an exception for a particular network connection in Windows Firewall.

5. On the Services tab, click Add.

   Windows displays the Service Settings dialog box.

6. Type a description of the service.

7. If the computer on which you are configuring Windows Firewall is an ICS host, you can configure Windows Firewall to forward traffic for the port to a particular computer on the network by typing that computer's IP address. If the computer is not an ICS host, you should enter the IP address for the local computer.

Tip   Instead of entering the IP address for the local computer, you can also use the loopback address 127.0.0.1, which always refers to the local computer. This is useful should the IP address of the local computer change.

8. Enter the port information for the service.

9. Click OK to close the Service Settings dialog box. Click OK to close the Advanced Settings dialog box. Click OK again to close the Windows Firewall dialog box.

▶   **ICMP Exceptions**

ICMP allows routers and host computers to swap basic error and configuration information. The information includes whether or not the data sent reaches its final destination, whether it can or cannot be forwarded by a specific router, and what the best route for the data is. ICMP tools such as Pathping, Ping, and Tracert are often used to troubleshoot network connectivity.

ICMP troubleshooting tools and their resulting messages are helpful when used by a network administrator, but harmful when used by an attacker. For instance, a network administrator sends a ping request in the form of an ICMP packet that contains an echo request message to the IP address that is being tested. The reply to that echo request message allows the administrator to verify that the computer is reachable. An attacker, on the other hand, can send a **storm** of specially formed pings that can overload a computer so that it cannot respond to legitimate traffic. Attackers can also use ping commands to determine the IP addresses of computers on a network. By configuring ICMP, you can control how a system responds (or does not respond) to such ping requests. By default, Windows Firewall blocks all ICMP messages.

Table 15-5 provides details about ICMP exceptions you can enable in Windows Firewall.

Table 15-5   ICMP Options

ICMP Option	Description
Allow Incoming Echo Request	Controls whether a remote computer can ask for and receive a response from the computer. Ping is a command that requires you to enable this option. When enabled (as with other options), attackers can see and contact the host computer.
Allow Incoming Timestamp Request	Sends a reply to another computer, stating that an incoming message was received and includes time and date data.
Allow Incoming Mask Request	Provides the sender with the subnet mask for the network of which the computer is a member. The sender already has the IP address; giving the subnet mask is all an administrator (or attacker) needs to obtain the remaining network information about the computer's network.
Allow Incoming Router Request	Provides information about the routes the computer recognizes and passes on information it has about any routers to which it is connected.

Table 15-5   ICMP Options

ICMP Option	Description
Allow Outgoing Destination Unreachable	The computer sends a Destination Unreachable error message to clients who attempt to send packets through the computer to a remote network for which there is no route.
Allow Outgoing Source Quench	Offers information to routers about the rate at which data is received; tells routers to slow down if too much data is being sent and it cannot be received fast enough to keep up.
Allow Outgoing Parameter Problem	The computer sends a Bad Header error message when the computer discards data it has received that has a problematic header. This message allows the sender to understand that the host exists, but that there were unknown problems with the message itself.
Allow Outgoing Time Exceeded	The computer sends the sender a Time Expired message when the computer must discard messages because the messages timed out.
Allow Redirect	Data that is sent from this computer will be rerouted if the path changes.

Security Alert   Generally, you should enable ICMP exceptions only when you need them for troubleshooting, and then disable them after you have completed troubleshooting. Make sure that you do not allow or enable these options without a full understanding of them and of the consequences and risks involved.

How to Enable ICMP Exceptions

To enable a global ICMP exception for all connections on a computer, use these steps:

1. Click Start, and then click Control Panel.

2. In the Control Panel window, click Network And Internet Connections.

3. In the Network And Internet Connections window, click Windows Firewall.

4. In the Windows Firewall dialog box, click the Advanced tab.

5. In the ICMP section, click Settings.

6. Select the check box for the exception you want to enable.

7. Click OK to close the ICMP Settings dialog box. Click OK again to close the Windows Firewall dialog box.

To enable an ICMP exception for a network connection, use these steps:

1. Click Start, and then click Control Panel.

2. In the Control Panel window, click Network And Internet Connections.

3. In the Network And Internet Connections window, click Windows Firewall.

4. In the Windows Firewall dialog box, click the Advanced tab.

5. In the Network Connection Settings section, click the connection for which you want to configure an exception, and then click Settings.

6. In the Advanced Settings dialog box, click the ICMP tab, shown in Figure 15-29.

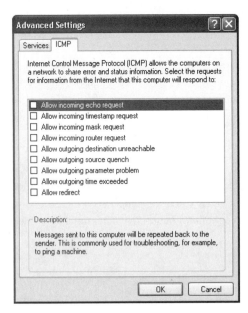

Figure 15-29   Create an ICMP exception for a connection.

7. Select the check box for the exception you want to enable.

8. Click OK to close the Advanced Settings dialog box. Click OK again to close the Windows Firewall dialog box.

Troubleshooting Windows Firewall

There are a few fairly common problems that end users encounter when using Windows Firewall, including the inability to enable or disable Windows Firewall on a connection, problems with file and print sharing, a network user's inability to access a server on the network (such as a Web server), problems with Remote Assistance, and problems running Internet programs.

When troubleshooting Windows Firewall, make sure that you remember to check the obvious first. The following are some basic rules that you must follow, and any deviation from them can cause many of the common problems that are encountered when using Windows Firewall:

■ Windows Firewall can be enabled or disabled only by administrators. ICF can be enabled or disabled by a Local Security Policy or Group Policy, as well—sometimes preventing access even by a local administrator.

■ To share printers and files on a local computer that is running Windows Firewall, you must enable the File And Printer Sharing exception.

■ If the local computer is running a service, such as a Web server, FTP server, or other service, network users cannot connect to these services unless you create the proper exceptions in Windows Firewall.

■ Windows Firewall blocks Remote Assistance and Remote Desktop traffic by default. You must enable the Remote Desktop exception for remote users to be able to connect to a local computer with Remote Desktop or Remote Assistance.

Practice: Configure Windows Firewall

In this practice, you will ensure that Windows Firewall is enabled on all connections on your computer. You will disable and then re-enable Windows Firewall on your LAN connection only. You will then enable an exception in Windows Firewall for all connections. The practices in this exercise require that you have a properly configured LAN connection.

Exercise 1: Ensure that Windows Firewall is Enabled For All Network Connections

1. Click Start, and then click Control Panel.

2. In the Control Panel window, click Network And Internet Connections.

3. In the Network Connections window, right-click your LAN connection, and then click Properties.

4. In the Local Area Connection Properties dialog box, on the Advanced tab, in the Windows Firewall section, click Settings.

5. In the Windows Firewall dialog box, ensure that On (Recommended) is selected. Also ensure that the Don't Allow Exceptions check box is cleared.

   Leave both the Windows Firewall dialog box and the Local Area Connection Properties dialog box open for the next exercise.

Exercise 2: Disable and Re-Enable Windows Firewall on Your Local Area Connection Only

1. In the Windows Firewall dialog box, click the Advanced tab.

2. In the Network Connection Settings section, in the list of connections, clear the check box next to Local Area Connection, and then click OK.

Windows Firewall is now disabled for the local area connection. A bubble appears in the notification area informing you that your computer is at risk because the firewall is disabled.

3. In the Network Connections window, right-click Local Area Connection, and then click Properties. In the Local Area Connection Properties dialog box, click the Advanced tab. In the Windows Firewall section, click Settings.

4. In the Windows Firewall dialog box, on the Advanced tab, select the check box next to Local Area Connection, and then click OK.

Windows Firewall is now enabled for the local area connection. Leave the Local Area Connection Properties dialog box open for the next exercise.

Exercise 3: Enable an Exception in Windows Firewall for all Connections

1. In the Local Area Connection Properties dialog box, on the Advanced tab, in the Windows Firewall section, click Settings.

2. In the Windows Firewall dialog box, on the Exceptions tab, select the File And Printer Sharing check box.

3. Click OK.

Windows Firewall is now configured to allow file and printer sharing traffic into your computer.

4. Click OK again to close the Local Area Connection Properties dialog box.

Lesson Review

Use the following questions to help determine whether you have learned enough to move on to the next lesson. If you have difficulty answering these questions, review the material in this lesson before beginning the next lesson. You can find answers to these questions in the "Questions and Answers" section at the end of this chapter.

1. You are troubleshooting a network connection and need to use the Ping command to see if a computer is reachable. Which ICMP exception must you enable on that computer? Choose the correct answer.

    a. Allow Incoming Router Request

    b. Allow Incoming Echo Request

    c. Allow Outgoing Source Quench

    d. Allow Redirect

2. By default, what two types of traffic does Windows Firewall allow into a computer?

_____

_____

_____

3. Windows Firewall protects a computer running Windows XP Professional even while the computer is starting up. (True/False)

_____

_____

Lesson Summary

- Windows Firewall is a software-based firewall built into Windows XP Professional. Windows Firewall blocks all incoming network traffic except for solicited traffic and excepted traffic.

- You can enable or disable Windows Firewall globally for all network connections on a computer, including LAN, dial-up, and wireless connections.

- You can also enable or disable Windows Firewall selectively for each network connection on a computer.

- Windows Firewall allows you to configure a number of advanced options, including the following:

    ❑ Enabling Windows Firewall logging to log network activity

    ❑ Creating an exception for a service or application to allow traffic through the firewall

    ❑ Creating a custom service definition when a built-in exception does not suit your needs

    ❑ Creating an ICMP exception so that the computer responds to traffic from certain network utilities

- Troubleshooting Windows Firewall typically involves enabling or disabling Windows Firewall and creating exceptions so that specific network traffic is allowed into the computer.

Case Scenario Exercise

In this exercise, you will read a scenario about configuring network connections and then answer the questions that follow. If you have difficulty completing this work, review the material in this chapter before beginning the next chapter. You can find answers to these questions in the "Questions and Answers" section at the end of this chapter.

Scenario

You are an administrator working for a company named Contoso, Ltd., a developer of custom networking applications based in Houston. Greta, a user in the Sales department, has contacted you for help in setting up a demonstration of one of the company's applications at a seminar in a hotel in Las Vegas. The hotel has provided a conference room with broadband Internet access via an Ethernet cable, but your staff must configure their own network when they get there. The company is sending five notebook computers running Windows XP Professional. Each computer has a built-in Ethernet network adapter and a built-in wireless network adapter, but none has been configured for networking.

All five of the computers will be used in demonstrations and must be networked together. In addition, all the computers will need access to the Internet. Because all the computers are running Windows XP Professional, you have configured each computer so that it is a member of a workgroup named Contoso.

Questions

1. Because each of the computers has a wireless network adapter, you have decided to create a wireless network to connect the computers. However, the company did not send any wireless networking devices. Can you create a wireless network without additional hardware? If so, what kind of wireless network can you create?

    _____

2. You want to secure the wireless network. What kind of security could you implement on the type of wireless network you can create?

    _____

    _____

    _____

3. Because there is only one Internet connection, and each computer must have Internet access, you have decided to use ICS to share Internet access among the computers. The connection you have been provided requires that the computer

be configured to accept a leased IP address from a DHCP server. How would you configure this?

_____

_____

_____

_____

_____

_____

_____

_____

4. After successfully establishing the Internet connection for the selected notebook computer, how would you enable ICS on the host computer?

_____

_____

_____

_____

5. After enabling Internet Connection Sharing, what IP address will the host computer assign itself for the wireless network connection on the private network?

_____

6. How should you configure the other notebook computers to connect to the host computer?

_____

_____

_____

_____

7. What range of IP addresses would you expect to see for the wireless network connections on the other notebook computers?

_____

8. After configuring the other notebook computers, all but one can connect to the Internet successfully. However, one of the computers does not connect. What two

methods could you use to determine the IP address assigned to that computer's wireless network connection?

_____

_____

_____

9. You determine that the computer's wireless connection has been assigned the IP address 169.254.003.322, which indicates that the computer has assigned itself an IP address rather than obtaining an address from the ICS host computer. In what two ways could you force the computer to attempt to obtain an IP address again?

_____

_____

Troubleshooting Lab

You are an administrator for a company named Contoso, Ltd., and are still working with Greta at her sales seminar. You have successfully configured the network so that all computers can connect to one another and to the Internet. Greta is now trying to demonstrate one of the company's custom networking applications. One notebook computer is running the custom application and is trying to connect to another note-book computer. The target computer does not need to have the application installed. However, the application cannot connect.

1. What do you suspect might be interfering with the network traffic from the custom application?

_____

_____

2. How would you solve this problem?

_____

_____

_____

_____

_____

_____

Chapter Summary

- You can view all network connections configured on a computer in the Network Connections window, which you can access through Control Panel. In the Network Connections window, you can right-click a connection to access command for renaming, disabling, and repairing a connection. You can also open a connection's Properties dialog box to configure advanced options.

- Dial-up connections work much like LAN connections, but they have additional options that let you control when the connection is dialed, the number for the connection, and other criteria for use. To create a dial-up connection, you use the New Connection Wizard. You can also configure Windows XP Professional to allow incoming dial-up connections.

- Windows XP Professional can operate in two wireless modes: ad-hoc wireless networking, in which there are multiple stations but no AP, and infrastructure wireless networking, in which stations connect to an AP. You can secure wireless networks in the following ways:

  - By filtering MAC addresses so that only specified computers can connect to an AP

  - By disabling SSID broadcasts so that casual intruders will not detect the wireless network

  - By using WEP encryption, which is widely supported but also has widely recognized flaws

  - By using WPA encryption, which provides stronger encryption than WEP

- ICS lets one computer with an Internet connection share that connection with other computers on the network. The computer running ICS always configures itself with the IP address 192.168.0.1. That computer also acts as a DHCP server and gives other computers on the network addresses in the 192.168.0.2 through 192.168.0.254 range.

- Windows Firewall is a software-based firewall built into Windows XP Professional. Windows Firewall blocks all incoming network traffic except for solicited traffic and excepted traffic. You can enable or disable Windows Firewall globally for all network connections on a computer, or enable and disable it on individual connections.

Exam Highlights

Before taking the exam, review the key points and terms that are presented in this chapter. You need to know this information.

Key Points

- Repairing a network connection forces several actions, the most important of which include renewing an IP address lease (which you can also do by typing **ipconfig /renew** at the command prompt) and flushing the DNS cache (which you can also do by typing **ipconfig /flushdns** at the command prompt).

- You can configure a wireless client to operate in two modes: ad-hoc mode, in which there is no AP, and infrastructure mode, in which an AP is used. An ad-hoc network offers little security or configurability, and is sometimes used in small workgroup environments. An infrastructure network, which provides greater security and configurability, is the most common mode for wireless networking.

- You should know where Windows Firewall log files are stored, whether logging is available, and what kind of information you can learn from log files.

Key Terms

ad-hoc wireless network   A wireless network mode in which multiple wireless stations can connect without requiring an AP.

dial-up connection   A connection that connects you to a private network or the Internet by using a device that transfers data over a public telephone network.

exception   Unsolicited network traffic that you have specifically configured Windows Firewall to allow.

IEEE 802.1x authentication   Authenticates users and computers for access to 802.11 wireless networks and wired Ethernet networks.

infrastructure wireless network   A wireless network mode in which multiple wireless stations communicate through an AP.

Internet Connection Sharing (ICS)   A feature of Windows XP Professional that allows you to share one connection to the Internet with all computers on your network.

Network Bridge   A feature that allows Windows XP Professional to connect network segments (groups of networked computers) without having to use a router or bridge.

New Connection Wizard   A wizard in Windows XP Professional that can perform much of the work of configuring a network connection for different situations.

Wi-Fi Protected Access (WPA)   A wireless encryption standard available in Windows XP Professional that provides increased security over the WEP standard—the other encryption standard supported by Windows XP Professional.

Windows Firewall   A stateful, host-based firewall provided with Windows XP Professional.

Wired Equivalent Privacy (WEP)   One of two wireless encryption standards available in Windows XP Professional. WEP is the encryption standard that is specified by the IEEE 802.11 standard. The other encryption standard available is WPA.

Questions and Answers

Lesson 1 Review

Page
15-17

1. What are the four outbound connection types that you can configure using the New Connection Wizard?

Connect To The Internet, Connect To The Network At My Workplace, Set Up A Home Or Small Office Network, and Set Up An Advanced Connection

2. In which two ways can you force a network connection to attempt to renew its DHCP lease?

You can type the **ipconfig /renew** command at the command prompt; or you can right-click a network connection in the Network Connections window, and then click Repair.

3. How can you tell the duration that a network connection has been successfully connected?

Right-click the network connection in the Network Connections window, and then click Status to open the Local Area Connection Status dialog box. The General tab shows the current connection status, including whether the connection is connected, the duration of the connection, the rated speed of the connection, and activity on the connection.

Lesson 2 Review

Page
15-28

1. A user complains to you that she does not want to hear her modem each time she connects to the company network from her portable computer. What should you do?

On the Modem tab of the modem's Properties dialog box, reduce the volume or disable the modem speaker entirely.

2. Other than allowing VPN connections, what does Windows XP Professional do when you configure a new connection to allow virtual private connections?

If you choose to allow VPN connections, Windows XP Professional configures Windows Firewall so that your computer can send and receive VPN traffic.

3. What is callback and why would you enable it?

Callback forces the remote server (in this case, your computer) to disconnect from the client calling in, and then call the client computer back. You would use callback to have the bill for a phone call charged to your phone number rather than to the phone number of the user who called in. You could also use callback to increase security because you can specify the number that the system calls back. If an unauthorized user calls in, the callback feature prevents the unauthorized user from accessing the system.

Lesson 3 Review

Page
15-40

1. Which two modes of networking are available for connecting to a wireless network in Windows XP Professional?

Ad-hoc wireless networking, in which there are multiple stations but no AP, and infrastructure wireless networking, in which stations connect to an AP.

2. What are four ways to protect a wireless network?

MAC address filtering, disabling SSID broadcasting, using WEP encryption, and using WPA encryption.

3. When you configure 802.1x authentication for wireless networking in Windows XP Professional, all wireless connections use the same authentication settings. (True/False)

False. Windows XP Professional allows you to configure 802.1x authentication on a per-connection basis.

Lesson 4 Review

Page
15-44

1. A user has set up ICS on a host computer that runs Windows XP Professional, but is experiencing problems with clients being able to connect to both the Internet and other computers on the network. Which of the following items could be the cause of the problems? Choose all that apply.

   a. There is a DHCP server on the network.

   b. There is a DNS server on the network.

   c. There are computers on the network with static IP addresses.

   d. There is a Windows 2000 server on the network.

A, B, and C are correct. DHCP and DNS servers as well as computers with static IP addresses all cause problems for ICS. D is not correct because Windows 2000 servers can be members of workgroups and work with ICS as long as they are not also domain controllers that provide DHCP or DNS services.

2. What IP address is assigned to the ICS host?

192.168.0.1

3. After enabling ICS on the host computer, how should you configure other computers in the workgroup to connect to the Internet through the ICS computer?

You should configure other computers to obtain an IP address automatically. The ICS host acts as DHCP server, assigning IP addresses in the range 192.168.0.2 through 192.168.0.254 to other computers on the network.

Lesson 5 Review

Page
15-58

1. You are troubleshooting a network connection and need to use the Ping command to see if a computer is reachable. Which ICMP exception must you enable on that computer? Choose the correct answer.

    a. Allow Incoming Router Request

    b. Allow Incoming Echo Request

    c. Allow Outgoing Source Quench

    d. Allow Redirect

The correct answer is B. The Allow Incoming Echo Request exception allows a computer to respond to ping requests. A is incorrect because this option provides information about connected routers and the flow of traffic from the computer. C is incorrect because this option allows the computer to send a message to slow the flow of data. D is incorrect because this option allows routers to redirect data to more favorable routes.

2. By default, what two types of traffic does Windows Firewall allow into a computer?

Solicited traffic, which is sent in response to a request by the local computer, and excepted traffic, which is unsolicited traffic that you have specifically configured the firewall to allow.

3. Windows Firewall protects a computer running Windows XP Professional even while the computer is starting up. (True/False)

True. Windows Firewall performs stateful packet filtering during startup so that the computer can perform basic network tasks and still be protected.

Case Scenario Exercise

Page
15-60

1. Because each of the computers has a wireless network adapter, you have decided to create a wireless network to connect the computers. However, the company did not send any wireless networking devices. Can you create a wireless network without additional hardware? If so, what kind of wireless network can you create?

Yes, you can create an ad-hoc network that does not require an AP.

2. You want to secure the wireless network. What kind of security could you implement on the type of wireless network you can create?

Because you are creating an ad-hoc network, you cannot configure the kind of security you could have if you had an AP, such as filtering MAC addresses or disabling SSID broadcasts. However, you can secure an ad-hoc network using WEP.

3. Because there is only one Internet connection, and each computer must have Internet access, you have decided to use ICS to share Internet access among the computers. The connection you have been provided requires that the computer be configured to accept a leased IP address from a DHCP server. How would you configure this?

You should designate one notebook computer to have the Internet connection. On that computer, you should connect the Ethernet cable to the built-in network adapter. You should then open the Properties dialog box for the LAN connection. In the Local Area Connection Properties dialog box, on the General tab, you should select the Internet Protocol (TCP/IP) component, and then click Properties to open the Internet Protocol (TCP/IP) Properties dialog box. You should configure the computer to obtain an IP address automatically.

4. After successfully establishing the Internet connection for the selected notebook computer, how would you enable ICS on the host computer?

   You would open the Properties dialog box for the local area connection that represents the Internet connection. On the Advanced tab of the Properties dialog box, you should select the Allow Other Network Users To Connect Through This Computer's Internet Connection check box.

5. After enabling Internet Connection Sharing, what IP address will the host computer assign itself for the wireless network connection on the private network?

   192.168.0.1.

6. How should you configure the other notebook computers to connect to the host computer?

   You should open the Properties dialog box for the wireless connection on each of the other notebook computers and ensure that the connection is configured to obtain an IP address automatically. The computers will obtain IP addresses from the host computer.

7. What range of IP addresses would you expect to see for the wireless network connections on the other notebook computers?

   ICS assigns IP addresses in the 192.168.0.2 through 192.168.0.254 range.

8. After configuring the other notebook computers, all but one can connect to the Internet successfully. However, one of the computers does not connect. What two methods could you use to determine the IP address assigned to that computer's wireless network connection?

   You could use the ipconfig command at the command prompt or you could right-click that connection in the Network Connections window and then click Status. The Support tab of the connection's Status dialog box indicates the IP address.

9. You determine that the computer's wireless connection has been assigned the IP address 169.254.003.322, which indicates that the computer has assigned itself an IP address rather than obtaining an address from the ICS host computer. In what two ways could you force the computer to attempt to obtain an IP address again?

   You could use the ipconfig /renew command at the command prompt or you could right-click the connection in the Network Connections window, and then click Repair.

Troubleshooting Lab

Page
15-62

1. What do you suspect might be interfering with the network traffic from the custom application?

Most likely, it is Windows Firewall that is interfering because it drops all unsolicited traffic by default unless you create an exception.

2. How would you solve this problem?

Although it would be tempting to disable Windows Firewall for the demonstration, a better solution is to create an exception on the target computer that allows the custom application to connect. This solution has the added advantage of showing Greta's customers how the application can work even when Windows Firewall is enabled. Because the application is not installed on the target computer, you must create an exception on the computer that allows the traffic on the particular port used by the application. To do this, you must know the port or ports that the application uses.

16 Configuring Security Settings and Internet Options

Exam Objectives in this Chapter:

- Configure, manage, and troubleshoot a security configuration and local security policy.
- Configure, manage, and troubleshoot local user and group accounts.
    - ❑ Configure, manage, and troubleshoot auditing.
    - ❑ Configure, manage, and troubleshoot account policy.
    - ❑ Configure, manage, and troubleshoot user and group rights.
- Configure, manage, and troubleshoot Internet Explorer security settings.
- Connect to resources by using Internet Explorer.

Why This Chapter Matters

A security policy is a combination of settings that affect a computer or a user. Policies that affect a computer also affect any user who logs on to that computer. Policies that affect a user affect that user no matter what computer the user logs on to.

In this chapter, you learn how Group Policy and Local Security Policy are applied to a computer running Windows XP Professional. You learn how to configure Local Security Policy and about the various settings that are available for configuration. In this chapter, you also learn how to configure Internet Options in Internet Explorer to view Internet resources and how to enhance security and privacy in Internet Explorer.

Lessons in this Chapter:

Before You Begin

To complete this chapter, you must have a computer that meets the minimum hardware requirements listed in the preface, "About This Book." You must also have Microsoft Windows XP Professional installed on a computer on which you can make changes.

Lesson 1: Overview of Security Policy

Security Policy in Windows XP Professional refers to two types of policies: **Local Security Policy** and **Group Policy**. Local Security Policy is applied to a specific computer, and is the only type of security policy you can use on computers that are members of a workgroup. The specific local policy that you create is referred to as a Local Group Policy Object (LGPO).

Group Policy is applied to sites, domains, and OUs in an Active Directory environment, and affects all computers or users that are members of the container to which the Group Policy is assigned. In a domain environment, administrators typically rely on Group Policy to apply security settings to computers, but Local Security Policy can also apply. The specific group policy that you create is referred to as a Group Policy Object (GPO).

After this lesson, you will be able to

- Configure Local Security Policy on a computer running Windows XP Professional.
- Describe how Group Policy affects a computer running Windows XP Professional.
- View policies that are in effect on a computer running Windows XP Professional.

Estimated lesson time: 40 minutes

How to Configure Local Security Policy

By using Local Security Policy, you can implement numerous security-relevant settings on a local computer, such as group membership, permissions and rights, password requirements, desktop settings, and much more. For computers in a workgroup environment, Local Security Policy offers a way to apply consistent restrictions across those computers.

What You Can Configure with Local Security Policy

Windows XP Professional allows you to configure security settings in the following areas by using Local Security Policy:

Account policies   **Account policies** include password policies, such as minimum password length and account lockout settings. You will learn about the account policies available for configuration in Lesson 2, "Configuring Account Policies."

Local policies   Local policies include three categories of policies, as follows:

   ❑ **Auditing policies** allow you to track the activities of users and the access of resources on a computer. Event log settings are used to configure auditing for security events, such as successful and failed logon attempts. You will learn about auditing in detail in Lesson 5, "Implementing an Audit Policy."

❑ **User rights** assignments allow you to control the basic system functions that a user can perform. You will learn about user rights in detail in Lesson 3, "Configuring User Rights."

❑ **Security options** allow you to control various security settings in Windows XP Professional. You will learn about security options in detail in Lesson 4, "Configuring Security Options."

Public key policies Public key policies are used to configure encrypted data recovery agents and trusted certificate authorities.

Software restriction policies Software restriction policies allow you to prevent unwanted applications from running.

IP security policy IP security policy is used to configure network Internet Protocol (IP) security.

System services System services settings are used to configure and manage security settings for areas such as network services, file and print services, and Internet services.

Registry Registry settings are used to manage the security descriptors on Registry subkeys and entries.

File system File system settings are used to configure and manage security settings on the local file system.

See Also This chapter focuses on using Local Security Policy to configure account policies (Lesson 2), user rights (Lesson 3), security options (Lesson 4), and auditing (Lesson 5). For more information on configuring other available settings, refer to Chapter 16 of the Microsoft Windows XP Professional Resource Kit Documentation, available at *http:// www.microsoft.com/resources/documentation/WindowsServ/2003/standard/proddocs/en-us/ prork_overview.asp*.

How to Modify Local Security Policy

To modify Local Security Policy, you use the Local Security Policy console (see Figure 16-1), which is found in the Administrative Tools folder. The Local Security Policy console provides a standard two-paned console window. The tree in the left pane shows the categories of policies you can assign. This chapter covers settings in the Account Policies folder, which allows you to configure password policy and account lockout policy; and the Local Polices folder, which allows you to configure audit policy, user rights assignments, and security options.

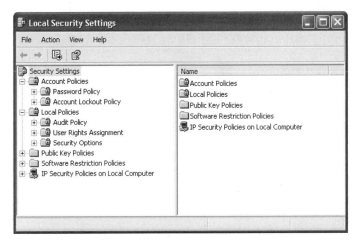

Figure 16-1   Use the Local Security Policy tool to set local policies.

When you select a policy folder (for example, the Password Policy folder), the right pane displays the available policies you can set, as shown in Figure 16-2. For each policy, the current setting is also shown.

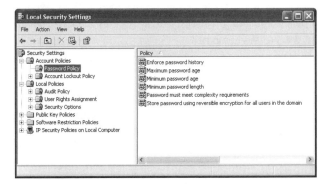

Figure 16-2   The Local Security Policy tool shows available policies and the current settings.

To change a policy with the Local Security Settings tool, use the following steps:

1. Click Start, and then click Control Panel.
2. In the Control Panel window, click Performance And Maintenance.
3. In the Performance And Maintenance window, click Administrative Tools.
4. In the Administrative Tools window, double-click Local Security Policy.
5. In the Local Security Policy window, select the folder containing the policy you want to edit.

6. In the right pane, double-click the policy you want to edit.

Windows displays the dialog box for the policy, as shown in Figure 16-3.

Figure 16-3   Change the settings for the policy.

7. Configure the settings for the policy, and then click OK.

> **Caution**   Settings you configure using the Local Security Policy tool occur immediately; you are not required to save the policy changes. Most of the settings that you make will take effect the next time a user logs on to the computer.

Security Templates

Windows XP Professional provides a number of predefined **security templates** that you can use as a starting point when configuring Local Security Policy. Each template is a collection of settings designed for a particular environment. You can use these templates as they come or you can customize them to suit your needs. There are two advantages of using administrative templates. The first advantage is that you can rely on preconfigured settings instead of having to configure all the settings yourself. The second advantage is that after you have configured a security template to suit your needs, you can use that template to quickly apply settings to other computers, saving you from having to configure the Local Security Policy yourself on each computer.

Predefined Security Templates   By default, the predefined security templates are stored in the %systemroot%\Security\Templates folder. The predefined templates available include the following:

Setup Security (Setup Security.inf)   This template defines the default level of security applied to all new installations of Windows XP Professional on an NTFS File System partition. This template is also intended for resetting security levels back to their default in disaster recovery situations.

Compatible (Compatws.inf)   This template provides a higher level of security than Setup Security, but still ensures that standard applications will run successfully. By default, this template allows all users to run Windows-certified applications, but allows only power users to run noncertified applications.

Secure (Securews.inf)   This template adds an additional layer of security to the Compatible level and can restrict some applications from functioning properly.

High Secure (Hisecws.inf)   This template provides a maximum level of security for network traffic and communication protocols without regard for application compatibility. The High Secure templates impose greater restrictions on the levels of encryption and signing required for authentication.

Root Directory Permissions (Rootsec.inf)   This template specifies the default Windows XP Professional permissions for the root of the system partition. You can use this template to reset the file permissions for the system partition root in disaster recovery situations.

> **Exam Tip**   The Setup Security template (Setup Security.inf) defines the default level of security applied to all new installations of Windows XP Professional on an NTFS partition. This template is useful resetting security levels back to their defaults.

How to Customize a Predefined Security Template   To customize a predefined security template, use these steps:

1. Click Start, and then click Run.

2. In the Run dialog box, type **mmc**, and then click OK.

   Windows opens the Microsoft Management Console (MMC) with a blank console window named Console1.

3. In the console, click File, and then click Add/Remove Snap-In.

4. In the Add/Remove Snap-In dialog box, click Add.

5. In the Add Standalone Snap-Ins dialog box, click Security Templates, and then click Add.

6. Click Close, and then click OK.

   In the console window, Windows displays the Security Templates add-in, as shown in Figure 16-4.

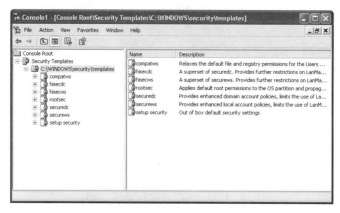

Figure 16-4   Add the Security Templates snap-in to a console.

7. Right-click the predefined template you want to customize, and then click Save As.

8. In the Save As dialog box, type a new name for your customized template, and then click OK.

   Windows adds the new template to the console window.

9. In the console window, expand the new template you just added.

10. Configure the policies the way you want them in your new template.

> **Note**   To configure a policy, double-click it, and then use the dialog box that opens to adjust settings. You will learn more about the settings you can adjust in the other lessons in this chapter.

How to Apply a Security Template   After creating a customized template, you must apply it to a computer for the template to take effect. You will do this by using a tool named Security Configuration And Analysis.

To apply a security template, use these steps:

1. Click Start, and then click Run.

2. In the Run dialog box, type **mmc**, and then click OK.

   Windows opens the MMC with a blank console window named Console1.

3. In the console, click File, and then click Add/Remove Snap-In.

4. In the Add/Remove Snap-In dialog box, click Add.

5. In the Add Standalone Snap-Ins dialog box, click Security Configuration And Analysis, and then click Add.

6. Click Close, and then click OK.

In the console window, Windows displays the Security Configuration And Analysis, as shown in Figure 16-5.

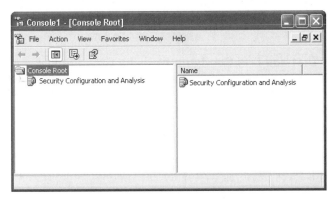

Figure 16-5   Add the Security Configuration And Analysis snap-in to a console.

7. In the console tree, right-click Security Configuration And Analysis, and then click Open Database.

8. In the Open Database dialog box, type the name of a database to create, and then click Open.

   Windows displays the Import Template dialog box.

9. In the Import Template dialog box, select the customized template you have created, and then click Open.

   Windows returns you to the console window. At this point, you can do two things with the template you have imported:

   ❑ Right-click Security Configuration And Analysis, and then click Configure Computer Now to apply the settings in the template to your computer. You are asked to specify a location for an error log file (which contains any errors encountered during the configuration), and then Windows applies the settings.

   ❑ Right-click Security Configuration And Analysis, and then click Analyze Computer Now to have Windows compare the current settings on your computer against the settings specified in the template. You can use this option to test your computer for weaknesses or security violations. After the analysis, you can browse through the policies in the Security Configuration And Analysis window to view the database setting and the computer setting for each policy.

What Is Group Policy?

Group Policy differs from Local Security Policy mainly in the way it is applied. Group Policy is available only in an Active Directory environment. When you create a GPO, you associate that object with a site, domain, or OU in Active Directory. All computers or users in that site, domain, or OU then have that policy applied to them.

> **Note**   This chapter does not cover how to create and apply GPOs because this topic is out of scope for this book and the exam it covers. Instead, this chapter covers how GPOs interact with and affect LGPOs.

Additional Settings That You Can Configure by Using Group Policy

You can use Group Policy to configure any of the settings that you can configure with Local Security Policy. In addition, you can also use Group Policy to do the following:

- Install software and software updates on desktop computers throughout an Active Directory network.

- Redirect special folders (such as users' My Documents folders) to a network location.

- Configure Remote Installation Services (RIS) options.

How Multiple Policies Are Combined

In an Active Directory environment, GPOs can come from different sources to apply to a single user or computer. For example, a computer might be a member of a domain, a site, and two levels of OUs. Each of them might have a GPO associated with it, meaning that four GPOs would affect the computer. In addition, the computer might have an LGPO in effect. There must be a way of determining how those GPOs and LGPOs are combined. GPOs and LGPOs are processed in the following order on a computer running Windows XP Professional.

1. The LGPO on the computer is processed, and all settings specified in that LGPO are applied.

2. Any GPOs that have been linked with the site in which the computer resides are processed. Settings made at this level override any conflicting settings made at the preceding level. For example, if the local GPO specifies that a computer does not have access to a printer, and a site GPO specifies that the computer does have access, the site GPO "wins."

3. GPOs linked to the domain in which the computer resides are processed, and any settings are applied. Settings made at the domain level override conflicting settings applied at the local or site level.

4. GPOs linked to any OUs that contain the user or computer object are processed. Settings made at the OU level override conflicting settings applied at the domain, local, or site level. It is possible for a single object to be in multiple OUs. In this case, GPOs linked to the highest level OU in the Active Directory hierarchy are processed first, followed by the next-highest level OU, and so on. If multiple GPOs are linked to a single OU, the administrator gets to specify the order in which they are processed.

Exam Tip   An easy way to remember the order in which GPOs are processed is that first the local GPO is processed, and then Active Directory GPOs are processed. Active Directory GPOs are processed starting with the farthest structure from the user (the site), then the next closer structure to the user (the domain), and finally the closest structure (the OU). You can also use the acronym LSDOU (local, site, domain, organizational unit) to help you remember.

Note   Administrators can configure the order in which GPOs are applied if multiple GPOs exist for a site, domain, or OU. In addition, administrators can control whether GPOs from higher levels are overridden or not, which might affect how GPOs are processed.

How Group Policy Is Applied

Obviously, processing policies when a user logs on is a pretty complicated endeavor. After all, a large number of GPOs might be linked (either directly or through inheritance) to the computer that a user is logging on to and to the user account being logged on with. The following steps describe how Group Policy is applied when a computer that is part of Active Directory starts and a user logs on.

1. During startup, the computer obtains an ordered list of GPOs, based on whether the computer is a member of Active Directory or not. If not, only the local GPO is processed. If the computer is a member of Active Directory, the list of GPOs to process is based on the Active Directory structure and inheritance, as discussed in the preceding sections.

2. If the GPOs linked to the computer have not changed since the last time the computer started, no processing is done. If the GPOs have changed, they are all processed again.

3. The computer applies any Computer Configuration settings, which occurs in the familiar order: local, site, domain, OU.

4. Startup scripts specified by any GPOs now run. Each script must complete or time out before the next script begins.

5. The logon screen is displayed to the user. The user presses CTRL+ALT+DEL and enters credentials to log on to the network.

6. Once the user is authenticated, the computer loads the user profile (which is governed by the GPOs in effect).

7. The computer receives an ordered list of GPOs that are linked to the user. Again, if no GPOs have changed since the last time the user logged on, no processing is done. If the GPOs have changed, they are all processed again.

8. The computer applies any User Configuration settings in this order: local, site, domain, OU.

9. The computer runs any logon scripts associated with GPOs, and then the desktop appears.

How to View Policies That Are in Effect On a Computer Running Windows XP Professional

Fortunately, Windows XP Professional provides ways to determine the policies that are in effect on a computer and to view the settings that result from those policies. Troubleshooting end user Group Policy is largely a matter of understanding how different policies are applied and how different levels of policy affect one another. You must take into consideration how multiple GPOs that affect the same computer or user are resolved and how GPO inheritance works.

Resultant Set of Policy Tool

The **Resultant Set of Policy** (RSoP) tool, which is new to Windows XP Professional, provides a way for you to simulate and test policy settings applied to computers or users. It shows you the policies applied to the object and order in which they are applied. This tool makes testing complicated policy structures much easier.

You can run RSoP in two modes:

Planning mode   Lets you query the existing GPOs for all policy settings that you can apply. Planning mode is available only on computers that are members of an Active Directory domain. This is helpful when you want to simulate the effect of implementing a new policy, simulate the effect of a slow network connection or a loopback, or test policy precedence when you plan to move a user or computer object to a new location.

Logging mode   Lets you review existing policy settings applied to computer and user objects. This mode is helpful for determining an existing structure, ferreting out problems with inheritance, or testing how security groups affect policy settings.

To start the RSoP tool, use these steps:

1. Click Start, and then click Run.

2. In the Run dialog box, type **mmc**, and then click OK.

   Windows opens the MMC with a blank console window named Console1.

3. In the console, click File, and then click Add/Remove Snap-In.

4. In the Add/Remove Snap-In dialog box, click Add.

5. In the Available Standalone Snap-Ins dialog box, click Resultant Set Of Policy, and then click Add.

6. Click Close, and then click OK.

   In the console window, Windows displays the Resultant Set Of Policy, as shown in Figure 16-6.

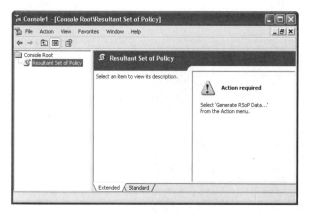

Figure 16-6   Use RSoP to view the settings in effect on a computer.

7. Right-click Resultant Set of Policy, and then click Generate RSoP Data.

   Windows opens the Resultant Set Of Policy Wizard.

8. On the Welcome page, click Next to continue.

9. On the Mode Selection page, ensure that Logging Mode is selected, and then click Next.

10. On the Computer Selection page, choose whether you want to display policy settings for This Computer or for Another Computer. If you want to view settings for a remote computer, you must enter the name of the remote computer. Click Next to continue.

11. On the User Selection page, choose whether you want to display policy settings for the Current User or Another User. Click Next to continue.

12. On the Summary Of Selections page, click Next to proceed.

    Windows analyzes the policy settings in effect, and then displays the Completing The Resultant Set Of Policy Wizard page.

13. Click Finish.

14. In the console window, browse the policy settings to determine the current computer settings and their source GPOs.

Group Policy Result Tool

Windows XP Professional also supplies a tool named **Group Policy Result Tool**, which is a command-line utility that helps you determine which policies are actually applied to a computer. You can start this tool by typing **Gpresult.exe** at the command prompt. The results, shown in Figure 16-7, show the policies in effect on the computer. Use the command **Gpresult.exe /?** to get information on other uses for this tool.

Figure 16-7   Use the Group Policy Result Tool to view polices in effect on a computer.

Lesson Review

The following questions are intended to reinforce key information presented in this lesson. If you are unable to answer a question, review the lesson materials and try the question again. You can find answers to the questions in the "Questions and Answers" section at the end of this chapter.

1. _____ is used to control settings on computers in a workgroup environment.

2. When multiple GPOs and the LGPO affecting a computer are combined, in what order are the policies resolved?

_____

_____

_____

_____

_____

3. You would use the _____ tool to view the actual settings affecting a computer and the source of those settings.

Lesson Summary

■ Local Security Policy is applied to a specific computer and is the only type of security policy you can use on computers that are members of a workgroup. You manage Local Security Policy by using the Local Security Policy tool found in the Administrative Tools folder.

■ Group Policy is applied to sites, domains, and OUs in an Active Directory environment, and affects all computers or users that are members of the container to which the Group Policy is assigned. When a computer running Windows XP Professional is affected by Local Security Policy and Group Policy, those policies are applied in the following order:

   a. The LGPO is processed first.

   b. GPOs linked to the site are processed.

   c. GPOs linked to the domain are processed.

   d. GPOs linked to the OU are processed.

■ Windows XP Professional provides two tools that help you work with policies. The RSoP tool lets you view the actual settings in effect on a computer and the source GPO of those settings. The Group Policy Result tool is a command-line utility that shows you the GPOs affecting a computer.

Lesson 2: Configuring Account Policies

In Chapter 7, "Setting Up and Managing User Accounts," you learned about assigning user account passwords and how to unlock an account that was locked by the system. In this lesson, you learn how to improve the security of your user's passwords and how to control when the system locks out a user account.

After this lesson, you will be able to

- Configure Password Policy.
- Configure Account Lockout Policy.

Estimated lesson time: 15 minutes

How to Configure Password Policy

Password Policy allows you to improve security on your computer by controlling how passwords are created and managed. You can specify the maximum length of time a password can be used before the user must change it. Changing passwords decreases the chances of an unauthorized person breaking into your computer. If an unauthorized user has discovered a user account and password combination for your computer, forcing users to change passwords regularly will cause the user account and password combination to eventually fail and lock the unauthorized user out of the system.

Other Password Policy options are available to improve a computer's security. For example, you can specify a minimum password length. The longer the password, the more difficult it is to discover. Another example is maintaining a history of the passwords used. If you also require passwords to be changed regularly, this prevents a user from having two passwords and alternating between them.

You can configure Password Policy on a computer running Windows XP Professional by using the Local Security Settings tool. To configure Password Policy, use these steps:

1. Click Start, and then click Control Panel.

2. In the Control Panel window, click Performance And Maintenance.

3. In the Performance And Maintenance window, click Administrative Tools.

4. In the Administrative Tools window, double-click Local Security Policy.

5. In the Local Security Settings window, expand Account Policies, and then click Password Policy.

6. Select the setting you want to configure, and then on the Action menu, click Properties.

The console displays the current Password Policy settings in the details pane, as shown in Figure 16-8.

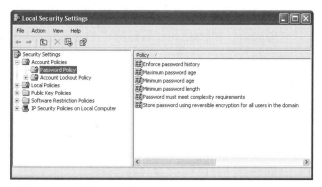

Figure 16-8   Configure Password Policy settings in the Local Security Settings window.

Table 16-1 explains the available Password Policy settings.

Table 16-1   Password Policy Settings

Setting	Description
Enforce Password History	The value you enter for this setting indicates the number of passwords to be kept in a password history. The default value of 0 indicates that no password history is being kept. You can set the value from 0 to 24, indicating the number of passwords to be kept in password history. This value indicates the number of new passwords that a user must use before he or she can reuse an old password.
Maximum Password Age	The value you enter for this setting is the number of days a user can use a password before he or she is required to change it. A value of 0 indicates that the password will not expire. The default value is 42 days, and the range of values is 0 to 999 days.
Minimum Password Age	The value you enter for this setting is the number of days a user must keep a password before he or she can change it. The default value of 0 indicates that the password can be changed immediately. If you are enforcing password history, this value should not be set to 0. The minimum password age must be less than the maximum password age. You can set the range of values from 0 to 999 days. This value indicates how long the user must wait before changing his or her password again. Use this value to prevent a user who was forced by the system to change his or her password from immediately changing it back to the old password.

Table 16-1 Password Policy Settings

Setting	Description
Minimum Password Length	The value you enter for this setting is the minimum number of characters required in a password. The value can range from 0 to 14 characters inclusive. The default value of 0 indicates that no password is required.
Passwords Must Meet Complexity Requirements	The options are Enabled or Disabled (the default). If enabled, all passwords must meet or exceed the specified minimum password length (or be at least 6 characters if no minimum length is otherwise enforced); must comply with the password history settings; must contain capitals, numerals, or punctuation; and cannot contain the user's account or full name.
Store Password Using Reversible Encryption For All Users In The Domain	The options are Enabled or Disabled (the default). This setting enables Windows XP Professional to store a reversibly encrypted password for all users in the domain. This option is only applicable if your computer running Windows XP Professional is in a domain.

How to Configure Account Lockout Policy

The Account Lockout Policy settings also allow you to specify that a user account be locked out after a certain number of unsuccessful logon attempts. While the idea behind this feature is to prevent unauthorized users from trying to break into a computer by repeatedly typing passwords, account lockout actually can be abused by attackers that try to perform denial of service (DoS) attacks (where the intent is to get Windows to lock accounts). For this reason, Microsoft recommends that you to not enable account lockouts. Nonetheless, you should understand how account lockout works.

You access the Account Lockout Policy settings using the Local Security Settings window, just as you did to configure the Password Policy settings. The console displaying the current Account Lockout Policy settings in the details pane is shown in Figure 16-9.

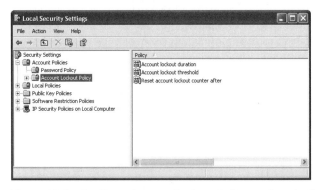

Figure 16-9 Configure Account Lockout Policy settings in the Local Security Settings window.

Table 16-2 explains the settings available in Account Lockout Policy.

Table 16-2   Account Lockout Policy Settings

Setting	Description
Account Lockout Duration	The value you enter for this setting indicates the number of minutes that the account is locked out. A value of 0 indicates that the user account is locked out indefinitely until an administrator unlocks the user account. You can set the value from 0 to 99,999 minutes. (The maximum value of 99,999 minutes is approximately 69.4 days.)
Account Lockout Threshold	The value you enter for this setting is the number of invalid logon attempts before the user account is locked out from logging on to the computer. A value of 0 indicates that the account will not be locked out, no matter how many invalid logon attempts are made. You can set the range of values from 0 to 999 attempts.
Reset Lockout Counter After	The value you enter for this setting is the number of minutes to wait before resetting the account lockout counter. You can set the range of values from 1 to 99,999 minutes.

Practice: Configuring Account Policies

In this practice you configure the Account Policy settings for your computer, and then test them to make sure that you set them correctly.

Exercise 1: Configure Minimum Password Length

In this exercise, you configure the minimum password length, one of the Account Policy settings for your computer. You then test the minimum password length to confirm that it was correctly configured.

1. Log on with an account that is a member of the Administrators group.

2. Click Start, and then click Control Panel.

3. In the Control Panel window, click Performance And Maintenance.

4. In the Performance And Maintenance window, click Administrative Tools.

5. In the Administrative Tools window, double-click Local Security Policy.

6. In the Local Security Settings window, expand Account Policies, and then click Password Policy.

7. In the details pane, right-click Minimum Password Length, and then click Properties.

   Windows XP Professional displays the Minimum Password Length Properties dialog box.

8. Type **8** to set the minimum password length to 8 characters, and then click OK.

9. Click File, and then click Exit to close Local Security Settings window.

10. Click Start, and then click Control Panel.

11. Click User Accounts, and then click Create A New Account.

12. In the Type A Name For The New Account text box, type **User13**, and then click Next.

13. Click Limited, and then click Create Account.

14. Click User13, and then click Change The Password.

15. In the Type A New Password and the Type The New Password Again To Confirm text boxes, type **water**.

16. Click Change Password.

    A User Accounts message box appears, indicating that your new password does not meet the password policy requirements. This test proves that you correctly configured the minimum password length account policy to eight characters.

17. Click OK to close the User Accounts message box.

18. Click Cancel to close the Change User13's Password window.

19. Close the User Accounts window, and then close Control Panel.

Exercise 2: Configure and Test Additional Account Policy Settings

In this exercise, you configure and test some additional Account Policy settings.

1. Click Start, and then click Control Panel.

2. In the Control Panel window, click Performance And Maintenance.

3. In the Performance And Maintenance window, click Administrative Tools.

4. In the Administrative Tools window, double-click Local Security Policy.

5. Use the Local Security Settings window to configure the following Account Policy settings:

    ❑ A user should have at least five different passwords before using a previously used password.

    ❑ After changing a password, a user must wait 24 hours before he or she can change it again.

    ❑ A user should change his or her password every three weeks.

6. What settings did you use for each of the three listed items?

_____

_____

_____

_____

_____

7. Close the Local Security Settings window.

8. Log on as User13 with no password.

   Windows XP Professional displays a Logon Message message box, indicating that you must change your password at first logon.

9. Click OK to close the message box.

10. Press TAB to move to the New Password text box and leave the Old Password text box blank.

11. In the New Password and Confirm New Password text boxes, type **hotwater**, and then click OK.

    Windows XP Professional displays a Change Password message box, indicating that your password was successfully changed.

12. Click OK to close the Change Password message box.

13. Click Start, and then click Control Panel.

14. Click User Accounts, and then click Change My Password.

15. In the Type Your Current Password text box, type **hotwater**.

16. In the Type A New Password and Type The New Password Again To Confirm text boxes, type **chocolate**.

17. Click Change Password.

18. Were you successful? Why or why not?

_____

_____

_____

19. Close any open dialog boxes and windows and log off.

Exercise 3: Configure Account Lockout Policy

In this exercise, you configure Account Lockout Policy settings, and then test them to make sure they are set up correctly.

1. Log on to your computer with a user account that is a member of the Administrators group.

2. Click Start, and then click Control Panel.

3. In the Control Panel window, click Performance And Maintenance.

4. In the Performance And Maintenance window, click Administrative Tools.

5. In the Administrative Tools window, double-click Local Security Policy.

6. In the Local Security Settings window, expand Account Policies, and then click Account Lockout Policy.

7. Use Account Lockout Policy settings to do the following:

   ❑ Lock out a user account after four failed logon attempts.

   ❑ Lock out user accounts until an administrator unlocks the user account.

> **Note**   If a Suggested Value Changes dialog box appears, click OK, and then verify that your settings are correct.

8. What Account Lockout Policy settings did you use for each of the two conditions?

   _____

   _____

   _____

   _____

   _____

   _____

9. Log off Windows XP Professional.

10. Try to log on as User13 with a password of **chocolate** four times.

11. Try to log on as User13 with a password of **chocolate** again and a dialog box appears, indicating that the account is locked out.

12. Click OK, and then log on as a user that is a member of the Administrators group.

Lesson Review

The following questions are intended to reinforce key information presented in this lesson. If you are unable to answer a question, review the lesson materials and try the question again. You can find answers to the questions in the "Questions and Answers" section at the end of this chapter.

1. What is the range of values Windows XP Professional allows you to set for the Enforce Password History setting, and what do those values mean?

    _____

    _____

    _____

2. The range of values Windows XP Professional allows you to set for the Maximum Password Age setting is _____ to _____ days. The default value is _____ days.

3. Which of the following selections are requirements for a password if the Passwords Must Meet Complexity Requirements setting is enabled? (Choose all that apply.)

    a. All passwords must exceed six characters in length.

    b. All passwords must comply with the password history settings.

    c. No passwords can contain capitals or punctuation.

    d. No passwords can contain the user's account or full name.

4. What is Account Lockout Duration, and what is the range of values?

    _____

    _____

    _____

Lesson Summary

- Password Policy allows you to manage the passwords used on your computer. For example, you can force users to change passwords on a regular basis and you can control the minimum length of a password.

- Account Lockout Policy allows you determine the number of invalid logon attempts before a user account is locked out of the computer.

Lesson 3: Configuring User Rights

In the Local Security Settings window, under the Local Policies folder, there are three categories of local policies available: Audit Policy, User Rights Assignment, and Security Options. Audit Policy and Security Options are covered in later lessons in this chapter. In this lesson, you learn how to assign user rights.

After this lesson, you will be able to

■ Configure user rights.

Estimated lesson time: 30 minutes

How to Configure User Rights

You can assign specific rights to groups or individual user accounts. To simplify the administration of user rights, Microsoft recommends that you assign user rights only to groups, not to individual user accounts. Each user right allows the members of the group or the individual users assigned the right to perform a specific action, such as backing up files or changing the system time. If a user is a member of more than one group, the user rights applied to that user are cumulative, so the user has all the user rights assigned to all the groups of which he or she is a member.

To configure user rights on a computer running Windows XP Professional, use these steps:

1. Click Start, and then click Control Panel.

2. In the Control Panel window, click Performance And Maintenance.

3. In the Performance And Maintenance window, click Administrative Tools.

4. In the Administrative Tools window, double-click Local Security Policy.

5. In the Local Security Settings window, expand Local Policies, and then click User Right Assignments.

6. In the details pane, click the user right you want to configure, and then on the Action menu, click Properties.

    The console displays the current groups and user accounts that have this user right assigned, as shown in Figure 16-10. To add groups or user accounts, click Add User Or Group. To remove a group or user, select the group or user, and then click Remove.

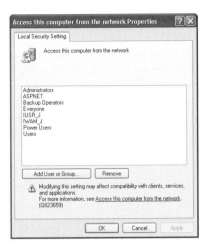

Figure 16-10   Assign user rights to a group or user account.

There are two types of user rights: privileges and logon rights.

What Are Privileges?

A privilege is a user right that allows the members of the group to which it is assigned to perform a specific task, usually one that affects an entire computer system rather than one object. Table 16-3 explains privileges you can assign in Windows XP Professional of which you should be aware.

Table 16-3   Privileges Available in Windows XP Professional

Privilege	Description
Act As Part Of The Operating System	Allows a process to authenticate like a user and thus gain access to the same resources as a user. Do not grant this privilege unless you are certain it is needed. Only low-level authentication services should require this privilege. Processes that require this privilege should use the Local-System account because it already has this privilege assigned. A separate user account with this privilege allows a user or process to build an access token, granting them more rights than they should have, and does not provide a primary identity for tracking events in the audit log.
Add Workstations To Domain	Allows a user to add a computer to a domain. The user specifies the domain being added on the computer, and an object is created in the Computer container of Active Directory in that domain. For this privilege to be effective, it must be assigned as part of the default domain controller policy for the domain.

Table 16-3   Privileges Available in Windows XP Professional

Privilege	Description
Back Up Files And Directories	Allows a user to back up the system without being assigned permissions to access all files and folders on the system. By default, members of the Administrators and Backup Operators groups have this privilege on workstations, member servers, and domain controllers. On domain controllers, members of the Server Operators group have this privilege.
Bypass Traverse Checking	Allows a user to move through folders that he or she has no permission to access. This privilege does not allow the user to view the contents of a folder, just to move through the folder. By default, members of the Administrators, Backup Operators, Power Users, Users, and Everyone groups have this privilege on workstations and member servers.
Change The System Time	Allows a user to set the time for the internal clock of the computer. By default, members of the Administrators and Power Users groups, as well as the LocalSystem and NetworkService accounts, have this privilege on workstations and member servers. By default, members of the Administrators and Server Operators groups, as well as the LocalSystem and NetworkService accounts, have this privilege on domain controllers.
Create A Pagefile	Allows a user to create a pagefile and modify the size of existing pagefiles. By default, members of the Administrators group have this privilege on workstations, member servers, and domain controllers.
Debug Programs	Allows a user to attach a debugger on any process. This privilege provides powerful access to sensitive and critical system operating components. By default, members of the Administrators group have this privilege on workstations, member servers, and domain controllers.
Enable Computer And User Accounts To Be Trusted For Delegation	Allows the user to set the Trusted For Delegation setting on a user or computer object. A server process running on a computer that is trusted for delegation or run by a user who is trusted for delegation can access resources on another computer. Do not assign this privilege unless you understand that this privilege and the Trusted For Delegation setting can open your network to attacks from Trojan horse programs that impersonate incoming clients and use their credentials to access network resources. This privilege is not assigned to anyone on workstations or member servers. On domain controllers, it is assigned by default to the members of the Administrators group.
Force Shutdown From A Remote System	Allows a user to shut down a computer from a remote computer on the network. By default, members of the Administrators group have this privilege on workstations and member servers. By default, members of the Administrators and Server Operators groups have this privilege on domain controllers.

Table 16-3   Privileges Available in Windows XP Professional

Privilege	Description
Load And Unload Device Drivers	Allows a user to install and uninstall Plug and Play device drivers. Non-Plug and Play device drivers are not affected by this privilege. By default, only Administrators have this privilege. Exercise caution when granting this privilege. Device drivers run as trusted programs, and only device drivers with correct digital signatures should be installed. By default, members of the Administrators group have this privilege on workstations, member servers, and domain controllers.
Manage Auditing And Security Log	Allows a user to specify object access auditing options for individual resources such as files, Active Directory objects, and Registry keys. A user with this privilege can also view and clear the security log from the Event Viewer. By default, members of the Administrators group have this privilege on workstations, member servers, and domain controllers. Be careful who you assign this privilege to because they have the power to cover their tracks by clearing the Security event log.
Modify Firmware Environment Values	Allows a user to use the System Properties program to modify system environment variables. Allows a process to use an API to modify the system environment variables.
Perform Volume Maintenance Tasks	Allows users to run disk tools such as Disk Cleanup or Disk Defragmenter. By default, members of the Administrators group have this privilege on workstations, member servers, and domain controllers.
Profile Single Process	Allows a user to use performance-monitoring tools to monitor the performance of nonsystem processes. By default, on workstations and member servers, Administrators and Power Users have this privilege. On domain controllers, only Administrators have this privilege.
Profile System Performance	Allows a user to use performance-monitoring tools to monitor the performance of system processes. By default, members of the Administrators group have this privilege on workstations, member servers, and domain controllers.
Remove Computer From Docking Station	Allows a user to undock a portable computer. By default, members of the Administrators, Power Users, and Users groups have this privilege on workstations and member servers.
Restore Files And Directories	Allows a user to restore backed up files and directories without being assigned the appropriate file and folder permissions, and allows a user to set any valid security principal as the owner of the object. By default, members of the Administrators and Backup Operators groups have this privilege on workstations, member servers, and domain controllers. On domain controllers, members of the Server Operators group also have this privilege.

Table 16-3   Privileges Available in Windows XP Professional

Privilege	Description
Shut Down The System	Allows a user to shut down the local computer. By default, members of the Administrators, Backup Operators, Power Users, and Users groups have this privilege on workstations.
Take Ownership Of Files Or Other Objects	Allows a user to take ownership of objects in the system, including Active Directory objects, files and folders, printers, Registry keys, processes, and threads. By default, members of the Administrators group have this privilege on workstations, member servers, and domain controllers.

What Are Logon Rights?

A **logon right** is a user right assigned to a group or an individual user account. Logon rights control the way users can log on to a system. Table 16-4 explains the logon rights you can assign in Windows XP Professional.

Table 16-4   Logon Rights Available in Windows XP Professional

Logon right	Description
Access This Computer From The Network	Allows a user to connect to the computer over the network. By default, members of the Administrators, Backup Operators, Power Users, Users, and Everyone groups are granted this logon right on workstations, member servers, and domain controllers.
Deny Access To This Computer From The Network	Prevents a user from connecting to the computer over the network. By default, this right is not granted to anyone.
Log On As A Batch Job	Allows a user to log on using a batch-queue facility. By default, members of the Administrators group are granted this logon right on workstations, member servers, and domain controllers. If Internet Information Services (IIS) is installed, the right is automatically assigned to the built-in account for anonymous access to IIS.
Deny Logon As A Batch Job	Prevents a user from logging on using a batch-queue facility. By default, this right is not granted to anyone.
Log On As A Service	Allows a security principal (an account holder such as a user, computer, or service) to log on as a service. Services can be configured to run under the LocalSystem, LocalService, or NetworkService accounts, which have the right to log on as a service. Any service that runs under a separate account must be granted this right. By default, this right is not granted to anyone.
Deny Logon As A Service	Prevents a security principal from logging on as a service. By default, this right is not granted to anyone.

Table 16-4   Logon Rights Available in Windows XP Professional

Logon right	Description
Log On Locally	Allows a user to log on at the computer's keyboard. By default, members of the Administrators, Account Operators, Backup Operators, Print Operators, and Server Operators groups are granted this logon right.
Deny Logon Locally	Prevents a user from logging on at the computer's keyboard. By default, this right is not granted to anyone.
Allow Logon Through Terminal Services	Allows a user to log on using Remote Desktop (also known as Terminal Services). By default, members of the Administrators and Remote Desktop Users groups are granted this logon right on workstations and member servers. On domain controllers, only Administrators are granted this logon right.
Deny Logon Through Terminal Services	Prevents a user from logging on using Remote Desktop. By default, this right is not granted to anyone.

> **Exam Tip**   For the exam, you should understand the user rights available and the default groups that are assigned the rights.

Lesson Review

The following questions are intended to reinforce key information presented in this lesson. If you are unable to answer a question, review the lesson materials and try the question again. You can find answers to the questions in the "Questions and Answers" section at the end of this chapter.

1. Which of the following statements about user rights are correct? (Choose all that apply.)

   a. Microsoft recommends that you assign user rights to individual user accounts.

   b. Microsoft recommends that you assign user rights to groups rather than individual user accounts.

   c. User rights allow users assigned the right to perform a specific action, such as backing up files and directories.

   d. There are two types of user rights: privileges and logon rights.

2. If your computer running Windows XP Professional is part of a domain environment and you configure the Local Security Policies on your computer so that you assign yourself the Add Workstation To A Domain user right, can you add additional workstations to the domain? Why or why not?

_____

_____

_____

3. What benefit does the Back Up Files And Directories user right provide?

_____

_____

_____

_____

4. What are logon rights and what do they do?

_____

_____

Lesson Summary

- User rights allow a user or group to perform a specific action, such as backing up files or changing the system time. There are two types of user rights:

  - A privilege is a user right that allows users to perform a specific task, usually one that affects an entire computer system rather than one object.

  - Logon rights are user rights assigned to a group or an individual user account to control the way users can log on to a computer. Logon rights control whether or not a user can connect to a computer over the network or sitting at the computer's keyboard.

Lesson 4: Configuring Security Options

In the Local Security Settings window, under the Local Policies folder, there is a Security Options folder. There are close to 60 additional security options grouped into the following categories: accounts, audit, devices, domain controller, domain member, interactive logon, Microsoft network client, network access, network security, recovery console, shutdown, system cryptography, and system objects. In this lesson, you learn about some of the more important security options available.

After this lesson, you will be able to

■ Configure security options.

Estimated lesson time: 15 minutes

How to Configure Security Options

To configure security options, use the Local Security Settings window to locate and select the Security Options node. In the details pane, double-click the option you want to configure and use the dialog box for the option to change settings.

Table 16-5 lists important security options you should be aware of.

Table 16-5   Important Security Options in Windows XP Professional

Security Option	Description
Accounts: Administrator Account Status	Enables or disables the Administrator account under normal operation. Under safe mode boot, the Administrator account is always enabled, regardless of this setting.
Accounts: Guest Account Status	Enables or disables the Guest account.
Accounts: Limit Local Use Of Blank Passwords To Console Logon Only	Determines whether remote interactive logons by network services (such as Remote Desktop, Telnet, and File Transfer Protocol) are allowed for local accounts that have blank passwords. If this setting is enabled, a local account must have a nonblank password to be used to perform an interactive or network logon from a remote client.
Accounts: Rename Administrator Account	Specifies a different account name to be associated with the Administrator account. You should use a name that does not identify it as the Administrator account to make it difficult for unauthorized users to break into the account.
Accounts: Rename Guest Account	Specifies a different account name to be associated with the Guest account.

Table 16-5   Important Security Options in Windows XP Professional

Security Option	Description
Audit: Audit The Use Of Backup And Restore Privilege	Determines whether to audit the use of all user privileges, including Backup and Restore, when the Audit privilege use setting is in effect. Enabling both policies generates an audit event for every file that is backed up or restored. See Lesson 5 for more information on auditing.
Devices: Prevent Users From Installing Printer Drivers	Enabling this setting allows only Administrators and Power Users to install a printer driver as part of adding a network printer. Disabling this setting allows any user to install a printer driver as part of adding a network printer.
Devices: Restrict CD-Rom Access To Locally Logged On User Only	Determines whether a CD-ROM is accessible to both local and remote users simultaneously. Enabling this setting allows only the interactively logged-on user to access removable CD-ROM media. If this setting is enabled and no one is logged on interactively, the CD-ROM can be accessed over the network.
Devices: Restrict Floppy Access To Locally Logged On User Only	Determines whether removable floppy media are accessible to both local and remote users simultaneously.
Devices: Unsigned Driver Installation Behavior	Determines what happens when an attempt is made to install a device driver that has not been digitally signed. You can configure Windows to allow unsigned drivers, to allow unsigned drivers but warn the user, or to not allow unsigned drivers.
Interactive Logon: Do Not Display Last User Name	Determines whether the Log On To Windows dialog box displays the name of the last user to log on to the computer.
Interactive Logon: Do Not Require CTRL+ALT+DEL	Determines whether pressing CTRL+ALT+DEL is required before a user can log on.
Interactive Logon: Message Text For Users Attempting To Log On	Specifies a text message displayed to users when they log on.
Interactive Logon: Prompt User To Change Password Before Expiration	Determines how many days in advance users are warned that their password is about to expire.
Network Access: Let Everyone Permissions Apply To Anonymous Users	Determines whether anonymous users receive the same permissions to resources that are assigned to the Everyone group.
Network Access: Shares That Can Be Accessed Anonymously	Determines which network shares anonymous users can access. When you enable this option, you generate the list of shares that are accessible.
Recovery Console: Allow Automatic Administrative Logon	Determines whether the Administrator account password must be given before access to the computer is granted in Recovery Console. Enabling this setting automatically logs on to the system in Recovery Console without requiring a password.

Table 16-5   Important Security Options in Windows XP Professional

Security Option	Description
Shutdown: Allow System To Be Shut Down Without Having To Log On	Determines whether a computer can be shut down without having to log on to Windows. Enabling this setting makes the Shut Down command available on the Windows logon screen.
Shutdown: Clear Virtual Memory Page File	Determines whether the virtual memory paging file is cleared when the system is shut down. This setting is especially useful on computers configured to allow booting to other operating systems, ensuring that sensitive information from process memory that might go into the paging file is not available to an unauthorized user.

Practice: Configuring Security Settings

In this practice, you configure the security setting that automatically renames the Guest account on your computer.

1. Log on with an account that is a member of the Administrators group.

2. Click Start, and then click Control Panel.

3. In the Control Panel window, click Performance And Maintenance.

4. In the Performance And Maintenance window, click Administrative Tools.

5. In the Administrative Tools window, double-click Local Security Policy.

6. In the Local Security Settings window, expand Local Policies, and then click Security Options.

7. In the right-hand pane, right-click Accounts: Rename Guest Account, and then click Properties.

8. In the Accounts: Rename Guest Account Properties dialog box, type **Fox**, and then click OK. Close the Local Security Settings window.

9. Click Start, and then click Control Panel.

10. In the Control Panel window, click User Accounts.

11. What is the name of the Guest account?

_____

12. Close the User Accounts window and the Control Panel window.

Lesson Review

The following questions are intended to reinforce key information presented in this lesson. If you are unable to answer a question, review the lesson materials and try the question again. You can find answers to the questions in the "Questions and Answers" section at the end of this chapter.

1. How can you require a user to be logged on to the computer to shut it down? (Discuss using the Welcome screen and using CTRL+ALT+DELETE to log on.)

_____

_____

_____

_____

_____

2. By default, Windows XP Professional does not clear the virtual memory pagefile when the system is shut down. Why can this be considered a security breach and what can you do to resolve it?

_____

_____

_____

_____

_____

3. Why does forcing users to press CTRL+ALT+DELETE improve security on your computer?

_____

_____

_____

_____

_____

4. By default, Windows XP Professional displays the last user name to log on to the computer in the Windows Security dialog box. Why is this considered a security risk, and what can you do to resolve it?

_____

_____

_____

_____

_____

Lesson Summary

■ Security Options represent many different categories of settings related to Windows XP Professional security. A few important security options you can configure are the following:

❑ You can prevent an unauthorized user from shutting down your computer by forcing users to log on before they can shut down the computer.

❑ You can force users to press CTRL+ALT+DELETE before they can log on to prevent a Trojan horse application from stealing user passwords.

❑ You can increase security by not displaying a valid user name for the last user account that logged on in the Windows Security dialog box.

Lesson 5: Implementing an Audit Policy

Auditing allows you to track both user activities and Windows XP Professional events on a computer. Through auditing, you can specify that Windows XP Professional records activities and events to a security log, which maintains a record of valid and invalid logon attempts and events related to creating, opening, or deleting files or other objects. An audit entry in the security log contains the following information:

- The action that was performed

- The user who performed the action

- The success or failure of the event and when the event occurred

---

After this lesson, you will be able to
- Describe the purpose of auditing.
- Determine what you should audit.
- Configure an audit policy.
- Enable auditing for files and folder.
- Enable auditing for printers.

Estimated lesson time: 60 minutes

Overview of Auditing

An audit policy defines the types of security events that Windows XP Professional records in the security log on each computer. The security log allows you to track the events that you specify.

Windows XP Professional writes events to the security log on the computer on which the event occurs. For example, you can configure auditing so that anytime someone tries to log on and the logon attempt fails, Windows XP Professional writes an event to the security log on that computer.

You can set up an audit policy for a computer to do the following:

- Track the success and failure of events, such as logon attempts by users, an attempt by a particular user to read a specific file, changes to a user account or to group memberships, and changes to your security settings

- Eliminate or minimize the risk of unauthorized use of resources

You use Event Viewer to view events that Windows XP Professional has recorded in the security log. You can also archive log files to track trends over time—for example, to determine the use of printers or files or to verify attempts at unauthorized use of resources. This lesson covers configuring an audit policy and enabling auditing of various resources and events. You will learn more about using Event Viewer in Chapter 18, "Using Windows XP Tools."

The requirements to set up and administer auditing are as follows:

- You must have the Manage Auditing And Security Log user right for the computer on which you want to configure an audit policy or review an audit log. By default, Windows XP Professional grants these rights to the Administrators group.

- The files and folders to be audited must be on NTFS volumes.

Setting up auditing for objects (files, folders, and printers) is a two-part process:

1. **Set the audit policy.** The audit policy enables auditing of objects but does not activate auditing of specific objects.

2. **Enable auditing of specific resources.** You designate the specific events to audit for files, folders, printers, and Active Directory objects. Windows XP Professional then tracks and logs the specified events.

What Should You Audit?

When you plan an audit policy, you must determine what you want to audit and the computers on which to set up auditing. Auditing is turned off by default. As you determine which computers to audit, you must also plan what to audit on each one. Windows XP Professional records audited events on each computer separately.

The types of events that you can audit include the following:

- Accessing files and folders
- Logging on and off
- Shutting down a computer running Windows XP Professional
- Starting a computer running Windows XP Professional
- Changing user accounts and groups

After you have determined the types of events to audit, you must also determine whether to audit the success of events, the failure of events, or both. Tracking successful events can tell you how often Windows XP Professional or users access specific files, printers, or other objects, and you can use this information for resource planning.

Tracking failed events can alert you to possible security breaches. For example, if you notice several failed logon attempts by a certain user account, especially if they are occurring outside normal business hours, you might conclude that an unauthorized person is attempting to break into your system.

Other guidelines in determining your audit policy include the following:

Determine how long you need to retain audit logs   Plan to archive event logs so that you can look back and determine when compromises occurred. Often, administrators do not realize that security has been breached for weeks or months, and important events may no longer be accessible in the log.

Review security logs frequently   You should set a schedule and regularly review security logs because configuring auditing alone does not alert you to security breaches.

Define an audit policy that is useful and manageable   Always audit sensitive and confidential data. Audit only those events that will provide you with meaningful information about your network environment, which minimizes usage of the computer's resources and makes essential information easier to locate. Auditing too many types of events can create excess overhead for Windows XP Professional.

How to Configure an Audit Policy

The first step in implementing an audit policy is selecting the types of events for Windows XP Professional to audit. For each event that you can audit, the configuration settings indicate whether to track successful or failed attempts. You set audit policies for a local computer in the Local Security Settings window. Under the Local Policies node, click Audit Policy to display a list of available audit policies.

Table 16-6 describes the types of events that Windows XP Professional can audit.

Table 16-6   Types of Events Audited by Windows XP Professional

Event	Description
Account Management	An administrator created, changed, or deleted a user account or group. A user account was renamed, disabled, or enabled; or a password was set or changed.
Logon Events	A user logged on or logged off, or a user made or canceled a network connection to the computer.
Object Access	A user gained access to a file, folder, or printer. You must configure specific files, folders, or printers for auditing. Object access is auditing a user's access to files, folders, and printers.
Policy Change	A change was made to the user security options, user rights, or audit policies.
Privilege Use	A user exercised a right, such as changing the system time (does not include rights that are related to logging on and logging off).
Process Tracking	A program performed an action. This information is generally useful only for programmers who want to track details of program execution.
System Events	A user restarted or shut down the computer, or an event occurred that affected Windows XP Professional security or the security log. (For example, the audit log is full and Windows XP Professional starts discarding entries.)

To set an audit policy on a computer that is running Windows XP Professional, use these steps:

1. Click Start, and then click Control Panel.

2. In the Control Panel window, click Performance And Maintenance.

3. In the Performance And Maintenance window, click Administrative Tools.

4. In the Administrative Tools window, double-click Local Security Policy.

5. In the Local Security Policy window, expand Local Policies, and then click Audit Policy.

   The console displays the current audit policy settings in the details pane, as shown in Figure 16-11.

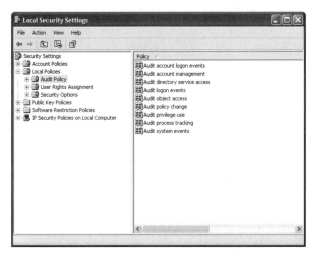

Figure 16-11   Select events that Windows XP Professional should audit.

6. Click the type of event to audit, and then, on the Action menu, click Properties.

   For example, if you select Audit Logon Events and on the Action menu you click Properties, the Audit Account Logon Events Properties dialog box appears, as shown in Figure 16-12.

Figure 16-12   Enable the Audit Account Logon Events policy.

7. Select the Success check box, the Failure check box, or both.

A check mark in the Success check box indicates that auditing is in effect for successful attempts. A check mark in the Failure check box indicates that auditing is in effect for failed attempts.

8. Click OK.

9. Restart your computer.

After you have set the audit policy, remember that the changes that you make to your computer's audit policy do not take effect immediately unless you restart your computer.

How to Enable Auditing for Files and Folders

If you have confidential files that you need to monitor, you can set up auditing for files and folders on NTFS partitions. To audit user access to files and folders, you must first set your audit policy to audit object access, which includes files and folders.

When you set your audit policy to audit object access, you enable auditing for files, folders, and printers. However, you must also enable auditing on the specific resources you want to audit.

To enable auditing for specific files and folders, use these steps:

1. Click Start, right-click My Computer, and then click Explore.

2. Right-click the file or folder for which you want to enable auditing and click Properties.

3. In the Properties dialog box for the file or folder, on the Security tab, click Advanced.

> **Tip**   If you do not have a Security tab on the Properties dialog box for your files and folders, you should first check to make sure that files and folders are located on a partition formatted as NTFS. You should also make sure that if your computer is not a member of a domain, you have turned off Simple File Sharing. To stop using Simple File Sharing, click Start, right-click My Computer, and then click Explore. On the Tools menu, click Folder Options. Click the View tab, clear Use Simple File Sharing (Recommended), and click OK.

4. In Advanced Security Settings For dialog box for the file or folder, click the Auditing tab. Click Add, select the users for whom you want to audit file and folder access, and then click OK.

5. In the Auditing Entry For dialog box for the file or folder, select the Successful check box, the Failed check box, or both for the events that you want to audit.

For a list of the events that can be audited for folders, see Figure 16-13. Table 16-7 describes the user activity that triggers these events so you can determine when you should audit these events.

Figure 16-13   Select events to be audited.

Table 16-7   User Events and What Triggers Them

Event	User Activity That Triggers the Event
Traverse Folder/Execute File	Running a program or gaining access to a folder to change directories
List Folder/Read Data	Displaying the contents of a file or a folder
Read Attributes And Read Extended Attributes	Displaying the attributes of a file or folder
Create Files/Write Data	Changing the contents of a file or creating new files in a folder
Create Folders/Append Data	Creating folders in a folder
Write Attributes and Write Extended Attributes	Changing attributes of a file or folder
Delete Subfolders And Files	Deleting a file or subfolder in a folder
Delete	Deleting a file or folder
Read Permissions	Viewing permissions for the file owner for a file or folder
Change Permissions	Changing permissions for a file or folder
Take Ownership	Taking ownership of a file or folder

6. Click OK to return to the Advanced Security Settings For dialog box for the file or folder.

   By default, any auditing changes that you make to a parent folder also apply to all child folders and all files in the parent and child folders.

7. To prevent changes that are made to a parent folder from applying to the currently selected file or folder, clear the Inherit From Parent The Auditing Entries That Apply To Child Objects check box.

8. Click OK twice.

How to Enable Auditing for Printers

Audit access to printers to track access to sensitive printers. To audit access to printers, set your audit policy to audit object access, which includes printers. Enable auditing for specific printers, and specify which types of access to audit and which users will have access. After you select the printer, you use the same steps that you use to set up auditing on files and folders, as follows:

1. Click Start, click Control Panel, and then click Printers And Other Hardware.

2. Click Printers And Faxes, right-click the printer you want to audit, and then click Properties.

3. In the Properties dialog box for the printer, click the Security tab, and then click Advanced.

The Advanced Security Settings dialog box appears.

4. In the Auditing tab, click Add, select the appropriate users or groups for whom you want to audit printer access, and then click OK.

5. In the Apply Onto box in the Auditing Entry dialog box, select where the auditing setting applies.

The options in the Apply Onto box for a printer are This Printer Only, Documents, and This Printer And Documents.

6. Under Access, select the Successful check box, the Failed check box, or both for the events that you want to audit (see Figure 16-14).

7. Click OK in the appropriate dialog boxes to exit.

Figure 16-14   Select printer events to be audited.

Table 16-8 describes audit events for printers and explains which user action triggers the event.

Table 16-8   Printer Events and What Triggers Them

Event	User Activity That Triggers the Event
Print	Printing a file
Manage Printers	Changing printer settings, pausing a printer, sharing a printer, or removing a printer
Manage Documents	Changing job settings; pausing, restarting, moving, or deleting documents; sharing a printer; or changing printer properties
Read Permissions	Viewing printer permissions
Change Permissions	Changing printer permissions
Take Ownership	Taking printer ownership

Lesson Review

The following questions are intended to reinforce key information presented in this lesson. If you are unable to answer a question, review the lesson materials and try the question again. You can find answers to the questions in the "Questions and Answers" section at the end of this chapter.

1. What is auditing?

_____

_____

2. What is an audit policy?

_____

_____

3. When you are auditing events on a computer running Windows XP Professional, where are the audited events being recorded?

_____

_____

4. What are the requirements to set up and administer auditing?

_____

_____

_____

5. What are the two steps in setting up auditing?

_____

6. By default, any auditing changes that you make to a parent folder _____ (are inherited/are not inherited) by all child folders and all files in the parent and child folders.

Lesson Summary

■ On a computer running Windows XP Professional, auditing helps ensure that your network is secure by tracking user activities and system-wide events. You must have the Manage Auditing And Security Log user right for the computer on which you want to configure an audit policy or review an audit log. By default, Windows XP Professional grants these rights to the Administrators group.

- You can audit the following types of events:

  - Accessing files and folders

  - Logging on and off

  - Shutting down a computer running Windows XP Professional

  - Starting a computer running Windows XP Professional

  - Changing user accounts and groups

  - Attempting to make changes to Active Directory objects (only if your Windows XP Professional computer is part of a domain)

- You set up an audit policy using the Local Security Settings window to specify which events to record. You can audit the success of events, the failure of events, or both.

- After enabling the Audit Object Access policy, you must configure particular files and folders to be audited. To do so, click the Advanced button on the Security tab of a file or folder's Properties dialog box. On the Auditing tab of the Advanced Security Settings dialog box for the file or folder, select the users and groups you want to audit, as well as the types of events to audit.

- If you enable the Audit Object Access policy, you can also configure auditing for specific printers. Configuring auditing for a printer follows the same procedure for configuring auditing for a file or folder.

Lesson 6: Configuring Internet Explorer Options

There are a number of options that you can configure in Internet Explorer, some of which deal with security, others of which deal with privacy, content, and how Internet Explorer connects to the Internet. You will configure these options using the Internet Options dialog box, which you can access in one of two ways:

- In the Control Panel window, click Network And Internet Connections. In the Network And Internet Connections window, click Internet Options. This method allows you to configure Internet Explorer options without running Internet Explorer.

- While Internet Explorer is running, on the Tools menu, click Internet Options.

After this lesson, you will be able to

- Configure Internet Explorer general options.
- Configure Internet Explorer security options.
- Configure Internet Explorer privacy options.
- Configure Internet Explorer content options.
- Configure Internet Explorer connection options.
- Configure Internet Explorer programs options.
- Configure Internet Explorer advanced options.

Estimated lesson time: 40 minutes

General Options

The General tab of the Internet Properties dialog box, shown in Figure 16-15, allows you to configure the following:

- The home page that Internet Explorer opens when you start the program. This is also the page you are returned to each time you click the Home icon on the toolbar.

- How Internet Explorer stores temporary files during browsing sessions. Internet Explorer automatically stores (or caches) copies of Web pages that you access to a folder on the local hard disk. These copies are called temporary Internet files. The next time you access the same page, Internet Explorer can load the page from the local cache rather than having to connect to the Web server and download it again. You can delete temporary Internet files by clicking the Delete Files button on the General tab of the Internet Options dialog box. You might want to delete temporary Internet files to make it more difficult for other users of the same computer to identify the Web sites you visited.

■ How long Internet Explorer tracks the history of Web pages you have visited. The History section of the General tab of the Internet Options dialog box allows you to manage how long Internet Explorer stores recent links. Use the Days To Keep Pages In History option to specify the number of days the history is maintained. The default value is 20 days. Setting this value to 0 disables the History feature. Use the Clear History button to clear the current history list. Similar to deleting temporary Internet files, clearing the history is an excellent way to improve your privacy.

The General tab also allows you to configure the colors, fonts, languages, and accessibility options used.

Figure 16-15   Configure general options in Internet Explorer.

How to Configure Security Options

The Security tab of the Internet Options dialog box (see Figure 16-16) allows you to assign Web sites to **security zones** and customize the security for each zone. The four zones provided are as follows:

■ **Internet**   Contains all Web sites that you have not placed in other zones.

■ **Local Intranet**   Contains all Web sites that are on the local network. By default, this zone includes all sites that bypass the proxy server (if a proxy server is being used) and all local network paths. You can add additional sites to this zone by selecting the zone and clicking Sites.

■ **Trusted Sites**   Contains Web sites that are believed to be safe. There are no sites in this zone by default. You can add sites to this zone as you see fit by selecting the zone and clicking Sites.

■ **Restricted Sites**   Contains Web sites that could potentially be harmful. There are no sites in this zone by default. You can add sites to this zone as you see fit by selecting the zone and clicking Sites.

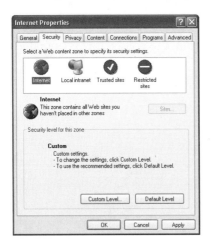

Figure 16-16   Configure security options in Internet Explorer.

The security levels that you can configure are as follows:

■ High, which is appropriate for sites that might have harmful content. The Restricted Sites zone has a High security level.

   ❏ Less-secure features are disabled.

   ❏ The safest way to browse, but functionality is potentially lost.

■ Medium, which is appropriate for most Internet sites. The Internet and Local Intranet zones have a Medium security level.

   ❏ Prompts before downloading potentially unsafe content.

   ❏ Unsigned ActiveX controls are not downloaded.

■ Medium-Low, which is appropriate for local sites.

   ❏ Most content is run without prompts.

   ❏ Unsigned ActiveX controls are not downloaded.

- Low, which is appropriate for sites that are trusted. The Trusted Sites zone has a Low security level.

  ❏ Minimal safeguards and warning prompts are provided.

  ❏ Most content is downloaded and runs without prompts.

  ❏ All ActiveX content can run.

The Security Level For This Zone section allows you to customize the security settings for each zone. To customize a zone's security level, click the zone and then click Custom Level. Windows XP Professional displays the Security Settings dialog box (see Figure 16-17), in which you can control what gets loaded onto your computer from the Internet. For example, for Download Signed ActiveX Controls you can choose one of the following three options:

- **Enable**   Allows you to download signed ActiveX controls

- **Disable**   Disables the downloading of ActiveX controls

- **Prompt**   Prompts you each time a page has an ActiveX control

Figure 16-17   Use the Security Settings dialog box to control security settings for a zone.

Other settings on the Security Settings dialog box include the following:

- File Download
- Font Download

- Access Data Sources Across Domains

- Allow META REFRESH

- Display Mixed Content

- Don't Prompt For Client Certificate Selection When No Certificates Or Only One Certificate Exists

- Drag And Drop Or Copy And Paste Files

- Installation Of Desktop Items

- Launching Programs And Files In An IFRAME

- Navigate Sub-Frames Across Different Domains

- Submit Nonencrypted Form Data

- User Data Persistence

- Active Scripting

- Allow Paste Operations Via Script

- Scripting Of Java Applets

- User Authentication Logon

Note   Internet Explorer 6.0 and Windows XP Professional do not contain the Sun Microsystems Java Virtual Machine (JVM). The first time you connect to a Web site that requires JVM support, you must download JVM.

How to Configure Privacy Options

The Privacy tab of the Internet Options dialog box allows you to control how Internet Explorer handles **cookies**, which are small text files stored on your computer by Web sites. Web sites use cookies to store user preferences for personalized sites, and cookies often contain personal information used to identify the user to the Web site.

Cookies can be either persistent (they remain after Internet Explorer is closed and can be reused) or temporary (they are deleted when Internet Explorer is closed). Also, there are first-party and third-party cookies. First-party cookies originate from the Web site that you are currently viewing. Third-party cookies originate from a site different from the one that you are currently viewing but are somehow related to the current Web site. For example, many sites use advertising from third-party sites that commonly use cookies to track your Web site usage for advertising purposes. Third-party cookies might compromise your privacy because advertisers can use them to track your Web site usage across multiple Web sites.

Table 16-9 explains the available privacy settings for handling cookies.

Table 16-9   Privacy Tab Settings

Setting	Description
Block All Cookies	Blocks cookies from all Web sites and makes existing cookies on your computer unreadable by Web sites.
High	Blocks cookies that do not have a compact privacy policy and those that use personally identifiable information without your explicit consent.
Medium High	Blocks third-party cookies that do not have a compact privacy policy and those that use personally identifiable information without your explicit consent. It also blocks first-party cookies that use personally identifiable information without your implicit consent.
Medium	Blocks third-party cookies that do not have a compact privacy policy and those that use personally identifiable information without your implicit consent. It also restricts first-party cookies that use personally identifiable information without your implicit consent.
Low	Restricts third-party cookies that do not have a compact privacy policy and those that use personally identifiable information without your implicit consent.
Accept All Cookies	Allows all cookies to be saved on the computer. Existing cookies on this computer can be read by the Web sites that created them.

> **Tip**   You can also click Advanced to override automatic cookie handling and manually define whether to accept, block, or prompt first-party and third-party cookies.

In addition to helping protect you from errant cookies, the Privacy tab also lets you enable Internet Explorer's built-in Pop-Up Blocker, which helps prevent Web pages from opening unexpected (and unwanted) pop-up windows. To enable the Pop-Up Blocker, select the Block Pop-Ups check box. After enabling the feature, click Settings to configure how the Pop-Up Blocker works. You can enter the names of sites for which you want to allow pop-ups, as well as have Internet Explorer play sounds when a pop-up is blocked. You can also control whether Internet Explorer announces blocked pop-up windows in its Information Bar.

Internet Explorer displays the Information Bar just below the address bar when certain activities occur, such as file downloads, blocked pop-up windows, and other alerts.

How to Configure Content Options

The Content tab of the Internet Options dialog box gives you access to the Content Advisor, which controls the display of Web sites based on rating levels defined by the

Recreational Software Advisory Council on the Internet (RSACi). The most common use for Content Advisor is on a home computer on which parents want to control the Web sites that their children can view. You can control access based on language, nudity, sex, and violence. Ratings for Web sites are based on voluntary ratings by Web site creators. However, by default, Content Advisor does not allow you to open sites that have not been rated. You can also create a list of Web sites that are always viewable or never viewable, no matter how they are rated.

How to Configure Connections Options

The Connections tab of the Internet Options dialog box, shown in Figure 16-18, allows you to control how Internet Explorer connects to the Internet. If the computer uses a dial-up or virtual private network (VPN) connection to connect to the Internet, those connections are shown in the Dial-Up And Virtual Private Network Settings section. Click Add to start the New Connection Wizard, which you use to configure networking connections (and which you learn more about in Chapter 15, "Configuring Network and Internet Connections"). When you select one of the displayed connections, you can also configure the following options for that connection:

Never Dial A Connection   Requires that you manually establish a connection before opening Internet Explorer.

Dial Whenever A Network Connection Is Not Present   Causes Internet Explorer to use the current default connection if it detects that there is no existing connection to the Internet.

Always Dial My Default Connection   Causes Internet Explorer to always dial the current default connection.

Figure 16-18   Configure the way Internet Explorer connects to the Internet.

To configure the default connection, select a connection from the list and click Set Default.

You can also use the Connections tab to configure proxy server settings. A proxy server is a centralized network device that provides Internet access to the client computers on the network, as shown in Figure 16-19. Proxy servers are used to centralize Internet connection settings, increase security by controlling which resources a client can access, and speed up Internet access by caching Web pages to the server. After you configure Internet Explorer to use a proxy server, Internet Explorer requests Internet content from the proxy server, which in turn connects to the actual Internet resource on the client's behalf, retrieves the information, and forwards it to the client.

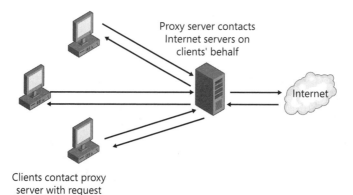

Figure 16-19   A proxy server enhances security and speeds up Internet access.

To configure Internet Explorer to use a proxy server for dial-up and VPN connections, select the connection, and then click Settings. To configure Internet Explorer to use a proxy server for local area network (LAN) connections, click LAN Settings.

Figure 16-20 shows the available proxy server configuration options, which are as follows:

Automatically Detect Settings   Allows the client to automatically receive proxy server configuration from a properly configured Dynamic Host Configuration Protocol (DHCP) or Domain Name System (DNS) server.

Use Automatic Configuration Script   Specifies the path to a configuration script containing proxy server information.

Use A Proxy Server For This Connection   Allows you to enter the address of the proxy server and the port that Internet Explorer should use to connect to the proxy server.

Bypass Proxy Server For Local Addresses   Allows the client to connect directly to address on the local network (such as an internal company Web server) instead of connecting to the proxy server.

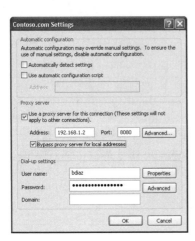

Figure 16-20   Configure proxy server settings.

How to Configure Programs Options

The Programs tab of the Internet Options dialog box, shown in Figure 16-21, allows you to configure the programs that are associated with particular services. For example, if a user is browsing a Web site and selects an e-mail address link, Internet Explorer must launch the appropriate e-mail program. Other configurable services include the HTML editor, the newsgroup client, the program to be used to establish a call across the Internet, and the programs to access the user's calendar and contact list.

Figure 16-21   Configure programs associated with certain services.

At the bottom of the Programs tab, you find an option named Internet Explorer Should Check To See Whether It Is The Default Browser. When you enable this option, Internet Explorer checks to see whether it is configured as the default browser each time you open the program. Windows XP opens the default browser when you open favorites from your desktop or from within e-mail messages.

How to Configure Advanced Options

The Advanced tab allows you to fine-tune accessibility, browsing, HTTP 1.1 settings, multimedia functionality, and security. Accessibility provides the following two check boxes:

Always Expand ALT Text For Images   Specifies whether the image size should expand to fit all the alternate text when the Show Pictures text box is cleared.

Move System Caret With Focus/Selection Changes   Specifies whether to move the system caret whenever the focus or selection changes. Some accessibility aids, such as screen readers or screen magnifiers, use the system caret to determine which area of the screen to read or magnify.

Browsing provides many options that allow control browsing, including the following check boxes:

Always Send URLs As UTF-8   Specifies whether to use UTF-8, a standard that defines characters so they are readable in any language. This enables you to exchange Internet addresses (URLs) that contain characters from another language. This option is selected by default.

Enable Folder View For FTP Sites   Specifies that FTP sites be shown in folder view. This feature might not work with certain types of proxy connections. If you clear this check box, FTP sites will display their contents in a Hypertext Markup Language (HTML)-based layout. This option is selected by default.

Enable Install On Demand (Other)   Specifies to automatically download and install Web components if a Web page needs them to display the page properly or perform a particular task. This option is selected by default.

The Multimedia section provides many options including the following check boxes:

Play Animations In Web Pages   Specifies whether animations can play when pages are displayed. Pages that contain animations display very slowly. To display pages faster, clear this check box. You can still play an individual animation even when this check box is not selected if you right-click the icon that represents the animation, and then click Show Picture. This option is selected by default.

Play Sounds In Web Pages   Specifies whether music and other sounds can play when pages are displayed. Some pages that contain sounds download very slowly. Clear this check box to speed up the downloading of these pages. This option is selected by default.

Show Pictures   Specifies whether graphical images should be included when pages are displayed. Pages that contain several graphical images can display very slowly. Clear this check box to speed up the downloading of these pages. You can still view an individual image even when this check box is not selected if you right-click the icon that represents the graphic, and then click Show Picture. This option is selected by default.

The Printing settings allow you to specify whether you want to print background colors and images.

The Security settings (see Figure 16-22) allow you to fine-tune your security settings.

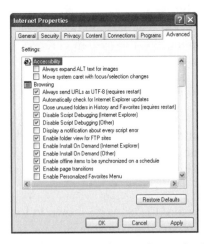

Figure 16-22   Configure advanced options in Internet Explorer.

The Security section provides many options, including the following check boxes:

Empty Temporary Internet Files Folder When Browser Is Closed   Specifies whether you want to empty the Internet Temporary Files folder when the browser is closed. This option is not selected by default.

Use SSL 2.0   Controls whether you want to send and receive secured information through Secure Sockets Layer Level 2 (SSL 2.0), the standard protocol for secure transmissions. All Web sites support this protocol. This option is selected by default.

Use SSL 3.0   Specifies whether you want to send and receive secured information through Secure Sockets Layer Level 3 (SSL 3.0), which is designed to be more secure than SSL 2.0. Some Web sites might not support SSL 3.0. This option is selected by default.

Warn About Invalid Site Certificates   Specifies whether Internet Explorer should warn you if the address (URL) in a Web site's security certificate is not valid. This option is selected by default.

Warn If Changing Between Secure And Not Secure Mode   Specifies whether Internet Explorer should warn you if you are switching between Internet sites that are secure and sites that are not secure.

> **Note**   For information about any of the other check boxes located in the Advanced tab of the Internet Properties dialog box, click the question mark in the upper-right corner of the dialog box, and then click the check box.

Lesson Review

The following questions are intended to reinforce key information presented in this lesson. If you are unable to answer a question, review the lesson materials and try the question again. You can find answers to the questions in the "Questions and Answers" section at the end of this chapter.

1. What is a cookie? How can you delete all the cookies that are stored on your computer?

_____

_____

_____

2. How can you control which cookies are stored on your computer?

_____

_____

3. As a concerned parent, how can you help protect your children from adult material found on the Internet?

_____

_____

_____

_____

_____

_____

4. How can you have the Internet Temporary Files folder emptied each time you close your browser?

_____

_____

_____

_____

_____

Lesson Summary

- Use the General tab of the Internet Options dialog box to configure your home page, temporary Internet file settings, history settings, and Internet Explorer appearance.

- Use the Security tab of the Internet Options dialog box to configure settings for the four security zones Internet Explorer uses to categorize sites: Internet, Local Intranet, Trusted Sites, and Restricted Sites. Web sites are placed into the Internet zone unless you place them into another zone.

- Use the Privacy tab of the Internet Options dialog box to configure how Internet Explorer handles cookies and to enable the Pop-Up Blocker.

- Use the Content tab of the Internet Options dialog box to configure the Content Advisor, which blocks Web sites based on their content.

- Use the Connections tab of the Internet Options dialog box to configure the connections that Internet Explorer uses to connect to the Internet. You can also use this tab to configure a proxy server.

- Use the Programs tab of the Internet Options dialog box to configure the programs that Internet Explorer uses by default for e-mail messages, newsgroups, contacts, and so on.

- Use the Advanced tab of the Internet Options dialog box to configure additional settings that govern the browsing experience.

Case Scenario Exercise

In this exercise, you will read a scenario about configuring Local Security Policy and then answer the questions that follow. If you have difficulty completing this work, review the material in this chapter before beginning the next chapter. You can find answers to these questions in the "Questions and Answers" section at the end of this chapter.

Scenario

You are working as an administrator for a company named Fourth Coffee, a distributor of gourmet coffees based in San Francisco. You are working with users in the Sales department who have 20 computers running Windows XP Professional in a workgroup environment. Your supervisor has given you the task of increasing security within the workgroup.

Specifically, you have been asked to do the following:

■ Ensure that the following password requirements are enforced:

❑ Passwords should be eight characters or more.

❑ Passwords should be complex.

❑ Users should be forced to change passwords after 30 days.

■ Users should be able to back up but not restore their own computers.

■ Users should be able to install device drivers for new devices.

■ The Administrator account on each computer should be renamed to CoffeeAdmin.

■ The Guest account should be disabled.

■ Computers should not display the last user name used to log on to a computer on the Welcome screen.

Questions

1. Although you could log on to each computer in person and use Local Security Policy to configure the settings for the computer, what would be an easier way to configure all computers in the workgroup?

_____

_____

2. List the specific policies you should configure to meet the requirements listed and how you would configure them.

You should configure the following policies:

_____

_____

_____

_____

_____

_____

_____

_____

3. After importing the custom template to a computer and restarting the computer, how could you verify that the appropriate settings were made?

_____

_____

_____

Troubleshooting Lab

In this troubleshooting lab, you will import a template to your computer that simulates a troubleshooting environment by enforcing certain security settings. You will then read a scenario and answer questions. If you have difficulty completing this work, review the material in this chapter before beginning the next chapter. You can find answers to these questions in the "Questions and Answers" section at the end of this chapter.

> **Caution**   Performing this procedure will import security settings to your computer that might result in loss of network connectivity to your computer. You should perform this procedure only on your test computer. The computer should be a member of a workgroup and not a domain.

To set up your computer for this troubleshooting lab, use these steps.

1. In Windows Explorer, open the Labs folder on the CD-ROM that accompanies this book, locate the 270template.inf file, and copy the file to your desktop.

2. Click Start, and then click Run.

3. In the Run dialog box, type **mmc**, and then click OK.

4. In the Console1 window that opens, maximize the Console Root window.

5. Click File, and then click Add/Remove Snap-In.

6. In the Add/Remove Snap-In dialog box, click Add.

7. In the Add Standalone Snap-Ins dialog box, click Security Configuration And Analysis, and then click Add.

8. Click Close, and then click OK.

9. In the console tree, right-click Security Configuration And Analysis, and then click Open Database.

10. In the Open Database dialog box, in the File Name text box, type **270.sdb**, and then click Open.

11. In the Import Template dialog box that opens, in the Look In drop-down list, click Desktop.

12. Click 270template.inf, and then click Open.

13. In the Console1 window, right-click Security Configuration And Analysis, and then click Configure Computer Now.

    Windows displays the Configure System dialog box.

14. What is the default error log file path?

    C:\Documents and Settings*username*\My Documents\Security\Logs\270.log

15. Click OK.

16. Close the Console 1 window.

    Windows displays the Microsoft Management Console dialog box, asking whether you want to save changes to the console.

17. Click Yes.

18. In the Save As dialog box, in the File Name text box, type **Security Configuration And Analysis.msc**, and then click Save.

Scenario

You are working as an administrator for Contoso, Ltd., a manufacturer of linen products. Tibor, a user in the Production department, is having trouble with his computer running Windows XP Professional. He has shared a folder named Bath Towels so that other users in the department can access the files he is working on for a new project, and he is pretty sure he shared the folder correctly. However, other users report that they cannot connect to his computer to access the shared folder. When they try, they see the following error message: Logon Failure: The User Has Not Been Granted The Requested Logon Type At This Computer.

You confirm that Tibor has shared the folder correctly and has granted the appropriate access to the Users group.

Questions

1. Given the error message that users are seeing when they try to access Tibor's computer, what do you suspect might be the problem?

    _____

    _____

2. Using the Local Security Settings window, list the users or groups that are granted the Access This Computer From The Network user right.

   _____

   _____

3. Recalling what you have learned in this chapter, does the list of groups that have been granted the Access This Computer From The Network user right seem like the default setting for a workstation? What groups should be granted this right on a workstation?

   _____

   _____

4. Open the Command Prompt window and at the command prompt, type **gpresult.exe.** Are there any group policies applied to this computer?

   _____

   _____

   _____

   _____

   _____

5. Open your Administrative Tools folder (in Control Panel) and then open the Security Configuration And Analysis console that you saved when setting up this lab. Use the following steps:

   a. Right-click Security Configuration And Analysis, and then click Import Template.

   b. In the Import Template window, browse to the %systemroot%\security\templates folder, click setup security.inf, and then click Open.

   c. Right-click Security Configuration And Analysis, and then click Analyze Computer Now. When asked, save the error log in the default location.

   d. After the analysis is done, expand the Local Policies node and click User Rights Assignment.

   e. For the Access This Computer From The Network user right, what are the database settings and what are the computer settings?

   _____

   _____

   _____

   _____

6. What other user rights are different from those in the Security Setup template?

_____

_____

_____

 Note   To restore your computer to the default settings after you finish this lab, right-click Security Configuration And Analysis, and then click Configure Computer Now. Save the error log in the default location. This action restores the default Windows user rights settings from the Security Setup template you have loaded.

Chapter Summary

■ Local Security Policy is applied to a specific computer, and is the only type of security policy you can use on computers that are members of a workgroup. You manage Local Security Policy by using the Local Security Policy tool found in the Administrative Tools folder. Group Policy, which is applied to sites, domains, and OUs in an Active Directory environment, affects all computers or users that are members of the container to which the Group Policy is assigned.

■ Windows XP Professional provides two types of account policies: Password Policy, which allows you to manage the passwords used on your computer, and Account Lockout Policy, which allows you determine the number of invalid logon attempts before a user account is locked out of the computer.

■ User rights allow a user or group to perform a specific action, such as backing up files or changing the system time. There are two types of user rights: privileges, which allow users to perform a specific task, and logon rights, which control the way users can log on to a computer.

■ Security Options represent many different categories of settings related to Windows XP Professional security.

■ On a computer running Windows XP Professional, auditing helps to ensure that your network is secure by tracking user activities and system-wide events. You set up an audit policy by using the Local Security Settings window to specify which events to record. You can audit the success of events, the failure of events, or both.

■ You can configure security and privacy options in Internet Explorer by using the Internet Options dialog box. You can also use this dialog box to configure how Internet Explorer connects to the Internet, manages temporary Internet files, and many other options.

Exam Highlights

Before taking the exam, review the key points and terms that are presented in this chapter. You need to know this information.

Key Points

- The Setup Security template (Setup Security.inf) defines the default level of security applied to all new installations of Windows XP Professional on an NTFS partition. This template is useful for resetting security levels back to their default in disaster-recovery situations.

- The order in which GPOs are processed is that first the local GPO is processed, and then Active Directory GPOs are processed. Active Directory GPOs are processed starting with the farthest structure from the user (the site), then the next closer structure to the user (the domain), and finally the closest structure (the OU).

- Auditing resource access on a computer running Windows XP Professional is a two-step process. First, you must configure the Audit Object Access Policy. Then, you must enable auditing for specific objects (such as files, folders, and printers).

Key Terms

account policy   A policy that enforces password restrictions and account lockout policy.

auditing   A process that tracks both user activities and Windows XP Professional activities on a computer and records these events in the security log.

auditing policies   Policies that allow you to track the activities of users and the access of resources on a computer.

Local Security Policy   A combination of settings, applied during startup, that affect a local computer.

logon right   A user right assigned to a group or an individual user account that controls the way users can log on to a system.

Group Policy   Combinations of security settings that are applied to users or computers based on membership in sites, domains, or OUs.

Group Policy Result Tool   A command-line utility that helps you determine which policies are actually applied to a computer.

privilege   A user right that allows the members of the group to which it is assigned to perform a specific task, usually one that affects an entire computer system rather than one object.

Resultant Set of Policy (RSoP)   A tool that provides a way for you to simulate and test policy settings applied to computers or users. It shows you the policies applied to the object and order in which they are applied.

security options   Policies that allow you to control various security settings in Windows XP Professional.

security templates   Preconfigured combinations of security settings that you can apply to computers or customize to suit your needs.

security zones   Categories of Web sites that Internet Explorer uses to allow or block access to particular types of activities. Zones include Internet, Local Intranet, Trusted Sites, and Restricted Sites.

user right   Allows the members of the group or the individual users assigned the right to perform a specific action, such as backing up files or changing the system time. User rights include privileges and logon rights.

Questions and Answers

Lesson 1 Review

Page
16-14

1. _____ is used to control settings on computers in a workgroup environment.

   Local Security Policy

2. When multiple GPOs and the LGPO affecting a computer are combined, in what order are the policies resolved?

   First, the LGPO on the computer is processed and all settings specified in that LGPO are applied. Next, any GPOs that have been linked with the site in which the computer resides are processed. Then, GPOs linked to the domain in which the computer resides are processed and any settings are applied. Finally, GPOs linked to any OUs that contain the user or computer object are processed. Settings made at each level override any conflicting settings made at the preceding levels.

3. You would use the _____ tool to view the actual settings affecting a computer and the source of those settings.

   RSoP or Gpresult.exe.

Lesson 2 Practice: Exercise 2

Page
16-20

1. What settings did you use for each of the three listed items?

   You should configure the Set Enforce Password History setting to 5 so that users must have at least 5 different passwords before they use a previously used password. Set Minimum Password Age to 1 day so that a user must wait 24 hours before he or she can change it again. Set Maximum Password Age to 21 days so that a user must change his or her password every three weeks.

18. Were you successful? Why or why not?

   No, because you must wait 24 hours (one day) before you can change your password a second time. A Change Password dialog box appears, indicating that you cannot change the password at this time.

Lesson 2 Practice: Exercise 3

Page
16-22

1. What Account Lockout Policy settings did you use for each of the two conditions?

   Set the account lockout threshold to 4 to lock out a user account after 4 failed logon attempts. When you set one of the three Account Lockout options and the other two options have not been set, a dialog box appears, indicating that the other two options will be set to default values. Set the account lockout duration to 0 to ensure that locked accounts remain locked until an administrator unlocks them.

Lesson 2 Review

Page
16-23

1. What is the range of values Windows XP Professional allows you to set for the Enforce Password History setting, and what do those values mean?

You can set the value from 0 to 24. A value of 0 indicates that no password history is being kept. All values indicate the number of new passwords that a user must use before he or she can reuse an old password.

2. The range of values Windows XP Professional allows you to set for the Maximum Password Age setting is _____ to _____ days. The default value is _____ days.

0; 999; 42

3. Which of the following selections are requirements for a password if the Passwords Must Meet Complexity Requirements setting is enabled? (Choose all that apply.)

   a. All passwords must exceed six characters in length.

   b. All passwords must comply with the password history settings.

   c. No passwords can contain capitals or punctuation.

   d. No passwords can contain the user's account or full name.

The correct answers are A, B and D. Password complexity requires that all passwords be at least six characters in length, no password contain the user's account or full name, and that the password contain upper and lowercase letters, numerals, and symbols. B is correct because setting complexity requirements does not affect password history settings. C is not correct because these are not complexity requirements.

4. What is Account Lockout Duration, and what is the range of values?

This value indicates the number of minutes that the system will prevent the user account from logging on to Windows XP Professional. You can set the value from 0 to 99,999 minutes.

Lesson 3 Review

Page
16-29

1. Which of the following statements about user rights are correct? (Choose all that apply.)

   a. Microsoft recommends that you assign user rights to individual user accounts.

   b. Microsoft recommends that you assign user rights to groups rather than individual user accounts.

   c. User rights allow users assigned the right to perform a specific action, such as backing up files and directories.

   d. There are two types of user rights: privileges and logon rights.

The correct answers are B, C, and D. A is not correct because Microsoft recommends that you assign user rights to groups, not to individual user accounts.

2. If your computer running Windows XP Professional is part of a domain environment and you configure the Local Security Policies on your computer so that you assign yourself the Add Workstation To A Domain user right, can you add additional workstations to the domain? Why or why not?

For the Add Workstation To A Domain privilege to be effective, it must be assigned as part of the default domain controller policy for the domain, not the Local Security Policy on your computer running Windows XP Professional.

3. What benefit does the Back Up Files And Directories user right provide?

The Back Up Files And Directories user right improves the security on your system. It allows a user to back up the system without being assigned file and folder permissions to access all files and folders on the system. In other words, the person backing up the files can back up secure files without being able to read them.

4. What are logon rights and what do they do?

A logon right is a user right assigned to a group or individual user account. Logon rights control the way users can log on to a system.

Lesson 4 Practice

Page 16-33

1. What is the name of the Guest account?

The Guest account is now named Fox.

Lesson 4 Review

Page 16-33

1. How can you require a user to be logged on to the computer to shut it down? (Discuss using the Welcome screen and using CTRL+ALT+DELETE to log on.)

If Windows XP Professional is configured to use the Welcome screen or CTRL+ALT+DELETE to log on, by default you do not have to log on to shut down the computer. In the console tree, expand Local Policies, and then click Security Options. In the details pane, right-click Shutdown: Allow System To Be Shut Down Without Having To Log On, and then click Properties and click Disabled.

2. By default, Windows XP Professional does not clear the virtual memory pagefile when the system is shut down. Why can this be considered a security breach and what can you do to resolve it?

The data in the pagefile might be accessible to users who are not authorized to view that information. To clear the pagefile each time the system is shut down, in the Local Security Settings window, expand Local Policies and click Security Options. Right-click Shutdown: Clear Virtual Memory Pagefile, and then click Properties. Select Enabled.

3. Why does forcing users to press CTRL+ALT+DELETE improve security on your computer?

Requiring users to press CTRL+ALT+DELETE to log on to the computer increases security on your computer because you are forcing users to use a key combination recognized only by Windows. Using this key combination ensures that users are giving the password only to Windows, not to a program waiting to capture user passwords.

4. By default, Windows XP Professional displays the last user name to log on to the computer in the Windows Security dialog box. Why is this considered a security risk, and what can you do to resolve it?

In some situations, displaying the last user name is considered a security risk because an unauthorized user can see a valid user account displayed onscreen, which makes it much easier to break into the computer. To resolve this security problem, in the Local Security Settings window, expand the Local Policies node, and then click Security Options. In the details pane, right-click Interactive Logon: Do Not Display Last User Name, click Properties, and select Enabled.

Lesson 5 Review

Page
16-44

1. What is auditing?

Auditing is a process that tracks both user activities and Windows XP Professional activities on a computer and records these events in the security log.

2. What is an audit policy?

An audit policy defines the types of security events that Windows XP Professional records in the security log on each computer.

3. When you are auditing events on a computer running Windows XP Professional, where are the audited events being recorded?

Windows XP Professional writes events to the security log on the computer on which the event occurs.

4. What are the requirements to set up and administer auditing?

You must have the Manage Auditing And Security Log user right for the computer for which you want to configure an audit policy or review an audit log. The files and folders you want to audit must be on an NTFS volume.

5. What are the two steps in setting up auditing?

Setting the audit policy and enabling auditing of specific resources

6. By default, any auditing changes that you make to a parent folder _____ (are inherited/are not inherited) by all child folders and all files in the parent and child folders.

Are inherited

Lesson 6 Review

Page
16-57

1. What is a cookie? How can you delete all the cookies that are stored on your computer?

   A cookie is a file created by a Web site; the cookie stores information about you on your computer. In the Temporary Internet Files section in the General tab, click Delete Cookies to delete all cookies now.

2. How can you control which cookies are stored on your computer?

   The Privacy tab of the Internet Properties dialog box allows you to determine how cookies will be handled on your computer.

3. As a concerned parent, how can you help protect your children from adult material found on the Internet?

   The Content tab gives you access to the Content Advisor, which allows you to control what can be viewed on the Internet. You can control access to Web sites based on language, nudity, sex, and violence based on voluntary ratings by Web site creators. By default, Content Advisor does not allow access to sites that have not been rated. You can also create a list of Web sites that are never viewable, no matter how they are rated.

4. How can you have the Internet Temporary Files folder emptied each time you close your browser?

   In the Security section of the Advanced tab in the Internet Properties dialog box, you can select the Empty Internet Temporary Files Folder When Browser Is Closed check box. Selecting this check box specifies that you want to empty the Internet Temporary Files folder when the browser is closed. This option is not selected by default.

Case Scenario Exercise

Page
16-58

1. Although you could log on to each computer in person and use Local Security Policy to configure the settings for the computer, what would be an easier way to configure all computers in the workgroup?

   You could customize an administrative template with the required settings, save the template, and then export it on each computer in the workgroup.

2. List the specific policies you should configure to meet the requirements listed and how you would configure them.

   You should configure the following policies:

   ❑ Configure the Minimum Password Length policy with a value of 8.

   ❑ Enable the Passwords Must Meet Complexity Requirements policy.

   ❑ Configure the Maximum Password Age with a value of 30.

❑ Add the Users group to the Back Up Files And Directories user right.

❑ Add the Users group to the Load And Unload Device Drivers user right.

❑ Configure the Accounts: Rename Administrator Account security option with the name CoffeeAdmin.

❑ Configure the Accounts: Guest Account Status security option as Disabled.

❑ Configure the Interactive Logon: Do Not Display Last User Name security option as Enabled.

3. After importing the custom template to a computer and restarting the computer, how could you verify that the appropriate settings were made?

You could use the Security Configuration And Analysis tool to analyze the computer against the template. The results would show you the security settings in effect on the computer and the setting specified in the template.

Troubleshooting Lab

Page 16-60

1. Given the error message that users are seeing when they try to access Tibor's computer, what do you suspect might be the problem?

The problem is likely that the Access This Computer From The Network user right is not configured to allow network access by the appropriate groups.

2. Using the Local Security Settings window, list the users or groups that are granted the Access This Computer From The Network user right.

Only the following groups are granted the Access This Computer From The Network user right: Administrators, Power Users, and Backup Operators.

3. Recalling what you have learned in this chapter, does the list of groups that have been granted the Access This Computer From The Network user right seem like the default setting for a workstation? What groups should be granted this right on a workstation?

No. The default groups that are granted this right are Administrators, Backup Operators, Power Users, Users, and Everyone.

4. Open the Command Prompt window and at the command prompt, type **gpresult.exe.** Are there any group policies applied to this computer?

Yes, the Local Group Policy. This computer should be a member of a workgroup, so no domain group policies are applied. If you are running the exercise on a computer that is connected to a domain, you might see group policies in effect. In addition, those policies might override the Local Security Policy you used to set up this lab.

5. Open your Administrative Tools folder (in Control Panel) and then open the Security Configuration And Analysis console that you saved when setting up this lab. Use the following steps:

   a. Right-click Security Configuration And Analysis, and then click Import Template.

   b. In the Import Template window, browse to the %systemroot%\security\templates folder, click setup security.inf, and then click Open.

   c. Right-click Security Configuration And Analysis, and then click Analyze Computer Now. When asked, save the error log in the default location.

   d. After the analysis is done, expand the Local Policies node and click User Rights Assignment.

   e. For the Access This Computer From The Network user right, what are the database settings and what are the computer settings?

   The database settings (the default Windows settings from the Security Setup template) include these groups: Administrators, Backup Operators, Power Users, Users, and Everyone. The computer settings (which were applied when you set up the lab) include these groups: Backup Operators, Power Users, and Administrators.

6. What other user rights are different from those in the Security Setup template?

   Change The System Time, Deny Access To This Computer From The Network, Deny Logon Locally, Load And Unload Device Drivers, Logon Locally, and Shut Down The System.

17 Monitoring and Managing Shared Folders by Using Computer Management

Exam Objectives in this Chapter:

- Manage and troubleshoot access to shared folders
- Create and remove shared folders

Why This Chapter Matters

This chapter prepares you to monitor network resources. You learn about using the Computer Management window to view and create shares. You also learn how to use view sessions, open files, and disconnect users from shared folders.

Lessons in this Chapter:

Before You Begin

To complete this chapter, you must have a computer that meets the minimum hardware requirements listed in the preface, "About This Book." You must also have Microsoft Windows XP Professional installed on a computer on which you can make changes.

Lesson 1: Monitoring Access to Shared Folders

Windows XP Professional includes the **Shared Folders snap-in**, which allows you to easily monitor access to network resources and send administrative messages to users. The Shared Folders snap-in is included in Computer Management, and you can also add the snap-in to your own custom console. You monitor access to network resources to assess and manage current usage on network servers. You monitor access to shared folders to determine how many users currently have a connection to each folder. You can also monitor open files to determine which users are accessing the files, and you can disconnect users from one open file or from all open files.

After this lesson, you will be able to

- Identify reasons for monitoring access to network resources
- Identify which users can monitor access to network resources
- View and monitor the shared folders on a computer
- Monitor open files on a computer
- Disconnect users from one or all open files

Estimated lesson time: 30 minutes

Reasons for Monitoring Network Resources

It is important that you understand why you should monitor the network resources in your computer environment. Some of the reasons why it is important to assess and manage network resources are included in the following list:

Maintenance   You should determine which users are currently using a resource so that you can notify them before making the resource temporarily or permanently unavailable. Additionally, you might be able to detect current or impending problems.

Security   You should monitor user access to resources that are confidential or need to be secure to verify that only authorized users are accessing them.

Planning   You should determine which resources are being used and how much they are being used so that you can plan for future system growth.

You can use Computer Management to monitor the resources on the local computer or a remote computer.

Who Can Monitor Access to Network Resources?

Not all users can monitor access to network resources. Table 17-1 lists the group membership requirements for monitoring access to network resources using Computer Management.

Table 17-1   Groups That Can Access Network Resources

A Member of These Groups...	Can Monitor...
Domain Administrators or Server Operators for the domain	All computers in the domain
Administrators or Power Users for a member server or a computer running Windows XP Professional	Local or remote computers in the workgroup

> **Exam Tip**   Members of the Domain Administrators or Server Operators domain groups can use Computer Management to monitor any computer that is a member of the domain. Members of the Administrators or Power Users local group can monitor a local computer, whether that computer is in a workgroup or domain.

How to Use the Shares Folder to View and Monitor Shared Folders

You use the **Shares folder** in Computer Management (located within System Tools\Shared Folders) to view a list of all shared folders on the computer and to determine how many users have a connection to each folder. In Figure 17-1, the Shares folder has been selected in the Computer Management console tree, and all the shared folders on that computer are shown in the details pane.

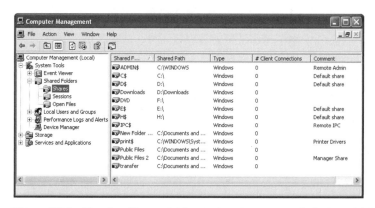

Figure 17-1   Use the Shares folder to view the status of all shared folders on a computer.

Table 17-2 explains the information provided in the details pane shown in Figure 17-1.

Table 17-2   Fields in the Details Pane of the Shares Folder

Column Name	Description
Shared Folder	The shared folders on the computer. This is the name that was given to the folder when it was shared.
Shared Path	The path to the shared folder.
Type	The type of network connection: Windows, Novell NetWare, or Apple Macintosh.
# Client Connections	The number of clients who have made a remote connection to the shared folder.
Comment	Descriptive text about the folder. This comment was provided when the folder was shared.

Note   Windows XP Professional does not update the list of shared folders, open files, and user sessions automatically. To update these lists, on the Action menu, click Refresh.

Real World   Monitoring Multiple Remote Computers Easily

The Microsoft Management Console (MMC) allows you to add multiple snap-ins that can connect to different remote computers. If you routinely monitor shared folders and users on several different remote computers, you can create a custom console that lets you switch between those computers easily. To create a custom console for monitoring multiple remote computers, follow these steps:

1. Click Start, and then click Run.

2. In the Run dialog box, type **mmc**, and then click OK.

   Windows XP displays an empty MMC console named Console 1.

3. Click File, and then click Add/Remove Snap-In.

4. In the Add/Remove Snap-In dialog box, click Add.

5. In the Add Standalone Snap-In dialog box, in the Available Standalone Snap-Ins list, click Shared Folders, and then click Add.

6. In the Shared Folders dialog box, click Another Computer, and then type the name of the remote computer (or click Browse to locate the computer on the network).

7. Repeat Steps 5 and 6 for each computer you want to add to the console.

> **8.** Click Close to close the Add Standalone Snap-In dialog box.
>
> **9.** Click OK to close the Add/Remove Snap-In dialog box,
>
> **10.** Click File, and then click Save to save the custom console.
>
> One thing to keep in mind as you set up a console for monitoring remote computers is that Windows Firewall prevents remote management in its default configuration. For information on allowing remote management in Windows Firewall, see the Knowledge Base article, "How to troubleshoot WMI-related issues in Windows XP SP2," available at *http://support.microsoft.com/ Default.aspx?kbid=875605*.

How to Specify the Maximum Concurrent Users Who can Access a Shared Folder

You can use Computer Management to specify the maximum number of users who are permitted to access a shared folder. To specify the maximum number of users, follow these steps:

1. Click Start, and then click Control Panel.

2. In the Control Panel window, click Performance And Maintenance.

3. In the Performance And Maintenance window, click Administrative Tools.

4. In the Administrative Tools folder, double-click Computer Management.

5. In the Computer Management window, expand the System Tools node, and then the Shared Folders node.

6. Click Shares.

7. In the right pane, right-click the shared folder for which you want to determine the maximum number of concurrent users, and then click Properties.

   Windows XP displays the Properties dialog box for the shared folder, with the General tab active. By default, the User Limit is set to Maximum Allowed, which in Windows XP Professional is 10 concurrent connections.

8. Click Allow This Number Of Users and specify the number of users (up to 10) that you want to be able to connect to the shared folder.

> **Exam Tip**   When troubleshooting connectivity problems when a user cannot connect to a share, do not forget to check the number of connections to the share and the maximum connections allowed on the share. If the maximum number of connections has already been made, the user cannot connect to the shared resource.

Shared Folder Properties

You can modify existing shared folders, including shared folder permissions, from the Shares folder. To change a shared folder's properties, right-click the shared folder, and then click Properties. The General tab of the Properties dialog box shows you the share name, the path to the shared folder, and any comment that has been entered. The General tab also allows you to view and set a user limit for accessing the shared folder. The Share Permissions tab lets you change the users and groups that have access to the shared folder and the permissions each user or group is assigned. The Security tab allows you to view and change the NTFS folder permissions for the folder that the shared folder is based on. (See Chapter 8, "Securing Resources with NTFS Permissions," for more on using the NTFS permissions. See Chapter 9, "Administering Shared Folders," for more on configuring shared folder permissions.)

How to Use the Open Files Folder to Monitor Files

Use the **Open Files folder** in Computer Management to view a list of open files that are located in shared folders and the users who have a current connection to each file. You can use this information when you need to contact users to notify them that you are shutting down the system. Additionally, you can determine which users have a current connection and should be contacted when another user is trying to access a file that is in use.

Table 17-3 describes the information that is available in the Open Files folder.

Table 17-3   Information Available in the Open Files Folder

Column Name	Description
Open File	The name of the open files on the computer.
Accessed By	The logon name of the user who has the file open.
Type	The operating system running on the computer in which the user is logged on.
# Locks	The number of locks on the file. Programs can request the operating system to lock a file to gain exclusive access and prevent other programs from making changes to the file.
Open Mode	The type of access that the user's application requested when it opened the file, such as Read or Write.

How to Disconnect Users from Open Files

You can disconnect users from one open file or from all open files. If you make changes to the NTFS File System permissions for a file that is currently opened by a user, the new permissions will not affect the user until he or she closes and then attempts to reopen the file.

You can force these changes to take place immediately by doing either of the following:

Disconnect all users from all open files   To disconnect all users from all open files, in Computer Management, click Open Files; on the Action menu, click Disconnect All Open Files.

Disconnect all users from one open file   To disconnect users from one open file, in Computer Management, click Open Files. In the details pane, select the open file; on the Action menu, click Close Open File.

> **Caution**   Disconnecting users from open files can result in data loss. You should disconnect users only when absolutely necessary and you should try to warn users first.

Practice: Monitoring Shared Folders

In this practice, you use Computer Management to view the shared folders and open files on your server. If there are any open files on your server and you want to disconnect them, use the Disconnect All Open Files selection. This selection will disconnect all users from all open files.

Exercise 1: View the Shared Folders on Your Computer

1. Log on with a user account that is a member of the Administrators group.

2. Click Start, point to All Programs, point to Administrative Tools, and then click Computer Management.

   Windows XP Professional displays Computer Management.

3. In the Computer Management window, expand the System Tools node, and then expand the Shared Folders node.

4. Under Shared Folders, click Shares.

   Notice that the details pane shows a list of the existing shared folders on your computer.

5. What information is displayed about each shared folder?

   _____

   _____

   _____

Exercise 2: View the Open Files on Your Computer

1. In the Computer Management window, under Shared Folders, click Open Files.

If you are working on a computer that is not connected to a network, there are not any open files because the open files show only connections from a remote computer to a share on your computer.

2. If there are any open files and you want to disconnect all of them, on the Action menu, click Disconnect All Open Files.

3. Leave Computer Management open and remain logged on for the next practice.

Lesson Review

The following questions are intended to reinforce key information presented in this lesson. If you are unable to answer a question, review the lesson materials and try the question again. You can find answers to the questions in the "Questions and Answers" section at the end of this chapter.

1. Why is it important to manage network resources?

   _____

   _____

   _____

   _____

   _____

2. On a computer running Windows XP Professional, members of the _____ and _____ groups can use Computer Management to monitor network resources.

3. How can you determine which files are open on a computer running Windows XP Professional?

   _____

   _____

4. Which of the following statements about monitoring network resources are correct? (Choose all that apply.)

   a. You can use Computer Management to disconnect all users from all open files.

   b. You can use Computer Management to disconnect one user from one file.

   c. If you change the NTFS permissions for an open file, the changes affect all users who have the file open immediately.

   d. If you make changes to the NTFS permissions for an open file, the changes do not affect the user who has that file opened until he or she closes and reopens the file.

Lesson Summary

- Monitoring network resources helps you determine whether a network resource is still needed and whether it is secure, and it helps you plan for future growth. Use Computer Management to monitor access to network resources on local or remote computers.

- In a workgroup, only members of the Administrators group or the Power Users group can monitor resources. In a domain, only members of the Administrators group or the Server Operators group for the domain can monitor resources on all the computers in the domain.

- Use the Shares folder in Computer Management to manage shared folders and open files on a computer.

- Use the Open Files folder to view currently open files on a computer.

- You can disconnect all users from a currently open file or you can disconnect all users from all open files. You cannot disconnect a single user from a single file.

Lesson 2: Creating and Sharing Local and Remote Folders

You can use Computer Management to share an existing folder or to create a new folder and share it on the local computer or on a remote computer. You can also modify the shared folder and NTFS permissions when you share the folder. Remember that to share folders on a computer on which Windows Firewall is running, you must enable the File And Printer Sharing exception (refer to Chapter 9 for details on how to do this).

After this lesson, you will be able to

- Create a new folder and share it by using Shared Folders
- Share a folder on a remote computer by using Shared Folders
- Stop sharing a folder

Estimated lesson time: 20 minutes

How to Create a New Folder and Share It by Using Shared Folders

From the Computer Management window, you can run the Create A Shared Folder Wizard to create a new folder and share it. To run the Create A Shared Folder Wizard, follow these steps:

1. Click Start, and then click Control Panel.

2. In the Control Panel window, click Performance And Maintenance.

3. In the Performance And Maintenance window, click Administrative Tools.

4. In the Administrative Tools folder, double-click Computer Management.

5. Expand the System Tools node, and then expand the Shared Folders node.

6. Under Shared Folders, click Shares.

7. On the Action menu, click New File Share.

   The Create A Shared Folder Wizard starts and displays the Welcome page.

8. Click Next to proceed.

   Windows displays the Set Up A Shared Folder page.

9. In the Folder To Share text box, type the path for the folder you want to share, or click the Browse button to locate an existing folder. If you type the name of a folder that does not already exist, Windows will display a dialog box asking whether you want to create the folder. You can create a new folder and share it in one process.

10. In the Share Name text box, type the share name of the folder. Optionally, you can also type a description for the folder.

11. Click Next to proceed.

    If you typed the name of a folder that does not exist in the Folder To Share text box, a dialog box appears that asks you if you want to create the new folder. If it does, click Yes.

    The Create A Shared Folder Wizard displays the Shared Folder Permissions page, which offers the options shown in Table 17-4.

12. Select the kind of permission you want to use for the shared folder, and then click Next.

13. Click Finish.

Table 17-4   Basic Share Permissions

Option	Description
All Users Have Read-Only Access	The Create A Shared Folder Wizard assigns the Full Control share permission to the Everyone group.
Administrators Have Full Control; Other Users Have Read-Only Access	The Create A Shared Folder Wizard assigns the Full Control share permission to the Administrators group and the Read share permission to the Everyone group.
Administrators Have Full Control; Other Users Have No Access	The Create A Shared Folder Wizard assigns the Full Control share permission to the Administrators group.
Customize Permissions	Select this option to create your own custom share permissions and NTFS permissions.

How to Share a Folder on a Remote Computer by Using Shared Folders

If you want to share a folder on a remote computer, you use the Computer Management window to connect to the remote computer.

> **Note**   Using Computer Management (or the Shared Folders snap-in) is the only way to share a folder on a remote computer. Otherwise, you need to be physically located at the computer where the folder resides to share it.

To share a folder on a remote computer, use these steps:

1. Click Start, and then click Control Panel.

2. In the Control Panel window, click Performance And Maintenance.

3. In the Performance And Maintenance window, click Administrative Tools.

4. In the Administrative Tools folder, double-click Computer Management.

5. In the Computer Management window, click Computer Management (Local).

6. Click Action, and then click Connect To Another Computer.

   Windows XP displays the Select Computer dialog box.

7. Type the Universal Naming Convention (UNC) of the computer to which you want to connect or click Browse to locate the computer on the network. Click OK when you have specified the computer.

8. Use the Create A Shared Folder Wizard (described in the previous section) to create a new folder and share it.

> **Note**   If you want to create and manage shared folders on remote computers and you are not in a domain, you must create the same user account with the same password on each computer. In workgroups, you do not have a central database that contains all user accounts. Instead, each computer in the workgroup has its own local security database. For more information on local security databases, see Chapter 7, "Setting Up and Managing User Accounts."

How to Stop Sharing a Folder by Using Shared Folders

You can also use the Shared Folders node in Computer Management to stop sharing a folder. To stop sharing a folder, follow these steps:

1. Click Start, and then click Control Panel.

2. In the Control Panel window, click Performance And Maintenance.

3. In the Performance And Maintenance window, click Administrative Tools.

4. In the Administrative Tools folder, double-click Computer Management.

5. Expand the System Tools node, and then expand the Shared Folders node.

6. Under Shared Folders, click Shares.

7. In the right-hand pane, right-click the folder you want to stop sharing and then click Stop Sharing.

   Windows displays a Shared Folders dialog box, asking whether you are sure you want to stop sharing the folder.

8. Click Yes.

Practice: Creating a Shared Folder

In this practice, you use Computer Management to create a new folder and share that folder on a local computer by using the Shared Folders node in Comptuer Management. You also use Shared Folders to stop sharing the folder.

Exercise 1: Create a Folder on a Local Computer and Share it by Using Shared Folders

1. Click Start, and then click Control Panel.

2. In the Control Panel window, click Performance And Maintenance.

3. In the Performance And Maintenance window, click Administrative Tools.

4. In the Administrative Tools folder, double-click Computer Management.

5. Expand the System Tools node, and then expand the Shared Folders node.

6. Under Shared Folders, click Shares.

7. On the Action menu, click New File Share.

   The Create A Shared Folder Wizard starts.

8. On the Create A Shared Folder Wizard page, in the Folder To Share text box, type **C:\Library**.

9. In the Share Name text box, type **Library**.

10. Click Next.

    A message box appears, asking you if you want to create C:\Library.

11. Click Yes.

    A message box appears, informing you that C:\Library has been created.

12. Click OK.

    The Create A Shared Folder Wizard displays a final page of three basic share permission options and a customizable permissions option, as described in Table 17-4. You can use one of the three basic permissions or you can choose Customize Share And Folder Permissions to create your own permissions.

13. Click Finish to accept the default permissions option All Users Have Full Control.

    The Create A Shared Folder Wizard displays a message box, telling you that the folder has been successfully shared and asking if you want to create another shared folder.

14. Click No.

    Leave the Computer Management window open for the next exercise.

Exercise 2: Stop Sharing a Folder

1. Under Shared Folders, click Shares.

2. Select the Library folder in the right pane.

3. On the Action menu, click Stop Sharing.

   Windows XP Professional displays a message box, asking if you are sure you want to stop sharing Library.

4. Click Yes.

   The Library share disappears from the list of shared folders.

 Caution   If you stop sharing a folder while a user has a file open, the user might lose data.

Lesson Review

The following questions are intended to reinforce key information presented in this lesson. If you are unable to answer a question, review the lesson materials and try the question again. You can find answers to the questions in the "Questions and Answers" section at the end of this chapter.

1. Which of the following tools can you use to create a shared folder on a remote computer? (Choose all that apply.)

   a. Windows Explorer

   b. Computer Management

   c. Administrative Tools

   d. Shared Folders snap-in

2. How do you create and share a folder on a remote computer?

   _____

   _____

   _____

Lesson Summary

■ You can use Computer Management (or the Shared Folders snap-in in a custom console) to share an existing folder or to create and share a new folder on the local computer.

■ You can also use Computer Management to create a shared folder on a remote computer.

Lesson 3: Monitoring Network Users

You can use Computer Management to monitor the users who are currently accessing shared folder resources on a server from a remote computer, and you can also view the resources to which the users have connections. You can disconnect users and send administrative messages to computers and users, including those not currently accessing network resources.

After this lesson, you will be able to

- Monitor user sessions
- Disconnect a specific user from his or her network connection
- Send administrative messages to users

Estimated lesson time: 20 minutes

How to Monitor User Sessions

You can use Computer Management to view the users who have a connection to open files on a server and the files to which they have a connection. This information enables you to determine which users you should contact when you need to stop sharing a folder or shut down the server on which the shared folder resides. You can disconnect one or more users to free idle connections to the shared folder, to prepare for a backup or restore operation, to shut down a server, or to change group membership and permissions for the shared folder.

You use the **Sessions folder** in the Computer Management window to view a list of the users with a current network connection to the computer that you are monitoring (see Figure 17-2).

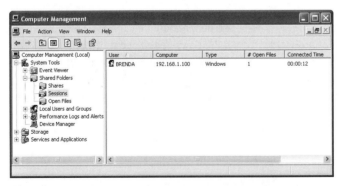

Figure 17-2   Use the Sessions folder to see a list of users with a current network connection to the computer.

Table 17-5 describes the information that is available in the Sessions folder.

Table 17-5 Information Available in the Sessions Folder

Column Name	Description
User	The users with a current network connection to this computer
Computer	The name of the user's computer
Type	The operating system running on the user's computer
# Open Files	The number of files that the user has open on this computer
Connected Time	The time that has elapsed since the user established the current session
Idle Time	The time that has elapsed since the user last accessed a resource on this computer
Guest	Whether this computer authenticated the user as a member of the built-in Guest account

How to Disconnect Users

You can disconnect one or all users with a network connection to a computer so that you can do any of the following:

- Have changes to shared folder and NTFS permissions take effect immediately. A user retains all permissions for a shared resource that Windows XP Professional assigned when the user connected to it. Windows XP Professional evaluates the permissions again the next time a connection is made.

- Free idle connections on a computer so that other users can make a connection when the maximum number of connections has been reached. User connections to resources might remain active for several minutes after a user finishes accessing a resource.

- Shut down a server.

> **Note** After you disconnect a user, he or she can immediately make a new connection. If the user gains access to a shared folder from a Windows-based client computer, the client computer automatically re-establishes the connection with the shared folder. This connection is established without user intervention unless you change the permissions to prevent the user from accessing the shared folder or you stop sharing the folder to prevent all users from accessing it.

To disconnect a specific user, use these steps:

1. In the Computer Management window, under Shared Folders, click Sessions.

2. In the list of users in the details pane, select the user that you want to disconnect, and on the Action menu, click Close Session.

> **Note**   If you want to disconnect all users, click Sessions in the console tree, and then, on the Action menu, click Disconnect All Sessions.

To prevent data loss, you should always notify users who are accessing shared folders or files that you are ready to stop sharing a folder or shut down the computer.

How to Send Administrative Messages to Users

You can send administrative messages to one or more users or computers. Send them to users with a current connection to a computer on which network resources are shared to notify them when there will be a disruption to the computer or resource availability. Some common reasons for sending administrative messages are to notify users when you intend to do any of the following:

- Perform a backup or restore operation
- Disconnect users from a resource
- Upgrade software or hardware
- Shut down the computer

> **Note**   Computers running Windows XP Professional can receive console messages only if the Messenger service is running on the computer. If a computer has Windows XP Service Pack 2 installed, the Messenger service is disabled by default. To enable the service, use the Services tool in the Administrative Tools folder.

To send an administrative message to one or more computers, follow these steps:

1. In the Computer Management window, right-click Shared Folders, point to All Tasks, and then click Send Console Message.

   Windows XP displays the Send Console Message dialog box.

2. In the Send Console Message dialog box, click Add.

   Windows XP displays the Select Computer dialog box.

3. In the Select Computer dialog box, type the names of the computers to which you want to send a message, and then click OK. (You can also click Advanced to browse through a list of available computers.)

> **Tip**   In Computer Management, you can determine the name of the computer that a user is logged on to by clicking the Sessions folder.

4. In the Send Console Message dialog box, in the Message box, type the message that you want to send.

5. Click Send to send the console message to the selected computers.

Lesson Review

The following questions are intended to reinforce key information presented in this lesson. If you are unable to answer a question, review the lesson materials and try the question again. You can find answers to the questions in the "Questions and Answers" section at the end of this chapter.

1. How can you determine which users have a connection to open files on a computer and the files to which they have a connection?

   _____

   _____

2. How can you disconnect a specific user from a file?

   _____

   _____

3. Why would you send an administrative message to users with current connections?

   _____

   _____

   _____

4. What can you do to prevent a user from re-establishing a network connection after you have disconnected that user from a shared folder?

   _____

   _____

   _____

   _____

Lesson Summary

- Use the Sessions folder in the Computer Management window to view which users have a connection to open files on a computer and the files to which they have a connection.

■ You can also use the Sessions folder to disconnect a specific user or all users with a network connection to a computer.

■ You can also use the Computer Management window to send administrative messages to the users on one or more computers.

Case Scenario Exercise

In this exercise, you will read a scenario about monitoring shared folders and then answer the questions that follow. If you have difficulty completing this work, review the material in this chapter before beginning the next chapter. You can find answers to these questions in the "Questions and Answers" section at the end of this chapter.

Scenario

You are working as an administrator for a company named Contoso, Ltd, a manufacturer of crystal glassware. You are working with Ray, a user in the Marketing department who has several shared folders on his computer running Windows XP Professional. One of these folders, Brochures, is used by many users in the department. Often, other users complain to Ray that they cannot gain access to the Brochures folder. Ray is aware that his computer supports only 10 concurrent connections, but he is sure that on many occasions, fewer than 10 people are actually using the files in the Brochures folder.

Questions

1. What misconception does Ray have about the connections to his computer?

   _____

   _____

   _____

2. Ray wants to be able to determine how many users are connecting to the Brochures folder at any given time. How could he do this? What requirements must he meet?

   _____

   _____

   _____

   _____

3. Ray also wants to be able to determine which users are connected to his computer. How could he do this?

_____

_____

4. Concerned that more than 10 users might need to connect to the shared folders on his computer at a time, Ray asks for your opinion. What should you tell him?

_____

_____

_____

_____

_____

Troubleshooting Lab

You are working as an administrator for a company named Lucerne Publishing, a publisher of electronic reference materials for government contracting firms. Sofia, one of the managing editors, calls to tell you that she is having trouble connecting to a shared folder on the network. The folder is located on a computer running Windows XP Professional that belongs to one of her junior editors, Kevin. Kevin is out of town for the week, and Sofia needs several files from Kevin's computer. You confirm that both Sofia's and Kevin's computers are both operational and are successfully connected to the network. Sofia is a member of the following groups: Users, Editors, and Managing Editors.

1. How can you confirm that Kevin's computer actually has a shared folder available?

_____

_____

_____

2. After confirming that the shared folder is indeed on Kevin's computer, how can you ensure that Sofia has the appropriate permissions to access the shared folder?

_____

_____

_____

_____

_____

3. After confirming that Sofia has the appropriate permissions to access the resource, you use Computer Management and discover that six users are currently accessing the computer, four of whom are connected to the resource that Sofia needs to access. You attempt to open the folder yourself and receive an error message, stating that there are too many connections to the folder. What should you suspect is the problem? How would you solve this problem?

_____

_____

_____

_____

Chapter Summary

■ Monitoring network resources helps you determine whether a network resource is still needed and whether it is secure, and it helps you plan for future growth. Use Computer Management to monitor access to network resources on local or remote computers.

■ You can use Computer Management (or the Shared Folders snap-in in a custom console) to share an existing folder or to create and share a new folder on a local or remote computer.

■ Use the Sessions folder in the Computer Management window to view which users have a connection to open files on a computer and the files to which they have a connection. You can also use the Sessions folder to disconnect a specific user or all users with a network connection to a computer.

Exam Highlights

Before taking the exam, review the key points and terms that are presented in this chapter. You need to know this information.

Key Points

■ Members of the Domain Administrators or Server Operators domain groups can use Computer Management to monitor any computer that is a member of the domain. Members of the Administrators or Power Users local group can monitor a local computer, whether that computer is in a workgroup or domain.

■ There is a quick and easy way to troubleshoot connectivity problems when a user cannot connect to a share. Determine the number of connections to the share and the maximum connections allowed. If the maximum number of connections has already been made, the user cannot connect to the shared resource.

Key Terms

Open Files folder   A folder in Computer Management that allows you to view a list of open files that are located in shared folders and the users who have a current connection to each file.

Sessions folder   A folder in Computer Management that allows you to view a list of the users with a current network connection to the computer that you are monitoring.

Shared Folders snap-in   An MMC snap-in that allows you to easily monitor access to network resources and send administrative messages to users

Shares folder   A folder in Computer Management that allows you to view a list of all shared folders on the computer and to determine how many users have a connection to each folder.

Questions and Answers

Lesson 1 Practice: Exercise 1

Page 17-7

1. What information is displayed about each shared folder?

The name of the share, the path to the folder that is being shared, the type of share, the number of client computers currently connected to the share, and any comment entered about the share.

Lesson 1 Review

Page 17-8

1. Why is it important to manage network resources?

You need to know which users access a network resource so that you can notify them if a resource becomes temporarily or permanently unavailable. You monitor confidential resources to verify that only authorized users are accessing them. You determine how much all resources are being used to help you plan for future system growth.

2. On a computer running Windows XP Professional, members of the _____ and _____ groups can use Computer Management to monitor network resources.

Administrators and Power Users

3. How can you determine which files are open on a computer running Windows XP Professional?

Use the Open Files folder in Computer Management to view a list of open files and the users who have a current connection to each file.

4. Which of the following statements about monitoring network resources are correct? (Choose all that apply.)

   a. You can use Computer Management to disconnect all users from all open files.

   b. You can use Computer Management to disconnect one user from one file.

   c. If you change the NTFS permissions for an open file, the changes affect all users who have the file open immediately.

   d. If you make changes to the NTFS permissions for an open file, the changes do not affect the user who has that file opened until he or she closes and reopens the file.

The correct answers are A and D. B is not correct because you cannot disconnect a single user from a file. You must disconnect all users from a file or disconnect all users from all files. C is not correct because if you change NTFS permissions for an open file, the changes are not applied until the next time the user logs on.

Lesson 2 Review

Page
17-14

1. Which of the following tools can you use to create a shared folder on a remote computer? (Choose all that apply.)

   a. Windows Explorer

   b. Computer Management

   c. Administrative Tools

   d. Shared Folders snap-in

   The correct answers are B and D. A is not correct because you cannot use Windows Explorer to create a shared folder on a remote computer—only on the local computer. C is not correct because Administrative Tools is a folder that provides access to several different tools.

2. How do you create and share a folder on a remote computer?

   You can create and share a folder on a remote computer by using Computer Management (or the Shared Folders snap-in), and connecting to the remote computer on which you want to manage shares.

Lesson 3 Review

Page
17-18

1. How can you determine which users have a connection to open files on a computer and the files to which they have a connection?

   The Sessions folder in Computer Management shows you a list of all users with a connection to an open file and the files to which they have a connection.

2. How can you disconnect a specific user from a file?

   In Computer Management, click Sessions. Select the user that you want to disconnect in the details pane. On the Action menu, click Close Session.

3. Why would you send an administrative message to users with current connections?

   To inform the users that you are about to disconnect them from the resource they are connected to so that you can perform a backup or restore operation, upgrade software or hardware, or shut down the computer.

4. What can you do to prevent a user from re-establishing a network connection after you have disconnected that user from a shared folder?

   To prevent all users from reconnecting, stop sharing the folder. To prevent only one user from re-establishing a connection, change the permissions for the folder so that the user no longer has access, and then disconnect the user from the shared folder.

Case Scenario Exercise

Page
17-19

1. What misconception does Ray have about the connections to his computer?

Ray is under the impression that 10 people can connect to the Brochures folder at a time. Actually, up to 10 people can connect to Ray's computer at a time, which includes connections to all shared folders (or printers) on the computer.

2. Ray wants to be able to determine how many users are connecting to the Brochures folder at any given time. How could he do this? What requirements must he meet?

Ray can use the Shares folder in the Computer Management window to determine the status of any shared folder on his computer, including the number of connections currently being made to the folder. To manage shared folders through Computer Management, Ray must be a member of the Administrators or Power Users local groups.

3. Ray also wants to be able to determine which users are connected to his computer. How could he do this?

Ray should use the Sessions folder in the Computer Management window, which shows all open connections to his computer.

4. Concerned that more than 10 users might need to connect to the shared folders on his computer at a time, Ray asks for your opinion. What should you tell him?

Ray should consider moving the shared folders to a computer running Windows Server 2003, which can support more than 10 concurrent connections. If he cannot do this (or if he is a member of a workgroup that does not contain a server), he should consider distributing the shared folders to other computers running Windows XP Professional.

Troubleshooting Lab

Page
17-20

1. How can you confirm that Kevin's computer actually has a shared folder available?

The easiest way to confirm this is to use Computer Management to connect remotely to Kevin's computer, and then use the Shares folder to determine what folders are shared.

2. After confirming that the shared folder is indeed on Kevin's computer, how can you ensure that Sofia has the appropriate permissions to access the shared folder?

You should right-click the share in the Shares folder, and then click Properties to open the Properties dialog box for the shared folder. Use the Share Permissions tab to make sure that Sofia is assigned the appropriate shared folder permissions to access the folder from the network (by permissions granted to a group that she is a member of or directly to her account). You should also use the Security tab to make sure that Sofia has the appropriate NTFS permissions to access the folder.

3. After confirming that Sofia has the appropriate permissions to access the resource, you use Computer Management and discover that six users are currently accessing the computer, four of whom are connected to the resource that Sofia needs to access. You attempt to open the folder yourself and receive an error message, stating that there are too many connections to the folder. What should you suspect is the problem? How would you solve this problem?

The problem is likely that Kevin has limited the number of connections that can access the folder to four. You could use Computer Management to disconnect current users or you could use the Properties dialog box for the shared folder to increase the number of connections allowed.

18 Using Windows XP Tools

Exam Objectives in this Chapter:

- Monitor, optimize, and troubleshoot performance of the Microsoft Windows XP Professional desktop.
  - ❏ Configure, manage, and troubleshoot Scheduled Tasks.
- Configure, manage, and troubleshoot Remote Desktop and Remote Assistance.

Why This Chapter Matters

In this chapter, you will learn about several of the tools available in Windows XP for configuring and troubleshooting the operating system. You will learn how to work with **services**, which are programs or processes that run in the background on a computer to perform particular system functions for other programs. You will also learn to use **Event Viewer** to monitor the events that Windows XP Professional records in various logs. You will learn to schedule tasks, and to use **System Restore** to save and restore system check points. Finally, you will learn to configure **Remote Desktop**, which allows you to control a computer from a remote location, and **Remote Assistance**, which allows a user to invite an administrator or other expert user to provide help remotely.

Lessons in this Chapter:

Before You Begin

To complete this chapter, you must have a computer that meets the minimum hardware requirements listed in the preface, "About This Book." You must also have Microsoft Windows XP Professional installed on a computer on which you can make changes.

Lesson 1: Working with Services

Services are programs or processes that start with Windows XP Professional and run in the background, providing necessary functions to other programs and operating system components. Services start prior to user logon, so a service can begin providing its functions without a user having to log on. Some services depend on other services, meaning that the other services must be running first for the dependent service to run. Windows XP Professional uses these dependencies to determine the order in which it starts services. You can disable services temporarily or even prevent services from running when Windows starts up by using the System Configuration Utility and the Services console.

After this lesson, you will be able to

- Manage services by using the Services console.
- Disable and enable services by using the System Configuration Utility.

Estimated lesson time: 40 minutes

How to Manage Services by Using the Services Console

The Services console is the primary method for managing services on a computer running Windows XP Professional. You can access the Services console in the following ways:

- Open the Administrative Tools folder (from Control Panel) and double-click Services.

- Open the Computer Management window, expand the Services And Applications node, and then click Services.

- Create a custom Microsoft Management Console (MMC) console and add the Services console.

No matter which way you open the Services console, shown in Figure 18-1, the interface is the same. In the right pane, you will see a long list of the available services along with a description, the current status of the service (Stopped or Started), the Startup Type (Automatic, Manual, or Disabled), and how the service logs on to the computer.

When you select a service (such as the DNS Client service selected in Figure 18-1), you are shown a detailed description that tells you what the service does. Some of these descriptions also tell you what happens if you stop or disable the service.

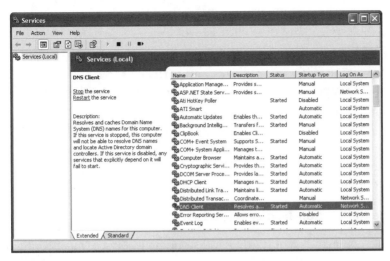

Figure 18-1   The Services console is the primary method for managing services in Windows XP Professional.

How to Stop, Start, Pause, Resume, and Restart a Service

After selecting a service in the Services console, you can control the service in the following ways:

Stop a service   When you stop a service, the service becomes unavailable. The service does not restart until you start the service again or until the next time Windows starts up (if the service is configured to start automatically during startup). The Services console does not let you stop a service on which other services depend. You must stop services in the correct order of dependency. To stop a service, click the service, and then click the Stop button (or right-click the service, and then click Stop).

Start a service   You can start a service that you have stopped or a service that is enabled, but for which the startup type is set to Manual. To start a service, click the service, and then click the Start button (or right-click the service, and then click Start).

Pause a service   Only some services can be paused. When you pause a service, the service refuses any new connections but does not disconnect existing connections to the service. An example of such a service is the World Wide Web Publishing service, which is the component of Internet Information Services (IIS) that allows users to connect to a Web site hosted on the local computer. When you pause this service, IIS no longer allows users to connect to any local Web sites, but it does not disconnect existing users from the Web site. Pausing a service allows you to shut down a service gracefully, without interrupting users or other services. After the users or services that are using a service stop using it, you can then stop the service. To pause a service, click the service, and then click the Pause button (or right-click the service, and then click Pause).

Resume a service   When you pause a service, the Resume command lets you resume the service without restarting it. To resume a paused service, click the service and the click the Resume button (or right-click the service, and then click Resume).

Restart a service   Restarting a service works just like stopping a service and then starting it again. To restart a service, click the service, and then click the Restart button (or right-click the service, and then click Restart). You might choose to restart a service during troubleshooting or when you need to immediately apply changed configuration settings.

How to Change the Startup Type of a Service

Aside from basic commands like starting and stopping a service, most configuration of a service happens by using the service's Properties dialog box. To open the Properties dialog box for a service, right-click the service and click Properties. The General tab of a service's Properties dialog box (see Figure 18-2) shows you information about the service, such as the service name, display name (what you see in the Services console), description, and path to the executable file for the service.

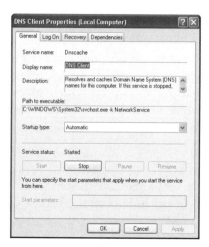

Figure 18-2   Use a service's Properties dialog box to control advanced options for a service.

You can use the Startup Type drop-down list on the General tab to configure a service for one of the following startup types:

Automatic   The service starts automatically during Windows startup.

Manual   The service is enabled, but does not start automatically during Windows startup. You must start the service by using the Services console or by using one of the other methods described later in this lesson.

Disabled   The service does not start automatically during Windows startup. In addition, the service cannot be started manually or by another service or program. You must set the service to the Automatic or Manual startup type before it can be started. You should disable unnecessary services to prevent them from accidentally starting and potentially introducing a security vulnerability.

> **Exam Tip**   When a service is disabled, you cannot start the service manually, and applications or other services cannot start the service programmatically. If you want a service not to run automatically when Windows starts, but need the service to be able to be started, set the service's startup type to Manual.

How to Change the Logon Properties of a Service

To start prior to user logon and to be able to access the system resources needed to perform its function, a service must be able to log on to a computer. Some services are configured by default to log on to the Local System account, which is a powerful account that has full access to a computer. Other services are configured to log on to LocalService or NetworkService accounts, which are special built-in accounts that are similar to authenticated user accounts. These accounts have the same level of access to resources and objects as members of the Users groups. Using this more limited access helps enhance security.

Most services running in Windows XP Professional log on using the Local System account, though a few use the Network Service account. For the most part, you will leave services configured to log on with the default account used for the service. If you need to specify a different account, use the Log On tab of the service's Properties dialog box, shown in Figure 18-3. Click This Account, and then type in the account name and password.

Figure 18-3   Use the Log On tab to specify the account under which a service logs on.

If you have more than one hardware profile configured on a computer (see Chapter 6, "Installing, Managing, and Troubleshooting Hardware Devices and Drivers," for more on hardware profiles), you can also use the Log On tab to control whether a service is enabled or disabled for a particular profile. Click a profile, and then click Enable or Disable.

How to Change the Recovery Options for a Service

By default, when a service fails to start, Windows XP Professional records an error in the System log file (see Lesson 2, "Using Event Viewer," for more about this), but takes no further action. Services that are dependent on the failed service also fail to start. You can configure certain recovery actions to occur when a service fails to start, though.

To set up recovery actions to take place when a service fails, use these steps:

1. In the Services console, right-click the service, and then click Properties.

2. In the Properties dialog box for the service, click the Recovery tab.

   The Recovery tab (see Figure 18-4) lets you configure an action to take on the first failure, the second failure, and on all subsequent failures. The actions you can configure include the following:

   ❏ **Take No Action**. This is the default choice.

   ❏ **Restart The Service**. Windows attempts to restart the service if the service does not start.

   ❏ **Run A Program**. Windows runs a custom program, which you can use to log error details or even send a notification of the failure. When you select this action, the options in the Run Program section of the Recovery tab become available. Type the path for the program and any command-line parameters you want to use, and indicate whether you want Windows to add the fail count (the number of times the service has failed) to the end of the command.

   ❏ **Restart The Computer**. Windows restarts the computer. This option provides a good last resort for recovery on important services. Often, a service does not start because services on which it is dependent failed. You should use this setting only on server computers. If a client computer automatically restarted, it could disturb the user's work.

3. Click OK.

Exam Tip   For the exam, remember the actions you can have Windows take should a service fail: Take No Action, Restart The Service, Run A Program, and Restart The Computer. Typically, you should have Windows attempt to restart the service on the first or second failure. You should have Windows attempt to restart the computer only when a service fails that is vital to the computer's role and when restarting will not interfere with the desktop environment.

Figure 18-4 Use the Recovery tab to specify the action Windows takes when a service fails.

How to Determine Service Dependency

Many services depend on other services, which means that the other services must start successfully for the services that depend on them to start. You can view the **service dependency** of any service by using the Dependencies tab of the service's Properties dialog box, shown in Figure 18-5.

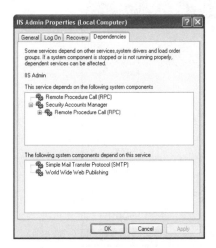

Figure 18-5 Use the Dependencies tab to view services that a service depends on and that depend on it.

The top list shows the services on which the current service depends. The bottom list shows the services that depend on the current service. For the IIS Admin service (the example shown in Figure 18-5), the service depends directly on the remote procedure call (RPC) service and the Security Accounts Manager service (which itself depends on the RPC service). The IIS Admin also has its own dependents: the Simple Mail Transfer Protocol (SMTP) and World Wide Web Publishing services.

How to Disable and Enable Services by Using the System Configuration Utility

The System Configuration Utility (which you can also use to control other startup parameters) allows you to disable system services individually or several at a time.

To disable a service by using the System Configuration Utility, use these steps:

1. Click Start, and then click Run.

2. In the Run dialog box, type **msconfig**, and then click OK.

   Windows displays the System Configuration Utility window. The Services tab, shown in Figure 18-6, displays a list of services on the computer along with the current status (Running, Stopped, or Paused) of each service.

3. To disable a service, clear the check box for the service. To enable a service, select the check box for the service.

   Windows displays the System Configuration dialog box, asking whether you want to restart your computer.

4. Click OK. When prompted, click Restart.

   When Windows restarts, the changes you have made take effect.

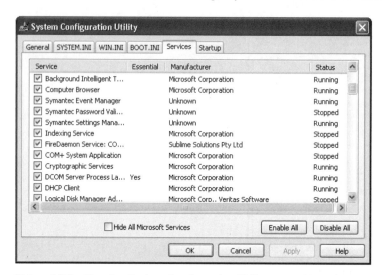

Figure 18-6   Use the System Configuration Utility to enable or disable services.

Note   If you change any startup setting by using the System Configuration Utility, Windows XP Professional prompts you to return to normal operations the next time you log on. A prompt and the System Configuration Utility appear each time you log on until you restore the original startup settings by clicking Normal Startup under Startup Selection on the General tab or until you tell Windows to not show you the dialog box any more. To permanently change a startup setting, use Control Panel, change a Group Policy setting, or uninstall the application that added the service.

Practice: Working with Services

In this practice, you will use the Services console to change, stop, and start a service. You will also change the startup type for a service. You will then use the System Configuration Utility to enable a service.

Exercise 1: Stop and Start a Service

1. Click Start, and then click Control Panel.

2. In the Control Panel window, click Performance And Maintenance.

3. In the Performance And Maintenance window, click Administrative Tools.

4. In the Administrative Tools window, double-click Services.

5. In the Services window, click Error Reporting Service.

6. What is the description provided for the Error Reporting Service?

   _____

   _____

7. Click the Stop toolbar button.

8. What do you see in the Status column for the Error Reporting Service?

   _____

9. Click the Start toolbar button.

   Leave the Services window open for the next exercise.

Exercise 2: Change the Startup Type of a Service

1. Right-click Error Reporting Service, and then click Properties.

2. In the Error Reporting Services Properties dialog box, on the General tab, on the Startup Type drop-down list, click Disabled.

3. Click OK.

4. In the Services window, is the service enabled or disabled? Is the service stopped or started?

   _____

5. Click Stop.

6. Close the Services window.

Exercise 3: Enable a Service with the System Configuration Utility

1. Click Start, and then click Run.

2. In the Run dialog box, type **msconfig**, and then click OK.

3. In the System Configuration Utility dialog box, on the Services tab, clear the check box next to the Computer Browser service.

4. Click OK.

5. In the System Configuration dialog box, click Restart.

   Windows restarts. After restarting, Windows displays the System Configuration Utility dialog box, warning you that Windows is running in Selective or Diagnostic mode.

6. Click OK.

7. On the Services tab, is the Computer Browser service stopped or started?

   _____

8. Select the check box next to the Computer Browser service, and then click OK.

9. In the System Configuration dialog box, click Restart.

Lesson Review

The following questions are intended to reinforce key information presented in this lesson. If you are unable to answer a question, review the lesson materials and try the question again. You can find answers to the questions in the "Questions and Answers" section at the end of this chapter.

1. What is a service?

_____

_____

2. What happens by default when a service fails? How can you change the default behavior?

_____

_____

_____

_____

3. What two tools does Windows XP Professional provide for enabling and disabling services?

_____

Lesson Summary

- The Services console allows you to perform basic commands on services such as stopping, starting, pausing, resuming, and restarting services. You can also use the Services console to configure options for services such as the startup type, the user account under which the service logs on, and recovery options.

- You can also use the System Configuration Utility to enable and disable services.

Lesson 2: Using Event Viewer

You use Event Viewer to perform a variety of tasks, including viewing the contents of log files, finding specific events within log files, and viewing the audit logs that are generated as a result of setting the audit policy and auditing events (which is covered in Chapter 16, "Configuring Security Settings and Internet Options").

After this lesson, you will be able to

- Identify the Windows XP Professional logs.
- View event logs by using Event Viewer.
- View an event.
- Locate events in a log.
- Configure logging options.
- Save and open logs.

Estimated lesson time: 30 minutes

Overview of Windows XP Professional Logs

You use Event Viewer to view information contained in Windows XP Professional logs. By default, Event Viewer has three logs available to view, as described in Table 18-1.

Table 18-1   Logs Maintained by Windows XP Professional

Log	Description
Application log	Contains errors, warnings, or information that programs (such as a database program or an e-mail program) generate. The program developer presets which events to record.
Security log	Contains information about the success or failure of audited events. The events that Windows XP Professional records are a result of your audit policy.
System log	Contains errors, warnings, and information that Windows XP Professional generates. Windows XP Professional presets which events to record.

 Exam Tip   For the exam, be sure you know that the three default logs in Windows XP Professional and the types of events recorded to each log.

How to View Event Logs by Using Event Viewer

To open Event Viewer and view a log, use these steps:

1. Click Start, and then click Control Panel.

2. In the Control Panel window, click Performance And Maintenance.

3. In the Performance And Maintenance window, click Administrative Tools.

4. In the Administrative Tools window, double-click Event Viewer.

5. In the left pane, click the log you want to view.

Windows displays the events in the log file in the right window, as shown in Figure 18-7.

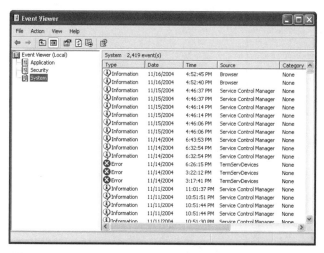

Figure 18-7   Use Event Viewer to view information contained in Windows XP Professional logs.

You will encounter five types of events in the logs you view in Event Viewer. A unique icon identifies each event type so that you can easily distinguish between entries. The five types of events you will encounter are as follows:

Error   This type of entry, indicated by an icon with a red X, means that a significant problem has occurred, such as a service that might not have started properly.

Warning   This type of entry, indicated by an icon with a yellow exclamation point, means that an event has occurred that is not currently detrimental to the system but might indicate a possible future problem.

Information   This type of entry, indicated by an icon with a blue "i," means that a successful operation has occurred. For example, a service starting successfully might trigger this type of event.

Audit Success   This type of entry, indicated by a key icon, means that an audited security access attempt—for example, a successful logon to the system—was successful.

Audit Failure   This type of entry, indicated by a lock icon, means that an audited security access attempt—for example, a failed attempt to open an audited file or directory—was not successful.

How to View an Event

Double-click any event in the right pane of Event Viewer to open the Event Properties dialog box (see Figure 18-8), which shows a description of the event. The up and down arrow buttons let you move through the events in the log without having to close the Event Properties dialog box and then reopen it for each event you want to view. The Copy button (showing the Copy icon) copies the information about the event to the Windows Clipboard.

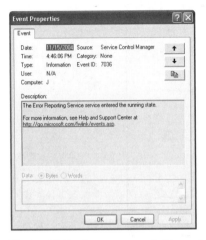

Figure 18-8   Open an event's Properties dialog box to see a description of the event.

The Event Properties dialog box contains the following information to help you identify an event:

Date and Time   The date and time that the event occurred.

Type   The type of event (Information, Warning, and so on).

User   The user with which the event is associated. Many events do not have an associated user.

Computer   The computer on which the event occurred.

Source   The service that experienced the event.

Category   The category associated with the event. Most events, particularly in the System log, do not have categories. Some application developers specify a category for events that concern the application, so you will see some events in the Application log that have an associated category. In the Security log, the category indicates the type of event that was audited.

Event ID   The Event ID number associated with the event. Microsoft keeps track of Event IDs and often makes solutions to problems available in the Microsoft Knowledge Base. To find out more about an event, use the Event ID as a keyword search in the Knowledge Base.

Description   A description of the event. The description often includes information on other services affected by the event and a link for finding out more information.

How to Locate Events In a Log

When you first start Event Viewer, it automatically displays all events that are recorded in the selected log. Because many events occur on a computer running Windows XP Professional, the number of events displayed can make it difficult to find the events you are looking for. To change what appears in the log, you can locate selected events by using the Filter command. You can also search for specific events by using the Find command.

To filter or find events, start Event Viewer, and then on the View menu, click Filter or click Find. The options provided by Filter and Find are almost identical. Figure 18-9 shows the options available on the Filter tab.

Figure 18-9   You can apply a filter to make it easier to locate certain types of events.

Table 18-2 describes the options for using the Filter tab to filter events and the Find command to find events.

Table 18-2   Options for Filtering and Finding Events

Option	Description
Event Types	The types of events to view
Event Source	The software or component driver that logged the event
Category	The type of event, such as a logon or logoff attempt or a system event
Event ID	An event number to identify the event. This number helps product support representatives track events.
User	A user logon name
Computer	A computer name
From And To	The date ranges for which to view events (Filter dialog box only)
Restore Defaults	Clears any changes in this tab and restores all defaults
Description	The text that is in the description of the event (Find dialog box only)
Search Direction	The direction (up or down) in which to search the log (Find dialog box only)
Find Next	Finds and displays the next occurrence defined by the Find Settings (Find dialog box only)

Logging Options

You can configure the properties of each individual log. To configure the settings for logs, right-click the log in Event Viewer, and then click Properties to display the Properties dialog box for the log.

Use the Properties dialog box for each type of audit log to control the following:

- The maximum size of each log, which can be from 64 KB to 4,194,240 KB (4 GB). The default size is 512 KB.

- The action that Windows XP Professional takes when the log fills up. To control this action, click one of the options described in Table 18-3.

Table 18-3   Options for Handling Full Audit Log Files

Option	Description
Overwrite Events As Needed	You might lose information if the log becomes full before you archive it. However, this setting requires no maintenance.
Overwrite Events Older Than X Days	You might lose information if the log becomes full before you archive it, but Windows XP Professional will lose only information that is at least x days old. Enter the number of days for this option. The default is seven days.
Do Not Overwrite Events	This option requires you to clear the log manually. When the log becomes full, Windows XP Professional will stop, but no security log entries will be overwritten.

How to Save and Open Logs

Saving logs allows you to maintain a history of events. Many companies have policies on archiving logs for a specified period—especially auditing-related events in the Security log.

To work with a log, right-click the log you want to configure in Event Viewer, and then click one of the options described in Table 18-4.

Table 18-4   Options to Archive, Clear, or View a Log File

To	Do this
Save the log	Click Save Log File As, and then type a filename.
Clear the log	Click Clear All Events to clear the log. Windows XP Professional creates a security log entry, stating that the log was cleared.
Open a saved log	Click Open Log File.
Open a new log view	Click New Log View to create a second view of the selected log. By default, this view is named the same as the original view with a copy number appended in parentheses. For example, if you create a new view of the System log, the default name for the new view is System (2). Right-click the new view and click Rename to change the name. You can use different views to look at log files filtered different ways or to open saved logs.

Lesson Review

The following questions are intended to reinforce key information presented in this lesson. If you are unable to answer a question, review the lesson materials and try the question again. You can find answers to the questions in the "Questions and Answers" section at the end of this chapter.

1. What are the three Windows XP Professional logs you can view with Event Viewer, and what is the purpose of each log?

_____

_____

_____

_____

_____

_____

_____

2. The two ways that Event Viewer provides for locating specific events are the
   _____ command and the _____ command. What does each of
   the commands allow you to do?

   _____

   _____

3. The size of each log can be from _____ KB to _____ GB, and the default size is _____
   KB.

4. If you select the Do Not Overwrite Events option, what happens when the log
   becomes full?

   _____

   _____

   _____

Lesson Summary

- Windows XP Professional has the following three logs by default: the application
  log, the security log, and the system log.

- You use Event Viewer to view the contents of the Windows XP Professional logs.

- Viewing the Event Properties dialog box shows you the date and time the event
  occurred, the user and service associated with the event, an Event ID that you can
  use to find more information about the event, and a detailed description of the
  event.

- You can use the Filter and Find commands in Event Viewer to easily locate specific
  events or types of events.

- For each log in Windows XP Professional, you can control the maximum size the
  log is allowed to reach and the action that Windows XP Professional takes when
  the log fills up.

- You can archive the Windows XP logs so that you keep an historical record of
  events and track trends over time.

Lesson 3: Using Scheduled Tasks

Use **Scheduled Tasks** to identify programs and batch files you want to run once, at regular intervals, or at specific times. You can schedule any script, program, or document to start at a specified time and interval, or when certain operating system events occur. This feature can complete many administrative tasks for you.

After this lesson, you will be able to

- Identify tasks that you can schedule.
- Schedule a task.
- Configure advanced options for a scheduled task.
- Troubleshoot scheduled tasks.

Estimated lesson time: 25 minutes

Overview of Scheduled Tasks

Windows XP Professional saves scheduled tasks in the Scheduled Tasks folder (see Figure 18-10), which you can access through the Control Panel under Performance And Maintenance. In addition, you can access Scheduled Tasks on another computer by browsing that computer's resources using My Network Places, which allows you to move tasks from one computer to another. For example, you can create task files for maintenance, and then add them to a user's computer as needed.

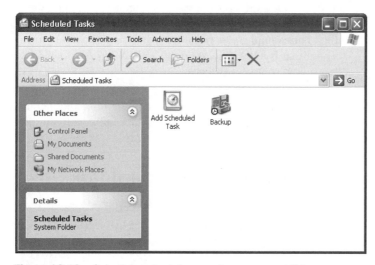

Figure 18-10   Schedule a task to run when you need it to.

Use Scheduled Tasks to perform the following tasks:

- Run maintenance programs at specific intervals.

- Run programs at a time when there is less demand for computer resources.

How to Schedule a Task

Use the Scheduled Task Wizard to schedule tasks. You access the wizard in the Scheduled Tasks folder by double-clicking Add Scheduled Task. Table 18-5 describes the options that you can configure in the Scheduled Task Wizard.

Table 18-5   Scheduled Task Wizard Options

Option	Description
Application	The applications to schedule. Select from a list of applications that are registered with Windows XP Professional, or click Browse to specify any program or batch file.
Name	A descriptive name for the task.
Perform This Task	How often Windows XP Professional will perform the task. You can select Daily, Weekly, Monthly, One Time Only, When My Computer Starts, or When I Log On.
Start Time	The start time for the task to occur.
Start Date	The start date for the task.
User Name And Password	A user name and password. You can enter your user name and password or another user name and password to have the application run under the security settings for that user account. If the user account that you used to log on does not have the rights required by the scheduled task, you can use another user account that does have the required rights. For example, you can run a scheduled backup by using a user account that has the required rights to back up data but does not have other administrative privileges.
Advanced Properties	Select this check box if you want the wizard to display the Advanced Properties dialog box so that you can configure additional properties after you click Finish. Advanced Properties are covered in the next section.

How to Configure Advanced Options for a Scheduled Task

In addition to the options that are available in the Scheduled Task Wizard, you can set several additional options for tasks. You can change options that you set with the Scheduled Task Wizard or set additional advanced options by configuring advanced properties for the task.

Table 18-6 describes the tabs in the Advanced Properties dialog box for the scheduled task.

Table 18-6 Scheduled Task Wizard Advanced Options

Tab	Description
Task	Change the scheduled task or change the user account that is used to run the task. You can also turn the task on and off.
Schedule	Set and display multiple schedules for the same task. You can set the date, time, and number of repeat occurrences for the task. For example, you can set up a task to run every Friday at 10:00 p.m.
Settings	Set options that affect when a task starts or stops, such as how long a backup can take, if the computer can be in use, or if the computer can be running on batteries when it runs the task.
Security	Change the list of users and groups that have permission to perform the task, or change the permissions for a specific user or group. This tab is available only if you have simple file sharing disabled.

How to Troubleshoot Scheduled Tasks

In general, troubleshooting the Scheduled Tasks involves checking the parameters that you have set up. In the Scheduled Tasks window, switch the view to Details view. Two columns, Status and Last Result, are useful in determining whether a task was successful or not.

The Advanced menu provides a few options to help you with troubleshooting. When you open Scheduled Tasks and click Advanced, the first option on the Advanced menu allows you to stop and start the Task Scheduler Service, and the selection is either Stop Using Task Scheduler or Start Using Task Scheduler. If your scheduled tasks are not starting, you can check this option to be sure that the Task Scheduler Service is running; if it is not, you can start it. The second option is similar to the first, only it pauses and continues the service. If the service is paused, scheduled tasks do not start.

The third option on the Advanced menu, Notify Me Of Missed Tasks, causes the system to send you a message when a scheduled task does not occur. The next option on the Advanced menu is the AT Service Account, which allows you to change the account being used from the System account. The next option, View Log, allows you to view a log of when the Task Scheduler Service started, stopped, paused, and continued. It also logs the name of each scheduled task, the application or task that started, and the time and date the task was started. The final option, View Hidden Tasks, allows you to view tasks created by Windows and applications that hide the tasks by default.

Practice: Using Task Scheduler

In this practice, you schedule Address Book to start at a predetermined time. You can use this as a reminder to review address information. You also configure Task Scheduler options.

1. Click Start, and then click Control Panel.

2. In the Control Panel window, click Performance And Maintenance.

3. In the Performance And Maintenance window, click Scheduled Tasks.

   Windows XP Professional opens the Scheduled Tasks folder.

4. Double-click Add Scheduled Task.

   The Scheduled Task Wizard appears.

5. Click Next.

   Windows XP Professional displays a list of currently installed programs. To schedule a program that is not registered with Windows XP Professional, click Browse to locate the program.

6. Click Browse.

   Windows XP Professional displays the Select Program To Schedule dialog box.

7. Double-click Program Files, and then double-click Windows NT.

8. Double-click Accessories, and then double-click WordPad.

9. Type **Launch WordPad** in the Type A Name For This Task text box.

   The Type A Name For This Task text box allows you to enter a description that is more intuitive than the program name. Windows XP Professional displays this name in the Scheduled Tasks folder when you finish the wizard.

10. Click One Time Only, and then click Next.

11. In the Start Time box, set the time to 4 minutes after the current system time and make a note of this time.

    To confirm the current system time, look at the Windows taskbar. Do not change the entry in the Start Date text box.

12. Click Next.

    The wizard requires you to enter the name and password of a user account. When Task Scheduler runs the scheduled task, the program receives all the rights and permissions of the user account that you enter here. The program is also bound by any restrictions on the user account. Notice that the user name you are currently using is already filled in as the default. You must type the correct password for the user account in both password boxes before you can continue.

You will schedule the console to run with your administrative privileges.

13. In both the Enter The Password text box and the Confirm Password text box, type your password.

14. Click Next.

Do not select the Open Advanced Properties For This Task When I Click Finish check box. You will review the Advanced properties in the next procedure.

15. Click Finish.

Notice that the wizard added the task to the list of scheduled tasks.

> **Note** The account that will run the task must have the Log On As A Batch Job user right in order to run a scheduled task. This right is normally added automatically when you create a scheduled task. If it is not, you should add the right to that account. See Chapter 16 for more information on user rights.

16. To confirm that you scheduled the task successfully, wait for the time that you configured in Step 11, and WordPad will start.

17. Close WordPad.

Lesson Review

The following questions are intended to reinforce key information presented in this lesson. If you are unable to answer a question, review the lesson materials and try the question again. You can find answers to the questions in the "Questions and Answers" section at the end of this chapter.

1. How can Scheduled Tasks help you monitor, manage, and maintain network resources?

_____

_____

_____

_____

_____

2. Which of the following are valid choices for the frequency with which Scheduled Tasks schedules programs to run? (Choose all that apply.)

    a. Daily

    b. One time only

    c. When the computer shuts down

    d. When a user logs off

3. Why do you have to assign a user account and password for each task that you schedule using the Scheduled Task Wizard?

_____

_____

_____

_____

_____

4. If none of your scheduled tasks is starting, what is one thing that you need to check?

_____

_____

_____

Lesson Summary

- You can use Scheduled Tasks to schedule programs and batch files to run once, at regular intervals, at specific times, or when certain operating system events occur.

- Windows XP Professional saves scheduled tasks in the Scheduled Tasks folder, which can be accessed through Performance And Maintenance in Control Panel.

- After you have scheduled a task to run, you can still modify any of the options or advanced features for the task, including the program to be run.

- You can access Scheduled Tasks on another computer by browsing that computer's resources using My Network Places, so you can move tasks from one computer to another.

Lesson 4: Using System Restore

System Restore is a feature that monitors changes to certain system and application files. System Restore functions like an "undo" feature for Windows XP Professional configuration changes, allowing you to recover from problems caused by incorrect system settings, faulty drivers, and incompatible applications. Windows XP Professional creates restore points automatically, and you can also create a restore point manually.

After this lesson, you will be able to

- Explain System Restore.
- Enable or disable System Restore.
- Create a restore point.
- Restore a restore point.

Estimated lesson time: 30 minutes

Overview of System Restore

System Restore works by creating **restore points** that contain a snapshot of the Registry (which includes user account, application, and hardware configuration) and a copy of certain system files that Windows XP Professional requires for startup, including those in the %systemroot% directory and boot files on the system partition. You can restore your computer to a particular restore point at any time.

By default, System Restore creates restore points when the following events occur:

- Every 24 hours if the computer is turned on or if it has been 24 hours since the computer was last turned on
- When you install an unsigned device driver
- When System Restore–compliant applications are installed
- When updates are installed through Automatic Updates or Windows Update
- When you restore data from backup media using Windows Backup
- When you restore a restore point
- When certain system or application files are changed
- When you create a restore point manually

System Restore also monitors file operations for a core set of system and application files. These files are specified in %systemroot%\System32\Restore\Filelist.xml. System Restore records changes to these file and sometimes copies them to a hidden archive before allowing the files to be overwritten, deleted, or changed.

System Restore does not monitor the following files and folders:

- The virtual memory paging file

- Personal user data, such as files in My Documents, Favorites, Recycle Bin, Temporary Internet Files, History, and Temp folders

- Image and graphics files, such as those with .bmp, .jpg, and .eps extensions

- Application data files with extensions not listed in systemroot\System32\Restore\ Filelist.xml, such as .doc, .xls, .mdb, and .pst

Restore point information is saved to a hidden folder on the volume in which a monitored file is located. The archive collects multiple restore points, each representing individual system states. The files, Registry snapshots, and logs associated with older restore points are purged on a first in, first out (FIFO) basis, optimizing System Restore disk space and making room for new restore points.

Real World   Changing System Restore Options in the Windows Registry

In most situations, the default System Restore operation is satisfactory. However, there might be situations in which you need to change how System Restore functions. There are four settings that you can change in the Windows Registry that affect the intervals System Restore uses when creating automatic restore points and the disk space it uses.

Each of these settings is located in the HKEY_LOCAL_MACHINE\SOFTWARE\Microsoft\Windows NT\CurrentVersion\SystemRestore subkey. These settings include the following:

- **RPSessionInterval** This setting specifies the intervals, in seconds, between scheduled restore-point creations during an active user session. The default value is 0 seconds (disabled).

- **RPGlobalInterval** This setting specifies the time interval, in seconds, at which scheduled restore points are created (regardless of whether or not there is an active user session). The default value is 86,400 seconds (24 hours).

- **RPLifeInterval** This setting specifies the time interval, in seconds, for which restore points are kept. System Restore deletes restore points older than the specified value. The default value is 7,776,000 seconds (90 days).

- **DiskPercent** This setting specifies the maximum amount of disk space on each drive that System Restore can use. This value is specified as a percentage of the total drive space. The default value is 12 percent.

> **Exam Tip**   Restoring to a restore point affects the Windows Registry and certain system and application files. The restoration does not affect user-created documents and data. Restoring to a restore point provides a safe means to reset the Windows configuration to an earlier time.

How to Enable or Disable System Restore

System Restore is enabled by default in Windows XP Professional to monitor all drives on the computer. You can disable System Restore entirely or you can disable it on any particular drive. The one exception to this is that you cannot disable System Restore on the system drive without disabling it on all drives.

To turn off System Restore for all drives, use these steps:

1. Click Start, and then click Control Panel.

2. In the Control Panel window, click Performance And Maintenance.

3. In the Performance And Maintenance window, click System.

4. In the System Properties dialog box, on the System Restore tab (see Figure 18-11), select the Turn Off System Restore On All Drives check box.

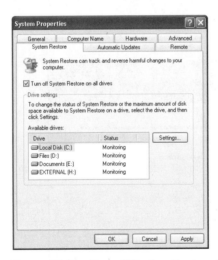

Figure 18-11   Turn off System Restore for all drives.

To turn off System Restore for a particular drive or to change the disk space that System Restore uses for a drive, use these steps:

1. In the System Properties dialog box, on the System Restore tab, in the Available Drives list, click the drive you want to configure, and then click Settings.

2. In the Settings dialog box for the drive, check the Turn Off System Restore On This Drive check box to disable file monitoring for that drive.

3. Use the Disk Space To Use slider to control how much disk space System Restore uses to save restore points on the drive.

4. Click OK.

How to Create a Restore Point

System Restore creates restore points automatically based on criteria you learned about earlier in this lesson. However, you should create a restore point manually if you are about to perform any major action, such as installing or removing an application, installing a new hardware device, or troubleshooting a problem.

To create a restore point, use these steps:

1. Click Start, point to All Programs, point to Accessories, point to System Tools, and then click System Restore.

   Windows displays the System Restore window, as shown in Figure 8-12.

2. Click Create A Restore Point, and then click Next.

3. In the Restore Point Description text box, type a name that describes the restore point, and then click Create.

4. Click Close.

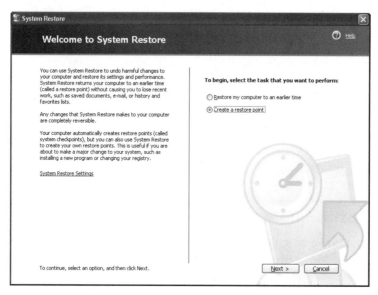

Figure 18-12   Create a restore point before making any major changes.

How to Restore a Restore Point

If you experience a problem in Windows, you can often solve that problem by restoring to an earlier restore point. You can also restore to a restore point to undo configuration changes that a user might not remember the details of. For example, if a user installs incompatible software that causes problems or makes changes to the Windows configuration, you can restore to a restore point created before the problem occurred.

To restore a restore point, use these steps:

1. Click Start, point to All Programs, point to Accessories, point to System Tools, and then click System Restore.

2. Click Restore My Computer To An Earlier Time, and then click Next.

   Windows displays the Select A Restore Point page (see Figure 8-13), which presents a simple, calendar-based way to browse available restore points. Dates in bold represent days when a restore point was created.

3. Click any date that is listed in bold, and then click a restore point on that day.

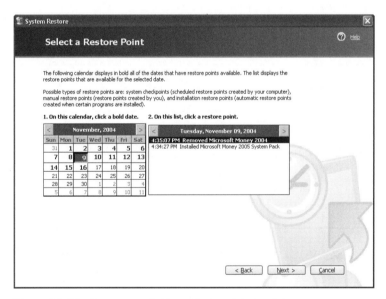

Figure 18-13   Browse available restore points by date.

4. Click Next to continue.

   Windows displays the Confirm Restore Point Selection page, which warns you that the computer will be shut down during the restoration process.

5. Click Next.

   Windows closes all open programs and logs off all users. Windows then restores the restore point and restarts.

6. Log on to Windows .

   After you log on, Windows displays the Restoration Complete page.

7. Click OK.

Lesson Review

The following questions are intended to reinforce key information presented in this lesson. If you are unable to answer a question, review the lesson materials and try the question again. You can find answers to the questions in the "Questions and Answers" section at the end of this chapter.

1. When does System Restore create restore points automatically?

   _____

   _____

   _____

   _____

   _____

   _____

2. Will System Restore recover a document that you accidentally delete from the My Documents folder?

   _____

   _____

   _____

3. How can you prevent System Restore from monitoring particular drives?

   _____

   _____

   _____

   _____

Lesson Summary

- System Restore works by creating restore points that contain a snapshot of the Registry (which includes user account, application, and hardware configuration) and a copy of certain system files that Windows XP Professional requires for startup. System Restore creates restore points automatically when certain events occur, and you can also create restore points manually.

- System Restore is enabled by default in Windows XP Professional to monitor all drives on the computer. You can disable System Restore entirely or you can disable it on any particular drive. You cannot disable System Restore on the system drive without disabling it on all drives.

- You should create a restore point manually if you are about to perform any major action, such as installing or removing an application, installing a new hardware device, or troubleshooting a problem.

- Windows provides access to restore points in a convenient date-based display. When you restore to a restore point, Windows must restart so that it can apply configuration changes.

Lesson 5: Using Remote Desktop and Remote Assistance

Remote Assistance and Remote Desktop are both Windows XP Professional features that allow remote access to a computer. Remote Desktop provides a user with a way to control a computer running Windows XP Professional from a remote location. Remote Assistance allows a user to invite an expert user in a remote location to assist with problems.

After this lesson, you will be able to

- Configure and use Remote Desktop.
- Configure and use Remote Assistance.

Estimated lesson time: 30 minutes

How to Configure and Use Remote Desktop

Remote Desktop is designed to allow users to remotely gain access to a Windows XP Professional desktop from another computer on the network. After connecting to the remote desktop, a user sees the remote desktop in a window and can access files, folders, and applications on the remote computer. After a connection is established, the local desktop is locked for security reasons, preventing anyone from viewing the tasks that are being performed remotely.

Remote Desktop is designed to allow a user to have full control over a Windows XP Professional desktop from another computer on the network or even from the Internet. This is useful when a user is working from home, another office, or another site and requires access to information or programs on a primary office computer. While a user is remotely accessing a computer, local access by another user is not permitted. An exception to this is an administrator; administrators are permitted to log on locally while another user is connected remotely, but the remote session is then terminated.

When you are connected to a computer via Remote Desktop, many of the resources on the host computer are available on the client computer. These resources include the following:

File System   While you are connected to the remote host, the file system on the client computer can be made available. If you open My Computer on the host computer, you will see the hard drives for the client computer. This feature allows you to copy information between the host and client computer.

Audio   Audio generated on the host computer plays through the client computer's sound system.

Port   The applications running within the session can have access to the ports on the client computer, which allows them to access and manipulate printers, scanners, and other peripheral devices.

Printer   The default local or network printer for the client computer becomes the default printing device for the Remote Desktop session. You print a document on the host computer to the printer connected to the client.

Clipboard   The Remote Desktop host and the client computer share a Clipboard, which allows data to be copied between applications running on the remote computer and applications running on the client computer.

Remote Desktop Requirements

Remote Desktop requires the following:

- A remote computer that is running Windows XP Professional and that is connected to a local area network (LAN) or the Internet. This is the computer to which you want to gain access remotely.

- A client computer with access to the host computer through a LAN, dial-up, or virtual private network (VPN) connection that has the Remote Desktop Connection program or the Terminal Services Client installed. A version of the Remote Desktop Connection program is available for most versions of Windows. Just insert the Windows XP Professional installation CD-ROM on the client computer and select the option to install the Remote Desktop Connection software.

- A user account with appropriate permissions. The user must be an administrator or a member of the Remote Users group, and have a password.

How to Configure a Computer to Accept Remote Desktop Connections

Remote Desktop configuration is a two-part process. First, you must configure the host computer to allow Remote Desktop connections. Then, you must configure the client computer with the Remote Desktop Connection client software.

To configure a computer running Windows XP Professional to allow Remote Desktop connections, follow these steps:

1. From the Start menu (or from the desktop or in Windows Explorer), right-click My Computer and select Properties.

2. On the Remote tab, in the Remote Desktop section, select Allow Users To Connect Remotely To This Computer, as shown in Figure 18-14.

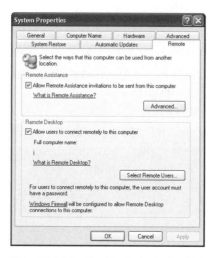

Figure 18-14   Enable Remote Desktop on a computer running Windows XP Professional.

3. If the user account to be used to connect remotely is not a member of the Administrators group, click Select Remote Users, add the appropriate user account, and then click OK.

4. Click OK again.

Verify that the user account to be used to connect remotely has a password assigned. User accounts used for remote connections must have passwords.

> **Note**   If you are using Windows Firewall, you must configure it to allow Remote Desktop connections. If you are using another software firewall, or if there is a hardware firewall on your network, you must enable inbound connections on TCP port 3389 to support Remote Desktop connections. You can also change the port on which Remote Desktop accepts connections. For more information on changing this port number, read the Knowledge Base article, "How to change the listening port for Remote Desktop," available at *http://support.microsoft.com/ kb/306759*.

How to Connect to a Remote Computer

After a computer running Windows XP Professional is configured to allow Remote Desktop connections, you can connect to that computer by using the Remote Desktop Connection client software on another computer. From the Start menu, select All Programs, then Accessories, then Communications, and then Remote Desktop Connection. In the Remote Desktop Connection dialog box, click the Options button to display configurable options, as shown in Figure 18-15. The only information that you must enter to establish a connection is the name or IP address of the computer. Other configurable options include the following:

■ General options, including the user name, password, and domain name used for authentication and the ability to save connection settings

■ Display options, including the configuration of the size of the remote connection display (all the way up to full screen) and color settings

■ Local Resources options, including sound and keyboard configuration, and which local devices to connect to when logged on the remote computer

■ Programs options, which provide the ability to automatically launch a program when a connection is established

■ Experience options, which allow the configuration of the connection speed to optimize performance, and provide the ability to control the display of the desktop background, themes, menu and windows animation, and other items that can affect performance

Figure 18-15   Configure options for connecting to a remote computer.

To use the Remote Desktop Connections client, use these steps:

1. From the Start menu, select All Programs, then Accessories, then Communications, and then Remote Desktop Connection.

2. In the Remote Desktop Connection dialog box, depicted in Figure 18-16, enter the name or IP address of the remote computer and click Connect.

Figure 18-16 Establish a Remote Desktop session.

3. When prompted, enter the appropriate user account and password, and then click OK.

4. If another user is currently logged on to the remote system, a Logon Message dialog box appears, indicating that in order to continue, that user must be logged off and any unsaved data will be lost. If this occurs, click Yes to continue.

5. The Remote Desktop session is established. Figure 18-17 displays a remote connection window.

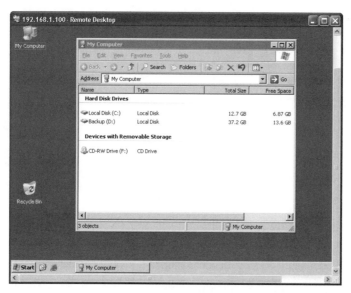

Figure 18-17 After connecting, you have complete control of the remote computer.

Key Combinations

After connecting to a remote desktop, you have complete control of the remote computer. However, there are certain key combinations that still affect the client computer instead of the host computer. For example, when you press CTRL+ALT+DELETE during a Remote Desktop session, either Task Manager or the Windows Security dialog box for the client computer appears—not for the host computer. There are key combinations you can use on the client computer to simulate special key combinations on the host computer. Table 18-7 describes the key combinations in a Remote Desktop Session.

Table 18-7   Key Combinations in Remote Desktop

Windows Key Combination	Equivalent Key Combination In Remote Desktop	Description
ALT+TAB	ALT+PAGE UP	Switches between programs from left to right.
ALT+SHIFT+TAB	ALT+PAGE DOWN	Switches between programs from right to left.
ALT+ESC	ALT+INSERT	Cycles through the programs in the order they were started.
CTRL+ESC	ALT+HOME	Displays the Windows menu.
ALT+PRTSCN	CTRL+ALT+MINUS (–) symbol on the numeric keypad	Places a snapshot of the active window in the Remote Desktop session on the Clipboard.
PRTSCN	CTRL+ALT+PLUS (+) symbol on the numeric keypad	Places a snapshot of the entire Remote Desktop session window on the Clipboard.
CTRL+ALT+DEL	CTRL+ALT+END	Displays the Task Manager or Windows Security dialog box.

How to End a Remote Session

There are two ways to end a remote session:

■ Log off from the remote computer normally, which closes all programs, logs the user off, and then closes the Remote Desktop connection.

■ Disconnect by either closing the Remote Desktop window or selecting Disconnect from the Start menu. Disconnecting leaves the user logged on at the remote computer, and all programs continue processing. The user will be reconnected to the same session the next time the user connects.

How to Configure and Use Remote Assistance

The **Remote Assistance** feature allows a user to request help from an expert user. Unlike with Remote Desktop, in Remote Assistance, the user needing help must issue an invitation to the other user and the other user must accept the invitation. After the connection is established, the expert user can take shared control of the user's desktop, chat with the user, and send and receive files. Taking shared control of the desktop requires the user's permission. Remote Assistance can minimize or eliminate the need to physically visit a remote computer to solve a problem.

How to Establish a Remote Assistance Session

A **Remote Assistance** session requires that both the user needing help and the expert user actively participate in establishing the connection. The session is established in the following phases:

1. The user that needs help sends a Remote Assistance invitation to the expert user.

2. The expert user responds to the invitation.

3. The user accepts the expert user's assistance.

To send a Remote Assistance invitation, use these steps:

1. From the Start menu, select Help And Support.

2. In the Help And Support Center, under Ask For Assistance, select Invite A Friend To Connect To Your Computer With Remote Assistance, and then select Invite Someone To Help You.

3. Select the method that you want to use to create the invitation, as shown in Figure 18-18. You can send invitations directly by using Windows Messenger, by using an e-mail attachment, or by saving an invitation file and transmitting it to the helper user (for example, you could save the file to a shared folder on the network).

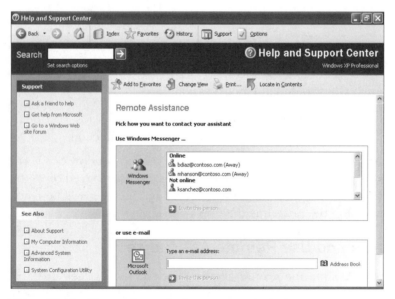

Figure 18-18   Choose the method to create an invitation.

4. When prompted, enter the requested information, including your name, a message, when the invitation should expire, and (optionally) a password to be used to establish the connection.

5. Click Send Invitation.

Note   When an invitation is sent through an e-mail attachment or saved as a file, the file has a .MsRcIndicent extension.

An expert user must respond to an invitation to continue the process. If the invitation is by using Windows Messenger, you must accept the invitation that is presented in the Messenger pop-up window. If the invitation is sent by e-mail, you must open the attached invitation. If the invitation file is transmitted in some other fashion, you must access and open it. If a password is required, you must enter the password in the Remote Assistance dialog box.

Tip   Using Windows Messenger to establish a Remote Assistance connection is the easiest method because the Windows Messenger connection can usually be established regardless of whether there are firewalls on either the user's or the expert helper's network. If you use another method of establishing a Remote Assistance session, you must configure a firewall to allow the connection. Like Remote Desktop, Remote Assistance uses TCP port 3389 by default.

Windows then notifies the user requiring assistance that the request has been accepted. The user must click Yes in the Remote Assistance dialog box as a final indication of acceptance, and Remote Assistance then establishes the connection.

Remote Assistance Console

After the Remote Assistance connection is established, the user needing help sees a User Console, and the expert user sees a Helper Console. The User Console has the following functionality:

Chat History and Message Entry windows   Used for online chatting.

Connection Status window   Displays the helper who has connected and the connection's capabilities (Screen View Only or In Control),

Stop Control (ESC)   Permits the user to regain control if the expert user has taken control (this can also be accomplished by pressing the ESC key).

Send A File   Sends a file from the user's computer or a network share to the helper's computer.

Start Talking   Enables voice communication on computers with voice capabilities.

Settings   Enables the user to adjust sound quality.

Disconnect   Ends the Remote Assistance connection.

Help   Provides access to Remote Assistance help features.

The Helper Console also provides Chat History and Message Entry windows for online chatting. The user's desktop is displayed on the right side of the display. The controls for the Helper Console are found across the top of the screen and include the following:

Take Control/Release Control   Sends a request to the user to take shared control of the user's desktop. The user must accept the request and can cancel it at any time by clicking Disconnect on the User Console or by pressing Esc.

Send A File   Sends a file from the helper's computer or a network share to the user's computer.

Start Talking   Enables voice communication on computers with voice capabilities.

Settings   Enables the user to adjust sound quality and console size.

Disconnect   Ends the Remote Assistance connection.

Help   Provides access to Remote Assistance help features.

How to Take Shared Control of the User's Computer

To take shared control, the expert user sends a request to the user by clicking Take Control. The user must accept the request and can cancel it at any time by clicking Disconnect on the User Console or by pressing Esc.

When the expert user establishes shared control of the user's system, the expert user can fully manipulate the computer, including loading and unloading drivers, starting applications, and viewing event logs. However, the expert user cannot copy files from the user's hard disk. The only way for the expert user to get a file from the user's computer is for the user to send it.

When shared control is established, both users can manipulate the mouse and keyboard simultaneously, so consider using the chat or voice communication functions to coordinate input device usage and minimize overlap. Also, the expert user must be careful not to do anything that might affect the network connection, or else the Remote Assistance connection might be disconnected.

Lesson Review

The following questions are intended to reinforce key information presented in this lesson. If you are unable to answer a question, review the lesson materials and try the question again. You can find answers to the questions in the "Questions and Answers" section at the end of this chapter.

   1. What are the requirements for running Remote Desktop?

   _____

   _____

   _____

2. How can you install the Remote Desktop Connection software on computers that are not running Windows XP Professional?

_____

_____

_____

3. What is the difference between Remote Desktop and Remote Assistance?

_____

_____

_____

_____

_____

_____

_____

Lesson Summary

- Remote Desktop allows users that are members of the Administrators or Remote Users groups to remotely gain access to a computer running Windows XP Professional. After a connection is established, the local desktop is locked for security reasons, preventing anyone from viewing the tasks that are being performed remotely.

- In Remote Assistance, the user needing help must issue an invitation to the other user, and the other user must accept the invitation. After the connection is established, the expert user can take shared control of the user's desktop, chat with the user, and send and receive files.

Case Scenario Exercise

In this exercise, you will read a scenario about using Windows XP tools, and then answer the questions that follow. If you have difficulty completing this work, review the material in this chapter before beginning the next chapter. You can find answers to these questions in the "Questions and Answers" section at the end of this chapter.

Scenario

You are working as an administrator for a company named Alpine Ski House, which owns a series of ski resorts in the Midwest. You work in the company headquarters in Boulder, Colorado. You are working with Ken, a supervising manager of a resort in

Jackson Hole, Wyoming. Ken has recently installed a non-Microsoft backup program on his computer running Windows XP Professional and is having some problems. He says that during the installation of the program, he was asked whether he wanted to install the backup program as a service or as a command-line utility. Not knowing what to choose, he installed the program as a service. Now, whenever he starts his computer, he gets an error message stating that one or more services failed to start. When he tries to run the new backup program, he receives an error message, and the program does not start. Ken wants to use the backup program because it is supposed to back up files to backup media in their original folder and file format, instead of backing up to a single proprietary-format file. This makes it easier for Ken to locate files in the backup location and restore them.

Questions

1. Ken is not an expert user and he wants you to help him solve his problem. He would also like to watch while you help him. What feature could you use to help Ken remotely while he watches?

   _____

   _____

2. After connecting to Ken's computer, you want to determine what service or services are failing to start. How would you do this?

   _____

   _____

3. You have determined that only one service is failing to start, and that service is related to Ken's backup program. You decide to use the Add/Remove Programs utility to remove the backup program from Ken's computer. After removing the program, Windows displays a message stating that some parts of the program could not be installed because they are running and that it needs to you restart the computer to finish the removal. When the computer restarts, you still see the error message stating that a service has failed to load, and the program is still listed in the Add/Remove Programs dialog box as being installed. What should you do?

   _____

   _____

   _____

   _____

4. After taking care of the service, you use Add/Remove Programs again to try to uninstall the program. However, the Add/Remove Programs utility tells you that the uninstallation file could not be found and that the removal process cannot continue. You suspect that during the previous removal attempt, the uninstallation

file was deleted. You decide that you need to restore Ken's computer to a configuration from before he installed the program. How can you do this?

_____

_____

_____

_____

5. You have managed to restore Ken's computer to a previous configuration. You no longer receive error messages about services not starting and are satisfied that the program has been removed from the computer. However, Ken still wants to use the backup program. After researching the program, you find that Ken was right about being able to install it as a command-line utility. When you perform this type of installation, no service is installed. You install Ken's program in this fashion. Ken is not familiar with using the command prompt, though, and wants to have the program back up his computer automatically each night. How can you set this up?

_____

_____

_____

_____

Troubleshooting Lab

In this troubleshooting lab, you will read a scenario and answer questions. If you have difficulty completing this work, review the material in this chapter before beginning the next chapter. You can find answers to these questions in the "Questions and Answers" section at the end of this chapter.

Scenario

You are working as an administrator for Contoso, Ltd., a manufacturer of laboratory equipment. Rebecca, an administrative assistant in the Production department, is having trouble with her computer running Windows XP Professional. When her computer starts, she sees the following message: At Least One Service Or Driver Failed During System Startup. Use Event Viewer To Examine The Event Log For Details.

Rebecca tells you that the last time the error message happened was at around 5:00 p.m. Central Time (US & Canada) on November 16, 2004. You walk Rebecca through the steps of opening Event Viewer and saving her System log as a file named **RebeccaSystem.evt**. You then ask her to e-mail you the saved log file. When you receive the file, you save it to your desktop.

> **On the CD** In the Labs folder of the CD-ROM accompanying this book, you will find a file named RebeccaSystem.evt. Copy this file to your desktop.

Using what you have learned in this chapter, perform the following actions:

1. In Event Viewer, create a new log view based on the System log.

2. Open the saved log named RebeccaSystem.evt in the new log view.

Questions

1. Given the date and time of the last error message that Rebecca saw, look through Rebecca's System log and use the following table to list the error events by their source name, time, and error ID. List only error events that occurred within 5 minutes of 5:00 p.m Central Time, and sort the list from oldest to newest. If you are not in the Central Time (US & Canada) time zone, change your computer's time zone to (GMT-06:00) Central Time (US & Canada).

Time	Source Name	Error ID

2. Examine the details of each of the error events. Using the following table of Sources and Event IDs, provide a brief description of each error and what (if any) service did not start as a result of the error.

Source and ID	Description	Service Not Started
W32Time–17		
W32Time–29		
NetBT–4321		
Netlogon–3095		
Server–2505		
Service Control Manager–7024		

3. Looking through these events, what do you suspect is the problem? How would you correct it?

_____

_____

_____

_____

Chapter Summary

- Services are programs or processes that start with Windows XP Professional and run in the background, providing necessary functions to other programs and operating system components. The Services console allows you to perform basic commands on services such as stopping, starting, pausing, resuming, and restarting services. You can also use the Services console to configure options for services such as the startup type, the user account under which the service logs on, and recovery options. You can also use the System Configuration Utility to enable and disable services.

- You use Event Viewer to view the contents of Windows XP Professional log files. By default, Windows keeps three log files: Application, which records events generated by programs; Security, which records audit events; and System, which records events generated by Windows services.

- You can use Scheduled Tasks to schedule programs and batch files to run once, at regular intervals, at specific times, or when certain operating system events occur. Windows XP Professional saves scheduled tasks in the Scheduled Tasks folder, which can be accessed through Performance and Maintenance in Control Panel.

- System Restore works by creating restore points that contain a snapshot of the Registry (which includes user account, application, and hardware configuration) and a copy of certain system files that Windows XP Professional requires for startup. System Restore creates restore points automatically when certain events occur, and you can also create restore points manually.

- Remote Desktop allows users that are members of the Administrators or Remote Users groups to remotely gain access to a computer running Windows XP Professional. Remote Assistance allows a user who needs help to invite an expert user to connect to the user's computer. After the connection is established, the expert user can take shared control of the user's desktop, chat with the user, and send and receive files.

Exam Highlights

Before taking the exam, review the key points and terms that are presented in this chapter. You need to know this information.

Key Points

- When a service is disabled, you cannot start the service manually, and applications or other services cannot start the service programmatically. If you want a service not to run automatically when Windows starts, but need the service to be able to be started, set the service's startup type to Manual.

- When a service fails, you can have Windows take the following actions: Take No Action, Restart The Service, Run A Program, and Restart The Computer. Typically, you should have Windows attempt to restart the service on the first or second failure. You should have Windows attempt to restart the computer only when a service fails that is vital to the computer's role.

- Windows XP Professional records events in three logs by default: Application, which records events generated by programs; Security, which records audit events; and System, which records events generated by Windows services.

- Restoring to a restore point affects the Windows Registry and certain system and application files. The restoration does not affect user-created documents and data. This provides a safe means to reset the Windows configuration to an earlier time.

Key Terms

Event Viewer   A utility that allows you to monitor the events that Windows XP Professional records in various logs.

Remote Assistance   A utility that allows a user to invite an administrator or other expert user to provide help remotely.

Remote Desktop   A utility that allows you to control a computer from a remote location.

restore points   A saved snapshot of the Registry and important system and application files that is created using the System Restore utility.

Scheduled Tasks   A feature of Windows XP Professional that lets you schedule programs, scripts, batch files, or documents to run once, at regular intervals, or at specific times.

service   A program or process that runs in the background on a computer to perform particular system functions for other programs.

service dependency   The other services that must be running for a service to start, as well as the services that cannot start until the service in question starts.

System Restore   A utility that monitors changes to certain system and application files and creates automatic restore points that contain a snapshot of the Registry and a copy of certain system files that Windows XP Professional requires for startup. You can also create restore points manually and restore the computer to any restore point.

Questions and Answers

Lesson 1 Practice: Exercise 1

Page
18-9

6. What is the description provided for the Error Reporting Service?

   Allows Error Reporting For Services And Applications Running In Non-Standard Environments.

8. What do you see in the Status column for the Error Reporting Service?

   The Status column is blank, indicating that the service is not started.

Lesson 1 Practice: Exercise 2

Page
18-10

1. In the Services window, is the service enabled or disabled? Is the service stopped or started?

   The service is disabled but is still started.

Lesson 1 Practice: Exercise 3

Page
18-10

1. On the Services tab, is the Computer Browser service stopped or started?

   Stopped.

Lesson 1 Review

Page
18-10

1. What is a service?

   A service is a program or process that runs in the background and provides functions to other programs and services.

2. What happens by default when a service fails? How can you change the default behavior?

   By default, Windows takes no action when a service fails. However, any services that depend on that service will also fail to start. You can use the Recovery tab of a service's Properties dialog box to change the action that Windows takes when a service fails the first time, the second time, and on subsequent failures.

3. What two tools does Windows XP Professional provide for enabling and disabling services?

   The System Configuration Utility and the Services console.

Lesson 2 Review

Page
18-17

1. What are the three Windows XP Professional logs you can view with Event Viewer, and what is the purpose of each log?

The application log contains errors, warnings, or information that programs such as database programs or e-mail programs generate. The program developer presets which events to record. The security log contains information about the success or failure of audited events. The events that Windows XP Professional records are a result of your audit policy. The system log contains errors, warnings, and information that Windows XP Professional generates. Windows XP Professional presets which events to record.

2. The two ways that Event Viewer provides for locating specific events are the _____ command and the _____ command. What does each of the commands allow you to do?

Filter; Find

The Filter command allows you to change what appears in the log. The Find command allows you to search for specific events.

3. The size of each log can be from ____ KB to ____ GB, and the default size is ____ KB.

64; 4; 512

4. If you select the Do Not Overwrite Events option, what happens when the log becomes full?

If you select the Do Not Overwrite Events option, you must clear the log manually. When the log becomes full, Windows XP Professional stops. However, no security log entries are overwritten.

Lesson 3 Review

Page 18-23

1. How can Scheduled Tasks help you monitor, manage, and maintain network resources?

Scheduled Tasks can be used to automatically launch any script, program, or document to start at a specified time and interval, or when certain operating system events occur. You can use Scheduled Tasks to complete many administrative tasks for you, run maintenance programs at specific intervals on the local or remote computers, and run programs when there is less demand for computer resources.

2. Which of the following are valid choices for the frequency with which Scheduled Tasks schedules programs to run? (Choose all that apply.)

  a. Daily

  b. One time only

  c. When the computer shuts down

  d. When a user logs off

The correct answers are A and B. C and D are not correct because you cannot configure a scheduled task to run when the computer shuts down or when a user logs off.

3. Why do you have to assign a user account and password for each task that you schedule using the Scheduled Task Wizard?

You enter a user name and password to have the task run under the security settings for that user account. For example, you can run a scheduled backup by using a user account that has the required rights to back up data but does not have other administrative privileges. The default is to use the user name of the person scheduling the task.

4. If none of your scheduled tasks is starting, what is one thing that you need to check?

If none of your scheduled tasks is starting, open the Task Scheduler and click Advanced to make sure that the Task Scheduler Service is running. If it is not running, you can use the Advanced menu to start it.

Lesson 4 Review

Page
18-30

1. When does System Restore create restore points automatically?

Every 24 hours (or if it has been 24 hours since the computer was last turned on), when you install an unsigned device driver, when System Restore-compliant applications are installed, when updates are installed through Automatic Updates or Windows Update, when you restore data from backup media using Windows Backup, when it detects changes to certain files, and when you restore a restore point.

2. Will System Restore recover a document that you accidentally delete from the My Documents folder?

No. System Restore does not monitor personal user data, such as files in My Documents, Favorites, Recycle Bin, Temporary Internet Files, History, and Temp folders.

3. How can you prevent System Restore from monitoring particular drives?

To turn off System Restore for a particular drive, in the System Properties dialog box, on the System Restore tab, in the Available Drives list, click the drive you want to configure, and then click Settings. Note that you cannot disable System Restore on the system drive without disabling it on all drives.

Lesson 5 Review

Page
18-32

1. What are the requirements for running Remote Desktop?

The remote computer must be running Windows XP Professional. After enabling Remote Desktop on this computer, you must make sure that the user who will connect remotely is a member of either the Administrators or Remote Users group.

2. How can you install the Remote Desktop Connection software on computers that are not running Windows XP Professional?

You can install the Remote Desktop Connection software by inserting the Windows XP Professional installation CD-ROM on the client computer. There is a version of the Remote Desktop Connection software for most Windows versions.

3. What is the difference between Remote Desktop and Remote Assistance?

Remote Desktop is designed to allow a user to have full control over a Windows XP Professional desktop from another computer on the network. Remote Desktop requires that a user be a member of the Administrators or Remote Users group on the host computer. Remote Assistance is designed to let a user request help from another user. To establish a Remote Assistance session, a user must send an invitation. When using Remote Assistance, both users can see the host computer's display.

Case Scenario Exercise

Page
18-41

1. Ken is not an expert user and he wants you to help him solve his problem. He would also like to watch while you help him. What feature could you use to help Ken remotely while he watches?

You could use Remote Assistance to help Ken. While you are connected to Ken's computer, you can take control of his desktop while he watches.

2. After connecting to Ken's computer, you want to determine what service or services are failing to start. How would you do this?

You should open Event Viewer and view the System log. Events marking services that fail to start are marked with a red icon that has an X.

3. You have determined that only one service is failing to start, and that service is related to Ken's backup program. You decide to use the Add/Remove Programs utility to remove the backup program from Ken's computer. After removing the program, Windows displays a message stating that some parts of the program could not be installed because they are running and that it needs to you restart the computer to finish the removal. When the computer restarts, you still see the error message stating that a service has failed to load, and the program is still listed in the Add/Remove Programs dialog box as being installed. What should you do?

You should stop the service and disable it. You can do this by using the Services console. Stopping the service should allow you to remove the program. Disabling the service will prevent it from running at startup in case the program needs to restart to finish the installation.

4. After taking care of the service, you use Add/Remove Programs again to try to uninstall the program. However, the Add/Remove Programs utility tells you that the uninstallation file could not be found and that the removal process cannot continue. You suspect that during the previous removal attempt, the uninstallation file was deleted. You decide that you need to restore Ken's computer to a configuration from before he installed the program. How can you do this?

You should use System Restore. Most likely, Ken did not create a manual restore point, and it is also unlikely that the setup program for the backup utility created one. You should find the most recent automatic restore point and restore the computer to that point.

5. You have managed to restore Ken's computer to a previous configuration. You no longer receive error messages about services not starting and are satisfied that the program has been removed from the computer. However, Ken still wants to use the backup program. After researching the program, you find that Ken was right about being able to install it as a command-line utility. When you perform this type of installation, no service is installed. You install Ken's program in this fashion. Ken is not familiar with using the command prompt, though, and wants to have the program back up his computer automatically each night. How can you set this up?

You should create a scheduled task that runs the executable command at the desired time each night. After creating the task, you can use the Properties dialog box for the task to specify the necessary command-line options for running the program.

Troubleshooting Lab

Page 18-43

1. Given the date and time of the last error message that Rebecca saw, look through Rebecca's System log and use the following table to list the error events by their source name, time, and error ID. List only error events that occurred within 5 minutes of 5:00 p.m Central Time, and sort the list from oldest to newest. If you are not in the Central Time (US & Canada) time zone, change your computer's time zone to (GMT-06:00) Central Time (US & Canada).

Time	Source Name	Error ID
4:55:14 PM	W32Time	17
4:55:14 PM	W32Time	29
4:55:14 PM	NetBT	4321
4:55:29 PM	W32Time	17
4:55:29 PM	W32Time	29
5:00:00 PM	NetBT	4321
5:00:01 PM	Netlogon	3095
5:00:01 PM	NetBT	4321
5:00:01 PM	Server	2505
5:00:03 PM	Service Control Manager	7024
5:00:17 PM	W32Time	17
5:00:17 PM	W32Time	29
5:00:33 PM	W32Time	17
5:00:33 PM	W32Time	29

2. Examine the details of each of the error events. Using the following table of Sources and Event IDs, provide a brief description of each error and what (if any) service did not start as a result of the error.

Source and ID	Description	Service Not Started
W32Time–17	Windows could not resolve a DNS lookup for a time server and will try again in 15 minutes.	
W32Time–29	Windows could not access a time server.	
NetBT–4321	The computer could not claim the name "Client1" because another computer on the network already has that name.	
Netlogon–3095	This computer is configured as a member of a workgroup, not as a member of a domain. The Netlogon service does not need to run in this configuration.	Netlogon service did not start.
Server–2505	The server could not bind to the transport \Device\NetBT_Tcpip_{DA411120-47FB-4F38-AC72-67AFC5649900} because another computer on the network has the same name.	Server service did not start.
Service Control Manager–7024	The Messenger service terminated with service-specific error 2270.	Messenger service did not start.

3. Looking through these events, what do you suspect is the problem? How would you correct it?

The problem is that Rebecca's computer has been given the same name as another computer on the network. When Rebecca's computer starts, the computer cannot claim its assigned name and as a result, neither the Messenger service nor Server service can start. To fix the problem, you should rename Rebecca's computer.

19 Monitoring and Optimizing System Performance

Exam Objectives in this Chapter:

- Monitor, optimize, and troubleshoot performance of the Microsoft Windows XP Professional desktop.
    - ❑ Optimize and troubleshoot memory performance.
    - ❑ Optimize and troubleshoot processor utilization.
    - ❑ Optimize and troubleshoot disk performance.
    - ❑ Optimize and troubleshoot application performance.
- Monitor and configure multiprocessor computers.

Why This Chapter Matters

> One of your responsibilities as an administrator is to help users keep their computer running well and to troubleshoot performance problems when they occur. This chapter covers the two major tools that Windows XP Professional provides for monitoring and troubleshooting performance: **Task Manager** and the **Performance console**.

Lessons in this Chapter:

Before You Begin

To complete this chapter, you must have a computer that meets the minimum hardware requirements listed in the preface, "About This Book." You must also have Microsoft Windows XP Professional installed on the computer.

Lesson 1: Using Task Manager

Task Manager provides information about the programs and processes running on your computer and the performance of your computer. You can use Task Manager to start programs, to stop programs and processes, and to see a current view of your computer's performance.

After this lesson, you will be able to

- Monitor programs by using Task Manager
- Monitor processes by using Task Manager
- Monitor system performance by using Task Manager
- Monitor networking by using Task Manager

Estimated lesson time: 25 minutes

How to Monitor Programs

Task Manager allows you to monitor applications and processes that are currently running on your computer. It also provides information about the processes, including the memory usage of each one. It provides statistics about the memory and processor performance and network usage. You start Task Manager in any of the following ways:

- Press CTRL+SHIFT+ESC
- Right-click the Windows taskbar, and then click Task Manager
- Press CTRL+ALT+DELETE

Note   Provided your computer running Windows XP Professional is in a domain environment, you can start Task Manager by pressing CTRL+ALT+DELETE. However, if your computer is in a workgroup environment, you might need to start Task Manager by selecting it, depending on how the logon and logoff options are configured.

The Task Manager dialog box shown in Figure 19-1 has four tabs: Applications, Processes, Performance, and Networking.

Figure 19-1 The Applications tab shows running applications and lets you terminate them.

You can use the buttons on the Applications tab of the Task Manager dialog box to stop a program from running (End Task), to switch to a program and bring the program into the foreground (Switch To), and to start a program (New Task). At the bottom of the display, Task Manager shows you the number of processes that are currently running, the CPU usage, and the memory usage.

How to Monitor Processes

The Processes tab in the Task Manager dialog box (see Figure 19-2) lists each **process** that is currently running on your computer that runs in its own address space, including all applications and system services. Task Manager also allows you to end processes.

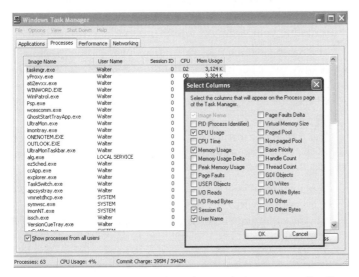

Figure 19-2 You can select the columns that appear on the Processes tab.

By default, the Processes tab shows you the processes, the users running each process, and the CPU and memory usage for each process that is running. You can add additional performance measures to those that are shown by default on the Processes tab. To add performance measures, on the View menu, click Select Columns (refer to Figure 19-2). Table 19-1 describes the columns that are displayed in Task Manager by default and some of the columns that can be added to the Processes tab.

Table 19-1 Processes Tab Columns

Column	Description
Image Name	The name of the process, displayed by default.
PID (Process Identifier)	The numeric identifier assigned to the process while it is running.
User Name	The name of the user that the process is running under, displayed by default.
CPU Usage	The percentage of time the threads of the process used the processor since the last update, displayed by default. If a process is consuming a large amount of processor time over a long period (other than when an application is first starting or is performing a particularly intensive task), the process might be having trouble. Try closing the application (by using the Applications tab).
CPU Time	The total processor time (in seconds) used by the process since it was started.
Memory Usage	The amount of memory (in kilobytes) used by the process, displayed by default. This column is particularly useful for determining which applications are using memory because it displays the total amount of physical and virtual memory used by an application. If an application seems to be using too much memory, there might be a problem with the application. Try closing the application and restarting it (or restarting your computer and then restarting the application).
Base Priority	The order in which threads are scheduled for the processor. The base priority is not set by the operating system; it is set by the code. You can use Task Manager to change the base priority of processes. To change the base priority of a process, right-click the process and click Set Priority.
Non-paged Pool	The amount of memory (in kilobytes) that is used by a process; operating system memory that is never paged (moved from memory) to disk.
Paged Pool	The amount of system-allocated virtual memory (in kilobytes) used by a process; virtual memory that can be paged to disk. Paging is the moving of infrequently used data from RAM to the paging file on the hard disk.

Table 19-1 Processes Tab Columns

Column	Description
Page Faults	The number of times that data had to be retrieved from the page file on the hard disk for this process because it had been paged out of physical memory. Windows XP Professional uses a page file stored on the hard disk to augment physical memory. When the physical memory is full, Windows swaps older information in physical memory to the swap file to make room for newer information. Too many page faults often indicate that you need more physical memory.
Peak Memory Usage	The maximum amount of physical memory resident in a process since it started.
Thread Count	The number of threads running in the process. This column can be useful for troubleshooting multithreaded applications.

Exam Tip For the exam, remember that Task Manager can show real-time information about the CPU, RAM, and virtual memory, but the measurements are fairly limited. To collect more detailed information, use the Performance console. The Performance console also allows you to collect performance data over a longer period.

How to Change the Base Priority of a Running Process

Changing the **base priority** of a process determines how much processor time Windows XP Professional devotes to the process compared with other processes. By default, most processes run at a base priority of Normal. However, you can change the base priority for a process by using the following steps:

1. In Task Manager, on the Processes tab, click the View menu and then click Select Columns.

2. In the Select Columns dialog box, select Base Priority and then click OK.

   The Base Priority column now appears in the Task Manager window.

3. Right-click the process for which you would like to change the base priority.

4. On the shortcut menu that appears, point to Set Priority, and then select one of the following commands:

   ❏ Realtime

   ❏ High

   ❏ AboveNormal

   ❏ Normal

   ❏ BelowNormal

   ❏ Low

Caution   You should change the priority of processes only when there is a process that needs priority over (or is less important than) other running processes; even then, you should try to use only the AboveNormal, Normal, and BelowNormal levels. Setting a process at too high a base priority (such as RealTime) can consume enough system resources that other vital processes cannot function properly.

How to Set Processor Affinity

Windows XP Professional can support two processors running on the same computer. When two processors are installed, Windows XP Professional does a good job of assigning processes to processors based on need. However, you can assign a particular process to a specific processor. (This is referred to as assigning **processor affinity** to a process; of course, it is available only on computers with two processors or on computers with a hyperthreaded processor in which multiple processes can run simultaneously on one processor.)

To assign a process to a processor, use the following steps:

1. In Task Manager, on the Processes tab, right-click a process and then click Set Affinity.

2. In the Processor Affinity dialog box, select the processors on which the process should be allowed to run. By default, both processors (CPU 0 and CPU 1) are selected for a processor.

Caution   Controlling processor affinity can improve performance by reducing the number of processor cache flushes that occur as threads move from one processor to another. This might be a good option for dedicated file servers. However, be aware that dedicating a program to a particular processor might not allow other program threads to migrate to the least-busy processor.

How to Monitor System Performance

You can use the Performance tab in the Task Manager dialog box (see Figure 19-3) to see a current overview of system performance that includes information about the CPU (or CPUs on a computer with two processors), physical memory, and virtual memory.

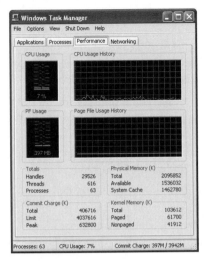

Figure 19-3   The Performance tab provides real-time performance data about the CPU, RAM, and virtual memory.

Table 19-2 describes the fields that are displayed by default on the Performance tab in Task Manager.

Table 19-2   Performance Tab Fields

Field	Description
CPU Usage	The percentage of time that the processor is busy. If this graph displays a high percentage continuously (and not when there is an obvious reason, such as a big application), your processor might be overloaded. If your computer has two processors, two graphs are shown. If this value runs continuously over 80 percent, you probably see a noticeable improvement in performance if you upgrade your processor.
CPU Usage History	The percentage of time that the processor is running a thread other than the idle thread shown over time. You can use the Update Speed command on the View menu to specify how often the values are refreshed. The High value updates about twice per second; Normal value updates once every two seconds; Low value updates once every four seconds. You can also pause the updates and update the view manually by pressing F5. This is a useful method if you want to monitor some specific activity. Note that Task Manager itself uses processor time. The more frequently you update the display, the more processor time it uses, which throws off the accuracy of whatever you are analyzing.
PF Usage	The amount of virtual memory used (in MB).
Page File Usage History	The amount of virtual memory used, shown over time. Values set using the Update Speed command affect this history as well.

Table 19-2   Performance Tab Fields

Field	Description
Total: Handles	The number of object handles in the tables of all processes. A handle represents a specific input/output (I/O) instance of a thread.
Threads	The number of running threads, including one idle thread per processor. A thread is an object within a process that runs program instructions.
Processes	The number of active processes, including the idle process. A process can have multiple threads, each of which in turn can have multiple handles.
Physical Memory (K): Total	The amount of physical RAM installed in the computer.
Available	The amount of physical memory available to processes.
System Cache	The amount of physical memory released to the file cache on demand.
Commit Charge: Total	The size of virtual memory in use by all processes.
Limit	The amount of virtual memory that can be committed to all processes without enlarging the paging file.
Peak	The maximum amount of virtual memory used in the session.
Paged	The size of the paged pool allocated to the operating system. The paged pool is data in physical memory that can be written to the page file if Windows needs to make space in physical memory for other data.
Nonpaged	The size of the nonpaged pool allocated to the operating system. Windows cannot page all memory to a page file. In particular, many threads created by the Windows kernel cannot be paged.
Kernel Memory (K): Total	The sum of the paged and nonpaged memory.

Note   When Task Manager is running, Windows XP Professional displays an accurate miniature CPU usage icon on the taskbar. If you point to the icon, Task Manager displays the percentage of processor usage in text format.

How to Monitor Networking

The Networking tab in Task Manager, shown in Figure 19-4, displays a visual interpretation of the current network traffic on various network connections on the computer. Although it is possible to get an idea about network performance from this tab, it is actually more useful for giving you a quick snapshot of network availability on each connection configured on your computer.

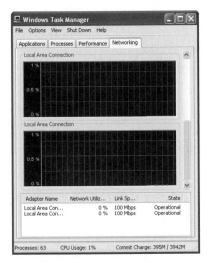

Figure 19-4   The Networking tab of Task Manager shows current network activity.

By default, the graph of network activity for each connection scales dynamically to show how much network utilization there is when compared with the theoretical maximum for the connection. For example, on a 100 Mbps connection, when there is no network activity on a connection, the vertical scale on the graph shows the values 0 percent, .5 percent, and 1 percent of the theoretical maximum. As network activity increases, the graph scales to show a greater percentage—up to 100 percent, indicating the full 100 Mbps potential. Because most people use this tab not to measure the exact network throughput, but rather to see whether there is network throughput (and sometimes what the maximum value is), this scale can be rather confusing. Fortunately, you have two options for controlling the way Task Manager displays the graph:

■ On the Options menu, click Show Scale to turn the vertical display of the scale on and off.

■ On the Options menu, click Auto Scale to turn the automatic scaling on and off. When the Auto Scale option is turned off, the graph always shows a range of 0 to 100 percent. This is usually a more useful view, unless you are trying to see very small amounts of network utilization.

The detailed information at the bottom of the tab displays current percent of network utilization and the theoretical link speed for each enabled adapter. When viewing the current percent of network utilization, you should keep the following in mind:

■ On wired Ethernet connections, you can usually expect to see a peak utilization value of 60 to 80 percent.

■ On wireless connections, you can expect to see peak utilizations of 30 to 50 percent, depending mostly on position of the wireless access point and structural interference (such as walls, heating ducts, or other devices).

When viewing network utilization and trying to figure out whether your connection is living up to its capacity, do not expect to see 100 percent utilization, even on the best of connections. However, if you see utilization considerably below the peak values listed previously, you should investigate the connection for potential problems.

Practice: Using Task Manager

In this practice, you use Task Manager to monitor programs, processes, and system performance. You use Task Manager to start a program and to stop a program. Finally, you add new columns to the Processes tab.

1. If necessary, log on with a user account that is a member of the Administrators group.
2. Press Ctrl+Shift+Esc to launch Task Manager.
3. Click the Applications tab. Which programs are currently running on your computer?

   _____

4. Click New Task.

   Windows XP Professional displays a Create New Task dialog box.
5. In the Open text box, type **wordpad.exe** and click OK.

   WordPad should start and be listed as a running application.
6. Click the Processes tab.
7. How many processes are running?

   _____

8. On the View menu, click Select Columns.

   The Select Columns dialog box appears.
9. Click Peak Memory Usage, and then click Page Faults. Click OK.

   Two new columns, Peak Memory Usage and Page Faults, are added to the Processes tab display. You might need to maximize Task Manager to see all columns.
10. Click the Performance tab.
11. What percentage of your CPU's capacity is being used? _____

    _____

12. Do you think that your CPU could be slowing down the performance on your computer?

    _____

    _____

    _____

13. Click the Applications tab.

14. Click WordPad, and then click End Task.

WordPad closes and is removed from the list of running applications.

15. Close Task Manager.

Lesson Review

Use the following questions to help determine whether you have learned enough to move on to the next lesson. If you have difficulty answering these questions, review the material in this lesson before beginning the next lesson. You can find answers to these questions in the "Questions and Answers" section at the end of this chapter.

1. Which of the following methods can you use to start Task Manager? (Choose all that apply.)

   a. Press CTRL+ALT+ESC

   b. Right-click the Desktop, and then click Task Manager

   c. Press CTRL+SHIFT+ESC

   d. Press CTRL+ALT+DELETE, and if necessary, click Task Manager

2. Which of the following tabs can be found in Task Manager? (Choose all that apply.)

   a. Networking tab

   b. Programs tab

   c. Processes tab

   d. General tab

3. What are page faults? Do you think a larger or smaller number of page faults indicates better system performance? Why?

   _____

   _____

   _____

   _____

   _____

4. What does CPU usage represent? In general, is system performance better with a high CPU usage value or a low value?

   _____

   _____

   _____

   _____

Lesson Summary

- Use the Applications tab of Task Manager to stop a program, switch to a program, and start a program.

- Use the Processes tab of Task Manager to view running processes. You can also end processes from the Processes tab.

- Use the Performance tab of Task Manager to view real-time performance information about your CPU, RAM, and virtual memory.

- Use the Networking tab of Task Manager to view current network traffic on various network connections on the computer.

Lesson 2: Using the Performance Console

Windows XP Professional provides two tools for monitoring resource usage: the **System Monitor** snap-in and the **Performance Logs And Alerts** snap-in. Both of these snap-ins are contained in the Performance console. You use the System Monitor snap-in to track resource use and network throughput. You use the Performance Logs And Alerts snap-in to collect performance data over time from the local or a remote computer or to have Windows XP alert you when a particular performance threshold is crossed.

After this lesson, you will be able to

- Use System Monitor to monitor resource usage
- Add counters to System Monitor
- Use Performance Logs And Alerts to track a computer's performance
- Establish a baseline for performance data
- Identify and resolve bottlenecks

Estimated lesson time: 30 minutes

How to Use System Monitor

To access the Performance console, click Start, click Control Panel, click Performance And Maintenance, click Administrative Tools, and then double-click the Performance shortcut. The Performance console contains the System Monitor snap-in and the Performance Logs And Alerts snap-in (see Figure 19-5).

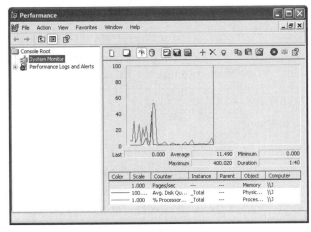

Figure 19-5   The System Monitor snap-in displays counter values in a graph by default.

You use System Monitor to collect and view real-time data about memory, disk, processor, network, and other activity on your computer or on remote computers. You can view this data in a graph, a histogram, or a report. To change the display, you can click the appropriate icon, as shown in Figure 19-5, or use the following key combinations: Ctrl+G for the graph, Ctrl+B for the histogram, and Ctrl+R for the report.

> **Note**   A *histogram* is a chart that consists of horizontal or vertical bars. The widths or heights of these bars represent the values of certain data.

Monitoring resources on your computer and overall system performance can help you to do the following:

■ Evaluate how well your computer is currently performing

■ Detect and eliminate bottlenecks to improve performance

■ Look for trends to plan for future growth and upgrades

■ Evaluate the effects of tuning and configuration changes on your computer

The Performance tool classifies information in the following areas:

Object   An **object** represents a major system component (hardware or software) of the computer or operating system. Examples of objects include physical disks, processor, and memory.

Instance   Each occurrence of an object is considered an **instance**. For example, if there are two processors on a computer, there are two processor instances. If there are three hard disks on a computer, each disk is represented by a separate instance. Not all objects have multiple instances. If there is only one instance, the Performance snap-in shows a dash for the Instance value.

Counter   A **counter** is a particular aspect of an object that System Monitor can measure. For example, the physical disk object contains the following counters:

❑ Percentage Disk Read Time

❑ Average Disk Bytes Per Read

❑ Disk Reads Per Second

System Monitor helps you gauge a computer's efficiency and locate and resolve current or potential problems. You monitor resources on your computer by selecting objects in System Monitor. A set of counters exists for each object; Table 19-3 describes some of the available objects.

Table 19-3   Partial List of Available Objects in System Monitor

Object	Description
Cache	Used to monitor the file system cache used to buffer physical device data
Memory	Used to monitor the physical and virtual memory on the computer
PhysicalDisk	Used to monitor a hard disk as a whole
Processor	Used to monitor CPUs

When you first start the Performance tool, the graph displays three counters by default:

Pages/sec   Represents the rate at which pages are read from or written to disk during virtual memory operations. Consistently high values can indicate that not enough memory is present on a computer.

Avg. Disk Queue Length   Represents the average number of read and write requests queued for the selected disk. Consistent values above 0 means that requests are backing up, which might indicate not enough memory or a slow disk system.

%Processor Time   Represents the percentage of elapsed time that the processor spends executing nonidle tasks. Consistently high values (exceeding approximately 80 percent) might indicate that the processor is slowing down your computer.

How to Add Counters

Adding counters to an object (such as those described in Table 19-3) allows you to track certain aspects of the object. The three default counters loaded with System Monitor actually do a very good job of representing the basic aspects of a computer's performance. Of course, they are only three of the hundreds of counters that are available. The counters that you monitor depend on whether you are trying to collect general baseline information, troubleshoot a performance problem, diagnose an issue with an application, and so on. The following steps allow you to add counters to an object in System Monitor:

1. At the bottom of the Performance console, right-click Counter and click Add Counters.

   The Add Counters dialog box appears.

2. In the Performance Object list box, select the object for which you want to add counters.

3. Ensure that Select Counters From List is selected.

   You can add all counters, but that usually provides more information than you need or can interpret.

4. Select a counter from the list, and click Add.

For an explanation of a counter, select it and then click Explain.

> **Tip**   If you want to add several counters at the same time, you can hold down Ctrl to select individual counters from the list. You can hold down Shift if you want to select several counters in a row, and click the first in the list you want and then click the last in the list that you want to select. All counters listed between the first and last you clicked are automatically selected.

5. When you have completed your selection of objects and counters, click Close to return to the Performance console.

Table 19-4 explains a few of the counters that you might find useful for evaluating your computer's performance.

Table 19-4   Partial List of Counters That Are Available in System Monitor

Counter	Description
Under Processor, choose %Processor Time	Indicates the percentage of time that the processor spends executing a nonidle thread, which is the percentage of time that the processor is active. During some operations this might reach 100 percent. Periods of 100 percent activity should occur only occasionally. This counter is the primary indicator of processor activity. Sustained values over 80 percent indicate a potential processor bottleneck.
Under Processor, choose %Interrupt Time	Indicates the time that the processor spends receiving and servicing hardware interrupts during sample intervals. This value is an indicator of the activity of devices that generate interrupts (such as the system clock, mouse, and disk drivers). Devices like these typically interrupt the processor when they complete a task or require the processor's attention. If the %Processor Time value is greater than 90 percent, and the %Interrupt Time value is greater than 15 percent, this processor is probably in need of assistance to handle the interrupt load.
Under Processor, choose % DPC Time	Indicates how much time the processor is spending processing DPCs. DPCs are software interrupts or tasks that require immediate processing, causing other tasks to be handled at a lower priority. DPCs represent further processing of client requests.
Under System, choose Processor Queue Length	Indicates the number of threads in the processor queue. There is a single queue for processor time, even on computers with multiple processors. A sustained processor queue of greater than two threads usually indicates that the processor is slowing down the overall system performance.

Table 19-4   Partial List of Counters That Are Available in System Monitor

Counter	Description
Under Memory, choose Pages/sec	Indicates the number of pages that were either read from disk or written to disk to make room in physical memory for other pages. This counter is the primary indicator of whether the computer has sufficient memory. An average value in excess of 20 can indicate insufficient memory in the computer.
Under Memory, choose Available Bytes	Indicates the amount of physical memory that is unallocated in the computer. Does not include any memory that is allocated to working sets or file system cache.
Under Paging File, choose %Usage	Indicates the percentage of the paging file that is currently in use.
Under Paging File, choose %Usage Peak	Indicates the peak percentage of the paging file in use.
Under Cache, choose Copy Read Hits %	Indicates the percentage of time that information was found in the file system cache and did not have to be read from disk during a file read operation (typically used by file systems and during small network transfers). A low value (lower than 70 percent) indicates that Windows might not have enough physical memory to keep up with the demands.
Under Logical Disk, choose %Free Space	Indicates the ratio of free disk space that is available to total usable disk space on a particular logical disk.
Under Physical Disk, choose %Disk Time	Indicates the percentage of time that the selected physical disk is busy servicing read or write requests. If this value is consistently over 50 percent, the hard disk is having trouble keeping up with the load that is being placed on it.
Under Physical Disk, choose Avg. Disk Queue Length	Indicates the average number of both read and write requests that are queued for the selected disk. If this value averages 2 or more, the disk is a bottleneck.

Exam Tip   Memorize the counters mentioned in this chapter, and understand the values of each counter that indicate a potential problem. In particular, you should remember the three default counters used in System Monitor: Pages/sec, Avg. Disk Queue Length, and %Processor Time.

How to Use Performance Logs And Alerts

Performance Logs And Alerts allows you to log counter information to a file and to trigger alerts that are based on configured events. You can automatically collect performance data from the local computer or from remote computers. You can view the logged data from System Monitor, or you can export it to a spreadsheet program or a database, such as Structured Query Language (SQL).

The Performance Logs And Alerts node in the Performance console (see Figure 19-6) contains three subsections:

Counter Logs   Log activity for selected counters at regular intervals

Trace Logs   Log activity for selected counters when a particular event occurs

Alerts   Log activity and can notify a user when a particular counter exceeds a certain threshold

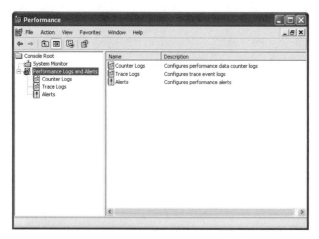

Figure 19-6   Use the Performance Logs And Alerts snap-in to track performance over time or alert you to performance problems.

How to Enable Performance Logging

To enable performance logging, use these steps:

1. In the Performance window, expand Performance Logs And Alerts.

2. Right-click Counter Logs, and select New Log Settings.

3. In the New Log Setting dialog box, enter the name for the log and click OK.

4. On the General tab, add the counters that you want to log. Modify the sampling interval if necessary.

5. On the Log Files tab, you can modify the name and location of the log file, as well as the type of file if desired.

6. On the Schedule tab, configure the start and stop times for logging. You can manually stop and start logging, or you can configure logging to start and stop at specified times.

7. Click OK to save the log configuration.

> ### Real World   Capture Performance Data from a Remote Computer
>
> To get a real picture of the performance of a computer, it is best if you use a different computer to monitor performance than the computer that is being monitored. The reason for this is that the Performance console itself uses some system resources. To use System Monitor or Performance Logs And Alerts to monitor a remote computer, all you have to do is select the remote computer when you add counters. In the Add Counters dialog box, click Select Counters From Computer, and then select the computer from the drop-down list (or type the UNC path for the computer).

How to View Performance Data from a Log

After you create a log, you can load the log into the Performance console and view it the same way that you would view real-time performance data. To view a performance log, follow these steps:

1. In the Performance console, click System Monitor, right-click the data display, and then select Properties.

2. In the System Monitor Properties dialog box, on the Source tab, select Log Files. Click Add, and enter the name of the log file that you want to view. Click OK to continue.

3. Right-click the data display, and then select Add Counters.

4. Add the counters that you want to view, and then click OK. The available counters are limited to those that are present in the log.

How to Configure an Alert

In addition to using other monitoring techniques, you can use alerts to notify users or administrators when conditions exceed preset criteria. For example, you can configure an alert to send a message to the administrator when processor utilization exceeds 80 percent.

When an alert is triggered, you can perform the following actions:

- Log an entry in the application event log. This option is enabled by default.

- Send a network message to a particular user.

- Start a performance log that can further monitor the alert condition.

- Run a program that can be used to launch any application program. You can use this option to launch a script that would send e-mail to the administrator.

To configure an alert, follow these steps:

1. In the Performance console, expand Performance Logs And Alerts.

2. Right-click the Alerts folder, and select New Alert Settings.

3. Enter a name for the alert, and click OK.

4. On the General tab, add the counter or counters and the alert value.

5. On the Action tab, configure the action or actions to be performed when an alert is triggered.

6. On the Schedule tab, configure the start and stop times for when the alert should be scanned. You can turn scanning on and off manually or configure scanning to occur on a schedule.

7. Click OK to create the alert.

How to Establish a Baseline for Performance Data

When you are ready to begin monitoring the resources on your computer, the first thing you need to do is establish a baseline. A baseline is a measurement derived from collecting data over an extended period of time. The data should reflect typical types of workloads and user connections but should also include any unusual activity that might occur. The baseline represents resource usage under normal conditions.

After you collect data on performance over an extended period of time, with data reflecting periods of low, average, and high usage, you can determine what is acceptable performance for your computer, and that determination becomes your baseline. You use the baseline to determine when bottlenecks are developing or to watch for changes in usage patterns. Determining bottlenecks will help you in troubleshooting problems that might arise. Watching for changes in usage patterns will help you plan for the future.

On the CD   At this point, you should watch the multimedia presentation "Creating a Performance Baseline" included in the Multimedia folder on the CD accompanying this book.

How to Identify and Resolve Bottlenecks

Deviations from your baseline are good indicators of performance problems. A bottleneck exists if a particular component's limitation is slowing the entire system performance. Even if one component in your computer is heavily used, if the other components or the system as a whole are not slowed down, there is no bottleneck.

If you discover a bottleneck on your computer, here are some basic suggestions to help you solve the problem:

■ If paging values are high (meaning that Windows is transferring pages of information from physical memory to disk more than you would expect), identify processes that are using the most memory. To do this, use the Processes tab of Task Manager and sort by the Mem Usage column. Stop any unnecessary applications or processes, and consider disabling the underlying service. For example, if a program running in the background uses a lot of memory and it is a program you do not really need, disable the program from starting with Windows.

■ If you see high processor utilization, see if you can determine which applications are consuming the most processor time. To do this, use the Processes tab of Task Manager and sort by the CPU column. If you do not need an application that is consuming processor time, close the application. If an application seems to be consuming too much processor time for a long period (in other words, not just when the program is starting up or performing an intensive process), there might be a problem with the application. Stop the application and start it again, or restart the computer and then restart the application. If the application continues to consume excessive amounts of processor time, there might be a problem with the application.

■ If you continue to see high processor utilization, and the programs consuming the most processor time are programs you use regularly, you should consider upgrading to a faster processor.

■ If you have programs consuming processor time that are multithreaded programs, consider installing a second processor. You can often gain more effective speed with a dual processor configuration than with a faster single processor.

■ If you see high processor utilization, but do not discover that programs are consuming too much processor time, you should use System Monitor to check the % Interrupts value. It is possible that a malfunctioning piece of hardware is trying too often to interrupt the processor.

■ If you see a high disk queue value, but do not see high paging file use, the bottleneck is more likely a slow hard disk than low memory. Consider adding a faster disk.

■ Never make more than one change at a time when trying to resolve a bottleneck, and always repeat monitoring to verify that the change you made actually improved the situation.

Practice: Using System Monitor

In this practice, you use System Monitor to monitor system resources. You add objects and counters to control what is being monitored, and you then view the three views—graph, histogram, and report—for output.

1. Click Start, click Control Panel, and then click Performance And Maintenance.

2. Click Administrative Tools, and then double-click the Performance shortcut.

   Windows XP Professional starts the Performance console with the System Monitor selected.

3. What objects and counters are monitored by default?

   _____

   _____

   _____

4. Under the graph, right-click Counter, and then click Add Counters.

   Windows XP Professional displays the Add Counters dialog box.

5. Which performance object and counter are selected by default?

   _____

6. In the Select Counters From list, select Interrupts/Sec, and then click Explain.

   Windows XP Professional displays an Explain Text dialog box indicating that Interrupts/Sec is the average number of hardware interrupts that the processor receives and services each second.

7. Close the Explain Text window.

8. Click Add to add the Interrupts/Sec counter to the Processor object.

9. In the Performance Object list box, select Paging File.

10. Under Select Counters From List, ensure that %Usage is selected, and then click Add to add the Paging File object with the %Usage counter.

11. Close the Add Counters dialog box.

12. Press Ctrl+B to view a histogram.

13. Press Ctrl+R to view a report.

14. Press Ctrl+G to return to a graph.

15. Close the Performance console.

Lesson Review

Use the following questions to help determine whether you have learned enough to move on to the next lesson. If you have difficulty answering these questions, review the material in this lesson before beginning the next lesson. You can find answers to these questions in the "Questions and Answers" section at the end of this chapter.

1. Which of the following monitoring tools are included in the Performance console? (Choose all answers that are correct.)

   a. System Monitor snap-in

   b. Task Manager snap-in

   c. Performance Logs And Alerts snap-in

   d. Task Scheduler

2. Why should you monitor resources and overall system performance?

   _____

   _____

   _____

   _____

3. What is a baseline, and what is a bottleneck?

   _____

   _____

   _____

4. Why do you need to determine a baseline when you monitor system resources and system performance?

   _____

   _____

   _____

   _____

   _____

Lesson Summary

■ The Performance console contains the System Monitor snap-in and the Performance Logs And Alerts snap-in. The System Monitor snap-in allows you to monitor the performance of your computer or other computers on the network.

- The System Monitor snap-in provides performance objects that consist of counters for collecting data. You can add any of hundreds of counters, each of which measures a particular aspect of system performance.

- The Performance Logs And Alerts snap-in records performance data and system alerts on your local computer or from remote computers.

- A baseline is a measurement derived from collecting data over an extended period of time that represents resource usage under normal conditions.

- A bottleneck is any component that slows down the entire system's performance.

Case Scenario Exercise

In this exercise, you will read a scenario about using System Monitor to measure system performance, and then answer the question that follows. If you have difficulty completing this work, review the material in this chapter before beginning the next chapter. You can find answers to these questions in the "Questions and Answers" section at the end of this chapter.

Scenario

You are an administrator working for a company named Fabrikam, Inc., a regional public relations firm with its headquarters in Dallas, Texas, and several branch locations throughout the country. You are working with Pat, a user in the company's accounting department (which is located in the main office). Pat recently noticed that her computer's performance has decreased, and it is functioning at unacceptably slow levels when running resource-intensive applications. The computer is configured as follows:

- Processor: Pentium 4 2.8 GHz

- RAM: 256 MB

- Hard disk: 12 GB

Questions

1. You want to monitor memory, processor, and disk usage over the course of a normal day's activity on Pat's computer. Which tool should you use to do this?

_____

_____

_____

_____

_____

2. What objects and counters would you select?

_____

_____

_____

_____

3. At the end of the day, you use System Monitor to view the log created on Pat's computer. You note the following key average counter values:

❑ Memory, Pages/sec: 92

❑ Processor, %Processor Time: 35 percent

❑ Physical Disk, %Disk Time: 73 percent

What do you suspect is causing the performance problem? How would you resolve it?

_____

_____

_____

_____

_____

_____

_____

_____

_____

_____

_____

Troubleshooting Lab

In this lab, you will create a performance log on your own computer and then read the results.

To create a performance log, use the following steps:

1. Click Start, and then click Control Panel.

2. In the Control Panel window, click Performance And Maintenance.

3. In the Performance And Maintenance window, click Administrative Tools.

4. In the Administrative Tools window, double-click Performance.

5. In the Performance window, expand Performance Logs And Alerts.

6. Right-click Counter Logs, and select New Log Settings.

7. In the New Log Setting dialog box, type **My Performance** for the name for the log and click OK.

8. In the My Performance dialog box, on the General tab, use the Add Counters button to add the following counters:

   ❑ Memory: Pages/sec

   ❑ Paging File (_Total): %Usage

   ❑ Processor: %Processor Time

   ❑ System: Processor Queue Length

   ❑ Physical Disk: Disk Reads/sec

   ❑ Physical Disk: Disk Writes/sec

   ❑ Physical Disk: Avg. Disk Queue Length

9. On the Schedule tab, configure the start time for five minutes in the future. In the Stop Log section, click After, and then set the stop time for one hour from now.

10. Click OK to save the log configuration.

    Windows displays a dialog box asking whether you want to create the new log file.

11. Click Yes.

12. In the Performance window, under Performance Logs And Alerts, click Counter Logs.

13. In the right-hand pane, what do you notice about the My Performance log?

    _____

    _____

14. While the log is recording, you should continue to use your computer as you normally would. Be sure to run multiple applications (you can even play pinball—a fairly resource-hungry program).

15. After one hour has elapsed, return to the Performance window.

    The My Performance log icon should now be red, indicating that the log is stopped.

16. Click System Monitor.

17. Press CTRL+L (or click the View Log Data button) to open the System Monitor Properties dialog box with the Source tab showing.

18. Click Log Files.

19. Click Add.

20. Locate the My Performance log file. The default location for log files is C:\PerfLogs. Click OK.

21. In the Performance window, add each of the counters that you configured the log to monitor.

22. Click the View Report button (or press CTRL+R).

23. Record the values for each counter in the following table.

Object: Counter	Value
Memory: Pages/sec	
Paging File (_Total): %Usage	
Processor: %Processor Time	
System: Processor Queue Length	
Physical Disk: Disk Reads/sec	
Physical Disk: Disk Writes/sec	
Physical Disk: Avg. Disk Queue Length	

24. Do you notice any values that indicate a bottleneck? If so, list the values and explain what you would do to troubleshoot the problem.

_____

_____

_____

_____

25. Close the Performance window.

Chapter Summary

- Task Manager provides information about the programs and processes running on your computer and the performance of your computer. You can use Task Manager to start programs, to stop programs and processes, and to see a current view of your computer's performance. Task Manager contains four tabs:

  - The Applications tab lets you view and terminate running applications.

  - The Processes tab lets you view and terminate running processes. You can also assign process priority and processor affinity on this tab.

  - The Performance tab provides a real-time view of CPU, RAM, and virtual memory performance.

  - The Networking tab indicates the current network traffic on various network connections on the computer.

- The Performance console consists of two tools: the System Monitor snap-in, which tracks resource use and network throughput in real time, and the Performance Logs And Alerts snap-in, which collects performance data over time and can have Windows XP alert you when a particular performance threshold is crossed.

Exam Highlights

Before taking the exam, review the key points and terms that are presented in this chapter. You need to know this information.

Key Points

- Task Manager can show real-time information about the CPU, RAM, and virtual memory, but the measurements are fairly limited. To collect more detailed information, use the Performance console. The Performance console also allows you to collect performance data over a longer period.

- Changing the base priority of an application can be useful on application or file servers, but you should use caution when changing priorities on a desktop computer. Setting the base priority too high can result in unstable system performance or loss of data.

- Memorize the counters mentioned in this chapter, and understand the values of each counter that indicate a potential problem. In particular, you should remember the three default counters used in System Monitor: Pages/sec, Avg. Disk Queue Length, and %Processor Time.

Key Terms

base priority   A setting made in Task Manager that determines how much processor time Windows XP Professional devotes to the process when compared with other processes.

counter   A particular aspect of an object that System Monitor can measure.

instance   A particular occurrence of an object.

object   A representation of a major system component (hardware or software) of the computer or operating system.

Performance console   A tool that is used to monitor resource usage on a computer running Windows XP Professional. The Performance console provides access to two snap-ins: System Monitor and Performance Logs And Alerts.

Performance Logs And Alerts   A snap-in that collects performance data over time from the local or a remote computer, or has Windows XP alert you when a particular performance threshold is crossed.

process   An operating system object that consists of an executable program, a set of virtual memory addresses, and one or more threads. When a program runs, a process is created.

processor affinity   A setting made in Task Manager that determines on which processors (on a multiple-processor computer) a process can run.

System Monitor   A snap-in that tracks resource use and network throughput in real time through the use of objects and counters.

Task Manager   A tool that provides information about the programs and processes running on your computer and the performance of your computer.

Questions and Answers

Lesson 1 Practice: Using Task Manager

Page
19-10

3. Click the Applications tab. Which programs are currently running on your computer?

Answers will vary, but no programs might be running.

7. How many processes are running?

Answers will vary.

11. What percentage of your CPU's capacity is being used?

Answers will vary but should be low.

12. Do you think that your CPU could be slowing down the performance on your computer?

Answers might vary, but if the CPU is barely being utilized (such as when WordPad is the only running application), the CPU does not slow down the performance of the computer.

Lesson 1 Review

Page
19-11

1. Which of the following methods can you use to start Task Manager? (Choose all that apply.)

a. Press CTRL+ALT+ESC

b. Right-click the Desktop, and then click Task Manager

c. Press CTRL+SHIFT+ESC

d. Press CTRL+ALT+DELETE, and if necessary, click Task Manager

The correct answers are C and D. A and B are not correct because you cannot launch Task Manager by using these methods.

2. Which of the following tabs can be found in Task Manager? (Choose all that apply.)

a. Networking tab

b. Programs tab

c. Processes tab

d. General tab

The correct answers are A and C. B is not correct because there is no Programs tab in Task Manager; programs are managed by using the Applications tab. D is not correct because there is no General tab in Task Manager.

3. What are page faults? Do you think a larger or smaller number of page faults indicates better system performance? Why?

Each time data has to be retrieved from the page file on the hard disk for a process, the data has been paged out of physical memory. This is known as a page fault. A smaller number of page faults indicates better system performance because it is faster to retrieve data from RAM than from a paging file on the hard drive.

4. What does CPU usage represent? In general, is system performance better with a high CPU usage value or a low value?

CPU usage is the percentage of time that the processor is running a thread other than the idle thread. You do not want the CPU to be a bottleneck to the computer. If the CPU usage is too high, it could indicate that the CPU is limiting system performance.

Lesson 2 Practice: Using System Monitor

Page 19-22

1. What objects and counters are monitored by default?

The objects and counters monitored by default are: Memory with the Pages/Sec counter; PhysicalDisk with the Average Disk Queue Length counter; and Processor with the %Processor Time counter.

5. Which performance object and counter are selected by default?

By default, the Processor object and the %Processor Time counter are selected.

Lesson 2 Review

Page 19-23

1. Which of the following monitoring tools are included in the Performance console? (Choose all answers that are correct.)

    a. System Monitor snap-in

    b. Task Manager snap-in

    c. Performance Logs And Alerts snap-in

    d. Task Scheduler

The correct answers are A and C. B is not correct because Task Manager is a stand-alone tool (not a snap-in) and is not part of the Performance console. D is not correct because Task Scheduler is a stand-alone tool and is not part of the Performance console.

2. Why should you monitor resources and overall system performance?

Monitoring resources and overall system performance helps you determine how well your computer is currently performing, detect and eliminate bottlenecks, recognize trends so that you can plan for future growth and upgrades, and evaluate the effects of tuning and configuration changes on your computer.

3. What is a baseline, and what is a bottleneck?

A baseline is a measurement derived from collecting data over an extended period of time that represents resource usage under normal conditions. A bottleneck is any component that slows down the performance of the entire system.

4. Why do you need to determine a baseline when you monitor system resources and system performance?

When you monitor system performance, you compare the current performance of the system with the baseline. If the current system performance is worse than the baseline, you need to check for bottlenecks. After you have resolved the problem, you again monitor system performance so that you can verify that the action you took actually resolved the bottleneck and improved system performance.

Case Scenario Exercise

Page
19-24

1. You want to monitor memory, processor, and disk usage over the course of a normal day's activity on Pat's computer. Which tool should you use to do this?

You should use the Performance Logs And Alerts snap-in. You should configure a performance log by using key objects and counters. Ideally, you should configure the Performance Logs And Alerts snap-in on a different computer from Pat's and monitor her computer remotely. After completing the log, you can view the results using System Monitor.

2. What objects and counters would you select?

Answers may vary, but you should consider monitoring at least the following objects and counters: Processor: %Processor Time; Processor: %Interrupts; System: Processor Queue Length; Memory: Pages/sec; Physical Disk: %Disk Time; and Physical Disk: Avg. Disk Queue Length.

3. At the end of the day, you use System Monitor to view the log created on Pat's computer. You note the following key average counter values:

   ❑ Memory, Pages/sec: 92

   ❑ Processor, %Processor Time: 35 percent

   ❑ Physical Disk, %Disk Time: 73 percent

   What do you suspect is causing the performance problem? How would you resolve it?

These values indicate that the computer is experiencing a shortage of memory. The acceptable level of Pages/sec is under 20. At the current average rate of 92 Pages/sec, the operating system is spending too much time moving data in and out of physical memory and the paging file. Also, the %Disk Time statistic indicates a potential hard disk performance issue (73 percent, and the acceptable maximum value is 50 percent). The hard disk could be a problem, but it is more likely that the increased paging is causing the hard disk to work much harder than it has to. Increasing the amount of memory in the computer decreases the amount of paging required, which in turn decreases the load on the hard disk, which will most likely cause the %Disk Time counter to drop below the acceptable threshold.

Troubleshooting Lab

Page
19-25

1. Do you notice any values that indicate a bottleneck? If so, list the values and explain what you would do to troubleshoot the problem.

Answers will vary.

20 Backing Up and Restoring Data

Exam Objectives in this Chapter:

- Restore and back up the operating system, System State data, and other user data.
  - ❏ Recover System State data and user data by using Windows Backup.
  - ❏ Recover System State data and user data by using the Recovery Console.

Why This Chapter Matters

Now that you have learned to install Microsoft Windows XP Professional and configure a network, it is important that you ensure that data is not lost. Windows XP Professional provides the **Backup Or Restore Wizard** to allow you to back up data. This chapter introduces you to backing up and restoring data, including **Automated System Recovery**.

Lessons in this Chapter:

Before You Begin

To complete this chapter, you must have a computer that meets the minimum hardware requirements listed in the preface, "About This Book." You must also have Microsoft Windows XP Professional installed on the computer.

Lesson 1: Using the Backup Utility

The efficient recovery of lost data is the end goal of all backup jobs. A **backup job** is a single process of backing up data. Regularly backing up the data on server hard disks and client computer hard disks prevents data loss caused by disk drive failures, power outages, virus infections, and other such incidents. If data loss occurs, and you have carefully planned and performed regular backups, you can restore the lost data, whether it is a single file or an entire hard disk.

After this lesson, you will be able to

■ Describe the Backup utility that is provided in Windows XP Professional

■ Identify the permissions and rights that are required to back up and restore data

■ Plan a backup

■ Select a type of backup operation

■ Change the default backup options in Windows XP Professional

Estimated lesson time: 30 minutes

What Is the Backup Utility?

The Windows **Backup** utility provides a simple interface for backing up and restoring data. To access the Backup Or Restore Wizard, on the Start menu, point to All Programs, point to Accessories, point to System Tools, and then click Backup. Alternatively, on the Start menu, you can click Run, type ntbackup, and then click OK.

You can use Backup in two modes:

Wizard mode   In Wizard mode, Backup steps you through the process of backing up or restoring your data.

Advanced mode   In Advanced mode, Backup presents a more traditional backup interface for selecting files and backup locations.

The Backup Or Restore Wizard

In Wizard mode, you will use the Backup Or Restore Wizard, shown in Figure 20-1, to back up or restore data. By default, Backup launches the Backup Or Restore Wizard when you launch the utility. You can use the Backup Or Restore Wizard to back up data manually or to schedule unattended backup jobs on a regular basis. You can back up data to a file or to a tape. Files can be stored on hard disks, in shared folders on a network, or on drives with removable media (such as Iomega Zip and Jaz drives or tape drives).

Note   Windows Backup does not support writing directly to a CD-ROM or DVD during the backup process. However, you can back up to a hard drive and then manually copy the backup file to optical media.

Figure 20-1   Use the Backup Or Restore Wizard to easily back up data.

On the Welcome To The Backup Or Restore Wizard page, click Next. The Backup Or Restore page allows you to specify whether you want to back up files and settings or restore files and settings.

Advanced Mode

You can also use the Backup utility in Advanced mode, shown in Figure 20-2, by clicking Advanced Mode on the Backup Or Restore Wizard's Welcome page. If you want to have Backup start in Advanced mode each time you start the program, clear the Always Start In Wizard Mode check box on the Welcome Page before clicking Advanced Mode.

As you will learn in Lesson 2, "Backing Up Data," Advanced mode provides access to a number of options that you cannot access by using the Backup Or Restore Wizard.

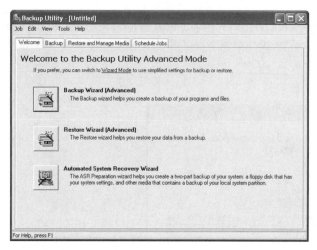

Figure 20-2 Use Advanced mode for a more traditional approach to backing up and restoring data.

Who Can Back Up and Restore Data?

To successfully back up and restore data on a computer running Windows XP Professional, you must have the appropriate permissions and user rights, as described in the following list:

- All users can back up their own files and folders. They can also back up files for which they have the Read, Read and Execute, Modify, or Full Control permission.

- All users can restore files and folders for which they have the Write, Modify, or Full Control permission.

- Any user who is assigned the Backup Files and Directories right can back up data. Any user who is assigned the Restore Files And Directories user right can restore backed up data.

- Members of the Administrators and Backup Operators groups can back up and restore all files (regardless of the assigned permissions). By default, members of these groups have the Backup Files And Directories and Restore Files And Directories user rights.

Exam Tip To back up all data on a computer regardless of the assigned permissions to that data, you must use a user account that has the Backup Files And Directories user right assigned. To restore data, you must use a user account that has the Restore Files And Directories user right assigned. Members of the Administrators and Backup Operators local groups have these rights by default.

How to Plan a Backup

You should plan your backup jobs to fit the needs of your company. The primary goal of backing up data is to be able to restore that data if necessary, so any backup plan that you develop should incorporate how you restore data. You should be able to quickly and successfully restore critical lost data. There is no single correct backup plan for all networks.

Consider the following guidelines in formulating your backup plan.

Determine What to Back Up

Always back up critical files and folders, such as user-created documents, sales and financial records, and the System State (the Windows Registry and a number of critical configurations). Also, identify application settings and documents that will be required to restore a user's desktop environment, including bookmarks, browser cookies, templates, and application settings.

Determine How Often to Back Up

If data is critical for company operations, back it up daily. If users create or modify reports once a week, backing up the reports weekly is sufficient. You need to back up data only as often as it changes. For example, there is no need to do daily backups on files that rarely change, such as monthly reports or the Windows XP Professional operating system files.

In summary, you should choose your backup frequency by thinking about how much data you can lose in the event of a hard disk failure. If you do not mind losing a week's worth of data, you can back up your data once per week. In environments in which data is extremely valuable, files can be backed up multiple times per day.

Determine Which Target Media to Use for Storing Backup Data

With the Backup Utility, you can back up to the following:

File   You can back up data to a backup file, which Backup can write to a hard drive, removable media drive (such as an Iomega Zip drive), or network location (such as a file server). The file that is created has the .bkf extension and contains the files and folders that you have selected to back up.

Tape   In the past, tape proved to be a more convenient and less expensive backup medium for large backup jobs because tapes had a high storage capacity and relatively low cost compared with other media. Today, with the higher capacity and lower cost of hard disks, a disk-based backup system is usually a more efficient and more cost-effective solution. Many networks use removable hard drive solutions instead of tape backup systems so that they can store backups offsite and create rotating backup systems. In addition to costing more than modern hard disks, tapes have a limited life and can deteriorate.

> **Note**   If you use a removable media device to back up and restore data, be sure that you verify that the device is supported in the Windows Catalog.

Determine Whether to Perform Network or Local Backup Jobs

A network backup can contain data from multiple computers on the network. This allows you to consolidate backup data from multiple computers to a single location. A network backup also allows one administrator to back up the entire network. Whether you perform a network or local backup job depends on the data that must be backed up. For example, you can back up the System State data only at the computer where you are performing the backup.

> **Exam Tip**   Backup allows you to back up data from or to shared folders on remote computers. Backup cannot write backup files directly to a CD-ROM or DVD.

If you decide to perform local backups, you must perform a local backup at each client computer. There are several issues to consider when performing local backups. First, you must move from computer to computer so that you can perform a backup at each computer, rely on users to back up their own computers, or schedule automated backups. Most users fail to back up their data on a regular basis.

A second consideration with local backups is the storage location. It is impractical to install removable storage media devices on every client computer, so backing up to a file server is often more appropriate. If you use removable storage media devices, such as tape drives, you must have one for each computer, or you must move the tape drive from computer to computer so that you can perform a local backup on each computer.

You might also choose to use a combination of network and local backup jobs. Do this when critical data resides on client computers and servers and you do not have a removable storage media device for each computer. In this situation, users should perform a local backup and store their backup files on a server. You then back up the server.

> ### Real World   **Backups on Large Networks**
>
> If you are working for a company with a large network, it is likely that a sophisticated backup infrastructure is already in place. More than likely, users store their important documents on file servers rather than on their local computers, and those file servers are backed up daily. Make sure you understand the backup system that exists on a network before you create a backup plan of your own.
>
> On large networks, you are more likely to use the Backup utility as a precaution before troubleshooting users' computers—an extra step to make sure that you can restore the computer should troubleshooting go wrong. On smaller networks, it may still be advantageous to centralize user documents on a file server, but more likely users will store documents on their own computers. In this case, you should consider backing up client computers to a file server daily and also backing up the data on the file server to a removable storage medium.
>
> Another challenge of backing up large networks is planning for notebook computers. Notebook users often disconnect their computer from the network to take their computers home at night or on trips with them. As a result, notebooks do not always fit into the same backup scheme as desktop computers. Although notebook users can connect to the network and initiate a more traditional backup to a network server, you should consider planning for a backup system that notebook users can use while they are disconnected from the main network. Depending on the amount of data that a notebook user stores, you might consider providing users with an external hard drive or a CD writer, or even have them connect to the company network (or an Internet backup location) periodically to back up data. If notebook users have small numbers of files that they work on while away, they can even back data up by e-mail.

Types of Backup Operations

The Backup Utility provides five types of backup operations that define which data is backed up, such as only those files that have changed since the last backup (see Figure 20-3).

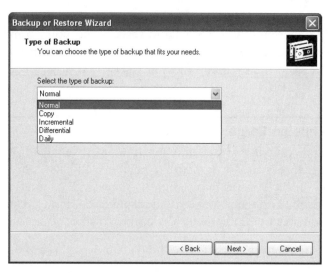

Figure 20-3   Choose one of the available backup types.

Some backup types use backup **markers**, also known as archive attributes, which mark a file as having changed. When a file changes, an attribute is set on the file that indicates that the file has changed since the last backup. When you back up the file, this clears or resets the attribute. Types of backups include the following:

Normal   During a **normal backup**, all the selected files and folders are backed up. A normal backup does not rely on markers to determine which files to back up. During a normal backup, any existing markers are cleared and each file is marked as having been backed up. Normal backups speed up the restore process because the backup files are the most current, and you do not need to restore multiple backup jobs.

Copy   During a **copy backup**, all the selected files and folders are backed up. A copy backup neither looks for nor clears markers. If you do not want to clear markers and affect other backup types, use a copy backup. For example, use a copy backup between a normal and an incremental backup to create an archival snapshot of network data.

Incremental   During an **incremental backup**, only the selected files and folders that have a marker are backed up, and then the backup clears markers. Because an incremental backup clears markers, if you did two consecutive incremental backups on a file and nothing changed in the file, the file would not be backed up the second time.

Differential   During a **differential backup**, only the selected files and folders that have a marker are backed up, but the backup does not clear markers. Because a differential backup does not clear markers, if you did two consecutive differential backups on a file and nothing changed in the file, the entire file would be backed up each time.

Daily   During a daily backup, all the selected files and folders that have changed during the day are backed up. This backup neither looks for nor clears markers. If you want to back up all files and folders that change during the day, use a daily backup.

Combining Backup Types

An effective backup strategy is likely to combine different backup types. Some backup types require more time to back up data but less time to restore data. Conversely, other backup types require less time to back up data but more time to restore data. If you combine backup types, markers are critical. Incremental and differential backups check for and rely on the markers.

The following are some examples of combining different backup types:

Normal and differential backups   On Monday, a normal backup is performed; on Tuesday through Friday, differential backups are performed. Differential backups do not clear markers, which means that each backup includes all changes since Monday. If data becomes corrupt on Friday, you need only to restore the normal backup from Monday and the differential backup from Thursday. This strategy takes more time to back up but less time to restore.

Normal and incremental backups   On Monday, a normal backup is performed; on Tuesday through Friday, incremental backups are performed. Incremental backups clear markers, which means that each backup includes only the files that changed since the previous backup. If data becomes corrupt on Friday, you need to restore the normal backup from Monday and all incremental backups, from Tuesday through Friday. This strategy takes less time to back up but more time to restore.

> **Off the Record**   Although you should remember for the exam that differential backups have the quickest restore time, and incremental backups have the quickest backup time, this is sometimes not true in practice. Because users tend to work on the same files each day for extended periods (particular documents or spreadsheets for a project, for example), differential and incremental backups end up backing up the same files. If this is the case for a particular user, you might as well save time during the restore and simply use differential backups.

Normal, differential, and copy backups   This strategy is the same as the first example that used normal and differential backups except that on Wednesday you perform a copy backup. Copy backups include all selected files and do not clear markers or interrupt the usual backup schedule. Therefore, each differential backup includes all changes since Monday. The copy backup done on Wednesday is not part of the Friday restore. Copy backups are helpful when you need to create a snapshot of your data and do not want to interrupt the normal backup routine.

> **Exam Tip** Performing regular normal backups takes the most time during the backup phase but the least time and effort during the restore phase. Using a normal backup and incremental backups takes the least time during the backup phase but takes the most time and effort during the restore phase. Using a normal backup plus differential backups takes more time to back up than using incremental backups (although less than using only normal backups) but takes less time during the restore phase than using incremental backups.

How to Change Default Backup Options

Backup allows you to change the default settings for all backup-and-restore jobs. These default settings are on the tabs in the Options dialog box. To access the Options dialog box, on the Welcome To The Backup Or Restore Wizard page, click Advanced Mode; then, on the Tools menu, click Options.

The following list provides an overview of the settings for the Backup Utility:

General tab These settings affect data verification, the status information for backup-and-restore jobs, alert messages, and what is backed up. Figure 20-4 shows the default settings for the options on the General tab. You should select the Verify Data After The Backup Completes check box because it is critical that your backup data not be corrupt.

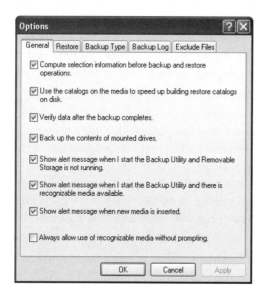

Figure 20-4 Change backup options on the General tab of the Options dialog box.

Restore tab   These settings affect what happens when the file to restore is identical to an existing file. Figure 20-5 shows the available settings; the default setting is selected.

Figure 20-5   Change restore options on the Restore tab of the Options dialog box.

Backup Type tab   These settings affect the default backup type when you perform a backup job. The settings that you select depend on how often you back up, how quickly you want to restore, and how much storage space you have. The backup types are Normal (which is the default), Copy, Differential, Incremental, and Daily.

Backup Log tab   These settings affect the amount of information that is included in the backup log. The default setting is Summary, which logs key operations such as loading the tape, starting the backup, or failing to open a file. Two additional settings are available: Detailed, which logs all information, including the names of the files and folders; and None, which turns off logging.

Exclude Files tab   These settings affect which files are excluded from backup jobs.

You can modify some default settings in the Backup Or Restore Wizard for a specific backup job. For example, the default backup type is normal, but you can change it to another backup type in the Backup Or Restore Wizard. However, the next time that you run the Backup Or Restore Wizard, the default backup type (normal) is selected.

Lesson Review

Use the following questions to help determine whether you have learned enough to move on to the next lesson. If you have difficulty answering these questions, review the material in this lesson before beginning the next lesson. You can find answers to these questions in the "Questions and Answers" section at the end of this chapter.

1. How do you access the Backup Or Restore Wizard?

_____

_____

_____

2. What two operations can you perform using the Backup Or Restore Wizard?

_____

_____

_____

3. What is the primary goal of backing up data?

_____

4. If you want to perform a backup but do not want to clear markers or affect other backup types, you should perform a(n) _____ backup.

5. During a(n) _____ backup, only selected files and folders that have a marker are backed up, but the backup does not clear markers. If you performed two of these backups in a row on a file and nothing changed in the file, the entire file would be backed up each time.

6. How can you change the default settings for backup-and-restores for all backup-and-restore operations by using the Backup Utility?

_____

_____

_____

_____

7. You performed a normal backup on Monday. For the remaining days of the week, you want to back up only files and folders that have changed since the previous day. Which backup type do you select? Why?

_____

_____

_____

Lesson Summary

- The Backup utility offers two modes: Wizard mode, which steps you through a backup or restore, and Advanced mode, which provides a more traditional backup interface and access to more options.

- To back up or restore data, you must have the appropriate rights and permissions. All users can back up files for which they have at least Read permissions and restore files for which they have at least Write permissions. Any user who is assigned the Backup Files and Directories right can back up data regardless of the assigned permissions. Any user who is assigned the Restore Files And Directories user right can restore backed up data. By default, members of the Administrators and Backup Operators groups have these rights.

- Planning backups includes determining what to back up, how often to back it up, and where the backup file is written.

- The Backup utility provides five types of backup: normal, copy, differential, incremental, and daily.

- The Backup Utility has default settings that apply to all backup-and-restore operations. The tabs in the Options dialog box for the Backup Utility allow you to change the default settings for the Backup Utility.

Lesson 2: Backing Up Data

After you have planned your backup, including planning the type of backup to use and when to perform backup jobs, the next step is to prepare to back up your data. You must complete certain preliminary tasks before you can back up your data. After completing these tasks, you can perform a backup or schedule an unattended backup.

After this lesson, you will be able to

- Identify preliminary tasks to accomplish prior to backing up
- Select files and folders to back up
- Specify a backup destination, media settings, and advanced settings
- Schedule a backup job

Estimated lesson time: 50 minutes

Preliminary Tasks

An important part of each backup job is performing the preliminary tasks, which includes ensuring that the files that you want to back up are closed. You should notify users to close files before you begin backing up data. You can use e-mail or the Send Console Message dialog box in the Computer Management snap-in to send administrative messages to users.

You can send a console message as follows:

1. On the Start menu, right-click My Computer, and then click Manage.

2. On the Action menu, click All Tasks, and then click Send Console Message.

The Send Console Message dialog box appears (see Figure 20-6).

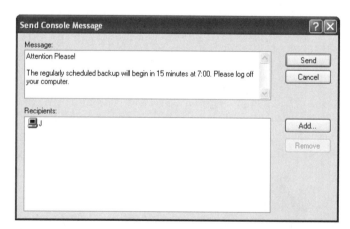

Figure 20-6   Use the Send Console Message dialog box to notify users before backing up.

1. Type the desired message in the Message text box. Note the recipients in the Recipients box. You can add or remove recipients.

2. Click Send to send the message to the listed recipients.

> **Note**   Sending a console message requires that the Messenger service be running on the computer that receives the message. In Windows XP with Service Pack 2, the Messenger service is disabled by default. You must enable the service on a computer before that computer can receive messages.

If you back up to a removable media device, make sure that the following preliminary tasks are complete:

- The backup device is attached to a computer on the network and is turned on. If you are backing up to tape, you must attach the tape device to the computer on which you run the Backup Utility.

- The media device is listed in the Windows Catalog.

- The media is loaded in the media device and properly prepared. For example, if you are using a tape drive, ensure that a tape is loaded in the tape drive. You might need to format a tape before backing up.

How to Select Files and Folders to Back Up

After you complete the preliminary tasks, you are ready to perform the backup. You can use the Backup Or Restore Wizard (refer to Figure 20-1). To start the Backup Or Restore Wizard, click Start, point to All Programs, point to Accessories, point to System Tools, and then click Backup. Click Next to close the Welcome To The Backup Or Restore Wizard page. On the Backup Or Restore page, ensure that Back Up Files And Settings is selected, and click Next to display the What To Back Up page, as shown in Figure 20-7.

Specify what to back up by choosing one of the following options:

My Documents And Settings   Backs up the My Documents folder, along with the Favorites folder, desktop, and cookies of the current user. This is the default selection.

Everyone's Documents And Settings   Backs up the My Documents folder, along with the Favorites folders, desktop, and cookies of all users.

All Information On This Computer   Backs up all files on the computer on which you are running the Backup Utility except those files that the Backup Utility excludes by default, such as certain power management files. Selecting this option also backs up the **System State** data, which includes the Windows Registry and important configuration files. Selecting this option also creates a system recovery disk that you can use to restore Windows in the case of a major failure. Read Lesson 4, "Using the Automated System Recovery Wizard," for more information about system recovery disks.

Let Me Choose What To Back Up Backs up selected files and folders. This includes files and folders on the computer where you run the Backup Utility and any shared file or folder on the network. When you click this option, the Backup Or Restore Wizard provides a hierarchical view of the computer and the network (through My Network Places).

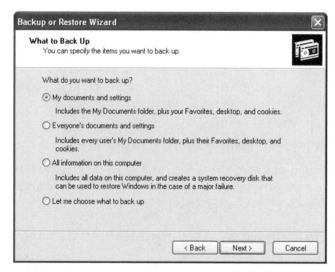

Figure 20-7 Select files and folders on the What To Back Up page.

How to Specify Backup Destination, Media Settings, and Advanced Settings

After you select what you want to back up, you must provide information about backup media. Table 20-1 describes the information that you must provide on the Backup Type, Destination, And Name page.

Table 20-1 Backup Type, Destination, And Name Page Options

Option	Description
Select The Backup Type	The target medium to use, such as a tape or file. A file can be located on any disk-based media, including a hard disk, a shared network folder, or a removable disk, such as an Iomega Zip drive.
Choose A Place To Save Your Backup	The location where the Backup Utility will store the data. For a tape, enter the tape name. For a file, enter the path for the backup file.
Type A Name For This Backup	The name of the backup. If it is a file name, the extension .bkf is appended automatically.

After you provide the media information, the Backup Or Restore Wizard displays the Completing The Backup Or Restore Wizard page, and you have the opportunity to do either of the following:

Start the backup   If you click Finish, during the backup process, the Backup Or Restore Wizard displays status information about the backup job in the Backup Progress dialog box.

Specify advanced backup options   If you click Advanced, the Backup Or Restore Wizard allows you to select the advanced backup settings listed in Table 20-2.

Table 20-2   Advanced Backup Settings

Advanced option	Description
Select The Type Of Backup	Allows you to choose the backup type that is used for this backup job. Select one of the following types: normal, copy, incremental, differential, or daily.
Verify Data After Backup	Confirms that files are correctly backed up. The Backup Utility compares the backup data and the source data to verify that they are the same. This option is recommended.
Use Hardware Compression, If Available	Enables hardware compression for tape devices that support it. If your tape device does not support hardware compression, this option is unavailable.
Disable Volume Shadow Copy	Allows files to be backed up even though they are in the process of being written to. By default, the Backup Utility will use volume shadow copies because this check box is cleared.
If The Archive Media Already Contains Backups:	
Append This Backup To The Existing Backups	Choose this option to store multiple backup jobs on a storage device.
or	
Replace The Existing Backups	Choose this option if you do not need to save previous backup jobs and you want to save only the most recent backup data.
Allow Only The Owner And The Administrator Access To The Backup Data And Any Backups Appended To This Medium	Allows you to restrict who can gain access to the completed backup file or tape. This option is available only if you choose to replace an existing backup on a backup medium, rather than appending to the backup medium. If you back up the Registry or Active Directory directory services, click this option to prevent others from getting copies of the backup job.
When To Backup	Allows you to specify Now or Later. If you select Later, you specify the job name and the start date. You can also set the schedule.

When you specify advanced backup settings that cover the backup media and characteristics of the backup job, you are changing the default backup settings for only the current backup job.

Depending on whether you chose to back up now or later, the Backup Or Restore Wizard provides you with the opportunity to do either of the following:

- If you chose to finish the backup process, the Backup Or Restore Wizard displays the Completing The Backup Or Restore Wizard page and then presents the option to finish and immediately start the backup. During the backup, the wizard displays status information about the backup job.

- If you chose to back up later, you are shown additional dialog boxes to schedule the backup process to occur later, as described in the next section.

Note   When the backup process is complete, you can choose to review the backup log, a text file that records backup operations. The backup log is stored on the hard disk of the computer on which you are running the Backup Utility.

How to Schedule Backup Jobs

Scheduling a backup job means that you can have an unattended backup job occur on a regular basis (or even occur just once at a later time). To enable this, Windows XP Professional integrates the Backup Utility with the Task Scheduler service. (See Chapter 18, "Using Windows XP Tools," for more on Task Scheduler.)

You can schedule a backup as follows:

1. Click Later on the When To Back Up page of the Backup Or Restore Wizard.

   Task Scheduler presents the Set Account Information dialog box, prompting you for your password. The user account must have the appropriate user rights and permissions to perform backup jobs on the selected data.

2. Enter your password in the Password text box and Confirm Password text box, and then click OK.

   Task Scheduler displays the When To Back Up page. You must provide a name for the backup job, and by default, the wizard displays the current date and time for the start date.

3. Type an appropriate name in the Job Name text box.

4. Click Set Schedule to set a different start date and time. This selection causes Task Scheduler to display the Schedule Job dialog box.

In the Schedule Job dialog box, you can set the date, time, and number of occurrences for the backup job to repeat, such as every Friday at 10:00 P.M. You can also display all of the scheduled tasks for the computer by selecting the Show Multiple Schedules check box. This helps prevent you from scheduling multiple tasks on the same computer at the same time.

You can also click Advanced to schedule how long the backup can last and for how many days, weeks, months, or years you want this schedule to continue.

After you schedule the backup job and complete the Backup Or Restore Wizard, the Backup Utility places the backup job on the calendar on the Schedule Jobs tab in Windows Backup. The backup job automatically starts at the time that you specified.

Offsite Backups

As you are learning in this chapter, backing up your data is a critical part of ensuring that you can recover from disaster. On many networks, administrators tend to leave backed up data close to the location where backups are created. Administrators might leave data on a network drive, assuming that because the data exists in two separate locations (in the original location and on drive where it is backed up), it is safe. Even when a removable backup medium is used, all too often administrators leave that medium in the same room as the backup server—tapes on a shelf or in a locking cabinet, for example.

Although this practice provides a certain level of assurance that you can recover data if a user's computer (or even the backup server itself) crashes, you should take the extra measure of keeping a copy of backed up data in an offsite storage location. It is best to keep a copy of data in a fire-resistant safe in a completely different building from your network. Keeping offsite backups requires more effort, but in the event of a true catastrophe (such as a fire or natural disaster), an offsite backup can be a real life saver.

Practice: Backing Up Data

In this practice, you use the Backup Or Restore Wizard to back up some files to your hard disk. You then create a backup job to perform a backup operation at a later time by using Task Scheduler.

Exercise 1: Back Up Files by Using the Backup Or Restore Wizard

1. Log on with an account that is a member of the Administrators or Backup Operators group or that has the Backup Files and Directories user right.

2. Click Start, point to All Programs, point to Accessories, point to System Tools, and then click Backup.

3. On the Welcome To The Backup Or Restore Wizard page, click Next.

   The Backup Or Restore Wizard displays the Backup Or Restore page.

4. Ensure that Back Up Files And Settings is selected, and click Next.

   The Backup Or Restore Wizard displays the What To Back Up page, prompting you to choose the scope of the backup job.

5. Click Let Me Choose What To Back Up, and then click Next to continue.

   The Backup Or Restore Wizard displays the Items To Back Up page, prompting you to select the local and network drives, folders, and files to be backed up.

6. Click the plus sign in front of My Computer to expand it, and then click drive C.

   Do not select the check box next to drive C. Selecting this check box would back up the entire drive.

7. In the details pane, select the check box next to the Autoexec.bat file.

   There should be a check mark in the check box in front of the file name Autoexec.bat.

8. Click Next to continue.

   The Backup Or Restore Wizard displays the Backup Type, Destination, And Name page.

> **Note**   If no tape drive is connected to your computer, Select The Backup Type is set to File and is unavailable for you to change.

9. Ensure that Select The Backup Type is set to File.

   The Choose A Place To Save Your Backup box is set to 3½ Floppy (A:) by default. The Type A Name For This Backup box is set to Backup by default.

10. For the Choose A Place To Save Your Backup box, click Browse.

11. If there is no floppy disk in drive A, Windows displays an Insert Disk dialog box asking you to insert a disk. Click Cancel.

12. In the Save As dialog box, click the down-pointing arrow at the end of the Save In text box and click Local Disk (C:).

13. In the File Name text box, type **backup1** and click Save.

> **Note**   You would not normally back up files from a drive to a file on that same drive, as is done in this exercise, unless you planned to transfer that file to another location.

14. Click Next to continue.

The Backup Or Restore Wizard displays the Completing The Backup Or Restore Wizard page, prompting you to finish the wizard and begin the backup job or to specify advanced options.

15. Click Advanced to specify additional backup options.

The Backup Or Restore Wizard displays the Type Of Backup page, prompting you to select a backup type for this backup job.

16. Ensure that Normal is selected in the Select The Type Of Backup list box, and click Next.

The Backup Or Restore Wizard displays the How To Back Up page.

17. Select the Verify Data After Backup check box to confirm that the files are correctly backed up.

> **Note**   If the Use Hardware Compression, If Available check box is unavailable, either you do not have a tape drive or your tape device does not support hardware compression.

18. Click Next.

The Backup Or Restore Wizard displays the Backup Options page.

19. Click Replace The Existing Backups.

20. Ensure that the Allow Only The Owner And The Administrator Access To The Backup Data And To Any Backups Appended To This Media check box is not selected, and then click Next.

The Backup Or Restore Wizard displays the When To Back Up page.

21. Make sure that Now is selected, and then click Next.

The Backup Or Restore Wizard displays the Completing The Backup Or Restore Wizard page.

22. Review the options and settings that you selected for this backup job, and then click Finish to start the backup job.

The Backup Utility briefly displays the Selection Information dialog box, indicating the estimated amount of data for, and the time to complete, the backup job. Because of the speed of your computer and the small number of files to back up, you might not see this dialog box. In the Backup Progress dialog box, the Backup Utility displays the status of the backup operation, statistics on the estimated and actual amount of data being processed, the time that has elapsed, and the estimated time that remains for the backup operation.

Exercise 2: Viewing a Backup Report

1. When the Backup Progress dialog box indicates that the backup is complete, click Report.

   Notepad starts, displaying the backup report. The backup report contains key details about the backup operation, such as the time that it started and how many files were backed up.

2. Examine the report, and when you are finished, quit Notepad.

3. In the Backup Progress dialog box, click Close.

Exercise 3: Creating and Running an Unattended Backup Job

1. Click Start, point to All Programs, point to Accessories, point to System Tools, and then click Backup.

2. On the Welcome To The Backup Or Restore Wizard page, click Next.

3. On the Backup Or Restore page, ensure that Back Up Files And Settings is selected, and click Next.

4. On the What To Back Up page, click Let Me Choose What To Back Up, and then click Next to continue.

5. On the Items To Back Up page, expand My Computer, expand drive C, and then select the System Volume Information check box.

6. Click Next to continue.

7. On the Backup Type, Destination, And Name page, in the Choose A Place To Save Your Backup list box, click Browse.

8. If there is no floppy disk in drive A, Windows displays an Insert Disk dialog box asking you to insert a disk. Click Cancel.

9. In the Save As dialog box, click the down-pointing arrow at the end of the Save In text box, and click Local Disk (C:).

10. In the File Name text box, type **backup2** and click Save.

11. Click Next.

12. On the Completing The Backup Or Restore Wizard page, click Advanced to specify additional backup options.

13. On the Type Of Backup page, ensure that Normal is selected in the Select The Type Of Backup list box, and then click Next.

14. On the How To Back Up page, select the Verify Data After Backup check box, and then click Next.

15. On the Backup Options page, click Replace The Existing Backups.

16. Ensure that the Allow Only The Owner And The Administrator Access To The Backup Data And To Any Backups Appended To This Medium check box is not selected, and then click Next.

17. On the When To Backup page, click Later.

    The Backup Or Restore Wizard makes the Schedule Entry box available.

18. In the Job Name text box, type **SysVol Info Backup** and then click Set Schedule.

    The Backup Or Restore Wizard displays the Schedule Job dialog box, prompting you to select the start time and schedule options for the backup job.

19. In the Schedule Task box, ensure that Once is selected, and in the Start Time text box, enter a time three minutes from the present time, and then click OK.

20. In the When To Back Up dialog box, click Next to continue.

    The Backup Or Restore Wizard displays the Set Account Information dialog box. For purposes of this exercise, use the Administrator account to run the scheduled backup job.

21. In the Set Account Information dialog box, enter the name of an account with the appropriate rights and permissions (for example, the Administrator account), enter and confirm the password, and then click OK.

22. Click OK.

    The Backup Or Restore Wizard displays the Account Information Warning dialog box.

23. Click OK to continue.

24. Review the information on the Completing The Backup Or Restore Wizard page, and then click Finish to schedule the backup job.

    When the time for the backup job is reached, the Backup Utility starts and performs the requested backup operation. To verify that the backup job was performed, locate the BACKUP2.BKF file on the root of the C drive.

Lesson Review

Use the following questions to help determine whether you have learned enough to move on to the next lesson. If you have difficulty answering these questions, review the material in this lesson before beginning the next lesson. You can find answers to these questions in the "Questions and Answers" section at the end of this chapter.

1. What are the four choices on the What To Back Up page of the Backup Or Restore Wizard and what does each choice allow you to do?

   _____

   _____

   _____

   _____

   _____

   _____

   _____

   _____

   _____

   _____

   _____

   _____

   _____

   _____

2. When should you select the Allow Only The Owner And The Administrator Access To The Backup Data And Any Backups Appended To This Media check box?

   _____

   _____

3. If your boss wants daily backups to occur at 1:00 A.M., what could you do to save yourself the trouble of having to go to the office each morning at 1:00 A.M. to do the backups?

   _____

   _____

   _____

4. If you do not have a tape drive, can you still perform backups? How?

   _____

   _____

   _____

5. Why should you e-mail or send a console message to users before you begin a backup?

_____

_____

_____

_____

_____

Lesson Summary

- Before beginning a backup, it is best to make sure that users have all files closed. If you are backing up to removable media, you might need to make sure that the media is properly prepared to receive a backup.

- The Backup Utility allows you to back up everything on the computer; to specify selected files, drives, or network data; or to back up only the System State data.

- The Backup Utility allows you to provide the target destination and the backup media or file name.

- The Backup Or Restore Wizard Advanced backup settings include the following options: selecting the type of backup operation to perform, verifying data after backup, using hardware compression, and scheduling the backup to run at a later time or to run at regularly scheduled times.

Lesson 3: Restoring Data

In this lesson, you learn about restoring data. The ability to restore corrupt or lost data is critical to all corporations and is the goal of all backup jobs. To ensure that you can successfully restore data, you should follow certain guidelines, such as keeping thorough documentation on all of your backup jobs and performing test restores on a regular basis.

After this lesson, you will be able to

- Prepare to restore data
- Select backup sets, files, and folders to restore
- Specify advanced restore settings

Estimated lesson time: 30 minutes

How to Prepare to Restore Data

To restore data, you must select the backup sets, files, and folders to restore. You can also specify additional settings based on your restore requirements. The Backup Or Restore Wizard helps you restore data.

When critical data is lost, you need to restore it quickly. Use the following guidelines to help prepare for restoring data:

- Base your restore strategy on the backup type that you used for the backup. If time is critical when you are restoring data, your restore strategy must ensure that the backup types that you choose for backups expedite the restore process. For example, use normal and differential backups so that you need to restore only the last normal backup and the last differential backup. If you have a reasonably fast backup device, you might want to perform daily normal backups so that you need to restore from only one backup set.

- Perform a trial restore periodically to verify that your backups are functioning correctly. A trial restore can uncover hardware problems that do not show up with software verifications. Restore the data to an alternate location, and then compare the restored data with the data on the original hard disk.

- Keep documentation for each backup job. Create and print a detailed backup log for each backup job, containing a record of all files and folders that were backed up. By using the backup log, you can quickly locate which piece of media contains the files that you need to restore without having to load the catalogs. A catalog is an index of the files and folders from a backup job that Windows XP Professional automatically creates and stores with the backup job and on the computer running the Backup Utility.

- Keep a record of multiple backup jobs in a calendar format that shows the days on which you perform the backup jobs. For each job, note the backup type and identify the storage that is used, such as a tape number or the name of the Iomega Zip disk. Then, if you need to restore data, you can easily review several weeks' worth of backup jobs to select which tape or disk to use.

How to Select Backup Sets, Files, and Folders to Restore

The first step in restoring data is to select the data to restore. You can select individual files and folders, an entire backup job, or a backup set, which is a collection of files or folders from one volume that you back up during a backup job. If you back up two volumes on a hard disk during a backup job, the job has two backup sets. You select the data to restore in the catalog.

To restore data, use the Restore Wizard, which you access through the Backup Utility, as follows:

1. In the Backup Or Restore Wizard, on the Backup Or Restore page, select Restore Files And Settings, and then click Next.

2. On the What To Restore page, expand the media type that contains the data that you want to restore. This can be either tape or file media.

3. Expand the appropriate media set until the data that you want to restore is visible. You can restore a backup set or specific files and folders.

4. Select the data that you want to restore, and then click Next.

   The Backup Or Restore Wizard displays the settings for the restore.

5. Do one of the following:

   ❑ Finish the restore process. If you choose to finish the restore job, during the restore, the Backup Or Restore Wizard requests verification for the source of the restore media and then performs the restore. During the restore, the Backup Or Restore Wizard displays status information about the restore.

   ❑ Specify advanced restore options. These options are covered in the following section.

How to Specify Advanced Restore Settings

The advanced settings in the Backup Or Restore Wizard vary, depending on the type of backup media from which you are restoring. Table 20-3 describes the advanced restore options.

Table 20-3   Advanced Restore Settings

Option	Description
Restore Files To	The target location for the data that you are restoring. The choices are as follows: ■ **Original Location** Replaces corrupted or lost data by copying files from the backup to their original location on the hard drive. ■ **Alternate Location** Restores files to a separate location from the original files but maintains the hierarchy of folders backed up. Use this option to restore an older version of a file or to perform a test restore. ■ **Single Folder** Consolidates the files from a tree structure into a single folder. For example, use this option if you want copies of specific files but do not want to restore the hierarchical structure of the files. If you select either an alternate location or a single directory, you must provide the path.
When Restoring Files That Already Exist On Your Computer	Determines whether Backup should overwrite existing files. The choices are as follows: ■ **Leave Existing Files (Recommended)** Prevents accidental overwriting of existing data. This setting is the default. ■ **Replace Existing Files If They Are Older Than The Backup Files** Verifies that the most recent copy exists on the computer. ■ **Replace Existing Files** The Backup Utility does not provide a confirmation message if it encounters a duplicate file name during the restore operation.
Select The Options You Want To Use	Determines whether Backup should restore security or special system files. The choices are as follows: ■ **Restore Security Settings** Applies the original permissions to files that you are restoring to an NTFS File System volume. Security settings include access permissions, audit entries, and ownership. This option is available only if you have backed up data from an NTFS volume and are restoring to an NTFS volume. ■ **Restore Junction Points, But Not The Folders And File Data They Reference** Restores junction points on your hard disk as well as the data that the junction points refer to. If you have any mounted drives, and you want to restore the data that mounted drives point to, select this check box. If you do not select this check box, the junction point is restored, but the data your junction point refers to might not be accessible. ■ **Preserve Existing Volume Mount Points** Prevents the operation from writing over any volume mount points that you have created on the partition or volume to which you are restoring data. This option is primarily applicable when you are restoring data to an entire drive or partition.

After you have finished the Backup Or Restore Wizard, the Backup Utility does the following:

- Prompts you to verify your selection of the source media to use to restore data. After the verification, the Backup Utility starts the restore process.

- Displays status information about the restore process. As with a backup process, you can choose to view the report (restore log) of the restore. It contains information about the restore, such as the number of files that have been restored and the duration of the restore process.

Practice: Restoring Data

In this practice, you restore the Backup1.bkf file that you created in Exercise 1 in the practice in Lesson 2 of this chapter.

Important   To complete this practice, you must have completed the practice in the previous lesson, or you must have some files you have backed up by using the Backup Utility that you can restore.

1. Log on with an account that has the permissions or rights to restore the file. For the purposes of this exercise, log on as a member of the Administrators group.

2. Click Start, point to All Programs, point to Accessories, point to System Tools, and then click Backup.

3. On the Welcome To The Backup Or Restore Wizard page, click Next.

4. On the Backup Or Restore page, click Restore Files And Settings, and then click Next.

   The Backup Or Restore Wizard displays the What To Restore page.

5. In the What To Restore box, expand the File node that you created.

   Notice that Backup1.bkf is listed.

6. Expand Backup1.bkf.

   Notice that drive C appears under Backup1.

7. Select the check box next to drive C, and then click Next.

   The Backup Or Restore Wizard displays the Completing The Backup Or Restore Wizard page. Notice that the file is being restored to its original location and that the existing files are not to be replaced.

8. Click Advanced.

   The Backup Or Restore Wizard displays the Where To Restore page.

9. In the Restore Files To list, select Alternate Location.

   The Backup Or Restore Wizard makes the Alternate Location box available.

10. In the Alternate Location text box, type **C:\Restored data** and then click Next.

    The Backup Or Restore Wizard displays the How To Restore page, prompting you to specify how to process duplicate files during the restore job.

11. Make sure that Leave Existing Files (Recommended) is selected, and then click Next.

12. On the Advanced Restore Options page, ensure that all check boxes are cleared, and then click Next.

13. Review the options that you specified on the Completing The Backup Or Restore Wizard page, and then click Finish to begin the restore process.

    The Backup Utility displays the Check Backup File Location dialog box, prompting you to supply or verify the name of the backup file that contains the folders and files to be restored.

14. Make sure that the file BACKUP1.BKF is entered in the Please Verify This Is The Correct Location For The Backup text box, and then click OK.

    The Backup Utility displays the Selection Information dialog box, indicating the estimated amount of data for, and the time to complete, the restore job. (This dialog box may appear very briefly because you are restoring only a single file.) The Backup Utility displays the Restore Progress dialog box, providing the status of the restore operation, statistics on estimated and actual amount of data that is being processed, the time that has elapsed, and the estimated time that remains for the restore operation.

15. Click Close.

Lesson Review

Use the following questions to help determine whether you have learned enough to move on to the next lesson. If you have difficulty answering these questions, review the material in this lesson before beginning the next lesson. You can find answers to these questions in the "Questions and Answers" section at the end of this chapter.

1. What is a trial restore, and why is it important that you perform it?

   _____

   _____

   _____

   _____

2. A(n) _____ is an index of the files and folders from a backup job that Windows XP Professional automatically creates and stores with the backup job and on the computer running the Backup Utility.

3. What is a backup set?

_____

_____

4. If you back up two volumes on a hard disk during a backup job, how many backup sets are created for the job?

_____

5. What are the three Advanced restore settings that allow you to specify how to restore files that already exist?

_____

_____

6. When do you use the Advanced restore setting Restore Security and when is it available?

_____

_____

_____

_____

Lesson Summary

- Before restoring data, you should ensure that you have access to the backup media. You should also document the restoration.

- The Backup Utility allows you to restore individual files and folders, an entire backup job, or a backup set.

- The Backup Utility's advanced settings for restoring data vary depending on the type of backup media from which you are restoring.

Lesson 4: Using the Automated System Recovery Wizard

In this lesson, you learn how to use the Automated System Recovery Wizard, which helps you back up your system partition so that you can restore it in case it is lost or damaged because of some type of disaster.

After this lesson, you will be able to

- Explain the use of the Automated System Recovery Wizard
- Use the Automated System Recovery Wizard to create an automated recovery disk
- Copy the System and Software files from backup by using Recovery Console

Estimated lesson time: 15 minutes

Overview of the Automated System Recovery Wizard

The Automated System Recovery Wizard is one of the three wizards provided by the Backup Utility (see Figure 20-8). Automated System Recovery (ASR) is intended to allow you to restore your computer after a major failure. The Automated System Recovery Wizard creates a backup in two parts:

- A floppy disk (referred to as a system recovery disk) that contains hard drive configuration information
- A full backup of your local system partition on tape or as a file located on a network server

After creating the system recovery disk and full backup, you can boot your computer by using the disk and run an automated system recovery process to restore your computer.

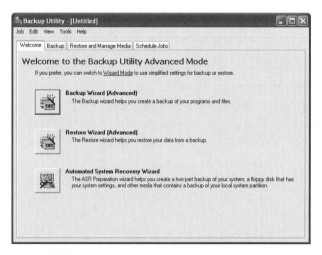

Figure 20-8   Use Advanced mode to access the Automated System Recovery Wizard.

How to Use the Automated System Recovery Wizard

To access the Automated System Recovery Wizard, click Start, point to All Programs, point to Accessories, point to System Tools, and then click Backup. On the Welcome To The Backup Or Restore Wizard page, click Advanced Mode.

To use the Automated System Recovery Wizard, use the following steps:

1. In the Advanced Mode window of the Backup Utility, click Automated System Recovery Wizard.

   The Backup Utility displays the Welcome To The Automated System Recovery Preparation Wizard page.

2. Click Next to continue.

   The Automated System Recovery Wizard begins and displays the Backup Destination page (see Figure 20-9). The options on the Backup Destination page are explained in Table 20-4.

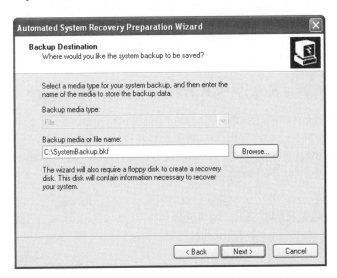

Figure 20-9   Enter the backup destination.

Table 20-4   Backup Destination

Option	Description
Backup Media Type	The target medium to use, such as a tape or file. A file can be located on any disk-based media, including a hard disk, a shared network folder, or a removable disk, such as an Iomega Zip disk.
Backup Media Or File Name	The location where the Backup Utility will store the data. For a tape, enter the tape name. For a file, enter the path for the backup file.

3. Select the appropriate media type and backup media name or file name, and then click Next.

   The Automated System Recovery Wizard verifies the information that you entered and displays the Completing The Automated System Recovery Preparation Wizard page.

4. Review the information on the Completing The Automated System Recovery Preparation Wizard page, and then click Finish.

   The Automated System Recovery Wizard makes a backup of your system files. This could take an hour or more.

5. When prompted, insert a floppy disk in your floppy disk drive.

6. When the backup completes, click Report to read the report. When you finish reviewing the report, close Notepad.

7. Click Close to close the Backup Progress dialog box, and then close the Backup Utility.

If you need to restore your system partition, you can use the floppy disk created by the Automated System Recovery Wizard. The backup of your local system partition on tape or as a file must be available to be restored. You would then use the Backup Or Restore Wizard to restore your data and applications.

How to Recover Important Registry Keys by Using Recovery Console

In Chapter 4, "Modifying and Troubleshooting the Startup Process," you learned how to install and start the Recovery Console, and also how to use the Recovery Console to help repair a Windows installation. If your recovery efforts do not allow you to start Windows, you can use the Recovery Console to replace two important system files:

■ The System file is used by Windows XP Professional during startup to create the HKEY_LOCAL_MACHINE\SYSTEM Registry key, which stores application settings that apply to all users of the computer.

■ The Software file is used during startup to create the HKEY_LOCAL_MACHINE\ SOFTWARE Registry key, which contains information about the local computer, including hardware data (such as bus type, system memory, and device drivers) and operating system data (such as startup control parameters).

In fact, if you are troubleshooting a computer that will not start, you should try to replace these files before going to the trouble of restoring the system using a recovery disk. The system and software files are stored in %systemroot%\System32\config. A backup copy is stored in the %systemroot%\repair folder, and this backup is refreshed each time you back up the System State data on the computer. You can use the Recovery Console to replace the current version of each file with the backed up copy.

When restoring the system or software files from backup with Recovery Console, you should replace one file at a time to see whether it fixes the problem you are having. If replacing both files does not fix the problem, you should then try to restore the computer using Automated System Recovery.

To replace the system or software file in the Recovery Console, use these steps:

1. Start your computer by using Recovery Console (see Chapter 4 for instructions on how to do this).

2. At the Recovery Console prompt, locate the config folder by typing **cd system32\config**.

3. Create backups of the current system or software file by typing **copy system** *<drive:\path\filename>* or **copy software** *<drive:\path\filename>*, where *<drive:\path\filename>* is the folder in which you want to store the backups.

4. Type **dir**.

5. Look through the list of files in the config folder and see whether any other files exist that start with "system" or "software" (such as System.sav). If you find such files, back them up to the same backup folder by using the copy command.

6. Replace the current system or software file by typing **copy ..\..\repair\system** (for the system file) or **copy ..\..\repair\softwar**e (for the software file).

    The Recovery Console displays the Answer The Overwrite System? (Yes/No/All): message.

7. Press Y, and then press ENTER.

8. Restart the computer.

Caution   The system and software files in the repair folder might not be current. If the files are not current, you might need to update drivers, reinstall applications and service packs, and perform other configuration to bring your computer up-to-date.

Lesson Review

Use the following questions to help determine whether you have learned enough to move on to the next lesson. If you have difficulty answering these questions, review the material in this lesson before beginning the next lesson. You can find answers to these questions in the "Questions and Answers" section at the end of this chapter.

1. What four wizards does the Backup Utility provide access to?

_____

_____

_____

2. What two things does the Automated System Recovery Wizard create during a backup?

_____

_____

3. What two pieces of information do you have to supply to the Automated System Recovery Wizard?

_____

Lesson Summary

- The Automated System Recovery Wizard creates a system recover disk (on a floppy disk) that contains your hard drive configuration, and a backup of your local system partition on tape or as a file.

- To start the Automated System Recovery Wizard, you must enable the Advanced mode of the Backup Utility. Because the Automated System Recovery Wizard includes a full backup, the process can take an hour or longer.

- The system and software files are stored in %systemroot%\System32\config. A backup copy is stored in the %systemroot%\repair folder, and this backup is refreshed each time you back up the System State data on the computer. You can use the Recovery Console to replace the current version of each file with the backed up copy.

Case Scenario Exercise

In this exercise, you will read a scenario about backing up a user's computer and then answer the questions that follow. If you have difficulty completing this work, review the material in this chapter before beginning the next chapter. You can find answers to these questions in the "Questions and Answers" section at the end of this chapter.

Scenario

You are an administrator working for a company named Blue Yonder Airlines, a company that rents charter airplanes to businesses across the country. You are working on a computer that belongs to Andrew, a user in the sales department. Like other employees in the department, Andrew saves all his documents to his local computer in the My Documents folder. Andrew keeps a relatively small number of files on his computer—about 225 MB. However, each user must back up data to a file server on the network if they want their documents to be included in the company's backup system. Your task today is to configure a nightly backup solution for Andrew.

Questions

1. Andrew wants to be able to restore his data as quickly and easily as possible if the time comes. Which type of backup would you suggest for Andrew's computer? Why?

_____

_____

_____

_____

_____

_____

2. If you want to minimize the time it takes to back up Andrew's computer instead of the time it takes to restore the data, which type(s) of backup would you recommend?

_____

_____

_____

_____

_____

_____

3. Andrew expresses his concern about being able to restore his system to working order if disaster strikes. What could you do to ensure that Andrew could recover the computer in the event of a major system failure?

_____

_____

_____

_____

Troubleshooting Lab

You are an administrator for a company named Contoso, Ltd., a manufacturer of fine dinnerware. You are working with a user named Ariane. Ariane's computer is configured to run a normal backup of her data each Saturday and to run an incremental backup every other evening. Backups are stored on a network file server. You are troubleshooting an intermittent hardware error on Ariane's computer. Before you begin troubleshooting, you want to create a backup of Ariane's data. Which type of backup should you perform to ensure that you do not interfere with the regular nightly back-ups already scheduled on Andrew's computer? Why?

_____

_____

_____

Chapter Summary

■ The Windows Backup utility provides a simple interface for backing up and restoring data. The Backup utility offers two modes: Wizard mode, which steps you through a backup or restore, and Advanced mode, which provides a more traditional backup interface and access to more options.

■ Before backing up data, it is best to make sure that users have closed all their files. To back up data, you can use the Backup And Recovery Wizard to select the files that you want to back up, the location to create the backup file, and any advanced backup options that you want to use (such as verifying files after they are backed up). You can also schedule backup jobs to occur at a later time or at regular intervals.

■ To ensure that you can successfully restore data, you should follow certain guidelines, such as keeping thorough documentation on all your backup jobs and performing test restores on a regular basis.

■ The Automated System Recovery Wizard creates a system recovery disk (on a floppy disk), which contains your hard drive configuration and a backup of your local system partition on tape or as a file.

Exam Highlights

Before taking the exam, review the key points and terms that are presented in this chapter. You need to know this information.

Key Points

■ To back up all data on a computer regardless of the assigned permissions to that data, you must use a user account that has the Backup Files And Directories user right assigned. To restore data, you must use a user account that has the Restore Files And Directories user right assigned. Members of the Administrators and Backup Operators local groups have these rights by default.

■ Backup allows you to back up data from or to shared folders on remote computers. Backup cannot write backup files directly to a CD-ROM or DVD.

■ Performing regular normal backups takes the most time during the backup phase but the least time and effort during the restore phase. Using a normal backup plus incremental backups takes the least time during the backup phase but takes the most time and effort during the restore phase. Using a normal backup plus differential backups takes more time to back up than using incremental backups (although less time than using only normal backups) but takes less time during the restore phase than using incremental backups.

Key Terms

Automated System Recovery   A feature of the Backup utility that creates a system recovery disk and performs a full normal backup of the system partition so that you can recover your computer in the event of a major failure.

Backup   A Windows utility that allows you to back up and restore data and to create a system recovery disk.

backup job   A single process of backing up data.

Backup Or Restore Wizard   A wizard that provides a simple, step-based interface for backing up or restoring data.

copy backup   A backup type in which all selected files and folders are backed up, regardless of their marker. During a copy backup, markers are not changed.

differential backup   A backup type in which only selected files and folders that have a marker are backed up. During a differential backup, markers are not cleared so that files are still backed up if they have changed since the last normal backup.

incremental backup   A backup type in which only selected files and folders that have a marker are backed up. During an incremental backup, markers are cleared so that the files are not backed up during subsequent incremental backups unless the files change.

markers   Archive attributes that mark a file as having been backed up. During incremental or differential backups, markers are used to determine whether a file has changed since the last backup.

normal backup   A backup type in which all selected files and folders are backed up, regardless of their marker. During a normal backup, all files are marked as having been backed up.

System State   Configuration information that includes the Windows Registry and important configuration files.

Questions and Answers

Lesson 1 Review

Page
20-12

1. How do you access the Backup Or Restore Wizard?

   To access the Backup Or Restore Wizard, on the Start menu, point to All Programs, point to Accessories, point to System Tools, and then click Backup; or, on the Start menu, click Run, type ntbackup, and then click OK.

2. What two operations can you perform using the Backup Or Restore Wizard?

   You use the Backup Or Restore Wizard to back up all or a portion of the files on your computer or network (using the Back Up Files And Settings option) and to restore data that you have backed up (using the Restore Files And Settings option).

3. What is the primary goal of backing up data?

   The primary goal of backing up data is to be able to restore that data if necessary.

4. If you want to perform a backup but do not want to clear markers or affect other backup types, you should perform a(n) _____ backup.

   Copy

5. During a(n) _____ backup, only selected files and folders that have a marker are backed up, but the backup does not clear markers. If you performed two of these backups in a row on a file and nothing changed in the file, the entire file would be backed up each time.

   Differential

6. How can you change the default settings for backup-and-restores for all backup-and-restore operations by using the Backup Utility?

   You can change the default settings for the Backup Utility for all backup-and-restore jobs by changing the settings on the tabs in the Options dialog box. To access the Options dialog box, on the Welcome To The Backup Or Restore Wizard page, click Advanced Mode. On the Tools menu, click Options.

7. You performed a normal backup on Monday. For the remaining days of the week, you want to back up only files and folders that have changed since the previous day. Which backup type do you select? Why?

   Incremental. The incremental backup type backs up changes since the last markers were set and then clears the markers. Thus, for Tuesday through Friday, you back up only changes since the previous day.

Lesson 2 Review

Page
20-23

1. What are the four choices on the What To Back Up page of the Backup Or Restore Wizard and what does each choice allow you to do?

The first choice is My Documents And Settings. Selecting this option backs up certain areas that pertain to the currently logged on user. All of the files located in the My Documents folder, your Favorites folder, desktop items, and cookies are backed up in this option.

The second choice is Everyone's Documents And Settings. Selecting this option backs up each user's My Documents folder, Favorites folder, desktop items, and cookies.

The third choice is All Information On This Computer. Selecting this option backs up all files on the computer except those files that the Backup Utility excludes by default, such as certain power management files.

The fourth choice is Let Me Choose What To Back Up. Selecting this option allows you to select the files and folders you want to back up, including files and folders on the computer where you run the Backup Utility and any shared file or folder on the network.

2. When should you select the Allow Only The Owner And The Administrator Access To The Backup Data And Any Backups Appended To This Media check box?

You should select this check box when you want to minimize the risk of unauthorized access to your data.

3. If your boss wants daily backups to occur at 1:00 A.M., what could you do to save yourself the trouble of having to go to the office each morning at 1:00 A.M. to do the backups?

You can use the Backup Or Restore Wizard to schedule the backup to occur automatically by clicking Later on the When To Back Up page of the Backup Or Restore Wizard and specifying that the backup should occur daily at 1:00 A.M.

4. If you do not have a tape drive, can you still perform backups? How?

Yes. You can use a tape or file as the target medium for the backup, and a file can be located on any disk-based media, including a hard disk, a shared network folder, or a removable disk, such as an Iomega Zip drive.

5. Why should you e-mail or send a console message to users before you begin a backup?

You should notify users to close files before you begin backing up data because the backup might not contain the correct data if users are still editing files while you perform the backup. Rather than skip the files that are being written to, the Backup Utility will back up these files unless you select the Disable Volume Shadow Copy check box. It is best to have all users log off before doing a backup.

Lesson 3 Review

Page 20-30

1. What is a trial restore, and why is it important that you perform it?

A trial restore involves restoring a backup to an alternate location and comparing the restored data with the data on the original hard disk. You should perform trial restores to verify that the Backup Utility is backing up your files correctly and that any hardware problems show up with software verifications.

2. A(n) _____ is an index of the files and folders from a backup job that Windows XP Professional automatically creates and stores with the backup job and on the computer running the Backup Utility.

Catalog

3. What is a backup set?

A backup set is a collection of files or folders from one volume that you back up during a backup job.

4. If you back up two volumes on a hard disk during a backup job, how many backup sets are created for the job?

Two

5. What are the three Advanced restore settings that allow you to specify how to restore files that already exist?

Leave Existing Files (Recommended), Replace Existing Files If They Are Older Than The Backup Files, and Replace Existing Files

6. When do you use the Advanced restore setting Restore Security and when is it available?

The Restore Security setting applies the original permissions, including access permissions, audit entries, and ownership, to files that you are restoring to an NTFS volume. The Restore Security option is available only if you have backed up data from an NTFS volume and are restoring to an NTFS volume.

Lesson 4 Review

Page 20-35

1. What four wizards does the Backup Utility provide access to?

The Backup Utility provides access to the Backup And Restore Wizard, the Backup Wizard (Advanced), the Restore Wizard (Advanced), and the Automated System Recovery Wizard.

2. What two things does the Automated System Recovery Wizard create during a backup?

The Automated System Recovery Wizard creates a floppy disk containing your hard drive configuration and a backup of your local system partition.

3. What two pieces of information do you have to supply to the Automated System Recovery Wizard?

The appropriate media type and the backup media or file name

Case Scenario Exercise

Page
20-36

1. Andrew wants to be able to restore his data as quickly and easily as possible if the time comes. Which type of backup would you suggest for Andrew's computer?

   Because Andrew is backing up each night and will be backing up over the network, the speed of the backup is not an issue. You should configure Andrew's computer to perform a normal backup each night to the file server. This way, Andrew will need to restore only one backup if there is a problem, instead of having to restore a normal backup and then a differential backup (or multiple incremental backups).

2. If you want to minimize the time it takes to back up Andrew's computer instead of the time it takes to restore the data, which type(s) of backup would you recommend?

   In this case, you should recommend that Andrew's computer perform a full normal backup occasionally (once each week is recommended) and then perform an incremental backup each day that backs up only the data that has changed since the last incremental backup. When it comes time to restore data, though, Andrew would have to first restore the most recent full backup, and then restore each incremental backup in turn.

3. Andrew expresses his concern about being able to restore his system to working order if disaster strikes. What could you do to ensure that Andrew could recover the computer in the event of a major system failure?

   You could use the Automated System Recovery Wizard on Andrew's computer to create a system recovery disk and a full system backup. This would allow Andrew to recover his computer in the event of a major failure.

Troubleshooting Lab

Page
20-37

You are an administrator for a company named Contoso, Ltd., a manufacturer of fine dinnerware. You are working with a user named Ariane. Ariane's computer is configured to run a normal backup of her data each Saturday and to run an incremental backup every other evening. Backups are stored on a network file server. You are troubleshooting an intermittent hardware error on Ariane's computer. Before you begin troubleshooting, you want to create a backup of Ariane's data. Which type of backup should you perform to ensure that you do not interfere with the regular nightly backups already scheduled on Andrew's computer?

   You should perform a copy backup on Ariane's computer. A copy backup does not reset the Backup attribute on files and so would not interfere with the regular nightly backups.

Part II
Prepare for the Exam

21 Installing Windows XP Professional (1.0)

Microsoft Windows XP Professional is designed to be deployed to a wide variety of environments, from stand-alone home computers to enterprise networks with thousands of computers. Because different environments have varying needs during deployment, Windows XP provides several different deployment methods. Home users and small businesses need a quick, user-friendly installation procedure. For these users, an attended installation is the most efficient. Enterprises might need to deploy hundreds or thousands of computers at a time, while minimizing the cost of that deployment. Computer manufacturers often build thousands of Windows XP Professional computers every day, with dozens of different hardware and software configurations. For these users, Windows XP provides several different unattended installation technologies, including Remote Installation Services (RIS), the System Preparation Tool (Sysprep.exe), and unattended answer files.

Upgrade scenarios are even more varied than new installation scenarios. As with new installations, many users need to upgrade many computers as efficiently as possible. There are two additional levels of complexity, however. Computers might have one of several different operating systems, including Windows NT Workstation 4.0, Windows 95, Windows 98, Windows Me, and Windows 2000 Professional. Additionally, users have documents, applications, and customized settings that they need access to after the upgrade has been completed.

The vast majority of new installations and upgrades complete without problems. However, when things do go wrong, you must understand how to resolve installation problems. Your job is not done when you complete the installation or upgrade of Windows XP, either. You must activate Windows XP, apply a service pack (or packs), and install critical updates to reduce the risk of security vulnerabilities or other problems.

This objective domain assesses your ability to prepare for and perform both attended (that is, manual) and unattended (automated) installations. You must determine whether existing operating systems and applications will be upgraded or will be removed and replaced with new installations. There are several methods for automated installations of Windows XP Professional, and you must be familiar with them all. Your ability to deploy service packs, diagnose installation failures, and correct installation failures will also be assessed. You will do a number of case studies that check your ability to identify the appropriate installation method when presented with detailed information about various computing environments. You will also need to understand the difference between activation and registration of Windows XP Professional and how to complete the activation process through all available methods.

Tested Skills and Suggested Practices

To successfully master the Installing Windows XP Professional objective domain on the *Installing, Configuring, and Administering Microsoft Windows XP Professional* exam, complete the following tasks.

> **Important**   For the following task, you should complete at least Practice 1. If you want a more well-rounded understanding of installation options, you should also complete Practice 2. If you want hands-on experience with every aspect of the exam and you have the extra lab resources needed to do Practice 3, complete Practice 3 as well.

■ Performing and troubleshooting an attended installation of Windows XP Professional.

❑ Practice 1: Become familiar with the various stages of the installation process by installing Windows XP Professional on computers with no operating system.

❑ Practice 2: Install Windows XP Professional on a computer running MS-DOS by using the 16-bit installation program (Winnt.exe).

❑ Practice 3: Install Windows XP Professional on a new computer, and then attempt to add it to an Active Directory service domain by using an account that is a member only of the Domain users group. Then, modify domain Group Policy settings until you can use the same account to successfully add the computer to the domain.

> **Important**   For the following task, you should complete at least Practice 1. If you want a more well-rounded understanding of installation options, you should also complete Practices 2 and 3. If you want hands-on experience with every aspect of the exam and you have the extra lab resources needed to do Practices 4 and 5, complete those practices as well.

■ Performing and troubleshooting an unattended installation of Windows XP Professional.

❑ Practice 1: Learn the command-line switches available with Winnt32.exe.

❑ Practice 2: Launch Setup Manager and create an answer file for an unattended installation of a single computer. Run Setup Manager again, but create a uniqueness database file (UDF) for automating the installation of Windows XP Professional on multiple computers. Verify that the answer file and UDF file created by Setup Manager work by running a Windows XP Professional installation with them.

❑ Practice 3: Download the latest Dynamic Update package from Microsoft, and configure a shared folder on your network with the Dynamic Update files. Perform an unattended installation that retrieves the Dynamic Update files from your local share rather than from Microsoft's Web site.

❑ Practice 4: Learn about cloning Windows XP Professional computers by using the SysPrep utility. If you have non-Microsoft imaging software available, use the image created to install Windows XP Professional.

❑ Practice 5: Build an RIS infrastructure by installing and configuring a Windows 2000 Server with RIS and Dynamic Host Configuration Protocol (DHCP). Build a Windows XP Professional system, use the Remote Installation Preparation Wizard (Riprep.exe) to prepare the system, and then use non-Microsoft software to create an image of the system. Upload the image to the RIS server. Create a Remote Boot Disk or use a Preboot Execution Environment (PXE)–capable computer to boot to the network, and then run a RIS-based installation. If you do not have access to non-Microsoft imaging software, you can copy the Windows XP Professional installation CD-ROM to the RIS server (the setup process will be similar to a normal CD-ROM-based installation).

Important   For the following task, you should complete at least Practice 1. If you want a more well-rounded understanding of installation options, you should also complete Practice 2. If you want hands-on experience with every aspect of the exam and you have the extra lab resources needed to do Practice 3, complete Practice 3 as well.

■ Upgrading from a previous version of Windows to Windows XP Professional.

❑ Practice 1: Perform upgrades from Windows 2000 Professional and Windows Me to Windows XP Professional. The simplest way to do this is to insert the Windows XP Professional installation CD-ROM into the target computer's CD-ROM drive and follow the prompts to upgrade the operating system. You can also run Winnt32.exe from the \I386 directory of the CD-ROM.

Tip   You probably do not have Windows NT 4.0 or Windows Me running on any computers that you can upgrade just for the sake of learning. (This is okay because most people do not have them.) I use Microsoft Virtual PC. I install earlier versions of Windows on a virtual PC, back up the virtual hard disk file, and then perform the Windows XP upgrade process. Later, I can return to my backup file if I want to try the upgrade by using a different technique. You can run multiple Virtual PCs simultaneously, and have the virtual computers communicate with each other over a network. Use this process to create a Windows Server 2003 Active Directory. Although this exam focuses on Windows XP, you absolutely must understand how changes to Group Policy settings affect what administrators and users can do on Windows XP computers.

❏ Practice 2: Use the Files And Settings Transfer Wizard to migrate the settings from one computer to another. The originating computer can be running Windows XP Professional, Windows 98, Windows Me, Windows NT Workstation 4.0, or Windows 2000 Professional; the destination computer must be running Windows XP Professional.

❏ Practice 3: Use the User State Migration Tool (USMT) to implement an automated migration of a user's settings from one computer to another. Customize the USMT process by making some changes to the .inf files used by the tool.

Important For the following task, you should complete at least Practices 1 and 2. If you want a more well-rounded understanding of installation options, you should also complete Practice 3. If you want hands-on experience with every aspect of the exam and you have the extra lab resources needed to do Practices 4 and 5, complete those practices as well.

■ Performing post-installation updates and product activation.

❏ Practice 1: Download and install the network package of the latest service pack for Windows XP Professional. Extract the package and run Update.exe with the -? switch, and then review the available command-line switches. Use the appropriate command-line switches to perform an unattended installation. Then, uninstall the service pack by using Add Or Remove Programs.

❏ Practice 2: Using an unpatched Windows XP Professional installation, use Internet Explorer to visit the Microsoft Windows Update site at *http://windowsupdate.microsoft.com/*. Choose to perform a custom installation of the available patches and explore each of the available updates to understand what changes they make. Bring your Windows XP installation up-to-date by installing the latest service packs and all available critical updates.

❏ Practice 3: Use the Microsoft Baseline Security Analyzer, available from *http://www.microsoft.com/technet/security/tools/mbsahome.mspx*, to identify any computers on your network that are missing critical updates.

❏ Practice 4: Install Microsoft Software Update Services (SUS), available from *http://www.microsoft.com/sus/*—on a Windows Server 2003 computer. Configure Automatic Updates on a Windows XP Professional computer to retrieve updates directly from SUS. Be familiar with how to configure Automatic Updates for Windows XP Professional stand-alone computers and members of an Active Directory domain.

❏ Practice 5: If you have time, install Windows XP Professional on a computer, but do not activate it. Wait until the 30-day grace period expires, and note the limited functionality that Windows XP provides you until you have activated it.

> **Important**   For the following task, you should complete at least Practice 1. If you want a more well-rounded understanding of installation options, you should also complete Practice 2. If you want hands-on experience with every aspect of the exam, complete Practice 3 as well.

- Troubleshooting failed installations.

  ❑ Practice 1: Locate and examine the log files created during installation in the computer's operating system folder (%systemroot%).

  ❑ Practice 2: Enable the highest level of error reporting during an install by using the /debug switch with Winnt32.exe. Examine the log file after installation is complete. The default location and filename is %systemroot%/Winnt32.log.

  ❑ Practice 3: Visit computer hardware vendors' Web sites and locate their support section. Study basic input/output system (BIOS) update procedures for motherboards, disk controllers, and other types of hardware that commonly have BIOS chips onboard.

Further Reading

This section lists supplemental readings by objective. We recommend that you study these sources thoroughly before taking exam 70-270.

Objective 1.1   "Deploying Windows XP Part I: Planning" by Microsoft Corporation (available online at *http://www.microsoft.com/technet/prodtechnol/winxppro/deploy/depovg/depxpi.mspx*).

"Deploying Windows XP Part II: Implementing" by Microsoft Corporation (available online at *http://www.microsoft.com/technet/prodtechnol/winxppro/deploy/depovg/depxpii.mspx*).

Microsoft Corporation. *Microsoft Windows XP Professional Resource Kit Documentation*. Redmond, WA: Microsoft Press, 2001. Read Chapter 1, "Planning Deployment," for an explanation of how to plan and prepare for deploying Windows XP Professional to meet the business needs of various types of organizations. Read Chapter 4, "Supporting Installations," for additional setup information. In particular, read the first two sections, "The Setup Process" and "Support Tools" (available online at *http://www.microsoft.com/resources/documentation/Windows/XP/all/reskit/en-us/prpt_pt1_fmjb.asp*).

Objective 1.2   "Deploying and Supporting Windows XP: Microsoft's IT Group shares its experiences" by Microsoft Corporation (available online at *http://www.microsoft.com/technet/itsolutions/msit/deploy/wxpdpsp.mspx*).

Read *Microsoft Windows XP Corporate Deployment Tools User's Guide* (DEPLOY.CHM), located on the installation CD-ROM or DVD in \Support\Tools\Deploy.cab. This file, which is formatted as a Windows Help file, contains extensive information about automating the deployment of Windows XP Professional in enterprise environments.

"Remote Operating System Installation" by Microsoft Corporation (available online at *http://www.microsoft.com/technet/prodtechnol/windows2000serv/deploy/depopt/remoteos.mspx*).

Microsoft Corporation. *Microsoft Windows XP Professional Resource Kit Documentation*. Redmond, WA: Microsoft Press, 2001. Read Chapter 2, "Automating and Customizing Installations." This chapter gives detailed information about creating unique automated installation routines (available online at *http://www.microsoft.com/resources/documentation/Windows/XP/all/reskit/en-us/prpt_pt1_fmjb.asp*).

Objective 1.3 "Upgrade or Wipe-and-Load" by Microsoft Corporation (available online at *http://www.microsoft.com/technet/prodtechnol/winxppro/deploy/upwpload.mspx*).

"Step-by-Step Guide to Migrating Files and Settings" by Microsoft Corporation (available online at *http://www.microsoft.com/technet/prodtechnol/winxppro/deploy/mgrtfset.mspx*).

"User State Migration in Windows XP" by Microsoft Corporation (available online at *http://www.microsoft.com/technet/prodtechnol/winxppro/deploy/usermigr.mspx*).

"Deploying Windows XP—Application Compatibility" by Microsoft Corporation (available online at *http://www.microsoft.com/technet/prodtechnol/winxppro/deploy/depxpapp.mspx*).

Microsoft Corporation. *Microsoft Windows XP Professional Resource Kit Documentation*. Redmond, WA: Microsoft Press, 2001. Read Chapter 1, "Planning Deployment." Focus on the third section, "Assessing Your Current Configuration" (available online at *http://www.microsoft.com/resources/documentation/Windows/XP/all/reskit/en-us/prpt_pt1_fmjb.asp*).

Objective 1.4 "Inside Update.exe—The Package Installer for Windows and Windows Components" by Microsoft Corporation (available online at *http://www.microsoft.com/technet/prodtechnol/windowsserver2003/deployment/winupdate.mspx*).

"Patch Management Process" by Microsoft Corporation (available online at *http://www.microsoft.com/technet/security/guidance/secmod193.mspx*).

"Deploying Updates with Windows Update and Automatic Updates" by Microsoft Corporation (available online at *http://www.microsoft.com/smallbusiness/gtm/securityguidance/articles/dep_patches_wu_au.mspx*).

"Software Update Services 2.0 Overview" by Microsoft Corporation (available online at *http://www.microsoft.com/technet/security/guidance/sus_2_0_overview.mspx*).

Microsoft Corporation. *Microsoft Windows XP Professional Resource Kit Documentation*. Redmond, WA: Microsoft Press, 2001. Read Chapter 1, "Planning Deployment." Focus on the third section, "Assessing Your Current Configuration." Read Chapter 4, "Supporting Installations." This chapter provides additional setup information. Read the third and fourth sections: "Installing Service Packs and Hotfixes" and "Uninstalling a Service Pack or Hotfix" (available online at *http://www.microsoft.com/resources/documentation/Windows/XP/all/reskit/en-us/prpt_pt1_fmjb.asp*).

Objective 1.5   "Windows Server 2003 Troubleshooting Disks and File Systems" by Tony Northrup (available online at *http://www.microsoft.com/technet/prodtechnol/windowsserver2003/operations/system/sptchtro.mspx*). The information applies equally well to Windows XP.

"Windows Server 2003 Tools for Troubleshooting" by Tony Northrup (available online at *http://www.microsoft.com/technet/prodtechnol/windowsserver2003/operations/system/sptcctol.mspx*). The information applies equally well to Windows XP.

Microsoft Corporation. *Microsoft Windows XP Professional Resource Kit Documentation*. Redmond, WA: Microsoft Press, 2001. Read Chapter 4, "Supporting Installations." This chapter provides additional setup information. Read the fifth and sixth sections: "Troubleshooting Windows XP Professional Setup" and "Additional Resources" (available online at *http://www.microsoft.com/resources/documentation/Windows/XP/all/reskit/en-us/prpt_pt1_fmjb.asp*).

Objective 1.1

Perform and Troubleshoot an Attended Installation of Windows XP Professional

You must prepare for installing Windows XP Professional by verifying that the target computer's hardware and software are compatible with Windows XP Professional. Although it is not mandatory, all hardware should appear in the **Windows Catalog** (previously known as the Hardware Compatibility List). You can view the current version of the Windows Catalog at *http://www.microsoft.com/windows/catalog/.*

Even if you have verified that all the hardware in the target computer is compatible with Windows XP Professional, there is a good chance that the CD-ROM does not contain drivers for hardware released after Windows XP was first released. If you have Internet access and are launching Setup from an existing version of Windows, the Windows XP Professional setup routine can attempt to download the latest installation files, including updated drivers, by using Dynamic Update.

If the computer has an existing operating system, you must know how to configure Windows XP for dual booting, how to upgrade the operating system, and how to perform a clean installation. Understand that Setup is launched from one of two programs: Winnt.exe when running a 16-bit operating system such as DOS 6.22 or Windows 3.*x*, or Winnt32.exe when running a 32-bit operating system such as Windows 2000 Professional or Windows Me. If the computer is to be part of a domain, you must know how to add the computer as a domain member and which domain privileges are required.

To successfully answer questions in this objective, you must be adept at manually installing Windows XP Professional on a range of computer systems, in both workgroup and domain environments. You must know how to prepare for the installation of Windows XP Professional and the phases of installation. You must also understand the differences between the various installation methods and how to use each method to install Windows XP Professional.

Objective 1.1 Questions

1. You want to perform a clean install of Windows XP Professional on a computer running Windows NT Workstation 3.51. The computer contains a Pentium II processor running at 350 MHz, 48 MB of RAM, a 4 GB hard disk formatted as two 2 GB FAT partitions (drive C has 1.5 GB of free space, whereas drive D has 900 MB of free space), a 24x CD-ROM drive, a mouse, a keyboard, and a Super Video Graphics Array (SVGA) video subsystem. All the hardware is in the Windows Catalog. Your desired results are to

- Replace the existing operating system with Windows XP Professional.

- Choose a file system that will enable you to ensure the greatest level of security possible.

- Rejoin the computer to the Active Directory domain.

- Retain the existing applications and user settings.

You perform the following tasks:

- Increase the amount of RAM to 128 MB.

- While logged on to the existing installation of Windows NT Workstation 3.51, run Winnt32.exe from the Windows XP Professional installation CD-ROM and choose to perform a New Installation.

- Answer the prompts during installation. When prompted, type the appropriate domain name.

Which goals does your proposed approach provide? Choose two correct answers.

A. Ensures that the computer meets the minimum hardware requirements for running Windows XP Professional

B. Replaces the existing installation of Windows NT Workstation 3.51 with a new installation of Windows XP Professional

C. Chooses a file system that enables you to ensure the greatest level of security possible

D. Rejoins the computer to the domain

E. Retains the existing applications and user settings

2. You want to perform a clean install of a Windows XP Professional computer running Windows NT Workstation 3.51. The computer contains a Pentium III processor running at 700 MHz, 32 MB of RAM, a 4 GB hard disk, a 24x CD-ROM drive, a mouse, a keyboard, and an SVGA video subsystem. The hard disk is formatted as two 2 GB partitions, both formatted with the FAT file system with 650 MB of free space. All the hardware is in the Windows Catalog. Your desired results are to

- Replace the existing operating system with Windows XP Professional.

- Choose a file system that enables you to ensure the greatest level of security possible.

- Rejoin the computer to the domain.

- Retain the existing applications and user settings.

- Allow for more efficient use of hard disk space by creating a single 4 GB partition.

You perform the following tasks:

- While logged on to the existing installation of Windows NT Workstation 3.51, run Winnt32.exe from the Windows XP Professional installation CD-ROM and choose to perform a New Installation.

- Answer the prompts during installation, but make certain to convert the existing boot partition to NTFS.

- When prompted, type the appropriate domain name, and then add the computer account to the domain by providing logon credentials for an account belonging to the Domain Administrators group.

- After Setup completes, open the Computer Management console, and then open the Disk Management snap-in and perform the appropriate actions to convert the second partition to NTFS.

Which goals does your proposal achieve? Choose three correct answers.

A. Ensures that the computer meets the minimum hardware requirements for running Windows XP Professional

B. Replaces the existing installation of Windows NT Workstation 3.51 with a new installation of Windows XP Professional

C. Chooses a file system that enables you to ensure the greatest level of security possible

D. Rejoins the computer to the domain

E. Retains the existing applications and user settings

F. Allows for more efficient use of hard disk space by creating a single 4 GB partition

3.   An account executive on your company's outside sales team just returned from a major networking conference. His laptop was stolen from him while he was passing through airport security. You have a new replacement computer available. His data was backed up to a network server before he left for the conference, so it is possible to restore a recent copy of his data to the new computer. You are more concerned that the thief might have compromised proprietary and sensitive information. You want to safeguard your firm's confidential data against potential theft in the future.

Which of the following steps do you take to protect the account executive's replacement computer when you install Windows XP Professional on it? Choose two correct answers.

A.   You configure the computer so that the Welcome Screen is enabled.

B.   During the installation of Windows XP Professional, you specify the FAT32 file system for the single partition on the hard disk.

C.   You add the computer to the corporate domain and issue user certificates for Secure/Multipurpose Internet Mail Extensions (S/MIME) and EFS from the Active Directory–integrated Certificate Services Certificate Authority. You install the certificates onto a smart card, and then instruct the user to keep the smart card in his wallet when not in use.

D.   Using EFS and the user's logon credentials, you encrypt the user's My Documents folders and other folders where the user stores data. You also enable S/MIME in e-mail client software and teach the user how to use both features.

E.   You install the Recovery Console and configure it for automatic administrative logon.

4.   Your current laptop computer is running Windows XP Professional, but you feel that its performance is unacceptable due to the speed of its central processing unit (CPU) and the amount of RAM installed. You acquire a new computer with significantly more RAM and a much faster CPU to replace your existing system. Which tool can you use to migrate your data and user settings from the old computer to the new one? Choose the correct answer.

A.   Setup Wizard

B.   SysPrep

C.   File And Settings Transfer Wizard

D.   RIS

5. Which of the following attended installation procedures best minimizes the risk of a successful network attack on a new Windows XP Professional installation? Choose the correct answer.

    A. Install Windows XP Professional from the installation CD-ROM. Connect to the Internet and activate Windows XP. Configure Automatic Updates to download and install updates without user intervention.

    B. Install Windows XP Professional from the installation CD-ROM. Connect to the Internet and activate Windows XP. Visit the Windows Update site, manually install the latest service pack, and then install all relevant critical updates.

    C. Install Windows XP Professional from the installation CD-ROM. Use another computer to create a CD-ROM containing the latest service pack and all critical updates released after the service pack. Connect to the Internet, and activate Windows XP. Install the latest service pack and all critical updates from the CD-ROM.

    D. Install Windows XP Professional from the installation CD-ROM. Use another computer to create a CD-ROM containing the latest service pack and all critical updates released after the service pack. Install the latest service pack and all critical updates from the CD-ROM. Connect to the Internet, and activate Windows XP.

6. You are the systems administrator for a branch of Humongous Insurance. Your organization has thousands of computers total, but your branch has only about 50. You do, however, have your own Windows Server 2003 Active Directory that you have hardened to reduce security risks. Recently, your manager informed you that executive management has assigned responsibility for another 10,000 customers to your branch. As a result, your organization needs to hire 20 additional customer support representatives, and each will need a Windows XP Professional desktop computer. You have too much work planned to install them yourself, so your manager calls a staffing agency, which sends over a systems administrator named Nicole Caron to perform the installs. You create a user account for Nicole and add it to the Domain Users group, hand her the Windows XP Professional CD-ROM and a set of manual installation instructions, and let her get started.

After about an hour, Nicole reports that she cannot join the computers to your domain because she receives an access denied error. What is the best way to resolve the problem? Choose the correct answer.

    A. Modify the Default Domain Security Settings Group Policy object and add Nicole's user account to the Add Workstations To Domain policy.

    B. Add Nicole's user account to the Domain Admins group.

    C. Modify the Default Domain Security Settings Group Policy object and add Nicole's user account to the Enable Computer And User Accounts To Be Trusted For Delegation policy.

    D. Add Nicole's user account to the Power Users group.

Objective 1.1 Answers

1. **Correct Answers: A and B**

A. Correct: By increasing the system RAM to 128 MB from 48 MB, you have guaranteed that the computer has enough memory for Windows XP Professional to install and run correctly. The computer already met all the other hardware requirements for Windows XP Professional, and you already knew that all the hardware was in the Windows Catalog.

B. Correct: Although you cannot upgrade directly from Windows NT Workstation 3.51 to Windows XP Professional, you can perform a clean install. By selecting a New Installation, you can replace the existing copy of Windows NT Workstation 3.51.

C. Incorrect: You can install Windows XP Professional onto a partition formatted with the file allocation table (FAT) file system, but that file system does not allow for file and folder level access controls. To ensure the greatest level of security possible, you need to convert each partition to NTFS. The version of NTFS included with Windows XP Professional also supports the Encrypting File System (EFS). EFS enables a user to encrypt files so that the data the files contain is protected—even if a hostile intruder obtains physical access to the hard disk. Nothing in the lists of tasks indicates that you converted each partition to NTFS.

D. Incorrect: Before a computer can join a domain, a computer account must be created in the domain. If a computer account already exists with the same name, it needs to be reset or deleted first. This can be accomplished before setup by adding the computer account into Active Directory—a domain administrator can do this. The computer can also be added to the domain during the installation of Windows XP Professional by anyone who has the right to add workstations to the domain. Nothing in the lists of tasks indicates that you created the account in the domain.

E. Incorrect: Performing a new installation on a computer with an existing operating system causes the loss of all user settings and forces you to reinstall all the applications. Performing an intermediate upgrade to Windows NT Workstation 4.0 or Windows 2000 Professional could have retained them.

2. **Correct Answers: B, C, and D**

A. Incorrect: The computer does not have 64 MB of RAM, which is the minimum requirement for Windows XP Professional to install and run correctly. The computer already met all the other hardware requirements for Windows XP Professional, and you knew that all the hardware was in the Windows Catalog.

B. Correct: Although you cannot upgrade directly from Windows NT Workstation 3.51 to Windows XP Professional, you can perform a clean install. By selecting a New Installation, you can replace the existing copy of Windows NT Workstation 3.51.

C. Correct: You can install Windows XP Professional onto a partition formatted with the FAT file system, but that file system does not allow for file- and folder-level access controls. To ensure the greatest level of security possible, you need to convert each partition to NTFS. The list of completed tasks indicates that you converted the boot partition to NTFS during installation. You also converted the second partition to NTFS after setup was complete. You cannot convert boot partitions from FAT or FAT32 to NTFS after setup by using the tools included with Windows XP Professional.

D. Correct: Before a computer can join a domain, a computer account must be created in the domain. If a computer account of that name already exists in the domain, it must be reset or deleted first. The list of tasks indicates that you provided logon information for an account with sufficient privileges to create a new computer account during the installation of Windows XP Professional and that you completed the required actions to add the computer to the domain.

E. Incorrect: Performing a new installation on a computer with an existing operating system causes the loss of all user settings and forces you to reinstall all the applications. In contrast, performing an intermediate upgrade to Windows NT Workstation 4.0 or Windows 2000 Professional could have retained them.

F. Incorrect: Nothing in the list of tasks performed indicates that the hard disk partitions were replaced with a single partition or somehow combined.

3.   Correct Answers: C and D

A. Incorrect: Windows XP Professional can be configured to automatically display the Welcome Screen at startup. The Welcome Screen lists the local user accounts so that users have to type only their password, not their user name when logging in. When the computer displays the user names, people who have gained physical access to it have useful information if they try to break into the installation of Windows XP Professional. It is more secure to require users to type both their user names and passwords when they log on to a computer.

B. Incorrect: NTFS supports folder- and file-level access controls. By carefully setting permissions on operating system and data files, you can ensure that only authenticated users can view files on the computer whether logged on locally or over the network. The FAT32 file system does not have any built-in security and is therefore a bad choice for computers that will contain sensitive data.

C. Correct: Public key encryption can greatly enhance security, especially for mobile users. Although user certificates can be stored on the computer's hard disk and can be password-protected, storing certificates on a smart card is more secure because it requires a thief to have access to both the smart card and the user's password.

D. Correct: By encrypting the user's data files, you ensure that if the replacement laptop computer is stolen and the hard disk is moved to another computer, the thief cannot view confidential information. S/MIME further enhances security by allowing the account executive to digitally sign sent e-mail and receive encrypted e-mail messages.

E. Incorrect: The Recovery Console can be a useful tool for diagnosing and repairing serious computer failures such as corrupted system files and unsupportable configuration changes. Configuring the Recovery Console for automatic logging on significantly decreases security on a system. This is especially true for mobile users whose laptop computers are at risk of theft. This configuration setting is appropriate only on computers that are physically secure or contain no sensitive data and cannot access any other important computers over the network. Use this setting with caution.

4.   Correct Answers: C

A. Incorrect: The Setup Wizard is part of the attended installation process; it does not include any features for migrating user settings from another computer to the system where Windows XP Professional is being installed.

B. Incorrect: You use SysPrep to prepare a computer running Windows XP Professional for imaging so that the disk image can be used to automate the deployment of similarly configured systems. It does not include any features for migrating user settings from one computer to another.

C. Correct: The File And Settings Transfer Wizard is a tool to help transfer a user's files and settings to a new installation of Windows XP Professional. It can copy many different types of files and settings for such things as the Desktop and Display, and for some applications (such as Microsoft Outlook). It is the ideal tool in this scenario.

D. Incorrect: You use RIS for automating the deployment of computers across the network. It leverages technologies such as Windows 2000 Server, Active Directory, GPOs, and Windows XP Professional. It does not include any features for migrating user settings between computers.

5.   Correct Answers: D

> **A. Incorrect:** This procedure does not minimize the risk of being successfully attacked because Windows XP has several vulnerabilities that are removed only after updates have been applied. Therefore, the computer might be exploited while Automatic Updates is downloading and installing the updates.

> **B. Incorrect:** This procedure does not minimize the risk of being successfully attacked because Windows XP has several vulnerabilities that are removed only after updates have been applied. Therefore, the computer might be exploited after it is connected to the Internet, but before the latest service packs and updates have been applied. Even if you might apply these updates as quickly as possible, your computer can be compromised within a few minutes of being connected to the Internet.

> **C. Incorrect:** This procedure does not minimize the risk of being successfully attacked because Windows XP has several vulnerabilities that are removed only after updates have been applied. Therefore, the computer might be exploited after it is connected to the Internet, but before the latest service packs and updates have been applied. Even if you might apply these updates as quickly as possible, your computer can be compromised within a few minutes of being connected to the Internet.

> **D. Correct:** This procedure reduces the risk of a successful network attack against the system by remaining disconnected from the network during the installation of Windows XP. Windows XP has many known vulnerabilities that are removed when the latest service pack and critical updates are applied. Even performing the installation behind a firewall is risky because the computer might be attacked by computers on the local network infected with worms or viruses. You should consider connecting to the Internet only after all updates have been applied.

6.   Correct Answers: A

> **A. Correct:** To add computers to a domain, the user must have the Add Workstations To Domain user right.

> **B. Incorrect:** Although it would solve the problem by allowing Nicole to add computers to the domain, it would also grant Nicole many unnecessary privileges, such as the ability to create a user account for herself that she could use to connect to network resources after she has finished her job. The security risks associated with this option are too great.

> **C. Incorrect:** This domain policy setting will not allow Nicole's account to add computers to the domain.

> **D. Incorrect:** The Power Users group exists only in the local user database, and being a member of the Power Users group grants no additional domain-level rights.

Objective 1.2

Perform and Troubleshoot an Unattended Installation of Windows XP Professional

Automation of the installation of Windows XP Professional, called **unattended installation**, is much more efficient and less prone to error when deploying large numbers of computers. To effectively automate the deployment of Windows XP Professional, you must know how to plan for deployment, build and configure the installation environment, create customized **answer files**, and distribute the operating system and applications to the target computers.

A number of methods for automating operating systems have been developed over time; consequently, there are several alternatives for preparing installation routines and deploying the installation packages. Preparation methods include

- Installation scripts that partially or completely automate setup.
- The SysPrep utility and disk imaging.
- The */syspart* switch available with Winnt32.exe.

Distribution methods include

- Bootable CD-ROM.
- RIS.
- Batch file and a network distribution folder.
- Systems Management Server (SMS).

To successfully answer questions in this objective, you must know how to use the Setup Manager Wizard to prepare for a Windows XP Professional installation and to create answer files and UDF files. You must also know how to create and edit these installation scripts manually by using a text editor. You need to be familiar with all the preparation and distribution methods and understand which ones are appropriate for different circumstances.

Objective 1.2 Questions

1. You were recently hired as part of a systems administration team at a medium-sized company. Your manager has asked you to install Windows XP Professional on 25 identical new desktop computers for the Accounts Receivable department in your firm. To date, your colleagues have been manually installing Windows XP Professional and the suite of applications on each computer as they arrive, carefully following written step-by-step instructions. The process has been tedious and slow, and users have had problems with new computers because of configuration errors caused by human error during the installation process. You want to deploy the computers as efficiently as possible with all the desktop applications that are required by the staff in Accounts Receivable installed and configured. You also want to ensure that all 25 computers are configured consistently.

You propose to do the following:

- Manually install and configure Windows XP Professional and the required applications on one of the new computers, meticulously following the existing step-by-step instructions.

- Use Setup Manager to fully automate the installation routine by creating an answer file called Sysprep.inf.

- Use a non-Microsoft imaging tool to create an image of the reference computer.

- Use the imaging tool to copy the image from the reference computer to the remaining computers.

What critical step is missing from your proposal? Choose the correct answer.

A. Use Setup Manager to create a UDF file with unique settings for each of the 25 computers.

B. Create RIS boot disks so that the computers can connect to the RIS server to download the disk image.

C. Use the SysPrep utility to prepare the reference computer for imaging.

D. Install PXE-compliant network cards into each computer so that they can connect to the RIS server to download the disk image.

2. You are creating an automated installation of Windows XP Professional for 30 computers. You want to accomplish the following.

- Assign a unique computer name to each computer

- Ensure that all computers have the same display settings, time zone configured, default user name, and organization name entered

- Install Microsoft Office Professional Edition 2003 on all the computers

- Configure the local Administrator account with a unique password on each system

- Modify the user interface so that the desktop icons are no longer visible

You plan to use Setup Manager to create a fully automated installation, combining an answer file and a UDF file with the preceding settings. Which goals does your approach achieve? Choose three correct answers.

A. You can assign a unique computer name to each computer.

B. You can ensure that all computers have the same display settings, time zone configured, default user name, and organization name entered.

C. You can install Office Professional Edition 2003 on all the computers.

D. You can configure the local Administrator account with a unique password on each system.

E. You can modify the user interface so that the desktop icons are no longer visible.

F. Your solution does not achieve any of the desired goals.

3. You want to perform an unattended installation of Windows XP Professional onto a computer with a bootable CD-ROM drive. You have already verified that the computer meets the minimum hardware requirements for Windows XP Professional and that all the hardware is in the Windows Catalog. You also have a bootable version of the Windows XP Professional installation CD-ROM.

Which of the following is correct? Choose the correct answer.

A. Ensure that the answer file has a section called [Winnt32] that contains the required keys and values. Save the answer file as **Sysprep.inf** and copy it to a floppy disk. Configure the target computer's BIOS so that it will boot from the CD-ROM drive, and then insert the Windows XP Professional installation CD-ROM and reboot the computer. Insert the floppy disk as soon as the computer boots from the CD-ROM.

B. Ensure that the answer file has a section called [Winnt32] that contains the required keys and values. Save the answer file as **Winnt.sif** and copy it to a floppy disk. Configure the target computer's BIOS so that it boots from the CD-ROM drive, and then insert the Windows XP Professional installation CD-ROM and reboot the computer. Insert the floppy disk as soon as the computer boots from the CD-ROM.

C. Ensure that the answer file has a section called [Data] that contains the required keys and values. Save the answer file as **Sysprep.inf** and copy it to a floppy disk. Configure the target computer's BIOS so that it boots from the CD-ROM drive, and then insert the Windows XP Professional installation CD-ROM and reboot the computer. Insert the floppy disk as soon as the computer boots from the CD-ROM.

D. Ensure that the answer file has a section called [Data] that contains the required keys and values. Save the answer file as **Winnt.sif** and copy it to a floppy disk. Insert the floppy disk into the target computer. Configure the target computer's BIOS so that it boots from the CD-ROM drive, and then insert the Windows XP Professional installation CD-ROM and reboot the computer.

4. During an unattended installation of Windows XP Professional, keys might have values set in the answer file, the UDF file, in both files, or in neither file. How does Setup handle the following scenarios? Choose four correct answers.

A. If a section or key is present in the UDF file, but there is no section or key of the same name in the answer file, Setup creates and uses the UDF section.

B. If a key is specified in the answer file and referenced by the unique ID in the UDF file, the value specified in the answer file is used.

C. If a key is specified in the UDF file but not in the answer file, the value specified in the UDF file is used.

D. If a key is not specified in the answer file, and it is in the UDF file but the value is left blank, the default value is supplied automatically by Setup.

E. If a key is not specified in the answer file, and it is in the UDF file but the value is left blank, no value is set.

F. If a key is specified in the answer file but not in the UDF file, the value specified in the answer file is used.

5. You will be performing an automated deployment of Windows XP Professional to 40 desktop computers. During testing, you discovered that the video driver causes Setup to fail unless the driver is updated by using Dynamic Update during the setup procedure. You want to use Dynamic Update, but you are using only a low-bandwidth dial-up connection while you wait for your Internet service provider (ISP) to provision your permanent Internet connection. What steps would you take to use Dynamic Update with an automated deployment of Windows XP? Choose the correct answer.

A. Download the latest Windows XP Dynamic Update package from Microsoft. Extract the files to a folder, and share that folder on your local area network. From your Windows XP CD-ROM, run the command *winnt32 /duprepare:path_to_shared_folder*. In the [Unattended] section of your Unattend.txt file, add the entry *Dushare: path_to_shared_folder*.

B. From your Windows XP CD-ROM, run the command *winnt32 /duprepare:path_to_shared_folder* to download the Dynamic Update files from Microsoft and store them in the specified shared folder. In the [Unattended] section of your Unattend.txt file, add the entry *Dushare:path_to_shared_folder*.

C. Download the latest Windows XP Dynamic Update package from Microsoft. Copy the file to a folder and share that folder on your local area network. In the [Unattended] section of your Unattend.txt file, add the entry *Dushare:path_to_shared_folder*.

D. Download the latest Windows XP Dynamic Update package from Microsoft. Extract the files to a folder, and share that folder on your local area network. From your Windows XP CD-ROM, run the command *winnt32 /duprepare:path_to_shared_folder*. In the [Unattended] section of your Unattend.txt file, add the entries *Dushare:local* and *Dupath:path_to_shared_folder*.

6.   You need to perform an unattended installation from a Windows XP Professional CD-ROM on a computer that does not currently have an operating system. You want to provide the computer name and Administrator password on a floppy disk. What do you name the answer file? Choose the correct answer.

A. Answer.txt

B. Winnt.sif

C. Winnt32.sif

D. Unattend.txt

7.   Which of the following components are required to install Windows XP Professional by using Remote Installation Services (RIS)? Choose three correct answers.

A. DNS server

B. WINS server

C. DHCP server

D. Web server

E. Active Directory

F. FTP server

Objective 1.2 Answers

1.   Correct Answers: C

> **A. Incorrect:** When using disk imaging to deploy Windows XP Professional, you do not need to create UDF files.

> **B. Incorrect:** RIS is another possible approach to deploying multiple computers, but you have already proposed using disk images. Copying the images to the disk drives of the new computers does not require RIS. In this scenario, non-Microsoft tools are used for distribution.

> **C. Correct:** Before you create an image of the reference computer, you must use SysPrep to remove security and user information unique to the system. SysPrep erases the computer's name, its globally unique identifier (GUID), and all other settings that might cause problems if they appear on multiple computers on the same network.

> **D. Incorrect:** RIS is another possible approach to deploying multiple computers, but you have already proposed using disk images. Copying the images to the disk drives of the new computers does not require RIS or PXE-enabled network cards. Additionally, the entire computer needs to be PXE-compliant, not just the network cards. Merely installing PXE-enabled network cards into a computer does not guarantee that it will be able to boot directly from the network. In this scenario, non-Microsoft tools are used for distribution.

2.   Correct Answers: A, B, and D

> **A. Correct:** With Setup Manager, you can create UDF files that can be used in conjunction with answer files. The settings in a UDF file take precedence over those in an answer file. You can specify unique values for many settings such as computer names so that each computer deployed has a distinct name.

> **B. Correct:** Setup Manager can create or modify answer files that can contain all the settings listed. An answer file is a customized script used to run an unattended installation of Windows XP Professional.

> **C. Incorrect:** Setup Manager cannot automate the installation of any version of Microsoft Office Professional Edition 2003 on its own. You can use Setup Manager to launch other programs and scripts, but you have to create an automated installation for Office Professional Edition 2003 by following the instructions included in the Office 2003 Editions Resource Kit.

> **D. Correct:** With Setup Manager, you can create UDF files that can be used in conjunction with answer files. The settings in a UDF file take precedence over those in an answer file. You can specify unique values for many settings, such as the password for the Local Administrator account.

E. **Incorrect:** Setup Manager does not include tools to modify user interface properties such as the appearance of desktop icons. Instead, you should configure the computers as Active Directory domain members, and use Group Policy settings to control the desktop environment.

F. **Incorrect:** Your solution does not achieve any of the desired goals.

3.   **Correct Answers: D**

A. **Incorrect:** The answer file must be named Winnt.sif, not Sysprep.inf. Sysprep.inf is the name given to the answer file when using SysPrep to deploy Windows XP Professional via disk imaging. The section with the required keys for automating installation from the bootable installation CD-ROM must be called [Data].

B. **Incorrect:** The section with the required keys for automating installation from the bootable installation CD-ROM must be called [Data].

C. **Incorrect:** The answer file must be named Winnt.sif, not Sysprep.inf. Sysprep.inf is the name given to the answer file when using SysPrep to deploy Windows XP Professional via disk imaging.

D. **Correct:** The [Data] section is an optional section needed only when installing Windows XP Professional in an unattended fashion directly from the product CD-ROM. If you use the Setup Manager Wizard to create the answer file and specify that the answer file will be used to install from a CD-ROM, it creates the [Data] section with the required keys and values: *AutoPartition=1*, *MsDosInitiated="0"*, and *UnattendedInstall="Yes"*. The answer file must be named Winnt.sif; by default, Setup Manager offers to name the file Unattend.txt. Be sure to name the file **Winnt.sif** before booting from the installation CD-ROM. Remember to insert the diskette into the floppy drive right after the computer boots from the CD-ROM.

4.   **Correct Answers: A, C, E, and F**

A. **Correct:** Setup automatically uses values within the UDF file when the corresponding values are not specified in the answer file.

B. **Incorrect:** The values specified in the UDF file take precedence over those in the answer file whenever they are in conflict.

C. **Correct:** Setup automatically uses values within the UDF file when the corresponding values are not specified in the answer file.

D. **Incorrect:** Setup does not automatically supply default values for any keys left blank. In this situation, it is possible that the user will be prompted for the missing information.

    E. Correct: If a key has a blank value in the UDF file and the answer file has no value specified for that key, no value is set and it is possible that the user will be prompted for the missing information.

    F. Correct: Any keys specified in the answer file that are not superseded by those in the UDF file are used.

5.   Correct Answers: A

    A. Correct: To use Dynamic Update, download the latest package, extract the files, and share them on a network. For unattended installations, you must add the *Dushare:* line to the Unattend.txt file to tell Setup where to retrieve the package. For attended installations, add the */dushare:path_to_shared_folder* option to the winnt32.exe command-line. For more information, refer to Microsoft Knowledge Base article 312110.

    B. Incorrect: Although winnt32.exe is capable of downloading the Dynamic Update files during installation, it is not capable of storing those files for later use. You must manually download and extract the files.

    C. Incorrect: Before Setup can use the Dynamic Update files, you must extract them, and then prepare them by running winnt32.exe with the */duprepare* command-line parameter.

    D. Incorrect: You need to add the Dushare entry only to the [Unattended] section of your Unattend.txt file. You should set the value to the path of the shared folder containing your Dynamic Update files.

6.   Correct Answers: B

    A. Incorrect: The correct filename is Winnt.sif.

    B. Correct: Winnt.sif has the same sections as an Unattend.txt file, and should be used when performing unattended installations on computers that do not currently have an operating system. Generally, you would place this file on a floppy disk and insert the floppy disk into the computer immediately after the computer begins to boot from the CD-ROM.

    C. Incorrect: The correct filename is Winnt.sif.

    D. Incorrect: The correct filename is Winnt.sif. Although Unattend.txt is often used for unattended installations where the computer currently has an operating system, you can specify any file name in this scenario.

7.   Correct Answers: A, C, and E

A. Correct: Remote installation relies on DNS for locating the directory service and client machine accounts.

B. Incorrect: RIS clients do not require a WINS server.

C. Correct: RIS requires a DHCP server to be present and active on the network. The remote boot–enabled client computers receive an Internet Protocol (IP) address from the DHCP server before contacting RIS.

D. Incorrect: RIS clients do not need to contact a Web server.

E. Correct: RIS relies on Active Directory for locating existing client machines as well as existing RIS servers.

F. Incorrect: RIS clients do not require FTP.

Upgrade from a Previous Version of Windows to Windows XP Professional

Often, Windows XP Professional is needed on systems that already have a version of Windows installed. The best way to minimize the impact on the applications running on that system is to perform an **in-place upgrade** to Windows XP. In-place upgrades can be performed on systems that have Windows 98, Windows Me, Windows NT Workstation 4.0 with Service Pack 6, or Windows 2000 Professional. Although this process is much more complex than performing a **clean installation,** the Windows XP setup procedures include many tools to make this process as painless as possible.

Systems running older Windows operating systems can also be upgraded, but not directly. For example, Windows 95 cannot be upgraded to Windows XP Professional simply by running Winnt32.exe; it must be upgraded to Windows 98 first. Similarly, a computer with Windows NT 4.0 and Service Pack 5 or earlier installed must be upgraded to Service Pack 6 before the Windows XP Professional setup routine can be run successfully.

In addition to verifying that the system's hardware resources meet the minimum requirements of Microsoft, you also need to verify that all applications installed on the system are compatible with Windows XP. To facilitate this process, Microsoft provides the Windows Application Compatibility Toolkit, which is available online at *http://msdn.microsoft.com/downloads/list/appcomp.asp.*

If you have ever replaced your personal desktop or laptop computer that you have been using for months or years with a new one, you understand how challenging it can be to copy all your data and user preferences over to the replacement system. Windows XP Professional includes two methods for migrating users' configuration settings and data between systems. The **Files And Settings Transfer Wizard (FSTW)** is intended for home users, small office users, and lightly managed users in an enterprise environment. The **User State Migration Tool (USMT)** is a command-line tool created for migrating large numbers of users in a corporate setting.

Objective 1.3 Questions

1. A newly hired CIO who understands the benefits of using a single desktop operating system for the entire company has hired you to upgrade all networked systems to Windows XP. Previously, local administrators with varying policies and procedures managed each remote office. Consequently, desktop systems have a mixture of Windows for Workgroups 3.11, Windows 95, Windows NT Workstation 4.0, and Windows 2000 Professional. You want to minimize the impact on each user's applications by performing an in-place upgrade whenever possible.

Which of these operating systems can be upgraded to Windows XP in a single step? Choose two correct answers.

   A. Windows for Workgroups 3.11

   B. Windows 95

   C. Windows NT Workstation 4.0 with no service pack

   D. Windows NT Workstation 4.0 with Service Pack 6

   E. Windows 2000 Professional

2. You are an administrator for a corporate network supporting 40 users. Your CEO recently learned about the many benefits that Windows XP Professional offers over the Windows 98 operating system that is currently installed on her laptop computer. You have been assigned the task of upgrading the CEO's laptop to Windows XP. It is critical that the computer be returned when the CEO returns from a business trip the following day; and all data, applications, and settings must be available.

Which is the best upgrade strategy? Choose the best answer.

   A. Perform a full system backup, scan for viruses, and uncompress any compressed drives. Document the user preferences and applications installed on the system. Run the Windows XP Professional setup procedure and repartition all drives with NTFS. After Setup has completed, restore the backup over the new installation. After Setup has completed, verify the functionality of all hardware and applications.

   B. Perform a full system backup, scan for viruses, and uncompress any compressed drives. Run the standard Windows XP Professional setup procedure and perform an in-place upgrade. After Setup has completed, verify the functionality of all hardware and applications. If Windows XP was unable to install drivers for some hardware components, download and install the updated drivers. If any of the applications do not function correctly, download and apply patches from the software vendors.

C. Perform a full system backup, scan for viruses, and uncompress any compressed drives. Generate a compatibility report by running the *Winnt32.exe /checkupgradeonly* command. Download any drivers that the compatibility report indicates are not provided by Windows XP, and patch any applications that have not been certified. Run the standard Windows XP Professional setup procedure and perform an in-place upgrade, providing updated drivers as prompted. After Setup has completed, verify the functionality of all hardware and applications.

D. Perform a full system backup, scan for viruses, and uncompress any compressed drives. Generate a compatibility report by running the *Winnt32.exe /checkupgradeonly* command. Download any drivers that the compatibility report indicates are not provided by Windows XP, and patch any applications that have not been certified. Run the standard Windows XP Professional setup procedure and perform a new install with a different system directory (that is, C:\WinXP\), providing updated drivers as prompted. After Setup has completed, verify the functionality of all hardware and applications. After the system is functioning correctly, delete the directory containing Windows 98.

3. You have several identical computers that you want to upgrade from Windows Me to Windows XP Professional. You have already verified that all the computers meet the minimum hardware requirements and that the hardware and subcomponents appear in the Windows XP Windows Catalog. You have also verified that each computer already has the current BIOS installed. The computers have been in operation for several months, and their users have installed their own applications. How can you quickly determine whether there will be any application-compatibility issues before proceeding with the upgrade? Choose the correct answer.

A. Run the Setup program from the Windows XP Professional installation media with the */checkupgradeonly* switch by typing **x:\i386\Winnt32.exe /checkupgradeonly** from a command prompt where *x:* is the drive letter assigned to the CD-ROM drive on each computer.

B. Create a list of the applications installed on each computer and then visit the Web site of the vendor for each application to find out whether the versions installed on the computers to be upgraded are compatible with Windows XP Professional.

C. Purchase the latest versions of each installed application.

D. Perform a clean installation of Windows XP Professional on each system, and then reinstall all the applications.

4. You are the administrator of a network that includes 50 users running Windows 2000 Professional and 4 servers running Windows 2000 Advanced Server and Active Directory in a domain setting. You are told to replace 20 of the users' desktop computers with new laptop computers that have Windows XP Professional preinstalled. You want to add the computers to the domain and transfer the users' data and settings from their current desktop computers to their new laptop systems. Which of the following solutions best accomplishes these goals? Choose the correct answer.

A. Name each of the computers appropriately, and then join them to the domain. Install the appropriate applications. Copy each user's User Profile from the old computer to the new computer.

B. Give each of the computers a unique name and then join them to the domain. Write a script that copies each user's My Documents folder from the old computer to the replacement computer. Write a script that exports each user's Registry from the old computer, and imports it to the replacement computer. Schedule the scripts to run on each of the replacement computers, and then reboot each computer.

C. Join each of the laptop computers to the domain. Install the appropriate applications. Write a script that uses the USMT ScanState tool to copy all users' settings from their old computers to a shared drive on one of the domain controllers. Write a script that launches the LoadState tool with the required settings to copy the files and settings from the shared network drive and schedule the script to run on each laptop computer.

D. Schedule a task to launch the FSTW on each laptop computer and be sure that the job is run in the context of an account with local administrative access on all the computers.

5. You are the administrator for a network that includes 80 users and 3 servers running Windows 2000 Advanced Server and Active Directory in a domain setting. You are preparing to migrate 15 users from their existing laptop computers that are running Windows Me to new laptop systems that will be running Windows XP Professional. You have automated most of the process, including installing Windows XP Professional, joining the computer to the domain, and installing the required applications. You are having trouble running USMT on your Windows Me test computer. How can you effectively troubleshoot the automated process of copying user data and settings to a shared folder on the network? Choose the correct answer.

A. Run the ScanState tool with verbose error logging enabled by adding the */l scanstate.log /v 7 /u /f* parameters to the command you use to run the tool.

B. Check the local system and application logs for error messages.

C. Run the LoadState tool with verbose error logging enabled by adding the */l scanstate.log /v 7* parameters to the command you use to run the tool.

D. Check the application and system logs on the domain controller where the shared network folder is located.

1.   Correct Answers: D and E

   A. Incorrect: Windows for Workgroups 3.11 cannot be upgraded directly to Windows XP Professional. After determining that the hardware and software are compatible with Windows XP, you must perform a full system backup and define a list of installed applications and document personalization settings such as wallpaper and color scheme. Then, perform a fresh install of Windows XP, reinstall all applications, and restore the user's data and settings. Alternatively, the system can be upgraded to Windows 95, and then Windows 98, and then Windows XP Professional. In practice, few people will choose to upgrade computers running this operating system because the hardware is not likely to meet the minimum requirements for Windows XP.

   B. Incorrect: You cannot upgrade directly from Windows 95 directly to Windows XP Professional. The suggested upgrade path is from Windows 95, to Windows 98, and then to Windows XP.

   C. Incorrect: You cannot upgrade Windows NT Workstation 4.0 to Windows XP Professional unless Service Pack 6 or later is installed.

   D. Correct: You can upgrade Windows NT Workstation 4.0 directly to Windows XP Professional, as long as Service Pack 6 is installed.

   E. Correct: You can upgrade Windows 2000 Professional directly to Windows XP Professional.

2.   Correct Answers: C

   A. Incorrect: Restoring Windows 98 system files over a Windows XP installation might return the system to its original state, or it might leave the system completely nonfunctional. Although it sometimes might be necessary to restore user data to a freshly upgraded system, applications and system settings cannot be transferred this way.

   B. Incorrect: This is a commonly used method that will work on many systems. However, it is very risky to not generate a compatibility report because there is a distinct possibility that the system will not function at all after the upgrade. Additionally, if you discover after the upgrade that a critical application cannot be patched to work properly with Windows XP, your only method of recovery is to perform a full system restore. It is more time-efficient to perform a *Winnt32.exe / checkupgradeonly* procedure and resolve any issues before running the full setup procedure.

C. Correct: This method is the correct choice because it proactively identifies system incompatibilities. Generating a compatibility report before performing the upgrade greatly improves the chance of a successful upgrade. If a system component or application is completely incompatible with Windows XP, this method identifies that weakness ahead of time.

D. Incorrect: Performing a new install of Windows XP preserves the user's data, but not applications and system settings. Although applications are not available from the Start menu, the application files still consume hard disk space. Applications need to be reinstalled, and system settings are completely lost.

3.   Correct Answers: A

A. Correct: This procedure will generate an application compatibility report for Windows XP Professional without actually installing the operating system; it is the most efficient way to check for application compatibility.

B. Incorrect: Although you might have to contact some of the vendors for upgrades to their applications after running the application compatibility report described in answer A, it is unlikely that you need to visit all their Web sites. This approach is unnecessarily cumbersome and time-consuming.

C. Incorrect: You might need to upgrade some of the installed applications, but it is unlikely that you have to upgrade all (or even most) of them. This approach is expensive and time-consuming.

D. Incorrect: This approach fails to accomplish the basic objective of upgrading the existing operating system on each computer. Additionally, you have done nothing to verify that the applications are compatible with Windows XP Professional, so you might find that you cannot install some of them.

4.   Correct Answers: C

A. Incorrect: The format and structure of user profiles are different between Windows 2000 and Windows XP. Copying a profile from a computer running one operating system to another will probably cause problems that can be serious, such as users not being able to log on (or to access certain applications after they have logged on).

B. Incorrect: Although a script is an efficient way to copy the My Documents folder, you cannot simply import the Registry from one computer to another. Additionally, many applications store data in the user profile but outside of the My Documents folder. With this approach, any user data stored outside the My Documents folder will not be copied to the new laptop computers.

C. Correct: These procedures accomplish all the stated goals in an efficient manner. The steps to add the computers to the domain can be partially automated through a script, but the laptop computers were delivered with Windows XP Professional already installed, so it might be faster do that manually. When scheduling the USMT tools to run, make sure that the scheduled job is run in the context of an account that belongs to the local Administrators group.

D. Incorrect: The FSTW is an interactive tool that cannot be run silently from a command line. In other words, scheduling the tool in this manner does not accomplish the goal of copying user data and settings. Additionally, there is nothing in this answer to suggest that the computers were added to the Active Directory domain.

5. **Correct Answers: A**

A. Correct: The /l switch enables logging for Scanstate.exe and requires you to provide a file name for the log. The /v switch specifies the level of verbosity for the logging—7 is the most verbose setting. The /u and /f switches provide additional information about the resources to be scanned.

B. Incorrect: The USMT does not record detailed error messages to the system or application logs.

C. Incorrect: The question states that you are having problems on the computer running Windows Me, which implies that the trouble involves the ScanState tool, not the LoadState tool. The LoadState tool would be run on the target computer that has Windows XP Professional installed.

D. Incorrect: The ScanState tool is run locally on the computer where data and settings are being transferred from; it is not likely that it will record any events on the domain controller's application or system log. It might generate events in the security log on the domain controller if auditing were enabled and you were trying to access a shared folder with an account that did not have sufficient permission to write files to that location.

Perform Post-Installation Updates and Product Activation

All operating systems require patches to be applied on a regular basis to fix problems, provide compatibility with new hardware, and resolve newly discovered security vulnerabilities. Microsoft distributes these updates in the form of **critical updates** and **service packs**. Microsoft releases critical updates with relative frequency to resolve security vulnerabilities. Service packs, which are released less frequently, include all critical updates released prior to the service pack, as well as other operating system improvements. These updates can be retrieved from the Windows Update Web site at *http://windowsupdate.microsoft.com/*.

If the only Windows XP system you are responsible for managing is your own personal computer, you will probably choose to configure Automatic Updates to automatically download and install updates when they become available. This method provides an easy and bandwidth-efficient method of keeping a single computer up-to-date. If you are responsible for managing a network of computers, you need to identify methods that scale to larger numbers of computers and give you tighter control over how patches are deployed.

The simplest way to distribute a service pack to your network is to download the network package from Microsoft. The network package contains the complete set of files required to install a service pack on any Windows XP computer. You can then copy this file to a shared folder on your network and launch the service pack installation without visiting Windows Update from each computer.

A more efficient (but complex) method of deploying both critical updates and service packs to computers on your network is to use SUS. When you deploy SUS, you can configure Automatic Updates to download updates from a server on your local network. This gives you control over which critical updates and service packs are deployed, which allows you to test each update thoroughly to detect compatibility problems with your custom applications. You can download SUS from *http://www.microsoft.com/sus/*.

Service packs can also be **slipstreamed** into a complete Windows XP Professional distribution point. Updating the Windows XP setup files with a service pack eliminates the need to install a service pack on a newly deployed system because the slipstreaming process integrates service pack updates into the Windows XP Professional setup files. Future systems built from the slipstreamed distribution point will contain all updates included in the service pack and reflect the updated build number, but will not require the additional step of manually installing a service pack.

Objective 1.4 Questions

1.   You are a systems administrator for a new service provider that plans to offer help desk services to 50 users. Although the users' desktop systems have been purchased, you need to install the latest version of Windows XP on each of them. Rather than installing Windows XP and then immediately upgrading to Service Pack 2, you want the initial deployment of Windows XP to include Service Pack 2.

Your Windows XP network distribution point is located at *server**winxp*\. Which command properly updates the distribution point to Service Pack 2? Choose the correct answer.

    A. *Update /copydir:\\server\winxp*

    B. *Update /syspart: \\server\winxp*

    C. *Update /integrate:\\server\winxp*

    D. *Update /o:\\server\winxp*

2.   You have a two-year-old computer from a well-known manufacturer that is currently running Windows Me and several dozen applications. The computer has 128 MB of RAM, a 500 MHz Pentium III CPU, and a 12 GB hard disk with 7 GB of free space. You have verified that the computer and its subcomponents are in the Windows XP Windows Catalog. You have also upgraded all the applications to versions that are compatible with Windows XP Professional except for the antivirus software you have temporarily uninstalled. You back up the current configuration to a removable hard drive and begin the upgrade process. The first phase of the upgrade appears to complete properly, but when the computer reboots, it crashes before the second phase begins. You reboot the computer several times with the same result. What is the most likely cause of this problem? Choose the correct answer.

    A. The Windows XP Professional installation CD-ROM is corrupt.

    B. One or more of the memory chips installed in the computer is faulty.

    C. You entered an invalid product key.

    D. The BIOS is incompatible with Windows XP Professional.

3.   You have a home office with a cable modem connection to the Internet. You install and configure all your own hardware and software. You have been using Windows XP Professional on a Pentium 4 computer for several months when the first service pack is released. You download and install the service pack from the Windows Update Web site and note that several minor problems have been resolved by the service pack. Later, you decide to add software from the Add/Remove Windows Components tool. After the installation of the new component is complete, what must you do to make sure that the new component has the latest updates applied? Choose the correct answer.

    A. Run Setupmgr.exe.

    B. Run Sysprep.exe.

    C. Reapply the service pack.

    D. Do nothing.

4.   What types of information are transmitted to Microsoft during product activation when performed over an Internet connection? Choose the correct answer.

    A. The Windows XP Professional product ID (PID), the product key, and details about the hardware present in the computer where the operating system is installed.

    B. The user's registration information, including name, address, city, state, and Zip code.

    C. The user's credit card information.

    D. The entire HKEY_LOCAL_MACHINE hive, several small files from the Application Data folder within the user's profile, the Windows XP Professional PID, and the serial number for each hard disk.

5.   Contoso, Inc. recently hired you as a system administrator for its small network of ten Windows XP Professional computers. After performing a security audit, you realize that two of the computers have not yet had Service Pack 2 for Windows XP installed. You use Internet Explorer to visit the Windows Update site, and are notified that the computers were activated with invalid product keys. Contoso has purchased additional valid product keys for these computers. What is the quickest way to resolve the problem to allow Service Pack 2 to be installed? Choose the correct answer.

    A. Insert the Windows XP Professional CD-ROM, and then restart the computer. Perform an upgrade installation over the existing Windows XP system directory. When prompted, provide the new valid product key, and then install Service Pack 2.

    B. Back up all files and settings on each computer. Insert the Windows XP Professional CD-ROM, and then restart the computer. Perform a new installation of Windows XP by reformatting the hard disk. When prompted, provide the new valid product key, and then install Service Pack 2. Restore the files and settings from the backup.

    C. Change the HKEY_LOCAL_MACHINE\Software\Microsoft\WindowsNT\Current Version\WPAEvents\OOBETimer Registry value, and then run the Msoobe.exe tool to reset the product activation key. Then install Service Pack 2.

    D. Right-click My Computer and then click Properties. Click the Advanced tab and click the Environment Variables button. Select the PRODUCT_KEY variable, and then click Edit to specify a new product activation key. Then restart the computer and install Service Pack 2.

6. Which of the following are valid techniques for removing Service Pack 2 for Windows XP? Choose two correct answers.

    A. Click Start, click All Programs, click Service Pack 2, and then click Uninstall.

    B. In Add Or Remove Programs, click Windows XP Service Pack 2, and then click Remove.

    C. From the command prompt, change to the %systemroot%\$NtservicepackUninstall$\spuninst folder. Run the command spuninst.exe.

    D. From the command prompt, change to the %systemroot%\$NtservicepackUninstall$\ folder. Run the command setup.exe.

7. You are a consultant hired by Fabrikam, Inc. to install Windows XP Professional on 45 desktop computers. At the beginning of your first day, your manager provided you with Fabrikam's volume license product key and the Windows XP Professional CD-ROM. You insert the CD-ROM into the first computer, but the installation fails after several minutes—indicating that the installation media could not be read. You remove the CD-ROM and examine it to discover a deep scratch in the surface of the media.

Your manager is nowhere to be found. His assistant reports that he will not return until the afternoon, and that he is the only person with keys to the media locker where backup copies of the Windows XP Professional CD-ROM are stored. However, you brought your laptop from home, and your Windows XP Professional retail CD-ROM is in the CD-ROM drive. What is the quickest way to begin your automated installations? Choose the correct answer.

    A. Use your personal Windows XP Professional retail CD-ROM, and provide the product key originally included with the disk.

    B. Use your personal Windows XP Professional retail CD-ROM and provide Fabrikam's product key.

    C. Copy the contents of your personal Windows XP Professional CD to a shared folder, and perform a network installation. Provide Fabrikam's product key.

    D. Wait for the manager to return, and get a backup copy of the Windows XP Professional volume licensing CD-ROM.

Objective 1.4 Answers

1.   Correct Answers: C

A. Incorrect: You use the */copydir* parameter with the Windows XP setup routine (Winnt32.exe) to copy an additional administrator-provided folder to a new instance of Windows XP.

B. Incorrect: You use the */syspart* parameter with Winnt32 only when preloading Windows XP Setup on a hard drive before moving it to another computer.

C. Correct: The */integrate:distribution_folder* is the correct syntax for updating a Windows XP network distribution point. When this command is issued, the update procedure identifies outdated files in the Windows XP setup files and replaces them with versions included in Service Pack 2. As installations are performed from this distribution point, the updated files are automatically used. Previous service packs used the */s* parameter to perform the same functionality, and Service Pack 2 still supports the use of */s* instead of */integrate*.

D. Incorrect: The */o* parameter is a valid parameter for the update command, but it does not perform slipstreaming. The */o* parameter is used to bypass prompting to overwrite original equipment manufacturer (OEM) drivers during the service pack install.

2.   Correct Answers: D

A. Incorrect: The first phase of the installation completed successfully, which strongly suggests that the installation media is in good working order.

B. Incorrect: Although this is a possible explanation, it is highly unlikely because the computer has been running for two years.

C. Incorrect: If you had entered an invalid product key during the information-gathering process, you would have seen an error message and been prompted to re-enter the correct key. If you had entered a valid product key that had already been assigned to a different computer, you would not see an error until you tried to activate Windows XP.

D. Correct: You performed most of the steps necessary before beginning the upgrade process, but you forgot to upgrade the BIOS with the latest version available from the manufacturer. An incompatible BIOS can render a computer unbootable. Recovering from this situation should not be too difficult if you have another system running that is connected to the Internet. Visit the manufacturer's Web site and download the latest BIOS. Follow the manufacturer's instructions to upgrade the BIOS on the target computer; typically this involves copying the BIOS update to a bootable floppy disk and booting the target computer from it. After the BIOS is upgraded, remove the floppy disk and reboot—the Windows XP Professional installation should proceed without further problems.

3.   **Correct Answers: D**

   A. **Incorrect:** Setup Manager is a tool for creating answer files to automate the installation of Windows XP Professional or to fully automate a SysPrep installation routine.

   B. **Incorrect:** The SysPrep tool is used for deploying Windows XP Professional onto multiple computers by using disk cloning. SysPrep assigns a unique security ID to each destination computer the first time the computer is restarted. This tool is not used for managing service packs or for adding and removing optional Windows components.

   C. **Incorrect:** In previous versions of Windows, you had to reapply the most recent service pack after installing any additional components from the installation media. Windows XP Professional overcomes this limitation by ensuring that all the files included with a service pack are installed to the appropriate folders on the hard disk, even those that are not currently needed. When an optional component is added to a system with a newer service pack, the most recent files are automatically retained, eliminating the need to reapply the service pack.

   D. **Correct:** For the reasons noted in answer C, it is not necessary to reapply the service pack.

4.   **Correct Answers: A**

   A. **Correct:** This is the only information sent to Microsoft.

   B. **Incorrect:** Although this information is sent to Microsoft during the registration process, it is not sent during product activation. Registration is a voluntary step that users can choose to bypass—product activation is required to continue running Windows XP Professional for more than 30 days after installation.

   C. **Incorrect:** No personal information, especially financial information, is sent to Microsoft.

   D. **Incorrect:** The Windows XP Professional PID is sent to Microsoft; however, only portions of the HKEY_LOCAL_MACHINE hive are sent.

5.   **Correct Answers: C**

   A. **Incorrect:** Performing an upgrade installation does not allow you to change the product activation key.

   B. **Incorrect:** Although this procedure does work, it would be extremely time-consuming.

   C. **Correct:** This procedure is the most efficient way to apply a valid product activation key to Windows XP. It is described more fully in Microsoft Knowledge Base article 328874.

   D. **Incorrect:** The product key is not an environment variable; it can be changed only by using the Msoobe.exe tool.

6.   Correct Answers: B and C

A. Incorrect: Service Pack 2 does not add a program group to the Windows XP Start menu.

B. Correct: The easiest way to manually remove Service Pack 2 is to use Add Or Remove Programs.

C. Correct: You can uninstall Service Pack 2 from a command line by running the Spuninst.exe application.

D. Incorrect: The Setup.exe application cannot be used to remove Service Pack 2.

7.   Correct Answers: D

A. Incorrect: Most retail product keys can be used to activate only a single computer, and you have already installed Windows XP Professional on your laptop. Additionally, this would allow you to complete the installation of only a single computer.

B. Incorrect: You cannot use volume licensing product keys to activate retail Windows XP installations. Similarly, you cannot activate retail Windows XP installations with volume licensing product keys.

C. Incorrect: You cannot use volume licensing product keys to activate retail Windows XP installations, regardless of whether the installation occurs across a network or directly from the media.

D. Correct: You must use the volume licensing CD-ROM with the volume licensing product key.

Troubleshoot Failed Installations

Setting up an operating system is an extremely complex procedure. The rich variety of hardware components provides an unlimited number of combinations that the setup routine must be able to accommodate. To make these procedures even more complex, Windows XP Professional is often installed on hardware that was designed after the release of the operating system.

These complexities lead to occasional failures of the setup routine. Although these failures are challenging to resolve, Windows XP Professional makes this a much simpler process by providing detailed logging and debugging information. Understanding how to interpret these log files is critical to quickly resolving failed installations. If you find that these log files are not providing enough information to effectively troubleshoot a failed installation, detailed debugging can be enabled.

The setup routine has three installation phases: the **Setup Loader** phase, the **Text-Mode Setup** phase, and the **GUI-Mode Setup** phase. Understanding which installation steps occur during each of these three stages is critical to troubleshooting a failed install.

Throughout these setup phases, text-based log files are written to the local hard disk for later reference. These log files are located in the %systemroot% directory and end with a log file extension. After every successful and unsuccessful step of the installation routine, a detailed description of the action is appended to the various log files for later reference. Referring to these log files will uncover the nature of any problems experienced, even if the installation routine could complete successfully. If the installation routine fails, identifying the last log entries written helps isolate the nature of the failure.

Objective 1.5 Questions

1. You are attempting to perform a new manual installation of Windows XP on a system that already has Windows Me installed. The setup routine fails, and you accidentally clear the error message box before reading it. Which log file do you view first to read the details of the error? Choose the correct answer.

    A. Setuperr.log

    B. Comsetup.log

    C. IIS6.log

    D. Tsoc.log

2. You are attempting to perform a new manual installation of Windows XP on a system that already has Windows Me installed. The setup routine succeeds, but afterward you cannot connect to the system with the Terminal Services client. Which log files do you view to determine whether errors were experienced during the installation of the terminal services? Choose two correct answers.

    A. Setuperr.log

    B. Comsetup.log

    C. IIS6.log

    D. Tsoc.log

    E. Oewablog.txt

3. After several installation failures, you determine that you need to examine a debug log for the setup routine. You want the setup routine to create the most detailed debug log possible. Which command do you use? Choose the correct answer.

    A. *Winnt32 /debug7:debug.log*

    B. *Winnt32 /debug4:debug.log*

    C. *Winnt32 /debug1:debug.log*

    D. *Winnt32 /debug0:debug.log*

4. You are a desktop administrator for the Graphic Design Institute, a small design firm. Your firm recently hired a new designer who insisted his workstation use a Small Computer System Interface (SCSI) drive because disk performance is critical to his work. You purchase a new computer without a hard disk, install a SCSI adapter, and connect the SCSI drive according to the manufacturer's instructions. You install Windows XP Professional manually from the installation CD-ROM. During the installation, you receive an error message indicating that Setup could not find a hard disk. After double-checking the SCSI connections, you attempt the installation again and again receive the error. Which of the following procedures would most likely solve the problem? Choose the correct answer.

A. Perform the installation by using the original Windows XP Professional setup files from a shared folder on the network.

B. Slipstream Service Pack 2 for Windows XP into the installation files and perform the installation from the slipstreamed files.

C. Restart installation again and provide the SCSI driver when prompted by Setup.

D. Reconfigure the computer's BIOS to boot from the SCSI hard disk instead of the CD-ROM drive.

Objective 1.5 Answers

1.   **Correct Answers: A**

    A. Correct: The Windows XP setup routine creates the Setuperr.log file during installation, and adds a description of every error encountered. This file is located in the %systemroot% directory.

    B. Incorrect: The Comsetup.log file contains a description of the progress of COM+ (Component Object Model) installation, but does not contain general error log information.

    C. Incorrect: The IIS6.log file contains a description of the progress of the IIS6 installation, but does not contain general error log information.

    D. Incorrect: The Tsoc.log file contains a description of the progress of the installation of terminal services, but does not contain general error log information.

2.   **Correct Answers: A and D**

    A. Correct: The Windows XP setup routine creates the Setuperr.log file during installation, and adds a description of every error encountered. This file is located in the %systemroot% directory.

    B. Incorrect: The Comsetup.log file contains a description of the progress of COM+ (Component Object Model) installation, but does not contain general error log information.

    C. Incorrect: The IIS6.log file contains a description of the progress of the IIS6 installation, but does not contain general error log information.

    D. Correct: The Tsoc.log file contains a description of the progress of the installation of terminal services. Examining this file in addition to the Setuperr.log file might reveal more detailed information about the nature of the problem experienced.

    E. Incorrect: The Oewablog.txt file contains information about the Microsoft Outlook Express installation, but does not contain general error log information.

3.   **Correct Answers: B**

    A. Incorrect: Although the */debug[level]:[filename]* syntax is correct, debug level 7 is not a valid option.

    B. Correct: The */debug[level]:[filename]* syntax is correct, and debug level 4 is the highest level of debugging available. Possible options vary from 0 to 4; 0 represents severe errors, 1 represents errors, 2 represents warnings, 3 represents informational messages, and 4 represents very detailed information. Naturally, each higher level of debugging includes information from all lower levels.

C. **Incorrect:** Although the */debug[level]:[filename]* syntax is correct, debug level 1 records only errors and severe errors.

D. **Incorrect:** Although the */debug[level]:[filename]* syntax is correct, debug level 0 records only severe errors.

4.   Correct Answers: C

A. **Incorrect:** Performing the installation from a shared folder would not solve this problem because the hardware detection would not be changed.

B. **Incorrect:** Slipstreaming is an excellent way to reduce the time spent updating Windows XP after installation completes, but it is not likely to solve the problem of missing SCSI drivers.

C. **Correct:** Windows XP Setup requires drivers for many types of SCSI adapters to write the operating system files to the hard disk. Although the setup routine prompts you to provide SCSI drivers, many administrators are accustomed to ignoring the prompt and tend to overlook it when they do need it.

D. **Incorrect:** Although the computer will need to be configured to boot from the hard disk at some point, it will probably do so with the default BIOS settings. Regardless, the problem occurred before the setup procedure could copy files to the hard disk and before the computer needed to boot from the hard disk. Therefore, changing this BIOS setting would not affect the detection of the hard disk.

22 Implementing and Conducting Administration of Resources

For the average user, managing disks, shared folders, and printers is self-explanatory because Microsoft Windows XP does an excellent job of making these resources simple to administer. Administrators who are expected to troubleshoot these resources must understand these management tasks in more detail, however. For example, understanding the differences between File Allocation Table (FAT), FAT32, and NT File System (NTFS) can mean the difference between having a system that successfully dual boots between Windows Me and Windows XP, and a system that must be rebuilt from scratch. Although most users can set up a locally attached printer, troubleshooting problems with network printers can be extremely challenging.

Network connectivity is critical for most users, yet it is not always possible for users who travel with portable computers. Offline Files minimize the problems users experience when disconnected from the network or accessing files across an unreliable network connection. Files in a shared folder can be automatically synchronized with the local hard disk when connected to a network, and users can access these files transparently when the network is not available. Files even can be edited while offline and automatically synchronized later.

Tested Skills and Suggested Practices

The skills you need to successfully master the Implementing and Conducting Administration of Resources domain on the *Installing, Configuring, and Administering Microsoft Windows XP Professional* exam include the following:

- Implementing and administering Windows XP file system features.

> **Important** You must perform these exercises only on a test computer. Modifying the disk configuration of production computers is very risky.

- ❑ Practice 1: Create a partition using the Disk Management snap-in.
- ❑ Practice 2: Convert a file system from FAT32 to NTFS using the Convert.exe command-line utility.

❏ Practice 3: Convert a basic disk to a dynamic disk using the Diskpart.exe command-line utility.

❏ Practice 4: Using the Disk Management snap-in, experiment with the different options available when accessing basic and dynamic disks.

❏ Practice 5: Create a striped disk by combining two dynamic disks.

❏ Practice 6: Use mount points to graft a dynamic volume into the file system of an existing volume.

❏ Practice 7: Move files between compressed and uncompressed folders on an NTFS volume, and notice whether the compression status is inherited from the source or destination folder.

❏ Practice 8: Move files between compressed and uncompressed folders on different NTFS volumes, and notice whether the compression status is inherited from the source or destination folder.

❏ Practice 9: Compress different types of files, and determine which file types benefit the most from compression.

❏ Practice 10: Create a share that only members of the Administrators group can access.

❏ Practice 11: Create a shared folder using the net share command.

❏ Practice 12: Remotely connect to a folder shared from a Windows XP Professional system. Then, from the system hosting the shared folder, open the Shared Folders snap-in. Use this tool to send all connected users a message warning them that their session will be disconnected. Finally, forcibly disconnect the user's session.

❏ Practice 13: Grant a user Full Control over a folder by using NTFS file permissions. Create a share, and grant that same user only Read access at a share level. Experiment with that user's ability to write files to the shared folder when accessing across the network. Do that user's rights differ when accessing the same folder when logged on locally?

❏ Practice 14: Stop the Workstation service and attempt to connect to a shared folder. Next, stop the Server service and attempt to create a shared folder.

Important   For the following task, you should complete at least Practices 1 through 4. If you want hands-on experience with every aspect of the exam and you have the extra lab resources needed to do Practice 5, then complete Practice 5 as well.

- Implementing and administering Windows XP printing.

  ❏ Practice 1: Add and share a new printer using the Add Printers Wizard.

  ❏ Practice 2: Stop the Workstation service and attempt to connect to a shared printer. Next, stop the Server service and attempt to create a shared printer.

  ❏ Practice 3: Remove the default right of the Power Users group to manage a printer.

  ❏ Practice 4: Print to a shared printer and immediately remove the document using the Printers And Faxes window.

  ❏ Practice 5: Connect to an Internet Printing Protocol (IPP) shared printer using a URL. Print a document and use Internet Explorer to remove the document before it has completed printing.

- Configuring offline files.

  ❏ Practice 1: Disable simple folder sharing—this is required for all following exercises.

  ❏ Practice 2: Create a shared folder and enable automatic caching of documents.

  ❏ Practice 3: Connect to a folder shared from a Windows XP system and pin individual documents to ensure synchronization.

  ❏ Practice 4: Change the default synchronization behavior so that files are synchronized nightly instead of when users log on and log off.

  ❏ Practice 5: Create a shared folder and configure it for automatic caching of programs. Connect to this share from a client system and pin files for synchronization. Disconnect from the network and modify the synchronized files. Reconnect to the network and attempt to synchronize the modified files to the shared folder.

Further Reading

This section lists supplemental readings by objective. We recommend that you study these sources thoroughly before taking exam 70-270.

Objective 2.1   Microsoft Corporation. *Microsoft Windows XP Professional Resource Kit Documentation*. Redmond, WA: Microsoft Press, 2001. Read Chapter 16, "Authorization and Access Control." This chapter provides an overview of file security concepts such as discretionary access control lists (available online at *http://www.microsoft.com/resources/documentation/Windows/XP/all/reskit/en-us/ prdd_sec_quni.asp*).

Objective 2.2   "Troubleshooting File and Printer Sharing in Microsoft Windows XP" by Microsoft Corporation (available online at *http://www.microsoft.com/downloads/ details.aspx?familyid=fd7fd48d-6b4a-448e-a632-076f98a351a2*).

"File and Printer Sharing with Microsoft Windows" by Microsoft Corporation (available online at *http://www.microsoft.com/downloads/details.aspx?FamilyID= 87C0A6DB-AEF8-4BEF-925E-7AC9BE791028*).

Objective 2.3   Microsoft Corporation. *Microsoft Windows XP Professional Resource Kit Documentation*. Redmond, WA: Microsoft Press, 2001. Read Chapter 11, "Enabling Printing and Faxing." This chapter provides detailed information about managing printers both locally and across a network (available online at *http:// www.microsoft.com/resources/documentation/Windows/XP/all/reskit/en-us/ prdl_pif_frpc.asp*).

"Troubleshooting File and Printer Sharing in Microsoft Windows XP" by Microsoft Corporation (available online at *http://www.microsoft.com/downloads/details .aspx?familyid=fd7fd48d-6b4a-448e-a632-076f98a351a2*).

"File and Printer Sharing with Microsoft Windows" by Microsoft Corporation (available online at *http://www.microsoft.com/downloads/details.aspx?FamilyID= 87C0A6DB-AEF8-4BEF-925E-7AC9BE791028*).

"Printing, Imaging, Fax, and All-in-One Frequently Asked Questions" by Bruce Sanderson (available online at *http://members.shaw.ca/bsanders/PrintingFAQ.HTM*).

Objective 2.4   "Choosing between NTFS, FAT, and FAT32" in Windows XP Help and Support Center (available online at *http://www.microsoft.com/windowsxp/home/ using/productdoc/en/choosing_between_NTFS_FAT_and_FAT32.asp*).

Objective 2.5   Microsoft Corporation. *Microsoft Windows XP Professional Resource Kit Documentation*. Redmond, WA: Microsoft Press, 2001. Read Chapter 5, "Managing Desktops," Chapter 6, "Managing Files and Folders," and Chapter 7, "Supporting Mobile Users." Pay particular attention to the sections that explain offline file synchronization and the suite of IntelliMirror technologies (available online at *http://www.microsoft.com/resources/documentation/Windows/XP/all/reskit/en-us/ prda_dcm_vdxa.asp*).

Monitor, Manage, and Troubleshoot Access to Files and Folders

Windows XP Professional administrators must understand the details behind NTFS compression precisely because it is so easy to use. As the feature increases in popularity, so will the number of users experiencing problems. Although any user can compress a folder using Windows Explorer, only the system administrators can explain exactly how compressed folders affect system performance and available disk space. Although Windows Explorer provides the most user-friendly interface into the details of compression, the Compact.exe utility is useful to administrators who need to compress multiple folders on a system or compress folders on many different systems.

NTFS file compression does not obey the same rules of inheritance as other aspects of Windows XP. For example, files that are copied always inherit the compression state of the destination folder. However, if you move files within a single volume, the compression state of the file is retained. To make things more confusing, files moved between different volumes inherit the compression state of the destination folder.

Windows XP Professional includes the ability to restrict users' access to files and folders using NTFS file permissions. For example, a user that has Full Control permission to a file might alter other users' rights to that file by modifying the discretionary access control list (DACL). Similar to the way Compact.exe provides a command-line alternative to enable compressing within Windows Explorer, Cacls.exe provides a command-line method for modifying file permissions.

Objective 2.1 Questions

1. You are moving files from the folder \OLD to the folder \NEW on the same volume. The \OLD folder is compressed using Windows XP NTFS compression, but the \NEW folder is not. What will the compression status of the files be after the move has completed?

    A. The files are uncompressed.

    B. The files are compressed.

    C. An error is returned because the files cannot be moved until their compression status matches that of the destination folder.

    D. The destination files are not compressed because Windows XP automatically changes the type of file transfer to copy instead of move to allow the transfer to complete.

2. You are copying files from the folder \OLD to the folder \NEW on the same volume. The \OLD folder is compressed using NTFS compression, but the \NEW folder is not. What will the compression status of the files be after the copy has completed?

    A. The files are uncompressed.

    B. The files will be compressed.

    C. An error is returned because the files cannot be copied until their compression status matches that of the destination folder.

    D. The destination files are not compressed because Windows XP automatically changes the type of file transfer to move instead of copy to allow the transfer to complete.

3. You need to copy a text-based log file that is compressed using NTFS compression to another volume. The file size of the log file is 2 GB; however, it consumes only 50 MB of the file system because it is compressed. The destination volume has only 1 GB of available space, so you enable compression on the folder that will receive the log file. During the file transfer, you receive an error indicating that there is not enough space to complete the copy. Which is the most likely explanation?

    A. Files copied between volumes are always written as uncompressed, regardless of the compression state of the source file or the destination folder.

    B. Files copied between volumes are first written to the disk uncompressed. NTFS then compresses the file only if the destination folder is compressed.

    C. Files copied between volumes inherit the compression state of the base volume, not the destination folder. Because the volume itself is not compressed, NTFS attempts to write the file uncompressed.

D. Compressed files must be written to unfragmented areas of the disk. Although the destination disk might have sufficient free space, the free space is fragmented and therefore unusable for compressed files.

4. You need to increase the free space on a Windows XP Professional system. Which of the following folders are good candidates for NTFS compression? Choose two correct answers.

   A. The system folder

   B. A folder of archived IIS log files

   C. A folder containing active IIS log files

   D. A folder containing images in the BMP format

   E. The %TEMP% folder

5. You need to grant Read access to files in the \Presentations folder for members of the Marketing user group in your Windows 2000 Active Directory. There is one exception, however, and his name is Todd. Todd is a member of the Marketing group, but must not be allowed access to your presentations. Which of these procedures provides the desired effect?

   A. Within the share permissions of the shared folder, grant Read access to the Marketing Read group. Using Windows Explorer, edit the NTFS file permissions and remove all existing permissions. Grant Change access to the Everyone group. Assign the members of the Marketing group Read access, and remove the rights from the user Todd.

   B. Within the folder share permissions, grant Everyone Full Control access. Using Windows Explorer, edit the NTFS file permissions and remove all existing permissions. Assign the No Access permissions to the Marketing group. Assign Read access to all members of the Marketing group with the exception of the user Todd.

   C. Within the folder share permissions, grant Marketing Read access. Using Windows Explorer, edit the NTFS file permissions and remove all existing permissions. Assign the No Access permissions to the user Todd.

   D. Within the folder share permissions, grant Everyone Full Control access. Using Windows Explorer, edit the NTFS file permissions and remove all existing permissions. Grant Read access to the Marketing group. Deny Read access permission to the user Todd.

Objective 2.1 Answers

1. **Correct Answers: B**

   A. **Incorrect:** Files that are moved within a single volume do not inherit the compression properties of the destination folder. This might seem confusing unless you understand that files are not rewritten when they are moved within a volume; only the pointer to the file is changed.

   B. **Correct:** When files are moved within a single volume, the compression status of the files does not change.

   C. **Incorrect:** Windows XP Professional does allow files to be moved to a destination folder that has a different compression status. However, the compression status of the files does not change and does not inherit the status of the destination folder.

   D. **Incorrect:** Although files that are copied *always* inherit the compression status of the destination folder, Windows XP Professional does not automatically change the type of file transfer from move to copy.

2. **Correct Answers: A**

   A. **Correct:** Files that are copied within a single volume always inherit the compression properties of the destination folder. This is in contrast to files that are moved within a single volume, which retain their compression status.

   B. **Incorrect:** When files are copied—either within a single volume or between volumes—the compression status of the files is inherited from the destination folder.

   C. **Incorrect:** Windows XP Professional does allow files to be copied to a destination folder that has a different compression status. The files inherit the compression status of the destination folder.

   D. **Incorrect:** Windows XP Professional has the capability to move and copy files between folders that have different compression settings. When files are copied, they always inherit the compression status of the destination folder.

3. **Correct Answers: B**

   A. **Incorrect:** Files copied between volumes inherit the compression property of the destination folder.

   B. **Correct:** Compression cannot occur on a file until the entire file has been received. Therefore, the file is written to the destination volume uncompressed. NTFS automatically compresses the file after the file transfer has completed. However, because the file is initially written uncompressed regardless of the compression state of the destination folder, the destination volume must have enough free space to store the entire uncompressed file.

    C. **Incorrect:** Files copied between volumes inherit the compression property of the destination folder, regardless of the compression status of the volume.

    D. **Incorrect:** Compressed files are written in blocks to the disk and can be fragmented like any other file. In fact, using compressed files necessitates more frequent disk defragmentation because of the way NTFS compresses files.

4.   Correct Answers: B and D

    A. **Incorrect:** NTFS compression negatively affects system performance, so you must avoid compressing files that are accessed frequently, such as system files.

    B. **Correct:** Old log files are an excellent candidate for NTFS compression. Log files compress significantly, and because they are not being regularly accessed, the compression will not negatively affect system performance.

    C. **Incorrect:** Windows XP Professional must perform processor-intensive calculations when writing to compressed files. These calculations can negatively affect system performance in situations where the processor is the performance bottleneck. Active IIS log files are written to regularly, making them a poor candidate for compression.

    D. **Correct:** BMP files compress extremely well because of the large amount of redundant information within a file. Unless bitmap files are being accessed continuously, they make an excellent candidate for compression.

    E. **Incorrect:** Many applications for Windows XP Professional use the %TEMP% folder continuously. The processor overhead associated with reading from and writing to compressed files can negatively affect system performance, so it is never advisable to compress the temp folder.

5.   Correct Answers: D

    A. **Incorrect:** This method does not accomplish the desired effect. Although the user Todd does not have explicit access to the folder, he has Change permissions because of his implicit membership in the Everyone group. His effective privileges are Read because of the restriction placed on the share.

    B. **Incorrect:** This method does not accomplish the desired effect. The No Access permission always overwrites all other permissions. So, all members of the Marketing group are restricted from accessing the files because the No Access right was assigned to the Marketing user group.

    C. **Incorrect:** This method does not accomplish the desired effect. The Marketing group has been assigned Read access to the folder share permissions, but this is not sufficient to enable members of that group to access files on the file system. For access to be granted to files accessed through a network share, a user must have access to both the share and the underlying file system. In this scenario, adding the Read right to the Marketing group within NTFS permissions accomplishes the desired effect.

D. Correct: This method accomplishes the desired effect. Members of the Marketing group have access to the shared folder through their implicit membership in the Everyone group. They have been explicitly assigned Read access to the folder at the NTFS level. Finally, Todd's access was removed by explicitly assigning Deny Read access rights. Assigning the Deny Read access right overrides the Read access that was granted to the Marketing group.

Manage and Troubleshoot Access to Shared Folders

Windows XP Professional is more than a desktop operating system; it is a peer-to-peer networking platform. Using Windows XP Professional, users can give other users carefully restricted access to files and printers across the network. Share permissions are similar to file permissions (when simple file sharing is disabled), but share permissions can be defined regardless of the underlying file system.

Besides traditional file sharing, Windows XP Professional users also have the option of creating Web shares. Users access Web shares in the same way as folder shares, or they can be accessed with a browser such as Microsoft Internet Explorer to present a more interactive Web interface. Web shares rely on the World Wide Web Publishing service instead of the Server service. The World Wide Web Publishing service is part of IIS, which is not installed during a standard Windows XP Professional installation.

Objective 2.2 Questions

1. Which Windows XP Professional built-in user groups have permissions to create shared folders? Choose two correct answers.

   A. Administrators

   B. Network Configuration Operators

   C. Backup Operators

   D. Power Users

   E. Users

2. You need to create a shared folder on your Windows XP Professional system, but you do not want users browsing the network to see the share. How do you name a share to ensure that it is not visible to users through My Network Places?

   A. PRIVATE#

   B. $PRIVATE

   C. #PRIVATE

   D. PRIVATE$

3. You are a domain administrator of your company's Windows 2003 Active Directory. You want to create a shared folder to allow one of your coworkers to view files on your Windows XP Professional system. You create an Active Directory user account named EricG, and grant it Change permissions to your \Presentations folder using Windows Explorer. You then share the folder as Presentations, remove all default share permissions, and assign the EricG user account Read permissions. What are EricG's effective permissions when connecting to the share across the network?

   A. No Access

   B. Read

   C. Change

   D. Full Control

4. What is the maximum number of users who can connect to a single folder shared on a Windows XP Professional system?

   A. 1

   B. 5

   C. 10

   D. 20

5.   You are the systems administrator for Margie's Travel, a travel agency with a small network based on Windows Server 2003 and Windows XP Professional. Recently, Kim Akers in Accounting created a spreadsheet that employees can use to automatically generate expense reports. Kim saved the spreadsheet to a share named ACCOUNTING on your organization's server (server.margiestravel.com) using the file name Expense-Reports.xls. Kim has a drive mapped to the shared folder, but nobody else at Margie's Travel understands how to access shared folders, so she wants to send out an e-mail with a Uniform Resource Locator (URL) that staff members can enter into Internet Explorer to open the file. Which URL do you recommend that Kim use?

   A. *ftp://server/accounting/expense-reports.xls*

   B. *http://server.margiestravel.com/accounting/expense-reports.xls*

   C. *file://server.margiestravel.com/accounting/expense-reports.xls*

   D. *http://server/accounting/expense%20reports.xls*

6.   As a favor to a friend, you are configuring two new Windows XP Professional computers to participate in a workgroup. Your friend needs to be able to share files between the two computers. After installing Windows XP Professional on both computers, and then installing Service Pack 2, what is the simplest procedure to allow one of the computers to share a folder?

   A. Simply share the folder.

   B. Share the folder. Then, select the File And Printer Sharing service on the list of Windows Firewall exceptions.

   C. Share the folder. Then, add TCP ports 389 and 445 and UDP ports 137 and 138 to the list of Windows Firewall exceptions.

   D. Share the folder. Then, add Services.exe to the list of Windows Firewall program exceptions.

7.   Which Windows component is required to share Web folders?

   A. Other Network File And Print Services

   B. Internet Information Services (IIS)

   C. Message Queuing

   D. Management and Monitoring Tools

Objective 2.2 Answers

1. **Correct Answers: A and D**

   A. Correct: Administrators, by default, can create shares on Windows XP Professional systems. Select the Computer Administrator account type to place a user only into the Administrators group when using the User Accounts Wizard. Grant this privilege only to users who understand the security implications associated with sharing folders across a network.

   B. Incorrect: The Network Configuration Operators group provides a member user with the ability to modify network parameters such as an IP address. However, it does not provide the ability to share folders.

   C. Incorrect: Although Backup Operators can access the entire file system for the purpose of backing up files, they do not have the ability to share folders.

   D. Correct: Power Users, by default, can create shares on Windows XP Professional systems. User accounts cannot be placed in the Power Users group directly from the Control Panel, however. To place a user account into the Power Users group, use the Computer Management administrative utility. Grant Power Users privilege only to users who understand the security implications associated with sharing folders across a network.

   E. Incorrect: One of the differences between the Power Users and the Users groups is that the Users group lacks the ability to create shared folders. Creating a shared folder provides access to the contents of that folder across the network, and, as a result, can weaken the security of a system if misused. Therefore, place users who do not understand the implications of shared folders only into the Users group. Select the Limited account type to place a user only into the Users group when using the User Accounts Wizard.

2. **Correct Answers: D**

   A. Incorrect: This answer is incorrect for the reasons stated in answer D.

   B. Incorrect: This answer is incorrect for the reasons stated in answer D.

   C. Incorrect: This answer is incorrect for the reasons stated in answer D.

   D. Correct: Hidden shares are created by ending the share name with a $.

3. **Correct Answers: B**

   A. Incorrect: Users have No Access rights to the share only if they are explicitly denied access or if neither they nor any group they belong to are named in the permissions. In this case, the user has been assigned Change file permissions and Read share permissions.

B. Correct: Share permissions override file permissions when the user accesses files across the network. Windows XP Professional restricts EricG's access to read-only because that user has only Read share permissions. If EricG were to log on locally to the system, he could modify files because Change permissions are assigned at an NTFS level. In other words, when users access files using a network share, only the most restrictive permissions are granted.

C. Incorrect: Although EricG has Change permissions at the NTFS level, the Read share permissions take precedence because Windows XP Professional uses the most restrictive permissions when comparing access at both the share level and file level.

D. Incorrect: The user EricG has Full Control permissions to the files in the shared folder only if the user were explicitly granted Full Control in both the file permissions and the share permissions.

4.   **Correct Answers: C**

   A. Incorrect: A maximum of 10 users can connect to a folder shared on a Windows XP Professional system.

   B. Incorrect: A maximum of 10 users can connect to a folder shared on a Windows XP Professional system.

   C. Correct: Only 10 users can simultaneously connect to a folder shared on a Windows XP Professional system. You need to use a member of the Windows Server 2003 family to provide access to more than 10 users simultaneously.

   D. Incorrect: A maximum of 10 users can connect to a folder shared on a Windows XP Professional system.

5.   **Correct Answers: C**

   A. Incorrect: The protocol specified in this URL, File Transfer Protocol (FTP), probably will not work because the question did not specify that FTP is running on the server. FTP is an optional component of Internet Information Server (IIS) that is available for both Windows Server 2003 and Windows XP Professional, but it is not enabled by default, and additional configuration would be required to enable files to be shared through FTP.

   B. Incorrect: The protocol specified in this URL, Hypertext Transfer Protocol (HTTP), probably will not work because the question did not specify that HTTP is running on the server. The HTTP protocol is the foundation for Web communications, and is implemented by the IIS and available for both Windows Server 2003 and Windows XP Professional. Although it would be possible to configure the server to share this file via HTTP, IIS does not share any files by default.

C. Correct: Specifying *file* for the protocol in the URL instructs Internet Explorer to access the file using shared folders. This URL is exactly equivalent to \\server.margiestravel.com\accounting\expense-reports.xls.

D. Incorrect: As with answer B, the protocol is incorrect. Additionally, the hyphen in the file name has been replaced with %20, a special sequence used in URLs to represent a space character, not a hyphen.

6. **Correct Answers: A**

A. **Correct:** Windows Firewall is enabled by default after Service Pack 2 is installed. However, Windows XP automatically configures Windows Firewall to allow file and printer sharing traffic when you create a share.

B. **Incorrect:** You do not need to manually select the File And Printer Sharing service because Windows XP automatically adds it to the Windows Firewall exception list.

C. **Incorrect:** Although this procedure does work, you do not need to manually add ports 389 and 445 to the list of Windows Firewall exceptions because Windows XP automatically adds the File And Printer Sharing service to the list of Windows Firewall exceptions.

D. **Incorrect:** As with answers B and C, you do not need to add any exceptions because Windows XP handles it automatically.

7. **Correct Answers: B**

A. **Incorrect:** This Windows component allows sharing printers with UNIX computers and does not relate to Web folders.

B. **Correct:** IIS is required for Web folders. Web folders use the HTTP protocol, which is provided by the World Wide Web Publishing service, a component of IIS.

C. **Incorrect:** Message Queuing is used by some applications to communicate across a network. However, it is not required by Web folders.

D. **Incorrect:** This component is primarily used by network administrators to manage and monitor Windows XP computers.

Connect to Local and Network Print Devices

Windows XP Professional allows users on the network to access a printer attached to a remote system in several different ways: standard file and printer sharing, Internet Printing Protocol (IPP), a Standard TCP/IP Port, and the Line Printer Remote (LPR) protocol. Controlling access to a shared printer is very different from controlling the security applied to file share. The primary rights available are Print, Manage Printers, and Manage Documents. By default, Everyone is allowed to print and manage their own documents, and only Power Users and Administrators are granted access to manage all documents and printers.

Connecting to remote printers is handled through the Add Printer Wizard—the same interface used to set up a directly connected printer. To connect to a network printer, users have the option of selecting the printer by browsing the network, typing a Universal Naming Convention (UNC) name in the form \\server\printer, or typing a URL in the form *http://server/printers/printer/.printer*. Local printers, networked LPR printers, and networked Standard TCP/IP printers are all configured as if they are connected directly to the computer.

Objective 2.3 Questions

1. Which services must be running to connect to and print to network printers? Choose two correct answers.

    A. Computer Browser

    B. Net Logon

    C. Network Connections

    D. Print Spooler

    E. Server

    F. Workstation

2. Which services must be running to share a printer on a network and allow network users to print? Choose two correct answers.

    A. Computer Browser

    B. Net Logon

    C. Network Connections

    D. Print Spooler

    E. Server

    F. Workstation

3. You are configuring your Windows XP Professional computer to connect to a printer that is shared by a UNIX server using the Line Printer Daemon (LPD) service. How should you connect to the printer?

    A. In Printers and Faxes, double-click Add A Printer. In the Add Printer Wizard, add a local printer. When prompted, create a new port of type LPR Port.

    B. In Printers and Faxes, double-click Add A Printer. In the Add Printer Wizard, add a network printer. When prompted, create a new port of type LPR Port.

    C. In Printers And Faxes, double-click Add A Printer. In the Add Printer Wizard, add a local printer. When prompted, create a new port of type Standard TCP/IP Port.

    D. In Printers And Faxes, double-click Add A Printer. In the Add Printer Wizard, add a network printer. When prompted, create a new port of type Standard TCP/IP Port.

4.   You are using a Windows XP Professional computer with Service Pack 2 installed and Internet Explorer's default security settings. You want to connect to a printer on the Internet by using Web-based printer management. How will Windows XP connect to the printer?

   A. Using Print Services for UNIX and LPR

   B. Using IPP and HTTP

   C. Using remote procedure call (RPC) true-connect

   D. Using LPT1 and the Standard TCP/IP Port

Objective 2.3 Answers

1.   Correct Answers: D and F

A. Incorrect: Although the Computer Browser service helps users find printers on a network, it is not required to explicitly connect to shared network printers.

B. Incorrect: The Net Logon service is used for pass-through authentication for computers in a domain, but is not required to connect to shared network printers.

C. Incorrect: The Network Connections service is used to manage objects in the Network and Dial-Up Connections folder and does not need to be running to connect to shared network printers.

D. Correct: The Print Spooler service is responsible for receiving files from applications and forwarding them to printers. Any time a user needs to print from a Windows XP Professional system, the Printer Spooler service must be running—including printing to a network printer.

E. Incorrect: The Server service is required only on the system hosting the shared printer. Windows XP Professional systems connecting to the shared printer across the network do not need to have the Server service running.

F. Correct: The Workstation service is responsible for establishing connections to shared files and printers. Therefore, although it is not required when printing to a local printer, it is required when printing to a shared network printer.

2.   Correct Answers: D and E

A. Incorrect: Although the Computer Browser service helps users find printers on a network, it is not required to explicitly share printers.

B. Incorrect: The Net Logon service is used for pass-through authentication for computers in a domain, but is not required to shared network printers. However, if the Net Logon service is not running, users must have an account on the Windows XP Professional system that is sharing the printer. For users authenticated using domain accounts, the Net Logon service is required because it enables pass-through authentication.

C. Incorrect: The Network Connections services is used to manage objects in the Network and Dial-Up Connections folder, and does not need to be running to share network printers.

D. Correct: The Print Spooler service is responsible for receiving files from applications and forwarding them to printers. Any time a user needs to print to a Windows XP Professional system, the Printer Spooler service must be running—including remote users printing to a shared printer.

E. Correct: The Server service is required on the system hosting the shared printer because it is responsible for receiving network connections from remote systems. The Server service interacts with the Workstation service, which acts as the client in the client-server relationship.

F. Incorrect: The Workstation service is responsible for establishing connections to shared files and printers. Although it is required for users connecting to a remote printer, it does not need to be running on the Windows XP Professional system sharing the printer.

3.   Correct Answers: A

A. Correct: Although you are connecting to a network printer, the Add Printer Wizard treats LPD-based printers as local printers with an LPR port.

B. Incorrect: This would seem to be the logical answer because the printer is shared across a network. However, the Add Printer Wizard treats LPD-based printers as local printers.

C. Incorrect: The Standard TCP/IP Port type is usually used by printers that connect directly to a network. You must use LPR Port to connect to LPD-based printers.

D. Incorrect: As with answer C, this is the incorrect port type. LPR Port must be used with LPD-based printers.

4.   Correct Answers: B

A. Incorrect: Although Windows XP does support using LPR, it does not automatically configure LPR from Web-based printer management.

B. Correct: If the client's Internet Explorer security settings for the print server are set to Medium or higher, Windows XP creates an IPP printer connection using an HTTP port. In this case, the print server is on the Internet, and therefore Internet Explorer will assign the print server the Medium security level by default.

C. Incorrect: Windows XP uses RPC true-connect only if the client's Internet Explorer settings are set to Medium-Low or lower. In this case, the print server is on the Internet, and therefore Internet Explorer will assign the print server the Medium security level by default.

D. Incorrect: Although Windows XP does support using a Standard TCP/IP Port, it will not automatically configure this port type from Web-based printer management.

Objective 2.4

Configure and Manage File Systems

Windows XP Professional supports both basic disks and dynamic disks. Basic disks are the only format available to Windows Me, Windows NT 4.0, and earlier operating systems. Dynamic disks support three different types of volumes: simple volumes, spanned volumes, and striped volumes. Simple volumes exist within a single disk. Spanned volumes concatenate multiple disks into a single volume. Striped volumes are similar to spanned volumes in that they combine multiple drives. However, striped volumes also improve performance because they enable data to be read from or written to both disks simultaneously.

Windows XP supports FAT and NTFS file systems for accessing local disks. The FAT16 and FAT32 file systems allow for dual booting with Windows 95, Windows 98, or Windows Me. NTFS is the preferred file system, however, and adds user-level file permissions, compression, encryption, disk quotas, volume mount points, directory junctions, and more. Windows XP provides the Convert.exe tool to convert from FAT to NTFS for users upgrading from previous operating systems.

Several additional file systems are available for accessing removable media. Floppy disks are formatted with FAT12, a version of FAT optimized for low-capacity media. The CD-ROM File System (CDFS) is the standard format for CD-ROMs. Universal Disk Format (UDF) is primarily used for digital video disc (DVD) access.

Objective 2.4 Questions

1. You are building a new Windows XP Professional system for a user in the imaging department of a publishing firm. Knowing that disk input/output (I/O) is critical for image editing, you decide to create a single volume striped across two Small Computer System Interface (SCSI) disks. Which disk and volume type must you use?

    A. Basic disks with spanned volumes

    B. Basic disks with striped volumes

    C. Dynamic disks with spanned volumes

    D. Dynamic disks with striped volumes

2. You are installing both Windows Me and Windows XP Professional onto a system with a single 36 GB hard disk. You need to dual boot between the two operating systems. Which file system must you use?

    A. FAT

    B. FAT32

    C. CDFS

    D. NTFS

3. On which operating systems can you create a RAID 5 volume? Choose four correct answers.

    A. Windows Me

    B. Windows NT Workstation 4.0

    C. Windows NT Server 4.0

    D. Windows 2000 Professional

    E. Windows 2000 Server

    F. Windows XP Professional

    G. Windows Server 2003

4. Which tools can be used to convert a disk from basic to dynamic? Choose two correct answers.

    A. Disk Management snap-in

    B. Fsutil.exe

    C. Format.exe

    D. Diskpart.exe

    E. Disk Defragmenter snap-in

5. You are a systems administrator for Lucerne Publishing. Editors store manuscripts on their local computers during the reviewing process, which consumes a large amount of disk space. One user, Lori Shea, ran out of disk space on her FAT32-formatted C:\ drive and purchased an external hard drive that connects to the computer via USB 2.0. She plugged it in and could immediately use it because it was preformatted with the FAT32 file system. The fact that it uses a separate drive letter (E:\) disturbs her folder organization, however. She would rather have the drive available as a subfolder of My Documents. Which of the following solutions would meet her requirements?

    A. Use the Disk Management snap-in in the Computer Management console to reformat the drive using the NTFS file system. Then, create a new subfolder in My Documents, and mount the new drive in that folder.

    B. Open a command prompt and run the command convert C:/fs:ntfs. Then, create a new subfolder in My Documents, and mount the new drive in that folder.

    C. Create a new subfolder in My Documents. Then, open a command prompt and run the command fsutil reparsepoint E: destination_folder.

    D. Create a new subfolder in My Documents. Then, open a command prompt and run the command format E /FS:NTFS /C: destination_folder.

Objective 2.4 Answers

1.   Correct Answers: D

   A. Incorrect: Basic disks cannot support spanned volumes. Regardless, spanned volumes do not improve disk I/O because data on the disk is not generally written to or read from multiple disks simultaneously.

   B. Incorrect: Although striped volumes are the correct choice for improving disk I/O when accessing multiple disks, basic disks cannot support striped volumes.

   C. Incorrect: Although dynamic disks can support spanned volumes, spanned volumes do not improve disk I/O because data on the disk is not generally written to or read from multiple disks simultaneously.

   D. Correct: Dynamic disks support striped volumes, whereas basic disks do not. Striped volumes combine multiple disks into a single logical volume. When files are written to or read from the volume, both disks are accessed simultaneously. When SCSI disks are used, disk I/O performance improves.

2.   Correct Answers: B

   A. Incorrect: Although both Windows Me and Windows XP Professional can access FAT partitions, FAT is not optimized for such large disk partitions.

   B. Correct: Both Windows Me and Windows XP Professional can access FAT32 partitions, and FAT32 can efficiently address 36 GB hard disks. For these reasons, FAT32 is the best choice for dual booting between Windows Me and Windows XP Professional.

   C. Incorrect: CDFS is a file system used only for CD-ROMs. It is not an option for hard disk drives.

   D. Incorrect: Although NTFS is an excellent choice for Windows XP Professional systems, NTFS partitions cannot be accessed from Windows Me.

3.   Correct Answers: B, C, E, and G

   A. Incorrect: Windows Me cannot support RAID 5 nor any NTFS volume.

   B. Correct: Windows NT Workstation 4.0 supports RAID 5 volumes across three or more disks using NTFS partitions. Windows NT Workstation 4.0 was the last desktop operating system from Microsoft to support RAID 5.

   C. Correct: Windows NT Server 4.0 supports RAID 5 volumes across three or more disks using NTFS partitions.

   D. Incorrect: Windows 2000 Professional supports NTFS, but does not support RAID 5 volumes.

E. Correct: Windows 2000 Server supports RAID 5 volumes across three or more disks using NTFS partitions.

F. Incorrect: Windows XP Professional supports NTFS, but does not support RAID 5 volumes.

G. Correct: The Windows Server 2003 family supports RAID 5 volumes across three or more disks using NTFS partitions.

4.   **Correct Answers: A and D**

A. Correct: The Disk Management snap-in is the preferred way to upgrade a disk from basic to dynamic. To do this, open the Disk Management snap-in or launch the Computer Management tool and select Disk Management. Right-click the disk to be upgraded, and select Convert To Dynamic Disk. Complete the process by following the instructions that appear.

B. Incorrect: Fsutil.exe is useful for modifying aspects of the file system, but it cannot be used to modify disk properties.

C. Incorrect: The Format.exe utility is used to add a file system to a disk that has already been configured. It cannot be used to change properties of a disk, such as whether the disk is basic or dynamic.

D. Correct: Diskpart.exe provides command-line access to functionality normally accessed using the Disk Management snap-in. To upgrade disk 0 from basic to dynamic, you must first open the Diskpart.exe shell by executing the command Diskpart.exe. At the *DISKPART>* prompt, type the command **select disk 0** to indicate that future disk-related commands will affect disk 0. Then, type the command **convert dynamic** to convert the disk from basic to dynamic.

E. Incorrect: The Disk Defragmenter utility is used to reorganize file segments on a disk to improve performance. It does not have the ability to upgrade disks from basic to dynamic.

5.   **Correct Answers: B**

A. Incorrect: Any volume type can be mounted only in an empty folder on an NTFS volume, but FAT does not support mounting a separate drive to an empty folder. Therefore, the external drive does not need to have the NTFS file system, but the C:\ drive does.

B. Correct: The C:\ drive must be converted to NTFS before external drive can be mounted to a folder. This answer has the proper syntax for converting the drive.

C. Incorrect: Fsutil.exe is useful for modifying aspects of the file system, but it cannot be used to create folder mount points.

D. Incorrect: The Format.exe utility is used to add a file system to a disk that has already been configured. It cannot be used to create folder mount points.

Manage and Troubleshoot Access to and Synchronization of Offline Files

Enterprise workers rely on the network to access information and exchange files. Users who always work at the office take this access for granted—but roaming users cannot. When users with portable computers disconnect from the network, their access to business-critical information is also disconnected. To ease the pain of being away from the network, users can synchronize important files to their portable computers for offline use.

Users control when their computer synchronizes files using the Synchronization Manager. This tool is useful for troubleshooting offline file problems because it displays when folders were last synchronized. It can also be used to configure offline files for synchronization when users log on or log off, while the computer is idle, or at specific times.

Objective 2.5 Questions

1. Which caching options are selected by default for folders shared from a Windows XP Professional system?

   A. Caching on shared folders is disabled by default.

   B. Manual Caching Of Documents is selected by default.

   C. Automatic Caching Of Documents is selected by default.

   D. Automatic Caching Of Programs And Documents is selected by default.

2. You have configured a shared network folder for offline use with your Windows XP Professional system. While you were disconnected from the network, you edited one of the synchronized files. At the same time, another user modified the network copy of this document. What happens when you reconnect your system to the network?

   A. The copy of the document on the network share is automatically overwritten with your cached copy.

   B. Changes you made to the cached document are automatically merged into the shared networked document.

   C. Windows XP Professional prompts you to choose which version to keep, and allows you to rename one of the copies of the document.

   D. The copy of the document that was modified most recently is kept. Changes to the older version of the document are discarded.

3. The vice president of marketing at your organization uses a Windows XP Professional laptop computer. While traveling, she needs to update a set of presentations located on a shared network folder. She will intermittently dial into your corporate network, but also plans to make updates while offline. Which synchronization strategy meets her needs?

   A. Disable simple file sharing. Enable automatic caching of documents by clicking the Caching button on the server's shared folder properties. From the Synchronization Manager settings, click the Setup button. Select the When I Log On To My Computer and When I Log Off My Computer check boxes for automatic synchronization for both her local area network (LAN) and dial-up connections.

   B. Disable simple file sharing. Enable automatic caching of programs and documents by clicking the Caching button on the server's shared folder properties. From the Synchronization Manager settings, click the Setup button. Select When I Log On To My Computer and When I Log Off My Computer for automatic synchronization for both her LAN and dial-up connections.

    C. Disable simple file sharing. Enable manual caching of documents by clicking the Caching button on the server's shared folder properties. From Windows Explorer, right-click the files and select the Make Available Offline check box to pin the files that she needs to access offline. From the Synchronization Manager settings, click the Setup button. Select When I Log On To My Computer and When I Log Off My Computer for automatic synchronization for both her LAN and dial-up connections.

    D. Disable simple file sharing. Enable manual caching of documents by clicking the Caching button on the server's shared folder properties. From Windows Explorer, right-click the files and select Make Available Offline to pin the files that she needs to access offline. From the Synchronization Manager settings, click the Setup button. Deselect the When I Log On To My Computer and When I Log Off My Computer check boxes for automatic synchronization for both her LAN and dial-up connections. Instead, select the Synchronize The Selected Items While My Computer Is Idle check box.

4. You are a systems administrator at a medium-sized company with 250 employees. All employees have Windows XP Professional computers, and all computers are members of your Windows Server 2003 domain. About 50 of those employees are salespeople who frequently travel with laptops. While connected to the internal network, these salespeople access shared folders containing presentations, spreadsheets, and databases to manage their contacts, gather information, and record notes. To enable these salespeople to work with these files when traveling, you have enabled offline file caching for the shared folder. However, during a recent security review, your manager noticed that there was extremely confidential financial information in the Excel spreadsheets. Your manager has asked you to ensure that these .XLS files are not stored on the salespeople's computers for offline use. What is the best way to accomplish this?

    A. On the Offline Files tab of the Folder Options dialog box on the client computers, select the Encrypt Offline Files To Secure Data check box.

    B. Modify the file permissions on all .XLS files so that salespeople are denied access.

    C. Modify the Computer Configuration\Administrative Templates\Network\Offline Files\Files Not Cached domain Group Policy setting to add the .XLS file name extension.

    D. Modify the share permissions for the shared folder containing the XLS files so that salespeople are denied Read access.

Obejective 2.5 Answers

1. **Correct Answers: B**

    A. Incorrect: Caching is enabled by default for folders shared from Windows XP Professional systems.

    B. Correct: By default, shared folders on a Windows XP Professional system have manual caching for documents enabled. Users connecting to the share must then specifically mark files as being available offline for the caching to be effective—no files are automatically cached with this setting.

    C. Incorrect: The Automatic Caching Of Documents setting on a shared folder causes the client system to cache documents in the folder after they have been accessed. Older and less frequently accessed cached documents are automatically removed to save space on the connecting user's hard disk. This option is not enabled by default.

    D. Incorrect: The Automatic Caching Of Programs And Documents setting on a shared folder is similar to the Automatic Caching Of Documents setting, but it does not allow files on the shared folder to be overwritten. This setting enables caching for read-only documents and applications, and ensures that changes made to a document offline are not synchronized back to the shared folder. This option is not enabled by default.

2. **Correct Answers: C**

    A. Incorrect: Windows XP never automatically overwrites a document that has been updated since synchronization, even if changes were made to a cached version of the document.

    B. Incorrect: Windows XP lacks the capability to merge changes. However, you can manually merge changes between multiple versions of documents.

    C. Correct: Windows XP Professional provides the user with the option of overwriting one version of the document. Avoid this, however, because changes to the discarded document are lost. Instead, choose the option of renaming one of the documents and manually merge the document's changes.

    D. Incorrect: Windows XP never automatically overwrites a document that has been updated since synchronization.

3. **Correct Answers: C**

    A. Incorrect: The automatic caching of documents setting meets the user's needs, but this synchronization strategy does not include pinning the files for offline use. Pinning files ensures that they are always synchronized. With this strategy, files are available offline only when the user accessed those files prior to disconnecting from the network.

B. Incorrect: The Automatic Caching Of Programs And Documents setting does not meet the user's needs because this is a read-only caching strategy. Files accessed through this type of shared folder cannot be edited offline and automatically synchronized the next time the user connects.

C. Correct: This synchronization strategy meets the user's needs. When manual caching is enabled on a folder, the user must pin files for them to be synchronized. Manual caching is enabled on shared folders by default, and Synchronization Manager is configured to synchronize files by default when users log on and log off.

D. Incorrect: The manual caching of documents setting meets the user's needs, except that the synchronization strategy was changed to happen when the computer was idle. This setting must not be used with users who are intermittently connected to the network because the computer is unlikely to be both connected and idle.

4.   Correct Answers: C

A. Incorrect: Although encrypting offline files does improve security, it does not ensure that .XLS files will not be stored on the salespeople's computers for offline use.

B. Incorrect: This would prevent salespeople from storing the files for offline use; however, it would also prevent them from accessing the files when they are connected to the network.

C. Correct: This Group Policy setting controls which file extensions can be cached on computers that apply the Group Policy Object (GPO). By default, several types of files are not cached to prevent multiuser databases from being cached.

D. Incorrect: This would prevent salespeople from storing the files for offline use; however, it would also prevent them from accessing the files when they are connected to the network.

23 Implementing, Managing, Monitoring, and Troubleshooting Hardware Devices and Drivers

Installing new hardware in a computer requires connecting it to the computer and then installing software, called a **device driver**, so that Microsoft Windows XP can communicate with the hardware. Usually, Windows XP finds the device and automatically installs the device driver. However, you must be prepared to troubleshoot problems with this process, particularly when working with hardware that is more than a few years old. You should be able to manually add, update, and roll back device drivers when problems arise.

The device driver is not always the only software you need. Computer motherboards and many other hardware devices have **firmware** that contain code independent of the operating system needed for startup and initialization of the device. If you have problems with a device that an updated device driver does not resolve, verify that the computer's firmware and the device's firmware are up-to-date and configured properly. Although you can use Device Manager to update device drivers, you will need a software tool provided by the hardware manufacturer to update a device's firmware.

Tested Skills and Suggested Practices

The skills that you need to successfully master the Installing Windows XP Professional objective domain on the *Installing, Configuring, and Administering Microsoft Windows XP Professional* exam include the following:

> **Important**   For the following task, you should complete at least Practices 1 through 3. If you want hands-on experience with every aspect of the exam and you have the extra lab resources needed to do Practice 4, complete Practice 4 as well.

- Implement, manage, and troubleshoot disk devices.
    - ❏ Practice 1: Configure Chkdsk to scan your C: drive and fix any problems that it finds. You will probably need to restart your computer.
    - ❏ Practice 2: Use the Disk Defragmenter to defragment your C: drive.

❑ Practice 3: Change the drive letter of your CD-ROM disk to T: and then change it back.

❑ Practice 4: On a test computer with multiple hard disks, upgrade a basic disk other than the system disk to a dynamic disk. Afterward, note whether you can downgrade the disk back to a basic disk.

Important For the following task, you should complete at least Practices 1 and 2. If you want hands-on experience with every aspect of the exam and you have the extra lab resources needed to do Practice 3, complete Practice 3 as well.

■ Implement, manage, and troubleshoot display devices.

❑ Practice 1: Change the refresh rate on your video adapter. Note the difference between high and low refresh rates. Afterward, reset the refresh rate to the highest rate supported by your monitor.

❑ Practice 2: Open Internet Explorer, maximize the window, and visit the *http:// www.microsoft.com* Web site. Then, use the Display Properties dialog box to adjust your monitor to several different resolutions. At each resolution, notice how the Web page appears different. Note the resolution that is the easiest to read while still enabling Internet Explorer to display the entire width of the Web page without scrolling left and right.

❑ Practice 3: On a test computer with one video adapter, install a second video adapter and video monitor; configure the computer for multiple monitors.

■ Configure Advanced Configuration Power Interface (ACPI).

❑ Practice 1: Check to see whether your computer is an ACPI system. Compare an ACPI-compatible with one that is not compatible.

❑ Practice 2: Review the various Power Schemes; create and test a custom Power Scheme.

❑ Practice 3: Enable hibernation, and then hibernate your computer.

■ Implement, manage, and troubleshoot input and output (I/O) devices.

❑ Practice 1: Install Plug and Play hardware such as a digital camera, scanner, and network card into an existing Windows XP Professional computer.

❑ Practice 2: Open Device Manager and inspect the properties of all the objects displayed there. Run the hardware troubleshooter for some of the devices by clicking the Troubleshoot button on the General tab of the device's Properties window.

❑ Practice 3: Familiarize yourself with the other tools available for troubleshooting hardware, such as Dxdiag.exe, Winmsd.exe, Sigverif.exe, and Verifier.exe.

- Manage and troubleshoot drivers and driver signing.

  ❑ Practice 1: Download updated drivers for one of the hardware devices and install them. Try installing updated drivers from the Windows Update Web site; also check the Web site of the hardware device manufacturer. Then, roll back the driver to the previous version.

  ❑ Practice 2: Download an updated driver for one of your hardware devices. Notice the current driver version before the upgrade using Device Manager. Next, install the updated driver. Restart your computer if necessary, and launch System Restore. Windows XP should have automatically created a restore point before you installed the driver. Restore to this point, and restart your computer. Use Device Manager to verify that the driver version was returned to the version before the update.

> **Important**   For the following task, you should complete at least Practice 1. If you want hands-on experience with every aspect of the exam and you have a test computer available, complete Practice 2 as well.

- Monitor and configure multiprocessor computers.

  ❑ Practice 1: Run the Performance snap-in to view and analyze data relating to the CPUs.

  ❑ Practice 2: On a test computer, use Recovery Console to replace the hardware abstraction layer (HAL) and kernel files with the original versions from the Windows XP Professional CD-ROM.

Further Reading

This section lists supplemental readings by objective. We recommend that you study these sources thoroughly before taking exam 70-270.

Objective 3.1   Microsoft Corporation. *Microsoft Windows XP Professional Resource Kit Documentation*. Redmond, WA: Microsoft Press, 2001. Read Chapter 12, "Disk Management," and Chapter 13, "File Systems." These chapters explain the various storage types and partition styles available in Windows XP Professional, the Disk Management snap-in, and the command-line utilities you can use to manage storage devices. Review Chapter 27, "Troubleshooting Disks and File Systems." This chapter outlines the troubleshooting tools available in Windows XP Professional, discusses many common problems relating to disk devices, and tells you how to correct them (available online at *http://www.microsoft.com/resources/documentation/Windows/XP/all/reskit/en-us/prork_overview.asp*).

Objective 3.2   Microsoft Corporation. *Microsoft Windows XP Professional Resource Kit Documentation*. Redmond, WA: Microsoft Press, 2001. Read Chapter 9, "Managing Devices," focusing on the sections about installing and configuring hardware and device drivers. Also read the sections called "Configuring the Display" and "Using Multiple Monitors." Review the list of error messages described in Appendix F, "Device Manager Error Codes" (available online at *http://www.microsoft.com/resources/documentation/Windows/XP/all/reskit/en-us/prdh_dmt_zehg.asp*).

Objective 3.3   Microsoft Corporation. *Microsoft Windows XP Professional Resource Kit Documentation*. Redmond, WA: Microsoft Press, 2001. Read Chapter 7, "Supporting Mobile Users," for a thorough look at all the challenges unique to managing mobile computers. Read Chapter 9, "Managing Devices" and review the section called "Power Management" (available online at *http://www.microsoft.com/resources/documentation/Windows/XP/all/reskit/en-us/prork_overview.asp*).

"Power Management in Windows XP," by Charlie Russel (available online at *http://www.microsoft.com/windowsxp/using/setup/learnmore/russel_02march25.mspx*).

Objective 3.4   Microsoft Corporation. *Microsoft Windows XP Professional Resource Kit Documentation*. Redmond, WA: Microsoft Press, 2001. Read the sections called "Other Hardware Support" and "Hardware Troubleshooting" in Chapter 9, "Managing Devices." Read Chapter 10, "Managing Digital Media" and review the "Digital Media Components Overview" section to ensure that you understand which features Windows XP Professional includes for creating and managing digital media. Read the "Troubleshooting Digital Media" section to learn about solving a wide range of typical problems. Read Chapter 26, "Troubleshooting Concepts and Strategies." This chapter provides a generalized troubleshooting methodology, steps to take for gathering information, additional online and print resources for technical information, and step-by-step troubleshooting instructions for a variety of common issues (available online at *http://www.microsoft.com/resources/documentation/Windows/XP/all/reskit/en-us/prork_overview.asp*).

"General USB troubleshooting in Windows XP," by Microsoft Corporation (available online at *http://support.microsoft.com/?kbid=310575*).

"How to troubleshoot wireless network connections in Windows XP Service Pack 2," by Microsoft Corporation (available online at *http://support.microsoft.com/?kbid=870702*).

"Wireless LAN Enhancements in Windows XP Service Pack 2," by Joseph Davies (available online at *http://www.microsoft.com/technet/community/columns/cableguy/cg0804.mspx*).

"Microsoft Windows XP: An Overview of Windows Image Acquisition," by William Keener (available online at *http://support.microsoft.com/?scid=%2Fservicedesks%2Fwebcasts%2Fen%2Ftranscripts%2Fwct042203.asp*).

Objective 3.5   Microsoft Corporation. *Microsoft Windows XP Professional Resource Kit Documentation*. Redmond, WA: Microsoft Press, 2001. Read Chapter 9, "Managing Devices," paying close attention to the sections titled "Device Drivers" and "Installing Drivers" (available online at *http://www.microsoft.com/resources/documentation/ Windows/XP/all/reskit/en-us/prdh_dmt_zehg.asp*).

"Troubleshoot Device Driver Problems," by Paul McFedries (available online at *http://www.microsoft.com/windowsxp/using/setup/expert/ mcfedries_03may12.mspx*).

"Digital Signature Benefits for Windows Users," by Microsoft Corporation (available online at *http://www.microsoft.com/winlogo/benefits/signature-benefits.mspx*).

"How to Troubleshoot Hardware and Software Driver Problems in Windows XP," by Microsoft Corporation (available online at *http://support.microsoft.com/ ?kbid=322205*).

Objective 3.6   Microsoft Corporation. *Microsoft Windows XP Professional Resource Kit Documentation*. Redmond, WA: Microsoft Press, 2001. Read Chapter 26, "Troubleshooting Concepts and Strategies." Study the "Check Firmware Versions" section (available online at *http://www.microsoft.com/resources/documentation/Windows/ XP/all/reskit/en-us/prma_trb_ersf.asp*).

Implement, Manage, and Troubleshoot Disk Devices

Windows XP Professional supports a wide range of fixed and removable storage devices. Common fixed disk technologies include **Small Computer System Interface (SCSI)**, **Intelligent Drive Electronics** or **Integrated Drive Electronics (IDE)**, and **Serial Advanced Technology Attachment (Serial ATA)**. **DVD-ROM**, floppy, **CD-ROM**, tape drives, and universal serial bus (USB) or Institute of Electrical and Electronics Engineers, Inc. (IEEE) 1394 (FireWire) external drives are popular removable storage devices. As with other hardware devices, a software device driver enables Windows XP to communicate with the storage hardware.

You use the Disk Management snap-in, part of the Computer Management console, and the Diskpart.exe command-line tool to convert storage types, create and extend volumes, and perform other disk-management tasks. Over time, the files on disks tend to become more and more fragmented. Windows XP Professional includes the Disk Defragmenter snap-in and the command-line version of the tool called Defrag.exe.

Windows XP Professional supports two types of fixed disk storage: **basic disks** and **dynamic disks**. If you want to dual boot Windows XP Professional with Windows NT 4.0, Windows Me, Windows XP Home Edition, or earlier Windows operating systems, you must use basic disks. Dynamic disks support many advanced features such as volume spanning, volume extending, and unlimited volumes per disk.

To successfully answer questions in this objective, you must be familiar with the common types of fixed and removable storage and know how to install, manage, and troubleshoot each type. You need to know how to use the tools included with Windows XP Professional for creating, managing, and modifying dynamic disks and basic disks. You must know how to enable and disable the different types of performance counters with Diskperf.exe, and know how to view performance data in the Performance Logs and Alerts snap-in.

Objective 3.1 Questions

1. Which of the following multiboot scenarios results in each operating system listed being fully functional with access to at least one hard disk? Choose two correct answers.

 A. Hard disk 1 configured as a basic disk with a single partition formatted as the NT File System (NTFS) with Windows XP Professional and Windows Me installed on it. Hard disk 2 configured as a basic disk with a single partition formatted as the 32-bit version of File Allocation Table (FAT32).

 B. Hard disk 1 configured as a basic disk with a single partition formatted as FAT32 with Windows XP Professional and Windows Me installed on it. Hard disk 2 configured as a basic disk with a single partition formatted as NTFS.

 C. Hard disk 1 configured as a dynamic disk with a single volume formatted as NTFS with Windows XP Professional installed on it. Hard disk 2 configured as a dynamic disk with a single volume formatted as NTFS with Windows 2000 Professional installed on it.

 D. Hard disk 1 configured as a dynamic disk with a single volume formatted as NTFS with Windows XP Professional and Windows 2000 Professional installed on it. Hard disk 2 configured as a basic disk with a single volume formatted as NTFS.

 E. Hard disk 1 configured as a dynamic disk with a single partition formatted as NTFS with Windows XP Professional and Windows XP Home Edition installed on it. Hard disk 2 configured as a basic disk with a single partition formatted as FAT32.

2. Your company uses a flexible workspace approach to organizing office space. You are replacing 30 desktop computers for the telemarketing department. You want to ensure that no individual user can monopolize local storage on these new computers, so you decide to apply disk quotas to them all. Which file system supports disk quotas? Choose the correct answer.

 A. FAT

 B. UDF

 C. FAT32

 D. NTFS

 E. CDFS

3. You have a 700 MHz Pentium III computer with 256 megabytes of RAM running Windows 2000 Professional. You want to retain the existing operating system while installing Windows XP Professional. You successfully configure the computer for dual booting and run a full backup using the NT Backup. You also create a new Automatic

Speech Recognition (ASR) disk and manually edit the Boot.ini file to change the order of the operating systems when you boot the computer. In doing so, you do not realize that you accidentally deleted the Boot.ini file.

The next time you start the computer, you receive an error message, and then it stops responding. What can you do to restore the computer to full functionality while retaining existing configuration settings? Choose all that apply.

 A. Reinstall Windows 2000 Professional and all the applications, and then reinstall Windows XP Professional.

 B. Use the Recovery Console to copy the Boot.ini file from a Windows XP Professional installation CD-ROM.

 C. Use the ASR disk to restore the Boot.ini file.

 D. Use the Recovery Console to copy the Boot.ini file from a Windows 2000 Professional installation CD-ROM.

 E. Use the Recovery Console and run the Bootcfg command to generate a new Boot.ini.

4. One of the graphics artists in your company's marketing department needs to access some multimedia files that were archived on an old removable storage device several years ago. You verify that the device is on the Windows XP Professional Windows Catalog and attach it to the artist's computer. You use the Add/Remove Hardware Wizard to install it, but receive a message that Windows could not detect it. You choose to manually select it from the list of hardware in the Add/Remove Hardware Wizard, but you cannot locate it.

What do you do to install it? Choose the correct answer.

 A. Click Have Disk in the Install New Hardware dialog box and specify the path to the driver files.

 B. Change the Driver Signing File signature verification setting to Ignore.

 C. Change the Driver Signing File signature verification setting to Block.

 D. The device cannot be installed.

 E. Reboot in safe mode and install the appropriate drivers.

Objective 3.1 Answers

1. **Correct Answers: B and C**

    A. **Incorrect:** Windows Me cannot read NTFS volumes; therefore, formatting hard disk 1 as NTFS would make it impossible to run the operating system on that computer.

    B. **Correct:** Both Windows Me and Windows XP Professional recognize partitions formatted with the FAT32 file system; therefore, both operating systems can be installed onto hard disk 1 in this scenario. Although Windows XP Professional can read NTFS drives, Windows Me cannot do so. Although Windows Me does not recognize hard disk 2 in this scenario, the requirement was for each operating system to be able to recognize at least one disk, not necessarily both disks.

    C. **Correct:** Both Windows XP Professional and Windows 2000 Professional support dynamic disks, but they store information about the disks in their Registry. If both operating systems are installed on the same disk and you use one to convert the disk to dynamic, the Registry of the other operating system becomes out-of-date and no longer boots. The proper method to use dynamic disks in a multiboot configuration with these operating systems is to install them on separate disks. For example, install Windows XP Professional on hard disk 1 and Windows 2000 Professional on hard disk 2. Use Windows XP Professional to convert hard disk 1 to dynamic, and then use Windows 2000 Professional to convert hard disk 2 to dynamic.

    D. **Incorrect:** Although both Windows XP Professional and Windows 2000 Professional support dynamic disks, they store information about the disks in their Registry. If both operating systems are installed on the same disk and you use one to convert the disk to dynamic, the Registry of the other operating system becomes out-of-date and no longer boots.

    E. **Incorrect:** Windows XP Home Edition does not recognize dynamic disks, so it cannot be installed on a dynamic disk.

2. **Correct Answers: D**

    A. **Incorrect:** The 16-bit FAT file system was created when disk drives were relatively small. FAT16 does not support large partitions, file and folder level security, disk quotas, and other advanced features.

    B. **Incorrect:** The Universal Disk Format (UDF) was introduced in Windows 2000. It is a standards-based file system for DVD and CD-ROM. You cannot format a hard disk with the UDF file system.

C. **Incorrect:** The 32-bit version of the FAT file system supports large partitions, but not other advanced features such as security, auditing, and disk quotas.

D. **Correct:** NTFS is a high-performance file system designed for modern computer systems. It supports per-user disk quotas, folder and file-level security, auditing, reparse points, and other advanced features.

E. **Incorrect:** The CD-ROM File System (CDFS) is used only for CD-ROM disks and cannot be used to format a hard disk.

3. **Correct Answers: C and E**

A. **Incorrect:** It is not necessary to reinstall the operating systems; there is a much quicker way to resolve this problem. Reinstalling the operating systems allows the computer to boot, but configuration settings are lost.

B. **Incorrect:** The Windows XP Professional installation CD-ROM does not contain a Boot.ini file. If no Boot.ini file is on a computer, it is created automatically by the Setup program; if one already exists, the Setup program automatically edits it.

C. **Correct:** You can boot from the Windows XP Professional installation CD-ROM and attempt to repair the existing installation. Selecting the Inspect Startup Environment option verifies and, if necessary, repairs the Windows XP Professional files in the system partition. A new Boot.ini file is automatically created. You are then able to boot from the hard disk into Windows XP Professional and manually edit the Boot.ini file to add Windows 2000 Professional to the boot menu.

D. **Incorrect:** The Windows 2000 Professional installation CD-ROM does not contain a Boot.ini file. If no Boot.ini file is on a computer, it is created automatically by the Setup program; if one already exists, the Setup program automatically edits it.

E. **Correct:** The *Bootcfg /rebuild* Recovery Console command is capable of scanning your hard disk for Windows installations and automatically rebuilding your Boot.ini file. Additionally, you can use *Bootcfg* to manually create or edit the Boot.ini file.

4. **Correct Answers: A**

A. **Correct:** You need to acquire device driver files compatible with Windows XP Professional from the vendor, and then use them to install the device. In this particular scenario, the most likely location for those files is on the vendor's Web site.

B. **Incorrect:** The issue is not Driver Signing; changing this setting does not correct the problem.

C. Incorrect: The issue is not Driver Signing; changing this setting does not correct the problem.

D. Incorrect: If the device appears in Windows Catalog, it should be possible to install it.

E. Incorrect: Safe mode is used for resolving problems caused by installing drivers that lead to system instability. You do not use safe mode to install new hardware devices.

Objective 3.2

Implement, Manage, and Troubleshoot Display Devices

In most circumstances, Windows XP automatically detects and configures display adapters and monitors. However, unusual hardware configurations do cause problems that require troubleshooting. For example, if the monitor, video adapter, or device driver does not support Plug and Play, Windows XP will detect your monitor as Default Monitor, and you will need to manually configure the monitor type. Even if all the display components are Plug and Play, connecting them to a keyboard-video-mouse switch box can block the Plug and Play signals from the monitor.

Windows XP generally prevents misconfigurations by testing updated settings and displaying a confirmation dialog box. If you do not confirm the new settings, Windows XP restores the old settings. If you, a user, or Windows XP does configure display settings that your monitor cannot support, or if you switch to a monitor that does not support your current settings, you might not be able to see the display to troubleshoot the problem. In this circumstance, you can use safe mode to start Windows XP with basic video settings and select an acceptable configuration.

If you plan to enable multiple monitors for a computer, install Windows XP Professional with only one adapter present. After you have completed the installation of the additional video adapters and video monitors, you use the Settings tab in the Display program in Control Panel to configure multiple monitor support.

To successfully answer questions in this objective, you must know how to use the Add Hardware Wizard, Device Manager, and the Display program in Control Panel to install, configure, and troubleshoot both legacy and Plug and Play video adapters and monitors. You must be able to install multiple video adapters and monitors, change the primary adapter, and move items between monitors.

Objective 3.2 Questions

1. You bought a new computer with recently released multimedia hardware including a video adapter with many advanced features. The computer was shipped with Windows XP Professional preinstalled, but the vendor's documentation indicates that the external television port on the video adapter did not have a functional driver at the time of shipping and that you must check with vendor's Web site for updates. Two weeks later, you find and download new drivers for the video adapter from the vendor's Web site. You install them and reboot when told to do so. The system restarts normally, and you log on. You see an error message indicating that the display settings have been restored to their defaults. You try to open the Display program in Control Panel, but the system freezes.

    What is the best way to return the computer to full functionality? Choose the best answer.

    A. Turn the computer off, unplug the power cord, and disconnect it from the video monitor. Physically move the video adapter to a different slot, and then reconnect the cables and restart the computer.

    B. Restart the computer using safe mode. Click the Roll Back Driver button from the video adapter's properties dialog box to restore the original device drivers for the video adapter.

    C. Restart the computer and use the ASR to restore the original drivers.

    D. Restart the computer using the Recovery Console to delete the new video device drivers.

2. You buy a new computer with an Accelerated Graphics Port (AGP) video adapter. You install Windows XP Professional from the installation CD-ROM, and the video adapter is automatically configured. You use the computer for several days at a resolution of 1600 x 1200 and decide that the text appears too small on-screen to be easily readable. You want to change the font size to 125 percent of its normal size. What do you do? Choose the correct answer.

    A. Edit the size manually in the system Registry using the Registry Editor tool.

    B. Open Device Manager from the Computer Management console.

    C. Select the List All Modes button from the Adapter tab of the display adapter's advanced properties dialog box.

    D. Adjust the DPI setting from the General tab of the display adapter advanced properties dialog box.

3. Recently, you discovered an old Pentium 233 MHz computer in a closet and decided to use it as a test system. During setup, the video adapter is not recognized, and the display is set to Video Graphics Adapter (VGA) resolution. You know that the adapter and video monitor support higher resolutions. What do you do to fully enable the video adapter? Choose the correct answer.

   A. Use the Registry Editor tool to manually modify the display settings in the system Registry.

   B. Use Dxdiag.exe to install the specified drivers from a floppy disk or CD-ROM.

   C. Windows XP Professional can support only VGA resolutions with legacy hardware devices; therefore, you must replace the computer's motherboard and processor.

   D. Obtain and manually install the correct device driver for the video adapter.

4. You are a desktop administrator at Contoso Pharmaceuticals. Recently, your organization hired a new employee named Dan Wilson who has special display requirements. Specifically, Dan needs his display adjusted so that window borders, buttons, and fonts are displayed using highly contrasting colors, rather than the Windows Standard color scheme other employees at your organization use. What is the best way to adjust Dan's display to meet his needs? Choose the best answer.

   A. Open Control Panel, and then open the Accessibility Options dialog box. Click the Display tab, select the Use High Contrast check box, and then apply the changes.

   B. Open Control Panel, and then open Display. Click the Accessibility Options tab, select the Use High Contrast check box, and then apply the changes.

   C. Launch Microsoft Narrator, and select the Read Typed Characters and Announce Events On Screen check boxes.

   D. Instruct Dan to enable high-contrast display settings by holding the Alt+Ctrl keys and pressing Print Screen.

Objective 3.2 Answers

1.   Correct Answers: B

A. Incorrect: These steps will not resolve the problem. If the video monitor is not displaying the Windows XP desktop or if the image is flickering, the video adapter might not be seated properly in its slot, or the slot's connectors might be damaged. If that is the case, moving the video adapter might resolve the problem. But the question stated that the image is viewable, so moving the card will not help.

B. Correct: This is the best way to repair the computer. In safe mode, Windows XP Professional starts with only basic files and drivers. If you still cannot access the display properties dialog box in safe mode, you might need to use the Recovery Console to manually replace the video driver. If you continue to have problems, you might need to restore the operating system files from a backup.

C. Incorrect: The ASR can be used to repair basic system files, the boot sector, and the startup environment, but it cannot help you to repair bad video drivers.

D. Incorrect: If you know the exact names and versions of each file that you need to delete and restore, it might be possible to manually correct this problem. This is a time-consuming and error-prone approach though; booting into safe mode and using the graphical tools to repair the computer are much more likely to succeed.

2.   Correct Answers: D

A. Incorrect: You do not need to manually edit the Registry to change the appearance of fonts on the Windows XP Professional desktop.

B. Incorrect: You use Device Manager to manage system resource configuration for hardware devices, but you cannot change the other video adapter and video monitor settings.

C. Incorrect: Use the Adapter tab to view detailed information about the display adapter, the list of modes that the adapter can display, and the adapter's properties. You cannot change the size of the fonts displayed on the Windows XP Professional desktop from the Adapter tab.

D. Correct: You can scale the fonts displayed in the Windows XP Professional desktop to be much smaller or larger than their default size by changing the value in the DPI list on the General tab of the display adapter's advanced properties dialog box. The specific font sizes available are determined by which fonts you have installed on your system. When you change the font size, you have to reboot for the new settings to take effect.

3. **Correct Answers: D**

A. Incorrect: Some of the earlier versions of Windows required you to manually edit the system Registry to resolve certain software problems; however, it is very easy to make a mistake and render Windows XP Professional unusable when you manually edit the Registry. Windows XP Professional allows you to manage virtually all aspects of the system through graphical tools and command-line tools. Whenever possible, use these built-in management tools to resolve issues such as this.

B. Incorrect: The DirectX Diagnostic Tool can be launched from a command line by typing **Dxdiag.exe**. This tool is used to review, configure, and troubleshoot the hardware in a computer that interacts with DirectX. The DirectX Diagnostic Tool is not used to install or update drivers for hardware devices.

C. Incorrect: Windows XP Professional is compatible with numerous legacy hardware devices. If the specific device does not appear on the list in the Add/Remove Hardware Wizard, verify that it is in Windows Catalog. If it is, contact the vendor to obtain up-to-date device drivers for Windows XP Professional.

D. Correct: Windows XP Professional is compatible with many legacy video adapters, even if they are not Plug and Play–compatible. During the installation of Windows XP Professional, the Setup program can detect many legacy hardware devices and then install appropriate drivers to enable them. However, Setup does not always recognize every installed hardware device. If appropriate drivers are not on the Windows XP Professional installation CD-ROM, you might be able to locate compatible drivers on the vendor's Web site.

4. **Correct Answers: A**

A. Correct: High-contrast display settings are well-suited to users who cannot easily distinguish user interface elements. The correct way to enable this setting is by using the Accessibility Options in Control Panel.

B. Incorrect: The Display properties dialog box does not have an Accessibility Options tab. Instead, you should use the Accessibility Options dialog box.

C. Incorrect: Narrator is a useful tool for users who prefer audio to visual feedback from the computer in response to events such as switching windows and typing characters. However, it does not meet Dan's needs because Dan prefers to view the monitor directly, but requires more contrasting colors.

D. Incorrect: High-contrast settings can be enabled by holding the left-Alt and left-Shift keys and pressing Print Screen.

Configure Advanced Configuration Power Interface

There are two ways to extend battery life in mobile computers: enhance battery technology and decrease power utilization. The vendors of batteries have been slowly improving their products since mobile computers were first introduced, but the greatest gains over the past few years have come from making mobile computer hardware and software more energy-efficient. **Advanced Configuration Power Interface (ACPI)** allows computers running Windows XP Professional to use electricity more efficiently than previous technologies. Windows XP Professional supports the ACPI for sophisticated power management. Windows XP Professional also supports the older and less-effective standard **Advanced Power Management (APM)**.

On an ACPI system, power consumption is determined by the power settings configured in the Power Options, the requirements of running services and applications, and the capabilities of the installed hardware. To put it another way, Windows XP Professional fully supports the ACPI standard, but applications and hardware must be designed to work with ACPI and Plug and Play for the power management system to be as effective as possible.

To successfully answer questions in this objective, you must know how to create, modify, and select power schemes. You need to know how to enable and disable hibernation; and how to configure power alarms, Standby mode, and advanced power settings. You must be able to install, configure, and troubleshoot PC Cards. You need to be able to unplug or eject hardware from the taskbar.

Objective 3.3 Questions

1.   You have installed Windows XP Professional on your laptop computer. You often carry the laptop around your company's campus while working, and periodically have to leave it unattended for extended periods of time. You do not want to drain the battery at all during these times, but you also do not want to close all your applications and shut down Windows XP. What do you do? Choose the correct answer.

   A. Shut down the computer.

   B. Enable Hibernation in the Power Options program in Control Panel. Then create a power scheme that causes the laptop computer to hibernate whenever the computer is not used for a suitable period of time.

   C. Use the Power Options in Control Panel to create a custom power scheme.

   D. Use the Power Options in Control Panel to select the Max Battery power scheme.

2.   Under which of the following scenarios do you not see the APM tab in the Power Options program located in Control Panel? Choose two correct answers.

   A. The APM-based basic input/output system (BIOS) is failing.

   B. The computer's BIOS is ACPI-compliant.

   C. The external Uninterruptible Power Supply (UPS) is not properly connected to the serial port of the computer.

   D. The computer's battery has been improperly charged.

   E. The computer's BIOS is not APM-based.

3.   A user in your organization has installed Windows XP Professional on his notebook computer, which supports APM. When the user tries to shut down the computer and it freezes during the shutdown process, pressing the power button does not resolve the problem. He has to unplug the computer and remove the battery to completely shut it off. How do you check to see whether the APM-based BIOS is the cause of the problem? Choose the correct answer.

   A. Restart the computer and run Acldiag.exe.

   B. Install a new copy of Windows XP Professional so that the APM-based BIOS can be properly detected and installed.

   C. Restart the computer in safe mode and disable as many of the power management options as possible.

   D. Turn the computer on and, after the desktop has appeared, run the Apmstat.exe tool from a command prompt.

Objective 3.3 Answers

1.   Correct Answers: B

   A. Incorrect: Shutting down the computer minimizes power drain on the battery, but takes a relatively long time to restart the computer from a complete shutdown.

   B. Correct: Hibernation must be enabled from the Hibernate tab in the Power Options program located in Control Panel first, and then you can create a custom power scheme that will automatically hibernate the computer after a period of inactivity that you specify. As an alternative, you could have your computer automatically go into Standby mode. However, Standby mode places a very slight drain on the battery, whereas hibernation uses no batteries.

   C. Incorrect: Until you enable hibernation, custom power schemes allow you to specify only when the monitor and hard disks will be turned off and when the system will go to Standby mode. Even when the system is in Standby mode with the disks and monitor powered-down, it continues to draw on the battery for power. In this state, the battery eventually runs out of power and it is possible to lose important data.

   D. Incorrect: This power scheme greatly reduces drain on the battery because the hard disks and monitor are turned off and the computer is left in Standby mode when unattended for just a few minutes. Nevertheless, when the system is in Standby mode with the disks and monitor powered down, it continues to draw on the battery for power. In this state, the battery eventually runs out of power, and it is possible for you to lose important data.

2.   Correct Answers: B and E

   A. Incorrect: If the motherboard's BIOS is failing, other more severe problems are apparent. The computer is probably not able to boot, and if it does boot, it probably crashes or freezes frequently.

   B. Correct: If a computer's BIOS is ACPI-complaint, the APM tab is not visible in the Power Options program.

   C. Incorrect: An external UPS is not required for either APM or ACPI support. You can use an UPS with a mobile computer, but it is an unlikely scenario because mobile computers already have built-in batteries. Many UPSs do provide protection against power surges and other quality-of-service problems possible on electrical outlets, but they are very expensive. A much more affordable solution appropriate for protecting a mobile computer is a surge suppressor.

D. Incorrect: As long as the computer is connected to a power source, the state of the battery is irrelevant to the question.

E. Correct: If a computer's BIOS is not APM-based or if it supports ACPI, the APM tab is not visible in the Power Options program.

3.   Correct Answers: D

A. Incorrect: Acldiag.exe is a command-line tool in the \Support\Tools\Support.cab file. It is used for checking security on objects and containers in Active Directory, and it has no relation to power management or APM technology.

B. Incorrect: It is doubtful that reinstalling Windows XP Professional will resolve the problem. A more effective approach to troubleshooting this issue is to determine why the BIOS is causing problems.

C. Incorrect: It is unlikely that these procedures will resolve the problem; a more effective approach to troubleshooting this issue is to determine why the BIOS is causing problems.

D. Correct: The Advanced Power Management Status tool (Apmstat.exe) is designed to check whether a computer's APM-based BIOS is compatible with Windows XP Professional. You install it by running Setup.exe in the \Support\Tools folder on the Windows XP Professional installation CD-ROM. If you do not have an APM-based BIOS, Apmstat.exe will inform you of this. You might determine that you need to update the BIOS, in which case you need to contact the manufacturer for tools to bring it up to date.

Implement, Manage, and Troubleshoot I/O Devices

Many of the hardware devices you might use with Windows XP Professional can be considered **I/O** devices. Other objectives in this domain discuss several classes of input and output (I/O) devices: network adapters, **PC Cards**, display adapters and monitors, and disks. This objective reviews many other I/O devices including modems, **smart card** readers and cards, **Universal Serial Bus (USB)**, IEEE 1394 (FireWire), wireless devices, and multimedia hardware. Multimedia hardware encompasses a broad array of devices such as **DVD-ROM** readers, Musical Instrument Digital Interface (MIDI) devices, scanners, digital cameras, digital video recorders, sound cards, and **CD-ROM** readers and writers. From a high level, the process of installing and managing each type of I/O device is similar: physically connect the device to the computer's bus; install software drivers; configure the device; maintain and troubleshoot the device as needed. The details vary between devices, especially when comparing Plug and Play devices to older models that do not fully support Plug and Play. Windows XP Professional usually detects Plug and Play hardware devices and automatically installs suitable drivers for them.

To successfully answer questions in this objective, you must be able to use the Add Hardware Wizard and Device Manager to install, manage, and troubleshoot I/O devices. You must also be able to use the individual device management applications in Control Panel such as Phone and Modem Options, Scanners and Cameras, Sounds and Audio Devices, and Wireless Link.

Objective 3.4 Questions

1. You are a desktop administrator at an organization with strict desktop security requirements that include software restrictions, the use of Windows Firewall, and the use of standard user accounts for day-to-day activities. A puzzled user in your organization asks you why he cannot install a flatbed scanner on his system. He previously successfully installed other hardware, such as his handheld Windows Mobile device and a digital camera that connect to his Windows XP Professional computer via the USB port. He tells you that he disconnected his personal laser printer; he then connected the scanner to the parallel port, turned it on, and launched the Add Hardware Wizard. He seems to think that Windows XP Professional might have detected the scanner, but he receives a series of error messages and cannot install the Windows XP drivers he just downloaded from the vendor's Web site.

What is preventing this user from installing the scanner? Choose the correct answer.

A. Someone who is a member of the local Administrators group on the computer must be logged on to install hardware devices that are not Plug and Play.

B. The scanner is not compatible with Windows XP.

C. The parallel cable is damaged.

D. There is an interrupt request (IRQ) conflict between the parallel port and another installed hardware device.

2. Your multimedia-capable computer seems to record and play back sound and voice at very low quality. When you try to conduct video conferences over the Internet, your colleagues cannot understand you, although they have no problems communicating with one another. You also notice that their voices sound distorted and you hear lots of pops and hisses.

When you use a different computer in your office, the video conferencing tools work great. You suspect that there is something wrong with your sound card or the drivers that interact with it; you want to examine the sound recording and playback devices installed in your computer. You also want to check driver versions and perform diagnostics. How do you do this? Choose the correct answer.

A. You run Sigverif.exe at a command prompt.

B. You open the Registry Editor tool (Regedt32.exe) and look for entries that might be related to audio devices installed in your computer.

C. You select the Hardware tab in the Sounds And Audio Devices program in Control Panel.

D. You open the DirectX Diagnostics tool.

3. You are listening to an audio CD on your desktop computer at work when you realize that the music might be disturbing your colleagues who are holding a small meeting in the cubicle next to yours. You turn off the speakers, put on your stereo headphones, and insert the plug into the jack on the front of the CD-ROM drive, but you hear no sound. You adjust the volume control on the front of the CD-ROM drive, but still hear no sound. You turn the speakers back on and can hear the music again.

Why is there no music through your headphones? Choose the correct answer.

    A. The CD-ROM drive is defective and must be replaced.

    B. Digital audio playback is enabled for your CD-ROM drive.

    C. One or more of the volume levels in the Volume Control program is muted or turned all the way down.

    D. The Hardware Sound Acceleration Level is set to No acceleration on the Sound tab of the DirectX Diagnostics tool.

4. You recently purchased an external USB hard disk. You plug the power cord in and connect the device to the USB hub that is already connected to your keyboard and Pocket PC. You insert the installation CD-ROM that came with the device, follow the prompts to install the device drivers, and reboot the computer when told to do so. You log back on to the desktop and open Windows Explorer. You do not see the new hard disk under My Computer where the other local disks are visible. You open Device Manager, but cannot locate the new hard disk there, either.

Which of the following are appropriate troubleshooting steps? Choose three correct answers.

    A. Install the device into another computer.

    B. Disconnect the Pocket PC and mouse.

    C. Disconnect the new disk drive from the hub and plug it directly into a USB port on the computer.

    D. Look for USB-related messages in the System event logs using Event Viewer.

    E. Verify that USB support is enabled in your computer's BIOS.

    F. Verify that you have not accidentally disabled USB support in Device Manager.

5. Which of the following are ways to install a modem in Windows XP Professional? Choose three correct answers.

    A. Use the Phone And Modem Options program in Control Panel.

    B. Use the Add Hardware program in Control Panel.

    C. Use the Printer And Faxes program in Control Panel.

    D. Boot into safe mode.

    E. Attach a Plug and Play modem.

    F. From the Start menu, click Run and type Winmsd.exe.

6. The president of your company just received a new laptop with a built-in 802.11g network adapter and Windows XP Professional with Service Pack 2. The CEO has asked you to configure it to connect to your corporate wireless network. You talk to the people responsible for managing the network, and they tell you that it uses Wired Equivalent Policy (WEP) encryption, and they give you the network name (SSID) and a network key. When you are adding the network, you realize that they did not tell you what to specify in the Network Authentication field, as shown in the following picture.

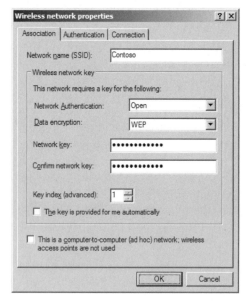

Which value do you select for the Network Authentication field? Choose the correct answer.

    A. Open

    B. Shared

    C. WPA

    D. WPA-PSK

Objective 3.4 Answers

1.   Correct Answers: A

A. Correct: Windows XP Professional installs Plug and Play devices automatically; an administrator does not need to be present. The puzzled user was able to use the Plug and Play devices because they were automatically detected and appropriate drivers were installed for him. Non–Plug and Play devices are installed in the context of the currently logged-on user, and only administrators can install device drivers and make other changes to critical system files and configuration settings. The user could not install the scanner because it is not Plug and Play–capable.

B. Incorrect: The user told you that he downloaded Windows XP Professional drivers from the firm that built the scanner.

C. Incorrect: The user believes that Windows XP Professional did detect the scanner and that he received the error messages after it had already been detected.

D. Incorrect: Nothing in the question suggests that there are any resource conflicts; additionally, the user had disconnected his personal laser printer from the parallel port before attempting to install the flatbed scanner. Because the user reported no problems with the printer, it is unlikely that there are resource conflicts between the parallel port and any other device.

2.   Correct Answers: C

A. Incorrect: The Signature Verification tool (Sigverif.exe) is used to scan the computer for critical files such as device drivers and system dynamic-link libraries (DLLs). It checks to see whether each file has a valid digital signature from Microsoft; it is not used for hardware or driver troubleshooting.

B. Incorrect: Manually searching the Registry is a haphazard and time-consuming approach to gathering the desired information. Launching the Sounds And Audio Devices program in Control Panel is much faster and more effective. Also, the Registry Editor tool does not include troubleshooting tools to help you resolve hardware and software problems.

C. Correct: You use the Sounds and Audio Devices program to adjust volume, specify the kind of speakers you are using, create and select Sound Schemes, select devices for sound and voice recording and playback, select devices for MIDI playback, view the properties of installed sound devices, and troubleshoot installed sound devices.

D. Incorrect: The DirectX Diagnostics tool is used to review, configure, and troubleshoot the hardware in a computer that interacts with DirectX. It does have a tab labeled Sound where you can test DirectSound, but it does not have detailed information about the sound card. You can launch the Sound Troubleshooter from the More Help tab in the DirectX Diagnostic tool or from the Hardware tab in the Sounds And Audio Devices program.

3.   Correct Answers: B

A. Incorrect: The CD-ROM drive plays audio CDs through the speakers, and the question gives no indication of other problems with the drive, so it is not clear that replacing it will solve the problem.

B. Correct: When digital playback of audio CDs is enabled, the headphone jack on the front of most CD-ROM drives is disabled. To use headphones to listen to audio CDs, you have to either connect the headphones to a jack attached to the sound card or to a headphone jack built into the speakers.

C. Incorrect: You can hear music through the speakers, so the CD volume and master volume controls must not be muted or turned down. There is no volume control specific to headphone jacks, so adjusting the volume levels in the Volume Control program does not resolve the problem.

D. Incorrect: The Hardware Sound Acceleration Level has no effect on the volume of audio CDs. Adjusting hardware acceleration on the Display and Sound tabs of the DirectX Diagnostic tools might help to resolve stability or performance issues relating to DirectX.

4.   Correct Answers: A, C, and D

A. Correct: If the problem reappears on a different computer system, it is likely that the USB hard disk is defective. If it performs as expected on the other computer, the problem is specific to the original computer.

B. Incorrect: It is possible that having too many USB devices connected can cause problems because there is not enough power available for all devices. There are limitations on how much power each individual USB device can draw from the USB chain; if a USB device tries to use more than 500 milliamps of current, the port is disabled until the system is rebooted. The total amount of power used by all the devices is also limited. However, the question states that you connected the USB disk drive's power plug, which means that it will not be using much current from the USB connection. Additionally, USB mouse devices and Pocket PCs normally use a trivial amount of electric current from the USB connection.

C. Correct: If this step resolves the problem, you have determined that the issue was caused by the USB hub or its connection to your computer. Try power cycling the hub and plugging it into an alternate port on your computer.

D. Correct: When Windows XP Professional detects problems with USB devices, it writes error messages to the System event log. These messages can provide useful troubleshooting information. Another important step to take when resolving

USB-related issues is to examine all the devices under the USB controller's tree in Device Manager. If a yellow exclamation point appears before a device, verify that the system firmware is configured to allocate an IRQ number to the USB controller.

E. Incorrect: The question stated that you had existing connections for your mouse and Pocket PC so USB support must already be enabled in your computer's BIOS.

F. Incorrect: The question stated that you had existing connections for your mouse and Pocket PC, so USB support was not disabled in Device Manager. For the USB disk drive to have been specifically disabled in Device Manager, it first must be installed.

5.   Correct Answers: A, B, and E

A. Correct: After opening the Phone And Modem Options program, select the Modems tab and click Add to open the Install New Modem page in the Add New Hardware Wizard. The wizard tries to automatically detect and install the modem; if automatic detection fails, the wizard allows you to select the manufacturer and model of the new modem.

B. Correct: After the Add New Hardware Wizard launches, click Next and then select Add A New Hardware Device From The List and click Next. You can then either allow the wizard to automatically detect and install the modem or manually select it from a list. If automatic detection succeeds, the wizard installs the modem and the appropriate device drivers; if automatic detection fails, the wizard allows you to select the manufacturer and model of the new modem.

C. Incorrect: The Printer And Faxes program is used to manage existing fax and printer connections; it also installs, removes, and configures printers and fax printers. It is not used to install new modems.

D. Incorrect: Booting Windows XP Professional in safe mode is a method to resolve stability problems with services and hardware devices; it is not an effective approach to installing new hardware.

E. Correct: After you connect a Plug and Play modem to the computer, the Install New Modem page in the Add New Hardware Wizard appears. The wizard tries to automatically detect and install the modem; if automatic detection fails, the wizard allows you to select the manufacturer and model of the new modem.

F. Incorrect: The System Information tool (Winmsd.exe) is not used to install or configure any hardware devices including modems. The System Information tool shows detailed information about the installed hardware and software and the allocation of resources such as IRQ, direct memory access (DMA), I/O ports, and memory.

6.   **Correct Answers: A**

A. **Correct:** Almost all WEP-based networks rely on open authentication.

B. **Incorrect:** WEP networks can use shared authentication. However, the shared authentication process actually decreases the security of the WEP network by giving more information to an attacker who is trying to crack your network key. Therefore, shared WEP authentication should not be used and is rarely used.

C. **Incorrect:** WPA provides similar functionality to WEP, but with improved security. However, WPA and WEP are mutually exclusive and therefore can never be used together.

D. **Incorrect:** As described in answer C, WPA-PSK and WEP cannot be used together.

Manage and Troubleshoot Drivers and Driver Signing

Drivers enable Windows XP to communicate with hardware devices. Drivers act as part of the operating system and, as a result, have the potential to cause Windows XP to fail with a Stop error, also known as a Blue Screen of Death (BSOD). This is the most disturbing type of error Windows XP can display, and it causes any work that has not yet been saved to be lost.

Most Stop errors are caused by problematic drivers. Although drivers act as part of the operating system, they are usually written by the hardware vendors, not by Microsoft. Hardware vendors might not use the same rigorous testing procedures as Microsoft and, as a result, unhandled errors that cause Stop errors can occur. With the proper skills, you can isolate the driver that is causing a problem and replace it with a more compatible driver.

To reduce the number of driver problems, Microsoft offers driver signing. Microsoft reviews and tests drivers written by hardware manufacturers to verify their stability. If a driver proves to be stable, Microsoft signs the driver, and users can install it with minimal risk. In fact, you might choose to block any unsigned drivers from being installed in your organization to prevent unpredictable driver problems.

To successfully answer questions in this objective, you must know how to configure and use Windows Update. You must be able to navigate to a specific hardware device in Device Manager; view its properties; and update, roll back, and uninstall its driver.

Objective 3.5 Questions

1. Members of which group can manually install, update, and roll back drivers on a computer running Windows XP Professional? Choose the correct answer.

    A. Network Configuration Operators

    B. Debugger Users

    C. Users

    D. Administrators

2. You have been using a film scanner connected to the USB port of your computer for several months. You learn that the manufacturer has released new drivers for the scanner that allow it to make multiple passes of a single negative and generate a higher resolution digital image. You download the drivers from the vendor's Web site, install them using the Update Hardware Wizard, and reboot when prompted. Now the scanner no longer works.

What is the easiest way to resolve this problem? Choose the correct answer.

    A. Use the Roll Back Driver feature available on the device's properties page.

    B. Uninstall the device drivers for the scanner, physically disconnect the printer, reboot, and then reconnect the printers and reinstall the new drivers when the Add Hardware Wizard prompts you.

    C. Uninstall the device drivers for the scanner, physically disconnect the printer, reboot, and then reconnect the printers and reinstall the original drivers when the Add Hardware Wizard prompts you.

    D. Use Drivers.exe to roll back to the previous version of the device driver.

3. You want to update the driver for your 3-D video adapter. Your computer has access to the Internet. Which of the following tools can you use to update the driver? Choose two correct answers.

    A. Run Drivers.exe from a command prompt.

    B. Run Device Manager.

    C. Use Windows Update.

    D. Open the WMI Control console.

    E. Open the System Information tool (Winmsd.exe).

    F. Launch the Add Hardware Wizard.

4.   Which command launches the File Signature Verification tool that is used to identify unsigned drivers installed on a Windows XP Professional system? Choose the correct answer.

   A. Winmsd.exe

   B. Fsutil.exe

   C. Sigverif.exe

   D. Regedit.exe

5.   Which of the following tools can produce a list of drivers installed on a Windows XP Professional computer? Choose two correct answers.

   A. Driverquery.exe

   B. Sigverif.exe

   C. Winmsd.exe

   D. Sfc.exe

   E. Getmac.exe

Objective 3.5 Answers

1. **Correct Answers: D**

    A. Incorrect: By default, the members of the Network Configuration Operators group have limited administrative privileges that allow them to manage networking features.

    B. Incorrect: By default, members of the Debugger Users group can debug processes on the computer.

    C. Incorrect: By default, members of the Users group are restricted from making system-wide changes including installing, updating, or rolling back device drivers.

    D. Correct: By default, members of the Administrators group have total control of the computer; therefore, they can install, update, and roll back device drivers.

2. **Correct Answers: A**

    A. Correct: The ability to roll back device drivers is a new feature in Windows XP Professional. You access it by clicking the Roll Back Driver button in the device's properties page. You can view the properties of a device by double-clicking it in Device Manager.

    B. Incorrect: You have already determined that the new drivers do not work with your system, so this series of steps does not resolve the problem.

    C. Incorrect: These procedures should resolve the problem, but it is much faster and easier to use the Driver Rollback feature available in Windows XP Professional.

    D. Incorrect: Drivers.exe is a Windows 2000 Resource Kit tool used for viewing information about the drivers currently running on a computer; it does not have the ability to roll back device drivers.

3. **Correct Answers: B and C**

    A. Incorrect: Drivers.exe is a Windows 2000 Resource Kit tool that lists information about all the drivers running; it is not used for updating device drivers.

    B. Correct: You can update device drivers from Device Manager in two ways. Navigate to the device and right-click it, and then select Update Driver from the menu. You can also double-click the device to open its properties dialog box, select the Driver tab, and click Update Driver. Both methods launch the Hardware Update Wizard, which guides you through the process of updating the driver.

    C. Correct: Although Windows Update is the simplest way to update device drivers, it requires access to the Web, might not have the most recent version of drivers, and does not offer drivers for all hardware vendors.

    D. Incorrect: Windows Management Instrumentation (WMI) provides a management infrastructure for monitoring and controlling system resources. The WMI Control console is used for configuring and controlling the WMI service; it is not used for managing device drivers.

    E. Incorrect: The System Information tool shows detailed information about the installed hardware and software and the allocation of system resources; it does not have the capability to update device drivers.

    F. Incorrect: The Add Hardware Wizard is used to install new hardware devices and to troubleshoot existing devices. It is not used to update drivers for existing devices.

4.   **Correct Answers: C**

    A. Incorrect: Winmsd.exe launches the Help And Support Services tool, which provides useful information about the system's configuration. Although this tool cannot be used to find unsigned drivers, it can be used to launch the File Signature Verification tool. To launch this tool, select File Signature Verification Utility from the Tools menu.

    B. Incorrect: Running the Fsutil.exe command-line utility is useful for modifying aspects of the file system. However, this tool cannot be used to verify driver signatures.

    C. Correct: Sigverif.exe is the correct command to launch the File Signature Verification utility. This tool can also be launched from the System Information program located in the Start menu in the folder called All Programs\Accessories\System Tools.

    D. Incorrect: The Regedit.exe command launches the Registry Editor, which is used to modify system configuration parameters. It cannot be used to verify driver signatures.

5.   **Correct Answers: A and C**

    A. Correct: Driverquery.exe is a command-line tool that lists drivers installed on a Windows XP computer. Because it is a command-line tool, you can conveniently redirect the output to a text file, which is useful for sending the drivers to technical support.

    B. Incorrect: The driver verifier is very useful for verifying driver signatures. It cannot, however, produce a list of drivers installed on the computer. Instead, it is capable only of listing unsigned drivers.

C. **Correct:** The System Information tool, launched by running Winmsd.exe, can display signed and system drivers. To display drivers, expand Software Environment, and then click System Drivers or Signed Drivers.

D. **Incorrect:** You can use the System File Checker to scan and replace important system files. It does not, however, list drivers.

E. **Incorrect:** This tool shows Machine Access Control (MAC) addresses assigned to network interface cards on the current computer. It does not list drivers.

Monitor and Configure Multiprocessor Computers

The operating system **kernel** in Windows XP can support one or two **CPUs**. Windows XP leverages the **hardware abstraction layer (HAL)** to bridge the gap between your computer's hardware and the operating system. This fundamental architecture facilitates porting the operating system to different hardware platforms.

Windows XP has a different HAL and kernel for uniprocessor and multiprocessor systems. Therefore, you must upgrade the HAL and kernel when adding a second processor to an existing Windows XP Professional computer. If you accidentally upgrade to an incompatible HAL, or if you forget to upgrade your HAL, the computer will probably be unable to boot. The only ways to recover from this situation are to restore your original hardware configuration, reinstall Windows XP Professional, or manually replace the kernel and HAL by using Recovery Console.

You can use the Performance console or Windows Task Manager to analyze processor performance. On each computer you manage, you must establish a baseline of satisfactory performance and monitor the system for diminished performance in an ongoing way. The major processor-related objects you must understand and monitor are Thread, Process, System, Processor, Job Object, and Job Object Details.

To successfully answer questions in this objective, you must know the different HAL versions available; how to upgrade from a single processor to a dual processor configuration; how to downgrade to a single processor configuration; and how to monitor system operation using the Performance snap-in.

Objective 3.6 Questions

1. You manage the computers for the graphic artists in your company, many of whom regularly use 3-D rendering software to create computerized special effects for promotional videos. Their standard workstations include dual CPUs running at 3 gigahertz, 1 gigabyte of RAM, and a high-end video card with built-in 3-D graphics acceleration. One of the artists complains that her workstation periodically performs poorly. You log performance data from several of the computers while the artist who is experiencing diminished performance continues to work. You see the following processor-related statistics for that system:

    ■ The Processor object's % Processor Time counter averages 85 percent.

    ■ The Processor object's Interrupts/Sec counter averages 6,500.

    ■ The Memory object's Pages/Sec counter averages 1.5.

    ■ The System object's Processor Queue Length counter averages 1.8.

    Which of the following is the likeliest cause of diminished performance? Choose the best answer.

    A. Processor object's % Processor Time

    B. Processor object's Interrupts per second

    C. Memory object's Pages/Sec

    D. System object's Processor Queue Length

2. Yesterday, one of the developers at your company purchased a second processor for his dual processor Windows XP Professional computer. Although he knows he should contact you for hardware upgrades, he was excited about the performance boost and installed the processor himself after hours. The first time he started his computer after adding the processor, he received a Stop error (which he referred to as a Blue Screen). He left his computer in that state until you arrived the next morning to help him troubleshoot the problem. The Stop error information was 0x00000079 MISMATCHED_HAL. He wants you to enable Windows XP to start successfully using both processors without opening the computer's case again. What is the best way to solve the problem? Choose the best answer.

    A. Start Windows XP in safe mode. Open the System Properties dialog box and click the Hardware tab. Click the Hardware Profiles button, and create a new profile for the multiprocessor configuration. Then, restart Windows XP in normal mode.

    B. Insert the Windows XP Professional CD-ROM and reinstall Windows XP Professional over the existing installation.

C. Replace the new processor with a functioning processor.

D. Start Recovery Console and insert the Windows XP Professional CD-ROM. Use Recovery Console to copy the multiprocessor kernel and HAL files that match the computer's hardware configuration. Rename the files as needed.

Objective 3.6 Answers

1.   Correct Answers: B

A. Incorrect: Although 85 percent is a very high sustained value for this counter, and the user probably could benefit from faster processors, the computer should continue to function acceptably because there is still 15 percent idle processor time. The average for the Interrupts per second suggests why the percent processor time might be running so high.

B. Correct: You must establish an acceptable baseline for Interrupts per second on a system performing nominally while under load. A generally considered acceptable starting point is 1,000 to 2,000 interrupts per second. 6,500 interrupts per second indicates a serious performance problem. You could further analyze the impact of the problem by watching the % Interrupt Time counter, which measures the percentage of the processor's time that is consumed by handling interrupt requests. Most likely, this problem is caused by a network adapter, although many different hardware devices could theoretically be responsible. Try updating the BIOS on the network adapter and the Windows XP Professional drivers for the adapter. If that procedure does not resolve the problem, replace the adapter.

C. Incorrect: This counter measures the number of times Windows XP has to access the paging file. If this counter were high, it would indicate that applications are using significantly more memory than the computer has physical RAM available. However, 1.5 is a very low count and is not indicative of a problem.

D. Incorrect: For this counter, 1.8 is an acceptable average. Because it is greater than 1, it indicates that the computer's processor is not handling instructions quite as fast as it is receiving them. However, the % Processor Time counter indicates that the computer should continue to function in an acceptable manner.

2.   Correct Answers: D

A. Incorrect: Even safe mode will fail to start when you have the incorrect kernel installed. Additionally, you cannot use hardware profiles to support both uniprocessor and multiprocessor configurations.

B. Incorrect: This would solve the problem because Setup would detect the second processor and install the multiprocessor kernel. However, it would also result in the user losing his operating system settings. It would be more efficient to replace the kernel file by using Recovery Console.

C. Incorrect: The question provides no information that should lead you to believe the processor is not functioning correctly. Windows XP does not automatically switch between uniprocessor and multiprocessor HALs, so the uniprocessor HAL and kernel files need to be replaced.

D. Correct: This process replaces the uniprocessor kernel with the multiprocessor kernel. The specific files you need vary depending on the exact hardware being used; contact your hardware manufacturer to determine which version of the HAL and kernel you need. You should name the HAL file **Hal.dll** and the kernel files **Ntoskrnl.exe** and **Ntkrnlpa.exe**.

24 Monitoring and Optimizing System Performance and Reliability

Windows XP gives administrators the ability to carefully monitor and tune system performance. Tools such as the Task Manager, the Performance utility, and a suite of command-line utilities allow for both real-time and historical performance data analysis. Trace logs function very similarly, and are used to troubleshoot system problems and debug applications.

Tuning the performance of portable computers is more complicated than tuning desktop systems because administrators must balance battery life with performance. Windows XP provides power schemes to allow users to quickly change a system's power consumption. Power schemes, combined with standby and hibernation features, dramatically increase battery life when a system is not in use.

Sometimes, problems are unavoidable. Windows XP provides a full set of troubleshooting tools to resolve these problems when they arise. The System Restore tool captures system configuration information, and can reapply a working configuration if the system later becomes unreliable. Functionality such as the Last Known Good Configuration can allow Windows XP to boot even if a faulty driver was installed. Safe mode and the Recovery Console provide administrators with the ability to repair even the most damaged Windows XP installations.

Tested Skills and Suggested Practices

The skills that you need to successfully master the Monitoring and Optimizing System Performance and Reliability objective domain on the *Installing, Configuring, and Administering Microsoft Windows XP Professional* exam include the following:

- Monitor, optimize, and troubleshoot performance of the Windows XP Professional desktop.
  - ❏ Practice 1: Use Task Manager to determine which process is currently consuming the most processor time.
  - ❏ Practice 2: Change the fields on the Processes tab of Task Manager so that every possible field is visible.
  - ❏ Practice 3: Use Task Manager to change the priority of an application so that it runs at high priority.

❑ Practice 4: Use the Performance console to monitor real-time performance information about several different counters simultaneously.

❑ Practice 5: Gather processor utilization information over several hours, and then analyze that information using the Performance console.

❑ Practice 6: Configure Scheduled Tasks to perform a complete disk defragmentation weekly, but only if the computer is idle. Configure the task to wake the computer if necessary.

❑ Practice 7: Run the AT command without any parameters to view scheduled tasks. Schedule a task to run daily using the AT command.

■ Manage, monitor, and optimize system performance for mobile users.

❑ Practice 1: On a portable computer, manually set the hardware profile for both docked and undocked configurations.

❑ Practice 2: Create a new hardware profile and disable noncritical drivers for that profile.

❑ Practice 3: Adjust the power scheme on a computer to a variety of different settings and observe how the computer's behavior is changed. Create a custom power scheme.

■ Restore and back up the operating system, System State data, and user data.

❑ Practice 1: Perform a complete system backup using the Backup Utility.

❑ Practice 2: Save the current system configuration using the System Restore tool, and then restore the system configuration to its previous state.

❑ Practice 3: Boot the computer using the Last Known Good Configuration.

❑ Practice 4: Boot the computer using safe mode.

❑ Practice 5: Install the Recovery Console as an option on the boot menu. Then, launch the Recovery Console using the Microsoft Windows XP Professional CD and examine the available commands by executing the HELP command. Examine each command in detail by typing the name of each command followed by /?. Finally, edit the Boot.ini system file using the Recovery Console.

Further Reading

This section lists supplemental readings by objective. We recommend that you study these sources thoroughly before taking exam 70-270.

Objective 4.1   Microsoft Corporation. *Microsoft Windows XP Professional Resource Kit Documentation*. Redmond, WA: Microsoft Press, 2001. Read sections covering Task Manager, Performance Monitor, and Disk Defragmenter in Appendix D, "Tools for Troubleshooting" (available online at *http://www.microsoft.com/ resources/documentation/Windows/XP/all/reskit/en-us/prmb_tol_cfbi.asp*).

"Support WebCast: Monitoring and Tuning System Performance in Microsoft Windows XP," by Dan Suehr (available online at *http://support.microsoft.com/ ?kbid=823887*).

"Solving Performance Problems," in the Windows XP Professional product documentation (available online at *http://www.microsoft.com/resources/documentation/ windows/xp/all/proddocs/en-us/sag_mpmonperf_28.mspx*).

Objective 4.2   Microsoft Corporation. *Microsoft Windows XP Professional Resource Kit Documentation*. Redmond, WA: Microsoft Press, 2001. Read Chapter 7, "Supporting Mobile Users," for information about power schemes, standby mode, and hibernation (available online at *http://www.microsoft.com/resources/documentation/Windows/ XP/all/reskit/en-us/prdc_mcc_gnml.asp*).

"Power Management in Windows XP," by Charlie Russel (available online at *http:// www.microsoft.com/windowsxp/using/setup/learnmore/russel_02march25.mspx*).

Objective 4.3   Microsoft Corporation. *Microsoft Windows XP Professional Resource Kit Documentation*. Redmond, WA: Microsoft Press, 2001. Read Chapter 4, "Supporting Installations," and Chapter 14, "Backup and Restore" (available online at *http://www.microsoft.com/resources/documentation/Windows/XP/all/reskit/en-us/ prork_overview.asp*).

"Microsoft Windows XP System Restore," by Bobbie Harder (available online at *http://msdn.microsoft.com/library/techart/windowsxpsystemrestore.htm*).

"Support WebCast: Microsoft Windows XP: Troubleshooting Startup and Shutdown Problems," by William Keener (available online at *http://support.microsoft.com/ ?kbid=326841*).

Objective 4.1

Monitor, Optimize, and Troubleshoot Performance of the Windows XP Professional Desktop

Windows XP Professional has been designed to provide the optimum performance on any hardware configuration without any adjustments. In fact, most users never need to monitor or modify the performance of their Windows XP system. There are also times when an administrator who has a detailed understanding of system performance monitoring and tuning can improve a system's performance. For these administrators, Windows XP provides a suite of tools useful for monitoring, analyzing, and tuning system performance characteristics.

The most commonly used tool is the Task Manager, which displays real-time information about network utilization and users in addition to monitoring applications, processes, and performance. The Performance console is a more powerful utility for analyzing system performance because it provides real-time information about hundreds of detailed aspects of the system's performance—including memory utilization, shared folders, and network errors. You can also use the Performance console to alert when counters reach a specific threshold, which enables you to detect impending problems such as low disk space or high memory utilization before they cause the computer to slow down.

Windows XP Professional provides the Scheduled Tasks to allow tasks to be executed when the computer is not being actively used. If you prefer, you can use the AT command-line utility to schedule tasks.

Objective 4.1 Questions

1. You are a systems administrator, and your responsibilities were recently increased to include a group of users at a remote office who have, up until now, been forced to maintain their own Windows XP computers. One of your users is complaining that his computer has grown slower over the past year. In particular, he notes that it takes Microsoft Word longer to open documents that have been recently created. Which of the following actions will improve the performance of this user's desktop? Choose the correct answer.

    A. Decrease the size of the paging file.

    B. Enable NTFS compression.

    C. Run Disk Defragmenter on the system's hard disk.

    D. Set the Performance Logs And Alerts service to start automatically.

2. Which of the following pieces of information can be gathered from the Windows Task Manager? Choose three correct answers.

    A. CPU utilization

    B. Network utilization

    C. Page file utilization

    D. Packet loss

    E. Memory usage

    F. Open files

3. A user is complaining of performance problems with his Windows XP Professional system, but he is not sure whether the problems are caused by an underpowered processor, a shortage of memory for the applications he uses, or a slow disk drive. To upgrade the system component that is limiting the system's performance, you need to log performance data over a period of several days while the user is working with the computer. Which of the following procedures begins the process of gathering performance data? Choose two correct answers.

    A. Log on to the user's computer. Launch the Computer Management console, expand System Tools, and then expand Performance Logs And Alerts. Select Counter Logs in the left pane. In the right pane, right-click System Overview and click Start.

    B. Log on to the user's computer. Launch Control Panel and select Performance And Maintenance. Click Consoles, and then double-click Performance. Select System Monitor in the left pane. In the right pane, right-click System Overview and click Start.

    C. Log on to the user's computer. Launch Windows Task Manager. From the File menu, select Log Data, and provide a file name.

    D. Log on to the user's computer. From a command prompt, type **Logman start "System Overview"**.

    E. Log on to the user's computer. From a command prompt, type **Relog System_Overview.blg -q -o System_Overview.txt**.

4. Which of the following tools can be used to set the priority of a process? Choose the correct answer.

    A. System Monitor

    B. Performance Logs And Alerts

    C. Computer Manager

    D. Task Manager

5. A user complains about slow system performance. You decide to improve performance by adjusting the Performance Options tool. You launch this tool by opening Control Panel, selecting Performance And Maintenance, and clicking Adjust Visual Effects task. Which of the following changes that can be applied to the Performance Options tool improves the system's responsiveness? Choose the correct answer.

    A. On the Visual Effects tab, click the Adjust For Best Appearance option.

    B. On the Visual Effects tab, click the Adjust For Best Performance option.

    C. On the Advanced tab, under Processor Scheduling, select optimization for Background Services.

    D. On the Advanced tab, under Memory Usage, select optimization for System Cache.

    E. On the Advanced tab, under Virtual Memory, reduce the paging file size by half.

6. You are the system administrator of a small network of end users who have both desktop and laptop Windows XP Professional systems. All systems participate in a Windows XP domain. You want to avoid the reduced performance that fragmented file systems cause by scheduling the disk defragmenter utility to run on all systems every Sunday at 01:00 Eastern Time (that is, at 1 A.M.). This task is important enough that systems must be brought out of power savings mode if necessary. However, you do not want the disk defragmentation to interfere with the users, nor do you want it to consume the batteries on laptop systems.

The proposed solution is as follows: Launch the Scheduled Tasks system tool and choose New Scheduled Task from the File menu. Name the task **File Defragmentation**, and then right-click the new task and select Properties. From the Task tab of the Properties dialog box, type **defrag C:** in the Run text box. In the Run As field, type the user name of a Domain Admin account that has local Administrator rights on all systems in the domain, and set the password using the Set Password button. From the Schedule tab, at the Schedule Task drop-down list, select Weekly. Set the Start Time to 1:00 A.M., and select only Sunday from the Schedule Task Weekly section. Create this task to all Windows XP Professional systems.

Which of your desired results does the proposed solution accomplish? Choose two correct answers.

    A. Schedule the Disk Defragmenter to run on Sundays at 1:00 A.M.

    B. Execute the Disk Defragmenter with an account that has proper privileges on all systems.

    C. Ensure that the Disk Defragmenter does not interfere with user sessions.

    D. Wake the computers from power savings mode to run the Disk Defragmenter, if possible.

    E. Ensure that the Disk Defragmenter does not consume the battery on laptop computers.

7. Using the AT command-line utility, you schedule a task to run nightly on your Windows XP Professional system. Immediately afterward, you decide that the task must run only weekly, so you launch the Scheduled Tasks administrative utility and modify the task properties. The next time you execute the AT command from the command-line, what does it display about your scheduled task? Choose the correct answer.

    A. The scheduled task appears and is scheduled to run daily.

    B. The scheduled task appears and is scheduled to run weekly.

    C. The scheduled task appears twice, and is scheduled to run both daily and weekly.

    D. The scheduled task does not appear.

8. You are a desktop administrator at the Graphic Design Institute. Currently, two dozen designers are adding an animated character to a digital film for an upcoming made-for-television movie. Each night, they render the animated characters using their desktop computers. The rendering process consumes their computer's processors for approximately nine hours. Tonight, one of the designers needs to work late, and the rendering process has slowed down other applications on his computer so much that his computer is barely usable. What is the most efficient way to improve the situation for him? Choose the correct answer.

    A. Change the priority of the rendering process to RealTime.

    B. Change the priority of all other applications to High.

    C. Change the priority of the rendering process to Low.

    D. Change the priority of all other applications to Low.

9.   You have recently upgraded a computer from Windows 98 to Windows XP. Although the computer meets the minimum requirements for Windows XP, the video card is out-dated by current standards. You enjoy the Windows XP visual effects and select the option to adjust visual effects for best appearance. Overall, performance is acceptable. However, when you select multiple items on your desktop by dragging a box around the items, it takes Windows XP several seconds to draw the box. What setting should you change to resolve this problem while retaining as many visual effects as possible? Choose the correct answer.

   A. Select Adjust For Best Performance.

   B. Deselect Show Shadows Under Mouse Pointer.

   C. Deselect Show Translucent Selection Rectangle.

   D. Deselect Smooth Edges Of Screen Fonts.

Objective 4.1 Answers

1.   **Correct Answers: C**

> **A. Incorrect:** Windows XP Professional uses the paging file to temporarily store data from the computer's memory. Decreasing the size of the paging file increases the free space on the system's hard disk, but it does not improve the system's performance.

> **B. Incorrect:** NTFS allows files and directories to be compressed at the file system level. This allows compressible files to consume less space on the hard disk. Although compressing files increases the free space on the hard disk, it does not improve the system's performance.

> **C. Correct:** Hard disks perform best when file data is written in contiguous blocks. Over time, however, file data can become broken into discontiguous fragments. Although the hard disk is still able to access fragmented files, they take longer to load. Because the user's performance problem was most noticeable when accessing files, and no maintenance had been done in at least a year, the cause of the problem is most likely disk fragmentation. Running the Disk Defragmenter utility resolves this problem and drastically improves disk performance on affected systems.

> **D. Incorrect:** The Performance Logs and Alerts service is used when logging data for performance analysis. Although it is necessary for logging performance data, simply starting the service does not improve system performance.

2.   **Correct Answers: A, B, and E**

> **A. Correct:** CPU utilization is shown both numerically and graphically on the Performance tab of the Windows Task Manager.

> **B. Correct:** Network utilization is shown both numerically and graphically on the Networking tab of the Windows Task Manager.

> **C. Incorrect:** Page file utilization information is not available from the Windows Task Manager.

> **D. Incorrect:** Packet loss cannot be viewed from the Windows Task Manager. However, executing the command NETSTAT -S -P TCP from the command line shows the Segments Retransmitted statistic, which is very similar to overall packet loss.

> **E. Correct:** Memory usage is shown both numerically and graphically on the Performance tab of the Windows Task Manager.

> **F. Incorrect:** Open files cannot be viewed from the Windows Task Manager.

3. Correct Answers: A and D

A. Correct: The Performance Logs And Alerts snap-in, available through the Computer Management console, is the correct graphical tool for creating performance logs.

B. Incorrect: The System Monitor snap-in is useful for monitoring real-time performance data, but it cannot log performance data.

C. Incorrect: Although the Windows Task Manager is useful for viewing a real-time snapshot of a system's performance, it cannot be used to log performance data.

D. Correct: Using the Logman utility is the correct way to start logging performance data from the command line.

E. Incorrect: Relog is useful for analyzing logged data, but it is not used for starting the logging process. Relog is used to resample logged data at a longer interval in order to reduce the amount of data being analyzed.

4. Correct Answers: D

A. Incorrect: The System Monitor is useful for viewing the processor utilization of a given process, but it cannot change a process' priority.

B. Incorrect: The Performance Logs And Alerts snap-in is useful for logging performance data, and allows you to record a given process' processor utilization. However, it cannot be used to change the priority of a process.

C. Incorrect: The Computer Manager provides access to both the System Monitor and the Performance Logs And Alerts snap-ins, but none of these tools can be used to change the priority of a process.

D. Correct: The Processes tab of the Task Manager is used to change the priority of a process. Right-click the name of a process, choose Set Priority, and select the desired level.

5. Correct Answers: B

A. Incorrect: The Adjust For Best Appearance option enables every visual feature of the Windows XP Professional operating system. This provides the best user experience on systems that have sufficient processing capability. However, it reduces system responsiveness and must not be used on systems experiencing performance problems.

B. Correct: The Adjust For Best Performance option disables all unnecessary visual effects. Choosing this option reduces the amount of work Windows XP needs to do to display the user's graphical interface, thereby improving system responsiveness. Changing this setting is the best way to make the computer seem faster.

C. **Incorrect:** Optimizing processor scheduling for background services is useful on servers because it ensures that interactive applications do not reduce the performance of a server's primary tasks. However, it does reduce system responsiveness for users working interactively with the computer because background services receive higher priority than interactive applications.

D. **Incorrect:** Optimizing memory usage for system cache improves the performance of file sharing and Web services. However, when you allocate more of the system RAM to these services, interactive applications suffer.

E. **Incorrect:** Windows XP uses virtual memory as an extension of the system's physical RAM. It is a slow process to page data from the physical memory to the virtual memory located on the system's hard disk, but decreasing the size of the paging file does not improve system performance.

6. **Correct Answers: A and B**

A. **Correct:** The settings selected on the Schedule tab are correct to launch the task every Sunday at 1:00 A.M.

B. **Correct:** Selecting a Domain Admin account is the best way to ensure that a scheduled task copied to many different systems has local Administrator rights on all systems. If a Domain Admin account is not used, a local Administrator account must be selected for each individual system—and account names and passwords might vary.

C. **Incorrect:** The proper method for ensuring that scheduled tasks do not interfere with user sessions is to select the Only Start The Task If The Computer Has Been Idle For At Least check box from the Settings tab of the Task Properties dialog box.

D. **Incorrect:** The Wake The Computer To Run This Task check box was not selected while the task was being configured. This check box is located on the Settings tab of the Task Properties dialog box.

E. **Incorrect:** This desired result was not accomplished. To ensure that the scheduled task does not consume the system's battery, select both the Don't Start The Task If The Computer Is Running On Batteries and Stop The Task If Battery Mode Begins check boxes from the Settings tab of the Task Properties dialog box.

7. **Correct Answers: D**

A. **Incorrect:** The Scheduled Tasks graphical administrative utility is capable of modifying tasks created with the AT command. Further, AT cannot display the task because tasks that have been modified by the Scheduled Tasks are not visible to AT.

B. **Incorrect:** The Scheduled Tasks graphical administrative utility can update tasks created with the AT command, but makes the tasks invisible to the AT command-line utility after they have been modified.

C. Incorrect: The Scheduled Tasks utility does not duplicate tasks when making a modification, but it does make them invisible to AT.

D. Correct: The Scheduled Tasks utility and the AT command maintain entirely separate lists of scheduled tasks. Although the Scheduled Tasks utility can display tasks created with the AT command, it cannot directly modify those tasks. To modify a task created with the AT command, the Scheduled Tasks utility removes the task from the AT command's list and adds the task to its own list. Therefore, tasks created with AT become invisible to AT after being modified with the Scheduled Tasks utility.

8.   Correct Answers: C

A. Incorrect: You should never use the RealTime priority level because it can interfere with normal system processing. Besides, increasing the priority of the rendering process would be opposite of the desired effect, and would make other applications even less usable by assigning them fewer processor cycles.

B. Incorrect: Technically, increasing the priority of other applications to High would improve their performance. However, because the designer might be using several different applications, it is more efficient to lower the priority of the rendering process.

C. Correct: This is the most efficient way to improve the performance of all interactive applications on the designer's computer. Setting the priority of the rendering process to Low will free up more processing time for other applications, achieving the desired effect.

D. Incorrect: This would have the opposite of the desired effect, making applications less usable by assigning them fewer processor cycles.

9.   Correct Answers: C

A. Incorrect: Although selecting this option would resolve the problem, it would also disable almost all visual effects.

B. Incorrect: If this were the source of the problem, performance would be bad any time the mouse cursor is displayed.

C. Correct: This visual effect displays a selection rectangle that uses a special video card capability. If the video card lacks the capability, Windows XP can still draw the translucent selection; however, it will take more processing capability. Deselecting this option should resolve the performance problem.

D. Incorrect: Deselecting this option would improve overall system performance. However, it would affect performance at all times, not simply when dragging a selection rectangle.

Manage, Monitor, and Optimize System Performance for Mobile Users

Thanks to recent improvements in portable computer hardware, battery life, and wireless networking, more and more users choose laptop computers that can travel with them. Windows XP Professional's mobile computing environment is so intuitive that mobile users do not need special training. Administrators need to have a detailed understanding of how the latest hardware and software work together to enable the mobile environment, however.

Power schemes, such as Always On, Presentation, and Max Battery, provide a simple way to adjust the balance between power consumption and performance. Power schemes define settings for power-saving features such as turning off hardware components, standby, and hibernation. Together, these features maximize battery life when a portable computer is used intermittently.

Hardware profiles were originally created to allow laptop computers to support different hardware configurations when connected to a docking station. You might never need to use hardware profiles, however, because Windows XP automatically detects the hardware that is currently connected to the computer. However, if a user wants to disable connected hardware, such as disabling a network interface adapter on a laptop when the computer is not connected to a network, you can create a hardware profile by using Device Manager.

Obejctive 4.2 Questions

1. You are configuring a new, fully PnP-compatible laptop for a user who will use the laptop both in a docking station and separate from the docking station. After installing Windows XP Professional, how must you configure the hardware profiles? Choose the correct answer.

   A. Make no changes to the hardware profiles.

   B. Insert the laptop into the docking station and boot the computer. View the current hardware profile properties, select the This Is A Portable Computer check box, and select the option labeled The Computer Is Docked.

   C. Create two new hardware profiles. Name the profiles **Docked** and **Undocked**.

   D. Insert the laptop into the docking station and boot the computer. Create a copy of the current profile and name it **Undocked**.

2. Which is the correct tool for specifying which drivers will be loaded in a given hardware profile? Choose the correct answer.

   A. Task Manager

   B. Device Manager

   C. Computer Manager

   D. System Monitor

3. Which power scheme is the correct choice for a mobile user who wants to maximize the lifetime of the battery, but needs the display to remain on at all times? Choose the correct answer.

   A. Home/Office Desk

   B. Portable/Laptop

   C. Presentation

   D. Always On

   E. Minimal Power Management

   F. Max Battery

4. Which of the following are advantages of standby mode over hibernation? Choose two correct answers.

   A. Shorter wake-up period

   B. Provides compliance with airline regulations regarding the use of electronic devices during takeoff and landing

    C. Lower power consumption

    D. No risk of data loss

    E. Does not consume hard disk space

5. You are a desktop administrator for City Power & Light. In the last several years, instant messaging has become the preferred technique for contacting people within your organization. Recently, Simon Rapier, your CEO, complained that nobody can instant message him when he closes the lid to his laptop computer because, in his words, "It seems to disconnect from the network." He wants his battery to last as long as possible, but needs to stay connected to the network when he closes his lid. How should you configure the Advanced Power Options on his computer? Choose the correct answer.

    A. Set When I Close The Lid Of My Portable Computer to Do Nothing, and set When I Press The Sleep Button On My Computer to Do Nothing.

    B. Set When I Close The Lid Of My Portable Computer to Do Nothing, and set When I Press The Sleep Button On My Computer to Stand By.

    C. Set When I Close The Lid Of My Portable Computer to Hibernate, and set When I Press The Sleep Button On My Computer to Shut Down.

    D. Set When I Close The Lid Of My Portable Computer to Stand By, and set When I Press The Sleep Button On My Computer to Hibernate.

Objective 4.2 Answers

1.   **Correct Answers: A**

  A. Correct: Hardware profiles are designed for computers that are not fully PnP-compatible. Computers with full PnP compatibility do not require hardware profiles to be configured.

  B. Incorrect: Hardware profiles do not need to be configured for laptops that are fully PnP-compatible. This is the correct procedure, however, if the computer is not PnP-compatible.

  C. Incorrect: Hardware profiles do not need to be configured for laptops that are fully PnP-compatible.

  D. Incorrect: Hardware profiles do not need to be configured for laptops that are fully PnP-compatible.

2.   **Correct Answers: B**

  A. Incorrect: The Task Manager is used to set process priorities and monitor processor performance, among other things. It cannot be used to specify which drivers are loaded in a given hardware profile.

  B. Correct: The Device Manager is used to disable drivers for the current profile. To disable a driver for the current profile, start Windows XP using the profile that you want to configure. Then, launch Device Manager to view the properties of a driver. From the Device Usage drop-down list, select Do Not Use This Device In The Current Hardware Profile (Disable).

  C. Incorrect: The Computer Manager is a set of snap-ins used to manage many aspects of a Windows XP Professional computer. However, it cannot be used to specify which drivers are loaded in a given hardware profile.

  D. Incorrect: The System Monitor is used to monitor hundreds of performance counters, but it cannot be used to specify which drivers are loaded in a given hardware profile.

3.   **Correct Answers: C**

  A. Incorrect: This power scheme does not meet the requirements. The Home/Office Desk scheme maintains constant power when the system is plugged in, but might turn off the display while on battery power.

  B. Incorrect: This power scheme does not meet the requirements. The Portable/Laptop scheme turns off all system components after a short period of inactivity. This causes the display to shut down.

C. **Correct:** The Presentation power scheme maximizes battery life by allowing any component except for the display to be turned off when not in use. When the system is plugged in, the Presentation power scheme maintains constant power to the hard disk and system.

D. **Incorrect:** This scheme does not meet the requirements. The Always On scheme disables all power-saving features, ensuring optimum performance at the cost of battery life.

E. **Incorrect:** This scheme does not meet the requirements. The Minimal Power Management scheme maintains constant power when the system is plugged-in, but might turn off the display while on battery power.

F. **Incorrect:** This scheme does not meet the requirements. The Max Battery scheme is excellent for conserving battery power, but might turn off the display.

4.   Correct Answers: A and E

A. **Correct:** Standby mode has a shorter wake-up period than hibernation mode. Waking from hibernation requires reading the contents of the system's memory from the hard disk.

B. **Incorrect:** A mobile computer running Windows XP Professional might wake up from standby mode to execute a scheduled task or switch to hibernation mode. This possibility restricts this mode from being used during the takeoff or landing of a commercial airplane.

C. **Incorrect:** Standby mode minimizes battery usage by shutting down as many components as possible. However, it maintains the state of the computer in the system's RAM, which requires small amounts of power. Hibernation writes the contents of the system's RAM to the hard disk and shuts the system down completely. Therefore, hibernation has a lower power consumption than standby mode.

D. **Incorrect:** Standby mode maintains the state of the computer in the system's RAM, which requires small amounts of power. If power is lost suddenly, for example if the battery is removed, data is lost. Hibernation does not have this limitation because no power is required to maintain that state.

E. **Correct:** Standby mode maintains the state of the computer in system's RAM—only hibernation mode writes the system's memory to the hard drive. As a result, you must have enough free disk space to store the contents of the system's memory to use hibernation mode.

5.   Correct Answers: B

A. Incorrect: Although this configuration would cause Simon's computer to stay online when he closes the lid, it does not allow him to manually put the computer into standby or hibernate mode to save power.

B. Correct: These settings enable Simon to stay connected to the network when the lid to his portable computer is closed and enable Simon to manually put the computer into standby mode when he needs to save power.

C. Incorrect: These settings would cause the computer to go into hibernate mode when Simon closes the lid. Hibernate mode saves the contents of the computer's memory to disk and shuts the computer down, which does cause the network to be disconnected.

D. Incorrect: These settings would cause the computer to go into standby mode when Simon closes the lid. Standby mode saves power by shutting down most of the computer's hardware resources, including the network interface cards. This would cause the network to be disconnected.

Restore and Back Up the Operating System, System State Data, and User Data

You cannot entirely prevent hardware failures, but you can be prepared for them. The most fundamental recovery tool is the Backup Utility, which includes wizards to back up files, restore files, and prepare your system for Automated System Recovery (ASR).

The System Restore utility enables you to recover from less-significant problems related to drivers and software configurations. Like the Last Known Good Configuration, the System Restore utility automatically creates a backup of vital system information. Unlike the Last Known Good Configuration, the System Restore utility keeps a history of system configurations and provides the user with the ability to restore the system state to a specific date.

For problems that result in the inability to boot normally, but cannot be resolved with the Last Known Good Configuration, use safe mode. If safe mode does not work correctly, the Recovery Console provides a useful set of command-line utilities that can be used to troubleshoot problems. Recovery Console, which is similar to a command prompt, allows you to view text files and replace system files, among other tasks.

Objective 4.3 Questions

1. Your Windows XP Professional system fails to boot after you add a new network card driver. Which feature of Windows XP Professional must you use to return the system to the state it was in prior to adding the driver? Choose the correct answer.

   A. Boot.ini

   B. System Restore

   C. Last Known Good Configuration

   D. Recovery Console

2. After an unexpected power outage, a user's Windows XP Professional system fails to boot successfully. The boot process allows you to select an instance of Windows XP Professional to boot from, but fails partially through the startup routine. Which tools can you use to diagnose and resolve this problem? Choose three correct answers.

   A. System Restore

   B. Last Known Good Configuration

   C. Safe mode

   D. Recovery Console

   E. ASR

   F. Device Manager

3. Which of the following tasks cannot be accomplished from the Windows XP Professional recovery console? Choose two correct answers.

   A. Format a hard disk.

   B. Boot to the Last Known Good Configuration.

   C. Set services to be disabled or start automatically.

   D. Reinstall Windows XP.

   E. Restore damaged system files from a CD.

   F. Restore damaged system files from a network share.

   G. Edit the Boot.ini file.

4. Which of the following tasks must you do before installing a new application that might cause a Windows XP Professional system to become unstable? Choose the correct answer.

    A. Create a new Restore Point using System Restore.

    B. Boot to the Last Known Good Configuration.

    C. Back up all files using the Backup Utility.

    D. Boot into safe mode.

    E. Boot into the Recovery Console.

5. You are designing a backup strategy for your Windows XP Professional system. You cannot afford to lose more than a single day's work, so you must back up the system every night. You want to minimize the tape backup media used to store your backups, but you do not want to use more than two backup tapes to perform a complete system restore. Which of the following backup procedures meets your needs? Choose the correct answer.

    A. Normal backup nightly

    B. Incremental backup nightly

    C. Differential backup nightly

    D. Normal backup weekly, incremental backup nightly

    E. Normal backup weekly, differential backup nightly

6. You are a desktop support technician at Litware, Inc., a financial organization with about 1,000 Windows XP Professional desktop computers. The desktop computing environment is tightly controlled, and users log on to their computers as members of the local Users group with no additional privileges. You receive a call from Jim Stewart, a traveling salesperson. You recognize his name because you recently replaced his hard drive after it failed while he was traveling. Jim lost several days of work when his laptop's hard drive failed because his computer is backed up only when attached to your corporate network. To prevent this from happening in the future, Jim's manager gave him a fairly old parallel port–based external tape backup drive. Although Jim seems to know how to run Windows Backup, when he reaches the Backup Type, Destination, And Name page of the Backup Or Restore Wizard, his external tape drive does not appear in the Choose A Place To Save Your Backup list. Jim has a floppy disk with drivers for the tape drive, but cannot seem to install the driver. The device seems to be in the Windows Catalog. Which of the following changes would be the best way to solve Jim's problem? Choose the correct answer.

    A. Contact the external tape drive vendor to acquire a driver signed by Microsoft.

    B. Add Jim's user account to the local Backup Operators group.

    C. Add Jim's user account to the local Administrators group.

    D. Restart Jim's computer and use the basic input/output system (BIOS) configuration to disable the laptop's serial port.

7. You are a desktop support technician at Northwind Traders, a firm with about 200 Windows XP Professional and Windows 2000 Professional desktop computers. You receive a call from James Van Eaton, a bookkeeper in your Accounting department. James recently installed an update to a non-Microsoft application. After he installed the update, his computer became very unreliable. Docking and undocking frequently failed, and his computer seemed to slow down and show a great deal of unexplained hard drive activity. James uninstalled the update, but the problems continue. What do you recommend for the next step in troubleshooting the problem? Choose the correct answer.

    A. Open System Restore and select the Create A Restore Point option.

    B. Open System Restore and select the Restore My Computer To An Earlier Time option.

    C. Boot to the Last Known Good Configuration.

    D. Boot into safe mode.

    E. Boot into the Recovery Console.

8. You are a desktop administrator for Trey Research, a small consulting firm. Recently, work that your firm did in 1999 has been subpoenaed for a lawsuit that one of your former clients is involved in. The files identified by the court order had been stored on a Windows 98 laptop computer that you decommissioned in 2001. However, you still have a copy of a backup file you made with the Windows 98 Msbackup tool. Unfortunately, the Backup Utility on your Windows XP Professional computer reports the following error message: Unrecognized Media: The Backup File Contains Unrecognized Data And Cannot Be Used. How can you restore the file? Choose the correct answer.

    A. You cannot restore the file because it has been corrupted.

    B. Install Windows 98 on a computer and use that computer to restore the backup.

    C. Use an administrator account to take ownership of the files and grant your user account Read permission.

    D. Decrypt the file using the administrator password from the Windows 98 computer, and then restore the file normally.

Objective 4.3 Answers

1. **Correct Answers: C**

   A. **Incorrect:** The Boot.ini file specifies the set of choices that are presented to the user before the operating system is loaded. The Boot.ini file can be configured to allow for booting between several different instances of Windows, but it cannot be used to modify the configuration of Windows XP.

   B. **Incorrect:** The System Restore tool is used to roll back the configuration of a Windows XP system. However, it can be used only after the operating system has booted. In this case, the System Restore tool is inaccessible because the operating system is unbootable.

   C. **Correct:** The Last Known Good Configuration is a copy of the system state stored in the HKEY_LOCAL_MACHINE\System\CurrentControlSet registry key when a user last successfully logged on. You can revert to this backup configuration by rebooting the computer and pressing F8 when prompted to select the operating system from which to start. From the Windows XP Professional Advanced Options menu, select the Last Known Good Configuration option.

   D. **Incorrect:** The Recovery Console can be a useful tool for recovering a system that does not boot correctly, but it is not useful for restoring the last working configuration of a system. Use the Recovery Console only when all other methods have failed.

2. **Correct Answers: C, D, and E**

   A. **Incorrect:** The System Restore utility is useful for troubleshooting problems caused by system misconfigurations. However, it can be used only if the system is bootable.

   B. **Incorrect:** The Last Known Good Configuration is a quick way to resolve problems caused by misconfigurations and faulty drivers. Although the Last Known Good Configuration is available at the boot menu and can therefore be used in this scenario, it would not resolve the problem because the problem is not related to a misconfiguration. Failure to boot after a power failure is generally caused by corrupted files or a damaged hard disk—neither of which Last Known Good Configuration is capable of repairing.

   C. **Correct:** Safe mode might or might not work in this scenario, but it is the first thing to try. Safe mode loads a minimal set of drivers, and as such, it has a higher chance of successfully booting than Windows XP Professional's standard boot mode. If safe mode does start successfully, you can use the graphical user interface to diagnose the hardware problems. If you determine that system files have been damaged, you can initiate a scan of the disk and, if necessary, restore files from the system CD.

    D. Correct: The Recovery Console is a useful tool for recovering a system that does not boot correctly. If the system has the recovery console installed, it is an option on the boot menu. If it is not installed, insert the Windows XP Professional CD and boot from the CD—the Recovery Console is an option. Recovery Console is command-line only, so it is not as convenient for diagnosis and troubleshooting as safe mode. However, because it can be loaded from a CD, it starts even if the system's hard disk is completely destroyed. In this scenario, use the Recovery Console to diagnose the extent of the damage. If you determine that system files have been damaged, you can initiate a scan of the disk and, if necessary, restore files from the system CD.

    E. Correct: You use ASR only after attempts to resolve the problem with safe mode and the Recovery Console have failed. If the hard disk is functional, but files have been damaged, ASR can make the Windows XP Professional installation bootable. If the hard disk itself is damaged, you need to fix those errors or replace the hard disk before using ASR.

    F. Incorrect: The Device Manager is a useful tool for diagnosing problems relating to hardware drivers. However, it is accessible only after the system has successfully booted. In this scenario, you cannot get access to the Device Manager tool unless you first start safe mode.

3.   **Correct Answers: B and D**

    A. Incorrect: The FORMAT recovery console command can be used to format a hard disk. This process erases all data on the hard disk and must be used only when all other recovery methods fail.

    B. Correct: You cannot boot the computer directly from the Recovery Console. The system must be rebooted before Windows XP can be started in any configuration.

    C. Incorrect: The Enable And Disable Recovery Console can be used to set the startup value of services.

    D. Correct: The Recovery Console cannot be used to launch the Windows XP setup routine.

    E. Incorrect: The Recovery Console can copy files from floppy drives and CDs using the COPY command.

    F. Incorrect: The Recovery Console can copy files across the network after a drive letter has been mapped using the Net Use command.

    G. Incorrect: Use the Bootcfg Recovery Console command to edit the Boot.ini file.

4.   Correct Answers: C

A. Incorrect: Creating a restore point prior to installing a new application enables you to restore the system's configuration if the new application causes problems. However, Windows XP creates a Restore Point automatically when you launch a Setup application.

B. Incorrect: Use the Last Known Good Configuration only if the system becomes unbootable. It might be a useful tool if the new application stops your system from starting successfully, but it must not be used prior to installing an application.

C. Correct: The Backup Utility enables you to back up all files and configuration settings to removable media. Having a valid backup allows a Windows XP Professional system to be completely rebuilt in the event of a complete failure. Always create a backup of a system before installing a potentially troublesome application.

D. Incorrect: Safe mode is a valuable tool for repairing a system that is having problems booting. Use it only after the system has failed, however.

E. Incorrect: The Recovery Console can salvage systems that are otherwise completely unbootable. Do not use it prior to installing an application, however, because it does not facilitate backing up files or configurations.

5.   Correct Answers: E

A. Incorrect: Performing a normal backup every night enables you to restore the entire system using only a single night's backup tape. However, it uses more tape backup media than is necessary because every file on the system is backed up every night.

B. Incorrect: The incremental backup makes a copy of all files marked with the archive attribute. After each file has been backed up, the file's archive attribute is cleared. Therefore, the incremental backup copies only files that were modified since the last backup. Performing only incremental backups would require restoring every single backup ever made in the event of a hard disk failure.

C. Incorrect: The differential backup makes a copy of all files marked with the archive attribute. Unlike the incremental backup, the differential backup does not modify the archive attribute of files after creating the backup. In this way, performing a differential backup every night ensures that every file modified since the last full backup can be restored. This is useful when combined with a normal backup, but using only differential backups results in a backup set that grows larger every night. Therefore, the differential backup does not meet the criteria of minimizing the backup media used.

D. Incorrect: This is a common backup strategy, but it does not meet the requirement of needing to restore only two sets of backups for a complete system recovery. Each incremental backup copies only those files that were modified since the prior night's backup. Therefore, every single incremental backup since the last normal backup must be restored to ensure total data recovery. For example, if a normal backup was performed on a Sunday and incremental backups thereafter, restoring the system on Thursday requires restoring Sunday's normal backup and Monday's, Tuesday's, and Wednesday's incremental backups.

E. Correct: This backup strategy meets all the requirements. Differential backups copy all files modified since the last normal backup, enabling a maximum of two separate restores to completely rebuild a file system. For example, if a normal backup was performed on a Sunday and differential backups thereafter, restoring the system on Thursday requires restoring only Sunday's normal backup and Wednesday's differential backup.

6.   Correct Answers: B

A. Incorrect: Although it is a good idea to contact the manufacturer for the latest drivers, a lack of a digital signature is not preventing Tom from installing the driver. Instead, he is restricted by the limited permission set granted by his membership in the Users group.

B. Correct: Normally, membership in the Backup Operators group is granted to allow a user to read files that the user would normally not be allowed to access. The group membership also gives the user the ability to install drivers for backup devices. In this scenario, Tom's user account lacks the necessary permissions to install drivers. Adding Tom's user account to the Backup Operators group gives him the permissions necessary to install the driver without granting excessive rights.

C. Incorrect: This would solve the problem because members of the Administrators group do have the right to install drivers. However, Administrators have many privileges that Tom does not need, which would create an unnecessary security vulnerability.

D. Incorrect: Prior to the introduction of Plug and Play, many hardware problems were resolved by disabling ports that used conflicting hardware interrupts. However, serial ports and parallel ports generally do not conflict. Additionally, Jim's problem is related to his restrictive user rights, not hardware conflicts.

7.   Correct Answers: B

A. Incorrect: Creating a restore point allows you to return to the current system configuration in the future if a problem occurs. In this case, the problem has already occurred, and it is too late to create a restore point.

B. Correct: By restoring the computer to an earlier restore point, you might be able to remove the settings that are causing problems on the computer. Hopefully, Windows XP automatically created a restore point when James ran the update.

C. Incorrect: Use the Last Known Good Configuration only if the system becomes unbootable. In this case, it could not possibly help because James has already logged into the computer. The Last Known Good Configuration settings are overwritten each time a user successfully logs in.

D. Incorrect: Safe mode is a valuable tool for repairing a system that is having problems booting. However, use it only after the system has failed and you can no longer boot normally.

E. Incorrect: The Recovery Console can salvage systems that are otherwise completely unbootable. Because James' computer does boot successfully, using Recovery Console is unnecessary. You can perform your troubleshooting from a standard Windows session.

8.   Correct Answers: B

A. Incorrect: Although it is possible for backup files to become corrupted, there is an incompatibility between the Windows 98 backup tool and the Windows XP backup tool that is causing this problem.

B. Correct: As described by Microsoft Knowledge Base article 305381, the Backup tool included with Windows XP cannot open compressed backups created in Windows 95, Windows 98, and Windows Me. The only way to access the backup file is to restore it by using one of those compatible operating systems.

C. Incorrect: In this scenario, the problem is not likely to be caused by insufficient file permissions.

D. Incorrect: Windows 98 did not provide encryption for backup files and did not have a dedicated administrator user account.

25 Configuring and Troubleshooting the Desktop Environment

The desktop environment in Microsoft Windows XP Professional is both flexible and customizable. It can be configured to meet the needs and tastes of a wide range of users and organizations, including those with employees and customers in different countries. Although flexibility is desirable in many situations, some organizations need to be able to enforce specific policies for the appearance and functionality of desktop elements because of security or supportability requirements.

This objective examines how to configure and manage a Windows XP Professional desktop, including configuring local and remote user profiles and multiple languages. Additionally, this objective requires you to understand how to distribute, install, and remove Windows Installer packages.

Tested Skills and Suggested Practices

The skills that you need to successfully master the Installing Windows XP Professional Objective Domain on the *Installing, Configuring, and Administering Microsoft Windows XP Professional* exam include the following:

> **Important** For the following task, you should complete at least Practices 1 through 8. If you want hands-on experience with every aspect of the exam and you have the extra lab resources needed, complete Practices 9 and 10 as well.

- Configure and manage user profiles and desktop settings.

  - Practice 1: Right-click the taskbar to open the Taskbar And Start Menu Properties dialog box. Customize the behavior and appearance of the taskbar and Start menu using the various options available on the Taskbar and Start Menu tabs.

  - Practice 2: Right-click the Start menu and select Explore. Right-click the Start menu and select Explore All Users. Compare the locations displayed in each Explorer window, and examine the subfolders and files contained within each location.

❑ Practice 3: Using the Display program from the Appearance And Themes group in Control Panel, select a different Theme for the desktop on the Theme tab.

❑ Practice 4: Select the Appearance tab in the Display Program located in the Appearance And Themes group in Control Panel and switch to Windows Classic from the drop-down list below Windows and buttons. Select different options from the drop-down list below Color Scheme. Click the Effects button and see how different choices affect the behavior of the user interface elements. Click the Advanced button and experiment with specifying custom colors for specific user interface elements.

❑ Practice 5: Create a blank Microsoft Management Console (MMC) and add the Group Policy snap-in and view the Local Computer Policy. Examine the configuration choices available under the Administrative Templates folder of the User Configuration node. Experiment with some of the settings available under these folders: Start Menu And Taskbar, Desktop, and Control Panel\Display.

❑ Practice 6: Launch Control Panel, click Performance And Maintenance, and then click System. Click the Advanced tab, and then click the Settings button in the User Profiles section of the dialog box. The User Profiles dialog box appears; use it to copy and delete a user profile.

❑ Practice 7: Create a new local user account and log on to the computer using that account. Type **set** at a command prompt to see a list of the configured environment variables. Make note of the value for the USERPROFILE variable. Log off the computer and log back on with an account that has local administrator privileges. Open the User Profiles dialog box, as discussed in Practice 1, and delete the user profile for this new local user. Log off the computer and back on with the new local user. Type **set** at the command prompt to see how the USERPROFILE variable has changed. Repeat these steps at least two more times with this user account.

❑ Practice 8: Launch Control Panel, click Performance And Maintenance, select System, click the Advanced tab, and then click the Environment Variables button to open the Environment Variables dialog box. Note which variables appear under the User Variables section and which appear under the Systems Variables section. Determine what happens when you create a new variable under each section and log on using different user accounts. Identify which environment variables are present regardless of which user account is logged on.

❑ Practice 9: Configure a roaming user profile on a workgroup computer, and then configure a fully functional roaming user profile using an Active Directory domain controller. Copy a local user profile to a network location and configure a domain account to use that roaming user profile; then log on to the network using that account.

❑ Practice 10: Using two Active Directory domain accounts, configure each type of mandatory user profile (Ntuser.man and *profile_folder*.man). Log on to a computer running Windows XP Professional with each of these accounts, and then disconnect the computer from the network. Attempt to log on again with each account and identify which mandatory user profile allows you to log on with the cached copy of the profile.

■ Configure support for multiple languages or multiple locations.

❑ Practice 1: Create a table showing which of the three versions of Windows XP Professional support the following features: ability to read and edit documents in multiple languages, language and regional support for 24 localized language versions, localized language user interface, ability to transact business primarily in English but to have access to additional languages, ability to transact business primarily in one or more languages besides English, and single worldwide rollouts for hot fixes and service packs.

❑ Practice 2: Install an additional Language Group on a computer running the International English version of Windows XP Professional. Visit two or more Web sites written in languages supported by the newly installed Language Group and copy the text into a text editor. Print a page from each Web site to verify that printing in the newly installed languages is possible. Enable the Language Bar and use it to quickly shift the keyboard from one language to another.

❑ Practice 3: Install the Windows XP Professional Multilingual User Interface Pack (MUI Pack), and use the Regional and Language Options application in Control Panel to select a non-English language. Open and use several of the applications included with Windows XP Professional (such as WordPad, Solitaire, and Calculator) to verify that the menus, dialog boxes, and other user interface elements appear in the language you selected.

❑ Practice 4: Select a different region, such as English (United Kingdom) or Italian (Italy), on the Regional Options tab of the Regional and Language Options dialog box. Open the Date and Time Properties program in Control Panel to see how the appearance of the calendar and clock changes when you specify a new region.

Important For the following task, you should complete at least Practices 1 and 2. If you want hands-on experience with every aspect of the exam and you have the extra lab resources needed to do Practice 3, complete Practice 3 as well.

■   Manage applications by using Windows Installer packages.

❑   Practice 1: Perform a Windows Installer–based routine (that is, from an .msi file) by downloading the Windows Server 2003 Administration Tools Pack from Microsoft.com and extracting the Adminpack.msi file from the executable file. Then, use the Add Or Remove Programs program in Control Panel to remove the newly installed tools.

❑   Practice 2: Repeat Practice 1, but perform all tasks from the command line by using the Msiexec.exe tool.

❑   Practice 3: On an Active Directory domain controller, use the Group Policy snap-in to assign and publish software applications to users. Be sure you understand which choice forces installation and which makes the installation optionally available. Use Group Policy to assign software to a client computer, and then reboot that computer and log on to it to verify that the software was installed automatically.

Further Reading

This section lists supplemental readings by objective. We recommend that you study these sources thoroughly before taking exam 70-270.

Objective 5.1   Open Help And Support from the Start menu; with the Help Index and the Help Search, look for the term *User Profile*. Scroll down to and view the articles about configuring user profiles such as "Assign a logon script to a profile," "Assign a mandatory user profile," "Creating a roaming or mandatory profile," and "Understanding User Profiles." Be sure to select additional articles from the Related Topics link available at the bottom of each of the articles you review.

Microsoft Corporation. *Microsoft Windows XP Professional Resource Kit Documentation*. Redmond, WA: Microsoft Press, 2001. Read Chapter 5, "Managing Desktops." This chapter examines options for configuring Windows XP desktops in workgroup and Active Directory domain environments; information relating to user profiles appears throughout the chapter (available online at *http://www.microsoft.com/resources/documentation/Windows/XP/all/reskit/en-us/prda_dcm_vdxa.asp*).

Microsoft Corporation. "User Data and Settings Management." 2002. This white paper is available at *http://www.microsoft.com/technet/prodtechnol/windowsserver2003/technologies/management/user01.mspx*. (If the white paper has moved, search for the title at *http://www.microsoft.com*.) Review this paper for a detailed look at managing user data and settings in Active Directory using IntelliMirror and Group Policy.

Objective 5.2   Microsoft Corporation. *Microsoft Windows XP Professional Resource Kit Documentation*. Redmond, WA: Microsoft Press, 2001. Read Chapter 3, "Multilingual Solutions for Global Business." This chapter examines the levels of support for multiple languages and locations available in the different versions of Windows XP Professional (available online at *http://www.microsoft.com/resources/ documentation/Windows/XP/all/reskit/en-us/prff_mul_wtws.asp*).

Objective 5.3   Microsoft Corporation. *Microsoft Windows XP Professional Resource Kit Documentation*. Redmond, WA: Microsoft Press, 2001. Read Chapter 5, "Managing Desktops." This chapter introduces desktop-management features in Windows XP Professional when running in workgroups or as part of Active Directory domains using IntelliMirror, Group Policy, and the Windows Installer Service (available online at *http://www.microsoft.com/resources/documentation/Windows/ XP/all/reskit/en-us/prda_dcm_vdxa.asp*).

Microsoft Corporation. "Group Policy Software Installation Overview." This is part of the Windows Server 2003 Help and Support Center documentation, and is available at *http://www.microsoft.com/resources/documentation/windowsserv/2003/ standard/proddocs/en-us/ADE.asp*. This topic describes how to use Active Directory GPOs to distribute software to computers and users that are members of a domain.

Configure and Manage User Profiles and Desktop Settings

Home users change desktop settings as a matter of convenience, and might never think about user profiles. To a business, however, desktop settings and user profiles are key tools for protecting the security of client systems. Businesses restrict desktop settings to enforce consistency between computers and reduce the occurrence of problems. On a network, a business might use roaming profiles to enable a user to use a different computer but keep the same documents and settings available.

In some environments, businesses use mandatory profiles to prevent users from making permanent changes to their profiles. Mandatory profiles are important in environments in which users change frequently, such as classroom environments and businesses that make use of temporary staff. To succeed at this objective, you must understand how to configure desktop settings on a local computer, create a roaming profile by moving a user's profile to a shared network folder, and configure mandatory profiles. Additionally, you should have a solid understanding of how domain administrators can use Active Directory Group Policy settings to control the desktop environment of domain member computers.

Objective 5.1 Questions

1. You are the administrator of a LAN consisting of Windows XP Professional computers and Windows 2003 Servers running Active Directory. All the systems belong to the same Active Directory domain. Some users periodically access more than one computer. You want to be sure that users retain their desktop settings, no matter which computer they use to log on to the network, and you want them to access their documents from a network file server. What do you do? Choose two correct answers.

   A. Have a domain administrator configure Group Policy settings to redirect personal folders to the file server.

   B. Configure the ClipBook service to redirect the personal folders to a network server.

   C. Configure each of the user accounts for roaming user profiles.

   D. Use the Accessibility Options program in Control Panel to specify the network location for user profiles.

   E. Use Windows Explorer to specify the network location for user profiles.

2. Your manager has asked you to find ways to lower support costs for maintaining desktop computers at your company. You want to restrict which configuration changes users can make to their computers. You also want to prevent users from modifying certain services local to their computers. You believe it will be easier to manage these restrictions if you can hide the administrative tools from the users so that they never even see them or their icons. Which of the following do you do? Choose the correct answer.

   A. Use the Add Or Remove Programs application in Control Panel to uninstall the programs you want to prevent users from accessing.

   B. Manually set permissions on the appropriate .cpl and .msc files from the file systems so that only administrators and the special local account called System have access to them on each computer you want to lock down.

   C. Have a domain administrator configure a Group Policy Object (GPO) that hides the desired Control Panel programs and MMC snap-ins. Link the GPO to the organizational units (OUs) containing the user accounts you need to restrict. Set permissions on the GPO so that it applies only to the users you want to lock down.

   D. Delete the appropriate .cpl and .msc files from the file systems of each computer you want to lock down.

3. You own a computer with a 300 MHz Pentium II microprocessor, 128 MB of RAM, and a 4 MB video adapter running Windows 2000 Professional. All the hardware components appear in Windows Catalog. You upgrade the computer to Windows XP Professional without any problems, but you notice that performance feels significantly slower than it used to. Short of upgrading the computer hardware, what can you do to improve the responsiveness of Windows XP Professional on your computer? Choose three correct answers.

A. Launch the Windows XP Professional installation routine again, but this time reformat the hard disk drive during the setup process and perform a clean installation of the operating system.

B. Reduce the size of the paging file to 2 MB.

C. Lower the screen resolution and reduce the color depth using the Display program in Control Panel.

D. Remove the paging file completely.

E. Run the Disk Defragmenter tool to reduce fragmentation on all the installed hard disks.

F. Use the Performance Options dialog box to set the display options to Adjust For Best Performance.

G. Use Task Manager to set the priority for the Explorer.exe process to Real Time.

4. John and Mary share the same computer running Windows XP Professional. You log on to their computer with an account that has administrative access and install a suite of internally developed applications used to access data on some of your firm's mainframe computers. You confirm that the applications were correctly installed by opening and testing each from their shortcuts on the Start menu. Later, they both report that they cannot find the icons for any of the programs. Which of the following is the quickest way to ensure that both John and Mary can easily access the suite of applications you just installed? Choose the correct answer.

A. Copy the program group for the suite of applications from your user profile to the Default User profile.

B. Copy the program group for the suite of applications from your user profile to John and Mary's user profiles.

C. Have John log on to the computer and install the suite of applications, and then have him log off. Have Mary perform the same installation while logged on with her user account.

D. Copy the program group for the suite of applications from your user profile to the All Users profile.

5. You have been told to increase security for your organization's network by designing a more tightly controlled approach to managing user desktop settings and data. The goals for your project are to do the following:

- Store user desktop settings in roaming profiles that will be available to users regardless of which computer they log on to.

- Prevent users from logging on with cached profiles when the network is unavailable.

- Minimize the amount of time required for mobile users to log on to their computers when away from the office.

- Ensure that all confidential user data is protected, even if a mobile user's laptop computer is stolen.

- Ensure that all critical user data is backed up regularly according to your organization's backup policy.

- Allow users to manage their own desktop settings.

You propose to do the following:

- Configure each user's account to employ a roaming user profile using the Active Directory Users And Computers snap-in.

- Make user profiles mandatory by appending .man to the root folder of each of the user profiles on the network.

- Use Group Policy to redirect the My Documents to a distributed file system (DFS) share located on several file servers that are secured and backed up according to your organization's policies.

- Implement Offline Folders so that users can work with their documents even when not connected to the network.

Which of the following goals does your proposed solution accomplish? Choose three correct answers.

A. Store user desktop settings in roaming profiles that will be available to users regardless of which computer they log on to.

B. Prevent users from logging on with cached profiles when the network is unavailable.

C. Minimize the amount of time required for mobile users to log on to their computers when away from the office.

D. Ensure that all confidential user data is protected, even if a mobile user's laptop computer is stolen.

E. Ensure that all critical user data is backed up regularly according to your organization's backup policy.

F. Allow users to manage their own desktop settings.

1.   Correct Answers: A and C

A.   Correct: Normally, a roaming user profile includes My Documents, My Pictures, and other personal folders. When you use Group Policy to redirect these folders, users work on the data contained in them as if the folders were still on their workstations. Another benefit of this approach is that when a user logs off the network, these folders are not synchronized with the roaming user profile. Because user data can become quite large, this approach might save users considerable time when logging on and off of their computers. You can further enhance this solution by configuring Offline Files for these folders, allowing mobile users to transparently synchronize the network-based folders with a locally cached copy of the files. When users are working from their computer while disconnected from the network, they can continue to work with the locally cached copies of their files. Changes are automatically resynchronized with the network copies the next time they connect their system to the network.

B.   Incorrect: The ClipBook service is for sharing documents copied to the Clipboard with other users via the network. The ClipBook service does not play a role in managing user profiles or folder redirection.

C.   Correct: When a user's account is set up to use a roaming user profile, that user's profile is stored on the network. When the user logs on to a computer, the user profile is cached to the local system. Any changes to the profile are written to the cached copy. When the user logs off the network, the changes in the cached copy are written back to the network copy. When a user logs on to a computer that has been disconnected from the network, the locally cached copy of the user profile is loaded transparently unless mandatory roaming profiles have been employed.

D.   Incorrect: The Accessibility Options program is for configuring keyboard, mouse, sound, and display settings to help people with mobility, vision, or hearing disabilities. The Accessibility Options program does not play a role in managing user profiles or folder redirection.

E.   Incorrect: Windows Explorer is not used to manage user profiles or folder redirection.

2.   Correct Answers: C

A.   Incorrect: Although the Add Or Remove Programs application can be used to remove some Windows components (such as the Indexing Service), it cannot be used to uninstall or reconfigure Control Panel programs or MMC snap-ins.

B.   Incorrect: Although this approach might accomplish the desired results, it is time-consuming, and doing it manually on many computers might result in errors on some systems. Using GPOs as described in answer C is a much more efficient and reliable approach.

C. Correct: GPOs are an extremely effective way to lock down the desktops of users. They are very flexible, allowing you to implement whatever degree of control that is appropriate for your particular environment.

D. Incorrect: This is a bad solution because the Windows File Protection feature in Windows XP Professional might automatically restore some or all the files that you manually remove. Any files that are not automatically restored are unavailable to all users who log on to those computers, including the system administrators who might need access to those files to do their jobs.

3.   **Correct Answers: C, E, and F**

A. Incorrect: This is a drastic approach that requires reinstalling all your applications and restoring your data from backup. Also, it is unlikely that you would notice a significant improvement in performance.

B. Incorrect: This step would probably result in even slower performance of Windows XP Professional.

C. Correct: Depending on the video card and how low you adjust these settings, the increase in performance might be subtle or dramatic. Dropping the resolution from 1280 × 1024 to 640 × 480 reduces the number of pixels by more than 75 percent. Cutting the color depth from 32 bits per pixel to 8 bits per pixel lowers the number of colors per pixel by 75 percent. Either of these steps reduces the workload on the video adapter by three-quarters, but it also decreases the quality of the display for the operating system and all applications.

D. Incorrect: This procedure would probably result in even slower performance.

E. Correct: Depending on the level of file fragmentation, the increase in performance might be imperceptible, moderate, or quite significant. It is a good idea to regularly defragment each hard disk on all your Windows XP systems. Disk Defragmenter can be launched from the Start menu by selecting All Programs, then Accessories, and then System Tools. You can also schedule the Defrag.exe command-line tool to run automatically by using Scheduled Tasks.

F. Correct: Slower systems such as the one described in this scenario often demonstrate much quicker responsiveness when the simpler graphical elements are selected for the user interface. The Performance Options dialog box is on the Advanced tab of the System program in Control Panel. You can enable or disable all the enhanced graphical user interface options together or specify settings for individual elements.

G. Incorrect: When tuning performance on busy systems running Windows XP Professional, it is possible to improve overall system efficiency considerably by specifying appropriate priority levels for individual processes. Be sure to have a thorough understanding of how the processes for the operating system, services, and applications interact and what effect each change will have before attempting this type of system tuning on production systems. It is extremely unusual to set any process to Real Time priority because that configuration might cause the process to consume 100 percent of the CPU's processing time, making it difficult or even impossible to do anything else on the computer.

4.   Correct Answers: D

A. Incorrect: Although copying the program group to the Default User profile ensures that any newly created profiles on the computer get a copy, existing user profiles do not.

B. Incorrect: These procedures ensure that both John and Mary have access to the new program group, but there is a quicker way to accomplish this.

C. Incorrect: It is possible that neither John nor Mary will be able to complete the installation if they do not have administrative privileges on the computer. Even if these procedures do work, it is an unnecessarily time-consuming solution.

D. Correct: This is the quickest way to resolve the problem. Program groups present in the All Users profiles are accessible to everyone who logs on to the computer. This type of issue is common with older applications and with internally developed programs that have not met all the requirements for the Certified for Windows logo program. Certified programs are required to recognize user profiles and to give the installer the option of making the program group accessible to all users or only the user logged on during the installation.

5.   Correct Answers: A, B, and E

A. Correct: By implementing roaming user profiles, your solution ensures that each user's profile will be available from any computer on the network.

B. Correct: By using the method of appending .man to the end of all users' Roaming User Profile folder, they cannot log on to computers using locally cached copies of their roaming profiles.

C. Incorrect: Appending .man to the end of each user's Roaming User Profile folder forces Windows XP Professional to download the entire user profile every time a user logs on. Although you are redirecting the My Documents to a location separate from each user's profile, the profiles can still grow large, leading to long logon times for remote users. It is important to note that this goal conflicts with the second goal—sometimes it is not possible to achieve all desired goals.

D. Incorrect: Nothing in your proposed solution addresses this goal. Implementing Encrypting File System (EFS) in combination with the Offline Files feature would allow you to better protect the data of the mobile users.

E. Correct: By redirecting the My Documents folder to a DFS share that is located on file servers that are backed up regularly, you have ensured that critical user data is backed up periodically.

F. Incorrect: If you implement mandatory profiles, users can no longer manage their desktop settings. Any changes users make to their desktops will be discarded when they log off.

Configure Support for Multiple Languages or Multiple Locations

Windows XP Professional is available in three versions that provide different levels of support for multiple languages.

- **International English Version.** This version includes the Multilingual Editing and Viewing feature, which allows the user to view, edit, and print information in more than 60 languages. This version is appropriate for occasional electronic communications in non-English languages.

- **Localized Language Versions.** This is a localized version that provides the same type of support as the English version, but all built-in menus, dialog boxes, Help files, wizards, and file systems appear in a non-English language. Implement this version when support for a few non-English languages is needed throughout the entire organization.

- **Multilingual User Interface Pack (MUI Pack).** Provides the same features as the other versions, but enables you to switch from one language to another on the fly. The MUI Pack is the best choice when support for numerous languages is needed across the organization.

The most important element of mastering this objective is to understand how to configure and deploy the MUI Pack.

Objective 5.2 Questions

1. Your organization has major offices in Spain, Portugal, France, Germany, Poland, Great Britain, and the United States. Many users do not speak or write English fluently. Users in many locations must regularly create and receive documents in two or more languages. Your organization has decided to migrate to Windows XP Professional, and it is up to you to recommend how to best support the multilingual needs of the users. Which of the following do you suggest? Choose the correct answer.

    A. Create a standard base desktop using the Windows XP Professional Multilingual User Interface (MUI) Pack. Be sure to install all the Input Languages used throughout your organization so that users can easily exchange documents in any language with one another.

    B. Create a standard base desktop using the English version of Windows XP Professional. Be sure to install all the Input Languages used throughout your organization so that users can easily exchange documents in any language with one another. Recommend to your manager that all users be signed up for extensive English language courses as soon as possible.

    C. Create a standard base desktop using the English version of Windows XP Professional. Recommend to your manager that all users be signed up for extensive English language courses as soon as possible. Require users to create all their documents in English.

    D. Create standard base desktops using the English version and the appropriate Translated versions of Windows XP Professional. Be sure to install all the Input Languages used throughout your organization so that users can easily exchange documents in any language with one another.

2. Your company has offices spread across the United States and Canada. Although all employees speak and write English fluently, your company occasionally does business with organizations in the Canadian province of Quebec. Some of these organizations do the majority of their business in French. What must you do at the Windows XP Professional computers of employees who will be working with these organizations? Choose the correct answer.

    A. Open WordPad and select the French (Canada) input locale.

    B. Install the French Translated version of Windows XP Professional.

    C. Install the French version of WordPad by downloading it from the Windows Update Web site.

    D. Use the Regional And Languages Options program by launching Control Panel and then choosing Date, Time, Language, And Regional Options to enable support for French (Canada) as an input language. If prompted, provide the location of the Windows XP Professional installation media and restart the computer.

3.   You are a consultant who was asked by a worldwide commercial property management firm to plan an upgrade program to deploy the MUI Pack throughout its organization. The firm has many offices around the globe, most of which have not been tightly managed by their information technology group. A thorough audit of the hardware and software reveals that the firm is running a variety of previous Windows versions on a multitude of hardware platforms. You determine that many systems will have to be replaced because that will be less expensive than trying to upgrade the hardware to the point where it could reliably run Windows XP Professional. Which of the following versions of Windows can be upgraded directly to the MUI Pack? Choose four correct answers.

   A. Windows 2000 Server

   B. Windows Me

   C. Windows NT Workstation 4.0

   D. Windows NT Server 4.0

   E. Windows NT Workstation 3.51

   F. Windows 2000 Professional

   G. Windows 98

Objective 5.2 Answers

1. **Correct Answers: A**

A. **Correct:** This is the easiest approach to this challenge because the information technology group within your organization has a single standard desktop to maintain and support.

B. **Incorrect:** Although this approach might be easier on your organization's information technology group, it does not fulfill the needs of your users. Forcing the users to learn a second language is expensive and time-consuming, and might cause resentment in some.

C. **Incorrect:** This solution is inappropriate for the same reasons noted in answer B.

D. **Incorrect:** Although this solution meets the multilingual requirements of the users, it will result in at least six versions of Windows XP Professional being deployed in your organization. That will cause an unnecessary challenge for your organization's information technology group.

2. **Correct Answers: D**

A. **Incorrect:** Although you can view and edit documents in WordPad using any installed Input Language, you cannot switch languages from within that program.

B. **Incorrect:** This is an inefficient and expensive solution for supporting the viewing, editing, and printing of documents in multiple languages.

C. **Incorrect:** There is no French version of WordPad available for download from the Windows Update Web site.

D. **Correct:** All versions of Windows XP Professional support viewing, editing, and printing documents in multiple languages as long as the proper language group is installed. The Western Europe and United States Language Group is installed by default in the English version of Windows XP Professional. It includes support for several languages such as French and English. Other language groups must be installed to support additional input languages, such as Greek. You must restart the computer after installing additional language groups.

3. **Correct Answers: B, C, F, and G**

A. **Incorrect:** Because it is not possible to upgrade Windows 2000 Server to Windows XP Professional, it is also not possible to upgrade this version of the operating system to Windows XP Professional MUI Pack.

B. **Correct:** Upgrade from Windows Me to Windows XP Professional, and then apply the MUI Pack files. You can simplify the process by creating an unattended answer file–based upgrade installation of Windows XP Professional. Then add

MUISETUP to the [GUIRunOnce] section of the answer file. Details of the procedure are available on the Windows XP MUI Pack installation media.

C. **Correct:** Like Windows Me, upgrade Windows NT Workstation 4.0 to Windows XP Professional English Version and then apply the MUI Pack files.

D. **Incorrect:** It is not possible to upgrade Windows NT Server 4.0 to Windows XP Professional; therefore, it is not possible to upgrade this version of the operating system to Windows XP Professional MUI Pack.

E. **Incorrect:** It is not possible to upgrade Windows NT Workstation 3.51 to Windows XP Professional; therefore, it is not possible to upgrade this version of the operating system to Windows XP Professional MUI Pack.

F. **Correct:** Like Windows Me, upgrade Windows 2000 Professional to Windows XP Professional English version and then apply the MUI Pack files.

G. **Correct:** Like Windows Me, upgrade Windows 98 to Windows XP Professional English version, and then apply the MUI Pack files.

Manage Applications by Using Windows Installer Packages

Software developers create Windows Installer packages for their products. For example, Microsoft distributes updates for Microsoft Office 2003 as Windows Installer packages. Developers within your organization can also create Windows Installer packages to simplify the deployment of the application. In particular, Windows Installer packages make it extremely easy to distribute an application by using Active Directory software distribution. Although you do not need to know exactly how to configure software distribution by using Active Directory Group Policy objects, you must understand it conceptually and be able to troubleshoot the problems that can arise.

To succeed at this objective, you must understand the purpose of Windows Installer packages. You should have hands-on experience installing, configuring, and removing Windows Installer packages using both graphical tools and the Msiexec.exe command-line tool. If you have an Active Directory domain controller at your disposal, having hands-on experience distributing Windows Installer packages using Active Directory software distribution will give you a deeper understanding of the capabilities.

Objective 5.3 Questions

1. You are a desktop administrator for a sports equipment manufacturing company. Yesterday, the engineers responsible for software distribution deployed Office 2003 to all computers in your domain. All users have local user profiles. The following day you discover that Office has not been deployed to most of the Windows XP Professional computers that you manage. Which Group Policy setting do the domain administrators need to modify to ensure that the application is distributed the next time users log in? Choose the correct answer.

    A. Enable the Always Wait For The Network At Computer Startup And Logon policy.

    B. Enable the Maximum Wait Time For Group Policy Scripts setting and set it to zero seconds.

    C. Enable the Wait For Remote User Profile setting.

    D. Enable Turn Off Background Refresh Of Group Policy.

2. You identify the source of a persistent problem with one of your user's computers: an application, installed by using a Windows Installer package, that is consuming a large amount of disk space. You are not sure where the user found the Windows Installer package to perform the original installation, however. What is the easiest way to uninstall the application? Choose the correct answer.

    A. msiexec /uninstall ProductCode

    B. Right-click the original .msi file and select Remove.

    C. Double-click the original .msi file. When prompted, click Remove

    D. Open Add Or Remove Programs. Click the application, and then click Remove.

3. You are a part-time desktop administrator for a small organization that consists of five users who work from home in different parts of the world. Each user has a Windows XP Professional computer that is not connected to an Active Directory domain. In fact, the organization has no servers. You have been working closely with one of your software vendors to resolve a bug in an application that the users depend on. After several weeks of support calls, the vendor posted a .msi file to its Web site for you to install on each of your computers. The location of the .msi file is *http://www.contoso.com/ patch.msi*. Users will need to install the update themselves.

Each user has a local administrator account to use for the installation. You want to send them a command that they can run to automatically install the patch. Which command would work? Choose the correct answer.

    A. msiexec /x "http://www.contoso.com/patch.msi"

    B. msiexec /update "http://www.contoso.com/patch.msi"

    C. msiexec /i "http://www.contoso.com/patch.msi"

    D. msiexec /url "http://www.contoso.com/patch.msi"

4. Which version of Windows Installer is included with Service Pack 2 for Windows XP? Choose the correct answer.

    A. Windows Installer 1.0

    B. Windows Installer 2.0

    C. Windows Installer 3.0

    D. Windows Installer 4.0

1. **Correct Answers: A**

   A. Correct: By default, Windows XP does not wait for the network to be fully initialized at startup and logon. Existing users are logged on using cached credentials, which results in shorter logon times. Windows XP applies Group Policy in the background after the network becomes available. As a result, software installations usually take two or three logons. Enabling this setting causes Windows XP to wait for the network before logon so that Group Policy can be immediately applied.

   B. Incorrect: Setting this policy to zero forces clients to wait indefinitely while Group Policy scripts run. It will not ensure that the application is installed at the next login, however.

   C. Incorrect: This setting directs the system to wait for the remote copy of the roaming user profile to load, no matter how long it takes. Waiting for the remote profile is appropriate when users move between computers frequently, and the local copy of their profile is not always current. However, the users in this scenario have local user profiles, so enabling this setting will have no effect.

   D. Incorrect: This setting prevents Group Policy from being updated while the computer is in use. If you enable this setting, the system waits until the user logs off the system before updating Group Policy settings instead of refreshing settings on a regular basis. This setting would have no effect on how software is distributed.

2. **Correct Answers: D**

   A. Incorrect: You can use the Msiexec tool to uninstall applications. However, it is easier to use Add Or Remove Programs.

   B. Incorrect: While you can uninstall a Windows Installer package by right-clicking the original .msi file and clicking Uninstall, the menu item is not named Remove. Additionally, this is typically not as easy as opening Add Or Remove Programs and uninstalling the package.

   C. Incorrect: This will work. However, because you do not know where the original .msi file is located, it would be more time-consuming than using Add Or Remove Programs.

   D. Correct: Windows Installer applications always add themselves to the Add Or Remove Programs list. Therefore, you should use Add Or Remove Programs to uninstall them.

3.   **Correct Answers: C**

> **A. Incorrect:** The /x parameter actually uninstalls a package, rather than installing it.
>
> **B. Incorrect:** The /update parameter requires a Windows Installer update file, which would have a .MSP file extension. The developer has provided you with a .msi file, which should be installed with the /i parameter.
>
> **C. Correct:** Use the /i parameter to install Windows Installer packages. You can specify a URL for the location of the file.
>
> **D. Incorrect:** Msiexec does not support the /url parameter.

4.   **Correct Answers: C**

> **A. Incorrect:** Windows XP includes Windows Installer 2.0, and Service Pack 2 upgrades it to version 3.0.
>
> **B. Incorrect:** Windows XP includes Windows Installer 2.0, and Service Pack 2 upgrades it to version 3.0.
>
> **C. Correct:** Windows XP includes Windows Installer 2.0, and Service Pack 2 upgrades it to version 3.0.
>
> **D. Incorrect:** Windows Installer 4.0 was not yet available when Service Pack 2 was released.

26 Implementing, Managing, and Troubleshooting Network Protocols and Services

Microsoft Windows XP makes it easy to stay connected while minimizing your exposure to attacks. Naturally, you can connect to traditional wired networks. You can also connect to wireless networks at your home or office, or at wireless hotspots. If you are away from the office, you can connect to any Internet connection and use Windows XP to create a virtual private network (VPN) connection to access resources on your internal network. If an Internet connection is not available, but you can access a telephone line, you can use dial-up networking to connect to your office network.

It is risky to connect to any network, especially the Internet. Windows XP helps protect you from network attacks by using Internet Connection Firewall (ICF) and, when Service Pack 2 is installed, Windows Firewall. Both ICF and Windows Firewall are capable of providing similar levels of protection by blocking all incoming connections that have not specifically been allowed. Windows Firewall is enabled by default, however, and is easier to configure. In Active Directory environments, domain administrators can configure Windows Firewall by using Group Policy settings.

For troubleshooting problems with remote computers and helping users across a network, Windows XP provides Remote Desktop and Remote Assistance, both of which display a remote computer's desktop on your own computer. Additionally, Windows XP can act as either a Web server or a Web client, thanks to Internet Information Services (IIS) and Microsoft Internet Explorer.

To complete this objective, you must understand how to install, configure, and troubleshoot all these technologies.

Tested Skills and Suggested Practices

The skills you need to successfully master the Implementing, Managing, and Troubleshooting Network Protocols and Services objective domain on the *Installing, Configuring, and Administering Microsoft Windows XP Professional* exam include the following:

- Configure and troubleshoot the TCP/IP protocol.
  - ❑ Practice 1: Install TCP/IP and configure the computer to use Automatic Private IP Addressing (APIPA).

❑ Practice 2: Connect a Windows XP computer to a network with a Dynamic Host Configuration Protocol (DHCP) server. Verify that the Windows XP Professional computer obtains its TCP/IP configuration from the DHCP server. Then use Ipconfig.exe to examine, release, and renew DHCP leases on the Windows XP Professional computer.

❑ Practice 3: Familiarize yourself with the other tools available for troubleshooting network connections such as Arp.exe, Hostname.exe, Ipconfig.exe, Ping.exe, Pathping.exe, Tracert.exe, Netstat.exe, and Route.exe.

❑ Practice 4: Configure a static TCP/IP address for a client computer that normally relies on DHCP-assigned Internet Protocol (IP) addresses.

❑ Practice 5: Use the Nslookup.exe utility to identify the IP addresses for *http:// www.microsoft.com*.

❑ Practice 6: Edit the HOSTS file in the %windir%\system32\drivers\etc directory so that the domain name *http://www.microsoft.com* resolves to the IP address 127.0.0.1. Save the HOSTS file, and use the command *ping www.microsoft.com* to verify that this domain name resolves to the IP address 127.0.0.1. Edit the HOSTS file again, remove the new entry, and save the file.

■ Connect to computers by using dial-up networking.

❑ Practice 1: Create a dial-up connection to an Internet service provider (ISP). After this connection is working properly, configure Internet Connection Sharing (ICS) to allow multiple computers to access the Internet across a single link.

❑ Practice 2: If you have a VPN server available, establish a VPN tunnel. Configure this connection with ICS to allow multiple computers to use the VPN simultaneously.

■ Connect to resources by using Internet Explorer.

❑ Practice 1: Configure offline Web pages to store several Web sites offline. Open the Synchronize dialog box, and adjust the properties to automatically download these sites at a specific time. After this time has passed, disconnect from the network and attempt to access one of the offline Web sites.

❑ Practice 2: Press Ctrl+H to open the history toolbar. Notice that all sites visited in the last several weeks are available for recall.

❑ Practice 3: Use the Internet Options dialog box to clear your temporary Internet files and history. This helps to protect your privacy if other people have access to your computer.

❑ Practice 4: Using the Security tab of the Internet Options dialog box, compare the security settings for the Internet and Trusted Sites zones. Consider how they differ, and how that improves the security of your computer.

- ❑ Practice 5: Using the Privacy tab of the Internet Options dialog, examine the settings for each of the six privacy levels. Temporarily set your privacy level to Block All Cookies, and then visit several of your favorite Web sites. Consider how your user experience was affected. Afterwards, set the privacy level to its original setting.

- ■ Configure, manage, and implement Internet Information Services (IIS).

  - ❑ Practice 1: If IIS was not installed with Windows XP, install it from Add/Remove Windows Components in Control Panel. Familiarize yourself with the different IIS components available for installation.

  - ❑ Practice 2: Edit the application configuration to remove unused script mappings. Although this does not change the site's existing functionality, it does dramatically reduce the risk of security vulnerabilities.

  - ❑ Practice 3: Add a virtual directory, and disable anonymous access to the virtual directory. Access the virtual directory using Internet Explorer and notice that you are prompted for authentication. Provide your user name and password, and verify that you have access.

  - ❑ Practice 4: Modify NTFS file permissions for Web content within the IIS home directory. Notice how removing Read file permissions for the IUSR_*computername* account affects your ability to anonymously access files.

  - ❑ Practice 5: Install an IIS security hot fixes if any are available.

Important   For the following task, you should complete at least Practice 1. If you want hands-on experience with every aspect of the exam and you have multiple networked Windows XP computers, complete Practices 2 and 3 as well.

- ■ Configure, manage, and troubleshoot Remote Desktop and Remote Assistance.

  - ❑ Practice 1: Use the Remote tab of the System Properties dialog box to allow both Remote Desktop and Remote Assistance incoming connections.

  - ❑ Practice 2: Open the Remote Desktop Connection tool, and use the Experience tab to optimize the performance for local area network (LAN) speeds. Connect to a remote computer by using Remote Desktop. Then disconnect, and optimize the performance of the connection for modem speeds. Reconnect, and notice how the experience is different.

  - ❑ Practice 3: Have another Windows XP user send you a Remote Assistance invitation, and then connect to the remote computer by using Remote Assistance.

- Configure, manage, and troubleshoot an ICF.

  ❑ Practice 1: First, disable Remote Desktop and Remote Assistance. Then install Service Pack 2, and open the Security Center. Notice whether Windows Firewall is enabled or not. View the Windows Firewall properties, and notice the programs and services listed on the Exceptions tab.

  ❑ Practice 2: Enable Remote Desktop. Then view the Windows Firewall properties, and notice that Remote Desktop has been added to the Exceptions tab.

  ❑ Practice 3: Manually add Windows Messenger to the list of Windows Firewall exceptions.

  ❑ Practice 4: Enable ICF or Windows Firewall with all default settings so that all incoming traffic is automatically filtered. Attempt to *ping* this system from a remote system, and notice the results. Attempt to map a connection to a shared folder, and notice the results. Disable ICF or Windows Firewall and repeat these steps.

Further Reading

This section lists supplemental readings by objective. We recommend that you study these sources thoroughly before taking exam 70-270.

Objective 6.1   Microsoft Corporation. *Microsoft Windows XP Professional Resource Kit Documentation*. Redmond, WA: Microsoft Press, 2001. Read Chapter 18, "Connecting Clients to Windows Networks." This chapter covers the fundamentals of installing and configuring network protocols and services in Windows XP Professional. Read Chapter 19, "Configuring TCP/IP," for a detailed look at all the configuration options available in the Windows XP Professional implementation of TCP/IP. Read Chapter 20, "Configuring IP Addressing and Name Resolution." This chapter provides detailed information about configuring IP addresses and names and how to identify and resolve problems (available online at *http:// www.microsoft.com/resources/documentation/Windows/XP/all/reskit/en-us/ prork_overview.asp*).

Microsoft Corporation. "How to Troubleshoot TCP/IP Connectivity with Windows XP." 2004. This Knowledge Base article provides important network troubleshooting information. This article is available at *http://support.microsoft.com/kb/314067*. (If the article has moved, search for the title at *http://www.microsoft.com*.)

Objective 6.2   Microsoft Corporation. *Microsoft Windows XP Professional Resource Kit Documentation*. Redmond, WA: Microsoft Press, 2001. Read Chapter 21, "Connecting Remote Offices," for background information about VPNs and Internet Connection Sharing (available online at *http://www.microsoft.com/resources/documentation/ Windows/XP/all/reskit/en-us/prcg_cnd_cgza.asp*).

Microsoft Corporation. "The Cable Guy - August 2001: Layer Two Tunneling Protocol in Windows 2000." 2001. Although this article was written for Windows 2000, it applies to Windows XP Professional as well. This article is available at *http://www.microsoft.com/technet/community/columns/cableguy/cg0801.mspx*. (If the article has moved, search for the title at *http://www.microsoft.com*.)

Objective 6.3 Microsoft Corporation. *Internet Explorer Administration Kit*. 2004. Read the Appendix, "Windows XP Service Pack 2 Enhancements to Internet Explorer 6." This appendix covers the very significant changes to Internet Explorer that Service Pack 2 adds (available online at *http://www.microsoft.com/windows/ieak/techinfo/deploy/60/en/appendix.mspx*).

Launch Internet Explorer, select the Help menu, and then select Contents And Index. Read through all the available topics, paying particular attention to the proxy settings, favorites, and history features.

Objective 6.4 Microsoft Corporation. *Microsoft Windows XP Professional Resource Kit Documentation*. Redmond, WA: Microsoft Press, 2001. Read "Internet Printing" in Chapter 11, "Enabling Printing and Faxing," for general information about how IIS facilitates sharing printers. Read "Broadcasting Digital Media Presentations over Your Intranet" in Chapter 10, "Managing Digital Media," for details about how IIS provides for streaming digital media (available online at *http://www.microsoft.com/resources/documentation/Windows/XP/all/reskit/en-us/prork_overview.asp*).

Microsoft Corporation. "Securing Internet Information Services 5.0 and 5.1." 2004. This white paper is available at *http://www.microsoft.com/smallbusiness/gtm/securityguidance/articles/sec_iis_5_0_5_1.mspx*. (If the white paper has moved, search for the title at *http://www.microsoft.com*.)

Objective 6.5 Microsoft Corporation. *Microsoft Windows XP Professional Resource Kit Documentation*. Redmond, WA: Microsoft Press, 2001. Read Chapter 8, "Configuring Remote Desktop," for detailed information about Remote Desktop. Also read Appendix D, "Tools for Troubleshooting," for information about remote assistance (available online at *http://www.microsoft.com/resources/documentation/Windows/XP/all/reskit/en-us/prork_overview.asp*).

Objective 6.6 Microsoft Corporation. *Microsoft Windows XP Professional Resource Kit Documentation*. Redmond, WA: Microsoft Press, 2001. Read "Internet Connection Firewalls" in Chapter 21, "Connecting Remote Offices" (available online at *http://www.microsoft.com/resources/documentation/Windows/XP/all/reskit/en-us/prcg_cnd_cgza.asp*).

Microsoft Corporation. "Troubleshooting Windows Firewall in Microsoft Windows XP Service Pack 2." 2004. This white paper is available at *http://www.microsoft.com/downloads/details.aspx?FamilyID=a7628646-131d-4617-bf68-f0532d8db131.* (If the white paper has moved, search for the title at *http://www.microsoft.com.*)

Tony Northrup. "Firewalls." 2002. This white paper is available at *http://www.microsoft.com/technet/security/topics/network/firewall.mspx.* (If the white paper has moved, search for the title at *http://www.microsoft.com.*)

Configure and Troubleshoot the TCP/IP Protocol

For two computers to communicate, they must agree to speak a common language. On the Internet, and most private networks, this common language is TCP/IP. Each device on a TCP/IP network is assigned one or more unique IP addresses. You can assign IP addresses in three ways: DHCP, Automatic Private IP Addressing (APIPA), or manually. Both DHCP and APIPA are enabled by default.

If a computer cannot communicate with another computer on the network, you must verify that the network adapter is installed and operational in Device Manager. Next, verify that it is physically connected to the network. Then run protocol-specific utilities designed to test network connections. Some of the tools for testing TCP/IP connectivity included with Windows XP Professional are Arp.exe, Hostname.exe, Ping.exe, Pathping.exe, Tracert.exe, Netstat.exe, Route.exe, and Ipconfig.exe.

To successfully answer questions in this objective, you must know how to install, configure, manage, and troubleshoot network adapters. You also need to know how to install, configure, manage, and troubleshoot TCP/IP connections.

Objective 6.1 Questions

1. Which of the following is the correct order Windows XP Professional uses for resolving a DNS host name? Choose the correct answer.

   A. (1) Check the local computer's host name for a match. (2) Check the NetBIOS name cache. (3) Send a WINS query if configured. (4) Send a broadcast query for a matching NetBIOS name. (5) Check the LMHOSTS file for a match. (6) Check the HOSTS file for a match. (7) Send a DNS query.

   B. (1) Check the local computer's host name for a match. (2) Send a DNS query. (3) Check the HOSTS file for a match. (4) Check the NetBIOS name cache. (5) Send a WINS query if configured. (6) Send a broadcast query for a matching NetBIOS name. (7) Check the LMHOSTS file for a match.

   C. (1) Check the local computer's host name for a match. (2) Check the HOSTS file for a match. (3) Send a DNS query. (4) Check the NetBIOS name cache. (5) Send a WINS query if configured. (6) Send a broadcast query for a matching NetBIOS name. (7) Check the LMHOSTS file for a match.

   D. (1) Check the local computer's host name for a match. (2) Check the HOSTS file for a match. (3) Send a DNS query. (4) Check the NetBIOS name cache. (5) Check the LMHOSTS file for a match. (6) Send a WINS query if configured. (7) Send a broadcast query for a matching NetBIOS name.

2. Your computer is able to connect to some network resources with no problem, but you feel that performance is abnormally slow when connecting to some specific servers located in remote offices. You suspect that there might be a routing issue on your network. Which tools included with Windows XP Professional are best for examining these types of problems? Choose two correct answers.

   A. Pathping.exe

   B. Arp.exe

   C. Tracert.exe

   D. Ping.exe

   E. Ipconfig.exe

3. You are a consultant and have just started working at the office of a new client. The company has a DHCP server on the network, so you should be able to plug your Windows XP laptop into the network and get immediate access to the Internet. You turn on your laptop computer, connect the network cable, and log on to the desktop. You open Microsoft Internet Explorer and receive a The Page Cannot Be Displayed Error no matter which Web page you try to access. You open a command prompt and run Ipconfig.exe. You notice that your computer has the IP address 169.254.0.2 and a subnet mask of 255.255.0.0. Choose the best answer.

Why are you unable to browse the Web from your laptop computer? Choose the best answer.

A. Your computer was unable to get an IP address from the DHCP server; therefore, it used APIPA to assign an address to itself.

B. The network adapter is malfunctioning.

C. The network cable is disconnected from either your computer's network adapter or the network port.

D. TCP/IP is not installed on your laptop computer.

4. Which of the following problems is resolved by clearing the ARP cache by typing the command **netsh interface ip delete arpcache**? Choose the best answer.

A. Clients cannot reach a server on the local subnet that has recently had the IP address changed.

B. Clients cannot reach a server on the local subnet that has recently had the network card replaced.

C. Clients cannot reach a server that has recently had the DNS entry changed.

D. Clients cannot reach a server that has moved to a different network segment.

5. You are a systems administrator at your organization's corporate headquarters. Your company is in the process of establishing a small remote office in another country. The local systems administrator calls you for assistance because his Windows XP desktop computer cannot connect to the company's wide area network (WAN). You gather information about the IP configuration of his network and draw the following diagram based on the information the systems administrator provides.

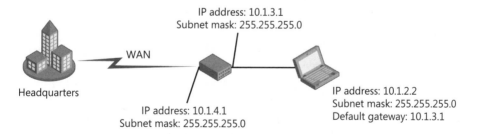

What setting does the administrator need to change? Choose the best answer.

A. Change the computer's subnet mask to 255.0.0.0.

B. Change the computer's default gateway to 10.1.4.1.

C. Change the computer's IP address to 10.1.3.2.

D. Set both of the router's IP addresses to 10.1.3.1.

Objective 6.1 Answers

1.   Correct Answers: C

   A. Incorrect: Windows XP Professional always attempts to resolve names using the HOSTS file and DNS first. NetBIOS name resolution methods such as WINS and the LMHOSTS file are used only as a last resort.

   B. Incorrect: Windows XP Professional checks the HOSTS file for host name resolution before sending a DNS query. However, the LMHOSTS file is not checked until after a WINS resolution request is attempted.

   C. Correct: Windows XP Professional first checks the specified host name against the local machine name. It then begins the DNS name resolution process, first checking the HOSTS file and then sending a DNS query. Finally, the NetBIOS name resolution process is used, which is as follows: check the NetBIOS name cache, send a WINS query, send a broadcast query, and scan the LMHOSTS file.

   D. Incorrect: A DNS query and the HOSTS file are very similar to a WINS query and the LMHOSTS file. Windows XP standard DNS name resolution scans the HOSTS file before sending a DNS query. However, by default, NetBIOS name resolution scans the LMHOSTS file *after* sending a WINS query.

2.   Correct Answers: A and C

   A. Correct: PathPing is a command-line tool for tracing routes through TCP/IP networks. It combines features of both Ping.exe and Tracert.exe and provides additional information that neither offers. It is an excellent tool for troubleshooting routing problems.

   B. Incorrect: You use the Arp tool to view, edit, and clear the Address Resolution Protocol (ARP) cache on the local computer. Arp is used to map IP addresses to media access control (MAC) addresses of specific network adapters on the same network segment. It does not provide any information about routing IP traffic to other network segments and therefore is not an appropriate tool for this scenario.

   C. Correct: Tracert is a command-line, route-tracing tool that repeatedly sends Internet Control Message Protocol (ICMP) Echo Request messages with increasingly larger time-to-live values to map out the route from the local computer to the one specified in the command. It is an ideal tool for diagnosing routing problems.

   D. Incorrect: Ping is a command-line tool for verifying IP connectivity. The Ping tool can be used to verify that your computer can communicate with another host on the network, but it does not provide information about the route taken across the network and therefore is not an appropriate tool to use in this scenario.

   E. Incorrect: Ipconfig is a command-line tool for reviewing the current IP addressing configuration for the local computer. It is not used for troubleshooting problems on the network.

3.   **Correct Answers: A**

   A. Correct: APIPA uses IP addresses from the range 169.254.0.1 through 169.254.255.254 and a subnet mask of 255.255.0.0, and your computer's address falls within that range. Your next step is to determine why your computer was unable to get an address from the DHCP server—likely reasons for that problem include the server being offline or the physical segment that your computer is connected to being unable to send DHCP messages to the DHCP server.

   B. Incorrect: If the network adapter was not working, you would see an error message when you ran Ipconfig.exe or no information would be displayed regarding your IP address.

   C. Incorrect: If the cable was not connected properly, you would see an error message when you run Ipconfig.exe stating that the media is disconnected.

   D. Incorrect: If TCP/IP were not installed correctly, you would not have had any IP address assigned.

4.   **Correct Answers: B**

   A. Incorrect: When Arp looks up an IP address' associated MAC address, this relationship is stored in the ARP cache for future reference. If a server's IP address changes, Arp issues a new request for the MAC address. Therefore, clearing the ARP cache does not resolve this problem.

   B. Correct: Every network card includes a unique MAC address. Therefore, when a network card is replaced on a system, that system's MAC address also changes. If clients attempt to reconnect to a system that has recently had the network card replaced, they may address network communications to the cached MAC address of the failed network card. The server does not respond to these communications because it is listening for requests addressed to the MAC address of the new network card. Clearing the ARP cache of the clients on the same subnet resolves this problem.

   C. Incorrect: Changing a server's DNS host name causes new communications addressed to the previous host name to fail. However, DNS resolution does not directly involve Arp. As a result, clearing the ARP cache does not resolve the problem.

   D. Incorrect: If a system moves between network segments, the IP address must also change. In this scenario, the ARP cache might still contain the IP address to MAC address mapping of the system's previous IP address. However, the new IP address of the server does not yet reside in the ARP cache. Therefore, clearing the ARP cache does not resolve the problem.

5.   **Correct Answers: C**

A.   **Incorrect:** In this scenario, the computer and both of the router's network interfaces have been configured with class A addresses. However, class A addresses can have a subnet mask of 255.255.255.0. In fact, a subnet mask of 255.0.0.0 would be extremely unusual.

B.   **Incorrect:** The computer's default gateway should be set to the IP address of the router's local network adapter. In other words, the default gateway must be set to the IP address that the router has been assigned on the local network. In this case, the default gateway is correct.

C.   **Correct:** The problem is that the computer's IP address and the router's local IP address are on different logical subnets. The computer has been configured with an IP address of 10.1.2.2, but the default gateway is 10.1.3.1. Because the default gateway is on a different logical subnet, the computer cannot send packets to it— even though it is on the same physical network segment. Assigning the computer an IP address of 10.1.3.2 places it on the same logical subnet as the router's 10.1.3.1 address, allowing it to send packets to the router.

D.   **Incorrect:** Each network interface must have a unique IP address. Therefore, you cannot configure two network adapters to have the same IP address.

Connect to Computers by Using Dial-Up Networking

There are two primary ways to gain remote access to your internal network: dial-up networking and a VPN. With dial-up networking, you connect your Windows XP computer to a telephone line and use the telephone line to connect to a remote access server at your office. With a VPN, you connect your Windows XP computer to the Internet and use the Internet to connect to a VPN server at your office.

ICS provides a convenient way for small business and home users to connect multiple systems to the Internet using a single connection. ICS combines three software services: DHCP, Network Address Translation (NAT), and DNS proxy. DHCP is used to assign private IP addresses to other computers on the local area network (LAN). NAT translates the private IP addresses used by the internal computers into the public IP address assigned by the ISP. DNS proxy enables systems residing on the LAN to resolve domain names to public IP addresses.

To successfully answer questions in this objective, you must know how to create dial-up and VPN connections. Additionally, you should understand how to configure and use ICS.

Objective 6.2 Questions

1. Which of the following accurately describes Layer Two Tunneling Protocol (L2TP) tunneling? Choose three correct answers.

    A. Supports Internet Protocol security (IPSec) authentication

    B. Supports header compression

    C. Automatically provides privacy using Point-to-Point Protocol (PPP) encryption

    D. Supported by Microsoft Windows NT 4.0

    E. Requires authentication of both the computer and the user

2. Which of the following remote access authentication protocols does not support sending encrypted password information? Choose the correct answer.

    A. PAP

    B. Shiva Password Authentication Protocol (SPAP)

    C. CHAP

    D. MS-CHAP

    E. MS-CHAP v2

3. In which of the following scenarios does ICS enable all computers to access the Internet? Choose the correct answer.

    A. A LAN with 100 computers and a routed T3 connection to the Internet. All the computers have IP addresses assigned by the ISP.

    B. A home network with four computers connected to the Internet with a cable modem. Each of the four computers has been assigned a public IP address by the ISP.

    C. A home network with four computers connected to the Internet with a single analog dial-up connection. All the computers currently use DHCP and do not have public IP addresses.

    D. A small office network with 300 computers and a single digital subscriber line (DSL) connection. All the computers currently use DHCP and do not have public IP addresses.

Objective 6.2 Answers

1.   Correct Answers: A, B, and E

    A. Correct: L2TP tunneling supports IPSec authentication. Point-to-Point Tunneling Protocol (PPTP) tunneling does not support this type of authentication.

    B. Correct: L2TP supports header compression, which reduces the number of bytes consumed by the header to four. PPTP does not perform header compression, and as a result, IP headers consume six bytes.

    C. Incorrect: Only PPTP automatically provides PPP encryption. L2TP can provide IPSec encryption.

    D. Incorrect: PPTP was the only method of tunneling included with Windows NT 4.0. Windows 2000 and later versions of Windows include both PPTP and L2TP capabilities.

    E. Correct: PPTP connections require only user-level authentication. L2TP/IPSec connections can require the same user-level authentication and, in addition, computer-level authentication through a computer certificate.

2.   Correct Answers: A

    A. Correct: Password Authentication Protocol (PAP) does not support encryption. As a result, PAP is more vulnerable to attack than other protocols and must be used only when the remote access client does not support any other method of authentication.

    B. Incorrect: The Shiva Password Authentication Protocol (SPAP) does support encryption. However, SPAP is not as secure as Challenge Handshake Authentication Protocol (CHAP) or Microsoft Challenge Handshake Authentication Protocol (MS-CHAP) because it sends the password across the remote access link using reversible encryption. Use SPAP only when it is the sole method of authentication that the client supports.

    C. Incorrect: The CHAP transmits authentication information using encrypted, one-way MD5 hashes. Using a one-way hash is more secure than using reversible encryption because the user can be authenticated without actually sending the password to the server.

    D. Incorrect: The MS-CHAP provides encrypted authentication in a very similar manner to CHAP. However, MS-CHAP can also use Microsoft Point-to-Point Encryption (MPPE) to encrypt data to the client or the server.

    E. Incorrect: The Microsoft Challenge Handshake Authentication Protocol version 2 (MS-CHAP v2) provides all the features of MS-CHAP, plus authentication of both the client and server using one-way encryption. Therefore, MS-CHAP v2 provides the highest level of security available to users of Windows XP Professional.

3. Correct Answers: C

A. Incorrect: The only aspect of this scenario that is not compatible with ICS is the public IP addressing. ICS can function only when the client computers on the LAN receive dynamically assigned IP addresses from the ICS computer. In this scenario, each of the 100 systems can reach the Internet directly, without requiring the assistance of ICS.

B. Incorrect: ICS is intended for use with small home networks and cable modems. However, in this scenario, the ISP is providing a block of four public IP addresses. Each system has its own IP address, so ICS is not needed for the systems to provide access.

C. Correct: ICS is the ideal method for providing all four systems in this scenario with Internet access. The computer that is connected to the dial-up connection must have ICS enabled. As soon as ICS is enabled, that system's LAN connection is assigned the private IP address 192.168.0.1. DHCP services are automatically initiated to assign the other systems IP addresses in the range 192.168.0.2 through 192.168.0.254. The next time the client computers reboot, they retrieve a DHCP-assigned IP address from the ICS system. When the ICS system connects to the Internet, it performs NAT services to provide all systems on the network with Internet access.

D. Incorrect: This scenario is perfect for ICS, except for one major detail: ICS can assign IP addresses to only 253 computers. ICS is intended to be used on small networks and is not designed to provide Internet access for larger quantities of computers. A more robust NAT/DHCP solution is required.

Connect to Resources Using Internet Explorer

The World Wide Web is the most widely used aspect of the Internet. The Web consists of Web servers, such as IIS, and Web clients, such as Internet Explorer. Windows XP provides Internet Explorer to allow users to access Web content while minimizing risk. After Service Pack 2 has been installed, Internet Explorer is much more resistant to attacks from malicious Web sites.

However, the fact that Internet Explorer attempts to protect users from malicious and annoying Web content can also cause problems. Many Web sites use Web content such as ActiveX objects and pop-up windows that may be blocked by default. To enable users to access these types of Web sites while minimizing their exposure to attack, you must understand how to configure Internet Explorer. In particular, pay attention to Internet Explorer's privacy and security features.

Objective 6.3 Questions

1. You are the desktop administrator of a 30-user LAN that connects to the Internet through a proxy server that the server management group configured. The proxy server is a Microsoft Windows Server 2003 computer running Microsoft ISA Server 2004. The server management group needs to closely monitor and control the public Internet sites that your users visit, so they have configured ISA Server to act as a Hypertext Transfer Protocol (HTTP) proxy for all Web requests, and they specifically do not want users to access public Web sites by using NAT.

   You are responsible for configuring the desktop computers to use the proxy server. In addition to using the ISA server to access public Web sites, you want Internet Explorer to bypass the proxy server for intranet Web sites on the local and wide area network. Which of the following solutions meets your requirements? Choose the best answer.

   A. Configure the ISA Server to not allow requests for sites on the local intranet.

   B. In each user's Internet Explorer Internet Options dialog box, select the Security tab. Select the Local Intranet Web content zone and click the Sites button. In the Local Intranet dialog box, add the URLs and IP addresses of the local intranet sites to the Web sites list.

   C. In each user's Internet Explorer Internet Options dialog box, select the Connections tab and click the LAN Settings button. Select the Use A Proxy Server For Your LAN check box, type the address and port number of your ISA server, and click the Advanced button. In the Proxy Settings dialog box, add the URLs and IP addresses of the local intranet sites to the Exceptions text box.

   D. In each user's Internet Explorer Internet Options dialog box, select the Privacy tab and click the Edit button. In the Per Site Privacy Actions dialog box, type the URL or the IP address of each local intranet site, and click the Block button.

2. Which of the following types of resources can be viewed from Internet Explorer without launching a separate application? Choose three answers.

   A. Web sites

   B. File Transfer Protocol (FTP) sites

   C. Gopher sites

   D. Hypertext Markup Language (HTML) files on the local computer

   E. Telnet sites

   F. Tagged Image File Format (TIFF) images

3.   As part of your effort to stay apprised of the latest security threats, you log on to a Web-based forum on the Internet that fellow systems administrators use to discuss security topics. This forum requires you to log in. Unfortunately, it makes you log in every day, which is not the case for most people. For other users, the forum seems to remember their user name and password. You are using Internet Explorer on Windows XP Professional with Service Pack 2. What is the most likely cause of the problem? Choose the best answer.

A. Internet Explorer security is configured to block cookies from the forum.

B. You have not granted appropriate file permission to allow the forum to store your user name and password.

C. The forum is presenting an invalid SSL certificate.

D. Windows Firewall is blocking authentication requests from the Web site.

Objective 6.3 Answers

1. **Correct Answers: C**

    A. **Incorrect:** This solution does not meet all the requirements because it does not configure Internet Explorer to directly access the intranet systems. Instead, users are completely unable to access local intranet sites.

    B. **Incorrect:** This solution does not meet any of the requirements. Placing URLs and IP addresses into the Local Intranet Web content zone increases the level of trust granted to those sites. However, it does not configure Internet Explorer for bypassing the proxy server for local intranet sites.

    C. **Correct:** This solution meets your requirements. Before a request is sent to a Web site, Internet Explorer checks the Web site's address against the list of exceptions. If that Web site's name appears on the list, requests are sent directly to the site instead of to the proxy server. To make deploying and maintaining these settings easier across a large user base, consider automating this process using an automatic configuration script.

    D. **Incorrect:** This solution does not meet any of the requirements. Adding the URLs and IP addresses of the local intranet sites to this list only blocks Internet Explorer from accepting cookies from those sites.

2. **Correct Answers: A, B, and D**

    A. **Correct:** Internet Explorer's primary purpose is to view sites on the Internet using HTTP.

    B. **Correct:** Internet Explorer can be used to navigate FTP sites, view directory contents, and transfer files.

    C. **Incorrect:** Gopher is a network protocol that was common during the early years of the Internet. Gopher's functionality has been replaced by HTTP. As a result, Internet Explorer does not support the Gopher protocol.

    D. **Correct:** Internet Explorer can be used to view HTML files on the local computer. The easiest way to access files on the local computer is to type the file path in the Address field. An alternative method is to choose Open from the File menu, click the Browse button, and select the file.

    E. **Incorrect:** Telnet is a text-based protocol used to issue commands on a remote system. An open telnet session resembles a command prompt. Although you can use Internet Explorer to launch a telnet session, Internet Explorer must launch a separate application—the telnet window. To launch a telnet session from the Internet Explorer address bar, type the address in the form **telnet://** *hostname.*

F. Incorrect: Internet Explorer is capable of viewing many types of images, including Graphics Interchange Format (GIF) and Joint Photographics Experts Group (JPEG) files. However, Internet Explorer cannot natively view TIFF images. TIFF is a common format for storing images that will be printed, but it is not common on the Internet because of the large file size.

3.   Correct Answers: A

A. Correct: Web sites store cookies on your computer, and under normal circumstances your Web browser presents the cookie to the Web site each time you visit it. Malicious Web sites can also abuse cookies to violate your privacy, however, so Internet Explorer has several different settings for cookies and will reject cookies under certain circumstances. Some of these circumstances are legitimate.

B. Incorrect: File permissions have no impact on whether a Web site will recognize your browser. That is handled by cookies.

C. Incorrect: SSL certificates have no impact on a Web site's ability to store your user settings.

D. Incorrect: Authenticating to Web sites uses the same network protocols that you use to visit the site. Therefore, if you are able to visit the site at all, Windows Firewall is not interfering with the connection.

Configure, Manage, and Implement Internet Information Services (IIS)

IIS is a robust, high-performance Web server included with Windows XP Professional. It is based on the same software included with the Windows Server 2003 family, used to host some of the largest sites on the Internet. The version of IIS included with Windows XP Professional has been scaled down for home and small office use, however. Understanding the features and limitations of this variety of IIS is critical for completing this objective.

To understand IIS, you must have some understanding of the underlying protocols. HTTP provides rich content to browsers, and is the only protocol most Internet and intranet Web sites require. File Transfer Protocol (FTP) is often used for downloading files, although HTTP is more common. Simple Mail Transfer Protocol (SMTP) is the protocol used to transfer messages between post offices. IIS uses SMTP to send outgoing mail—for example, to forward the results of a form to the site administrator.

Security is a critical aspect of every Web site. To protect IIS from attack, you should restrict NTFS file permissions, configure authentication requirements, and restrict the types of access available to users. You can configure each of these types of protection separately for different virtual directories. Optimally, you would follow the security principal of least privilege and grant only the minimal access required to each virtual directory.

Objective 6.4 Questions

1. By default, which TCP port is IIS is configured to use for HTTP? Choose the correct answer.

    A. 25

    B. 443

    C. 80

    D. 21

2. What is the maximum number of users who can connect to an IIS Web site installed on Windows XP Professional? Choose the correct answer.

    A. 1

    B. 10

    C. 100

    D. No enforced limitation

3. Which of the following features are available with IIS included with Windows XP Professional? Choose two correct answers.

    A. ISAPI filters

    B. Application recycling

    C. Bandwidth throttling

    D. IP address and domain name restrictions

    E. Content expiration

4. You configure IIS on your Windows XP Professional system to allow a coworker on the Internet to view HTML files located on your computer. Windows Firewall is enabled on your computer, and you create an exception for HTTP traffic. You create a user account with the name Kevin for your coworker and make that account a member of your local Users group. The Users group currently has Change NTFS permissions to the IIS home directory and all subdirectories. On the Home Directory tab of the Web site Properties, you enable Read access, and disable Script Source Access, Write access, and Directory Browsing. What are Kevin's effective permissions to the HTML files in your IIS home directory? Choose the correct answer.

    A. Read access only

    B. Write access only

    C. Read and write access

    D. Full control

5.   A Windows XP Professional user is attempting to share files with other computers on your local network. He has installed IIS, and configured IIS following some security guidelines he read in a magazine article. Windows Firewall is enabled, but it is configured to allow IIS traffic as an exception. His computer's IP address is 192.168.10.152.

When he tries to connect from another computer, he receives an error message indicating that the server could not be found. You examine his IIS Web site configuration, as shown in the following figure.

You suspect that he is using the wrong URL to access the Web site. What is the correct URL? Choose the correct answer.

A. *http://192.168.10.152/*

B. *ftp://192.168.10.152/*

C. *http://www.192.168.10.152/*

D. *http://192.168.10.152:81/*

E. *https://192.168.10.152/*

Objective 6.4 Answers

1.   Correct Answers: C

    A. **Incorrect:** TCP port 25 is the IIS default port for SMTP. SMTP is used for transferring e-mail messages.

    B. **Incorrect:** TCP port 443 is the IIS default port for Hypertext Transfer Protocol Secure (HTTPS). HTTPS adds SSL encryption to the standard HTTP protocol.

    C. **Correct:** IIS uses port 80, the Internet standard, as the default for HTTP. Web browsers automatically connect to Web servers on port 80. Therefore, if you specify a port other than 80 for Web services, you need to specify the port number as part of the Web site's URL. For example, if you change the port number to port 8080, the URL for the Web site becomes *http://<your URL>:8080/*.

    D. **Incorrect:** TCP port 21 is the IIS default port for FTP services. Port 21 is used only to authenticate users and accept commands—FTP uses TCP port 20 for all file transfers.

2.   Correct Answers: B

    A. **Incorrect:** The version of IIS included with Windows XP Professional can support up to 10 simultaneous incoming connections.

    B. **Correct:** IIS, when installed on Windows XP Professional, can support a maximum of 10 simultaneous users. There is no limit to the number of incoming connections that IIS can support when installed on Windows 2000 Server or the Windows Server 2003 family.

    C. **Incorrect:** The version of IIS included with Windows XP Professional can support up to 10 simultaneous incoming connections. To support more than 10 connections, you must upgrade to Windows 2000 Server or the Windows Server 2003 family.

    D. **Incorrect:** The version of IIS included with Windows XP Professional can support up to 10 simultaneous incoming connections. To support more than 10 connections, you must upgrade to Windows 2000 Server or the Windows Server 2003 family.

3.   Correct Answers: A and E

    A. **Correct:** The version of IIS included with Windows XP Professional does support ISAPI filters. ISAPI filters process incoming requests before IIS default processing and are capable of dramatically changing the way IIS behaves.

B. Incorrect: Only the Windows Server 2003 family includes application recycling as a feature of IIS. This feature automatically restarts IIS applications and ensures that active users do not get disconnected during this process.

C. Incorrect: Only the Windows Server 2003 and the Windows 2000 Server families include bandwidth throttling as a feature of IIS. This feature limits the amount of traffic that IIS can generate. It is useful for ensuring that Web services do not consume an Internet connection, thereby reducing performance for users and other Web sites.

D. Incorrect: Only the Windows Server 2003 and the Windows 2000 Server families include IP address and domain name restrictions. Using this capability, it is possible to allow or disallow users based on their source IP address. Alternatively, filtering can be done based on the results of a reverse DNS lookup of the source IP address.

E. Correct: The version of IIS included with Windows XP Professional does support content expiration. This feature improves the performance of the Web site by instructing the client and proxy servers to cache specified content. Cached content can be retrieved from the local system, without issuing a request to the Web server. Content expiration must be enabled only on content that does not change frequently, to ensure clients always retrieve an up-to-date version of the content.

4.   Correct Answers: A

A. Correct: If Kevin logs on interactively, he has Change permission to the files in the IIS home directory. However, because Kevin can access the Web content only using HTTP, IIS controls access and limits rights to Read access only. NTFS permissions do not override limitations enforced by IIS. Instead, effective permissions are always equal to the lesser access allowed by IIS and NTFS. As a result, the Full Control provided by the file permissions has no effect.

B. Incorrect: Kevin is not capable of updating files using HTTP because IIS does not have Write access enabled.

C. Incorrect: Kevin is able to read files in the home directory because IIS has read access enabled. However, write access is not enabled. NTFS permissions do not override limitations enforced by IIS. Instead, effective permissions are always equal to the lesser access allowed by IIS and NTFS. As a result, the Full Control provided by the file permissions has no effect.

D. Incorrect: Kevin is able to read files in the home directory because IIS has read access enabled. However, write access is not enabled. Full control also allows for file permissions to be changed, which is never possible when access to files is through IIS. NTFS permissions do not override limitations enforced by IIS. Instead, effective permissions are always equal to the lesser access allowed by IIS and NTFS. As a result, the Full Control provided by the file permissions has no effect.

5.   Correct Answers: D

A. Incorrect: This URL would cause the Web browser to attempt to connect to the Web site by using the default HTTP port of 80. The figure shows that IIS has been configured to use port 81, however.

B. Incorrect: FTP is a separate protocol from HTTP. You cannot use FTP to connect to Web sites. Instead, you must specify HTTP.

C. Incorrect: Adding *www* to the URL will not solve the problem. Instead, you need to specify that the Web browser use port 81 to connect to the Web server.

D. Correct: The figure shows that the Web site has been configured to use port 81 for HTTP. This is different from the default port of 80. Therefore, you must explicitly append the port number to the URL.

E. Incorrect: HTTPS is the correct protocol to use when accessing Web sites protected by an SSL certificate. However, this Web site does not have an SSL certificate, which is evident because the SSL Port box is disabled.

Objective 6.5

Configure, Manage, and Troubleshoot Remote Desktop and Remote Assistance

Remote Desktop enables users to interact with a computer across a network as if they were sitting directly in front of it. Essentially, keyboard and mouse commands are transmitted from the client computer across the network to the Remote Desktop server running Windows XP Professional. The Remote Desktop server returns video and sound to the client, recreating the experience of working directly with the remote system. A variation of the Remote Desktop is the Remote Desktop Web connection. Installed as an option in the World Wide Web Service of IIS, the Remote Desktop Web Connection enables users to connect to the Remote Desktop without installing the Remote Desktop client utility.

Remote assistance leverages the abilities of the Remote Desktop to enable administrators to provide technical support to remote users. If the user has enabled remote control, the administrator can even take control of the keyboard and mouse to guide the user through the problem. To ensure privacy, all communications are encrypted.

Objective 6.5 Questions

1. Which of the following Remote Desktop performance options must be enabled to optimize performance across slow dial-up connections? Choose the best answer.

    A. Desktop Background

    B. Show Contents Of Window While Dragging

    C. Menu And Window Animation

    D. Themes

    E. Bitmap Caching

2. Remote Desktop Web connection requires which of the following protocols to establish a connection? Choose two correct answers.

    A. HTTP (TCP port 80)

    B. RDP (TCP port 3389)

    C. SMTP (TCP port 25)

    D. LDAP (TCP port 389)

    E. POP (TCP port 110)

3. Which of the following methods of communication can be used to send an invitation for remote assistance? Choose two correct answers.

    A. Internet Explorer

    B. Internet newsgroups

    C. E-mail

    D. Windows Messenger

    E. FTP

4. Which user groups have permissions to connect to control the Remote Desktop of a Windows XP Professional computer that has Remote Desktop enabled? Choose two correct answers.

    A. Administrators

    B. Power Users

    C. Users

    D. Guests

    E. Remote Desktop Users

5. Remote Desktop could be used for which of the following scenarios? Choose two correct answers.

    A. Connecting to your Windows XP Professional computer at home to access your personal e-mail.

    B. Connecting to your Windows XP Home Edition computer at home to edit a Microsoft Word document stored on your home computer.

    C. Training a remote user by interactively walking him or her through the steps required to perform a task on his or her Windows XP Professional computer.

    D. Connecting to a computer in a remote office after hours to install the latest updates.

    E. Controlling a remote Windows XP Professional computer behind a firewall that allows only traffic using TCP port 80.

Objective 6.5 Answers

1. **Correct Answers: E**

A. **Incorrect:** Enabling the Desktop Background option on Remote Desktops decreases performance because the image must be transmitted across the network to the Remote Desktop client. Therefore, this option must not be enabled when a slow dial-up connection is being used.

B. **Incorrect:** The Show Contents Of Window While Dragging option must be disabled when a slow dial-up connection is being used because it causes unnecessary traffic across the network connection.

C. **Incorrect:** Menu And Window Animation must be disabled when a slow dial-up connection is being used. Although this option provides the Remote Desktop with a richer graphical user interface, it causes unnecessary traffic to be sent across the network.

D. **Incorrect:** Enabling the Themes performance option for a Remote Desktop connection causes the client to retrieve customized aspects of the user interface, such as fonts and colors. This transfer causes less traffic than the other performance options, but must still be disabled for best performance. Enabling the Themes option does not automatically cause the desktop background to be transferred, even if the background is part of the theme.

E. **Correct:** Enabling Bitmap Caching reduces the number of times a single image must be sent between the Remote Desktop client and server. Therefore, enabling this option reduces network traffic and can dramatically improve performance on slow dial-up connections.

2. **Correct Answers: A and B**

A. **Correct:** HTTP is the protocol used by IIS and Internet Explorer for exchanging files. Remote Desktop Web connection uses HTTP to prompt the user to connect. By default, HTTP uses port 80, though that can be changed. After the connection has been established, Remote Desktop Protocol (RDP) is used exclusively.

B. **Correct:** RDP is used by the Remote Desktop, Remote Desktop Web connection, and Remote Assistance for exchanging video, sound, keyboard, and mouse data. By default, RDP uses TCP port 3389. Though you can change the TCP port used for RDP on the Remote Desktop server computer, the Remote Desktop Web connection client must always use the default port. Remote Desktop Web connection also requires HTTP to initiate the session from a browser.

C. **Incorrect:** SMTP is the protocol used to exchange messages between post offices. Remote Desktop Web connection does not require SMTP.

D. Incorrect: Lightweight Directory Access Protocol (LDAP) is the protocol used by Windows clients to communicate with the Active Directory service. Remote Desktop Web connection does not require LDAP.

E. Incorrect: Post Office Protocol (POP) is a common protocol used by e-mail clients to retrieve messages from a post office. Remote Desktop Web connection does not require POP.

3.   Correct Answers: C and D

A. Incorrect: Invitations for remote assistance can be sent using either e-mail or Windows Messenger. Internet Explorer cannot be used to send invitations.

B. Incorrect: Internet newsgroups are a common message-based method for seeking assistance with technical problems. However, remote assistance cannot send an invitation to an Internet newsgroup. Invitations for remote assistance can be sent using either e-mail or Windows Messenger.

C. Correct: When remote assistance is initiated, it prompts the novice to send an invitation via e-mail or Windows Messenger. After the expert receives the e-mail message, clicking the link establishes a connection to the novice's computer. At that point, the novice is prompted to accept the incoming connection.

D. Correct: When remote assistance is initiated, it prompts the novice to send an invitation via e-mail or Windows Messenger. After the expert receives the real-time message, clicking the link establishes a connection to the novice's computer. At that point, the novice is prompted to accept the incoming connection.

E. Incorrect: FTP is commonly used to transfer files across the Internet. However, it cannot be used to send remote assistance invitations. Invitations for remote assistance can be sent using either e-mail or Windows Messenger.

4.   Correct Answers: A and E

A. Correct: Members of the Administrators group have permission to connect to the Remote Desktop.

B. Incorrect: Members of the Power Users group do not have permissions to connect to the Remote Desktop unless they are also a member of the Administrators or Remote Desktop Users groups.

C. Incorrect: Members of the Users group do not have permissions to connect to the Remote Desktop unless they are also a member of the Administrators or Remote Desktop Users groups.

D. Incorrect: Users authenticating with only Guest permissions do not have permissions to connect to the Remote Desktop.

E. Correct: Members of the Remote Desktop Users group have permission to connect to the Remote Desktop.

5.   Correct Answers: A and D

A.   Correct: If you have enabled Remote Desktop and properly configured Windows Firewall and any other firewalls that might be present, you can use Remote Desktop to control your home computer from your office.

B.   Incorrect: Although you could use Remote Desktop to edit a document using Word, Windows XP Home Edition does not support acting as a Remote Desktop server.

C.   Incorrect: Connecting with Remote Desktop blocks users sitting in front of the computer from accessing the computer. Remote Assistance would be the better choice for this scenario

D.   Correct: Remote Desktop is perfect for remote administration scenarios such as this one.

E.   Incorrect: Remote Desktop Web Connection does use TCP port 80 to transfer the ActiveX Remote Desktop Client to the client's browser. However, Remote Desktop Web Connection also requires the use of TCP port 3389, exactly like the standard Remote Desktop client.

Objective 6.6

Configure, Manage, and Troubleshoot an Internet Connection Firewall

Windows XP Professional is a client operating system, but it has many server capabilities. It can share folders and printers, host a Web site, and receive messages from other computers on the network. Unfortunately, by listening for inbound connections, Windows XP is vulnerable to network attacks against those services.

Firewalls help protect against network attacks by blocking any network requests that have not specifically been allowed. Windows XP includes a built-in firewall named Internet Connection Firewall (ICF). Unfortunately, ICF is not enabled by default. When you install Service Pack 2, ICF is upgraded to Windows Firewall. Windows Firewall is enabled by default, and greatly reduces the risk of network attacks.

To successfully answer questions in this objective, you must know how to configure both ICF and Windows Firewall. Additionally, you should understand how to configure exceptions to selectively enable applications that must receive incoming connections.

Objective 6.6 Questions

1. Enabling Windows Firewall can prevent which of the following types of network intrusions? Choose the best answer.

   A. A hacker who exploits a vulnerability in IIS by sending malformed HTTP requests to your publicly accessible IIS Web server

   B. A hacker who initiates a distributed denial of service (DoS) intrusion to saturate the bandwidth on your DSL connection, which is connected directly to your Windows XP computer

   C. A user who opens a virus disguised as an e-mail attachment

   D. A hacker who uploads a Trojan horse into a directory on an FTP server that was accidentally started

2. Which of the following types of information is collected in the Windows Firewall security log? Choose two correct answers.

   A. Source IP address

   B. Destination port

   C. Source host name

   D. Packet contents

   E. Source user name

3. You are a systems administrator at a small office with 10 Windows XP Professional computers organized in a workgroup. All computers at your office have Service Pack 2 installed. Your home computer is running Windows XP Professional with Service Pack 1 installed and is connected to the Internet with a cable modem and a static IP address. The ISP you use at home provides no packet filtering, and you do not have Internet Connection Firewall enabled, which allows you to use Remote Desktop to connect directly to your home computer to check your personal e-mail.

   You upgrade your home computer to Service Pack 2 for Windows XP. The next day at work, you are unable to connect to your home computer with Remote Desktop. What should you do to fix the problem? Choose the best answer.

   A. Contact your ISP and request that they allow packets using port 3389.

   B. Reselect the Allow Users To Remotely Connect To This Computer check box on the Remote tab of the System Properties dialog.

   C. Re-enable Remote Desktop.

   D. Add Remote Desktop to the list of Windows Firewall exceptions.

Objective 6.6 Answers

1. Correct Answers: D

    A. Incorrect: Windows Firewall cannot prevent this type of intrusion because the Web server must be able to receive HTTP requests from legitimate users on the public Internet. Windows Firewall is capable of stopping all HTTP requests, but cannot distinguish between legitimate and malicious requests within a single protocol.

    B. Incorrect: Windows Firewall filters packets as they are processed by a Windows XP Professional network adapter. This particular scenario saturates your bandwidth with incoming packets. The packets sent during the DoS intrusion saturate the Internet connection before they reach hosts on the destination network. Windows Firewall can filter the packets when they reach the Windows XP Professional system; however, it cannot stop the Internet connection from being saturated.

    C. Incorrect: Windows Firewall is capable of filtering connections only where the Windows XP Professional computer is acting as the server. When users retrieve e-mail messages, the connection is initiated by the Windows XP Professional computer. Further, Windows Firewall is capable of filtering only an entire protocol. ICF is incapable of differentiating between legitimate and malicious requests within a single protocol.

    D. Correct: By default, Windows Firewall filters incoming FTP requests. In this scenario, the FTP server was accidentally started. Windows Firewall is designed to prevent this type of vulnerability. When Windows Firewall is enabled, only those services explicitly enabled can receive traffic—even if they are accidentally started.

2. Correct Answers: A and B

    A. Correct: The source IP address is one of the fields of data collected in the Windows Firewall security log.

    B. Correct: The destination port is one of the fields of data collected in the Windows Firewall security log.

    C. Incorrect: The Windows Firewall security log does not contain the source's host name. The source IP address is included, however, so you can perform a reverse DNS lookup based on the source IPs in the log.

    D. Incorrect: Windows Firewall security logs do not contain the data that was contained in the dropped packets. Only information contained in the header of packets is recorded.

E. Incorrect: Although some protocols do pass user name information, the Windows Firewall security log does not attempt to record this information. Indeed, in the case of malicious intrusions, the user name information included is never accurate.

3.   Correct Answers: D

A. Incorrect: Nothing in this scenario indicates that the ISP would start filtering. In this case, the packet filtering is occurring on the home computer itself.

B. Incorrect: Although this check box should be selected, upgrading to Service Pack 2 for Windows XP will not disable it.

C. Incorrect: Service Pack 2 does not disable Remote Desktop. Therefore, if it worked previously, it would still be enabled.

D. Correct: To enable incoming Remote Desktop connections, you will have to add Remote Desktop to the Exception tab of the Windows Firewall properties dialog box.

27 Configuring, Managing, and Troubleshooting Security

Computers are constantly under attack. Although Microsoft Windows XP (especially with Service Pack 2 installed) is designed to protect against most attacks, the default configuration might not meet your organization's security needs. Depending on how users make use of their computers and the confidentiality of the data on your computers, you might need to adjust the default security settings.

You will start by configuring Users and Groups for the people who will need to access resources on each Windows XP computer. Then, you can use tools such as the Computer Management console and the Local Security Policy console to grant rights to those users. Users who do not have accounts will have a very difficult time gaining access to resources on your computer, which will protect you against most attacks.

Some attacks might come from users with legitimate user accounts, however. In fact, the most damaging attacks come from people within your own organization. You can reduce the risk of this type of attack by tightly configuring user rights. Ideally, you will follow the principle of least privilege and assign users only the bare minimum rights they need to do their jobs.

You might still be vulnerable to attacks from threats without valid user accounts, however. To protect against people who might physically steal a computer (especially a laptop), use Encrypting File System (EFS). EFS encrypts files, requiring the attacker to log on with a user account that has a private key that can decrypt the files. To protect against malicious Web sites, you can configure Internet Explorer to prevent risky types of communications, such as transmitting unencrypted data across the Internet or accepting third-party cookies without privacy policies.

To complete this objective, you must understand how to install, configure, and troubleshoot all these security technologies.

Tested Skills and Suggested Practices

The skills you need to successfully master the Configuring, Managing, and Troubleshooting Security objective domain on the *Installing, Configuring, and Administering Microsoft Windows XP Professional* exam include the following:

- Configure, manage, and troubleshoot Encrypting File System (EFS).
    - ❑ Practice 1: Encrypt and decrypt files and folders on a storage volume formatted with NTFS by using Microsoft Windows Explorer.

❑ Practice 2: Use the command-line tool CIPHER.EXE to view the encryption settings on some files encrypted in Practice 1. Use CIPHER.EXE to encrypt and decrypt additional files and folders. Type **cipher /?** at a command prompt to view all the command-line switches for this tool.

❑ Practice 3: Use the command-line tool EFSINFO.EXE from the Windows XP Professional Resource Kit to view the encryption settings on some of the files and folders used in Practices 1 and 2. Type **efsinfo /?** at a command prompt to view all the command-line switches for this tool.

❑ Practice 4: Recover encrypted files from a Windows XP Professional computer in a workgroup. If you have a domain available, perform an EFS recovery by using the domain administrator account.

■ Configure, manage, and troubleshoot a security configuration and local security policy.

❑ Practice 1: Open the Local Security Policy console and expand the Local Policies folder. Select the Audit Policy folder and review each of the settings available. Select the Security Options folder and examine all the settings.

❑ Practice 2: Open the Local Security Policy console and expand the Account Policies folder. Select and configure settings available under both the Password Policy and Account Lockout Policy folders.

❑ Practice 3: Open the Local Security Policy console snap-in and expand the Software Restriction Policies folder. Right-click the Software Restriction Policies folder and click Create New Policies from the context menu. Configure a new policy so that Notepad.exe is restricted from execution. Verify that you can no longer launch Notepad from the Start menu. Carefully review all the other options available under the Software Restriction Policies folder.

■ Configure, manage, and troubleshoot local user and group accounts.

❑ Practice 1: Open the Computer Management console and expand the Local Users and Groups node. Create several test accounts and groups, and then make some of the accounts members of some of the groups.

❑ Practice 2: Use the Local Security Policy console to enable success and failure auditing for the Audit Logon Events policy.

❑ Practice 3: Log off Windows XP, and then attempt to log on with an incorrect password. Afterwards, log back onto Windows XP, and open Event Viewer. Click the Security node, and examine the events that were generated during your successful and unsuccessful logon attempts.

■ Configure, manage, and troubleshoot Internet Explorer security settings.

❑ Practice 1: Launch Internet Explorer and visit some Web sites that include active content. Open the Internet Options dialog box from the Tools menu in

Internet Explorer. Click the Security tab, click the Internet zone, and then click the Custom Level button. On the Security Settings dialog box, set the Reset To list to High and click the Reset button. Click Yes when prompted. Restart Internet Explorer and revisit the same Web sites. What happens? Restore the security settings in Internet Explorer to their defaults. Note that you can add specific sites to the predefined site collections: Internet, Local Intranet, Trusted Sites, and Restricted Sites. You can also customize the security settings for each of these collections.

❏ Practice 2: Launch Internet Explorer. Open the Internet Options dialog box from the Tools menu and click the Privacy tab to review the options for customizing how Internet Explorer handles cookies.

❏ Practice 3: Launch Internet Explorer, and then open the Internet Options dialog box from the Tools menu and click the Content tab. Click the Certificates button to open the Certificates dialog box. View all the tabs available in this dialog box. With a certificate selected, click the Advanced button to examine the purpose of the certificate. Close this dialog box and click the View button to examine the certificate itself.

❏ Practice 4: Launch Internet Explorer, and then open the Internet Options dialog box from the Tools menu and click the Advanced tab. Scroll to the bottom of the list to examine the additional security settings that can be configured for Internet Explorer, such as enabling or disabling Secure Sockets Layer (SSL) 2 and SSL 3.

Further Reading

This section lists supplemental readings by objective. We recommend that you study these sources thoroughly before taking exam 70-270.

Objective 7.1   Microsoft Corporation. *Microsoft Windows XP Professional Resource Kit Documentation*. Redmond, WA: Microsoft Press, 2001. Read Chapter 17, "Encrypting File System." This chapter takes a close look at how to implement and resolve common problems with EFS (available online at *http://www.microsoft.com/resources/documentation/Windows/XP/all/reskit/en-us/prnb_efs_qutx.asp*).

Microsoft Corporation. "Protecting Data by Using EFS to Encrypt Hard Drives." 2004. This article is available at *http://www.microsoft.com/smallbusiness/gtm/securityguidance/articles/protect_data_efs.mspx*. (If the article has moved, search for the title at *http://www.microsoft.com*.)

Objective 7.2   Microsoft Corporation. *Microsoft Windows XP Professional Resource Kit Documentation*. Redmond, WA: Microsoft Press, 2001. Read Chapter 13, "File Systems," focusing on the sections that discuss NTFS. Read Chapter 15, "Logon and Authentication," for information about configuring account policies and other security settings relating to user authentication. Review Chapter 16, "Authorization and Access Control," and Appendix B, "User Rights." Chapter 16 explains how objects in Windows XP have ACLs, and how to use the permissions available with different types of objects to secure them from unauthorized access. Appendix B defines all the user rights available under Windows XP Professional (available online at *http://www.microsoft.com/resources/documentation/Windows/XP/all/ reskit/en-us/prork_overview.asp*).

Objective 7.3   Microsoft Corporation. *Microsoft Windows XP Professional Resource Kit Documentation.* Redmond, WA: Microsoft Press, 2001. Read Chapter 15, "Logon and Authentication," for information about creating and managing user accounts and groups. Review Chapter 16, "Authorization and Access Control." This chapter explains how to configure and troubleshoot permissions on objects in Windows XP Professional (available online at *http://www.microsoft.com/resources/ documentation/Windows/XP/all/reskit/en-us/prork_overview.asp*).

Microsoft Corporation. "Windows XP Security Guide." 2004. Read Chapters 3, 4, 5, and 6 for detailed information about Windows XP Professional security settings. Then, read Appendix A for information about new security settings included in Service Pack 2. This documentation is available at *http://www.microsoft.com/ technet/security/prodtech/winclnt/secwinxp/*. (If the documentation has moved, search for the title at *http://www.microsoft.com.*)

Objective 7.4   Launch Internet Explorer, click the Help menu, and then click Contents and Index. Read all the articles and related topics under the headings "Sending Information over the Internet" and "Understanding Security and Privacy on the Internet."

Microsoft Corporation. "Windows XP Service Pack 2: What's New for Internet Explorer and Outlook Express." 2004. This article is available at *http:// www.microsoft.com/windowsxp/sp2/ieoeoverview.mspx.* (If the article has moved, search for the title at *http://www.microsoft.com.*)

Configure, Manage, and Troubleshoot Encrypting File System (EFS)

Security experts say, "If an attacker can touch your computer, it is not your computer anymore." The rationale behind this is that an attacker with physical access to your computer can bypass your operating system's security measures. For example, an attacker could start your computer with a bootable CD and access your files directly from the hard disk, regardless of how you had configured file permissions.

EFS can protect your files from this type of attack. EFS encrypts files on your hard disk, and they can be decrypted only with your private key. The operating system protects your private key, making it very difficult for an attacker to access your files with a bootable CD. To effectively use EFS, you must understand how to configure, manage, and troubleshoot EFS. Troubleshooting is particularly important because EFS problems often result in users not being able to access their most important files.

Objective 7.1 Questions

1. You are the administrator for a network of computers running Windows XP Professional. You want to write a script and schedule it to run once on each system. The script encrypts each user's My Documents folder using EFS. What tool must you call from the script to encrypt the desired folder? Choose the correct answer.

   A. Windows Explorer

   B. Efsinfo

   C. Syskey

   D. Cipher

2. You are the administrator of an Active Directory directory service domain with 50 Windows XP Professional desktop computers. All users have their own home folder on a file server in which they save their documents. John leaves the company, and his manager, April, asks you to move John's documents to her home folder. You log on to the network with your account that belongs to the Domain Admins group and move the files. When April tries to open the files, she sees an Access Denied error message. How can you give April access to the encrypted files? Choose the best answer.

   A. Grant April the Full Control NTFS permission.

   B. Log on by using the domain Administrator account and recover the files.

   C. Log on as a local administrator and recover the files.

   D. Restore the files from the most recent backup tape.

3. Which of the following file systems supports EFS? Choose the correct answer.

   A. FAT (also known as FAT 16)

   B. FAT32

   C. CDFS

   D. NTFS

4. You are a desktop systems engineer at the Graphic Design Institute. At a recent board meeting your CEO had a conversation with a board member who had his laptop stolen at the airport while on the way to the meeting. Although the board member was not concerned about the cost of replacing the laptop hardware, she was extremely concerned about the confidentiality of the documents stored on her laptop. Your CEO asks you how to best protect the confidentiality of the files in his My Documents\Confidential\ folder in the event his laptop is stolen, while minimizing any negative performance impacts. What do you recommend that he do? Choose the best answer.

A. In Windows Explorer, right-click the Confidential folder and click Properties. Click the Advanced button and select the Compress Contents To Save Disk Space check-box.

B. In Windows Explorer, right-click the Confidential folder and click Properties. Then, click the Security tab. Remove all user accounts from the Group Or User Names List. Then, add the CEO's user account to the list and grant the account Full Control permissions.

C. In Windows Explorer, right-click the Confidential folder and click Properties. Then, click the Advanced button and select the Encrypt Contents To Secure Data check box.

D. In Windows Explorer, select the Confidential folder and then press Ctrl+A to select all files in the folder. Right-click the selected files and then click Properties. Then, click the Advanced button and select the Encrypt Contents To Secure Data check box.

Objective 7.1 Answers

1.   Correct Answers: D

A. Incorrect: Although you can use Windows Explorer to manually encrypt files and folders, it is a graphical tool that cannot be easily incorporated into a script.

B. Incorrect: Efsinfo (EFSINFO.EXE) is a command-line tool that displays information about encrypted files and folders—you cannot use it to encrypt or decrypt files or folders.

C. Incorrect: Syskey (SYSKEY.EXE) is the graphical Startup Key tool for encrypting sensitive operating system files—it cannot be used to encrypt user's data files.

D. Correct: Cipher (CIPHER.EXE) is a command-line tool for creating file encryption keys, viewing encryption settings, encrypting files and folders, and decrypting files and folders. It is the best tool to use in a script for encrypting files and folders.

2.   Correct Answers: B

A. Incorrect: Encryption is separate from NTFS permissions. As a member of the Domain Admins group, you can modify the permissions on Jim's documents, but giving April Full Control will still not enable her to decrypt the files because she is not a recovery agent.

B. Correct: Windows XP Professional computers that are members of an Active Directory domain automatically specify the domain administrator account (*domain_name*\Administrator) as EFS recovery agents because those accounts are designated as encryption recovery agents in the Default Domain Policy Group Policy Object (GPO).

C. Incorrect: When a Windows XP Professional computer joins an Active Directory domain, the domain administrator account (*domain_name*\Administrator) becomes the default recovery agent. Whether the computer is a stand-alone system or a member of an Active Directory domain, the local Administrator account is never automatically made a recovery agent. Note that there is an alternative solution to this situation: If John's domain account has not been deleted yet, you can reset the password for that account and then log on with her account and decrypt the files.

D. Incorrect: Files encrypted via EFS remain encrypted when backed up to tape—the restored files are still encrypted and inaccessible to April.

3.   Correct Answers: D

A. Incorrect: Neither FAT nor FAT32 supports EFS. Only NTFS supports EFS.

B. Incorrect: FAT32 does not support EFS. Only NTFS supports EFS. As a result, operating systems that do not support NTFS, such as Windows 98 and Windows ME, cannot use EFS.

C. Incorrect: CDFS is the file system used for CD-ROM media. You cannot use EFS on CD-ROM drives.

D. Correct: NTFS is the only file system that supports EFS.

4.   Correct Answers: C

A. Incorrect: Although compression and encryption can be combined, compressing files does nothing to improve confidentiality.

B. Incorrect: Creating restrictive file permissions does improve the security of files when a user is logged on. However, file permissions are not sufficient to deter an attacker with physical access to the system. An attacker who can access the computer's hard disk can bypass file security. Encryption is the best way to deter attackers with physical access to a computer.

C. Correct: Choosing to encrypt the contents of a folder enables EFS. All files and subfolders can be automatically encrypted, and new files and subfolders will be automatically encrypted. Because the files are encrypted, the security cannot be bypassed as easily as file security.

D. Incorrect: Although encrypting existing files and folders would make it much more difficult for a thief to gain access to those files, new files would not be encrypted because the parent folder properties were not modified.

Objective 7.2

Configure, Manage, and Troubleshoot a Security Configuration and Local Security Policy

You can greatly reduce the risk of your computer being compromised by carefully configuring security settings. To simplify this configuration task, Windows XP uses local security policy, which you can configure by using the Local Security Policy tool in Administrative Tools. The Local Security Policy tool provides access to a wide variety of security settings, including password policies, audit policies, user rights assignments, and software restrictions.

Configuring multiple computers in a network can be difficult. The simplest way to control the security configuration of multiple Windows XP Professional computers is to join them to a domain, and configure domain GPOs. If you do not have a domain, you can create security templates, and apply the security template to each of your computers. Windows XP even includes default security templates that might meet your needs.

To configure, manage, and troubleshoot security configuration, you should understand how to use the different settings available in local security policy. You should also understand how to use security templates and how domain GPOs might override your local security policy settings.

Objective 7.2 Questions

1.   Jim and Lisa share the same desktop computer running Windows XP Professional. They log on to the system with their own local accounts that are members of the local Users group. While trying to tighten security on the computer, Jim resets the permissions on many of the files and folders located on the local hard drive. Both Jim and Lisa can still log on to the system, but they cannot launch some programs that they were using previously, such as Microsoft Word and Microsoft Outlook. You want to use auditing to locate the files and folders that have their permissions set too restrictively. What do you do? Choose two correct answers.

A. Configure auditing in Event Viewer.

B. Open the Local Security Policy console and enable Failure auditing for the Audit Object Access setting.

C. Open the Local Security Policy console and configure Software Restriction policies on the programs that Jim and Lisa need to use.

D. Load the Security Configuration And Analysis snap-in, import the HISECWS.INF security template, and analyze the computer.

E. Use Windows Explorer to configure failure auditing for the desired groups or accounts on the files and folders you believe Jim might have configured incorrectly.

2.   You manage a handful of Windows XP Professional computers in a workgroup environment. You want to specify how many failed logon attempts are allowed before an account is locked out and how long before the account is automatically reset. How can you do this? Choose the best answer.

A. Open the Local Security Policy console, expand the Account Settings folder, select the Account Lockout Policy folder, and configure the appropriate settings located there.

B. Open the Local Users And Groups snap-in located in the Computer Management console by launching Control Panel, clicking Performance And Maintenance, and then clicking Administrative Tools.

C. Launch Control Panel and click User Accounts.

D. Launch Control Panel, click Accessibility Options, click Accessibility Options again, and click the General tab when the Accessibility Options program window appears.

3.   Your company's legal department has decided that all corporate computer systems must display a brief message when users log on to the computers interactively. You are responsible for a half-dozen Windows XP Professional computers that are set up as a workgroup separate from the company's Active Directory domain. A member of the legal department provides you with the text that she wants displayed on these systems. How do you configure them? Choose the correct answer.

A. Open the Services And Applications group from the Computer Management console, expand the Services folder, scroll down the list, and double-click the Workstation service. Configure the startup parameters for the Workstation service to display the message text.

B. Launch Control Panel, click Appearance And Themes, click Display, and click the Settings tab.

C. Open the Local Security Policy console, expand the Local Policies folder, and then select the Security Options folder. Scroll down the list of policies and double-click Interactive Logon: Message Text For Users Attempting To Log On and type the desired text.

D. Open Notepad, copy the text message into the document, and then save the document as a file called **LOGON.TXT** into the %systemroot% folder.

4. Which of the following tools *cannot* be used to apply the settings in a security template to a computer? Choose all that apply.

A. The Resultant Set Of Policy snap-in

B. The Secedit command-line tool

C. The Security Templates snap-in

D. The Security Configuration And Analysis snap-in

E. The Local Security Policy console

5. You are a consultant setting up four new desktop computers for a dental office on its local area network that is set up as a workgroup. The computers all have Windows XP Professional preinstalled. You want to design a secure configuration and apply it to all four computers. What is the most efficient and effective way to accomplish this goal? Choose the best answer.

A. Open the Local Security Policy console and configure the desired settings on each of the computers. Next, open Windows Explorer and configure the desired permissions on each folder.

B. Write a script in VBScript that makes all the desired changes; copy and run the script on each of the four computers.

C. Use the System program located in Control Panel to configure the desired settings on one computer, and then export the settings to a text file and import them into each of the other computers using the System program.

D. Open the Security Templates snap-in and create a new security template with the desired settings on one of the computers. Save the template and copy it to each of the other computers. Open the Security Configuration And Analysis snap-in, import the template, and then apply the template on each computer.

Objective 7.2 Answers

1. **Correct Answers: B and E**

   A. Incorrect: Although you use Event Viewer to view the Security log, you cannot configure auditing settings here.

   B. Correct: This is one of the two steps you must perform to enable failure auditing for specific files and folders. In this scenario, this setting is stored in the LGPO; it can also be configured in a Windows 2000 domain environment by using Active Directory-based GPOs.

   C. Incorrect: The problems described in this scenario were caused by improperly set NTFS permissions—configuring Software Restriction policies does not correct them.

   D. Incorrect: You can use this snap-in to compare the current NTFS permissions with those contained in a security template, but the HISECWS.INF security template does not include any NTFS permissions settings. Also, the scenario states that you want to configure auditing, which you cannot accomplish by analyzing the computer.

   E. Correct: This is the second step you must perform to enable failure auditing for specific files and folders. When this step is combined with setting auditing policy, an event is written to the local Security log each time an account attempts an unauthorized access on an audited object.

2. **Correct Answers: A**

   A. Correct: The Local Security Policy console contains the Security Settings extension of the LGPO. You configure settings for stand-alone and workgroup computers using this console; the settings made apply to the local computer, therefore you must log on to each targeted computer to make the settings.

   B. Incorrect: You can add and remove users and groups, set properties for users and groups, and reset passwords for users using the Local Users and Groups snap-in, but you cannot configure account lockout policies with this tool.

   C. Incorrect: The User Accounts program located in Control Panel includes some of the features available through the Local Users And Groups snap-in, but you cannot use it to configure account lockout policies.

   D. Incorrect: The Accessibility Options program is for configuring Windows XP for people with disabilities; it is not used for configuring account lockout policies.

3.   Correct Answers: C

   A. Incorrect: The startup parameters field is located on the General tab in the Properties dialog box for each service. The parameters in this field are included in the command that launches the service when the service is started from this dialog box; there are no command-line parameters for configuring the logon message text.

   B. Incorrect: The Display program is used for configuring desktop appearance, screen saver options, display resolution, color depth, and other display-related options; you cannot configure a logon message from this tool.

   C. Correct: This is how you configure this setting on stand-alone and workgroup computers. There is a second setting usually configured with this one called Interactive Logon: Message Title For Users Attempting To Log On that is displayed in the title bar for the dialog box displaying the logon message. When you are configuring this setting on large numbers of Windows XP Professional computers, it is more efficient to apply this setting via a domain-based GPO.

   D. Incorrect: Windows XP Professional does not use a text file to determine whether it should display a text message when users attempt to log on interactively, nor does Windows XP store a logon message in a text file.

4.   Correct Answers: A and C

   A. Correct: The Resultant Set Of Policy snap-in is a very useful tool for determining what a computer's effective security settings will be when security settings are defined by multiple layers of policy, such as both GPOs and local security policy. However, you cannot change a computer's configuration settings by using this tool.

   B. Incorrect: You can use the Secedit command-line tool to apply a security template to a computer by using the /configure parameter.

   C. Correct: You can use the Security Templates snap-in to create and edit security templates. However, it cannot be used to apply a security template to a computer.

   D. Incorrect: You can use the Security Configuration And Analysis snap-in to apply a security template by first importing the security template into a database, right-clicking Security Configuration And Analysis, and then clicking Configure Computer Now.

   E. Incorrect: You can use the Local Security Policy console to apply a security template to a computer by right-clicking Security Settings and then clicking Import Policy.

5.   Correct Answers: D

A.   **Incorrect:** Although this approach will get security configured on each of the computers, it is a time-consuming and error-prone approach. It is unlikely that all four computers will have the same settings when the process is completed.

B.   **Incorrect:** This approach will result in a consistent security configuration across all four computers but writing and debugging a complex script will take a great deal of time.

C.   **Incorrect:** The System program is not used for configuring security settings.

D.   **Correct:** For computers that are not members of an Active Directory domain, this is the best way to apply consistent computer settings across multiple computers.

Configure, Manage, and Troubleshoot Local User and Group Accounts

Windows XP stores a list of users that can be assigned rights to access resources in a local user database. To make it easier to assign rights, you can place those users into groups and assign the rights to these groups.

User management is a complex topic, however. First, you need to be able to keep track of who has accessed, or attempted to access, your computers. To enable this, Windows XP provides auditing. Second, you must be able to control what users can do on your computer because not all users should have the same rights. To enable you to configure user rights, Windows XP provides account settings, account policies, and user and group rights.

To configure, manage, and troubleshoot local user and group accounts, you must understand how to use the Computer Management console to manage accounts. You must also understand how to use the Local Security Policy console to configure user privileges. Finally, make sure that you understand how to assign users and groups rights to access resources such as files, printers, and the Registry.

Objective 7.3 Questions

1. You are a network administrator for a manufacturing company. You have been told to remove Richard and Anthony from the Accounting1 group, which has access to the Overdue shared folder. You notice that Richard and Anthony are the only members of the Accounting1 group, so you remove their accounts from the group and then delete the group. Several weeks later, you are told that Richard once again needs access to the Overdue folder. What steps can you take to restore his access? Choose two correct answers.

    A. Re-create Richard's user account.

    B. Re-create the Accounting1 group and add Richard's account to it.

    C. Give Richard's user account the user right Create Permanent Shared Objects.

    D. Re-create the Accounting1 group.

    E. Grant the Accounting1 group the proper permissions to the Overdue shared folder.

2. You work for a small law firm. Dave, Jenny, and Joe are attorneys at the same firm who have been assigned a laptop computer to share. The laptop is delivered with Windows XP Professional and Office 2003 Professional preinstalled. You install the remaining applications that your firm uses, but you want to make sure that Dave, Jenny, and Joe have their data and user preferences stored and maintained separately from one another. What do you do? Choose the best answer.

    A. Run the Sysprep tool.

    B. Manually create a new local user profile for each attorney.

    C. Create separate hardware profiles for each attorney.

    D. Create local user accounts for each attorney.

3. You work at a small law office that upgraded its network to an Active Directory–based domain. All user accounts and computers have been migrated to the domain. An attorney named Dave recently left the company and is being replaced by a temporary attorney named Scott. What is the easiest way to give Scott the exact same access to the network that Dave had? Choose the best answer

    A. Rename Dave's account to Scott and reset the password.

    B. Create a new user account called **Scott** and then copy the Dave user profile to Scott's account.

    C. Create a new account for Scott and manually grant it access to all the resources that Dave's account had access to. Delete Dave's account.

    D. Create a new account for Scott and manually grant it access to all the resources that Dave's account had access to. Disable Dave's account.

4. You recently took a position as desktop systems engineer at The Phone Company. The Phone Company currently has about 500 Windows XP Professional desktop computers and a single Windows Server 2003 Active Directory domain. During a meeting with members of the Human Resources team to discuss its IT needs, the members mention that they employ a large staff of temporary employees. They emphasize that it is critical that those users cannot log on to their computers after their accounts have been removed. You want to ensure that no user can log on unless the domain controller is available and authenticates the user. What is the best way to accomplish this? Choose the best answer.

   A. In the Local Security Policy console, set the Log On Locally security policy to only Authenticated Users.

   B. In the Local Security Policy console, disable the Interactive Logon: Do Not Require CTRL+ALT+DEL security policy.

   C. In the Local Security Policy console, enable the Interactive Logon: Require Domain Controller Authentication To Unlock Workstation security policy.

   D. In the Local Security Policy console, set the Interactive Logon: Number Of Previous Logons To Cache security policy to 0.

5. Bob is a Web developer in your organization. He has installed Internet Information Services (IIS) on his Windows XP Professional computer for testing and development purposes. He is writing a Web application that will access files stored on Windows Server 2003 computers and he wants the IIS service on his computer to be able to access those other systems across the network. He asks you to create an account in the domain called **BobIIS**. He adds the account to the local Power Users group and then configures the World Wide Web Publishing service to start with the new domain account. However, when he tries to start the service, he receives a logon failure message. When he reboots the computer, the service still fails to start. What do you do? Choose the best answer.

   A. Add the domain account to the local Administrators group.

   B. Open the Local Security Policy console, expand the Local Policies folder, select the User Rights Assignment folder, and scroll down the list of user rights until you see Log On As A Service. Double-click Log On As A Service and add the new domain account to the list of accounts that have this user right.

   C. Configure the IIS Admin service's startup so that it runs under the BobIIS domain account as well.

   D. Open the Local Security Policy console, expand the Local Policies folder, select the User Rights Assignment folder, and scroll down the list of user rights until you see Log On Locally. Double-click Log On Locally and add the new domain account to the list of accounts that have this user right.

Objective 7.3 Answers

1. **Correct Answers: B and E**

   A. **Incorrect:** There is no need to re-create Richard's account because it has not been deleted.

   B. **Correct:** Merely creating a group and calling it **Accounting1** does not restore its members and permissions. You must manually add the members that need to belong to it and explicitly grant permissions to the resources it must be able to access.

   C. **Incorrect:** User accounts do not require this user right to access resources shared over the network.

   D. **Incorrect:** This answer is incorrect for the reasons noted in answer B.

   E. **Correct:** This answer is correct for the same reasons noted in answer B.

2. **Correct Answers: D**

   A. **Incorrect:** The Sysprep tool is used for creating installation images of Windows XP Professional that include other applications such as Office 2003; it is not used for creating user accounts or user profiles.

   B. **Incorrect:** It is not necessary to manually create local user profiles for the reasons explained in answer D.

   C. **Incorrect:** Hardware profiles are used when computers are regularly moved between markedly distinct hardware environments, for example, docked and undocked profiles for a laptop computer. Hardware profiles have nothing to do with individual user data or settings, so creating unique hardware profiles does not address the requirements outlined in the question.

   D. **Correct:** When the users log on to the computer for the first time, a new user profile is created for them under the Documents And Settings folder located on the system volume. The profile automatically retains their user settings, and a folder called My Documents is created within their profile. Most Windows-compatible programs automatically try to store documents at this location.

3. **Correct Answers: A**

   A. **Correct:** Each user account has a unique Security Identifier (SID). The SID is granted access to resources but is typically represented by the friendlier user name for the account. Changing the account name does not change the SID, so Scott will have access to everything that Dave had access to. Changing the password ensures that Dave can longer connect to the network with that account.

B. Incorrect: This procedure would ensure that Scott's profile settings match Dave's, but Scott's account would not have access to shared folders and printers, NTFS files and folders, and other resources that Dave's account had access to. Also, if Dave were still able to connect to the network, perhaps via a dial-up or virtual private network (VPN) connection, he would still be able to gain access to data on the network—this is a significant security risk.

C. Incorrect: These procedures would accomplish the desired goals, but there is a much simpler way to give Scott the appropriate access to resources on the network.

D. Incorrect: These procedures would accomplish the desired goals, but there is a much simpler way to give Scott the appropriate access to resources on the network.

4.   Correct Answers: D

A. Incorrect: This security setting would not prevent users from logging on if they previously had logged on to the computer, had their domain account removed, and disconnected the computer from the network. In this scenario, the user could authenticate by using locally cached credentials.

B. Incorrect: Requiring users to press Ctrl+Alt+Del does improve the security of the system, but it might still allow users to log on without being authenticated by a domain controller if that domain controller is unavailable.

C. Incorrect: The Interactive Logon: Require Domain Controller To Unlock Workstation security policy causes Windows XP to reauthenticate a user with a domain controller when he unlocks the workstation. The primary purpose of this security setting is to prevent an attacker from guessing a user's password when the workstation has been locked by a screen saver. When this setting is disabled, authentication attempts made at a locked workstation do not count against failed logon attempts. Although enabling this security policy is an important security best practice, it does not accomplish the goal outlined in this scenario.

D. Correct: Setting this security policy to 0 means that no user can log on unless a domain controller is available to authenticate the user.

5.   Correct Answers: B

A. Incorrect: Although adding the account to that group ensures that it has access to all the local files, folders, and other resources that it might need, it probably already had sufficient access because it was added to the Power Users group. This step is unlikely to resolve the problem.

B. Correct: Services that run on Windows XP must run in the context of accounts that have the user right called Log On As A Service. The account must also have access to files, folders, and other resources utilized by that service.

C. Incorrect: These procedures do not resolve the problem; the account used to launch the IIS Admin service will not impact the behavior of the World Wide Web Publishing service. You will also see the same logon failure for this service when you try to start it.

D. Incorrect: This user right is required for any accounts that will log on to the system interactively. It is also needed for any users, including the built-in account for anonymous Web access, that will access any Web sites running on the computer. The Log On Locally user right is not needed for the account used to launch services, though, so this procedure will not resolve the problem.

Objective 7.4

Configure, Manage, and Troubleshoot Internet Explorer Security Settings

When Web browsers were new, they were simple tools for displaying HTML files. As time went on, Web browsers gained more and more functionality. Today, Internet Explorer is an extremely complex tool that requires a great deal of knowledge to configure, manage, and troubleshoot.

Especially after installing Service Pack 2 for Windows XP, you must have a detailed understanding of Internet Explorer security settings. If security settings are too restrictive, users cannot access Web sites that they need for their jobs. If security settings are too permissive, malicious Web sites will install spyware or other types of malicious software on the computers you manage. To successfully maintain Internet Explorer, you must understand not only how to configure, manage, and troubleshoot it, but also how to protect it from malicious Web content.

Objective 7.4 Questions

1. By default, which of the following Web content zones prompts the user to download an unsigned ActiveX control? Choose the correct answer.

   A. Internet

   B. Local Intranet

   C. Trusted Sites

   D. Restricted Sites

2. You work for Humongous Insurance, a company that has a strong partnership with Contoso Pharmaceuticals. Users on your network can access some Web servers on Contoso's intranet via a VPN connection that travels across the network. For an added level of security, the administrators of Contoso's network require HTTPS for all connections to its intranet Web servers. These servers use SSL certificates issued from Contoso's own certificate authority (CA). Every time users on your network visit one of the Web servers on Contoso's intranet, they receive an error message stating that the SSL certificate was not issued from a trusted root CA. What is the easiest way to allow users on your network to access Web servers on Contoso's intranet without having to view these error messages? Choose the best answer.

   A. Ask an administrator from Contoso to provide you with a copy of the issuing certificate from its root CA. Use the Internet Options program located in Control Panel to import the certificate as a trusted root authority on each computer used for visiting the Contoso intranet.

   B. Ask an administrator from Contoso to send the issuing certificate from its CA to Microsoft so it can be incorporated into the next service pack for Windows XP.

   C. Instruct the administrators at Contoso to purchase a new certificate from an existing trusted root CA, and then rebuild its internal CA using the new certificate for the first server.

   D. Use the Registry Editor tool (REGEDT32.EXE) to manually add Contoso's issuing certificate to the list of trusted root CAs on each computer that visits the Contoso intranet.

3. You regularly visit a hardware vendor's Web site to order computers, computer parts, and network equipment online. You have been satisfied with this arrangement for many months until the vendor introduces a revamped Web site that uses ActiveX controls to present its catalog, inventory, account information, past orders, and pending orders. When you visit the overhauled Web site, you can see many text and graphic elements, but large sections appear to be blank. When you click some links, more

pages with blank sections appear. What is the easiest way to allow yourself to access all the functionality on the vendor's new Web site? Choose the best answer.

A. Contact the vendor and explain that its Web site is down.

B. Ask the vendor to e-mail the ActiveX controls to you so you can manually install them on your computer.

C. Add the vendor's URL to the list of Trusted sites by using the Security tab in the Internet Options program located in Control Panel.

D. Ask the vendor to provide you with a link to its old Web site.

4.   In response to an increased number of attackers using malicious Web sites to attack visitors' browsers, you have hardened your organization's Internet Explorer security settings. During testing, you notice that you can no longer search at any popular Web directory. What change should you make to resolve the problem while minimizing security risks? Choose the best answer.

A. Searching is inherently risky, so hardened versions of Internet Explorer refuse to submit information to Internet search directories.

B. Change Internet Explorer's default protocol from HTTP to HTTPS.

C. Edit the Internet Explorer access control list (ACL). Add the Authenticated Users special group to the Permit Unencrypted Form Data resource.

D. In Internet Explorer, click the Tools menu, and then click Internet Options. Click the Security tab, and then click the Internet zone. Click the Custom Level button. Scroll down to Submit Nonencrypted Form Data, and then click Enable.

Objective 7.4 Answers

1. **Correct Answers: C**

    A. **Incorrect:** By default, sites that are placed in the Internet zone have unsigned ActiveX controls disabled. If an ActiveX control has been signed, the user is prompted to download it. This ensures that the user is kept safe from potentially dangerous unsigned ActiveX controls on the public Internet. Users can change this default by choosing Internet Options in Internet Explorer, clicking the Security tab, clicking the Internet zone, and clicking the Custom Level button.

    B. **Incorrect:** By default, sites that are placed in the Local Intranet zone have unsigned ActiveX controls disabled. If an ActiveX control has been signed, the user is prompted to download it, which ensures that users are kept safe from potentially dangerous unsigned ActiveX controls on their local intranet. Users can change this default by choosing Internet Options in Internet Explorer, clicking the Security tab, clicking the Local Intranet zone, and clicking the Custom Level button.

    C. **Correct:** By default, sites that have been placed in the Trusted Sites zone prompt the user to download an unsigned ActiveX control. Signed ActiveX controls are automatically downloaded, which provides users with the convenience of skipping prompts to install controls from a Web server that they feel confident will never present potentially dangerous ActiveX controls for download.

    D. **Incorrect:** Restricted Sites have both signed and unsigned ActiveX controls disabled. The user is not prompted to download any ActiveX controls, ever. Sites placed in the Restricted Sites zone are assumed to have potentially dangerous code. Users can change this default by choosing Internet Options in Internet Explorer, clicking the Security tab, clicking the Restricted Sites zone, and clicking the Custom Level button.

2. **Correct Answers: A**

    A. **Correct:** This is the best choice among the answers given. This process would be greatly simplified if the network were running Active Directory. The certificate from Contoso can be added to the list of trusted root CAs using domain-based GPOs instead.

    B. **Incorrect:** Microsoft has tough requirements that must be met before adding new trusted root CAs to the list shipped with its operating systems. There must be compelling evidence that a wide range of users from many different organizations will benefit from the new CA being added to the list.

C. Incorrect: If Contoso were just starting to deploy its first CA this option might make sense, but because the CA is already in operation it would be very time consuming to scrap it and start all over again.

D. Incorrect: It is not possible to import SSL certificates in this manner.

3. **Correct Answers: C**

A. Incorrect: Although it is possible that the Web site is having problems, it is not the most likely cause of the behavior described in the question. Because parts of the pages are rendered correctly, and links to other pages function, the Web server is probably working. The issues might be caused by a failing database server or application server that is supposed to feed data to the Web server, but you do not have enough information to determine whether this is the case.

B. Incorrect: ActiveX, Java, and other Web-based applets are designed to be downloaded by visitors to the Web site as they go along, not to be repackaged and deployed via installation routines. Resolving the problem in this manner would add a great deal of overhead to the vendor's Web management team and force you to spend time manually installing its software.

C. Correct: This is an easy way around the problem. By default, sites in the Internet zone do not allow unsigned ActiveX controls. This restrictive setting can cause problems for some downloadable ActiveX controls. The default setting for Trusted sites is Low Safety, which should allow any thoroughly debugged Java applet to run correctly. Be careful when adding URLs to your list of Trusted Sites because malicious or poorly written programs might be downloaded and run by Internet Explorer without your knowledge. This could lead to lost or compromised data or even a damaged installation of Windows XP Professional. However, there is little risk when adding sites with content you trust to our list of Trusted Sites.

D. Incorrect: It is unlikely that the vendor will want to maintain two different versions of its Web site simultaneously; therefore, this approach is not feasible.

4. **Correct Answers: D**

A. Incorrect: Although unencrypted data transmitted across the Internet is vulnerable to capture and analysis, Internet Explorer can be configured to allow it. In fact, Internet Explorer transmits unencrypted data by default.

B. Incorrect: In this scenario, Internet Explorer refuses to transmit unencrypted data. The HTTPS protocol would encrypt the data prior to transmission, allowing Internet Explorer to function properly. However, you cannot configure HTTPS to be the default protocol, and many Internet Web sites do not support HTTPS.

C. Incorrect: Internet Explorer does not use ACLs to restrict actions that users are allowed to take.

D. Correct: Although not enabled by default, Internet Explorer can be configured to refuse to send unencrypted form data across the Internet to reduce the likelihood of an attacker capturing your traffic and identifying the data you typed into the form.

Glossary

A

AC-3   The coding system used by Dolby Digital. A standard for high-quality digital audio that is used for the sound portion of video stored in digital format.

Accelerated Graphics Port (AGP)   A type of expansion slot that is solely for video cards. Designed by Intel and supported by Microsoft Windows XP Professional, AGP is a dedicated bus that provides fast, high-quality video and graphics performance.

access control entry (ACE)   The entries on the access control list (ACL) that control user account or group access to a resource. The entry must allow the type of access that is requested (for example, Read access) for the user to gain access. If no ACE exists in the ACL, the user cannot gain access to the resource or folder on an NTFS partition. See also access control list (ACL).

access control list (ACL)   A list of all user accounts and groups that have been granted access for the file or folder on an NTFS partition or volume, as well as the type of access they have been granted. When a user attempts to gain access to a resource, the ACL must contain an entry, called an access control entry (ACE), for the user account or group to which the user belongs. See also access control entry (ACE).

access permissions   Features that control access to shared resources in Windows XP Professional.

access token   A data structure containing security information that identifies a user to the security subsystem on a computer running Windows XP Professional, Windows 2000, or Windows NT. An access token contains a user's security ID, the security IDs for groups that the user is a member of, and a list of the user's privileges on the local computer.

account   See user account.

account lockout   A Windows XP Professional security feature that locks a user account if a number of failed logon attempts occur within a specified amount of time, based on account policy lockout settings. Locked accounts cannot log on.

account policy   Controls how passwords must be used by all user accounts on an individual computer or in a domain.

ACE   See access control entry (ACE).

ACL   See access control list (ACL).

ACPI   See Advanced Configuration and Power Interface (ACPI).

Active Directory directory service   The directory service included in Windows 2000 Server products that identifies all resources on a network and makes them accessible to users and applications.

Active Directory schema   The structure of the tables and fields and how they are related to one another. In Active Directory, the schema is a collection of data (object classes) that defines how the real data of the directory (the attributes of an object) is organized and stored.

Address Resolution Protocol (ARP)   Determines hardware addresses (MAC addresses) that correspond to an Internet Protocol (IP) address.

ad-hoc wireless network   A wireless network mode in which multiple wireless stations can connect without requiring an access point.

administrative share   A hidden share that Windows XP Professional creates automatically so that administrators can access resources on a computer.

ADSL   See asymmetric digital subscriber line (ADSL).

Advanced Configuration and Power Interface (ACPI)   An open industry specification that defines power management on a wide range of mobile, desktop, and server components and peripherals. ACPI is the foundation for the OnNow industry initiative that allows system manufacturers to deliver computers that will start at the touch of a keyboard. ACPI design is essential to take full advantage of power management and Plug and Play in Windows XP Professional. Check the manufacturer's documentation to verify that a computer is ACPI-compliant.

Advanced Power Management (APM)   A software interface designed by Microsoft and Intel used between hardware-specific power management software, such as that located in a system BIOS and an operating system power management driver.

agent   A program that performs a background task for a user and reports to the user when the task is done or when some expected event has taken place.

AGP   See Accelerated Graphics Port (AGP).

American National Standards Institute (ANSI)   An organization of American industry and business groups dedicated to the development of trade and communication standards. ANSI is the American representative to the International Organization for Standardization (ISO). See also International Organization for Standardization (ISO).

analog   A system that encodes information using frequency modulation in a nonbinary context. Modems use analog encoding to transmit data through a phone line. An analog signal can be any frequency, allowing many possibilities. Because of this ambiguity of signal, a device has to interpret the signal, often finding errors. See also digital, modem.

analog line   A communication line that carries information using frequency modulation. See also digital line.

ANSI   See American National Standards Institute (ANSI).

answer file   A text file that supplies Windows XP Professional Setup with information necessary during the installation process.

API   See application programming interface (API).

APIPA   See Automatic Private IP Addressing (APIPA).

APM   See Advanced Power Management (APM).

application layer   The top (seventh) layer of the OSI reference model. This layer serves as the window that application processes use to access network services. It represents the services that directly support user applications, such as software for file transfers, database access, and e-mail. See also Open Systems Interconnection (OSI) reference model.

application programming interface (API)   A set of routines that an application program uses to request and carry out lower-level services performed by the operating system.

application protocols   Protocols that work at the higher end of the OSI reference model, providing application-to-application interaction and data exchange. Popular application protocols include File Transfer Access and Management (FTAM), a file access protocol; Simple Mail Transfer Protocol (SMTP), a TCP/IP protocol for transferring e-mail; Telnet, a TCP/IP protocol for logging on to remote hosts and processing data locally; and NetWare Core Protocol (NCP), the primary protocol used to transmit information between a NetWare server and its clients.

ARP   See Address Resolution Protocol (ARP).

ASCII (American Standard Code for Information Interchange)   A coding scheme that assigns numeric values to letters, numbers, punctuation marks, and certain other characters. By standardizing the values used for these characters, ASCII enables computers and programs to exchange information.

asymmetric digital subscriber line (ADSL)   A recent modem technology that converts existing twisted-pair telephone lines into access paths for multimedia and high-speed data communications. These new connections can transmit more than 8 Mbps to the subscriber and up to 1 Mbps from the subscriber. ADSL is recognized as a physical layer transmission protocol for unshielded twisted-pair media.

Asynchronous Transfer Mode (ATM)   An advanced implementation of packet switching that provides high-speed data transmission rates to send fixed-size cells over local area networks (LANs) or wide area networks (WANs). Cells are 53 bytes—48 bytes of data with 5 additional bytes of address. ATM accommodates voice, data, fax, real-time video, CD-quality audio, imaging, and multimegabit data transmission. ATM uses switches as multiplexers to permit several computers to put data on a network simultaneously. Most commercial ATM boards transmit data at about 155 Mbps, but theoretically a rate of 1.2 Gbps is possible.

asynchronous transmission A form of data transmission in which information is sent one character at a time, with variable time intervals between characters. Asynchronous transmission does not rely on a shared timer that allows the sending and receiving units to separate characters by specific time periods. Therefore, each transmitted character consists of a number of data bits (which compose the character itself) preceded by a start bit and ending in an optional parity bit followed by a 1-, 1.5-, or 2-stop bit.

ATM See Asynchronous Transfer Mode (ATM).

auditing A process that tracks network activities by user accounts and is a routine element of network security. Auditing can produce records of users who have accessed—or attempted to access—specific resources; help administrators identify unauthorized activity; and track activities such as logon attempts, connection and disconnection from designated resources, changes made to files and directories, server events and modifications, password changes, and logon parameter changes.

audit policy Defines the types of security events that Windows XP Professional records in the security log on each computer.

authentication Verification based on user name, passwords, and time and account restrictions.

automated installation An unattended setup using one or more of several methods such as Remote Installation Services, bootable CD, and Sysprep.

Automated System Recovery A feature of the Backup utility that creates a system recovery disk and performs a full normal backup of the system partition so that you can recover your computer in the event of a major failure.

Automatic Private IP Addressing (APIPA) A feature of Windows XP Professional that automatically configures a unique Internet Protocol (IP) address from 169.254.0.1 to 169.254.255.255, and a subnet mask of 255.255.0.0 when the Transmission Control Protocol/Internet Protocol (TCP/IP) is configured for dynamic addressing and a Dynamic Host Configuration Protocol (DHCP) server is not available.

Automatic Updates A Windows service that scans for, downloads, and installs available updates for Windows XP and other Microsoft programs

B

back end In a client/server application, the part of the program that runs on the server.

backup A duplicate copy of a program, a disk, or data made to secure valuable files from loss.

backup job A single process of backing up data.

Backup Or Restore Wizard A wizard that provides a simple, step-based interface for backing up or restoring data.

bandwidth In analog communication, the difference between the highest and lowest frequencies in a given range.

Bandwidth Allocation Protocol (BAP) A Point-to-Point Protocol (PPP) control protocol that helps provide bandwidth on demand. BAP dynamically controls the use of multilinked lines and is a very efficient mechanism for controlling connection costs while dynamically providing optimum bandwidth.

BAP See Bandwidth Allocation Protocol (BAP).

base I/O port Specifies a channel through which information is transferred between a computer's hardware, such as the network interface card (NIC) and its CPU.

baseline A measurement derived from the collection of data over an extended period of time. The data should reflect varying but typical types of workloads and user connections. The baseline is an indicator of how individual system resources or a group of resources are used during periods of normal activity.

base memory address Defines the address of the location in a computer's memory (RAM) that is used by the network interface card (NIC). This setting is sometimes called the RAM start address.

base priority A setting made in Task Manager that determines how much processor time Windows XP Professional devotes to the process compared to other processes.

basic disk A physical disk that contains primary partitions or extended partitions with logical drives used by Windows XP Professional, Windows 2000, and all versions of Windows NT. Basic disks can also contain volume, striped, mirror, or RAID-5 sets that were created using Windows NT 4.0 or earlier versions. As long as a compatible file format is used, basic disks can be accessed by MS-DOS, Windows 95, Windows 98, and all versions of Windows NT.

basic input/output system (BIOS) The set of essential software routines that tests hardware at startup, assists with starting the operating system, and supports the transfer of data among hardware devices. The BIOS is stored in read-only memory (ROM) so that it can be executed when the computer is started. Although critical to performance, the BIOS is usually invisible to computer users.

baud A measure of data-transmission speed named after the French engineer and telegrapher Jean-Maurice-Emile Baudot. It is a measure of the speed of oscillation of the sound wave on which a bit of data is carried over telephone lines. Because baud was originally used to measure the transmission speed of telegraph equipment, the term sometimes refers to the data transmission speed of a modem. However, current modems can send at a speed higher than one bit per oscillation, so baud is being replaced by the more accurate bps (bits per second) as a measure of modem speed.

baud rate Refers to the speed at which a modem can transmit data. Often confused with bps (the number of bits per second transmitted), baud rate actually measures the number of events, or signal changes, that occur in one second. Because one event can actually encode more than one bit in high-speed digital communication, baud rate and bps are not always synonymous, and the latter is the more accurate term to apply to modems. For example, the 9600-baud modem that encodes four bits per event actually operates at 2400 baud but transmits at 9600 bps (2400 events times 4 bits per event), so it should be called a 9600-bps modem. See also bits per second (bps).

bind To associate two pieces of information with one another.

binding A process that establishes the communication channel between network components on different levels to enable communication between those components—for example, the binding of a protocol driver (such as TCP/IP) and a network adapter.

BIOS See basic input/output system (BIOS).

bisync (binary synchronous communications protocol) A communications protocol developed by IBM. Bisync transmissions are encoded in either ASCII or EBCDIC. Messages can be of any length and are sent in units called frames, optionally preceded by a message header. Because bisync uses synchronous transmission, in which message elements are separated by a specific time interval, each frame is preceded and followed by special characters that enable the sending and receiving machines to synchronize their clocks.

bit Short for binary digit: either 1 or 0 in the binary number system. In processing and storage, a bit is the smallest unit of information handled by a computer. It is represented physically by an element such as a single pulse sent through a circuit or small spot on a magnetic disk capable of storing either a 1 or 0. Eight bits make a byte.

bits per second (bps) A measure of the speed at which a device can transfer data. See also baud rate.

bit time The time it takes for each station to receive and store a bit.

bootable CD An automated installation method that runs Setup from a CD-ROM. This method is useful for computers at remote sites with slow links and no local IT department.

BOOT.INI A file used to build the operating system choices that are displayed during startup.

boot partition The disk partition that possesses the system files required to load the operating system into memory.

boot sector   A critical disk structure for starting your computer, located at sector 1 of each volume or floppy. It contains executable code and data that is required by the code, including information used by the file system to access the volume. The boot sector is created when you format the volume.

boot-sector virus   A type of virus that resides in the first sector of a floppy disk or hard drive. When the computer is booted, the virus executes. In this common method of transmitting viruses from one floppy disk to another, the virus replicates itself onto the new drive each time a new disk is inserted and accessed.

bottleneck   A device or program that significantly degrades network performance. Poor network performance results when a device uses noticeably more CPU time than it should, consumes too much of a resource, or lacks the capacity to handle the load. Potential bottlenecks can be found in the CPU, memory, network interface card (NIC), and other components.

bps   See bits per second (bps).

broadcast   A transmission sent simultaneously to more than one recipient. In communication and on networks, a broadcast message is one distributed to all stations or computers on the network.

broadcast storm   An event that occurs when there are so many broadcast messages on the network that they approach or surpass the capacity of the network bandwidth. This can happen when one computer on the network transmits a flood of frames, saturating the network with traffic so it can no longer carry messages from any other computer. Such a broadcast storm can shut down a network.

buffer   A reserved portion of RAM in which data is held temporarily, pending an opportunity to complete its transfer to or from a storage device or another location in memory.

built-in group   One type of group account used by Windows XP Professional. Built-in groups, as the name implies, are included with the operating system and have been granted useful collections of rights and built-in abilities. In most cases, a built-in group provides all the capabilities needed by a particular user. For example, if a user account belongs to the built-in Administrators group, logging on with that account gives the user administrative capabilities. See also user account.

bus   Parallel wires or cabling that connect components in a computer.

byte   A unit of information consisting of 8 bits. In computer processing or storage, a byte is often equivalent to a single character, such as a letter, numeral, or punctuation mark. Because a byte represents only a small amount of information, amounts of computer memory are usually given in kilobytes (1024 bytes or 2 raised to the 10th power), megabytes (1,048,576 bytes or 2 raised to the 20th power), gigabytes (1024 megabytes), terabytes (1024 gigabytes), petabytes (1024 terabytes), or exabytes (1024 petabytes).

C

cache   A special memory subsystem or part of RAM in which frequently used data values are duplicated for quick access. A memory cache stores the contents of frequently accessed RAM locations and the addresses where these data items are stored. When the processor references an address in memory, the cache checks to see whether it holds that address. If it does hold the address, the data is returned to the processor; if it does not, regular memory access occurs. A cache is useful when RAM accesses are slow compared with the microprocessor speed.

CAL   See client access license (CAL).

callback   A setting in Windows XP Professional that causes the remote server to disconnect and call back the client attempting to access the remote server. This reduces the client's phone bill by having the call charged to the remote server's phone number. The callback feature can also improve security by calling back the phone number that you specified.

central processing unit (CPU)   The computational and control unit of a computer; the device that interprets and carries out instructions. Single-chip CPUs, called microprocessors, made personal computers possible. Examples include the 80286, 80386, 80486, and Pentium processors.

Check Disk   A command-line utility that verifies and repairs the integrity of the file system on a volume.

Cipher   A command-line utility that provides the capability to encrypt and decrypt files and folders from a command prompt.

client   A computer that accesses shared network resources provided by another computer, called a server.

client access license (CAL)   A CAL gives client computers the right to connect to computers running one of the Windows Server family of products.

client/server   A network architecture designed around the concept of distributed processing in which a task is divided between a back end (server) that stores and distributes data and a front end (client) that requests specific data from the server.

codec (compression/decompression)   Compression/decompression technology for digital video and stereo audio.

Color Quality   A setting that affects the number of colors used to display objects on the Desktop.

compressed folders   A feature that allows you to compress folders on volumes formatted with NTFS or FAT. Compressed folders are compatible with other ZIP programs.

compression state   Each file and folder on an NTFS volume has a compression state, either compressed or uncompressed.

Computer Management   A console that provides access to a number of management utilities for administering a computer, including the ability to create, manage, and monitor shared folders.

control set   A Windows XP Professional installation contains control sets stored as subkeys in the registry. The control sets contain configuration data used to control the system, such as a list of which device drivers and services to load and start.

copy backup   A backup type in which all selected files and folders are backed up, regardless of their marker. During a copy backup, markers are not changed.

counter   A particular aspect of an object that System Monitor can measure.

CPU   See central processing unit (CPU).

D

database management system (DBMS)   A layer of software between the physical database and the user. The DBMS manages all requests for database action from the user, including keeping track of the physical details of file locations and formats, indexing schemes, and so on. In addition, a DBMS permits centralized control of security and data integrity requirements.

data encryption   See encryption.

Data Encryption Standard (DES)   A commonly used, highly sophisticated algorithm developed by the U.S. National Bureau of Standards for encrypting and decoding data. This encryption algorithm uses a 56-bit key and maps a 64-bit input block to a 64-bit output block. The key appears to be a 64-bit key, but one bit in each of the 8 bytes is used for odd parity, resulting in 56 bits of usable key. See also encryption.

data frames   Logical, structured packages in which data can be placed. Data being transmitted is segmented into small units and combined with control information such as message start and message end indicators. Each package of information is transmitted as a single unit, called a frame. The data-link layer packages raw bits from the physical layer into data frames. The exact format of the frame used by the network depends on the topology. See also frame.

data-link layer   The second layer in the OSI reference model. This layer packages raw bits from the physical layer into data frames. See also Open Systems Interconnection (OSI) reference model.

data stream   An undifferentiated, byte-by-byte flow of data.

DBMS   See database management system (DBMS).

defragmenting   The process of finding and consolidating fragmented files and folders. Defragmenting involves moving the pieces of each file or folder to one location so that each occupies a single, contiguous space on the hard disk. The system can then access and save files and folders more efficiently.

DES   See Data Encryption Standard (DES).

Desktop Cleanup Wizard   A wizard that runs every 60 days by default, offering to remove unused Desktop icons.

device   A generic term for a computer subsystem. Printers, serial ports, and disk drives are referred to as devices.

Device Manager   An administrative tool that you can use to manage the devices on your computer. Using Device Manager, you can view and change device properties, update device drivers, configure device settings, and uninstall devices.

DHCP   See Dynamic Host Configuration Protocol (DHCP).

dial-up connection   A connection that connects you to a private network or the Internet by using a device that transfers data over a public telephone network.

differential backup   A backup type in which only selected files and folders that have a marker are backed up. During a differential backup, markers are not cleared so that files are still backed up if they have changed since the last normal backup.

digital   A system that encodes information numerically, such as 0 and 1, in a binary context. Computers use digital encoding to process data. A digital signal is a discrete binary state, either on or off. See also analog, modem.

digital line   A communication line that carries information only in binary-encoded (digital) form. To minimize distortion and noise interference, a digital line uses repeaters to regenerate the signal periodically during transmission. See also analog line.

digital video disc (DVD)   An optical storage medium with higher capacity and bandwidth than a compact disc. A DVD can hold a full-length film with up to 133 minutes of high-quality video, in MPEG-2 format, and audio. Also known as digital versatile disc.

DIP (dual inline package) switch   One or more small rocker or sliding switches that can be set to one of two states—closed or open—to control options on a circuit board.

direct memory access (DMA)   Memory access that does not involve the microprocessor; frequently employed for data transfer directly between memory and an "intelligent" peripheral device such as a disk drive.

direct memory access (DMA) channel   A channel for direct memory access that does not involve the microprocessor, providing data transfer directly between memory and a disk drive.

directory   Stores information about network resources, as well as all the services that make the information available and useful. The resources stored in the directory—such as user data, printers, servers, databases, groups, computers, and security policies—are known as objects. The directory is part of Active Directory.

directory service   A network service that identifies all resources on a network and makes them accessible to users and applications.

Disk Cleanup   A utility that calculates the amount of space that you can gain by deleting certain types of files, such as temporary files and downloaded program files.

Disk Defragmenter   The program used in Windows XP to defragment a disk.

disk duplexing   See disk mirroring, fault tolerance.

disk duplication   An automated installation in which you use the System Preparation tool to create an image from a computer running Windows XP Professional, and then clone that image on other computers. Using disk duplication usually requires third-party software.

diskless computers   Computers that have neither a floppy disk nor a hard disk. Diskless computers depend on special ROM to provide users with an interface through which they can log on to the network.

Disk Management   The name of the Windows XP utility used to manage fixed and removable disks, as well as to create and manage volumes and partitions.

disk mirroring   A technique, also known as disk duplicating, in which all or part of a hard disk is duplicated onto one or more hard disks, each of which ideally is attached to its own controller. With disk mirroring, any change made to the original disk is simultaneously made to the other disk or disks. Disk mirroring is used in situations in which a backup copy of current data must be maintained at all times. See also disk striping, fault tolerance.

Diskpart   A command used to execute disk-management tasks from a command prompt and to create scripts for automating tasks that you need to perform frequently or on multiple computers.

disk quota   A feature that allows you to allocate disk space to users based on the files and folders that they own.

disk striping   Divides data into 64-Kb blocks and spreads it equally at a fixed rate and in a fixed order among all disks in an array. However, disk striping does not provide any fault tolerance because there is no data redundancy. If any partition in the set fails, all data is lost. See also disk mirroring, fault tolerance.

distinguished name (DN)   A name that uniquely identifies an object within Active Directory and contains sufficient information for a client to retrieve the object from the directory.

distribution server   Stores the distribution folder structure, which contains the files needed to install a product, for example Windows XP Professional.

DLL   See dynamic-link library (DLL).

DMA   See direct memory access (DMA).

DMA channel   See direct memory access (DMA) channel.

DN   See distinguished name (DN).

DNS   See Domain Name System (DNS).

domain   For Microsoft networking, a collection of computers and users that share a common database and security policy stored on a computer running Windows 2000 Server and configured as a domain controller. Each domain has a unique name. See also workgroup.

domain controller   For Microsoft networking, the Windows 2000 Server-based computer that authenticates domain logons and maintains the security policy and master database for a domain.

Domain Name System (DNS)   A general-purpose, distributed, replicated, data-query service used primarily on the Internet and on private Transmission Control Protocol/Internet Protocol (TCP/IP) networks for translating host names into Internet addresses.

domain namespace   The naming scheme that provides the hierarchical structure for the DNS database.

downtime   The amount of time a computer system or associated hardware remains nonfunctioning. Although downtime can occur because hardware fails unexpectedly, it can also be a scheduled event, such as when a network is shut down to allow time for maintaining the system, changing hardware, or archiving files.

drive letter   Used to access the volume through Windows Explorer and other applications. Hard disks, floppy drives, CD-ROM and DVD drives, removable drives, and tape devices are assigned drive letters.

driver   A software component that permits a computer system to communicate with a device. For example, a printer driver is a device driver that translates computer data into a form understood by the target printer. In most cases, the driver also manipulates the hardware to transmit the data to the device.

driver signing   A process in which device drivers that have passed a series of tests by Microsoft are digitally signed, enabling the operating system to determine whether the drivers are acceptable for use.

duplex transmission   Also called full-duplex transmission. Communication that takes place simultaneously and in both directions. See also full-duplex transmission.

DVD   See digital video disc (DVD).

dynamic disk   A physical disk that is managed by Disk Management. Dynamic disks can contain only dynamic volumes, which are created by using Disk Management. Dynamic disks cannot contain partitions or logical drives, nor can they be accessed by MS-DOS.

Dynamic Host Configuration Protocol (DHCP)   A protocol for automatic TCP/IP configuration that provides static and dynamic address allocation and management. See also Transmission Control Protocol/Internet Protocol (TCP/IP).

dynamic-link library (DLL)   A feature of the Microsoft Windows family of operating systems and the OS/2 operating system. DLLs allow executable routines, generally serving a specific function or set of functions, to be stored separately as files with .dll extensions and to be loaded only when needed by the program that calls them.

E

EAP   See Extensible Authentication Protocol (EAP).

effective permissions   The sum of the NTFS permissions assigned to the user account and to all of the groups to which the user belongs. If a user has Read permission for a folder and is a member of a group with Write permission for the same folder, then the user has both Read and Write permission for the folder.

EFS   See Encrypting File System (EFS).

EISA   See Extended Industry Standard Architecture (EISA).

Encrypting File System (EFS)   A feature of Windows 2000 and Windows XP Professional that protects sensitive data in files that are stored on disk using the NTFS file system. It uses symmetric key encryption in conjunction with public key technology to provide confidentiality for files. It runs as an integrated system service, which makes it easy to manage, difficult to attack, and transparent to the file owner and applications.

encryption   The process of making information indecipherable to protect it from unauthorized viewing or use, especially during transmission or when the data is stored on a transportable magnetic medium. A key is required to decode the information. See also Data Encryption Standard (DES).

End-User License Agreement (EULA)   An agreement that dictates the terms of service for using an application or service.

Enhanced Small Device Interface (ESDI)   A standard interface for hard drives before the IDE/ATA interface became mainstream.

environment variables   Settings that define the system and user environment information; they contain information such as a drive, path, or file name.

ESDI   See Enhanced Small Device Interface (ESDI).

EULA   See End-User License Agreement (EULA).

event   An action or occurrence to which a program might respond. Examples of events are mouse clicks, key presses, and mouse movements. Also, any significant occurrence in the system or in a program that requires users to be notified or an entry to be added to a log.

Event Viewer   A utility that allows you to monitor the events that Windows XP Professional records in various logs.

exabyte   See byte.

exception   Unsolicited network traffic that you have specifically configured Windows Firewall to allow.

Extended Industry Standard Architecture (EISA)   A 32-bit bus design for x86-based computers introduced in 1988. EISA was specified by an industry consortium of nine computer companies (AST Research, Compaq, Epson, Hewlett-Packard, NEC, Olivetti, Tandy, Wyse, and Zenith). An EISA device uses cards that are upwardly compatible from ISA. See also Industry Standard Architecture (ISA).

extended partition   A partition that provides a way to exceed the four primary partition limit. You cannot format an extended partition with any file system. Rather, extended partitions serve as a shell in which you can create any number of logical partitions.

Extensible Authentication Protocol (EAP)   An extension to the Point-to-Point Protocol (PPP) that works with dial-up, PPTP, and L2TP clients. EAP allows for an arbitrary authentication mechanism to validate a dial-up connection. The exact authentication method to be used is negotiated by the dial-up client and the remote access server.

F

FAT   See file allocation table (FAT).

FAT32   A derivative of the file allocation table file system. FAT32 supports smaller cluster sizes than FAT in the same given disk space, which results in more efficient space allocation on FAT32 drives. See also file allocation table (FAT).

fault tolerance   The capability of a computer or an operating system to respond to an event such as a power outage or a hardware failure so that no data is lost and any work in progress is not corrupted.

FDDI   See Fiber Distributed Data Interface (FDDI).

Fiber Distributed Data Interface (FDDI)   A standard developed by the ANSI for high-speed, fiber-optic local area networks. FDDI provides specifications for transmission rates of 100 Mbps on networks based on the Token Ring standard.

file allocation table (FAT)   A table maintained by some operating systems, including Windows NT, Windows 2000, and Windows XP Professional, to keep track of the status of various segments of disk space used for file storage.

Files And Settings Transfer Wizard   One of two methods used by administrators to transfer user configuration settings and files from systems running Windows 95 or later to a clean Windows XP installation.

File Signature Verification utility (Sigverif.exe)   A utility that is used to scan a Windows XP system for unsigned files, providing a simple method to identify unsigned drivers.

File Transfer Protocol (FTP)   A process that provides file transfers between local and remote computers. FTP supports several commands that allow bidirectional transfer of binary and ASCII files between computers. The FTP client is installed with the TCP/IP connectivity utilities. See also ASCII (American Standard Code for Information Interchange), Transmission Control Protocol/Internet Protocol (TCP/IP).

firewall   A security system, usually a combination of hardware and software, intended to protect a network against external threats coming from another network, including the Internet. Firewalls prevent an organization's networked computers from communicating directly with computers that are external to the network, and vice versa. Instead, all incoming and outgoing communication is routed through a proxy server outside the organization's network. Firewalls also audit network activity, recording the volume of traffic and information about unauthorized attempts to gain access. See also proxy server.

firmware   Software routines stored in read-only memory (ROM). Unlike random access memory (RAM), ROM stays intact even in the absence of electrical power. Startup routines and low-level input/output (I/O) instructions are stored in firmware.

fixed storage device   A storage device that is not removable, such as a hard drive.

forest   A grouping or hierarchical arrangement of one or more domain trees that form a disjointed namespace.

formatting   Preparing a hard disk to accept data by creating a file system (such as NTFS or FAT) on that disk.

fragmentation   The scattering of the parts of a file over different parts of the disk rather than having all parts of the file located in contiguous space. When a hard disk contains numerous fragmented files and folders, the computer takes longer to gain access to files and folders because it requires several additional reads to collect the various pieces. Creating new files and folders also takes longer because the available free space on the hard disk is scattered.

frame   A package of information transmitted on a network as a single unit. Frame is a term most often used with Ethernet networks. A frame is similar to the packet used in other networks. See also data frames, packet.

frame preamble   Header information added to the beginning of a data frame in the physical layer of the OSI reference model.

frame relay   An advanced, fast-packet, variable-length, digital, packet-switching technology. It is a point-to-point system that uses a private virtual circuit (PVC) to transmit variable-length frames at the data-link layer of the OSI reference model. Frame relay networks can also provide subscribers with bandwidth, as needed, that allows users to make nearly any type of transmission.

front end   In a client/server application, the part of the program carried out on the client computer.

FTP   See File Transfer Protocol (FTP).

full-duplex transmission   Also called duplex transmission. Communication that takes place simultaneously, in both directions. See also duplex transmission.

G

gateway   A device used to connect networks using different protocols so that information can be passed from one system to the other. Gateways function at the network layer of the OSI reference model.

Gb   See gigabit (Gb).

GB   See gigabyte (GB).

gigabit (Gb)   1,073,741,824 bits. Also referred to as 1 billion bits.

gigabyte (GB)   Commonly, 1000 megabytes. However, the precise meaning often varies with the context. A gigabyte is 1 billion bytes. In the context of computing, bytes are often expressed in multiples of powers of two. Therefore, a gigabyte can also be either 1000 megabytes or 1024 megabytes, where a megabyte is considered to be 1,048,576 bytes (2 raised to the 20th power).

Global Catalog   A service and a physical storage location that contains a replica of selected attributes for every object in Active Directory.

global group   One type of group account used by Windows 2000 Server. Used across an entire domain, global groups are created on domain controllers in the domain in which the user accounts reside. Global groups can contain only user accounts from the domain in which the global group is created. Members of global groups obtain resource permissions when the global group is added to a local group. See also group.

globally unique identifier (GUID)   A 128-bit number, guaranteed to be unique, that is assigned to an object created in Active Directory.

group   In networking, an account containing other accounts that are called members. The permissions and rights granted to a group are also provided to its members; thus, groups offer a convenient way to grant common capabilities to collections of user accounts. For Windows XP Professional, groups are managed with the Computer Management snap-in. For Windows 2000 Server, groups are managed with the Active Directory Users And Computers snap-in.

Group Policy   An administrator's tool for defining and controlling how programs, network resources, and the operating system operate for users and computers in an organization. In an Active Directory environment, Group Policy is applied to users or components on the basis of their membership in sites, domains, or organizational units (OUs).

Group Policy Result Tool   A command-line utility that helps you determine which policies are actually applied to a computer.

GUID   See globally unique identifier (GUID).

H

handshaking   A term applied to modem-to-modem communication. Refers to the process by which information is transmitted between the sending and receiving devices to maintain and coordinate data flow between them. Proper handshaking ensures that the receiving device will be ready to accept data before the sending device transmits it.

hard disk   One or more inflexible platters coated with material that allows the magnetic recording of computer data. A typical hard disk rotates at up to 7200 revolutions per minute (RPM), and the read/write heads ride over the surface of the disk on a cushion of air 10- to 25-millionths of an inch deep. A hard disk is sealed to prevent contaminants from interfering with the close head-to-disk tolerances. Hard disks provide faster access to data than floppy disks and are capable of storing much more information. Because platters are rigid, they can be stacked so that one hard-disk drive can access more than one platter. Most hard disks have between two and eight platters.

hardware   The physical components of a computer system, including any peripheral equipment such as printers, modems, and mouse devices.

Hardware Compatibility List (HCL)   See Windows Catalog.

hardware loopback   A connector on a computer that is useful for troubleshooting hardware problems, allowing data to be transmitted to a line and then returned as received data. If the transmitted data does not return, the hardware loopback detects a hardware malfunction.

header   In network data transmission, one of the three sections of a packet component. It includes an alert signal to indicate that the packet is being transmitted, the source address, the destination address, and clock information to synchronize transmission.

hertz (Hz)   The unit of frequency measurement. Frequency measures how often a periodic event occurs, such as the manner in which a wave's amplitude changes with time. One hertz equals one cycle per second. Frequency is often measured in kilohertz (KHz, 1000 Hz), megahertz (MHz, 1000 KHz), gigahertz (GHz, 1000 MHz), or terahertz (THz, 1000 GHz).

hibernate mode   A state where Windows saves the current system state (including open programs and windows) to your hard disk and then shuts the computer down. When you restart the computer, the open programs and windows are restored.

HID   See Human Interface Device (HID).

hidden share   A method of preventing users who are browsing the network from viewing the share. If you append the dollar sign ($) to a share name, it becomes hidden. Built-in administrative shares are examples of hidden shares.

histogram   A chart consisting of horizontal or vertical bars. The widths or heights of these bars represent the values of certain data.

host   See server.

host ID   The portion of an IP address that identifies the network segment on which a host is located.

hot fixing   See sector sparing.

HTML   See Hypertext Markup Language (HTML).

HTTP   See Hypertext Transfer Protocol (HTTP).

Human Interface Device (HID)   A firmware specification standard for input and output devices such as drawing tablets, keyboards, universal serial bus (USB) speakers, and other specialized devices designed to improve accessibility.

Hypertext Markup Language (HTML)   A language developed for writing pages for the World Wide Web. HTML allows text to include codes that define fonts, layout, embedded graphics, and hypertext links. Hypertext provides a method for presenting text, images, sound, and videos that are linked together in a nonsequential web of associations.

Hypertext Transfer Protocol (HTTP)   The method by which World Wide Web pages are transferred over the network.

I

ICM   See Image Color Management (ICM) 2.0.

ICMP   See Internet Control Message Protocol (ICMP).

ICS   See Internet Connection Sharing (ICS).

IDE   See Integrated Device Electronics (IDE).

IEEE   See Institute of Electrical and Electronics Engineers (IEEE).

IEEE 802   A networking model developed by the IEEE. Named for the year and month it began (February 1980), Project 802 defines local area network (LAN) standards for the physical and data-link layers of the OSI reference model. Project 802 divides the data-link layer into two sublayers: media access control (MAC) and Logical Link Control (LLC).

IEEE 802.1x authentication   Authenticates users and computers for access to 802.11 wireless networks and wired Ethernet networks.

IEEE 802.11a   a Wireless network standard that offers data transfer rates up to 54 Mbps and operates in the 5.8 GHz frequency.

IEEE 802.11b   A wireless network standard that offers data transfer rates of 5.5 Mbps and 11 Mbps and operates in the 2.45 GHz frequency.

IEEE 802.11g   A wireless network standard that offers data transfer rates up to 54 Mbps and operates in the 2.4 GHz frequency.

IEEE 1394 Firewire   A standard for high-speed serial devices such as digital video and digital audio editing equipment.

IIS   See Internet Information Services (IIS).

Image Color Management (ICM) 2.0   The API that applications use to take advantage of color management capabilities in Windows.

incremental backup   A backup type in which only selected files and folders that have a marker are backed up. During an incremental backup, markers are cleared so that the files are not backed up during subsequent incremental backups unless the files change.

Industry Standard Architecture (ISA)   An unofficial designation for the bus design of the IBM Personal Computer (PC) PC/XT. It allows various adapters to be added to the system by inserting plug-in cards into expansion slots. Commonly, ISA refers to the expansion slots themselves; such slots are called 8-bit slots or 16-bit slots. See also Extended Industry Standard Architecture (EISA).

infrared transmission   Electromagnetic radiation with frequencies in the electromagnetic spectrum in the range just below that of visible red light. In network communications, infrared technology offers extremely high transmission rates and wide bandwidth in line-of-sight communications.

infrastructure wireless network   A wireless network mode in which multiple wireless stations communicate through an access point.

input language   Language installed on a computer running Windows XP Professional from which the computer can accept input.

instance   A particular occurrence of an object in System Monitor.

Institute of Electrical and Electronics Engineers (IEEE)   An organization of engineering and electronics professionals; noted in networking for developing the IEEE 802.x standards for the physical and data-link layers of the OSI reference model, applied in a variety of network configurations.

Integrated Device Electronics (IDE)   A type of disk drive interface in which the controller electronics reside on the drive itself, eliminating the need for a separate network interface card. The IDE interface is compatible with the Western Digital ST-506 controller.

Integrated Services Digital Network (ISDN)   A worldwide digital communication network that evolved from existing telephone services. The goal of the ISDN is to replace current telephone lines, which require digital-to-analog conversions, with completely digital switching and transmission facilities capable of carrying data ranging from voice to computer transmissions, music, and video. The ISDN is built on two main types of communications channels: B channels, which carry voice, data, or images at a rate of 64 Kbps (kilobits per second); and a D channel, which carries control information, signaling, and link management data at 16 Kbps. Standard ISDN Basic Rate desktop service is called 2B+D. Computers and other devices connect to ISDN lines through simple, standardized interfaces.

interfaces   Boundaries that separate layers from each other. For example, in the OSI reference model, each layer provides some service or action that prepares the data for delivery over the network to another computer.

International Organization for Standardization (ISO)   An organization made up of standards-setting groups from various countries. For example, the United States member is the American National Standards Institute (ANSI). The ISO works to establish global standards for communications and information exchange. Primary among its accomplishments is development of the widely accepted OSI reference model. Note that the ISO is often wrongly identified as the International Standards Organization, probably because of the acronym *ISO*; however, ISO is derived from *isos*, which means *equal* in Greek, rather than an acronym.

Internet Connection Sharing (ICS)   A feature of Windows XP Professional that allows you to share one connection to the Internet with all computers on your network.

Internet Control Message Protocol (ICMP)   Used by Internet Protocol (IP) and higher level protocols to send and receive status reports about information being transmitted.

Internet Information Services (IIS)   Web server software built into Windows XP Professional that allows you to easily publish information on the Internet or on your or your company's intranet.

Internet Protocol (IP)   The TCP/IP protocol for packet forwarding. See also Transmission Control Protocol/Internet Protocol (TCP/IP).

Internet Protocol Security (IPSec)   A framework of open standards for ensuring secure private communications over IP networks by using cryptographic security services.

Internet service provider (ISP)   A company that provides individuals or companies access to the Internet and the World Wide Web. An ISP provides a telephone number, a user name, a password, and other connection information, so users can connect their computer to the ISP's computers. An ISP typically charges a monthly or hourly connection fee.

internetworking   The intercommunication in a network that is made up of smaller networks.

interoperability   The ability of components in one system to work with components in other systems.

interrupt request (IRQ)   An electronic signal sent to a computer's CPU to indicate that an event has taken place that requires the processor's attention.

intranet   A network within an organization that uses Internet technologies and protocols but is available only to certain people, such as employees of a company. An intranet is also called a private network.

IP   See Internet Protocol (IP), Transmission Control Protocol/Internet Protocol (TCP/IP).

IP address   A 32-bit address used to identify a node on an Internet Protocol (IP) internetwork. Each node on the IP internetwork must be assigned a unique IP address, which is made up of the network ID plus a unique host ID. This address is typically represented with the decimal value of each octet separated by a period (for example, 192.168.7.23). In Windows XP Professional, the IP addresses can be configured manually, or if you have a computer running Windows 2000 Server and DHCP, the IP addresses can be configured dynamically. See also Dynamic Host Configuration Protocol (DHCP).

ipconfig A diagnostic command that displays all current TCP/IP network configuration values. It is of particular use on systems running DHCP because it allows users to determine which TCP/IP configuration values have been configured by the DHCP server.

IPSec See Internet Protocol Security (IPSec).

IRQ See interrupt request (IRQ).

ISA See Industry Standard Architecture (ISA).

ISDN See Integrated Services Digital Network (ISDN).

ISO See International Organization for Standardization (ISO).

ISP See Internet service provider (ISP).

J

jumper A small, plastic-and-metal plug or wire for connecting different points in an electronic circuit. Jumpers are used to select a particular circuit or option from several possible configurations. Jumpers can be used on network interface cards to select the type of connection through which the card will transmit, either DIX or BNC.

K

K See kilo (K).

KB See kilobyte (KB).

Kbit See kilobit (Kbit).

Kerberos authentication protocol An authentication mechanism used to verify user or host identity. The Kerberos v.5 authentication protocol is the default authentication service for Windows XP Professional. Internet Protocol security and the QoS Admission Control Service use the Kerberos protocol for authentication.

key In database management, an identifier for a record or group of records in a data file. Most often, the key is defined as the contents of a single field (called the key field in some database management programs and the index field in others). Keys are maintained in tables and are indexed to speed record retrieval. Keys also refer to code that deciphers encrypted data.

kilo (K) Refers to 1000 in the metric system. In computing terminology, because computing is based on powers of 2, kilo is most often used to mean 1024 (2 raised to the 10th power). To distinguish between the two contexts, a lowercase k is often used to indicate 1000 and an uppercase K indicates 1024. A kilobyte is 1024 bytes.

kilobit (Kbit) 1024 bits. See also bit, kilo (K).

kilobyte (KB) 1024 bytes. See also byte, kilo (K).

L

L2TP   See Layer Two Tunneling Protocol (L2TP).

LAN   See local area network (LAN).

LAN requester   See requester (LAN requester).

Last Known Good configuration   A hardware configuration that is available by pressing the F8 key during startup. The Last Known Good configuration contains the configuration information saved after the last successful logon.

LAT   See local area transport (LAT).

layering   The coordination of various protocols in a specific architecture that allows the protocols to work together to ensure that the data is prepared, transferred, received, and acted on as intended.

Layer Two Tunneling Protocol (L2TP)   Its primary purpose is to create an encrypted tunnel through an untrusted network. L2TP is similar to Point-to-Point Tunneling Protocol (PPTP) in that it provides tunneling but not encryption. L2TP provides a secure tunnel by cooperating with other encryption technologies such as IPSec. L2TP functions with IPSec to provide a secure virtual private network solution.

line printer   A connectivity tool that runs on client systems and is used to print files to a computer running an LPD server.

Line Printer Daemon (LPD)   A service on the print server that receives documents (print jobs) from Line Printer Remote (LPR) tools running on client systems.

link   The communication system that connects two local area networks (LANs). Also refers to Equipment that provides the link, including bridges, routers, and gateways.

local area network (LAN)   Computers connected in a geographically confined network, such as in the same building, campus, or office park.

local area transport (LAT)   A nonroutable protocol from Digital Equipment Corporation.

local computer   A computer that can be accessed directly without using a communications line or a communications device, such as a network adapter or a modem.

local group   One type of group account used by Windows XP. Implemented in each local computer's account database, local groups contain user accounts and other global groups that need to have access, rights, and permissions assigned to a resource on a local computer. Local groups cannot contain other local groups.

local printer   A printer that is connected to a physical port on the print server.

local security database   A database on a computer running Windows XP Professional that holds local user accounts and groups.

Local Security Policy   A combination of settings applied during startup that affect a local computer.

local user account   An account that allows you to log on to a specific computer to access resources on that computer.

logical drive   A volume created within an extended partition on a basic disk. You can format and assign a drive letter to a logical drive. Only basic disks can contain logical drives. A logical drive cannot span multiple disks.

Logical Link Control (LLC) sublayer   One of two sublayers created by the IEEE 802 project out of the data-link layer of the OSI reference model. The LLC is the upper sublayer that manages data-link communication and defines the use of logical interface points, called service access points (SAPs), used by computers to transfer information from the LLC sublayer to the upper OSI layers. See also media access control (MAC) sublayer, service access point (SAP).

logical printer   The software configuration that is created in Windows and displayed in Printers And Faxes.

logical structure   The administrative structure of Active Directory that includes domains, trees, organizational units, and objects.

logon right   A user right assigned to a group or an individual user account that controls the way users can log on to a system.

logon script   Files that can be assigned to user accounts. Typically a batch file, a logon script runs automatically every time the user logs on. It can be used to configure a user's working environment at every logon, and it allows an administrator to influence a user's environment without managing all aspects of it. A logon script can be assigned to one or more user accounts.

loopback address   A special reserved IP address that represents the local computer.

LPD   See Line Printer Daemon (LPD).

M

marker   An archive attribute that marks a file as having been backed up. During incremental or differential backups, markers are used to determine whether a file has changed since the last backup.

Master Boot Record (MBR)   The first sector on a hard disk, this data structure starts the process of booting the computer. The MBR contains the partition table for the disk and a small amount of executable code called the master boot code.

MB   See megabyte (MB).

Mb   See megabit (Mb).

Mbps   See millions of bits per second (Mbps).

MBR   See Master Boot Record (MBR).

media   The vast majority of local area networks (LANs) today are connected by some sort of wire or cabling that acts as the LAN transmission medium, carrying data between computers. The cabling is often referred to as the media.

media access control (MAC) driver   The device driver located at the media access control sublayer of the OSI reference model. This driver is also known as the NIC driver. It provides low-level access to network interface cards (NICs) by providing data-transmission support and some basic NIC management functions. These drivers also pass data from the physical layer to transport protocols at the network and transport layers.

media access control (MAC) sublayer   One of two sublayers created by the IEEE 802 project out of the data-link layer of the OSI reference model. The MAC sublayer communicates directly with the network interface card and is responsible for delivering error-free data between two computers on the network. See also Logical Link Control (LLC) sublayer.

megabit (Mb)   Usually, 1,048,576 bits (2 raised to the 20th power); sometimes interpreted as 1 million bits. See also bit.

megabyte (MB)   1,048,576 bytes (2 raised to the 20th power); sometimes interpreted as 1 million bytes. See also byte.

Member server   A computer running Windows 2000 Server or Windows Server 2003 that is a member of an Active Directory domain but is not a domain controller.

Microsoft Technical Information Network (TechNet)   Provides informational support for all aspects of networking, with an emphasis on Microsoft products.

millions of bits per second (Mbps)   The unit of measure of supported transmission rates on the following physical media: coaxial cable, twisted-pair cable, and fiber-optic cable. See also bit.

mobile computing   Incorporates wireless adapters using cellular telephone technology to connect portable computers with the cabled network.

modem   A communications device that enables a computer to transmit information over a standard telephone line. Because a computer is digital, it works with discrete electrical signals representing binary 1 and binary 0. A telephone is analog and carries a signal that can have many variations. Modems are needed to convert digital signals to analog and back. When transmitting, modems impose (modulate) a computer's digital signals onto a continuous carrier frequency on the telephone line. When receiving, modems sift out (demodulate) the information from the carrier and transfer it in digital form to the computer.

mounted volume   A volume to which you assign a path on an existing volume rather than a drive letter.

multitasking   A mode of operation offered by an operating system in which a computer works on more than one task at a time. There are two primary types of multitasking: preemptive and nonpreemptive. In preemptive multitasking, the operating system can take control of the processor without the task's cooperation. In nonpreemptive multitasking, the processor is never taken from a task—the task itself decides when to give up the processor. A true multitasking operating system can run as many tasks as it has processors. When there are more tasks than processors, the computer must "time slice" so that the available processors devote a certain amount of time to one task and then move on to the next task, alternating between tasks until all are completed.

N

namespace   Any bounded area in which a name can be resolved. Name resolution is the process of translating a name into some object or information that the name represents. The Active Directory namespace is based on the Domain Name System (DNS) naming scheme, which allows for interoperability with Internet technologies.

naming convention   An organization's established standard for identifying users.

nbtstat   A diagnostic command that displays protocol statistics and current Transmission Control Protocol/Internet Protocol (TCP/IP) connections using NetBIOS over TCP/IP (NetBT). This command is available only if the TCP/IP protocol has been installed. See also netstat.

NDIS   See Network Device Interface Specification (NDIS).

NetBEUI (NetBIOS Extended User Interface)   A protocol supplied with all Microsoft network products. NetBEUI advantages include small stack size (important for MS-DOS-based computers), speed of data transfer on the network medium, and compatibility with all Microsoft-based networks. The major drawback of NetBEUI is that it is a local area network (LAN) transport protocol and therefore does not support routing. It is also limited to Microsoft-based networks.

NetBIOS (network basic input/output system)   An application programming interface (API) that can be used by application programs on a local area network (LAN) consisting of IBM-compatible microcomputers running MS-DOS, OS/2, or some version of UNIX. Primarily of interest to programmers, NetBIOS provides application programs with a uniform set of commands for requesting the lower level network services required to conduct sessions between nodes on a network and transmit information between them.

NetBIOS over TCP/IP   The session-layer network service that performs name-to-IP address mapping for name resolution.

NetBT   See NetBIOS over TCP/IP.

netstat   A diagnostic command that displays protocol statistics and current Transmission Control Protocol/Internet Protocol (TCP/IP) network connections. This command is available only if the TCP/IP protocol has been installed. See also nbtstat.

network   In the context of computers, a system in which a number of independent computers are linked together to share data and peripherals, such as hard disks and printers.

network adapter card   See network interface card (NIC).

Network Device Interface Specification (NDIS)   A standard that defines an interface for communication between the media access control (MAC) sublayer and protocol drivers. NDIS allows for a flexible environment of data exchange. It defines the software interface, called the NDIS interface, which is used by protocol drivers to communicate with the network interface card. The advantage of NDIS is that it offers protocol multiplexing so that multiple protocol stacks can be used at the same time. See also Open Data-link Interface (ODI).

Network Bridge   A feature that allows Windows XP Professional to connect network segments (groups of networked computers) without having to use a router or bridge.

network ID   The portion of the IP address that identifies a particular host on a network segment.

network interface card (NIC)   An expansion card installed in each computer and server on the network. The NIC acts as the physical interface or connection between the computer and the network cable.

network interface printer   A printer that is connected directly to the network via an internal network adapter.

network layer   The third layer in the OSI reference model. This layer is responsible for addressing messages and translating logical addresses and names into physical addresses. This layer also determines the route from the source to the destination computer. It determines which path the data should take based on network conditions, priority of service, and other factors. It also manages traffic problems such as switching, routing, and controlling the congestion of data packets on the network. See also Open Systems Interconnection (OSI) reference model.

network monitors   Monitors that track all or a selected part of network traffic. They examine frame-level packets and gather information about packet types, errors, and packet traffic to and from each computer.

New Connection Wizard   A wizard in Windows XP Professional that can perform much of the work of configuring a network connection for different situations.

NIC   See network interface card (NIC).

node On a local area network (LAN), a device that is connected to the network and is capable of communicating with other network devices. For example, clients, servers, and repeaters are called nodes.

nonpreemptive multitasking A form of multitasking in which the processor is never taken from a task. The task itself decides when to give up the processor. Programs written for nonpreemptive multitasking systems must include provisions for yielding control of the processor. No other program can run until the nonpreemptive program gives up control of the processor. See also multitasking, preemptive multitasking.

normal backup A backup type in which all selected files and folders are backed up, regardless of their marker. During a normal backup, all files are marked as having been backed up.

NTFS compression A function of the NTFS file system that performs dynamic compression and decompression on folders and files marked with the compression attribute.

NTFS permissions Assignments that specify which users and groups can access files and folders and what they can do with the contents of the files or folders. NTFS permissions are available only on NTFS volumes.

NTLDR A file used to control the Windows startup process until control is passed to the Windows kernel.

O

object A distinct, named set of attributes that represent a network resource. Object attributes are characteristics of objects in the Active Directory directory. For example, the attributes of a user account might include the user's first and last names, department, and e-mail address.

ODI See Open Data-link Interface (ODI).

Offline Files A feature of Windows XP Professional that makes temporary copies of shared network files on a local computer so that you can access those files when the local computer is disconnected from the network.

Open Data-link Interface (ODI) A specification defined by Novell and Apple to simplify driver development and to provide support for multiple protocols on a single network interface card. Similar to Network Device Interface Specification (NDIS) in many respects, ODI allows Novell NetWare drivers to be written without concern for the protocol that will be used on top of them.

Open Systems Interconnection (OSI) reference model   A seven-layer architecture that standardizes levels of service and types of interaction for computers exchanging information through a network. It is used to describe the flow of data between the physical connection to the network and the end user application. This model is the best-known and most widely used model for describing networking environments.

organizational unit (OU)   A container used to organize objects within a domain into logical administrative groups. An OU can contain objects such as user accounts, groups, computers, printers, applications, file shares, and other OUs.

OSI   See Open Systems Interconnection (OSI) reference model.

OU   See organizational unit (OU).

Owner   The user who created a file, folder, or printer.

P

packet   A unit of information transmitted as a whole from one device to another on a network. In packet-switching networks, a packet is defined more specifically as a transmission unit of fixed maximum size that consists of binary digits representing data; a header containing an identification number, a source, and destination addresses; and sometimes error-control data. See also frame.

Packet Internet Groper (ping)   A simple tool that tests if a network connection is complete, from the server to the workstation, by sending a message to the remote computer. If the remote computer receives the message, it responds with a reply message. The reply consists of the remote workstation's Internet Protocol (IP) address, the number of bytes in the message, how long it took to reply—given in milliseconds (ms)—and the length of Time to Live (TTL) in seconds. Ping works at the IP level and often responds even when higher level TCP-based services cannot respond.

packet switching   A message delivery technique in which small units of information (packets) are relayed through stations in a computer network along the best route available between the source and the destination. Data is broken into smaller units and then repacked in a process called packet assembly/disassembly (PAD). Although each packet can travel along a different path, and the packets composing a message can arrive at different times or out of sequence, the receiving computer reassembles the original message. Packet-switching networks are considered fast and efficient. Standards for packet switching on networks are documented in the CCITT recommendation X.25.

page-description language (PDL)   A language that communicates to a printer how printed output should appear. The printer uses the PDL to construct text and graphics to create the page image. PDLs are like blueprints in that they set parameters and features such as type sizes and fonts, but leave the drawing to the printer.

page fault   An error that occurs when the requested code or data cannot be located in the physical memory that is available to the requesting process.

paging   The process of moving virtual memory back and forth between physical memory (RAM) and the disk. Paging occurs when physical memory becomes full.

paging file   A special file on one or more of the hard disks of a computer running Windows XP Professional. Windows XP Professional uses virtual memory to store some of the program code and other information in RAM and to temporarily store some of the program code and other information on the computer's hard disks. This increases the amount of available memory on the computer.

parity   An error-checking procedure in which the number of 1s must always be the same—either odd or even—for each group of bits transmitted without error. Parity is used for checking data transferred within a computer or between computers.

partition   A logical division of a hard disk that functions as if it were a physically separate unit. Each partition can be formatted for a different file system.

password-protected share   Access to a shared resource that is granted when a user enters the appropriate password.

password reset disk   A removable disk on which is stored a file that allows a user to recover a user account when the user forgets his or her password.

Pathping   A command-line tool that is a combination of both Ping and Tracert, displaying information about packet loss at every router between the host computer and the remote one.

PCI   See Peripheral Component Interconnect (PCI).

PDA   See personal digital assistant (PDA).

PDL   See page-description language (PDL).

PDN   See public data network (PDN).

peer-to-peer network   A network in which there are no dedicated servers or hierarchy among the computers. All computers are equal and therefore known as peers. Generally, each computer functions as both client and server.

Performance Console   A tool that is used to monitor resource usage on a computer running Windows XP Professional. The Performance Console provides access to two snap-ins: System Monitor and Performance Logs And Alerts.

Performance Logs And Alerts   A snap-in that collects performance data over time from the local or a remote computer or that has Windows XP alert you when a particular performance threshold is crossed.

peripheral A term used for devices such as disk drives, printers, modems, mouse devices, and joysticks that are connected to a computer and controlled by its microprocessor.

Peripheral Component Interconnect (PCI) 32-bit local bus used in most Pentium computers and in the Apple Power Macintosh. Meets most of the requirements for providing Plug and Play functionality.

permanent virtual circuit (PVC) A permanent logical connection between two nodes on a packet-switching network; similar to leased lines that are permanent and virtual, except that with PVC the customer pays only for the time the line is used. This type of connection service is gaining importance because both frame relay and ATM use it. See also packet switching, virtual circuit.

permissions See access permissions.

permissions inheritance The process of a file or folder receiving permissions based on the permissions assigned to the object's parent folder.

personal digital assistant (PDA) A type of handheld computer that provides functions including personal organization features—such as calendar, note-taking device, database manipulation, calculator, and communications functions. For communication, a PDA uses cellular or wireless technology that is often built into the system but can be supplemented or enhanced by means of a PC card.

petabyte See byte.

phase change rewritable (PCR) A type of rewritable optical technology in which the optical devices come from one manufacturer (Matsushita/Panasonic) and the media come from two manufacturers (Panasonic and Plasmon).

physical layer The first (bottom) layer of the OSI reference model. This layer addresses the transmission of the unstructured raw bitstream over a physical medium (the networking cable). The physical layer relates the electrical/optical, mechanical, and functional interfaces to the cable and also carries the signals that transmit data generated by all of the higher OSI layers. See also Open Systems Interconnection (OSI) reference model.

ping See Packet Internet Groper (ping).

Plug and Play A set of specifications developed by Intel that allows a computer to automatically detect and configure a device and install the appropriate device drivers.

point of presence (POP) The local access point for a network provider. Each POP provides a telephone number that allows users to make a local call for access to online services.

point-to-point configuration   Dedicated circuits that are also known as private, or leased, lines. They are the most popular wide area network (WAN) communication circuits in use today. The carrier guarantees full-duplex bandwidth by setting up a permanent link from each end point, using bridges and routers to connect local area networks (LANs) through the circuits. See also Point-to-Point Protocol (PPP), Point-to-Point Tunneling Protocol (PPTP), duplex transmission.

Point-to-Point Protocol (PPP)   A data-link protocol for transmitting Transmission Control Protocol/Internet Protocol (TCP/IP) packets over dial-up telephone connections, such as between a computer and the Internet. PPP was developed by the Internet Engineering Task Force in 1991.

Point-to-Point Tunneling Protocol (PPTP)   An extension of the Point-to-Point Protocol (PPP) used for communications on the Internet. It was developed by Microsoft to support virtual private networks (VPNs), which allow individuals and organizations to use the Internet as a secure means of communication. PPTP supports encapsulation of encrypted packets in secure wrappers that can be transmitted over a Transmission Control Protocol/Internet Protocol (TCP/IP) connection. See also virtual private network (VPN).

POP   See point of presence (POP).

Power scheme   Allows you to configure Windows XP Professional to turn off the power to your monitor and your hard disk, conserving energy.

Preboot eXecution Environment (PXE)   A standard for network booting that is supported by some network adapters. Using a PXE-compliant network adapter is one of three configurations that will allow a RIS client to boot from the network and locate a RIS server. (RIS clients can also be compliant with the Net PC specification or use an RIS boot disk.)

preemptive multitasking   A form of multitasking (the capability of a computer's operating system to work on more than one task at a time). With preemptive multitasking—as opposed to nonpreemptive multitasking—the operating system can take control of the processor without the task's cooperation. See also nonpreemptive multitasking.

presentation layer   The sixth layer of the OSI reference model. This layer determines the form used to exchange data between networked computers. At the sending computer, this layer translates data from a format sent down from the application layer into a commonly recognized, intermediary format. At the receiving end, this layer translates the intermediary format into a format useful to that computer's application layer. The presentation layer manages network security issues by providing services such as data encryption, provides rules for data transfer, and performs data compression to reduce the number of bits that need to be transmitted. See also Open Systems Interconnection (OSI) reference model.

primary display   The default display in a multiple display configuration. You can often change which video adapter controls the primary display by changing settings in the computer's BIOS.

primary partition   A partition that you can configure as the active, or bootable, drive. You can configure up to four primary partitions on a computer running a Windows operating system (three partitions if you also have an extended partition on the disk).

print job   A document that Windows has prepared for printing.

print permissions   Permissions that enable you to control which users can access a printer and which actions they can perform.

print processor   Software that is responsible for processing print documents into a format that is suitable to be sent to the printer. Windows XP contains only the Win-Print processor by default.

print queue   A buffer in which a print job is held until the printer is ready to print it.

print server   The computer on which the printers reside. The print server receives and processes documents from client computers. You set up and share network printers on print servers.

print spooling   The process of saving a print job to the hard disk before sending it to the printer.

printer   The physical device used for printing. This device is usually a standard printer, but it can also be a fax device, a plotter, or a file. It might also refer to the combination of the physical and logical printer.

printer driver   One or more files containing information that Windows XP Professional requires to convert print commands into a specific printer language, such as PostScript. A printer driver is specific to each print device model.

printer pool   A printing option that permits you to attach two or more printers to a single printer configuration.

printer port   The software interface through which a computer communicates with a print device by means of a locally attached interface. These supported interfaces include LPT, COM, USB, and network-attached devices such as the HP JetDirect and Intel NetPort.

printer priority   Governs the order in which print jobs are printed relative to other logical printers configured for the same printer.

printer redirecting   The process of sending a document to another printer. You can redirect only all documents for a printer, not individual documents. Also, you can redirect documents only to printers that use the same printer driver as the original printer.

private key The secret half of a cryptographic key pair that is used with a public key algorithm. Private keys are typically used to digitally sign data and to decrypt data that has been encrypted with the corresponding public key.

privilege A user right that allows the members of the group to which it is assigned to perform a specific task, usually one that affects an entire computer system rather than one object.

process An operating system object that consists of an executable program, a set of virtual memory addresses, and one or more threads. When a program runs, a process is created.

processor affinity A setting made in Task Manager that determines on which processors (on a multiple-processor computer) a process can run.

protocol The system of rules and procedures that govern communication between two or more devices. Many varieties of protocols exist, and not all are compatible, but as long as two devices are using the same protocol, they can exchange data. Networking software usually implements multiple levels of protocols layered one on top of another. Windows XP Professional includes TCP/IP- and IPX/SPX-compatible protocols.

protocol driver The driver responsible for offering four or five basic services to other layers in the network while "hiding" the details of how the services are actually implemented. Services performed include session management, datagram service, data segmentation and sequencing, acknowledgment, and possibly routing across a wide area network (WAN).

protocol stack A layered set of protocols that work together to provide a set of network functions.

proxy server A firewall component that manages Internet traffic to and from a local area network (LAN). The proxy server decides whether it is safe to let a particular message or file pass through to the organization's network, provides access control to the network, and filters and discards requests as specified by the owner—including requests for unauthorized access to proprietary data. See also firewall.

public data network (PDN) A commercial packet-switching or circuit-switching wide area network (WAN) service provided by local and long-distance telephone carriers.

public key The nonsecret half of a cryptographic key pair that is used with a public algorithm. Public keys are typically used to verify digital signatures or decrypt data that has been encrypted with the corresponding private key.

PVC See permanent virtual circuit (PVC).

PXE See Preboot eXecution Environment (PXE).

Q

QoS   See quality of service.

quality of service (QoS)   A set of quality assurance standards and mechanisms for data transmission.

R

RADIUS   See Remote Authentication Dial-In User Service (RADIUS).

RAID   See redundant array of independent disks (RAID).

RAM   See random access memory (RAM).

random access memory (RAM)   Semiconductor-based memory that can be read and written to by the microprocessor or other hardware devices. The storage locations can be accessed in any order. Note that the various types of read-only memory (ROM) are also capable of random access. However, RAM is generally understood to refer to volatile memory, which can be written as well as read. See also read-only memory (ROM).

RDN   See relative distinguished name (RDN).

read-only memory (ROM)   Semiconductor-based memory that contains instructions or data that can be read but not modified. See also random access memory (RAM).

recovery agent   A user account that is given the capability to decrypt an encrypted file or folder in case the owner of the resource loses the file encryption certificate that allows decryption.

Recovery Console   A command-line console interface that provides access to the hard disks and a limited set of administrative commands useful for recovering a computer.

redirector   Networking software that accepts input/output (I/O) requests for remote files, named pipes or mail slots, and sends (redirects) the requests to a network service on another computer.

Reduced Instruction Set Computing (RISC)   A type of microprocessor design that focuses on rapid and efficient processing of a relatively small set of instructions. RISC architecture limits the number of instructions that are built into the microprocessor, but it optimizes each so it can be carried out very rapidly, usually within a single clock cycle.

redundancy system   A fault-tolerant system that protects data by duplicating it in different physical sources. Data redundancy allows access to data even if part of the data system fails. See also fault tolerance.

redundant array of independent disks (RAID)   A standardization of fault-tolerant options in five levels. The levels offer various combinations of performance, reliability, and cost. Formerly known as redundant array of inexpensive disks.

redundant array of inexpensive disks (RAID)   See redundant array of independent disks (RAID).

Registry   In Windows XP Professional, Windows 2000, Windows NT, Windows 98, and Windows 95, a database of information about a computer's configuration. The Registry is organized in a hierarchical structure and consists of subtrees and their keys, hives, and entries.

relative distinguished name (RDN)   A name that uniquely identifies an object within a particular OU.

Remote Assistance   A utility that allows a user to invite an administrator or other expert user to provide help remotely.

Remote Authentication Dial-In User Service (RADIUS)   A security authentication protocol widely used by Internet service providers (ISPs). RADIUS provides authentication and accounting services for distributed dial-up networking.

remote-boot PROM (programmable read-only memory)   A special chip in the network interface card that contains the hardwired code that starts the computer and connects the user to the network, used in computers for which there are no hard disk or floppy drives. See also diskless computers.

Remote Desktop   A utility that allows you to control a computer from a remote location.

remote installation   The process of connecting to a server running Remote Installation Services (RIS), called the RIS server, and then starting an automated installation of Windows XP Professional on a local computer.

Remote Installation Services (RIS)   Software that stores images of Windows XP installations and makes those images available over the network.

remote user   A user who dials in to the server over modems and telephone lines from a remote location.

removable storage device   A storage device that allows you to remove either the device itself or the storage media that the device uses.

replication   The process of copying information from one location to another. In Active Directory, replication of directory information happens automatically between domain controllers in the same site.

requester (LAN requester)   Software that resides in a computer and forwards requests for network services from the computer's application programs to the appropriate server. See also redirector.

Request for Comments (RFC)   A document that defines a standard. RFCs are published by the Internet Engineering Task Force (IETF) and other working groups.

resource publishing   The process of making an object visible and accessible to users in a Windows 2000 domain.

resources   Any part of a computer system. Users on a network can share computer resources, such as hard disks, printers, modems, CD-ROM drives, and even the processor.

restore point   A saved snapshot of the Registry and important system and application files that is created using the System Restore utility.

Resultant Set of Policy   A tool that provides a way for you to simulate and test policy settings applied to computers or users. It shows you the policies applied to the object and the order in which they are applied.

RFC   See Request for Comments (RFC).

rights   Authorization with which a user is entitled to perform certain actions on a computer network. Rights apply to the system as a whole, whereas permissions apply to specific objects. For example, a user might have the right to back up an entire computer system, including the files that the user does not have permission to access. See also access permissions.

RIP   See Routing Information Protocol (RIP).

RIS   See Remote Installation Services (RIS).

RISC   See Reduced Instruction Set Computing (RISC).

Roll Back Driver   A feature in Windows XP that permits you to reinstall (roll back) a previously installed driver. The uninstalled drivers are stored in the system-root\system32\reinstallbackups folder.

ROM   See read-only memory (ROM).

routable protocol   The protocol that supports multipath LAN-to-LAN communications. See also protocol.

router   A device used to connect networks of different types, such as those using different architectures and protocols. Routers work at the network layer of the OSI reference model. They can switch and route packets across multiple networks, which they do by exchanging protocol-specific information between separate networks. Routers determine the best path for sending data and filter broadcast traffic to the local segment.

Routing Information Protocol (RIP)   A protocol that uses distance-vector algorithms to determine routes. With RIP, routers transfer information among other routers to update their internal routing tables and use that information to determine the best routes based on hop counts between routers. TCP/IP and IPX support RIP.

RS-232 standard   An industry standard for serial communication connections. Adopted by the Electrical Industries Association (EIA), this recommended standard defines the specific lines and signal characteristics used by serial communications controllers to standardize the transmission of serial data between devices.

S

safe mode   A method of starting Windows XP Professional using basic files and drivers only, without networking. Safe mode is available by pressing the F8 key when prompted during startup. Safe mode allows the computer to start when a problem prevents it from starting normally.

SAP (service access point)   See service access point (SAP).

SAP (Service Advertising Protocol)   See Service Advertising Protocol (SAP).

Scheduled Tasks   A feature of Windows XP Professional that lets you schedule programs, scripts, batch files, or documents to run once, at regular intervals, or at specific times.

schema   Contains a formal definition of the contents and structure of Active Directory, including all attributes, classes, and class properties. For each object class, the schema defines what attributes an instance of the class must have, what additional attributes it can have, and what object class can be a parent of the current object class.

Screen Resolution   A setting that allows you to set the number of pixels Windows uses to display the Desktop.

SCSI   See Small Computer System Interface (SCSI).

SDLC   See Synchronous Data Link Control (SDLC).

Secondary Logon Service   A service in Windows XP Professional that allows a user to run a program (using the Run As command) with different credentials from the currently logged-on user.

sector   A portion of the data-storage area on a disk. A disk is divided into sides (top and bottom), tracks (rings on each surface), and sectors (sections of each ring). Sectors are the smallest physical storage units on a disk and are of fixed size—typically capable of holding 512 bytes of information each.

sector sparing   A fault-tolerant system also called hot fixing. It automatically adds sector-recovery capabilities to the file system during operation. If bad sectors are found during disk I/O, the fault-tolerant driver will attempt to move the data to a good sector and map out the bad sector. If the mapping is successful, the file system is not alerted. It is possible for SCSI devices to perform sector sparing, but AT devices (ESDI and IDE) cannot.

security   Making computers and the data stored on them safe from harm or unauthorized access.

Security Center   A feature of Windows XP Professional with Service Pack 2 that provides at-a-glance security status for a computer, including information on Windows Firewall, Automatic Updates, and antivirus software.

Security Identifier (SID)   A data structure of variable length that uniquely identifies user, group, service, and computer accounts within an enterprise. Every account is issued an SID when the account is first created. Access control mechanisms in Windows XP Professional and Windows 2000 identify security principals by SID rather than by name.

security log   Records security events, such as valid and invalid logon attempts, and events relating to creating, opening, or deleting files or other objects.

Security options   Policies that allow you to control various security settings in Windows XP Professional.

security templates   Preconfigured combinations of security settings that you can apply to computers or customize to suit your needs.

security zones   Categories of Web sites that Internet Explorer uses to allow or block access to particular types of activities. Zones include Internet, Local Intranet, Trusted Sites, and Restricted Sites.

segment   The length of cable on a network between two terminators. A segment can also refer to messages that have been broken up into smaller units by the protocol driver.

separator page   A file that contains print device commands. Separator pages identify and separate print jobs and can also be used to switch a printer to a different print mode.

serial transmission   One-way data transfer. The data travels on a network cable with one bit following another.

server   A computer that provides shared resources to network users. See also client.

server-based network   A network in which resource security and most other network functions are provided by dedicated servers. Server-based networks have become the standard model for networks serving more than 10 users. See also peer-to-peer network.

Server Message Block (SMB)   The protocol developed by Microsoft, Intel, and IBM that defines a series of commands used to pass information between network computers. The redirector packages SMB requests into a network control block (NCB) structure that can be sent over the network to a remote device. The network provider listens for SMB messages destined for it and removes the data portion of the SMB request so that it can be processed by a local device.

service   A program or process that runs in the background on a computer to perform particular system functions for other programs.

service access point (SAP)   The interface between each of the seven layers in the OSI protocol stack that has connection points, similar to addresses, used for communication between layers. Any protocol layer can have multiple SAPs active at one time.

Service Advertising Protocol (SAP)   Allows service-providing nodes (including file, printer, gateway, and application servers) to advertise their services and addresses.

service dependency   The other services that must be running for a service to start, as well as the services that cannot start until the service in question starts.

Service Pack   A software upgrade to an existing software distribution that contains updated files consisting of patches and fixes.

session   A connection or link between stations on a network.

session layer   The fifth layer of the OSI reference model. This layer allows two applications on different computers to establish, use, and end a connection called a session. This layer performs name recognition and functions, such as security, needed to allow two applications to communicate over the network. The session layer provides synchronization between user tasks. This layer also implements dialog control between communicating processes, regulating which side transmits, when, for how long, and so on. See also Open Systems Interconnection (OSI) reference model.

session management   Establishing, maintaining, and terminating connections between stations on the network.

shared folder   A folder made accessible to users on the network.

shared folder permissions   Permissions assigned to shared folders that control access to the folder over the network. Shared folder permissions include Read, Change, and Full Control.

sharing   Means by which files of folders are publicly posted on a network for access by anyone on the network.

shell   A piece of software, usually a separate program, that provides direct communication between the user and the operating system. This usually, but not always, takes the form of a command-line interface. Examples of shells are Macintosh Finder and the MS-DOS command interface program COMMAND.COM.

SID   See Security Identifier (SID).

Simple File Sharing   A type of sharing that is used when a Windows XP computer has not joined a domain or is running Windows XP Home Edition.

Simple Mail Transfer Protocol (SMTP)   A TCP/IP protocol for transferring e-mail. See also application protocols, Transmission Control Protocol/Internet Protocol (TCP/IP).

Simple Network Management Protocol (SNMP)   A network management protocol installed with TCP/IP and widely used on TCP/IP and IPX networks. SNMP transports management information and commands between a management program run by an administrator and the network management agent running on a host. The SNMP agent sends status information to one or more hosts when the host requests it or when a significant event occurs.

simple volume   A dynamic volume that contains disk space from a single disk and can be extended if necessary.

simultaneous peripheral operation on line (spool)   Facilitates the process of moving a print job from the network into a printer.

site   A combination of one or more Internet Protocol (IP) subnets, typically connected by a high-speed link.

Small Computer System Interface (SCSI)   A standard, high-speed parallel interface defined by the ANSI. A SCSI interface is used for connecting microcomputers to peripheral devices, such as hard disks and printers, and to other computers and LANs. Pronounced "scuzzy."

smart card   A credit card–sized device that is used with a PIN number to enable certificate-based authentication and single sign on to the enterprise. Smart cards securely store certificates, public and private keys, passwords, and other types of personal information. A smart card reader attached to the computer reads the smart card.

SMB   See Server Message Block (SMB).

SMDS   See Switched Multimegabit Data Services (SMDS).

SMP   See symmetric multiprocessing (SMP).

SMTP   See Simple Mail Transfer Protocol (SMTP).

SNMP   See Simple Network Management Protocol (SNMP).

software   Computer programs or sets of instructions that allow the hardware to work. Software can be grouped into four categories: system software, such as operating systems, which control the workings of the computer; application software, such as word processing programs, spreadsheets, and databases, which perform the tasks for which people use computers; network software, which enables groups of computers to communicate; and language software, which provides programmers with the tools they need to write programs.

SONET   See Synchronous Optical Network (SONET).

spanned volume   A dynamic volume that contains disk space from 2 or more (up to a maximum of 32) disks. The amount of disk space from each disk can vary. There is no fault tolerance in spanned volumes. If any of the disks containing the spanned volume fails, you lose all data in the entire spanned volume.

spanning tree algorithm (STA)   An algorithm (mathematical procedure) implemented to eliminate redundant routes and avoid situations in which multiple local area networks (LANs) are joined by more than one path by the IEEE 802.1 Network Management Committee. Under STA, bridges exchange certain control information in an attempt to find redundant routes. The bridges determine which is the most efficient route, and then use that one and disable the others. Any of the disabled routes can be reactivated if the primary route becomes unavailable.

SQL   See structured query language (SQL).

STA   See spanning tree algorithm (STA).

stand-alone computer   A computer that is not connected to any other computers and is not part of a network.

stand-alone environment   A work environment in which each user has a personal computer but works independently, unable to share files and other important information that would be readily available through server access in a networking environment.

stealth virus   A variant of the file-infector virus. This virus is so named because it attempts to hide from detection. When an antivirus program attempts to find it, the stealth virus tries to intercept the probe and return false information, indicating that it does not exist.

stop error   Also referred to as a blue-screen error, a stop error occurs when the system detects a condition from which it cannot recover.

striped volume   A dynamic volume that contains disk space from 2 or more (up to a maximum of 32) disks. Unlike spanned volumes, striped volumes require that you use an identical amount of disk space from each disk. Striped volumes provide increased performance because it is faster to read or write two smaller pieces of a file on two drives than to read or write the entire file on a single drive. However, you cannot extend striped volumes and they provide no fault tolerance.

structured query language (SQL)   A widely accepted standard database sublanguage used in querying, updating, and managing relational databases.

subnet   A subdivision of an Internet Protocol (IP) network. Each subnet has its own unique subnetted network ID.

subnet mask   A 32-bit value expressed as four decimal numbers from 0 to 255, separated by periods (for example, 255.255.255.0). This number allows TCP/IP to determine the network ID portion of an IP address.

Switched Multimegabit Data Services (SMDS)   A high-speed, switched-packet service that can provide speeds of up to 34 Mbps.

switched virtual circuit (SVC)   A logical connection between end computers that uses a specific route across the network. Network resources are dedicated to the circuit, and the route is maintained until the connection is terminated. These are also known as point-to-multipoint connections. See also virtual circuit.

symmetric multiprocessing (SMP)   SMP systems, such as Windows 2000, use any available processor on an as-needed basis. With this approach, the system load and application needs can be distributed evenly across all available processors.

Synchronization Manager   In Windows XP Professional, the tool used to ensure that a file or folder on a client computer contains the same data as a matching file or folder on a server.

Synchronous Data Link Control (SDLC)   The data link (data transmission) protocol most widely used in networks conforming to IBM's Systems Network Architecture (SNA). SDLC is a communications guideline that defines the format in which information is transmitted. As its name implies, SDLC applies to synchronous transmissions. SDLC is also a bit-oriented protocol and organizes information in structured units called frames.

Synchronous Optical Network (SONET)   A fiber-optic technology that can transmit data at more than one gigabit per second. Networks based on this technology are capable of delivering voice, data, and video. SONET is a standard for optical transport formulated by the Exchange Carriers Standards Association (ECSA) for the ANSI.

System Monitor   A snap-in that tracks resource use and network throughput in real time through the use of objects and counters.

system partition   Normally the same partition as the boot partition, this partition contains the hardware-specific files required to load and start Windows XP.

System Preparation   A utility that allows you to prepare master images of an existing Windows XP installation for distribution to other computers by removing machine-specific information from the computer.

System Restore   A utility that monitors changes to certain system and application files, and creates automatic restore points that contain a snapshot of the Registry and a copy of certain system files that Windows XP Professional requires for startup. You can also create restore points manually and restore the computer to any restore point.

systemroot   The path and folder name where the Windows XP Professional system files are located. Typically, this is C:\Windows, although a different drive or folder can be designated when Windows XP Professional is installed. The value of %systemroot% can be used to replace the actual location of the folder that contains the Windows XP Professional system files. To identify your systemroot folder, click Start, click Run, type **%systemroot%**, and click OK.

System State   Configuration information that includes the Windows Registry and important configuration files.

T

Task Manager   A tool that provides information about the programs and processes running on your computer and the performance of your computer.

TCO   See total cost of ownership (TCO).

TCP   See Transmission Control Protocol (TCP).

TCP/IP   See Transmission Control Protocol/Internet Protocol (TCP/IP).

TDI   See transport driver interface (TDI).

Technet   See Microsoft Technical Information Network (TechNet).

Telnet   The command and program used to log on from one Internet site to another. The Telnet command and program brings the user to the logon prompt of another host.

terabyte   See byte.

thread   A type of object within a process that runs program instructions. Using multiple threads allows concurrent operations within a process and enables one process to run different parts of its program on different processors simultaneously.

throughput   A measure of the data transfer rate through a component, connection, or system. In networking, throughput is a good indicator of the system's total performance because it defines how well the components work together to transfer data from one computer to another. In this case, the throughput would indicate how many bytes or packets the network could process per second.

topology   The arrangement or layout of computers, cables, and other components on a network. Topology is the standard term that most network professionals use when referring to the network's basic design.

total cost of ownership (TCO)   The total amount of money and time associated with purchasing computer hardware and software and deploying, configuring, and maintaining the hardware and software. It includes hardware and software updates, training, maintenance and administration, and technical support. One other major factor is lost productivity caused by user errors, hardware problems, software upgrades, and retraining.

tracert   A Trace Route command-line tool that shows every router interface through which a TCP/IP packet passes on its way to a destination.

trailer   One of the three sections of a packet component. The exact content of the trailer varies depending on the protocol, but it usually includes error checking in the form of a cyclical redundancy check (CRC).

Transmission Control Protocol (TCP)   The TCP/IP protocol for sequenced data. See also Transmission Control Protocol/Internet Protocol (TCP/IP).

Transmission Control Protocol/Internet Protocol (TCP/IP)   An industry standard suite of protocols providing communications in a heterogeneous environment. In addition, TCP/IP provides a routable enterprise networking protocol and access to the Internet and its resources. It is a transport layer protocol that actually consists of several other protocols in a stack that operates at the session layer. Most networks support TCP/IP as a protocol. See also Internet Protocol (IP).

transport driver interface (TDI)   An interface that works between the file-system driver and the transport protocols, allowing any protocol written to TDI to communicate with the file-system drivers.

transport layer   The fourth layer of the OSI reference model. It ensures that messages are delivered error-free, in sequence, and without losses or duplications. This layer repackages messages for efficient transmission over the network. At the receiving end, the transport layer unpacks the messages, reassembles the original messages, and sends an acknowledgment of receipt. See also Open Systems Interconnection (OSI) reference model.

transport protocol   A protocol that provides for communication sessions between computers and ensures that data can move reliably between computers.

Traverse Folder   A permission that allows or denies moving through folders to access other files or folders, even when the user has no permissions for the traversed folder (the folder that the user is moving through).

tree   A grouping of hierarchical arrangements of one or more Windows 2000 domains that share a contiguous namespace.

Trojan horse virus   A type of virus that appears to be a legitimate program that might be found on any system. A Trojan horse virus can destroy files and cause physical damage to disks.

trust relationship   A trust relationships is a link between domains that enables pass-through authentication, in which a user has only one user account in one domain but can access the entire network. User accounts and global groups defined in a trusted domain can be given rights and resource permissions in a trusting domain, even if those accounts do not exist in the trusting domain's database. A trusting domain honors the logon authentication of a trusted domain.

U

UDF   See uniqueness database file (UDF).

UDP   See User Datagram Protocol (UDP).

unattended installation   An automated installation in which the Winnt32 and Winnt commands are used along with an unattended answer file to script the installation.

UNC   See Universal Naming Convention (UNC).

Uniform Resource Locator (URL)   Provides the hypertext links between documents on the World Wide Web (WWW). Every resource on the Internet has its own URL that specifies the server to access as well as the access method and the location. URLs can use various protocols including File Transfer Protocol (FTP) and Hypertext Transfer Protocol (HTTP).

uninterruptible power supply (UPS)   A device connected between a computer or another piece of electronic equipment and a power source, such as an electrical outlet. The UPS ensures that the electrical flow to the computer is not interrupted because of a blackout and, in most cases, protects the computer against potentially damaging events such as power surges and brownouts. All UPS units are equipped with a battery and loss-of-power sensor. If the sensor detects a loss of power, it immediately switches to the battery so that users have time to save their work and shut off their computers. Most higher-end models have features such as power filtering, sophisticated surge protection, and a serial port so that an operating system capable of communicating with a UPS (such as Windows XP Professional) can work with the UPS to facilitate automatic system shutdown.

uniqueness database file (UDF)   A text file that is used in conjunction with an answer file and contains the settings that are unique to each computer.

Universal Naming Convention (UNC)   A convention for naming files and other resources beginning with two backslashes (\\), indicating that the resource exists on a network computer. UNC names conform to the \\Servername\Sharename syntax.

universal serial bus (USB)   A serial bus with a data transfer rate of 12 megabits per second (Mbps) for connecting peripherals to a microcomputer. USB can connect up to 127 peripheral devices to the system through a single general-purpose port. This is accomplished by daisy chaining peripherals together. USB is designed to support the ability to automatically add and configure new devices as well as the ability to add such devices without having to shut down and restart the system.

UPN   See user principal name (UPN).

UPS   See uninterruptible power supply (UPS).

URL   See Uniform Resource Locator (URL).

USB   See universal serial bus (USB).

user account   Consists of all of the information that defines a user on a network. This includes the user name and password required for the user to log on, the groups in which the user account has membership, and the rights and permissions the user has for using the system and accessing its resources. See also built-in group.

User Datagram Protocol (UDP)   A connection-less protocol that is responsible for end-to-end data transmission.

user groups   Groups of users who meet online or in person to discuss installation, administration, and other network challenges for the purpose of sharing and drawing on each other's expertise in developing ideas and solutions.

user principal name (UPN)   A "shorthand" name representing the user account and the DNS name of the tree where the user account object resides.

user profile   A collection of user-specific settings, such as a customized desktop or personalized application settings.

User rights   Rights that allow the members of a group or an individual user to perform a specific action, such as backing up files or changing the system time. User rights include privileges and logon rights.

User State Migration Tool (USMT)   A tool that lets administrators transfer user configuration settings and files from systems running Windows 95 or later to a clean Windows XP installation.

V

virtual circuit   A logical connection between two nodes on a packet-switching network. Similar to leased lines that are permanent and virtual, except that with a virtual circuit, the customer pays only for the time the line is used. This type of connection service is gaining importance because both frame relay and ATM use it. See also packet switching, permanent virtual circuit (PVC).

virtual memory   The space on one or more of a computer's hard drives used by Windows XP Professional as if it were random access memory (RAM). This space on the hard drives is known as a paging file. The benefit of virtual memory is being able to run more applications at one time than is possible by using just the RAM (physical memory) on the computer.

virtual private network (VPN)   Computers on a public network such as the Internet that communicate among themselves by using encryption technology. In this way, their messages are safe from being intercepted and understood by unauthorized users. VPNs operate as if the computers were connected by private lines.

virus Computer programming, or code, that hides in computer programs or on the boot sector of storage devices such as hard disk drives and floppy disk drives. The primary purpose of a virus is to reproduce itself as often as possible; a secondary purpose is to disrupt the operation of the computer or the program.

Visual Effects Desktop display features that look nice but often degrade a computer's performance.

volume set A collection of hard-disk partitions that are treated as a single partition, thus increasing the disk space available in a single drive letter. Volume sets are created by combining between 2 and 32 areas of unformatted free space on one or more physical drives. These spaces form one large logical volume set that is treated like a single partition.

VPN See virtual private network (VPN).

W

WAN See wide area network (WAN).

WEP See Wired Equivalent Privacy (WEP).

wide area network (WAN) A computer network that uses long-range telecommunication links to connect networked computers across long distances.

Wi-Fi Protected Access (WPA) A wireless encryption standard available in Windows XP Professional that provides increased security over the Wired Equivalent Privacy (WEP) standard—the other encryption standard supported by Windows XP Professional.

Windows Catalog A Web site that lists all hardware and software tested for compatibility with Windows XP by Microsoft.

Windows Firewall A software-based firewall built into Windows XP Service Pack 2 that replaces the Internet Connection Firewall built into Windows XP prior to Service Pack 2.

Windows Product Activation (WPA) The process of activating a copy of Windows with Microsoft after installation. Windows XP Professional requires that the operating system be activated with Microsoft within 30 days of installation.

Windows Setup Manager A wizard-based program that allows you to quickly create a script for an unattended installation of Windows XP Professional.

Windows Update An Internet-based service that allows you to download and install updates provided by Microsoft for the Windows operating system.

Windows XP Service Pack 2 A major update to Windows XP that includes all the critical updates released for Windows XP to date. In addition, Service Pack 2 includes a large number of new enhancements to Windows XP—enhancements aimed at increasing the default level of security for the operating system.

Winnt.exe   The command used for starting Windows XP Professional installation in MS-DOS and Windows 3.0/3.1.

Winnt32.exe   The command used for starting Windows XP Professional installation in Windows 95, Windows 98, Windows Me, Windows NT 4.0, or Windows 2000 Professional.

Wired Equivalent Privacy (WEP)   One of two wireless encryption standards available in Windows XP Professional. WEP is the encryption standard that is specified by the IEEE 802.11 standard. The other encryption standard available is Wi-Fi Protected Access (WPA).

workgroup   A collection of computers grouped for sharing resources such as data and peripherals over a local area network (LAN). Each workgroup is identified by a unique name. See also domain, peer-to-peer network.

World Wide Web (WWW)   Also known as the Web, the Internet multimedia service that contains a vast storehouse of hypertext documents written in Hypertext Markup Language (HTML). See also Hypertext Markup Language (HTML).

WORM   See Write-Once Read-Many (WORM).

WPA   See Wi-Fi Protected Access (WPA).

WPA   See Windows Product Activation (WPA).

Write-Once Read-Many (WORM)   Any type of storage medium to which data can be written only once but can be read any number of times. Typically, this is an optical disc whose surface is permanently etched using a laser to record information.

WWW   See World Wide Web (WWW).

Z

zone   A zone represents a discrete portion of the domain namespace. Zones provide a way to partition the domain namespace into discrete manageable sections.

Index

Q

System Requirements

While following the practices in this book, it is recommended that you use a computer that is not your primary workstation because you will be called on to make changes to the operating system and application configuration. The computer you use must have the following minimum configuration. All hardware should be listed in the Microsoft Windows Catalog.

Hardware Requirements

- Personal computer with an Intel Pentium 233 megahertz (MHz) or faster processor (300 MHz or faster processor recommended)
- 64 megabytes (MB) of RAM or higher (128 MB or higher recommended)
- 1.5 gigabytes (GB) of available hard disk space
- CD-ROM drive or DVD drive
- Super VGA (800 x 600) or higher resolution monitor
- Keyboard and Microsoft Mouse or compatible pointing device

Additionally, several chapters have practices that require you to have an Internet connection.

Software Requirements

- Microsoft Windows XP Professional Edition with Service Pack 2 (SP2)

Caution The 180-day Evaluation Edition of Windows XP Professional with SP2 provided with this training is not the full retail product and is provided only for the purposes of training and evaluation. Microsoft Technical Support does not support these evaluation editions. For additional support information regarding this book and the CD-ROMs (including answers to commonly asked questions about installation and use), visit the Microsoft Press Technical Support Web site at http://www.microsoft.com/learning/support/default.asp/. You can also e-mail tkinput@microsoft.com, or send a letter to Microsoft Press, Attn: Microsoft Press Technical Support, One Microsoft Way, Redmond, WA 98502-6399.

Inside *security information* you can trust

Microsoft® Windows® Security Resource Kit
ISBN 0-7356-1868-2   Suggested Retail Price: $49.99 U.S., $72.99 Canada

Comprehensive security information and tools, straight from the Microsoft product groups. This official RESOURCE KIT delivers comprehensive operations and deployment information that information security professionals can put to work right away. The authors—members of Microsoft's security teams—describe how to plan and implement a comprehensive security strategy, assess security threats and vulnerabilities, configure system security, and more. The kit also provides must-have security tools, checklists, templates, and other on-the-job resources on CD-ROM and on the Web.

Microsoft Encyclopedia of Security
ISBN 0-7356-1877-1   Suggested Retail Price: $39.99 U.S., $57.99 Canada

The essential security reference for computer professionals at all levels. Get the single resource that defines—and illustrates—the rapidly evolving world of computer and network security. The MICROSOFT ENCYCLOPEDIA OF SECURITY delivers more than 1000 cross-referenced entries detailing the latest security-related technologies, standards, products, services, and issues—including sources and types of attacks, countermeasures, policies, and more. You get clear, concise explanations and case scenarios that deftly take you from concept to real-world application—ready answers to help maximize security for your mission-critical systems and data.

Microsoft Windows Server™ 2003 Security Administrator's Companion
ISBN 0-7356-1574-8   Suggested Retail Price: $49.99 U.S., $72.99 Canada

The in-depth, practical guide to deploying and maintaining Windows Server 2003 in a secure environment. Learn how to use all the powerful security features in the latest network operating system with this in-depth, authoritative technical reference—written by a security expert on the Microsoft Windows Server 2003 security team. Explore physical security issues, internal security policies, and public and shared key cryptography, and then drill down into the specifics of the key security features of Windows Server 2003.

Microsoft Internet Information Services Security Technical Reference
ISBN 0-7356-1572-1   Suggested Retail Price: $49.99 U.S., $72.99 Canada

The definitive guide for developers and administrators who need to understand how to securely manage networked systems based on IIS. This book presents obvious, avoidable mistakes and known security vulnerabilities in Internet Information Services (IIS)—priceless, intimate facts about the underlying causes of past security issues—while showing the best ways to fix them. The expert author, who has used IIS since the first version, also discusses real-world best practices for developing software and managing systems and networks with IIS.

To learn more about Microsoft Press® products for IT professionals, please visit:

microsoft.com/mspress/IT

Microsoft Press products are available worldwide wherever quality computer books are sold. For more information, contact your book or computer retailer, software reseller, or local Microsoft Sales Office, or visit our Web site at **microsoft.com/mspress.** To locate your nearest source for Microsoft Press products, or to order directly, call 1-800-MSPRESS in the United States. (In Canada, call 1-800-268-2222.)

In-depth technical information and tools for
Microsoft Windows Server 2003

Microsoft® Windows Server™ 2003 Deployment Kit: A Microsoft Resource Kit
ISBN 0-7356-1486-5

Plan and deploy a Windows Server 2003 operating system environment with expertise from the team that develops and supports the technology—the Microsoft Windows® team. This multivolume kit delivers in-depth technical information and best practices to automate and customize your installation, configure servers and desktops, design and deploy network services, design and deploy directory and security services, implement Group Policy, create pilot and test plans, and more. You also get more than 125 timesaving tools, deployment job aids, Windows Server 2003 evaluation software, and the entire Windows Server 2003 Help on the CD-ROMs. It's everything you need to help ensure a smooth deployment—while minimizing maintenance and support costs.

Internet Information Services (IIS) 6.0 Resource Kit
ISBN 0-7356-1420-2

Deploy and support IIS 6.0, which is included with Windows Server 2003, with expertise direct from the Microsoft IIS product team. This official RESOURCE KIT packs 1200+ pages of in-depth deployment, operations, and technical information, including step-by-step instructions for common administrative tasks. Get critical details and guidance on security enhancements, the new IIS 6.0 architecture, migration strategies, performance tuning, logging, and troubleshooting—along with timesaving tools, IIS 6.0 product documentation, and a searchable eBook on CD. You get all the resources you need to help maximize the security, reliability, manageability, and performance of your Web server—while reducing system administration costs.

To learn more about the full line of Microsoft Press® products for IT professionals, please visit:

microsoft.com/mspress/IT

Microsoft Press products are available worldwide wherever quality computer books are sold. For more information, contact your book or computer retailer, software reseller, or local Microsoft Sales Office, or visit our Web site at **microsoft.com/mspress.** To locate your nearest source for Microsoft Press products, or to order directly, call 1-800-MSPRESS in the United States. (In Canada, call 1-800-268-2222.)

© 2004 Microsoft Corporation. All rights reserved. Microsoft, Microsoft Press, Windows, and Windows Server are either registered trademarks or trademarks of Microsoft Corporation in the United States and/or other countries.

Work smarter—*conquer your software from the inside out!*

Microsoft® Windows® XP Inside Out, Second Edition
ISBN: 0-7356-2044-X
U.S.A. $44.99
Canada $64.99

Microsoft Office System Inside Out— 2003 Edition
ISBN: 0-7356-1512-8
U.S.A. $49.99
Canada $72.99

Microsoft Office Access 2003 Inside Out
ISBN: 0-7356-1513-6
U.S.A. $49.99
Canada $72.99

Microsoft Office FrontPage® 2003 Inside Out
ISBN: 0-7356-1510-1
U.S.A. $49.99
Canada $72.99

Hey, you know your way around a desktop. Now dig into the new Microsoft Office products and the Windows XP operating system and *really* put your PC to work! These supremely organized software reference titles pack hundreds of timesaving solutions, troubleshooting tips and tricks, and handy workarounds into a concise, fast-answer format. They're all muscle and no fluff. All this comprehensive information goes deep into the nooks and crannies of each Office application and Windows XP feature. And every INSIDE OUT title includes a CD-ROM packed with bonus content such as tools and utilities, demo programs, sample scripts, batch programs, an eBook containing the book's complete text, and more! Discover the best and fastest ways to perform everyday tasks, and challenge yourself to new levels of software mastery!

Microsoft Press has other INSIDE OUT titles to help you get the job done every day:

Microsoft Office Excel 2003 Programming Inside Out
ISBN: 0-7356-1985-9

Microsoft Office Word 2003 Inside Out
ISBN: 0-7356-1515-2

Microsoft Office Excel 2003 Inside Out
ISBN: 0-7356-1511-X

Microsoft Office Outlook 2003® Inside Out
ISBN: 0-7356-1514-4

Microsoft Office Project 2003 Inside Out
ISBN: 0-7356-1958-1

Microsoft Office Visio® 2003 Inside Out
ISBN: 0-7356-1516-0

Microsoft Windows XP Networking Inside Out
ISBN: 0-7356-1652-3

Microsoft Windows Security Inside Out
for Windows XP and Windows 2000
ISBN: 0-7356-1632-9

To learn more about the full line of Microsoft Press® products, please visit us at:

microsoft.com/mspress

Microsoft Press products are available worldwide wherever quality computer books are sold. For more information, contact your book or computer retailer, software reseller, or local Microsoft Sales Office, or visit our Web site at **microsoft.com/mspress**. To locate your nearest source for Microsoft Press products, or to order directly, call 1-800-MSPRESS in the United States. (In Canada, call 1-800-268-2222).

In-depth technical information for
Microsoft Windows Server 2003

Microsoft® Windows® TCP/IP Protocols and Services Technical Reference
ISBN 0-7356-1291-9

The in-depth technical guide to TCP/IP protocols and services and their implementation in Windows .NET Server 2003. Get the in-depth details you need to support TCP/IP on the Windows .NET Server 2003 platform with this comprehensive technical guide. Combining concepts with packet examples, it steps layer by layer through the TCP/IP protocols and services that Windows .NET Server 2003 supports to help you understand how they work and how they're implemented in the operating system. With the latest information about Point-to-Point Protocol (PPP), Remote Authentication Dial-In User Service (RADIUS), IP Security (IPSec), and Virtual Private Networks (VPNs), it's a must-have for any technical professional who works with Windows .ENT Server 2003 and TCP/IP.

Active Directory® Services for Microsoft Windows Server 2003 Technical Reference
ISBN 0-7356-1577-2

The in-depth reference for network architects and administrators implementing enterprise directory services. Get the focused, in-depth technical expertise you need to implement and optimize your Microsoft directory services infrastructure. As two Active Directory experts guide you through advanced design and deployment issues for the Windows Server 2003 environment, you'll develop a thorough understanding of the underlying concepts, architectural components, and real-world functionality of Active Directory directory service. Whether you're upgrading from Microsoft Windows NT® 4.0 or later, or performing a clean installation, you'll learn the best ways to exploit Active Directory capabilities for your organization—and deliver new levels of network performance and productivity.

Deploying Virtual Private Networks with Microsoft Windows Server 2003 Technical Reference
ISBN 0-7356-1576-4

The essential guide to designing and deploying Windows based VPN solutions. Get the focused, in-depth technical expertise you need to deploy virtual private networks (VPNs) using the Windows Server 2003 operating system. The authors—networking specialists from the Microsoft Windows Server team—thoroughly detail VPN components, capabilities, and security considerations for remote access and site-to-site connections. From planning and design to deploying and troubleshooting your solution, you get expert technical guidance through all key decision points and procedures. This guide also features an end-to-end deployment example and best practices information, with additional resources on CD.

To learn more about the full line of Microsoft Press® products for IT professionals, please visit

microsoft.com/mspress/IT

Microsoft Press products are available worldwide wherever quality computer books are sold. For more information, contact your book or computer retailer, software reseller, or local Microsoft Sales Office, or visit our Web site at **microsoft.com/mspress**. To locate your nearest source for Microsoft Press products, or to order directly, call 1-800-MSPRESS in the United States. (In Canada, call 1-800-268-2222.)

In-depth learning solutions *for every software user*

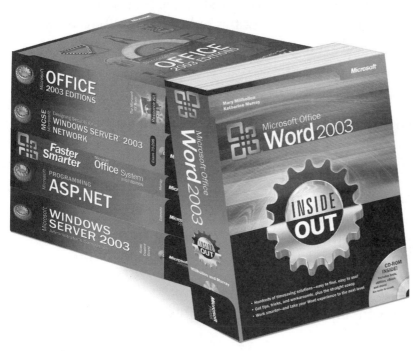

The tools you need to put technology to work.

Microsoft Press produces in-depth learning solutions that empower home and corporate users, IT professionals, and software developers to do more exciting things with Microsoft technology. From beginning PC how-to's to developer reference titles to IT training and technical resources, we offer hundreds of computer books, interactive training software, and online resources, all designed to help build your skills and knowledge—how, when, and where you learn best.

To learn more about the full line of Microsoft Press® products, please visit us at:

microsoft.com/mspress

Microsoft Press products are available worldwide wherever quality computer books are sold. For more information, contact your book or computer retailer, software reseller, or local Microsoft Sales Office, or visit our Web site at **microsoft.com/mspress**. To locate your nearest source for Microsoft Press products, or to order directly, call 1-800-MSPRESS in the United States. (In Canada, call 1-800-268-2222).

What do you think of this book? We want to hear from you!

Do you have a few minutes to participate in a brief online survey? Microsoft is interested in hearing your feedback about this publication so that we can continually improve our books and learning resources for you.

To participate in our survey, please visit:

www.microsoft.com/learning/booksurvey

And enter this book's ISBN, 0-7356-2152-7. As a thank-you to survey participants in the United States and Canada, each month we'll randomly select five respondents to win one of five $100 gift certificates from a leading online merchant.* At the conclusion of the survey, you can enter the drawing by providing your e-mail address, which will be used for prize notification *only*

Thanks in advance for your input. Your opinion counts!

Sincerely,

Microsoft Learning

Learn More. Go Further.

To see special offers on Microsoft Learning products for developers, IT professionals, and home and office users, visit: *www.microsoft.com/learning/booksurvey*

* No purchase necessary. Void where prohibited. Open only to residents of the 50 United States (includes District of Columbia) and Canada (void in Quebec). Sweepstakes ends 6/30/2005. For official rules, see: *www.microsoft.com/learning/booksurvey*